MAKING America

A History of the United States

Brief Second Edition

BERKIN ◆ MILLER ◆ CHERNY ◆ GORMLY ◆ MAINWARING

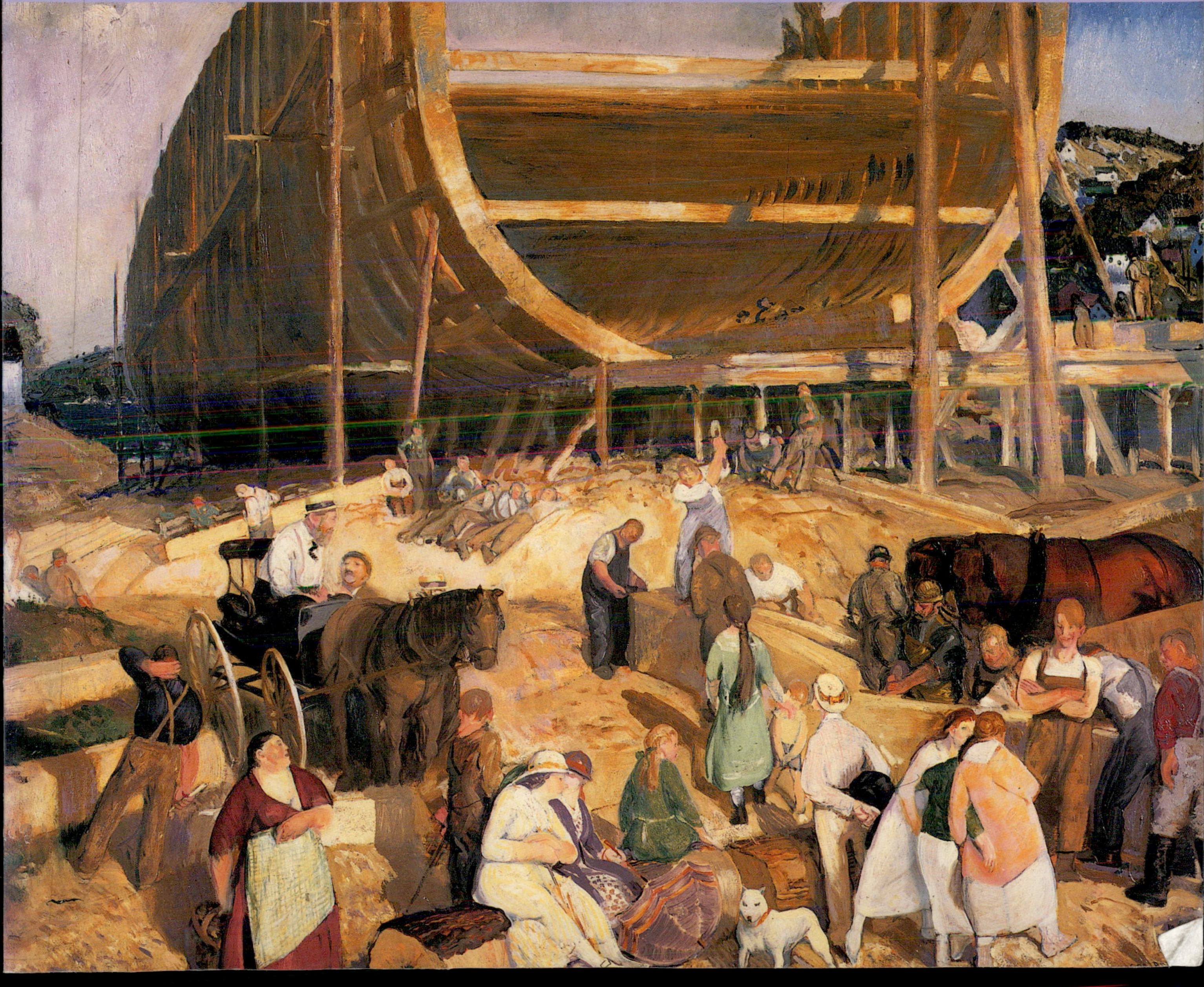

Making America
A History of the United States

Making America

A History of the United States

Brief Second Edition

Carol Berkin
Baruch College, City University of New York

Christopher L. Miller
The University of Texas, Pan American

Robert W. Cherny
San Francisco State University

James L. Gormly
Washington and Jefferson College

and

W. Thomas Mainwaring
Washington and Jefferson College

HOUGHTON MIFFLIN COMPANY
Boston New York

Editor-in-chief for history and political science: Jean L. Woy
Sponsoring editor: Colleen Kyle Shanley
Senior project editor: Carol Newman
Senior production/design coordinator: Jill Haber
Senior manufacturing coordinator: Priscilla Bailey
Senior marketing manager: Sandra McGuire

Cover design: Design Associates Inc., Chicago, IL
Cover image: *Shipyard Society* by George Bellows, 1916. Virginia Museum of Fine Arts, Richmond, VA. The Adolph D. and Wilkins C. Williams Fund.

Text credits
Page 198: *Map 9.2:* "Removal of Native Americans from the South, 1820–1840" from *American History Atlas* by Martin Gilbert. Copyright © Routledge Limited. Used with permission.
Page 504: "First Fig" by Edna St. Vincent Millay. From *Collected Poems,* HarperCollins. Copyright © 1922, 1950 by Edna St. Vincent Millay. Reprinted by permission of Elizabeth Barnett, literary executor.
Page 506–507: "Song for a Dark Girl," from *Selected Poems* by Langston Hughes. Copyright © 1927 by Alfred A. Knopf Inc. and renewed 1955 by Langston Hughes. Reprinted by permission of the publisher. "I, Too" from *Selected Poems* by Langston Hughes. Copyright © 1926 by Alfred A. Knopf Inc. and renewed 1954 by Langston Hughes. Reprinted by permission of the publisher.
Page 624: Six lines from "Howl" from *Collected Poems 1947–1980* by Allen Ginsberg. Copyright © 1955 by Allen Ginsberg. Reprinted by permission of HarperCollins Publishers, Inc.

Printed in the U.S.A.

Library of Congress Catalog Card Number: 00-103016

ISBN: 0-618-04427-2

1 2 3 4 5 6 7 8 9—VH—04 03 02 01 00

BRIEF CONTENTS

CONTENTS

MAPS

**Note: Maps listed in boldface type indicate chapter opener maps.*

FEATURES

Individual Choices

Making History

Chronologies

Figures

PREFACE

Our aim in producing this second brief edition has again been to be as faithful as possible to the narrative of American history contained in the full version of *Making America*. Although the brief edition has reduced the length of *Making America* by one third, we have sacrificed very few sections and none of the features of the long edition. The clear chronology, straightforward narrative, and strong thematic structure remain. In addition, all the learning features, including chapter-opening maps and timelines, chapter outlines with focus questions, and in-text glossaries, have been retained.

Wherever possible, we have cut words and avoided excising larger sections to retain the book's narrative flow. Of necessity, the brief edition provides fewer examples and details. Where there were four examples, this edition may contain only two. We have also followed Mark Twain's advice about the adjective: "When in doubt, strike it out." We trust that in pruning the text with a discerning eye that we have allowed the major themes of *Making America* to stand out clearly.

The biggest change in this second brief edition of *Making America* is that, in response to reviewer requests, we have published it in full color. Maps, illustrations, and photographs are now more illustrative and contribute to a much livelier, visually appealing second edition.

The brief edition of *Making America* carries the story of American history through the impeachment trial of President Clinton. It also includes NATO's intervention in Kosovo.

This edition is well suited for use in courses in which additional reading is assigned or where the course is shorter than usual. It is available in a one-volume and two-volume format: Volume A covers American history from prediscovery through Reconstruction, and Volume B covers Reconstruction to Clinton's impeachment. The chapter on Reconstruction is contained in both volumes.

The Approach

Professors and students who have used the first brief edition of *Making America* will recognize that we have preserved many of its central features. We have again set the nation's remarkable and complex story within a political chronology, relying on a basic and familiar structure that is broad enough to accommodate generous attention to the social, economic, and diplomatic aspects of our national history. We remain confident that this political framework allows us to integrate the experiences of all Americans into a meaningful and effective narrative of our nation's development.

Making America continues to be built on the premise that all Americans are historically active figures, playing significant roles in creating the history that we and other authors narrate. Once again, we have written the text on the basis of our understanding that history is a dynamic process resulting from the decisions and actions of all women and men in our American past. Thus, our second brief edition continues the tradition of ECCO, our acronym for four fundamental aspects of the historical process: expectations, constraints, choices, and outcomes. In each chapter, *Making America* examines the variety of *expectations* people held about their futures; the *constraints* of time, place, and multiple social and economic factors that these historical figures faced; the *choices* they made, given the circumstances of their lives; and the expected and unexpected *outcomes* flowing from their decisions.

In this revised edition, we have chosen to retain ECCO as an explicit device in each chapter introduction and summary but have made it implicit within the chapter narrative. This strategy allows students to recognize the dynamic ECCO elements as providing an underlying structure and organizing principle rather than as a surface device.

Themes

This edition continues to thread five central themes through *Making America*. The first of these themes, the political development of the nation, is evident in the text's coverage of the creation and revision of the federal and local governments, the contests waged over domestic and diplomatic policies, the internal and external crises faced by the United States and its political institutions, and the history of political parties. The second theme is the diversity of a national citizenry created by immigrants. To do justice to this theme, *Making America* explores not only English and European immigration but immigrant communities from Paleolithic times to the present. The text attends to the tensions and conflicts that arise in a diverse population, but it also examines the shared values and aspirations that define the majority of ordinary, middle-class American lives.

Making America's third theme is the significance of regional economies and cultures. This regional theme is developed for society before European colonization and for the colonial settlements of the seventeenth and eighteenth centuries. It is evident in our attention to the striking social and cultural divergences that existed between the American Southwest and the Atlantic coastal regions as well as between the antebellum South and North. A fourth theme is the rise and impact of the large social movements, from the Great Awakening in the 1740s to the rise of youth cultures in the post–World War II generations, prompted by changing material conditions or by new ideas challenging the status quo.

The fifth theme is the relationship of the United States to other nations. In *Making America* we explore in depth the causes and consequences of this nation's role in world conflict and diplomacy. This examination includes the era of colonization of the Americas, the eighteenth-century independence movement, the removal of Indian nations from the their traditional lands, the impact of the rhetoric of manifest destiny, American policies of isolationism and interventionism, and the modern role of the United States as a dominant player in world affairs.

Learning Features

The chapters in *Making America* follow a format that provides students essential study aids for mastering the historical material. Each chapter begins with a map that sets the scene for the most significant events and developments in the narrative that follows. Accompanying the map is a chronological chart of these significant events and a time line that illustrates where these events fit in a broader time frame. On the chapter-opening page, there is a topical outline of the new material students will encounter in the chapter, along with several new and, we think, thought-provoking critical thinking questions to help students focus on the broad, overarching themes of the chapter.

Each chapter offers an introduction in which we apply the ECCO model to the subject matter the students are about to explore. Each chapter ends with a summary, also structured in accordance with the ECCO model. At the end of the chapter students will also find suggestions for further reading on the events, movements, or people covered in that chapter. There is as well a selected bibliography at the end of the text citing the best scholarship in the field, old and new.

To ensure that students have full access to the material in each chapter, we provide a page-by-page glossary, defining terms and explaining their historically specific usage the first time they appear in the narrative. This running glossary will help students build their vocabularies and review for tests.

The illustrations in each chapter provide a visual connection to the past, and their captions analyze the subject of the painting, photograph, or artifact and comment on its significance. For this edition we have selected many new illustrations to reinforce or illustrate the themes of the narrative.

More than half the chapters contain an "Individual Choices" feature, which helps students understand an important point raised in the chapter. The "Individual Choices" provide intimate portraits of famous people such as President Grover Cleveland and ordinary people such as the twentieth-century farmers' advocate Milo Reno. By exploring how individuals arrived at decisions that shaped their lives, "Individual Choices" dramatize the fact that history is not inevitable but is the result of real people making real choices.

New to This Edition

In this new edition we have preserved what our colleagues and their students considered the best and most useful aspects of the first brief edition of *Making America.* We also have replaced what was less successful, revised what could be improved, and added new elements to strengthen the book.

A new chapter places the English colonial world and the empire of which it was a part in their broad historical context. Chapter 2, "A Continent on the Move, 1400–1725," prepares students to see the origins of the Anglo-American world in the expansionist ideology of western Europe, to recognize that the colonies were part of a transatlantic community of ideas and policies, and to understand that Indians, Europeans, and the English were all critical players in the development of the seventeenth- and eighteenth-century society that became the United States.

Changes that improve the coverage of content in *Making America* are evident in every chapter. The newest contributions to scholarship in American history have been integrated throughout the text. There is, for example, more coverage of the West throughout the text, and the coverage of the Kennedy and Johnson presidencies has been revised to reflect the insights of the best new work in this field. Chapters 7 through 9 have been recast into two chapters to make for more continuity in the story of the Federalists' decline and the Jeffersonian Republicans' ascendancy.

This new edition also offers a new feature: "Making History: Using Sources from the Past." This feature encourages students to work with primary documents in order to answer important historical questions. In each, "Making History" feature, the student is presented with a brief background statement entitled "The Context." This is followed by the statement of a problem, "The Historical Question." Then students are given "The Challenge" to write an essay or hold a discussion on the challenge question, drawing on knowledge and information that they have gained from reading the text and the primary sources that accompany the feature. There is no single, correct answer, of course; students will come to different conclusions just as historians do. This feature is flexible enough to provide teachers the opportunity to hone students' essay-writing skills, critical thinking abilities, and understanding of historical methods of inquiry and standards of proof.

We the authors of *Making America* believe that this new edition will be effective in the history classroom. Please let us know what you think by sending us your views through Houghton Mifflin's American history web site, located at college.hmco.com.

Study and Teaching Aids

A number of useful learning and teaching aids accompany the second brief edition of *Making America.* They are designed to help students get the most from the course and to provide instructors with some useful teaching tools.

@history: an interactive American history source is a multimedia teaching/learning package that combines a variety of material on a cross-platformed CD-ROM—primary sources (text and graphic), video, and audio—with activities that can be used to analyze, interpret, and discuss primary sources; to enhance collaborative learning; and to create multimedia lecture presentations. @history also has an accompanying web site, located at college.hmco.com, where additional primary sources, online resources for *Making America,* and links to relevant sites can be found.

An ***On-line Study Guide*** is available at no charge for students. Accessible through Houghton Mifflin's @history web site (college.hmco.com), it functions as a tutorial, providing rejoinders to all multiple-choice questions that explain why the student's response is or is not correct. The online Study Guide also offers chapter outlines and other learning resources for students.

The ***Instructor's Resource Manual with Test Items,*** prepared by Kelly Woestman of Pittsburgh State University, includes for every chapter instructional objectives that are drawn from the textbook's critical thinking questions, a chapter summary and annotated outline, and three lecture topics that include resource material and references to the text. Each chapter also includes discussion questions, answers to the critical thinking questions that follow each major heading in the text, cooperative and individual learning activities, map activities, ideas for paper topics, and a list of audiovisual resources. The test items provide twenty key terms and definitions, forty to fifty multiple-choice questions, five to ten essay questions with answer guidelines, and an analytical exercise to test critical thinking skills.

A ***Computerized Test Items File*** is available for IBM PC or compatible and Macintosh computers. This computerized version of the printed Test Items file allows professors to create customized tests by editing and adding questions.

A set of over 150 full-color ***American History Map Transparencies*** is available in two-volume sets upon adoption.

Please contact your local Houghton Mifflin representative for more information about the ancillary items or to obtain desk copies.

Acknowledgments

The authors have benefited from the critical reading of the manuscript by our generous colleagues. We thank the following instructors for the advice they provided on the second brief edition:

Shirley Eoff, Angelo State University

Larry Hartzell, Brookdale Community College

Daniel Lewis, California State Polytechnic University, Pomona

Pamela Riney-Kehrberg, Illinois State University

Theresa Kaminski, University of Wisconsin—Stevens Point

Pamela Robbins, Florida State University

Cornelia L. Dopkins, Fredonia State College

Ted M. Kluz, Auburn University—Montgomery

Gary L. Huey, Ferris State University

W. Thomas Mainwaring, the abridging editor of *Making America,* would like to thank Colleen Kyle at Houghton Mifflin for her faith in this project. He would like to reiterate his gratitude to James Gormly at Washington and Jefferson College for suggesting that he take on this task. He would also like to voice appreciation to his colleague Robert H. Dodge for tolerating countless interruptions to discuss many fine points of history, grammar, and style. They usually agreed. Carol Newman at Houghton Mifflin did her usual fine job of turning the manuscript into a polished book. He thanks Deborah, Amy, and Philip for everything else.

TO THE STUDENTS

To most students, the authors of a textbook are little more than names on the spine of a heavy book. We the authors of *Making America,* however, hope you'll give us a chance to be more than "Berkin et al." If you'll give us a moment, we'll introduce ourselves—and our book—to you. We also want to give you some solid suggestions about how to get the most out of this text and out of the study of American history it is designed to assist.

We—Carol Berkin, Robert Cherny, James Gormly, Christopher Miller, and Thomas Mainwaring—have been historians, teachers, and colleagues for many years. Carol and Bob went to graduate school together; Jim and Chris taught at University of Texas—Pan American together; Jim and Tom teach at Washington and Jefferson College. As scholars, we spend much of our time in libraries or historical archives, leafing through centuries-old letters from a wife to a husband, looking at letters to an abolitionist, reading government reports on Indian policy, analyzing election returns from the 1890s, or examining newspaper editorials on the Cold War. At those moments, immersed in the past, we feel as if we have conquered time and space, traveling to eras and to places that no longer exist. This experience is part of the reason why we are historians. But we also are historians because we believe that knowing about the past is critical for anyone who hopes to understand the present and chart the future.

Our goal for this textbook is deceptively simple: we want to tell the story of America from its earliest settlement to the present, to make that story complex and interesting, and to tell it in a language and format that will help students enjoy learning that history. Achieving those goals has been hard work, and with each edition of *Making America,* we hope we move closer to success.

This textbook is organized and designed to help you master American history. Our narrative is chronological, telling the story as it happened, decade by decade or era by era. If you look at the table of contents, you can see that the chapters cover specific time periods rather than large themes. This does not mean that themes are absent; it means that we present them to you in the context of specific moments in time.

Each chapter follows the same pattern. It begins with a map of the United States on which vital information is provided. For instance, the chapter on English settlement in the colonial era shows you the boundaries of each colony, gives you the date it was founded, and tells you what type of colony it was. The map locates for you in space what the chronological narrative locates in time. Below the map you will see a time line, which gives you the dates of important events and a sense of where in the larger history of the nation these events fit. On the opposite page, you will see a chapter outline with focus questions, and when you turn the page, you will see a chart that lists in chronological order the significant events that we describe in the chapter. Together, the map, time line, outline, and chronology provide an overview of what you will be reading in the pages that follow.

The introduction to each chapter sets the scene and tells you what major themes and issues you will find as you read on. You will notice that the introductions present the story in a very particular way: as a series of *expectations,* or hopes and desires held by the people of the era; of *constraints,* or limitations that they confronted as they tried to fulfill their expectations; of *choices,* or decisions that they finally made; and of *outcomes,* or consequences of the actions prompted by those choices. Our shorthand name for this approach is ECCO, an acronym formed from the first letter of each of the four elements. Expectations, constraints, choices, outcomes—ECCO—are the dynamic elements of history. ECCO is a way to remind you that what we call "the past" was "the present" to the people who lived it. They could not know what would happen as a result of their actions—and this is the excitement of the story we have to tell.

Then the chapter itself begins. It consists of sections that you can read as mini-narratives. A summary at the end of each chapter recaps the material in the text. If you want to make sure you have focused on the important points in the chapter, you can review by reading the summary and then trying to answer the focus questions at the beginning of the chapter.

Because a serious examination of a history as rich and complex as our nation's requires us to introduce you to many new people, places, events, and ideas, it is easy to get lost in details or panic over what is most important to remember. You may also encounter words that are unfamiliar or words that seem to be used in a different way from the way you use them in everyday speech. Both problems can distract you from learning what happened—and why—and enjoying the story. To prevent this distraction, we have provided a glossary on each page to define key terms and possibly unfamiliar words. Each chapter also has suggestions for further reading on the subjects covered in the text, so that you can explore other viewpoints or look in depth at subjects that interest you.

Because students learn from visual as well as written sources, each chapter provides reproductions of paintings, photographs, artifacts, cartoons, and maps. These are not intended just to be decorative. They are there to give faces to the people you are reading about, to show you what the environment, both natural and constructed, was like in the era under discussion, and to provide images of objects from the era that make clear their similarity to or difference from material objects in the world around you today. In the captions we identify each visual aid and suggest ways to interpret it.

More than half the chapters have a feature called "Individual Choices." In this feature we present a man or woman from the past who needed to make a choice. After all, individuals, including you, shape their history at the same time that history is shaping their lives. We believe that by reading about real people—some famous, some not—as they face an important choice and an uncertain outcome, you will better understand the era in which they lived.

A feature called "Making History" also appears throughout the text. It gives you the opportunity to work with the raw materials of history: the primary sources that help historians reconstruct the past. This feature is designed to answer, the most common question students ask a history professor: "How do you know what happened or how it happened or why?" In "Making History," we pose a question to you, provide a variety of primary sources on the topic, then challenge you to offer your interpretation of the issue. "Making History" gives you a chance to be a historian, not just to read history. You will quickly see that your conclusions are not the same as those of your classmates, and these discrepancies will demonstrate why historians often disagree about issues in the past.

At the back of the textbook, you will find some additional resources. In the Appendix you will find a bibliography listing the books on which we relied in writing the chapters. You will also find reprinted two of the most important documents in American history: the Declaration of Independence and the Constitution. Here, too, are tables that give you quick access to important data on the presidents and the states. Finally, you will see the index, which will help you locate a subject quickly if you want to read about it.

We the authors of *Making America* hope that our textbook conveys to you our own fascination with the American past and sparks your curiosity about the nation's history. We invite you to share your feedback on the book: you can reach us through Houghton Mifflin's American history web site, which is located at college.hmco.com.

ABOUT THE AUTHORS

Carol Berkin

Born in Mobile, Alabama, Carol Berkin received her undergraduate degree from Barnard College and her Ph.D. from Columbia University. Her dissertation won the Bancroft Award. She is now professor of history at Baruch College and the Graduate Center of City University of New York, where she serves as deputy chair of the Ph.D. program in history. She has written *Jonathan Sewall: Odyssey of an American Loyalist* (1974) and *First Generations: Women in Colonial America* (1996). She has edited *Women in America: A History* (with Mary Beth Norton, 1979), *Women, War and Revolution* (with Clara M. Lovett, 1980), and *Women's Voices, Women's Lives: Documents in Early American History* (with Leslie Horowitz, 1998). She was contributing editor on southern women for *The Encyclopedia of Southern Culture* and has appeared in the PBS series *Liberty! The American Revolution* and The Learning Channel series *The American Revolution*. Professor Berkin chaired the Dunning Beveridge Prize Committee for the American Historical Association, the Columbia University Seminar in Early American History, and the Taylor Prize Committee of the Southern Association of Women Historians, and she served on the program committees for both the Society for the History of the Early American Republic and the Organization of American Historians. In addition, she has been a historical consultant for the National Parks Commission and served on the Planning Committee for the U.S. Department of Education's National Assessment of Educational Progress.

Christopher L. Miller

Born and raised in Portland, Oregon, Christopher L. Miller received his undergraduate degree from Lewis and Clark College and his Ph.D. from the University of California, Santa Barbara. He is currently associate professor of history at the University of Texas—Pan American. He is the author of *Prophetic Worlds: Indians and Whites on the Columbia Plateau* (1985), and his articles and reviews have appeared in numerous scholarly journals. In addition to his scholarship in the areas of American West and American Indian history, Professor Miller has been active in projects designed to improve history teaching, including programs funded by the Meadows Foundation, the U.S. Department of Education, and other agencies.

Robert W. Cherny

Born in Marysville, Kansas, and raised in Beatrice, Nebraska, Robert W. Cherny received his B.A. from the University of Nebraska and his M.A. and Ph.D. from Columbia University. He is now professor of history at San Francisco State University. His books include *American Politics in the Gilded Age, 1868–1900* (1997), *San Francisco, 1865–1932: Politics, Power, and Urban Development* (with William Issel, 1986), *A Righteous Cause: The Life of William Jennings Bryan* (1985, 1994), and *Populism, Progressivism, and the Transformation of Nebraska Politics, 1885–1915* (1981). His articles on politics and labor in the late nineteenth and early twentieth centuries have appeared in scholarly journals, anthologies, and historical dictionaries and encyclopedias. He has been an NEH fellow, Distinguished Fulbright Lecturer at Moscow State University (Russia), and Visiting Research Scholar at the University of Melbourne (Australia). He has also served as president of the Society for Historians of the Gilded Age and Progressive Era and of the Southwest Labor Studies Association.

James L. Gormly

Born in Riverside, California, James L. Gormly received a B.A. from the University of Arizona and his M.A. and Ph.D. from the University of Connecticut. He is now professor of history and chair of the history department at Washington and Jefferson College. He has written *The Collapse of the Grand Alliance*

(1970) and *From Potsdam to the Cold War* (1979). His articles and reviews have appeared in *Diplomatic History, The Journal of American History, The American Historical Review, The Historian, The History Teacher,* and *The Journal of Interdisciplinary History.*

W. Thomas Mainwaring

Born in Pittsburgh, Pennsylvania, W. Thomas Mainwaring received his B.A. from Yale University and his M.A. and Ph.D. from the University of North Carolina at Chapel Hill. Currently an associate professor of history at Washington and Jefferson College, he is interested in local and community history. He has edited a collection of essays on the Whiskey Rebellion and has written about a variety of topics on local and community history. He is currently engaged in a study of the Underground Railroad.

Making America
A History of the United States

ARCTIC OCEAN
EUROPE
ENGLAND
FRANCE
SPAIN
AFRICA
Greenland
Bering Strait
INUIT
ALEUT
ARCTIC
DOGRIB
TLINGIT
NORTHWEST COAST
KWAKIUTL
CHINOOK
CHIPEWYAN
Hudson Bay
SUBARCTIC
CREE
MONTAGNAIS
BLACKFEET
PLATEAU
CROW
MANDAN
SIOUX
GREAT PLAINS
CHIPPEWA
SAUK
FOX
ALGONQUIN
OTTAWA
HURON
IROQUOIS
WAMPANOAG
GREAT BASIN
POMO
CALIFORNIA
CHEYENNE
ARAPAHO
ILLINOIS
MIAMI
EASTERN WOODLANDS
DELAWARE
POWHATAN
SHAWNEE
TUSCARORA
CHEROKEE
CHICKASAW
CREEK
MOHAVE
SOUTHWEST
APACHE
WICHITA
COMANCHE
SOUTHEAST
CHOCTAW
PACIFIC OCEAN
ATLANTIC OCEAN
GRAND BANKS
VIKINGS 1000 A.D.
CABOT 1497
CARTIER 1534–35
NORMAN AND BRETON
BASQUE
1534
1535
VERRAZZANO 1524
COLUMBUS 1492
PONCE DE LEON 1513
SEMINOLE
MEXICO AND MIDDLE AMERICA
Gulf of Mexico
AZTEC EMPIRE
MAYA EMPIRE
CORTES 1519–21
TAINO
COLUMBUS 1493
COLUMBUS 1502–03
VESPUCCI 1499
COLUMBUS 1498
CARIBBEAN
Caribbean Sea
BALBOA 1510–13
CABRILLO 1542–43
ARAWAK
CARIB
PIZARRO 1530–33
INCA EMPIRE
AMAZON
SOUTH AMERICA
Spanish exploration
French exploration
English exploration
Viking exploration
Fishing expeditions
PLATEAU Culture area
CROW Indian nation
0 400 800 Km.
0 400 800 Mi.

TWO WORLDS MEET For convenience sake, scholars have divided New World societies into broad culture groups, though each group was actually composed of many different specific cultures. This map shows those culture groups and traces the routes of early explorers who opened these new worlds up to European contact and colonization.

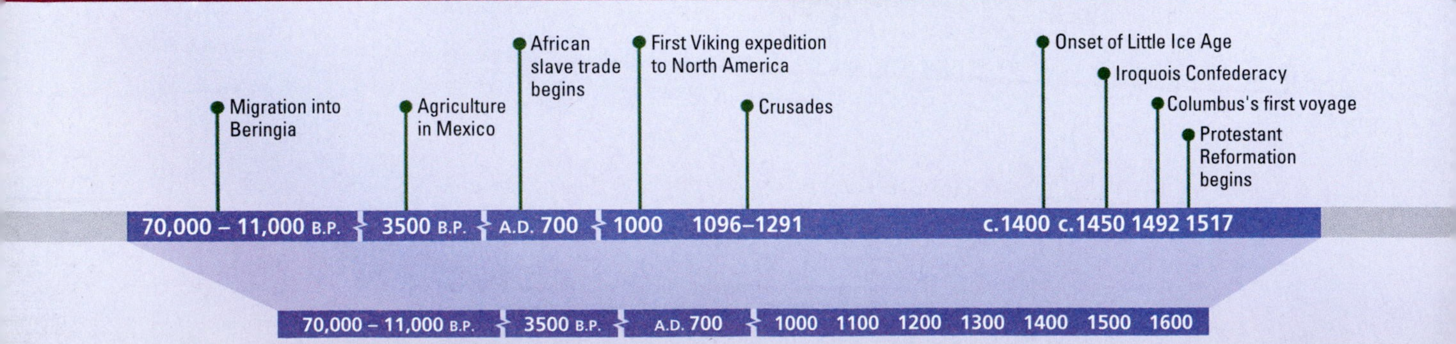
Migration into Beringia
Agriculture in Mexico
African slave trade begins
First Viking expedition to North America
Crusades
Onset of Little Ice Age
Iroquois Confederacy
Columbus's first voyage
Protestant Reformation begins
70,000 – 11,000 B.P.
3500 B.P.
A.D. 700
1000
1096–1291
c.1400
c.1450
1492
1517
70,000 – 11,000 B.P.
3500 B.P.
A.D. 700
1000 1100 1200 1300 1400 1500 1600

*Note: B.P. means before present time.

CHAPTER 1

Making a "New" World, to 1558

American Origins

- Before the arrival of Columbus, what constraints did environmental conditions impose on native cultures?
- What kinds of choices did American Indians make, and what were the outcomes of those choices for Indians living in various parts of the continent?

European Outreach and the Age of Exploration

- What expectations led Europeans into extensive exploration and outreach?
- What geographical and political constraints stood in their way?
- How did they choose to overcome those constraints?

The Challenges of Mutual Discovery

- How did American Indians choose to respond to European contact?
- How did Europeans choose to respond to Indians and Africans?
- What were some outcomes of the Columbian Exchange?

INTRODUCTION

Expectations
Constraints
Choices
Outcomes

The first people to come to America *chose* to come here a very long time ago, *expecting* to find improved hunting. These Americans subsequently faced natural, cultural, and economic *constraints* that gave peculiar shape to their societies. As their numbers grew, these hunters were *constrained* by the rapid rise of their own population and the simultaneous decline of the large game animals they depended on for food. Many *chose* to increase their reliance on plants. The *outcome* for these societies was the eventual development of agriculture. Other societies responded differently to the decline and ultimate extinction of big game because of different *constraints* and *expectations.* The overall *outcome* was a broadly diverse cultural universe in North America.

In the meantime, people in Africa, the Middle East, and Europe were making their own *choices.* Muslim traders, following routes first taken by the ancient Egyptians, spread knowledge and goods that presented a new set of *expectations* and *choices* to Africans. One *outcome* was the rise of rich and sophisticated African kingdoms. Another was the establishment of a systematic slave trade by Africans and Muslims.

The influence of Viking and Muslim traders led to changed *expectations* in Europe as well. The wealth of these traders lured Europeans into increasing adventurousness. At first, their neighbors' military strength was a large *constraint,* but gradually Europeans *chose* to challenge Islam's control over large parts of Europe and the Asian and African trade. Italian merchants formed partnerships with their Islamic neighbors, bringing new wealth and knowledge into their cities. Farther west, the Portuguese and then the Spanish swept the Muslims from their lands. They then explored new trade routes to escape the Italian-Muslim monopoly of the Far Eastern and African trade. Their successes led other European nations to *choose* exploration as a way of bringing new riches to their lands.

The *outcome* of these *expectations, constraints,* and *choices* was a collision among Europeans, Africans, and American Indians in the Western Hemisphere. This collision of worlds transformed life on both sides of the Atlantic. Thus the story of making America must begin with the first discovery of the New World, long before Columbus, and trace the development of the people who were already here when Columbus arrived. Then we must consider what was happening in the rest of the world so we can understand why others eventually came to this land. Only then will we be prepared to see how the *expectations, constraints,* and *choices* made by the people who came together in the New World following Columbus had the particular *outcomes* we call America.

American Origins

The settlement of the **Western Hemisphere** took place fairly recently in human history. Although human culture began about 4 million years ago in what is now northern Tanzania, anthropologists hold that the peopling of the Americas did not begin until at least 70,000 years ago. Some theorize that this process did not begin until about 20,000 years ago.

The movement of people from Asia to North America is intimately connected to the advance and retreat of glaciers during the Great Ice Age, which began about 2.5 million years ago and

Western Hemisphere The half of the earth that includes North America, Mexico, Central America, and South America.

CHRONOLOGY

The New World

c. 70,000–10,000 B.P.	Human migration from Asia into Beringia
c. 7000 B.P.	Plant cultivation begins in North America
c. 3500 B.P.	Agriculture begins in central Mexico
c. A.D. 500	Agriculture extends into present-day New Mexico and Arizona
c. 500–1000	Rise of Hopewell culture
c. 700	Islamic caravans to West Africa and African slave trade begin
800–1100	Vikings extend trade network
800–1700	Rise of Mississippian culture
1096–1291	The Crusades to the Holy Land
c. 1200	Aztecs invade central Mexico
c. 1400	Beginning of the Little Ice Age
c. 1450	Hiawatha founds the Iroquois Confederacy
1492	Reconquista completed Columbus's first voyage
1500	Portuguese begin to control the African slave trade
1517	Protestant Reformation begins
1527–1535	Henry VIII begins English Reformation
1558	Elizabeth I becomes queen of England

ended only about 10,000 years ago. During the Wisconsin glaciation, the last major advance of glaciers, a sheet of ice over 8,000 feet thick covered the northern half of both Europe and North America. So much water was frozen into this massive glacier that sea levels dropped as much as 450 feet.

This drop in sea levels created a land bridge called **Beringia** between Siberia and Alaska. During the Ice Age, Beringia was a dry, frigid grassland that was free of glaciers. It was a perfect grazing ground for animals such as giant bison and huge-tusked woolly mammoths. Hunters of these animals, including large wolves, saber-toothed cats, and humans, followed them across Beringia into North America.

Geologists believe that sea levels were low enough to expose Beringia between 70,000 and 10,000 years ago. Archaeological evidence yields a wide variety of dates for when people first moved southward into North America, ranging from about 40,000 to about 12,000 years ago.

Other evidence, from blood DNA, tooth shapes, and languages, suggests that the majority of North America's original inhabitants descended from three separate migrating groups. The first of these, the Paleo-Indians, probably arrived 30,000 to 40,000 years ago. Their descendants ultimately occupied the entire Western Hemisphere. The second group the Na-Dene people, arrived near the end of the Wisconsin era, between 10,000 and 11,000 years ago. Their descendants are concentrated in subarctic regions of Canada and in the southwestern United States. The final group, the Arctic-dwelling

B.P. An abbreviation for "before the present"; 70,000 B.P. means "70,000 years ago."

Beringia An expanse of land between present-day Siberia and Alaska, now covered by water; an avenue for migration between Asia and North America in prehistoric times.

Inuits, or Eskimos, probably arrived after the land bridge between North America and Asia disappeared (see Map 1.1).

About 9,000 years ago, a warming trend began that ended the Ice Age and brought temperatures to what we now consider normal. As temperatures warmed and grasslands disappeared, the gigantic Ice Age creatures that had supplied early hunters with their primary source of meat, clothing, and tools began to die out. The hunters faced the unpleasant prospect of following the large animals into extinction if they kept trying to survive by hunting big game.

Seedtime for Native Cultures in North America

The constraints imposed by the changing environment forced the American Indians to make a series of choices. The first phase of adaptation, called the **Archaic phase,** lasted until about 3,000 years ago. During this period, people in North America abandoned **nomadic** big-game hunting and began to explore new sources of food, clothing, and tools and new places to live.

Archaic culture emerged at different times in different places. It appears that western North America was hit earliest and hardest by the changing climate. At Fort Rock Cave in southern Oregon, archaeologists have unearthed evidence dating from 9,600 years ago of people abandoning big-game hunting and adapting to local conditions. Three findings at Fort Rock Cave mark it as an important transitional site between the big-game and Archaic cultures. First, investigators found many different tools for grinding seeds. The tools were signs that these people were eating less meat and more local grass seeds, nuts, and other vegetable foods. Second, investigators found baskets, sandals, and clothing woven from grasses and reeds, also indications of a greater reliance on plants. Third, investigators found small spear points and fishing and bird-hunting equipment. These early Indians had apparently stopped chasing after mammoths and had begun to hunt and fish for animals that they could find close by.

Over the next several thousand years, people throughout North America made similar choices, differing only in the specific foods and types of materials they employed. In the forests that grew up to cover the eastern half of the continent, Archaic Indians developed finely polished stone tools, which they used to make functional and beautiful implements out of wood, bone, shell, and other materials. There and along the Pacific shore, people hollowed out massive tree trunks to make boats. During this time domesticated dogs were introduced into North America, probably by newly arriving migrants from Asia. With dogs to help carry loads on land and boats for river transportation, Archaic people were able to make the best use of their local environments by moving from camp to camp over the year, perhaps collecting shellfish for several weeks in one spot and then wild strawberries in another.

Such efficient use of local resources caused an enormous increase in population. Nomadic hunting had involved dangerous animals and occasional famines that helped keep human populations small. Archaic life was much safer and food supplies more reliable. Freed from the constant need to track and kill big game for meat, Archaic people also had more spare time. One outcome was the continuing invention of new tools and craft skills. Another was the emergence of art, which played a prominent role in the elaborate burial practices that emerged everywhere in North America during this period.

Early Indians left their mark on their local environments. They used fire to clear forests of unwanted scrub and to encourage the growth of berries and other plants that they found valuable. In this way they produced vegetables for themselves and also provided food for browsing animals like deer, which increased in number, while other species, less useful to people, declined.

Archaic phase In Native American culture, the period when people began to shift away from hunting big game and turn to agriculture and other food sources in local environments.

nomadic Having no fixed home and wandering from place to place in search of food or other resources.

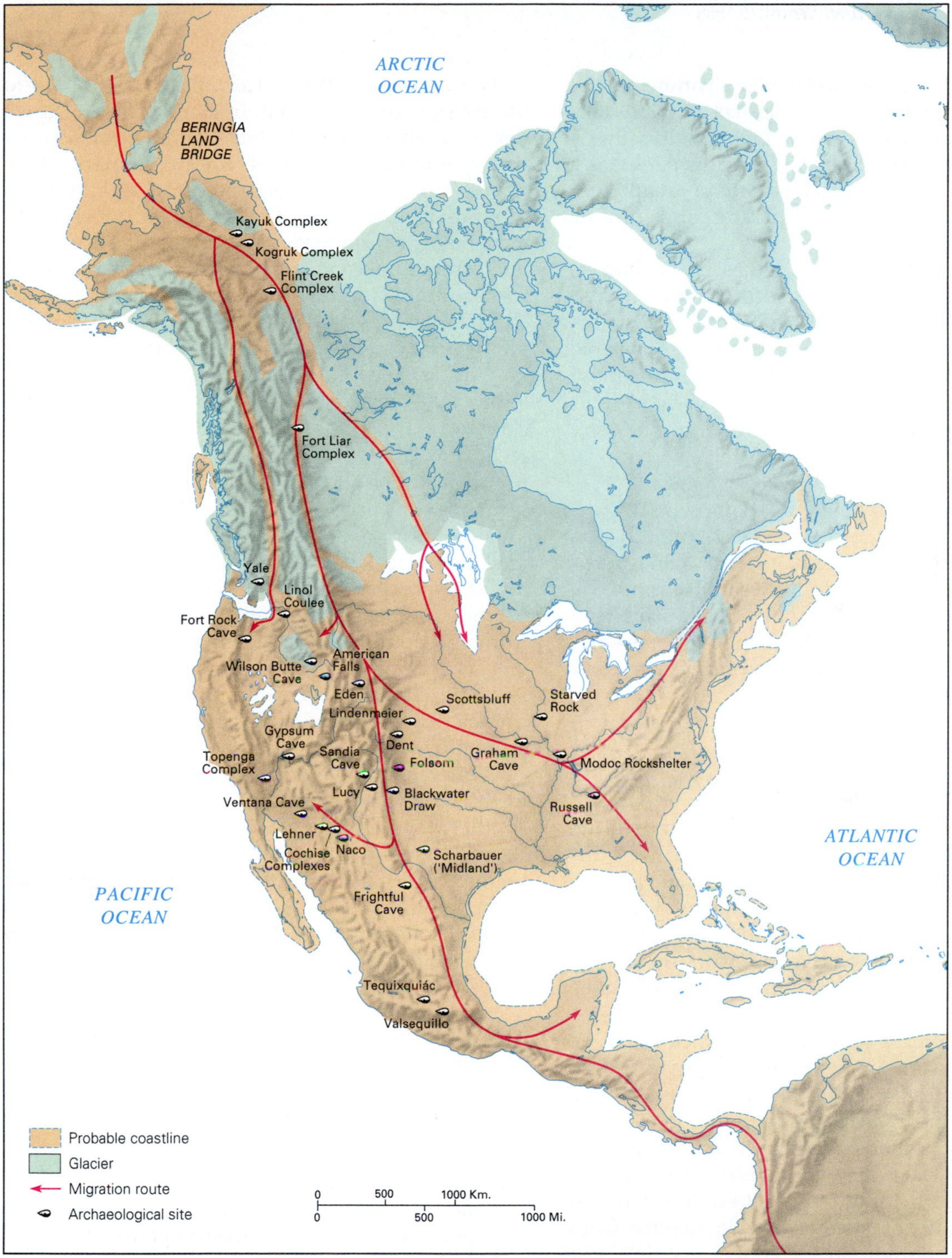
ARCTIC OCEAN
BERINGIA LAND BRIDGE
Kayuk Complex
Kogruk Complex
Flint Creek Complex
Fort Liar Complex
Yale
Linol Coulee
Fort Rock Cave
Wilson Butte Cave
American Falls
Eden
Scottsbluff
Starved Rock
Lindenmeier
Gypsum Cave
Dent
Topenga Complex
Sandia Cave
Folsom
Graham Cave
Modoc Rockshelter
Lucy
Blackwater Draw
Ventana Cave
Russell Cave
Lehner
Naco
Cochise Complexes
Scharbauer ('Midland')
ATLANTIC OCEAN
PACIFIC OCEAN
Frightful Cave
Tequixquiác
Valsequillo
Probable coastline
Glacier
Migration route
Archaeological site
0 500 1000 Km.
0 500 1000 Mi.

♦ **MAP 1.1 First Americans Enter the New World** Although DNA evidence indicates that all early migrants to the Western Hemisphere were genetically related, at least two cultural groups moved into North America approximately 40,000 years ago. The Old Cordilleran group entered to the west of the Rocky Mountains, and the Clovis group, to the east of the Rockies. Both groups left records of their passing at numerous sites, the most prominent of which are labeled here.

A significant example of such environmental engineering comes from north-central Mexico. Perhaps 7,000 years ago, humans began cultivating a wild strain of grass. Such cultivation eventually transformed a fairly unproductive plant into **maize,** an enormously nourishing and prolific food crop.

Maize, along with beans, squash, and chilies, formed the basis for an agricultural revolution in America. Although it is not clear how or why this revolution got started, about 3,500 years ago people near what is now Mexico City began planting these vegetables. Shortly thereafter, they stopped their annual round of hunting and gathering. They settled down into villages near their fields and moved away only when these fields were exhausted.

Maize spread like wildfire. From central Mexico, it found its way to New Mexico and Arizona about 1,000 or 2,000 years ago and then spread northward and eastward. Between 500 and 800 years ago, the Woodland Indians of eastern North America, who had been cultivating wild sunflowers and other foods, incorporated maize into their economy.

The Complex World of Indian America

Although the broad shape of American Indian life was similar throughout North America, vast differences existed among various Indian groups. This variety of cultures developed in direct response to local environmental conditions. The map at the beginning of the chapter shows the eleven major culture areas that anthropologists have identified.

Lifestyles differed greatly from one culture area to another. The language and technology of Arctic peoples were unlike those anywhere else on the continent. In the eastern half of what is now the United States, Indians were agriculturalists who supplemented their diet of corn, beans, and squash by hunting and fishing. On the Western Plains, an Archaic lifestyle persisted as people traveled from one camp to another on an annual hunting and gathering cycle. On the Pacific coast, Indians lived in permanent villages and harvested the riches of the sea. Clearly North America was socially and culturally complex.

The spread of agriculture allowed Indians to build large, ornate centers in many parts of North America. These centers were generally not residential cities but trading and ceremonial centers where people congregated periodically. Large earthen mounds in the shape of huge animals, pyramids, or geometrical patterns characterize these trading and ceremonial centers. Archaeologists have called these **mound builder** societies. The map of late Archaic America is dotted with such centers (see Map 1.1). Along the Ohio River, a complex of sites known as the Adena culture was constructed about 3,000 years ago. Adena cities were centers of ceremony and trade, as is evidenced by the artifacts from all over North America that have been found at Adena sites.

In the Eastern Woodlands, **Hopewell culture** took the place of Adena culture. Hopewell culture reached its peak between 1,500 and 1,000 years ago at Cahokia, near the modern city of East St. Louis, Illinois. Archaeologists have found the distinctive forms of pottery, tools, and religious and artistic objects that originated there over much of North America. About 800 years ago, Cahokia and the entire Hopewell complex fell into decline for unknown reasons.

While ceremonial and trading centers declined in the North, their development continued in the southern Mississippi River valley. Between 1,200 years ago and the time of European entry into the region in the 1700s, peoples speaking Siouan, Caddoan, and Muskogean languages formed a vibrant agricultural and urban society, named the **Mississippian culture.**

maize Corn, a tall plant with a solid stem and narrow leaves that bears seeds on large ears; the word *maize* comes from an Indian word for this plant.

mound builder Name applied to a number of Native American societies that constructed earthen mounds as monuments and building fundations.

Hopewell culture An early American Indian culture centered in the Ohio River valley; it is known for its burial mounds, tools, and pottery.

Mississippian culture An American Indian culture centered in the southern Mississippi River valley; influenced by Mexican culture, it is known for its pyramid building and its urban centers.

♦ Cahokia was the largest city in pre-Columbian North America, occupying over 6 square miles and containing more than 120 earthen mounds, including several gigantic pyramids. The largest, Monk's Mound (the huge structure in the upper right corner), was larger than the Great Pyramids of Egypt. Despite being a significant ceremonial and trading center, Cahokia probably did not have a large permanent population. *Cahokia Mounds State Historic Site/painting by L. K. Townsend.*

Although the Mississippian culture had ties with the earlier Adena and Hopewell cultures, it was more directly influenced by contacts with adventurous traders from Mexico. The Mississippian culture featured fortified cities such as the one at present-day Natchez. These cities contained gigantic pyramids. Unlike the earlier Hopewell centers, these were true cities in that they housed a large residential population.

Farther north, in the Eastern Woodlands, people lived in smaller villages where they combined agriculture with hunting and gathering. The **Iroquois,** for example, lived in towns containing three thousand or more people. They moved their towns when soil fertility, firewood, and game became exhausted. Each town was made up of a group of **longhouses,** which often were more than 60 feet long. Family apartments ranged down both sides of a long central hallway. This hallway was the center of social and political life. In it, babies crawled, children played, men swapped hunting stories, and women cooked and cleaned.

A dominant **matriarch** supervised the daily tasks of running the household. Women occupied places of high social and economic status in Iroquois society. Families were matrilineal, meaning that they traced their descent through the mother's line, and matrilocal, meaning that a man left his home to move in with his wife's family upon marriage. Women distributed the rights to cultivate specific fields and controlled the harvest. Clan matriarchs chose the men who would sit as judges and political council members.

Variations on the Iroquois pattern were typical throughout the Northeast and in the Great Plains and Southwest. Agricultural village life dominated in each region before the arrival of Europeans.

Iroquois Collective name for six Indian tribes that lived in present-day New York State whose cultures and languages were closely related.

longhouse A long communal dwelling, usually built of poles and bark, having a central hallway with family apartments on either side.

matriarch A woman who rules a family, clan, or tribal group.

Migrants into the plains probably came from the East, carrying seed corn from the declining Hopewell settlements. Groups like the Mandans began settling on bluffs overlooking the many streams that fed the Missouri River. By 1300, such villages could be found on every stream from North Dakota to Kansas.

Indians in the Southwest were closely tied to Mexico. Corn appears to have been brought into this region as early as 3,200 years ago. But the Southwestern Indians, unlike their counterparts in Mexico, continued to engage in hunting and gathering for a long time thereafter. Not until about A.D. 400 did the Southwestern Indians begin building larger, more substantial permanent houses.

A drastic climatic change in the eighth century prompted two different responses among the Southwestern Indians. Generally, this new climate was drier, but it also brought violent late-summer thunderstorms that often caused flash floods. One group of Indians, whom later residents called the Anasazi, protected their homes by building dams that channeled runoff through irrigation canals. The cooperative labor required for such projects resulted in much larger communities.

Another Southwestern group, called the Chichimecs, responded to climatic change by moving southward into Mexico. There they built on the declining fortunes of highly urbanized societies, borrowing architectural and agricultural skills from such established city-states as Teotihuacán. The most famous of these Chichimec groups was the Aztecs, who established themselves on a small island in the middle of a lake in the Valley of Mexico in about 1200.

Still another change in climate in the thirteenth century spelled the demise of the Anasazi people. Prolonged droughts and bitterly cold winters forced the Anasazi to abandon their cities and to split into much smaller communities. These smaller communities, which ultimately became the various Pueblo tribes, were able to survive by mixing agriculture, hunting, and gathering.

In the rest of North America, agriculture was practiced only marginally. Areas like the **Great Basin** were too dry for agriculture. In California, the Pacific Northwest, and the **Plateau region,** the bounty of wild food made agriculture unnecessary. The Nez Perces and their neighbors in the Plateau region, for example, moved around from season to season, hunting, fishing, and gathering plants. Although they occupied permanent village sites in the winter, they did not stay together in a single group all year. Members of the village went their separate ways during the rest of the year to fish for salmon or to dig for roots. Political authority in such tribes was based on skills such as salmon fishing, and thus passed from individual to individual on a seasonal basis.

Variations in daily life and social arrangements in **pre-Columbian** North America thus reflected variations in climate, soil conditions, food supplies, and cultural heritage. The only generalization we can make is that pre-Columbian Indians adopted economic strategies, social conventions, and political systems that were well suited to their ecological and historical circumstances.

European Outreach and the Age of Exploration

While the Aztecs were expanding into Mexico, Europeans were feeling a similar restlessness. The **Vikings** extended their holdings throughout many parts of Europe and even into North America. In

Great Basin A desert region of the western United States that includes most of present-day Nevada and parts of Utah, California, Idaho, Wyoming, and Oregon.

Plateau region A region of the United States and Canada bounded on the east by the Rocky Mountains, on the west by the Cascade range of mountains, on the north by the subartic plains, and on the south by the Great Basin.

pre-Columbian Existing in the Americas before the arrival of Columbus.

Vikings Medieval Danish, Swedish, and Norwegian groups, who responded to land shortages in Scandanavia by taking to the sea and establishing communities in western Europe, Iceland, Greenland, and North America.

the **Middle East,** Christian monarchs and church leaders launched a series of **Crusades** to wrest control of the **Holy Land** from the **Muslims.** In the Holy Land, the Crusaders came into contact with fine silks, exotic spices, and precious stones and metals that they had known only through myth and rumor. Subsequently, enterprising individuals began looking for ways to profit by providing Europeans with such luxuries. These movements ultimately led to the establishment of transatlantic ties and the creation of a new world.

Change and Restlessness in the Atlantic World

Around 800, Vikings from the northern frontier of Europe began sweeping down along the continent's western coasts. They captured the British Isles and seized Normandy, a large province in western France. Simultaneously, another group of Vikings pushed south through Russia along Europe's eastern frontier. Eventually they extended their influence all the way to the eastern Mediterranean.

Accomplished seamen, the Vikings also sailed westward, colonizing Iceland, Greenland, and eventually North America. According to Viking sagas, Bjarni Herjolfsson first sighted North America in 986 when he was blown off course during a storm. In about 1000, Viking chieftain Leif Ericson led an expedition to the new land, touching shore at Baffin Island and later at Labrador. During the next few decades, Vikings established several colonies in North America.

Although the Vikings' discovery went unnoticed in Europe, it did have important consequences for Native Americans. As the Vikings were expanding westward, a group of Inuit hunters known as the Thule people was expanding eastward. The Thule Inuits appear to have become middlemen between the Vikings and the subarctic Indians. The Thule people brokered ivory from walrus tusks obtained from other Native Americans for Viking coins and other metal objects. They guarded access to their Indian trading partners jealously and prevented the Vikings from expanding their holdings.

The Vikings were ultimately forced to retreat from North America and Greenland. The most likely cause of their departure was a change in climate known as the Little Ice Age. At some point between 1350 and 1450, temperatures fell worldwide. In the Arctic and the subarctic region, sea ice became a major hazard to navigation. It soon became impossible for the Vikings to practice the herding, farming, and trading that supported their economy in Greenland, and Iceland became the westernmost outpost of the Viking world.

Crusading, Trading, and the Rise of Nation-States

While the Vikings were expanding to the west and to the south, an economic, religious, and political empire controlled by Muslim Arabs, Turks, and **Moors** was taking over Europe's southern and eastern frontiers (see Map 1.2). The Vikings and the Muslims often made life miserable for Europeans but also eventually benefited them. Both groups helped Europeans expand their knowledge and broaden their culture. Europeans became participants in a trading system that extended from Viking outposts in Greenland to Islamic trading posts in India and China.

In 1096, European Christians launched the first of several Crusades designed to sweep the Muslims from their strongholds in the Holy Land in the eastern Mediterranean. The Europeans proclaimed

Middle East The region of the eastern Mediterranean, including modern Turkey, the Persian Gulf area, the Arabian Peninsula, and the Holy Land.

Crusades Military expeditions undertaken by European Christians in the eleventh through the thirteenth centuries to recover the Holy Land from the Muslims.

Holy Land The region in which the events in the Old Testament of the Bible took place; it is sacred to Christians, Jews, and Muslims.

Muslims People who practice the religion of Islam, a monotheistic faith that accepts Mohammed as the chief and last prophet of God.

Moors The Muslim rulers of the Iberian Peninsula.

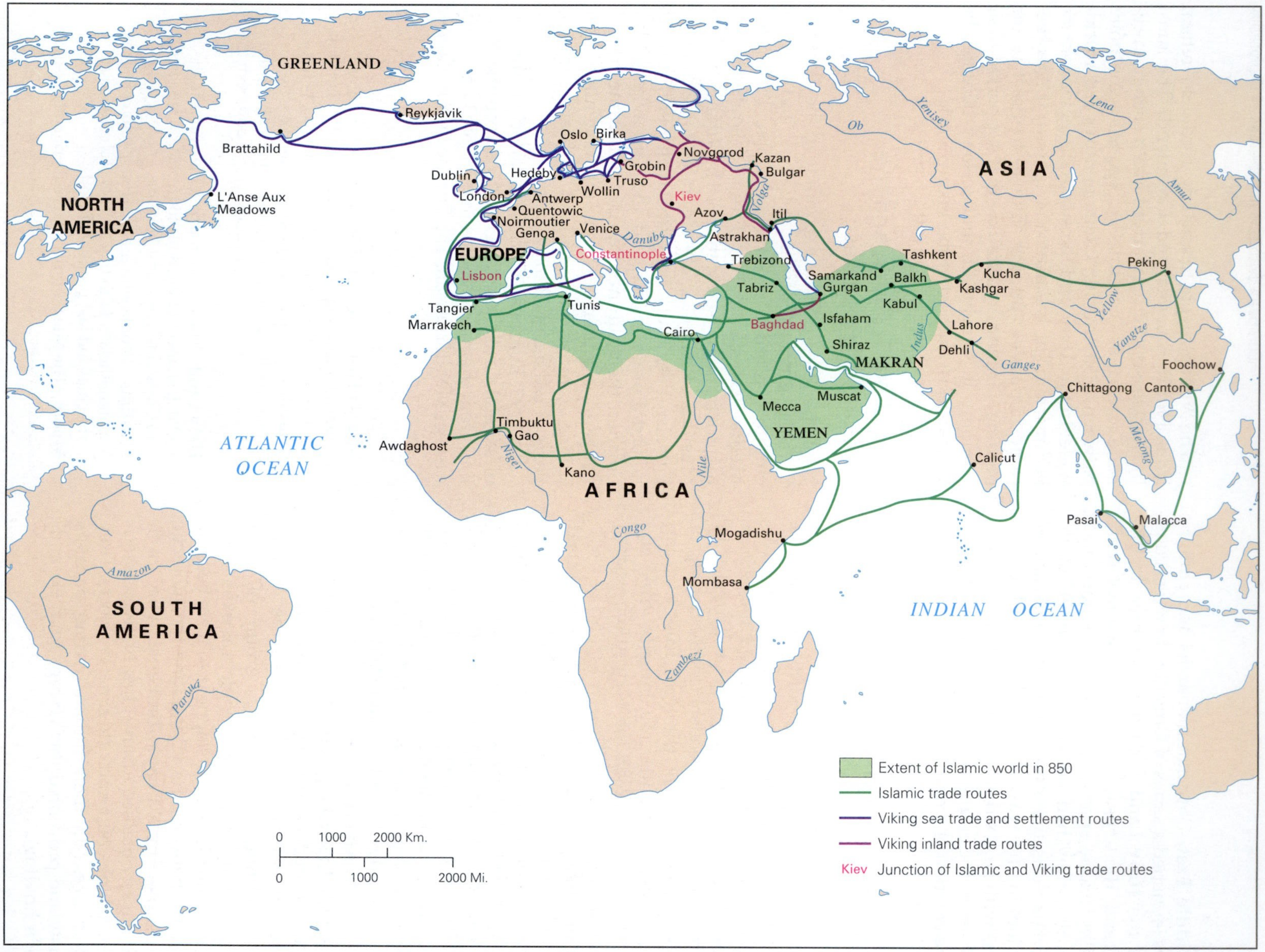

♦ **MAP 1.2 Europe and Its Neighbors,** C. A.D. **1000** Europe was not isolated during medieval times. As shown here, Viking and Islamic empires surrounded Western Europe, and their trade routes crisscrossed the region.

that they were seeking to destroy what they claimed was the false religion of Islam, but they also were hoping to break Islamic control of the eastern and African trade. Over the next two centuries, hordes of Crusaders invaded the area, capturing key points, only to be expelled by Muslim counterattacks. In the process, however, the Europeans gained more knowledge, technical skill, and access to trade. By the time the Crusades ended in 1291, trading families from city-states such as Venice had edged their way into the trade between Europe and the East.

The **Reconquista,** or reconquest of the Muslim-held areas of the Iberian Peninsula by Christian Europeans, began at about the same time as the Crusades. Portugal attained independence from Islamic rule in 1147, and by 1380 Portugal's King John I had united that country's various principalities under his rule. Spanish unification took much longer because feuding local states could not settle their differences. But in 1469, **Ferdinand and Isabella,** heirs to the rival thrones of Aragon and Castile, married and created a united state in Spain. Twenty-three years later, the Spanish subdued the last Islamic stronghold on the peninsula.

Northern European rulers also attempted to create national states in the face of local and regional rivalries. Consolidation finally occurred in France around 1480, when Louis XI took control of five rival provinces to create a unified kingdom. Five years later, Henry Tudor became king of a unified England when he defeated his rivals in the Wars of the Roses.

Portuguese Exploration, Africa, and the Quest for Asia

Portugal, the first of the European national states, was also the first to contest the hold of Italian merchants and their Islamic trading partners on eastern commerce. **Henry the Navigator,** the son of Portugal's John I, took the decisive step by establishing a school of navigation and ordering expeditions to sail west and south to look for new sources of wealth. By the 1430s, the Portuguese had discovered and taken control of the Azores, the Canaries, and Madeira, islands off the western shore of Africa. Within thirty years, Portuguese captains had pushed their way to sub-Saharan Africa, where they came into contact with the **Songhay Empire.**

The Songhay Empire combined various kingdoms along the Niger River. Timbuktu, the Songhay capital, was a cosmopolitan center where African and Islamic influences met. It was a showplace of art, architecture, and scholarship. From Timbuktu, Muslim traders shipped goods across the Sahara by means of caravans. The Portuguese, however, offered speedier shipment and higher profits, carrying trade goods directly to Europe by sea.

By the end of the fifteenth century, Portuguese navigators had gained control over the flow of gold, ivory, and spices out of West Africa, and Portuguese colonizers were growing sugar and other crops on the newly conquered Azores and Canary Islands. Gradually, Portuguese plantation owners borrowed an institution from their former Islamic rulers and their African trading partners: slavery. Slaves had formed a crucial part of Islamic caravans in West Africa since about A.D. 700. From the beginning of the sixteenth century, the Portuguese became increasingly involved in slave trafficking, at first to their own plantations and then to Europe itself. By 1550, Portuguese ships were carrying African slaves throughout the world.

The Portuguese took a major step toward becoming world traders when Bartholomew Dias became the first European to reach the **Cape of Good Hope** at the southern tip of Africa in 1487. Ten

Reconquista The campaign undertaken by European Christians to recapture the Iberian Peninsula from the Muslims.

Ferdinand and Isabella Joint rulers of Spain; their marriage in 1469 created a united Spain from the rival kingdoms of Aragon and Castile.

Henry the Navigator Prince who founded an observatory and school of navigation and directed voyages that helped build Portugal's colonial empire.

Songhay Empire A large empire in West Africa; its capital was Timbuktu; its rulers accepted Islam in about A.D. 1000.

Cape of Good Hope A point of land projecting into the ocean at the southern tip of Africa; European mariners had to sail around the cape to pass from the Atlantic to the Indian Ocean.

♦ Ferdinand and Isabella were the king of Aragon and queen of Castille—the two dominant Christian states in Spain. Their marriage in 1469 created a new nation powerful enough to drive out the Muslims and launch Spain on an expansive new course. Within a hundred years, the kingdom they created became one of the richest and most powerful nations in the world. *ARXIU MAS.*

years later, Vasco de Gama sailed around the cape and launched the Portuguese exploration of eastern Africa and the Indian Ocean.

By the end of the fifteenth century, England, Spain, and France were vying with Portugal for access to the riches of the East. Borrowed technologies from China and the Arab world aided these new competitors. From China, Europeans acquired the magnetic compass, which allowed mariners to know the direction in which they were sailing. An Arab invention, the **astrolabe,** allowed navigators to determine their latitude. These inventions, together with improvements in steering mechanisms and in hull design, improved captains' control over their ships' direction, speed, and stability.

Columbus's Folly

An impoverished but ambitious sailor from the Italian city of Genoa was eager to capitalize on the new technology and knowledge. In 1484, **Christopher Columbus** approached John II of Portugal and asked him to support a risky voyage across the Atlantic. When John's geographers warned that Columbus had probably underestimated the distance of the trip, the king refused to support the enterprise. Undaunted, Columbus peddled his idea to various European governments over the next several years but found no backers. Finally, in 1492, Ferdinand and Isabella's defeat of the remaining Muslim enclave in Spain provided Columbus with an opportunity.

The Spanish monarchs, eager to break the domination of the Italians and their Arab partners in the east and of the Portuguese in the south and west, agreed to equip three ships and granted Columbus 10 percent of any returns from the voyage. On August 3, 1492, Columbus and some ninety sailors departed on the *Niña, Pinta,* and *Santa Maria* for Asia.

After ten weeks at sea, the three ships finally made landfall on a small island on October 12, 1492. Columbus thought he had reached the Indies, but he had really reached the **Bahamas.** Celebrating his escape from disaster, Columbus named the place San Salvador (Holy Savior).

Over the next ten weeks, Columbus sailed around the Caribbean, stopping at Cuba and Hispaniola. He collected spices, coconuts, bits of gold, and some native captives. He called these people

astrolabe An instrument that navigators used to measure the height of the sun and stars and calculate their position of latitude.

Christopher Columbus Italian explorer in the service of Spain who attempted to reach Asia by sailing west from Europe, thereby discovering America in 1492.

Bahamas A group of islands in the Atlantic Ocean east of Florida and Cuba.

"Indians" because he believed that he had reached the Indies. Columbus then returned to Spain and was welcomed home with great celebration. His account of the trip and the goods he brought back helped gain him support for three more voyages. Over the next several decades, the Spanish gained a permanent foothold in the region that Columbus had discovered and became aware that the area was not the Indies or Japan but an entirely new world.

Columbus's discovery opened unprecedented opportunities for Europeans. Taking to heart stories of new lands, new goods, new peoples, and new possibilities for acquiring wealth, kings, sailors, and merchants began eyeing the New World with enormous interest.

A New Transatlantic World

Initially, North America posed more of an obstacle than an opportunity for Europeans. Exploration efforts for several decades after Columbus's landfall aimed at finding a sea route around or through the continent to the riches of the East. Though fruitless, the search for the Northwest Passage led to the gradual charting of the North American coast.

The English were the first to search for an alternate route to India. In 1497, King Henry VII commissioned an Italian mariner, Giovanni Caboto, known to the English as **John Cabot,** to investigate a northern passage. Cabot explored the area that Leif Ericson had colonized five centuries before. Another Italian, **Amerigo Vespucci,** sailing shortly thereafter under a Spanish flag, explored the northeastern coast of South America and the Caribbean. The French entered into the quest in 1524, when they commissioned Giovanni da Verrazzano to chart the Atlantic coast of North America. A decade later, **Jacques Cartier** explored the Canadian coast for the French government. In 1542, he established a short-lived colony near present-day Quebec, primarily to trade for furs.

It was the fish of the Grand Banks, however, that became the first staple of North American commerce. Historians continue to debate when the English, French, and **Basque** fishermen first took advantage of the prolific fishing grounds off the North American coast. Some have argued that they were harvesting cod and mackerel even before Columbus set sail. What is clear is that by the early 1500s, such fishermen were making annual voyages to the Grand Banks and were conducting a lively trade in copper pots, knives, jewelry, and other goods in exchange for Indian ivory, furs, and food. The Micmacs, Hurons, and other northeastern tribes welcomed the newcomers and were eager to trade, in part to gain advantages over their rivals.

The nearly simultaneous arrival of Europeans and the Little Ice Age had several effects. Tribes pressured by the Thule Inuits withdrew to the south, thereby coming into conflict with the Algonquins and Iroquois. Deteriorating corn harvests in turn prompted the Iroquois to expand their holdings. Warfare thus increased among the northeastern tribes. As war became more common, some Indian groups began to form formal alliances for defense. The most prominent of these was the Iroquois Confederacy, organized by a Mohawk leader named Hiawatha in about 1450.

The Challenges of Mutual Discovery

It is usually said that Europeans discovered America, but it is also true that America discovered Europeans. The relationship between Europeans and American Indians ran in two directions. Europeans approached the inhabitants of the New World based on what they already knew. American Indians approached Europeans in the same way. Both

John Cabot Italian explorer who led the English expedition that sailed along the North American mainland in 1497.

Amerigo Vespucci Italian explorer of the South American coast; America was named after him.

Jacques Cartier Frenchman, who in 1534, explored the St. Lawrence River, giving France its primary claim to territories in the New World.

Basques An ethnic group from north central Spain that was heavily involved in early North American fishing activities.

groups had many of their fundamental assumptions challenged. Mutual discovery in America influenced the choices people were to make on a global scale.

A Meeting of Minds in America

Initially, most Europeans were content to fit what they found in the New World with their prior expectations. Columbus expected to find the Indies and Indians, and he believed that was precisely what he had found. Europeans understood only later that America was a new land and that the natives there were a new people.

Europeans were of a divided mind about the people they encountered in America. Columbus's comments about the American Indians set the tone for many of those to follow. "They are so **ingenuous** and free with all they have," Columbus wrote, "that no one would believe it who has not seen it. Of anything that they possess, if it be asked of them, they never say no; on the contrary, they invite you to share it and show as much love as if their hearts went with it, and they are content with whatever trifle be given them, whether it be a thing of value or of petty worth." Such writings led to a perception of the Indians as noble savages, men and women free from the temptations and conceits of modern civilization. Many Europeans praised the Indians' apparent ignorance of private property.

Not all Europeans held this view of American Indians. Amerigo Vespucci shared the opinion that Indians were savage, but he found them less than noble. "They marry as many wives as they please," he explained. "The son cohabits with mother, brother with sister, male cousin with female, and any man with the first woman he meets. . . . Beyond the fact that they have no church, no religion and are not **idolaters,** what more can I say?"

From the European point of view, the native populations lacked "true" religion. But Columbus was optimistic that this lack could be remedied. "I maintain," he wrote to Ferdinand and Isabella, "that if they had access to devout religious persons knowing the language, they would all turn Christian." He added, "It appeared to us that these people were very poor in everything." Thus although Indians were savages, they could be made civilized through European religion and trade.

The arrival of Europeans may have been easier for American Indians to understand than the existence of American Indians was for the Europeans. To Indians, Europeans did not appear to be either superhuman or even particularly strange. Their mode of arrival, manners, speech, and dress no doubt seemed odd, but no odder than the language, behavior, and appearance of traders from the Valley of Mexico. Indians accepted Europeans as simply another new group to be added to the already complex social cosmos.

The Columbian Exchange

Although Europeans and American Indians found some similarities in each other, their natural environments differed greatly. The passage of people, plants, and animals among Europe, Africa, and North America wrought profound changes in all three continents. Historians call this process the **Columbian Exchange.**

Perhaps the most tragic trade among the three continents was in disease. The Indian peoples whom Columbus and other explorers encountered lived in an environment in which contagious diseases that were common in Europe (such as smallpox, measles, and typhus) did not exist. Thus they had no **acquired immunity** to the various bacteria and viruses that Europeans carried. As a result, new diseases spread very rapidly among the native peoples and were much more deadly than they were among Europeans.

ingenuous Lacking in sophistication; artless.

idolater A person who worships idols or false gods.

Columbian Exchange The exchange of people, plants, and animals among Europe, Africa, and North America that occurred after Columbus's discovery of the New World.

acquired immunity Resistance or partial resistance to a disease; it develops in a population over time, after exposure to harmful bacteria and viruses.

Controversy rages over the number of Indians killed by imported European diseases, but most scholars agree that the number was enormous. An estimated 3 million to 10 million people lived in America north of Mexico in 1492. Between 90 and 95 percent of this native population appears to have died of European diseases during the first century of contact.

This exchange of microorganisms created a distinctive pattern of contagion and immunity in North America. American Indians appear to have been less devastated physically by **syphilis,** which may have originated in the Western Hemisphere, than other groups were. Africans were largely unaffected by various **malarial** fevers, transplanted from their home continent, that ravaged both European and native populations. For Europeans mumps was a mild childhood disease, but for Africans and Indians it was a mass killer and left many survivors sterile. The march of exchanged diseases across the North American landscape played an important role in the continent's history.

Less immediate effects arose from the exchange of plants, but the long-term consequences were profound. Asian transplants such as bananas, sugar cane, and rice, which came to America by way of Africa, became **cash crops** on New World plantations, as did cotton, **indigo,** and coffee. Wheat, barley, and millet were readily transplanted to suitable areas in North America. So were grazing grasses and vegetables such as turnips, spinach, and cabbage.

The most important North American plant in the Columbian Exchange was tobacco, a stimulant used widely in North America for ceremonial purposes and broadly adopted by Europeans and Africans as a recreational drug. Another stimulant, cocoa, also enjoyed significant popularity among Old World consumers. New World vegetables helped to revolutionize world food supplies. Maize was remarkably easy to grow and thrived in Europe, the Middle East, and Africa. In addition, the white potato, tomato, manioc, squash, beans, and peas native to the Western Hemisphere were transplanted throughout the world.

The Columbian Exchange also involved animals. Animal populations in North America were very different from those in the Old World. The continent teemed with deer, bison, elk, and moose, but they had to be hunted rather than herded and were useless as draft animals. Europeans brought a full complement of Old World domesticated animals to America. Horses, pigs, cattle, oxen, sheep, goats, and domesticated fowl did well in the new environment.

The exchange of plants and animals altered the natural environments in North America. The transplanting of European grain crops and domesticated animals led to the reshaping of the land itself. Clearing trees, plowing, and fencing changed the flow of water, the distribution of seeds, the nesting of birds, and the movement of native animals. Gradually, imported livestock pushed aside native animals, and imported plants choked out native ones.

Probably the most far-reaching environmental impact of the Columbian Exchange was on human populations. Although exchanged diseases killed many millions of Indians and lesser numbers of Africans and Europeans, the transplantation of animals and plants significantly expanded food production in Europe and Africa. The environmental changes that Europeans caused in eastern North America permitted the region to support many more people than it had under Indian cultivation. The result was a population explosion in Europe and Africa that eventually spilled over to repopulate a devastated North America.

New Worlds in Africa and America

The Columbian Exchange did more than redistribute plants, animals, and populations among Europe, Africa, and North America. It permanently altered the history of both hemispheres.

syphilis An infectious disease usually transmitted through sexual contact; if untreated, it can lead to paralysis and death.

malarial Related to malaria, an infectious disease characterized by chills, fever, and sweating; it is often transmitted through mosquito bites.

cash crop A crop raised in large quantities for sale rather than for local or home consumption.

indigo A plant that yielded a blue dye used for coloring textiles; in the mid-eighteenth century, it was a staple crop in the Lower South.

♦ Parties of captured villagers from Africa's interior were bound together and marched to trading centers on the coast, where they were sold to Europeans or Muslims. The slave drivers were heavily influenced by outside contact. One of those shown here is wearing a Muslim turban, while the clothing of the other is more European. Note, too, that the slave driver carries both a gun and a traditional African spear. *The Granger Collection.*

Imported disease had the most devastating influence on the lives of Indians. Those who escaped epidemics were often faced with a struggle for survival because too few able bodies were left to perform tasks that had been done cooperatively. Wholesale death by disease sometimes wiped out the elders and storytellers who stored the entire practical, religious, and cultural knowledge of these **nonliterate** societies. The result of this loss was confusion and disorientation among survivors.

The devastation wrought by European diseases also made it easier for Europeans to penetrate the North American continent. Such devastation prompted some Indians to seek alliances with the newcomers. Others adopted European tools, which helped make smaller work forces more productive. Still others turned to European religions for spiritual explanations and possible remedies for the hardships they faced. Together, economic and spiritual forces pushed the Indians into an increasingly tangled alliance with Europeans.

The Columbian Exchange also severely disrupted life in Africa. The depopulation of America and the suitability of America for crops such as sugar cane created a huge demand for African slave labor. The Portuguese were well prepared to meet that demand, having taken over much of the African slave trade from North African Muslims in the fifteenth century. They supplied aggressive tribes like the Ashanti with European firearms, thereby enabling coastal tribes to raid deep into the Niger and Congo River regions. These raiders captured millions of prisoners, whom they herded back to the coast and sold to European traders to supply labor for New World mines and plantations.

It is difficult to determine the number of people sold in the West African slave trade from 1500 to 1800. The most recent estimates suggest that over 9.5 million enslaved Africans arrived in the New World during this period. But these estimates do not include the 10 to 20 percent of the slaves who died on ships, those who died on the march to the African coast, and those who remained as slaves in Africa and elsewhere. Africa sacrificed a great deal to the Columbian Exchange.

A New World in Europe

The discovery of America and the Columbian Exchange also had repercussions in Europe. Along with new economic opportunities and foodstuffs, the opening of the Western Hemisphere brought new ideas and demanded new kinds of political and economic organization. The discovery of the New World clearly forced a new and more modern society onto Europeans, and in the process, it produced a sense of crisis.

nonliterate Lacking a system of reading and writing.

Europe's population was already rising when potatoes, maize, and other New World crops began to revolutionize food production. The population of Europe in 1500 was about 81 million. It grew to 100 million by 1600 and 120 million by 1700. This growth occurred despite nearly continuous wars and a flood of thousands of people to the New World each year.

The development of centralized states under leaders such as John I of Portugal, Louis XI of France, Ferdinand and Isabella of Spain, and Henry VII of England appeared to offer the most promising avenue for harnessing the riches of the New World while controlling ever-increasing numbers of people at home. The sons and daughters of these monarchs continued the centralization of authority begun by their parents.

They did so even as traditional sources of authority broke down. Martin Luther, a German monk, dealt a devastating blow to religious authority by preaching that Christians could achieve salvation without the intercession of the Catholic church. Salvation, he said, was God's gift to the faithful. In 1517, Luther attacked the sale of **indulgences** by Catholic priests. He presented ninety-five arguments ("theses") against this practice, maintaining that only individual repentance and the grace of God, not the purchase of a pardon, could save sinners.

Luther's ideas took root among a generation of theologians who were dissatisfied with the corruption that permeated the medieval Catholic church. A Frenchman, John Calvin, further undermined the authority of the Catholic church. Like Luther, Calvin believed that salvation was a gift from God and that God had chosen the souls to be saved and the souls to be damned when he created the world. Calvin likewise concurred that no human actions could alter God's plan. Calvin differed from Luther in calling attention to **the elect,** the small elite God had chosen to save. Although only God knew who was among the saved and who among the damned, Calvin urged Christians to engage in constant meditation, prayer, and scriptural study and to live as though they were among the chosen.

The doctrines of Luther, Calvin, and others who wanted to reform the Catholic church collectively became known as **Protestantism.** Their ideas appealed to a broad audience in the rapidly changing world of the sixteenth century. The new doctrines were most attractive to the middling classes of lawyers, bureaucrats, merchants, and manufacturers, groups that stood to gain from the questioning of entrenched authority. Some in the ruling classes also found the new theology attractive for similar reasons. In Germany, Luther's challenge to the Catholic church led many local princes eager to establish a German national church to question the **divine right** to authority claimed by the ruler of the **Holy Roman Empire.**

Similarly, **Henry VIII** of England found Protestantism convenient when he wanted to divorce his wife. Henry VIII was the first undisputed heir to the English throne in several generations, and he was consumed with the desire to have a son who could inherit the crown. When his wife, Catherine of Aragon, daughter of Ferdinand and Isabella of Spain, failed to bear a boy, Henry demanded in 1527 that Pope Clement VII grant him an annulment of his marriage. Fearful of Spanish reprisals on Catherine's behalf, Clement refused. In desperation, Henry launched the English Reformation by seizing the Catholic church in England. By 1535, he had gained complete control of it.

Henry was not a staunch believer in the views aired by Luther and others. But he reluctantly opened the door to Protestant practices in his newly created Church of England to win the support of

indulgence A pardon issued by the pope absolving the purchaser of a particular sin.

the elect According to Calvinism, the people chosen for God for salvation.

Protestantism The religion and religious beliefs of Christians who accept the Bible as the only source of revelation, believe salvation to be God's gift to the faithful, and believe the faithful can form a direct, personal relationship with God.

divine right The idea that monarchs derive their right to rule directly from God and are accountable only to God.

Holy Roman Empire A political entity authorized by the Catholic church in 1356 unifying Central Europe under an emperor elected by four princes and three Catholic archbishops.

Henry VIII King of England (r. 1509–1547); his desire to divorce his first wife led him to break with Catholicism and establish the Church of England.

Protestants. Henry also seized the extensive and valuable lands that the Catholic church owned in England, thereby adding to his wealth and power.

The Protestants gained substantially during the short reign of Henry's young son Edward VI from 1547 to 1553. When Mary, Edward's oldest sister, succeeded him, however, she attempted to reverse the Protestant tide. The daughter of Henry's first wife, Catherine of Aragon, Mary had married Philip II of Spain and was a devout Catholic. She burned several hundred of the leading reformers at the stake in her effort to suppress Protestantism. Her brutality only drove the movement underground and made it more militant. When Mary died in 1558 and was succeeded by her half sister Elizabeth, who had been raised as a Protestant, militant Protestantism resurfaced. Elizabeth spent much of her long reign attempting to moderate the demands of Protestant reformers. The desire of Protestant **dissenters** to worship freely clashed with her desire to control church and state. This tension between fervent reformers and the Anglican church would significantly affect English settlement in the New World.

dissenters People who do not accept the doctrines of an established or national church.

SUMMARY

E xpectations
C onstraints
C hoices
O utcomes

Making America began perhaps as long as 70,000 years ago, when the continent's first human occupants started adapting to the land. *Expecting* better conditions than they had left behind in Asia, they migrated across Beringia and then overcame or adapted to *constraints* presented by the new environment. Over thousands of years, they continually made *choices* to preserve and enhance their lives. The eventual *outcome* of these *choices* was a rich and flourishing world of different cultures, linked by common religious and economic bonds.

The Atlantic crossing by Europeans presented the natives of America with *constraints* that they had never dreamed of. Disease, then war, and then environmental changes wrought by the Europeans who followed Columbus soon limited the *choices* open to Native Americans.

At the same time, however, Europeans knew full well that American Indians were an important key to making America. Thus Indians exerted a powerful *constraint* on Europeans' freedom of *choice.*

Influences from the New World accelerated processes that were already changing *expectations* and *constraints* in the Old World. Wealth and food from the New World fostered the growth of population, of powerful kings, and of strong nations, but led in turn to continuing conflict over New World resources. In Africa, strong coastal states *chose* to raid weaker neighboring tribes, more than doubling the flow of slaves out of Africa. Meanwhile, as disease destroyed millions of Indians, newcomers came pouring in. These newcomers came from a very different physical environment and brought drastic changes to the face of the land. The *outcome* of these continuing interactions among newcomers, and between them and the survivors of America's original people, would be the making of America.

SUGGESTED READINGS

Becker, Marvin B. *Civility and Society in Western Europe, 1300–1600* (1988).

A brief but comprehensive look at social conditions in Europe during the period leading up to and out of the exploration of the New World.

Crosby, Alfred W. *The Columbian Exchange: Biological and Cultural Consequences of 1492* (1972).

The landmark book that brought the Columbian impact into focus for the first time. Parts of the book are technical, but the explanations are clear and exciting.

Fagan, Brian M. *The Great Journey: The Peopling of Ancient America* (1987).

An excellent recounting of the peopling of North America during the last stages of the Ice Age.

Laslett, Peter. *The World We Have Lost Further Explored* (1983).

Updated third edition of the author's well-respected characterization of British society before colonization. Highly readable and interesting.

McNeill, William H. *Plagues and Peoples* (1976).

A fascinating history of disease and its impact on people throughout the period of European expansion and New World colonization.

Oliver, Roland, and J. D. Fage. *A Short History of Africa* (1988).

The most concise and understandably written comprehensive history of Africa available.

EUROPEANS AND INDIANS IN NORTH AMERICA Although Europeans did not realize immediately that Columbus had encountered an entirely new world in 1492, they quickly came to understand the economic, political, and military potential involved in American colonization. As this map shows, exploration continued into the seventeenth century as Europeans scrambled to claim individual pieces of New World real estate.

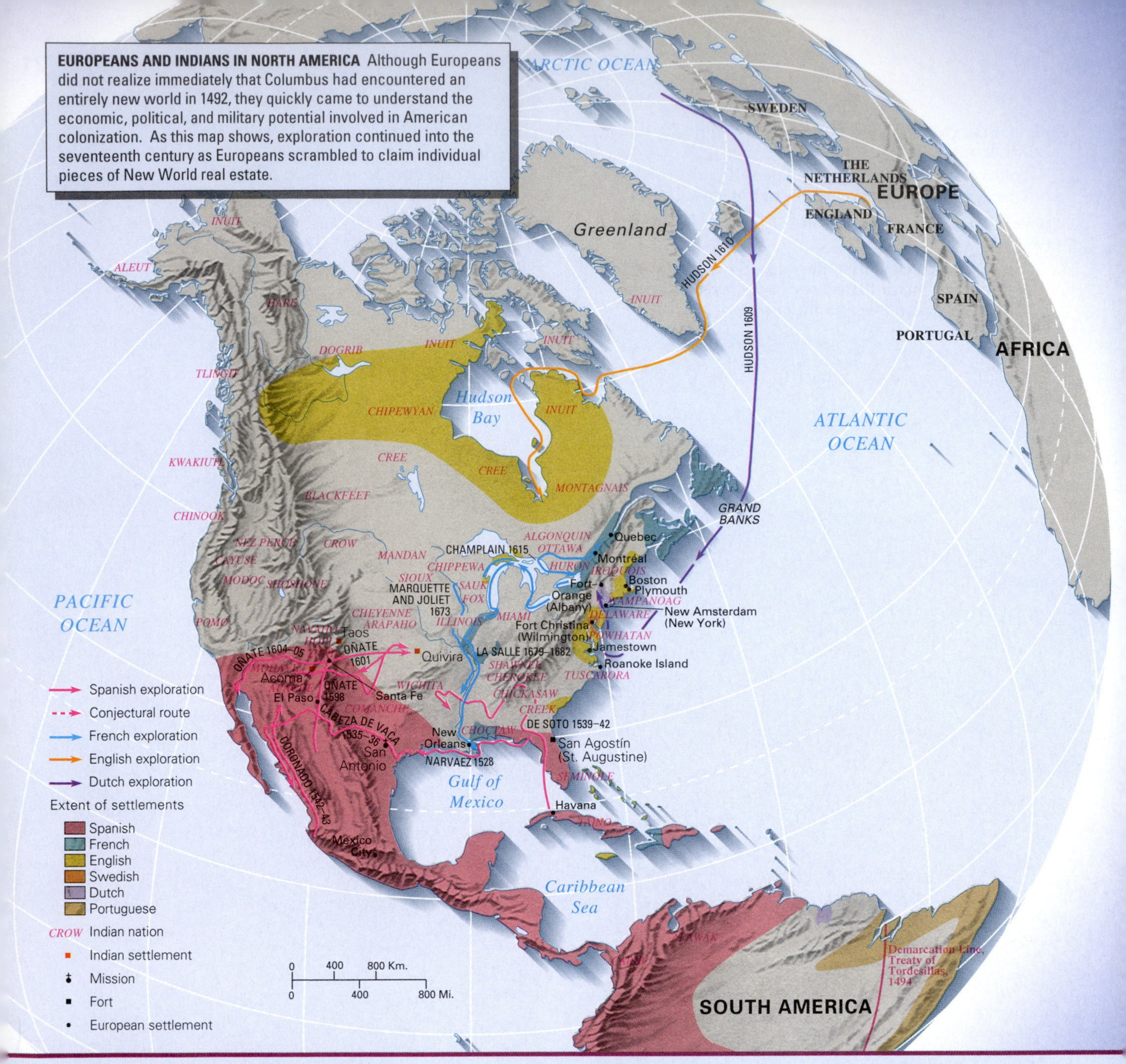

ARCTIC OCEAN
SWEDEN
THE NETHERLANDS
EUROPE
ENGLAND
FRANCE
SPAIN
PORTUGAL
AFRICA
Greenland
HUDSON 1610
HUDSON 1609
ATLANTIC OCEAN
GRAND BANKS
PACIFIC OCEAN
Hudson Bay
INUIT
ALEUT
HARE
DOGRIB
TLINGIT
CHIPEWYAN
CREE
KWAKIUTL
BLACKFEET
MONTAGNAIS
CHINOOK
NEZ PERCE
CROW
CAYUSE
MODOC
SHOSHONE
MANDAN
SIOUX
CHIPPEWA
SAUK
FOX
ALGONQUIN
OTTAWA
HURON
IROQUOIS
WAMPANOAG
DELAWARE
POWHATAN
TUSCARORA
MIAMI
ILLINOIS
CHEYENNE
ARAPAHO
POMO
NAVAHO
HOPI
MOHAVE
COMANCHE
WICHITA
SHAWNEE
CHEROKEE
CHICKASAW
CREEK
CHOCTAW
SEMINOLE
TAINO
CHAMPLAIN 1615
MARQUETTE AND JOLIET 1673
LA SALLE 1679–1682
Quebec
Montreal
Boston
Plymouth
Fort Orange (Albany)
New Amsterdam (New York)
Fort Christina (Wilmington)
Jamestown
Roanoke Island
Taos
OÑATE 1604–05
OÑATE 1601
OÑATE 1598
Quivira
Acoma
El Paso
Santa Fe
CABEZA DE VACA 1535–36
CORONADO 1540–42
San Antonio
New Orleans
NARVAEZ 1528
DE SOTO 1539–42
San Agostín (St. Augustine)
Havana
Gulf of Mexico
Mexico City
Caribbean Sea
SOUTH AMERICA
Demarcation Line, Treaty of Tordesillas, 1494
Spanish exploration
Conjectural route
French exploration
English exploration
Dutch exploration
Extent of settlements
Spanish
French
English
Swedish
Dutch
Portuguese
CROW Indian nation
Indian settlement
Mission
Fort
European settlement
0 400 800 Km.
0 400 800 Mi.

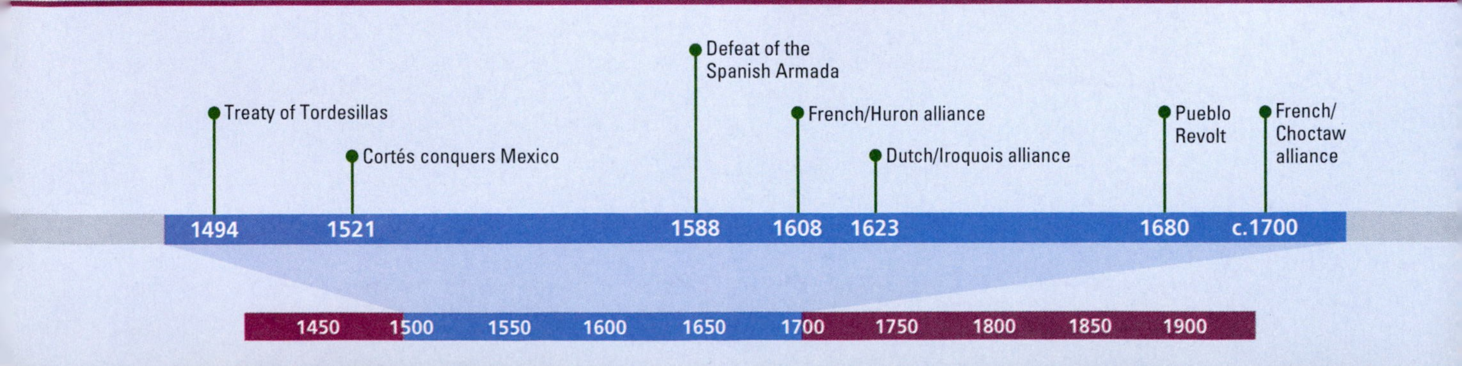

1494 Treaty of Tordesillas
1521 Cortés conquers Mexico
1588 Defeat of the Spanish Armada
1608 French/Huron alliance
1623 Dutch/Iroquois alliance
1680 Pueblo Revolt
c.1700 French/Choctaw alliance
1450 1500 1550 1600 1650 1700 1750 1800 1850 1900

CHAPTER 2

A Continent on the Move, 1400–1725

The New Europe and the Atlantic World

- What were some economic constraints that pushed European rulers to promote exploration and colonization in North America?
- What political and religious rivalries influenced European choices regarding New World colonization?

European Empires in America

- What similarities and differences characterized the choices that Spanish, French, and Dutch officials made in starting their empires in North America?
- What constraints did the choices made by colonists themselves place on administrative policies?

Indians and the European Challenge

- What constraints did environmental changes place on Indians?
- What constraints and opportunities came with the arrival of Europeans?
- What social and political choices did Indians make in response to these changes?

Conquest and Accommodation in a Shared New World

- What constraints most affected the lives of settlers in New Mexico, Louisiana, and New Netherland?
- How did choices made by settlers and American Indians help both groups to deal with these constraints?

INTRODUCTION

Expectations
Constraints
Choices
Outcomes

The European powers that colonized the New World intended to impose their own political, economic, and cultural stamp on the regions they occupied. But they encountered many *constraints.* New World environments did not resemble those in the Old World, and Native Americans had their own agendas for dealing with the newcomers. As the colonizers and the colonized confronted each other and changing conditions, they found themselves making *choices* and witnessing *outcomes* that neither group ever expected.

As Spain's rulers moved in to capitalize on the unexpected return from their investment in Columbus's voyages, they found themselves embroiled in an emerging crisis. Portugal already claimed vast holdings to the west of Europe and feared Spanish competition, making some sort of accommodation necessary. Also, France, Holland, and England were not content to watch Spain and Portugal divide the world between themselves. Stirred by *expectations* of increasing wealth and power, each of the leading European nations launched colonizing enterprises.

Spain capitalized on its lead by sending adventurous military captains on exploring tours throughout the Aztec realm they had conquered and into South America and the unknown frontiers to the north. By 1700, the Spaniards controlled more New World real estate than any other power. Their empire stretched from the tip of South America up through and around the Gulf of Mexico and into the high deserts of the North American Southwest.

France was determined not to be outdone. Following up on the early trading between fishermen and Indians along the Atlantic shore, French explorers moved inland along riverways that teemed with valuable fur-bearing animals and provided a highway for carrying on commerce. Although France's early efforts at establishing large settlements in America's interior were largely unsuccessful, fur hunters continued to trace the continent's rivers. They eventually found and traveled the Mississippi River, giving France a claim to the vast midsection of North America.

Even the recently created nation of the Netherlands got into the colonizing game, establishing a fur-trading station at the mouth of the Hudson River. Radiating outward from there, Dutch fur traders and farmers began to place their own particular stamp on the land.

One *constraint* that all the European nations had to face was the large and powerful presence of Native Americans. Although they were in the midst of a serious historical crisis, Indians continued to make *choices* that influenced North American life profoundly. The Pueblo Indians drove Spain out of New Mexico altogether for a period of time. In New France and New Netherland, different Indian groups seriously endangered European occupation. At all times, Europeans had to be sharply aware of the *constraints* that Indian *expectations* imposed.

The *outcome* of this constant interplay among European traditions, a novel physical environment, and a dynamic Indian presence was a series of new societies across the North American continent. Throughout the colonial era and beyond, these hybrid societies continued to influence historical development and color the life of the people and the nation.

CHRONOLOGY

New World Colonies and American Indians

1494	Treaty of Tordesillas
1512	Creation of the encomienda system
1519–1521	Cortés invades Mexico
1558	Elizabeth I becomes queen of England
1565	Spanish found St. Augustine in present-day Florida
1588	Defeat of the Spanish Armada
1598	Defeat of Ácoma pueblo by Don Juan de Oñate
1608	French/Huron alliance, completing the confederacy encompassing the Great Lakes and St. Lawrence River
1609	Henry Hudson sails up the Hudson River Spanish found the town of Santa Fe in present-day New Mexico
1623	Beginning of Dutch/Iroquois alliance
1626	Dutch lease Manhattan Island
1634	Creation of the French West India Company
1680	Pueblo Revolt
1683	La Salle expedition down the Mississippi River to the Gulf of Mexico
c. 1700	Beginning of French/Choctaw alliance

The New Europe and the Atlantic World

Expansion into the New World aggravated the crisis of authority in Europe. The crisis, however, also helped to promote overseas enterprises. Eager to enlist political allies against Protestant dissenters, popes during this era used land grants in the New World as rewards to faithful monarchs. At the same time, England's Protestant rulers, constantly fearful of being outflanked by Catholic adversaries, promoted the development of a powerful navy and geographical exploration as defensive measures.

The Spanish Empire in America

Spain's Atlantic explorations created a diplomatic crisis with Portugal. In 1493, the pope settled the dispute by drawing a line approximately 300 miles west of Portugal's westernmost holdings in the Atlantic. Spanish exploration was to be confined to areas west of the line (that is, to the New World) and Portuguese activity to the eastern side (to Africa and India). A year later, Spain and Portugal revised the agreement in the **Treaty of Tordesillas,** which moved the line 1,000 miles westward. This revision unwittingly gave Portugal a claim in the New World because part of Brazil bulged across the line. Most of the Western Hemisphere, however, fell to Spain.

With the pope's blessing, Ferdinand and Isabella in 1493 issued Columbus instructions that set the

Treaty of Tordesillas The treaty, signed by Spain and Portugal in 1494, that moved the line separating Spanish and Portuguese territory in the non-Christian world and gave Portugal a claim to Brazil.

tone for Spanish colonization in America. They told him to make the conversion of the natives to Catholicism his first priority. In addition, they authorized Columbus to establish a trading center. He would receive one-eighth of the profits, and the rest would go directly to the Spanish Crown. Ferdinand and Isabella also told Columbus to continue exploring the Caribbean region for "good things, riches, and more secrets."

Although Columbus was a skillful navigator and sailor, he was not a particularly gifted leader. Spanish officials and settlers could never forget that he was a foreigner, and they gave him only grudging loyalty. Only after Columbus was removed from office did Ferdinand and Isabella's vision of missionary outreach and riches begin to materialize.

Hernando Cortés helped to realize that vision. In 1519, he and an army of six hundred Spanish soldiers landed in Mexico. Within three years, Cortés and his small force had conquered the mighty Aztec Empire. Smallpox and other deadly diseases, the Spaniards' armor and guns, and help from numerous native enemies of the Aztecs contributed to this quick and decisive victory. Establishing themselves in Mexico City, the Spanish took over the Aztecs' tributary empire, quickly bringing the Indian groups to the south under their rule.

The Spanish Crown supported many other exploratory ventures. In 1513 and again in 1521, Juan Ponce de León led expeditions to Florida. (For an account of a later expedition to Florida, see Individual Choices: Cabeza de Vaca.) The Spanish sent Hernando de Soto to claim the Mississippi River in 1539. De Soto penetrated into the heart of the mound builders' territory in present-day Louisiana and Mississippi. One year later, Francisco Vásquez de Coronado left Mexico to look for some supposedly very wealthy Indian towns. Coronado crossed what are now New Mexico, Arizona, Colorado, Oklahoma, and Kansas in his unsuccessful quest for these rumored "cities of gold." These explorations were but a few of the ambitious undertakings of Spanish **conquistadors.**

Increasingly, the conquistadors' hunger for riches outstripped the quest for souls or trade. In Bolivia, Colombia, and north-central Mexico, explorers unearthed rich silver deposits. In 1533, **Francisco Pizarro** conquered the **Inca Empire,** an advanced civilization that glittered with gold. Enslaving local Indians to provide labor, Spanish officials moved quickly to rip precious metals out of the ground. Between 1545 and 1660, Indian and African slaves dug over 7 million pounds of silver from these mines—twice the volume of silver held by all of Europe before 1492. In the process, Spain became the richest nation in Europe.

Philip, Elizabeth, and the English Challenge

Spain's early successes in the New World stirred conflict in Europe, particularly with England. Tension between Spain and England had been running high ever since Henry VIII divorced his Spanish wife. That he quit the Catholic church to do so and began permitting Protestant reforms in England deepened the affront. Firmly wedded to the Catholic church, Spain was aggressive in denouncing England. For his part, Henry was concerned primarily with domestic issues and steered away from direct confrontations with Spain.

The Spanish threat could no longer be ignored after Henry VIII's daughter Elizabeth came to the throne in 1558. Relations between Spain and England deteriorated after Elizabeth rejected Philip II's offer of marriage. (The Spanish monarch had been married to Elizabeth's half sister, Mary, a Catholic, who ruled England between 1553 and

Hernando Cortés Spanish soldier and explorer who conquered the Aztecs and claimed Mexico for Spain.

conquistadors Spanish soldiers who conquered the Indian civilizations of Mexico, Central America, and Peru.

Francisco Pizarro Spanish soldier and explorer who conquered the Incas and claimed Peru for Spain.

Inca Empire The Indian civilization, based in present-day Peru, that ruled peoples in the lands from northern Ecuador to central Chile until the Spanish conquest.

1558.) Elizabeth was determined to be her own ruler and to steer England on a Protestant course. That course resulted in a collision when Philip II in 1567 sent an army of twenty thousand soldiers to the Low Countries to crush Protestantism there. To counter Philip's threat just across the English Channel, Elizabeth began providing secret aid to the Dutch Protestants, supporting a revolt against Spanish rule.

She also struck at Philip's New World empire. In 1577, Elizabeth secretly authorized the English **privateer** Francis Drake to attack Spanish ships in the area reserved for Spain under the Treaty of Tordesillas. Drake raided Spanish ships and seized tons of gold and silver during a three-year cruise around the world. Philip demanded that Drake be hanged for piracy, but Elizabeth rewarded the captain on his return in 1580 by knighting him.

The conflict between Elizabeth's England and Philip's Spain escalated during the 1580s. In 1585, Elizabeth incensed the Spanish king by sending an army of six thousand troops across the Channel to aid Dutch rebels. Philip retaliated by supporting a plot within England to have the Catholic Mary Stuart—Mary Queen of Scots—usurp Elizabeth's throne. Elizabeth was outraged when the plot was exposed and executed her cousin for treason. Philip, in turn, was incensed that Elizabeth would behead a legitimate Catholic queen. As tensions increased, so did Drake's piracy. In 1586, Drake not only raided Spanish ships at sea but looted settlements in the New World. By 1586 war between England and Spain loomed on the horizon.

Elizabeth was open to whatever ventures might vex her troublesome brother-in-law. New World colonies promised to do precisely that. Like the rest of Europe, sixteenth-century England was experiencing a population boom that put great stress on traditional economic institutions. Farmland was becoming extremely scarce, and there was a clamor for overseas expansion. The English began eyeing the New World for this purpose.

Thus in 1578, Elizabeth granted her friend and political supporter Sir Humphrey Gilbert permission to found a colony in America. In 1583 he set out with two hundred colonists for what is today Newfoundland. Gilbert and his party were ultimately lost at sea.

Gilbert's vision lived on with his half brother, **Sir Walter Raleigh,** a great favorite of Queen Elizabeth. Petitioned by Raleigh, the queen gladly gave the dashing young man Gilbert's former land grant. To repay her kindness, Raleigh named the proposed colony Virginia, in honor of the unwed queen.

For his initial settlement, Raleigh chose an island off the coast of present-day North Carolina. He advertised **Roanoke Island** as an "American Eden" where the Indians were friendly innocents and "the earth bringeth forth all things in abundance, as in the first Creation, without toile or labour." Encouraged by such rosy promises, 108 settlers sailed to Roanoke in 1585. The venture started out peacefully enough, as the Indians and Europeans labored to understand each other. A dispute over a silver cup, however, led to a series of English raids against Indian villages and an armed confrontation between the two societies. Before the conflict was resolved, trust and friendship had broken down. Thus when Francis Drake visited Roanoke in the late summer of 1586 to warn of a Spanish raid, most of the settlers chose to go back to England with him. Fifteen men remained on the island to protect Raleigh's claim, but none survived.

Despite this loss, Raleigh sent John White, another English courtier, with a new party of settlers in 1587. Remaining only a month, White concluded that his community of ninety-one men, seventeen women, and nine children was safe and well established and set sail for England to get supplies and additional colonists. White's return was delayed considerably by a new threat from Spain.

privateer A captain who owned his own ship and hired his own crew and was authorized by his government to attack and capture enemy ships.

Sir Walter Raleigh English courtier, soldier, and adventurer who attempted to establish the Virginia Colony.

Roanoke Island English colony that Raleigh planted on an island off North Carolina in 1585; the colonists who did not return to England had disappeared without a trace by 1590.

INDIVIDUAL CHOICES

Escape and Exploration

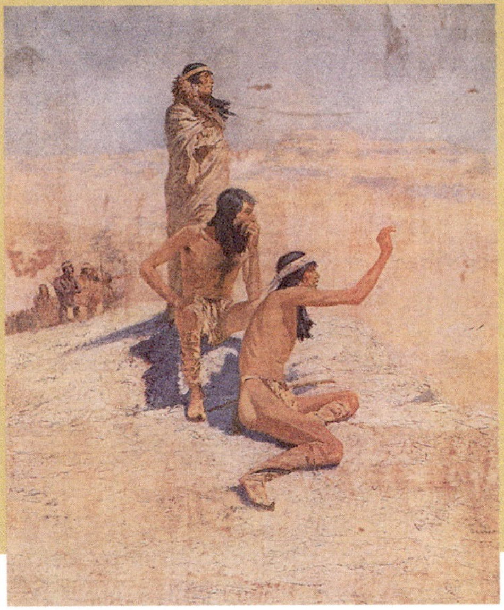

Cabeza de Vaca

Captured by Indians along the Gulf Coast of Spanish Florida, Álvar Núñez Cabeza de Vaca was made a slave. Most of his companions were afraid to resist or run away, but Cabeza de Vaca chose freedom over safety, eventually leading a small party of men all the way back to Mexico. Courtesy of Frederic Remington Art Museum, Ogdensburg, NY.

Ever since leaving Spain in June 1527, Álvar Núñez Cabeza de Vaca had survived one disaster after another. But in November 1528, this heir to a long line of Spanish nobles found himself in a sorrier state than he ever could have imagined: he was a slave belonging to a tribe of Indians along the Gulf Coast of America.

Hardship was nothing new to Núñez. Like so many others in his generation of young nobles, he had chosen a military career and, during this time of intense competition among European powers, had often been in great danger. Early in his career, he had fought in the Battle of Ravenna, in which twenty thousand men were killed, and he had earned a reputation for bravery and good sense under fire. Since that time, he had established such a name for himself that he was made second-in-command of the expedition that was to colonize Florida in 1527. His future appeared bright.

But the expedition seemed cursed from the start. Arriving in the West Indies, the small fleet was hit by a hurricane, and most of the vessels were destroyed. Finally landing somewhere near Tampa Bay in May 1528, the commander, Pánfilo de Narváez, chose to divide his force, leading a small detachment overland in order to explore the country. The unfamiliar and rough terrain along the coast made travel difficult, and the Indians the Spaniards met were not friendly. After a series of running battles, the Spanish expedition was all but wiped out, and the survivors were enslaved by their Indian captors.

Escape seemed impossible. The Indians held the few surviving Spaniards at sites distant from each other, eliminating any chance for them to plan a getaway. And the natives' hostility, combined with the unfamiliar terrain, promised certain death to anyone escaping alone. Most of the Spaniards settled dejectedly into life as servants. But not Núñez. He chose strategy over surrender. He later wrote, "I set to contriving how I might transfer to the forest-dwellers, who looked more propitious [agreeable]." He hit upon the notion of serving as a trader, striving always "to making my traffic profitable so I could get food and good treatment." In this way, he earned a degree of freedom to travel among various tribes, and although he experienced great hardship, he was able to contact other survivors and explore for escape routes.

Núñez served as a traveling trader among the Gulf Coast Indians for six years. He tried to escape, but his masters chased him down and recaptured him. He needed companions, but other survivors fearfully refused to join him. Finally, in 1534, Núñez encountered Andres Dorantes, Alonso del Castillo, and Castillo's black servant, Estevanico. For six months, Núñez pleaded and planned with these three, but only when the Indians announced they were splitting up and taking their Spanish slaves in different directions did the whole company resolve to escape. "Although the season was late and the prickly pears nearly gone, we still hoped to travel a long distance on acorns which we might find in the woods," Núñez recalled.

Having made this fateful choice, Núñez and his companions were forced to see things through. For fourteen months, the four Spaniards traveled from village to village, exchanging their skills as healers for food, clothing, and other necessities. Finally, in the early spring of 1536, the little party overtook a Spanish exploring and slave-raiding company. "They were dumbfounded at the sight of me, strangely undressed and in company with Indians," Núñez reported. "They just stood staring for a long time, not thinking to hail me or come closer to ask questions." Over the next several months, Núñez and his companions rested up and composed a memoir of their experiences, which they presented to the king himself.

The outcome of Núñez's choice to escape was not only his own freedom and that of his companions but a new season of territorial expansion and exploration for Spain. In the course of his travels, he visited places that no other European had ever seen, he saw things that would dazzle those who eventually followed his course, and he heard about treasure that prompted generations of Spaniards and others to search for gold, silver, and other riches in the deserts of the American Southwest. Núñez's stories of vast amounts of gold, silver, and precious gems located just to the north of Spain's New World frontier captured the imagination of a new generation of conquistadors and stirred enormous new interests in America's interior.

Spain's Crisis and England's Opportunity

Each New World claim asserted by England, France, or some other country represented the loss of a piece of treasure that Spain considered necessary for its continued survival. Philip finally undertook a gamble designed to remove the Protestant threat, rid him of Elizabeth's vexing harassment, and demonstrate to the rest of Europe that Spain intended to exercise absolute authority over the Atlantic world. In the spring of 1585, Philip decided to invade England.

He began massing the largest marine force the world had ever witnessed. Finally in the spring of 1588 he launched an **armada** of 132 warships carrying over 3,000 cannons and an invasion force of 30,000 men. Arriving off England in July, the Spanish Armada ran up against small, maneuverable English ships commanded by Elizabeth's pirate captains. Drake and his fleet seriously crippled the sluggish Spanish fleet. Then a fierce storm scattered the remaining Spanish ships and destroyed Philip's chance to end English advances into his New World realm. Although Spanish power remained great, the Armada disaster ended Spain's near monopoly over New World colonization.

John White returned to Roanoke in 1590, only to find the colony abandoned. The only clue to what had happened was the word "Croatoan" carved on a doorpost. The Croatoan Indians lived on a neighboring island. The carving led to speculation that the colonists had either gone to live with this tribe or had been attacked by them. Neither theory has ever been confirmed. White returned to England, but found that Raleigh's fortune had been exhausted. Only after Elizabeth's death in 1603 did Englishmen return to carry out Raleigh's dream of an English empire in the New World.

European Empires in America

In the seventeenth and eighteenth centuries, Spain, France, England, and a number of other European nations vied for control of the Americas and for domination of transatlantic trade. By the time England became deeply involved in New World ventures, Spain, France, and Holland had already made major progress toward establishing empires in America. These European settlements not only affected England's colonization process profoundly, but through their interactions among themselves and with the Native Americans, they also created unique societies in North America whose presence influenced the entire course of the continent's history.

The Troubled Spanish Colonial Empire

Although the destruction of the Armada in 1588 struck a terrible blow at Spain's military power, the Spanish Empire continued to grow. By the end of the seventeenth century, it stretched from New Mexico southward through Central America and much of South America into the Caribbean islands and northward again into Florida. Governing such a vast empire was difficult. Two agencies in Spain, the House of Trade and the Council of the Indies, set Spanish colonial policy. In the colonies, Crown-appointed viceroys wielded military and political power in each of the four divisions of the empire. The Spanish colonies had local governments as well, and each town had a ***cabildo secular,*** a municipal council, as well as judges and other minor officials. The colonial administrators were appointed rather than elected; most came from Spain.

Over the centuries, as the layers of bureaucracy developed, corruption and inefficiency developed too. The Spanish government made efforts to regulate colonial affairs, sending *visitadores* to inspect local government operations. Despite these safeguards, colonial officials ignored their written instructions and failed to enforce laws.

One major source of corruption was a persistent shortage of labor. The Spanish adapted their traditional institutions to address the demand for work-

armada A fleet of warships.

cabildo secular Secular municipal council that provided local government in Spain's New World empire.

ers in mines and on plantations. In Spain, **feudal** landlords, called *encomenderos,* were entitled by their military service to the king to harness the labor of peasants. In New Spain, Indians took the place of the peasants in what was called the **encomienda system.** Under a law passed in 1512, administrators gave to the Spanish colonists Indian workers, who were required to labor for nine months each year. The *encomendero* paid a tax to the Crown for each Indian he received and agreed to teach his workers the Catholic faith, Spanish language and culture, and a "civilized" vocation.

Such workers came from among Indians who peacefully acknowledged Spanish rule. For Indians who did not, a completely different labor system prevailed. Under Spanish law, any Indian who resisted Spanish rule "had no rights save such as the conqueror might freely choose to concede to them." Thus any Indian rebels who survived an uprising against Spanish authority could be put to death or enslaved.

As a result of church pressure, the Spanish government issued a law that required the conquistadors to explain to Indians the obligations they owed to the Spanish king and to the Catholic church, and to offer to absorb them peacefully if they would acknowledge those obligations. Thereafter, all conquistadors had to take with them a priest who would certify that they had read (in Spanish, of course) a document called the **Requerimiento** to each Indian group they encountered. Indians who acknowledged the king's authority were to receive the "protection" of the encomienda system. Those who did not could be enslaved.

Colonists and conquistadors often ignored even these slim protections. Conquistadors frequently stood outside an Indian village, read the Requerimiento in a whisper, and then attacked when the community made no immediate response. Some simply forged a priest's signature, anticipating that by the time the document reached administrators in faraway Madrid, no one would know the difference. Others ignored the law altogether.

As such behavior demonstrates, a degree of tension always existed between New Spain and old. Bureaucratic and church interference in the labor system was one source of tension. Taxes were another. Spanish colonists were taxed to support the huge and largely corrupt, unrepresentative, and self-serving imperial bureaucracy. But for many decades, the wealth produced within this empire overshadowed all governing problems. The gold, silver, and copper mined by Indian and later by African slaves satisfied the Spanish government until the end of the seventeenth century.

The French Presence in America

If the Spanish overgoverned their New World provinces, the French may have erred in the opposite direction. Despite the long existence of the fur trade in Canada, French colonial authorities at first took little interest in it. **Samuel de Champlain,** the "father of **New France,**" established trading posts in Nova Scotia and elsewhere, founded the city of Quebec, and in 1608 formed an enduring alliance with the Huron Indians. But officials in France did little to capitalize on the achievements of Champlain and other enterprising individuals.

In 1627, the king awarded a group of his favorites a charter to develop resources in New France. The resulting Company of One Hundred Associates failed for several reasons. Few French

feudal Relating to a system in which landowners held broad powers over peasants or tenant farmers in exchange for their loyalty and for protection from abuse by others.

encomienda system A system of bonded labor in which Indians were assigned to Spanish plantation and mine owners in exchange for the payment of a tax and an agreement to "civilize" and convert them to Catholicism.

Requerimiento A statement delivered in Spanish explaining the obligations of Indian people to the king of Spain and to the church and requiring their cooperation; Indians who failed to accept the statement could be killed or enslaved.

Samuel de Champlain French explorer who traced the St. Lawrence River inland to the Great Lakes, founded the city of Quebec, and formed the French alliance with the Huron Indians.

New France The colony established by France in what is now Canada and the Great Lakes region of the United States.

Catholics showed any interest in migrating to New France. French Protestants, who might have emigrated to avoid religious persecution, were forbidden to move to the colony. Thus the Company of One Hundred Associates did not attract enough rent-paying tenants to make the envisioned estates profitable. Equally important, the few French peasants and small farmers who did venture to the New World found life in the woods preferable to life as tenant farmers. So-called ***coureurs de bois,*** or "runners of the woods," married Indian women and lived among the tribes, returning to the French settlements only when they had enough furs to sell to make the trip worthwhile. Because of their activity, the fur trade gradually came to dominate French Canada's culture and economy.

Frustrated by the lack of profits from the Company of One Hundred Associates, the king revoked its charter in 1633 and in the following year created the **French West India Company.** This company became quite profitable by focusing on the fur trade. Setting up posts in Quebec, Montreal, and some more remote locations, the French West India Company became the primary outfitter of and buyer from the coureurs de bois.

Local officials exercised considerable control over colonial affairs in New France. The governor of New France was in charge of Indian matters and military decisions. An ***intendant*** directed the judicial and commercial affairs of the colony, and a Catholic bishop supervised religious affairs. Colonists had no representative assembly, although the governor did call on colonists for their opinion when he wished.

Only after 1663 did the French Crown begin to intervene seriously in Canadian affairs. In that year, the king revoked the French West India Company's charter and took direct control of New France. While the king continued to reap enormous profits from the fur trade, his interests ranged beyond this single source of income. In 1673, a French expedition led by Louis Joliet and Jacques Marquette set out to explore the riverways that had long been the domain of the Indians and the coureurs de bois. Leaving Green Bay on Lake Michigan, Marquette and Joliet eventually located the Fox and Wisconsin rivers and from there traced the origins of the Mississippi. Although they did not follow the great river all the way to its mouth, they speculated, correctly, that it led to the Gulf of Mexico.

An ambitious French nobleman, **Robert Cavelier, Sieur de La Salle,** recognized the strategic and economic promise in Joliet and Marquette's discovery. In 1683, he and a party of French coureurs de bois and Indians followed the Mississippi all the way to the Gulf of Mexico. La Salle immediately claimed the new territory for Louis XIV of France, naming it **Louisiana** in his honor. In 1698, the king sent settlers to the lower Mississippi valley under the leadership of Pierre LeMoyne d'Iberville. In 1718, French authorities built the city of New Orleans to serve as the capital of the new territory.

The acquisition of Louisiana was a major accomplishment for France. The newly discovered riverway gave the French a rich, unexploited source of furs as well as a warm-water port. But perhaps of greatest importance was Louisiana's strategic location between Spain's claims in the Southwest and England's colonies along the eastern seaboard. Controlling this piece of real estate gave Louis a valuable bargaining chip.

The Dutch Enterprise

Another source of competition to Spain's New World monopoly came from a former colony of Spain: the Netherlands. The Armada disaster tipped the scales in favor of Dutch Protestant

coureurs de bois Independent French fur traders who lived among the Indians and sold furs to the French; literally, "runners of the woods."

French West India Company Company of investors that became profitable by ignoring royal orders and engaging in the fur trade in Canada.

intendant A French government official who directed colonial judicial and commercial affairs.

Robert Cavelier, Sieur de La Salle French explorer who followed the Mississippi River from its origin in present-day Illinois to the Gulf of Mexico in 1683, giving France a claim to the entire riverway and adjoining territory.

Louisiana French colony south of New France, it included the entire area drained by the Mississippi River and all its tributary rivers.

♦ New Amsterdam's location at the mouth of the Hudson River made the Dutch settlement a particularly important colonial trading center. Furs flowed down the river from Fort Orange (near modern Albany, New York), while guns, tools, and other trade goods traveled the other way. Both river and sea traffic were central to the city's existence, as shown in this 1679 painting of the Dutch statehouse, which stood overlooking the harbor. *Prints Collection, Miriam and Ira D. Wallach Division of Art, Prints and Photography. The New York Public Library, Astor, Lenox, and Tilden Foundation.*

rebels in 1588, and the newly independent nation quickly developed a thriving commercial economy. Dutch privateers outshone Queen Elizabeth's in the profitable raiding of Spanish and Portuguese treasure ships, and by the 1630s the Dutch dominated the African slave trade. In 1634, Dutch forces overcame weak Spanish and Portuguese resistance, conquering a number of islands in the Caribbean. Holland's next goal was to establish an empire on the North American mainland.

Henry Hudson established Holland's first serious claim to American territory in 1609, when he explored the east coast in search for the Northwest Passage. He sailed up a large river that he hoped would lead him west to the Pacific. After realizing that he had not found the hoped-for Northwest Passage, he returned to Holland and reported that the Hudson valley was very pleasant country. But the region attracted little immediate attention.

In 1621, the **Dutch West India Company** was formed for planting colonies on mainland America. The company's director, Peter Minuit, negotiated a lease for the entire island of Manhattan from the Manhates Indians in 1626. For three more years, the company did nothing to attract settlers.

But in 1629, the Dutch West India Company drew up a comprehensive plan to maximize profits and minimize dependence on local Indians for food and other support. To encourage the agricultural development necessary to support the fur industry, the company offered huge estates called **patroonships** to any company stockholder willing and able to bring fifty colonists to **New Netherland** at his own expense. The patroons would enjoy broad powers over their tenants. However, few prosperous Dutchmen were interested in becoming New World pioneers. Rensselaerswyck, the estate of Kilian Van Rensselaer, was the only patroonship to develop in accordance with the company's plan.

Settlers seeking land did come on their own. At first, people from just about anywhere were welcome in New Netherland, including German and

Henry Hudson Dutch ship captain and explorer who sailed up the Hudson River in 1609, giving the Netherlands a claim to the area now occupied by New York.

Dutch West India Company Dutch investment company formed in 1621 to develop colonies in North America.

patroonship A huge grant of land given to any Dutchman who, at his own expense, brought fifty colonists to New Netherland; the colonists became the tenants of the estate owner.

New Netherland The name of the colony founded by the Dutch West India Company in present-day New York; its capital was New Amsterdam on Manhattan Island.

♦ **MAP 2.1 Indian Economies in North America** Indian economic activities helped to shape patterns of European settlement and investment in the New World. Regions that were primarily agricultural, like the Atlantic shoreline, lent themselves to European farming activities. Farther north and west, however, where hunting played a more prominent role in native life, the fur trade was a more attractive investment for European settlers.

French Protestants, free and enslaved Africans, Catholics, Jews, and Muslims. In 1638, four hundred Swedish immigrants gained financial support and political blessings from the Dutch company to establish a colony called **New Sweden** within the boundaries of New Netherland along the Delaware River. For about seventeen years, New Sweden existed peacefully and independently as a fur-trading community. By 1655, however, the Swedes had become so successful as fur traders that they aroused the jealousy of New Netherland governor Peter

New Sweden Swedish fur-trading community established with the assistance of the Dutch on the Delaware River in 1638 and absorbed by New Netherland in 1655.

Stuyvesant. He sent a militia force larger than the entire Swedish population to demand their submission. The Swedes had little choice but to agree.

Indians and the European Challenge

Native Americans did not sit idly by while the European powers carved out empires in North America. Some joined the newcomers, serving as advisers and companions. Others sought to use the Europeans as allies to accomplish their own economic, diplomatic, or military goals (see Map 2.1). Still others, overwhelmed by the onset of European diseases, withdrew into the interior. The changes in native America created both obstacles and opportunities, giving shape to the patterns of expansion and conflict that characterized the colonial world.

The Indian Frontier in New Spain

Indian assistance had been critical in Spain's successful military campaigns throughout the Americas. In Mexico, for example, groups who had been forced to pay tribute to the Aztec Empire gladly allied themselves with the Spanish to win their independence. Their hopes were soon dashed when the Spanish simply replaced the Aztecs as the new lords of a tributary empire.

A similar pattern occurred wherever the Spanish went in North America. The rumors of great wealth that spread after Cabeza de Vaca's adventure pulled conquistadors northward. The Spanish repeatedly encountered new Indian populations, read the Requerimiento, and placed the Indians under Spanish rule as either **serfs** or slaves.

Spanish expansion met little native resistance until 1598, when a particularly brutal conquistador named **Don Juan de Oñate** led a large expedition to the Rio Grande region of New Mexico. Many of the Pueblo people soon found themselves subjected to Spanish and Catholic authority. Some, however, resisted Oñate's efforts to force Spanish culture and religion onto them. The conquistador chose to make an example of the **Ácoma pueblo.** It took Oñate's troops three days to subdue the settlement. When the battle was over, Oñate ordered eight hundred Indians executed and made slaves of the nearly seven hundred remaining survivors, mostly women and children. In addition, each male survivor over the age of 25 had one foot chopped off to prevent his escape from slavery.

Despite Oñate's excesses, New Mexico remained relatively peaceful for nearly a century. Then, in 1680, the Pueblo Indians rebelled against Spanish attempts to destroy their native religion. Led by a religious prophet named Popé, the **Pueblo Revolt** left 400 Spaniards dead. The rebels captured **Santa Fe** and drove the surviving Spaniards from the land. The Spanish needed more than a decade to regroup sufficiently to reinvade New Mexico and recapture the territory.

Elsewhere along the northern frontier of New Spain, the unsettled nature of Indian life and the arid and uninviting character of the land made settlement unappealing to the Spaniards. Efforts at mining, raising livestock, and missionizing in Arizona and Texas were largely unsuccessful until after 1700.

The Indian World in the Southeast

Members of Spanish exploring expeditions under would-be conquistadors like Ponce de León and de Soto were the first Europeans to contact the mound builder societies and other Indian groups in the

serfs Peasants who were bound to a particular estate but, unlike slaves, were not the personal property of the estate owner and received traditional feudal protections.

Don Juan de Oñate Spaniard who conquered New Mexico and claimed it for Spain in the 1590s.

Ácoma pueblo Pueblo Indian community that resisted Spanish authority in 1598 and was destroyed by the Spanish.

Pueblo Revolt Indian rebellion against Spanish authority in 1680 led by Popé; succeeded in driving the Spanish out of New Mexico for nearly a decade.

Santa Fe Spanish colonial town established in 1609; eventually the capital of the province of New Mexico.

Southeast. Although their great cities impressed the Spaniards, the Cherokees, Creeks, and other agricultural groups had no gold and could not be enslaved easily. The conquistadors moved on without attempting to impose Spanish rule or the Catholic religion on these peoples. Given sufficient incentive, however, the Spanish were quick to strike at Indian independence and culture.

In Florida, for example, the need to protect Spanish ships from English and other raiders led Spain to establish garrisons like **St. Augustine,** founded in 1565. Using these military posts as staging areas, Jesuit and Franciscan missionaries ranged outward to bring Catholicism to Indians in the region. By 1600, they had established missions from the Gulf coast of Florida all the way to Georgia.

Although the Spanish presence in the region was small, its impact was enormous. The Spanish introduced European diseases into the densely populated towns in the Mississippi River region. Epidemics wiped out entire Native American civilizations and forced survivors to abandon their cities and entirely modify their ways of life.

Epidemic diseases forced the Cherokees, Creeks, and other groups to abandon city life in favor of a village-based economy that combined agriculture, hunting, and gathering. The consequences in the Southeast were similar to those in the Northeast; warfare became increasingly common. Groups became more inclined to join in formal alliances for mutual support. And when new Europeans arrived in the seventeenth and eighteenth centuries, Indians found it beneficial to welcome them as trading partners and allies.

For example, the **Creek Confederacy,** a union of many groups who had survived the Spanish epidemics, played a careful diplomatic game. The confederacy balanced the competing demands of the Spanish and French, and later the English, taking as much advantage as possible of the competition among the European powers.

The Indian World in the Northeast

By the time Europeans had begun serious exploration and settlement of the Northeast, the economic and cultural changes among Indians that had begun between 1350 and 1450 had resulted in the creation of two massive alliance systems. On one side were the Hurons, Algonquins, Abenakis, Micmacs, Ottawas, and several smaller tribes. On the other was the Iroquois Confederacy.

The costs and benefits of sustained European contact first fell to the Hurons and their allies. The Abenakis, Micmacs, and others who lived along the northern shore of the Atlantic were the first groups drawn into trade with French and other fishermen. As the coureurs du bois pushed farther into Indian territory, these were the Native American groups they met in the woods and with whom they settled and intermarried. These family ties became firm economic bonds when formal French exploration brought these groups into more direct contact with the European trading world.

The strong alliance between these Indians and the French posed a serious threat to Iroquois plans for expansion. The arrival of the Dutch in the Albany area, however, offered the Iroquois an attractive diplomatic opportunity. In 1623, the Dutch West India Company invited representatives from the Iroquois Confederacy to a meeting at **Fort Orange,** offering them friendship and trade. The Iroquois responded enthusiastically but sought to dominate this trade by imposing their authority over all of the Indian groups already trading with the Dutch. They began a bloody war with the **Mohicans,** who had been the Dutch traders' main source for furs in the Hudson valley. By 1627, the Iroquois had driven the Mohicans away from the river and had taken control over the flow of furs.

Recognizing the value of a powerful alliance, the Dutch abandoned a long-standing policy of

St. Augustine First colonial city in the present-day United States; located in Florida and founded by Pedro Menéndez de Aviles for Spain in 1565.

Creek Confederacy Confederacy of Indians living in the Southeast; formed after the spread of European diseases to permit a cooperative economic and military system among survivors.

Fort Orange Dutch trading post established near present-day Albany, New York, in 1614.

Mohicans Algonkian-speaking Indians who lived along the Hudson River. They were dispossessed in a war with the Iroquois Confederacy, and eventually were all but exterminated.

♦ Alfred Jacob Miller based this 1837 painting of eighteenth-century mounted buffalo hunters on interviews with Shoshone Indians he met on a trip through the American West. It illustrates the enormous impact the arrival of horses had on Plains Indian life. Note how few mounted men it took to drive vast numbers of animals over a cliff to their deaths. The meat, bones, and hides that would be taken from the butchered bison would provide food, clothing, tools, tents, and trade goods sufficient to support an entire band of Indians for some time. The arrival of the horse on the plains in the late 1600s marked the beginning of 150 years of unprecedented wealth and power for the Indians in the region. *Alfred Jacob Miller, Walter's Art Gallery, Baltimore.*

neutrality in Indian wars and a prohibition against the sale of guns to the natives. Throughout the 1630s, guns flowed up the Hudson and into the hands of the Mohawks and other Iroquois tribes, while furs from northern and western New York flowed down to Manhattan.

The Iroquois soon wiped out fur supplies in their own territory and began an even more serious push to acquire new lands. Beginning in the late 1630s, the Iroquois Confederacy entered into a long-term war against the Hurons and their allies in New France; against the Munsees, Delawares, and other groups in the Susquehanna and Delaware river valleys to the south; and even against the Iroquois-speaking Eries to the west.

Through it all, the Dutch maintained a pro-Iroquois policy. Following the massacre of a Mohican party by a joint Dutch/Mohawk force in 1643, non-Iroquois Indians living along the lower Hudson valley finally became disgusted with Dutch policies. They raided outlying Dutch settlements and maintained a light siege on Manhattan itself. The Dutch responded with a winter campaign, staging surprise attacks against Indian settlements, burning houses and food stores, killing those who resisted, and capturing and enslaving those who did not. By the spring of 1644, Indian resistance was broken.

The New Indian World of the Plains

Though largely unexplored and untouched by Europeans, the vast area of the Great Plains also underwent profound change during the period of initial contacts. Climate change, the pressure of shifting populations, and the introduction of novel European goods created an altogether new culture and economy among the Indians in this region.

Before about 1400, Indians living on the plains rarely strayed far from the riverways that form the Missouri River drainage. The climate change that affected their neighbors to the east had a similar effect on them: growing seasons became shorter, and the need to hunt became greater. But this climatic force that undermined their existing way of life provided an attractive alternative as well: buffalo.

The **buffalo,** or American bison, is particularly well adapted to survival in cold climates. Unlike European cattle, which often starve when snow buries the grasses on which they graze, buffalo use their hooves to dig out the grass they need. Although buffalo were always a presence on the plains, the cold weather during the Little Ice Age spurred a massive increase in their numbers. Between 1300 and 1800, herds numbering in the millions roamed the new environment created by the climate change.

The Wichitas, Pawnees, and Arikaras virtually abandoned their agricultural villages and became hunters. The Hidatsas split into factions: those called Hidatsas remained in their villages, and those called Crows went off to the grasslands to hunt. The Mandans and several other groups remained in their villages and established a thriving trade with hunters like the Arikaras.

The increase in buffalo not only provided an attractive resource for the Indians already on the Great Plains but also drew new groups to the area. As the climate farther north became unbearably severe, the **Blackfeet** and other Indians swept down from the subarctic northeast to hunt on the plains. Other Algonkian-speaking Indians, such as the Gros Ventres, Cheyennes, and Arapahos, soon followed.

As the climate change affected the Northeast and groups like the Hurons and Iroquois expanded their territories, many other groups chose to flee rather than fight or be absorbed by the warring confederacies. These pressures became even more severe as the coureurs du bois carried the fur trade farther west. Experiencing such pressure, groups like the **Lakotas** moved into the plains to hunt but maintained trading relations with their **Dakota** neighbors in Minnesota, who continued to farm and harvest wild rice and other crops.

The buffalo also began to play an important role on the southern plains. The Apaches, Comanches, and Kiowas specialized in hunting the ever-increasing herds and then exchanging part of their take for village-based products from their neighbors and kinsmen the Navajos, Hopis, and Pueblos.

Although buffalo hunting was attractive to many of the groups displaced by climate change and population pressure, at first the life of a hunter was extremely difficult. Lacking any draft animals larger than dogs, early plains hunters had to travel light and on foot. That changed after the Pueblo Revolt in New Mexico in 1680.

One unintentional outcome of the Pueblo Revolt was the liberation of thousands of Spanish horses. The Pueblos had little use for these animals, but the Kiowas and Comanches quickly put the animals to use. Horses could move much larger loads than dogs and could survive on a diet of grass rather than taking a share of the meat. In less than a generation, horses became a mainstay of the buffalo-hunting culture on the southern plains. From there, horses spread quickly to other hunting peoples.

Northern plains dwellers like the Shoshones quickly began acquiring horses from their southwestern kinsmen and trading partners. Following a northward path along the eastern flank of the Rocky Mountains, horses were passed from one group to another. Well adapted to grasslands and virtually free from natural predators or diseases, horses greatly increased in number. By 1730, virtually all of the plains hunting peoples had some horses and were clamoring for more.

The continual demand for horses and the need for space in which to hunt created a new dynamic on the Great Plains (see Map 2.2). After the Spanish reconquest of New Mexico, Indians could obtain horses only through warfare and trade, and both increased significantly. Surprise raids to steal horses from neighboring Indian groups and European settlements brought both honor and wealth to those who were successful. As groups raided back and forth, human captives also became valuable prizes. In exchange for horses, human cap-

buffalo The American bison, a large member of the ox family, native to North America and the staple of the Plains Indian economy between the fifteenth and mid-nineteenth centuries.

Blackfeet Algonkian-speaking Indians from the Canadian subarctic who moved onto the Great Plains in the sixteenth century.

Lakotas/Dakotas Collectively the Sioux Nation; Lakotas were the western branch, living mostly on the Great Plains, and Dakotas were the eastern branch, living mostly in the prairie and lakes region of the Upper Midwest.

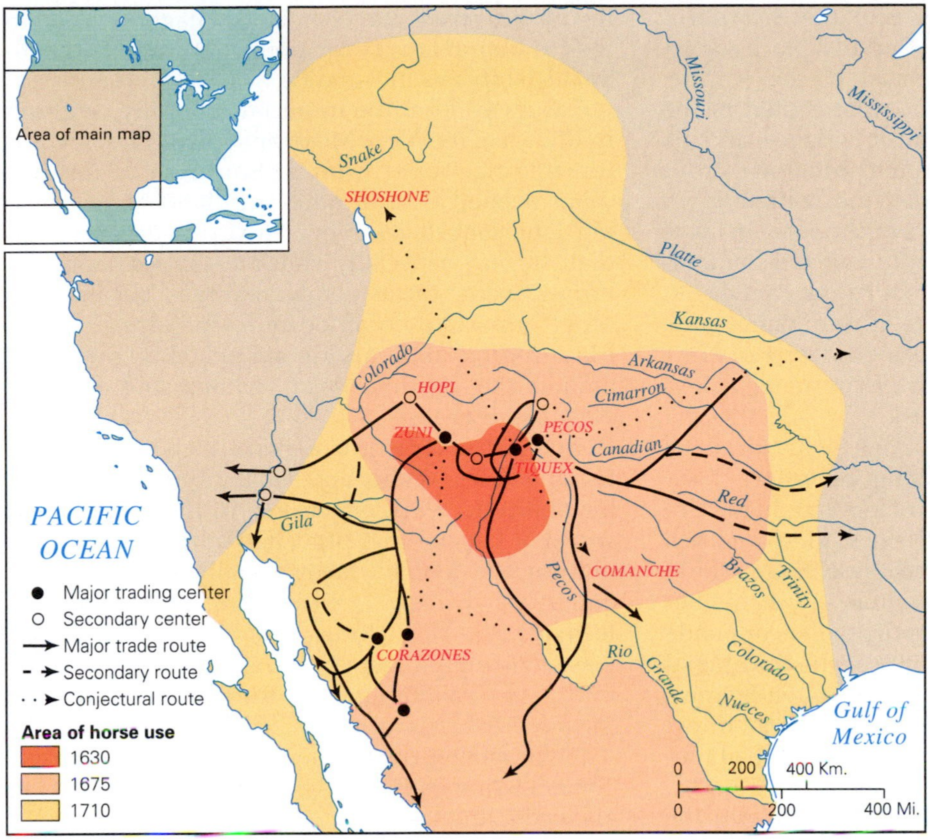

♦ **MAP 2.2 Intergroup Trading on the Southern Plains** Located on New Spain's northern frontier and Louisiana's western frontier, the southern plains became a hotbed of cultural and economic interchange among Indian groups and between them and Europeans. As this map shows, trade routes that had existed before Europeans entered the region acquired added importance in distributing the novel technologies and ideas that the newcomers brought with them. The most important of these contributions was horses, which followed these trade routes and became the single most important feature in Plains Indian life.

tives might be sold as slaves to the Spanish. Thus horse trading and slave trading became linked.

Conquest and Accommodation in a Shared New World

Old World cultures, Native American historical dynamics, and New World environmental conditions combined to create new societies in European pioneer settlements. Despite the regulatory efforts of Spanish bureaucrats, French royal officials, and Dutch company executives, life in the colonies developed in its own peculiar ways. Entire regions in what would become the United States assumed cultural contours that would shape all future developments in each.

New Spain's Northern Frontiers

Daily life along the Spanish frontier in New Mexico combined the formality of Spain's highly organized imperial structure and the disorderliness that one might expect to find in a place so distant and different from the rest of the empire. Spanish notions of civil order were rooted in the local community—city, town, or village—and its ruling elite. Responsibility for maintaining order belonged to the *cabildo secular,* the secular town council composed of members of the elite. In all of its colonies, Spain established towns and immediately turned authority over to a ruling cabildo. In Mexico, Peru, and elsewhere, this practice was usually successful, but in the high desert of New Mexico, it was at odds with environmental and cultural conditions.

Although economic conditions were far from ideal, Spaniards began drifting back into New Mexico after the Pueblos had been subdued. Unlike areas to the south, New Mexico offered no rich deposits of gold or silver, and the climate would not support large-scale agriculture. With neither mines nor plantations to support the encomienda system, the basic underpinnings of the traditional ruling order never emerged. Even so, the Spanish colonial bureaucracy followed conventional imperial procedures and made Santa Fe the official municipal center for the region.

As in the days before the Pueblo Revolt, the most attractive economic enterprise in the region was ranching. During the period of control by the Pueblos, the small flocks of sheep abandoned by the fleeing Spanish grew dramatically. By the time the Spanish returned, sheep ranching had become a reliable way to make a living. Thus, rather than concentrating near the municipal center in Santa Fe, the population in New Mexico spread out across the land. South of Santa Fe, people settled on scattered ranches. Elsewhere, they gathered in small villages established along streams, and they pooled their labor to make a living from irrigated **subsistence farming.**

Like colonists elsewhere in Spain's New World empire, the New Mexico colonists were almost entirely male. Isolated on the sheep ranch or in small villages, these men sought Indian companionship and married into local populations. The marriages brought into being lines of kinship, trade, and authority that were in sharp contrast to the imperial ideal. For example, when Navajo or Apache raiding parties struck, ranchers and villagers turned to their Indian relatives for protection rather than to Spanish officials in Santa Fe.

Far away from the imperial economy centered in Mexico City, New Mexicans looked northward for trading opportunities. Southern Plains Indians needed a continuous supply of horses. Facing labor shortages New Mexicans accepted Indian slaves—especially children—in exchange for horses. Soon these young captives became another important commodity in the already complex trading and raiding system that prevailed among the southwestern Indians and Spanish New Mexicans.

In this frontier world, a man's social status came to depend less on his Spanish background than on his ability to work effectively in the complicated world of kinship that prevailed in the Indian community. The people who eventually emerged as the elite class in New Mexico were those who perfected these skills. Under their influence, Santa Fe was transformed from a traditional imperial town into a cosmopolitan frontier trading center. During the next two centuries, this multiethnic elite absorbed first French and then Anglo-American newcomers while maintaining its own social, political, and economic style.

Life in French Louisiana

France's colony in Louisiana faced many of the same problems as Spain's North American possessions. Like most European settlements, Louisiana suffered from a critical shortage of labor. Few Frenchmen showed any interest in settling in Louisiana in the seventeenth century. In the first years of the colony's existence, the population consisted primarily of three groups: military men, who were generally members of the lower nobility; coureurs de bois from Canada looking for new sources of furs; and French craftsmen seeking in the New World the economic and social opportunities that

subsistence farming Farming that produces enough food for survival but does not produce a surplus that can be sold.

were denied them in France. These men had no knowledge of or interest in food production.

Recognizing the problem, the French government tried everything it could think of to make the colony more attractive to French farmers. In the late 1690s, officials in Louisiana proposed that the government pay the passage of young women of good character to the colony. Agents in France were able to attract only about twenty-four women, who arrived in the colony in 1704. But they were ill suited for the primitive life offered by Louisiana and entirely unprepared to work as farm laborers. By 1708, even officials who had been enthusiastic about the project were advising that it be discontinued. As a result, French men, like their Spanish neighbors, married Indians and, later, African slaves, creating a hybrid **creole** population.

In the absence of an agricultural establishment, the settlers in Louisiana depended at first on imported food, but war in Europe frequently interrupted this source. In desperation, the colonists turned to the Indians.

The **Natchez, Chickasaws,** and **Choctaws** were all well provisioned and close by. The Chickasaws refused to deal with the French, and the Natchez were sometimes helpful and sometimes hostile. But the Choctaws, locked into a war with the Chickasaws and a tense relationship with the Natchez, found the prospect of an alliance with the French quite attractive.

Despite the Choctaw alliance, which guaranteed ample food supplies and made territorial acquisitions possible, Louisiana remained unattractive to French farmers. Although Louisiana officials advised against it, the French government finally resorted to recruiting German refugees, paupers, and criminals to people the new land. But even with these newcomers, there was not enough labor to ensure survival. Increasingly, settlers in Louisiana imported slaves to do necessary work. By 1732, slaves made up two-thirds of the population.

The Dutch Settlements

The existence of Rensselaerswyck and other great landed estates made the New Netherland colony seem prosperous and secure, but in actuality it was neither. Few of the wealthy stockholders in the Dutch West India Company wanted to trade their lives as successful gentleman investors for a pioneering existence on a barely tamed frontier. The economy in Holland was booming, and only the most desperate or adventurous wanted to leave. But having no one to pay their way, most could not afford to emigrate to the colony.

Desperate to draw settlers, the Dutch West India Company offered a tract of land to any free man who would agree to farm it. This offer appealed to many groups in Europe who were experiencing hardships in their own countries but were prohibited from moving to other colonies. French Protestants, for example, were forbidden to go to France's New World provinces. Roman Catholics, Quakers, Jews, Muslims, and a wide variety of others chose to migrate to New Netherland. Most settled on small farms, called *bouweries* in Dutch. Thus New Netherland was dotted with little settlements, each having its own language, culture, and internal economy.

Farming was the dominant activity of the emigrants, but some followed the example of the French coureurs du bois. Called ***bosch loopers,***

creole In colonial times, a term referring to anyone of European or African heritage who was born in the colonies; in Louisiana, a term referring to the ethnic group that was the result of intermarriage by people of mixed languages, races, and cultures.

Natchez An urban, mound-building Indian people who lived on the lower Mississippi River until they were destroyed in a war with the French in the 1720s; survivors joined the Creek Confederacy.

Chickasaw An urban, mound-building Indian people who lived on the lower Mississippi River and became a society of hunters after the change in climate and the introduction of disease after 1400; they were successful in resisting French aggression throughout the colonial era.

Choctaw Like the Chickasaws, a mound-building people who became a society of hunters after 1400; they were steadfast allies of the French and helped them in wars against the Natchez and Chickasaws.

bosch loopers Independent Dutch fur traders; literally, "woods runners."

these independent traders traveled through the forests, trying to intercept Indian parties on their way to Dutch West India Company posts. They traded cheap brandy and rum for the Indians' furs, which they then sold to the company for enormous profits. Although both tribal leaders and company officials complained about the bosch loopers' illegal activities, the authorities could not control them.

In fact, the Dutch West India Company was unable to control much of anything in New Netherland. Poor leadership and unimaginative policies contributed to the disorder. Following Peter Minuet's dismissal by the company in 1631, a long line of incompetent governors ruled the colony. One of these governors, William Kieft, was not only incompetent but dangerously hot tempered. He personally ordered the massacre that touched off a disastrous Indian war in 1643 and 1644. The company finally replaced Kieft in 1647 with the much more competent Peter Stuyvesant, but his authoritarian style alienated settlers who were used to doing things in their own way.

SUMMARY

Expectations
Constraints
Choices
Outcomes

Spain's opening ventures in the Americas were wildly successful, making the Iberian kingdom the envy of the world. With *expectations* of cashing in on similar finds, other European nations began to contest Spain's monopoly on American colonization, creating an outward explosion of exploring energy. Although slow to consolidate an imperial presence in North America, England was the first to confront the Spanish in force, wounding them severely. France and the Netherlands took advantage of the situation to begin building their own American empires.

For Native Americans, the entry of Europeans into their realms combined with other forces to create an air of crisis. Presented with a series of new *constraints,* Indians created altogether new societies and sought new ways to solve their problems. This often involved difficult *choices,* perhaps allying with the newcomers, resisting them, or fleeing. As different groups exercised different options, the *outcome* was a historically dynamic world of interaction involving all the societies that were coming together in North America.

This dynamic interaction yielded interesting fruit. In New Spain, New France, Louisiana, New Netherland, and throughout the Great Plains, new societies emerged. These were truly cosmopolitan societies, bearing cultural traits and material goods taken from throughout the world. As we will see in Chapter 3, societies on the Atlantic coast also were evolving as English colonists interacted with the land and its many occupants. The *outcome* of such interchange, over the centuries, was the emergence of a multicultural, multiethnic, and extraordinarily rich culture—an essential element in the making of America.

SUGGESTED READINGS

Boxer, Charles R. *The Dutch Seaborne Empire, 1600–1800* (1965).

A comprehensive overview of Dutch colonial activities and the trading economy that evolved in the Netherlands following its independence from Spain.

Eccles, W. J. *France in America* (rev. ed., 1990).

A newly revised version of the classic work on France's activities in the New World; inclusive and readable.

Richter Daniel K., and James H. Merrell. *Beyond the Covenant Chain: The Iroquois and Their Neighbors in Indian North America* (1987).

Two leading ethnohistorians collaborated to write this excellent study of the changing Indian world of the Northeast during the colonial era.

Weber, David. *The Spanish Frontier in North America* (1992).

A broad synthesis of the history of New Spain by the foremost scholar in the field.

White, Richard. *The Middle Ground: Indians, Empires, and Republics in the Great Lakes Region, 1650–1815* (1991).

Although it covers material far beyond the chronological scope of this chapter, students interested in the relations between Indians and Europeans in the colonial era will find this book extraordinarily rich.

THE COLONIES AND THEIR MAJOR CITIES The creation of the English mainland colonies spanned almost 150 years, from the first settlement at Jamestown, Virginia, in 1607 to the founding of the last colony of Georgia in 1732. This map indicates the year each colony was founded, the type of charter governing it, and the date in which eight of these colonies came directly under royal control. The map also locates the major colonial cities in each region.

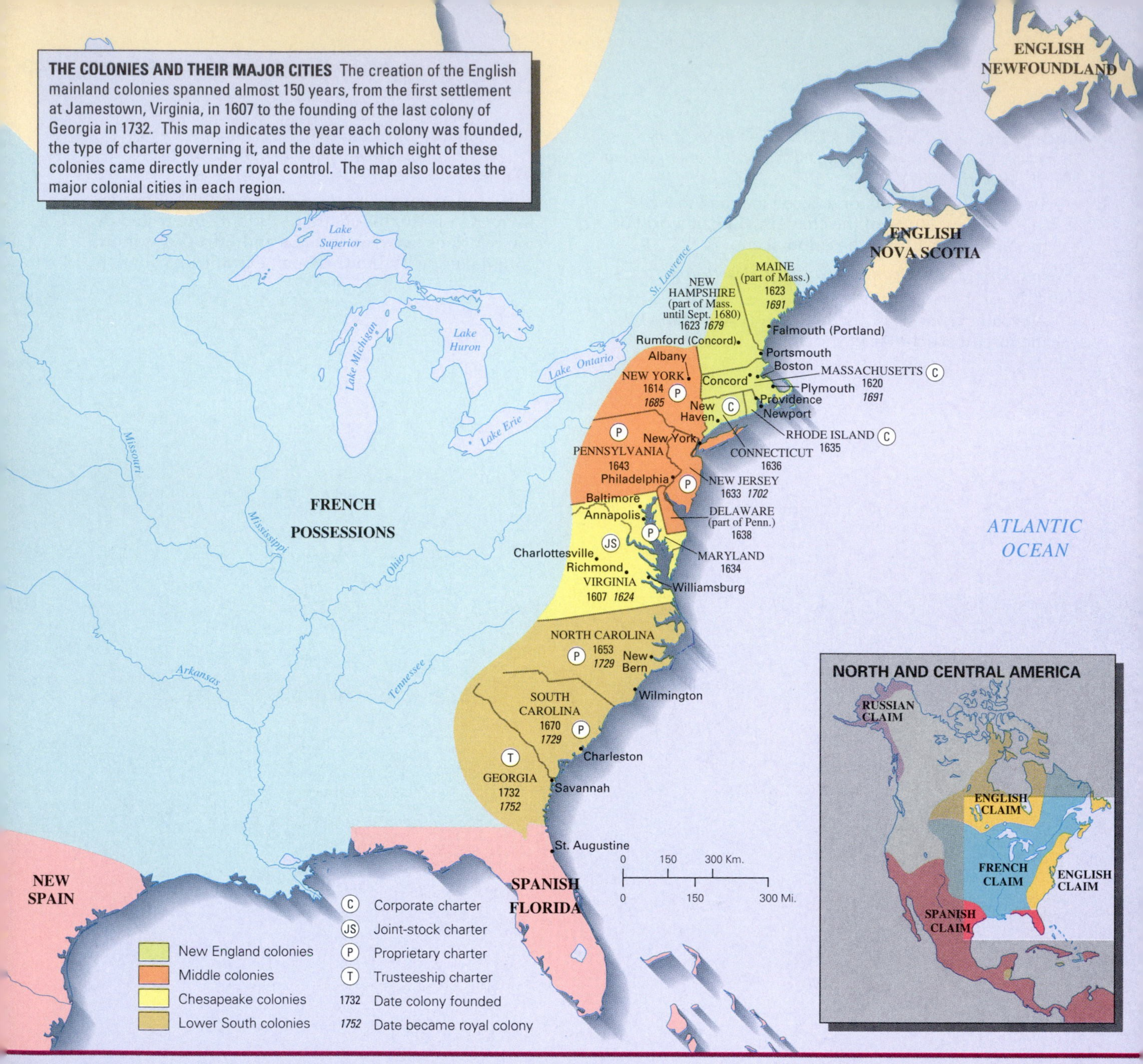

ENGLISH NEWFOUNDLAND
ENGLISH NOVA SCOTIA
Lake Superior
Lake Michigan
Lake Huron
Lake Ontario
Lake Erie
St. Lawrence
Missouri
Mississippi
Ohio
Arkansas
Tennessee
FRENCH POSSESSIONS
MAINE (part of Mass.) 1623 1691
NEW HAMPSHIRE (part of Mass. until Sept. 1680) 1623 1679
Falmouth (Portland)
Rumford (Concord)
Portsmouth
Boston
MASSACHUSETTS 1620 1691
Plymouth
Concord
Albany
NEW YORK 1614 1685
New Haven
Providence
Newport
RHODE ISLAND 1635
New York
CONNECTICUT 1636
PENNSYLVANIA 1643
Philadelphia
NEW JERSEY 1633 1702
Baltimore
Annapolis
DELAWARE (part of Penn.) 1638
MARYLAND 1634
Charlottesville
Richmond
VIRGINIA 1607 1624
Williamsburg
NORTH CAROLINA 1653 1729
New Bern
Wilmington
SOUTH CAROLINA 1670 1729
Charleston
GEORGIA 1732 1752
Savannah
St. Augustine
ATLANTIC OCEAN
NEW SPAIN
SPANISH FLORIDA
0 150 300 Km.
0 150 300 Mi.
New England colonies
Middle colonies
Chesapeake colonies
Lower South colonies
C Corporate charter
JS Joint-stock charter
P Proprietary charter
T Trusteeship charter
1732 Date colony founded
1752 Date became royal colony
NORTH AND CENTRAL AMERICA
RUSSIAN CLAIM
ENGLISH CLAIM
FRENCH CLAIM
ENGLISH CLAIM
SPANISH CLAIM

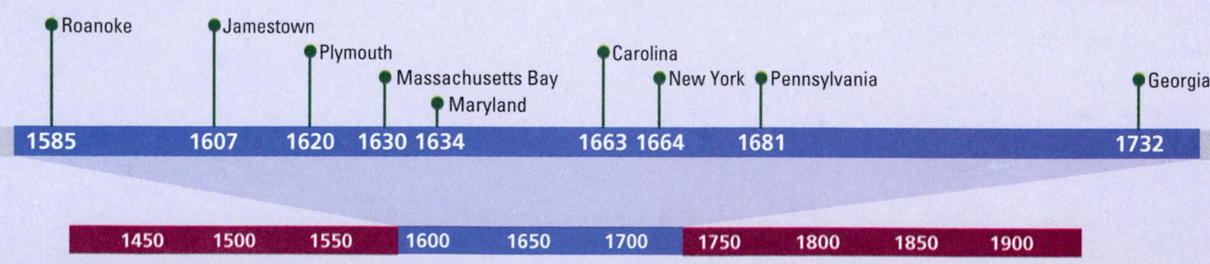

Roanoke
Jamestown
Plymouth
Massachusetts Bay
Maryland
Carolina
New York
Pennsylvania
Georgia
1585
1607
1620
1630
1634
1663
1664
1681
1732
1450
1500
1550
1600
1650
1700
1750
1800
1850
1900

CHAPTER 3

Founding the English Mainland Colonies, 1607–1732

England and Colonization

- What constraints in England encouraged people to migrate to America?

Settling the Chesapeake

- What expectations did the Virginia Company and the Calvert family have for their Chesapeake colonies? Did the outcomes satisfy or disappoint these founders?
- How did Chesapeake colonists choose to resolve conflicts within their communities?

New England: Colonies of Dissenters

- Why did English religious dissenters choose to settle in America?
- What kind of society did the Puritans expect to create?
- What constraints did Puritan authorities impose to discourage dissent? What was the outcome of dissenters' actions?

The Pluralism of the Middle Colonies

- Why did the Dutch and the English choose to encourage a multicultural population in New York?
- What made the expectations for Pennsylvania so distinctive?

The Colonies of the Lower South

- What type of society did the founders of Carolina expect to create? How did the outcome differ from their expectations?
- Why did philanthropists choose to create Georgia? Why did the king choose to support this project?

INTRODUCTION

Expectations
Constraints
Choices
Outcomes

Beginning in the early seventeenth century, many English men and women set out on the adventure of their lives: colonizing a new world. Whatever their *expectations*, the *choice* to begin life anew on the mainland of North America shaped their fates. *Constraints* in England such as poverty, religious persecution, terrifying civil war, and confusing economic transformations drove many to emigrate. The love of danger or dreams of sudden fame or fortune spurred others to come. Still others pursued the promise of land, even if they first had to work as servants for several years. Only the slaves who arrived from Africa, often by way of the Caribbean, had no *choice* about coming to the English mainland colonies.

The *constraints* and dangers facing the colonists proved fatal to many. Some did not survive the ocean voyage. Others died of diseases they had never encountered in their homeland. Many died in the recurrent warfare that raged between Indians and Europeans and among rival European powers. But circumstances in England and Europe continued to prompt new groups to come to North America. By 1732, there were thirteen colonies. Although each colony had its own individual history, groups of colonies shared regional characteristics. The colonies of the Chesapeake, New England, the Middle Colonies, and the Lower South usually possessed a common economy, labor system, and religious heritage. Whether established by a group of investors, by wealthy proprietors, by conquest, or by the division of another colony, each colony grew through experimentation, adjustment, cooperation, and conflict.

The colonists and their leaders faced a seemingly endless series of critical *choices* about where to settle, how to organize their communities, and how to sustain themselves. Through trial and error, they began to *choose* the crops they would grow, the labor force they would employ, and the rules that would govern them. Although the colonists *expected* to re-create the world they had left behind, most had to adapt to the *constraints* imposed by their new environment and situation. The earliest settlers often lacked the resources and skills needed to achieve their goals. Because the American Indians often opposed their efforts to push farther inland or to cultivate more land, deadly conflict was often the *outcome*. Nevertheless, by the eighteenth century it was clear that the American colonies were no longer outposts but permanent communities.

No matter how wide the Atlantic seemed, events in England affected the lives of all the colonists. English law and governmental policy cut across colonial borders, placing *constraints* on colonial behavior and altering colonial *expectations*.

England and Colonization

Following the death of Queen Elizabeth in 1603 and the establishment of peace with Spain, Englishmen again began to entertain Sir Walter Raleigh's dream of a New World colony. A host of motives caused English men and women to look across the Atlantic. The lure of easy riches attracted the attention of those who sought to emulate Spain's early colonizers. Religious persecution and economic uncertainties combined to cause some groups to flee England to establish colonies. The prospect of owning land and of economic opportunities attracted still others who faced a dismal future in England. To understand the motives, hopes, and fears of those willing to uproot themselves from England and venture into the unknown, we need to look first at

CHRONOLOGY

Settling the Mainland Colonies

1585	English colonize Roanoke Island
1603	James I becomes king of England
1606	Creation of the London (later Virginia) Company
1607	Jamestown founded
1608	Pilgrims flee to Holland from England
1612	Tobacco cultivation begins in Virginia
1619	Virginia House of Burgesses meets
1620	Pilgrims found Plymouth Plantations
1630	Puritans found Massachusetts Bay Colony
1634	First English settlements in Maryland
1636	Roger Williams founds Providence
1637	Anne Hutchinson banished from Massachusetts Pequot War in New England
1642–1648	English Civil War
1649	Charles I executed Cromwell and Puritans come to power in England
1660	Restoration of English monarchy
1662	Half-Way Covenant
1663	Carolina chartered
1664	English capture New Netherland New Jersey chartered
1675	King Philip's War in New England
1676	Bacon's Rebellion in Virginia
1681	Pennsylvania chartered
1685	James II becomes king of England
1686	Dominion of New England established
1688	Glorious Revolution in England
1691	Massachusetts becomes royal colony
1692	Salem witch trials
1732	Georgia chartered

the prevailing political, social, and religious conditions of seventeenth-century England.

Religious and Political Tensions in Seventeenth-Century England

Between 1603 and 1688, the English people lived through periods of intense religious conflict, economic upheavals and dislocations, civil war, and the removal of two kings from the throne. In the midst of these dramatic events, wealthy men found ways to finance risky colonizing ventures, religious sects established communities in America, and impoverished men and women sought their fortunes across the ocean.

The political unrest began soon after the death of the childless Queen Elizabeth in 1603, when first the son (James I) and then the grandson (Charles I) of Mary Stuart, a Catholic, came to the throne. Neither was committed to Protestantism, and both were thought to be secret Catholics. Their religious background disturbed many who wanted to see further Protestant reforms within the **Church of England.** Elizabeth had listened politely to the demands of **Puritans** who wanted to purge the church of all vestiges of Catholicism and then ignored them. James was not the diplomat that Elizabeth was. He responded to the Puritans' calls for further reforms by harassing them. He succeeded only in provoking more Puritan opposition.

James and Charles did not welcome challenges to their political authority either. They had little respect for **Parliament,** the legislative body that claimed important powers for itself and set limits on royal authority. James was not shy about declaring his commitment to **absolutism,** the doctrine that the king alone held all power. Parliament did not take kindly to James's lectures on the subject.

The Stuart kings underestimated the determination of Parliament to insist on its rights. Because Parliament controlled how taxes were raised and spent, it had a powerful weapon against these kings. Although James had clashes with Parliament, open conflict did not emerge until Charles's reign began in 1625. His solution to the problem of an uncooperative Parliament, which included many Puritans, was to dismiss that body. Charles attempted to rule alone, financing his rule by the imposition of arbitrary taxes.

In 1640, however, a rebellion in Scotland forced Charles to call Parliament back into session in order to raise an army. The legislature quickly challenged the king. In 1642, civil war erupted between those loyal to the Stuart monarchy and the political and religious dissenters represented by Parliament. Led by Oliver Cromwell, the rebels won, ultimately executing Charles in 1649. For the next eleven years, England was ruled by Cromwell and his followers. Cromwell's increasingly dictatorial rule, however, led to great popular dissatisfaction. His death in 1658 paved the way for a restoration of the monarchy and the return of the house of Stuart in 1660.

The Catholic sympathies of Charles II and the open Catholicism of James II revived tensions that had existed between the earlier Stuart monarchs and Parliament. Charles II avoided a confrontation by generally cooperating with Parliament during his twenty-five-year reign, but James's commitment to Catholicism led to his overthrow only three years into his rule. Parliament deposed him in 1688 in favor of James's Protestant daughter, Mary, and her Dutch husband, William of Orange. This bloodless revolution established William and Mary as king and queen of England, with the clear understanding that their rule was subject to Parliament. The **Glorious Revolution** was a victory for English Protestantism and a defeat for arbitrary government.

Colonizers and Colonies

For most of the seventeenth century, the people of England had to endure turbulent, sometimes violent, and very rapidly changing circumstances. Those in power had harassed and persecuted religious dissenters. The shift from an agricultural society to a more commercial one had made some people very wealthy but had left others in poverty or in fear of poverty. The political disputes over the rights of king and Parliament and over the liberties of Englishmen had led to such remarkable events as the execution of a king and a civil war. These precarious conditions at home provided compelling motives for thousands of English men and women to seek a new life across the Atlantic.

Initially, England's merchant **entrepreneurs** provided these men and women with the means and the great sums needed for colonizing North America. Early in the seventeenth century, they

Church of England The Protestant church that King Henry VIII established as England's official church in the sixteenth century; also known as the Anglican church.

Puritans English Protestants who wanted to reform the Church of England.

Parliament The lawmaking branch of the English government, composed of the House of Lords, representing English nobility, and the House of Commons, an elected body of untitled English citizens.

absolutism The exercise of complete and unrestricted power in government.

Glorious Revolution The events in 1688 that resulted in the removal of James II from the throne of England and the crowning of the Protestant monarchs William and Mary.

entrepreneur A person who organizes and manages a business enterprise that involves risk and requires initiative.

formed **joint-stock companies** that pooled the resources of numerous individuals and that protected investors from losing their entire fortunes (as Sir Walter Raleigh had) to finance England's first North American colonies. After the Restoration, the king played an increasingly important role in colonization. He gave his friends and supporters large grants of land that became **proprietary colonies.** Eventually, the English monarchs themselves established colonies or took control of existing ones, making them **royal colonies.**

By the early eighteenth century, the English colonists who lived in the North American settlements had come to think of themselves not as members of a single society but as residents of four distinct regions. The Chesapeake, consisting of Virginia and Maryland, was the site of the first successful English foothold on the continent. New England followed soon after. The Middle Colonies of New York, Pennsylvania, and New Jersey came about through the conquest of earlier Dutch settlements. The Lower South—consisting of North Carolina, South Carolina, and ultimately Georgia—carried the English flag to the borders of Spanish Florida.

Settling the Chesapeake

In 1606, James granted royal **charters** to two groups of merchants. The Plymouth Company was given the right to colonize a northern area stretching all the way from present-day Maine to Virginia. Its single venture, the Popham Colony in Maine, failed almost immediately in 1607. The wealthier London Company received permission to create settlements from present-day New York to South Carolina. Its outpost near the Chesapeake Bay became England's first successful colony in the New World.

The Planting of Jamestown

The London Company's investors expected a quick profit from their venture because the settlers were instructed to "dig, mine, and search for all Manner of Gold, Silver, and Copper." Many of the 144 initial colonists were gentlemen adventurers more interested in the excitement of gathering precious metals than in starting life over in a new world.

The exclusively male colonists set sail from England in December 1606. Before land was sighted, sixteen people had died at sea. But **Jamestown,** the camp they established on a small peninsula on the James River, near the Chesapeake Bay, would prove to be more deadly than the transatlantic voyage.

The colonists chose the site because it was easy to defend against attack by Spanish ships or local Indians. What they did not realize was that the swampy area around Jamestown was an unhealthy environment. "Swelling Fluxes" and "Burning Fevers" (probably caused by typhoid and dysentery) killed many Englishmen that summer.

By winter, starvation had replaced disease as the primary danger. The English gentlemen in the camp, unaccustomed to working, refused to clear fields or to do any manual labor at all. The personal servants of these gentlemen were inept pioneers as well. By January 1608, only thirty-eight of these helpless settlers were still alive.

Among the survivors of the nightmare winter was a 27-year-old soldier of fortune, **Captain John Smith.** With the settlement in crisis, Smith took charge. He immediately imposed military discipline on the colonists. Smith forced the gentlemen, their servants, and the newcomers who arrived in the spring of 1608 to build, plant, and fish. Even with these sensible efforts, the deaths continued.

joint-stock company A business financed through the sale of shares of stock to investors, who share both the profits and the losses from a risky venture.

proprietary colonies Colonies owned by an individual or group of individuals who determined how settlement would take place and the rules and laws under which the colonists would live.

royal colonies Colonies under the direct authority of the king or queen.

charter An official document in which a sovereign or a governing body grants rights or privileges.

Jamestown The first permanent English settlement in America; it was founded in Virginia in 1607.

Captain John Smith English colonist at Jamestown who imposed military discipline when disease and famine threatened the settlement.

By October 1608, almost 150 of the original and new Virginia colonists had died.

Terrible as the first winters had been, Virginians remembered 1609 as "the starving time." When new settlers arrived in the spring of 1610, they found only sixty ragged survivors. The Virginia Company, as it was now known, continued to send new colonists annually to replace the dead and the dying. But the survival of the colony remained in doubt.

Tobacco proved to be Virginia's salvation. Since the 1560s, when Indian tobacco was introduced, smoking had become a steady English habit. Native Virginia tobacco was too harsh for English tastes, but colonist John Rolfe experimented successfully with a milder West Indian strain. By 1612, Rolfe and most of his neighbors had begun a mad race to plant and harvest as many acres of tobacco as possible.

Tobacco became the colony's obsession. "Brown gold" grew to dominate every aspect of Virginia life. Colonists dispersed themselves over vast areas, rather than settling in towns or farming communities, because planters needed large tracts of land for a crop that rapidly depleted the soil. Planters fanned out along the Virginia river system because the waterways provided transportation for their tobacco. One outcome was a life of isolation rather than a sense of community. Another was improved health, for tobacco drew Virginians away from Jamestown's deadly environment.

"Brown gold" may have made Rolfe and his neighbors prosperous, but the Virginia Company continued to struggle. To cut its expenses, in 1618 the company introduced the **headright system.** Under this system, any man who paid the cost of transporting and supplying a settler—whether himself, a family member, or a servant—had the right to obtain fifty acres per settler for himself. The system shifted the cost of populating and developing the colony to the residents, but it also diminished the company's control over its primary resource: land. The company made other significant concessions to its colonists. The tight military discipline begun by Captain John Smith gave way to civil government. The planters won decision-making powers over local issues in 1619, when the company created an elected, representative law-making body called the **House of Burgesses.**

The company made costly errors in its Indian policy. Its governors in Virginia chose confrontation rather than compromise or negotiation with the local Powhatan Indians. The outcome was a deadly Indian raid on Jamestown on Good Friday in 1622. News of the attack and of other mismanagement prompted King James to revoke the company's charter and to assume control of the colony in 1624. By that time, only 1,275 of the 8,500 settlers who had arrived since 1607 remained alive.

Creating a Refuge for Catholics

As Virginians spread out along the riverways of their colony, George Calvert, a wealthy Catholic, began making plans for a second southern colony. The first Lord Baltimore, Calvert was a Catholic who turned his attention to America to accomplish two aims. First, he wanted to create a refuge for English Catholics. Second, he wanted to establish a peaceful, orderly society where aristocrats would rule over respectful commoners much as he believed they had in medieval England. Charles I, who had ascended the English throne when James I died in 1625, was happy to oblige his friend's request for a colonial charter.

Calvert died before the charter was actually drawn up in 1632. Thus it fell to his son Cecilius to realize his father's dreams for Maryland, a vast tract of southern land. The second Lord Baltimore soon discovered, however, that very few of England's remaining Catholics wanted to go to Maryland to become **tenant farmers.** Ironically, most of Maryland's first settlers in 1634 were Protestants from England's middle and lower classes. Few Protestants or Catholics joined the colony subsequently because of the lack of prospects to own land. By 1640, Calvert had to abandon his father's

headright system Virginia Company program under which colonists who paid their own expenses or the expenses of another person got 50 acres of land per settler in return.

House of Burgesses The representative lawmaking body of Virginia; it was established by the Virginia Company in 1618.

tenant farmer A person who farms land owned by someone else and pays rent either in cash or by giving up a share of the crops.

vision in favor of the headright system that Virginia used to attract colonists.

Maryland's colonists immediately turned to tobacco growing. They repeated Virginians' scramble for good riverfront land and used trickery, threats, or violence to pry acres away from resisting Indians. Virginians did not welcome their new neighbors despite the fact that most were fellow Protestants. They resented the competition of Maryland tobacco planters, and they disliked the constraints on their own acquisition of land that Calvert's colony imposed.

Troubles on the Chesapeake

The Catholics who came to Maryland did not find a peaceful haven from religious problems. Both Protestant and Catholic Marylanders brought religious hatreds with them to the New World. When the English Civil War broke out in 1642 between the Puritan-dominated Parliament and King Charles I, the conflict spread to this Catholic colony.

The triumph of the parliamentary forces, led by Oliver Cromwell, and the subsequent beheading of the king in 1649 spelled trouble for Calvert. In 1654, the militantly Protestant Parliament took Maryland away from the Calvert family and established a Protestant Assembly in the colony. The Assembly began persecuting Catholics and ultimately provoked Catholics to take up arms. At the Battle of Severn River in 1655, a smaller Puritan force routed a Catholic army of two hundred men. When Cromwell died in 1658, the local balance of power shifted once again as the English government returned Maryland to the Calverts. Still no peace followed. Protestants in Maryland organized rebellions in 1659, 1676, 1681, and 1691, the last of which was successful.

Seventeenth-century Virginia also witnessed a revolt, although for different reasons. By the 1670s, a planter aristocracy was entrenched in Virginia. Governor William Berkeley ran the colony for the benefit of himself and a group of planter cronies. They faced little opposition until Nathaniel Bacon arrived in the colony. Although Bacon was as well educated and refined as the local elite, he found himself outside the governor's circle of friends. Unable to acquire choice coastal land, he had no choice but to take up land in the backcountry among poor neighbors, who were often freed white servants. Indian resistance to white expansion and high taxes on the backcountry posed serious constraints for Bacon and his neighbors.

Bacon's growing anger at the government erupted in 1676 when the Susquehannock Indians retaliated for the settlers' killing of five of their tribe. The Indians killed several dozen colonists, leading western planters to demand protection and reprisals. Governor Berkeley refused to send troops or to permit the westerners to raise an army of their own. Bacon then led a large number of armed planters in a march on Jamestown, threatening to demolish the capital unless the governor changed his mind. Furious but frightened, Berkeley gave in to Bacon's demand for a military commission. As soon as Bacon's army headed west, however, Berkeley revoked the military **commission** he had just given Bacon. He declared Bacon and his men "rebells and traytors" and ordered them to disband at once.

Bacon responded by turning his army around and heading back to Jamestown. Poor farmers, servants, craftsmen, artisans, and black slaves, to whom Bacon promised freedom, swelled the army's ranks as it neared Jamestown. What began as an uprising by a group of **vigilantes** was rapidly turning into a social revolution against a privileged elite.

Governor Berkeley tried desperately to rally his supporters, but to no avail. When Bacon's army reached Jamestown, even the governor fled. The rebels looted the town and then headed home to fight the Indians. Before Bacon could do so, however, he fell victim to a fatal attack of dysentery.

Without Bacon's leadership, the rebellion fell apart. Berkeley took revenge for all the insults and humiliations he had suffered by executing twenty-three of the rebels. **Bacon's Rebellion** was over,

commission Authorization to carry out a particular task or duty.

vigilantes People who take the law into their own hands.

Bacon's Rebellion A revolt of backcountry farmers against the colonial government of Virginia; it was triggered by inland taxes and strife with the Indians, and it collapsed after the death of Nathaniel Bacon.

♦ Nathaniel Bacon came to Virginia as a gentleman in the 1670s, but his resentment of the economic and political domination of the colony by a small group of planters transformed him into a backwoods rebel. In 1676, Bacon led an army of discontented farmers, servants, and slaves against the powerful coastal planters—and almost won. In this stained-glass window, discovered and restored in the twentieth century, Bacon's social class and his commanding presence are both evident. *The Association for the Preservation of Virginia Antiquities at Bacon's Castle, Library of Virginia.*

but resistance to the old planter government continued sporadically until 1683, when royal troops flushed the last of Bacon's men out of hiding.

Colonial Chesapeake Life

Tobacco established rhythms of work, play, and life in Virginia and Maryland that differed dramatically from those in England. Planting, tending, harvesting, and drying tobacco took almost ten months of the year, beginning in late winter and ending just before Christmas. In the short period between the holiday and the beginning of the new planting season, Chesapeake planters frantically tried to catch up on other neglected farm chores. They mended fences, built new cabins and sheds, and cut timber and firewood. They also compressed their meager social life into these winter months. Courtships were not long in the Chesapeake.

Because tobacco exhausted the soil quickly, planters moved often to new fields on their land or acquired new land. With each move, they left drying sheds and workers' shacks behind. Planters placed little value on permanent homes until well into the eighteenth century. They were willing to sacrifice comfort and permanence to the profits of growing tobacco.

Planters searched endlessly for a large and cheap labor force. During the seventeenth century, economic hard times in England sent thousands of landless and jobless young men and women to them as **indentured servants.** Such servants worked for planters for four to seven years in exchange for their passage across the Atlantic and the promise of land at the end of their service. The planters' decided preference for male laborers resulted in very lopsided sex ratios in the Chesapeake. In many areas, there were more than three males for every female.

More than three-quarters of the white immigrants to the Chesapeake in the seventeenth century arrived as indentured servants. They spent long, backbreaking days stooped down among tobacco plants. Food rations were meager and whippings frequent. A shocking number did not survive their term of service. Malnutrition took a severe toll. Diseases to which the English had little or no immunity struck down planters as well as their servants. Life was so uncertain in the first century of settlement in the Chesapeake that the white population was unable to reproduce itself. Only immigration sustained the population.

Improving economic conditions in England during the second half of the seventeenth century meant

indentured servant Someone obligated to compulsory service for a fixed period of time, usually from four to seven years, most often agreed to in exchange for passage to the colonies. A labor contract called an indenture spelled out the terms of the agreement.

a declining number of people were willing to immigrate to the harsh conditions that prevailed in Maryland and Virginia. Tobacco planters turned increasingly to African slaves to meet their labor needs.

New England: Colonies of Dissenters

Shortly after the founding of Jamestown, religious dissenters in a small English village began preparations to escape King James I's wrath. These residents of Scrooby Village were people of modest means. But they had angered the king by their declaration that the Church of England was hopelessly corrupt and that they intended to separate from it. James vowed to drive these **Separatists** out of England.

Founding Plymouth

In 1608, a small group of Separatists took this threat to heart. These **Pilgrims** went to the city of Leyden, Holland, where they found religious freedom and prosperity. But **William Bradford,** a leader of the exiles, saw hidden dangers in this comfortable new life. He worried that the Pilgrims were being "drawn away by evil examples into extravagant and dangerous courses." Bradford decided it was time to become a pilgrim once more, this time to America.

In 1620, Bradford led thirty-five supporters back to England. There they joined a second, smaller group of Separatists and set sail for Virginia aboard an old, creaky ship. Nine weeks later, the *Mayflower* delivered them to Cape Cod, hundreds of miles north of their destination of Jamestown. Although many of the Pilgrims were disheartened by the captain's faulty piloting and the approach of winter, Bradford saw distinct advantages to the accident that had taken them so far from Virginia. In an isolated settlement, the Pilgrims would be able to pursue their own religious ideas without interference. Bradford's problem was to persuade the loudly complaining passengers to remain where they were.

To prevent a mutiny, Bradford negotiated an unusual contract with all the men aboard the *Mayflower.* The **Mayflower Compact** granted political rights to any man willing to remain and abide by the new colony's laws. Given such an unheard-of opportunity to participate in political decisions, the men chose to remain in what came to be called Plymouth Plantations.

Half of the colonists died during that first winter. The colony survived thanks to **Squanto,** a Patuxet Indian who came upon the struggling settlement in the spring of 1621. Squanto became the Pilgrims' teacher and adviser. He taught them how to plant corn, squash, and pumpkins. He acted as translator for William Bradford when he and Massasoit, leader of the local Wampanoag Indians, sat down to negotiate a treaty of friendship. The summer of cooperation between the Wampanoags and the Pilgrims saved Plymouth Plantations. In the fall of 1621, the English settlers and Indians sat down to a harvest feast of thanksgiving.

Over the next decades, Plymouth Plantations grew at a steady, modest pace. When William Bradford died in 1657, after a long career as governor, the colony had over thirteen hundred people. Most of the colonists lived comfortably by farming, fishing, or cutting timber. A few grew wealthy from the fur trade. Much of the of the colony's success was probably due to the alliance with the Wampanoags. For forty years, Plymouth Plantations grew peacefully by purchasing land from Massasoit's people. By the time of Bradford's death, however, the intense religious piety of the original Pilgrims had faded. Bradford had recognized the dangers of a comfortable life in Holland but not in America.

Separatists English Protestants who chose to leave the Church of England because they believed it was corrupt.

Pilgrims A small group of Separatists who left England in search of religious freedom and sailed to America on the *Mayflower* in 1620.

William Bradford Pilgrim leader who organized the *Mayflower* journey and became governor of the Plymouth colony.

Mayflower Compact An agreement drafted in 1620, when the Pilgrims reached Cape Code, granting political rights to all male colonists willing to abide by the colony's laws.

Squanto A Patuxet Indian who taught the Pilgrims how to survive in America and acted as a translator.

Massachusetts Bay and Its Settlers

When Charles I came to the throne in 1625, the persecution of religious dissenters became unrelenting. William Laud, whom the king appointed as archbishop of Canterbury, was determined to rid the Church of England of all would-be purifiers. This persecution and a deepening economic depression in England led many Puritans who had opposed the Pilgrims' separatism to reconsider their choice to remain critics within the Church of England. The outcome was the planting of new colonies in America (see Map 3.1).

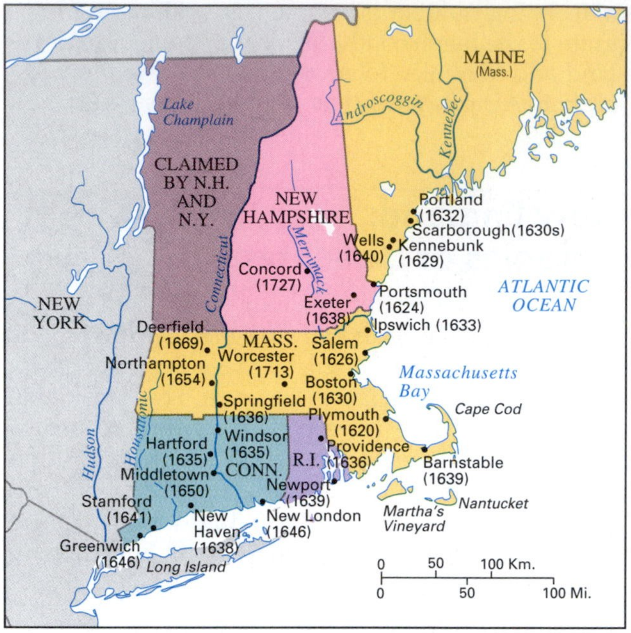

♦ **MAP 3.1 New England Settlement in the Seventeenth and Early Eighteenth Centuries** This map shows the major towns and cities of New England and their settlement dates. By the end of the seventeenth century, the region had four colonies. Colonists seeking land moved west and south toward the New York border and north toward French Canada. Those involved in trade, shipping, and crafts migrated to the seaport cities.

A young Puritan lawyer named **John Winthrop** agonized over the Puritans' increasingly desperate situation. His solution was to propose that the Puritans leave England yet retain their ties to the Anglican church. This proposal would free the Puritans from the taint of separatism yet allow them to create a truly godly community far from the prying eyes of the king's officials, especially Archbishop Laud. This ideal Puritan community would serve as a model for others and show England the error of its sinful ways.

King Charles I, who was more than willing to help dissenters leave England, approved the request by Winthrop's Massachusetts Bay Company for a northern colony. The company immediately began to recruit devout Puritan families to join in the religious experiment. Winthrop spoke of the colony in biblical terms, comparing the American "Wilderness Zion" of the Puritans to the desert wilderness in which the Hebrews wandered before reaching their "Promised Land." Winthrop's vision and the king's dismissal of Parliament in 1629 produced the **Great Migration** of nearly twenty thousand Puritans in the 1630s. Many more Puritans, however, remained in England.

The first years of the Massachusetts Bay Colony stood in sharp contrast to the lean and lonely beginnings of nearby Plymouth Plantations or Jamestown. An advance crew traveled to Massachusetts in early 1629 to prepare shelters and to clear fields for planting. Winthrop and over a thousand more colonists followed in 1630 in seventeen sturdy ships loaded with livestock, tools, supplies, and food. There was no "starving time" in the colony.

Aboard his flagship, the *Arbella,* John Winthrop preached a sermon in which he urged his audience to create a model Protestant community. "We shall be a city upon a hill," he pointed out, observing that "the eyes of all peoples are upon us." God would protect and nurture their settlement if they kept their promises to Him. To falter in their mission, or to forget their purpose, however, would bring punishment from God.

The first government of the colony, called the General Court, consisted of Winthrop and the

John Winthrop English Puritan who was one of the founders of Massachusetts Bay Colony and served as its first governor.

Great Migration The movement of Puritans from England to America in the 1630s; it was caused by political conflict in England and by fear of persecution.

eleven other stockholders in the Massachusetts Bay Company who had decided to emigrate. No man was permitted to vote or hold office unless he was an acknowledged church member, not simply a churchgoer. To be a church member, or **saint,** a person had to testify to an experience of "saving faith"—a moment of intense awareness of God's power that offered an assurance of salvation. Slowly, however, free white males who could not claim sainthood did win the right to vote on local matters, and by the mid-1630s the Puritan saints had wrested important political power from Winthrop and his fellow shareholders with the creation of a representative assembly.

Puritan authorities intended to enforce biblical laws as well as English civil law. A colonist's religious beliefs and practices, style of dress, sexual conduct, and personal behavior were all legally subject to regulation by the community. Every colonist was required to attend church, and the church joined the government in supervising business dealings, parent-child relationships, and marital life. The Puritan desire to create a godly community on earth led the colony's leaders to create standards of behavior that they imposed on every individual.

Massachusetts Bay developed into a society of small farming villages and small seaport towns. The Puritans believed that these close-knit settlements would help them create model Christian communities. In contrast to the Chesapeake settlers, the Puritans in Massachusetts largely re-created the village life they had known in England. They built their homes in clusters around a village green, where they also located the church. Farms were within walking distance of the village center. As town populations grew and the walking distance to fields lengthened, those who had to walk the farthest requested and were usually granted permission to start new communities for themselves.

The Bay Colony and other later Puritan colonies in New England were societies based on families. Because the Puritans arrived in family groups, roughly the same number of men and women lived in the Puritan settlements. Unlike the Chesapeake colonists, men and women in New England could expect to find marriage partners. Puritan couples could expect to raise a family of five to seven children and to see their children marry and produce children. Cool temperatures, good drinking water, and an ample diet provided much more favorable conditions for a long life and for families than existed in the Chesapeake.

Family was also the building block for the larger society in New England. The Puritans and Pilgrims believed that it was the duty of families to teach children to obey and to be respectful. In Massachusetts Bay, criticizing a parent was a crime punishable by death, although the punishment was rarely enforced. Family government extended to wives. Puritan ministers reinforced the ideal of a **hierarchy** within a family by saying, "Wives are a part of the House and Family, and ought to be under a Husband's Government: they should obey their own Husbands." In return, the husband was expected to be loving, kind, and tender. But the man was the undisputed head of the household. He was owed obedience by all its members and had control over all its economic resources. Wives, no matter how wise or wealthy, had no property or political rights.

Dissenters in Zion

Despite being victims of persecution, the Puritans did not favor religious toleration. They saw no reason to welcome **Quakers,** Jews, Catholics, or Anglicans into their midst. The Bay Colony dealt harshly with non-Puritans who came to Massachusetts. When Quaker missionaries arrived and attempted to convert the Puritans, they were flogged, beaten, imprisoned, and branded with hot irons. Some persistent Quakers were even hanged.

Puritan leaders showed just as little tolerance toward fellow Puritans who criticized or challenged them. Winthrop and his cofounders tried to

saint A person who was granted full membership in a Puritan church after testifying to an experience of "saving faith."

hierarchy A system in which people or things are ranked one above another.

Quakers Members of the Religious Society of Friends, a Protestant sect; Quakers believe in the equality of men and women, refuse to bear arms, and seek divine inspiration from the "inner light" within each individual.

enforce orthodoxy, or religious agreement, by labeling their critics **heretics.**

One of the most powerful challenges came from **Roger Williams,** the assistant minister in the Salem congregation, who was highly critical of every aspect of the colony's life. Williams condemned the government's seizure of Indian lands through intimidation and warfare as a "National Sinne." He insisted that true religious belief was a matter of personal commitment and could not be compelled by the government. "Forced religion," he said bluntly, "stinks in God's nostrils."

Williams's evident popularity and his dissident views led the General Court to banish him from the Bay Colony in the middle of the winter of 1635. Williams sought refuge with the Narragansett Indians, who lived south of the colony. In the spring, many of his most faithful followers joined him in exile. Providence, the community they established, became a magnet for Puritan dissenters, Quakers, and Jews. John Winthrop tolerated Providence, for he saw it as a dumping ground for troublemakers. In 1644, Providence Plantations acquired a colonial charter from England's new Puritan government. This charter clearly established Williams's principle of separation of church and state. The colony later became known as Rhode Island.

Another challenge to Winthrop's authority came from **Anne Hutchinson,** who arrived in the Bay Colony with her husband in 1634. Soon after their arrival, the Hutchinsons began to host meetings in their home to discuss their minister's sermons. The meetings were immediately popular. The brilliant Anne Hutchinson, who had been trained by her minister father to interpret the Scriptures, quickly acquired a reputation as a critic of the colony's clergy. She contended that the vast majority of the colony's clergy had slipped into what Calvinists considered a Catholic heresy: the belief that good works earned a person salvation. Hutchinson reemphasized the original Calvinist doctrine that only God's grace, not good behavior or obedience to biblical laws, could save a person's soul. Puritan ministers conceded this point but could not agree with Hutchinson that proper behavior had no place in a Christian community. They feared her thinking might lead to sin and anarchy.

The fact that Hutchinson was a woman made the challenge to Puritan authorities seem worse. Men like John Winthrop believed that women had no business criticizing ministers and government officials. A surprising number of Puritans, however, were untroubled by Hutchinson's outspokenness. She developed a strong following among women and among merchants and artisans who were not saints. They appreciated her attacks on men who had political rights that they themselves lacked. Hutchinson also attracted Puritan saints who disliked the tight reins on business, personal, and social life that Winthrop and the clergy maintained.

In the end, however, none of Hutchinson's supporters could protect her. In 1637, she was arrested and brought to trial before the General Court. Although she was in the last stages of a troubled pregnancy, the judges forced her to stand throughout the long, exhausting, repetitive examination. Hutchinson was a clever defendant and seemed to be winning until she claimed that she had had direct communication with God. Such a claim was counter to Puritan teachings that God spoke to individuals only through the Bible, and it justified her conviction as a heretic. Triumphantly, Winthrop and his court ruled her "unfit to our society" and banished her from the Bay Colony.

Some Puritans left Massachusetts voluntarily. In 1636, Reverend Thomas Hooker and his entire Newton congregation resettled in the Connecticut River valley. Other Puritan congregations followed. By 1639, the Connecticut valley towns had drafted their own government, and in 1664 they joined to create the colony of Connecticut. A number of Bay colonists searching for new or better lands made their way north to what later became Maine and New Hampshire. New Hampshire became a separate colony in 1679, but Maine remained part of Massachusetts until 1820.

heretic A person who publicly dissents from an officially accepted doctrine or religion.

Roger Williams A minister who was banished from Massachusetts for criticizing the Puritan leaders of the colony; in 1636 he founded Providence, a community based on religious freedom.

Anne Hutchinson A religious leader who was banished from Massachusetts in 1637 because of her heretical beliefs.

♦ King Philip's War was one of the bloodiest conflicts in colonial history. One out of every sixteen adult male colonists was killed, and local tribes like the Wampanoags and Narragansetts were virtually exterminated. The Puritan victory at the Battle of Hadley, depicted in this nineteenth-century drawing, was a turning point in this bitter struggle. Soon afterward, the leader of the Indian uprising, Metacomet (King Philip), was trapped and killed. *"General Goffe Repulsing the Indians at Hadley." Library of Congress.*

Indian Suppression

The Puritans' commitment to building a godly community did not mean that they were pacifists or that they were always altruistic. Their treatment of the New England Indians offers ample proof that the Puritans were all too often motivated by greed.

In 1637, the Puritans used trumped-up murder charges against Sassacus, the leader of the **Pequots** in Connecticut, as an excuse to declare war on the tribe. The Puritans were often the "savages" in the Pequot War, as is evidenced by their attack on the civilian Indian population at Mystic Village. The Bay Colony's Captain John Underhill noted with satisfaction that there were "about four hundred souls in this fort, and not above five of them escaped out of our hands." The Pequot War did not end until all the men had been killed and the women and children sold into slavery in the Caribbean.

In 1675, the long alliance between the Plymouth colonists and the Wampanoag Indians broke down when colonists encroached on Wampanoag lands. The Narragansetts and other smaller tribes joined Chief Metacomet (known to the English as King Philip) in **King Philip's War.** Indian resistance was dealt a crushing blow when the governor of New York sent Iroquois troops into battle against Metacomet's exhausted army. Metacomet escaped immediate capture, only to be killed in 1676 by an Indian ally of the English.

Metacomet's death ended Indian resistance in New England. Some tribes had been entirely wiped out, or the survivors had been sold into slavery. Indians who escaped death or capture scattered to the north and the west. The outcome was a New England virtually depopulated of its original inhabitants.

Religious and Political Change in New England

New England Puritans discovered that the Atlantic Ocean did not free them from English politics. The start of the English Civil War in 1642 affected New England profoundly. As Puritans seized control of England's government, England itself became a grand Puritan experiment. Massachusetts lost its special place as a "city upon a hill," and the sense of mission among its inhabitants declined.

The war affected New England in mundane ways as well. Population fell as many settlers returned to England to fight beside Oliver Cromwell. The end of the Great Migration dried up the flow

Pequots An American Indian people inhabiting eastern Connecticut; when the Pequots resisted colonial expansion, the Massachusetts Bay colonists declared war on them.

King Philip's War War between settlers and Indians in New England from 1675 through 1676; it ended after the Wampanoag chief Metacomet was killed.

of funds and supplies from England. New England's remaining colonists, who had profited by selling livestock and foodstuffs to immigrants, now had to find a new way to pay for the imported goods that they needed. When English fishing fleets could not make their usual voyages to New England's waters because of the war, colonists created local fishing fleets. By the end of the seventeenth century, Bay colonists were actively involved in transatlantic and Caribbean trade, and Boston had grown into the largest of the English mainland colonial cities.

Massachusetts faced new religious problems after the English Civil War. Puritan colonists who had been born in America lacked the religious intensity that marked their parents' sainthood. Perhaps their growing interest in trade and commerce lessened their zeal. Whatever the cause, fewer young Puritans became saints. The declining number of new church members led to the **Half-Way Covenant** of 1662. This allowed children of church members to be baptized even if they could not make a convincing declaration of their salvation. The Half-Way Covenant allowed those baptized to become halfway members of the church and thus to participate in church affairs.

Meanwhile, external political pressures were growing. After the restoration of the monarchy in 1660, King Charles II insisted that Anglicans and other Protestants be allowed to settle in New England. A growing number did so. Charles II also pressured Massachusetts to conform to English law. He revoked the colony's charter in 1683 when the colony refused to end its restriction of voting to church members. This marked the beginning of an effort to centralize royal control over the growing American empire.

King James II, who assumed the throne after his brother's death in 1685, took the next step in this process. He revoked the charter of every English mainland colony and combined the New England colonies as well as New Jersey and New York into the Dominion of New England.

James hoped the Dominion would increase the land grants and other political favors that he could distribute to loyal supporters. He also expected to increase the royal revenues by imposing duties and taxes on colonial goods. What he may not have foreseen was the strength of popular resistance to his new Dominion and to the man he chose to govern it, Sir Edmund Andros. Andros offended New England's Puritans immediately by establishing the Church of England as the Dominion's official church. Then he alienated the non-Puritans by abolishing the General Court in Massachusetts. Nonsaints had been struggling for inclusion in this representative body, not for its destruction. So when Andros imposed new taxes, many saints and nonsaints refused to pay.

In 1689, when news of James II's downfall in the Glorious Revolution reached Boston, New Englanders imprisoned Andros and shipped him back to England for trial as a traitor. Puritans hoped that their new English rulers, William and Mary, would reward them by restoring their charter. But under the new charter of 1691, Massachusetts became a royal colony whose governor was appointed by the Crown. The charter did call for a popularly elected assembly. Potential voters, however, would now have to meet the standard English **property requirement.** Church membership was no longer relevant to the exercise of political rights in New England. The Puritan experiment had largely ended.

The Salem witch trials occurred in the context of these wrenching and bewildering changes in New England life. In 1692, a group of young women and girls in Salem began to show signs of "bewitchment." They fell into violent fits and their bodies contorted. Under questioning, they named several local women, including Tituba, a slave acquired from the West Indies, as their tormentors. The conviction that the devil had come to Massachusetts spread quickly, and the number of accused witches grew. By summer, over a hundred women, men, and even children filled local jails. Testimony of the alleged victims led to the execution of twenty witches, most by hanging, before the new royal governor, Sir William Phips, arrived in Massachusetts and forbade any further arrests. In January

Half-Way Covenant An agreement that gave partial membership in Puritan churches to the children of church members even if they had not had a "saving faith" experience.

property requirement The limitation of voting rights to people who own certain kinds of property.

♦ Although often described as an African, Tituba was probably a West Indian. Tituba's accounts of witchcraft in Massachusetts were a powerful combination of her own Indian background, African traditions learned on the Barbadian plantation where she was a slave, and the Puritan beliefs acquired in the household of a local minister. *Tituba, Reluctant Witch of Salem by Elaine G. Breslaw.*

♦ **MAP 3.2 The Middle Colonies** This map shows the major towns, cities, and forts in the colonies of New York, Pennsylvania (including Delaware), and New Jersey. The prosperity of the region was based on the thriving commerce of its largest cities, Philadelphia and New York, and on the commercial production of wheat.

1693, the governor assembled a new court that quickly acquitted the remaining prisoners.

Economic change and local resentments apparently played a role in the Salem witchcraft hysteria as well as uncertainties about the end of Puritan government. Those leveling the accusations typically lived on small farms outside the town of Salem; those accused of witchcraft were wealthier and lived in the rising seaport of Salem.

The Pluralism of the Middle Colonies

Between the Chesapeake and New England lay a vast stretch of forests and farmland claimed by the Dutch. In the early seventeenth century, settlers from Holland, Sweden, Germany, and France made New Netherland their home. But in the 1660s, the Dutch lost this American empire to England. The English divided the conquered territory into three colonies: New York, New Jersey, and Pennsylvania (see Map 3.2).

From New Amsterdam to New York

New Netherland in 1664 had only about eight thousand people, the majority of whom were not Dutch. The colony grew slowly because it was not very prosperous, thanks largely to the poor management of the Dutch West India Company.

The company was also unable to defend its colony. Eager to gain an advantage over the Dutch, England's main commercial rival, King Charles II in 1664 granted New Netherland to his brother James, the duke of York. All James had to do was take this prize from the Dutch. When the duke's four armed ships arrived in New Amsterdam harbor, the colonists refused to defend the town. The Dutch had done little for them. Governor Peter Stuyvesant was forced to surrender the colony without a shot being fired, and New Netherland became New York.

New York grew rapidly under James's rule. Its population doubled between 1665 and 1685. Religious refugees, including French Protestants, English Quakers, and Scottish **Presbyterians,** found New York attractive because it offered religious toleration. The result was a remarkably diverse colonial population.

Diversity did not ensure harmony in the colony. English, Dutch, and German merchants in New York City competed fiercely for control of the colony's trade and for domination of the city's cultural life. Fierce rivalries also existed between New York City's merchants and Albany's fur traders.

New Yorkers were united only in their resentment of James's political control of the colony. Except for a brief period, New York lacked a representative assembly under his rule. Thus when King James II merged New York with the surrounding colonies in his Dominion of New England in 1686, local opposition was as great as it was in Massachusetts. In 1689, news of the Glorious Revolution prompted a revolt in New York City similar to the revolt in Boston. New Yorkers were also successful in deposing the king's officials.

The Founding of New Jersey

In 1664, James granted the area west of Manhattan and east of the Delaware River to two loyal supporters. Sir George Carteret and Lord John Berkeley were never able to profit from their New Jersey holdings. They did not anticipate the rush of Puritans, Quakers, and Baptists into New Jersey that began as soon as the Dutch surrendered New Netherland. The settlers refused to recognize the authority of the governor appointed by the proprietors or to pay rents.

Exasperated, Berkeley sold his half-interest in New Jersey to a group of Quaker merchants in 1672. Carteret held on to his half until his death in 1681, when a second group of Quaker merchants acquired it. The liberal policies of the Quakers drew great numbers of dissenters to the colony. The Quaker proprietors granted **suffrage** to all male inhabitants and established a representative assembly with broad powers. Colonists were ensured full religious freedom and the right to a trial by jury. These policies promoted a thriving and prosperous pair of communities. In 1702, West Jersey and East Jersey combined to form New Jersey.

Pennsylvania: Another Holy Experiment

William Penn was eager to create a refuge for his fellow Quakers, who had been severely persecuted in England. Penn was in a unique position to accomplish this end. His father, Admiral Sir William Penn, who was not a Quaker, had been one of England's naval heroes and one of King Charles II's political advisers. Although Charles II disliked the Quakers, by the 1670s they had become the largest dissenting sect in England, and he wanted their political support in his battles with Parliament. He looked to the younger Penn to secure that support. For a decade, Penn combined political loyalty with generous loans to the king just as his father had done. As a reward, in 1681 Charles granted Penn a charter to a huge area west of the Delaware River, which Penn named Pennsylvania ("Penn's Woods"). King Charles gave Penn the same sweeping powers as proprietor that he gave others, but Penn did not intend to govern by whim. He planned a holy experiment based on Quaker values and principles.

Quakers believed that the divine spirit—or "inner light"—resided in every human being. They there-

Presbyterians Members of a Calvinist sect that eventually became the established church of Scotland; in the seventeenth century, it was sometimes opposed by Scotland's rulers.

suffrage The right to vote.

William Penn English Quaker who founded the colony of Pennsylvania in 1681.

fore respected all individuals and maintained a highly egalitarian church structure. The **Quaker meeting** was strikingly simple, without ceremony or ritual. Any congregation member who felt moved to speak was able to participate. Within the meetinghouse, distinctions of wealth and social status were not recognized. Women as well as men were welcome to speak in the meeting. In their plain dress and their refusal to remove their hats in the presence of their social "betters," Quakers demonstrated their belief that all men and women were equal.

Quaker egalitarianism influenced the political structure of Pennsylvania as well. All free male residents had the right to vote, and the legislature had full governing powers. William Penn, unlike his patron Charles II, did not interfere in the colony's lawmaking process. He honored the legislature's decisions even when they disturbed him. The political quarrels that developed in Pennsylvania's assembly actually shocked Penn, but his only action was to urge political leaders not to be "so noisy, and open, in your dissatisfactions."

Penn's land policy promoted a thriving colony of small, independent, landowning farmers. He wanted no politically powerful landlords and no economically dependent tenant farmers. He insisted that all land be purchased fairly from the Indians, and he strived for peaceful coexistence between Indian and English societies. Penn recruited settlers from outside England by publishing pamphlets that stressed the freedom and the economic opportunity available in Pennsylvania. Over eight thousand immigrants poured into the colony in the first four years. Many came from England, but Irish, Scottish, Welsh, French, Scandinavian, and German settlers came as well. To their English neighbors, German newcomers such as the Mennonites and Amish became known as the "Pennsylvania Dutch."

When William Penn died in 1717, he left behind a successful, dynamic colony. Philadelphia had already emerged as a great shipping and commercial center, rivaling Boston and New York City. But this success was achieved at some cost to Penn's original vision and to his Quaker principles. Most of the eighteenth-century settlers were not Quakers and had no strong commitment to egalitarianism, pacifism, or other Quaker principles. Penn's welcome to all immigrants ultimately jeopardized his holy experiment.

The Colonies of the Lower South

In 1663, Charles II granted eight of his favorite supporters several million acres of land south of Virginia. Gratitude certainly influenced Charles's grant, but so did his desire to secure an English foothold in this region that was also claimed by France, Spain, and Holland (see Map 3.3).

The new proprietors named their colony Carolina. Their plan for Carolina was similar to Lord Baltimore's, and to this end the *Fundamental Constitution of Carolina* sought to create a society of great landowners, **yeoman farmers,** and serfs. Like the Calverts, the Carolina proprietors found out that few Englishmen and women were willing to travel 3,000 miles to become serfs. The proprietors soon had to abandon their scheme and to adopt the headright system used in Virginia and Maryland.

The Carolina Colony

A fine natural harbor, fertile land, and the short distance to England's overcrowded possessions in the West Indies attracted settlers to Charleston in southeastern Carolina. Charleston (Charles Town before 1782) became the most important city in the southern colonies. The colony supported itself initially by trading with the local Indians for deerskins and for other Indians captured in tribal warfare. The deerskins were shipped to England, the Indians to the Caribbean as slaves. Other colonists took advantage of the region's pine forests to produce **naval stores** such as tar, resin, pitch, and turpentine, which were used in maintaining wooden ships.

Carolinians tried, unsuccessfully, to develop sugar cane, tobacco, silk, cotton, ginger, and olives

Quaker meeting A gathering of Quakers for reflection and silent or oral prayer.

yeoman farmers Owners of small landholdings who were entitled to vote.

naval stores Products such as timber, tar, resin, pitch, and turpentine, used in the building of wooden ships.

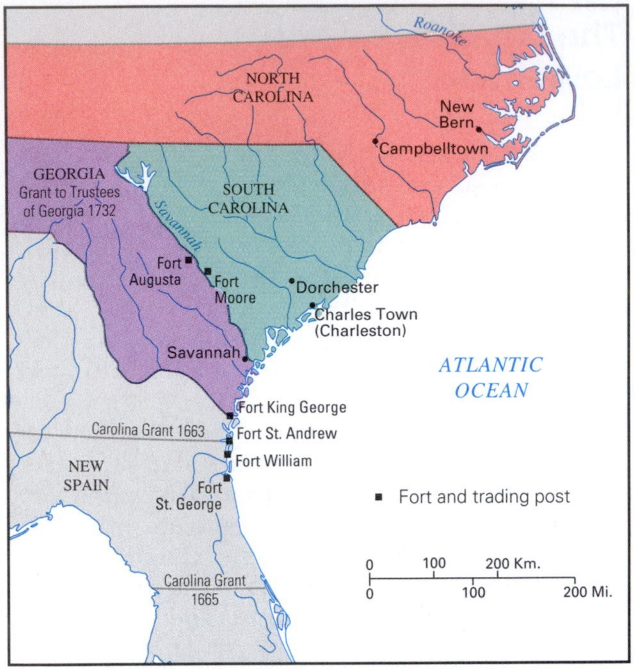

♦ **MAP 3.3 The Settlements of the Lower South** This map shows the towns and fortifications of North Carolina, South Carolina, and Georgia, as well as the overlapping claims by the Spanish and the English to the territory south and west of Fort King George. The many Georgia forts reflect that colony's role as a buffer state between rice-rich South Carolina and the Spanish troops stationed in Florida.

as cash crops. Cattle raising, which the settlers learned from African slaves imported from the West Indies, was successful. Later, rice planting, another African borrowing, proved even more profitable. The rice grown in swampy lowlands by African slaves quickly made Carolina planters the richest English colonists on the mainland. By 1708, African Americans outnumbered Europeans in the rice region.

In 1719, the Charleston planter elite wrested control of the southern half of Carolina from the original proprietors. In South Carolina, as it was now called, a small white elite dominated and controlled the lives of thousands of black slaves.

The northern region of Carolina around Albemarle Sound was economically unpromising and isolated. It was bordered by swamps to the north and south. A chain of barrier islands blocked access to oceangoing vessels. Despite all these constraints, settlers had begun drifting into the area about 1660. These poor farmers and freed white servants from Virginia were searching for unclaimed land and a fresh start. They grew tobacco and produced naval stores from the pine forests around them.

In 1729, the Albemarle colonists overthrew proprietary rule and officially separated from the southern part of the colony to form North Carolina. Both South Carolina and North Carolina became royal colonies.

Georgia: The Last Colony

In 1732, a group of wealthy English social reformers received a charter for an unusual social experiment. They hoped to reform the lives of thousands of imprisoned English debtors by giving them a new start in America.

James Oglethorpe and his colleagues gave few political rights to their colonists in Georgia. Georgians were not given a representative assembly or a voice in the selection of political or military officers. The reformers established many other restrictions. For example, no Georgian was allowed to buy or sell property in the colony, and slave labor was banned. Clearly, Oglethorpe felt that the ideal colonist was a hardworking farmer of permanently modest means.

Oglethorpe, however, could find few English debtors whom he considered as "deserving poor." Thus Georgia actually filled with South Carolinians searching for new land and with English men and women of the middling ranks. These colonists soon challenged all the land and labor policies imposed on Georgians. They won the right to buy and sell land. They introduced slave labor even though the founders refused to lift the ban on slavery. In 1752, Oglethorpe and his friends abandoned their reform project and turned Georgia over to the king.

James Oglethorpe Englishman who established the colony of Georgia as an asylum for debtors.

SUMMARY

Expectations
Constraints
Choices
Outcomes

The Virginia Company established Jamestown in *expectation* of profits from gold and silver. But the Virginians found no precious metals. *Constrained* for years by illness and the Powhatan Indians, they *chose* to cultivate tobacco. The *outcome* was a small coastal planter elite that ruled over a struggling frontier population.

Though intended as a refuge for Catholics, Maryland attracted mostly Protestant immigrants. Marylanders *chose* to cultivate tobacco through servant and slave labor as Virginians had done. One *outcome* was a tobacco-growing society throughout the Chesapeake.

The Pilgrims sought a refuge from religious persecution. Initially, they faced two main *constraints* on the New England coast: discontent among the settlers and the cold. They *chose* cooperation by offering political participation to all adult males and by establishing peaceful relations with the local Indians. The *outcome* was a society that attracted other religious dissenters.

The Puritan founders of New England *expected* to create a perfect religious society. Colonists were to obey biblical laws, and only church members were to participate in politics. The *outcome* of this experiment was not what the Puritans *expected.* No uniformity existed, and the colony had to exile its dissenters. The Puritan experiment ended in 1691, when King William issued a new Massachusetts charter.

The region between the Chesapeake and New England was colonized by the Dutch and later conquered by the English. Tolerant policies there led a diverse population to *choose* to settle in New York, New Jersey, and Pennsylvania.

In the Lower South, the proprietors of Carolina *expected* to create a medieval society, but settlers would not volunteer to live in such a colony. Carolinians eventually developed a thriving rice economy built on slave labor. The *outcome* in South Carolina was that a small planter elite dominated the culture. Georgia, the last of England's mainland colonies, was founded by philanthropists who *expected* to reform "worthy debtors." In Georgia too, labor supply *constraints* led to a reliance on slavery.

SUGGESTED READINGS

Barbour, Philip. *Pocahontas and Her World* (1970).

A factual account of the life of an American Indian princess celebrated in folklore.

Breslaw, Elaine G. *Tituba, Reluctant Witch of Salem: Devilish Indians and Puritan Fantasies* (1996).

The author reconstructs the life of the West Indian slave who was a central figure in the Salem witch trials.

Demos, John. *A Little Commonwealth: Family Life in Plymouth Colony* (1970).

A beautifully written and very engaging portrait of family and community life in Plymouth Plantations.

Erikson, Kai T. *Wayward Puritans: A Study in the Sociology of Deviance* (1966).

The author discovers the values and ideals of Massachusetts Puritan society by examining the behavior and ideas these Puritans condemned, including witchcraft and Quakerism.

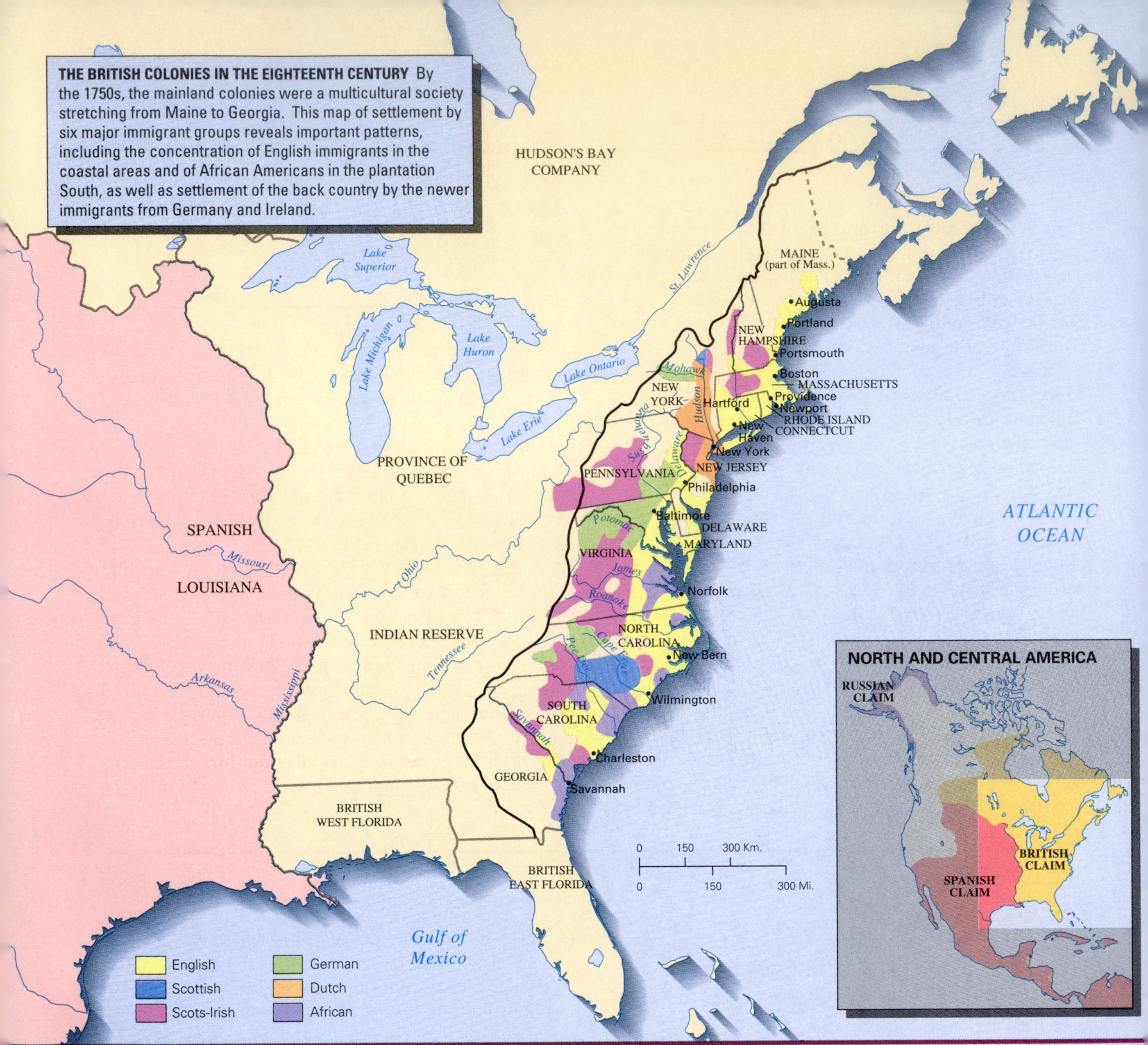
HUDSON'S BAY COMPANY
Lake Superior
Lake Michigan
Lake Huron
Lake Ontario
Lake Erie
St. Lawrence
PROVINCE OF QUEBEC
SPANISH
LOUISIANA
Missouri
Ohio
Arkansas
Mississippi
Tennessee
INDIAN RESERVE
BRITISH WEST FLORIDA
BRITISH EAST FLORIDA
Gulf of Mexico
ATLANTIC OCEAN
MAINE (part of Mass.)
Augusta
Portland
NEW HAMPSHIRE
Portsmouth
Boston
MASSACHUSETTS
Providence
Newport
RHODE ISLAND
CONNECTCUT
Hartford
New Haven
Mohawk
Hudson
NEW YORK
New York
NEW JERSEY
PENNSYLVANIA
Susquehanna
Delaware
Philadelphia
Baltimore
DELAWARE
MARYLAND
Potomac
VIRGINIA
James
Roanoke
Norfolk
NORTH CAROLINA
New Bern
Cape Fear
Pee Dee
Wilmington
SOUTH CAROLINA
Savannah
Charleston
GEORGIA
Savannah
0 150 300 Km.
0 150 300 Mi.
English
Scottish
Scots-Irish
German
Dutch
African
NORTH AND CENTRAL AMERICA
RUSSIAN CLAIM
BRITISH CLAIM
SPANISH CLAIM

THE BRITISH COLONIES IN THE EIGHTEENTH CENTURY By the 1750s, the mainland colonies were a multicultural society stretching from Maine to Georgia. This map of settlement by six major immigrant groups reveals important patterns, including the concentration of English immigrants in the coastal areas and of African Americans in the plantation South, as well as settlement of the back country by the newer immigrants from Germany and Ireland.

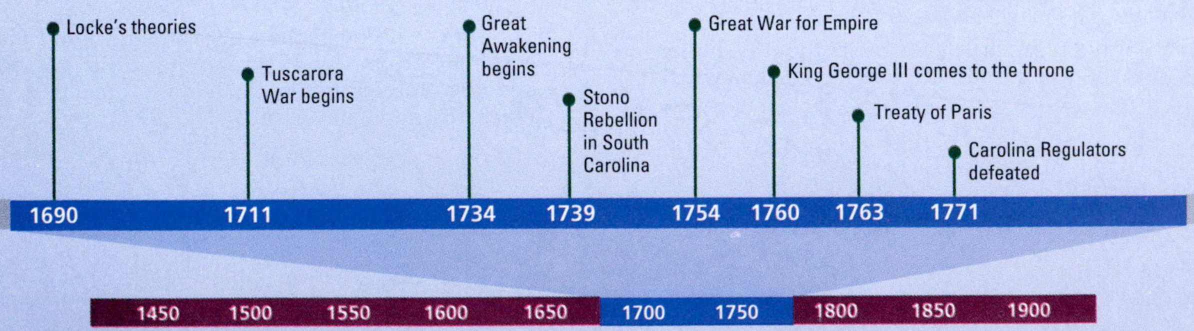
1690 Locke's theories
1711 Tuscarora War begins
1734 Great Awakening begins
1739 Stono Rebellion in South Carolina
1754 Great War for Empire
1760 King George III comes to the throne
1763 Treaty of Paris
1771 Carolina Regulators defeated
1450 1500 1550 1600 1650 1700 1750 1800 1850 1900

CHAPTER 4

The British Colonies in the Eighteenth Century, 1689–1763

The British Transatlantic Communities of Trade

- What variations in commercial activity could someone traveling from Maine to Georgia expect to find?
- In which region did new immigrants seem to have the best economic choices?

Community and Work in Colonial Society

- What was the outcome of changes in New England society?
- Why did colonists in the Chesapeake and Lower South choose to shift from indentured servants to slaves as their primary labor force? What choices and constraints did African Americans face in slavery?
- What was distinctive about life in the Middle Colonies?
- What expectations led most immigrants to the backcountry?

Reason and Religion in Colonial Society

- What political and personal expectations arose from Enlightenment philosophy?
- What were the significant outcomes of the Great Awakening?

Government and Politics in the Mainland Colonies

- What constrained a colonial governor's exercise of royal power?
- What was the outcome of the struggle for power between the colonial assemblies and the colonial governors?

North America and the Struggle for Empire

- What did Europeans and American Indians expect to gain from diplomacy and warfare in North America?
- How did the outcome of the French and Indian War affect people in North America?

INTRODUCTION

Expectations
Constraints
Choices
Outcomes

In 1748, a European traveler named Peter Kalm arrived in Philadelphia, one of his many stops in the colonies. Like tourists in every century, Kalm jotted down his impressions while traveling. Unlike most travelers, however, he *chose* to publish his diary. His *Travels in North America* is filled with remarkable details on how eighteenth-century Americans lived and worked.

Kalm was clearly impressed with Pennsylvania's "City of Brotherly Love," whose "fine appearance" and "agreeable situation" rivaled much older European cities. He attributed Philadelphia's sudden rise to prominence to the liberty that its residents enjoyed. Men and women from distant lands chose to undertake difficult journeys there not to become rich but so that they might reside in a city where everyone lived secure in his rights and enjoyed the fruits of his labors.

Few of the European elite were influenced by such glowing reports of colonial life. They continued to think of the colonies as a crude backwater. But Kalm's report and others stirred the hearts of many less prosperous Europeans. Faced with the *constraints* of poverty, religious persecution, or political oppression, they marveled at accounts of colonial liberty and prosperity. Thousands *chose* to emigrate to the British mainland colonies.

Emigrants found distinct regional variations in the colonies. To the north, where land and climate *constrained* agriculture, New Englanders had created a commercially oriented society. Their cities and towns were filled with wealthy merchants, impoverished widows, struggling dockworkers, and ambitious shopkeepers. In the more fertile Middle Colonies, comfortable family farms were common, but vast estates worked by tenant farmers could be found in New York's Hudson valley. In the Chesapeake and Lower South, a planter aristocracy dominated social and political life. There a growing slave labor force contradicted Kalm's reports of a land of liberty and opportunity. The struggling frontiersmen and embattled Indians of the backcountry that stretched from Pennsylvania southward likewise did not fit well with Kalm's colonial portrait. The *outcome* of these regional patterns of life was a complex, contradictory society that even an observant visitor such as Kalm could not fully grasp.

British colonial policy and rivalries among European powers for territory and control of trade placed *constraints* on all the colonists (see Map 4.1). Wars among Britain, France, and Spain disrupted the lives of most colonists and cast a long shadow from Maine to Georgia.

The British Transatlantic Communities of Trade

British America did not have a single, unified economy. The mainland colonies consisted of five distinctive regional economies: four along the Atlantic coast and a **subsistence** society along the western edge of settlement. To the south, the sugar islands of the Caribbean made up a sixth regional economy.

Regions of Commerce

The sugar-producing islands of the West Indies were the brightest jewels in the British colonial crown. Spain had first laid claim to these islands,

subsistence Supported by the minimum amount of food and other resources necessary to sustain life.

CHRONOLOGY

From Settlements to Societies

1690 John Locke publishes *Two Treatises on Government*

1690s Sharp increase in slave importation

1696 English colonial administration reorganized

1701 Yale College founded

1702 Queen Anne's War begins

1715 Colonists defeat Creek and Yamasee Indians of Georgia

1734 Great Awakening begins in New England

1739 Stono Rebellion in South Carolina

1754 Great War for Empire (French and Indian War) begins

1759 British capture Quebec

1760 George III becomes king of Great Britain

1763 Treaty of Paris ends Great War for Empire
Paxton Boys revolt in Pennsylvania

1771 Carolina Regulator movement defeated

but by the eighteenth century the British flag flew over St. Kitts, Barbados, Nevis, Montserrat, and Jamaica. On each island, British plantation owners built fabulous fortunes on the sugar and molasses produced by African slaves. While the absentee planters lived in luxury in England, black slaves lived and died—in staggering numbers—on the islands.

Few mainland colonists enjoyed the wealth of the "Sugar Interest." Still, the planters of South Carolina and Georgia amassed considerable fortunes by growing rice in the coastal lowlands. Planters profited also by growing indigo, which was used to make a blue dye. Like the sugar planters, Carolina and Georgia rice growers made their fortunes from the forced labor of African slaves, but the mainland planters never became permanent **absentee landowners.**

Tobacco continued to dominate the economy of the eighteenth-century Chesapeake. Beginning about 1700, however, overproduction locally and Mediterranean competition caused tobacco prices to fall. Many **tidewater** planters chose crop diversification. They began producing wheat and other grains for export. One outcome was a westward shift in tobacco production to the area along the Potomac, the James River valley, and the **piedmont.** Tobacco remained the biggest export of the mainland colonies.

The New England regional economy depended far less than the Lower South and the Chesapeake did on Britain as an export market. Except in the Connecticut River valley where tobacco was grown, rocky soil constrained New Englanders from large-scale farming. They therefore concentrated on fishing, logging, shipbuilding, and trading. These colonists found a market for dried fish and timber in the West Indies, but New England's greatest profits came from its extensive shipping network. New Englanders carried colonial exports

absentee landowner An estate owner who collects profits through farming or rent but does not live on the land or help cultivate it.

tidewater Low coastal land drained by tidal streams.

piedmont Land lying at the foot of a mountain range.

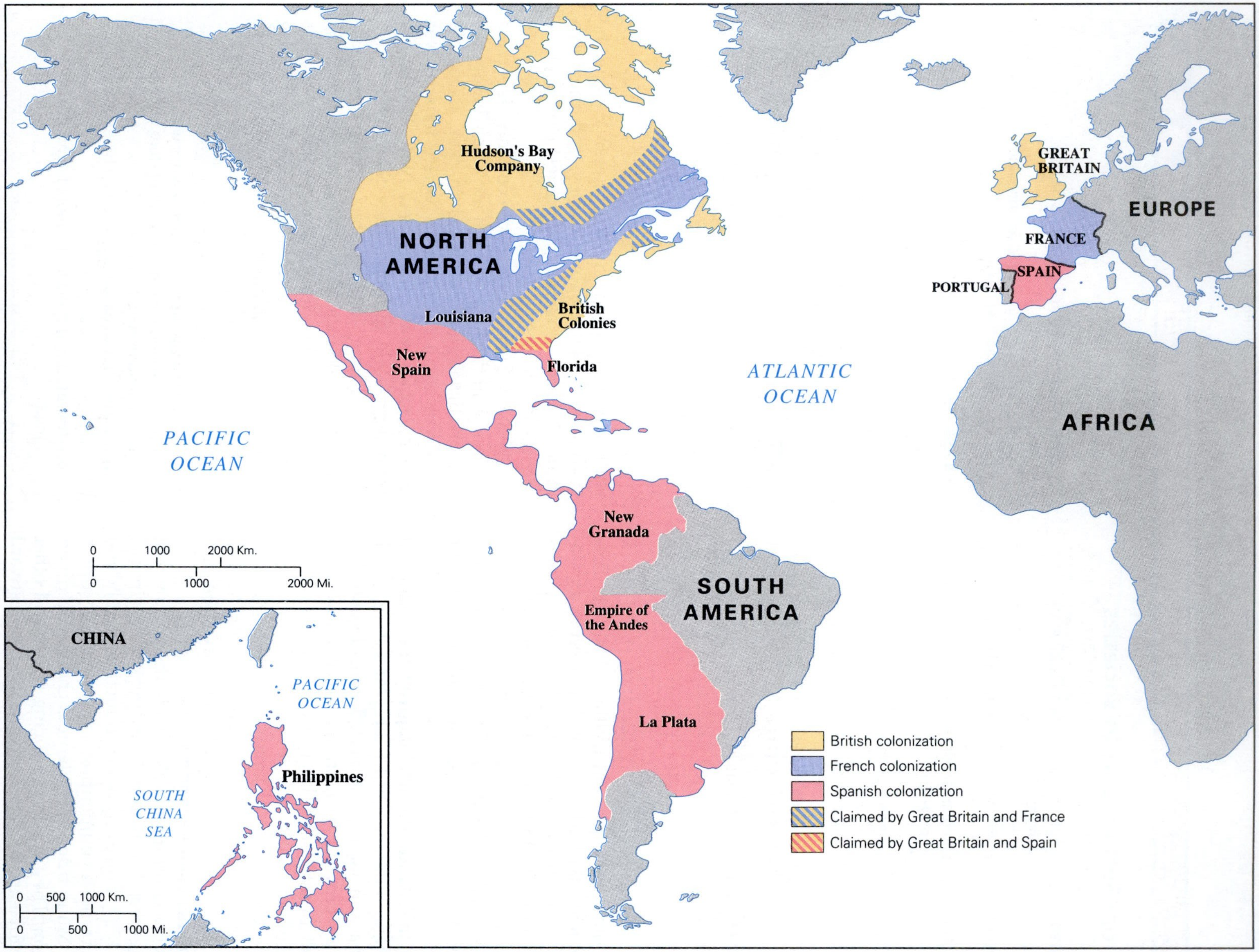
Hudson's Bay Company
NORTH AMERICA
Louisiana
British Colonies
New Spain
Florida
PACIFIC OCEAN
ATLANTIC OCEAN
GREAT BRITAIN
EUROPE
FRANCE
SPAIN
PORTUGAL
AFRICA
New Granada
Empire of the Andes
SOUTH AMERICA
La Plata
0 1000 2000 Km.
0 1000 2000 Mi.
CHINA
PACIFIC OCEAN
SOUTH CHINA SEA
Philippines
0 500 1000 Km.
0 500 1000 Mi.
British colonization
French colonization
Spanish colonization
Claimed by Great Britain and France
Claimed by Great Britain and Spain

♦ **MAP 4.1 The European Empires in Eighteenth-Century America** This map shows the colonization of the Americas and the Philippines by three rival powers. It is clear from the map why British colonists felt vulnerable to attack by Britain's archenemies, France and Spain, until British victory in the Great War for Empire in 1763.

across the Atlantic and distributed foreign goods and British-manufactured products to the colonies. The regional emphasis on shipping made New Englanders the rivals of British merchants rather than useful sources of profit for the mother country.

The middle colonies of New York, New Jersey, and Pennsylvania combined trade and farming. The heart of the region's commerce was wheat production. These colonists benefited from the steady rise of wheat prices during the eighteenth century. Trade was equally important in this mixed regional economy. Ships carried grain and flour as exports and brought back British manufactured goods and luxury items through the region's two major port cities, New York and Philadelphia. By 1775, Philadelphia was the second-largest city in the British Empire.

Inland from the coastal farms, towns, and cities was a sparsely settled backcountry that was farmed by European immigrants, former servants, or landless sons from older communities. These settlers struggled for survival. Even if they could grow a marketable crop, they lacked the means to get that crop to market. Thus a subsistence economy ran from Maine to inland Carolina.

The Cords of Commercial Empire

Colonists traded with many European nations and their colonies. Salt, wine, and spices reached colonial tables from southern Europe. Sugar, rum, molasses, and cotton came to them from the West Indies. But the deepest and broadest channels in the transatlantic trade were those that connected the mother country and the colonies. The British purchased over half of all the crops and furs that the colonists produced for market and supplied the colonists with 90 percent of their imported goods.

The mainland colonies were also bound to each other by trade, despite a deserved reputation for endless rivalries. New Englanders might exchange insults with Pennsylvanians, but in the shops and on the wharfs, Pennsylvania flour and Massachusetts mackerel changed hands in a lively and profitable commerce. Domestic trade was greater in volume, although lower in value, than all foreign trade in this eighteenth-century world.

Community and Work in Colonial Society

Visitors to eighteenth-century America could see enormous physical differences as they traveled from the carefully laid-out towns of New England into the isolated rural worlds of the plantation South. If they were observant, they would see cultural differences as well. Although political loyalties and economic exchanges linked the colonists, they lived and worked in societies that had some striking differences.

New England Society and Culture

In the early eighteenth century, New England's seaport towns and cities grew steadily in size and economic importance. The growing role of commerce in New England produced a shift from a Puritan to what became known as a "Yankee" culture in the eighteenth century. Economic competition and the pursuit of wealth replaced older, communal values. Still, certain traditions remained, including the concern for the creation and maintenance of public institutions, such as schools and colleges. As early as 1647, the Massachusetts government had ordered towns with fifteen families or more to support an elementary school through local taxes. Literacy was consequently widespread, even among women. In 1636, in the Bay Colony's first decade of existence, Harvard College was established to educate the sons of the local elite. In 1701, Yale College was established in Connecticut. Whether Puritan or Yankee, New England sustained local newspapers, publishers, and a vibrant intellectual life.

Even in more traditional New England villages, changes were evident. In the eighteenth century, the scarcity of land in the oldest communities sent younger sons whose prospects for inheriting land were slim or nonexistent away from their localities in search of opportunities. They ventured to relatively undeveloped areas of New England such as Maine and New Hampshire, or to the commercial cities of the region. Inequalities of wealth and political power increased, as poor widows and landless young men sought employment and sometimes public charity in Boston or Salem. Aware that good land was scarce, eighteenth-century immigrants generally avoided New England.

Planter Society and Slavery

Southern society, like New England, changed slowly but dramatically between the early seventeenth century and the middle of the eighteenth century. By the 1680s, improved economic conditions in England halted the steady flow of indentured servants to the Chesapeake tobacco fields (see Individual Choices: James Revel, page 72). At about the same time, the English established their control over the African slave trade. The outcome was a dramatic shift in the tobacco labor force from white servants to enslaved Africans.

Although Africans had been brought to Virginia as early as 1619, black workers remained few until late in the seventeenth century. The legal difference between black and white servants was vague until the 1660s. Although some black servants were then being held for life terms, their children were still considered free. In 1662, Virginia made slavery a hereditary condition by declaring that "all children born in this country shall be held bond or free according to the condition of the mother." This natural increase of slaves was supplemented by slaves imported by England's Royal African Company, which broke the Dutch monopoly on the slave trade in the 1680s. The price of slaves dropped dramatically. By 1700, 13 percent of the Chesapeake population was black. At the end of the colonial period, 40 percent of Virginians were of African-American descent.

Colonists who could not afford slaves were at an economic disadvantage. Unable to compete with the planter elite, poorer Virginians and Marylanders moved west. New immigrants, merchants, and skilled craftspeople avoided the Chesapeake because of the lack of opportunities there and competition from slave labor. Few towns or cities developed in the region. The Chesapeake remained a rural society, dominated by a slaveowning class made prosperous by the labor of African-American men, women, and children.

If tobacco provided a comfortable life for an eighteenth-century planter, rice provided a luxurious one. The Lower South, too, was a plantation society, dominated by the rice growers of coastal Carolina and Georgia. This planter elite concentrated their social life in elegant Charleston, where they moved each summer to avoid the heat, humidity, and unhealthy environment of their lowland plantations. With its beautiful townhouses, theaters, and parks, Charleston was the only truly cosmopolitan city of the South. Its prosperity rested on the backs of the majority of South Carolina's population—black slaves.

Slave Experience and Slave Culture

A slave's experience of bondage began when African slavers, armed with European weapons, captured him or her. The slavers then marched this slave and other captives from the interior of Africa and delivered them to European ships anchored along the West African coast. Many slaves died on this forced march. Others committed suicide by leaping into the ocean as they were being canoed out to the waiting ships.

The transatlantic voyage, or **middle passage,** was a nightmare of death, disease, suicide, and sometimes mutiny. The packed ships were breeding grounds for scurvy, yellow fever, malaria, dysentery, smallpox, measles, and typhus. One crew member recorded hauling eight or ten dead slaves out of the hold every morning during a smallpox epidemic. "The flesh and skin peeled off their wrists when taken hold of," he wrote. About 18 percent of all the Africans who began the middle passage died on the ocean.

Until the 1720s, most Chesapeake slaves worked alone or in small groups of two or three on tobacco farms. This isolation made both marriage and sustaining a slave community almost impossible. Even on larger plantations, the steady influx of newly imported slaves made it difficult for African Americans to work together to create mutual support in the early eighteenth century. Speaking different languages, practicing different religions,

middle passage The crowded, often deadly voyage in which indentured servants or slaves were transported across the Atlantic Ocean from Europe or Africa.

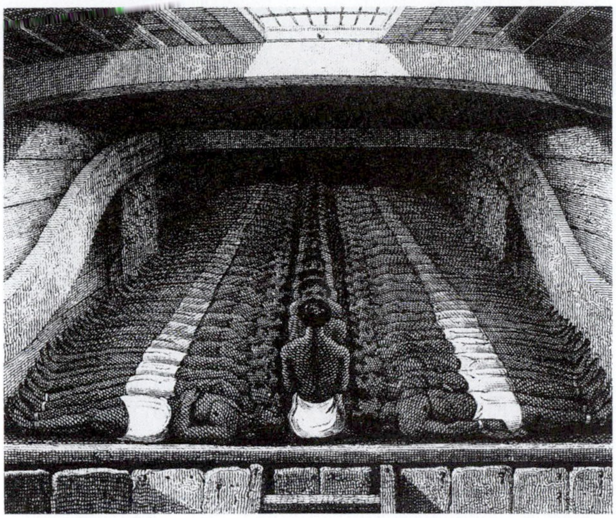

♦ This drawing shows the interior of the slave ship *Vigilante.* On board, 227 male slaves were confined to a 37-by-22-foot room, and 120 female slaves were crowded into a 14-by-19-foot room. The ceilings were less than 5 feet high. Although this was an 1822 slave ship captured off the coast of Africa by the British navy, the conditions shown here differed little from those described in the eighteenth century by slaves and by commentators on slavery. *Courtesy, American Antiquarian Society.*

and attempting to survive under oppressive conditions, African-American slaves were able only slowly to create a sense of community. This community gave meaning to and created a sense of identity within the slaves' world.

In the Lower South, slaves were concentrated on large plantations where they had limited contact with white society. This isolation gave them the opportunity very early to create their own culture. Local languages that mixed English with a variety of African tongues evolved. Gullah, spoken on the Sea Islands off South Carolina and Georgia, remained a local dialect until the end of the nineteenth century.

For many slaves, the creation of a distinctive culture represented a form of resistance to slavery. African Americans also showed their resistance in other ways. Slaves challenged orders, broke tools, pretended sickness, stole supplies, and damaged property. Slaves of all ages ran away to the woods for a day or two or to the slave quarters of a neighboring plantation. African Americans understood the odds against escape and sought to undermine the slave system rather than risk open rebellion.

Even so, white masters feared slave revolts. In the 1720s, rumors of revolts were thick in Virginia and South Carolina, although most of these plots existed only in the planters' imaginations. Despite the odds against success, some rebellions did occur. The most famous, the **Stono Rebellion,** began near the Stono River, just south of Charleston, in 1739. About twenty slaves seized guns and killed several planter families. Other slaves joined the rebels as they headed south toward Spanish Florida and killed other white settlers. The Carolina militias, however, soon caught up to the rebels and surrounded them. Ultimately every rebel was killed or put to death. Although the retaliation against the rebels was quick and bloody, the Stono Rebellion struck deep fear into white planters for a long time thereafter.

The Urban Culture of the Middle Colonies

Small family wheat farms earned Pennsylvania its reputation as the "best poor man's country." Although tenant farmers and hired laborers were not unknown in eastern Pennsylvania, their numbers were much fewer than in neighboring New York, where great estates along the Hudson River monopolized much of the colony's best farmland.

The region's distinguishing feature, however, was the dynamism of its two major cities, New York and Philadelphia. By 1770, Philadelphia's forty thousand residents made it the second-largest city in the British Empire, after London. In the same year, twenty-five thousand people crowded onto the tip of Manhattan Island in New York.

The attractions of a colonial city were powerful to a farmer's daughter or son. Cities offered a range of occupations and experiences that simply did not exist in the countryside. Young men could

Stono Rebellion Slave rebellion that occurred in South Carolina in 1739; it prompted the colony to pass harsh laws governing the movement of slaves and the capture of runaways.

INDIVIDUAL CHOICES

Choosing Between Prison and Servitude

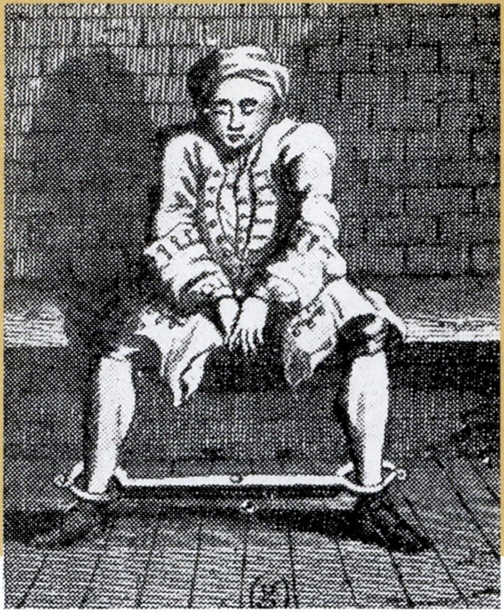

James Revel

This illustration of a young man shackled in a leg brace and handcuffs and sitting in a bare prison cell in 1728 suggests why James Revel chose to serve his sentence as an indentured servant rather than in jail. Marshalsea Prison, 18th c. print. Fotomas Index Public Library.

James Revel was one of the thousands of impoverished men and women who made their way to London in the 1690s in search of work. But Revel found little there that gave him hope. Unemployment was high, competition for wages was fierce, and modest expectations of a decent life had given way to a desperate struggle to survive. Many of these landless, homeless, and poverty-stricken people turned to crime. Revel did likewise and was caught and imprisoned. English authorities offered him one more choice: he could sell himself and his labor for several years to a stranger in the colonies, or he could serve his long term in prison.

Revel was only one of thousands who had to make this fateful decision, but the fact that he recorded his choice—and that this record has survived—makes him unique. Revel tells his story in a remarkable autobiographical poem, which he wrote after surviving his term as an indentured servant in Virginia. He describes his life of crime, his capture, and his experiences in the Chesapeake tobacco colony. Whatever fears the 17-year-old boy had, nothing prepared him

seek training as **apprentices** in scores of trades ranging from blacksmithing to goldsmithing. The poorest might find work on the docks or as servants, or they might go to sea.

Young women had more limited choices because few trades were open to them. Some might become dressmakers or **milliners,** but domestic service or prostitution were more likely. A widow or an unmarried woman who had a little money could open a shop, set up a tavern, or run a boarding house.

Slavery was not common in New England or on the family farms of the middle colonies, but slaves

apprentice A person bound by legal agreement to work for an employer for a specific length of time in exchange for instruction in a trade, art, or business.

milliner A maker or designer of hats.

for the reality of a servant's life in America. He wrote about his arrival in Virginia:

At length a grim old man unto me came
He ask'd my trade, and likewise ask'd my Name:
I told him I a Tin-man was by trade
And not quite eighteen years of age I said.
At last to my new master's house I came,
All the town of Wicoccomoco call'd by name,
Where my European clothes were took from me,
Which never after I again could see.
A canvas shirt and trowsers that they gave,
With a hop-sack frock in which I was to slave:
No shoes or stockings had I for to wear,
Thus dressd into the field I next must go,
Amongst tobacco plants all day to hoe,
At day break in the morn our work began,
And so held to the setting of the Sun.

Revel worked beside African slaves, whom he found more sympathetic and kind than the countryman who was his master. He describes the constraints that they shared in common:

We and the Negroes both alike did fare,
Of work and food we had an equal share;
But in a piece of ground we call our own,
The food we eat first by ourselves were sown,
Six days we slave for our master's good,
The seventh day is to produce our food.
And if we offer for to run away,
For every hour we must serve a day:
Much hardships then in deed I did endure,
No dog was ever nursed so I'm sure,
More pity the poor negroe slaves bestowed
Than my inhuman brutal master showed.

Revel was in his thirties when his term of service ended. A free man, he chose to return to England rather than remain to seek his fortune in the colonies. He clearly hoped that his choices in life would serve as a lesson to others:

At length my fourteen years expired quite,
Which fill'd my very soul with fine delight
To think I should no longer there remain,
But to old England once return again.
My country men take warning e'er too late,
Lest you should share my hard unhappy fate;
Altho' but little crimes you here have done,
Consider seven or fourteen years to come.

were used on New York City's docks as manual laborers. The city also attracted free African-American men and women who eked out a living as laborers, servants, and sailors. Only perhaps 5 percent of all colonial African Americans were free.

Life in the Backcountry

The population of the mainland colonies jumped from 225,000 in 1688 to over 2.5 million in 1775 (see chapter opener map). Natural increase accounted for much of this growth, for over half of the colonists were under age 16 in 1775. But almost 650,000 white immigrants risked hunger, thirst, frost, heat, dampness, fear, and misery on the transatlantic voyage to start life over in eighteenth-century America. While some were pushed out of Europe by oppressive landlords, unemployment, and poverty, many were pulled toward the colonies by opportunities for landownership and religious freedom. The majority found their way to the backcountry of the colonies.

The **Scots-Irish** and German Protestants who fled persecution by the tens of thousands in the first half of the eighteenth century saw their best opportunities in western Pennsylvania, Virginia's Shenandoah valley, and the Carolina backcountry. Those were the favored destinations as well of the younger sons of the tidewater Chesapeake. For descendants of Puritan settlers, western New York and the sparsely settled regions of New Hampshire, Vermont, and Maine beckoned. Many of these settlers were squatters who cleared a few acres of a promising piece of land and lay claim to it by their presence. A backcountry family was likely to move several times before settling down.

Backcountry settlers frequently clashed with American Indians and the established political powers of their own colony over Indian policy. Eighteenth-century colonial governments preferred diplomacy to military action, but western settlers wanted Indians pushed out of the way. Even when there was bloodshed between settlers and Indians, easterners were reluctant to spend tax money to provide protection to the inland region. Consequently, western settlers sometimes took matters into their own hands, as they had in Bacon's Rebellion.

The revolt by Pennsylvania's **Paxton Boys** was the most dramatic episode of vigilante action in the eighteenth century. Pennsylvania's Quaker-dominated government expected settlers to live peacefully with local Indian tribes. Scots-Irish settlers did not share this expectation. When Indians responded to their provocations, the Scots-Irish demanded but did not get protection from the government. In 1763, frustrated settlers from Paxton, Pennsylvania, attacked a village of Conestoga Indians who had done nothing to these white colonists. Hundreds of colonists from the Pennsylvania frontier joined the Paxton Boys' dubious cause and marched on Philadelphia to press their demands for an aggressive Indian policy. The popular Benjamin Franklin met the Paxton Boys on the outskirts of the city and negotiated a truce. As a result of this vigilante uprising, Pennsylvania's government abandoned its long commitment to peaceful relations with the Indians and agreed to establish a bounty for Indian scalps.

In South Carolina, the conflict between old and new settlements similarly led to vigilante action; in North Carolina, it resulted in a brief civil war. South Carolina's lowland planters refused to provide government for the backcountry. Although settlers in western South Carolina paid their taxes, their counties had no courts. The government sent no sheriffs either, allowing outlaws to prey on these communities. In the 1760s, backcountry settlers chose to "regulate" their own affairs. These **Regulators** pursued and punished backcountry outlaws, dispensing justice without the aid of courts or judges.

The Regulator movement in North Carolina was organized against corrupt local officials who had been appointed by the colony's slaveholding elite. These officials awarded contracts for building roads to their friends, charged exorbitant fees to register deeds and surveys, and set high poll taxes on voters. The legislature ignored backcountry demands for the removal of these officials. The outcome was a taxpayers rebellion. The governor squelched this rebellion by leading eastern militiamen into battle near the Alamance River in 1771. The governor's army of twelve hundred easily defeated the two thousand poorly armed Regulators. He subsequently hanged six of the Regulator leaders. The conflict between Regulators and colonial governments left a bitter legacy for decades to come.

Scots-Irish Scottish settlers in northern Ireland, many of whom migrated to the colonies in the eighteenth century.

Paxton Boys Settlers from Paxton, Pennsylvania, who massacred Conestoga Indians in 1763 and then marched on Philadelphia to demand that the colonial government provide better defense against the Indians.

Regulators Frontier settlers in the Carolinas who protested their lack of representation in the colonial governments; they were suppressed by the government militia in North Carolina in 1771.

Reason and Religion in Colonial Society

Trade routes, language, and custom tied the eighteenth-century colonial world to parent societies across the Atlantic. The flow of ideas and religious beliefs helped sustain a transatlantic community.

The Impact of the Enlightenment

At the end of the seventeenth century, a new intellectual movement called the **Enlightenment** arose in Europe. Enlightenment thinkers argued that reason, or rational thinking, rather than divine revelation, tradition, intuition, or established authority, was the true basis for reliable knowledge and human progress. The French thinkers known as *philosophes*—Voltaire, Rousseau, Diderot, Buffon, and Montesquieu, to name a few—were the central figures of the Enlightenment. These philosophers, political theorists, and scientists believed that nature can provide for all human wants and that human nature is basically good rather than flawed by original sin. Humans, they insisted, are capable of making progress toward a perfect society if they study nature, unlock its secrets, and carefully nurture the best human qualities in their children. This belief in progress became a central Enlightenment theme.

The colonial elite had the best access to these Enlightenment ideas. They were particularly drawn to the religious philosophy of deism and the political theory of the social contract. **Deism** is the belief that God created a rational universe that operates in accordance with logical, natural laws. Deists deny the existence of any miracles after Creation and reject the value of prayer in this rational universe. Deism appealed to Benjamin Franklin, George Washington, Thomas Jefferson, and other colonists who were intensely interested in science and scientific methods.

The most widely accepted Enlightenment ideas in the colonies were those of the seventeenth-century English political theorist John Locke. In his *Two Treatises on Government* (1690), Locke argued that human beings are born with certain natural rights that cannot be given or taken away. These include the rights of life, liberty, and property. Locke believed that government originates in a **social contract** designed to protect the people's natural rights against the powerful. Government is thus founded by the consent of the people and represents their interests through an elected legislature. Locke went on to say that the people have a right to rebel if government violates their rights.

Religion and Religious Institutions

Eighteenth-century Americans became increasingly tolerant of religious differences as Protestant sects proliferated in the colonies. Colonists began to see religious toleration in a practical light. Toleration did not extend to everyone. No colony, even Maryland, allowed Catholics to vote or to hold elective office. And religious tolerance did not mean the separation of church and state. **Established churches,** supported by public taxes, were the rule in the southern colonies and in Massachusetts and Connecticut.

The Great Awakening

Despite the spread of deism and religious toleration, one of the most notable religious developments in eighteenth-century America was the Great Awakening, a religious revival that swept

Enlightenment An eighteenth-century philosophical movement that emphasized the pursuit of knowledge through reason and refused to accept ideas on the strength of religion or tradition alone.

deism The belief that God created the universe in such a way that no divine intervention is necessary for its continued operation.

social contract An agreement among members of an organized society, or between the government and the governed, which defines and limits the rights and duties of each.

established church The official church of a nation or state.

through the colonies. **Charismatic** preachers denounced the materialism and commercialism they saw growing around them and called for a revival of basic Calvinist belief.

The **Great Awakening** was based on a new approach to preaching. Ministers "awakened" their audiences to the awful condition of their plight as sinners by preaching fiery sermons that vividly depicted the fate of those who were doomed to the fires of hell. These awakeners condemned ministers who delivered dry, literary sermons for their "cold" preaching. This new style of preaching first appeared in New Jersey and Pennsylvania in the 1720s.

Probably the most famous of the awakeners was **Jonathan Edwards,** a Congregational minister who began a local revival in Northampton, Massachusetts, in 1734. He roused terror in his listeners with such powerful sermons as "Sinners in the Hands of an Angry God." Edwards compared mortals to spiders, dangling by a fragile thread over the deadly hellfire. The revival sparked by people like Edwards spread rapidly throughout the colonies, carried from town to town by wandering ministers.

The greatest awakener of all, however, was **George Whitefield,** an Anglican minister who came to the colonies in 1740. Crowds gathered to hear the young preacher wherever he went, from Charleston to Maine. Often the audience grew so large that Whitefield had to finish his service in a nearby field. His impact was electric. "Hearing him preach gave me a heart wound," wrote one colonist. Even Benjamin Franklin, America's most committed deist, was moved by Whitefield's sermons. By the end of a Whitefield sermon, his audience was "crying to God for mercy."

The Great Awakening provoked tension and conflict. Many ministers were angered by the criticisms of their preaching and launched a counterattack against the revivalists. Bitter fights within congregations and **denominations** developed over preaching styles and the worship service. Congregations split, and minority groups hurriedly formed new churches. Many awakened believers left their own denominations entirely, joining the Baptists, the Methodists, or the Presbyterians. Antirevivalists sometimes left their strife-ridden churches and became Anglicans. These religious conflicts became intertwined with other, secular issues. For example, poor, "awakened" colonists expressed hostility to their rich neighbors through a religious vocabulary that condemned luxury, dancing, and gambling.

The Great Awakening led to the establishment of new colleges. The complicated theological arguments between Old Lights (those who opposed the revivalism of the Awakening) and awakeners led the revivalists to found Rutgers, Brown, Princeton, and Dartmouth to prepare their clergy properly. One of the most important outcomes of the Great Awakening was also one of its least expected. All the debate, argument, and resistance to authority promoted a belief that protest was acceptable, not just in religious matters but in political matters as well.

Government and Politics in the Mainland Colonies

From a British perspective, colonial governments had been created largely for the convenience of handling the day-to-day affairs of a colony. The real authority for governing still lay in Great Britain. In the eighteenth century, however, colonial assemblies became increasingly powerful at the expense of colonial governors, who repre-

charismatic Having a spiritual power or personal quality that stirs enthusiasm and devotion in large numbers of people.

Great Awakening Series of religious revivals characterized by fiery preaching that swept over the American colonies during the second quarter of the eighteenth century.

Jonathan Edwards Congregational minister whose sermons threatening sinners with damnation helped begin the Great Awakening.

George Whitefield British evangelist in the Great Awakening; he drew huge crowds during his preaching tours through the colonies.

denomination A group of religious congregations that accept the same doctrines and are united under a single name.

sented the king or the proprietor, and increased their control over local matters.

Imperial Institutions and Policies

In 1696, the British government reorganized its colonial administration and formed what became known as the Board of Trade. On paper, the Board of Trade had responsibility for most aspects of colonial administration. In practice, it was simply an advisory board. Authority over the colonies thus remained divided. For example, an admiralty board, not the Board of Trade, had the authority to enforce trade regulations.

Parliament's policy for colonial administration in the eighteenth century was largely one of **benign neglect.** This meant that most regulations would be enforced loosely, if at all, as long as the colonies remained loyal in military and economic matters. As long as colonial raw materials continued to flow into British hands and the colonists continued to rely on British manufactured goods, benign neglect suited the British government.

Benign neglect did not mean that the colonists were free to do exactly as they pleased. Intense political conflicts had arisen in the first half of the eighteenth century over the constraints royal authority placed on the power of the colonial assemblies.

Local Colonial Government

The mainland colonies were strikingly similar in the structure and operation of their governments. Each had a governor, usually appointed by the king or proprietor. (The governor was elected in Connecticut and Rhode Island.) Each colony had a council, usually appointed by the governor, though sometimes elected by the assembly, that served as an advisory body to the governor. Each also had an elected representative assembly with lawmaking and taxing powers.

The governor's powers were impressive in theory. He alone could call the legislature into session, and he had the power to dismiss it. He could veto any act that it passed. He had the sole power to appoint and dismiss all government officials. He made all land grants, oversaw all aspects of colonial trade, and conducted diplomatic negotiations with the Indians. He was commander in chief of the colony's military forces. Armed with such extensive powers, the man who sat in the British colonial governor's seat ought to have been obeyed.

On closer look, however, much of the governor's authority evaporated. First, he was not free to act on his own because he was bound by a set of instructions written back in Great Britain by the Board of Trade. Second, the governor's skills and experience were often limited. Few men in the prime of their careers wanted to be sent 3,000 miles from Great Britain to the provinces. Governorships therefore often went to **bureaucrats** who were either old and incompetent or young and inexperienced. Third, most governors served too briefly to learn how to govern a particular colony effectively. Often they did not want to be in the colonies and were willing to surrender much of their authority to the local assembly in exchange for a calm, uneventful, and profitable term in office.

Colonial governors also lacked the patronage to grease the wheels of colonial assemblies. The kings of Great Britain had learned that political favors could buy political loyalty in Parliament. By mid-century, over half of Parliament held Crown offices or had received government contracts. Colonial governors had few such favors to hand out.

The greatest constraint on the governor, however, was the fact that the assembly paid his salary. Governors who challenged the assembly soon encountered unaccountable delays in the payment of their salaries. Compliant governors were rewarded with cash or land grants.

While the governors realized that their great powers were less than they seemed, assemblies learned how to broaden their powers. They gained the right to elect their own speaker of the assembly and to make their own procedural rules governing

benign neglect The British policy of lax enforcement of most regulations on the American colonies as long as the colonies remained loyal and were a source of economic benefit.

bureaucrat A government official, usually non-elected, who is rigidly devoted to the details of administrative procedure.

the operation of the assembly. They also increased their power of the purse over taxation and the use of revenues.

Colonial political leaders had several advantages besides the governor's weaknesses. They came from a small social and economic elite that was regularly elected to office. Although from 50 to 80 percent of adult free white males in a colony could vote, few met the high property qualifications to hold office. The elite also benefited from the **deference** or respect shown by lesser folks toward the well educated and wealthy. Thus generations of fathers and sons from elite families dominated colonial political offices. These men knew each other well. Although they fought among themselves for positions and for power, they could effectively unite against outsiders like a governor.

Conflicting Views of the Assemblies

The king and Parliament expected local assemblies to raise taxes, to pay government salaries, and to maintain bridges and roads. To the colonists, this set of expectations indicated acceptance of two levels of government. One level was the central government in Great Britain, which created and executed imperial policy. The other level was the various colonial governments, which managed local domestic affairs. The colonists regarded both levels of government as legitimate.

The British did not agree. They saw only one government ruling a vast empire. British leaders did not believe the colonial governments had acquired any share of the British government's sovereign power. They viewed colonial assemblies as inferior to Parliament and as having no real authority.

North America and the Struggle for Empire

During the seventeenth century, most of the violence and warfare in colonial America arose from struggles between Indians and colonists or from disputes between colonists. After 1688, however, the most persistent danger to colonial peace came from fierce rivalries among the French, the Spanish, and the British. Between that date and 1763, these European powers waged five bloody and costly wars that ultimately spilled over into the colonies. These wars left their mark on every generation of colonists, for periods of peace were short and the shadow of war hung over colonial society until Britain's major triumph in 1763.

Indian Alliances and Rivalries

From the earliest days of settlement, many Indian tribes had formed alliances with European colonists for a variety of motives. The long alliance between the Wampanoags and the Pilgrims had helped the tribe fend off its enemies. Although this alliance had unraveled during King Philip's War, other seventeenth-century alignments remained intact. The Huron-dominated confederacy (see Map 4.2) and the French continued to find a strong bond in the profits from the fur trade. Like many eastern Indians, the Hurons were also increasingly dependent on European manufactured goods and weapons. The Iroquois, bitter rivals of the Hurons over access to the Great Lakes fur trade, formed a similar strategic alliance with the British. Consisting of the Mohawks, Senecas, Onondagas, Oneidas, Cayugas, and Tuscaroras, the **Iroquois League** enjoyed an advantage over other Indians in resisting expansion because of its strength in numbers and in organization.

In the South, the **Creek Confederacy** and the British established common ground for agreement. The two parties established a trade in deerskins

deference Yielding to the judgment or wishes of another person, usually seen as a social superior.

Iroquois League An American Indian confederacy in New York, originally composed of the Mohawk, Oneida, Onondaga, Cayuga, and Seneca peoples; in 1722 the Tuscaroras joined the confederacy.

Creek Confederacy An American Indian confederacy made up of the Creeks and various smaller southeast tribes.

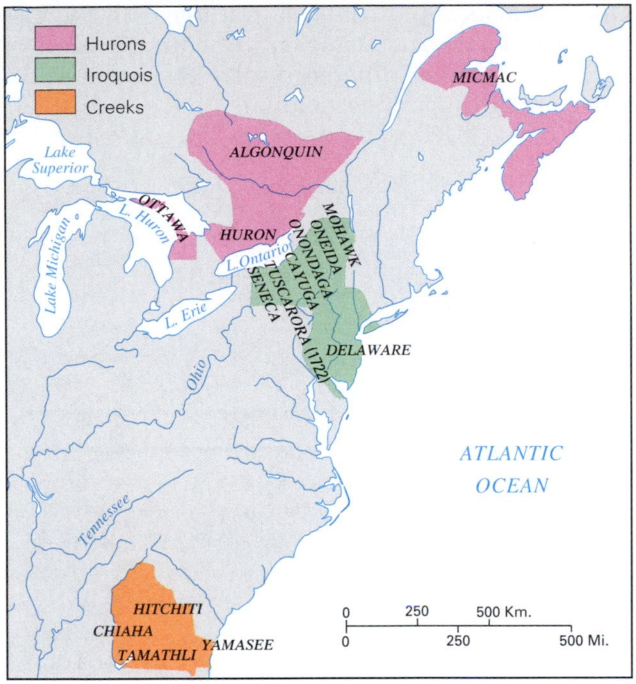
Hurons
Iroquois
Creeks
Lake Superior
OTTAWA
L. Huron
Lake Michigan
ALGONQUIN
HURON
L. Ontario
L. Erie
MOHAWK
ONEIDA
ONONDAGA
CAYUGA
TUSCARORA (1722)
SENECA
DELAWARE
MICMAC
Ohio
Tennessee
ATLANTIC OCEAN
HITCHITI
CHIAHA
TAMATHLI
YAMASEE
0 250 500 Km.
0 250 500 Mi.

♦ **MAP 4.2 The Indian Confederacies** This map shows the three major Indian military and political coalitions—the Huron, Iroquois, and Creek confederacies. Unlike the squabbling British mainland colonies, these Indian tribes understood the value of military unity in the face of threats to their land and safety and the importance of diplomatic unity in negotiating with their European allies.

and in captive Indians, whom the Creeks sold as slaves to South Carolinians. The Creeks later joined the British in attacks on Spanish Florida and helped capture runaway slaves. Land-hungry colonists severed the alliance when they attacked the Creeks and the Yamasees in 1715. The defeated Creeks moved west, while the Yamasees sought Spanish protection in Florida. When European rivalries led to warfare, southern tribes often sided with the French or Spanish to recover lost tribal lands.

The Great War for Empire

Between 1688 and 1763, the rivalry among Spain, France, and Great Britain produced five bloody and costly wars. No matter why or where these wars began, colonists were drawn into them. The first four of these wars did little to change the map of Europe. The fifth changed the map of the world.

In the 1740s, as the population explosion in British America sent thousands of settlers westward, the French began to build trading posts and forts in the Ohio valley. The neutral zone between the two empires shrank, and in 1754 the fifth and most dramatic war among the European rivals began: the Great War for Empire, known in the colonies as the **French and Indian War.** That year, a young Virginia planter and militia officer, Major George Washington, led an expedition against Fort Duquesne, the newest French garrison in the Ohio valley. When Washington was badly defeated, colonial leaders attempted to organize a unified defense. The colonial assemblies, however, proved too jealous of their independence to approve this **Albany Plan of Union.**

By 1755, British and French armies were battling in America. The conflict soon involved every major European power and spread to the Caribbean, the Philippines, Africa, and India. The war in North America did not go well for the British initially. Led by General Louis Joseph Montcalm, French and Indian forces by 1757 controlled western and central New York and were threatening Albany and New England.

At that critical juncture William Pitt became Britain's prime minister. Pitt committed the British treasury to the largest war expenditures the nation had ever known and then assembled the largest military force that North America had ever seen: twenty-five thousand colonial troops and twenty-four thousand British regulars. In September 1759, General James Wolfe led this army in a daring attack on Quebec. After scaling the steep cliffs that

French and Indian War A war in North America (1754–1763) that was part of a worldwide struggle between France and Great Britain; it ended with France's defeat.

Albany Plan of Union A proposal that the colonies form a union with a representative government and an army; Benjamin Franklin drafted it in 1754, but it was never ratified by the colonies.

protected the walled city, Wolfe's army met Montcalm's in front of the city on the Plains of Abraham. Both generals died in this short but decisive battle won by the British. Within five days, Quebec had surrendered.

In 1760, Montreal fell to the British. The French governor subsequently surrendered the whole of New France, effectively ending the war in North America. The fighting continued elsewhere until 1763. French hopes had risen briefly when Spain enlisted as their ally in 1761, but British victories in India, the Caribbean, and the Pacific squelched any expectations the French had. The **Treaty of Paris** (1763) established the supremacy of the British Empire. The reign of George III, which began in 1760, had started in glory.

The Outcomes of the Great War for Empire

At the peace table, the map of the world was redrawn. The French Empire shriveled. Nothing remained of New France but St. Pierre and St. Miquelon, two tiny islands between Nova Scotia and Newfoundland used by French fishing fleets. The only other remnants of the French Empire in the Western Hemisphere were the sugar islands of Guadeloupe, Martinique, and St. Domingue. Great Britain's sugar interest did not want to add these islands to the British Empire, for they would then be competitors in the British market. Across the Atlantic, France lost trading posts in Africa. On the other side of the world, the French presence in India vanished. The Treaty of Paris dismantled the French Empire but left France and its borders intact.

The victorious British did not escape unharmed. Their government was now deeply in debt and faced new problems in managing and protecting its greatly enlarged empire.

The American colonists lit bonfires and staged parades to celebrate their victory, but the war left scars. The British military had been arrogant toward provincial soldiers, had arbitrarily seized colonial goods, and had quartered British soldiers at colonial expense. The resentments were not one-sided. British officials could not understand how the colonists could continue trading with the enemy in wartime. Suspicion, resentment, and a growing sense of difference were the unexpected outcomes of a glorious victory.

Treaty of Paris Treaty that ended the French and Indian War in 1763; it gave all of French Canada and the Spanish Floridas to Great Britain.

SUMMARY

Expectations
Constraints
Choices
Outcomes

Each colonial region developed its own unique culture and society in response to varying regional *constraints*. New England life was centered on the family and community. The men and women of the small farming communities there were *expected* to live godly and harmonious lives. No single religious tradition bound the colonists of the southern or middle regions together. The *choice* to focus on cash crops led to the rise of a planter elite in the Chesapeake and the Lower South. In those regions, *choices* and opportunities were great for those who controlled the labor of others, especially of enslaved African Americans. The Middle Colonies developed a lively urban culture. Most people who immigrated to British North America after 1700, however, *chose* to settle in the backcountry, where there were greater opportunities.

Intellectual life in the eighteenth century changed dramatically as Enlightenment ideas encouraged reliance on reason. Colonial elites *chose* to adopt John Locke's theory of natural rights as well as skepticism about religious dogma. The Great Awakening exposed an opposing intellectual current. Revivalist George Whitefield and other evangelicals carried the religious revival throughout the colonies. "Awakeners" challenged all authority except the individual spirit, and many colonists *chose* to embrace those beliefs.

A similar challenge to authority spread to politics and imperial relations. Colonial assemblies *chose* to assert their own claim to power against appointed governors and other British officials. Strains in the relationship between colonial assemblies and imperial officers ran deep.

Rivalries among Spain, France, and Great Britain produced five major wars between 1688 and 1763 whose *outcome* damaged their empires. French power diminished greatly; Spain was put on the defensive. Despite their sweeping victory in the Great War for Empire, the British were forced to go deeply into debt and to face a new challenge to their empire.

SUGGESTED READINGS

Bailyn, Bernard. *Voyagers to the West: A Passage in the Peopling of America on the Eve of the Revolution* (1986).

Bailyn won a Pulitzer Prize for this survey of the character of, and motives for, emigration from the British Isles to America during the eighteenth century.

Hofstadter, Richard. *America at 1750: A Social Portrait* (1971).

This highly accessible work includes chapters on indentured servitude, the slave trade, the middle-class world of the colonies, the Great Awakening, and population growth and immigration patterns.

Lewis, Thomas A. *For King and Country: The Maturing of George Washington, 1748–1760* (1993).

This look at the early career of George Washington follows him as a colonial soldier of the Crown, a Virginia planter, and a young man of ambition.

Steele, Ian Kenneth. *"Betrayals," Fort William Henry and the Massacre* (1980).

Dramatized in James Fenimore Cooper's popular novel *The Last of the Mohicans*, this horrific attack on the garrison of a New York frontier outpost after its surrender was carried out by Indian allies of the French. Steele finds the roots of the massacre in radically different European and Indian concepts of warfare and victory.

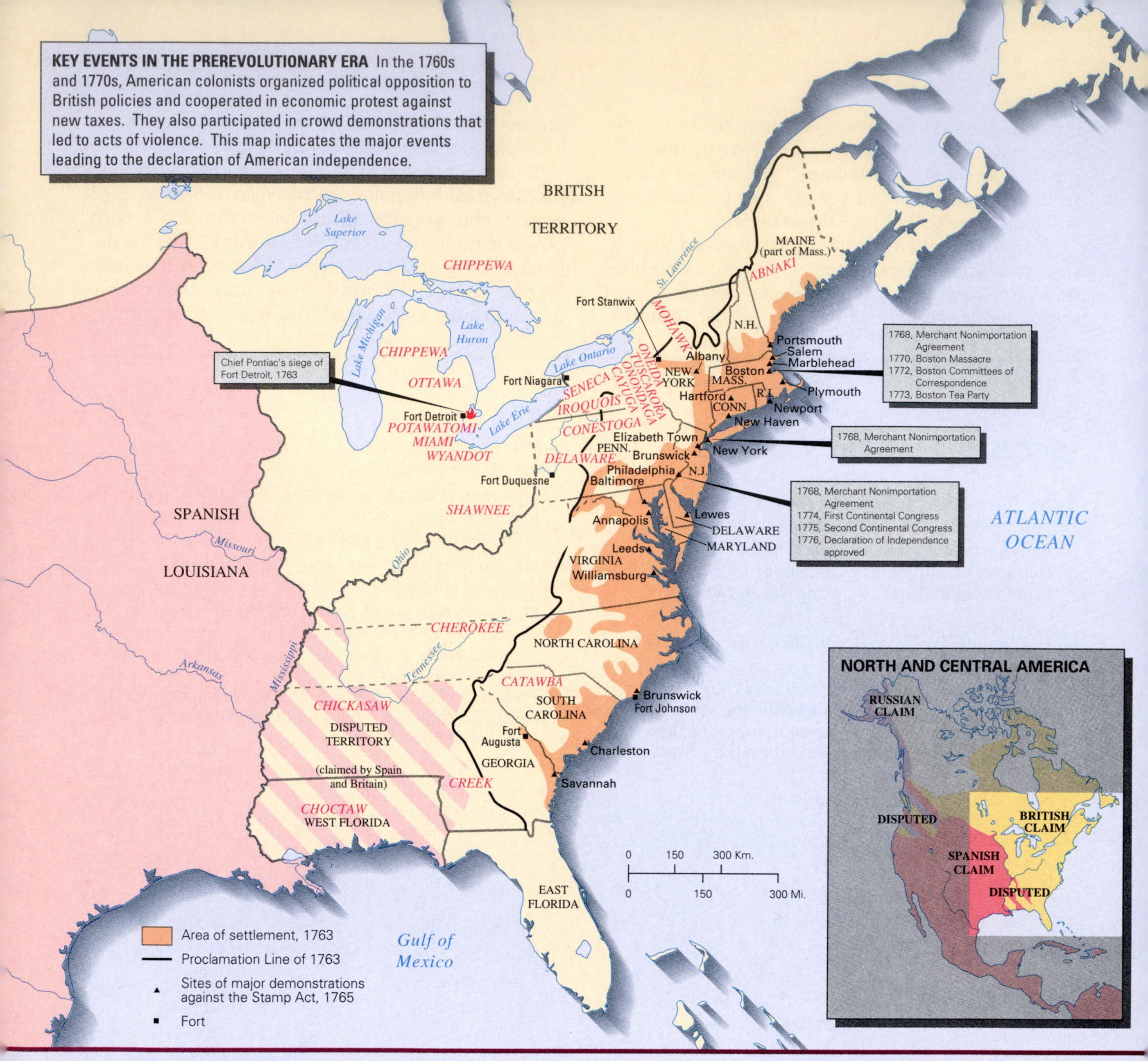

BRITISH
TERRITORY
Lake Superior
Lake Michigan
Lake Huron
Lake Ontario
Lake Erie
St. Lawrence
CHIPPEWA
CHIPPEWA
OTTAWA
POTAWATOMI
MIAMI
WYANDOT
SENECA
IROQUOIS
ONEIDA
TUSCARORA
ONONDAGA
CAYUGA
MOHAWK
CONESTOGA
DELAWARE
SHAWNEE
ABNAKI
CHEROKEE
CATAWBA
CHICKASAW
CREEK
CHOCTAW
Chief Pontiac's siege of Fort Detroit, 1763
Fort Detroit
Fort Niagara
Fort Stanwix
Fort Duquesne
MAINE (part of Mass.)
N.H.
Portsmouth
Salem
Marblehead
Boston
MASS.
Plymouth
R.I.
Newport
Albany
NEW YORK
Hartford
CONN
New Haven
Elizabeth Town
PENN.
Brunswick
New York
N.J.
Philadelphia
Baltimore
Lewes
DELAWARE
MARYLAND
Annapolis
Leeds
VIRGINIA
Williamsburg
NORTH CAROLINA
Brunswick
Fort Johnson
SOUTH CAROLINA
Fort Augusta
GEORGIA
Charleston
Savannah
DISPUTED TERRITORY
(claimed by Spain and Britain)
WEST FLORIDA
EAST FLORIDA
SPANISH
LOUISIANA
Missouri
Ohio
Tennessee
Arkansas
Mississippi
Gulf of Mexico
ATLANTIC OCEAN
1768, Merchant Nonimportation Agreement
1770, Boston Massacre
1772, Boston Committees of Correspondence
1773, Boston Tea Party
1768, Merchant Nonimportation Agreement
1768, Merchant Nonimportation Agreement
1774, First Continental Congress
1775, Second Continental Congress
1776, Declaration of Independence approved
0 150 300 Km.
0 150 300 Mi.
Area of settlement, 1763
Proclamation Line of 1763
Sites of major demonstrations against the Stamp Act, 1765
Fort
NORTH AND CENTRAL AMERICA
RUSSIAN CLAIM
DISPUTED
BRITISH CLAIM
SPANISH CLAIM
DISPUTED

KEY EVENTS IN THE PREREVOLUTIONARY ERA In the 1760s and 1770s, American colonists organized political opposition to British policies and cooperated in economic protest against new taxes. They also participated in crowd demonstrations that led to acts of violence. This map indicates the major events leading to the declaration of American independence.

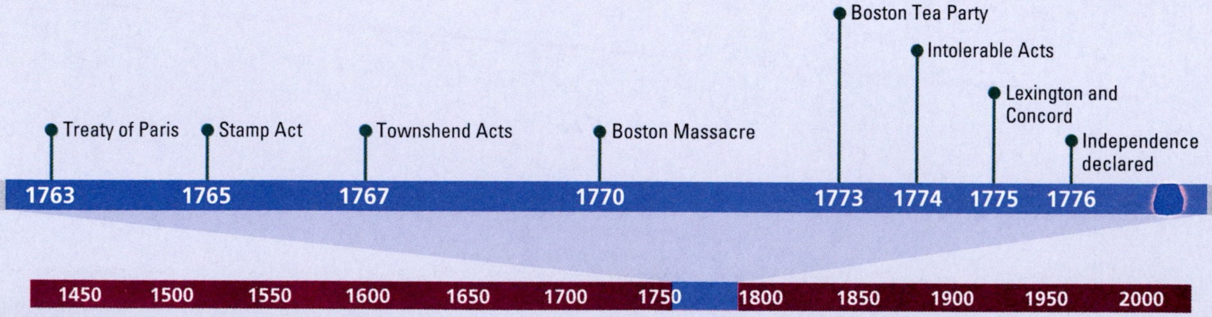

Treaty of Paris
Stamp Act
Townshend Acts
Boston Massacre
Boston Tea Party
Intolerable Acts
Lexington and Concord
Independence declared
1763
1765
1767
1770
1773
1774
1775
1776
1450
1500
1550
1600
1650
1700
1750
1800
1850
1900
1950
2000

CHAPTER 5

Choosing Loyalties, 1763–1776

Victory's New Problems

- Why did George Grenville expect the colonists to accept part of the burden of financing the British Empire in 1764?
- Why were the colonists alarmed by Grenville's choice to impose a stamp tax in 1765?
- How did the colonists choose to respond to direct taxation by Parliament?

Asserting American Rights

- Why did Charles Townshend expect his revenue measures to be successful?
- What form of protest did the colonists choose in response?
- What was the outcome of that protest?

The Crisis Renewed

- What British choices led Americans to see a plot against their rights and liberties?
- What constraints did the king place on Massachusetts to crush resistance there?
- How did the Continental Congress choose to respond?

The Decision for Independence

- Could the Revolutionary War have been avoided?
- What choices on both sides might have kept compromise alive?
- What different expectations and constraints influenced some colonists to become loyalists and others to become patriots?

INTRODUCTION

Expectations
Constraints
Choices
Outcomes

The British victory over France in 1763 raised *expectations* for an era of prosperity and cooperation between mother country and colonies. But less than two years later, Britain's mainland colonists had risen in protest against the *constraints* placed on them by British policies and regulations. Fundamental political differences then emerged between the British government and the colonists. They could not agree on the rights and obligations of the colonists. Americans who had once toasted the king *chose* instead to drink to resistance to tyrants. By 1775, a new *choice* faced the colonists: loyalty or rebellion.

The *outcome* of the troubled years between 1763 and 1775 was the American Revolution. However, the colonists who *chose* to protest taxation in 1765 did not know they were laying the groundwork for a revolution. We can look back on their *expectations, constraints,* and *choices* and see that the likely *outcome* was indeed a break with Britain. But the people who made that revolution did not know it was coming.

Events between 1763 and 1776 forced many colonists to *choose* between loyalty to Great Britain and loyalty to colonial independence. The war that resulted set neighbor against neighbor, father against son, and wife against husband. For thousands, the *outcome* of this crisis of loyalty was exile from home and family. For others, it meant death or injury on the battlefield. In 1776, however, the *outcome* was unclear.

Victory's New Problems

When **George Grenville** became King George III's chief minister in 1763, he appeared to face a much easier task than William Pitt had confronted six years earlier. The battles of the Great War for Empire had been won, and all that remained to be done was to negotiate a treaty with an exhausted and defeated France.

Grenville soon discovered the costs of glory. Pitt had spent vast sums without hesitation to secure his nation's victory, and he had left the new minister with an enormous war debt. British taxpayers, who had groaned under the wartime burden, were expecting tax relief, not tax increases. There were also serious problems in governing the new Canadian territory because some American Indian tribes were unwilling to pledge their allegiance to King **George III.**

Dealing with Indian Resistance

The former Indian allies of France and Spain were threatened by Britain's recent victory. For decades, they had protected their lands by playing European rivals against each other. Now the French had been ousted from Canada and the Spanish from Florida. The Creeks and the Cherokees of the Southeast had felt the effects of Spanish withdrawal even before the war ended, when settlers from the southern colonies poured into Creek and

George Grenville British prime minister who sought to tighten British control over the colonies and impose taxes on colonial trade.

George III King of Great Britain (r. 1760–1820); his government's policies fed colonial discontent and helped start the American Revolution in 1776.

CHRONOLOGY

Loyalty or Rebellion?

1763	Treaty of Paris ends French and Indian War Pontiac's Rebellion Proclamation Line
1764	Sugar Act
1765	Stamp Act Sons of Liberty organized Stamp Act Congress Nonimportation of British goods
1766	Repeal of the Stamp Act Declaratory Act
1767	Townshend Acts John Dickinson's *Letters from a Farmer in Pennsylvania*
1768	Nonimportation of British goods
1770	Boston Massacre Repeal of the Townshend Acts
1772	Burning of the *Gaspée*
1773	Tea Act Boston Tea Party
1774	Intolerable Acts First Continental Congress Declaration of Rights and Grievances Suffolk Resolves
1775	Battles of Lexington and Concord Second Continental Congress Olive Branch Petition
1776	Tom Paine's *Common Sense* Declaration of Independence

Cherokee territory. When the Cherokees launched a full-scale war along the southern frontier, the British crushed their rebellion and forced the Cherokees to open up their lands to settlement.

In 1763, settlers began a similar invasion of Indian territory in the upper Ohio valley and Great Lakes region. In response, the Ottawa chief, **Pontiac,** created an intertribal alliance known as the **Covenant Chain** to oppose white expansion. Throughout the summer and early fall of 1763, this alliance of Senecas, Ojibwas, Potawatomis, Hurons, Ottawas, Delawares, Shawnees, and Mingos mounted attacks on Fort Detroit and other frontier forts in what became known as Pontiac's Rebellion. The British forts held, however, and by winter Pontiac had to acknowledge British control of the Ohio valley.

The British recognized that this victory did not ensure permanent peace in the West. Indian resistance would not end as long as settlers continued to pour into Indian territories. Thus, in late 1763, Grenville issued a proclamation that temporarily banned settlement west of the Appalachian Mountains (see Map 5.1). Colonists in the backcountry, were outraged by this **Proclamation Line of 1763.** They generally ignored the proclamation and continued to take land they wanted. Over the next decade, homesteaders poured into areas such as western Pennsylvania and Kentucky.

Pontiac Ottawa chief and former French ally who organized the Covenant Chain; he mounted an unsuccessful siege of Fort Detroit in 1763.

Covenant Chain An alliance of American Indian peoples formed to resist colonial settlement in the Northwest and British trading policy.

Proclamation Line of 1763 British policy that banned white settlement west of the Appalachian Mountains; it was intended to reduce conflict between Indians and settlers, but it angered settlers.

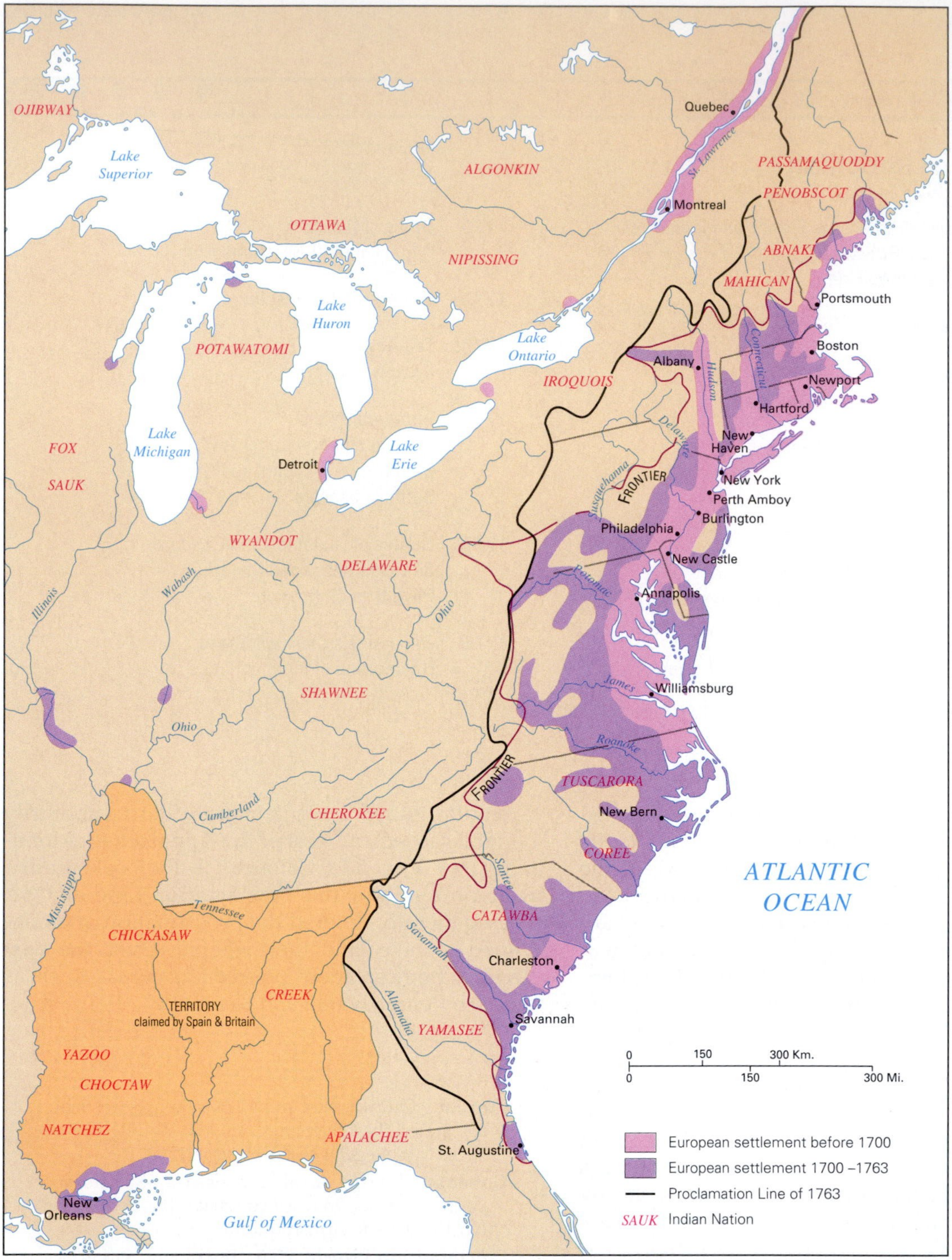
OJIBWAY
Lake Superior
ALGONKIN
Quebec
St. Lawrence
PASSAMAQUODDY
PENOBSCOT
Montreal
OTTAWA
NIPISSING
ABNAKI
MAHICAN
Portsmouth
Lake Huron
Lake Ontario
POTAWATOMI
Albany
Boston
Hudson
Connecticut
Newport
IROQUOIS
Hartford
Lake Michigan
FOX
SAUK
Detroit
Lake Erie
Delaware
New Haven
FRONTIER
Susquehanna
New York
Perth Amboy
Burlington
Philadelphia
WYANDOT
DELAWARE
New Castle
Wabash
Illinois
Potomac
Annapolis
Ohio
SHAWNEE
James
Williamsburg
Ohio
Roanoke
FRONTIER
TUSCARORA
Cumberland
CHEROKEE
New Bern
COREE
ATLANTIC OCEAN
Santee
Mississippi
Tennessee
CATAWBA
CHICKASAW
Savannah
Charleston
CREEK
TERRITORY claimed by Spain & Britain
Altamaha
YAMASEE
Savannah
YAZOO
CHOCTAW
0 150 300 Km.
0 150 300 Mi.
NATCHEZ
APALACHEE
St. Augustine
European settlement before 1700
European settlement 1700 –1763
Proclamation Line of 1763
SAUK Indian Nation
New Orleans
Gulf of Mexico

♦ **MAP 5.1 The Proclamation Line of 1763** This map shows European settlement east of the Appalachian Mountains and the numerous Indian tribes with territorial claims to the lands between the Appalachians and the Mississippi River. The Proclamation Line, which roughly followed the crest of these mountains, was the British government's effort to halt colonial westward expansion and thus to prevent bloodshed between settlers and Indians. This British policy was deeply resented by land-hungry colonists.

Demanding More from the Colonies

Grenville's examination of the economic relationship between mother country and colonies revealed that Great Britain had not benefited greatly from her American colonies. Grenville singled out illegal colonial trade as the primary reason why the expected benefits had not materialized. Americans traded for illegal goods with Britain's rivals and avoided paying **import duties** for legal foreign goods whenever they could.

The results of such avoidance were apparent from the imperial trade books. By the 1760s, the Crown was collecting less than £2,000 in customs duties while spending more than £7,000 to collect those duties annually. In 1764, Grenville proposed new policies to correct this problem and thereby ended the long era of benign neglect.

To end American smuggling, Grenville first had to reform the **customs service.** He took steps to stop customs officers from taking bribes from smugglers. He then gave customs men the power to use blanket warrants, or **writs of assistance,** to search ships and warehouses for smuggled goods. Grenville's next step was to reform the import regulations. The 1764 American Revenue Act, known popularly as the **Sugar Act,** showed that Grenville was a practical man. His intent was to make it cheaper to pay the import duties on foreign molasses and sugar than it was to bribe customs officials or to evade the duty by landing a cargo on an isolated beach. The act cut the duty on foreign molasses in half, from six to three pence per gallon, but Grenville was determined that this duty be paid.

To ensure that it was, Grenville changed the way smuggling cases were handled in court. Until 1764, a colonist accused of smuggling was brought before a jury of neighbors in a **civil court.** He expected, and usually got, a favorable verdict. Grenville now declared that smugglers would be tried in a **vice-admiralty court,** where there were no sympathetic colonial juries. Once smuggling became too costly and too risky, Grenville reasoned, American shippers would bow to trade regulations and pay the Crown for the privilege of importing French molasses.

The Colonial Response

Grenville's reforms could not have come at a worse time for the colonists. They took effect during the economic **depression** that followed the French and Indian War. The depression was largely the result of an abrupt decline of British military spending in the colonies. Unemployment among artisans, dockworkers, and sailors ran high. Merchants found themselves unable to pay their debts to British suppliers because the merchants' customers had no money to pay their bills. The merchants blamed this situation on Grenville's **Currency Act** of 1764, which outlawed the printing of paper money in the colonies.

Ironically, some colonists welcomed the hard times. They believed that Americans had become overly fond of luxuries and that this had weakened their spirit, sapped their independence, and corrupted their morals. They warned that moral decay had ruined Britain, where extravagance and corruption infected society. Such colonists appealed to their neighbors to embrace simplicity and to sacrifice by **boycotting** all British manufactured goods.

import duty A tax on imported goods.

customs service A government agency authorized to collect taxes on foreign goods entering a country.

writs of assistance General search warrants issued to customs officers by colonial courts, giving them the authority to search ships and warehouses for smuggled goods.

Sugar Act British law (1764) that taxed sugar, molasses, and other colonial imports to defray British expenses in protecting the colonies.

civil court Any court that hears cases regarding the rights of private citizens.

vice-admiralty court British court that heard cases involving shipping.

depression A period of drastic economic decline, characterized by decreasing business activity, falling prices, and unemployment.

Currency Act British law (1764) that banned the printing of paper money in the American colonies.

boycott A protest in which people refuse to buy goods from or otherwise deal with a nation or group of people whose actions they object to.

Colonial newspapers, however, focused on the political dimensions of Grenville's reforms. Those reforms raised disturbing questions about the rights of the colonists and the relationship between Parliament and the colonial governments. But in 1764, Americans were far from agreement over how they should respond to the Sugar Act.

The Stamp Act

Grenville's next proposal to Parliament startled the colonists even more. He suggested that Parliament approve the first internal tax, or **direct tax,** ever levied on the colonies. Until 1765, Parliament had passed many acts regulating colonial trade, some of which taxed imported goods. It had never, however, levied direct taxes on the colonists. Such taxes had previously been approved only by their local assemblies. From a colonial perspective, this proposed tax would change the traditional relationship between the colonial assemblies and Parliament dramatically.

Colonists greeted news of Parliament's approval of the **Stamp Act,** passed in February 1765, with outrage and anger. Come November, when the act would go into effect, virtually every free man and woman would be affected by this tax that required the use of government "stamped paper" on legal documents, newspapers, pamphlets, and even playing cards. Grenville's Stamp Act united northern merchants and southern planters, rural women and urban workingmen, and it riled the most argumentative of all Americans: lawyers and newspaper publishers.

The Popular Response

Many colonists were determined to resist the new legislation. During the summer of 1765, a group of Bostonians formed a secret organization called the **Sons of Liberty.** Although one of its founders was the socially prominent, Harvard-educated **Samuel Adams,** most members were artisans and shopkeepers. They had been hit hard by the postwar depression and would suffer further from the stamp tax. They took to the streets to make their protests known.

Such protests soon made the position of government stamp agent a hazardous occupation in Boston. On August 14, 1765, the Sons of Liberty and gentlemen disguised in working-class garb paraded an **effigy** of Andrew Oliver, a wealthy merchant and newly appointed stamp agent, through the city. The Sons not only hung the effigy on a tree near Oliver's wharf but also destroyed Oliver's warehouse and later broke all the windows in his home. The following day, Oliver resigned his position as stamp agent. The Sons of Liberty celebrated by declaring the tree on which they had hanged Oliver's effigy the "liberty tree."

The Sons then harassed other Crown officials living in Boston. **Thomas Hutchinson,** lieutenant governor of Massachusetts, became the chief target of abuse when a false rumor spread that he had written to British officials in support of the Stamp Act. The rumor encouraged a large crowd of artisans and others to trash the lieutenant governor's elegant brick mansion later that August of 1765.

Hutchinson appears to have been a political and a social target for the working people of Boston. He represented the privilege and power of the few and the well placed. The destruction of his home caused many of Boston's elite merchants to withdraw their support from popular protests. They reasoned that the tensions aroused between rich

direct tax Tax explicitly imposed to raise revenues.

Stamp Act British law (1765) that levied direct taxes on a large variety of items, including newspapers, almanacs, and legal documents.

Sons of Liberty A secret organization formed in Boston to oppose the Stamp Act; its leaders included Samuel Adams and Paul Revere.

Samuel Adams Massachusetts revolutionary leader and propagandist who organized opposition to the Stamp Act and took part in the Boston Tea Party.

effigy A representation of a hated or despised person.

Thomas Hutchinson Boston merchant who served as lieutenant governor of Massachusetts and later as governor; his efforts to enforce the Stamp Act prompted a mob to destroy his house.

and poor were perhaps more dangerous than the tensions between Parliament and the colonies.

The campaign against stamp agents spread like a brush fire throughout the colonies. Colonists who had agreed to take the position of agent had not expected to endure hatred or to suffer harm. They believed that a British law would be obeyed. But no stamp agent was safe. When the stamps reached colonial ports that fall, only the young colony of Georgia could produce anyone willing to distribute them.

The British responded to this explosion of violence and political protest by refusing to allow colonial ships to leave port. They hoped that the disruption of trade would force colonial merchants to use their influence to end the resistance. The strategy backfired. Hundreds of angry, unemployed sailors took to the streets to join in the resistance to the stamp tax.

Political Debate

The Stamp Act raised a fundamental issue: whether Parliament had the right to tax the colonists. As the young Virginia lawyer Patrick Henry put it, the Stamp Act was a matter of "liberty or death." A basic British principle held that no citizen could be taxed by a government in which he was not represented. "No taxation without representation" was a principle shared on both sides of the Atlantic. The real question was whether Parliament represented the colonists, even though no colonist sat in that body or voted in parliamentary elections.

To Massachusetts lawyer **James Otis,** the answer to this question was clearly no. Otis took the position that the colonists should be given representation in the House of Commons. Few colonial political leaders took Otis's demand for American representation seriously because they realized that a small contingent of colonists could be easily ignored or defeated in Parliament. Therefore most leaders declared that taxation was the right of local assemblies and that American rights and liberties were under attack. After much debate, most assemblies issued statements condemning the Stamp Act and demanding its repeal.

The Stamp Act produced the first stirrings of intercolonial unity. Until 1765, the colonies had been more prone to disagree with each other than to cooperate. When Massachusetts called for an intercolonial meeting to discuss the Stamp Act, however, nine colonies sent delegates to New York in the fall of 1765. The **Stamp Act Congress** conceded in a **petition** to the king that Parliament had authority over the colonies but boldly denied that Parliament had the right to impose a direct tax on them. "No taxes," they said, "ever have been, or can be Constitutionally imposed" on the colonies "but by their respective Legislatures." Americans expected that tradition to be honored.

Repeal of the Stamp Act

Neither the intimidation of the Sons of Liberty nor the arguments of the Stamp Act Congress prompted the repeal of the stamp tax. But economic pressure did work. American merchants applied this pressure when they announced that as of November 1, 1765, when the Stamp Act went into effect, they would refuse to import any more British manufactured goods. More than patriotic motives were at work here, for the warehouses of these merchants were bulging with unsold goods because of the postwar depression. Economic motives also prompted artisans to support these **nonimportation agreements** wholeheartedly, for their products competed with British goods. Regardless of motive, much of colonial America endorsed a boycott of British goods.

James Otis Boston lawyer who argued that writs of assistance violated colonists' rights under British law and who called for colonial representation in Parliament.

Stamp Act Congress A meeting of colonial delegates in New York in 1765, which drew up a declaration of rights and grievances for presentation to the king and Parliament.

petition A formal written request to a superior authority.

nonimportation agreements Colonial policy of refusing to import British goods, undertaken as a protest against the Stamp Act.

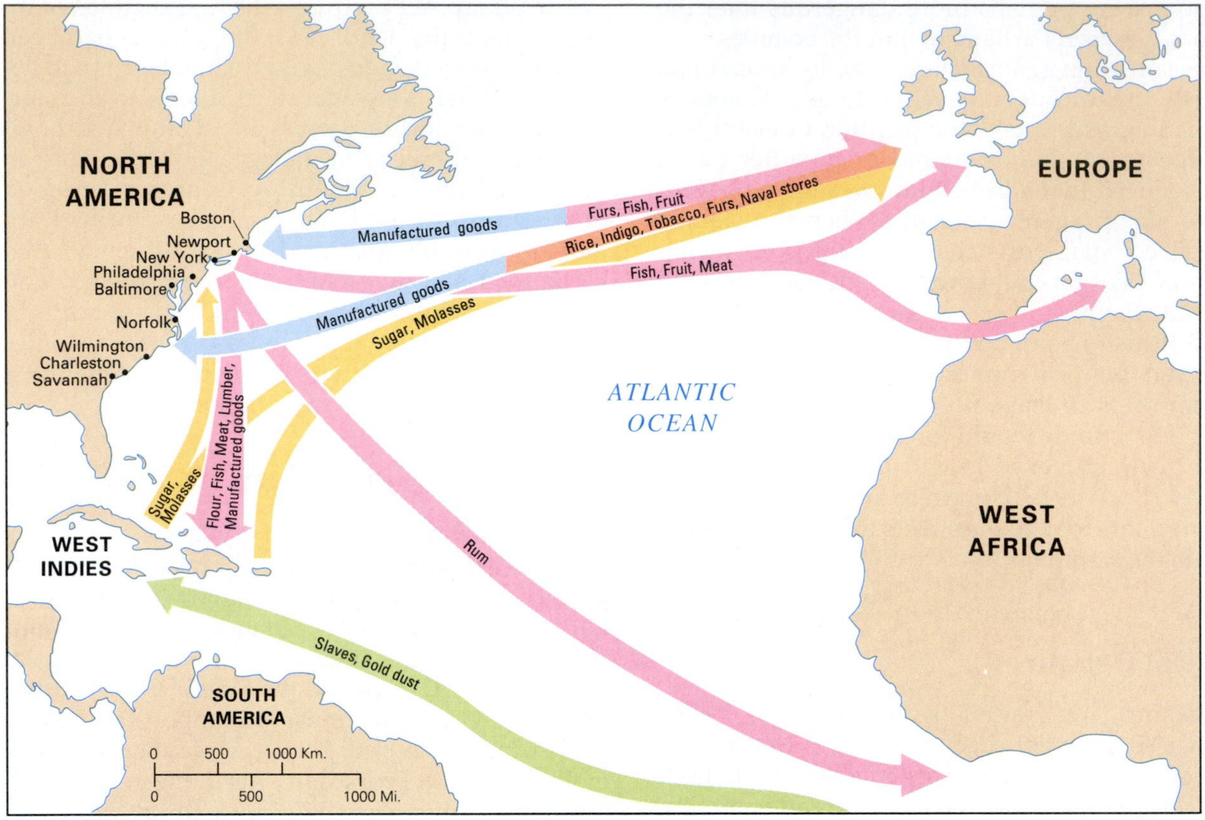

♦ **MAP 5.2 Colonial Transatlantic Trade in the 1760s** This map shows the major trade routes among the British mainland colonies, West Africa, the Caribbean, and Europe and the most important export and import cargoes carried along these routes. The central role northern seaport cities played in carrying colonial agricultural products across the Atlantic and bringing British manufactured goods into the colonies is clear. Note also the role the northern colonies played in the slave trade.

Because the mainland colonies constituted the largest market for goods made in Britain, British exporters consequently saw a huge downturn in their business (see Map 5.2). Parliament listened to the bitter complaints of these exporters, and talk of repeal grew within its halls. The Grenville government had to concede that enforcement of the Stamp Act had failed miserably. Americans continued to sue their neighbors, publish their newspapers, and buy their playing cards as if the Stamp Act did not exist.

By winter's end, a new prime minister, Lord Rockingham, had replaced Grenville. Rockingham had opposed the Stamp Act from the start. For him, the critical issue now was how to repeal the Stamp Act without appearing to cave in to colonial pressure. His solution was to have Parliament repeal the Stamp Act but at the same time pass the **Declaratory Act.** This act reasserted Parliament's absolute right to legislate for and to tax the colonies.

Declaratory Act British law (1766) that asserted Parliament's right to make laws for and impose taxes on the American colonies.

Colonists celebrated news of the repeal with public displays of loyalty to the mother country that were as impressive as their protests had been. There were cannon salutes, bonfires, parades, speeches, and public toasts to the king and Rockingham. The crisis seemed to have passed.

Asserting American Rights

In their celebrations of repeal, the colonists overlooked the Declaratory Act and its clear assertion of parliamentary power. They soon had to take notice of it. By the summer of 1766, William Pitt had replaced Lord Rockingham. The aging and ailing Pitt, however, could not direct the government. So the **chancellor of the exchequer,** Charles Townshend, became the effective head of government. By 1767, Townshend had imposed new taxes on the colonies.

The Townshend Acts and Colonial Protest

During the Stamp Act crisis, Pennsylvania's **colonial agent,** Benjamin Franklin, had assured Parliament that American colonists opposed direct taxes (such as stamp taxes) but did not object to indirect taxes (such as import duties). Franklin's hard distinction between direct and indirect taxes was not shared by many colonists. But Charles Townshend took Franklin at his word. The **Townshend Acts** of 1767 placed an import tax on tea, glass, paper, paint, and lead products. These acts differed from previous customs duties in that they were levied on imported British goods instead of on foreign products.

Townshend took every precaution to avoid a repetition of the Stamp Act disaster. He expanded the scope and powers of the customs service. He transferred British troops from the western frontier to the major port cities. He expected the presence of uniformed soldiers, known as "redcoats" because of their scarlet uniforms, to allow customs officers to perform their duties and to keep the peace.

But Townshend made a serious error in accepting Franklin's assurances about taxes on imported goods. When news of the import duties reached the colonies, the response was immediate, determined, and well-organized resistance. The British government was once again trampling on the principle of "no taxation without representation."

John Dickinson, a well-respected landowner and lawyer, laid out the basic American position on taxes in 1767 in his *Letters from a Farmer in Pennsylvania.* Both direct and indirect taxation without representation violated the colonists' rights as British citizens, Dickinson wrote. Parliament did have the right to regulate foreign trade, and thus to levy duties on foreign imports—but not on British goods. An import duty on British products was merely a tax in disguise.

Dickinson also rejected the British argument that Americans were represented in Parliament. According to this argument, the colonists enjoyed **virtual representation** because the House of Commons represented the interests of all citizens in the empire, whether they participated directly in elections to the House or not. Dickinson insisted that the colonists were entitled to **actual representation** by men

chancellor of the exchequer The head of the British government department in charge of collecting taxes; the exchequer is a treasury department.

colonial agent Person chosen by each colonial assembly to represent each colony's interests in Parliament.

Townshend Acts British laws (1767) that required the colonials to pay duties on manufactured goods—such as glass, lead, and tea—imported from Britain.

John Dickinson Philadelphia lawyer who drafted the Articles of Confederation and argued for the rights of small states.

virtual representation Parliamentary representation that stems from people's status as citizens, regardless of whether they have directly elected delegates to look out for their specific interests.

actual representation Parliamentary representation by delegates directly elected to speak for voters' interests.

whom they elected to Parliament and who were dedicated to protecting their interests. To Dickinson, virtual representation was only a weak excuse for exploitation. As one American quipped, "Our privileges are all virtual, our sufferings are real."

While political theorists set out the American position in newspaper essays and pamphlets, activists organized popular resistance. Samuel Adams initiated nonimportation agreements of British goods that were to take effect on January 1, 1768. Some colonists again welcomed the chance to "mow down luxury and high living." Economic interests also affected support for the boycott. Underemployed artisans remained enthusiastic about any action that stopped the flow of inexpensive British goods to America. Merchants and shippers who made their living smuggling goods from the West Indies supported the boycott because it cut out competing products. The affluent merchants who had led the nonimportation movement in 1765, however, were reluctant supporters of this new boycott. By 1767, their warehouses no longer overflowed with unsold British stock, and they were not eager to cut off their own livelihoods. Some never signed the new agreements.

The biggest critics of the boycott were colonists in royal offices. These Americans shared their neighbors' attachment to the rights of Englishmen, but they were sworn to uphold and to carry out the policies of the British government. Because their careers and their identities were closely tied to the Crown, they were inclined to accept British policy as a patriotic duty. Despite their prestige and authority, these Crown officers were unable to prevent the boycott.

Just as the Sons of Liberty brought common men into the political arena, the 1768 boycott brought politics more dramatically into the lives of women. By the mid-eighteenth century, any colonial woman with the means bought ready-made British cloth instead of making her own. In 1768, however, British textiles became boycotted goods. Suddenly, an old and neglected domestic skill became both a real and a symbolic element in the American political strategy. The Daughters of Liberty staged large public **spinning bees** to support the boycott, boost morale, and pool their resources. Wearing cloth spun at home became a mark of honor. Politics had entered the domestic circle.

The British Humiliated

Townshend faced sustained defiance of British authority in almost every colony, but nowhere was it as great as in Massachusetts. Enforcers of the boycott roamed the streets of Boston, intimidating pro-British merchants and harassing anyone wearing British-made clothing. Mobs openly threatened customs officials, and the Sons of Liberty protected smuggling operations. Despite more customs officers, the illegal importation of British and foreign goods was thriving. One of the most notorious smugglers, **John Hancock,** seemed to grow more popular each time he unloaded his illegal cargoes of French and Spanish wines or West Indian molasses. Customs officers finally seized his vessel the *Liberty* in June 1768. Their action led mobs to beat up senior customs men and to threaten other royal officials. Governor Francis Bernard sent an urgent plea for help to the British government.

In October 1768, the Crown responded by sending four thousand troops to Boston. These soldiers, many of them young, far from home, and surrounded by a hostile citizenry, worsened the situation. The soldiers passed their idle hours courting local women who would speak to them and pestering those who would not. They angered local dockworkers by moonlighting in the shipyards. In turn, civilians taunted and insulted the soldiers. News of street-corner fights and tavern brawls inflamed feelings on both sides. Samuel Adams and his friends fanned the flames by publishing accounts of confrontations (both real and imagined) between hostile soldiers and innocent townspeople.

These confrontations culminated in what became known as the **Boston Massacre.** On March 5, 1770, an angry crowd began throwing snowballs at

spinning bee A meeting of women to compete or work together in spinning thread or yarn.

John Hancock Patriot who became president of the First Continental Congress and was the first to sign the Declaration of Independence.

Boston Massacre Incident in Boston on March 5, 1770, in which British troops fired on a crowd, killing five colonists; it increased colonial resentment of British rule.

British sentries guarding the custom house. The redcoats issued a frantic call for help. Captain Thomas Preston arrived with troops to rescue the sentries, but he and his men were soon enveloped by the growing crowd. Preston's men panicked and opened fire, killing five colonists.

Accounts of the Boston Massacre appeared in colonial newspapers everywhere. Although a jury of colonists later cleared Preston and all but two of his men of the charges against them, nothing that was said at the trial could erase the image of British brutality against British subjects.

On the very day that Captain Preston's men fired on the crowd at Boston, the new British prime minister, **Lord North,** repealed the Townshend Acts. Like Rockingham, North wanted to give no ground on the question of parliamentary control of the colonies. For this reason, he kept the tax on tea.

Success Weakens Colonial Unity

Repeal of the Townshend Acts allowed the colonists to return to their ordinary routines. But the boycott that began in 1768 exposed growing divisions between the merchant elite and the coalition of small merchants, artisans, and laborers. Despite the boycott, many wealthy merchants had secretly imported and sold British goods whenever possible. When repeal came in 1770, artisans and laborers still faced poor economic prospects and were reluctant to abandon the boycott. But few merchants, large or small, would agree to continue it. The boycott collapsed.

Many elite colonists abandoned the radical **activism** they had shown in the 1760s in favor of social **conservatism.** Their fear of British tyranny dimmed as their fear of the lower classes' demand for political power grew. Artisans and laborers continued to press for broader participation in local politics and for more representative political machinery. "Many of the poorer People," observed one supporter of expanded political participation, "deeply felt the Aristocratic Power, or rather the intolerable Tyranny of the great and opulent." The new political language employed by these common men made their social superiors uneasy. The colonial elite found its impassioned appeals to rights and liberties returning to haunt it.

The Crisis Renewed

Lord North's government took care not to disturb the calm that followed the repeal of the Townshend Acts. Between 1770 and 1773, North proposed no new taxes on the colonists and made no major changes in colonial policy. American political leaders took equal care not to make any open challenges to British authority. But this political truce had its limits. It certainly did not extend to smugglers and customs men.

Disturbing the Peace of the Early 1770s

Despite the repeal of the Townshend duties, the British effort to crack down on American smuggling continued. Rhode Island merchants were especially angry and frustrated by the highly effective customs operation in their colony. They took their revenge in June 1772 by burning a customs patrol boat, the *Gaspée,* that had run aground as it chased an American vessel.

Rhode Islanders interpreted the burning of the *Gaspée* as an act of political resistance. The British called it vandalism. The British government appointed a royal commission to investigate the raid but could find no witnesses or evidence to support an **indictment.** The British found the conspiracy of silence among the Rhode Islanders appalling.

In turn, American political leaders found the royal commission appalling. They were convinced that the British had intended to take suspects back to Britain for trial and thus deprive them of a jury of their peers. They read this as further evidence of the plot to destroy American liberty.

Lord North British prime minister during the American Revolution.

activism The assertive use of militant action, such as demonstrations and strikes, to support a controversial position.

conservatism The desire to maintain the existing or traditional order.

indictment A formal written statement that charges someone with the commission of a crime.

The *Gaspée* incident convinced leaders of the American resistance that they needed to coordinate their efforts to monitor British moves throughout the colonies. They organized **committees of correspondence** that were instructed to circulate reports of any incidents to the other committees. These committees were also a good mechanism for coordinating protest or resistance. Thus the colonists put in place their first permanent machinery of protest.

The Tea Act and the Tea Party

During the early 1770s, colonial activists worked to keep the political consciousness of the 1760s alive. They commemorated American victories over British policy and observed the anniversary of the Boston Massacre with solemn speeches and sermons. Without major British provocation, however, any new mass action was unlikely.

In 1773, Parliament provided that provocation when it rescued the East India Tea Company from bankruptcy. To bail out the company, Parliament offered it a government loan and permission to ship tea directly from its warehouses in India to the colonies. This arrangement would bypass British middlemen, cut shipping costs, and allow the company to lower the price of its tea in America. Even with the three-penny tax on tea that remained from the Townshend era, British tea would be cheaper than the Dutch tea smuggled into the colonies. Lord North supported the **Tea Act** when he realized that if Americans purchased the cheaper British tea, they would also pay the tea tax and confirm Parliament's right to tax the colonies.

The Tea Act galvanized American protest. Colonists read it as another sign of a conspiracy against their well-being and their liberty. They were troubled that the government had altered its colonial trade policy to suit the needs of a special interest, the East India Tea Company. They feared that the cheaper prices for tea were a temporary measure that would last only until all foreign teas had been driven off the market. And they perceived the snare that Lord North had set for them: if they drank cheap tea, they would be legitimizing Parliament's right to tax them.

Colonists mobilized their resistance in 1773 with the skill acquired from a decade of experience. In many colonies, crowds met the ships carrying the East India Company tea and used violent threats to persuade ship captains to return to Britain with the tea still on board. But in Massachusetts, Governor Thomas Hutchinson refused to allow the tea ships to leave Boston harbor without unloading. Boston's activists took him at his word. On December 16, 1773, some sixty men, thinly disguised as Indians, boarded the tea ships. They dumped 342 chests of tea, worth almost £10,000, into Boston harbor.

The Intolerable Acts

The **Boston Tea Party** delighted colonial activists everywhere, especially in New England. The Crown, however, failed to see the humor in this deliberate destruction of valuable private property. Lord North decided to make an example of Boston and Massachusetts. The four harsh acts that Parliament passed in 1774 soon became known in the colonies as the **Intolerable Acts.** The Port Act closed the port of Boston until the city paid for the destroyed tea. The Massachusetts Government Act transferred much of the power of the colony's assembly to the royal governor. The colony's **town meetings,** which had served as forums for anti-British sentiment and protest, also came under the governor's direct control. A third measure, the Justice Act, allowed royal officials charged with **capital crimes** to stand trial in

committees of correspondence Groups formed throughout the colonies in 1772 to quickly circulate news of British oppression.

Tea Act British law (1773) that lowered the price of British tea but kept the tax on tea sold to America.

Boston Tea Party Protest against the Tea Act staged by Boston patriots in 1773; they boarded ships carrying British tea and dumped the tea into Boston harbor.

Intolerable Acts The name colonists gave to four laws that Parliament passed in 1774 to punish Boston for the Boston Tea Party.

town meeting A legislative assembly of townspeople characteristic of local government in New England.

capital crime An offense punishable by death.

London rather than before local juries. A new Quartering Act gave military commanders the authority to quarter troops in private homes. To see that these laws were enforced, the king named Thomas Gage, commander of the British troops in North America, as the acting governor of Massachusetts.

At the same time that those punitive measures were passed, the British government issued a comprehensive plan for the government of Canada. The timing of the **Quebec Act** may have been a coincidence, but its provisions angered Americans. The Quebec Act granted the French in Canada the right to worship as Catholics, to retain their language, and to keep many of their legal practices. The Quebec Act also expanded the borders of Canada into the Ohio valley at the expense of the English-speaking colonies' claims. This act seemed to be one more blow in the attack on American liberty.

The king expected the harsh punishment of Massachusetts to isolate that colony from its neighbors. But in every colony, newspapers urged readers to see Boston's plight as their own. "This horrid attack upon the town of Boston," said the *South Carolina Gazette*, "we consider not as an attempt upon that town singly, but upon the whole Continent." George Washington declared that "the cause of Boston now is and ever will be the cause of America." Indeed the Intolerable Acts produced a wave of sympathy for the beleaguered Bostonians, and relief efforts sprang up across the colonies. The residents of Surry County, Virginia, for example, sent 150 barrels of corn and wheat to their fellow patriots in Boston.

For many colonists, the Intolerable Acts provided conclusive evidence that Great Britain was systematically oppressing them and robbing them of their liberties. Political writers began referring to the British government as the "enemy" and urged the colonists to defend themselves. In Boston, Samuel Adams and his radical followers formed a "solemn league and covenant" when they organized another boycott of British goods. As most Bostonians knew, the words "solemn league" referred to the pact made between Scottish Presbyterians and English Puritans when they challenged royal authority with arms in the 1640s. Adams and his allies had made armed rebellion their choice.

Creating a National Forum: The First Continental Congress

On September 5, 1774, delegates from every colony but Georgia gathered in Philadelphia for the First Continental Congress. Few of the delegates thought of themselves as revolutionaries. "We want no revolution," a North Carolina delegate bluntly stated. Yet he and other colonists were getting dangerously close to treason. Neither the king nor Parliament had authorized this Congress, which intended to resist acts of Parliament and to defy the king. People had been hanged as traitors for far less.

Radicals such as Samuel Adams wanted the Congress to endorse a total boycott of British goods. Conservatives wanted to be more conciliatory and to petition Parliament to pay attention to American grievances. The radicals won this struggle when the Congress approved a boycott of all British goods to begin on December 1, 1774, and demanded the repeal of the Intolerable Acts.

Still, many delegates hoped for a course in between the radicals and conservatives that would bring a peaceful resolution to the crisis. Pennsylvania's Joseph Galloway offered one way out by proposing a drastic restructuring of imperial relations. His **Plan of Union** called for a Grand Council, elected by each colonial legislature, that would share with Parliament the right to originate laws for the colonies. The Grand Council and Parliament would have the power to veto or disallow each other's decisions. A governor-general, appointed by the Crown, would oversee the Grand Council and preserve imperial interests.

After much debate, the Congress rejected Galloway's compromise by the narrowest of margins. Then it was John Adams's turn to propose a

Quebec Act British law (1774) that aimed to reform the government of the former French colony of Canada; some of its provisions angered Americans.

Plan of Union Joseph Galloway's plan to restructure relations between the colonies and the mother country to give the colonies a greater say about local laws while preserving their basic colonial relationship with Britain.

solution. Under his skillful urging and direction, the Congress adopted the **Declaration of Rights and Grievances.** The declaration politely but firmly established the colonial standard for acceptable legislation by Parliament. Colonists, said the declaration, would consent to acts meant to regulate "external commerce." But they absolutely denied the legitimacy of a "taxation, internal or external, for raising a revenue on the subjects of America, without their consent."

To add teeth to Adams's declaration, the delegates endorsed the **Suffolk Resolves.** These resolves, which originated in Suffolk County, Massachusetts, urged citizens to arm themselves and to prepare to resist British military action. Congressional support for these resolutions was a clear message that American leaders were willing to rebel if politics failed.

The delegates adjourned and headed home to wait for the Crown's response. When it came, it was electric. "Blows must decide," declared King George III, "whether they are to be subject to this country or independent."

The Decision for Independence

While Americans were waiting for the king's response, a peaceful transfer of political power occurred in most colonies. Americans withdrew their support for royal governments and recognized the authority of anti-British, or **patriot,** governments. Independent local governments became a reality before any shots were fired.

Taking Charge and Enforcing Policies

The transition from royal to patriot political control was peaceful in communities where anti-British sentiment was strong. Where it was weak or where the community was divided, radicals used persuasion, pressure, and open intimidation to advance the patriot cause. These radicals became increasingly impatient with dissent, disagreement, or even indecision among their neighbors. They demanded that loyalties be declared.

In most colonial cities and towns, patriot committees enforced compliance with the boycott of British goods. These committees published violators' names in local newspapers and called on the community to shun them. If public shaming did not work, most committees were ready to use threats of physical violence and to make good on them.

Suspected British sympathizers were brought before committees and made to swear oaths of support for the patriot cause. Such political pressure often gave way to violence. In New England, many pro-British citizens, or **loyalists,** came to fear for their lives. Hundreds fled to Boston, where they hoped General Gage could protect them.

The Shot Heard Round the World

As the spring of 1775 approached, General Gage decided that it was time to take action against the Massachusetts rebels. Gage planned to dispatch a force of redcoats from Boston to Concord, just twenty miles away, where the patriots had stockpiled arms.

The patriots, however, had anticipated Gage's action. When British troops began to move out of Boston in supposed secret on the night of April 18, spies in the bell tower of Old North Church signaled that movement to waiting riders. Within minutes, Paul Revere and his fellow messengers, William Dawes and Samuel Prescott, galloped off to sound the alarm to the militias in the surrounding countryside (see Map 5.3).

Around sunrise on April 19, an advance guard of a few hundred redcoats reached Lexington,

Declaration of Rights and Grievances A resolution, passed by the First Continental Congress in 1774, that denied Parliament's right to tax the colonies without their consent.

Suffolk Resolves Resolutions adopted in 1774 by Boston and other towns in Suffolk County, Massachusetts, calling on the colonists to take up arms against the British.

patriot An American colonist who opposed British rule and fought for independence.

loyalist An American colonist who supported the British side during the Revolution.

♦ British troops came to Concord in April 1775 to destroy the cache of arms and ammunition stored there. In this painting, soldiers carry out the mission while their commanding officers keep watch for the local militia. They found the Minutemen at the North Bridge, where, in a three-minute exchange of fire, five men were killed. For New Englanders, the Revolutionary War had begun. *"A View of the Town of Concord," 1775. Attributed to Ralph Earle. Concord Museum, Concord, MA.*

where they saw about seventy colonial militiamen waiting on the village green. Militia captain John Parker ordered his men to disperse. Some, however, stood their ground. No one ordered the redcoats to fire, but shots rang out, killing eight Americans. Later, Americans would insist that the first musket fired at Lexington sounded a "shot heard round the world."

The British troops marched next to Concord. They searched the nearly deserted town for weapons but found little of military value. At the appropriate moment, the Concord militia launched a surprise attack from their position above the town's North Bridge. The shocked redcoats fled in a panic back toward Boston. The Concord militia followed, gathering more so-called **Minutemen** along the path of pursuit. These American farmers, artisans, servants, and shopkeepers terrorized the young British soldiers, firing on them from behind barns, stone walls, and trees. When the shaken troops reached the British encampment across the Charles River from Boston, 73 of their comrades were dead, 174 were wounded, and 26 were missing. The next day, thousands of New England militiamen poured in from the surrounding countryside and laid siege to Boston. The war had begun.

The Second Continental Congress

When the Second Continental Congress convened in Philadelphia in May 1775, it began to ready the colonies for war. It approved the creation of the Continental Army and selected George Washington, the Virginia veteran of the French and Indian War, as its commander in chief.

Even after Lexington and Concord, some delegates still hoped to find a peaceful solution to the crisis. This sentiment led the Congress to draft the **Olive Branch Petition.** In this petition, the colonists offered to end their armed resistance if the king would withdraw the British military and revoke the Intolerable Acts. Few expected him to do so, for the very next day the Congress issued a public statement in defense of war preparations.

Across the Atlantic, Lord North struggled to find room for negotiations. Before receiving news of Lexington, he had proposed that Parliament suspend its taxation of the colonies if Americans would raise the money to pay for their own defense. North was not willing, however, to concede Parliament's right to tax the colonists.

Americans rejected Lord North's proposals in July 1775. George III rejected the Olive Branch Petition in turn and instead persuaded Parliament to pass the **American Prohibitory Act.** This act instructed the Royal Navy to seize American ships

Minutemen Nickname first given to the Concord militia and then applied generally to colonial militia at the time of the Revolution.

Olive Branch Petition Resolution adopted by the Second Continental Congress in 1775 that offered to end armed resistance if the king would withdraw his troops and revoke the Intolerable Acts.

American Prohibitory Act British law (1775) that authorized the Royal Navy to seize all American ships engaged in trade; it amounted to a declaration of war.

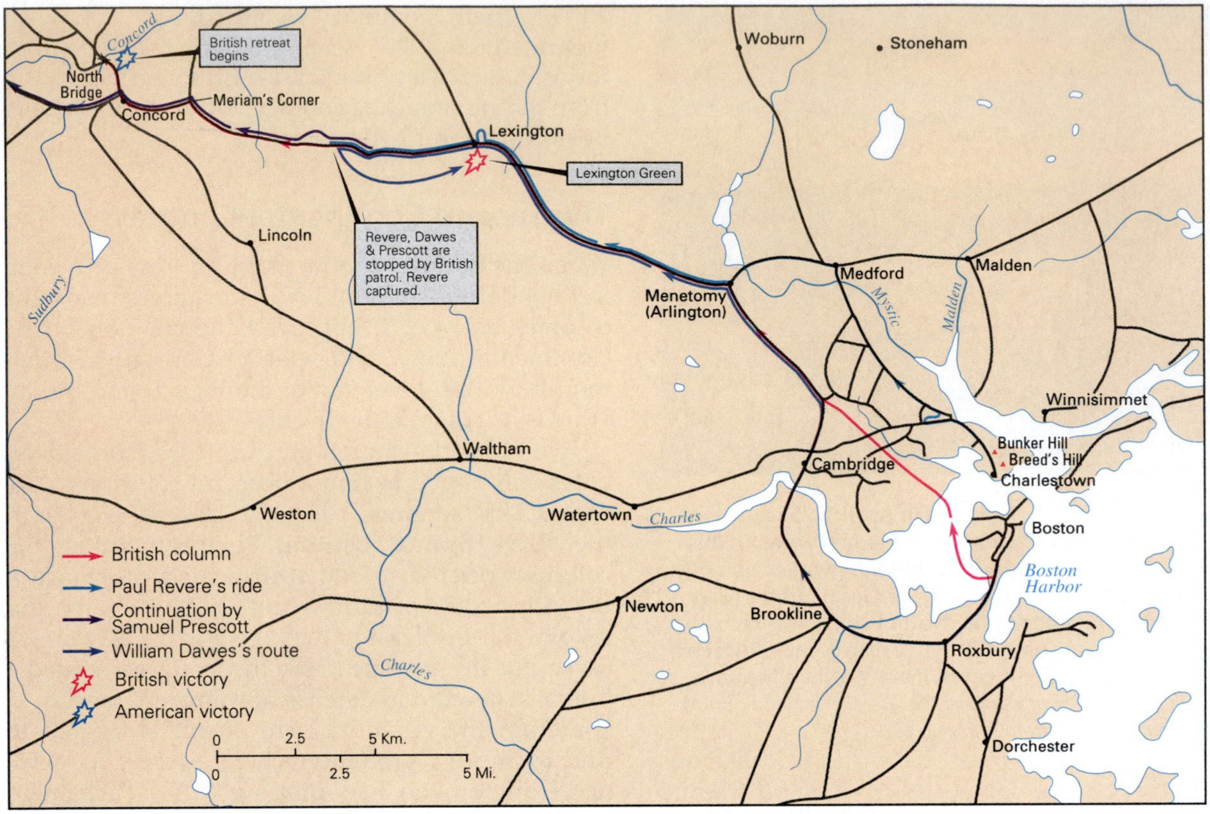

♦ **MAP 5.3 The First Battles in the War for Independence, 1775** This map shows the British march to Concord and the routes taken by the three Americans who alerted the countryside of the enemy's approach. Although Paul Revere was captured by the British and did not complete his ride, he is the best remembered and most celebrated of the riders who spread the alarm.

"as if the same were the ships . . . of open enemies." King George III had effectively declared war.

The Impact of *Common Sense*

Although war was now a fact, few Americans called for a complete political break with Britain. Even the most ardent patriots continued to justify their actions as a means to preserve the rights guaranteed to British citizens, not to establish an independent nation.

Few colonists had yet traced the source of their oppression to George III. Then, in January 1776, Thomas Paine, an Englishman who had immigrated to Philadelphia several years earlier, published ***Common Sense.*** In this pamphlet, Paine attacked the monarchy in the plain language of the common people. He challenged the idea of a hereditary ruler, questioned the value of monarchy as an institution, and criticized the personal character of kings. The common man, Paine insisted, had the ability to be his own king and was surely

Common Sense Revolutionary pamphlet written by Thomas Paine and published in 1776; it attacked George III and argued against the monarchical form of government.

more deserving of that position than most actual kings. He dismissed George III as a "Royal Brute." *Common Sense* sold 120,000 copies in its first three months of publication.

Paine's defiance of royal authority and open criticism of the man who wielded it helped many of his readers to discard the last shreds of loyalty to the king and to the empire. The impact of Paine's words could be seen in the taverns and coffeehouses, where ordinary farmers, artisans, shopkeepers, and laborers took up his call for independence and the creation of a republic.

Declaring Independence

The Second Continental Congress had lagged far behind popular sentiment in moving toward independence. Then, on June 7, 1776, Virginia lawyer Richard Henry Lee rose on the floor of the Congress and offered this straightforward motion: "That these United Colonies are, and of right ought to be, free and independent States, that they are absolved from all allegiance to the British Crown, and that all political connection between them and the State of Great Britain is, and ought to be, totally dissolved." The Congress postponed its final vote until July to give members time to win over fainthearted delegates and give the committee appointed to draft a formal declaration of independence time to complete its work.

Four of the men appointed to the committee to draft this declaration were well-known figures: Massachusetts's John Adams, Pennsylvania's Benjamin Franklin, Connecticut's Roger Sherman, and New York's Robert Livingston. But these men delegated the task of writing the document to the fifth and youngest member of the committee, Thomas Jefferson. They chose well. The 32-year-old Virginian lacked the reputation of fellow Virginians George Washington and Richard Henry Lee, but he could draw on a deep and broad knowledge of political theory and philosophy. He had read the works of Enlightenment philosophers, classical theorists, and seventeenth-century English revolutionaries. He was also a master of written prose.

Jefferson began the **Declaration of Independence** with a defense of revolution based on "self-evident truths" about humanity's "unalienable rights" to "life, liberty, and the pursuit of happiness." Jefferson argued that these natural rights came from the "Creator" rather than from human law, government, or tradition. Thus they were broader and more sacred than the specific "rights of Englishmen." With this philosophical groundwork in place, Jefferson moved on to list the colonists' grievances, focusing on the king's abuse of power rather than on Parliament's oppressive legislation. All government rested on the consent of the governed, he asserted, and the people had the right to overthrow any government that tyrannized them.

Declaring Loyalties

Delegates to the Second Continental Congress approved the Declaration of Independence in July 1776. Now all Americans had to choose their loyalties. For Americans of every region, religion, social class, and even race, this choice weighed heavily. Many wavered in the face of such a critical decision. A surprising number clung to neutrality, hoping that the conflict could be resolved without their having to participate or take sides.

Those who did commit themselves based their decisions on many deeply held beliefs, personal considerations, and fears (see Individual Choices: Esther Quincy Sewall). For loyalists, tradition and common sense argued for acknowledging parliamentary supremacy and the king's right to rule. Respect for the British government tied these Americans to the empire. The advantages of remaining within the protective circle of the most powerful nation in Europe and the dangers of waging war against it seemed too obvious to debate. Loyalists who were members of the colonial elite also feared that a revolution would unleash the "madness of the multitude."

Economic and social interests brought men and women to the loyalist camp as much as political

Declaration of Independence Document adopted by the Second Continental Congress in 1776 that listed the rights of man, described the abuses of George III, and declared the American colonies independent of Britain.

INDIVIDUAL CHOICES

Choosing Loyalty

Esther Quincy Sewall

This is the home Esther Sewall chose to leave in 1775 when she accompanied her loyalist husband, Jonathan, to England on the eve of the Revolutionary War. Faced with an uncertain life abroad, she nevertheless chose to stay with her husband rather than remain in Boston and enjoy the safety and certainty her friends and family provided. Harvard University Archives.

On November 13, 1790, Esther Quincy Sewall took up her pen to answer a letter from her brother-in-law, the famous patriot John Hancock. Hancock had pleaded with her to return to her family and friends in their native city, Boston. "I wish it was in my power to accept of your kind invitation," Esther wrote from the isolated loyalist settlement in New Brunswick, Canada; "however this is a pleasure I must post pone for a future day."

Esther Quincy Sewall's exile from her beloved Massachusetts was voluntary. Unlike her husband, Jonathan Sewall, she had not been named a political enemy of the newly independent state. Yet despite the encouragement of her sisters and brothers, she chose to continue her exile. For Esther, the choice was a matter of personal loyalties and commitments as strong as the political ones that shaped her husband's life.

Esther Quincy first met Jonathan Sewall at a boating party in 1759. He was struck by her beauty and her good humor and placed her immediately in "the rank of the Agreeables." She was, he observed, a woman of "unaffected Modesty," with good judgment, delicate manners, and "real Good sense." Their courtship

theory did. Royal officials and merchants who traded with British manufacturers joined the loyalists. Small farmers and tenant farmers from the "multitude" gave their support to the Crown because their foes—the great planters of the South or the manor lords of New York—became patriots. The choosing of sides often hinged on local and economic conflicts rather than on imperial issues.

African-American slaves viewed the conflict in terms of their opportunities for freedom. The royal governor of Virginia, Lord Dunmore, struck a blow began at once, but the couple did not marry until 1764, when Jonathan's legal career was better established. Esther's family and friends approved of the match, for although Jonathan was from a poor branch of a distinguished family, his talent and ambition led them to predict a good future for the couple. Their predictions were correct. By the eve of the Revolution, Jonathan Sewall held several highly prized positions in the colony's royal government, and Esther lived in quiet elegance with her husband and two sons in their Cambridge home.

The escalating conflicts of 1775 put a sudden end to the life the Sewalls knew. Jonathan Sewall was among the first loyalists to leave America for England in 1775. Esther said goodbye to her patriot relatives and went with him. As the war dragged on, the Sewalls' finances grew strained. They moved from rooming house to rooming house, finally settling in the port city of Bristol.

Exile and the American victory made Jonathan Sewall bitter and emotionally distant. Esther Sewall bore the brunt of his despair. He vented his anger and frustration on his wife, sarcastically wishing her "tyed to the Tail of the Comet of 1668." Esther did not hide her homesickness, and this provoked her husband's anger. He railed against the "deviltry and matrimony" that had ruined his life—and insisted that Esther return to America and leave him in peace.

Despite his accusations and insults, Esther never considered leaving her physically ailing and depressed husband. She accompanied him to Canada in 1787, joining a small community of loyalist exiles in Nova Scotia. As Jonathan's condition deteriorated, Esther became his constant companion and nurse. On September 25, 1796, she began a three-day vigil by his bedside, remaining with him until he died on September 27. Having done her duty as a wife, Esther Sewall felt free to choose her own future. After twenty-one years in exile, she packed her few belongings and went home. Whatever her private regrets or satisfactions, she never recorded a word of regret at the choice of loyalties that shaped her life.

against slaveowning patriots when he offered freedom in 1775 to "all indentured Servants, negroes or others . . . able and willing to bear Arms" who escaped their masters. Dunmore's policy had mixed results. It drove many uncommitted southern slaveholders into the revolutionary camp. At the same time, between six hundred and two thousand slaves escaped from their masters in 1775–1776, enough to form an "Ethiopian Regiment" of soldiers. In the long war that followed, perhaps as many as fifty thousand slaves gained their freedom.

Most Indian tribes saw their interests best served by the Crown. Colonial territorial ambitions threatened the Indians along the southern and northwestern frontiers. The Continental Congress knew that the Indians were unlikely allies and did little to win their support.

Fewer than half of the colonists sided with the revolutionaries. Among them were people whose economic interests made independence seem worth the risk: artisans and urban laborers, merchants who traded outside the British Empire, large and small farmers, and many members of the southern planter elite. Many colonists affected by the Great Awakening's message of egalitarianism chose the patriot side. Many who became revolutionaries wanted to live under a government that encouraged its citizens to be virtuous and live simply.

As Americans armed themselves or fled from the violence they saw coming, they realized that the conflict was both a war for independence and a civil war. In the South, it pitted master against slave and backcountry farmer against the tidewater elite. In New England, it set neighbor against neighbor, forcing scores of loyalist families to flee. In some families, children were set against parents and wives against husbands. Whatever the outcome of the struggle, Americans knew that it would come at a great cost.

SUMMARY

Expectations
Constraints
Choices
Outcomes

Victory in the Great War for Empire made Great Britain the most powerful European nation. The victory also exposed conflicts between British and colonial *expectations* about the colonists' rights and responsibilities. The British had to pay an enormous war debt while maintaining a strong army and navy. Given these *constraints,* the British government *chose* to impose taxes on the colonies. The *outcome* was growing tension between mother country and colonies.

The Sugar Act of 1764 tightened customs collections, the Stamp Act of 1765 taxed legal documents, and the Townshend Acts of 1767 set import taxes on British products such as paint and tea. In response to these *constraints,* the colonists *chose* protest. Colonists boycotted British goods, crowds attacked royal officials, and civilians clashed with British troops. American colonists saw Parliament's acts as an abuse of power and as a threat to American liberties.

Protest led to the repeal of the Townshend Acts, but political activists *chose* to prepare themselves for any new crises by creating committees of correspondence. In 1773, the British passed the Tea Act, *expecting* little American opposition. The *outcome* was immediate protest. Activists in Boston dumped tea worth thousands of pounds into the harbor.

The British moved to punish the colonists by closing the port of Boston to all trade. This action and other Intolerable Acts infuriated the colonists, who decided to take united action in support of Massachusetts. In 1774, the First Continental Congress met to debate the colonies' relationship to Great Britain and to issue united protests. The Congress sent a Declaration of Rights and Grievances to the king. The king *chose* to reject the colonists' appeal for compromise. Instead he declared that "blows must decide."

After the battles at Lexington and Concord, the Second Continental Congress began to prepare for war. Tom Paine's pamphlet *Common Sense* pushed many reluctant colonists into the revolutionary camp. In July 1776, the Congress issued the Declaration of Independence. The Declaration defended the colonists' right to resist the destruction of their liberty by a tyrannical king. In 1776, Americans faced the difficult task of *choosing* between loyalty to the Crown and revolution. The *outcome* was both a war for colonial independence and a civil war that divided families and communities across America.

SUGGESTED READINGS

Calloway, Colin G. *The American Revolution in Indian Country: Crisis and Diversity in Native American Communities* (1995).

A well-written account of the variety of Indian experiences during the American revolutionary era.

Countryman, Edward. *The American Revolution* (1985).

An excellent narrative of the causes and consequences of the Revolutionary War.

Fast, Howard. *Citizen Tom Paine* (1943).

This novel traces Tom Paine's life from his early English roots to his radical politics during the Revolutionary War.

Fischer, David Hackett. *Paul Revere's Ride* (1994).

This lively account details the circumstances and background of the efforts to rouse the countryside in response to the march of British troops toward Lexington.

"Liberty!" PBS series on the American Revolution.

Using the acutal words of revolutionaries, loyalists, and British political leaders, this six-hour series follows events from the Stamp Act to the Constitution.

TURNING POINTS IN THE REVOLUTIONARY WAR

Although every battle or diplomatic negotiation was important in deciding the victor in the Revolutionary War, six major turning points stand out between 1776 and 1781. This map shows these critical moments that shaped the course of the war.

BRITISH
CANADA
Quebec
Montreal
St. Lawrence
MAINE (part of Mass.)
Lake Superior
Lake Michigan
Lake Huron
Lake Ontario
Lake Erie
General John Burgoyne surrenders at Saratoga, October 17, 1777.
British abandon Boston, March 17, 1776, after Americans place cannon on the heights overlooking the city.
Fort Ticonderoga
N.H.
Fort Oswego
Fort Edward
Saratoga
Fort Stanwix
Albany
Bunker Hill
Boston
Lexington
NEW YORK
MASS.
Kingston
CONN.
R.I.
British occupy New York, August 27, 1776, following American defeat after the battle of Brooklyn Heights.
New York
N.J.
Brooklyn Heights
PENNSYLVANIA
Trenton
Valley Forge
Philadelphia
American army winters at Valley Forge, 1777–1778.
Franco-American Treaty of Amity and Commerce and Treaty of Alliance signed in Paris, France, February 1778.
Baltimore
DELAWARE
MARYLAND
ATLANTIC OCEAN
SPANISH
LOUISIANA
Missouri
Ohio
Charlottesville
Richmond
VIRGINIA
Yorktown
Cornwallis surrenders at Yorktown, October 17, 1781.
Tennessee
Arkansas
Mississippi
NORTH CAROLINA
Wilmington
SOUTH CAROLINA
Augusta
GEORGIA
Charleston
Savannah
WEST FLORIDA
EAST FLORIDA
Gulf of Mexico
0 150 300 Km.
0 150 300 Mi.
British victory
American victory
NORTH AND CENTRAL AMERICA
RUSSIAN CLAIM
DISPUTED
BRITISH CLAIM
SPANISH CLAIM

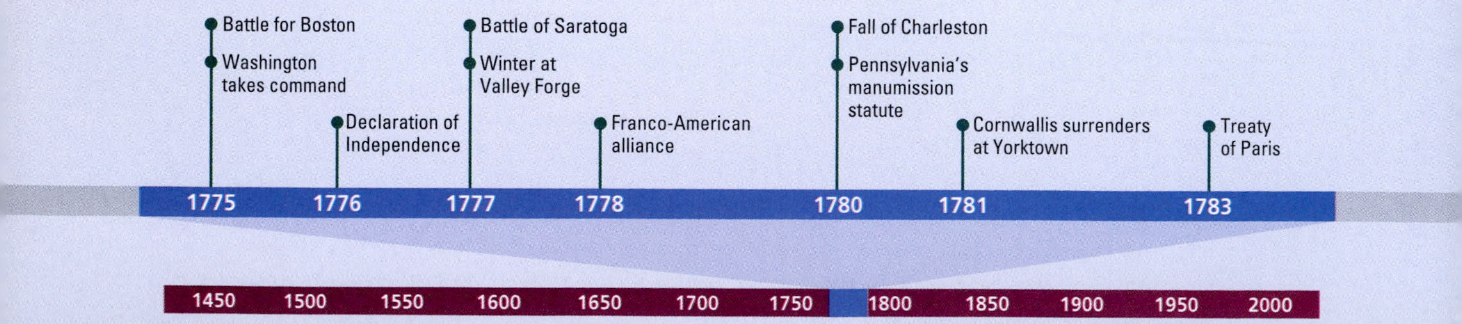

Battle for Boston
Washington takes command
Declaration of Independence
Battle of Saratoga
Winter at Valley Forge
Franco-American alliance
Fall of Charleston
Pennsylvania's manumission statute
Cornwallis surrenders at Yorktown
Treaty of Paris
1775
1776
1777
1778
1780
1781
1783
1450
1500
1550
1600
1650
1700
1750
1800
1850
1900
1950
2000

CHAPTER 6

Re-creating America: Independence and a New Nation, 1775–1783

The First Two Years of War

- What expectations shaped the British and American strategies in the early years of the war?
- What choices and constraints kept the British from achieving the quick victory many expected?

Influences away from the Battlefield

- Why did the French choose to assist the Americans secretly in the early years of the war?
- Why did they choose to enter the war after Saratoga?

From Stalemate to Victory

- What choices led to General Cornwallis's surrender at Yorktown?
- What were the most important outcomes of the peace treaty negotiations?

Republican Expectations in a New Nation

- How did the Revolution affect Americans' expectations regarding individual rights, social equality, and the role of women in American society?
- What choices were open to African Americans during and after the Revolution?
- What choices were open to loyalists?

INTRODUCTION

E xpectations
C onstraints
C hoices
O utcomes

What began as a skirmish at Concord in April 1775 grew into an international war costing millions of pounds and thousands of lives. Great Britain *expected* victory over the colonial rebels, while the Americans' *expectations* were far less confident. Even George Washington frequently expressed his doubts that independence could be won.

To crush the rebellion, Great Britain *chose* to commit vast human and material resources. Between 1775 and 1781, it deployed over fifty thousand British soldiers and hired thirty thousand German mercenaries to fight in North America. The well-trained British troops were assisted and supplied by the most powerful navy in the world. Many Indian tribes, including the Iroquois, *chose* to fight as allies of the British. The Crown *expected* that thousands of white and black loyalists would fight beside them as well.

The Americans, by contrast, labored under many *constraints.* The Continental Congress had a nearly empty treasury. The country lacked the foundries and factories to produce arms and ammunition. Through most of the war, American soldiers could *expect* to be underpaid or unpaid, poorly equipped, hungry, and dressed in rags. Unlike the British, these Americans had little military training. Although some officers proved to have a feel for military strategy and tactics, many were just rash young men dreaming of glory. Even the size of this poorly equipped and badly prepared American army was uncertain. Washington and his fellow commanders seldom knew how many soldiers would be marching with them on a campaign.

The British advantage was great but not absolute. They had to transport arms, provisions, and men across thousands of miles of ocean. The Americans were fighting on familiar terrain, and their vast society could not be easily conquered. European rivalries also worked to the Americans' advantage. Holland, France, and Spain supported the rebellion in the *expectation* that Britain's loss would be their gain. When France and Spain *chose* to recognize American independence, the war expanded into an international struggle. French naval support transformed General Washington's strategy. The *outcome* was victory at Yorktown.

Even though the *outcome* of the war was often in doubt, its impact on American men and women was not. No matter which side eighteenth-century Americans supported or what role they played in the war, they shared the experience of extraordinary events and the need to make extraordinary *choices.* In this most personal and immediate sense, the *outcome* was revolutionary.

The First Two Years of War

Thomas Gage, the British general who was military governor of Massachusetts, surely wished he were anywhere but Boston in the spring of 1775. The town was unsophisticated by British standards and unfriendly. Gage's army was restless, and his officers were bored. The thousands of colonial **militiamen** gathering on the hills surrounding Boston were clearly hostile. Yet in 1775, they were still citizens of the British Empire rather than foreign invaders or foes. Gage was caught up in the dilemma of an undeclared war.

Thomas Gage British general who was military governor of Massachusetts; he commanded the British army of occupation at the beginning of the Revolution.

militamen Soldiers who were not members of a regular army but were ordinary citizens ready to be called out in case of an emergency.

CHRONOLOGY

Rebellion and Independence

1775	Battle for Boston George Washington takes command of the Continental Army
1776	British campaigns in the Middle Colonies George Mason's Declaration of Rights Declaration of Independence
1777	Burgoyne's New York campaign Battle of Saratoga Winter at Valley Forge
1778	Alliance between France and America British begin southern campaign
1780	Fall of Charleston Treason of Benedict Arnold Pennsylvania's manumission statute
1781	Cornwallis surrenders at Yorktown Loyalists evacuate the United States
1782	British Parliament votes to end war
1783	Treaty of Paris

The Battle for Boston

In early June, Gage proclaimed that all armed colonists were traitors but offered **amnesty** to any rebel who surrendered. The militiamen responded to this offer by expanding their hillside fortifications. Observing this activity, Gage decided it was time to teach the colonials a lesson. He ordered General **William Howe** to take Breed's Hill, across the Charles River from Boston, on June 17, 1775.

Despite the heat and humidity, General Howe ordered his twenty-four hundred soldiers to climb the hill in full-dress uniform. Howe also insisted on making a frontal attack on the Americans. The outcome was a near massacre of redcoats by Captain William Prescott's militiamen. When the Americans ran out of ammunition, however, the tables turned. Most of Prescott's men fled in confusion. The British bayoneted the few who remained to defend their position.

The British suffered more casualties that June afternoon than they would suffer in any other battle of the war. The Americans, who retreated to the safety of nearby Cambridge, learned the cost of a poor supply system that left fighting men without fresh powder and shot. Little was gained by either side in the misnamed **Battle of Bunker Hill** (an adjacent hill).

On July 3, 1775, **George Washington** arrived to take command of the rebel forces at Cambridge. He could find no signs of military discipline. Instead, a carnival atmosphere prevailed. Men fired their muskets at random inside the camp, using their weapons to start fires and to shoot at geese flying overhead. They accidentally wounded and killed themselves and others. The men were dirty, and the camp resembled a pigpen. The general was disturbed but

amnesty A general pardon granted by a government, especially for political offenses.

William Howe British general in command at the Battle of Bunker Hill; three years later, he was appointed commander in chief of British forces in America.

Battle of Bunker Hill British assault on American troops on Breed's Hill near Boston in June 1775; the British won the battle but suffered heavy losses.

George Washington Commander in chief of the Continental Army; he led the Americans to victory in the Revolutionary War and later became the first president of the United States.

not surprised by what he saw. Many of these country boys were away from home for the first time in their lives. The prevailing chaos resulted from a combination of fear, excitement, boredom, inexperience, and plain homesickness, all brewing freely under poor leadership. Washington immediately set about reorganizing the militia units, replacing incompetent officers, and tightening discipline.

The siege of Boston ended when cannon captured from the British at Fort Ticonderoga, New York, reached Washington's army after being hauled some 300 miles across country. Once positioned on Dorchester Heights, which overlooked the city, these cannon made Gage's situation hopeless. In March 1776, a fleet of British ships carried Gage, the British army, and almost a thousand loyalist refugees away from Boston and north to Halifax, Nova Scotia. There Gage turned over command to General William Howe.

The British Strategy in 1776

Howe immediately set to work on devising a strategy for subduing the rebellious colonies. The heart of his strategy was to locate areas of loyalist support, to establish a military occupation of these areas with the cooperation of loyalists, and then to expand the British area of influence.

Howe correctly identified New York, New Jersey, Pennsylvania, and the backcountry of the Carolinas as loyalist strongholds. The Middle Colonies had been slow to take up the cause of independence. In the Carolinas, the coastal planters' support of the revolution had led the majority of backcountry farmers into the loyalist camp. Although the British did make one attempt in 1776 to capture Charleston, South Carolina, Howe concentrated his attention on New York.

Shortly after the American declaration of independence in July 1776, General William Howe and his brother, Admiral **Richard Howe,** sailed into New York harbor with the largest **expeditionary** force of the eighteenth century (see Map 6.1). With thirty thousand men, this British army was larger than the peacetime population of New York City. Washington had anticipated Howe's move and marched his twenty-three thousand troops to defend New York in April 1776.

The British began their advance on August 22, 1776, moving toward the Brooklyn neck of Long Island. Confronted with this large, well-armed British landing force and confused by the sound and the sight of battle, almost all the American troops surrendered or ran. Only Howe's slowness and poor planning prevented a fiasco for the Americans. Had Howe stationed ships to guard the East River, Washington's troops would have been trapped on Long Island, and the war might have ended there. But Washington and most of his army escaped to Manhattan and lived to fight another day.

Washington and his army survived primarily by retreating. Howe's troops chased him off Manhattan as well. Watching his men flee in disorder, Washington at one point threw his hat to the ground and shouted, "Are these the men with whom I am to defend America!"

Concerted British pursuit might have put an end to Washington's inexperienced army. But after pushing Washington's force out of Manhattan, Howe spent a month consolidating his position in New York City. It was October 12 before he engaged Washington again. Howe's haphazard pursuit allowed Washington's army to escape to New Jersey and ultimately across the Delaware River to the safety of Pennsylvania before the arrival of winter.

Winter Quarters and Winter Victories

Following European custom, General Howe established winter quarters before the cold set in. The Redcoats and **Hessians** made their camps in the New York area and in Rhode Island that December. Washington did not follow this custom. Enlistment terms in what was left of his army would soon be up, and without some encouraging military suc-

Richard Howe British admiral who commanded British naval forces in America; General William Howe was his brother.

expeditionary Designed for military operations abroad.

Hessians German mercenaries known as Hessians after the German state of Hesse.

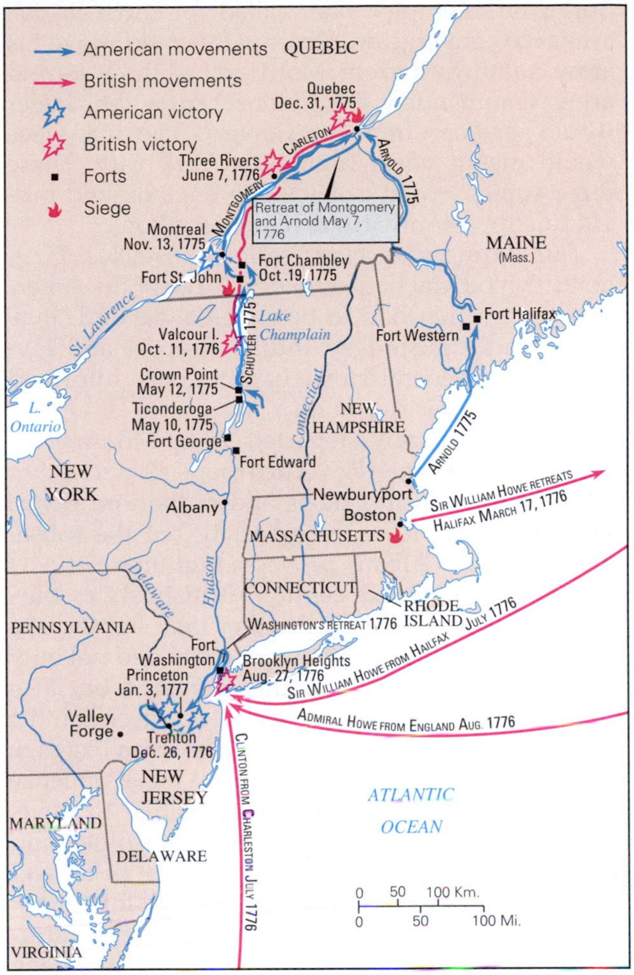
American movements
British movements
American victory
British victory
Forts
Siege
QUEBEC
Quebec
Dec. 31, 1775
CARLETON
ARNOLD 1775
Three Rivers
June 7, 1776
MONTGOMERY
Retreat of Montgomery and Arnold May 7, 1776
Montreal
Nov. 13, 1775
MAINE
(Mass.)
Fort Chambley
Oct .19, 1775
Fort St. John
St. Lawrence
Lake Champlain
Valcour I.
Oct . 11, 1776
SCHUYLER 1775
Fort Western
Fort Halifax
Crown Point
May 12, 1775
Ticonderoga
May 10, 1775
Fort George
L. Ontario
Connecticut
NEW HAMPSHIRE
ARNOLD 1775
NEW YORK
Fort Edward
Albany
Newburyport
Boston
MASSACHUSETTS
SIR WILLIAM HOWE RETREATS HALIFAX MARCH 17, 1776
Delaware
Hudson
CONNECTICUT
RHODE ISLAND
WASHINGTON'S RETREAT 1776
JULY 1776
PENNSYLVANIA
Fort Washington
Brooklyn Heights
Aug. 27, 1776
SIR WILLIAM HOWE FROM HALIFAX
Princeton
Jan. 3, 1777
ADMIRAL HOWE FROM ENGLAND AUG. 1776
Valley Forge
Trenton
Dec. 26, 1776
NEW JERSEY
CLINTON FROM CHARLESTON JULY 1776
ATLANTIC OCEAN
MARYLAND
DELAWARE
0 50 100 Km.
0 50 100 Mi.
VIRGINIA

♦ **MAP 6.1 The War in the North, 1775–1777** The American attempt to capture Canada and General George Washington's effort to save New York from British occupation were failures, but Washington did manage to stage successful raids in New Jersey before retreating to safety in the winter of 1777. This map details the movements of both British and American troops during the northern campaign, and it indicates the victories and defeats for both armies.

cess, he expected that few of his soldiers would reenlist.

Washington took a large gamble in his quest for a resounding victory. On Christmas night, in the midst of a howling storm, he and twenty-four hundred troops recrossed the Delaware River and then marched nine miles to Trenton, New Jersey. The hostile weather worked to Washington's ultimate advantage. The several thousand Hessian troops garrisoned near Trenton, never expecting anyone to venture out on such a night, drank heavily before falling into their beds. They were in poor shape to resist when the Americans caught them by surprise the following morning, and quickly surrendered. Washington did not lose a single man in capturing nine hundred prisoners and many badly needed supplies, including six German cannon. Washington then made a rousing appeal to his men to reenlist. Washington had been correct in taking the Christmas night risk, for about half of the soldiers agreed to remain.

Washington enjoyed his next success even more. In early January, he again crossed into New Jersey and made his way toward the British garrison at Princeton. En route, his advance guard ran into two British regiments. As both sides lined up for battle, Washington rode back and forth in front of his men, shouting encouragement and urging them to stand firm. His behavior was reckless, for it put him squarely in the line of fire, but it was also effective. When the British turned in retreat, Washington rode after them, delighted to be in pursuit for once.

The Trenton and Princeton victories raised the morale of the Continental Army as it settled into winter quarters near Morristown, New Jersey. Those successes also stirred popular support. Still, the revolutionary forces had done little to stop the Howes. And neither Washington's polite requests nor his angry demands could get the Second Continental Congress to provide the assistance he needed. The Congress met his requests for supplies that winter with "permission" to **commandeer** what was needed from nearby residents. Washington refused, for he knew that seizing civilian property might turn potential patriots into enemies.

Burgoyne's New York Campaign

In July 1777, General William Howe sailed with fifteen thousand men up Chesapeake Bay toward Philadelphia, causing the Continental Congress to

commandeer To seize for military use.

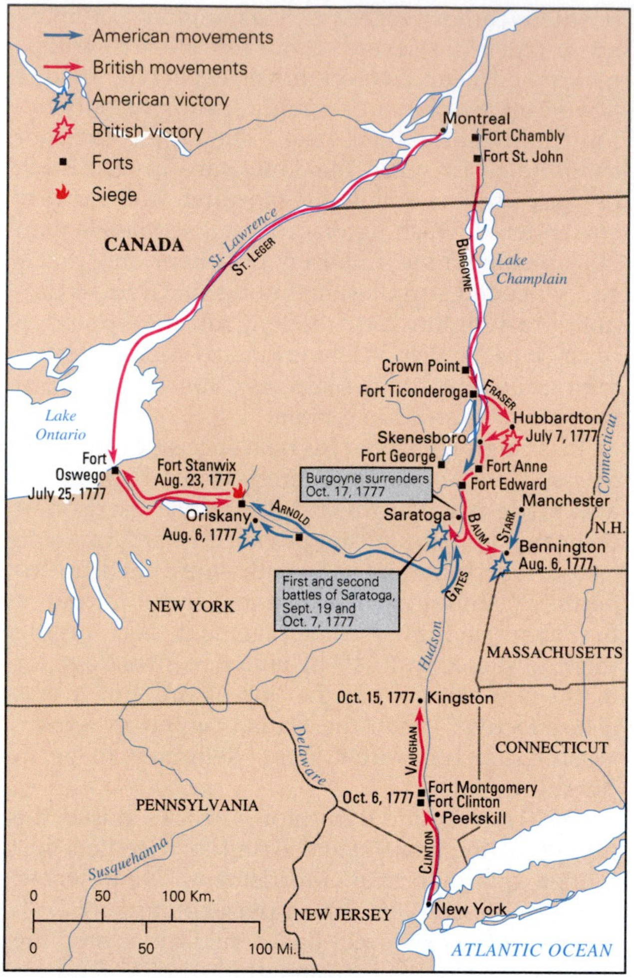
American movements
British movements
American victory
British victory
Forts
Siege
CANADA
St. Lawrence
St. Leger
Montreal
Fort Chambly
Fort St. John
Burgoyne
Lake Champlain
Crown Point
Fort Ticonderoga
Fraser
Hubbardton
July 7, 1777
Skenesboro
Fort George
Fort Anne
Fort Edward
Manchester
Connecticut
N.H.
Bennington
Aug. 6, 1777
Lake Ontario
Fort Oswego
July 25, 1777
Fort Stanwix
Aug. 23, 1777
Burgoyne surrenders
Oct. 17, 1777
Arnold
Oriskany
Aug. 6, 1777
Saratoga
Baum
Stark
First and second
battles of Saratoga,
Sept. 19 and
Oct. 7, 1777
Gates
NEW YORK
Hudson
MASSACHUSETTS
Oct. 15, 1777
Kingston
Delaware
Vaughan
CONNECTICUT
Fort Montgomery
Oct. 6, 1777
Fort Clinton
Peekskill
PENNSYLVANIA
Susquehanna
Clinton
0
50
100 Km.
0
50
100 Mi.
NEW JERSEY
New York
ATLANTIC OCEAN

♦ **MAP 6.2 The Burgoyne Campaign, 1777** The defeat of General John Burgoyne and his army at Saratoga was a major turning point in the war. It led to the recognition of American independence by France and later by Spain and to a military alliance with both these European powers. This map shows American and British troop movements and the locations and dates of the Saratoga battles leading to the British surrender.

flee. Although the American forces did challenge Howe at Brandywine Creek, they could not stop the British from occupying the capital.

While Howe was settling in at Philadelphia, a British campaign was getting under way in northern New York. This campaign was part of General **John Burgoyne's** scheme to sever New England from the rest of the American colonies (see Map 6.2). Burgoyne's complex plan called for three British armies to converge on Albany. He would move his army southward from Montreal, while a second army commanded by Colonel Barry St. Leger would head east from Fort Oswego. The third force would march north from New York City. These three armies would isolate New England and provide an opportunity to crush the rebellion.

This daring plan faced serious obstacles. First, no British official had any knowledge of the American terrain that had to be covered. Second, Burgoyne badly misjudged Indian support and loyalty. Third, General Howe had not been informed of the plan or his role in it.

Burgoyne's army departed from Montreal in high spirits in June 1777. The troops floated down Lake Champlain in canoes and flatbottom boats. They took Fort Ticonderoga easily, but the subsequent march to Albany proved a nightmare.

In true eighteenth-century British style, Burgoyne chose to travel well rather than lightly. The 30 wagons he brought with him contained not only 138 pieces of artillery for the campaign but also Burgoyne's mistress, her personal wardrobe, and a generous supply of champagne. The extra baggage might have been only a minor inconvenience across mild terrain, but the wagons had to travel through swamps and forests, across gullies and ravines. Movement slowed to a snail's pace, and food supplies began to run dangerously low.

The Americans took full advantage of Burgoyne's circumstances. Ethan Allen and the **Green Mountain Boys** harassed the British as they entered what is now Vermont. A confrontation with Allen near Bennington slowed his army even more. When Burgoyne finally reached Albany in mid-September, he was disturbed to discover neither St. Leger nor Howe waiting there.

St. Leger had counted on the support of the entire Iroquois League in his eastward march to Albany. He discovered, however, that some Iroquois

John Burgoyne British general who recaptured Fort Ticonderoga but was forced to surrender his entire army at Saratoga in October 1777.

Green Mountain Boys Vermont militiamen led by Ethan Allen.

♦ As Burgoyne's army moved south, Catherine Van Rensselaer rushed from Albany to rescue the furnishings of her country estate in Saratoga. Although panicked refugees fled past her, Van Rensselaer refused to turn back. She not only saved her furniture but set fire to her wheat fields to prevent the enemy from harvesting the grain. Such acts of sabotage were frequently carried out by patriot and loyalist women. *Los Angeles County Museum of Art; bicentennial gift of Mr. and Mrs. J. M. Schaaf, Mr. and Mrs. Charles C. Shoemaker, and Mr. and Mrs. Julian Ganz, Jr.*

had allied with the Americans. St. Leger faced resistance that grew fiercer the closer he got to the rendezvous point. When he learned that **Benedict Arnold** and an army of a thousand Americans were on their way to challenge him, St. Leger decided to retreat to the safety of Fort Niagara.

St. Leger's retreat and William Howe's ignorance of his role in this military operation left Burgoyne stranded. As his supplies dwindled, Burgoyne had few choices left by mid-September 1777. He could attempt to break through the American lines and retreat northward to Canada, or he could surrender. On September 19, Burgoyne attacked American forces commanded by Horatio Gates at Saratoga. But "Granny" Gates, as the general was affectionately called, held his ground. He again shut the door on Burgoyne on October 7. On October 17, 1777, Burgoyne was forced to surrender.

News of Burgoyne's defeat gave a powerful boost to American confidence and an equally powerful blow to British self-esteem. The stunning victory at Saratoga also raised hopes that France might openly acknowledge American independence and join the war against Britain.

Winter Quarters in 1777

For General Washington, Saratoga was a mixed blessing. The victory fueled expectations—which he did not share—that the war was practically at an end. Congress consequently ignored his urgent requests for money to support the Continental Army in its winter quarters some 20 miles from Philadelphia. The result was a long and dreadful winter at **Valley Forge.**

Rations were a problem from the start. Most soldiers at Valley Forge lived entirely on a diet of fire cakes, made of flour mixed with water and baked in the coals or over the fire on a stick. Keeping warm occupied these soldiers even more than

Benedict Arnold A Philadelphian whose acts of daring and bravery made him a favorite of George Washington until he committed treason in 1780.

Valley Forge Winter encampment (1777–1778) of Washington's army in Pennsylvania, where soldiers were poorly supplied and suffered terribly from cold and hunger.

keeping fed, for blankets were scarce, coats were rare, and firewood was precious. They sometimes traded their muskets for the momentary warmth provided by liquor.

The enlisted men at Valley Forge shared a common background. Most were unmarried farm boys, farm laborers, servants, apprentices, artisans, or even former slaves. Although some had wives and children, the majority had few dependents and few hopes of economic advancement. Yet poverty had not driven them into Washington's army. There were other, easier choices than soldiering. They could have secured more money, better food, and greater comfort if they had taken up begging. Those who preferred a military life could have served as substitutes for wealthy men in their local militia units and been well paid. Instead, they had chosen Washington's Continental Army out of their dedication to liberty and independence and intended to see the war to its conclusion.

What these soldiers needed, besides new clothes and hot baths, was professional military training. That is exactly what they got when an unlikely Prussian volunteer arrived at Valley Forge in the spring of 1778. Baron **Friedrich von Steuben** was almost 50 years old, dignified, and elegantly dressed. Although von Steuben was not the grand aristocrat that he claimed to be, he was a talented military drillmaster.

All spring, the baron drilled Washington's troops, alternately shouting in rage and applauding with delight. He expected instant obedience, set high standards, and criticized freely. But he also gave lavish praise when it was due and revealed a genuine affection and respect for the men. To Washington, Baron von Steuben was an invaluable surprise.

The spring of 1778 brought many changes besides a better-trained American army. General William Howe had been called home and replaced by his second-in-command, **Henry Clinton.** The most welcome news to reach Washington was that France had formally recognized the independence of the United States. He immediately declared a day of thanks, ordering cannon to be fired in honor of the new alliance and calling for an inspection of his troops. That day, the officers feasted with their commander, and Washington issued brandy to each enlisted man at Valley Forge.

Influences away from the Battlefield

The American Revolution, like most other wars, was not confined to the battlefield. Diplomacy in foreign capitals played a crucial role in its outcome. So did American popular support for the revolutionary government. In the end, diplomatic and political concerns could not be separated from the fate of the armies on the battlefield.

The Long Road to Formal Recognition

In 1776, Great Britain's rivals in Europe thought the American Revolution would fail. Thus France, Spain, and the Netherlands were willing to provide aid secretly to the colonial rebels but unwilling to risk war with Britain by formally recognizing American independence. Even **Benjamin Franklin,** the American minister to France who had charmed everyone in Paris, could not produce a diplomatic miracle of this magnitude.

Burgoyne's surrender changed everything. After Saratoga, the French government immediately reassessed its diplomatic position. The comte de Vergennes, the chief minister of King Louis XVI, suspected that the British would quickly send a peace commission to America. France would gain nothing if the American Congress agreed to a compromise ending the rebellion. But if France gave Americans reason to hope for total victory, perhaps it could recoup some of the territory and prestige lost to Britain in the Great War for Empire. This meant,

Friedrich von Steuben Prussian military officer who volunteered to drill Washington's army at Valley Forge, giving the Continental troops much-needed military training at a pivotal period in the war.

Henry Clinton General who replaced William Howe as commander of the British forces in America in 1778; the change of command was in response to the British defeat at Saratoga.

Benjamin Franklin American writer, inventor, and diplomat who negotiated French support for the American Revolution in 1778.

of course, recognizing the United States and entering a war against Britain. Vergennes wavered.

Meanwhile, the British government was indeed preparing a new peace offer. George III believed that he was offering the Americans two great concessions. First, Parliament would renounce all intentions of ever taxing the colonies again. Second, Parliament would repeal the Intolerable Acts, the Tea Act, and any other objectionable legislation passed since 1763. For the American government, these concessions were too late in coming. By 1778, a voluntary return to colonial status was unthinkable.

Benjamin Franklin knew that Congress would reject the king's offer, but the comte de Vergennes did not. Franklin shrewdly played upon Vergennes's fears of compromise. He secured French recognition of American independence and a military alliance. Spain followed with recognition in 1779, and the Netherlands in 1780.

The Revolution thus grew into an international struggle that taxed British resources and made it impossible for Britain to concentrate all its military might and naval power in America. With ships diverted to the Caribbean and the European coast, the British no longer enjoyed the mastery of American waters.

War and the American Public

In America, the most striking consequence of the treaty with France was an orgy of spending. Conditions were ripe for this in 1778. The value of government-issued paper money was dropping steadily, and spending rather than saving seemed more sensible. The profits that some farmers and civilians were making from supplying the American armies meant that there were more Americans with money to spend. Finally, some of the credit that American diplomats negotiated with European allies went to purchase foreign manufactured goods. Fear of a long and unsuccessful war had kept Americans wary of spending. When the treaty spurred new confidence that victory was on the way, the combination of optimism, **cheap money,** and the availability of foreign goods led to a wartime spending spree.

Many of these goods were actually made in Britain. Such products often found their way into American hands by way of British-occupied New York City, where imports had reached their prewar levels by 1780. American consumers apparently saw no contradiction between patriotism and the purchase of enemy products such as tea.

The spirit of self-indulgence infected the government and the military. Corruption and **graft** were common, especially in the department of the **quartermaster** and in the **commissaries.** Administrators in these divisions sold government supplies for their own profit or charged the army excessive rates for shoddy goods and services. Civilians cheated the government too. Soldiers became accustomed to defective weapons, shoes, and ammunition. They were not immune to the lure of easy money. Some soldiers sold army-issued supplies to any buyers they could find.

Although American expectations of victory rose after Saratoga, victory itself remained out of reach. By 1778, the war effort was in financial crisis. Both Congress and the states had exhausted their meager sources of hard currency, leaving the Continental Army in desperate straits. Congress and the state governments met the crisis by printing more paper money. The result was a further lowering of the value of paper currency and complaints from soldiers that they were being cheated out of their pay. Congress acknowledged the justice of these complaints by giving soldiers pay raises in the form of certificates that could be redeemed after the war.

From Stalemate to Victory

The entrance of France into the war did not immediately alter the strategies of British or American

cheap money Loans obtainable at a low rate of interest.

graft Unscrupulous use of one's position to derive profit or advantage.

quartermaster An officer responsible for purchasing the food, clothing, and equipment used by troops.

commissary A supplier of food and other essentials to the Continental Army. Members of a commissary received a commission for their services.

military leaders. After Burgoyne's surrender at Saratoga, British generals continued to be cautious. Washington, who was waiting for help from the French navy, was unwilling to take risks either. The result was a stalemate.

The War Stalls in the North

Sir Henry Clinton, William Howe's successor as British military commander in America, was painfully aware that the French fleet could pose a serious problem for his army. Philadelphia was an easy target for a naval blockade. Clinton accordingly decided to abandon Philadelphia and to return to the safety of New York. By the spring of 1778, Clinton's army was marching east toward New York.

♦ Mohawk chief Thayendanegea (Joseph Brant) believed that Iroquois lands would be lost if the Americans were victorious. He urged an Iroquois alliance with the British, fought for the British, and directed a series of deadly raids against settlements in Pennsylvania and New York. After the war—as Brant had feared—his people were forced to relocate to Canada. *"Joseph Brant" by Wilhelm von Moll Berczy c. 1800. National Gallery of Canada, Ottawa.*

Washington decided that the retreating British forces, with their long and cumbersome supply lines, were a ripe target. But **Charles Lee,** the American who commanded this attack, called for a retreat almost as soon as the enemy began to return fire. Only Washington's personal intervention rallied the retreating Americans. Trained by von Steuben, the men responded well. They held their lines and then drove the redcoats back. The **Battle of Monmouth** was not the decisive victory Washington had dreamed of, but it was a fine recovery after what appeared to be certain defeat.

The missed opportunity at Monmouth was followed by others. An early joint operation with the French was particularly upsetting. In August 1778, a combined French and American force landed to attack the large British base at Newport, Rhode Island. The French commander, Admiral d'Estaing, lost his nerve, abruptly gathered up his own men, and sailed to safety on the open seas. The Americans were left stranded, forced to retreat as best they could.

General Washington could hardly contain his frustration with the new allies. He was eager to map out a joint strategy using American military strengths and French naval resources to their best advantage. But no French admiral contacted him. All Washington could do was wait.

He did that as patiently as he could through the summer of 1779. That fall he learned that d'Estaing and his fleet had sailed for the West Indies to protect French possessions and perhaps to acquire new islands from the British. Washington understood the French priorities, but he was discouraged. D'Estaing's departure meant more months of inactivity for the general and his restless troops.

Charles Lee Revolutionary general who was envious of Washington and allowed his egotism to dictate his decisions on the battlefield; he was eventually dismissed from service.

Battle of Monmouth Battle fought in New Jersey in June 1778, in which the American retreat ordered by Charles Lee was stopped by General Washington.

The War Moves South

By 1778 it had become apparent to the British that their campaigns in the northern colonies were a failure. Although they could occupy any port they selected, the countryside remained in patriot hands. And when British troops ceased their occupation of places such as Philadelphia, the rebels quickly resumed control. The British had little to show for three years of fighting in the North. General Henry Clinton decided to shift his attention to the South, where he hoped to find a stronger base of loyalists.

The southern campaign began in earnest with an assault on Savannah, Georgia, in the fall of 1778 (see Map 6.3). When Savannah fell that December, all resistance in Georgia collapsed. For once the British controlled the countryside. Clinton's next target was Charleston, South Carolina. Clinton sailed for Charleston, accompanied by eight thousand troops, in late 1779. After a month-long bombardment, Charleston fell in May 1780. The loss of Charleston was the costliest one of the entire war for the Americans: the whole garrison of fifty-four hundred soldiers surrendered.

Clinton then returned to New York, leaving the ambitious and able General **Charles Cornwallis** in charge. Cornwallis and his regular army were joined by loyalist militias who were eager to take revenge on their enemies. Since 1776, small roving bands of loyalist guerrillas had kept alive resistance to the Revolution. After the British victory at Charleston, these guerrillas increased their attacks, and a bloody civil war of ambush, arson, and brutality on both sides resulted. By the summer of 1780, the revolutionaries were now the resistance, and the loyalists were in control.

The revolutionary resistance produced legendary guerrilla leaders. None was more loved, or feared, than Francis Marion, known as the "Swamp Fox." Marion recruited both blacks and whites to his raiding bands. They steadily harassed Cornwallis's army and effectively cut British communication between Charleston and the interior of South Carolina.

When guerrillas and loyalists met in battle, few rules of war were honored. In October 1780, for example, in the **Battle of Kings Mountain,** revolutionaries surrounded loyalist troops and picked them off one by one. As this bitter civil war continued, civilians were terrorized and their farms and homes plundered. Outlaws posing as soldiers often did the worst damage.

The regular American army, under the command of the Saratoga hero, "Granny" Gates, enjoyed little success against Cornwallis. In August 1780, Gates suffered a crushing defeat at Camden, South Carolina. Washington ordered Gates's removal that fall, replacing him with **Nathanael Greene,** a younger, more energetic officer from Rhode Island.

Greene was shocked when he arrived in South Carolina. Not only were his fourteen hundred troops tired, hungry, and poorly clothed, but they were "without discipline and so addicted to plundering that the utmost exertions of the officers cannot restrain them." Greene's first steps were to ease the strains caused by civil war and plundering by offering pardons to loyalists and proposing alliances with local Indian tribes. He managed to win all but the Creeks away from the British.

Greene's military strategy was to wear the British out by having them chase his small army. He boldly split his military force in half, sending six hundred soldiers to western South Carolina under the able command of Virginian Daniel Morgan. Cornwallis countered by sending Lieutenant Colonel Banastre Tarleton in pursuit. Morgan led the British officer on a hectic chase across rugged terrain. By the time Tarleton's men cornered the Americans on an open meadow called Cowpens, the British were tired and frustrated. There the smaller American force stood its ground and

Charles Cornwallis British general who was second-in-command to Henry Clinton; his surrender at Yorktown in 1781 brought the Revolutionary War to a close.

Battle of Kings Mountain Battle fought in October 1780 on the border between the Carolinas; revolutionary troops forced the British to retreat to South Carolina.

Nathanael Greene American general who took command of the Carolinas campaign in 1780.

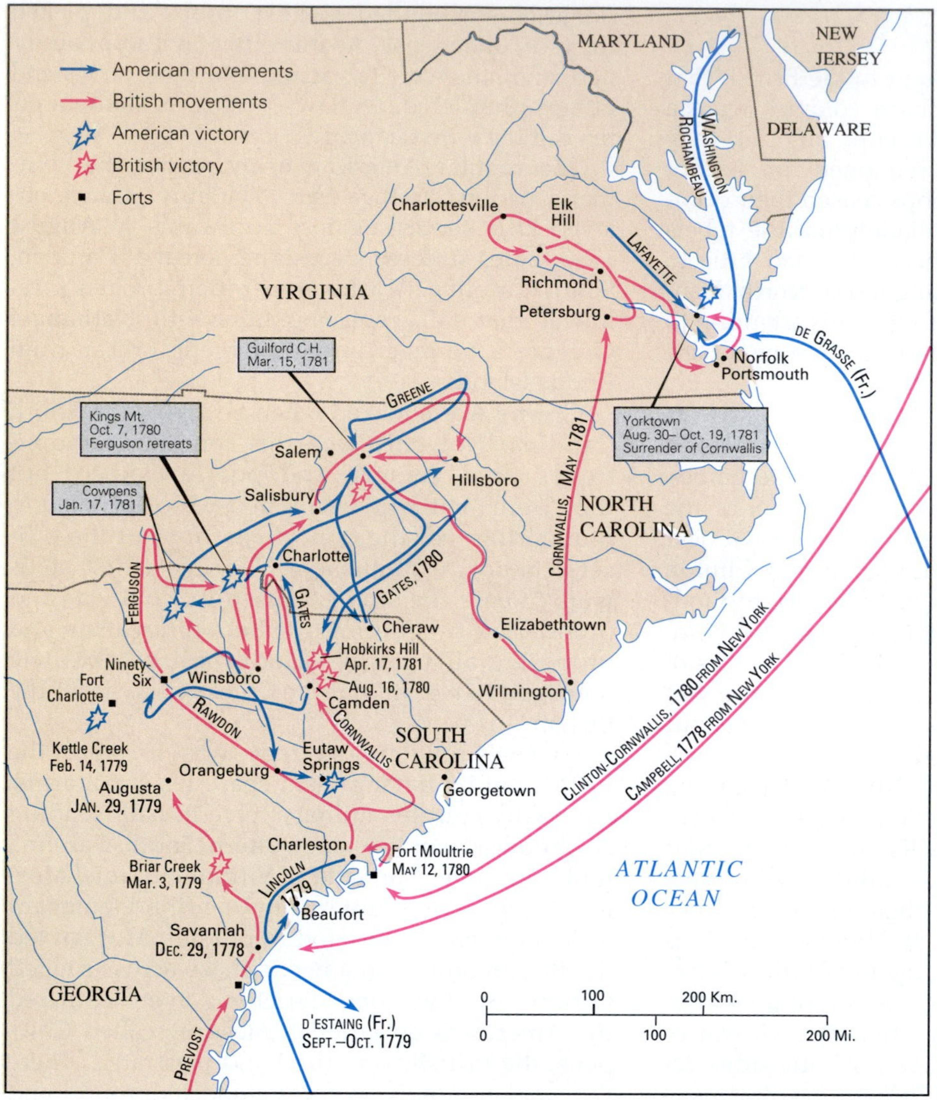

American movements
British movements
American victory
British victory
Forts
MARYLAND
NEW JERSEY
DELAWARE
WASHINGTON
ROCHAMBEAU
Charlottesville
Elk Hill
Richmond
Petersburg
LAFAYETTE
VIRGINIA
DE GRASSE (Fr.)
Norfolk
Portsmouth
Guilford C.H. Mar. 15, 1781
GREENE
Yorktown Aug. 30– Oct. 19, 1781 Surrender of Cornwallis
Kings Mt. Oct. 7, 1780 Ferguson retreats
Salem
Hillsboro
CORNWALLIS, MAY 1781
NORTH CAROLINA
Cowpens Jan. 17, 1781
Salisbury
Charlotte
GATES, 1780
FERGUSON
GATES
Cheraw
Elizabethtown
Hobkirks Hill Apr. 17, 1781
Ninety-Six
Fort Charlotte
Winsboro
Aug. 16, 1780
Camden
Wilmington
RAWDON
CORNWALLIS
SOUTH CAROLINA
Kettle Creek Feb. 14, 1779
Eutaw Springs
Orangeburg
Augusta JAN. 29, 1779
Georgetown
CLINTON-CORNWALLIS, 1780 FROM NEW YORK
CAMPBELL, 1778 FROM NEW YORK
Charleston
Fort Moultrie MAY 12, 1780
ATLANTIC OCEAN
Briar Creek Mar. 3, 1779
LINCOLN 1779
Beaufort
Savannah DEC. 29, 1778
GEORGIA
PREVOST
D'ESTAING (Fr.) SEPT.–OCT. 1779
0 100 200 Km.
0 100 200 Mi.

◆ **MAP 6.3 The Southern Campaign, 1778–1781** This map of the British attempt to crush the rebellion in the South shows the many battles waged in the Lower South before Cornwallis's encampment at Yorktown and his surrender there. This decisive southern campaign involved all the military resources of the combatants, including British, loyalist, French, and American ground forces and British and French naval fleets.

inflicted heavy casualties on the British, taking six hundred prisoners. Morgan and his soldiers then reunited with General Greene.

Cornwallis subsequently took the offensive against Greene. But the American general led the British commander on a long, exhausting chase into North Carolina. In March 1781, Greene decided it was time to stop running and to fight. Although the Americans withdrew from the Battle of Guilford Courthouse in North Carolina, British losses were so great that Cornwallis was compelled to retreat to coastal Wilmington, where he could obtain fresh supplies and troops. Cornwallis then headed north into Virginia.

♦ John Trumbull celebrated the surrender of Cornwallis at Yorktown in this painting. However, neither Cornwallis nor Washington actually participated in the surrender ceremonies. The British commander claimed illness and sent his general of the guards as his deputy. Washington, always sensitive to status as well as to protocol, promptly appointed an officer to equal rank, General Benjamin Lincoln, to serve as his deputy. *"Surrender of Lord Cornwallis" by John Trumbull. Yale University Art Gallery. Trumbull Collection.*

Triumph at Yorktown

In May 1781, Washington's impatient wait for French action ended. Meeting with the French naval commander, the comte de Rochambeau, Washington pressed his case for an attack on New York. Rochambeau, however, had already decided to move against Cornwallis in Virginia and ordered Admiral de Grasse's fleet to Chesapeake Bay. Washington had little choice but to concur with Rochambeau's plan. On July 6, 1781, a French army joined Washington's forces just north of Manhattan for the long march to Virginia.

General Cornwallis, unaware that a combined army was marching toward him, busied himself fighting skirmishes with local Virginia militia units. His first clue that trouble lay ahead came when a force of regulars, led by Baron von Steuben and the **marquis de Lafayette,** appeared in Virginia. Soon afterward, Cornwallis settled his army at the peninsula port of **Yorktown** to prepare for more serious battles ahead.

marquis de Lafayette French aristocrat who served on Washington's staff during the Revolution.

Yorktown Port town in Virginia on the York River near Chesapeake Bay; its location on a peninsula allowed American and French forces to trap the British in their encampment there.

By September 1781, French and American troops coming from New York had joined forces with von Steuben's and Lafayette's men to surround Cornwallis. Meanwhile, Admiral de Grasse's twenty-seven ships had arrived at Chesapeake Bay to seal the trap. General Clinton, still in New York, had been slow to realize what the enemy intended. He could send only a small number of ships from New York to rescue the trapped Cornwallis because most of the British fleet was in the Caribbean.

Admiral de Grasse had little trouble fending off Clinton's rescue squad. Then he and Washington turned their guns on the redcoats. For Cornwallis, there was no escape. On October 17, 1781, he admitted the hopelessness of his situation and surrendered.

Despite the surrender at Yorktown, loyalists and patriots continued to fight each other in the South for another year. Indian warfare continued in the backcountry. The British occupation of Charleston, Savannah, and New York continued. But after Yorktown, the British gave up all hope of military victory against the revolutionaries. On March 4, 1782, Parliament voted to cease "the further prosecution of offensive war on the Continent of North America, for the purpose of reducing the Colonies to obedience by force." The war for independence had been won.

Winning Diplomatic Independence

What Washington and his allies had won on the battlefield had to be preserved by American diplomats. Three men represented the United States at the peace talks in Paris: Benjamin Franklin, John Jay, and John Adams. Each was a veteran of wartime negotiations with European governments. They knew that their chief ally, France, had its own agenda and that Great Britain still wavered about the degree of independence America was to enjoy.

Despite firm orders from Congress to rely on France at every phase of the negotiations, the American diplomats quickly put their own agenda on the table. They issued a direct challenge to Britain: you must recognize American independence as a precondition to negotiations. The British commissioner reluctantly agreed.

In the **Treaty of Paris** of 1783, the Americans emerged with two clear victories. First, the boundaries of the new nation were to be extensive, going all the way to the Mississippi River. The British did not, however, give up Canada as the Americans had hoped. Second, the treaty granted the United States unlimited access to the fisheries off Newfoundland, a particular concern of New Englander John Adams. But the treaty was vague about many other matters. For example, Britain ceded the Northwest to the United States, but the treaty set no timetable for British evacuation of this territory. In some cases, the vague language worked to the Americans' advantage. The treaty contained only the most general promise that the American government would not interfere with Britain's efforts to receive payment for the large prewar debts owed to British merchants. The promise to urge the states to return confiscated property to loyalists was equally vague. The American peacemakers were aware of the treaty's lack of clarity on some issues. But they had gained their major objectives and were willing to accept vagueness as the cost of avoiding stalemate.

Republican Expectations in a New Nation

As an old man, John Adams reminisced about the American Revolution with his family and friends. The Revolution, Adams said, took place "in the hearts and the minds of the people." What he meant was that changes in American social values and political ideas were as critical as artillery, swords, and battlefield strategies in the making of the new nation. Significant changes certainly did take place in American thought and behavior during the war years. Many of these changes reflected the growing identification of the new American

Treaty of Paris Treaty that ended the Revolutionary War in 1783; it gave the Northwest to the United States, set boundaries between the United States and Canada, and called for the payment of prewar debts.

nation as a **republic**—that is, a nation in which supreme power rests in the people, not kings or aristocrats. Republican values could be seen in the emphasis on individual rights, in the establishment of representative and **limited government,** and in the ideals of civic-mindedness, patriotism, and a simple, unpretentious lifestyle.

Protection of Individual Rights

After 1763, the debates over British colonial policy brought about a new emphasis on individual rights. By 1776, many Americans expected their government to protect fundamental rights such as life, liberty, and property. The belief that Britain had to respect and protect individual rights had been critical in justifying the Revolution. No government, Americans believed, had the authority to abuse or threaten their fundamental rights. Whatever form Americans chose for their new, independent government, they would demand that it protect their rights.

The emphasis on individual rights opened the door to a reform of laws affecting religion. Although individual dissenters such as Roger Williams in the seventeenth century had risked their lives for freedom of conscience, most colonists did not question the value of established churches until the Revolutionary era.

In 1776, the Virginia House of Burgesses approved George Mason's Declaration of Rights, which ensured the right to "the free exercise of religion." Virginia, however, continued to use tax monies to support the Anglican church. Not until the passage of the Statute of Religious Freedom in 1786 did the state sever its ties with the Anglican church and allow for complete freedom of conscience, even for atheists. Other southern states followed Virginia's lead.

New Englanders proved more resistant to **disestablishment.** Many wished to continue government support of the Congregational church. Others wished to retain the principle of an established church. As a compromise, the New England states allowed towns to decide which denomination would be the established church. New England did not separate church and state entirely until the nineteenth century.

Protection of Property Rights

The American revolutionaries were very vocal about the importance of private property. They expected government to protect people's rights to own property. In the decade before the Revolution, much of the protest against British policy had focused on this issue. For property holders and aspiring property holders, life, liberty, and happiness were interwoven with the right of ownership.

The property rights of some, however, infringed on the freedoms of others. Slavery's reduction of human beings to private property produced a stark contradiction in values. Masters wielded control over the lives of indentured servants, including the power to forbid a servant to marry or to bear children. Constraints could be seen in the white community's denial of Indian claims to the land. Laws placed restrictions on women's property rights as well. Unless special contracts were drafted before marriage, a woman's property, including her clothing and personal items, fell under the control of her husband.

Although all free white males had the right to own property, not all of them were able to acquire it. When the Revolution began, at least one-fifth of the American people lived in poverty or depended on public charity. The uneven distribution of wealth among white colonists was obvious on the streets of colonial Boston and in the rise in the number of **almshouses** in Philadelphia.

Social Equality and Legal Reforms

Despite wide variations in wealth, American republicans did believe in social equality. In particular, they aimed to create a society free of artificial

republic A nation in which supreme power resides in the citizens, who elect representatives to govern them.

limited government Government that guarantees the security and freedom of the people and interferes as little as possible with their lives.

disestablishment Depriving a church of official government support.

almshouse A public shelter for the poor.

privileges that benefited a few at the expense of the many. They eliminated **primogeniture** and **entail** for this reason. In Britain, primogeniture and entail together had created a landed aristocracy. Although the danger of the formation of a similarly privileged aristocracy in the United States was small, the revolutionaries repealed these laws.

The passion for social equality extended to national heroes. George Washington and his fellow Revolutionary War officers ran afoul of public opinion when they organized the Society of the Cincinnati in 1783 to sustain wartime friendships. Critics warned that the society's hereditary memberships, which were to pass from officer fathers to their eldest sons, would create a military aristocracy and pose a threat to republican government. Washington and his comrades were forced to revise the offending bylaws.

In some states, the principle of social equality had concrete political consequences. Pennsylvania and Georgia eliminated all property qualifications for voting among free white males. Other states lowered their property requirements for voters but refused to go as far as universal manhood suffrage.

Women in the New Republic

American women would remember the war years as a time of shortages, worry, harassment, and difficult responsibilities. Men going off to war left women and children to manage the farm or the shop, to cope with shortages of food and supplies, and to survive on meager budgets. Many women faced these new circumstances with great anxiety. After the war, however, they remembered with satisfaction how well they had adapted to new roles. They expressed their sense of accomplishment in letters to husbands that spoke no longer of "your farm" and "your crop" but of "our farm" and even "my crop."

What struck many women most vividly was their sudden independence from men. Even women whose circumstances were difficult experienced a new sense of freedom. Grace Galloway, wife of loyalist exile Joseph Galloway of Pennsylvania, remained in America during the war in an effort to preserve her family property. Reduced from wealth to painful poverty, Grace Galloway nevertheless confided to her diary that "Ye liberty of doing as I please Makes even Poverty more agreeable than any time I ever spent since I married."

Galloway's new self-confidence and her newfound liberty were certainly not characteristic of all women. For many, the war meant age-old experiences of vulnerability. Occupying armies, guerrilla bands, and outlaws posing as soldiers left trails of rape and physical attack, particularly in New Jersey, the Carolinas, and along the frontier.

For women, the war also meant adapting traditional behavior and skills to new circumstances. Women who joined husbands or fathers in army camps took up the familiar domestic chores of cooking, cleaning, laundering, and providing nursing care. On some occasions, however, they crossed gender boundaries. Women such as Mary Ludwig Hays (better known as "Molly Pitcher") carried water and ammunition to their husbands and took up the men's guns when they fell wounded. After the war, a number of these women applied to the government for pensions, citing evidence of wounds they had received in battle.

Both loyalist and patriot women served as spies, sheltered soldiers, and hid weapons in their cellars. Sometimes they burned their crops or destroyed their homes to prevent the enemy from using them. These were conscious acts of patriotism rather than wifely duties. The same was true of the small number of women who disguised themselves as men and fought in the military.

Such novel experiences created a new role for women in the family and in a republican society. This new role of **republican motherhood** called for women to be actively involved in the preservation of a republican society. Republican motherhood

primogeniture The legal right of the eldest son to inherit the entire estate of his father.

entail A legal limitation that prevents property from being divided, sold, or given away.

republican motherhood A role for women that stressed the importance of instructing children in republican virtues such as patriotism and honor.

stressed the importance of women as educators of the next generation of republicans. Republican motherhood did not arise solely from women's wartime experience. It had roots in the growth during colonial times of a prosperous urban class that could purchase many household necessities. These prosperous urban wives and mothers had more time to devote to raising children. Yet the Revolution did give republican motherhood its particular qualities. The republican woman was expected to possess an independence of mind and an ability to survive in times of crisis and disaster.

This new civic role for American mothers had profound implications for education. Women could not raise proper republican citizens if they themselves were ignorant and uneducated. It suddenly became important to teach women not just domestic skills but geography, philosophy, and history as well. By the 1780s, public education had come to include girls, and private academies had opened to educate the daughters of wealthy American families.

The War's Impact on Slaves and Slavery

The protection of liberty and the fear of enslavement were major themes of the Revolution. The denial of liberty was a central reality in the lives of most African Americans. Ironically, the desire for freedom set many slaves against the Revolution. Of the fifty thousand or so slaves who won their freedom in the war, half did so by escaping to the British army. Only about five thousand African-American men joined the Continental Army. In both armies, however, African-American troops were paid less than white soldiers.

Slaves found other routes to freedom besides military service during the war. They escaped from farms and plantations to the cities, where they passed as free people. Or they fled to the frontier, where they joined sympathetic Indian tribes.

The long war also affected the lives of those who remained in slavery. Control and discipline broke down when the southern campaigns disrupted work routines. Slave masters complained loudly and bitterly that their slaves "all do now what they please every where" or that slaves "pay no attention to the orders of the overseer."

In the northern states, the revolutionaries' demand for liberty undermined black slavery. Loyalists taunted patriots, asking, "How is it that we hear the loudest yelps for liberty among the drivers of negroes?" The question made the contradiction between revolutionary ideals and American reality painfully clear. In Boston, a young African-born slave named **Phillis Wheatley,** whose literary talents were encouraged by her master, called on the revolutionaries to acknowledge the universality of the wish for freedom. "In every human breast," Wheatley wrote, "God had implanted a Principle, which we call love of freedom; it is impatient of Oppression, and pants for Deliverance."

Free black Americans joined with white reformers to mobilize antislavery campaigns in Pennsylvania, Massachusetts, Rhode Island, and Connecticut. The broadly based antislavery sentiment in these states was not entirely a matter of moral commitment, however, for the region had few slaves outside New York City (see Figure 6.1).

Manumission increased during the 1770s, especially in the North. In 1780, Pennsylvania became the first state to pass an emancipation statute. Pennsylvania lawmakers, however, compromised on a gradual rather than an immediate end to slavery. Only persons born after 1780 were to be free, and only after they had served a twenty-eight-year term of indenture. By 1804, all northern states except Delaware had committed themselves to a slow end to slavery.

Slavery was far more deeply embedded in the South. In the Lower South, white Americans ignored the debate over slavery and continued to maintain the institution as if nothing had changed. Manumission did occur in the Upper South, where planters debated the morality of slavery in a republic. They did not all reach the same conclusions.

Phillis Wheatley African-born poet who became the first widely recognized black writer in America.

manumission The legal act of giving a slave freedom.

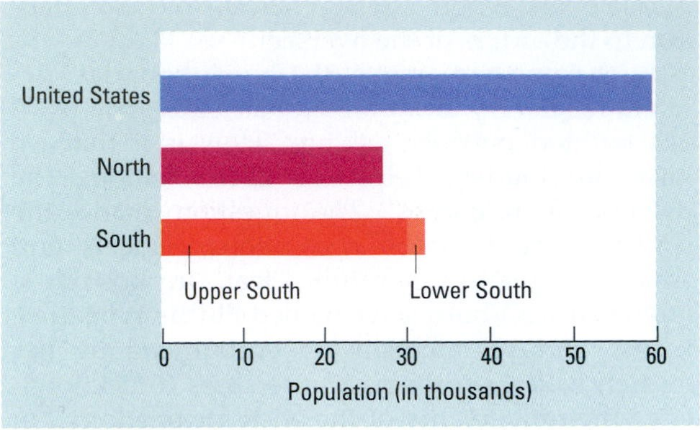
United States
North
South
Upper South
Lower South
0
10
20
30
40
50
60
Population (in thousands)

♦ **FIGURE 6.1 Free Black Population, 1790** This graph shows the number of free African Americans in the United States in 1790, as well as their regional distribution. These almost sixty thousand free people were less than 10 percent of the African-American population of the nation. Although 40 percent of northern African Americans were members of this free community, only about 5.5 percent of Upper South blacks and less than 2 percent of Lower South blacks lived outside the bounds of slavery.

George Washington freed all his slaves when he died. In 1765, Patrick Henry had stirred the souls of his fellow Virginia legislators by shouting, "Give me liberty or give me death!" But after the war, he justified his decision to continue slavery with blunt honesty. Freeing his slaves, he said, would be inconvenient.

The Fate of the Loyalists

After 1775, Americans loyal to the Crown flocked to the safety of British-occupied cities—first Boston and later New York City and Philadelphia. When the British left an area, most of the loyalists went with them. Over a thousand Massachusetts loyalists boarded British ships when the British abandoned Boston in 1776. Fifteen thousand sailed out of New York when the fighting ended in 1781. As many as a hundred thousand men, women, and children left America to take up new lives in Great Britain, Canada, and the West Indies.

Wealth often determined a loyalist's destination. Rich and influential men like Thomas Hutchinson of Massachusetts took refuge in Great Britain. But even wealthy colonials discovered that the cost of living there was so great that they could not live comfortably. Some were reduced to passing their days in seedy boarding houses. Even those who fared better lost their status and prestige. Ironically, many loyalists in Britain grew homesick.

When the war ended, most loyalists in Britain departed for Nova Scotia, New Brunswick, or the Caribbean. Some were specifically forbidden to return to the United States, while others had no desire to return. Those who did return adjusted slowly. Less prosperous loyalists, and especially those who had served in the loyalist battalions during the war, went to Canada after 1781. The separation from family and friends at first caused depression and despair in some exiles. One woman who had bravely endured the war and its deprivations cried when she landed in Nova Scotia. Like the revolutionaries, these men and women had based their political loyalty on a mixture of principles and self-interest. Unlike the revolutionaries, they had chosen the losing side. They would suffer the consequences for the rest of their lives.

Canada became the refuge of another group of loyalists: Indian tribes that had supported the Crown. The British ceded much of the Iroquois land in the United States in the Treaty of Paris, and American hostility toward "enemy savages" led the Iroquois to settle in new communities along the Grand River in Ontario in the 1780s.

SUMMARY

Expectations
Constraints
Choices
Outcomes

At the start of the American Revolution, both sides had *expectations* that proved incorrect. The British *expected* a short war from the inexperienced Americans. The Americans *expected* the British to abandon a war fought so far from home. The war, however, dragged on for seven years.

The British *chose* initially to invade New York, *expecting* to find strong loyalist support there. But the British were unable to deliver a crushing blow, and Washington's retreat across the Delaware saved the Americans from surrender.

A dramatic turning point in the war came in 1777, when British general John Burgoyne was forced to surrender at Saratoga, New York. The *outcome* of this American victory was an alliance between France and the United States that expanded the war into an international conflict. When the British *chose* to invade the South in 1778, their campaign ended in disaster. French and American forces together defeated General Cornwallis at Yorktown, Virginia, in October 1781. Fighting continued for a time, but in March 1782 the British Parliament *chose* to end the conflict. The war for American independence had been won.

Independence from British rule was not the only *outcome* of the war. Victory led to transformations in American society. Individual rights were strengthened for free white men. Many white women developed a new sense of the importance of their domestic role as "republican mothers." Black Americans also made some gains. Fifty thousand slaves won their freedom during the war. Some northerners moved to outlaw slavery, but southern slaveholders *chose* to preserve the institution. Loyalists, having made their political *choices*, had to live with the consequences of defeat. The *outcome* for most was exile in Ontario, Nova Scotia, New Brunswick, or the Caribbean.

SUGGESTED READINGS

Martin, Joseph Plumb. *Ordinary Courage: The Revolutionary War Adventures of Joseph Plumb Martin*, ed. James Kirby Martin (1993).

The military experiences of a Massachusetts soldier who served with the Continental Army during the American Revolution.

Nelson, William. *The American Tory* (1961).

An account of those who chose to align themselves with the British during the war.

Randall, Wallace Sterne. *Benedict Arnold: Patriot and Traitor* (1990).

The author tries to make sense of a man who might have been remembered as a great hero of the Revolution but whose name is synonymous in American history with *traitor.*

Revolution.

This feature-length film starring Al Pacino is available in most well-stocked video stores. Although it is a romance, the film captures some of the mood and spirit of the Revolutionary era.

A Revolution in Women's Education

The Context

In 1787, the Young Ladies Academy of Philadelphia opened its door to the daughters of America's revolutionary generation, offering a rigorous course of study that included literature, composition, sciences, arithmetic, oratory, and rhetoric. In the three decades that followed, similar schools appeared across the United States, in major cities like New York, Boston, and New Haven, and in smaller towns like Medford, Massachusetts; Litchfield, Connecticut; and Warrenton, North Carolina. The result, many believed, was a revolution in female education. (For further information on the context, see pages 120–121.)

The Historical Question

Modern historians have traced the rapid growth of educational institutions for women in the young republic. The significance of this "rise of the female academy" is debated, however. Did this educational trend reflect a change in ideas about women's intellectual capacities? Did it arise from or lead to a major shift in women's roles in American society?

The Challenge

Using the sources provided, along with other information you have read, write an essay or hold a discussion on the following question. Cite evidence in the sources to support your conclusions.

What new ideas about women's intellectual abilities and their role in society may have found expression in the growth of women's educational institutions?

The Sources

1 In 1635, John Winthrop, the Puritan governor of Massachusetts, recorded in his journal this judgment on the illness suffered by a woman:

Mr. Hopkins . . . came to Boston and brought his wife with him . . . who was fallen into a sad infirmity, the loss of her understanding and reason, which had been growing upon her . . . by occasion of her giving herself wholly to reading and writing . . . if she had attended to her household affairs, and such things as belong to women, and not . . . meddle[d] in such things as are proper for men, whose minds are stronger . . . she [would have] kept her wits.

2 This colonial advertisement, appearing in the *Virginia Gazette* in 1772, describes a curriculum the school mistress believed appropriate for female students:

E. Armston . . . continues the Schools at Point Pleasant, Norfolk Borough, where [there] is a large and convenient House proper to accommodate young Ladies as Boarders; at which School is taught Petit Point in Flowers, Fruit, Landscapes, and Sculpture, Nuns Work, Embroidery in Silk, Gold, Silver, Pearls, or embossed, Shading of all Kinds, in the various Works in Vogue, Dresden Point Work, Lace, Catgut in different Modes, Muslin after the Newest Taste, and most elegant Pattern, Waxwork in Figure, Fruit, or Flowers, Shell ditto, or grotesque, Painting in Water Colours and Mezzotints . . . Specimens of the Subscriber's Work may be seen at her House, as also of her Scholars; having taught several Years in Norfolk, and elsewhere to general Satisfaction. She flatters herself that those Gentlemen and Ladies who have hitherto employed her will grant her their further indulgence, as no endeavors shall be wanted to complete what is above mentioned, with a strict attention to the Behavior of those Ladies entrusted to her Care.

3 Wealthy Philadelphia matron Esther DeBerdt Reed helped organize women's voluntary associations to raise funds and supplies for the American army during the Revolution. In "The Sentiments of an American Woman," printed in 1780, Reed discusses female patriotism:

On the commencement of actual war, the Women of America manifested a firm resolution to contribute as much as could depend on them, to the deliverance of this country. Animated by the purest patriotism . . . they aspire to render themselves more really useful; and this sentiment is universal from the north to the south of the Thirteen United States . . . if the weakness of our [women's] Constitution, if opinion and manners did not forbid us to march to glory by the same paths as the Men, we should at least equal and sometimes surpass them in our love for the public good. I glory in all that which my sex has done great and commendable . . . Who knows if persons disposed to censure, and sometimes too severely with regard to us, may not disapprove . . . we are at least certain, that he cannot be a good citizen who will not applaud our efforts for the relief of the armies which defend our lives, our possessions, our liberty.

4 Like other advocates of female advancement, poet Susanna Haswell Rowson argued that nurture, not nature or divine dictates, created women's moral and intellectual inferiority to men. In "The Virtues of an Educated Wife," she wrote:

When the creator formed this world in common,
His last, best work, his master-piece, was woman.
Taken from the side of man, and next his heart,
Of all his virtues she partakes a part;
And from that source, poor woman got a share
Of vice and folly, mingled here and there.
But would you treat us, scorning custom's rules,
As reasonable beings, not as fools,
And from our earliest youth, would condescend
To form our minds, strengthen, correct, amend:
Teach us to scorn those fools, whose only joys,
Are placed in trifling idleness and noice.
Teach us to prize the power of intellect;
And whilst inspiring love, to keep respect;
You'd meet the sweet reward of all your care;
Find in us friends, your purest joys to share.

5 In July 1787, Dr. Benjamin Rush, one of Philadelphia's leading intellectuals and social reformers, addressed the entering class of the Young Ladies Academy of Philadelphia. Rush said:

I know that the elevation of the female mind, by means of moral, physical, and religious truth, is considered by some men as unfriendly to the domestic character of a woman. But this is the prejudice of little minds and springs from the same spirit which opposes the general diffusion of knowledge among the citizens of our republic. If men believe that ignorance is favorable to the government of the female sex, they are certainly deceived, for a weak and ignorant woman will always be governed with the greatest difficulty . . . It will be in your power, LADIES, to correct the mistakes and practices of our sex upon these subjects by demonstrating that the female temper can only be governed by reason and that the cultivation of reason in women is alike friendly to the order of nature and to private as well as public happiness.

THE FEDERALIST AND ANTIFEDERALIST STRUGGLE OVER THE CONSTITUTION The battle over ratification of the Constitution was fiercely fought throughout 1787 and 1788. This map shows the areas of strong antifederalism, the areas of Federalist strength, and the scattered pockets where opinion was evenly divided. The map also provides the final ratification vote for each state. Note that Rhode Island did not ratify the Constitution until after the new government went into effect.

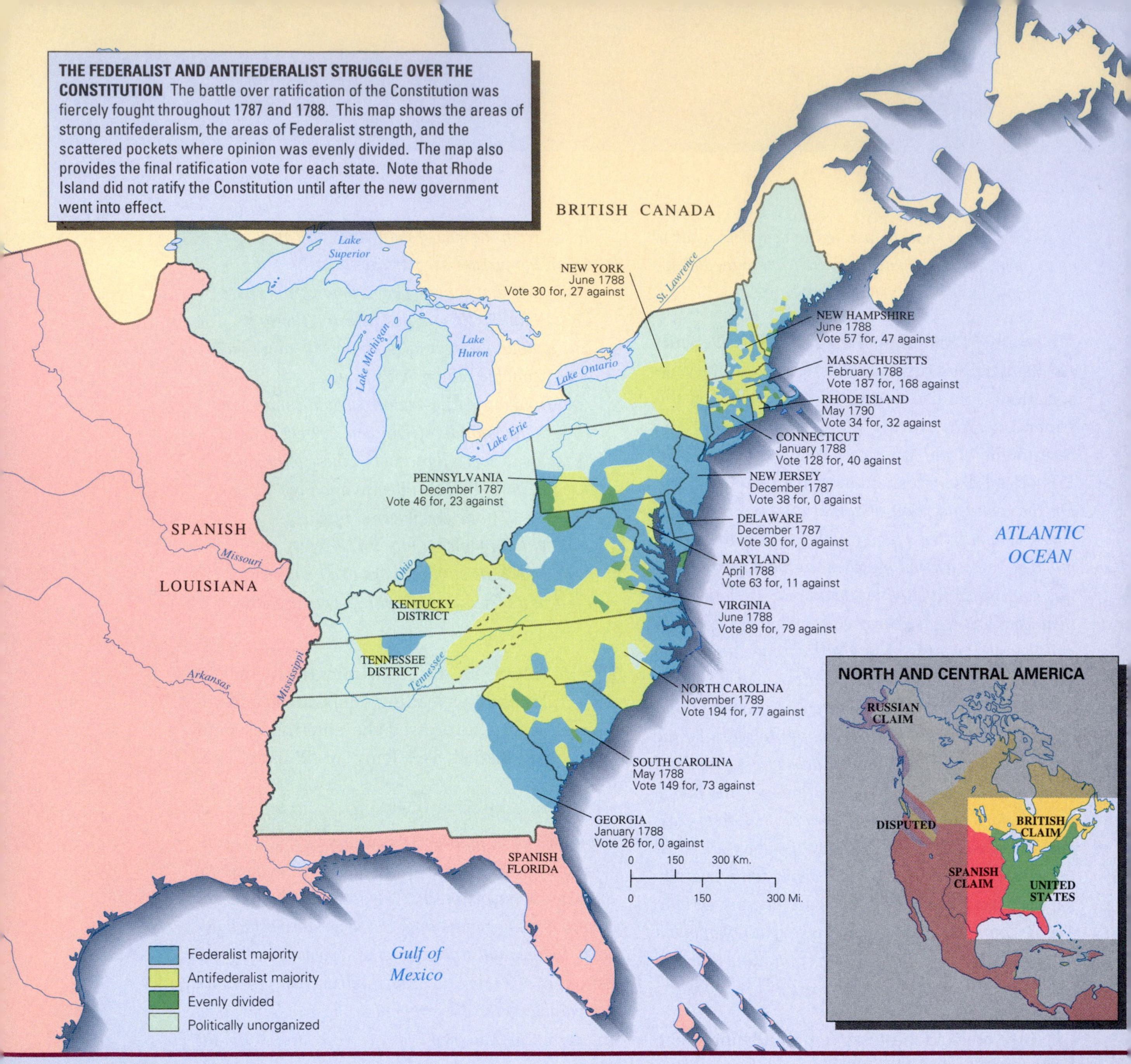

BRITISH CANADA
Lake Superior
Lake Michigan
Lake Huron
Lake Ontario
Lake Erie
St. Lawrence
NEW YORK
June 1788
Vote 30 for, 27 against
NEW HAMPSHIRE
June 1788
Vote 57 for, 47 against
MASSACHUSETTS
February 1788
Vote 187 for, 168 against
RHODE ISLAND
May 1790
Vote 34 for, 32 against
CONNECTICUT
January 1788
Vote 128 for, 40 against
NEW JERSEY
December 1787
Vote 38 for, 0 against
PENNSYLVANIA
December 1787
Vote 46 for, 23 against
DELAWARE
December 1787
Vote 30 for, 0 against
MARYLAND
April 1788
Vote 63 for, 11 against
VIRGINIA
June 1788
Vote 89 for, 79 against
NORTH CAROLINA
November 1789
Vote 194 for, 77 against
SOUTH CAROLINA
May 1788
Vote 149 for, 73 against
GEORGIA
January 1788
Vote 26 for, 0 against
SPANISH
LOUISIANA
Missouri
Ohio
KENTUCKY DISTRICT
TENNESSEE DISTRICT
Tennessee
Arkansas
Mississippi
ATLANTIC OCEAN
SPANISH FLORIDA
Gulf of Mexico
0 150 300 Km.
0 150 300 Mi.
Federalist majority
Antifederalist majority
Evenly divided
Politically unorganized
NORTH AND CENTRAL AMERICA
RUSSIAN CLAIM
DISPUTED
BRITISH CLAIM
SPANISH CLAIM
UNITED STATES

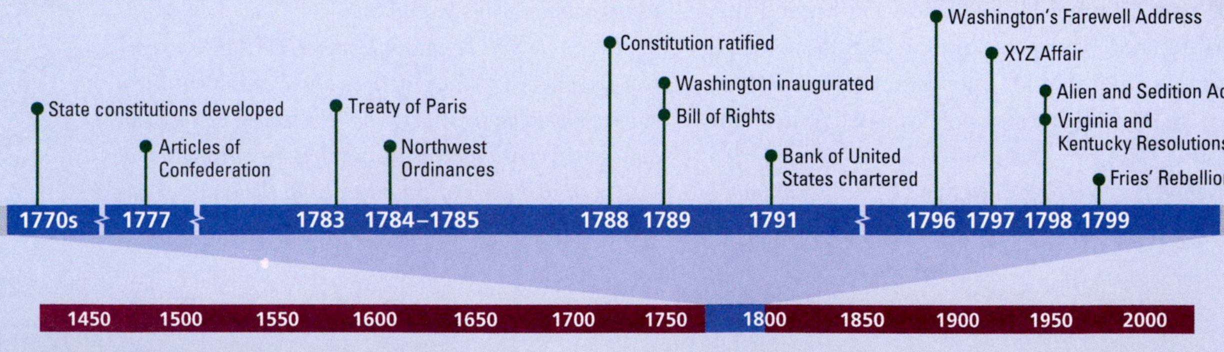

State constitutions developed
Articles of Confederation
Treaty of Paris
Northwest Ordinances
Constitution ratified
Washington inaugurated
Bill of Rights
Bank of United States chartered
Washington's Farewell Address
XYZ Affair
Alien and Sedition Acts
Virginia and Kentucky Resolutions
Fries' Rebellion
1770s 1777 1783 1784–1785 1788 1789 1791 1796 1797 1798 1799
1450 1500 1550 1600 1650 1700 1750 1800 1850 1900 1950 2000

CHAPTER 7

Competing Visions of a Virtuous Republic, 1776–1800

What Kind of a Republic?

- How did Americans define a good citizen of the republic?
- How did colonial experience influence the outcome of drafting state constitutions?
- What constraints did the Articles of Confederation place on the central government?

Challenges to the Confederation

- What constraints undermined the Confederation, and what was the outcome?
- What was the outcome of Shays' Rebellion for national politics?
- What gains did nationalists expect from a stronger national government?

Creating a New Government

- What major compromises did the framers choose to make in writing a new constitution?
- What positive outcome did James Madison see in his "checks and balances" system?

Resolving the Conflict of Visions

- How did the Federalists' and Antifederalists' expectations of the Constitution differ?
- What was the outcome of the ratification process?

Competing Visions Reemerge

- How did Alexander Hamilton's expectations for the new nation differ from Thomas Jefferson's? What were the outcomes of their conflict?
- How did the French Revolution affect diplomatic choices during Washington's presidency?

Conflict in the Adams Administration

- What did the Federalists hope to accomplish by declaring war on France in 1798?
- How did the Republicans respond to the constraints that the Federalists imposed during the Quasi-War?

INTRODUCTION

Expectations
Constraints
Choices
Outcomes

Most Americans of the revolutionary generation rejected monarchy and *expected* to live in a republic. They disagreed, however, on what form of republic best suited their new nation. As a consequence, the transition from revolution to nationhood was neither smooth nor uncontested.

In the great political contests that occurred during this transition, fundamental *choices* were made about how power should be divided between local and national governments, how laws should be made and by whom, and who should administer those laws. Americans also had to *choose* the best way to protect their unalienable individual rights.

Americans made these political *choices* within the context of serious postwar *constraints.* After the Revolution, the nation struggled with economic depression, unpaid war debts, and vanishing credit. There were rivalries among the states over trade and territory, diplomatic problems with foreign nations and Indians, and disputes among Americans that sometimes erupted into violence.

The first national government, established by the Articles of Confederation, guided Americans through the last years of the war and the peace negotiations. The Articles, however, did not survive the decade of postwar adjustment. The nation *chose* to replace them with the Constitution. The Constitution greatly strengthened and expanded the role of the central government in matters such as regulating trade. The Constitution also provided the central government with powers that the Confederation government had lacked, including the right to levy taxes.

The creation of a new federal government was controversial. Its opponents, the Antifederalists, argued that the Constitution rejected basic revolutionary ideals such as the commitment to local representative government and the guarantee of protection from the dangers of centralized authority. Its supporters, the Federalists, argued that it would save America from economic disaster, international scorn, and domestic unrest. Leading patriots of the 1760s and 1770s could be found on both sides of this debate, but the Federalists carried the day.

The framers of the Constitution knew they had left many problems unresolved. Tensions remained between people who supported an active, strong central government and those who believed strong local governments offered the best protection of their liberties. The framers did not *expect,* however, that these tensions would soon lead to the formation of rival political parties. Both the Republican followers of Thomas Jefferson and the Federalist followers of Alexander Hamilton believed that their vision of American republicanism was correct, and they exercised few *constraints* against their political enemies.

Although George Washington appealed for national unity in his Farewell Address in 1796, the victorious Federalists *chose* to ignore his advice. The *outcome* was a series of repressive laws and nearly a war with France.

CHRONOLOGY

From Revolution to Nationhood

1770s	State constitutions developed
1776	New Jersey constitution gives some women the right to vote Declaration of Independence
1777	Articles of Confederation adopted by Congress
1780	Massachusetts constitution establishes bicameral legislature
1781	Articles of Confederation ratified Surrender at Yorktown
1783	Treaty of Paris
1784	Ordinance of 1784 approved
1785	Land ordinance of 1785 approved
1786	Annapolis conference
1786–1787	Shays' Rebellion in Massachusetts
1787	Constitutional Convention Northwest Ordinance enacted
1788	Constitution ratified First congressional elections
1789	Washington becomes first president Judiciary Act Bill of Rights adopted by Congress French Revolution begins
1791	Hamilton's *Report on Manufactures* First Bank of the United States chartered Bill of Rights ratified
1793	Genêt affair Jefferson resigns as secretary of state
1794	Whiskey Rebellion in Pennsylvania
1795	Jay's Treaty
1796	Washington's Farewell Address First contested presidential election
1797	XYZ affair
1798	Alien and Sedition Acts Virginia and Kentucky Resolutions
1799	Fries' Rebellion Napoleon seizes control in France Convention of Mortefontaine

What Kind of a Republic?

To late eighteenth-century Americans, a republic had three basic elements. First and most important, political power rested with the people rather than with a monarch. Second, the people elected those who governed them. Finally, officeholders were expected to represent the people's interests and to protect individual rights. Although there was broad agreement on these basics, Americans disputed much else about republican government.

Competing Notions of Republicanism

Tom Paine spoke for many when he declared that republicanism was a moral code of behavior as well as a system of government. No representative government could survive without virtuous citizens who led simple, industrious lives and who were willing to make sacrifices in the best interests of the community. If citizens became selfish or corrupt, a republic would succumb to tyranny. After all, history demonstrated that the **Roman republic,** which Americans greatly admired, had degenerated into a despotism when its formerly simple citizens adopted a luxurious and **decadent** lifestyle.

The belief that a republic depended on individual virtue was widespread but not universally held in eighteenth-century America. For some Americans, republicanism meant that individuals should be free to pursue their own self-interest. Advocates of this notion of republicanism drew their inspiration from economists and philosophers such as **Adam Smith.** They believed that a government that did not interfere with the individual's pursuit of wealth and success would win the enduring loyalty of its citizens. Thus, whereas one vision of republicanism held that the pursuit of self-interest would lead to the downfall of republican government, a conflicting vision argued that the purpose of government was to allow individuals to better themselves economically.

Creating Republican Governments: The State Constitutions

The drafting of state constitutions after 1776 offers a revealing look at the many differences in how Americans defined republican government. The states were a laboratory for republican experiments. They came up with many different answers to such fundamental questions as who should be allowed to vote, who should be allowed to hold office, and what the structure of a republican government should be.

Pennsylvania passed the most democratic of the state constitutions. Its constitution abolished all property qualifications and granted the vote to all white males. Maryland, by contrast, continued to link property ownership to voting and required officeholders to possess considerable property.

The state constitutions also reflected disagreements over how political power should be distributed in a republic. Pennsylvania's constitution concentrated all power in a **unicameral** assembly. Pennsylvania had neither a governor nor an upper house in the legislature. To ensure that the assembly remained responsive to popular will, the constitution required the annual election of all legislators. Maryland chose to divide power among a governor, an upper house requiring high property qualifications for its members, and a lower house. In this manner, Maryland ensured a voice for its elite.

Pennsylvania and Maryland represented two ends of the democratic spectrum. The remaining states fell somewhere between them. New Hampshire, North Carolina, and Georgia followed the democratic tendencies of Pennsylvania. New York, South Carolina, and Virginia chose Maryland's more conservative approach. New Jersey and Delaware took the middle ground. New Jersey's constitution was unusual in extending **suffrage** to white women who met modest property qualifications. New Jersey rescinded this right in 1807.

A state's history as a colony was likely to influence its constitution. New Hampshire, South Carolina, Virginia, and North Carolina had all been dominated by coastal elites. Their first state constitutions corrected this injustice by giving more representation to small farmers in the interior. In Massachusetts, the memory of highhanded colonial governors and elitist upper houses led citizens to demand limited powers for their new government.

Revisions of the state constitutions in the 1780s generally expanded the powers of the state governments and curbed democratic tendencies. The Massachusetts constitution of 1780 became a model for these constitutional reforms. It called for

Roman republic A republic in ancient Rome that lasted from 500 to 31 B.C., when it was replaced by the Roman Empire.

decadent Being in a state of moral decay.

Adam Smith Scottish economist (1723–1790) and advocate of the principles of free trade.

unicameral Consisting of a single legislative house.

suffrage The right to vote.

a system of **checks and balances** among the legislative, judicial, and executive branches and for a **bicameral** legislature. Wealth returned as a qualification to govern in these revised constitutions, but the wealthy were not allowed to tamper with the basic individual rights of citizens. In seven states, a **bill of rights** guaranteed freedom of speech, religion, the press, and other rights.

The Articles of Confederation

After declaring American independence, political leaders realized that some form of national government was needed. Popular sentiment, however, ran against a powerful central government. As John Adams later recalled, Americans wanted "a Confederacy of States, each of which must have a separate government."

Congress adopted the first national framework of government, the **Articles of Confederation,** in 1777 and submitted the plan to the state governments for their approval. The plan called for a **confederation** that preserved the rights and privileges of the states and that had few powers. This arrangement reflected the revolutionaries' fears that a strong central government was the enemy of liberty.

The Confederation government consisted of a unicameral legislature. It had no executive branch and no separate **judiciary.** Believers in democracy such as Tom Paine and Samuel Adams praised this concentration of powers in the hands of an elected assembly. John Adams, however, thought it "too democratical."

The Confederation government had no power to tax. The states retained this crucial power. Thus the Confederation government had to rely on the states for funds. It had no legal right to compel states to provide funds and no practical means of forcing them to contribute.

Voting in the Confederation Congress was to be done by states. Each state, whether large or small, had one vote. This jealous protection of state sovereignty also determined the amendment process for the Articles of Confederation. An amendment required the consent of all the states.

Fierce arguments developed over how each state's share of the federal budget was to be determined. Proposals that everyone in a state be counted brought southern political leaders to their feet, for their states had large slave populations. If slaves were included, southern whites would have to shoulder a heavier tax burden. Congress ultimately decided to count slaves for tax purposes.

Such debates delayed ratification of the Articles. The biggest delay, however, was caused by the battle over western land claims. Based on their colonial charters, Virginia, Massachusetts, and Connecticut claimed the Pacific as their western boundary (see Map 7.1). Consequently, they could assert rights to the Northwest Territory, the region north of the Ohio River and east of the Mississippi River. States with fixed western boundaries such as Maryland feared that they would be dwarfed by their neighbors that claimed western lands for expansion. Maryland advocated that western lands be set aside as part of a national domain controlled by Congress, not by the individual states. Although most states without western claims reluctantly ratified the Articles, Maryland would not endorse them without the establishment of a national domain.

To avoid further delays in ratification, Virginia ceded all its claims to Congress. The other states with western claims followed suit. In 1781, Maryland became the thirteenth and final state to ratify the Articles.

checks and balances Separation of the powers of government into executive, legislative, and judicial branches, each of which is intended to prevent the others from getting out of control.

bicameral Consisting of two legislative houses.

bill of rights A formal summary of essential rights and liberties.

Articles of Confederation The first constitution of the United States; it created a central government with limited powers and was replaced by the Constitution in 1788.

confederation An association of states or nations united for joint action in matters that affect them all.

judiciary A system of courts of law for the administration of justice.

♦ **MAP 7.1 Western Land Claims After American Independence** This map indicates the claims made by several of the thirteen original states to land west of the Appalachian Mountains and in the New England region. The states based their claims on the colonial charters that governed them before independence. Until this land was ceded to the federal government, new states could not be created here as they were in the Northwest Territory.

Challenges to the Confederation

Members of the first Confederation Congress had barely taken their seats when Lord Cornwallis surrendered at Yorktown in 1781. Even the most optimistic could see, however, that the new nation faced monumental challenges. The physical, psychological, and economic damage caused by the long and brutal war was extensive. New York and Charleston had been burned. Communities in New Jersey and Pennsylvania bore the scars of rape and looting by the British armies. In the South, where civil war had raged, plantations had been destroyed and slaves had fled. A steady stream of refugees filled the cities.

Depression and Financial Crisis

Americans were hard hit by a postwar depression. By the time peace was declared, small farmers who had lost barns and livestock and planters who had lost slaves or seen their tobacco warehouses go up in smoke were desperate. Wages plummeted in the 1780s for urban workers and farm laborers. Soldiers waited without hope for their back pay.

Financial problems also plagued wealthy Americans. Many merchants feared ruin because they had overextended their credit to import foreign goods after the war. Land **speculators** had borrowed too heavily in order to grab up confiscated loyalist land or secure claims in the Northwest Territory. Independence hurt those who had once lived well by supplying British markets. Rice planters saw the demand for their crop fall dramatically after the war.

British policy also hurt the economy. Parliament banned the sale of American farm products in the West Indies and limited the rights of American ships to carry goods to and from Caribbean ports. These restrictions hit New England shipbuilders so hard that whole communities faced poverty.

This economic depression made it extremely difficult for the Confederation government to pay its debts. To finance the war, the Continental Congress had printed over $240 million in paper money backed by "good faith" rather than by gold and silver. As expectations that the national government would ever **redeem** the paper for hard currency fell, the value of paper money declined rapidly. The phrase "not worth a Continental" indicated the low regard Americans had for it. Congress was equally embarrassed by substantial debts to foreign nations that it could not repay.

Congress appointed Robert Morris, a Philadelphia merchant who had earned a reputation during the war for his financial genius, to raise money to pay these debts. Morris knew from experience that he could not rely on the states for contributions. Instead, he asked the states for permission to impose a 5 percent federal **tariff** on imported goods. The states refused to give their unanimous permission in 1782, 1783, and again in 1784. Morris resigned in disgust in 1784.

The Northwest Ordinances

The Confederation Congress turned next to western land sales as a way to raise money. Here at least Congress did not need state approval. It had the exclusive authority to set policy for the settlement and governance of national territory.

National land policy took shape in three **Northwest Ordinances** enacted in 1784, 1785, and 1787. These ordinances had a significance far beyond their role in raising money. They guaranteed that men and women who moved west would not be colonial dependents of the original states. The 1784 ordinance prescribed that five new states would be carved out of the region and that each new state would be equal in status to the original thirteen. Settlers in the region could expect to acquire the rights of self-government quickly. Initially, each territory would have a governor appointed by Congress. As soon as there were enough voters, settlers were entitled to a representative assembly. Finally, the territory's voters would draft a state constitution and elect representatives to the Confederation Congress. Ohio, Illinois, Indiana, Michigan, and Wisconsin followed this path to statehood (see Map 7.2).

The ordinance of 1785 spelled out the terms for the sale of government land. It called for Congress to auction off 640-acre plots to individual settlers at a minimum price of a dollar per acre. When the original price proved too high for the average farm family, Congress lowered the price but also began to sell to wealthy speculators.

The ordinance of 1787 specified that any territory with sixty thousand white males could apply for admission as a state. Thomas Jefferson, who drafted this ordinance, took care to protect the liberties of the settlers with a bill of rights and to ban slavery forever north of the Ohio River.

speculator A person who buys or sells land or some other commodity in hopes of making a profit.

redeem To pay a specified sum in return for something.

tariff A tax on imported or exported goods.

Northwest Ordinances Three laws (1784, 1785, 1787) that dealt with the sale of public land in the Northwest Territory and established a plan for the admission of new states to the Union.

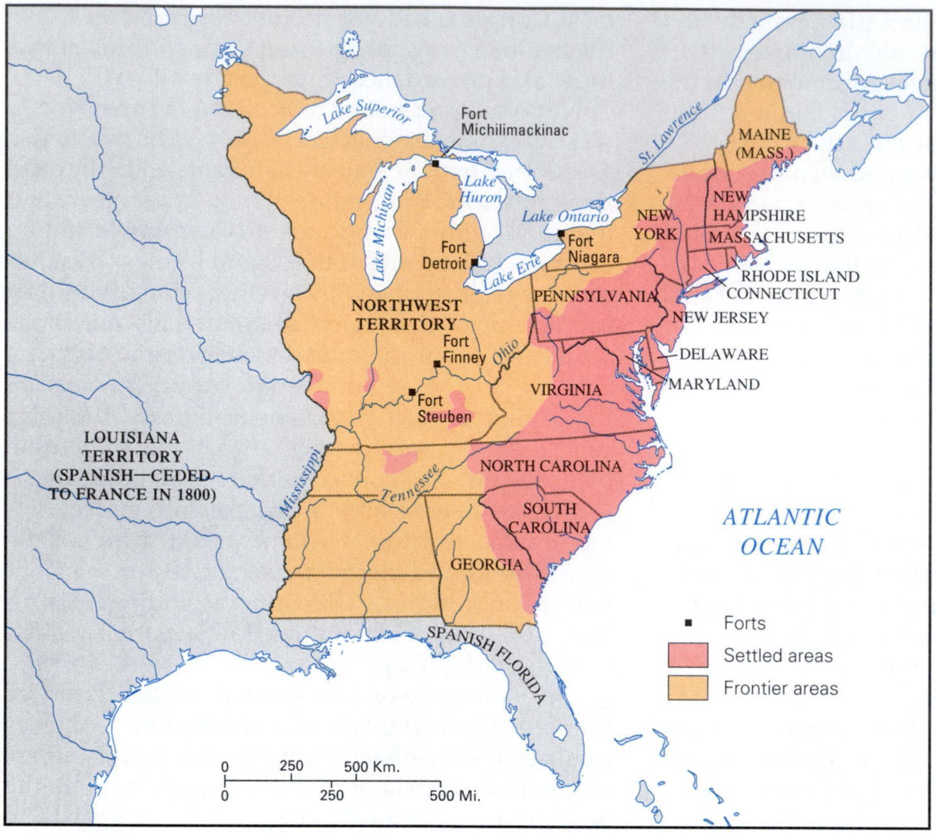

♦ **MAP 7.2 The United States in 1787** This map shows the extent of American westward settlement in 1787 and the limits placed on that settlement by French and Spanish claims west of the Mississippi and in Florida. Plans for the creation of three to five states in the Northwest Territory were approved by Congress in 1787, ensuring that the settlers in this region would enjoy the same political rights as the citizens of the original thirteen states.

Diplomatic Problems

Despite the Treaty of Paris, diplomatic relations between the new nation and its former mother country remained sour. The British refused to evacuate their western forts until the Americans repaid their war debts and allowed loyalists to recover confiscated property. Meanwhile, the British supported Indian resistance to American settlement in the Ohio valley by providing a steady supply of weapons to the Shawnees, the Miamis, the Delawares, and other tribes that refused to recognize the 1784 **Treaty of Fort Stanwix.** Made with the remnants of the Iroquois League, the treaty opened up all Iroquois lands to white settlement, according to Americans. Tribes that were not party to the treaty disagreed and, with British assistance, waged warfare along the frontier for a decade.

Americans got little satisfaction from the British on this or other issues. John Adams, the American

Treaty of Fort Stanwix Treaty signed in 1784 that opened all Iroquois lands to white settlement.

minister to Britain, was unable to persuade the British to abandon their northwestern forts, to stop their aid to Indians, or to open up their markets to American goods.

The United States also experienced difficulties with its former allies. When Spain saw a steady stream of Americans heading into Kentucky and Tennessee, it became alarmed that Americans might soon threaten its interests west of the Mississippi. Aware that the Mississippi provided the only practical way for Americans west of the mountains to export their surplus goods, Spain banned all American traffic on the Mississippi to discourage migration into the trans-Appalachian area. American negotiator **John Jay** reported that talks with Spain produced no promise of access to the Mississippi.

The Confederation's failures in dealing with the **Barbary pirates** were military rather than diplomatic in nature. For many years, rulers along the Barbary Coast of North Africa had attacked ships engaged in Mediterranean trade. Most European nations paid blackmail to these pirates or provided naval escorts for their ships. Now sailing without British protection, American ships traveled at their own risk.

In 1785, the Barbary pirates captured an American ship, seized its cargo, and sold its crew into slavery. Despite outcries, the Confederation Congress could do nothing. It had no navy and no authority to create one. It could not even raise enough money to ransom the enslaved crew. Lack of resources and authority plagued the Confederation government in this and other efforts to conduct foreign affairs.

A Farmers' Revolt

Among those hardest hit by the postwar depression were the farmers of western Massachusetts. Many were deeply in debt to creditors who held mortgages on their farms and land. When they asked the state government for debt relief, however, it turned a deaf ear. Instead, the legislature raised taxes to pay the state's war debts.

Farmers protested this additional burden by petitioning the legislature to lower their taxes. Their protests again went unheeded. Hundreds of farmers led by Daniel Shays, a 39-year-old veteran of the Battle of Bunker Hill, then turned to armed resistance in the western part of the state.

In 1786, Shays' followers closed down several courts in which debtors were tried and freed their fellow farmers from debtors' prison. Fear of a widespread uprising prompted the Massachusetts government to order General William Sheperd and six hundred men to Springfield, where over a thousand farmers, most of them armed with pitchforks, had gathered to close the local courthouse. Sheperd let loose a cannon barrage that killed four rebels and set the rest to flight. In February 1787, a government force surprised the remaining rebels in the village of Petersham. Daniel Shays managed to escape, but the revolt was over.

Shays' Rebellion revealed the temper of the times. When the government did not respond to their needs, the farmers acted as they had before the Revolution. They organized; they protested; and when the government did not respond, they took up arms. Across the country, many Americans sympathized with these farmers.

But many did not. Among the southern planter elite and the prosperous commercial class of the North, the revolt raised the fear that other local insurrections would follow. Rebellions by slaves, pitched battles between debtors and creditors, and wars between the haves and have-nots could easily be imagined. Such anxieties led many Americans to wonder if their state and national governments were strong enough to preserve the rule of law.

John Jay New York lawyer and diplomat who negotiated with Great Britain and Spain on behalf of the Confederation; he later became the first chief justice of the Supreme Court.

Barbary pirates Pirates along the Barbary Coast of North Africa who attacked European and American vessels engaged in Mediterranean trade.

Shays' Rebellion Uprising by farmers in western Massachusetts who wanted to protest the indifference of the state legislature to the plight of farmers; the rebellion was suppressed by the state militia in 1787.

In 1786, western Massachusetts farmers began an agrarian revolt against high taxes and mortgage foreclosures that soon spread to other New England states. Most of the leaders of the uprising, known as Shay's Rebellion, were veteran officers of the American Revolution; many had participated in the protest and resistance that preceded the war itself. The government of Massachusetts crushed the rebellion, driving Shays to seek asylum in Vermont. News of the uprising prompted elite political leaders like George Washington and Alexander Hamilton to press for a more powerful central government, able to ensure "law and order" throughout the nation. *National Portrait Gallery, Washington, D.C.*

The Revolt of the "Better Sort"

Even before Shays' Rebellion, many Americans had come to believe that a crisis was enveloping their young nation. They pointed to the Confederation's lack of power to solve critical problems as a major cause of this crisis. In the words of George Washington, "I predict the worst consequences from a half-starved, limping government, always moving upon crutches and tottering at every step."

To Washington, the solution was clear: a stronger national government. Support for a revision of the Articles grew in the key states of Virginia, Massachusetts, and New York, especially among the elite. They urged that the central government be given taxing powers and that some legal means of enforcing national government policies be instituted. These reforms would help improve the young republic's diplomatic and trade relations with foreign countries. But these reforms would also create a national government able to protect their property and to preserve their peace of mind.

The **nationalists'** agenda began to take shape in 1786 when they obtained approval from Congress for a conference at Annapolis, Maryland. Their stated purpose was to discuss trade restrictions and conflicts among the states. But the organizers also meant to test support for revising the nation's constitution. Although only a third of the states participated, the nationalists were convinced that they had strong support. They asked Congress to call a convention for the following year in Philadelphia to discuss remedies for the Confederation's problems. News of Shays' Rebellion convinced doubters of the need for a convention. Leaders of the "better sort" thus won an opportunity to reopen debate on the nature of the republic.

Creating a New Government

Late in May 1787, George Washington welcomed delegates from twelve of the thirteen states to the Constitutional Convention. Rhode Island had declined to attend, declaring that this was a meeting to revise the Articles masquerading as a discussion of interstate trade. The accusation was correct. The

nationalist A person devoted to the interests of a particular nation and favoring a strong central government.

fifty-five men in attendance intended to consider significant changes in their national government. The seriousness of their task explained their willingness to meet in a tightly closed room in the sweltering heat of Philadelphia.

Revise or Replace?

Most of the delegates were nationalists, but they did not agree about whether to revise or abandon the Articles of Confederation. For five days, the convention debated this issue. Then Edmund Randolph of Virginia presented a plan that essentially scrapped the Articles of Confederation.

Although Randolph introduced the **Virginia Plan, James Madison** was its guiding spirit. The plan reflected the 36-year-old Madison's deep consideration of the following question: what kind of government was best for a republic? He concluded that a strong central government could serve a republic well. Fear of tyranny should not rule out a powerful national government. Abuse of power could be avoided, Madison believed, if internal checks and balances were built into the government's structure.

The Virginia Plan embodied this conviction. It called for a government with three distinct branches: legislative, executive, and judicial. The Confederation Congress had performed all three of these functions. By dividing power, Madison intended to ensure that no group or individual could wield too much authority. And by allowing each branch of government some means to check the other branches, Madison intended to protect the interests of citizens.

Although the delegates supported the broad principles of the Virginia Plan, they were in sharp disagreement over many specific issues. The greatest controversy centered on representation in the legislative branch. Madison had proposed that membership in each house of the bicameral legislature be based on proportional representation. Large states supported the plan, for representation based on population was to their advantage. Small states objected that the Virginia Plan would leave them helpless in a federal government dominated by large states. They supported the **New Jersey Plan,** which proposed that every state have an equal voice within a unicameral legislature.

The hopeless deadlock over the Virginia and New Jersey plans threatened to destroy the convention. Roger Sherman of Connecticut then introduced the **Great Compromise.** It called for **proportional representation** in the lower house (the House of Representatives) and equal representation in the upper house (the Senate).

The Great Compromise resolved the first major controversy at the convention. Another compromise settled the issue of how representatives were to be chosen. State legislatures would select senators, and a state's eligible voters would elect members of the House of Representatives.

The final stumbling block over representation was the question of who was to be counted in determining a state's population. Southern delegates argued that slaves should be counted for the purposes of representation but not for the purposes of taxation. Northern delegates countered that slaves should be considered property, and not people, for both purposes. The **Three-fifths Compromise** settled this issue. It stipulated that three-fifths of the slave population be included in a state's critical head count.

Virginia Plan A plan for a federal government submitted by the Virginia delegation; it gave states representation in a bicameral legislature in proportion to their population.

James Madison Virginia planter and political theorist who supported ratification of the Constitution; he later became the fourth president.

New Jersey Plan A plan for a federal government giving all states equal representation in a unicameral legislature.

Great Compromise A plan for a federal government that set up a bicameral legislature, with one house providing equal representation to all states and the other providing proportional representation based on population.

proportional representation Representation in the legislature based on population; it gives large states more power than small states.

Three-fifths Compromise An agreement to count three-fifths of a state's slaves to determine a state's representation in the House of Representatives.

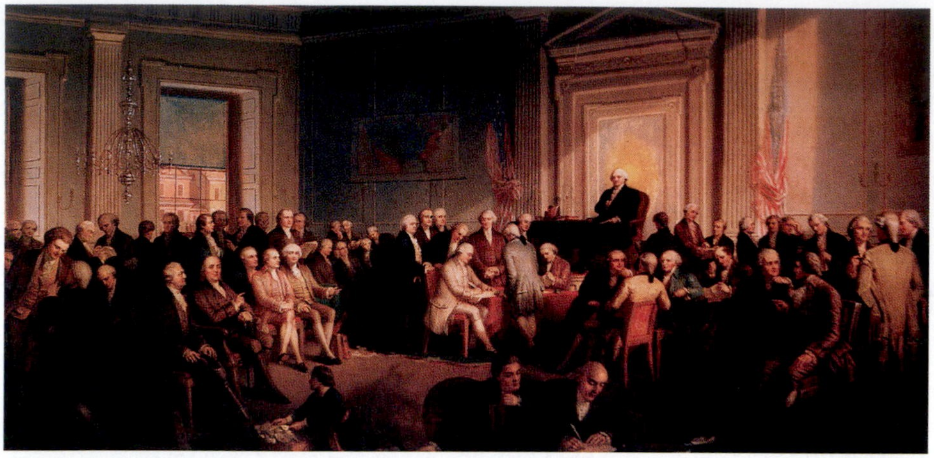

♦ In 1867, Thomas Pritchard Rossiter painted his *Signing of the Constitution of the United States* honoring a group of statesmen that included James Madison, Alexander Hamilton, and George Washington, who presided over the Constitutional Convention. Thomas Jefferson, absent because of his duties as ambassador to France, referred to the fifty-five delegates who crafted the Constitution as a gathering of "demigods." *"Signing of the Constitution of the United States" by Thomas Pritchard Rossiter, 1867. Fraunces Tavern Museum.*

Drafting an Acceptable Document

The Three-fifths Compromise ended the long, exhausting debate over representation. No other issue provoked such controversy, and the Constitutional Convention proceeded calmly to implement the principle of checks and balances. For example, the president was named commander in chief of the armed forces and given primary responsibility for the conduct of foreign affairs. To balance the president's executive powers, the rights to declare war and to raise an army were given to Congress. Congress was also given the critical power to tax, but this power was checked by the president's power to veto congressional legislation. Congress in turn could override a presidential veto by the vote of a two-thirds majority.

The procedure for electing a president reflected the delegates' fears that the ordinary people could not be trusted to perform such an important task. Their solution was to elect the president indirectly, through the **Electoral College.** This body consisted of electors chosen by the states to vote for presidential candidates. Each state was entitled to as many electors as it had senators and representatives in Congress. (No one serving in Congress was eligible to be an elector.) If two candidates received the same number of votes in the Electoral College, or if no candidate received a majority of the Electoral College votes, the House of Representatives would select the new president.

The proposed Constitution won nearly unanimous support from the delegates. A weary George Washington at last declared the convention adjourned on September 17, 1787.

Resolving the Conflict of Visions

For the new Constitution to go into effect, special state **ratifying conventions** had to approve of the proposed change of government. The framers of the

Electoral College A body of electors chosen by the states to elect the president and vice president; each state gets a number of electors equal to the number of its senators and representatives in Congress.

ratifying conventions Meetings in each state attended by delegates to determine whether that state would support the Constitution.

Constitution argued that these conventions would give citizens a more direct role in making this important political decision. This procedure also gave the framers two advantages. First, it allowed them to bypass the state legislatures, which stood to lose power under the new government and were thus likely to oppose it. Second, it allowed the framers to nominate their supporters and to campaign for their election to the state conventions. The framers added to their advantage by declaring that the approval of only nine states was necessary for ratification. Fortunately, the Confederation Congress agreed to all these terms and procedures. By the end of September 1787, Congress had passed the proposed Constitution on to the states, triggering the next debate over America's political future.

The Ratification Controversy

The framers were leading figures in their states. These men of wealth, political experience, and frequently great persuasive powers put their skills to the task of ratifying the Constitution. But many revolutionary heroes and political leaders strongly opposed the Constitution, most notably Patrick Henry and Samuel Adams. Leadership on both sides of the issue was drawn from the political elite of the revolutionary generation.

Pro-Constitution forces won an early and important victory by calling themselves **Federalists.** This name had originally been associated with those who supported strong state governments and a limited national government. This shrewd tactic robbed opponents of the Constitution of their rightful name. The pro-Constitution forces then dubbed their opponents **Antifederalists.**

Although the philosophical debate over the best form of government for a republic was important, voters considered practical factors in choosing a Federalist or an Antifederalist position. Voters in states with a stable economy were likely to oppose the Constitution because the Confederation system gave their states greater independent powers. Voters in small states, by contrast, were likely to favor a strong central government that could protect them from their competitive neighbors. Thus the small states of Delaware and Connecticut ratified the Constitution quickly.

To some degree, the split between Federalists and Antifederalists matched the divisions between the urban, market-oriented communities of the Atlantic coast and the rural, inland communities. For example, the backcountry of North and South Carolina saw little benefit in a strong central government that might tax them. However, commercial centers such as Boston, New York City, and Charleston were eager to see an aggressive national policy regarding foreign and interstate trade. Artisans, shopkeepers, and even laborers in these urban centers joined forces with wealthy merchants and shippers to support the Constitution.

Antifederalists developed a number of arguments against the proposed Constitution. They rejected the claim that the nation was facing economic and political collapse. As one New Yorker put it, "I deny that we are in immediate danger of anarchy and commotions." Antifederalists struck hard as well against the dangerous **elitism** that they saw in the Constitution. They portrayed the Federalists as a privileged minority, ready to oppress the people if a powerful national government were ratified.

The Antifederalists' most convincing evidence of their opponents' potential for tyranny was that the Constitution lacked any bill of rights. Unlike many of the state constitutions, the Constitution did not contain written guarantees of the people's rights. Antifederalists asked what this glaring omission revealed about the intentions of the framers. The only conclusion, Antifederalists argued, was that the Constitution was a threat to republican principles of representative government, a vehicle for elite rule, and a document unconcerned with the protection of individual liberties.

The Federalists' strategy was to portray America in crisis. They pointed to the stagnation of the

Federalists Supporters of ratification of the Constitution; they believed in a strong central government.

Antifederalists Opponents of ratification of the Constitution; they feared that a strong central government would be an instrument of tyranny.

elitism The belief that certain people deserve favored treatment because of their social, intellectual, or financial status.

American economy, to the potential for revolt and social anarchy, and to the contempt that other nations showed toward the young republic. They also argued that the Constitution could preserve the republican ideals of the Revolution far better than the Articles of Confederation.

That was the primary argument of the ***Federalist Papers,*** a series of essays that appeared in New York newspapers. Signed by "Publius," they were actually written by **Alexander Hamilton,** James Madison, and John Jay in an effort to persuade New Yorkers of the merits of ratification. The essays linked American prosperity and a strong central government. They countered Antifederalist claims that a strong central government would endanger individual liberties by arguing that a system of checks and balances would protect those liberties. And as Madison pointed out in *The Federalist, No. 10,* a large republic with an effective national government offered far better protection against tyranny than the state governments, where it was far easier to form a permanent majority.

The Federalist Victory

Practical politics influenced the decision of most state ratifying conventions. Delaware, New Jersey, Georgia, and Connecticut—all states with small populations—quickly approved the Constitution. Although there was more opposition in Pennsylvania, Federalists won a quick victory there as well. In the remaining states, the two sides were more evenly matched.

Antifederalists had the majority initially in the Massachusetts convention. Many delegates were small farmers from the western counties, more than twenty of whom had participated in Shays' Rebellion. The Federalist strategy in Massachusetts was to woo key Antifederalists such as Samuel Adams and John Hancock with promises that a bill of rights would be added to the Constitution. This strategy yielded the Federalists a narrow 19-vote margin of victory out of the more than 350 votes cast.

After Massachusetts ratified, the Federalists in New Hampshire carried the day by a small majority. Rhode Island, true to its history of opposition to strong central authority, refused to hold a convention. But Maryland and South Carolina ratified. Thus, as of June 1788, the requisite number of nine states had given their assent to the new plan of government. But this new government could not function effectively in the absence of such large and populous states as New York and Virginia. In Virginia, Antifederalist leaders Richard Henry Lee, Patrick Henry, and James Monroe focused on the absence of a bill of rights in the proposed Constitution. Edmund Randolph, James Madison, and George Washington directed the Federalist counterattack. In the end, Washington's presence and promises of a bill of rights proved decisive. Virginians expected this war hero to be the first president of the United States if the Constitution went into effect. Virginia became the tenth state to ratify the new government. Aware that the new government had already become a reality, New York's strongly Antifederalist convention followed Virginia's course. North Carolina ratified the Constitution in 1789, and a reluctant Rhode Island followed suit in 1790, two years after the first congressional elections.

President George Washington

George Washington's unanimous selection by the Electoral College to become the nation's first president took no one by surprise. He was the hero of the Revolution. The celebrations surrounding Washington's inauguration in the temporary capital of New York in April 1789 bore witness to the genuine affection Americans of all classes and regions felt for the Virginian.

Washington's popularity served the new government well, for it softened general suspicion of

Federalist Papers Essays written by Alexander Hamilton, James Madison, and John Jay in defense of the Constitution; they helped establish the basic principles of American government.

Alexander Hamilton New York lawyer and political theorist who worked to win ratification of the Constitution; he later became the first U.S. secretary of the treasury.

executive power. The new president understood that he symbolized a new national experiment in government and that his behavior in office would be watched carefully. Because he was the first person to hold the presidency, every action he took had the potential to set a precedent for those who followed.

Washington took particular care in selecting the men to head the four executive departments—Treasury, War, Attorney General, and State—created with approval from Congress. Naming his **protégé** Alexander Hamilton to head the Treasury Department was probably Washington's easiest decision. He asked Henry Knox of Massachusetts to head the War Department and fellow Virginians Edmund Randolph to serve as attorney general and Thomas Jefferson as secretary of state. Over time, the president established a pattern of meeting with these advisers regularly to discuss policy. Thus, although the Constitution made no provision for a **cabinet,** Washington established the precedent of cabinet meetings with the department heads and the vice president.

Competing Visions Reemerge

A remarkable spirit of unity marked the early days of Washington's administration. Federalists had won the overwhelming majority of seats in the new Congress, and this success enabled them to work quickly and efficiently. This unity also proved to be fragile. As the government debated foreign policy and domestic affairs, two distinct groups slowly emerged. Alexander Hamilton's vision for America guided one; Thomas Jefferson's guided another.

Unity's Achievements

One of the first Congress's major accomplishments was the creation of a federal judiciary. The **Judiciary Act of 1789** established a Supreme Court, thirteen district courts, and three circuit courts. It also empowered the Supreme Court to review the decisions of state courts and to nullify state laws that violated either the Constitution or any treaty made by the federal government. Washington chose John Jay as the first chief justice of the Supreme Court.

The spirit of cooperation during Washington's first term enabled Congress to break the stalemate on the tariff issue. Discussion of tariffs had previously become snarled by regional interests. But James Madison was able to negotiate an import tax on items such as rum, cocoa, and coffee that was acceptable to northerners and southerners.

Madison also prodded Congress to draft the promised bill of rights. He gathered eighty suggested amendments and honed them down to nineteen for Congress to consider. Congress narrowed these to ten amendments and submitted them to the states for ratification in 1789. The required approval by three-fourths of the states came quickly, and by December 1791 the **Bill of Rights** had become part of the Constitution. Eight of these amendments spelled out the government's commitment to protect the **civil liberties** of individuals such as free speech and freedom of religion. The Ninth Amendment made clear that the inclusion of these rights did not imply the exclusion of others. The Tenth Amendment stated that any powers not given to the federal government or denied to the states belonged solely to the states or the people.

protégé One whose welfare or career is promoted by an influential person.

cabinet A body of officials appointed by the president to run the executive departments of the government and to act as his advisers.

Judiciary Act of 1789 Law establishing the Supreme Court and the lower federal courts; it gave the Supreme Court the right to review state laws and state court decisions to determine constitutionality.

Bill of Rights The first ten amendments to the U.S. Constitution, added in 1791 to protect certain basic rights of American citizens.

civil liberties Fundamental individual rights such as freedom of speech and religion, protected by law against interference by the government.

Hamilton's and Jefferson's Differences

Alexander Hamilton dreamed of transforming an agricultural America into a manufacturing society that would rival Great Britain. His blueprint for achieving this goal included tariffs designed to protect developing American industry and government **subsidies** for new enterprises. It also called for close economic and diplomatic ties with Great Britain.

Thomas Jefferson and his ally James Madison had a different vision for America's future. They hoped America would remain a prosperous agrarian society. They favored a national policy of **free trade** rather than one employing protective tariffs. Jefferson was willing to tolerate commerce and industry as long as they complemented agrarian society. A dominant commercial society constituted a threat because it could exploit citizens or lead to the love of luxury, which every republican knew was bad.

Hamilton's group spoke of themselves as true **Federalists.** Those who agreed with Jefferson and Madison spoke of themselves as **Republicans.** The emergence of these two political camps troubled even the men who helped create them. The revolutionary generation had been taught that **factions** or parties were great political evils.

Hamilton's Economic Plan

As secretary of the treasury, Alexander Hamilton was responsible for solving the young republic's **fiscal** problems, particularly its foreign and domestic debts. For Hamilton, these problems were as much an opportunity as a challenge. His solutions, however, bitterly divided Congress in the early 1790s.

In January 1790, Hamilton submitted the *Report on Public Credit* to Congress. In it, he argued that the public debt fell into three categories, each requiring attention:

1. Foreign debts, owed primarily to France
2. State debts, incurred by the individual states to finance their war efforts
3. A national debt in the form of government notes (the notorious paper Continentals) that the Second Continental Congress had issued to finance the war

To establish its credit and trustworthiness, Hamilton said, the nation must find a way to pay each type of debt. Hamilton proposed that the federal government assume responsibility for all three types. He insisted that the Continentals be redeemed at their face value, which was much greater than their current market value. And he proposed that the current holders of Continentals should receive that payment. These recommendations raised a storm of debate within Congress.

Before Hamilton's *Report*, James Madison had been the voice of unity in Congress. Now Madison leaped to his feet in protest. The government's debt, he argued, was not to the current holders of the Continentals but to the original bondholders. Many of the original holders were ordinary citizens and Continental soldiers who had sold their bonds to speculators at a tremendous loss during the postwar depression. If Hamilton's plan were adopted, Madison warned, these speculators rather than the nation's true patriots would reap enormous profits.

Hamilton responded by pointing out the difficulty of identifying and finding the original holders of the Continentals. Madison's solution was simply impractical. With some misgivings, Congress supported Hamilton.

Madison was still not prepared to accept Hamilton's proposal that the federal government as-

subsidy Financial assistance granted by a government in support of an enterprise regarded as being in the public interest.

free trade Trade between nations without protective tariffs.

Federalists Political group led by Alexander Hamilton that formed during Washington's first administration; they favored commercial growth and a strong central government.

Republicans Political group led by Thomas Jefferson that favored limited government and envisioned the United States as a nation of independent farmers.

faction A group of people with shared opinions and goals who split off from a larger group.

fiscal Relating to government finances.

sume, or take over, the states' debts. A fierce nationalist, Hamilton wanted to concentrate political and economic power in the federal government. He knew that creditors, who included America's wealthiest citizens, would take a particular interest in the welfare and success of any government that owed them money. Hamilton intended to tie the material interests of America's elite to the federal government.

Maryland and Virginia, which had already paid their war debts, led the fight against assumption. If the national government assumed state debts and raised taxes to repay them, then the citizens of Maryland and Virginia would have to be burdened with debts that other states had not paid.

The Senate approved assumption, but the House deferred action. To ensure success, Hamilton conducted some behind-the-scenes negotiations with Madison and Jefferson. Hamilton's bargaining chip was the location of the national capital. Although the new government had made New York its temporary home in 1789, a permanent site for the national capital had not yet been decided on. Hamilton was willing to put the capital in Madison's and Jefferson's backyard in exchange for their support of federal assumption of state debts. The bargain appealed to the two Virginians, and they threw their support behind assumption. The future capital was to be located on a site between Maryland and Virginia.

Hamilton made still another proposal in 1791 to further his vision for America. This time he proposed chartering a national bank. The bank, modeled on the Bank of England, would serve as fiscal agent for the federal government, although it would not be an exclusively public institution. The bank would be funded by the government and by private sources in a partnership that would further tie national prosperity to the interests of private wealth.

Although James Madison questioned the constitutionality of this proposal, Congress nevertheless passed the legislation. Madison's argument did cause President Washington to consult Secretary of State Jefferson and Treasury Secretary Hamilton for their views on the constitutionality of the Bank of the United States before signing the bill.

Jefferson, like Madison, was a **strict constructionist** regarding the Constitution. Jefferson argued that there were grave dangers in interpreting the government's powers broadly: "To take a single step beyond the boundaries . . . specifically drawn around the powers of Congress is to take possession of a boundless field of power." Hamilton saw no such danger in the proposed bank. A **broad constructionist,** Hamilton countered with Article I, Section 8, of the Constitution. This section grants Congress the right to "make all Laws which shall be necessary and proper" to exercise its legitimate powers. Hamilton believed that this language "ought to be construed liberally in advancement of the public good." Since the bank would serve a useful purpose in tax collections, Hamilton believed there could be no reasonable constitutional objection to it. Hamilton's argument persuaded the president.

Hamilton outlined the next phase of his economic development program for the United States in his *Report on Manufactures* in 1791. This report called for protective tariffs, government subsidies, and other policies that would make the country into an industrial power. These proposals, however, were too extreme for Congress. Still, Hamilton had done much to realize his dream of a commercial and manufacturing republic. The Bank of the United States and the establishment of sound national credit did much to create and to attract **capital** for new enterprises.

Foreign Affairs and Deepening Divisions

The first signs of division in American politics had appeared in response to Hamilton's economic program. Those divisions hardened into permanent

strict constructionist A person who believes the government has only those powers that the Constitution specifically grants to it.

broad constructionist A person who believes the government has not only the powers specifically listed in the Constitution but whatever implied powers are in keeping with the spirit of the Constitution.

capital Money needed to start a commercial enterprise.

political parties when Americans were forced to respond to the **French Revolution** and its international repercussions. When the French Revolution broke out in 1789, Americans had almost universally applauded it. The American Revolution and the French Revolution seemed close cousins in their shared political rhetoric and ideals. Like most Americans, Washington was pleased to be identified with this newest struggle for the "rights of man."

By 1793, however, American public opinion had begun to divide sharply on the French Revolution. Popular support weakened when the Revolution's most radical party, the **Jacobins,** imprisoned and then executed the king and queen. Shocked Americans denounced the Revolution when the Jacobins began the **Reign of Terror** against their opponents.

Meanwhile, France had become involved in a war with Great Britain, Spain, Austria, and Prussia. France expected the Americans to honor the terms of the 1778 alliance, which bound the United States to protect French possessions in the West Indies. Since the British were likely to strike these possessions, a second war between Britain and the United States loomed as a possibility.

American opinion about such a war was contradictory and complex. Some thought American honor dictated that the United States should aid France, its Revolutionary War ally. Others, including Thomas Jefferson, did not want the United States to become embroiled in a European war. Hamilton favored maintaining close ties with the British. While Americans struggled with these contradictory views, the French decided to mobilize American support directly.

In 1793, the French republic sent a diplomatic minister to the United States. When **Edmond Genêt** arrived in Charleston, he did not present his credentials as an official representative from France. Instead he launched a campaign to recruit Americans for the war effort. Genêt's flagrant disregard for formal procedures infuriated Washington. But popular support for the colorful Genêt was strong. Prominent citizens welcomed and entertained him when he arrived in Philadelphia, the new temporary capital.

Washington responded to Genêt's provocations by declaring American **neutrality** on April 22, 1793. He avoided a formal **repudiation** of the 1778 alliance with France but made it clear that the United States would not give the French military support. When Genêt ignored Washington's proclamation of neutrality and commissioned several Americans as officers in the French army, even Jefferson thought that he had gone too far. Genêt's influence declined rapidly, and the Genêt affair was over.

The Genêt affair had domestic as well as diplomatic consequences. For the first time, George Washington came under attack. A Republican newspaper editor questioned the president's integrity in refusing to honor the Franco-American treaty. Washington was furious with this assault. Federalist newspapers struck back, accusing Jefferson and his friends of encouraging Genêt's outrageous behavior. By the end of 1793, Jefferson had resigned from Washington's cabinet.

More Domestic Disturbances

Following Washington's election to a second term in 1792, both Federalists and Republicans tried to rouse popular sentiment in favor of their programs and policies and against those of their opponents. These appeals to popular opinion broadened participation in the debate over the future of the na-

French Revolution Political upheaval against the French monarchy and aristocratic privileges; it began in 1789 and ended ten years later; its republican ideals gradually gave way to violence and disorder.

Jacobins Radical republican party during the French Revolution.

Reign of Terror The period from 1793 to 1794 in the French Revolution, during which thousands of people were executed because the revolutionary government considered them to be enemies of the state.

Edmond Genêt Diplomat whom the French revolutionary government sent to the United States to try to draw it into France's war against Britain and Spain.

neutrality The policy of not favoring either side in a conflict but treating both sides in the same way.

repudiation The act of rejecting the validity or authority of something.

tion. Ordinary citizens began to form organizations to make demands on the government. The most troubling of these to President Washington were the **Democratic-Republican societies.**

Consisting primarily of craftsmen and men of "the lower orders," thirty-five of these pro-French political groups formed between 1793 and 1794. The societies also included some professional men, merchants, and planters. The Philadelphia society, for example, included the noted scientist and inventor David Rittenhouse. Regardless of their composition, the societies insisted that political officeholders were "agents of the people" and should act as the people wished.

In 1794, many western farmers believed that government was not responding to the people's needs. Kentuckians complained about not being able to navigate the Mississippi, while farmers all along the frontier protested a new federal excise tax on whiskey. Although the Democratic-Republican societies denied playing any role in creating unrest in these areas, Federalists saw the societies behind the tarring and feathering of government tax agents, the burning of the barns of tax supporters, and the intimidation of other government officials. The most determined resistance to the whiskey excise tax came from western Pennsylvania. In July 1794, a crowd burned the home of a tax collector and later made a threatening but largely peaceful march on Pittsburgh, where some supporters of the excise tax lived.

President Washington, fearful that the radical spirit of the French Revolution was spreading throughout America, was determined to crush the **Whiskey Rebellion.** Calling up thirteen thousand militiamen, the president accompanied these troops as far as Cumberland, Maryland, before handing command to General Henry Lee. The whiskey rebels quickly dispersed in the face of such an overwhelming force.

Washington blamed the Democratic-Republican societies for the western insurrection, and Federalists in Congress passed resolutions condemning them. Fisher Ames of Massachusetts, for example, accused the societies of spreading "jealousies, suspicions, and accusations" against the government. The Jeffersonians, generally believed to be sympathetic to the societies, were forced to remain silent in the aftermath of the Whiskey Rebellion.

By 1796, Democratic-Republican societies had disappeared. Washington's condemnation and Congress's criticism certainly damaged the organizations' reputation. But improved conditions on the western frontier also diminished farmers' interest in protest. In October 1795, Thomas Pinckney was able to secure free navigation of the Mississippi River in the Treaty of San Lorenzo with Spain. This treaty not only gave western farmers an outlet for their produce through New Orleans but also ensured their protection from Indian attacks launched from Spanish-held territories.

Jay's Treaty

Washington was far less successful in securing a favorable treaty with Great Britain. The British believed that Washington's 1793 proclamation of American neutrality in the dispute between Britain and France, as well as American assertions of the right to free trade, favored the French. The British accordingly began seizing American ships that were trading with the French Caribbean islands.

These seizures posed serious difficulties for the largely pro-British Washington administration. Many people were calling for war against the British, and the situation worsened when the governor of British Canada encouraged Indian violence against American settlers in the Northwest. The House of Representatives considered trade restrictions against the British. Mobs even attacked British seamen and tarred and feathered Americans expressing pro-British views.

Washington's response to the growing domestic crisis was to send Supreme Court Chief Justice John Jay to Britain as his special **envoy** early in

Democratic-Republican societies Political organizations formed in 1793 and 1794 to demand greater responsiveness by the state and federal governments to the needs of the people.

Whiskey Rebellion An uprising by grain farmers in western Pennsylvania in 1794 over a federal tax on whiskey; Washington led militias from nearby states to quell the rebellion.

envoy A government representative who is sent on a special diplomatic mission.

1794. The treaty that Jay negotiated was not a great victory for American diplomacy, but it did resolve some old, nagging issues. The British agreed to evacuate the western forts and to grant some small trade concessions in the West Indies. The United States in return agreed to see that all prewar debts to British merchants were at last paid. But Jay was forced to abandon America's demand for freedom of the seas and conceded the Royal Navy's right to remove French property from any neutral ship. Jay returned home to strong public criticism and very little praise. The Federalists credited **Jay's Treaty** with preserving the peace, but the Republicans condemned it. The treaty squeaked through the Senate in 1795. Neutrality, compromised and shaky, continued to be the nation's policy.

The Washington administration did far better in military and diplomatic affairs in the West. In August 1794, at the **Battle of Fallen Timbers,** General "Mad" Anthony Wayne's army decisively defeated Indians from several tribes in the Northwest Territory. In the **Treaty of Greenville** in August 1795, the Indians ceded most of the land that later became Ohio.

Washington's Farewell

The bitter political fight over Jay's Treaty, nagging press criticism of his policies, and the hardening of party lines between Federalists and Republicans helped George Washington decide not to seek a third term as president. In 1796, he retired to Mount Vernon, his beloved Virginia home, and resumed the life of a gentleman planter.

When Washington retired, he left behind a nation very different from the one whose independence he had helped win. The postwar economic depression was over. The economy of the United States had moved decisively in the direction that Alexander Hamilton had envisioned. The pursuit of profit and of individual success had captured the imaginations of many white Americans. Hamilton's policies as secretary of the treasury had promoted the expansion of trade, the growth of markets, and the development of American manufacturing and industry. In its political life, the republic had seen the relationships between the states and the central government redefined. America's political leadership, taught that factions were dangerous, had nevertheless created and begun to work within an evolving party system.

In his **Farewell Address** to the public, Washington reflected on these changes. He spoke against political parties, urging the nation to return to nonpartisan cooperation. He also warned America not to "entangle our peace and prosperity in the toils of European ambition." An honorable country must "observe good faith and justice toward all nations," said the aging Virginian, but not let any alliance draw it into a foreign war.

Conflict in the Adams Administration

Although retiring president George Washington had warned of the "baneful effects of the spirit of party" in his Farewell Address, few in the newly organized parties listened to him. The Republicans were eager to unseat the politicians who were responsible for causing the Whiskey Rebellion and for tying the United States to Great Britain. The Federalists were eager to rid the nation of those who might pull down Hamilton's economic pro-

Jay's Treaty Treaty between the United States and Britain negotiated in 1794 by John Jay; it addressed issues such as British refusal to evacuate forts in the Northwest and British seizure of American ships.

Battle of Fallen Timbers Battle in August 1794 in which Kentucky riflemen defeated Indians of several tribes, hastening the end of Indian resistance in the Northwest.

Treaty of Greenville Treaty of 1795 under which Northwest Indians were paid about $10,000 to cede land that later became the state of Ohio.

Farewell Address Speech that George Washington made at the end of his second term as president; in it he called for nonpartisan cooperation and warned against entanglements with foreign nations.

gram and the philosophy of government by the well-to-do.

The Split Election of 1796

Thomas Jefferson was the Republican party's logical choice to represent the party in the presidential election of 1796. **Aaron Burr,** a brilliant young New York attorney and member of the U.S. Senate, was chosen to balance the ticket. Both Jefferson and Burr were veterans of the revolutionary struggles in 1776 and outspoken champions of democracy.

The unity of the Republicans contrasted sharply with the disunity of the Federalists. Most Federalists favored John Adams from Massachusetts, but many preferred South Carolinian **Thomas Pinckney** because of his diplomatic success in opening the Mississippi River to American commerce (see page 145). Alexander Hamilton, to whom the majority of Federalists looked for leadership, supported Pinckney's candidacy in large part because he felt that he could influence the mild-mannered southerner more than he could the stiff-necked Yankee. Many old revolutionaries viewed Adams, like Washington, as a **statesman** above politics whose conscience would help the new nation avoid the pitfalls of party.

Hamilton's scheming nearly lost the election for the Federalists. He was counting on a peculiarity in the election process. According to Article II, Section 1, of the Constitution, each member of the Electoral College could vote for two candidates. The highest vote getter (regardless of party) became president, and the runner-up (again regardless of party) became vice president. Hamilton urged Pinckney supporters to withhold votes from Adams so that Pinckney would win more votes than the former vice president. Adams's supporters learned of the plot, however, withheld their votes from Pinckney, and gave them to Jefferson. Jefferson ended up with more votes than Pinckney. The first truly contested presidential election thus produced a president (Adams) and a vice president (Jefferson) who belonged to different political parties.

Never known for charm, subtlety, or willingness to compromise, Adams was ill-suited to lead a deeply divided nation. The new president did little to put Republicans' fears to rest. He retained Secretary of Treasury Oliver Wolcott, Secretary of War James McHenry, and Secretary of State Timothy Pickering from Washington's cabinet—all Hamilton men. Republicans had hoped Hamilton's influence would wane now that he had retired from government service to practice law, but the selection of these ardent Federalists dashed that hope.

XYZ: The Power of Patriotism

The revolutionary government in France had been angry with the Federalists ever since the signing of the pro-British Jay Treaty of 1795. Under the terms of that treaty, American ships bound for French territory that were carrying food and naval stores—not just military supplies—were considered to be carrying contraband and were thus subject to British seizure. In the wake of the Jay Treaty, France applied the same logic to America's trade with Great Britain. By Adams's inauguration in 1797, France had confiscated cargoes from some three hundred American ships and broken diplomatic relations with the United States.

Faced with this diplomatic crisis, Adams wisely pursued two courses simultaneously. Asserting that the United States would not be "humiliated under a colonial spirit of fear and a sense of inferiority," he pressed Congress to build up America's military defenses. At the same time, he dispatched John Marshall of Virginia and Elbridge Gerry of Massachusetts to join **Charles Cotesworth Pinckney** in Paris to arrange a peaceful settlement of differences.

Aaron Burr New York lawyer who became Thomas Jefferson's vice president after the House of Representatives broke a deadlock in the Electoral College.

Thomas Pinckney South Carolina politician and diplomat who was an unsuccessful Federalist candidate for president in 1796.

statesman A political leader who acts out of concern for the public good and not out of self-interest.

Charles Cotesworth Pinckney Federalist politician and brother of Thomas Pinckney; he was sent on a diplomatic mission to Paris in 1797 during a period of unfriendly relations between France and the United States.

French foreign minister Talleyrand declined to receive Pinckney and the peace delegation. As weeks passed, three Parisian businessmen suggested a way to meet with Talleyrand. If the Americans were willing to pay a bribe to key members of the French government and to guarantee an American loan of several million dollars to France, the businessmen would be able to get them a hearing. Offended at such treatment, Pinckney reportedly responded, "No, no, not a sixpence." In relating the affair to President Adams, Pinckney refused to name the three businessmen, calling them only "X," "Y," and "Z."

Americans' response to the **XYZ affair** was overwhelming. In Philadelphia, people paraded in the streets to protest France's arrogance, chanting Pinckney's response to X, Y, and Z. "Millions for defense but not a cent for tribute!" became the rallying cry of the American people. The president vowed not to resume diplomatic relations with France until the U.S. envoy was "received, respected and honored as a representative of a great, free, powerful and independent nation."

The patriotic response to the XYZ affair overcame the divisions that had plagued the Adams administration, giving the president a virtually unified Congress. Adams pressed for increased military forces, and in short order Congress created the Department of the Navy, appropriated the money to build a fleet of warships, and authorized a standing army of twenty thousand troops. Washington came out of retirement to lead the new army. Although the old general saw no action, sea battles between French and American ships resulted in the sinking or capture of many vessels. This undeclared war became known as the Quasi-War.

Despite the combat, Adams continued to press for a peaceful solution. In doing so, he clashed with Hamilton's wing of the party, which wanted desperately to declare war. Hamilton and his supporters dreamed of crushing the French revolutionary state, which they regarded as the evil fruit of democracy. Hamilton also saw war with France as a way to destroy the Jeffersonian opposition, which had been sympathetic to the French Revolution.

The War at Home

The Quasi-War led the Federalists to identify the Republican party as an enemy nearly as great as France. The Federalists attacked foreigners living in the United States (especially those from Ireland and France, who detested the Federalists' pro-British stance) and the Jeffersonian press, which showed little restraint in attacking the Adams administration.

In 1798, Federalists in Congress passed three acts designed to counter the influence of immigrants. The Naturalization Act extended the residency requirement for citizenship from five to fourteen years. The **Alien Act** authorized the president to deport any foreigner he judged "dangerous to the peace and safety of the United States." Another bill, the Alien Enemies Act, permitted the president to imprison or banish any foreigner he considered dangerous during a national emergency. The Naturalization Act was designed to prevent recent immigrants from supporting the Republican cause. The other two acts served as a constant reminder that the president could arbitrarily imprison or deport any resident alien who stepped out of line.

Later in 1798, the Federalist Congress passed the Sedition Act to silence the Jeffersonian press. The **Sedition Act** outlawed the publication or utterance of any criticism of the government that might be regarded as "false, scandalous and malicious" or that would bring the government "into contempt or disrepute." In the words of one Federalist newspaper, "It is patriotism to write in favour

XYZ affair A diplomatic incident in which American envoys to France were told that the United States would have to loan France money and bribe government officials as a condition for negotiation.

Alien Act Law passed by Congress in 1798 authorizing the president to order out of the United States any alien regarded as dangerous to the public peace or safety.

Sedition Act Law passed by Congress in 1798 outlawing any criticism of the U.S. government that might bring the government into disrepute; the law was enforced mainly against Republicans.

of our government, it is **sedition** to write against it." Federalists brandished the law against criticism directed toward the government or the president. Not surprisingly, most of the defendants were prominent Republican newspaper editors.

One case involved a Republican journalist named James Thompson Callender, a notorious radical who had been forced to flee Britain in 1793. In the United States, he wielded his pen in support of Jefferson and became widely disliked by the Federalists. In 1798, Callender was arrested for writing a pamphlet that attacked Adams and the Federalists. Federalist judge Samuel Chase fined Callender $200, sentenced him to nine months in jail, and ordered him to post a bond of $1,200 to ensure his continued compliance with the Sedition Act.

Republicans complained that the Alien and Sedition Acts violated the Bill of Rights, but the Federalist Congress and judiciary paid no attention. Jefferson and Madison had little choice but to take their case to the states. In 1798, Madison submitted a resolution to the Virginia legislature, and Jefferson submitted one in Kentucky.

The **Virginia and Kentucky Resolutions** argued that the national government was simply a compact that the individual states had created and that the states could declare inappropriate federal laws null and void. In the Virginia Resolution, Madison asserted that the collective will of the states should overrule federal authority. Jefferson went further in the Kentucky Resolution, arguing that each individual state had the "natural right" to interpose its own authority to protect the rights of its citizens.

The Virginia and Kentucky Resolutions passed in the respective state legislatures in 1798, but no other states followed suit. Nevertheless, the resolutions brought the disputed relationship between federal law and **states' rights** into national prominence. This relationship would be a major bone of contention in the decades to come.

Another dispute arose over the methods used to finance the Quasi-War with France. Although tariffs and **excises** were the primary sources of revenue, the Federalists also imposed a tax on land, hitting cash-poor farmers especially hard. In 1799, farmers in Northampton County, Pennsylvania, used the tactics employed during the Whiskey Rebellion to avoid paying the land tax. After several tax resisters had been arrested and jailed, John Fries raised an armed force to break them out of jail. The federal troops sent by Adams to subdue Fries' Rebellion arrested Fries and two of his associates. A federal court found them guilty and condemned them to death.

Settlement with France

Shortly after the XYZ affair, George Logan, a Quaker friend of Jefferson, secretly departed for France to seek a peaceful solution to the diplomatic crisis. Logan gained quick admission to see Foreign Minister Talleyrand, who told him that France would gladly receive an American peace **overture.** When Logan returned to America, Adams ignored his party's advice and met with him. Soon thereafter, without consulting his cabinet, Adams instructed the American minister to the Netherlands, William Vans Murray, to lead a delegation to Paris.

Hamilton and his supporters were furious, and the fissure that had opened between Adams and Hamilton during the 1796 election widened. Adams responded to his Federalist critics by firing Hamilton's supporters in the cabinet. In addition, he pardoned the Pennsylvanians who had been condemned after Fries' Rebellion.

Adams's diplomatic appeal to France was well timed. On November 9, 1799, **Napoleon Bonaparte** overthrew the government that was responsible for the XYZ affair. Napoleon was more interested

sedition Conduct or language inciting rebellion against the authority of a state.

Virginia and Kentucky Resolutions Statements issued by the Virginia and Kentucky legislatures in 1798 asserting their right to declare the Alien and Sedition Acts unconstitutional.

states' rights Limited federal powers and the greatest possible autonomy for the states.

excise A tax on the production, sale, or consumption of a commodity or the use of a service.

overture A proposal or the actions that lead up to a proposal.

Napoleon Bonaparte General who took control of the French government at the end of the revolutionary period and eventually proclaimed himself emperor of France.

in establishing an empire in Europe than in continuing a conflict with the United States. Murray and Napoleon negotiated the Convention of Mortefontaine, which ended the Quasi-War. All prisoners captured during the conflict were released. French restrictions on trade with the United States were removed, and France was forgiven for seizing American property worth $20 million.

SUMMARY

Expectations
Constraints
Choices
Outcomes

After winning independence, Americans faced the challenge of creating a new nation out of thirteen distinct states. *Constrained* by enormous debt and still surrounded by real and potential enemies, the United States appeared dangerously vulnerable. To many Americans and foreigners, *expectations* for its survival seemed doubtful.

During the Revolution and immediately after, the states drafted their own constitutions. Some *chose* relatively democratic forms of government. Others *chose* to retain less democratic features such as high property qualifications for voting. A major *constraint* on state cooperation was the Articles of Confederation. The Articles guaranteed state representatives the right to withhold important powers from the national governing body. The *outcome* of this weak central government was continuing financial crises and debt.

The Confederation *chose* the sale of western lands as one solution to its financial problems. The *outcome* was conflict with the British, Indians, and Spanish. Farmers, too, felt the *constraints* of economic depression and indebtedness, and Massachusetts farmers rose in revolt during Shays' Rebellion. The continuing national crisis convinced many of the nation's elite that critical *choices* had to be made about revising the system of government.

In the summer of 1787, experienced political leaders met in Philadelphia to draft the Constitution of the United States. This document steered a middle course between a central government that was too powerful and one that was too weak. The states ratified the Constitution after a vigorous battle between Federalists and Antifederalists. George Washington was elected the nation's first president.

Although harmony prevailed initially, sharp differences in political opinion soon emerged between Alexander Hamilton's Federalists and Thomas Jefferson's Republicans. Federalists wanted an industrial nation and opposed the French Revolution. Republicans *expected* the United States to remain agrarian and generally supported the Revolution. The *outcome* was deeper divisions between these two political groups. The United States remained neutral, however, when France and Britain went to war.

By the end of Washington's second term, the United States had expanded its borders, negotiated with Spain for access to the Mississippi River, and established a national bank that promoted economic growth. The departing Washington warned Americans not to allow competing visions of America's future to harm their republic.

Washington's advice went unheeded. Federalists *expectations* of a war with France in the wake of the XYZ affair led them to regard the Republican opposition as an enemy fully as dangerous as France. They passed laws intended to act as major *constraints* on the Republicans.

President John Adams, however, *chose* to break with his party when it came to the issue of war with France. The *outcome* was negotiations that led to peace with France.

SUGGESTED READINGS

Butterfield, Lyman, et al. *The Book of Abigail and John: Selected Letters of the Adams Family, 1762–1784* (1975).

The editors of the Adams Papers have collected part of the extensive correspondence between John and Abigail Adams during the critical decades of the independence movement.

Morris, Richard B. *Witness at the Creation* (1985).

A distinguished scholar re-creates the drama of the Constitutional Convention by focusing on the personalities and motives of the framers.

Slaughter, Thomas P. *The Whiskey Rebellion* (1986).

A vivid account of the major challenge to the Washington government.

Wills, Gary. *Cincinnatus: George Washington and the Enlightenment* (1984).

A beautifully written biography of our first president and his times.

Restraining Federal Power

The Context

The Alien and Sedition Acts raised serious questions about Congress's right to pass laws affecting free speech and free assembly. They also raised questions about who had the right to determine whether acts of Congress violated the Constitution. Kentucky and Virginia passed legislative resolutions, written by Thomas Jefferson and James Madison respectively, laying out two approaches to this issue. Other states responded, outlining their views on this fundamental problem in the checks-and-balances system and the separation of powers. (For further information on the context, see pages 148–149.)

The Historical Question

Historians continue to debate the constitutional issues relating to the Alien and Sedition Acts. Now, as then, the question hinges on interpreting exactly what the Constitution means. Madison and Jefferson offered slightly different opinions, and others challenged their interpretations. What were the most appropriate avenues for questioning the constitutionality of the acts? What legitimate recourse could individuals have pursued? What responsibilities did various branches of government have to protect individual rights from potential violation? What, really, did the Constitution say?

The Challenge

Using the sources provided, the Constitution, (printed as an appendix at the end of this book), and other information you have read, write an essay or hold a discussion on the following question. Cite evidence in the sources to support your conclusions.

If you were an interested and impartial citizen living in the United States in 1798, which of the arguments presented here would you find most convincing? Why?

The Sources

1 Thomas Jefferson was sure that the Sedition Act was unconstitutional, but there was no clear mechanism for challenging a federal law. In the first Kentucky Resolution, written in October 1798, Jefferson came to the following conclusion:

. . . the government created by this compact [the Constitution] was not made the exclusive or final judge of the extent of the powers delegated to itself; since that would have made its discretion, and not the Constitution, the measure of its powers; but that as in all other cases of compact among parties having no common judge, each party has an equal right to judge for itself, as well of infractions as of the mode and measure of redress. . . .

. . ."the powers not delegated to the United States by the Constitution, nor prohibited by it to the States, are reserved to the States respectively or to the people"; and that no power over the freedom of religion, freedom of speech, or freedom of the press being delegated to the United States by the Constitution, nor prohibited by it to the States, all lawful powers respecting the same did of right remain, and were reserved to the States, or to the people. . . . Therefore [the Sedition Act], which does abridge the freedom of the press, is not law, but is altogether void and of no effect.

2 James Madison was particularly concerned that with Federalists in control of all three branches of the national government, the separation of powers he had built into the Constitution had broken down. Some other check seemed to be necessary in the "checks and balances" system. Madison said:

. . . the [Alien Act] exercises a power nowhere delegated to the Federal Government, and which, by uniting legislative and judicial powers to those of [the] executive, subverts the general principles of free government, . . .

. . . the good people of this commonwealth, having ever felt and continuing to feel the most sincere affection for their brethren of the other states, the truest anxiety for establishing and perpetuating the union of all and the most scrupulous fidelity to that Constitution . . . doth solemnly appeal to the like dispositions of the other states, in confidence that they will concur with this Commonwealth in declaring, as it does hereby declare, that the acts aforesaid are unconstitutional; and that the necessary and proper measures will be taken by each for co-operating with this state, in maintaining unimpaired the authorities, rights, and liberties reserved to the states respectively, or to the people.

3 No other state joined Kentucky and Virginia in challenging the constitutionality of the Alien and Sedition Acts. Several, in fact, issued proclamations criticizing the resolutions. The Rhode Island legislature had this to say:

"The judicial power shall extend to all cases arising under the laws of the United States,"—vests in the Federal Courts, exclusively, and in the Supreme Court of the United States, ultimately, the authority of deciding on the constitutionality of any act or law of the Congress of the United States.

That for any state legislature to assume that authority would be—

1st. Blending together legislative and judicial powers;

2d. Hazarding an interruption of the peace of the states by civil discord, in case of a diversity of opinions among the state legislatures; each state having, in that case, no resort, for vindicating its own opinions, but the strength of its own arm;

3d. Submitting most important questions of law to less competent tribunals; and

4th. An infraction of the Constitution of the United States, expressed in plain terms.

4 Timothy Pickering, Adams's secretary of state and a stalwart Federalist, denied that the acts were in any way unreasonable. He wrote:

The Sedition Act has . . . been shamefully misrepresented as an attack upon the freedom of speech and of the press. But we find, on the contrary, that it prescribes a punishment only for those pests of society and disturbers of order and tranquillity "who write, print, utter, or publish any false, scandalous, and malicious writings against the government of the United States, or either house of the Congress of the United States, or the President, with intent to defame, or bring them into contempt or disrepute, or to excite against them the hatred of the good people of the United States; or to stir up sedition, or to abet the hostile designs of any foreign nation."

What honest man can justly be alarmed at such a law, or can wish unlimited permission to be given for the publication of malicious falsehoods, and with intentions the most base?

AMERICAN EXPANSION AND INDIAN LAND CESSIONS, TO 1800
Growth was a dominant characteristic of the United States during the late 1700s. As this map shows, population was becoming increasingly dense and pushing westward. At the same time, Indians were forced to withdraw, ceding large expanses of land, often under threat of violence.

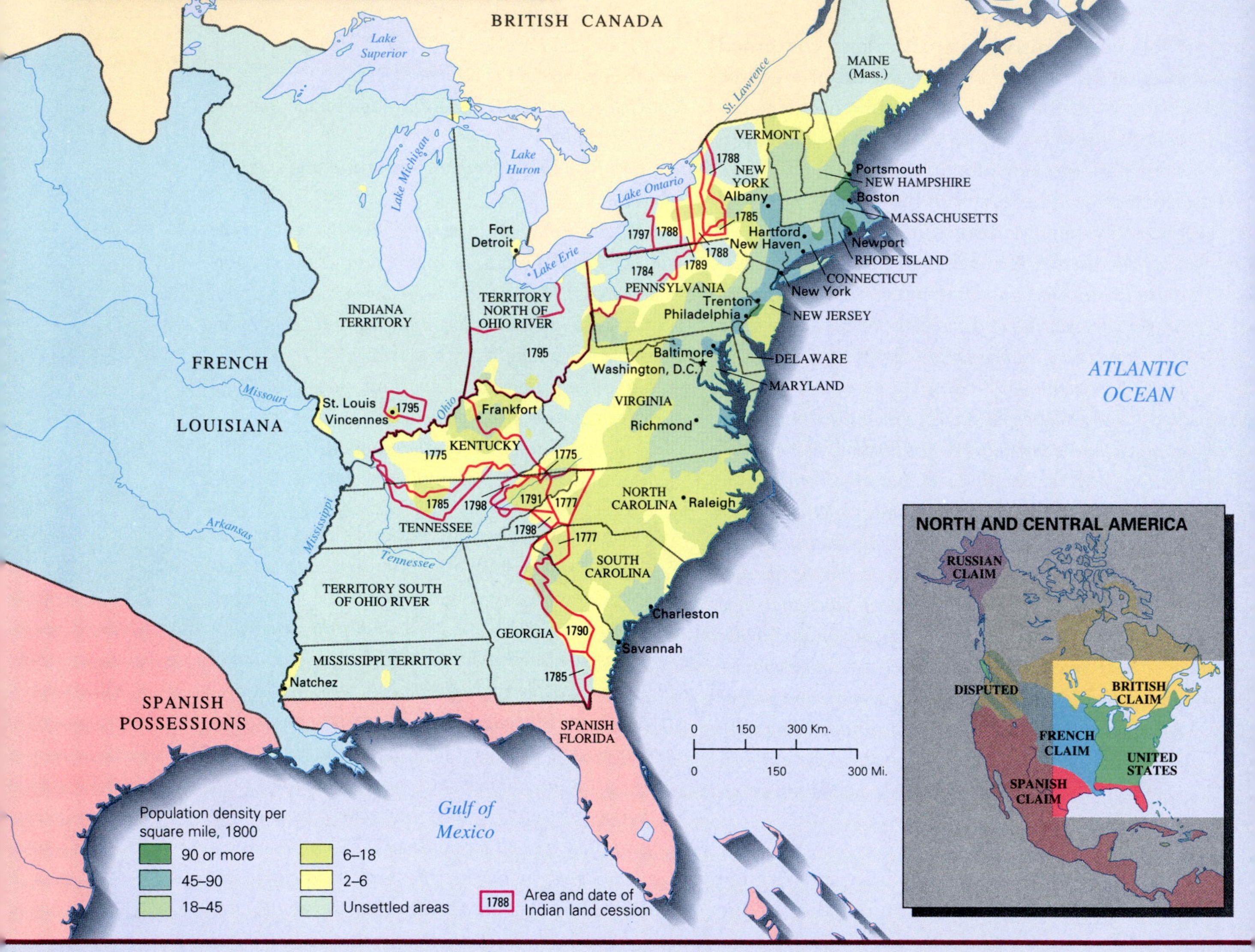

BRITISH CANADA
Lake Superior
Lake Michigan
Lake Huron
Lake Ontario
Lake Erie
St. Lawrence
MAINE (Mass.)
VERMONT
NEW YORK
NEW HAMPSHIRE
MASSACHUSETTS
RHODE ISLAND
CONNECTICUT
NEW JERSEY
DELAWARE
MARYLAND
PENNSYLVANIA
VIRGINIA
NORTH CAROLINA
SOUTH CAROLINA
GEORGIA
KENTUCKY
TENNESSEE
Portsmouth
Boston
Albany
Hartford
New Haven
Newport
New York
Trenton
Philadelphia
Baltimore
Washington, D.C.
Richmond
Raleigh
Charleston
Savannah
Frankfort
Fort Detroit
St. Louis
Vincennes
Natchez
INDIANA TERRITORY
TERRITORY NORTH OF OHIO RIVER
TERRITORY SOUTH OF OHIO RIVER
MISSISSIPPI TERRITORY
FRENCH
LOUISIANA
SPANISH POSSESSIONS
SPANISH FLORIDA
Missouri
Ohio
Mississippi
Arkansas
Tennessee
Gulf of Mexico
ATLANTIC OCEAN
1775
1777
1784
1785
1788
1789
1790
1791
1795
1797
1798
0 150 300 Km.
0 150 300 Mi.
Population density per square mile, 1800
90 or more
45–90
18–45
6–18
2–6
Unsettled areas
1788 Area and date of Indian land cession
NORTH AND CENTRAL AMERICA
RUSSIAN CLAIM
DISPUTED
BRITISH CLAIM
FRENCH CLAIM
UNITED STATES
SPANISH CLAIM

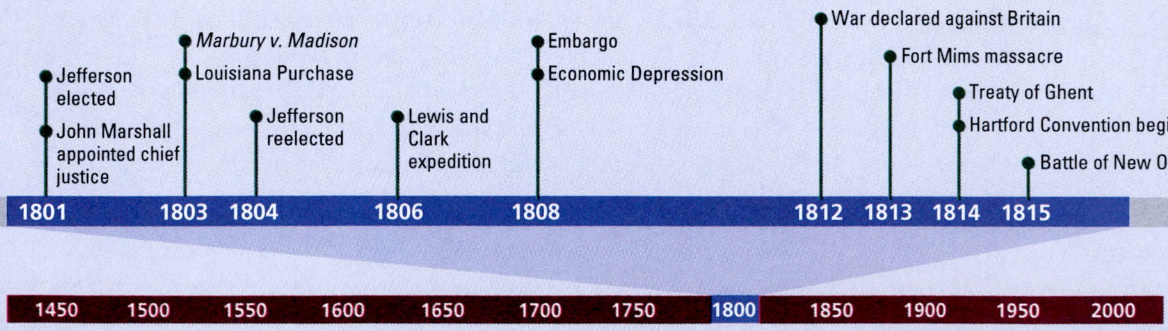

1801 Jefferson elected
1801 John Marshall appointed chief justice
1803 Marbury v. Madison
1803 Louisiana Purchase
1804 Jefferson reelected
1806 Lewis and Clark expedition
1808 Embargo
1808 Economic Depression
1812 War declared against Britain
1813 Fort Mims massacre
1814 Treaty of Ghent
1814 Hartford Convention begins
1815 Battle of New Orleans
1450
1500
1550
1600
1650
1700
1750
1800
1850
1900
1950
2000

CHAPTER 8

The Triumphs and Trials of Jeffersonianism, 1800–1815

The "Revolution of 1800"

- What constraints did the Federalists attempt to impose on Jefferson's presidency?
- How did Republicans choose to deal with Federalist constraints?

Republicanism in Action

- What were Jefferson's expectations for American development?
- What policies did he choose to meet those expectations?

Challenge and Uncertainty in Jefferson's America

- How did the expectations of most Americans change during Jefferson's presidency?
- What were Jefferson's expectations concerning Native Americans and African Americans?

Troubling Currents in Jefferson's America

- How did regional interests constrain Jefferson's political and economic expectations?

Crises in the Nation

- What constraints arose from Jefferson's economic and Indian policies?
- How did the expectations of frontier politicians such as William Henry Harrison help lead to war in 1812?

The Nation at War

- What developments finally convinced the United States to choose war against Great Britain in 1812?
- Why were American military choices successful or unsuccessful?

The War's Strange Conclusion

- What constraints on American national development did the outcome of the War of 1812 remove?
- How did the war change Americans' expectations about politics, economics, and national expansion?

INTRODUCTION

E xpectations
C onstraints
C hoices
O utcomes

The *outcome* of Federalist efforts to maintain power at any cost was the loss of voter support. In 1800, voters *chose* to remove Federalists from office, turning the government over to Thomas Jefferson. But enough people remained faithful to the Federalist position to maintain that faction's existence and to ensure that it would act as a continuing *constraint* on Republican political activity.

Although Jefferson claimed that he distrusted and disapproved of federal power, he used his power as president to pursue his policy goals. Jefferson purchased the Louisiana Territory despite the fact that there was no constitutional provision permitting such a purchase.

The entire direction of national development changed during Jefferson's presidency. The Louisiana Purchase and the elimination of internal taxes indicated that the days of eastern-dominated mercantilism were at an end. Now the nation's future would be tied to the West. Most Americans saw significant improvement in their *expectations* thanks to a thriving economy, and the nation became increasingly optimistic. But prosperity was a product of international problems as much as it was of Jefferson's *choice.* The nearly constant war in the Old World allowed Americans to make money by selling grain to Europeans. National security and economic prosperity depended on Jefferson's ability to keep America a neutral player on the world stage, a role that became harder to sustain in his second term.

After 1804, increasing *constraints* on American trade forced Jefferson and his successor, James Madison, to make hard *choices.* Believing that Europe needed American food more than America needed European manufactures, Republicans *chose* to prohibit American ships from trading with Europe. The *outcome* was economic depression in the United States. Adding to the problem were widening cracks in Jefferson's party support. Some Republicans thought Jefferson had overstepped his bounds in *choosing* to make the Louisiana Purchase. Federalists too were upset, especially in the Northeast. They believed that Jefferson had *chosen* to serve southern and western interests exclusively.

The *expectations* and *choices* of others played havoc with Jefferson's hopes for a peaceful and prosperous nation. French and British policymakers *chose* not to respect American neutrality. American politicians of various stripes *chose* to oppose the president. In the West, whites seeking land for expansion *expected* that war against the Indians and the British would best serve their ends, while Indians increasingly *chose* to stop retreating. The *outcome* of these *choices* was another war with Great Britain in 1812.

Ill prepared and underfinanced, the United States initially fared badly against Great Britain and its Indian allies. An economic crisis and political infighting divided the nation even more. But a series of improbable American victories prompted a war-weary British public to demand peace.

Officially, the outcome of the war changed nothing. The Treaty of Ghent simply restored relations between the United States and Great Britain to what they had been before hostilities broke out. But in reality, much had changed. Americans emerged from the conflict with a new sense of national pride and purpose and a new set of *expectations* about the future.

CHRONOLOGY

Domestic Expansion and International Crisis

1800	Jefferson and Burr tie in Electoral College
1801	Judiciary Act of 1801 Jefferson elected president by House of Representatives John Marshall becomes chief justice
1803	Louisiana Purchase Renewal of war between France and Britain *Marbury v. Madison*
1804	Thomas Jefferson re-elected president Britain steps up impressment Duel between Alexander Hamilton and Aaron Burr
1804–1806	Lewis and Clark expedition
1805	Beginning of Shawnee religious revival
1807	Burr conspiracy trial Founding of Prophetstown *Chesapeake* affair
1808	Embargo goes into effect Economic depression begins James Madison elected president
1809	Fort Wayne Treaty Non-Intercourse Act
1810	Macon's Bill No. 2 Formation of the War Hawks
1811	United States breaks trade relations with Britain Destruction of Prophetstown
1812	United States declares war against Britain United States invades Canada Madison re-elected
1813	Fort Mims massacre Battle of Put-in-Bay Embargo of 1813 Battle of the Thames
1814	Battle of Horseshoe Bend Napoleon defeated Battle of Plattsburgh British capture and burn Washington, D.C. Treaty of Ghent Hartford Convention begins
1815	Battle of New Orleans

The "Revolution of 1800"

The partisan press portrayed the election of 1800 in terms of stark contrasts. The Republican press characterized Adams as a monarchist who planned to rob citizens of their freedom and to turn the United States back into a British colony. By contrast, Federalist newspapers painted Vice President Jefferson as a dangerous, atheistic radical who shared French tastes for violent politics and loose sexual morals.

The Lesser of Republican Evils

As the election of 1800 approached, the split within the Federalist party widened. Disgusted by the president's failure to declare war on France, Hamilton schemed to elevate Charles Cotesworth Pinckney, hero of the XYZ affair, to the presidency over Adams. Hamilton's methods backfired. They drove southern Federalists into supporting Jefferson. Bitter factional disputes within the Federalist party and hatred of the taxes the Federalists had imposed in 1798 led to a Republican victory in 1800.

Still, it was not clear who would be the next president. Jefferson and his running mate, Aaron Burr, emerged with the same number of electoral votes, thereby throwing the election into the House of Representatives. The majority of the House consisted of hard-line Federalists elected during the Quasi-War hysteria in 1798. These Federalists were forced to choose between two men, both of whom they regarded as dangerous radicals. Neither Jefferson nor Burr could win a clear majority of House votes. Burr could have ended the deadlock at any time by withdrawing, but he sat silent.

Hamilton helped to break the deadlock by convincing several Federalists that Jefferson was far more conservative than his rhetoric implied. Another development that tipped the scales in Jefferson's favor was the mobilization of the Virginia and Pennsylvania militias. These states feared that the Federalists might attempt to steal the election from Jefferson. As Delaware senator James Bayard described the situation, Federalists had to admit "that we must risk the Constitution and a Civil War or take Mr. Jefferson." Finally, on the thirty-sixth ballot, Jefferson emerged with a clear majority.

The Jefferson-Burr deadlock of 1801 led to the passage of the **Twelfth Amendment.** Ratified in 1804, this amendment separated balloting in the Electoral College for president and vice president and thereby eliminated the confusion that had nearly wrecked the nation in 1800.

♦ Suffering a lifelong sensitivity to cold as well as a dislike for formality, Thomas Jefferson usually chose to dress practically, in fairly plain clothes that kept him warm. This 1822 portrait by Thomas Sully captures the former president in his customary greatcoat, unadorned suit, and well-worn boots. *"Thomas Jefferson" by Thomas Sully, West Point Museum, United States Military Academy, West Point, N.Y.*

Federalist Defenses and Party Acceptance

The Federalists were not about to leave office without erecting a strong bulwark against the Republicans. During its last days in office, the Federalist Congress passed the **Judiciary Act of 1801,** which created sixteen new federal judgeships, six additional circuit courts, and many federal marshalships and clerkships. President Adams filled all these positions with loyal Federalists, signing appointments right up to midnight on his last day in office. Adams appointed his secretary of state, **John Marshall,** as chief justice of the Supreme Court.

Twelfth Amendment Constitutional amendment ratified in 1804 that provides for separate balloting in the Electoral College for president and vice president.

Judiciary Act of 1801 Law that the Federalist Congress passed to increase the number of federal courts and judicial positions; President Adams rushed to fill these positions with Federalists before his term ended.

John Marshall Virginia lawyer and politician made chief justice of the Supreme Court by President Adams; his legal decisions helped shape the role of the Court in American government.

Despite these last-minute Federalist appointments, Jefferson's inaugural address was conciliatory. "We are all Republicans; we are all Federalists," Jefferson said. In his mind, all Americans shared the same fundamental principles established in 1776. Yet even Jefferson considered the election of 1800 "a revolution in the principles of our government."

Jefferson sought to restore the republic envisioned by revolutionaries twenty-five years before. Unlike the Federalists, Jefferson was unalterably opposed to sedition acts or other government restraints directed against political opponents. The Republican Congress endorsed Jefferson's commitment to free speech by letting the Sedition Act and the Alien Acts expire. Congress also repealed the Naturalization Act, replacing its fourteen-year naturalization period with one of five years.

Jefferson's **conciliatory** policies and tone led Americans to see political parties in a new light. Many concluded that people in opposite political camps could hold different positions and not be enemies. As Jefferson observed, "Every difference of opinion is not a difference of principles." Even extreme Federalists like Fisher Ames of Massachusetts came to realize that a "party is an association of honest men for honest purposes." Such realizations marked the beginnings of accepting political parties in the United States.

Madison Versus the Midnight Appointments

The power of the judicial branch to interpret and enforce federal law became a major issue during Jefferson's first administration. His secretary of state, James Madison, had held back the appointment letters that had not been delivered before the expiration of Adams's term. One jilted appointee was William Marbury, who was to have been justice of the peace for the newly created District of Columbia. Marbury filed suit in the Supreme Court, claiming the Judiciary Act of 1789 gave the Court the power to demand that Madison deliver Marbury's appointment letter.

In considering ***Marbury v. Madison,*** Chief Justice Marshall believed that the Judiciary Act did require Madison to deliver the letter. He was keenly aware, however, that the Court had no power to enforce its orders. Ordering Madison to appoint Marbury justice of the peace could lead to a confrontation between the executive and judicial branches, a confrontation that Marshall was sure the Court would lose. He thus ruled in 1803 that the Constitution contained no provision for the Supreme Court to issue orders such as the Judiciary Act of 1789 required. Therefore the 1789 act was unconstitutional.

Jefferson and Madison accepted Marshall's decision because it meant they did not have to place Adams's handpicked men in powerful judicial positions. But it also meant that they would have to acknowledge that the Supreme Court, not the individual states or the branches of the federal government, had the right to determine the **constitutionality** of federal laws. Most Republicans endorsed Marshall's decision, which asserted the principle of **judicial review** over acts of Congress. Because of their experience with the Alien and Sedition Acts, however, many southerners continued to assert that states had the fundamental right to determine the constitutionality of the laws.

Having blocked the appointment of many new Federalists to judicial posts, some Republicans in Congress chose to wage a partisan war against those already on the bench. Their first target was New Hampshire Federalist John Pickering, an alcoholic who used his federal judgeship to rail against Republicanism. Brought before the Senate on **impeachment** charges, the Republican majority

conciliatory Striving to overcome distrust or to regain someone's good will.

Marbury v. Madison Supreme Court decision (1803) declaring part of the Judiciary Act of 1789 unconstitutional and thus establishing the principle of judicial review.

constitutionality Agreement with the principles or provisions of the Constitution.

judicial review The power of the Supreme Court to review the constitutionality of laws passed by Congress and the states.

impeachment The presentation of formal charges of wrongdoing against a public official.

quickly found him guilty and removed him from office. Flushed by that success, staunch Republicans decided to go after bigger game: Supreme Court Justice Samuel Chase. Though extremely competent as a jurist, Chase was notorious for making partisan decisions. There was no evidence, however, that Chase had committed the "high crimes and misdemeanors" required for the removal of a federal judge. Even so, House Republicans ordered a bill of impeachment and sent Chase to trial before the Senate. Many expected the Senate, chaired by radical Republican Aaron Burr, to make quick work of disrobing Chase, but Burr surprised his colleagues by conducting a fair trial during which Chase presented a convincing defense. The war on the courts came to a sudden end when both Federalists and the majority of Republicans chose to dismiss the charges against Chase, marking an important precedent against the partisan use of impeachment powers.

Republicanism in Action

When Jefferson assumed office, he brought a new spirit to national politics and the presidency. He was the first president to be inaugurated in the new national capital of Washington City. He led a much simpler life than his predecessors had. He refused, for example, to ride in a carriage, preferring to go by horseback through Washington's muddy and rutted streets. He abandoned the fashion of wearing a wig, letting his red hair stand out.

Jefferson's Vision for America

Jefferson had a strong, positive vision for the nation that was guided by his fears and hopes for the American experiment in republican government. The greatest dangers to a republic, he believed, were high population density and the concentration of money in the hands of a few. These led to corruption and the rise of tyrants like George III. Accordingly, Jefferson wanted to steer America away from the large, publicly supported industries that Hamilton advocated. Jefferson wanted America to be a nation of farmers who owned their own land, produced their own food, and were beholden to no one. Such yeoman farmers, Jefferson believed, could make political decisions based solely on reason and good sense.

Jefferson did not want Americans to be deprived of the benefits of industry and commerce. But he did want to preserve American independence and freedom from corruption. His solution was simple: America's vast surpluses of food should be traded for European manufactures.

Jefferson was also an advocate of free trade. He believed that businesses should make their own decisions and succeed or fail in a marketplace free of government interference. This belief contrasted with the mercantilist theory that governments should control prices and restrict trade to benefit the nation-state.

Responsibility for implementing this economic policy fell to Treasury Secretary **Albert Gallatin.** Gallatin's first goal was to make the United States free of debt by 1817. He cut the budget drastically, even closing several American embassies. At home, he pared administrative costs by reducing staff and putting an end to fancy receptions and balls. The administration reduced the army from four thousand to twenty-five hundred men and the navy from twenty-five ships to a mere seven. In making these cuts, Gallatin subtly weakened the central government's economic presence, putting more responsibilities back onto the states, where he thought they belonged.

Gallatin's plan also called for a significant change in how the government raised revenue. In 1802, the Republican Congress repealed all internal taxes, including the hated whiskey excise tax, leaving customs duties and the sale of western lands as the sole sources of federal revenue. With this one gesture, Gallatin struck a major blow for Jefferson's economic vision by tying the nation's financial future to westward expansion and foreign trade.

The success of Jefferson's economic policy depended greatly on his handling of foreign affairs. During Jefferson's presidency, two foreign issues

Albert Gallatin Treasury secretary in Jefferson's administration; he favored limited government and reduced the federal debt by cutting spending.

loomed large. One was the need to improve navigation on North America's inland waterways. The other was the need to ensure free navigation of the open seas. France and Spain posed a major challenge to the first of these, and pirates threatened the other.

War in the Mediterranean

The challenge to free navigation came from pirates who patrolled the northern coast of Africa from Tangier to Tripoli. Ever since the 1790s, the United States had paid the Barbary pirates not to attack American ships. By 1800, fully a fifth of the federal budget was earmarked for this purpose. Gallatin wanted to eliminate this expense. For Jefferson, the principle of free navigation of the seas was just as important. Noting that "tribute or war is the usual alternative of these Barbary pirates," Jefferson decided on war and dispatched navy ships to the Mediterranean in 1801.

The war that followed was far from successful. The American navy suffered a major defeat when the warship *Philadelphia* and its entire crew were captured. Lieutenant Stephen Decatur, Jr.'s bold raid left the *Philadelphia* in ashes so it could not be used by the ruler of Tripoli, but the ship's crew remained in captivity. The United States finally negotiated peace terms in 1805, paying $60,000 for the release of the hostages, while Tripoli promised to halt pirate raids on American shipping.

Crisis in America's Interior

As settlers continued to pour into the region west of the Appalachian Mountains, the commercial importance of the Mississippi River increased. Whoever controlled the mouth of the Mississippi would have the power to make or break the economy of the interior.

In Pinckney's treaty of 1795 (see page 145), Spain had granted American farmers the right to ship cargoes down the Mississippi. In 1800, however, Napoleon had exchanged some French holdings in southern Europe for Spain's land in North America. The deal between Spain and France threatened to scuttle American commerce on the river. Such fears took on substance when Spanish officials suspended free trade in New Orleans.

Jefferson responded by dispatching James Monroe to talk with the British about a military alliance. He also had Monroe instruct the American minister to France, Robert Livingston, to purchase New Orleans and as much adjacent real estate as he could get for $2 million.

Napoleon may have been considering the creation of a North American empire when he acquired Louisiana from Spain. **Santo Domingo,** a French colony in the Caribbean, would likely have been the hub for such an empire. But Napoleon's invasion force that was sent in 1802 to reclaim Santo Domingo from rebellious slaves was unsuccessful.

The Louisiana Purchase

Having failed in the Caribbean, Napoleon turned his full attention to conquest in Europe. Desperate for money, the French emperor greeted Monroe and Livingston with an offer to sell the whole of Louisiana for $15 million. Although Livingston and Monroe had been authorized to spend only $2 million, they jumped at the deal. The president not only approved of their action but was overjoyed. The deal offered three important benefits. It saved him from having to ally the United States with Britain. It secured the Mississippi River for shipments of American agricultural products to Europe. And it doubled the size of the United States, opening up uncharted expanses for settlement by yeoman farmers. Jefferson recommended that the Senate ratify the purchase, even though the Constitution was silent on the acquisition of new territories. The Senate approved the **Louisiana Purchase** overwhelmingly in November 1803.

Jefferson subsequently sent a small party to explore this area (see Map 8.1). **Meriwether Lewis,**

Santo Domingo Island shared by the modern nations of Haiti and the Dominican Republic.

Louisiana Purchase The U.S. purchase of Louisiana from France for $15 million in 1803; the Louisiana Territory extended from the Mississippi River to the Rocky Mountains.

Meriwether Lewis Jefferson aide who was sent to explore the Louisiana Territory in 1803; he later served as its governor.

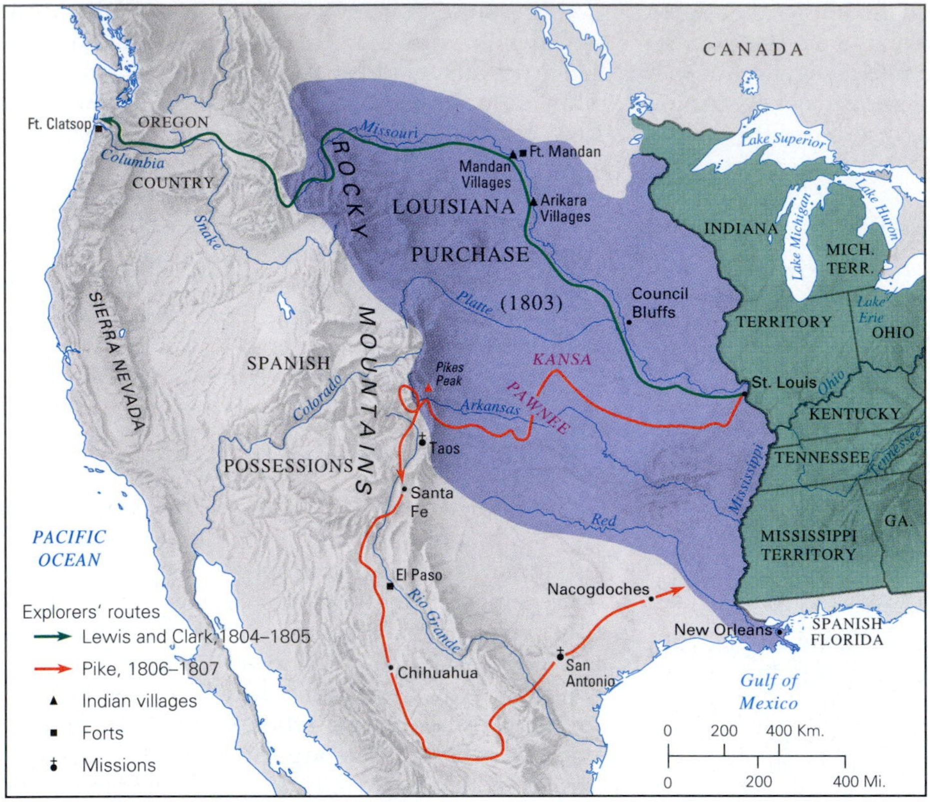

♦ **MAP 8.1 Louisiana Purchase and the Lewis and Clark Expedition** As this map shows, President Jefferson added an enormous tract of land to the United States when he purchased Louisiana from France in 1803. The president was eager to learn as much as possible about the new territory and sent two exploration teams into the West. In addition to collecting information, Lewis and Clark's and Pike's expeditions sought to commit Indian groups along their paths to alliances with the United States and to undermine French, Spanish, and British relations with the Indians, even in those areas that were not officially part of the United States.

Jefferson's private secretary, and his co-commander, Indian fighter **William Clark,** were to note the numbers of French, Spanish, and Indians in the area and to chart major waterways and other important strategic sites. They were also to undermine the Indians' relations with the Spanish and French.

The expedition set out by boat in the spring of 1804, arriving among the Mandan Indians in present-day North Dakota in the late fall. The explorers spent the winter there, gathering information from the Mandans and from French Canadian fur traders. The next spring, they set out across the mountains, led by a French trapper named Charbono and his Shoshone wife, **Sacajawea.** With the

William Clark Soldier and explorer who joined Meriwether Lewis on the expedition to explore the Louisiana Territory; he was responsible for mapmaking.

Sacajawea Shoshone woman who served as guide and interpreter on the Lewis and Clark expedition.

help of Sacajawea's people and other Indians, the expedition reached the Pacific Ocean in November 1805, wintering near the mouth of the Columbia River. When spring came, the party retraced its steps eastward. Finally, after nearly three years, Lewis and Clark arrived back in Washington carrying the information they had been asked to gather. They had also obtained promises from many Indian tribes to join in friendship with the new American republic.

Challenge and Uncertainty in Jefferson's America

Jefferson's policies brought a new spirit into the land. The Virginian's commitment to opportunity and progress, to openness and frugality, offered a stark contrast to the policies of his predecessors. Nevertheless, some disturbing social and intellectual developments began to surface. In particular, rapid westward expansion strained conventional social institutions. The economic opportunities in the West caused a quiet rebellion of young adults against the authority of their parents.

The Heritage of Partisan Politics

The popularity of Jefferson's Republican party was abundantly clear by the 1804 election. The Republicans had virtually eclipsed the Federalists in the congressional elections of 1802, and by 1804 the Federalists were in disarray. Prominent Federalists such as Fisher Ames and John Jay had withdrawn from public life altogether. In the absence of more prominent alternatives, the Federalists chose Charles Cotesworth Pinckney to face off against Jefferson.

In launching their campaign, the Federalists focused on the Louisiana Purchase, charging that Jefferson had overstepped his constitutional authority. Most Americans, however, considered this technicality unimportant compared to the benefits of opening up the West. Also, Jefferson had eliminated internal taxes, encouraged westward migration, eliminated the hated Alien and Sedition Acts, and fostered hope in the hearts of many disaffected Americans. He had also proved that he was no threat to national commerce. America's international earnings grew at the same pace during Jefferson's tenure in office as they had in the 1790s. This substantial record won Jefferson a resounding victory in 1804. He captured 162 electoral votes to Pinckney's 14, carrying every state except Connecticut and Delaware.

Westward Expansion and Social Stress

By 1810, vast numbers of young adults had grabbed at Jefferson's frontier vision. The population of Ohio, for example, grew from 45,000 in 1800 to 231,000 in 1810. Similar spurts occurred in Tennessee and Kentucky. Although such rapid growth was a source of pride, it was also a source of anxiety to westerners trying to establish order in new communities.

Social instability was common in the West. The odd mixture of ethnic, religious, and national groups that made their way west did little to bring cohesiveness to community life. Most of the population consisted of young men. There were few women or older people to encourage stable behavior.

The expansion of the American West had an unsettling effect on communities in the East as well. During the eighteenth century, older people had maintained their authority by controlling the distribution of land to their children. Sons and daughters lived with and worked for their parents until their elders saw fit to deed property to them. As a result, children living in the East generally did not marry or operate their own farms and businesses until they were in their thirties. Economic opportunities on the frontier lessened young people's need to rely on their parents for support and lowered the age at which they began to break away from their parents.

During the early nineteenth century, the age at which children attained independence fell steadily. By the 1820s, children were marrying in their early to mid-twenties. Breathing the new air of independence, intrepid young people moved out of their parents' homes, migrating westward to find land and new opportunities.

The Religious Response to Social Change

The changes taking place in the young republic stirred conflicting religious currents. One was **rationalism** in religious thought. The other was a new **evangelicalism.**

Jefferson, Franklin, Paine, and many others of the revolutionary generation had embraced the **deism** of the Enlightenment (see page 75). They viewed God as a vague "first cause" whose universe was a perfectly crafted machine that had been left to run itself according to rational laws. Religion had to be plain, reasonable, and verifiable to be acceptable to such rationalists. Jefferson, for example, edited his own version of the Bible, keeping only the moral principles and the solid historical facts and discarding anything that he regarded as supernatural. Thomas Paine rejected Christianity altogether, calling it the "strangest religion ever set up."

Rationalism also permeated some mainstream denominations during the Revolutionary era. Some New England Congregationalists began to question predestination and to emphasize instead the individual's role in salvation, especially the significance of reason in that pursuit. Like Jefferson, these rationalist reformers rejected much of the mystery in Christian faith, including the ideas of the **Trinity** and Christ's divinity. Unitarianism, as this form of Christian worship came to be called, grew by leaps and bounds during and after the Revolution.

Unitarianism held great appeal for the young generation in fast-growing port cities like Boston, New York, and Baltimore. In a nation where young people were carving out economic lives for themselves in the worlds of commerce and manufacturing, the notion that they were powerless to effect their own salvation seemed increasingly ridiculous.

While deism and Unitarianism were gaining footholds in eastern cities, a very different kind of religious response was taking shape in the West. There Methodists, Baptists, and Presbyterians emphasized the centrality of conversion in the life of a Christian. Conversion was that emotional moment during which one realizes that one is damned and can be saved only by the grace of God. Typically, conversions were brought about by spirited preaching. These denominations concentrated on training a new, young ministry and sending it to preach in every corner of the nation. The Second Great Awakening, which began in Cane Ridge, Kentucky, in 1801, spread throughout the country.

Like the rationalist sects, the evangelicals stressed individuals' roles in their own salvation and de-emphasized predestination. However, the new awakeners breathed new life into the old Puritan notion of God's plan for the world and the role that Americans were to play in this plan. They also emphasized the importance of Christian community in areas where other forms of community were lacking.

Presbyterian, Baptist, and Methodist churches provided ideological underpinnings for the expansive behavior of westerners and a sense of mission to ease the insecurities produced by venturing into the unknown. They also provided some stability for communities in which traditional controls were lacking. These attractive features helped evangelicalism sweep across the West.

The Problem of Race in Jefferson's Republic

Jefferson's policies enabled many Americans to benefit from the nation's development, but they certainly did not help everyone. Neither Indians nor African Americans had much of a role in Jefferson's America.

A slaveholder, Jefferson doubted the capabilities of blacks. In his *Notes on the State of Virginia* (1785), he asserted that blacks were "inferior to whites in the endowments both of body and mind." Although Phillis Wheatley had won acclaim for her

rationalism The theory that the exercise of reason, rather than the acceptance of authority or spiritual revelation, is the only valid basis for belief and the best source of spiritual truth.

evangelicalism Protestant movements that stress personal conversion and salvation by faith.

deism The belief that God created the universe in such a way that no divine intervention was necessary for its continued operation.

Trinity The Christian belief that God consists of three divine persons: Father, Son, and Holy Spirit.

poetry (see page 121), Jefferson dismissed her work as "below the dignity of criticism." He similarly refused to accept the accomplishments of the black mathematician, astronomer, and engineer **Benjamin Banneker** as proof that blacks were the intellectual equals of whites.

Throughout the Jeffersonian era, the great majority of blacks in America were slaves in the southern states. From the 1790s onward, the number of free blacks increased steadily. Emancipation did not bring equality, however, even in northern states that had mandated the gradual abolition of slavery (see page 121). Many states did not permit free blacks to testify in court, to vote, or to exercise other fundamental freedoms accorded to whites. Public schools often refused admission to African-American children. Even churches were often closed to blacks.

Free blacks began to respond to systematic exclusion by forming their own institutions. In Philadelphia, tension between white and free black Methodists led former slave Richard Allen to form the Bethel Church for Negro Methodists in 1793. Ongoing tension with the white Methodist hierarchy eventually led Allen to secede from the church and to form his own **African Methodist Episcopal church** (Bethel) in 1816. Similar controversies in New York led James Varick to found the African Methodist Episcopal church (Zion) in 1821.

The African Methodist Episcopal (AME) church grew rapidly. Besides providing places of worship and centers for cultural and social activities, AME churches joined with other African-American churches to provide schools and other services withheld by whites. Bishop Allen's organization launched the first black magazine in America and eventually founded its own college, Wilberforce University.

The place of Indians in Jeffersonian thought was somewhat paradoxical. Jefferson considered Indians to be savages but was not convinced that they were biologically inferior to Europeans. Jefferson attributed the differences between Indians and Europeans to the Indians' cultural retardation. He argued that harsh economic conditions and lack of a written language had kept the Indians in a condition of "barbarism." Jefferson was confident that whites could help lift Indians out of their uncivilized state.

Jefferson's Indian policy reflected this attitude. As president, he created government-owned trading posts at which Indians were offered goods at cheap prices. He believed that Indians who were exposed to white manufactures would recognize the superiority of white culture and adopt that culture. Until this process was complete, the Indians, like children, were to be protected from those who would take advantage of them. Also like children, the Indians were not to be given the full rights and responsibilities of citizenship. What rights they had were not to be protected by the Constitution but were to be subject to the whims of the Senate.

The chief problem for Jeffersonian Indian policy was not the Indians' supposed cultural retardation but their rapid progress and acculturation. This was particularly true of the Cherokees and Creeks. Alexander McGillivray of the Creeks, for example, deftly played American, French, and Spanish interests off against each other while building a strong economic base founded on both communal and privately owned plantations. In similar fashion, the Cherokee elite in 1794 established a centralized government that brought the Cherokees wealth and power.

The Indians' white neighbors generally did not think that this represented the right kind of progress. From their perspective, the Indians' destiny was to vanish along with the receding wilderness. Eyeing Cherokee lands, Georgia contended that Indians within its borders were no concern of the federal government. Jefferson insisted, however, that federal authority over Indian affairs was essential for maintaining peace and ensuring the Indians' future welfare.

Jefferson nonetheless feared that an all-out war between the states and the Indians might develop. He accordingly suggested that large reserves in the Louisiana Territory be created for Indians. This

Benjamin Banneker African-American mathematician and astronomer who published an almanac that calculated the movements of stars and planets.

African Methodist Episcopal church African-American branch of Methodism established in Philadelphia in 1816 and in New York in 1821.

would remove Indians from state jurisdictions and from the corrupting influence of the baser elements of white society. He made many efforts, largely unsuccessful, to convince the Indians to exchange traditional lands for new lands west of the Mississippi.

Troubling Currents in Jefferson's America

Racial problems were not the only ones that beset Jefferson's party following its success in the 1804 election. Factions that would challenge Jefferson's control were forming. A small but vocal coalition of disgruntled Federalists threatened to **secede** from the Union. Even within his own party, voices were raised against Jefferson. Diplomatic problems also would trouble Jefferson's second administration.

Emerging Factions in American Politics

The Federalists' failure in the election of 1804 nearly spelled their demise. With the West and the South firmly in Jefferson's camp, New England Federalists found themselves powerless. Federalist leader Timothy Pickering was so disgruntled that he advocated the secession of the northeastern states from the Union. He formed a political coalition called the **Essex Junto** to carry out his scheme, which came to nothing at this time.

Rifts appeared in Jefferson's party as well. Throughout Jefferson's first administration, some southerners had criticized the president for expanding federal power and interfering with states' rights. One of Jefferson's most vocal critics was his cousin, congressman **John Randolph** of Roanoke. Randolph considered himself the last true Republican, and he opposed any legislation that violated his principles.

The tension between the two Virginia Republicans came to a head in 1804 over the **Yazoo affair,** a scandal stemming from Georgia's sale of most of present-day Alabama and Mississippi to political insiders in 1795. Outraged voters forced the Georgia legislature to overturn the sale the following year, but lawsuits were still pending when Georgia ceded the area to the United States in 1802. Jefferson advocated federal compensation for those who had lost money because of the overturned sale. Randolph claimed that would violate Republican principles and plain morality, and he used his power in Congress to block Jefferson's efforts.

In 1806, Randolph broke with Jefferson completely. He regarded Jefferson's requesting Congress for a $2 million gift to France for trying to influence Spain to part with its claims in Florida as nothing more than bribery. Randolph formed a third party, the **Tertium Quids,** fracturing Jefferson's united political front.

A second fissure in the Republican party opened over Vice President Aaron Burr. Burr's failure to renounce the presidency in the election of 1800 had deeply angered Jefferson. Jefferson snubbed Burr throughout his first term and then dropped Burr from the ticket in 1804. Burr then ran for governor of New York with the support of the Essex Junto, which was scheming to have New York join a northern confederacy. Alexander Hamilton was furious when he perceived Burr's intentions and loudly denounced Burr as "a dangerous man . . . who ought not to be trusted with the reins of government." Burr lost the election in a landslide.

Steaming with resentment, Burr blamed Hamilton for his defeat and challenged him to a duel. Although Hamilton hated dueling, he accepted

secede To withdraw formally from membership in an alliance or association.

Essex Junto Group of Federalists in Essex County, Massachusetts, who called for New England and New York to secede from the Union during Jefferson's second term.

John Randolph Virginia politician who was a cousin of Thomas Jefferson; he believed in limited government and opposed the acquisition of Florida.

Yazoo affair Notorious deal in which the Georgia legislature sold a huge tract of public land to speculators for a low price; the sale was overturned by a new legislature a year later.

Tertium Quids Republican faction formed by John Randolph in protest against Jefferson's plan for acquiring Florida from Spain.

Burr's challenge. The vice president wounded Hamilton mortally in July 1804. Burr was indicted for murder and fled. While in hiding, he hatched a plot with James Wilkinson, a Revolutionary War commander who had become something of a soldier of fortune. The nature of this plot remains obscure. Whatever they had in mind, rumors that Burr and Wilkinson intended to seize Louisiana soon surfaced. Federal authorities began investigating when they received a letter from Wilkinson in December 1806.

Double-crossing Burr and playing innocent, Wilkinson warned of a "deep, dark, wicked, and widespread conspiracy" against America. Burr, learning that Wilkinson had turned him in, tried to reach Spanish Florida but was captured early in 1807 and put on trial for treason. Chief Justice John Marshall instructed the jury that treason, according to the Constitution, consisted of "levying war against the United States or adhering to their enemies." Because Burr had not waged war and because neither Spain nor Britain was then an enemy of the United States, the jury acquitted the former vice president.

The Problem of American Neutrality

Shortly after the conclusion of the Burr trial, new concerns about the possibility of war with Great Britain emerged. The impressment of American seamen and violations of American neutrality had led to deteriorating relations with Great Britain since 1803, when war resumed between Britain and France. Britain, strapped for mariners by renewed warfare and by thousands of desertions, pursued a vigorous policy of reclaiming British sailors, even if they were on neutral American ships and, more provocatively, even if they had become naturalized American citizens. The British abducted as many as eight thousand sailors from American ships between 1803 and 1812. The loss of so many seamen hurt American shippers, but it wounded American pride even more. Like the XYZ affair, impressment insulted national honor.

The escalating economic warfare between France and Britain quickly involved Americans. A pivotal event occurred in June 1807. A British frigate fired on the American warship *Chesapeake* inside American territorial waters when the latter refused to hand over British sailors. The British **broadsides** crippled the American vessel, killing three men. The British then boarded the *Chesapeake* and dragged off four men, three of them naturalized American citizens. Americans were outraged.

Napoleon responded to more aggressive British enforcement by declaring economic war against neutrals. In the **Milan Decree,** he vowed to seize any neutral ship that even carried a license to trade with Britain. Ships that had been boarded by the British would be subject to immediate French capture.

Many Americans viewed the escalating French and British sanctions as extremely insulting. The *Washington Federalist* observed, "We have never, on any occasion, witnessed . . . such a thirst for revenge." If Congress had been in session, it probably would have called for war. But Jefferson stayed calm. War would bring his whole political program to a crashing halt. He had insisted on inexpensive government, lobbied for American neutrality, and hoped for renewed prosperity through continuing trade with Europe. War would destroy all those things. But doing nothing also would put the country in great peril.

Believing that Europeans were far more dependent on American goods than Americans were on European manufactures, Jefferson issued an **embargo**—an absolute ban—on all American trade with Europe in December 1807. It went into effect at the beginning of 1808.

Crises in the Nation

While impressment, blockade, and embargo plagued America's Atlantic frontier, a combination of European and Indian hostility along the western

broadside The simultaneous discharge of all the guns on one side of a warship.

Milan Decree Napoleon's order authorizing the capture of any neutral vessels sailing from British ports or submitting to British searches.

embargo A government order that bans trade with another nation or group of nations.

frontier added to the air of national emergency. The resulting series of domestic crises played havoc with Jefferson's vision of a peaceful, prosperous nation.

The Depression of 1808

Jefferson's embargo resulted in the worst economic depression since the founding of the American colonies. Trade slumped disastrously. American exports fell from $109 million to $22 million, and net earnings from shipping plummeted by almost 50 percent. During 1808, earnings from legitimate business enterprise in America declined to less than a quarter of their value in 1807.

The depression shattered economic and social life in many eastern towns. Some thirty thousand sailors were thrown out of work. In New York City alone, 120 businesses went bankrupt, and 1,200 New Yorkers were imprisoned for debt in 1808. New England, where the economy had become almost entirely dependent on foreign trade, was hit harder still. The Federalists enjoyed a comeback, not in spite of but because of their rhetoric calling for disobedience of federal law and the possibility of secession.

New Englanders screamed loudest about the embargo, but southerners and westerners were just as seriously hurt by it. The economy of the South had depended on the export of staple crops like tobacco since colonial times. The embargo meant near death to all legitimate trade. The loss of foreign markets caused tobacco prices to fall from $6.75 per hundredweight to $3.25, and cotton from 21 to 13 cents per pound. In the West, wholesale prices for agricultural products also spiraled downward.

Although trading interests in New England suffered during the depression, a new avenue of economic expansion opened there as a result of the embargo. Cut off from European manufactured goods, Americans started to make more textiles and other items for themselves. The expansion in cotton spinning is a case in point. Prior to 1808, only fifteen cotton mills had been built in the United States. Between the passage of the embargo and the end of 1809, eighty-seven mills sprang up, mostly in New England.

The Prophet and Tecumseh

The crisis along the Atlantic frontier was echoed by a problem along the nation's western frontier. Relations with Indians in the West had been peaceful since the Battle of Fallen Timbers in Ohio in 1794, but only because the Indians had been crushed into submission. The Shawnees and other groups had been thrown off their traditional homelands in Ohio by the Treaty of Greenville and forced to move to new lands in Indiana. Food shortages, disease, and continuing encroachment by settlers caused many young Indians to lose faith in their traditional beliefs and in themselves as human beings. A growing number turned to alcohol to escape feelings of helplessness and hopelessness. Traditional leaders seemed unable to halt the growing tide of white expansion.

In the midst of the crisis, one disheartened, diseased alcoholic rose above his sickness to lead the Indians into a brief new era of hope. A young Shawnee named Lalawathika claimed that he remembered dying and meeting the Master of Life, who showed him the way to lead his people out of degradation. He then returned to the world of the living and awoke, cured of his illness. He immediately adopted the name Tenskwatawa ("The Way") and launched a revival in 1805 to teach the ways revealed to him by the Master of Life. Whites called him "the Prophet."

The Prophet preached a message of ethnic pride, nonviolence, and passive resistance. Blaming the decline of his people on their adoption of white ways, the Prophet taught them to discard whites' clothing, religion, and especially alcohol and to live as their ancestors had. Whites, he said, were dangerous witches, and Indians must avoid them. He also urged his followers to unify against the white exploiters and to hold on to what remained of their lands. If they followed his teachings, the Indians would regain control of their lives

The Prophet Shawnee religious visionary who called for a return to Indian traditions and founded the community of Prophetstown on Tippecanoe Creek in Indiana.

and their lands, and the whites would vanish from their world.

In 1807, the Prophet established a new community, Prophetstown, on the banks of Tippecanoe Creek in Indiana. This community was to serve as a model for revitalized Indian life. Liquor, guns, and other white goods were banned from the settlement. The residents of Prophetstown worked together, using traditional forms of agriculture, hunting, and gathering.

The Prophet's message of passive resistance underwent a significant change in the face of continuing white opposition. He began to advocate more forceful solutions to the Indians' problems. In April 1807, the Prophet suggested that warriors unite to resist white expansion. Although he did not urge his followers to attack whites, he claimed that the Master of Life would protect his followers in the event of war.

Whereas the Prophet continued to stress spiritual means for stopping white aggression, his older brother **Tecumseh** advocated a political course of action. A brave fighter and a persuasive political orator, Tecumseh traveled the western frontier working out alliances with other Indian tribes. Although he did not want to start a war against white settlers, Tecumseh exhorted Indians to defend every inch of their remaining land.

Tecumseh's success in organizing Indian groups caused confusion among whites. British authorities in Canada were convinced that the Prophet and Tecumseh were French agents trying to divert British attention from the war in Europe. Americans were equally convinced that the brothers were British agents. Both the British and the Americans were wrong. Like many other gifted Indian leaders, Tecumseh played whites off against each other to gain what he wanted for his people. He did go to Canada in 1807 and secured promises of British support, but he did not become a British agent. Rather, Tecumseh wanted the Americans to believe that he had a powerful ally.

Identifying Tecumseh as a British spy, however, served the purposes of some Americans. Indiana Governor William Henry Harrison, for example, had built a military career and then a political career as an advocate of westward expansion. Harrison, who had first made his reputation at the Battle of Fallen Timbers, believed nothing should stand in the way of American control of all of North America.

War with Britain and its supposed Indian allies was an attractive option to American expansionsists for at least three reasons. First, a war could justify Americans' invading and seizing Canada. Taking Canada from the British would open up rich timber, fur, and agricultural lands for Americans. More important, it would secure American control of the Great Lakes and St. Lawrence River, the primary shipping route for agricultural produce from upper New York, northern Ohio, and the newly opening areas of the Old Northwest.

Second, many believed that the British in Canada stirred up Indian conflict on America's frontiers. A war could remove this source of trouble and remove obstacles to American expansion. It would further provide an excuse to attack the Shawnees and break up their emerging confederacy.

Finally, frontiersmen, like other Americans, blamed Britain for the economic depression that began in 1808. They believed that eliminating British interference would restore a boom economy for western farmers. Thus westerners banded together to raise their voices in favor of American patriotism and war against Britain.

Choosing War

In 1808, Jefferson followed Washington's lead and left the presidency after two terms. When he stepped down from the presidency, he pegged fellow Virginian James Madison as his successor. Madison easily defeated his Federalist opponent, Charles Cotesworth Pinckney. But the one-sided election disguised deep political divisions in the nation. Federalist criticism of Jefferson's embargo found a growing audience as the depression deepened, and the Republicans lost twenty-four congressional seats to the Federalists.

Internal dissent also weakened the Republican party. In 1810, sixty-three mainstream Republicans lost their congressional seats to dissident

Tecumseh Shawnee leader and brother of the Prophet; he tried to establish an Indian confederacy along the frontier as a barrier to white expansion.

Republicans who did not agree with Madison's conciliatory policy toward the British. The newcomers' increasingly strident demands for aggressive action against Britain earned them the nickname **War Hawks.**

Henry Clay and **John C. Calhoun** quickly assumed the leadership of this group of young southerners and westerners. Clay was the dominant voice among the younger representatives. Born in Virginia in 1777, Clay at the age of 20 had moved to Kentucky to practice law and carve out a career in politics. He became Speaker of the Kentucky state assembly when he was only 30 years old and won a seat in the House of Representatives four years later.

A year younger than Clay, John C. Calhoun of South Carolina was a dedicated nationalist who wanted to break Britain's stranglehold on the American agricultural economy. Together, he and Clay called for aggressive action against British provocations. Events soon played into their hands.

In 1809, Congress revoked the Embargo Act and replaced it with the **Non-Intercourse Act,** which forbade trade only with Britain and France. Even though this act was much less restrictive than the embargo, American merchants were relieved when it expired in 1810. Congress then passed an even more liberal boycott, **Macon's Bill No. 2.** Under this new law, merchants could trade even with the combatants if they wanted to take the risk. Also, if either France or Britain lifted its blockade, the United States would stop trading with the other.

Napoleon responded to Macon's Bill in August by promising to suspend French restrictions on American shipping. Although the French emperor had no intention of living up to his promise, Madison sought to use it as a lever against Great Britain. Madison instructed the American mission in London to tell the British that France's action would force the president to close down trade with Britain unless Britain ended its trade restrictions. Sure that Napoleon was lying, the British refused. In February 1811, the provisions of Macon's Bill forced Madison to end trading with Britain.

Events in the West added the final element to the unfolding diplomatic crisis. In August 1810, Tecumseh and a delegation of Indians had told **William Henry Harrison** that they regarded the Fort Wayne Treaty, signed a year earlier, as fraudulent. Tecumseh claimed that the three tribes that had sold millions of acres in Indiana and Illinois to the government had no right to sell this land. Harrison insisted that the Fort Wayne Treaty was legitimate. Tecumseh countered that "bad consequences" would follow if whites attempted to settle on the disputed lands. The meeting resulted in a stalemate.

The meeting with Harrison convinced the Indians that they must prepare for a white attack. The Prophet increasingly preached that the Master of Life would support the faithful in battle against the whites. Tecumseh traveled the frontier to enlist additional allies for his confederacy.

Convinced that war was imminent, Harrison determined to attack the Indians before they could unite. He got his chance in the fall of 1811 when Potawatomis raided a village in Illinois. Harrison assembled over a thousand soldiers and militiamen to march on Prophetstown, even though the Indians there had had nothing to do with the raid.

The Prophet ignored Tecumseh's advice to avoid confrontation and unleashed the Indians on Harrison's army. Prepared for the assault, the white soldiers routed the attackers and made a mockery of the Prophet's assurance that the Mas-

War Hawks Members of Congress from the West and South who campaigned for war with Britain in the hopes of stimulating the economy and annexing new territory.

Henry Clay Congressman from Kentucky who was a leader of the War Hawks; he helped negotiate the treaty ending the War of 1812.

John C. Calhoun Congressman from South Carolina who was a leader of the War Hawks; he later became an advocate of states' rights.

Non-Intercourse Act Law passed by Congress in 1809 reopening trade with all nations except France and Britain and authorizing the president to reopen trade with them if they lifted restrictions on American shipping.

Macon's Bill No. 2 Law passed by Congress in 1810 that offered exclusive trading rights to France or Britain, whichever recognized American neutral rights first.

William Henry Harrison Indiana governor who led U.S. forces at the Battle of Tippecanoe; he later became the ninth president of the United States.

ter of Life would make the Indians victorious. Disheartened, most of the warriors from Prophetstown deserted the settlement, which enraged frontiersmen then burned.

Tecumseh was away trying to win southwestern Indians over to his cause when Harrison's men burned Prophetstown. When he learned that hope for a peaceful settlement had vanished, he gathered an army of Indian allies to defend Indian territory. Harrison immediately called on the federal government for military support against what he portrayed as a unified Indian and British declaration of war. He had no doubt that the British stood behind Tecumseh.

The **Battle of Tippecanoe** provided the War Hawks with the excuse they had been looking for. John C. Calhoun declared that Great Britain had left Americans with the choice between "the base surrender of their rights, and a manly vindication of them." Calhoun was out to vindicate American rights, and he introduced a war bill in Congress in 1812. His bill declaring war on Great Britain passed by a vote of 79 to 49 in the House and 19 to 13 in the Senate. Representatives from heavily Federalist regions that depended the most on overseas trade—Massachusetts, Connecticut, and New York—voted against war. Republican western and southern representatives voted in favor.

The Nation at War

Although the prospect of war had been likely for some time, the United States was woefully unprepared when the breach with Great Britain finally came. With virtually no army or navy, the United States was taking a terrible risk in confronting the world's most formidable military power. Not surprisingly, defeat and humiliation were the early fruits of the War of 1812.

The Fighting Begins

In line with War Hawk ambitions, the first military campaign was a three-pronged drive toward Canada (see Map 8.2). Harrison's force was successful in raiding undefended Indian villages but was unable to make any gains against British troops. Farther east, Major General Stephen Van Rensselaer's force was defeated by a small British and Indian army. Meanwhile, Henry Dearborn's troops lunged at Montreal but withdrew into U.S. territory after an inconclusive battle.

American sailors fared much better. Leading the war effort at sea were the *Constitution* (popularly known as **Old Ironsides**), the *President*, and the *United States*. In mid-August, the *Constitution* outmaneuvered a British **frigate** and sank it. The *United States* enjoyed a similar victory.

The biggest threat to British seafaring, however, came from armed American privateers. During the first six months of the war, privateers captured 450 British merchant ships valued in the millions. American naval victories were all that kept the nation's morale alive in 1812. One observer commented, "But for the gallantry of our noble Tar's [sailors], we should be covered with shame and disgrace." Vowing to reverse the situation, Congress increased the size of the army to fifty-seven thousand men and offered a $16 bonus to encourage enlistments.

Madison thus stood for re-election at a time when the nation's military fate appeared uncertain and his own leadership seemed shaky. Although the majority of his party's congressional caucus supported him for re-election, nearly a third of the Republican congressmen—mostly those from New York and New England—rallied around New Yorker DeWitt Clinton. Clinton was a Republican who favored Federalist economic policies and agreed that the war was unnecessary. Most Federalists supported Clinton and did not field a candidate of their own.

Battle of Tippecanoe Battle near Prophetstown in Indiana Territory in 1811; American forces led by William Henry Harrison defeated Shawnee followers of the Prophet.

Old Ironsides Nickname of the *Constitution*, the forty-four-gun American frigate whose victory over the *Guerrière* bolstered sagging morale in the War of 1812.

frigate A very fast warship rigged with square sails and usually carrying thirty guns on its gun deck.

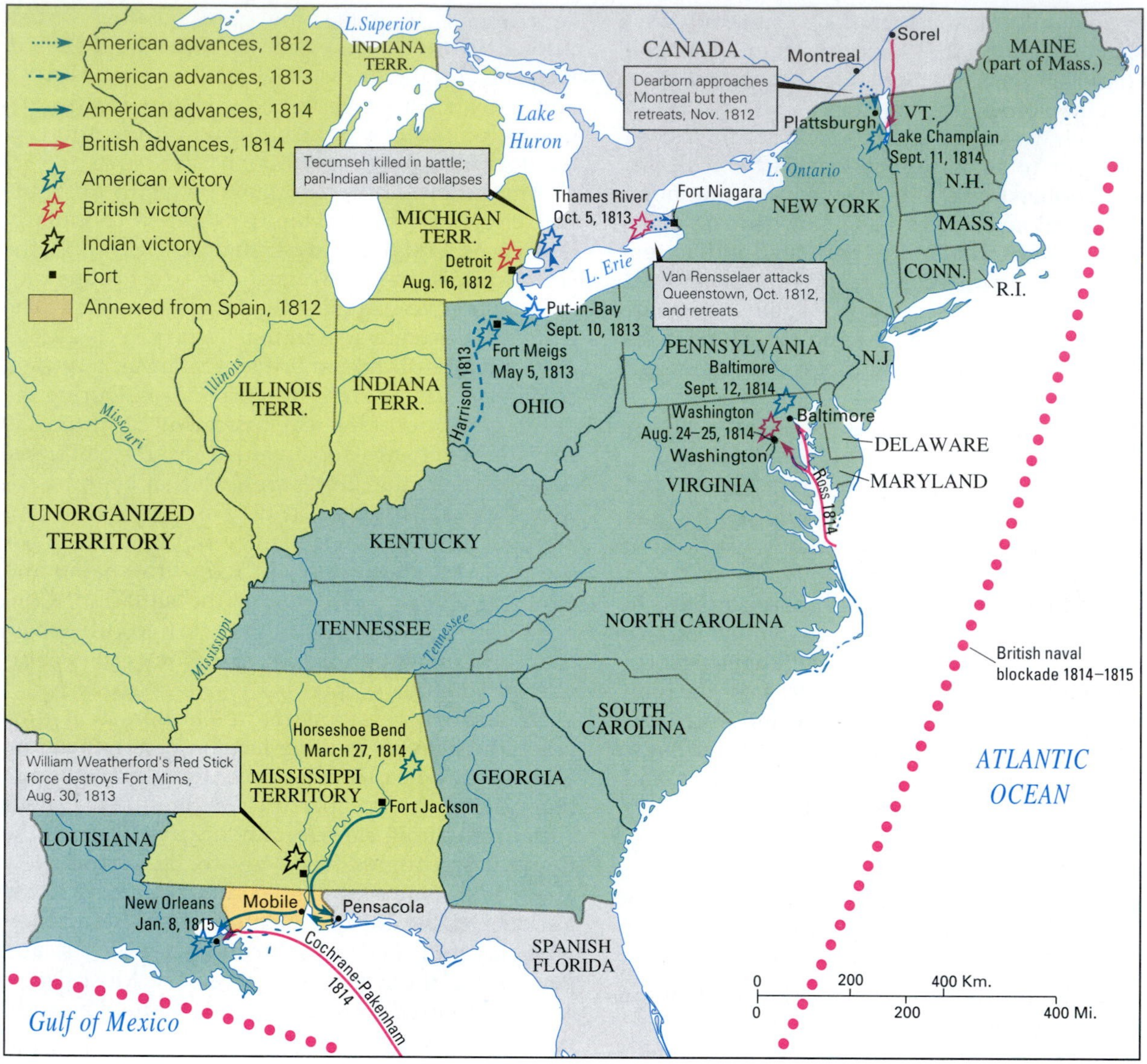

♦ **MAP 8.2 The War of 1812** The heaviest action during the first two years of the War of 1812 lay along the U.S./Canadian border. In 1814, the British sought to knock the United States out of the war by staging three offensives: one along the northern frontier at Plattsburgh, New York; one into the Chesapeake; and a third directed at the Mississippi River in New Orleans. All three offensives failed.

The outcome of the election was nearly the same as that of the congressional vote on the war bill earlier in 1812. New York and New England rallied behind Clinton; the South and West supported Madison, the Republicans, and war. Madison won, but his share of electoral votes fell from 72 percent in 1808 to 59 percent in 1812. The Republicans also lost strength in the House and the Senate.

The War's Fruitless Second Year

In the spring of 1813, American forces challenged British control of the Great Lakes and the uninterrupted supply line those lakes afforded. On Lake Ontario, the Americans met with frustration; on Lake Erie, they met with success. **Oliver Hazard Perry** met the British at the Battle of Put-in-Bay on Lake Erie in September 1813. After two hours of cannon fire, Perry's **flagship,** the *Lawrence,* had been nearly destroyed. Still, Perry refused to surrender. He slipped off his damaged vessel and took command of a nearby ship. What remained of his command then cut the enemy to pieces and captured six British vessels. "We have met the enemy and they are ours," Perry reported to William Henry Harrison.

Harrison's land campaign was not going nearly so well. In the spring of 1813, Tecumseh and the British general Henry Procter had surrounded Harrison's camp on the Maumee Rapids in Ohio. Finally, on May 5, Kentucky militiamen arrived to drive the enemy off. However, they lost nearly half of their number in pursuing the British and Indian force.

After harassing American forces throughout the summer of 1813, Procter and Tecumseh withdrew to Canada in the fall. Harrison pursued them. His army surprised the British and Indian forces at the Thames River, about 50 miles east of Detroit, on October 5. The British surrendered quickly, but the Indians abandoned the fight only after Tecumseh was killed. His body was torn apart by the victorious Americans following the Battle of the Thames.

Another war front opened up during 1813. Although the Creek Confederacy as a whole remained neutral, the Red Stick faction had allied with Tecumseh in 1812. When war broke out, the Red Sticks raided settlements in what are now Alabama and Mississippi. Alexander McGillivray's heir, William Weatherford, led a Red Stick army against Fort Mims, 40 miles north of Mobile (see Individual Choices: William Weatherford). The attackers overran the fort, killing all but about thirty of the more than three hundred people there.

The Fort Mims massacre enraged whites in the Southeast. In Tennessee, twenty-five hundred militiamen enlisted under the command of **Andrew Jackson.** Nicknamed "Old Hickory" because of his toughness, Jackson promised that "the blood of our women & children shall not call for vengeance in vain." Along with other volunteers from Tennessee and Georgia, Jackson's troops hounded the Red Sticks throughout the summer and fall.

Meanwhile, the British shut down American forces at sea. Embarrassed by the success of *Old Ironsides* and other American frigates, the British sent sufficient ships to bottle up the American fleet and **merchant marine** in port. British control over the Atlantic was so complete that they decided to bring the war home to Americans living near the shore. Admiral Sir George Cockburn raided the countryside around Chesapeake Bay during the spring of 1813. In Maryland, Cockburn burned an American fleet in Frenchtown and then burned Georgetown, Fredericktown, and Havre de Grace. The Americans seemed powerless against these raids.

The War's Strange Conclusion

The War of 1812 assumed a new character when Britain and its European allies defeated Napoleon's army in the fall of 1813. By the end of March 1814, they had forced Napoleon's abdication and

Oliver Hazard Perry American naval officer who led the fleet that defeated the British in the Battle of Put-in-Bay during the War of 1812.

flagship The ship that carries the fleet commander and bears the commander's flag.

Andrew Jackson General in the War of 1812 who defeated the British at New Orleans in 1815; he later became the seventh president of the United States.

merchant marine A nation's commercial ships.

INDIVIDUAL CHOICES

Choice in Civil War

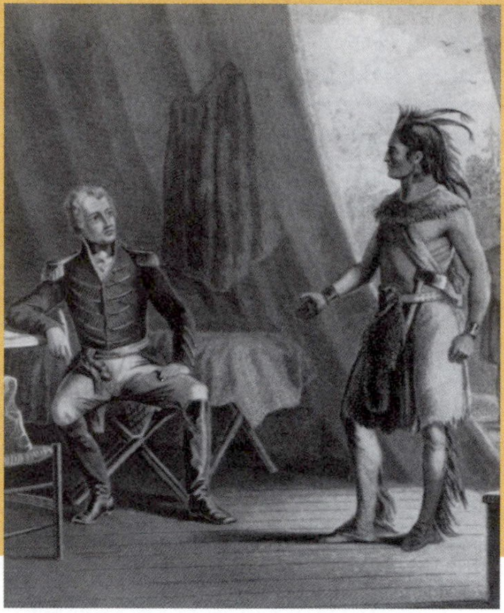

William Weatherford

Tecumseh's effort to unite all Indians into a single political military alliance split the Creek Confederacy into two warring factions. At first, William Weatherford tried to mediate between the two, but he encountered serious constraints and finally chose to lead the Red Stick faction into war against the United States. Tennessee State Library & Archives.

William Weatherford had the potential to be the most powerful man in the Creek Nation. Like his maternal uncle Alexander McGillivray, Weatherford was part white and part Indian. But among the Creeks, family roots were traced back only through the mother's line, making him fully Creek in the tribe's eyes. The Creek tradition also marked him to inherit McGillivray's position as the dominant chief in the confederacy. But by 1800, historical pressures on the Creeks had eroded traditional ways of doing things, and Weatherford's position was far from secure. In 1812, he found himself facing a difficult choice: he had to choose sides in a Creek Nation split in two by civil war.

The Creek Nation was a confederacy consisting of a variety of Indian groups that spoke a variety of languages, had different customs, and practiced quite different economies. Over time, these groups had aligned themselves into two large organizations: the Lower Towns—villages in the low-lying southern portion of the Creek territory in modern-day Georgia and Alabama—and the Upper Towns—villages in the more mountainous and heavily wooded northern part of the region. Geographical and cultural diversity was part of what held the Creek confederacy together: the many different resources controlled by different Creek member villages led them to depend on each other.

By the end of the eighteenth century, the mutually dependent economy that had kept the Creek towns aligned had given way to greater dependence on the Europeans. In the Upper Towns, where Weatherford was born, the fur trade distracted hunters from providing meat and other necessities for the confederacy. In the Lower Towns, the lure of growing cotton and tobacco for sale to the whites distracted the people from providing corn. In many villages, essential commodities now had to be purchased outside the confederacy.

The economic separation between the two areas became a source of major conflict after 1808, when President Jefferson's embargo triggered a depression. Suddenly, Creeks in the Upper Towns had no market for their furs. Blaming whites for their dependence on the fur trade, and the fur trade for their dire economic situation, many in the Upper Towns found the Prophet's message of turning away from white ways appealing. More appealing still was Tecumseh's suggestion of empowerment through joint action. Not surprisingly, when Tecumseh visited the Creeks in 1811, he was well received in the Upper Towns. Many chose to follow his red war stick.

It appears that Weatherford was leery of Tecumseh, but the response of the Lower Towns to Tecumseh's visit forced Weatherford's hand. Allied by common economic interests with southern white planters, Creeks in the Lower Towns feared that an alliance between Creeks in the Upper Towns and the Shawnees might ruin their economy further and, more important, close off avenues of improvement through political cooperation with their white neighbors. The Lower Towns began putting enormous pressure on the Upper Towns to turn away from Tecumseh's message. Weatherford and other responsible leaders tried to keep the peace, but when war broke out between the Americans and the British in 1812, that became hard to do. In February 1813, rogue bands of Red Sticks went on forays against settlements, aiming to punish whites for attacks or rumored attacks on Indians.

Bent on preventing war with the Americans, the Creeks in the Lower Towns sent an armed party against the Upper Towns to put an end to Red Stick violence, but the situation only worsened. Determined to defend themselves, the Upper Towns sent a party under Red Stick leader Peter McQueen to the Spanish post at Pensacola to buy guns and ammunition. Though not yet committed to the Red Stick position, Weatherford accompanied this party, possibly hoping to prevent further violence. A combined force of white militiamen and Creeks from the Lower Towns stumbled on them at midday on July 27, attacking them while they ate lunch. Most of McQueen's party was able to escape, but the bodies of the twenty men who were killed in the surprise attack were brutally mutilated. For Weatherford, that was the last straw. An honorable peace no longer seemed possible, so he chose war.

A little over a month later, Weatherford led about seven hundred Red Sticks on a raid against Fort Mims, a post jointly occupied by Creeks from the Lower Towns and white militiamen with their families. Weatherford and his force launched their assault as the lunch bell rang at noon on August 30. Within minutes, they swept into the surprised post, and a general melee began. When the fighting stopped, between three hundred and five hundred people lay dead, and the fort was in flames. Major Joseph P. Kennedy, who arrived at the fort ten days after the battle, reported, "Indians, negroes, white men, women, and children lay in one promiscuous ruin."

Although he preferred peace and was no convert to the teachings of Tecumseh, Weatherford had seen his choices narrow as differing interests among the Creeks pulled the confederacy apart. His decision to join Tecumseh irreversibly altered the Creek Nation's future. After the massacre at Fort Mims, there was no going back: the destiny of the Creeks would depend on Tecumseh's plan and British military success.

imprisoned him. Napoleon's defeat left the United States as Great Britain's sole military target. Republican Joseph Nicholson expressed a common lament when he said, "We should have to fight hereafter not for 'free Trade and sailors rights,' not for the Conquest of the Canadas, but for our national Existence."

The Politics of Waging War

American choices in the war were complicated by the British offer in December 1813 to open peace negotiations. President Madison responded by forming an American peace commission. The British peace overture made the unruly Congress even more difficult to deal with. Federalist William Gaston of North Carolina proclaimed it "inexpedient to prosecute military operations against the Canadas" while negotiations were pending. Fellow Federalists joined him in supporting bills to limit American military operations to "the defence of the territories and frontiers of the United States." Madison's supporters objected. John C. Calhoun proclaimed that the entire war was "defensive."

While this debate was going on, Madison turned his attention to diplomacy. He proposed another embargo to hasten negotiations with the British. Madison had two objectives in mind: (1) to stop the flow of American flour and other supplies to British military commissaries in Canada and (2) to stop the drain of American currency from the country. He asked and obtained Congress's approval to prohibit American ships and goods from leaving port and to ban British imports.

The **Embargo of 1813** was the most far-reaching trade restriction bill ever passed by the American Congress. It had a devastating economic impact. The embargo virtually shut down the economies of New England and New York and crippled the economy of nearly every other state.

A Stumbling British Offensive

As combat-hardened British veterans began arriving in North America after Napoleon's fall, the survival of the United States was in jeopardy (see Map 8.2). By September 1814, the British had thirty thousand troops in Canada. From this position of strength, they prepared three offensives to bring the war to a quick end.

The main thrust of the British offensive in the North was against eastern New York. Sir George Prevost, governor-general of Canada, massed ten thousand troops for an attack against Plattsburgh, New York. Prevost's plans were upset when a small American fleet shredded British naval forces on Lake Champlain on September 11. Prevost broke off his attack when he learned about the fate of the British lake fleet and ordered a retreat. The New Yorkers gave chase and turned the retreat into a rout. Prevost's failure in the Battle of Plattsburgh marked the end of the major fighting on the Canadian frontier.

The British opened a second front farther south in August 1814. It began when twenty British warships and several troop transports sailed up Chesapeake Bay. British General Robert Ross landed a force outside Washington, D.C., on August 24. Some seven thousand Maryland militiamen held off the experienced British regulars for several hours, but when they ran out of ammunition, the British broke their defensive line and seized the capital.

The defenders did stop the British long enough to allow most of the civilians in the capital, including the president, to escape. Dolley Madison, the president's wife, managed to save a number of treasures from the presidential mansion, as well as important cabinet documents. Department clerks succeeded in moving most of the government's vital papers. Even so, much of value was lost. The British looted many buildings, including the White House, and then torched most of the structures, including the Capitol, which housed the Library of Congress. The British finally abandoned the ruins of Washington on August 25, marching toward Baltimore.

At Baltimore, the British navy had to knock out Fort McHenry and control the harbor before they could take the city. On September 12, British ships armed with heavy **mortars** and rockets attacked

Embargo of 1813 An absolute embargo on all American trade and British imports.

mortar A portable, muzzle-loading cannon.

the fort. During a twenty-five-hour bombardment, the British fired more than fifteen hundred rounds at the American post. Despite the pounding, the American flag continued to wave over Fort McHenry. The sight moved a young volunteer named **Francis Scott Key,** who had watched the shelling as a prisoner aboard a British ship, to record the event in a verse that later became the national anthem of the United States.

The Gulf Coast Campaign

On the third front, the British pressed an offensive against the Gulf coast designed to take the pressure off Canada and to close the Mississippi River. The campaign began in May 1814 when the British occupied the Spanish port city of Pensacola, Florida. From there the British began working their way toward New Orleans and the Mississippi.

The defense of the Gulf coast fell to Andrew Jackson and his Tennessee volunteers. Having spent the winter raising troops and collecting supplies, Jackson was determined to punish the Red Sticks. At the **Battle of Horseshoe Bend** on the Tallapoosa River in Alabama, Jackson's forces killed nearly eight hundred Red Sticks, destroying the Creeks' power.

Jackson then moved on the British depot at Pensacola. Although ordered to stay out of Florida to avoid war with Spain, he ignored the order. He attacked Pensacola on November 7, 1814. The Spanish did nothing, and the overmatched British withdrew.

Jackson immediately left Pensacola and raced his army to New Orleans, where the main British force was closing in. When he arrived on December 1, he found the city ill prepared to defend itself. The local militia, consisting mostly of French and Spanish residents, would not obey American officers. Local banks and businesses refused to support government efforts, fearing a collapse in the nation's economy.

A man of forceful action, Jackson permitted no opposition or apathy. "Those who are not for us are against us, and will be dealt with accordingly," he proclaimed. Through the example of his own energy and enthusiasm he transformed the community. "General Jackson electrified all hearts," one observer said. Soon volunteers flooded to the general's assistance. Free blacks in the city formed a regular army corps, and Jackson created a special unit of black refugees from Santo Domingo. Proper white citizens protested when Jackson armed runaway slaves and when he accepted a company of Baratarian pirates under the command of **Jean Laffite,** but Jackson ignored them. The pirate commander became Jackson's constant companion during the campaign.

Having pulled his ragtag force together, Jackson settled in to wait for the British attack. On January 7, 1815, it came. Jackson's men waited until the British were only five hundred yards away before they fired their cannon. When the British got to within three hundred yards, riflemen opened fire. And when the British were within one hundred yards, the men armed with muskets began to shoot. One British veteran said that it was "the most murderous fire I have ever beheld before or since." General Edward Pakenham tried to keep his men from running but was cut in half by a cannon ball. General John Lambert, who took over command, raised a white flag immediately.

The **Battle of New Orleans** was by far the most successful battle fought by Americans during the War of 1812. The British lost over two thousand men, the Americans only seventy. Ironically, the war was already officially over before the battle began.

Francis Scott Key Author of "The Star-Spangled Banner," which chronicles the British bombardment of Fort McHenry at Baltimore in the War of 1812; it became the official U.S. national anthem in 1916.

Battle of Horseshoe Bend Battle in 1814 between Tennessee militia and Creek Indians in Alabama; the American victory marked the end of Indian power in the South.

Jean Laffite Leader of a band of pirates off Barataria Bay in southeast Louisiana; he offered to fight for the Americans at New Orleans in return for the pardon of his men.

Battle of New Orleans Battle in the War of 1812 in which American troops commanded by Andrew Jackson repulsed the British attempt to seize New Orleans.

♦ The nearly miraculous American victory in the Battle of New Orleans—fought two weeks after the Americans and British had signed a peace treaty—helped launch a new era in American nationalism. As this illustration from a popular magazine shows, it also made Andrew Jackson, shown waving his hat to encourage his troops, a national hero of greater than human proportions. *Library of Congress.*

The Treaty of Ghent

While the British were closing in on Washington in August 1814, treaty negotiations were beginning in Ghent, Belgium. Confident of victory, the British refused to enter meaningful negotiations. They declined to discuss impressment and insisted that the security of Canada be ensured by the formation of an Indian buffer state between Canada and the United States.

The Americans, however, were anxious for a peaceful settlement. Madison ordered the delegation to drop impressment as an issue. He justified this decision by saying that the end of the war in Europe had so greatly reduced Britain's need for sailors that impressment was no longer an important issue. Far more important was the British plan for an Indian buffer state.

When Prevost lost the Battle of Plattsburgh and the Lake Champlain fleet, however, the British demand for an Indian buffer zone suddenly became negotiable. The sticking point then became what territories each country would retain when the war ended. The British proposed that each nation keep whatever land it held when the hostilities stopped. The Americans rejected this because it would require giving up much of Maine, some territory around the Great Lakes, and perhaps even New Orleans and the nation's capital.

At that point, domestic politics in Britain intervened. After two decades at arms, the British people were weary of war and wartime taxes. The failure at Plattsburgh made it appear that the war would drag on endlessly. Moreover, the American war interfered with Britain's European diplomacy. Still trying to arrive at a peace settlement for Europe at the Congress of Vienna, a British official commented, "We do not think the Continental Powers will continue in good humour with our Blockade of the whole Coast of America." Like the proposed Indian buffer state, British territorial demands fell before practical considerations.

♦ Following the War of 1812 and the death of Tecumseh, aggressive American expansionists put great pressure on Indians living on the east side of the Mississippi River to move farther west. Artist James Otto Lewis was present at the 1825 Prairie du Chien treaty meetings, where various Sauk and Fox, Menominee, Iowa, Winnebago, Ojibwa, and Sioux bands gave up much of their land. He was present the following year at similar talks at Fond du Lac, where he painted these three Chippewa (Ojibwa) women. *"Chippeway Squaws at the Treaty of Fond du Lac" by James Otto Lewis, 1826. Chicago Historical Society.*

In the end, the **Treaty of Ghent,** completed on December 24, 1814, restored diplomatic relations between Britain and the United States to what they had been before the war. The treaty said nothing about impressment, blockades, or neutral trading rights. It left Canada in British hands. Although the Americans had not fulfilled any of the initial goals for which the war was fought, they still considered it a victory. They had secured national survival against the world's most formidable military power and could point to the Battle of New Orleans with justifiable pride.

The War of 1812 also proved to be a pivotal experience in American history. First, the conflict entirely discredited Jefferson's plan for an agricultural nation that would exchange raw materials for European manufactures. Americans now meant to steer clear of entanglement in European affairs and tried to become more self-sufficient. Pioneering developments in American manufacturing during the embargo of 1808 helped make this course possible. The pace of industrialization quickened considerably during the war. In the years to come, factories in New England and elsewhere would supply more and more of America's consumer goods. Industrial areas in turn offered an enlarging market for the nation's harvests. In an economic sense, the War of 1812 truly was a second war for independence.

Second, relations between the United States and the Indian nations changed profoundly. When Harrison's soldiers burned Prophetstown and later killed Tecumseh, they wiped out all hopes for a pan-Indian confederacy. Jackson's victories against the Red Sticks destroyed the power of the Creeks and the other southern tribes. As a result, no serious Indian resistance occurred for decades. During that time, white settlers occupied most of the eastern half of the continent.

Third, the failure to take Canada and its water routes convinced Americans that they had to improve inland transportation. British control of the Great Lakes had demonstrated how poor American transportation was. The lack of roads and the resulting shortage of men and equipment in the interior had ruled out any significant American vic-

Treaty of Ghent Treaty ending the War of 1812, signed in Belgium in 1814; it restored peace but was silent on the issues over which the United States and Britain had clashed.

tories on the Canadian front. In the following decades, Americans built canals, national roads, and other transportation links to tie the expanding West to the rest of the nation.

Finally, the war's conclusion helped bring an end to political factionalism. As the war dragged on, the Essex Junto grew in strength. From mid-December 1814 until January 5, 1815, New England Federalists met in Hartford, Connecticut. At the Hartford Convention, party members finally went public with their threat to secede. If Madison did not repeal the Embargo of 1813 and submit constitutional amendments that protected New England's minority rights, New England was ready to leave the Union. News of the Treaty of Ghent and the Battle of New Orleans, however, made the Federalists appear to be traitors. Madison and the Republicans were able to drive their political opponents into retreat. The Federalists managed to hold on in hard-core areas of New England until the 1820s, but the party as a whole was on a steepening decline. They vanished altogether in 1825.

Thus, after 1815, a new surge of hopefulness and national pride engulfed Americans. The United States had fought the greatest military power in the world to a standstill and in the process had launched new ventures in manufacturing, swept away Indian resistance, and restored political unity.

SUMMARY

Expectations
Constraints
Choices
Outcomes

Many Americans *expected* a political revolution when Jefferson and the Republicans triumphed in the 1800 election. In the waning days of the Adams administration, however, the Federalists erected a formidable *constraint* against the Republicans by filling the federal courts with their appointees. As Alexander Hamilton *expected*, Jefferson also *chose* to be much more moderate in his actions while in office than his former radical rhetoric had led many to believe.

The *outcome* of the first transfer of power from one political party to another was a redirection of government, not a revolution. Jefferson did have the much-despised excise taxes repealed, and he did pare down the expenses of government. He also cherished the *expectation* that he had secured the future for America's yeoman farmers when he authorized the Louisiana Purchase and doubled the size of the nation.

Jefferson and his Republican successor, James Madison, faced increasingly difficult diplomatic *constraints* after 1803 when renewed warfare broke out between Great Britain and France. Both chose to steer a neutral course and to avoid becoming entangled in a war with either European power. The War Hawks, however, regarded British violations of American neutrality and British incitement of the Indians living in the Northwest as insults to the national honor. The *outcome* was the War of 1812.

Although there were moments of glory for the Americans, the war was mostly a disaster. The Americans were fortunate that a war-weary British public chose peace in 1814. The Treaty of Ghent restored diplomatic relations to what they had been before 1812. Nevertheless, news of peace and of Andrew Jackson's stunning victory at New Orleans produced an unlikely *outcome*—a surge of national pride, confidence, and unity.

SUGGESTED READINGS

Edmunds, R. David. *The Shawnee Prophet* (1983); *Tecumseh and the Quest for Indian Leadership* (1984).

Each of these biographies is a masterpiece. They present the most complete recounting of the lives and accomplishments of these two fascinating brothers and their historical world.

Hickey, Donald. *The War of 1812: A Forgotten Conflict* (1989).

Arguably the best single-volume history of the war; encyclopedic in content but so colorfully written that it will hold anyone's attention.

Hofstadter, Richard. *The Idea of a Party System* (1969).

The classic account of the rise of legitimate opposition in the American party system.

McCoy, Drew. *The Last of the Fathers; James Madison and the Republican Legacy* (1989).

Hailed by most critics as the best book on Madison and his role in making the early republic.

McCoy, Drew. *The Elusive Republic* (1980).

The best summary of Jefferson's agrarian vision; engagingly written and forcefully argued.

Miller, John C. *The Wolf by the Ears: Thomas Jefferson and Slavery* (1977).

A master historian confronts the dichotomy between Jefferson's attitudes about race and the actuality of slavery.

Ronda, James. *Lewis and Clark Among the Indians* (1984).

A bold retelling of the expedition's story, showcasing the Indian role in both Lewis and Clark's journey and the nation's successful expansion into Louisiana.

Sheehan, Bernard W. *Seeds of Extinction: Jeffersonian Philanthropy and the American Indian* (1973).

An evaluation of Jefferson's attitudes toward Indians and his Indian policy, beautifully written by one of the nation's best Indian policy historians.

Stagg, J. C. A. *Mr. Madison's War: Politics, Diplomacy, and Warfare in the Early American Republic, 1783–1830* (1983).

An excellent view of the politics and diplomacy surrounding the War of 1812.

CANADA
OREGON COUNTRY
LOUISIANA TERRITORY
NEW SPAIN
ALTA CALIFORNIA
BAJA CALIFORNIA
MICHIGAN TERR.
ILLINOIS TERR.
INDIANA TERR.
MISSISSIPPI TERR.
ORLEANS TERR.
SPANISH FLORIDA
PACIFIC OCEAN
ATLANTIC OCEAN
Gulf of Mexico
San Francisco Bay
Tampa Bay
Ft. La Reine
Ft. Charles
Ft. St. Pierre
Ft. Kaministiquia
Mandan Villages
Arikara Villages
St. François Xavier
Ft. Pontchartrain (Detroit)
Ft. St. Joseph
Ft. St. Louis
Ft. Crèvecoeur
Ft. Miami
Ft. Orléans
Pawnee Village
Cahokia
St. Louis
Independence
Ft. Massiac
Chillicothe
Shawnee Village
Cumberland Gap
Nashville
Arkansas Post
Comanche Village
Caddodachos
Ft. Toulouse
Natchez
Nacogdoches
Natchitoches
New Orleans
Pensacola
St. Augustine
San Antonio
La Bahia
Laredo
San Juan Baptista
Mier
Reinosa
Serralvo
Matamoros
Queretaro
Mexico City
Veracruz
Chihuahua
El Paso
Santa Fe
Albuquerque
Taos
Oraibi
Zuñi
Acoma
Casa Grande (ruins)
Tubac
Mojave Villages
Yuma Villages
San Francisco
Monterey
Santa Barbara
San Gabriel
Los Angeles
San Diego
Loreto
Montreal
Frontenac
Ft. Niagara
Ft. Sandusky
Portland
Boston
Worcester
Providence
Albany
New York
Pittsburgh
Philadelphia
Lancaster
Baltimore
Washington
Staunton
Richmond
Williamsburg
Raleigh
Charlotte
Wilmington
Charleston
Savannah
Apalachicola Fort
Mississippi
Missouri
Platte
Arkansas
Red
Ohio
Tennessee
Colorado
Rio Grande
St. Lawrence
OLD SPANISH TRAIL
SANTA FE TRAIL
MISSION TRAIL
CHIHUAHUA TRAIL
MAIN POST ROAD
MOHAWK TRAIL
GREAT GENESEE ROAD
BOSTON POST ROAD
GREAT TRAIL
SCIOTO TRAIL
LANE'S TRACE
FORBES ROAD
CUMBERLAND ROAD
BRADDOCK'S ROAD
GREAT VALLEY ROAD
WARRIOR'S PATH
GREAT TRADING PATH
WILDERNESS ROAD
AVERY'S TRACE
WESTERN ROAD
NICKAJACK TRAIL
CHARLESTON PATH
VIRGINIA ROAD
CAPE FEAR ROAD
POST ROAD
TRADER'S PATH
CHICKASAW TRACE
NATCHEZ TRACE
SURVEYED TRAIL
Inland waterways
Roads
Trails
Towns, camps, and missions
Forts
Indian villages
States
Territories
0 200 400 Km.
0 200 400 Mi.

TRANSPORTATION IN AMERICA As this map shows, before 1820 roads and trails crisscrossed the United States. However, most of the roads shown here were little more than dirt tracks, with no bridges and few accommodations for travelers. It was impossible to ship large loads of goods along such roads, limiting economic expansion.

- 1813 — First mechanized textile factory
- 1819 — Panic of 1819
- 1820 — Missouri Compromise
- 1823 — Monroe Doctrine
- 1828 — Jackson elected
- 1832 — Bank War; Nullification crisis; Jackson reelected
- 1838 — Trail of Tears

1450 1500 1550 1600 1650 1700 1750 1800 1850 1900 1950 2000

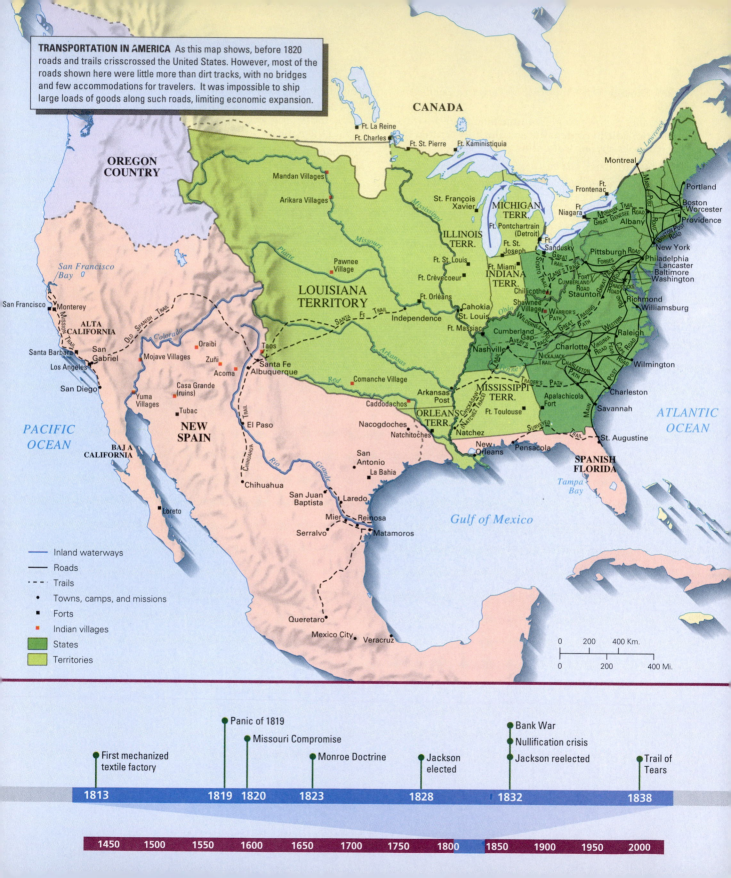

CHAPTER 9

The Rise of a New Nation, 1815–1836

The Emergence of New Expectations

- How did the end of the War of 1812 foster new expectations for Americans?
- What choices did each region make to realize those expectations?

Politics and Diplomacy in an "Era of Good Feelings"

- What choices did the Republicans make to help create a market economy?
- How did new expectations influence American diplomacy?

Dynamic Growth and Political Consequences

- How did expectations of economic prosperity lead to a financial panic in 1819?
- How did economic issues contribute to choices that led to sectional conflict and political contention?

The "New Man" in Politics

- What factors helped change Americans' political expectations during the 1820s?
- How did the election of Andrew Jackson in 1828 reflect those new expectations?

The Presidency of Andrew Jackson

- Analyze the choices Andrew Jackson made in his Indian policy.
- What constraints influenced the regional divisions reflected in the nullification crisis and the Bank War?

INTRODUCTION

Expectations
Constraints
Choices
Outcomes

The United States emerged from the War of 1812 with new confidence. "The veterans of Wellington attest the prowess of our troops," one Protestant preacher declared at war's end, "and the world is astonished at the facility with which our naval heroes have conquered . . . those who have conquered all other nations." The United States had finally become a nation to be reckoned with, and nationalism emerged as the dominant force in domestic and international affairs.

Confident *expectations* for national development led to *choices* that would greatly influence the country's future. Both James Madison and his successor, James Monroe, sought to develop a national market economy. Nationalists like Henry Clay and John C. Calhoun steered bills through Congress designed to strengthen the nation's currency and encourage economic development. Others, like John Quincy Adams and Andrew Jackson, expanded the boundaries of the nation itself.

Expanding economic opportunities created optimistic business and financial *expectations.* Initial *constraints* were brushed aside as a confident generation developed new technologies and organizational innovations. The entire country felt the pressure to modernize. Paradoxically, the *outcome* of efforts to promote economic interdependence was a regional economic specialization that bred sectional cultures and conflict.

Politics also underwent a profound change after the War of 1812. The old generation of Revolutionary statesmen was dying out and being replaced by a new, restless generation of politicians. This younger generation called for freer access to government, even for those who owned no property. General Andrew Jackson became their champion. Sweeping from the backwoods of Tennessee into the White House, Jackson brought a new kind of politics onto the national scene. Assuming greater presidential powers than even Alexander Hamilton had imagined, Jackson placed his own personal stamp on the era and the nation.

The Emergence of New Expectations

The War of 1812 imposed some severe restrictions on the American economy and revealed the shortcomings of that economy. Consequently, the war did much to change Americans' thinking about economic matters. For example, the war exposed the liabilities of relying on other countries to produce manufactured goods. Thomas Jefferson's vision of a nation of yeoman farmers trading for foreign manufacturers died with the war.

The war also accelerated economic trends already under way in the nation's regions. The disruption of trade in New England, for example, prompted an extensive redirection of investment from shipping into textile factories and other enterprises. The economic boom that immediately followed the war reinforced trends toward regional economic specialization.

New Expectations in the Northeastern Economy

Although trading interests in the Northeast suffered during Jefferson's embargo and were nearly ruined by the war, a new avenue of economic expansion opened in New England. Cut off from European manufactured goods, Americans started to make more textiles and other items for themselves.

Samuel Slater, an English immigrant, had introduced the use of machines for spinning cotton

CHRONOLOGY

New Optimism and a New Democracy

1794	Eli Whitney patents the cotton gin
1814	Treaty of Ghent ends War of 1812
1816	Tariff of 1816 James Monroe elected president
1817	Second Bank of the United States opens for business Rush-Bagot Agreement
1818	Convention of 1818 Andrew Jackson invades Spanish Florida
1819	Adams-Onís Treaty Missouri applies for statehood Panic of 1819
1820	Monroe re-elected Missouri Compromise
1823	Monroe Doctrine
1825	House of Representatives elects John Quincy Adams president Prairie du Chien treaties
1826	Disappearance of William Morgan; beginning of Antimasonry
1827	Ratification of Cherokee constitution
1828	Tariff of Abominations Publication of *The South Carolina Exposition and Protest* Andrew Jackson elected president
1830	Webster-Hayne debate Indian Removal Act
1831	*Cherokee Nation v. Georgia*
1832	*Worcester v. Georgia* Bank War Nullification crisis Jackson re-elected
1836–1838	Federal removal of Creeks, Chickasaws, and Cherokees

thread to the United States in 1790. Although Slater's mill was successful, it was not widely emulated. British cloth was inexpensive, and the risks of manufacturing were high. The Embargo of 1807 suddenly made British cloth very expensive and the risks more acceptable. The number of American textile mills jumped from 15 in 1807 to 102 in 1809.

It was Francis Cabot Lowell, however, who revolutionized the American textile industry by combining all the processes of converting raw cotton into finished cloth under one roof. Lowell then mechanized every stage in the production process at the Boston Manufacturing Company, organized in 1813.

Thanks in part to Lowell's inventiveness and in part to the unavailability of British goods, textile manufacturing spread even more rapidly during the War of 1812. By 1816, perhaps as many as one hundred thousand people worked in the industry. In the years to come, factories in New England and elsewhere supplied more and more of the nation's consumer goods. In the process, they changed the economic roles and hopes of many Americans.

The Emergence of the Old South

Before the War of 1812, the southern economy had been sluggish and the future of the region's single-crop agricultural system doubtful. Tobacco was no longer the glorious profit maker it had been during the colonial period. Sea Island cotton, rice, sugar, and other products continued to find markets,

♦ Before the transportation revolution, traveling was highly risky and uncomfortable. This painting by Russian traveler Pavel Svinin shows a rather stylish stagecoach, but its well-dressed passengers are clearly being jostled. Note how the man in the front seat is bracing himself, while the man behind him has lost his hat under the wheels. *"Travel by Stagecoach Near Trenton, NJ" by Pavel Svinin. The Metropolitan Museum of Art, Rogers Fund, 1942, (42.95.11).*

but they could be grown only in limited areas. Now, though, postwar technological and economic changes pumped new energy into the South's economy. In only a few decades, an entirely new South emerged, one that became known to history as the Old South.

Although southern planters had grown cotton since colonial times, the demand for it was small until the **mechanization** of the British textile industry in the 1780s. The production of cotton cloth rapidly increased, and the need for raw cotton fiber grew.

Planters along the Carolina coast had responded by growing long-staple, or Sea Island, cotton for the British market. This variety could be grown only in warm, wet, semitropical climates like that of the Carolina Sea Islands. Short-staple cotton could be grown throughout much of the South, but the difficulty of separating the sticky seeds from the fibers made it unprofitable. A worldwide shortage of cotton threatened Britain's textile industry.

Eli Whitney, a 1792 graduate of Yale College, found a solution. In 1793, while a guest at a Georgia plantation, he learned about the difficulty of removing the seeds from short-staple cotton. In a matter of weeks, Whitney designed a machine that quickly combed out the seeds without damaging the fibers. He obtained a **patent** for the cotton gin (short for "engine") in 1794.

Whitney's inventiveness allowed short-staple cotton to spread rapidly throughout inland South Carolina and Georgia. With the arrival of peace and the end of the British blockade, cotton spread westward rapidly into land once fiercely defended by the Red Stick Creeks (see page 173), into Alabama and Mississippi, and later into Arkansas, northern Louisiana, and east Texas. Between 1790 and 1840, the South's annual cotton crop grew from about 3,000 bales to nearly 1.5 million bales.

Most of the South's cotton was initially exported to Britain, but a significant and growing amount went to New England's textile factories (see pages 211–215). Cotton from the South thus helped spur industrialization in the North. Northern demand in turn encouraged southern suppliers to plant more cotton. This dynamic interaction between North and South pushed their regional economies in dif-

mechanization The substitution of machinery for hand labor.

Eli Whitney American inventor and manufacturer; his cotton gin revolutionized the cotton industry.

patent A government grant that gives the creator of an invention the sole right to produce, use, or sell that invention for a set period of time.

ferent directions. Although both remained predominantly rural, the North moved toward mechanization and urbanization, and the South depended more and more on the labor of people rather than on the power of machines. These transformations are discussed in detail in Chapter 10.

New Opportunities in the West

Cotton growers were not the only people who saw new opportunities in the West after the war. Many Americans rushed to the frontier to seek their fortunes.

One of the most important outcomes of the War of 1812 was the change brought about between the United States and various Indian nations. When William Henry Harrison's soldiers burned Prophetstown and killed Tecumesh (see page 169), they wiped out any hope for a pan-Indian confederacy. Furthermore, Jackson's decisive victory against the Red Stick Creeks removed all meaningful resistance to westward expansion in the South. The Creeks were forced to sell 20 million acres of their land.

A similar but more gradual assault on Indian land began in the Northwest in 1815. Although the United States signed peace accords with tribes that had sided with the British during the war, national policy was directed at wresting lands east of the Mississippi from tribes such as the Kickapoos, Sauks, Foxes, Chippewas, and Dakotas. The Prairie du Chien treaties of 1825 secured an enormous cession of land from them. Pioneer farmers subsequently came pouring into the Northwest. The population of Ohio more than doubled between 1810 and 1820. Indiana, Illinois, and Michigan experienced similar growth.

The war also opened up the interior of the continent to American fur traders. Even before the war, John Jacob Astor, a German immigrant, had attempted to establish a series of trading posts along the route followed by Lewis and Clark. The key to Astor's vision of a fur empire was an outpost at the mouth of the Columbia River, from which he intended to ship furs directly across the Pacific to Asia. Although the British seized Astor's outpost during the war, this proved to be only a temporary setback. After the war, Astor expanded his fur business and Asian trade to become a leading figure in world commerce. When he died in 1848, he was the richest man in the United States.

August Chouteau, a French frontiersman, played a similar role in organizing the fur trade in the Southwest. Changing nationality as circumstances demanded, he and his brother employed an extensive kinship network that included French, Spanish, and Indian connections to collect furs. Chouteau's trading network reached deep into the Missouri region and as far as Spanish Santa Fe. After the war, Chouteau branched into other businesses, including banking, flour milling, distilling, and real estate.

The examples set by Astor and Chouteau proved to many that great fortunes were to be made on the frontier. Although the promise was almost always greater than the reality, the allure of the West was unmistakable. After the War of 1812, the nation's aspirations became more firmly tied to that region's growth and development.

Politics and Diplomacy in an "Era of Good Feelings"

The nationalism that arose after the War of 1812 caused the Federalists to be seen as traitors or fools, and they disappeared from politics. For the first time since Washington's administration, the air was free of party politics, prompting a Boston newspaper to proclaim the dawn of an **Era of Good Feelings.**

The "American System" and New Economic Direction

The nationalism that characterized the Era of Good Feelings was evident in the Republican economic plan, which Henry Clay called the

Era of Good Feelings The period from 1816 to 1823 when the decline of the Federalist party and the end of the War of 1812 gave rise to a time of political cooperation.

American System. The American System depended on three essential developments. First, a national bank was needed to promote the country's economic growth. Although Republicans had opposed Alexander Hamilton's Bank of the United States, they came to appreciate the need for a national bank after the difficulties of financing the recent war. In 1816, the overwhelmingly Republican Congress chartered the Second Bank of the United States for twenty years. The Second Bank, which opened in Philadelphia in 1817, had many of the same powers and responsibilities as Hamilton's bank. Congress provided $7 million of its initial $35 million capital and appointed one-fifth of its board of directors.

Second, the war had shown that improvements in communication and transportation were needed. Poor lines of supply and communication had spelled disaster for American military efforts. Congress approved legislation to finance a national transportation program that would include building roads and canals.

Finally, Republicans advocated **protective tariffs** to help the fledgling industries that had hatched during the war. Incubated by trade restrictions, American cotton-spinning plants had mushroomed between 1808 and 1815. But with the reopening of trade at war's end, British merchants dumped accumulated inventories of cotton cloth below cost, hampering further American development. Although most southerners and westerners remained leery of tariffs, Clay and Calhoun were able to gain enough support to pass the Tariff of 1816.

The American System was designed to create a national **market economy.** Since colonial times, local market economies had existed in the trading centers of the Northeast. Individuals in these areas produced items for cash sale and used the cash they earned to purchase goods produced by others. Economic specialization was the natural outcome. Farmers, for example, chose to grow only one or two crops and sell the whole harvest for cash, which they used to buy goods that they had once grown or made for themselves.

But outside such commercial centers, people generally **bartered** goods and labor. Families tried to make or grow as much of what they needed as they could and exchanged some surplus goods for sugar, tea, metal goods, and other items they could not produce. Little cash changed hands in this economic world.

Advocates of the American System envisioned a time when whole regions would specialize in producing commodities for which they were most suited. Agricultural regions in the West, for example, would produce food for the industrializing Northeast and the fiber-producing South. The North would depend on the South for cotton, and both the South and the West would look to the Northeast for manufactured goods. Improved transportation systems would make this flow of goods possible, and a strong national currency would ensure orderly trade. Advocates of the American System were confident that regional specialization would free the nation from economic dependence on manufacturing centers in Europe.

The popularity of Madison's programs was apparent in the 1816 election. His handpicked successor, fellow Virginian James Monroe, won 184 electoral votes to Federalist Rufus King's 34. Republicans swept over three-fourths of the seats in both the House of Representatives and the Senate.

James Monroe and the Nationalist Agenda

Monroe's first diplomatic goal was to solve important issues not settled by the Treaty of Ghent, which ended the War of 1812. He assigned this task to Secretary of State John Quincy Adams. Adams first helped establish peaceful borders with British Canada. In the 1817 Rush-Bagot Agreement, both

American System An economic plan sponsored by nationalists in Congress; it was intended to spur U.S. economic growth and the domestic production of goods previously bought from foreign manufacturers.

protective tariff Tax on imported goods intended to make them more expensive than similar domestic goods and thus to protect domestic producers.

market economy An economic system based on the buying and selling of goods and services, with money as the primary medium of exchange and the forces of supply and demand setting prices.

barter To trade goods or services without the exchange of money.

nations agreed to cut back their Great Lakes naval fleets to a few vessels. A year later, the two nations drew up the Convention of 1818. The British agreed to honor American fishing rights in the Atlantic, to recognize a boundary between the Louisiana Territory and Canada at the 49th parallel, and to occupy the Oregon Territory jointly with the United States.

With these northern border issues settled, Adams set his sights on defining the nation's southern and southwestern frontiers. Conditions in Spanish Florida had been extremely unsettled since Napoleon had deposed the king of Spain in 1808. Pirates, runaway slaves, and Indians used Florida as a base for launching raids against American settlements and shipping. By December 1817, matters in Florida seemed critical. General Andrew Jackson urged the president to take possession of Spanish Florida by invading it.

A short time later, Secretary of War John C. Calhoun ordered Jackson and his troops to patrol Georgia's border with Spanish territory. Claiming that he had received secret authorization from Monroe, Jackson crossed into Spanish territory, where his troops brutally destroyed peaceful Seminole villages. He then invaded the Spanish capital at Pensacola on May 24, 1818, forcing the governor to flee to Cuba. The zealous general capped his already reckless venture by executing two British citizens for conspiring with the Indians.

In response to Spanish and British protests, Calhoun and others recommended privately that the general be severely disciplined. Adams, however, saw Jackson's raid as an opportunity to settle the Florida border issue. Jackson's raid, he claimed, was an act of self-defense, and he warned that it would be repeated unless Spain could police the area adequately. Fully aware that Spain could not do that, Adams proposed that Spain give up Florida. Understanding his country's precarious position, Spanish minister Don Luis de Onís ceded Florida in the Adams-Onís Treaty of 1819. The United States in return released Spain from $5 million in damage claims resulting from pirate and Indian raids.

The Monroe Doctrine

Spain's declining power posed a more general diplomatic problem. In the early nineteenth century, many of its colonies in Latin America had rebelled and established themselves as independent republics. Fearful that their own colonists might follow this example, Austria, France, Prussia, Russia, and other European powers considered helping Spain reclaim its overseas empire.

Neither Great Britain nor the United States wanted European intervention in the Western Hemisphere. The British had developed a thriving trade with the new Latin American republics. Americans supported Latin American independence for various reasons. Some hoped the new countries would follow in America's footsteps and move toward greater democracy. Others favored an independent Latin America as a fertile ground for American expansion.

In 1823, British foreign minister George Canning proposed that the United States and Britain form an alliance to end European meddling in Latin America. Most of Monroe's cabinet supported this proposal, but Adams, who disliked the British intensely, protested that America would be reduced to a "cock-boat in the wake of the British man-of-war." In other words, Adams feared that the United States would always be following the British lead. Instead, he suggested that the United States should act **unilaterally** in declaring the Western Hemisphere off-limits to "future colonization by any European power."

Monroe ultimately supported Adams's position. In December 1823, he announced that the United States would regard any effort by European countries "to extend their system to any portion of this hemisphere as dangerous to our peace and safety." European intervention in the hemisphere would be seen as an act of war against the United States.

The **Monroe Doctrine,** as this statement was later called, announced the arrival of the United States on the international scene as a nation to be

unilateral Undertaken or issued by only one side and thus not involving an agreement made with others.

Monroe Doctrine President Monroe's 1823 statement declaring the Americas closed to further European colonization and discouraging European interference in the affairs of the Western Hemisphere.

contended with. Both Europeans and Latin Americans, however, thought it was a meaningless statement. Despite proud assertions, the policy depended on the British navy and on Britain's informal commitment to New World autonomy.

Dynamic Growth and Political Consequences

During the **Napoleonic wars,** massive armies had drained Europe's manpower, laid waste to crops, and tied up ships, making European nations dependent on America. Although those wars ended in 1815, a war-torn Europe continued to need American food and manufactures. Encouraged by a ready European market and easy credit, southern planters, northern manufacturers, and western farmers embarked on a frenzy of speculation. They rushed to borrow money to buy equipment, land, and slaves for what they were sure was a golden future.

Entrepreneurs in the North, West, and South, however, had different ideas about the best course for the American economy. As the American System drew the regions together into increasing mutual dependency, the tensions among them began to swell. As long as economic conditions remained good, there was little reason for conflict, but when the speculative boom collapsed, sectional tensions increased dramatically.

The Panic of 1819

Developments in Europe undermined the foundations of postwar American prosperity. When Europe began to recover several years after the Napoleonic wars, its demand for American products, particularly foodstuffs, dropped rapidly. The bottom fell out of the international market that had fueled land speculation in the United States.

Congress tried to head off disaster by tightening credit. In 1817, it stopped **installment** payments on new land purchases and demanded that land be paid for in hard currency. The Second Bank of the United States in 1818 tightened credit further by demanding immediate repayment of loans in either gold or silver. State banks and land speculators followed suit. Instead of curing the problem, however, tightening credit and recalling loans burst the speculative balloon, creating the **Panic of 1819.**

Six years of economic depression followed. As prices declined, individual farmers and manufacturers, unable to repay loans for land and equipment, faced **repossession** and imprisonment for debt. Bankruptcy sales were a daily occurrence. Factories fell idle, and the ranks of the unemployed grew steadily. The number of paupers in New York more than doubled between 1819 and 1820.

Although the financial panic was the result of Americans' own reckless speculation, they tended to point the finger of blame elsewhere. Many blamed the national bank and called for the destruction of this "Monster Bank." Some understood that controlling credit was the only way to prevent similar crises, but the Second Bank's critics prevented any meaningful financial reforms.

Economic Woes and Political Sectionalism

The Panic of 1819 drove a wedge between the nation's geographical sections. The depression touched each region differently, and for several years the halls of Congress rang with debates rooted in sectional economic needs.

The issue that pitted section against section more violently than any other was protective tariffs. Before 1816, the tariffs enacted by Congress were designed to produce tax revenue. The goal of President Madison's **Tariff of 1816,** however, was

Napoleonic wars Wars in Europe waged by or against Napoleon between 1803 and 1815.

installment Partial payment of a debt to be made at regular intervals until the entire debt is repaid.

Panic of 1819 A financial panic that began when the Second Bank of the United States tightened credit and recalled government loans.

repossession The reclaiming of land or goods by the seller after the purchaser fails to pay installments due.

Tariff of 1816 First protective tariff in U.S. history; its purpose was to protect America's fledgling textile industry.

the protection of American industry. As the Panic of 1819 spread economic devastation throughout the country, the coal, iron, and textile industries began clamoring for more protection against foreign competition.

Farmers were split on the issue. Small farmers favored a free market that would keep the price of manufactures low. By contrast, commercial farmers who specialized in cash crops such as wheat and wool joined industrialists, factory managers, and industrial workers in supporting protection against the foreign dumping of such products. Southern cotton and tobacco farmers did not favor protection.

After supporting the Tariff of 1816, John C. Calhoun and other southerners became firm opponents of tariffs. Cotton growing had slowed the development of industry in the South, so protection offered small benefit to southerners. Also, Britain, not the United States, was the South's main supplier of manufactured goods and its primary market for raw cotton. Protective tariffs raised the price of the former and might cause Britain to enact a tariff on southern cotton. If that happened, southerners would pay more for manufactures but receive less for cotton.

In 1820, northern congressmen proposed a major increase in the tariff. Small farmers in the West and cotton growers defeated the measure. Northerners then wooed western congressmen by supporting bills favorable to westerners. These bills lowered the minimum price of public land from $2 to $1.25 per acre and authorized the extension of the national road into the West. Western congressmen reciprocated in 1824 by favoring a greatly increased tariff.

The Missouri Compromise

As all three regions sought solutions to the nation's economic woes, the regional balance of power in Congress became a matter of crucial importance. The delicate balance began to tip when the Missouri Territory applied for statehood in 1819. New York congressman James Tallmadge, Jr., provoked the crisis when he proposed that no new slaves be taken into Missouri and that those already in the territory be emancipated gradually. His amendment generated a moral and political debate that nearly led to national collapse.

The political issue in the Missouri controversy was straightforward. If Missouri was admitted as a slave state, its congressional **bloc** would undoubtedly support the southern position on tariffs and other key issues. But if Missouri was admitted as a free state, its congressmen would be inclined to support the position taken by representatives from the Old Northwest.

Both sides in the debate about Missouri were deeply entrenched. In 1820, Henry Clay suggested a compromise. He proposed that Missouri be admitted as a slave state and that Maine, which had separated from Massachusetts in 1819, be admitted as a free state. Clay also proposed that slavery be banned in the rest of the Louisiana Territory above 36°30′ north latitude, the line that formed Missouri's southern border (see Map 9.1). Congress approved the **Missouri Compromise,** and the issue of slavery in the territories quieted down for a while.

New Politics and the End of Good Feelings

Conducted in the midst of the Missouri crisis, the presidential election of 1820 went as smoothly as could be expected. Monroe faced no meaningful political opposition. The people's faith in Jefferson's party and his handpicked successors remained firm. As the election of 1824 approached, however, it became clear that the Panic of 1819 and the Missouri crisis had broken Republican unity.

In 1824, the southern-dominated Republican caucus named Georgia states' rights advocate William Crawford as its presidential candidate. As nationalists, Henry Clay and John Quincy Adams were so disappointed with this selection that each defied party discipline by deciding to run without the approval of the caucus. The Tennessee legislature then named its own candidate, Andrew Jackson.

bloc A group of people united for common action.

Missouri Compromise Law proposed by Henry Clay in 1820 admitting Missouri to the Union as a slave state and Maine as a free state and banning slavery in the Louisiana Territory north of latitude 36°30′.

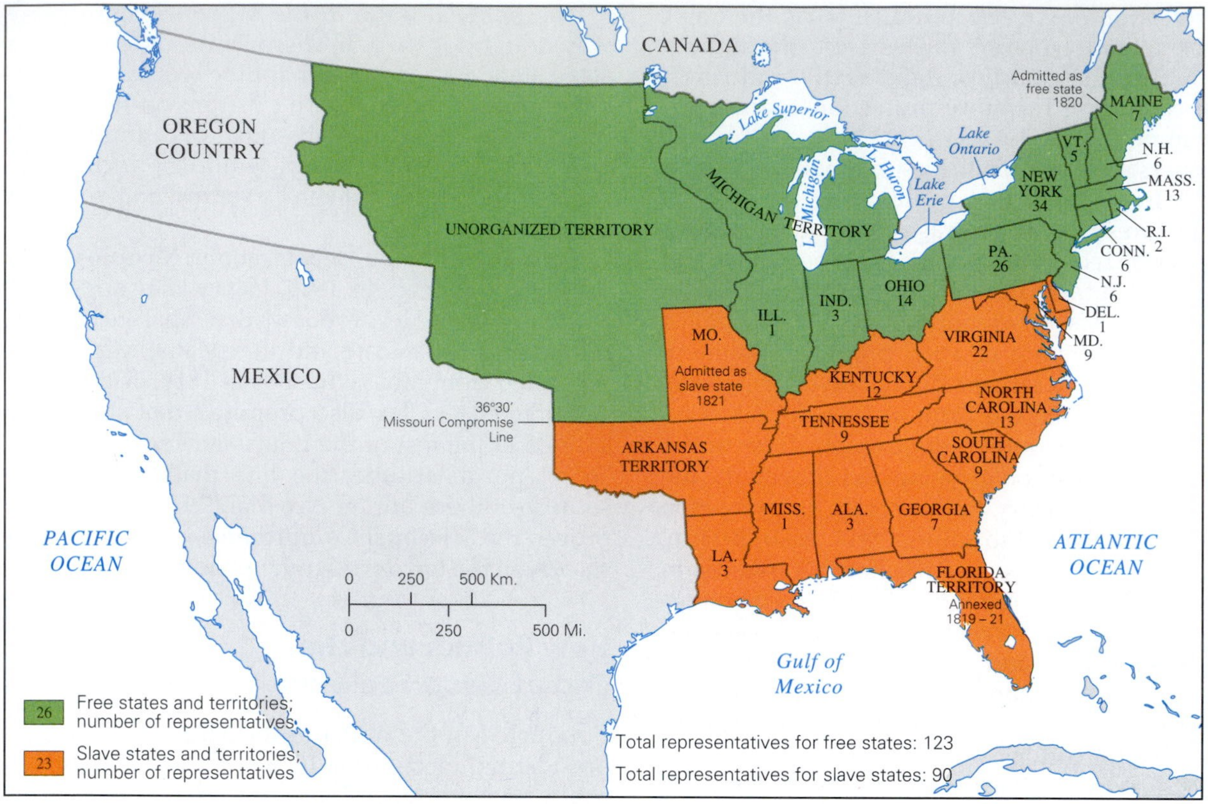

♦ **MAP 9.1 Missouri Compromise and Representative Strength** The Missouri Compromise fixed the boundary between free and slave territories at 36°30′. This map shows the results in both geographical and political terms. While each section emerged from the compromise with the same number of senators (twenty-four), the balance in the House of Representatives and Electoral College tilted toward the North.

The 1824 election brought home how deeply divided the nation had become. Northern political leaders rallied behind Adams, southerners supported Crawford, and northwestern commercial farmers and other supporters of the American System lined up behind Clay. Many independent yeoman farmers, traditional craftsmen, and immigrants supported Jackson.

The Tennessean said little during the campaign, but his reputation as the hero of the Battle of New Orleans spoke louder than words. Jackson won the most popular votes, capturing 153,544 to Adams's 108,740, Clay's 47,136, and Crawford's 46,618. Jackson also received more electoral votes than any other candidate, but he did not have the majority needed to win the election. The Constitution specifies that in such cases a list of the top three vote getters be passed to the House of Representatives for a final decision.

By the time the House convened to settle the election, Crawford had suffered a disabling stroke and was no longer a contender. Clay's name was not put before the House because he had finished fourth. As Speaker of the House, however, he had considerable influence over the outcome of the election. Backers of both candidates asked him for support. Seeing himself as the leading spokesman for western interests, Clay viewed Jackson as a rival rather than a kindred spirit. Although Clay had no great love for the New Englander either, their views on tariffs, manufacturing, and foreign affairs were quite compatible. Clay therefore threw his support to Adams, who won the House election and in 1825 became the nation's sixth president.

Adams subsequently named Clay as his secretary of state, the position that had been the springboard to the presidency for every past Republican who had held it. Although Adams had done nothing illegal, Jacksonians accused him of having made a "corrupt bargain" with Clay, whom they dubbed the "Judas of the West." In anger and disgust, Jackson supporters withdrew from the party of Jefferson, bringing an end to the Era of Good Feelings.

The "New Man" in Politics

Since Washington's day, Americans had expected their presidents to be gentlemen. The social changes unleashed after the War of 1812, however, altered those expectations. New voters with radically varying political and economic views began making political demands. Many felt isolated from a political system that permitted the presidency to pass from one propertied gentleman to another. Clearly, changing times called for political change.

Adams's Troubled Administration

John Quincy Adams may have been the best prepared man ever to assume the office of president. The son of a former president, he had been a diplomat, a U.S. senator, a Harvard professor, and an exceptionally effective secretary of state. But he was singularly lacking in the personal warmth and political skill that might have made him a successful chief executive.

Rigidly idealistic, the new president believed himself to be above partisan politics. Apart from his appointment of Henry Clay as secretary of state, he refused to distribute political favors, and so he had few political followers. Adams was thereby exposed to the constant sniping of his critics, and his administration floundered.

Adams's policies also alienated many. He proposed increased tariffs to protect American manufacturers and wanted the Second Bank of the United States to provide ample loans to finance new manufacturing ventures. Southerners opposed these measures because they feared the increase in federal power that Adams's policies implied and because they disliked tariffs.

The **Tariff of Abominations,** passed in 1828, illustrates Adams's difficulties as president. Manufacturers insisted on raising the tariff even higher than Adams had recommended. Some of Adams's opponents also supported the bill so that it would pass and thereby discredit Adams in the fall election. Only southerners universally opposed the proposed legislation.

Democratic Styles and Political Structure

Adams's political style added to his problems. The detached style appropriate in his father's era became a liability in his own. The easy informality of Adams's archrival, Andrew Jackson, was better suited to an increasingly democratic age than Adams's stiff reserve.

Adams's demeanor would not have been so damaging if a huge increase in voter turnout had not framed his presidency. In the election of 1824, 356,038 people cast votes for the presidency. In 1828, over three times that number voted. These numbers reflect the mobilization of a new **electorate.** Voting rights in the early republic had been restricted to landowners. This restriction had raised no controversy earlier because a majority of white Americans owned land. The expansion of a commercial and industrial economy, however, meant that an increasing number of people did not own land and were therefore not entitled to vote. The emerging middle class clamored for suffrage reform. In 1800, only three of the sixteen states had no qualifications for voting. Three other states permitted taxpayers who were not landowners to vote. By 1830, only six of the twenty-four states continued to demand property qualifications. Nine others required tax payment only, and the remaining nine

Tariff of Abominations Tariff passed by Congress in 1828 that outraged the southern states by placing high duties on raw materials.

electorate The portion of the population that is qualified to vote.

had no qualifications. As a result, the number of voters grew enormously and rapidly. The United States was evolving from a republic into a democracy in which all white males could vote.

Changes in the structure of politics accompanied this expansion of the electorate. Among the most important was the popular selection of members of the Electoral College. By 1828, only two states continued to name electors. Another important change was that government jobs that had been appointive became elective. States increasingly dropped property qualifications for officeholding, opening new fields for political participation.

Opportunists quickly took advantage of the new situation. Men like New Yorker **Martin Van Buren** organized political factions into tightly disciplined local and statewide units. A long-time opponent of Governor DeWitt Clinton, Van Buren molded disaffected Republicans into the so-called Bucktail faction. In 1820, the Bucktails' charges that the Clintonians were corrupt and aristocratic swept Clinton out of office. The new politics practiced by the Bucktails had clearly triumphed. This new politics combined political patronage and fiery speeches to draw newly qualified voters into the political process.

These new voters were often frustrated that their voting had little impact. The "corrupt bargain" that had denied the presidency to Andrew Jackson in 1824 was a prime example. Secret, elite societies such as the **Masons** also appeared to thwart the popular will. The most notorious case of Masonic influence concerned William Morgan, a New York bricklayer and Mason who mysteriously disappeared in 1826 after threatening to publish some Masonic secrets. Morgan's presumed murder caused an outcry. When an investigation turned up no clues, many suspected that the Masons had used their political clout to suppress the facts. Within a year, young politicians such as New Yorkers Thurlow Weed and William Seward and Pennsylvanian Thaddeus Stevens had exploited the Morgan case to form a new political organization. Based on the resentments felt by craftsmen, small farmers, and others, the **Antimasonic party** had no platform beyond a disapproval of politics as usual.

New York typified political developments throughout the country. As the party of Jefferson dissolved, a rash of political factions broke out. It was Van Buren who forged an alliance that would fundamentally alter American politics.

The Rise of Andrew Jackson

By 1826, Van Buren had brought together political outsiders and dissidents from all over the country into a new political party, the Democratic-Republicans, or the **Democrats.** The Democrats in some ways looked to the past. They denounced the National Republicans by calling for a return to Jeffersonian simplicity, states' rights, and democratic principles. But they relied on the modern political tactics and organization that Van Buren had perfected in New York. The appeal to Jeffersonian ideals and the use of tight party discipline attracted new voters and political outsiders. In the congressional elections of 1826, Van Buren's coalition gained a majority in the House of Representatives and in the Senate.

Perhaps the key to the Democrats' electoral success was their use of Andrew Jackson's name. Jackson became synonymous with the new party. Thus voters who identified with him identified with the new party. In many ways, Jackson was a perfect reflection of the new voters. He had been born into humble circumstances and had lost his family as a youngster. Jackson epitomized the self-made man who, through sheer will and hard work, had risen far above his modest beginnings. Voters did not begrudge the fact that by the 1820s Jackson had become one of the wealthiest men in Tennessee and owned over two hundred slaves. They admired

Martin Van Buren New York politician known for his skillful handling of party politics; he helped found the Democratic party and later became eighth president of the United States.

Masons An international fraternal organization with many socially and politically prominent members, including a number of U.S. presidents.

Antimasonic party Political party formed in 1827 to capitalize on popular anxiety about the influence of the Masons; it opposed politics as usual without offering any particular substitute.

Democrats Political party that brought Andrew Jackson into office; it harked back to Jeffersonian principles of limited government and drew its support from farmers and small businessmen.

him for his accomplishments and hoped to emulate his example. Despite fame and fortune, Jackson remained a common man with the common touch. He had become a man of substance without becoming a snob. Jackson was also a military hero. His exploits along the southern frontier during the War of 1812, culminating in the Battle of New Orleans, had become legendary (see page 177).

The images of Jackson and Adams, not substantive issues, dominated the election of 1828. Jackson forces accused Adams of diverting public funds to buy personal luxuries, providing the Russian tsar with a young American mistress to win his diplomatic support, and bowing to **special interests** in defining his tariff and land policies. Adams's supporters charged Jackson with being a dueler, an insubordinate military adventurer, and a rustic backwoodsman who had lived with a married woman before she had divorced her first husband.

The charges of corruption were entirely untrue. The charges against Jackson were all too true, but voters saw them as irrelevant. Rather than damaging Jackson's image, such talk made him appear romantic and daring. The Tennessean polled a hundred thousand more popular votes than did the New Englander and won the majority of states, taking every one in the South and the West.

Jackson's inauguration on March 4, 1829, was cause for celebration among his supporters and for contempt among his detractors. A crowd of ten thousand well-wishers packed the capital to witness Jackson take the oath of office. Boisterous supporters then followed him into the presidential mansion, where they climbed over furniture, broke glassware, and generally frolicked. The new president was finally forced to flee the near riot by climbing out a back window. A new spirit was alive in the nation's politics.

The Presidency of Andrew Jackson

Jackson had promised the voters "retrenchment and reform." He gave them retrenchment, but reform was more difficult to manage. Jackson tried to reform (1) Indian affairs, (2) internal improvements and public land policy, (3) the collection of revenue and the enforcement of federal law, and (4) the nation's banking and financial system. The steps that he took to reform the nation nearly tore it apart.

Jackson had courted public support with the implied promise that he would run the nation for the benefit of the people against the manipulations of the privileged. He had pulled together a coalition from all three sections of the nation, but keeping the coalition together was not easy in a time of increasing sectional tension.

Launching Jacksonian Politics

Jackson faced a novel problem in that he suspected he could not trust the ten thousand **civil servants** his Republican predecessors had appointed. Jackson's supporters also claimed that many of these government employees were incompetent and had been retained only because of their political connections. Jackson's solution was to introduce the principle of rotation in office for federal officials. Appointments in his administration, he promised, would last only four years. After that, civil servants would have to return to "making a living as other people do."

Rotation in office was intended to accomplish several goals. First, it would rid the government of entrenched bureaucrats and replace them with honest, publicly minded men. The average citizen, Jackson believed, was fully capable of carrying out public responsibilities. Such duties were "so plain and simple that men of intelligence may readily qualify themselves for their performance." Second, rotation in office opened up many federal jobs. The Jacksonian adage became, "To the victor belong the **spoils.**" The Jacksonian practice of distributing government jobs to loyal party members became known as the spoils system.

special interest A person or organization that attempts to influence legislators to support one particular interest or issue.

civil servants Workers in government administration, excluding the courts, the legislature, and the military; they are usually appointed rather than elected.

spoils Jobs and other rewards for political support.

Patronage appointments extended to the highest levels of government. Jackson selected cabinet members not for their experience but for their political loyalty. The president abandoned his predecessors' practice of holding regular cabinet meetings and of giving cabinet members a vote on major issues. Jackson called virtually no meetings and seldom asked for his cabinet's opinion. Instead, he surrounded himself with an informal network of friends and advisers known as the **Kitchen Cabinet.**

Jackson conducted himself in office unlike any of his predecessors. He raged, pouted, and stormed at those who disagreed with him. Earlier presidents had at least pretended to believe in the equal distribution of power among the three branches of government. Jackson, however, believed that the executive should be supreme because the president was the only member of the government elected by all the people. (This belief conveniently ignored the fact that the Electoral College actually elected the president.) The president was to be the people's advocate in the face of entrenched interests, whether in banks, factories, or the halls of Congress. One sign of his testy relationship with the legislative branch was that he vetoed twelve bills while in office, three more than all his predecessors combined. Through his policies and his style, Jackson changed the presidency profoundly.

Jackson and the Indians

Immediately after the War of 1812, the federal government began pressuring eastern tribes to give up their lands and to resettle west of the Mississippi River. Between 1815 and 1820, a number of smaller northern tribes exchanged their land for reservations west of the Mississippi. During the 1820s, many other tribes, plied with money from the federal government, followed suit. Factions within the tribes, however, often fought to stay on ancestral lands.

The **Five Civilized Tribes**—the Cherokees, Choctaws, Seminoles, Creeks, and Chickasaws—were also pressured to relocate. They were able to resist the lure of money more successfully than their smaller northern neighbors. These more powerful southern tribes numbered nearly seventy-five thousand people and occupied large areas of Georgia, North and South Carolina, Alabama, Mississippi, and Tennessee. Although these tribes had made significant strides in becoming acculturated to European ways, most southern whites saw them merely as obstacles to obtaining rich cotton land.

John Quincy Adams had at least paid lip service to honest dealings with the Indians, and on one occasion he even overturned a fraudulent treaty. Jackson, however, had never been troubled by such niceties. "I have long viewed treaties with the Indians an absurdity not to be reconciled to the principles of our government," he proclaimed in 1817. Indians were subjects of the United States, he said, and there was no point in negotiating treaties with them. His policy was to remove all the eastern Indians west of the Mississippi (see Map 9.2). If persuasion did not accomplish this goal, Jackson advocated the use of force. Congress gave Jackson this authority when it passed the **Indian Removal Act** in 1830.

The case of the Cherokees provides an excellent illustration of the new, more aggressive Indian policy. By 1830, the Cherokees had shown considerable progress in following Jefferson's advice to become as much like white Americans as possible. They had created a formal government with a bicameral legislature and a court system. They ratified their written constitution, modeled on the U.S. Constitution, in 1827. The next year they began publication of a newspaper, the *Cherokee Phoenix,* written in English and in the eighty-six-character Cherokee alphabet invented by tribal member **George Guess (Sequoyah).**

Kitchen Cabinet President Jackson's informal advisers, who helped him shape both national and Democratic party policy.

Five Civilized Tribes Term used by whites to describe the Cherokee, Choctaw, Seminole, Creek, and Chickasaw Indians, many of whom were Europeanized farmers and merchants.

Indian Removal Act Law passed by Congress in 1830 providing for the removal of all Indian tribes east of the Mississippi and the purchase of western lands for their resettlement.

George Guess (Sequoyah) Cherokee silversmith and trader who created an alphabet that made it possible to transcribe the Cherokee language according to the sounds of its syllables.

♦ Andrew Jackson always presented himself as a friend of the Indians, but this satirical drawing captures his attitude that they were as unimportant as dolls. The engraving shown in the upper right corner depicts his approach to Indian resistance: Liberty with her foot on the neck of a conquered enemy. *William L. Clements Library, University of Michigan, Ann Arbor.*

None of these accomplishments won the acceptance of their white neighbors. From the frontiersmen's point of view, Indians were supposed to be dying out, not flourishing. The Georgia legislature responded by **annulling** the Cherokee constitution in 1828 and, when gold was found on Cherokee land in 1829, ordering all tribal lands seized.

Subsequently, Georgia passed a series of laws to make life as difficult as possible for the Cherokees. When Christian missionaries living with the tribe encouraged the Cherokees to seek federal assistance, Georgia passed a law that required teachers among the Indians to obtain state licenses. When Samuel Austin Worcester and Elizar Butler refused to apply for the licenses, a company of Georgia militia invaded the Cherokee country and arrested them.

Two notable lawsuits came out of these arrests. In ***Cherokee Nation v. Georgia*** (1831), the Cherokees claimed that Georgia's enforcement of a state law within Cherokee territory was entirely illegal because they were a sovereign nation. The U.S. Supreme Court refused to hear this case on the grounds that the Cherokee Nation was not sovereign. As American citizens, however, Worcester and Butler did have a standing in federal law. In 1832, Chief Justice John Marshall held that Georgia did not have legitimate power to pass laws regulating Indian behavior or to invade Indian land. The court thus declared that all the laws Georgia had passed to harass the Cherokees were null and void and ordered Georgia to release Worcester and Butler from jail (see Individual Choices: Samuel Austin Worcester, page 200).

The Cherokees' joy was brief. When Jackson heard the verdict in ***Worcester v. Georgia,*** he refused to use federal troops to carry out Marshall's order. Jackson reportedly fumed, "John Marshall has made his decision, now let him enforce it."

Jackson's refusal to act broke the back of tribal unity. Most Cherokees stood fast with their leader, John Ross. But another faction advocated relocation. Federal Indian agents named this faction as the true representative of the tribe and convinced it

annul To declare a law or contract invalid.

Cherokee Nation v. Georgia Supreme Court case (1831) concerning Georgia's annulment of all Cherokee laws; Chief Justice John Marshall ruled that Indian tribes did not have the right to appeal to the Supreme Court.

Worcester v. Georgia Supreme Court case (1832) concerning the arrest of two missionaries living among the Cherokees in Georgia; the Court found that Georgia had no right to rule in Cherokee territory.

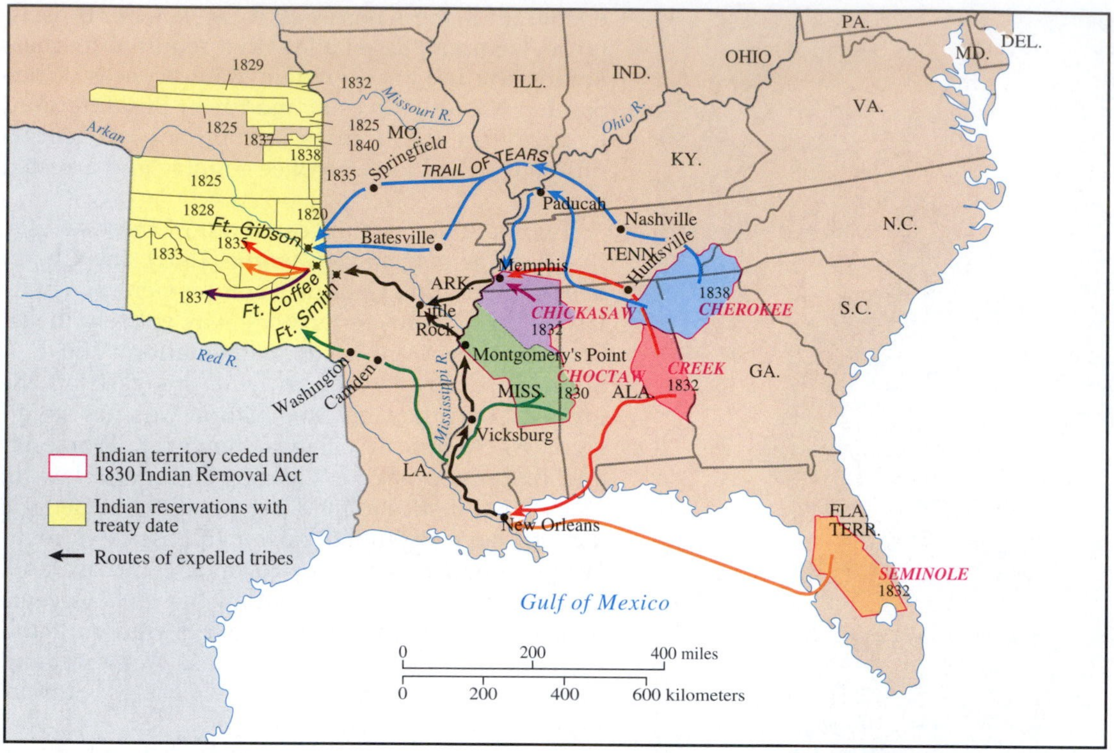

♦ **MAP 9.2 Indian Removal** The outcome of Andrew Jackson's Indian policy appears clearly on this map. Between 1830 and 1838, all the Civilized Tribes except Osceola's faction of Seminoles were forced to relocate west of the Mississippi River. Thousands died in the process.

to sign the **Treaty of New Echota** (1835), which sold the last 8 million acres of Cherokee land in the East for $5 million.

A similar combination of pressure, manipulation, and outright fraud led to the dispossession of the other Civilized Tribes. During the winter of 1831–1832, the Choctaws were removed forcibly from their lands in Mississippi and Alabama to Indian Territory, in what is now Oklahoma. They were joined by the Creeks in 1836 and by the Chickasaws in 1837. In 1838, President Martin Van Buren ordered federal troops to round up the entire Cherokee tribe, nearly twenty thousand people, and force-march them to Indian Territory. The Cherokees suffered terribly in the course of the long trek known as the **Trail of Tears** (see Map 9.2). Nearly a fourth of the Cherokees died of disease, exhaustion, or heartbreak on this march.

The only Civilized Tribe to adopt a policy of military resistance was the Seminoles. Like the other tribes, the Seminoles were deeply divided. Some chose peaceful relocation, but a group led by **Osceola** declared war on the protreaty group and

Treaty of New Echota Treaty in 1835 that gave all Cherokee land east of the Mississippi to the U.S. government in return for $5 million and land in Indian Territory.

Trail of Tears Forced march of the Cherokee people from Georgia to Indian Territory in the winter of 1838; thousands of Cherokees died.

Osceola Seminole leader in Florida who opposed removal of his people to the West and led resistance to U.S. troops; he was captured by treachery while bearing a flag of truce.

on the United States. After years of guerrilla swamp fighting, Osceola was finally captured in 1837. The antitreaty faction fought on until 1842, when the United States withdrew its troops. Eventually, even Osceola's followers agreed to move west, though a small faction of the Seminoles remained in Florida's swamps.

Jackson and the West

Jackson's Indian policy enhanced his popularity in the West, but two other western demands proved troublesome for Old Hickory. The demand for federally funded internal improvements clashed with his notions of small and frugal government, and the demand for more liberal public land policies endangered government revenues and Jackson's relationship with supporters outside the West.

Jackson's views on federal spending for roads, canals, and other internal improvements were influenced more by political than by regional considerations. For example, Jackson vetoed a bill appropriating money to build a road from Maysville, Kentucky, on the Ohio border, to Lexington. He claimed that it would benefit only one state and was therefore unconstitutional. But political considerations clearly influenced this decision. Lexington was the hub of Henry Clay's political district, and Jackson wanted to do nothing that would aid his rival. In this case, Jackson's constitutional scruples coincided with his political interests.

The issue of public land policy proved more difficult for Jackson. Many aspiring farmers could not afford to pay $1.25 per acre for public land and clamored for a price reduction. Jackson's response was to propose that federal land be offered for sale at what it cost to **survey** the land and process the sale. This proposal represented a departure from previous land policy, which assumed that land sales should profit the government. Easterners and southerners were alarmed at proposals to sell federal land at cost. They feared that migration would drain their population and give the West an even bigger voice in the nation's economics and politics. Southerners were also concerned that Congress would replace revenues lost from the sale of public land by raising tariffs. Northern employers were afraid that westward migration would drive up the price of labor. The result was nearly three years of debate in Congress that hinted at the difficulties that sectionalized politics could cause.

The Nullification Crisis

Southern concerns about rising tariffs were felt most keenly in South Carolina. Soil exhaustion and declining agricultural prices left many planters in the state in an economic pinch. South Carolina had protested loudly in 1828 when Congress passed the Tariff of Abominations. Calhoun, who had turned away from Clay's nationalist program to support southern interests and states' rights as the economy turned sour in 1819, led the protest.

In 1828, Calhoun wrote an anonymous pamphlet, *The South Carolina Exposition and Protest.* In it he argued that tariffs benefited only one part of the country rather than the nation at large and should be considered unconstitutional. More important, Calhoun echoed the Virginia and Kentucky Resolutions of 1798 in asserting that the states were the ultimate judge of the national government's legitimate power. The states had given up none of their sovereignty when they signed the Constitution. It was thus reserved for the states, not the Supreme Court, to judge the constitutionality of any law.

This reasoning led Calhoun to assert that the Tariff of Abominations could not be imposed on a state that believed it unjust. Such a state had the right to call a popular convention to consider a disputed law. If the state convention decided against the law, the law would not be binding within the state. In other words, a state had the right to declare the law invalid within the state's jurisdiction. This idea came to be called **nullification.**

As Calhoun's pamphlet circulated, nationalists like Clay and Jackson became more anxious about the potential threat to federal power. The first test came in 1830, when Senator Robert Y. Hayne of

survey To determine the area and boundaries of land through measurement and mathematical calculation.

nullification Refusal of a state to recognize or enforce a federal law within its boundaries.

INDIVIDUAL CHOICES

Choosing Justice or Union

Samuel Austin Worcester

Samuel Austin Worcester chose to help the Cherokee Indians when Georgia passed a series of discriminatory laws. This aid led to Worcester's imprisonment. He took his case all the way to the Supreme Court, which sided with him. But he chose to back away from his position when it became clear that civil war would be the result of defending Cherokee rights. From "Cherokee Messenger" by Althea Bass, University of Oklahoma Press.

During the waning days of 1830, two very different groups met in Georgia to discuss the impact of the Indian Removal Act. One, the Georgia state legislature, was flush with victory: when enforced, the new federal law would sweep the Cherokees out of western Georgia, freeing up the tribe's rich lands. The other was a group of missionaries. At its head was the frail-looking and scholarly heir to seven generations of New England ministers, Reverend Samuel A. Worcester, who, with his associates, vowed to resist Cherokee removal.

Announcing their vow in the *Cherokee Phoenix,* Worcester stated that Andrew Jackson's Indian policy had moral as well as political implications "inasmuch as it involves the maintenance or violation of the faith of our country." Moreover, the American Board of Commissioners for Foreign Missions had declared in 1810 that it would bring about the Christian conversion of the entire world within a single generation, and removing the Cherokees would delay their conversion and imperil the board's agenda.

For their part, the Georgia state legislators had spent years attempting to drive the Cherokees out of the state, and they regarded missionary support for the Indians as an irritation. Now, with victory nearly at hand, the legislators wanted to cut off missionary assistance. They passed a new law ordering the missionaries to sign a loyalty oath to the state promising to comply with Georgia law. If they signed the oath, Georgia could legally order them to stop helping the Indians. If they did not sign the oath, they would be imprisoned.

The new law became effective on March 1, 1831, and shortly thereafter Worcester and his colleagues were arrested. Because Worcester was the federal postmaster for the community of New Echota, a Georgia judge released him. But on May 15, Worcester received notice from Georgia governor George R. Gilmer that politicians had pulled strings in Washington to have his postmaster's commission suspended. The governor told Worcester that he had ten days to sign the oath, leave the state, or face arrest. Writing back to the governor, Worcester asserted that he did not believe the state of Georgia had the authority to enforce its will within the Cherokee Nation. Even if it did, he said, he was answerable to a higher law.

On July 7, Worcester was arrested again. He posted a bond and regained his freedom, but threats of further harassment forced him to move to neighboring Tennessee, leaving his ailing wife and baby at the mission in New Echota. On August 14, his baby daughter died, and when he rushed home to be with his family, he was arrested. When the court learned why he had returned to Georgia, he was released but was forced to return to exile in Tennessee.

Worcester thus lived like a fugitive, separated from his family and subject to legal harassment, until his case finally came to trial on September 16. The facts were clear. Worcester's own letter to the governor had declared his guilt, and the jury quickly made it official. Samuel Worcester and ten other missionaries were sentenced to four years at hard labor in the Georgia state penitentiary.

After refusing to hear the case of *Cherokee Nation v. Georgia,* Chief Justice John Marshall informed Cherokee tribal lawyers that he was eager for them to bring a stronger case. Worcester's case filled the bill, and the Cherokee Nation and the American Board jointly appealed Worcester's conviction before the Supreme Court. The Court agreed to hear the case, and in a landmark decision ordered Worcester and his co-defendants released, declaring all the laws passed to harass the Cherokees null and void.

Technically, Worcester should have been a free man, but President Jackson refused to acknowledge Marshall's decision and would not order Georgia to release him. The American Board's attorneys had to return to Marshall and ask for a federal court order instructing Jackson to force Worcester's release. In the meantime, however, the Bank War and the nullification crisis had hit the nation with full force, threatening the fabric of the Union. Hoping to avoid yet another blow, newly elected Georgia governor Wilson Lumpkin told Worcester and his associates that he would grant them a pardon if they chose not to press their case. The American Board instructed the missionaries to accept the pardon and end the legal struggle. Their decision to follow the board's instruction is understandable, but there is truth to the charge leveled by historian William G. McLoughlin that Worcester and the American Board chose to "sacrifice the Cherokees to save the Union."

South Carolina and Senator **Daniel Webster** of Massachusetts debated Calhoun's ideas. Hayne supported Calhoun's ideas completely. Webster countered with one of the most stirring orations ever delivered in the Senate. He concluded his speech by proclaiming, "Liberty and Union, now and for ever, one and inseparable!"

Jackson soon made his position clear. At a political banquet, he offered a toast: "Our Federal Union—it must be preserved." Calhoun then rose and countered Jackson's toast with one of his own: "The Union—next to our liberty most dear. May we always remember that it can only be preserved by distributing evenly the benefits and burthens of the Union." These toasts marked a complete rift between Jackson and Calhoun, who had been elected as Jackson's vice president in 1828.

Two years passed before the crisis finally came to a head. In 1832, Jackson sought to enhance his re-election prospects by asking Congress to lower tariff rates. (Jackson dropped Calhoun as his running mate in favor of Martin Van Buren.) It gladly complied. This action still did not satisfy the nullifiers in South Carolina. They called for a special convention to consider the matter of the tariff. The convention met in November 1832 and voted overwhelmingly to nullify the tariff.

Jackson quickly proved true to his toast of two years before. Bristling that nullification violated the Constitution, Jackson immediately reinforced federal forts in South Carolina and sent warships to enforce the collection of the tariff. He also asked Congress to pass a "force bill" giving him the power to invade the rebellious state if necessary. In hopes of placating southerners and winning popular support in the upcoming election, Clay proposed and Congress passed a lowered tariff, but it also voted to give Jackson the power he asked for.

Passage of these measures prompted South Carolina to repeal its nullification of the tariff. But it then nullified the force bill. Although Jackson ignored this action, the problem was not resolved. The issue of federal versus states' rights continued to fester throughout the antebellum period.

Jackson and the Bank War

Jackson faced another major crisis related to federal power in 1832, this one involving the Second Bank of the United States. Casting about for an issue that might dampen Jackson's popularity in an election year, Webster and Clay seized on the bank. Although the bank's twenty-year charter was not due for renewal until 1836, several considerations led Jackson's political enemies to press for renewal on the eve of the 1832 election. First, Jackson was a known opponent of the bank. Second, the country was prosperous at the time, and the bank was apparently popular. Many attributed this prosperity to the economic stability provided by the bank under the leadership of **Nicholas Biddle,** who had been its president since 1823. Proponents of the bank reasoned that Democratic unity might break down if Jackson opposed renewing the bank's charter.

Jackson's opponents were partially right. Congress passed the renewal bill and Jackson vetoed it, but the envisioned rift between Jackson and congressional Democrats did not open. The president stole the day by delivering a powerful veto message. Jackson launched the **Bank War** by denouncing the Second Bank as an example of vested privilege and monopoly power that served the interests of "the few at the expense of the many" and injured "humbler members of society—the farmers, the mechanics, and laborers—who have neither the time nor the means of securing like favors to themselves." Jackson further asserted that foreign interests, many of which were seen as enemies to American rights, had used the bank to amass large blocks of American securities.

Although the charter was not renewed, the Second Bank could operate for four more years on its existing charter. Jackson, however, wanted to kill the bank immediately. He withdrew federal funds from the bank and redeposited the money in state banks.

Daniel Webster Massachusetts senator and lawyer who was known for his forceful speeches and considered nullification a threat to the Union.

Nicholas Biddle President of the Second Bank of the United States; he struggled to keep the bank functioning when President Jackson tried to undermine its powers.

Bank War The political conflict that occurred when Andrew Jackson tried to destroy the Second Bank of the United States, which he thought represented special interests at the expense of the common man.

Powerless to stop the withdrawal of federal funds, Biddle sought to replace dwindling assets by calling in loans owed by state banks and by raising interest rates. In this way, the banker believed, he would not only head off the Second Bank's collapse but also trigger a business panic that might force the government to reverse its course. By the time this panic occurred, however, Andrew Jackson was no longer in the White House.

SUMMARY

Expectations
Constraints
Choices
Outcomes

With the end of the War of 1812, President Madison and the Republicans *chose* to promote an agenda for an expansive America. They championed a national market economy and passed federal legislation to create a national bank and to protect American industry. Madison gave free rein to nationalists such as John Quincy Adams and Andrew Jackson, who expanded the nation's sphere of influence.

Ironically, the *outcome* of postwar economic expansion was an increase in tensions among regions. During the economic hard times that followed the Panic of 1819, the nation's geographical sections *chose* to wrestle for control over federal power in an attempt to solve their economic ills. The political contention over the admission of Missouri reflected these economic tensions and marked the end of the Era of Good Feelings.

Meanwhile, newly politicized voters *chose* to sweep the gentlemanly John Quincy Adams out of office and replace him with the presumably more democratic Andrew Jackson. Backed by a machine that reflected sectional interests, Jackson had to juggle all the regions' financial, tariff, and Indian policy demands while trying to hold his political alliance and the nation together. The *outcome* was a series of regional crises—Indian removal, nullification, and the Bank War—that alienated the regions.

SUGGESTED READINGS

Dangerfield, George. *The Era of Good Feelings* (1952).

A book so well written and informative that it deserves its status as a classic. All students will enjoy this grand overview.

Rogin, Michael Paul. *Fathers and Children: Andrew Jackson and the Subjugation of the American Indian* (1975).

A controversial and enjoyable psychoanalysis of Andrew Jackson. Focuses on his Indian policy but gives an interesting view of his entire personality.

Taylor, George Rogers. *The Transportation Revolution, 1815–1860* (1951).

The only comprehensive treatment of changes in transportation during the antebellum period and their economic impact. Nicely written a nd comprehensive in treating the topic.

Ward, John William. *Andrew Jackson: Symbol for an Age* (1955).

A classic and fascinating view of how Jackson was shaped as a man and the reasons for his dramatic hold on the American imagination.

ROADS, CANALS, RAILWAYS, AND TELEGRAPH LINES, 1850 A transportation and communications revolution took place between 1820 and 1850 as roads, canals, rails, and telegraph lines reached out to bind the many parts of the nation together. The intimate connections made possible by the new lines of communication shown here ensured economic growth but also increased tensions between the nation's sections by making it difficult to ignore the vast differences between regional cultures.

CANADA
Lake Superior
Lake Michigan
Lake Huron
L. Ontario
Lake Erie
St. Lawrence
MAINE
NEW YORK
VT.
N.H.
MASS.
R.I.
CONN.
PENNSYLVANIA
N.J.
DEL.
MD.
Washington D.C.
VIRGINIA
NORTH CAROLINA
SOUTH CAROLINA
GEORGIA
ALABAMA
MISSISSIPPI
LOUISIANA
TENNESSEE
KENTUCKY
OHIO
INDIANA
ILLINOIS
MICHIGAN 1837
WISCONSIN TERRITORY 1836
IOWA TERRITORY 1838
UNORGANIZED TERRITORY
MISSOURI 1837
ARKANSAS 1836
REPUBLIC OF TEXAS
FLORIDA TERRITORY 1822
MEXICO
ATLANTIC OCEAN
Gulf of Mexico
Portland
Lowell
Boston
Worcester
Providence
New Haven
New York
Springfield
Albany
Utica
Rochester
Buffalo
Erie
Cleveland
Toledo
Akron
Pittsburgh
Harrisburg
Trenton
Philadelphia
Hagerstown
Baltimore
Winchester
Columbus
Dayton
Cincinnati
Indianapolis
South Bend
Ft. Wayne
Evanston
Chicago
St. Louis
Louisville
Lexington
Lynchburg
Richmond
Norfolk
Raleigh
Fayetteville
Wilmington
Nashville
Knoxville
Chattanooga
Memphis
Little Rock
Atlanta
Augusta
Charleston
Macon
Savannah
Montgomery
Vicksburg
Jackson
Natchez
Mobile
New Orleans
St. Augustine
Erie Canal
CATSKILL TPK.
POST RD.
BOSTON
Pennsylvania
State Canal
PENNSYLVANIA RD.
NATIONAL
PIKE
VALLEY TPK.
GREAT VALLEY RD.
NASHVILLE RD.
NATCHEZ TRACE
GENERAL JACKSON'S MILITARY RD.
Missouri
Ohio
Mississippi
Arkansas
Tennessee
0 150 300 Km.
0 150 300 Mi.
Roads
Railroads
Canals
Telegraph lines
Settled areas
1820
1840
Principal manufacturing city
NORTH AND CENTRAL AMERICA
RUSSIAN CLAIM
CANADA
OREGON COUNTRY
UNITED STATES
MEXICO
REPUBLIC OF TEXAS

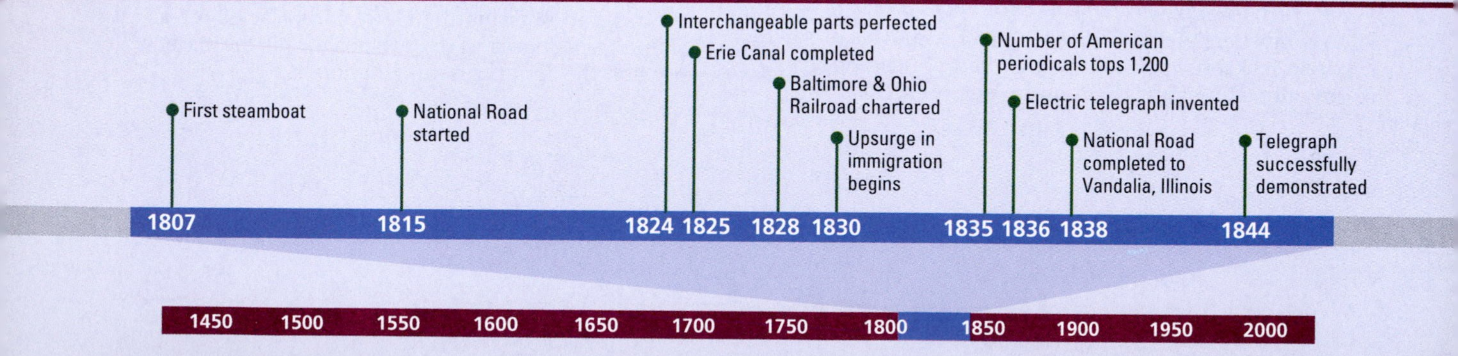

First steamboat
National Road started
Interchangeable parts perfected
Erie Canal completed
Baltimore & Ohio Railroad chartered
Upsurge in immigration begins
Number of American periodicals tops 1,200
Electric telegraph invented
National Road completed to Vandalia, Illinois
Telegraph successfully demonstrated
1807
1815
1824
1825
1828
1830
1835
1836
1838
1844
1450
1500
1550
1600
1650
1700
1750
1800
1850
1900
1950
2000

CHAPTER 10

The Great Transformation, 1815–1840

The Transportation Revolution

- How did newly emerging networks of transportation and communication change the expectations of Americans in the North, West, and South?

The Manufacturing Boom

- How did new manufacturing techniques following the adoption of interchangeable parts change the nature of work?
- How did the developing factory system affect the expectations of artisans and elite and middle-class Americans?

The New Cotton Empire in the South

- How did the expectations of southerners—black and white—change after 1820?
- How did white southerners chose to respond to these changing expectations, and what new constraints resulted for slaves, free blacks, and poor whites?

INTRODUCTION

Expectations
Constraints
Choices
Outcomes

In the quarter century after the War of 1812, the United States underwent a profound economic transformation that affected the lives of virtually all Americans. Although most Americans *chose* to remain farmers as of 1840, it was clear that the agrarian republic of the Founding Fathers was rapidly disappearing, particularly in the Northeast, where an industrial revolution was well under way.

The effects of this economic transformation were felt even in regions where farming remained the mainstay. Whether growing cotton or corn, farmers by 1840 expected to sell their crops in distant markets rather than subsisting on the fruits of their toil. Most had become thoroughly integrated into a national market economy. Jefferson's ideal of the isolated, self-sufficient yeoman farmer had largely vanished.

The spread of commercial farming and the proliferation of manufacturing were made possible by a revolution in transportation that occurred after the War of 1812. Although some *constraints* on transportation still remained as of 1840, a network of roads, canals, and railroads connected the nation in a way that had been unimaginable in 1815. The improving transportation system encouraged the *expectations* of manufacturers, farmers, and businessmen that they could sell products profitably in faraway markets.

In the North, new techniques of manufacturing such as the invention of interchangeable parts and new methods of organizing work led to a host of unexpected *outcomes.* Skilled workers were no longer needed to make complicated machines, and the value of labor declined along with the range of *choices* open to workers. Factory owners and their families *chose* to live in fashionable neighborhoods far away from their factories, leaving daily operations of the workplace in the hands of clerks and managers.

The American South underwent a profound transformation during this era as well. The hunger that British and American textile mills shared for raw cotton gave southerners great *expectations* for enormous prosperity. The astounding growth of cotton agriculture led to the equally explosive growth of slavery. The *outcome* was a political and social economy in the South that would shape every soul in the region.

Each step in this great transformation generated waves of change, altering *expectations,* removing old *constraints,* and then creating new ones. A whole generation was forced to make *choices* the likes of which no previous generation of Americans had faced. One long-term *outcome* of the choices these people made was that the foundation for a modern America was set firmly in place.

The Transportation Revolution

The movement to improve transportation after the War of 1812 had two origins. The first was the recognition that the poor state of American roads had been a considerable handicap for American troops during the war. The second was the rapid settlement of the Old Northwest and the Old Southwest. As farmers moved into these fertile lands, they began producing huge agricultural surpluses. It quickly became apparent that improved transportation was needed to take advantage of the agricultural bounty being produced in these regions.

Before the War of 1812, travel on the nation's roads was a wearying, bone-rattling experience. Those who could afford to travel by stagecoach were bounced along over muddy, rutted roads at the pace of 4 miles per hour. The enjoyment of such

CHRONOLOGY

A Revolution in Transportation

1807	Robert Fulton tests the *Clermont*
1815	Government funding for the National Road
1812	First successful steamboat run from Pittsburgh to New Orleans
1817	Construction of Erie Canal begins
1819	*Dartmouth College v. Woodward* *McCulloch v. Maryland*
1824	John H. Hall perfects interchangeable parts for gun manufacturing *Gibbons v. Ogden*
1825	Erie Canal completed
1830	Steam locomotive *Tom Thumb* beaten by a horse in a race
1830–1840	Immigration approaches 600,000 for the decade
1834	Main Line Canal from Philadelphia to Pittsburgh completed
1836	Samuel F. B. Morse invents electric telegraph
1838	National Road completed to Vandalia, Illinois

dubious luxury cost the equivalent of a pint of good whiskey for each mile traveled.

Although some private **turnpikes** had existed since the 1790s, the road-building business took on new energy after the War of 1812 when the federal and state governments began financing road improvements. The federal commitment began in 1815 when President Madison supported the government-funded National Road between Cumberland, Maryland, and Wheeling, Virginia. Such a road was a military and postal necessity, Madison declared. By 1838, the government had spent in excess of $7 million on this road, also known as the **Cumberland Road,** extending it all the way to Vandalia, Illinois.

New roads helped to alleviate the transportation problems faced by the growing nation, but they hardly solved them. Some small manufactured goods could be hauled west along the roads, and relatively lightweight items like whiskey could move the other way. But heavy, bulky products were still difficult and expensive to move. At a minimum, hauling a ton of **freight** along the nation's roads cost 15 cents per mile.

Water transportation remained the most economical means for shipping large loads. Unfortunately, navigable rivers and lakes seldom formed usable transportation networks. Holland and other European countries had solved this problem by digging canals. After the War of 1812, the state governments opened an era of canal building.

New York State was the most successful at canal development. In 1817, the state started work on a canal that would run more than 350 miles from Lake Erie at Buffalo to the Hudson River at Albany.

turnpike A highway on which tolls are collected at barriers set up along the way; companies that hoped to make a profit from the tolls built the first turnpikes.

Cumberland Road A national highway built with federal funds; it eventually stretched from Cumberland, Maryland, to Vandalia, Illinois, and beyond.

freight Any goods or cargo carried in commercial transport.

This canal would tap the rich agricultural regions of western New York and the Great Lakes. When completed in 1825, the Erie Canal revolutionized shipping. The cost of shipping a ton of oats from Buffalo to Albany fell more than 80 percent, and the transit time dropped from twenty days to eight. The canal enabled a flood of goods from America's interior to reach New York City and made that city the nation's commercial center.

The spectacular success of the **Erie Canal** prompted state governments to offer all manner of financial incentives to canal-building companies. The result was an explosion in canal building that lasted through the 1830s.

Pennsylvania's experiences were typical. Jealous of New York's success, Pennsylvania proposed a system of canals and roads that would make it the commercial hub of the Western Hemisphere. At the center of this system was the Main Line Canal connecting Philadelphia and Pittsburgh. The problem was that the two cities were separated by mountains over two thousand feet high. Using **locks** to raise boats over this height was a technological impossibility. Engineers finally designed a **portage** railroad over the Allegheny Mountains.

The Allegheny Portage Railroad permitted passengers and cargo to make the trip across the mountains on land but without leaving canal boats. The canal boats were floated onto submerged railcars. Steam power was then used to pull the railcars, which were attached to a cable, up a series of inclined planes. After being pulled up five steep inclines, the railcars began the descent to the canal at the other side of the mountains. At the bottom of the last incline, the boats were unloaded and placed in the canal to continue the trip to Philadelphia or Pittsburgh.

The portage railroad was an engineering marvel. The completion of the Main Line system in 1834 allowed a family to travel relatively quickly and comfortably all the way from Philadelphia to Pittsburgh. The tolls alone, however, cost as much as six acres of prime farmland. In the long run, the Main Line Canal was a dismal financial failure, never earning investors one cent of profit.

Despite Pennsylvania's experience, nearly every state in the North and West undertook some canal building between 1820 and 1840. States and private individuals invested over $100 million on nearly 3,500 miles of canals during the heyday of canal building. Nearly all experienced the same sad financial fate as Pennsylvania's Main Line Canal.

Steam Power

Canals solved one problem of water transportation but did not address the issue of how to move people and goods upstream on America's great rivers. While a barge could make it downstream from Pittsburgh to New Orleans in about a month, the return trip took over four months, if it could be made at all. As a result, most shippers barged their freight downriver, sold the barges for lumber in New Orleans, and walked back home along the **Natchez Trace.**

In 1807, Robert Fulton perfected a design that made steam-powered shipping practical. His *Clermont* used steam-driven wheels mounted on the sides of the vessel to push it up the Hudson River from New York City to Albany. Unfortunately, the *Clermont* was not well suited to most of America's waterways. Heavy and narrow-beamed, Fulton's ship needed deep water to carry a limited **payload.** It did not take long, however, for engineers to design broader-beamed, lighter vessels that could

Erie Canal A 350-mile canal stretching from Buffalo to Albany; it revolutionized shipping in New York.

lock An enclosed section of a canal, with gates at each end, used to raise or lower boats from one level to another by admitting or releasing water; locks allow canals to compensate for changes in terrain.

portage The carrying of boats or supplies overland between two waterways.

Natchez Trace A road connecting Natchez, Mississippi, with Nashville, Tennessee; it evolved from a series of Indian trails and had commercial and military importance in the late eighteenth and early nineteenth centuries.

payload The part of a cargo that generates revenue, as opposed to the part needed to fire the boiler or supply the crew.

♦ Though painted many years after the event, this picture captures the excitement of the historic race between the steam-powered *Tom Thumb* and a stagecoach horse that took place in the summer of 1830. The horse won, leading the Baltimore and Ohio Railroad to scrap steam power and hitch horses to their cars rather than locomotives. *"The Race of the Tom Thumb" by Herbert D. Stitt. The Chessie System, B&O Railroad Museum Archives.*

carry heavy loads in shallow western rivers. By 1812 the *New Orleans* had made a successful run from Pittsburgh to New Orleans.

Steam power took canal building's impact on inland transportation a revolutionary step further. Between 1816 and 1840, the cost of shipping a ton of goods down American rivers fell from an average of 1¼ cents per mile to less than half a cent. The cost of upstream transport fell from over 10 cents per mile to about half a cent. In addition, steamboats could carry bulky and heavy objects that could not be hauled upstream for any price by any other means. Dependable river transportation drew cotton cultivation farther into the nation's interior and allowed fur trappers and traders to press up the Missouri River. Only the development of steam railroads would ultimately have a greater impact on nineteenth-century transportation.

Merchants from cities without extensive navigable rivers, such as Baltimore, took the lead in developing this new technology. In 1828, the state chartered the Baltimore and Ohio (B&O) Railroad. The B&O soon demonstrated its potential when inventor Peter Cooper's steam locomotive *Tom Thumb* sped 13 miles along B&O tracks. Ironically, the B&O abandoned steam power and replaced it with horses temporarily after a stagecoach horse beat the *Tom Thumb* in a widely publicized race held in 1830.

Despite this race, South Carolina invested in steam technology and chartered a 136-mile rail line from Charleston to Hamburg. Here the first full-size American-built locomotive was used to pull cars. Even the explosion of this engine did not deter the Charleston and Hamburg Railroad from continuing to use steam engines.

Rail transport could not rival water-based transportation systems during this early period. By 1850, individual companies had laid approximately 9,000 miles of track, but not in any coherent network. Also, the distance between tracks varied from company to company. As a result, cargoes had to be unloaded from the cars of one company's trains at line's end, lugged to the railhead of another line, and reloaded onto the other company's cars. There were other problems too. Boiler explosions, fires, and derailments were common. Entrenched interest groups used their power in state legislatures to limit the extension of railroads. These obstacles prevented railroads from becoming a major factor in American life until the 1850s.

The Information Revolution

Since the nation's founding, American leaders had feared that the sheer size of the country would make true federal democracy impractical. During the 1790s, it took a week for a letter to travel from Virginia to New York City and three weeks from Cincinnati to the Atlantic coast. Thomas Jefferson speculated that the continent would become a series of allied republics, each small enough to operate efficiently given the slow speed of communication. The transportation revolution, however, made quite a difference in how quickly news got around.

The Erie Canal enabled letters posted in Buffalo to reach New York City within six days and New Orleans in about two weeks. The increased flow of information caused an explosion in the number of newspapers and magazines published in the country. In 1790, the 92 American newspapers had a total **circulation** of around 4 million. By 1835, the number of periodicals had risen to 1,258, and circulation had surpassed 90 million.

Samuel F. B. Morse's invention of the **electric telegraph** greatly enhanced the speed of the communications revolution. His invention, first tested in 1836, consisted of a transmitter and receiver of electrical impulses. The transmitter sent either a short electrical pulse (a dot) or a long electrical pulse (a dash), from which Morse devised his famous code. The major obstacle that Morse faced was sending these electrical pulses long distances over wires. By 1843, he had worked out this problem, and Congress agreed to finance an experimental line between Washington, D.C., and Baltimore. On May 24, 1844, he sent his first message over the line: "What hath God wrought!"

Legal Anchors for New Business Enterprise

Before wholesale changes could take place in American transportation and business, some thorny legal issues needed to be resolved. The American System made questions of authority over finance and interstate commerce increasingly important. In three landmark legal cases, John Marshall, chief justice of the U.S. Supreme Court, resolved such questions and cleared the way for the expansion of interstate trade.

If businesses were going to build and operate large enterprises, they had to have confidence in the sanctity of legal contracts. In the case of *Dartmouth College v. Woodward* (1819), the Supreme Court made contracts secure. The 1769 charter for Dartmouth College specified that the college's board of trustees would be self-perpetuating. In 1816, to gain control over the college, the New Hampshire legislature passed a bill allowing the state's governor to appoint board members. The board sued, claiming that the charter was a legal contract that the legislature had no right to alter. Marshall concurred that the Constitution protected the sanctity of contracts and that state legislatures could not interfere with them.

In *McCulloch v. Maryland* (1819), Marshall established the superiority of the federal government over state authorities in matters of finance. The case involved the cashier of the Baltimore branch of the Bank of the United States, who refused to put state revenue stamps on federal bank notes as required by Maryland law. McCulloch (the cashier) was **indicted** by the state but appealed to federal authorities. Marshall ruled that the states could not impose taxes on federal institutions and that McCulloch was right in refusing to comply with Maryland's law. As he wrote, "The Constitution and the laws made in pursuance thereof are supreme."

The supremacy of federal authority was demonstrated again in *Gibbons v. Ogden* (1824). This case involved a New York charter given to Robert Fulton and Robert Livingston that granted them exclusive rights to run steamboats on rivers in that state. Thomas Gibbons also operated a

circulation The number of copies of a publication sold or distributed.

electric telegraph Device used to send messages in the form of electrical signals.

indict To make a formal accusation against someone.

steamboat service in the same area, but under the authority of the federal Coasting Act. When a conflict between the two companies ended up in court, Marshall ruled in favor of Gibbons, arguing that the **monopoly** that New York had granted conflicted with federal authority and was therefore invalid.

Those three cases helped ease the way for the development of new businesses. With contracts free from state and local meddling and the superiority of Congress in banking and interstate commerce established, businesses had the security they needed to turn Henry Clay's dream of a national market economy into a reality.

The Manufacturing Boom

During the opening years of the nineteenth century, manufacturing in America was largely a home-based affair. Before the 1820s, American households produced most of the manufactured goods they used. More than 60 percent of the clothing Americans wore was spun from raw fibers and sewn by women in their homes. Craftsmen also worked in their homes, assisted by family members and an extended family of **apprentices** and **journeymen.**

Beginning during the War of 1812, textile manufacturing led the way in moving production out of the home and into the factory. The intimate ties between manufacturers and workers were severed, and both found themselves surrounded by strangers in new and unfamiliar urban environments.

The "American System" of Manufacturing

At first, mechanized production played only a small part in the manufacturing of textiles. Even Samuel Slater (see pages 184–185), depended on the **putting-out system** to finish the manufacturing process. In this system, manufacturers provided thread and other materials to women artisans, who then wove, dyed, and sewed the final products at home. During slack times in the agricultural year, entire families participated in this home industry. When the householders had used all the thread, they took the finished goods to the manufacturer and were paid for their work.

A radical departure in cloth manufacturing took place in 1813, when the Boston Manufacturing Company mechanized all the stages in the production of finished cloth, bringing the entire process under one roof. By 1822, the factory's success led the company to build a larger one in Lowell, Massachusetts, a town named after one of the company's founders, Francis Cabot Lowell.

The design of the Lowell factory was widely copied during the 1820s and 1830s. Spinning and weaving on machines located in one building cut the time and the cost of manufacturing significantly. **Quality control** became easier because employees were under constant supervision. As a result, the putting-out system for turning thread into cloth went into serious decline, as did home production of clothes for family use. Ready-made clothing became standard wearing apparel in the 1830s and 1840s.

A major technological revolution helped to push factory production into other areas of manufacturing during these same years. In traditional manufacturing, individual artisans crafted each item one at a time. A clockmaker, for example, either cast or carved individually by hand all

monopoly The right to exclusive control over a commercial activity; it may be granted by the government.

apprentices Individuals who work for a master craftsman in order to learn a trade or skill.

journeyman A person who has finished an apprenticeship in a trade or craft and is a qualified worker in the employ of another.

putting-out system A system of production in which manufacturers provided artisans with materials such as thread and dye for use in producing goods at home.

quality control The effort to ensure that all goods produced meet consistent standards.

the gears, levers, and wheels. As a result, the innards of a clock worked together only in the clock for which they had been made. If that clock ever needed repair, new parts had to be custom-made for it. The lack of **interchangeable parts** made manufacturing extremely slow and repairs difficult.

Eli Whitney, inventor of the cotton gin (see page 186), was the first American to propose the large-scale use of interchangeable parts, to manufacture guns in 1798. Whitney's efforts failed because of a lack of start-up money and precision machine tools. But his former partner, John H. Hall, proved that manufacturing guns from interchangeable parts was practical at the federal armory in Harpers Ferry, Virginia, in 1824. This "American system of manufacturing" spread to the Springfield Armory in Massachusetts and then to private gun manufacturers like Samuel Colt. Within twenty years, products ranging from sewing machines to farm implements were being made from interchangeable parts.

The use of interchangeable parts speeded up the manufacture of important products and improved their dependability. The new technology also made repairing guns and other standardized mechanisms easy and relatively cheap. Like the textile mills, factories assembling interchangeable parts slashed the production costs. The use of interchangeable parts allowed employers to hire unskilled workers to assemble those parts. Extensive training became irrelevant. A gunsmith with years of experience was likely to find himself working on equal terms alongside a youngster or recent immigrant with no craft experience at all.

New Workplaces and New Workers

Moving manufacturing from the home to the factory changed the nature of work and altered the traditional relationship between employers and employees. To attract workers, some entrepreneurs developed **company towns.** Families recruited from the economically depressed New England countryside were installed in neat row houses, each with its own small vegetable garden. Each family member was employed by the company. Women worked on the production line. Men ran heavy machinery and worked as **millwrights,** carpenters, haulers, or day laborers. Children did light work in the factories and tended gardens at home.

Lowell's company developed another system. Hard-pressed to find enough families to work in the factories, it recruited unmarried farm girls. Because most of the girls saw factory work as a transitional stage between girlhood and marriage, the company assured them and their families that the moral atmosphere in its dormitories would be strictly controlled to maintain the girls' reputations.

In New York, Philadelphia, and other cities, enterprising manufacturers found an alternative source of labor in the immigrant slums. In the shoe industry, for example, they assigned one family to make soles, another to make heels, and so forth. Making shoes this way was not as efficient as making them in a factory, but it did have advantages. Such manufacturers did not have to build factories and could pay rock-bottom wages to desperate slum dwellers.

Machine production and the growing pool of labor proved economically devastating to the working class. No longer was the employer a master craftsman who felt some responsibility toward his workers. Factory owners had obligations to investors and bankers, but not to their workers. Owners kept wages low, regardless of the workers' cost of living. As the supply of labor swelled and wages declined, increasing numbers of working people faced poverty and squalor.

The increasing number of immigrants who came to America after 1820 contributed signifi-

interchangeable parts Parts that are identical and can be substituted for one another.

company town A town built and owned by a single company; its residents depend on the company not only for jobs but for stores, schools, and housing.

millwright A person who designs, builds, or repairs mills or mill machinery.

♦ Women who worked in the new textile factories complained about the noise, tedium, and dangers. This engraving, from the *Memoir of Samuel Slater* (1836), shows the conditions under which they worked. *Museum of American Textile History.*

cantly to the desperate situation of the working class. Between 1820 and 1830, for example, slightly more than 151,000 people immigrated to the United States. In the following decade, that number increased to nearly 600,000; between 1840 and 1850, it soared to more than a million and a half people (see Map 10.1). This enormous increase in immigration changed the cultural and economic face of the nation. Immigrants flocked to the port and manufacturing cities of the Northeast, where they joined Americans fleeing the countryside after the Panic of 1819. Former master craftsmen, journeymen, and apprentices combined with immigrants and refugees from the farm to form a new social class and culture in America.

Nearly half of all immigrants to the United States between 1820 and 1860 came from Ireland, a nation beset with poverty, political strife, and, after the potato blight appeared in 1841, starvation. Few Irish had marketable skills or more money than the voyage to America cost. They arrived penniless and virtually unemployable. Many of them spoke not English but Gaelic.

The same was true of many Germans, the second most numerous immigrant group. Radical economic change and political upheaval put peasants and skilled craftsmen into flight. Like Irish peasants, German farmers arrived in America destitute and void of opportunities. Trained German craftsmen had a better chance at finding employment, but mechanization threatened their livelihoods as well. Adding to their difficulties was their lack of fluency in English.

Not only were the new immigrants poor and unskilled, but most were culturally different from native-born Americans. Catholicism separated most from the vast majority of Americans, who were Protestants. In religion, language, dress, eating and drinking habits, and social values, the new immigrants were very different from the people whose culture dominated American society.

Poverty, cultural distinctiveness, and the desire to live among fellow immigrants created ethnic neighborhoods in New York, Philadelphia, and other cities. Here, people with the same culture and religion built churches, stores, pubs, beer halls, and other familiar institutions to help themselves cope with the shock of transplantation and to adapt to life in the United States. They started fraternal organizations and clubs to overcome loneliness and isolation. Living conditions were crowded, uncomfortable, and unsanitary.

Desperate for work, the new immigrants were willing to do nearly anything to earn money. For

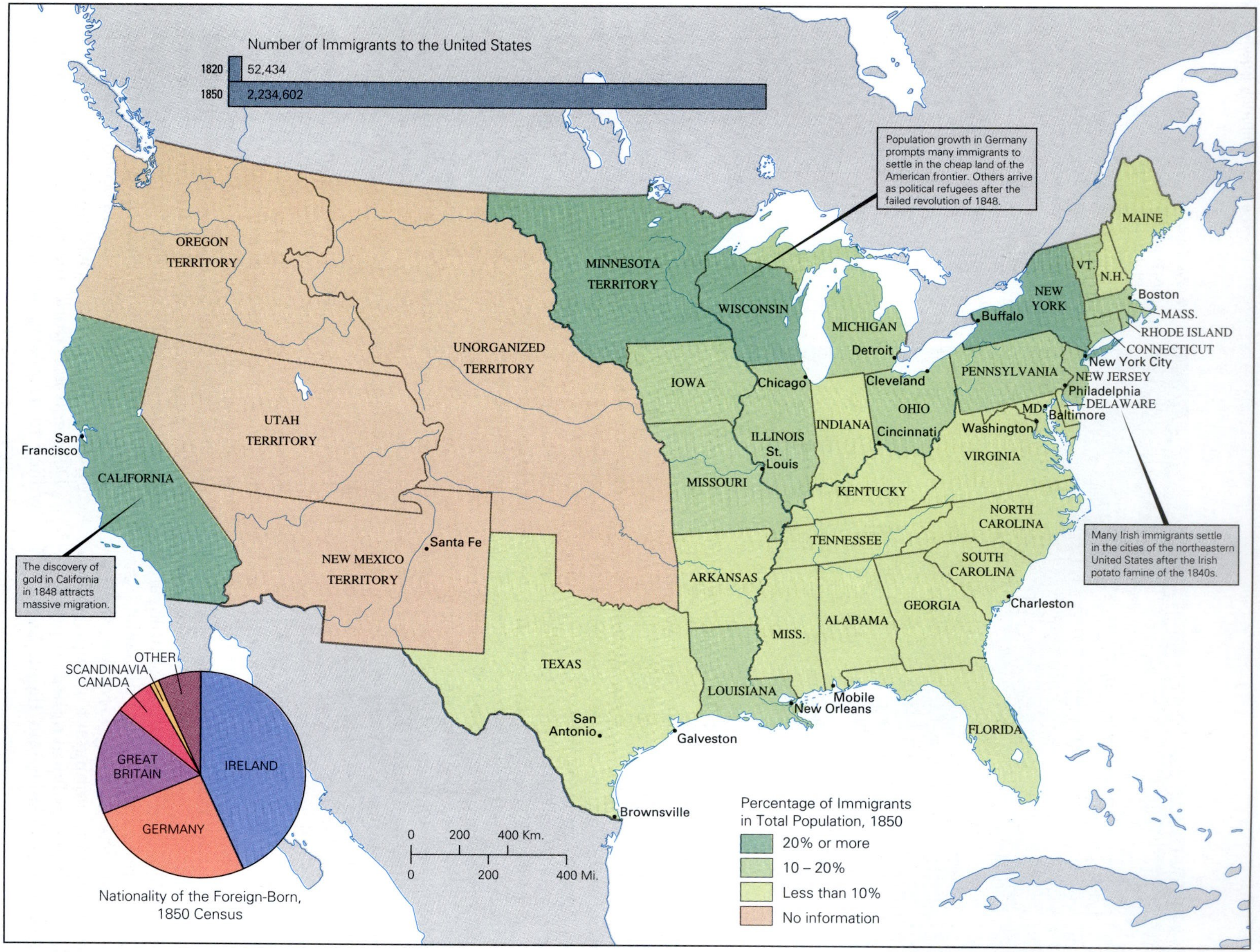

Number of Immigrants to the United States
1820
52,434
1850
2,234,602
Population growth in Germany prompts many immigrants to settle in the cheap land of the American frontier. Others arrive as political refugees after the failed revolution of 1848.
Many Irish immigrants settle in the cities of the northeastern United States after the Irish potato famine of the 1840s.
The discovery of gold in California in 1848 attracts massive migration.
OREGON TERRITORY
MINNESOTA TERRITORY
WISCONSIN
MICHIGAN
MAINE
VT.
N.H.
NEW YORK
MASS.
RHODE ISLAND
CONNECTICUT
NEW JERSEY
DELAWARE
MD.
PENNSYLVANIA
UNORGANIZED TERRITORY
UTAH TERRITORY
CALIFORNIA
IOWA
ILLINOIS
INDIANA
OHIO
VIRGINIA
MISSOURI
KENTUCKY
NORTH CAROLINA
TENNESSEE
SOUTH CAROLINA
NEW MEXICO TERRITORY
ARKANSAS
GEORGIA
ALABAMA
MISS.
TEXAS
LOUISIANA
FLORIDA
Boston
Buffalo
Detroit
Chicago
Cleveland
New York City
Philadelphia
Baltimore
Washington
Cincinnati
St. Louis
San Francisco
Santa Fe
Charleston
Mobile
New Orleans
San Antonio
Galveston
Brownsville
OTHER
SCANDINAVIA
CANADA
GREAT BRITAIN
IRELAND
GERMANY
Nationality of the Foreign-Born, 1850 Census
0 200 400 Km.
0 200 400 Mi.
Percentage of Immigrants in Total Population, 1850
20% or more
10 – 20%
Less than 10%
No information

♦ **MAP 10.1 Origin and Settlement of Immigrants, 1820–1850** Immigration was one of the most important economic, political, and social factors in American life during the antebellum period. As this map shows, with the exception of Louisiana, immigration was confined almost exclusively to areas where slavery was not permitted. This gave the North, Northwest, and California a different cultural flavor than the rest of the country and affected the political balance between those areas and the South.

manufacturers, they were the perfect work force. As immigration increased, the traditional labor shortage in America was replaced by a **labor glut,** and the social and economic status of all workers declined accordingly.

Living Conditions in Industrializing America

Working conditions for factory workers reflected the labor supply, the manufacturing company's capital, and the personal philosophy of the factory owner. Girls at Lowell's factories described an environment of familiar paternalism. Factory managers and boarding-house keepers supervised every aspect of their lives. As for the work itself, one mill girl commented that it was "not half so hard as . . . attending the dairy, washing, cleaning house, and cooking." What bothered her most was the repetitive work and the resulting boredom.

Boredom could have disastrous consequences. Inattentive factory workers were likely to lose fingers, hands, arms, or even lives to whirring, pounding, slashing mechanisms. Some owners tried to make the workplace safe, but investors discouraged many from buying safety devices. Samuel Slater complained bitterly to investors after a child was chewed up in a factory machine. "You call for yarn," he declared, "but think little about the means by which it is to be made."

Such concern became increasingly rare as factory owners withdrew from overseeing daily operations. The influx of laborers from the countryside and foreign lands wiped out the decent wages and living conditions that manufacturing pioneers had offered. Laborers were increasingly expected to provide their own housing, food, and entertainment.

Large areas in cities became working-class neighborhoods. Factory workers, journeymen, and day laborers crammed into the boxlike rooms of **tenements.** Large houses formerly occupied by domestic manufacturers and their apprentices were broken up into tiny apartments and were rented to laborers. In some working-class areas of New York City, laborers were crowded fifty to a house. Sewage disposal, drinking water, and trash removal were sorely neglected in such areas.

Social Life for a Genteel Class

The factory system also altered the daily lives of manufacturers. In earlier years, journeymen and apprentices had lived with master craftsmen and their families. Craftsmen exercised great authority over their workers but felt obligated to care for them almost as parents would. Such working arrangements blurred the distinction between employee and employer. The factory system ended this relationship. The movement of workers out of owners' homes permitted the emerging elite class to develop a **genteel** lifestyle that set them apart from the rest of the population.

Genteel families aimed at the complete separation of their private and public lives. Men in the elite class spent their leisure time socializing with each other in private clubs and organizations instead of drinking and eating with their employees. The lives of genteel wives also changed. The wife of a traditional craftsman had been responsible for important tasks in the operation of the business. Genteel women, by contrast, were expected to leave business dealings to men. They became immersed in what is called the **cult of domesticity,** which encouraged women to focus their lives completely on their homes and children. Women who did so believed they were performing an important duty for God and country and fulfilling their natural calling.

labor glut Oversupply of labor in relation to the number of jobs available.

tenement Urban apartment house, usually with minimal facilities for sanitation, safety, and comfort.

genteel The manner and style associated with the elite classes, usually characterized by elegance, grace, and politeness.

cult of domesticity The belief that women's proper role lay in domestic pursuits.

Motherhood consumed genteel women during the antebellum period. The new magazines and advice manuals of the 1820s and 1830s urged mothers to nurture rather than punish their children. Influential author Bronson Alcott helped to convince an entire generation of the need for a gentle and supporting hand and for a departure from harsh, Puritan methods of child rearing.

Despite the demands of motherhood, many genteel women found themselves isolated with time on their hands. They sought activities that would provide a sense of accomplishment without imperiling their genteel status. Many found outlets in fancy needlework, reading, and art appreciation societies. But some wished for more challenging activities. As Sarah Huntington Smith complained in 1833, "To make and receive visits, exchange friendly salutations, attend to one's wardrobe, cultivate a garden, read good and entertaining books, and even attend religious meetings for one's own enjoyment; all this does not satisfy me." Smith chose to become a missionary. Other genteel women during the 1830s and 1840s used their nurturing and purifying talents to reform what appeared to be a chaotic and immoral society by involving themselves in crusades against alcohol and slavery.

Life and Culture Among the New Middle Class

The new class of clerks, bookkeepers, and managers that helped to run the factories owned by the genteel elite sought to find their own cultural level. This middle class had many of the same prejudices and ideals as the elite class. They read the same advice magazines, often attended the same churches, and sometimes belonged to the same civic and reform societies. Nevertheless, the lives of these two classes were different in many respects.

One distinguishing characteristic of the new middle class was its relative youth. These young people had flocked from the countryside to newly emerging cities in pursuit of formal education and employment. While middle-class men found employment as clerks, bookkeepers, and managers, middle-class women parlayed their education and perceived gift for nurturing children into work as teachers. It became acceptable for women to work as teachers for several years before marriage. Some avoided marriage altogether to pursue their hard-won careers.

Middle-class men and women tended to put off marriage until they had established themselves socially and economically. They also tended to have fewer children than their parents had. Because middle-class children were sent to school to prepare them to pursue careers, they were an economic liability rather than an asset. Late marriage and birth control kept middle-class families small.

Middle-class city life cut people off from the comforting sociability of farm families and the church-centered communities that shaped and directed rural life. Many unmarried men and women seeking their fortunes in town boarded in private homes or rooming houses. After marriage, they emulated the closely knit isolation of the elite. Accordingly, these couples looked to each other for companionship and guidance.

Like the elite class, this new group sought bonds in voluntary associations. College students formed discussion groups, preprofessional clubs, and benevolent societies. For those out of school, groups like the Odd Fellows and the Masons brought people together for companionship. Such organizations helped enforce traditional values through rigid membership standards stressing moral character, upright behavior, and, above all, order.

The New Cotton Empire in the South

While increasing multitudes packed into the industrializing cities of the North, the South exploded outward seeking new land on which to grow cotton. By 1850, cotton was being grown from the southeastern corner of Virginia to eastern Texas. The ascendancy of King Cotton affected the outlook and experiences of everyone

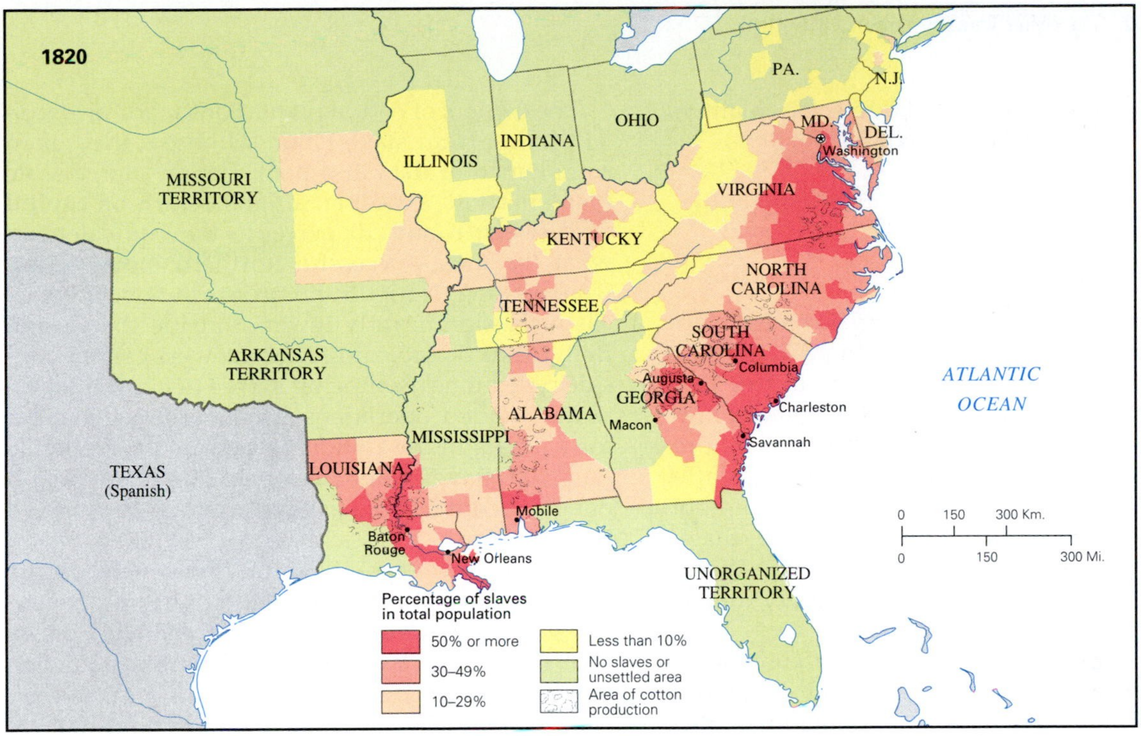

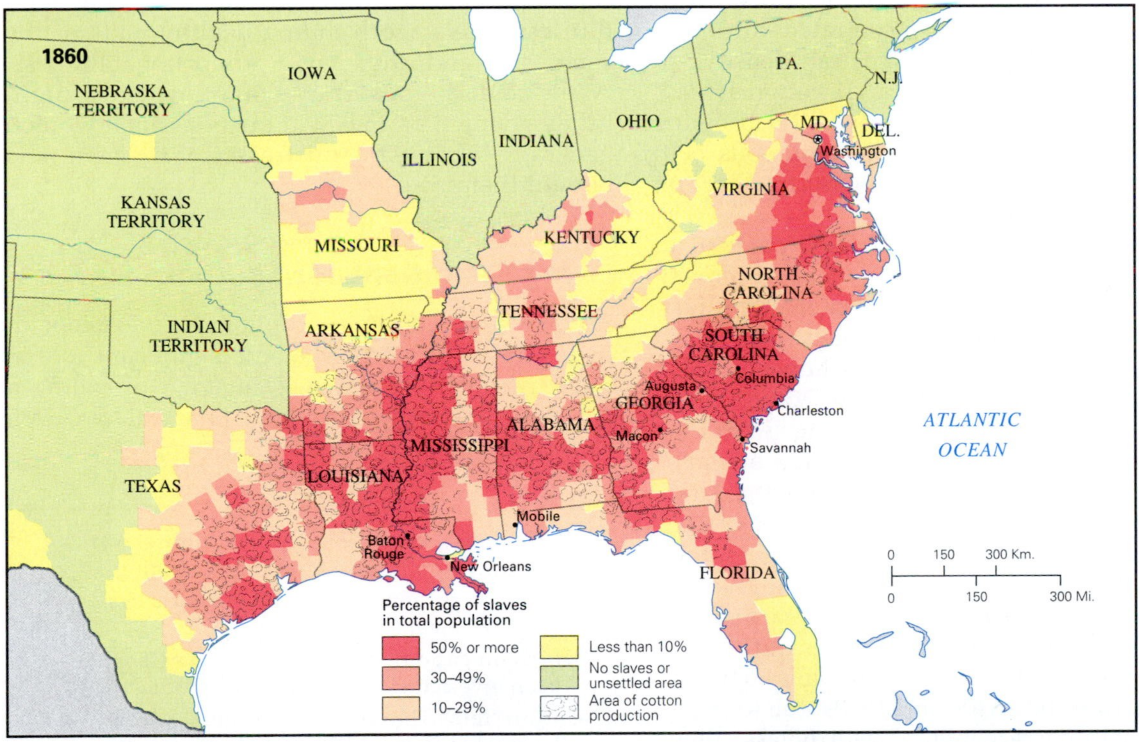

♦ **MAP 10.2 Cotton Agriculture and Slave Population** Between 1820 and 1860, the expansion of cotton agriculture and the extension of slavery went hand in hand. As these maps show, cotton production was an isolated activity in 1820, and slavery remained isolated as well. By 1860, both had extended westward.

who lived in the region—large-scale planters, slaves, free blacks, and poor whites.

A New Birth for the Slavery System

Before the emergence of King Cotton, many southerners questioned slavery. In 1782, Virginia made it legal for individual masters to free their slaves, and many did so. In 1784, Thomas Jefferson proposed an ordinance that would have prohibited slavery in all the nation's territories after 1800. Some southern leaders advocated abolishing slavery and transporting freed blacks to Africa. But the cotton boom after the War of 1812 required the expansion of slavery, not its elimination.

The rapid expansion of cotton production revived the slave system. A map showing cotton production and one showing slave population appear nearly identical (see Map 10.2). In the 1820s, when cotton was most heavily concentrated in South Carolina and Georgia, the greatest density of slaves occurred in the same area. As cotton spread west, so did slavery. By 1860, both cotton growing and slavery would appear as a continuous belt stretching from the Carolinas to the Brazos River in Texas.

Although a majority of slaves—58 percent of men and 69 percent of women—were employed as **field hands,** slaves did much more than just pick cotton. Two percent of slave men and 17 percent of women were employed as **house slaves.** The remaining 14 percent of slave women were employed in occupations like sewing, weaving, and food processing. Seventeen percent of slave men drove wagons, piloted riverboats, and herded cattle. The remaining 23 percent of the male slaves on plantations were managers and craftsmen. This percentage was even higher in cities, where slave artisans such as carpenters were often allowed to hire themselves out on the open job market. The number of slave artisans declined during the 1840s and 1850s due to pressure from white craftsmen. Nevertheless, they remained a significant proportion of the slave population.

The owners of cotton plantations made an excellent living from slave labor. Although they often complained of debt and poor markets, large-scale planters could expect an annual **return on capital** of between 8 and 10 percent—the equivalent of what the most successful northern industrialists were making. Agricultural profits in noncotton areas were significantly lower. Outside the **Cotton Belt,** tobacco, rice, and sugar growers earned considerable money selling off slaves that were not essential to their operations. The enormous demand for workers in the Cotton Belt created a profitable interstate slave trade. Thus even planters who did not grow cotton came to have a significant stake in its cultivation.

Slaves were a major capital investment. In the 1850s, a healthy male field hand in his mid-twenties sold for an average of $1,800, a skilled craftsman for $2,500. Even a male child too young to work in the fields or a man in his fifties cost anywhere from $250 to $500. The price for female slaves was more variable. A female field hand did less heavy work than a healthy male of the same age and thus cost proportionately less. A particularly beautiful young woman might bring as much as $5,000 at auction. Such women generally became the mistresses of the men who bought them.

Living Conditions for Southern Slaves

Slaveowners' enormous economic investment in their human property played a significant role in their treatment of slaves. Damaging or killing a healthy slave resulted in a large financial loss, even

field hands People who did agricultural work, such as planting, weeding, and harvesting.

house slaves People who did domestic work, such as cleaning and cooking.

return on capital The yield on money that has been invested in an enterprise or product.

Cotton Belt The region in the southeastern United States in which cotton is grown (see Map 10.2).

♦ This early photograph, taken on a South Carolina plantation before the Civil War, freezes slave life in time, giving us a view of what slave cabins looked like, how they were arranged, how slaves dressed, and how they spent what little leisure time they had. *Collection of William Gladstone.*

if **slave codes** allowed an owner to do anything to his property. A delicate balance between power and profit shaped planters' policies toward slaves and set the tone for slave life.

Housing for slaves was seldom more than adequate. Generally, slaves lived in a one-room log cabin with a dirt floor and a fireplace or stove. The cabin was usually about 16 by 18 feet and housed five or six people. Slaveowners seldom crowded people into slave quarters. As one slaveowner explained, "In no case should two families be allowed to occupy the same house. The crowding [of] a number into one house is unhealthy. It breeds contention; is destructive of delicacy of feeling, and it promotes immorality between the sexes."

Slave quarters were not particularly comfortable. The windows had only wooden shutters and no glass, so they let in flies in summer and cold in winter. An open fireplace or stove provided light as well as heat for cooking. The need for a cooking fire required slaves to build fires even at the hottest time of year. Furnishings were usually crude. Bedding consisted of straw pallets stacked on the floor. Equally simple rough-hewn wooden benches and plank tables could sometimes be found.

Clothing, too, was basic. "The proper and usual quantity of clothes for plantation hands is two suits of cotton for spring and summer, and two suits of woolen for winter; four pair of shoes and three hats," a Georgia planter observed in 1854. On many plantations, slave women made a durable but rough cotton fabric called osnaburg, which was uncomfortable to wear. One slave complained that the material was "like needles when it was new." Children often went naked in the summer and were fitted with long, loose-hanging osnaburg shirts during the colder months.

Whether slaves were fed an adequate diet remains a controversial issue among historians. Some historians have claimed that slaves were actually fed better—in terms of how much meat they ate—than contemporary workers in the North, in Germany, and in Italy. Although they concede that the slaves' typical fare of corn and pork was monotonous, these historians point out that it was

slave codes Laws that established the status of slaves, denying them basic rights and classifying them as the property of slaveowners.

quite adequate. As one slave noted, there was "plenty to eat sich as it was."

Other historians, however, have pointed to high infant mortality rates and low birth weights among slaves as evidence that slave mothers did not receive adequate nutrition. It would also appear that at least until the age of six, slave children as well were not fed a sufficient diet. American slaves at that age were shorter than their contemporaries in Europe, Africa, North America, and the Caribbean—evidence of "disastrous malnutrition." Yet by the age of 17 American male slaves were taller than factory workers in England and German peasants. This evidence suggests that American slaves began to be fed much better once they were capable of working.

What is clear is that diet-related diseases plagued slave communities. These diseases were probably no more common among slaves than among their owners, who also lived on meals consisting mostly of corn and pork. Such a diet often led to diseases such as pellagra that were caused by vitamin deficiencies. Because of the lack of proper sanitation, slaves did suffer from dysentery and cholera more than southern whites.

With the possible exception of sexual exploitation, no other aspect of slavery has generated more controversy than violence. The image of sadistic white men beating slaves permeates the dark side of the southern myth. Such behavior was not unknown, but it was far from typical. Slaves represented money, and damaging slaves was expensive. Still, given the need to keep up production, slaveowners were not shy about using measured force. "When picking cotton I never put on more than 20 stripes [lashes with a whip] and verry frequently not more than 10 or 15," one plantation owner observed. But not all owners were so practical when it came to discipline.

The significant number of slaves who lived on small farms probably did not live much better than plantation slaves. Owners of such farms saw slaves as vehicles for social and economic advancement and were willing to overwork or sell their slaves if it would benefit themselves. When all was going well, slaves might be treated like members of a farmer's family. But when conditions were bad, slaves were the first victims.

A New Planter Aristocracy

Few other images have persisted in American history longer than that of courtly southern planters in the years before the Civil War. Songs and stories have immortalized the myth of a southern aristocracy of enormous wealth and polished manners upholding a culture of romantic chivalry. Charming though this image of the **antebellum South** is, it is not accurate.

Statistics indicate that the great planters of popular myth were few and far between. In the early nineteenth century, only about a third of all southerners owned slaves. Large-scale planters were a tiny minority of these. Nearly three-fourths of these slaveholders were small farmers who owned fewer than ten slaves. Another 15 percent of slaveholders owned between ten and twenty slaves. The true planters, who possessed more than twenty slaves, constituted just 12 percent of all slaveholders. Only the very wealthy—less than 1 percent—owned more than one hundred slaves.

Even among true southern planters, the aristocratic manners and trappings of the idealized plantation were rare. King Cotton brought a new sort of man to the forefront. These new aristocrats were generally not related to the old colonial plantation gentry. Most had begun their careers as land speculators, financiers, and rough-and-tumble yeoman farmers. They had parlayed ruthlessness, good luck, and dealings in the burgeoning cotton market into large landholdings and armies of slaves.

The wives of these planters bore little resemblance to their counterparts in popular fiction. Far from being frail, helpless creatures, southern plantation mistresses carried a heavy burden of responsibility. A planter's wife supervised large staffs of

antebellum South The South in the period from 1815 to 1860 before the Civil War; *antebellum* means "before the war."

slaves, organized and ran schools for the white children on the plantation, looked out for the health of everyone, and managed the plantation in the absence of her husband.

All those duties were complicated by a sex code that relegated southern women to a peculiar position in the plantation hierarchy. On the one hand, white women were expected to exercise absolute authority over their slaves. On the other, they were to be absolutely obedient to white men. "He is master of the house," said Mary Boykin Chesnut about her husband. "To hear [him] is to obey."

This is not to say that the image of grand plantations and aristocratic living is entirely false. Enormous profits from cotton in the 1840s and 1850s permitted some planters to build elegant mansions and to affect the lifestyle that they had read about in romantic literature. Planters assumed what they imagined were the ways of medieval knights, adopting courtly manners and the nobleman's **paternalistic** obligation to look out for their social inferiors, both black and white. Women decked out in the latest gowns flocked to formal balls and weekend parties. Young men were sent to academies where they could learn the aristocratic virtues of militarism and honor. Courtship became highly ritualized, a modern imitation of imagined medieval court manners.

Plain Folk in the South

Another enduring myth about the South holds that society there was sharply divided between two kinds of people: slaveholders and slaves. If the planter myth is only partially true, this myth is totally false.

Fully two-thirds of southern white families owned no slaves. A small number of these families owned stores, craft shops, and other businesses in Charleston, New Orleans, Atlanta, and other southern cities. The great majority, however, were proud and independent small farmers.

Often tarred with the label "poor white trash," most of these yeomen were actually productive stock raisers and farmers. They concentrated on growing and producing what they needed to live, but all aspired to produce small surpluses of grain, meat, and other commodities that they could sell. Many grew small crops of cotton to raise cash. Whatever money they made was usually spent on needed manufactured goods, land, and, if possible, slaves.

These small farmers had a troubled relationship with white planters. On the one hand, many yeoman farmers yearned to join the ranks of the great planters. On the other, they resented the aristocracy and envied the planters' exalted status and power.

Free Blacks in the South

Free blacks are entirely absent from the myth of the South. The Lower South had very few free blacks, but in states such as Virginia free blacks amounted to 10 percent of the black population. Some could trace their origins back to the earliest colonial times, when African Americans had served limited terms of indenture. The majority, however, had been freed since the late 1700s. Most worked for white employers as day laborers.

Some opportunities were available to free blacks. In the Upper South, they could become master carpenters, coopers, painters, brick masons, blacksmiths, boatmen, bakers, and barbers. Black women had few opportunities as skilled laborers. Some became seamstresses, washers, and cooks. A few grew up to run small groceries, taverns, and restaurants. Folk healing and **midwifery** might also lead to economic independence for black women. Some resorted to prostitution.

Mounting restrictions on free blacks during the first half of the nineteenth century limited their freedom of movement, their economic freedom, and their legal rights. Skin color left them open to abuses and forced them to be extremely careful in their dealings with whites.

paternalistic Treating social dependents as a father treats his children, providing for their needs without allowing them rights or responsibilities.

midwifery Assistance in childbirth.

SUMMARY

E xpectations
C onstraints
C hoices
O utcomes

Although seemingly the most old-fashioned region of the country, the South that emerged during the years leading up to 1840 was a profoundly different place than it had been before. As an industrial revolution overturned the economies in Great Britain and the American Northeast, *expectations* for southerners changed radically. Although they clothed their new society in romanticized medieval garb, they were creating an altogether new kind of economy and society. The efficient production of cotton by the newly reorganized South was an essential aspect of the emerging national market economy and a powerful force in a great transformation.

Change in the North was more obvious. As factories replaced craft shops and cities replaced towns, the entire fabric of northern society seemed to come unraveled. The new economy and new technology created wonderful new *expectations* but also imposed serious *constraints.* A new social structure replaced the traditional order as unskilled and semiskilled workers, a new class of clerks, and the genteel elite made *choices* concerning their lives. As in the South, the *outcome* was a great transformation in the lives of everyone in the region.

And tying these two regions together was a new network of roads, waterways, and communications systems that accelerated the process of change. After 1840, it was possible to ship goods from any one section of the country to any other, and people in all sections were learning more about conditions in far distant parts of the growing country. Often this new information raised *expectations* of prosperity, but it also made more and more people aware of the enormity of the transformation taking place and the glaring differences between the nation's various regions. The twin *outcomes* would be greater integration in the national economy and increasing tension as mutually dependent participants in the new marketplace struggled with change and with each other.

SUGGESTED READINGS

Berlin, Ira. *Slaves Without Masters* (1975).

A masterful study of a forgotten population: free African Americans in the Old South. Lively and informative.

Cecil-Fronsman, Bill. *Common Whites: Class and Culture in Antebellum North Carolina* (1992).

A pioneering effort to describe the culture, lifestyle, and political economy shared by the antebellum South's majority population: nonslaveholding whites. Though confined in geographical scope, the study is suggestive of conditions that may have prevailed throughout the region.

Cott, Nancy M. *The Bonds of Womanhood: "Woman's Sphere" in New England, 1780–1835* (1977).

A classic work on the ties that held the women's world together but collectively bound them into a secondary position in American life.

Dublin, Thomas. *Women at Work: The Transformation of Work and Community in Lowell, Massachusetts, 1826–1860* (1979).

An interesting look at the ways in which the nature of work changed and the sorts of changes that were brought to one manufacturing community.

Eisler, Benita, ed. *The Lowell Offering: Writings by New England Mill Women, 1840–1845* (1977).

Firsthand accounts of factory life and changing social conditions written by the young women who worked at Lowell's various factories.

Fox-Genovese, Elizabeth. *Within the Plantation Household* (1988).

A look at the lives of black and white women in the antebellum South. This study is quite long but is well written and very informative.

Mitchell, Margaret. *Gone with the Wind* (1936).

Arguably the most influential book in conveying a stereotyped vision of antebellum southern life. The film version, directed by Victor Fleming in 1939, was even more influential.

Ryan, Mary P. *Cradle of the Middle Class: The Family in Oneida County, New York, 1790–1865* (1981).

A marvelous synthesis of materials focusing on the emergence of a new social and economic class in the midst of change from a traditional to a modern society.

Taylor, George Rogers. *The Transportation Revolution, 1815–1860* (1951).

The only comprehensive treatment of changes in transportation during the antebellum period and their economic impact. Nicely written.

POPULATION GROWTH AND CHANGING SUFFRAGE QUALIFICATIONS Two of the most important changes that accompanied the great transformation in American society were population growth and the extension of political suffrage. As this map shows, population density was going up in virtually every part of the country. At the same time, most states were easing their requirements for voter qualifications. These two forces together changed the face of American politics as the number of people participating in the political system expanded explosively.

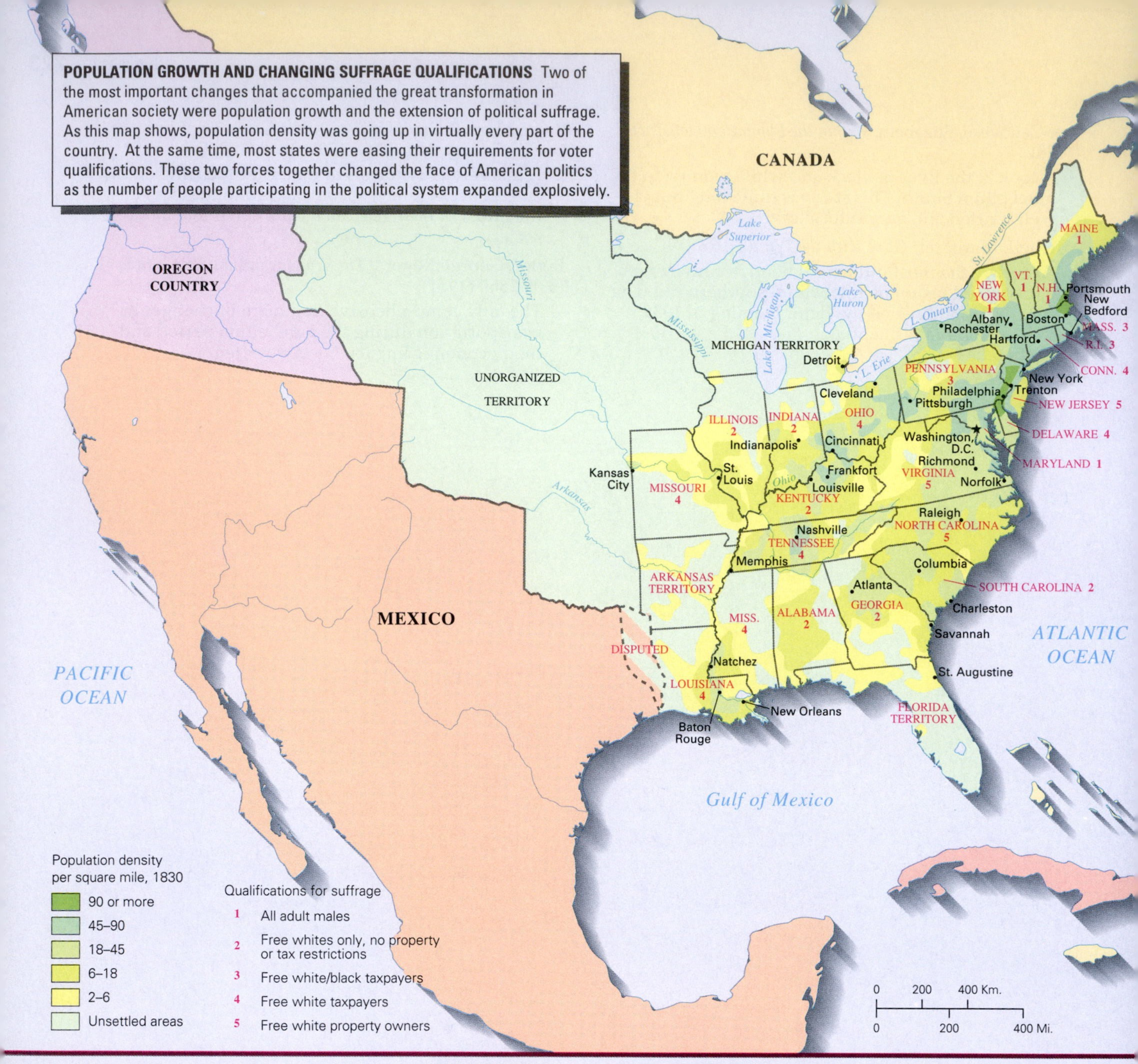

CANADA
OREGON COUNTRY
UNORGANIZED TERRITORY
MICHIGAN TERRITORY
MEXICO
PACIFIC OCEAN
ATLANTIC OCEAN
Gulf of Mexico
Lake Superior
Lake Michigan
Lake Huron
L. Ontario
L. Erie
St. Lawrence
Missouri
Mississippi
Arkansas
Ohio
MAINE 1
VT. 1
N.H. 1
NEW YORK 1
MASS. 3
R.I. 3
CONN. 4
PENNSYLVANIA 3
NEW JERSEY 5
DELAWARE 4
MARYLAND 1
OHIO 4
INDIANA 2
ILLINOIS 2
MISSOURI 4
KENTUCKY 2
VIRGINIA 5
NORTH CAROLINA 5
TENNESSEE 4
SOUTH CAROLINA 2
GEORGIA 2
ALABAMA 2
MISS. 4
LOUISIANA 4
ARKANSAS TERRITORY
FLORIDA TERRITORY
DISPUTED
Portsmouth
New Bedford
Boston
Albany
Rochester
Hartford
New York
Trenton
Philadelphia
Pittsburgh
Detroit
Cleveland
Cincinnati
Indianapolis
Washington, D.C.
Richmond
Norfolk
Frankfort
Louisville
St. Louis
Kansas City
Nashville
Raleigh
Memphis
Columbia
Atlanta
Charleston
Savannah
Natchez
St. Augustine
New Orleans
Baton Rouge
Population density per square mile, 1830
90 or more
45–90
18–45
6–18
2–6
Unsettled areas
Qualifications for suffrage
1 All adult males
2 Free whites only, no property or tax restrictions
3 Free white/black taxpayers
4 Free white taxpayers
5 Free white property owners
0 200 400 Km.
0 200 400 Mi.

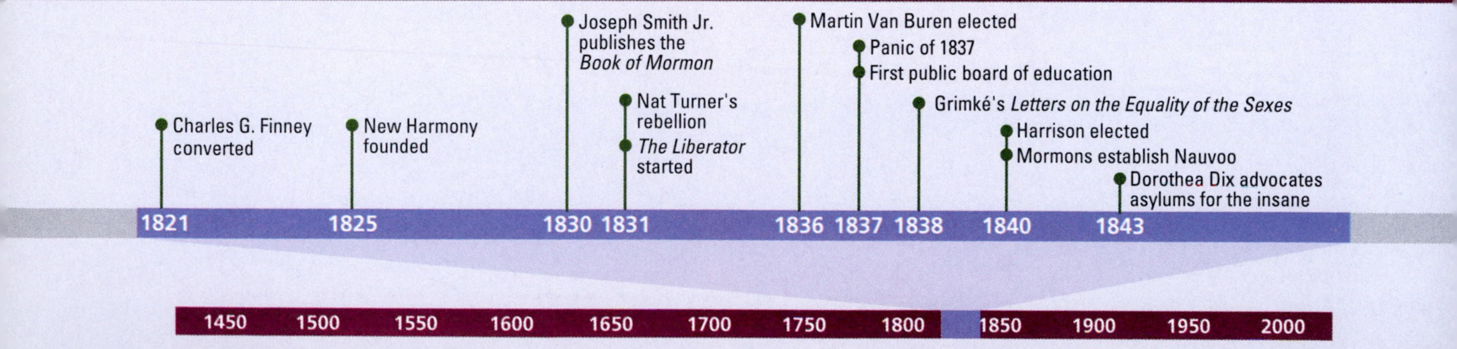

1821 Charles G. Finney converted
1825 New Harmony founded
1830 Joseph Smith Jr. publishes the *Book of Mormon*
1831 Nat Turner's rebellion
The Liberator started
1836 Martin Van Buren elected
1837 Panic of 1837
First public board of education
1838 Grimké's *Letters on the Equality of the Sexes*
1840 Harrison elected
Mormons establish Nauvoo
1843 Dorothea Dix advocates asylums for the insane
1450 1500 1550 1600 1650 1700 1750 1800 1850 1900 1950 2000

CHAPTER 11

Responses to the Great Transformation, 1815–1840

Reactions to Changing Conditions

- What choices did Americans make in dealing with the stresses created by rapid change during the Jacksonian era?
- What was the cultural outcome?

Toward an American Culture

- How did the choices made in American arts and letters reflect the spirit of change during the Jacksonian era?
- What were some other cultural outcomes of the stresses of rapid change during the era?

The Whig Alternative to Jacksonian Democracy

- What expectations did Jackson's opponents have when they built their coalition to oppose the Democrats?
- Was the outcome what they expected? Why or why not?

INTRODUCTION

E xpectations
C onstraints
C hoices
O utcomes

The great transformation in American economics and society created vast new opportunities and *expectations* for people during the antebellum period. But new *constraints* arose as quickly as new hopes. A man could amass a fortune one day and find a place among the genteel elite, only to lose it the next and find himself among the mass of hourly wage workers. Some entrepreneurs experienced this cycle many times during their careers. Others experienced no mobility at all; they were stuck either as underpaid urban workers or, worse yet, as slaves.

Different groups of Americans reacted differently to this precarious situation, as their *choices* attest. Some found relief in a new evangelical faith that empowered them to rule their own souls while forging them into close-knit congregations. Others responded more violently, attacking those they believed were responsible for the *constraints* on their lives. Some banded together in tightly organized societies bent on removing from the world sinfulness, drunkenness, ignorance, and a thousand other evils. Others *chose* to escape the world altogether, isolating themselves in communes devoted to anything from socialism to celibacy to free love. The *outcome* was a peculiar mixture of emerging societies that often were at odds with each other, frequently adding to the tensions that had driven them to make particular *choices*.

At the same time, various American cultures were coming into being. The elite and the middle class could *choose* to sip tea and read romantic poems or the novels of Nathaniel Hawthorne and James Fenimore Cooper. But the economic and social *constraints* that working-class people faced led them to choose cheap whiskey and rowdy theater performances or athletic competitions. Slaves faced even more serious *constraints*, *choosing* to stave off the worst effects of their condition by crafting a creative African-American culture. The *outcome* of these various *choices* was the foundation for the rich culture the United States enjoys today.

In politics, too, change was in the air. Old-line nationalists like Henry Clay and Daniel Webster chafed under Andrew Jackson's personal political style. Southerners like John C. Calhoun found Jackson's forcefulness discomforting and a dangerous threat to states' rights. And many Americans, like those who flocked to the Antimasonic movement, were skeptical of politics in general and of Jackson's politics in particular. Seeking to unseat Jackson, these disaffected groups invited reforming evangelicals to join them in a new coalition. In 1840, the Whig party used every political trick it could to woo voters away from the Democrats. The *outcome* of that election was a Whig victory and a new kind of politics that forever changed the way Americans conducted their public business.

CHRONOLOGY

Modernization and Rising Stress

1806	Journeyman shoemakers strike in New York City
1821	Charles G. Finney experiences a religious conversion
1823	James Fenimore Cooper's *The Pioneers*
1825	Thomas Cole begins Hudson River school of painting Robert Owen establishes community at New Harmony, Indiana
1826	Shakers have eighteen communities in the United States
1828	Weavers protest and riot in New York City Andrew Jackson elected president
1830	Joseph Smith, Jr., publishes the Book of Mormon
1831	Nat Turner's Rebellion William Lloyd Garrison begins publishing *The Liberator*
1832	Jackson reelected
1834	Riot in Charlestown, Massachusetts, leads to the destruction of a Catholic convent
1835	Protestants and Catholics clash in New York City streets
1836	Congress passes the gag rule Martin Van Buren elected president
1837	Horace Mann heads the first public board of education Panic of 1837 Ralph Waldo Emerson's "American Scholar" speech
1838	Emerson articulates transcendentalism
1840	Log-cabin campaign William Henry Harrison elected president Mormons build Nauvoo, Illinois
1841	Brook Farm established
1842	*Commonwealth v. Hunt*
1843	Dorothea Dix advocates state-funded asylums for the insane

Reactions to Changing Conditions

In the grasping, competitive conditions that were emerging in the dynamic new America, an individual's status, reputation, and welfare seemed to depend exclusively on his or her economic position. "It is all money and business, business and money which make the man now-a-days; success is everything," failed entrepreneur Chauncey Jerome lamented. The combination of rapid geographical expansion and new opportunities in business produced a highly precarious social world for all Americans. Desperate for some stability, many pushed for various reforms to bring the fast-spinning world under control.

A Second Great Awakening

Popular religion was a major counterbalance to rapid change. Beginning in the 1790s, Protestant theologians sought to create a new Protestant creed that would maintain Christian community in an era of increasing individualism and competition.

Mirroring tendencies in society, Protestant thinking during the early nineteenth century emphasized the role of the individual. Traditional

♦ Marking his triumphant arrival in New York City, evangelist Charles G. Finney had this massive tabernacle built to his own specifications. Here he held the same sort of revival meetings he had been leading in rural tents and village churches for years before arriving in the city. *Oberlin College Archives.*

Puritanism had emphasized **predestination,** the idea that individuals can do nothing to win salvation. Nathaniel Taylor of Yale College created a theology that was consistent with the new secular creed of individualism. According to Taylor, God offered salvation to all who sought it. Thus the individual had "free will" to choose or not choose salvation. Taylor's ideas struck a responsive chord in a restless and expanding America. Hundreds of ministers carried his message of a democratic God.

Most prominent among the evangelists of the **Second Great Awakening** was Charles Grandison Finney. A former schoolteacher and lawyer, Finney experienced a soul-shattering religious conversion in 1821 at the age of 29. Finney performed on the pulpit as a spirited attorney might argue a case in court. Seating those most likely to be converted on a special "anxious bench," he focused his whole attention on them. Many of those on the anxious bench fainted, experienced bodily spasms, or cried out in hysteria. Such dramatic results brought Finney enormous publicity, which he and an army of imitators used to gain access to communities all over the West and the Northeast. This religious revival spread across rural America like wildfire until Finney carried it into Boston and New York in the 1830s.

Revival meetings were remarkable affairs. Usually beginning on a Thursday and continuing until the following Tuesday, they drew crowds of up to twenty-five thousand people. Those attending listened to spirited preaching in the evenings and engaged in religious study during the daylight hours.

The revivals led to the breakdown of traditional church organizations and the creation of various Christian denominations. The Presbyterians, Baptists, and Methodists split between those who supported the new theology and those who clung to more traditional notions. Such fragmentation worried all denominations that state support of any

predestination The doctrine that God has predetermined everything that happens, including the final salvation or damnation of each person.

Second Great Awakening Series of religious revivals that began around 1800 and were characterized by emotional public meetings and conversions.

revival meeting A meeting for the purpose of reawakening religious faith, often characterized by impassioned preaching and emotional public testimony by converted sinners.

one church might give that denomination an advantage in the continuing competition for souls. Oddly, those most fervent in their Christian beliefs joined deists and other Enlightenment-influenced thinkers in arguing for even more stringent separation of church and state.

Although religious conversion had become an individual matter, revivalists did not ignore the notion of community. At revival meetings, for example, when individuals were overcome by the power of the spirit, those already saved began "surrounding them with melodious songs, or fervent prayers for their happy resurrection, in the love of Christ." Finney put great emphasis on creating a single Christian community to stand in opposition to sin. As he observed, "Christians of every denomination generally seemed to make common cause, and went to work with a will, to pull sinners out of the fire."

The intimacy forged during revivals gave a generation of isolated individuals a sense of community and a sense of duty. According to the new theology, it was each convert's obligation to carry the message of salvation to the multitudes still in darkness. New congregations, missionary societies, and a thousand other **benevolent** groups rose up to lead America in the continuing battle against sin.

The Middle Class and Moral Reform

The missionary activism that accompanied the Second Great Awakening dovetailed with the inclination toward reform among genteel and middle-class people. The Christian benevolence movement gave rise to voluntary societies that aimed to outlaw alcohol and a hundred other evils. These organizations provided both genteel and middle-class men and women with a purpose missing from their lives. Such activism drew them together in common causes and served as an antidote to the alienation and loneliness common in early nineteenth-century America.

As traditional family and village life broke down, voluntary societies pressed for public intervention to address social problems. The new theology emphasized that even the most depraved might be saved if proper means were applied. This idea had immediate application to crime and punishment. Criminals were no longer characterized as evil but were seen as lost and in need of divine guidance.

Mental illness underwent a similar change in definition. Rather than being viewed as hopeless cases suffering an innate spiritual flaw, the mentally ill were now spoken of as lost souls in need of help. **Dorothea Dix,** a young, compassionate, and reform-minded teacher, learned firsthand about the plight of the mentally ill when she taught a Sunday school class in a Boston-area prison. "I tell what I have seen," she said to the Massachusetts legislature in 1843. "Insane persons confined within the Commonwealth, in cages, closets, cellars, stalls, pens! Chained, naked, beaten with rods, and lashed into obedience!" For the balance of the century, Dix toured the country pleading the cause of the mentally ill.

Middle-class Protestant activists targeted many other areas for reform. They insisted on stopping mail delivery and closing canals on Sundays. Others joined Bible and tract societies that distributed Christian literature. They founded Sunday schools or opened domestic missions to win the **irreligious** and Roman Catholics to what they regarded as the true religion.

Many white-collar reformers were genuinely interested in forging a new social welfare system. A number of their programs, however, appear to have been aimed more at achieving control over others than social reform. Such reformers often tried to force people to conform to a middle-class standard of behavior. Reformers believed that immigrants should willingly discard their traditional customs and learn American ways. Immigrants who clung to familiar ways were suspected of disloyalty. Social control was particularly prominent in public education and **temperance.**

benevolent Concerned with doing good or organized for the benefit of charity.

Dorothea Dix Philanthropist, reformer, and educator who was a pioneer in the movement for specialized treatment of the mentally ill.

irreligious Hostile or indifferent to religion.

temperance Avoidance of alcoholic drinks.

Some communities, like Puritan Boston, had always emphasized compulsory education for children. Most communities, however, did not require children to attend school. The apprenticeship system rather than schools often provided the rudiments of reading, writing, and figuring. But as the complexity of life increased during the early nineteenth century, **Horace Mann** and others came out in favor of formal schooling.

Mann, like Charles Finney, was trained as a lawyer but believed that ignorance, not sin, lay at the heart of the nation's problems. He became the nation's leading advocate of publicly funded education for all children. "If we do not prepare children to become good citizens," Mann proclaimed, "if we do not enrich their minds with knowledge, then our republic must go down to destruction, as others have gone before it."

Massachusetts took the lead in formalizing schooling in 1837 when the state founded the country's first public board of education. Appointed head of the board, Mann extended the school year to a minimum of six months and increased teachers' salaries. Gradually, the state board changed the curriculum in Massachusetts schools, replacing classical learning and ministerial training with courses like arithmetic, practical geography, and physical science.

Education reformers were interested in more than knowledge. Mann and others were equally concerned that new immigrants and the urban poor be trained in Protestant values and middle-class habits. Thus schoolbooks emphasized promptness, persistence, discipline, and obedience to authority. In cities with numerous Roman Catholics, Catholic parents resisted the Protestant-dominated school boards by establishing **parochial schools.**

Social control was also evident in the crusade against alcohol. Before the early nineteenth century, the consumption of alcohol was not broadly perceived as a significant social problem. Two factors contributed to a new perception. One was the increasing visibility of drinking and its consequence, drunkenness, as populations became more concentrated in cities. By the mid-1820s, Rochester, New York had nearly a hundred drinking establishments that included groceries, barbershops, and even candy stores.

The changing taste of genteel and middle-class people was the second factor that contributed to a new view of alcohol. As alternatives to alcohol such as clean water and coffee became available or affordable, these people reduced their consumption of alcohol and disapproved of those who did not. By 1829, the middle class saw strong drink as "the cause of almost all of the crime and almost all of the misery that flesh is heir to." Drinking made self-control impossible and endangered morality and industry. Thus behavior that had been acceptable in the late eighteenth century was judged to be a social problem in the nineteenth.

Like most of the reform movements, the temperance movement began in churches touched by the Second Great Awakening and spread outward. Drunkenness earned special condemnation from reawakened Protestants, who believed that people besotted by alcohol could not possibly gain salvation. Christian reformers believed that stopping the consumption of alcohol was necessary not only to preserve the nation but to save people's souls.

The religious appeal of temperance was enhanced by a powerful economic appeal. Factory owners recognized that workers who drank heavily threatened the quantity and quality of production. They rallied around temperance as a way of policing their employees in and out of the factory. By promoting temperance, reformers believed they could increase production and turn the raucous lower classes into clean-living, self-controlled, peaceful workers.

The Rise of Abolitionism

Another reform movement that had profound influence in antebellum America was **abolitionism.**

Horace Mann Educator who called for publicly funded education for all children and was head of the first public board of education in the United States.

parochial school A school supported by a church parish.

abolitionism A reform movement favoring the immediate freeing of all slaves.

Although Quakers had long opposed slavery, there was little organized opposition to it before the American Revolution. During the Revolution, many Americans saw the contradiction between asserting the "unalienable rights" of "life, liberty, and the pursuit of happiness" and holding slaves (see page 121). By the end of the Revolution, Massachusetts and Pennsylvania had taken steps to abolish slavery. And by the mid-1780s, most states, except those in the Lower South, had active antislavery societies. In 1807, when Congress voted to outlaw the importation of slaves, little was said in defense of slavery. But by 1815, the morality of slavery had begun to emerge as a national issue. The profits to be made in cotton made it impossible for many white southerners to even think about ending slavery.

The **American Colonization Society,** founded in 1817, reflected public feeling about slavery. Humanitarian concern for slaves' well-being was not the only reason for the society's existence. Many members believed that the black and white races could not live together and advocated that emancipated slaves be sent back to Africa. Although the American Colonization Society began in the South, its policies were particularly popular in the Northeast and West. In eastern cities, workers feared that free blacks would lower their wages and take their jobs. Western farmers similarly feared economic competition.

Most evangelical preachers supported colonization, but a few individuals advocated more radical reforms. The most vocal leader was **William Lloyd Garrison.** A Christian reformer from Massachusetts, Garrison in 1831 founded the nation's first prominent abolitionist newspaper, *The Liberator.* In it he advocated immediate emancipation for blacks and no compensation for slaveholders. Garrison founded the American Anti-Slavery Society in 1833.

At first, Garrison had few followers. Some Christian reformers joined his cause, but the majority supported colonization. At this early date, radical abolitionists were almost universally ignored or, worse, attacked. Throughout the 1830s, riots often accompanied abolitionist rallies as angry mobs stormed stages and pulpits to silence abolitionist speakers. Still, support for the movement gradually grew. In 1836, petitions demanding an end to the slave trade in the District of Columbia flooded Congress. Congress responded by passing a **gag rule,** which lasted until 1844, to avoid any discussion of the issue. But debate over slavery could not be silenced.

The Beginnings of Working-Class Culture and Protest

Wretched living conditions and dispiriting poverty encouraged working-class people in northern cities to choose social and cultural outlets that were very different from those of upper- and middle-class Americans. Offering temporary relief from unpleasant conditions, drinking was the social distraction of choice among working people. Whiskey and gin were cheap and available during the 1820s and 1830s as western farmers used the new roads and canals to ship distilled spirits to urban markets. In the 1830s, consumers could purchase a gallon of whiskey for 25 cents.

Even activities that did not center on drinking tended to involve it. While genteel and middle-class people remained in their private homes reading, working people attended popular theaters. **Minstrel shows** featured fast-paced music and raucous comedy. Plays, such as Benjamin Baker's *A Glance at New York in 1848,* depicted caricatures of working-class "Bowery B'hoys" and "G'hals" and of the well-off Broadway "pumpkins" they poked fun at. To put the audience in the proper

American Colonization Society Organization established in 1817 to send free blacks from the United States to Africa; it used government money to buy land in Africa and found the colony of Liberia.

William Lloyd Garrison Abolitionist leader who founded and published *The Liberator,* an antislavery newspaper.

gag rule A rule that limits or prevents debate on an issue.

minstrel show A variety show in which white actors made up as blacks presented jokes, songs, dances, and comic skits.

mood, theater owners sold cheap drinks in the lobby or in basement pubs. Alcohol was usually also sold at sporting events such as bare-knuckle boxing contests.

Stinging from their low status in the urbanizing and industrializing society, and freed from inhibitions by hours of drinking, otherwise rational workingmen pummeled one another to let off steam. Fistfights often turned into brawls and then into riots, pitting Protestants against Catholics, immigrants against the native-born, and whites against blacks.

Working-class women experienced the same dull but dangerous working conditions and dismal living circumstances as working-class men, but their lives were even harder. Single women were particularly bad off. They were paid significantly less than men but had to pay as much and sometimes more for living quarters, food, and clothing. Marriage could reduce a woman's personal expenses—but at a cost. While men congregated in the barbershop or pub during their leisure hours, married women were stuck in tiny apartments caring for children and doing household chores. Social convention banned women from many activities that provided their husbands, boyfriends, and sons some relief.

In view of their working and living conditions, it is not surprising that some manufacturing workers began to organize in protest. Skilled journeymen took the lead in making their dissatisfaction with new methods of production known to factory owners.

Journeyman shoemakers staged the first labor strike in America in 1806 to protest the hiring of unskilled workers to perform work that the journeymen had been doing. The strike failed, but it set a precedent for labor actions for the next half-century. The replacement of skilled workers remained a major cause of labor unrest in the 1820s and 1830s. Journeymen bemoaned the decline in craftsmanship and their loss of power to set hours, conditions, and wages. Industrialization was costing journeymen their independence and forcing some to become wage laborers.

Instead of attacking or even criticizing industrialization, however, journeymen simply asked for decent wages and working conditions. To achieve these goals, they banded together in **trade unions.** During the 1830s, trade unions from different towns formed the beginnings of a national trade union movement. In this way, house carpenters, shoemakers, hand-loom weavers, printers, and comb makers attempted to enforce national wage standards in their industries. In 1834, many of these merged to form the **National Trades' Union,** which was the first labor union in the nation's history to represent many different crafts.

The trade union movement accomplished little during the antebellum period. Factory owners, bankers, and others who wanted to keep labor cheap used every device available to prevent unions from gaining the upper hand. Employers formed their own associations to resist union activity. They also used the courts to keep unions from disrupting business. A series of local court decisions upheld employers and threatened labor's right to organize.

A breakthrough for trade unions finally came in 1842. The Massachusetts Supreme Court decided in *Commonwealth v. Hunt* that Boston's journeyman boot makers had the right to organize and to call strikes. By that time, however, the Panic of 1837, which threw many people out of work for long periods of time, had so undermined the labor movement that legal protection became somewhat meaningless.

Not all labor protests were peaceful. In 1828, for example, immigrant weavers protested the low wages paid by Alexander Knox, New York City's leading textile employer. Demanding higher pay, they stormed and vandalized his home. The weavers then marched to the homes of weavers who had not joined the protest and destroyed their looms.

More frequently, however, working men took out their frustrations not on their employers but on other ethnic groups. Ethnic riots shook New York, Philadelphia, and Boston during the late 1820s and 1830s. In 1834, rumors that innocent girls were be-

trade union A labor organization whose members work in a specific trade or craft.

National Trades' Union The first national association of trade unions in the United States; it was formed in 1834.

ing held captive and tortured in a Catholic convent near Boston led a Protestant mob to burn the convent to the ground. A year later, as many as five hundred native-born Protestants and immigrant Irish Catholics clashed in the streets of New York. These ethnic tensions were the direct result of declining economic power and terrible living conditions. Native-born journeymen blamed immigrants for lowered wages and loss of status. Immigrants hated being treated like dirt.

Apart from drinking and fighting among themselves, working people in America during the early nineteenth century did little to protest their fate. Why were American workers so unresponsive? One reason may be that as poor as conditions were, life was better than in Ireland and Germany. Another reason is that workers did not see themselves staying poor. As one English observer commented, women in America's factories were willing to endure boring twelve-hour days because "none of them consider it as their permanent condition." Men expected to "accumulate enough to go off to the West, and buy an estate at 1¼ dollar an acre, or set up in some small way of business at home."

Culture, Resistance, and Rebellion Among Southern Slaves

Like their northern counterparts, slaves fashioned for themselves a culture that helped them survive and maintain their humanity under inhumane conditions. The degree to which African practices endured in America is remarkable, for slaves seldom came to southern plantations directly from Africa. That many African practices were passed on from one generation to another demonstrates the strength of slave families, religion, and folklore. What evolved was a unique African-American culture.

Traces of African heritage were visible in slaves' clothing, entertainment, and folkways. Often the plain garments that masters provided were supplemented with colorful head scarves and other decorations similar to those worn in Africa. Hairstyles often resembled those characteristic of African tribes. Music, dancing, and other forms of public entertainment and celebration also showed strong African roots. Musical instruments were copies of traditional ones, modified only by the use of New World materials. Other links to Africa abounded. Healers used African ceremonies, Christian rituals, and both imported and native herbs to effect cures. These survivals and adaptations of African traditions provided a strong base on which blacks erected a solid African-American culture.

Strong family ties helped make possible this cultural continuity. Slave families endured despite a precarious life. Husbands and wives could be sold to different owners or be separated at the whim of a master, and children could be taken away from their parents. Families that remained intact, however, remained stable. When families did suffer separation, the **extended family** of grandparents, uncles, aunts, and other relatives offered emotional support and helped maintain some sense of continuity.

Relationships within slave families closely resembled relationships among white families. As in southern white families, black women, when not laboring at the assigned tasks of plantation work, generally performed domestic work and tended children while the men hunted, fished, did carpentry, and performed other "manly" tasks. Children were likely to help out by tending family gardens and doing other light work until they were old enough to join their parents in the fields or learn skilled trades.

Religion was another means for preserving African-American traits. White churches virtually ignored the religious needs of slaves until the Great Awakening (see pages 75–76), when many white evangelicals turned their attention to the spiritual life of slaves. In the face of slaveowners' negligence, evangelical Presbyterians, Baptists, and Methodists took it upon themselves to carry the Christian message to slaves.

The Christianity that slaves practiced resembled the religion practiced by southern whites but also differed from it in many ways. Slave preachers

extended family A family group consisting of various close relatives as well as the parents and children.

untrained in white theology often equated Christian and African religious figures, creating unique African-American religious symbols. The joining of African musical forms with Christian lyrics gave rise to a new form of Christian music: the **spiritual.** Masters often encouraged such worship, thinking that the Christian emphasis on obedience and meekness would make slaves better and more peaceful servants. Some, however, discouraged religion among their slaves, fearing that large congregations of slaves might be moved to rebellion. Thus some religious slaves had to meet in secret to practice their own particular form of Christianity.

Despite the hopes of white masters, slaves did resist and rebel, sometimes subtly and sometimes quite openly and violently. Slaves adopted clever strategies for getting extra food, clothing, and other supplies and developed sly techniques for manipulating their masters. Slaves often stole food simply to fluster their masters. Farm animals disappeared mysteriously, tools broke in puzzling ways, and people fell ill from unknown diseases.

The importance of clever resistance is evident in the tales that slaves told among themselves. Perhaps the best known are the stories of Br'er Rabbit (Brother Rabbit), the physically weak but shrewd character who uses deceit to get what he wants. One particularly revealing tale tells of Br'er Rabbit's being caught by Br'er Fox. Unable to get a fire started to cook the helpless rabbit, Fox threatens Rabbit with all sorts of horrible tortures. Rabbit replies that Fox can do anything he wants so long as he does not throw him into the nearby briar patch. Seizing on Rabbit's apparent fear, Fox pitches him deep into the briar patch, expecting to see Rabbit die amid the thorns. But Br'er Rabbit had been raised in a briar patch, and so he scampers away, laughing at how he has tricked Br'er Fox into doing exactly what he wanted him to do. Such stories taught slaves how to deal with powerful adversaries.

Not all slave resistance took covert forms. Perhaps the most common form of active resistance was running away (see Map 11.1). An average of about a thousand slaves made their way to freedom each year between 1840 and 1860. Most of them lived in the **border states** or Texas, where freedom lay not far away. Most were also young male slaves between the ages of 16 and 35. Artisans and other slaves with special skills became fugitive slaves more frequently than other slaves.

Runaway slaves left few documents explaining why they were willing to face hounds, patrollers, hunger, and other dangers. Frederick Douglass, who became a famous abolitionist leader, ran away because he grew tired of turning his wages over to his master. Many ran away to be with wives who had been sold. But contemporary observers thought that fear of punishment was the most common motivation for running away. One former slave disagreed with this explanation: "They didn't do something and run. They run before they did it, 'cause they knew that if they struck a white man there wasn't going to be a nigger."

To southerners, the most frightening form of slave resistance was armed revolt. The nineteenth-century South saw very few actual rebellions, although a number of planned uprisings were betrayed before they could take place. Such was the fate of Gabriel Prosser's rebellion in Richmond, Virginia, in 1800, and the Denmark Vesey conspiracy in Charleston in 1822.

Nat Turner, a black preacher, carried out the most serious and violent of the antebellum slave revolts. In 1831, Turner led about seventy slaves in a predawn raid against the slaveholding households in Southampton County, Virginia. During the four days of Nat Turner's Rebellion, the slaves slaughtered fifty-five white men, women, and children. Angry whites finally captured and executed Turner and sixteen of his followers.

In the wake of such frightening revolts, southern courts and legislatures clapped stricter controls on slaves and free blacks. In most areas, free blacks were denied the right to own guns, to buy liquor, and to hold public assemblies. Slaves were forbidden to attend unsupervised worship services and to learn reading and writing. The new

spiritual A religious folksong originated by African Americans, often expressing a longing for deliverance from the constraints and hardships of their lives.

border states The slave states of Delaware, Maryland, Kentucky, and Missouri, which shared a border with states in which slavery was illegal.

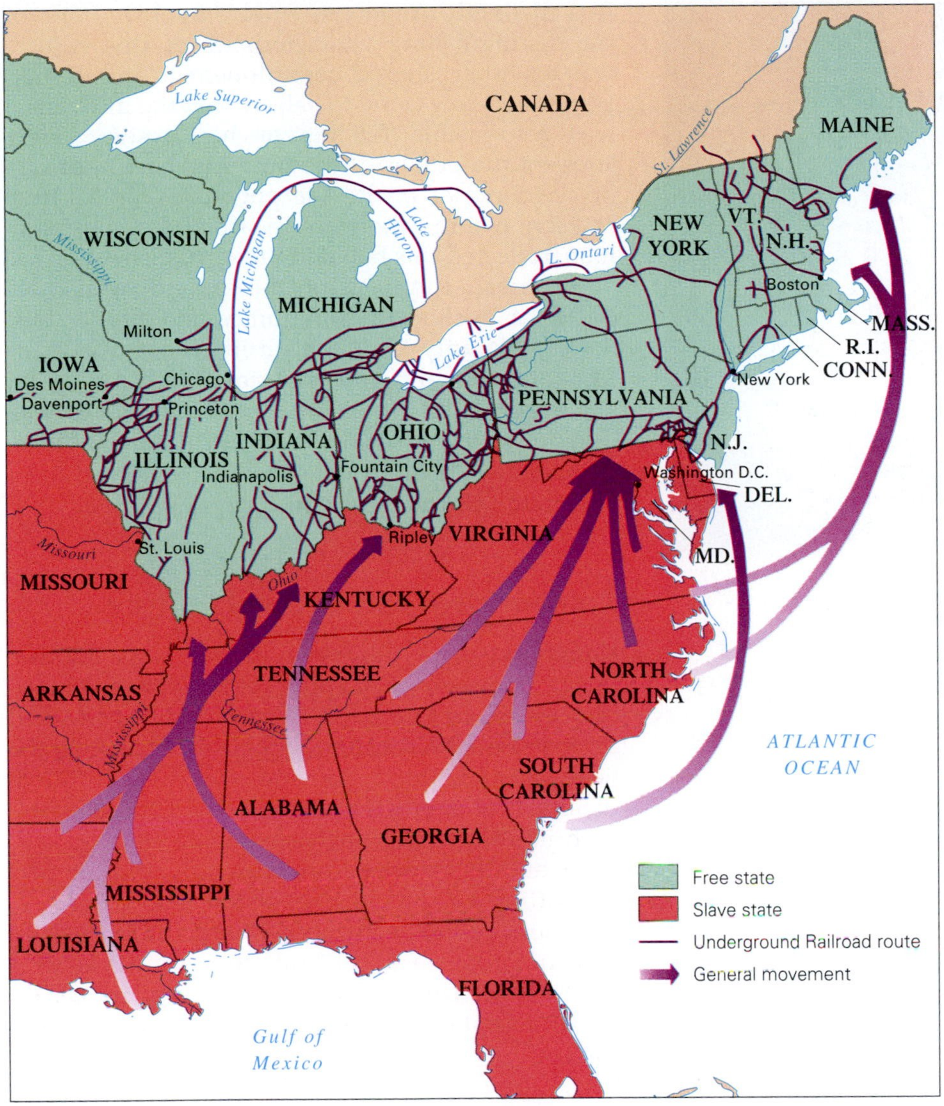

♦ **MAP 11.1 Escaping from Slavery** Running away was one of the most prominent forms of slaves resistance during the antebellum period. Success often depended on help from African Americans who had already gained their freedom and from sympathetic whites. Beginning in the 1820s, an informal and secret network called the Underground Railroad provided escape routes for slaves who were daring enough to risk all for freedom. The routes shown here are based on documentary evidence, but the network's secrecy makes it impossible to know whether they are all drawn accurately.

♦ No pictures of famed slave revolt leader Nat Turner are known to exist, but this nineteenth-century painting illustrates how one artist imagined the appearance of Turner and his fellow conspirators. White southerners lived in terror of scenes such as this and passed severe laws designed to prevent African Americans from having such meetings. *Library of Congress.*

laws virtually eliminated slaves as unsupervised urban craftsmen after 1840.

Fear of slave revolts reached paranoid levels in areas where slaves outnumbered whites. Whites felt justified in passing strong restrictions and using harsh methods to enforce them. White citizens formed local **vigilance committees,** which rode armed through the countryside to intimidate slaves. Local authorities pressed court clerks and ship captains to limit the freedom of blacks. White critics of slavery, who had been numerous and well respected before the birth of King Cotton, were harassed and sometimes beaten into silence. Increasingly, the extension of slavery limited the freedom of both whites and blacks.

Toward an American Culture

The profound political, social, and economic changes of the early nineteenth century gave birth to a distinctly American culture by 1840. One of the distinguishing characteristics of this culture was a widely shared commitment to individualism. Americans came to believe that the individual was responsible for his or her destiny. They stressed the power of the individual self, not fate or accidents of birth. The popularity of Andrew Jackson, whom Americans regarded as a self-made man, reflected this belief in individualism.

American emphasis on the individual also reflected a decline in community and family ties. Such ties simply could not survive the corrosive effects of social and geographical mobility. The desire to get ahead often took precedence over everything else. As the visiting French nobleman **Alexis de Tocqueville** observed, Americans seemed to be "animated by the most selfish cupidity [greed]."

Romanticism and Genteel Culture

Romanticism, a European import, was another major ingredient in shaping contemporary American culture. In Europe, the Romantics had rebelled against Enlightenment rationalism, stressing the heart over the mind, the wild over the controlled, the mystical over the mundane. The United States, with its millions of uncharted acres, its wild animals, and its colorful frontier myths, was the perfect setting for romanticism to flourish.

American intellectuals combined individualism and romanticism to celebrate the positive aspects of life in the United States. This combination won broad acceptance among the genteel and middle classes.

vigilance committees Groups of armed private citizens who use the threat of mob violence to enforce their own interpretation of the law.

Alexis de Tocqueville French aristocrat who toured the United States in 1830–1831 to investigate and write about political and social conditions in the new democracy.

romanticism Artistic and intellectual movement characterized by interest in nature, emphasis on emotion and imagination, and rebellion against social conventions.

Romanticism and individualism had their greatest spokesman in **Ralph Waldo Emerson.** Emerson by 1829 had become pastor of the prestigious Second Unitarian Church in Boston. He was thrown into a religious crisis, however, when his young wife, Ellen Louisa, died in 1831 after only two years of marriage.

Emerson could find no consolation in the rationalism of **Unitarianism.** He sought alternatives in Europe, where he met the famous Romantic poets William Wordsworth and Thomas Carlyle. They taught Emerson to seek truth in nature and spirit rather than in reason and order. Building from their insights, Emerson created a new philosophy and religion called **transcendentalism.** Recovered from his grief, he returned to the United States to begin a new career as an essayist and lecturer.

The problem with historical Christianity, Emerson told students at the Harvard Divinity School in 1838, is that it treated revelation as "long ago given and done, as if God were dead." Emerson, however, believed that revelation could happen at any time and that God was everywhere. Only through direct contact with the **transcendent** power in the universe could men and women know the truth. "It cannot be received at second hand," Emerson insisted, but only through the independent working of the liberated mind.

Although Emerson emphasized **nonconformity** and dissent in his writings, his ideas were in tune with the economic currents of his day. In celebrating the individual, Emerson validated the surging individualism of Jacksonian America. Rather than condemning the "selfish cupidity" that Alexis de Tocqueville said characterized Jacksonian America, Emerson stated that money represented the "prose of life." Little wonder, then, that Emerson's ideas found a wide following among young people of means in the Northeast.

Emerson's declaration of literary independence from European models in an 1837 address titled "The American Scholar" set a bold new direction for American literature. During the next twenty years, Henry David Thoreau, Walt Whitman, Henry Wadsworth Longfellow, and others spread the transcendentalist message, emphasizing the uniqueness of the individual and the role of literature as a vehicle for self-discovery. "I celebrate myself, and sing myself," Whitman proclaimed in *Leaves of Grass,* published in 1855. Like the romantics, the transcendentalists celebrated the primitive and the common. Longfellow wrote of the legendary Indian chief Hiawatha and sang the praises of the village blacksmith. In "I Hear America Singing," Whitman made poetry of the everyday speech of mechanics, carpenters, and other common folk.

Perhaps the most radical of the transcendentalists was Emerson's good friend **Henry David Thoreau.** Emerson advocated self-reliance, but Thoreau embodied it. He lived for several years at Walden Pond near Concord, Massachusetts, where he did his best to live independently of the rapidly modernizing market economy. "I went to the woods because I wished to live deliberately," Thoreau wrote, "and not, when I came to die, discover that I had not lived."

James Fenimore Cooper, Herman Melville, Nathaniel Hawthorne, and Edgar Allan Poe pushed American literature in a romantic direction. Even before Emerson's "American Scholar," Cooper had launched a new sort of American novel and American hero. In *The Pioneers* (1823), Cooper introduced Natty Bumppo, a frontiersman whose honesty, independent-mindedness, and skill as a

Ralph Waldo Emerson Philosopher, writer, and poet whose essays and poems made him a central figure in the transcendentalist movement and an important figure in the development of literary expression in America.

Unitarianism Christian religious association that considers God alone to be divine; it holds that all people are granted salvation and that faith should be based on reason and conscience.

transcendentalism A philosophical and literary movement asserting the existence of God within human beings and in nature and the belief that intuition is the highest source of knowledge.

transcendent Lying beyond the normal range of experience.

nonconformity Refusal to accept or conform to the beliefs and practices of the majority.

Henry David Thoreau Writer, naturalist, and friend of Ralph Waldo Emerson; his best-known work is *Walden* (1854).

marksman represented the rough-hewn virtues so beloved by romantics. Altogether, Cooper wrote five novels featuring the plucky Bumppo.

Like Cooper, Herman Melville emphasized primitive scenes and noble savages in his adventure novels. Beginning with *Typee* (1846), Melville's semiautobiographical accounts of an American seaman among the natives of the South Pacific became overnight best sellers. Melville followed these with his most famous novel, *Moby Dick* (1851), an **allegorical** tale of a good man turned bad by his obsession for revenge against a whale he believed to be evil. Literary critics and the public hated *Moby Dick.*

Nathaniel Hawthorne had more financial success than Melville in exploring the contest between good and evil. In his first famous work, *Twice-Told Tales* (1837), Hawthorne presented readers with a collection of moral allegories stressing the evils of pride, selfishness, and secret guilt. He brought these themes to fruition in his 1850 novel *The Scarlet Letter,* in which adulteress Hester Prynne overcomes shame to gain redemption and her secret lover, Puritan minister Arthur Dimmesdale, is destroyed by his hidden sins.

Edgar Allan Poe excelled in telling **Gothic** tales of pure terror. For Poe, the purpose of writing was to stir the passions of the reader. Poe tried to instill fear, which he believed was the strongest emotion. Haunting short stories like "The Tell-Tale Heart," "The Masque of the Red Death," and "The Pit and the Pendulum" did precisely that.

The drive to celebrate America and American uniqueness also influenced the visual arts during this period. Greek and Roman themes had dominated American art through the first decades of the nineteenth century. Horatio Greenough's statue of George Washington, for example, depicted the nation's first president wrapped in a toga.

After 1825, however, American scenes gradually replaced classical ones. Thomas Cole, a British immigrant painter, was the dominant force in this movement. Cole fell in love with the landscapes he saw in New York's Hudson River valley. The refreshing naturalness and Americanness of Cole's paintings created a large following known as the **Hudson River school,** who lived in and painted landscapes of this valley.

George Caleb Bingham started a different artistic trend in his realistic pictures of common people engaged in everyday activities. He departed from traditional portrait artists, who painted the well-to-do posed in their finery. The flatboatmen, marketplace dwellers, and electioneering politicians in Bingham's paintings were artistic testimony to the emerging democratic style of America in the Jacksonian period.

The Jacksonian era also saw a proliferation of women writers. Some, like Sarah Moore Grimké, the sister of abolitionist Angelina Grimké, deplored the status of women in American society in her *Letters on the Equality of the Sexes and the Condition of Women* (1838). Margaret Fuller, who edited the influential transcendentalist magazine *The Dial,* explored the same theme in *Women in the Nineteenth Century* (1845). The most popular women writers of the day, however, depicted the new genteel woman in an approving, sentimental fashion. Lydia Sigourney, one of the first women to carve out an independent living as a writer, was contributing regularly to more than thirty popular magazines by 1830. Poe, who dismissed her work as shallow, nevertheless solicited her to write for his magazine. She wrote two best sellers in 1833, *How to Be Happy* and *Letters to Young Ladies,* both of which glorified women in their domestic roles.

Radical Attempts to Regain Community

Some religious groups and thinkers tried to ward off the excesses of Jacksonian individualism by

allegorical Having the characteristics of an allegory, a literary device in which characters and events stand for abstract ideas.

Gothic A style of fiction that emphasizes mystery, horror, and the supernatural; it is so named because the action often takes place in gloomy, ghost-infested castles built in the medieval Gothic style of architecture.

Hudson River school The first native school of landscape painting in the United States (1825–1875); it attracted artists rebelling against the neoclassical tradition.

forming communities that experimented with various living arrangements and ideological commitments. Nearly all of these experiments were in the North, where the unsettling effects of a market-driven economy were felt most acutely. Those who joined these communes hoped to strike a new balance between self-sufficiency and community support.

Brook Farm, a commune near Boston founded by transcendentalist George Ripley in 1841, was such a community. Ripley's goal in establishing Brook Farm was to "permit a more wholesome and simple life than can be led amidst the pressure of our competitive institutions." Each member of the community was expected to work on the farm to make the group self-sufficient. Brook Farm attracted few residents during its first few years. The adoption in 1844 of the **socialist** ideas of Frenchman Charles Fourier, however, attracted numerous artisans and farmers. **Fourierism** emphasized community self-sufficiency but also called for the equal sharing of earnings among members of the community. A disastrous fire in 1845 cut the experiment short. Brook Farm was one of nearly a hundred Fourierist communities founded during this period from Massachusetts to Michigan. All ended in failure.

So did Robert Owen's community at New Harmony, Indiana. Owen, a wealthy Welsh industrialist, believed that the solution to poverty was to collect the unemployed into self-contained and self-supporting villages. In 1825, Owen attempted to put his ideas into practice when he purchased an existing agricultural commune. At **New Harmony,** Owen opened a textile factory in which ownership was held communally and decisions were made by group consensus. Despite such innovations, internal dissent and economic difficulties forced New Harmony to close in 1827.

Communal experiments based on religious ideas fared much better than those founded on secular theories. The **Oneida Community,** established in central New York in 1848, reflected the religious ideas of its founder, John Humphrey Noyes. No church was willing to ordain him because of his beliefs that Christ had already returned to earth and had commanded his followers to live communally and to practice group marriage. Unlike Brook Farm and New Harmony, the Oneida Community was financially successful, establishing thriving logging, farming, and manufacturing businesses. It finally disbanded in 1881 because of local outcries about the "free love" practiced by its members.

The **Shakers** avoided the Oneida Community's problems by banning sex altogether. Called the "Shaking Quakers" because of the ecstatic dances they performed as part of their worship services, they grew steadily after their founder, Ann Lee, emigrated from Great Britain in 1774. By 1826, there were eighteen Shaker communities in eight states. The Shakers at one time claimed nearly six thousand members. Their emphasis on celibacy stemmed from their belief that sexuality promoted selfishness and sinfulness. Farming activities and the manufacture and sale of widely admired furniture and handicrafts brought them success. After 1860, however, recruiting new members became difficult. The Shakers' rules of celibacy ultimately spelled their demise.

Brook Farm An experimental farm based on cooperative living; established in 1841, it first attracted transcendentalists and then serious farmers before fire destroyed it in 1845.

socialist Someone who believes in the public ownership of manufacturing, farming, and other forms of production so that they benefit society rather than create individual profit.

Fourierism Social system advanced by Charles Fourier, who argued that people were capable of living in perfect harmony under the right conditions, which included communal life and republican government.

New Harmony Utopian community that Robert Owen established in Indiana in 1825; economic problems and discord among members led to its failure two years later.

Oneida Community A religious community established in central New York in 1848; its members shared property, practiced group marriage, and reared children under communal care.

Shakers A mid-eighteenth-century offshoot of the Quakers, the Shakers practiced communal living and strict celibacy; they gained members only by conversion or adoption.

By far the most successful of these communal groups were the Mormons. They harnessed the religious fervor of the Second Great Awakening, the romantics' appeal to the primitive, and the inclination to communal living displayed by the Shakers and other groups. This peculiarly American movement was founded by **Joseph Smith, Jr.,** a New York farmer. Smith claimed in 1827 that an angel had led him to a set of golden plates inscribed in a strange hieroglyphic language. Smith's translation of these plates resulted in the Book of Mormon, printed in 1830.

Smith then founded the Church of Jesus Christ of Latter-Day Saints, also called the Mormon church, after the prophet Mormon, who had written the golden plates. A revelation inspired Smith in 1831 to lead his congregation out of New York to Kirtland, Ohio. Stressing community, faith, and hard work, the **Mormons** thrived there for a while. More traditional Protestants, however, regarded Smith's followers with suspicion, envy, and hostility. Their misgivings increased markedly after 1840, when Smith and other elders in the church began to practice **polygamy.** Increasing persecution convinced Smith to lead his followers farther west into Missouri.

The Mormons found Missouri frontiersmen no less resentful than easterners. Smith then decided to lead his congregation to Illinois, founding the city of Nauvoo in 1840. Continuing conversions to the new faith brought a flood of Mormons to Smith's Zion in Illinois. In 1844, Nauvoo, with a population of fifteen thousand Mormons, dwarfed every other Illinois city.

The Whig Alternative to Jacksonian Democracy

Although Andrew Jackson was perhaps the most popular president since George Washington, not all Americans agreed with his philosophy, policies, or political style. Men like Henry Clay and Daniel Webster opposed Jackson in and out of Congress. Gradually, anger over Jackson's policies and anxiety about the changing character of the nation convinced dissidents to combine into a new national party.

The End of the Old Party Structure

Jackson's enemies were deeply divided among themselves. Henry Clay had started the Bank War (see page 202) to rally Jackson's opponents behind a political cause. Southern politicians like John C. Calhoun, however, feared and hated Clay's nationalistic policies as much as they did Jackson's assertions of federal power. And political outsiders like the Antimasons distrusted all political organizations.

The Antimasons kicked off the anti-Jackson campaign in September 1831 when they held a national nominating convention in Baltimore. The convention drew a wide range of people who were disgusted with politics as usual. Thurlow Weed cajoled the convention into nominating William Wirt, a respected lawyer from Maryland, as its presidential candidate. Weed fully expected that the Republicans would later rubber-stamp the Antimasonic nomination and present a united front against Jackson. But the Republicans, fearful of the Antimasons' odd combination of **machine politics** and antiparty philosophy, nominated Clay for president.

Even having two anti-Jackson parties in the running did not satisfy some. Distrustful of the Antimasons and hating Clay's nationalist philosophy, some southerners refused to support any of the announced candidates. They backed nullification advocate John Floyd of Virginia.

Lack of unity spelled disaster for Jackson's opponents. The president received 219 electoral votes to Clay's 49, Wirt's 7, and Floyd's 11. Despite un-

Joseph Smith, Jr. Founder of the Church of Jesus Christ of Latter-Day Saints, also known as the Mormon church; he led his congregation westward from New York to Illinois, where he was murdered by an anti-Mormon mob.

Mormons Members of the church founded by Joseph Smith in 1830; Mormon doctrines are based on the Bible, the Book of Mormon, and revelations made to church leaders.

polygamy The practice of having more than one husband or wife at a time.

machine politics The aggressive use of influence, favors, and tradeoffs by a political organization, or "machine," to mobilize support among its followers.

BORN TO COMMAND.
OF VETO MEMORY.
HAD I BEEN CONSULTED.
VETO
CONSTITUTION of the UNITED STATES
Internal Improvements
U.S. Bank
KING ANDREW THE FIRST.

♦ Calling themselves Whigs after the British political party that opposed royal authority, Henry Clay, John C. Calhoun, and Daniel Webster joined forces to oppose what they characterized as Andrew Jackson's kingly use of power. This lithograph from 1834, depicting Jackson in royal dress stepping on the Constitution, expresses their view quite vividly. *Tennessee Historical Society.*

settling changes in the land and continuing political chaos, the people still wanted the hero of New Orleans as their leader.

The New Political Coalition

If one lesson emerged clearly from the election of 1832, it was that Jackson's opponents needed to unite if they expected to challenge the Democrats successfully. By 1834, the various factions opposing Jackson had formed the **Whig party.** The term "Whig" referred to the party in opposition to the British king. In adopting it, Clay and his associates called attention to Jackson's growing power and what they saw as his monarchical pretensions. They took to calling Jackson "King Andrew."

Clay's supporters formed the heart of the Whigs. The nullifiers, however, quickly came around. Late in 1832, Clay and Calhoun joined forces in opposing Jackson's appointment of Martin Van Buren, whom Jackson had picked as his political successor, as American minister to Britain. The Antimasons joined the Whig coalition prior to the 1834 congressional elections. Not only was Jackson a Mason, but his use of patronage and back-alley politics disgusted the Antimasons sufficiently to overcome their distrust of Clay's party philosophy. Christian reformers who wanted to eliminate alcohol, violations of the Sabbath, and dozens of other perceived evils also joined the Whigs. Evangelicals disapproved of Jackson's lifestyle and his views on issues ranging from slavery to alcohol.

The new Whig coalition proved its ability to challenge Jacksonian Democrats in the 1834 election. In their first electoral contest, the Whigs won nearly 40 percent of the seats in the House and over 48 percent in the Senate.

Van Buren in the White House

Jackson had seemed to be a tower of strength when he was first elected to the presidency in 1828, but he was aging and ill by the end of his second term. Nearly 70 years old and plagued by various ailments, Old Hickory decided not to run for a third term. Instead, he did all that was within his power to ensure that Martin Van Buren would win the Democratic presidential nomination in 1836.

Meanwhile, Clay and the Whigs were hatching a novel strategy. Rather than holding a national

Whig party Political party that came into being in 1834 as an anti-Jackson coalition and that charged "King Andrew" with executive tyranny.

convention and nominating one candidate, the Whigs let each region's party organization nominate its own candidates. As a result, four **favorite sons** ran on the Whig ticket: Daniel Webster of Massachusetts, Hugh Lawson White of Tennessee, W. P. Mangum of North Carolina, and William Henry Harrison of Ohio. Whig leaders hoped the large number of candidates would confuse voters and throw the election into the House of Representatives. This strategy failed narrowly. Van Buren squeaked by in the Electoral College, winning by a margin of less than 1 percent.

Van Buren's entire presidency was colored by the economic collapse that occurred just weeks after he took office. Although the Panic of 1837 was a direct outcome of the Bank War and Jackson's money policies, Van Buren bore the blame. The crisis had begun with bank president Nicholas Biddle's manipulation of credit and interest rates in an effort to have the Second Bank rechartered. Jackson had added to the problem by issuing the **Specie Circular** on August 15, 1836. The intent of the Specie Circular was to make it more difficult for speculators to obtain public land by requiring payment in specie, or hard money. The effect was to remove paper money from the economy.

The contraction in credit and currency had the same impact in 1837 as in 1819: the national economy collapsed. By May 1837, New York banks were no longer accepting any paper currency, a policy soon followed by all other banks. Hundreds of businesses, plantations, farms, factories, canals, and other enterprises were thrown into bankruptcy by the end of the year. Over a third of Americans lost their jobs. Those fortunate enough to keep their jobs found their pay reduced by as much as 50 percent. The nation sank into an economic and an emotional depression.

As credit continued to collapse through 1838 and 1839, President Van Buren tried to address the problems but only made them worse. His first mistake was to continue Jackson's hard-money policy of accepting payment only in specie. The outcome was more contraction in the economy. Then, to keep the government solvent, Van Buren cut federal spending to the bone, accelerating the downward economic spiral. The public began referring to him as Martin Van Ruin.

The Log-Cabin and Hard-Cider Campaign of 1840

The Whigs had learned their lesson in 1836: only a party united behind one candidate could possibly beat the Democrats. For that candidate, they selected William Henry Harrison, the hero of Tippecanoe. The general had a distinguished military record and few enemies. **John Tyler,** a Virginian who had bolted from the Democrats during the Bank War, was chosen as his running mate.

Although the economy was in bad shape, the Whigs avoided addressing any serious issues. Instead, they launched a smear campaign against Van Buren. The Whig press portrayed Van Buren, the son of a tavern keeper, as an aristocrat with expensive tastes in clothes, food, and furniture. Harrison, by contrast, had been born into the Virginia aristocracy, but the Whigs characterized him as a simple frontiersman who had risen to greatness through his own efforts. Whig claims were so extravagant that the Democratic press soon satirized Harrison in political cartoons as a rustic hick rocking on the porch of a log cabin and swilling hard cider. The satire backfired. Whig newspapers and speechmakers sold Harrison, the long-time political insider, as a simple man of the people who truly lived in a log cabin. At campaign rallies, Whigs passed out cider to voters while they chanted, "Van, Van, Van, Oh! Van is a used-up man."

Unfortunately for Van Buren, the slogan was on target. By the time the cider had been drunk and the votes counted, Harrison was swept out of his log cabin and into the White House.

favorite son A candidate nominated for office by delegates from his or her own region or state.

Specie Circular Order issued by President Jackson in 1836 stating that the federal government would accept only gold and silver as payment for public land.

John Tyler Virginia senator who left the Democratic party after conflicts with Andrew Jackson; he was elected vice president in 1840 and became president when Harrison died.

SUMMARY

Expectations
Constraints
Choices
Outcomes

William Henry Harrison inherited a deeply troubled country from outgoing president Martin Van Buren. Economic *constraints* triggered by Andrew Jackson's unwise *choice* in issuing the Specie Circular were worsened by Van Buren's error in revamping the treasury system, and both were compounded by Nicholas Biddle's malevolence. The new party system that emerged promised excitement but not much in the way of solutions. Still, Americans must have had great *expectations* from the new politics: nearly twice as many men *chose* to vote in the 1840 election as had done so in any other presidential contest.

This *outcome* came on top of a number of other *choices* Americans made in response to the many unsettling changes that had been taking place as part of the great transformation. Different economic classes responded by creating their own cultures and by *choosing* specific strategies for dealing with anxiety. Some *chose* violent protest, some passive resistance. Some looked to heaven for solutions and others to earthly utopias. And out of this complex swirl of new *expectations* and *constraints*, something entirely new and unexpected emerged. The *outcome* was a new America, on its way to being socially, politically, intellectually, and culturally modern.

In the election of 1840, a man who had become a national figure by fighting against Indian sovereignty and for westward expansion swept a new sentiment into national politics. Increasingly, Americans shared the *expectation* that the West would provide the solutions to the problems raised by the great transformation. In the short term, the *outcome* was an exciting race by Americans toward the Pacific. But new *constraints* pared down available *choices*, propelling the nation toward a sectional crisis.

SUGGESTED READINGS

Genovese, Eugene D. *From Rebellion to Revolution: Afro-American Slave Revolts in the Making of the Modern World* (1979).

Although it focuses somewhat narrowly on confrontation, as opposed to more subtle forms of resistance, this study traces the emergence of African-American political organization from its roots in antebellum slave revolts.

Haltunen, Karen. *Confidence Men and Painted Women: A Study of Middle-Class Culture in America, 1830–1870* (1982).

A wonderfully well-researched study of an emerging class defining and shaping itself in the evolving world of early-nineteenth-century urban space.

Pessen, Edward. *Most Uncommon Jacksonians: The Radical Leaders of the Early Labor Movement* (1967).

A look at the early labor movement and reform by one of America's leading radical scholars.

Wallace, Anthony F. C. *Rockdale: The Growth of an American Village in the Early Industrial Revolution* (1978).

A noted anthropologist's reconstruction of a mill town and the various class, occupational, and gender cultures that developed there during its transition from a traditional village.

Walters, Ronald G. *American Reformers, 1815–1860* (1978).

The best overview of the reform movements and key personalities who guided them during this difficult period in American history.

Wilentz, Sean. *Chants Democratic: New York City and the Rise of the American Working Class, 1788–1850* (1984).

An insightful view of working-class culture and politics in the dynamic setting of New York City during the heyday of the Erie Canal.

Prescribing Middle-Class Expectations

The Context

Chapter 11 discusses the emergence of a new economic and social class in the United States: the middle class. Being a new class and living under new circumstances, these people had to figure out new rules for appropriate behavior, proper appearance, and desirable relationships. Those rules then had to be communicated. What emerged was a flood of what historians call "prescriptive literature," writing that recommends certain modes of behavior, dress, and social conduct. Through mass-publishing syndicates like the American Tract Society, literature prescribing middle-class cultural values spread to every class in America. (For further information on the context, see pages 229–230.)

The Historical Question

Few historians would dispute that a major cultural shift took place during the forty-six years that separated the War of 1812 and the Civil War, but many questions remain concerning the causes for this shift, the exact nature of it, and the media by which it spread. Examining prescriptive literature from the period is one way to approach those questions. What did the prescriptive literature have to say about class roles, gender roles, and roles for different age groups? How does advice given to one such group help to inform us about desirable roles for the other groups? What expectations were being formed about people's behavior, dress, and social relations?

The Challenge

Using the sources provided, along with other information you have read, write an essay or hold a discussion on the following question. Cite evidence in the sources to support your conclusions. **What roles and responsibilities were being prescribed for middle-class men, women, and children during the early nineteenth century? How do these roles reflect new economic and social realities during the period?**

The Sources

1 Prescriptive literature for young women took many forms—ranging from parables to sentimental poetry. Catherine Beecher was inclined to write manifestoes. In *The Duty of American Women to Their Country* (1845), she said: *Women, then, are to be educated for teachers, and sent to the destitute children of this nation by hundreds and by thousands. This is the way in which a* profession *is to be created for women—a profession as honourable and as lucrative for her as the legal, medical, and theological are for men. . . .*

And who else, in such an emergency as this, can so appropriately be invoked to aid? It is woman who is the natural and appropriate guardian of childhood. It is woman who has those tender sympathies which can most readily feel for the wants and sufferings of the young. . . . It is woman, too, who has that conscientiousness and religious devotion which, in any worthy cause, are the surest pledges of success.

Every woman has various duties pressing upon her attention. It is right for her, it is her duty, to cultivate her own mind by reading and study, not merely for her own gratification or credit, but with the great end in view of employing her knowledge and energies for the good of others. It is right, and a duty for a woman to attend to domestic affairs; but, except in cases of emergency, it is not right to devote all her time to this alone. It is a duty for her to attend to religious efforts and ordinances; but it is not right for her to give all her time to these alone. . . .

2 Prescriptive literature for men usually avoided the sentimental and took on an air of friendly conversation. T. S. Arthur's *Advice to Young Men on Their Duties and Conduct in Life* (1853) was one such advice manual. Arthur wrote:

. . . It is no light task which a man takes upon himself—that of sustaining, by his single efforts, a whole family. . . . You have an education that enables you to take a respectable position in society; you have a groundwork of good principles; habits of industry; in fact, all that a young man need ask for in order that he may rise in the world; and for these you are indebted to your father. To give you such advantages, cost him labor, self-denial, and much anxious thought. Many times has he been pressed down with worldly difficulties. . . . He has seen his last dollar, it may be, leave his hand, without knowing certainly where the next was to come from. But still, his love for his children has urged him on. . . .

. . . you should make it a point of duty always to go with your sisters into company, and to be their companion, if possible, on all public occasions. By so doing, you can prevent the introduction of men whose principles are bad; or, if such introductions are forced upon them in spite of you, can throw in a timely word of caution. . . . The great thing is to guard, by every means in your power, these innocent ones from the polluting presence of a bad man. You cannot tell how soon he may win the affections of the most innocent, confiding, and loving of them all, and draw her off from virtue. And even if his designs be honorable . . . he cannot make her happy, for happy no pure-minded woman ever has been, or even can be made by a corrupt, evil-minded, and selfish man.

. . . But not only should you seek to guard them from the danger just alluded to,—your affection for them should lead you to enter into their pleasures as far as in your power to do so; to give interest and variety to the home circle; to afford them, at all times, the assistance of your judgment in matters of trivial as well as grave importance.

3 Probably more prescriptive words were written to and about children than about any other subject during the antebellum period. An anonymous pamphlet issued by the American Tract Society advised:

Be careful in the formation of intimate friendships. Attach yourself to those chiefly who are diligent, thoughtful, and amiable. Behave always in the most respectful manner to your teachers, and to all that occasionally visit you. Avoid the extremes of bashfulness and bold presumption; frankness and modesty form a happy union. In diet be moderate; in apparel neat; among your companions, cheerful and kind. . . . Never tell a lie, nor conceal the truth when it is your duty to make it known; at the same time remember that a tale-bearer in a school is an odious character.

GEOGRAPHICAL EXPANSION AND POPULATION GROWTH During the 1840s, population growth and westward expansion were celebrated as never before in American history. This map shows the results. By 1850, population density was increasing in most of the settled portions of the country, and huge new regions were coming under American control.

CANADA
Treaty Line 1846
Treaty Line of 1842
Treaty Line of 1842
Lake Superior
St. Lawrence
MAINE 1842
Portland
Fort Vancouver
Columbia
OREGON TERRITORY 1848
Oregon Country 1846
OREGON TRAIL
ROCKY MTS.
Missouri
MINNESOTA TERRITORY 1849
UNORGANIZED TERRITORY
Lake Huron
NEW YORK
Albany
Syracuse
Rochester
Buffalo
VT.
N.H.
Portland
Boston
MASS.
R.I.
CONN.
L. Ontario
Snake
WISCONSIN 1848
Lake Michigan
MICHIGAN
Detroit
Milwaukee
L. Erie
Erie
PENNSYLVANIA
Philadelphia
Pittsburgh
Baltimore
New York
Trenton
NEW JERSEY
DELAWARE
MARYLAND
Washington, D.C.
Richmond
VIRGINIA
Norfolk
LASSEN'S TRAIL
CALIFORNIA TRAIL
OREGON TRAIL
Fort Laramie
IOWA 1846
MORMON TRAIL
Chicago
Cleveland
ILLINOIS
Nauvoo
INDIANA
OHIO
Cincinnati
Sutter's Fort
Sutter's Mill
UTAH TERRITORY 1850
Salt Lake City
SALT LAKE TO LOS ANGELES TRAIL
Fort Kearney
San Francisco
CALIFORNIA 1850
OLD SPANISH TRAIL
Colorado
MISSOURI
St. Louis
Independence
Evansville
Ohio
Frankfort
Louisville
KENTUCKY
SANTA FE TRAIL
CIMARRON CROSSING TRAIL
Arkansas
Missouri Compromise Line, 36°30′ N
Nashville
TENNESSEE
Tennessee
Raleigh
NORTH CAROLINA
Los Angeles
Mexican Cession 1848
NEW MEXICO TERRITORY 1850
Santa Fe
SANTA FE TRAIL
Red
ARKANSAS
SOUTH CAROLINA
Atlanta
GEORGIA
Charleston
Columbus
Savannah
ALABAMA
MISS.
Texas Annexation 1845
TEXAS 1845
Natchez
LOUISIANA
Baton Rouge
New Orleans
St. Augustine
FLORIDA 1845
PACIFIC OCEAN
ATLANTIC OCEAN
Rio Grande
Chihuahua
MEXICO
Gulf of Mexico
Western trail
Treaty or cession boundary
Population density per square mile, 1850
90 or more
45–90
18–45
6–18
2–6
Unsettled areas
0 200 400 Km.
0 200 400 Mi.

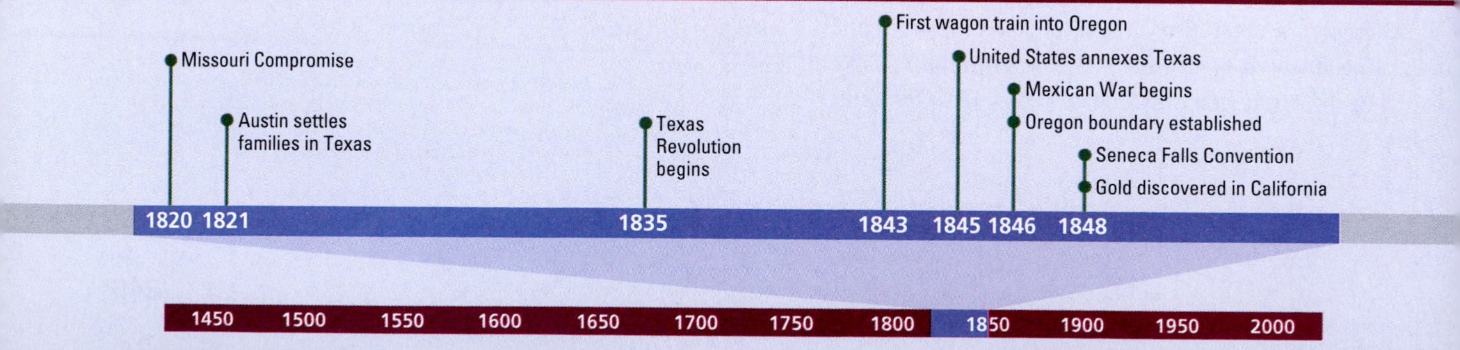

Missouri Compromise
Austin settles families in Texas
Texas Revolution begins
First wagon train into Oregon
United States annexes Texas
Mexican War begins
Oregon boundary established
Seneca Falls Convention
Gold discovered in California
1820 1821 1835 1843 1845 1846 1848
1450 1500 1550 1600 1650 1700 1750 1800 1850 1900 1950 2000

CHAPTER 12

Westward Expansion and Manifest Destiny, 1841–1849

The Explosion Westward

- What expectations pulled Americans westward between 1820 and 1848?

The Social Fabric in the West

- To what extent did people in the West expect to create new and different societies in that region?
- What sorts of cultures emerged in response to western constraints?

The Triumph of "Manifest Destiny"

- What expectations contributed to the idea of manifest destiny?
- Did choices by American settlers in Oregon and Texas reflect those expectations? Why or why not?

Expansion and Sectional Crisis

- How did expansionist and economic expectations shape Americans' positions on slavery in the 1840s?

INTRODUCTION

The election of frontier hero William Henry Harrison to the presidency in 1840 was but one milestone in a progressive westward tilt in the nation's political and cultural focus. As transportation systems extended the American frontier and as industrialization generated new capital, speculators invested in the newly opened West. Americans looking for economic opportunities, places to transplant particular religious or political beliefs, or simply adventure followed those entrepreneurs. They *expected* to find a wide-open land of opportunity.

But men and women moving into the West faced many *constraints.* The land itself was often not what they *expected.* Water was frequently in short supply, and wild animals were a constant threat to crops and livestock. In addition, most of the land in the West was already claimed by Indians, the Spanish, or the British.

Environmental and cultural *constraints* forced change on pioneers and led to the creation of new societies. Mormon farmers in the Utah deserts, for example, had to learn to cooperate with each other in building irrigation systems. Pioneers in the Southwest had to learn about the Spanish language and culture.

Westward expansion brought great pressure to bear on the nation's political and economic institutions. Easterners disagreed about what institutions should be planted in the new territories. Southerners *expected* to spread cotton agriculture. Northerners were equally convinced that a diversified entrepreneurial economy was the wave of the future. And each region had specific notions about tariffs, taxes, the money supply, and the role of the federal government in the economy.

Each section *chose* to push for its own vision of westward expansion, but each met *constraints.* The United States fought a war with Mexico and then faced a national crisis over what to do with newly acquired territories. The *outcome* was a political dispute that rocked the halls of Congress and moved some to call for outright civil disobedience.

At the core of the debate lay the issue of slavery. Although only a few Americans were disturbed about its moral implications, slavery symbolized the cultural, economic, and political differences between northerners and southerners. Independent farmers and businessmen feared the *constraint* of competition from wealthy southern planters. Workers, too, wondered how they could compete successfully against slave laborers. While more and more people in the North and the Old Northwest *chose* to raise their voices against the expansion of slavery, southerners worked all the harder to ensure their freedom to take slaves anywhere they *chose.*

As the debate over slavery and expansion broadened, another group of Americans chafed under discrimination. Evangelical women had *chosen* to join a wide variety of reform movements, including abolitionism, but they found that their sex was a major *constraint* to their participation. Few men were willing to give them the political and economic voice they believed they needed to carry out their mission. Increasing frustration was the *outcome* for such women.

Expectations
Constraints
Choices
Outcomes

CHRONOLOGY

Expansion and Crisis

1820	Missouri Compromise
1821	Stephen F. Austin settles Americans in Texas
1834	Mexican government begins seizure of California mission lands
1835	Texas Revolution begins
1836	Rebellion against Mexican rule in California
1838	John Quincy Adams filibusters against annexation of Texas Armed confrontation between Maine and New Brunswick
1839	John Sutter founds New Helvetia
1840	William Henry Harrison elected president
1841	John Tyler becomes president Congress passes preemption bill
1842	Elijah White named federal Indian agent for Oregon
1843	First wagon train into Oregon First Organic Laws adopted in Oregon
1844	James K. Polk elected president Murder of Joseph Smith
1845	United States annexes Texas Term "manifest destiny" coined
1846	Mexican War begins Oregon boundary established; United States and Britain end joint occupation California declares itself a republic
1847	Whitman massacre Mormons arrive in Utah
1848	Gold discovered in California Zachary Taylor elected president Seneca Falls Convention Treaty of Guadalupe Hidalgo
1855	Indians in the Pacific Northwest settled on reservations

The Explosion Westward

Western pioneers seldom sought to create new and different lifestyles for themselves, but the physical and cultural environments in the West shaped their society in peculiar ways. Thus cultures that contrasted sharply with those in the industrializing North and the plantation South emerged in the new West.

The Complicated Worlds of the West

Two views of the West dominated the popular imagination in the 1840s. One, traceable to Zebulon Pike's expedition in 1806–1807, envisioned the West as a "great American desert" unsuitable for habitation by any but the hardiest Indians. The other, traceable to the Lewis and Clark expedition, imagined a verdant region rich in resources. Common to both was the notion that the West was a virgin land free for the taking.

Realities in the **Far West** were much more complex than the myths suggested. Indeed, vast areas of the region had extremely dry and fragile ecologies largely unsuitable for the sort of economic

Far West In North America, the lands west of the Mississippi River.

exploitation nineteenth-century Americans desired. At the other extreme, some regions were so wet that their rain forests were virtually impassable. But nowhere was there virgin land.

For thousands of years, various Indian groups had extracted a rich living from the many different environments in the Far West. By moving from place to place and trading, Indians had taken advantage of the West's diversity, receiving what each ecological zone had to offer. This flexible approach to the complicated and often fragile ecology of the Far West provided an excellent living and did minimal damage to natural resources. If the land appeared to expansionists in the United States to be unoccupied, it was only because they would not, or could not, recognize a system of land use with which they were unfamiliar.

With the arrival of Spanish, French, Russian, and other Europeans, the complex world of intergroup relations in the West became even more complicated. Indians on the Great Plains used the mobility provided by European horses to expand not just their hunting range but also their trading range. Goods from the Plains made their way regularly to Spanish settlements in New Mexico, and replacement horses, guns, and other European goods flooded northward in return. This was the world into which early western entrepreneurs like John Jacob Astor and Auguste Chouteau had entered earlier in the century. No unexploited land or great American desert could have supported their monumental visions of an inland fur empire. What both men did was to tap into an already complicated trading world.

The image of the solitary trapper braving a hostile environment and even more hostile Indians is the stuff of American adventure novels and movies. Although characters like Christopher ("Kit") Carson and Jeremiah ("Crow Killer") Johnson really did exist, these men were merely advance agents for an **extractive industry** geared to the efficient removal of animal pelts.

What drew men like Carson and Johnson into the Far West in the 1830s and 1840s was an innovation instigated by a former Astor employee and one-time partner of Chouteau, William Henry Ashley. Taking advantage of the presence of large numbers of underemployed young men seeking fortune and adventure in the West, Ashley in 1825 set up the highly successful **rendezvous system** for collecting pelts. Under this arrangement, individual trappers like Carson combed the upper Missouri for furs. Once each year, Ashley conducted a fur rendezvous in the mountains, where the trappers brought their furs and exchanged them for goods.

Ashley's, Chouteau's, and Astor's strategies for harvesting wealth from the Far West inadvertently led to the decline of the fur trade. Astor's Asian trade opened the way for vast silk imports. Soon silk hats became a fashion rage in both America and Europe, replacing beaver hats, which had sustained the fur trade. In addition, the efficiency of these enterprises virtually wiped out beaver populations in the Rocky Mountains. By the 1830s, the beaver business had slowed to a near standstill.

Many beaver hunters stayed in the West to become founding members of new communities. As early as 1840, fur trapper Robert ("Doc") Newell reportedly told his companion Joe Meek, "The fur trade is dead in the Rocky Mountains, and it is no place for us now, if ever it was." The two men then headed to the Willamette Valley in Oregon to become settlers.

Often the first to join the former fur trappers in the West were not rugged yeoman farmers but highly organized and well-financed land speculators. Liberalization of the land laws during the first half of the nineteenth century had put smaller tracts within reach of more citizens, but speculators continued to play a role in land distribution by offering even smaller tracts and more liberal credit.

A third group of expectant fortune hunters was lured into the Far West by the discovery of gold. Most fortune hunters did not find gold, but many stayed to establish trading businesses, banks, and

extractive industry An industry, such as fur trapping, logging, or mining, that removes natural resources from the environment.

rendezvous system A system in which trappers gathered furs independently in their own territories and met traders once a year to exchange the furs for goods.

farms. Others moved on, still seeking their fortunes. But usually they too eventually settled down to become shopkeepers, farmers, and entrepreneurs.

The Attraction of the West

The underlying cause for westward migration was the hope of economic opportunity. The promise of cheap land was especially enticing after the panics of 1819 and 1837.

Although the promise of economic opportunity pulled most people westward, some were pushed in that direction, particularly New Englanders. Two sources of land pressure combined to uproot these descendants of the Puritans. First, the New England tradition of dividing family holdings equally among adult children had created a shortage of workable farms in the region. Second, innovations in spinning and weaving wool had created a sheep-raising craze after 1824. Sheep required little labor but a lot of land. Between 1825 and 1840, sheep displaced people throughout much of the New England countryside as smaller, poorer farmers sold out.

Thus young people in New England faced a choice between moving into cities or heading west. Those who opted to migrate west sought an environment friendly to their moral and religious outlook in areas like upper New York, Michigan, and Oregon, where Protestant missionaries were establishing little New Englands in the wilderness.

The image of the independent farmer fleeing the restrictions of civilized life and hewing out a living on the frontier is a persistent myth in American history. Although a few antisocial sorts moved to the frontier to escape neighbors, most went west as part of a larger community.

Most migrants to Texas in the 1820s and 1830s came in large groups under the direction of men like **Stephen F. Austin.** Beginning in 1821, the Spanish government in Mexico gave these **empresarios** land grants and the right to assess fees in exchange for encouraging settlement in its northern colony. Spanish authorities stipulated that all the families had to be Roman Catholic or be willing to convert.

Austin offered families land for a filing fee of only 12½ cents per acre and had no trouble finding willing settlers. He led his first overland party from Louisiana into Texas in 1821. After Mexico became independent of Spain in 1822, Austin convinced the Mexican government to extend his license.

The first permanent agricultural settlements in the Pacific Northwest were begun by Protestant missionaries to the Indians. These missionaries encouraged mass migration to the new territory. Their calls appealed to people eager for economic opportunity in familiar cultural surroundings. When the Methodist church issued a call for a "great reinforcement" for its mission in Oregon, it received a flood of applications. Three separate reinforcements arrived in Oregon by ship in 1840, but it was not until 1843 that large-scale migration began.

Beginning in the spring of 1843 and every spring thereafter for decades, families from all over the East gathered in Missouri to start the overland trek by wagon train. Although trail life was novel for most of the Oregon-bound migrants, the division in domestic labor remained much as it was at home. "Everybody was supposed to rise at daylight, and while the women were preparing breakfast, the men rounded up the cattle, took down the tents, yoked the oxen to the wagons and made everything ready for an immediate start after the morning meal was finished," one young pioneer woman remembered. Even social customs remained the same. "We were expected to visit our neighbors when we paused for rest," the same woman noted. "If we did not, we were designated as 'high-toned' or 'stuck-up.'"

And so life went on during the six months it took to cross the more than 2,000 miles to the **Oregon Country.** Families arriving in Oregon tended to settle in rings around the existing missions,

Stephen F. Austin American colonizer in Texas who was imprisoned by the Mexican government on suspicion of revolutionary sympathies and who later took part in the Texas Revolution.

empresario In the Spanish colonies, a person who organized and led a group of settlers in exchange for land grants and the right to assess fees.

Oregon Country The region to the north of Spanish California extending from the crest of the Rocky Mountains to the Pacific coast.

♦ With two wives and several children to help share the burden of work, this Mormon settler was in a good position to do well, even in the harsh conditions that prevailed in the near-desert environment of Utah. Sensitive to disapproval from more traditional Christians, families like this tended to associate exclusively with other Mormons and pressured outsiders to leave as quickly as possible. *Denver Public Library.*

which soon became the hubs for transplanted New England–style villages.

The Mormons established another migration pattern into the **Great Basin.** Persecution continued to haunt Joseph Smith's followers after their move to Illinois and became much worse when the church leadership declared polygamy acceptable. In 1844, Smith was murdered by a mob in Carthage, Illinois, leading many Mormon leaders to conclude that the community would never be safe until they moved far from mainstream American civilization. **Brigham Young,** Smith's successor, led sixteen hundred Mormons beyond the Rocky Mountains in search of a refuge. On July 24, 1847, Young's advance party finally pushed into the valley of the **Great Salt Lake.**

Despite their differences, pioneers shared the fundamental problem of being short of hard cash. Western farmers barely made ends meet when conditions were good and fell into debt when weather or other hazards interrupted farming. Still, those who were lucky and exercised careful management could carve out an excellent living. Strongly centralized authority and a deeply felt sense of community helped the Mormons to prosper. Many people in other communities, however, had their land repossessed or had to sell out to pay off creditors.

Many pioneers had no legal claim to their farms. People often settled wherever they could find unoccupied land. Thousands of squatters living on unsold federal land were a problem for the national government when the time came to sell off the public domain. Western politicians frequently advocated bills guaranteeing "squatter rights." They finally maneuvered the passage of a **preemption bill** in 1841 that gave squatters the right to settle on unsurveyed federal land. Squatters still had to buy the land once it came up for sale.

The Social Fabric in the West

Migrants to Texas, Oregon, and Utah seldom intended to create a new social order in the West. Rather, they intended to re-create the society they

Great Basin A desert region including most of present-day Nevada and parts of Utah, California, Idaho, Wyoming, and Oregon.

Brigham Young Mormon leader who took over in 1844 after Joseph Smith's death and guided the Mormons from Illinois to Utah, where they established a permanent home for the church.

Great Salt Lake A shallow, salty lake in the Great Basin, about 83 miles long and 51 miles wide; the Mormons established a permanent settlement near it in 1847.

preemption bill A temporary law that gave squatters the right to buy land they had settled on before it was offered for sale at public auction.

were leaving behind. The physical and cultural environments into which they moved, however, forced change on them. Pioneers had to accommodate themselves to the geography and people they found there. Thus some significant differences in the culture and society of the Far West emerged.

The New Cotton Country

Migrants to cotton country in Texas and Arkansas often started out as landless herders. These families carved out claims beyond the **frontier line** and worked as herders until they could put the land into production. Frequently, they did not have to clear land because Indians had already done so.

Although some areas were cleared and extremely fertile, others were swampy, rocky, and unproductive. Differences in the quality of land helped recreate the southern class system in the new areas. Those fortunate enough to get profitable land might become great planters; those less fortunate had to settle for lesser prosperity.

Southern pioneers devoted most of their time to the tasks necessary for survival. Even their social and recreational life tended to center on practical tasks. House building, planting, and harvesting were often done in cooperation with neighbors. On such occasions, plenty of food and homemade whiskey were consumed. Women gathered together separately for large-scale projects like group quilting. Another community event for southwestern settlers was the periodic religious revival, which might last for days. Here they could make new acquaintances, court sweethearts, and discuss the common failings in their souls and on their farms.

Westering Yankees

The frontier experience for migrants to Michigan and Oregon differed from that of southwesterners. In the Old Northwest, as Indians such as the Winnebagos were pushed out, pioneers snatched up their deserted farms. Settlers quickly established villages like those left behind in New England. Law courts, churches, and schools were likely to be the first institutions set up in northwestern towns. These institutions and the similarity of this region to New England helped prevent the growth of class distinctions that had developed so quickly along the southern frontier.

Conditions in the Oregon Country resembled those farther east in most respects, but some significant differences did exist. Most important, the Indians in the Oregon Country had never practiced agriculture. Their environment was so rich in fish, meat, and wild vegetables that farming was unnecessary. Large, open prairies flanking the Columbia, Willamette, and other rivers provided fertile farmland.

Much like the Indians in colonial New England, the Nez Perces, Cayuses, and Kalapuyas of the Oregon Country made whites welcome. In 1831, the Nez Perces and the Flatheads even issued an appeal for whites to come live among them. Although occasional tensions arose between white settlers and Indians, no serious conflict took place until 1847, when a disillusioned group of Cayuse Indians killed missionaries Marcus and Narcissa Whitman. The so-called Whitman massacre triggered the Cayuse War and a concerted effort by white Americans to confine all the northwestern tribes to reservations. By 1855, this effort had succeeded.

The Hispanic Southwest

Frontier life in California was unique in many ways. One major reason was that the Spanish left a lasting cultural imprint on California. Spanish exploration into what is now California did not begin until 1769. Prompted by Russian expansion into North America, the Spanish established garrisons at San Diego and Monterey. Eventually, Franciscan monks established twenty-one missions, each placed one day's travel from the next, extending from San Diego to the town of Sonoma, north of San Francisco.

The mission system provided a skeleton for Spanish settlement in California. The missions were soon surrounded by groves, vineyards, and lush farms, all tended by California Indians, who

frontier line The outer limit of agricultural settlement bordering on the wilderness.

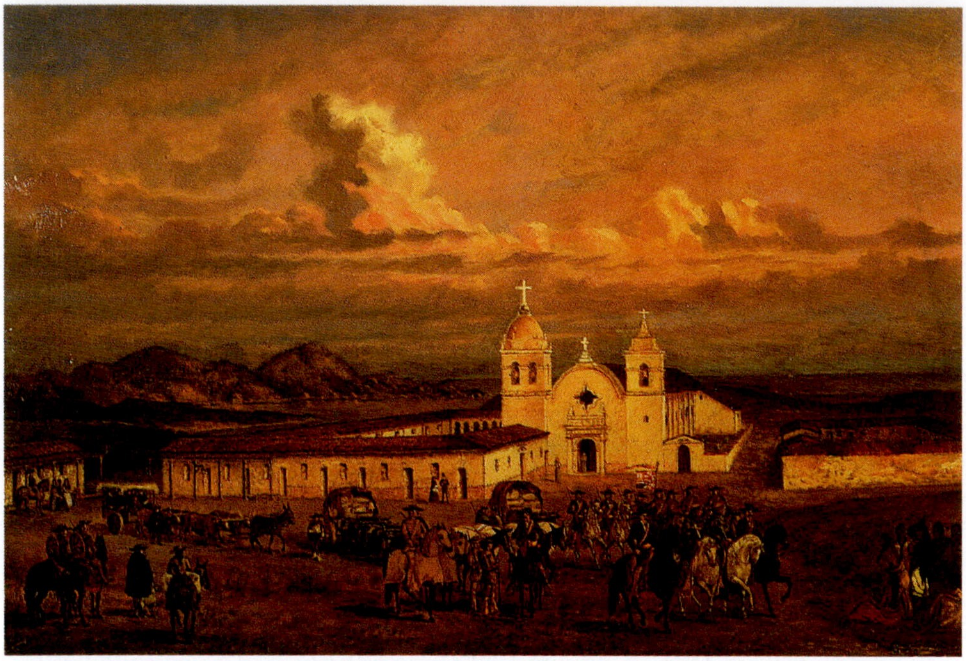

♦ Using Indian labor, Franciscan missionaries transformed the dry California coastal plain into a blooming garden and built beautiful missions in which to celebrate their religion. This early nineteenth-century painting by Oriana Day shows the Carmel Mission at the peak of its prosperity. *"Mission San Carlos Borromeo de Carmelo" by Oriana Day, oil on canvas 20″ × 30″. The Fine Arts Museum of San Francisco. Gift of Mrs. Eleanor Martin.*

often became virtual slaves. California's coastal plain became a vast and productive garden at the cost of thousands of Indian lives.

The Franciscans continued to control these missions after Mexico won its independence from Spain. Between 1834 and 1840, however, the Mexican government seized the California missions and sold them off to private citizens. An elite class of Spanish-speaking Californians snatched up the rich lands. Never numbering more than about a thousand people, this Hispanic elite eventually owned some 15 million acres of California's richest land. In 1836, the **Californios** and non-Hispanic newcomers rebelled against Mexico to place Californio Juan Bautista Alvarado in the governorship of California. The landholding elite never ended California's official relationship with Mexico but nevertheless ran the region's government.

At first, the Californios welcomed outsiders as neighbors and trading partners. Ships from the United States called regularly at California ports, picking up cargoes of beef **tallow** and cowhides. The settlers they brought were given generous grants and assistance to open up new lands and businesses. **John Sutter,** for example, a Swiss immigrant, was given a grant of land in the Sacramento valley, where he established a colony called New Helvetia in 1839. This settlement drew trappers, traders, Indians, and other settlers like a magnet.

Californios Spanish colonists in California in the eighteenth and early nineteenth centuries.

tallow Hard fat obtained from the bodies of cattle and other animals and used to make candles and soap.

John Sutter Swiss immigrant who founded a colony in California; in 1848 the discovery of gold on his property attracted hordes of miners who seized his land and left him financially ruined.

In New Helvetia, San Francisco, and other centers in northern California, a cosmopolitan society developed. Farther south, however, in the heartland of Spanish California, the Hispanic landholding elite resented intrusions by lower-class Mexicans and other newcomers. Governor Alvarado had a number of American and British citizens arrested on the suspicion that they were plotting to overthrow his government.

A more harmonious pattern of interracial cooperation existed in Santa Fe, where an elite class emerged from the intermingled fortunes and intermarriages among Indian, European, and American populations. Thus the Hispanic leaders of New Mexico, unlike those of California, consistently worked with their kinsmen.

In Texas, the economic desperation of impoverished southern frontiersmen combined with cultural insensitivity and misunderstanding to create the sort of tensions that were rare in New Mexico. **Texians** (non-Hispanic settlers) tended to cling to their own ways, and **Tejanos** (migrants from Mexico) did the same.

The Mormon Community

Physical conditions in the Great Basin led to a completely different social and cultural order in that area. Utah is a high desert plateau where water is scarce and survival depends on its careful management. The tightly knit community of Mormons was perfectly suited to that hostile environment.

Mormons followed the principle that "land belongs to the Lord, and his Saints are to use so much as they can work profitably." The church measured off plots of up to 40 acres and assigned them to settlers on the basis of need. Thus a man with several wives, many children, and enough wealth to hire help might receive a grant of 40 acres, but a man with one wife, few children, and little capital might receive only 10. Community work parties among the Mormons were more rigidly controlled and formal than in other settlements. Men had to supply labor in direct proportion to the amount of land they were granted. A man who had been granted 40 acres had to provide four times the amount of labor as one who had been granted 10.

Because of their bad experiences in Missouri and Illinois, the Mormons were unaccepting of strangers. The **General Authorities** of the church made every effort to keep Utah an exclusively Mormon society. The one exception was American Indians. Because Indians occupied a central place in Mormon sacred literature, the Mormons practiced an accepting and gentle Indian policy. The Mormon hierarchy used its enormous power in Utah to prevent private violence against Indians whenever possible.

The Triumph of "Manifest Destiny"

Economic opportunity was the primary reason for westward movement before the Civil War erupted in 1861, but it was not the only reason people ventured west. Cultural and religious issues also pushed people west. So did the idea of **manifest destiny.**

The Rise of Manifest Destiny

To some extent, manifest destiny was as old as the Puritan idea of a "wilderness Zion" (see pages 54–56). Like John Winthrop, many early nineteenth-century Americans believed they had a mission to go into new lands. During the antebellum period, romantic nationalism, land hunger, and the Second Great Awakening shaped this sense of divine mission into a powerful incentive to expand westward.

Evangelical Protestants came to believe that the westward movement was part of a divine plan for

Texians Non-Hispanic settlers in Texas in the nineteenth century.

Tejanos Mexican settlers in Texas in the nineteenth century.

General Authorities Leaders in the Mormon church hierarchy; the prophet, his two assistants, twelve apostles, and several full-time administrators.

manifest destiny Term first used in the 1840s to describe the inevitability of the continued westward expansion of the United States.

North America and the rest of the world. The earliest and most aggressive proponents of expansion were Christian missionary organizations, whose many magazines, newsletters, and reports were the first to give it formal voice. Politicians were not far behind. Democrat Thomas Hart Benton of Missouri quickly adopted the missionary rhetoric in promoting liberal land policies, territorial acquisition, and overseas expansion. By 1845, when journalist John L. O'Sullivan coined the expression "manifest destiny," the idea that the United States should occupy all of North America was already an established one.

Expansion to the North and West

One major obstacle to manifest destiny was that Spain, Britain, Russia, and other countries already owned large parts of North America. The continued presence of the British proved to be a constant irritation.

The disputed border between Maine and Canada threatened to lead to a major confrontation in 1838, when Canadian loggers moved into the disputed region and began cutting trees. Fighting broke out when American lumberjacks attempted to drive them away. The Canadian province of New Brunswick and the state of Maine then mobilized their militias; Congress called up fifty thousand men; and President Van Buren ordered General Winfield Scott to the scene. Scott arranged a truce, but tensions continued to run high.

Another source of conflict with Britain was the **Oregon Question.** At the close of the War of 1812, the two countries had been unable to settle their claims and had agreed to joint occupation of Oregon for ten years. This arrangement was extended indefinitely in 1827.

Joint occupation began to be undermined when American settlers in the Willamette Valley held a series of meetings in 1843 to create a civil government. A constitutional convention was called for May 2. Although the British tried to prevent the convention, the assembly passed the First Organic Laws of Oregon on July 5, 1843, making Oregon an independent republic in all but name. Independence, however, was not the settlers' long-term goal. They desired **annexation** by the United States of America.

Revolution in Texas

Unlike the situation in Maine and the Oregon Country, the ownership of the Southwest was fairly clear. Present-day Texas, New Mexico, Arizona, California, Nevada, and portions of Colorado, Oklahoma, Kansas, and Wyoming belonged to Spain prior to Mexico's successful revolution in 1821. After that revolution, title presumably passed to Mexico. But owning this vast region and controlling it were two different matters. The distance between the capital in Mexico City and the northern provinces made governing the region difficult.

Anglo-American settlers in the Southwest generally ignored Mexican customs, including their pledge to practice Roman Catholicism. The distant and politically unstable Mexican government could do little to enforce laws and customs. In addition, many Tejanos desired greater autonomy from Mexico City as much as their American counterparts did.

In an effort to forge a peaceful settlement with the Mexican government, Stephen F. Austin went to Mexico City in 1833. While Austin was there, **Antonio López de Santa Anna** seized power. A key figure in the adoption of a republican constitution in 1824, Santa Anna had come to the conclusion that Mexico was not ready for democracy. He suspended the constitution, dismissed congress, and declared himself the "Napoleon of the West."

Austin pressed several petitions advocating reforms and greater self-government in Texas upon

Oregon Question The question of the national ownership of the Pacific Northwest; the United States and Great Britain renegotiated the boundary in 1846, establishing it at 49° north latitude.

annexation The incorporation of a territory into an existing political unit such as a neighboring country.

Antonio López de Santa Anna Mexican general who was president of Mexico when he led an attack on the Alamo in 1836.

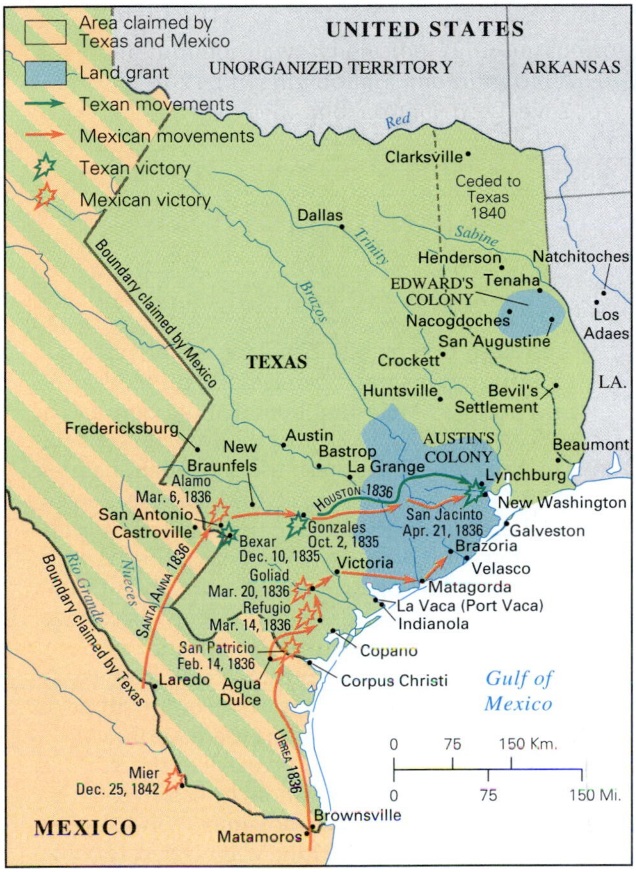

♦ **MAP 12.1 The Texas Revolution** This map shows troop movements and the major battles in the Texas Revolution, as well as the conflicting boundary claims made by Texans and the Mexican government. The Battle of San Jacinto and the Treaty of Velasco ended the war, but the conflicting land claims continued when Mexico repudiated the treaty.

the Mexican president. Believing that Santa Anna agreed with him, Austin departed for home, only to be arrested and dragged back to Mexico City in chains on charges of advocating revolution in Texas. Though finally cleared of all charges in 1835, Austin had decided by the time he arrived back in Texas that "war is our only recourse." In early September, he called for a convention of delegates from all over Texas to discuss what should be done.

By the time this convention met in November 1835, the first shots of the **Texas Revolution** had already been fired. The convention formed itself into a provisional government but refrained from declaring its independence from Mexico.

The first major confrontation of the rebellion occurred at San Antonio (see Map 12.1). Santa Anna personally led the Mexican army against that city, which had been captured by the rebels. Knowing that Santa Anna was on his way, Texas commander William Travis moved his troops into a former mission called the **Alamo**. On March 6, 1836, Santa Anna ordered an all-out assault on the Alamo. Storming the walls, the Mexican army sustained staggering casualties but captured it nevertheless. Most of the post's defenders were killed in the assault. Santa Anna executed those who survived the battle, including former congressman and frontier celebrity Davy Crockett.

Texas rebels elsewhere were consolidating the revolution. On March 2, a convention met at Washington-on-the-Brazos and issued a declaration of independence. The convention also ratified a constitution, based largely on the Constitution of the United States, on March 16. It elected David G. Burnet president of the new republic and Lorenzo de Zavala, one of the many Tejanos who had joined the rebellion, as vice president (see Individual Choices: Lorenzo de Zavala). **Sam Houston** had earlier been named commander of the army.

Despite the loss at the Alamo, Texans continued to underestimate Santa Anna's strength. On March 18, a large Mexican detachment under General José Urrea captured the town of Goliad and its defenders. Over the next several days, Urrea scoured the countryside for additional prisoners. On Palm

Texas Revolution A revolt by American colonists in Texas against Mexican rule; it began in 1835 and ended with the establishment of the Republic of Texas in 1836.

Alamo A Franciscan mission that the Mexican commander at San Antonio fortified; rebellious Texas colonists were besieged there by Santa Anna's forces in 1836.

Sam Houston American general and politician who fought in the struggle for Texas's independence from Mexico and became president of the Republic of Texas.

INDIVIDUAL CHOICES

Choosing Texas and Independence

Lorenzo de Zavala

Lorenzo de Zavala fought against tyranny in his native Mexico. When the government he helped establish after a successful revolution against Spain refused to create a democracy, de Zavala moved to Texas. In 1835, he chose to join the Texas Revolution against Mexico and was elected vice president of the Republic of Texas. "Lorenzo de Zavala" by C. E. Proctor. Archives Division, Texas State Library. Photo by Eric Beggs.

Although Lorenzo de Zavala was a physician by training, his heart persistently pulled him into politics. An ardent liberal and federalist, he was elected to the Mérida city council in his native Yucatán, in southern Mexico, when he was only 23 years old. Then, in 1814, he was elected a delegate to the Spanish parliament, though he never assumed his seat. The young liberal was imprisoned by Spain's King Ferdinand VII for antimonarchial sentiments. Gaining his release in 1817, de Zavala returned to Yucatán.

De Zavala chafed at Spanish rule, and as revolutionary movements broke out in all parts of Mexico in 1820, he again entered politics, winning election as the secretary of the Yucatán assembly. From this position, he assisted the Mexican independence movement. Shortly after it succeeded in 1821, he was elected to the Mexican constituent congress, serving there and in the national senate until 1827, when he was made governor of the province of Mexico.

By 1829, de Zavala was having doubts about how things were going in Mexico. The independent government had proved far from stable, and the ruling authorities seemed just as reactionary as the Spaniards. The liberals' demand to allocate farmland to peasants, for example, was continually refused by the government. Seeking some way to help the peasants, de Zavala resigned his governorship and secured an empresario grant to settle five hundred poor Mexican families in Texas.

For the next several years, de Zavala traveled and wrote a history of the revolutionary movement in Mexico, which he published in 1831. Then, finding himself in Paris, de Zavala accepted a post as Mexico's ambassador to France in 1833, returning to public service and politics. In 1834, Antonio López de Santa Anna pushed his way into power, suspending the constitution, dissolving the national congress, and assuming dictatorial control. Watching events unfold from his post in Paris, de Zavala became increasingly disaffected with Santa Anna. In 1835, he resigned as ambassador and sailed for Texas, where, he believed, he might join with others to oppose Santa Anna and restore the constitution. When Stephen F. Austin called for a "general consultation of the people" in the fall of 1835, de Zavala sought and won a seat.

Like many settlers in Texas—whether they were originally from the United States, Europe, or Mexico—de Zavala wanted reform, but not necessarily independence. Thus he agreed with the consultation's decision in November 1835 to form a provisional government using the Mexican constitution of 1824—a document he had helped write—as a legal foundation. But when Santa Anna declared all members of the consultation traitors and ordered troops into Texas, de Zavala gave up hope of a peaceful settlement. On March 2, 1836, he chose to join his colleagues in signing a declaration of independence and then threw himself into the task of writing a constitution for Texas. The resulting document was an interesting hybrid: a mixture of de Zavala's and James Madison's views concerning liberal federalism.

The Texas consultation ratified the new constitution on March 16, 1836. Then, in recognition of de Zavala's strong political voice and the significant role he had played in helping to launch the revolution, the consultation unanimously elected him vice president of the Republic of Texas.

The revolution and the establishment of the Texas republic represented a victory for views that de Zavala and many Mexican-born Texans had held for a lifetime. Throughout his political career, de Zavala had fought for reform in Mexico, helping to win independence from Spain and pushing for liberal federalism. His expectations had been dashed by the harsh constraints imposed by self-interested political factions, which had created such instability that Santa Anna had bullied his way to the top and ended liberal government. For de Zavala and many others, the choice was clear: if Mexico could not be reformed, they would throw their lot in with a new state where their views might be brought into reality. The Republic of Texas became the seat for their dreams.

Sunday, Urrea ordered all 445 able-bodied prisoners to be marched out of town, where their guards shot and killed them.

The Texans had their vengeance on April 21 after Santa Anna ordered his troops to pause at the San Jacinto River. Arriving in the vicinity undetected, Houston's force of just over nine hundred formed up quietly. Shouting "Remember the Alamo" and "Remember Goliad," the Texans stormed the Mexican camp. In just eighteen minutes, 630 Mexican soldiers lay dead. Santa Anna attempted to escape but was captured. In exchange for his release, the Mexican president signed the **Treaty of Velasco,** in which he agreed to withdraw his troops south of the Rio Grande.

Many leaders in Texas hoped for annexation by the United States. In 1838, Houston, by then president of the Republic of Texas, invited the United States to annex Texas. He was forced to withdraw the invitation when John Quincy Adams, elected to Congress after his loss in the presidential election of 1828, **filibustered** in the House of Representatives for three weeks against the acquisition of such a big bloc of potentially slave territory.

The Politics of Manifest Destiny

Adams certainly did not speak for the majority of Whigs on the topic of national expansion. The party of manufacturing, revivalism, and social reform inclined naturally toward manifest destiny. William Henry Harrison, the party's first national candidate, had been a prominent War Hawk and Indian fighter, and his political campaign in 1840 had celebrated the virtues of frontier life. When Harrison died only a month after taking office in 1841, his vice president, John Tyler, picked up the torch of American expansionism.

Tyler was an atypical Whig. A Virginian and a states' rights advocate, he had been a staunch Democrat until the nullification crisis. Although he had objected to Jackson's use of presidential power, Tyler as president was as unyielding as Old Hickory where political principles were concerned. He vetoed high protective tariffs, internal improvements bills, and attempts to revive the Second Bank of the United States. Tyler's refusal to promote Whig economic policies led to a general crisis in government in 1843, when his entire cabinet resigned over his veto of a bank bill.

Tyler did share his party's desire for expansion. He assigned Secretary of State Daniel Webster to settle the Maine border dispute with Britain. The resulting **Webster-Ashburton Treaty** (1842) gave over half of the disputed territory to the United States and finally established the nation's northeastern border with Canada. Tyler adopted an aggressive stance on the Oregon Question by appointing Elijah White as the federal Indian agent for the region in 1842. This action flew in the face of the mutual occupation agreement between the United States and Great Britain. Historians have speculated that Tyler also encouraged migration to Oregon to strengthen the U.S. claim to the region.

Tyler similarly pushed a forceful policy toward Texas and the Southwest. He opened negotiations with Sam Houston that led to a proposed treaty of annexation in 1844. Proslavery and antislavery forces in the Senate fiercely debated the treaty, however, and failed to ratify it. The issue of Texas's annexation then joined the Oregon Question as a major campaign issue in the presidential election of 1844.

The issue of expansion put the two leading presidential contenders, Democrat Martin Van Buren and Whig Henry Clay, in an uncomfortable position. Van Buren had opposed the extension of slavery and was therefore against the annexation of Texas. Clay, a slaveholder, was opposed to any form of expansion that would fan sectional ten-

Treaty of Velasco Treaty signed by Santa Anna in May 1836 after his capture at the San Jacinto River; it granted recognition to the Republic of Texas but was later rejected by the Mexican congress.

filibuster To use obstructionist tactics, especially prolonged speechmaking, to delay legislative action.

Webster-Ashburton Treaty Treaty negotiated by Secretary of State Daniel Webster and British minister Lord Ashburton in 1842 that established the present border between Canada and northeastern Maine.

sions. Both candidates stated that they favored annexation only if Mexico agreed.

President Tyler's constant refusal to support the larger Whig political agenda led the party to nominate Clay as its candidate in 1844. Van Buren was not so lucky. The strong southern wing of the Democratic party was so put off by Van Buren's position on slavery that it nominated Tennessee congressman **James K. Polk.**

The Democrats proclaimed in their platform that they stood for "the re-occupation of Oregon and the re-annexation of Texas at the earliest practicable period." Polk vowed to stand up to the British by claiming the entire Oregon Country up to 54°40′north latitude and to defend the territorial claims of Texas. The Democrats appealed to the expansionist sentiments of northerners and southerners. Clay ignored expansionism, emphasizing economic policies instead.

The temper of the people was evident in the election's *outcome.* Clay was a national figure, well respected and regarded as one of the nation's leading statesmen. Polk was barely known outside Tennessee. Even so, Polk captured the presidency by sixty-five electoral votes.

Outgoing president Tyler accomplished one of the Democrats' platform goals before Polk assumed the presidency. In a special message to Congress in December 1844, Tyler proposed a **joint resolution** annexing Texas. Congressmen who had opposed annexation could not ignore the clear mandate given to manifest destiny in the presidential election. The bill to annex Texas passed in February 1845, just as Tyler was about to leave the White House.

Often called "Young Hickory" because of his political resemblance to Andrew Jackson, Polk promoted expansion by asking Congress to end the joint occupation of Oregon and by negotiating with Mexico to purchase much of the Southwest. The president urged Congress to pursue exclusive control over the Oregon Country and to obtain the Southwest even if doing so meant war.

Neither the United States nor Britain intended to go to war over Oregon. The only issue was where the border would be. Polk insisted on 54°40′. The British lobbied for the Columbia River, but their position softened quickly. The fur trade along the Columbia had become unprofitable by the early 1840s. As a result, in the spring of 1846, the British foreign secretary offered Polk a compromise boundary at the 49th parallel. The Senate recommended that Polk accept the offer, and a treaty settling the Oregon issue was ratified on June 15, 1846.

Expansion and Sectional Crisis

Significant political controversy accompanied the extension of the nation's borders. At the heart of the matter lay slavery. Although only a few radicals were totally opposed to southern slavery, many people in the North and West were strongly opposed to its expansion. For them this was less a moral than an economic issue. The expansion of slavery meant economic competition with slaves or slaveholders for jobs and profits. Southerners, by contrast, demanded that slavery be allowed to expand as far as economic opportunity permitted. Not surprisingly, southerners believed that the nation should expand into areas where cotton would grow and slavery would be profitable. Given these strong economic motives, the debate over expansion turned into a debate over slavery.

The Texas Crisis and Sectional Conflict

In annexing Texas, the United States had offended Mexico, which immediately severed diplomatic relations and threatened war. The Mexican government held that Texas was still a province of Mexico, not an independent republic, and that Texas's southern boundary was the Nueces River, not the Rio Grande. Polk responded by blustering that the entire Southwest should be annexed.

James K. Polk Tennessee congressman who was a leader of the Democratic party and the dark-horse winner of the presidential campaign in 1844.

joint resolution A special resolution adopted by both houses of Congress and subject to approval by the president; if approved, it has the force of law.

Polk sought his objectives peacefully but was prepared to use force. Late in 1845, he dispatched John Slidell to Mexico City to negotiate the boundary dispute, authorizing Slidell to purchase New Mexico and California. He also sent American troops to Louisiana, ready to strike if Mexico resisted Slidell's offers. And he notified the American consul in California that American naval ships had orders to seize California ports if war broke out with Mexico.

The Mexican government refused to receive Slidell. In January 1846, Slidell reported that his mission was a failure. Polk then ordered **Zachary Taylor** to lead troops into the disputed area between the Nueces River and the Rio Grande. Shortly thereafter, an American military exploration party led by **John C. Frémont** violated Mexican territory by crossing the mountains into California's Salinas Valley.

On April 22, Mexico responded by declaring war. Two days later, Mexican troops engaged a detachment of Taylor's army at Matamoros on the Rio Grande, killing eleven and capturing the rest. When news of this action reached Washington on May 9, Polk asked Congress for a declaration of war, charging that Mexico had "invaded our territory, and shed American blood upon American soil." Although the nation was far from united, Congress declared war on May 13, 1846 (see Map 12.2).

The outbreak of war disturbed many Americans. In New England, protest ran high. Henry David Thoreau chose to be jailed rather than pay taxes that would support the war. The United States had lost its reputation as a "refuge of liberty," he wrote, when it held a sixth of its population as slaves and engaged in an unjust war with Mexico. Other protesters also made the connection between the war with Mexico and slavery.

The annexation of Texas brought slavery to the attention of the American people like nothing before. To southerners, this land represented economic and political power. Proslavery constitutions in these newly acquired territories would ensure the immigration of friendly voters and the strengthening of the South's interests in Congress. Northerners saw something much more alarming in the southern expansion movement. Since the Missouri Compromise in 1820, some northerners had come to believe that a slaveholding **oligarchy** controlled life and politics in the South. Abolitionists warned that this "Slave Power" sought to expand its reach until it controlled every aspect of American life. Many viewed Congress's adoption of the gag rule in 1836 and the drive to annex Texas as evidence of the Slave Power's influence. Thus debates over Texas pitted two regions of the country against each other in what champions of both sides viewed as mortal combat.

The contenders joined battle in earnest over appropriations for the war effort. In August 1846, David Wilmot, a Democratic representative from Pennsylvania, proposed an amendment to a military appropriations bill specifying that "neither slavery nor involuntary servitude shall ever exist" in any territory gained in the Mexican War. The **Wilmot Proviso** passed in the House of Representatives but failed in the Senate. The vote on the proviso was an ominous one, for it followed sectional and not party lines. After several more efforts to pass the proviso, the House finally decided in April 1847 to appropriate money for the war without stipulating whether slavery would be permitted in territories acquired from Mexico.

War with Mexico

Americans quickly took control of the Southwest from Mexico. In California, American settlers in

Zachary Taylor American general whose defeat of Santa Anna at Buena Vista in 1847 made him a national hero and the Whig choice for president in 1848.

John C. Frémont Explorer, soldier, and politician who explored and mapped much of the American West and Northwest; he later ran unsuccessfully for president.

oligarchy Government by a small group of people or families.

Wilmot Proviso Amendment to an appropriations bill in 1846 proposing that any territory acquired from Mexico be closed to slavery; it was defeated in the Senate.

♦ **MAP 12.2 The Southwest and the Mexican War** When the United States acquired Texas, it inherited the Texans' boundary disputes with Mexico. This map shows the outcome: war with Mexico in 1846 and the acquisition of the disputed territories in Texas as well as most of Arizona, New Mexico, and California through the Treaty of Guadalupe Hidalgo.

the Sacramento Valley captured the town of Sonoma in June 1846 and declared themselves independent. They crafted a flag depicting a grizzly bear and announced the birth of the Republic of California, also called the Bear Flag Republic. Frémont's force joined the Bear Flag rebels and marched south toward Monterey. There they found that the American navy had already seized the city. The Mexican forces were in full flight southward.

Polk had also ordered Colonel Stephen Kearny to invade New Mexico on May 15. After leading his men across 800 miles of desert to Santa Fe, Kearny found a less-than-hostile enemy force facing him. The interracial upper class of Santa Fe, which had already expressed interest in joining the United States, surrendered without firing a shot. Within a short time, all of New Mexico and California were securely in the hands of U.S. forces.

Zachary Taylor faced more serious opposition in Mexico. After marching across the Rio Grande, Taylor captured the Mexican city of Monterrey in September 1846, but then allowed the enemy garrison to retreat through his lines. From Monterrey,

Taylor planned to turn southward toward Mexico City, but politics intervened.

After Taylor's victory at Monterrey, Polk feared that Taylor might use his military success to challenge him for the presidency. That Taylor had allowed the Mexican garrison to escape also convinced the president that Taylor was not aggressive enough to win the war quickly. Thus Polk ordered General **Winfield Scott** to lead American troops in the assault against Mexico City.

Polk complicated the military situation by plotting with deposed Mexican president Santa Anna, who had been exiled to Cuba after his defeat at San Jacinto. Santa Anna promised that he would help end the war in America's favor if Polk would help him return to Mexico. The American president agreed, and Santa Anna soon resumed the presidency of Mexico. To Polk's dismay, however, Santa Anna vowed to resist American expansion. Thus Mexico's most able general was back in command.

Santa Anna and his numerically superior army encountered Taylor at Buena Vista in February 1847. Tired from marching across the desert, the Mexican army was in no shape to fight, but Santa Anna ordered an attack anyway. Although the **Battle of Buena Vista** was a draw, Santa Anna was compelled to withdraw into the interior of Mexico.

Scott's forces captured the port of Veracruz on March 9 and then moved relentlessly toward Mexico City. An ambush at Cerro Gordo turned into a disaster for Santa Anna. Scott's forces captured three thousand Mexican troops, most of Santa Anna's equipment and provisions, and even the president's personal effects. By May 15, however, Scott had run into trouble. Nearly a third of his army went home when their twelve-month enlistments expired on that date. Three months later, Scott received reinforcements and resumed his march on Mexico City. Leading a brilliant assault, Scott captured the city on September 13, 1847.

Scott's enormous success caused Santa Anna's government to collapse, leaving no one to negotiate with American peace commissioner Nicholas Trist. After a month had passed with no settlement, Polk concluded that Trist was not pressing hard enough and removed him as peace commissioner. But by the time Polk's orders arrived, the Mexican government had elected a new president and told Trist that Mexico was ready to begin negotiations. Trist ignored Polk's orders and pressed on with negotiations. On February 2, 1848, Trist and the Mexican delegation signed the **Treaty of Guadalupe Hidalgo,** granting the United States all the territory between the Nueces River and the Rio Grande and all the territory between there and the Pacific. In exchange, the United States would pay Mexico $15 million and all claims made by Texans for war damages.

Polk was very angry when he heard the terms of the treaty. He felt that Scott's sweeping victory at Mexico City should have gained the United States more territory for less money. Political realities in Washington, however, prevented Polk from trying to get a more aggressive treaty ratified by the Senate. Although the president had strong support for annexing all of Mexico, antislavery voices loudly protested the acquisition of so much land south of the Missouri Compromise line. Others opposed the annexation of Mexico because they feared that the largely Roman Catholic population of Mexico might threaten Protestant institutions in the United States. Still others had moral objections to taking any territory by force. Congress was also unwilling to appropriate more money for war if peace was within reach. Thus Polk submitted the treaty Trist had negotiated, and the Senate approved it by a vote of 38 to 14.

Winfield Scott Virginia soldier and statesman who led troops in the War of 1812 and the war with Mexico; he was still serving as a general at the start of the Civil War.

Battle of Buena Vista Battle in February 1847 during which U.S. troops led by Zachary Taylor forced Santa Anna's forces to withdraw into the interior of Mexico.

Treaty of Guadalupe Hidalgo Treaty signed in 1848 under which Mexico gave up Texas above the Rio Grande and ceded New Mexico and California to the United States in return for $15 million.

The Antislavery Crusade and Women's Rights

As the debates over the Mexican War indicate, abolitionist voices were getting louder in the 1840s. Despite sometimes violent opposition, the abolition movement had continued to grow, especially among the privileged and educated classes in the Northeast. Throughout the 1830s, evangelicals increasingly stressed the sinful nature of slavery and broke away from the **gradualism** of the American Colonization Society. Men and women steeped in evangelical zeal joined with William Lloyd Garrison and Angelina Grimké in urging the immediate, uncompensated liberation of slaves.

Garrison, however, consistently alienated his followers. Calling the Constitution "a covenant with death and an agreement with hell," Garrison burned a copy of it, and he urged his followers to have no dealings with a government that permitted so great an evil as slavery. Citing the reluctance of most organized churches to condemn slavery outright, Garrison urged his followers to break with them as well. He also alienated many of his white, evangelical supporters by associating with and supporting free black advocates of violent abolition. In 1840, moderates in the American Anti-Slavery Society withdrew from Garrison's organization to found the American and Foreign Anti-Slavery Society.

Garrison's persistent insistence that women should play a key role in the abolition effort also fragmented the movement. Having assumed the burden of eliminating sin from the world, many evangelical women rallied around Garrison and the antislavery cause. Their growing prominence in the movement led Garrison to insist that they play a more equal role. In 1841, women were members of Garrison's delegation to the first World's Anti-Slavery Convention in London. British antislavery advocates, like their American counterparts, considered the presence of women inappropriate and refused to seat them. Garrison's group walked out in protest. Increasingly in the 1840s, slights like that made women in the abolition movement feel there was a similarity between their condition and that of the slaves they were seeking to free.

Angelina Grimké was one of the first to make a public proclamation of the frustration women were feeling. In her speech before the Massachusetts state assembly in 1838, she had asked, "Have women *no* country—*no* interests staked in public weal—no liabilities in the common peril—no partnership in a nation's guilt and shame?" That same year, her sister Sarah wrote a powerful indictment against the treatment of women in America. In *Letters on the Equality of the Sexes and the Condition of Woman,* Sarah proclaimed, "The page of history teems with woman's wrongs . . . and it is wet with woman's tears."

Many women began backing away from the male-dominated abolitionist cause and instead advanced their own cause. In 1848, two women who had been excluded from the World's Anti-Slavery Convention, **Lucretia Mott** and **Elizabeth Cady Stanton,** called women to a convention at Seneca Falls, New York, to discuss their common problems. At Seneca Falls, they presented the Declaration of Sentiments based on the Declaration of Independence, citing "the history of repeated injuries and usurpations on the part of man toward woman, having in direct object the establishment of an absolute tyranny over her." The convention adopted eleven resolutions relating to equality under the law, rights to control property, and other prominent issues. A twelfth resolution, calling for the right to vote, failed to receive unanimous endorsement.

Issues in the Election of 1848

The presidential election of 1848 came along at the peak of national tension. Sectional differences

gradualism The belief that slavery in the United States should be abolished gradually by methods such as placing territorial limits on slavery or settling free blacks in Africa.

Lucretia Mott Quaker minister who founded the Philadelphia Female Anti-Slavery Society (1833) and co-organized the Seneca Falls Women's Rights Convention in 1848.

Elizabeth Cady Stanton Pioneering woman-suffrage leader and co-organizer of the first Women's Rights Convention, held in Seneca Falls, New York, in 1848.

were reaching crisis proportions. Rather than offering solutions, however, both major parties continued to practice the politics of avoidance.

In poor health, Polk declined to run for a second term. The Democrats chose Lewis Cass of Michigan, a long-time moderate on slavery issues, as their candidate. The Whigs hoped to ride a wave of nationalism following the Mexican War by running military hero Zachary Taylor, a Louisianan and a slaveholder, for president. During the campaign, Cass tried to avoid offending anyone by advocating the policy of **popular sovereignty.** Under this policy, territories would choose for themselves whether to admit slavery. Taylor echoed Calhoun's opinion that Congress did not have the authority to control slavery in the territories.

A third party cut to the heart of the slavery issue. A number of northern Democrats and northern Whigs joined forces with members of the former **Liberty party** to form the **Free-Soil party.** The party acquired this name because it wanted to exclude slavery from the territories. It named Martin Van Buren as its candidate.

Although the Free-Soilers won 10 percent of the votes cast in the election, Taylor emerged as the victor. Congress remained split between Whigs and Democrats. Sectional issues had not yet fragmented the political system, but large cracks were showing.

These fissures widened noticeably when the question of admitting California to the Union arose. During the winter of 1847–1848, workmen had discovered gold while digging a ditch for John Sutter. Word soon reached San Francisco that huge gold deposits had been discovered at New Helvetia. By mid-May 1848, prospectors were swarming into the Sacramento Valley from all over California and Oregon. By September, the news had reached the East. Over a hundred thousand **forty-niners** took up residence in California the next year.

The twin issues of expansion and slavery were raised once again. Southerners wanted California to be open for slavery. But northerners were not about to turn the richest source of gold yet discovered over to the Slave Power. Thus although the discovery of gold in California seemed to announce God's approval of American expansionism, it drove an enormous wedge into an already cracking political system.

popular sovereignty The doctrine that the people of a territory had the right to determine whether slavery would exist within their territory.

Liberty party The first antislavery political party; it was formed in Albany, New York, in 1840.

Free-Soil party A political party that opposed the extension of slavery into any of the territories newly acquired from Mexico.

forty-niners Prospectors who streamed into California in 1849 after the discovery of gold at New Helvetia in 1848.

SUMMARY

Expectations
Constraints
Choices
Outcomes

During the first half of the nineteenth century, the westward movement of Americans steadily gained momentum. Successful fur traders like William Henry Ashley made enormous profits from their *choice* to move west. Land speculators and gold seekers also helped open areas to settlement.

Communities in Texas, Oregon, California, Utah, and elsewhere in the West sprang up like weeds. One *outcome* was the development of a variety of cultures and economies, which evolved from the interplay of old habits, new ideals, and environmental *constraints.*

Conflicting *expectations* about the country's manifest destiny promoted an air of crisis in the nation at large. Northerners wanted a West that would be free for diversified economic development. Southerners wanted the West to be open to slavery and staple crops. And people from each region *chose* to use expansion to add to their power in Congress.

Slavery began to eclipse all other issues in symbolizing the differing demands made by North and South. For northerners, the idea of going to war to win Oregon was acceptable because the Missouri Compromise prohibited slavery there, but the idea of going to war to acquire Texas was quite another matter. The possibility of many new southern senators and representatives filled northerners with dread. Nevertheless, the nation *chose* to fight a war with Mexico between 1846 and 1848. It thereby gained California and vast territories in the Southwest. The discovery of gold in California in 1848 made that region a new bone of contention in the sectional debate.

Meanwhile, radical abolitionists like William Lloyd Garrison still labored for acceptance. What made Garrison's message hard for many to accept was his insistence on an equal role for women. But severely discriminatory conditions *constrained* the many women who participated in abolition and other reform movements. One *outcome* was the Seneca Falls conference in 1848, where politically active women called for greater equality with men.

SUGGESTED READINGS

Billington, Ray Allen. *America's Frontier Heritage* (1966).

A broad overview of America's western experience.

Hietala, Thomas R. *Manifest Design* (1985).

An interesting and well-written interpretation of the Mexican War and the events leading up to it.

Limerick, Patricia Nelson. *The Legacy of Conquest* (1988).

This wonderfully written interpretation of events in the West challenges many assumptions and stereotypes.

Meinig, Donald W. *Imperial Texas* (1969).

A fascinating look at Texas history by a leading historical geographer.

Miller, Christopher L. *Prophetic Worlds* (1985).

Critics have called this a seductive reinterpretation of the history of Indians and whites in the Oregon Country.

Rodman, Paul. *California Gold* (1947; reprint 1965).

A classic account of the Gold Rush and its impact on life in California.

Stegner, Wallace E. *The Gathering of Zion* (1964).

A masterfully written history of the Mormon Trail by one of the West's leading literary figures.

Unruh, John David. *The Plains Across* (1979).

Arguably the best one-volume account of the overland passage to Oregon. The author captures the adventure of the Oregon Trail.

THE COMPROMISE OF 1850 The acquisition of Texas and California brought a showdown between North and South over representation in the national government. As this map shows, the Compromise of 1850 permitted California to be admitted to the Union, giving the North a one-state majority in the Senate. In the House of Representatives, however, the balance heavily favored the North.

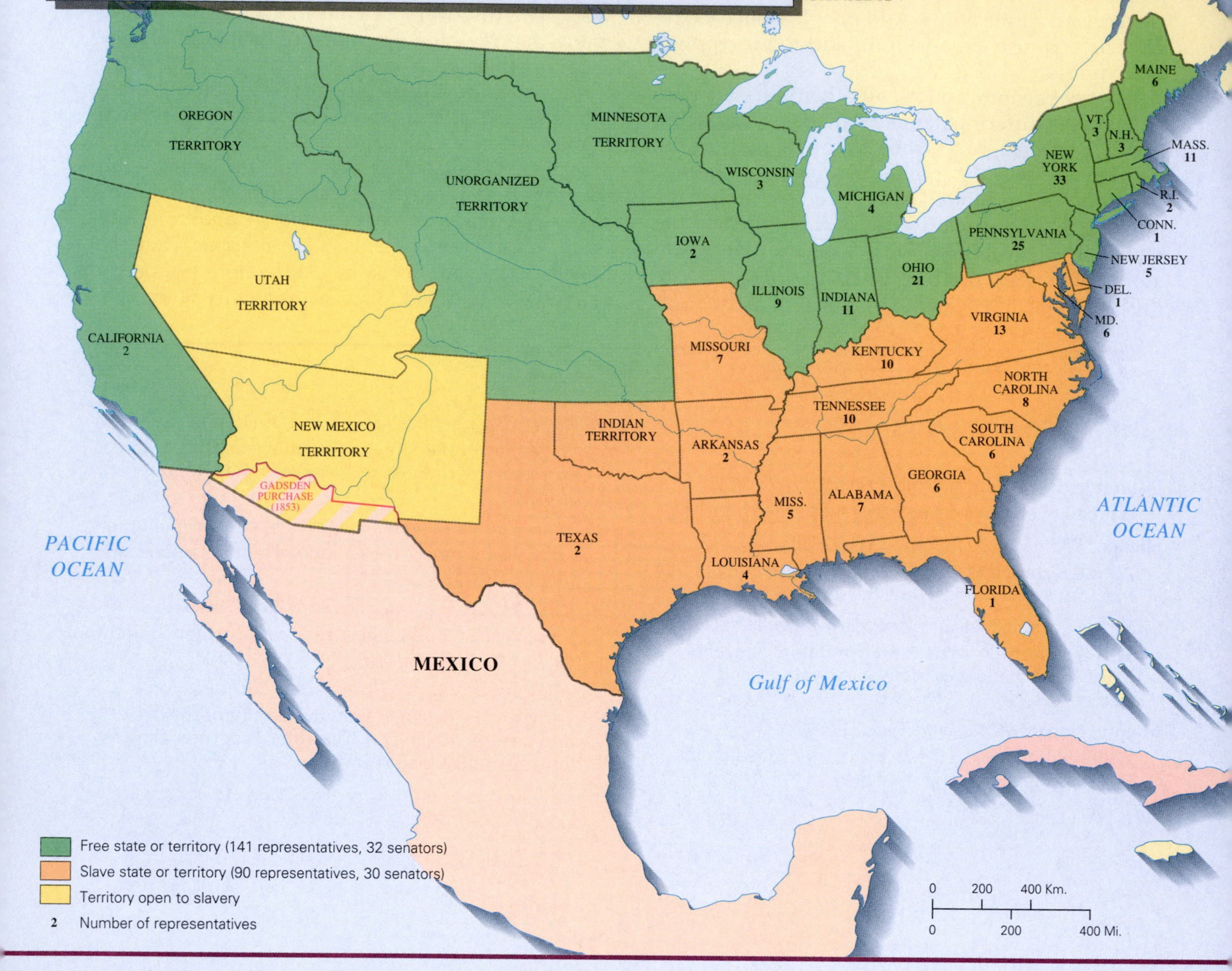

CANADA
OREGON TERRITORY
MINNESOTA TERRITORY
UNORGANIZED TERRITORY
WISCONSIN 3
MICHIGAN 4
MAINE 6
VT. 3
N.H. 3
MASS. 11
NEW YORK 33
R.I. 2
CONN. 1
PENNSYLVANIA 25
NEW JERSEY 5
DEL. 1
MD. 6
IOWA 2
ILLINOIS 9
INDIANA 11
OHIO 21
VIRGINIA 13
KENTUCKY 10
NORTH CAROLINA 8
TENNESSEE 10
SOUTH CAROLINA 6
GEORGIA 6
ALABAMA 7
MISS. 5
LOUISIANA 4
FLORIDA 1
ARKANSAS 2
MISSOURI 7
INDIAN TERRITORY
TEXAS 2
UTAH TERRITORY
CALIFORNIA 2
NEW MEXICO TERRITORY
GADSDEN PURCHASE (1853)
PACIFIC OCEAN
ATLANTIC OCEAN
Gulf of Mexico
MEXICO
Free state or territory (141 representatives, 32 senators)
Slave state or territory (90 representatives, 30 senators)
Territory open to slavery
2 Number of representatives
0 200 400 Km.
0 200 400 Mi.

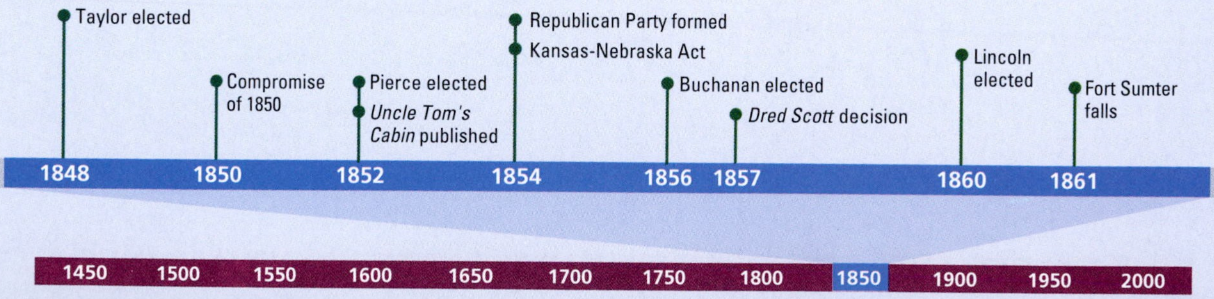

Taylor elected
Compromise of 1850
Pierce elected
Uncle Tom's Cabin published
Republican Party formed
Kansas-Nebraska Act
Buchanan elected
Dred Scott decision
Lincoln elected
Fort Sumter falls
1848
1850
1852
1854
1856
1857
1860
1861
1450
1500
1550
1600
1650
1700
1750
1800
1850
1900
1950
2000

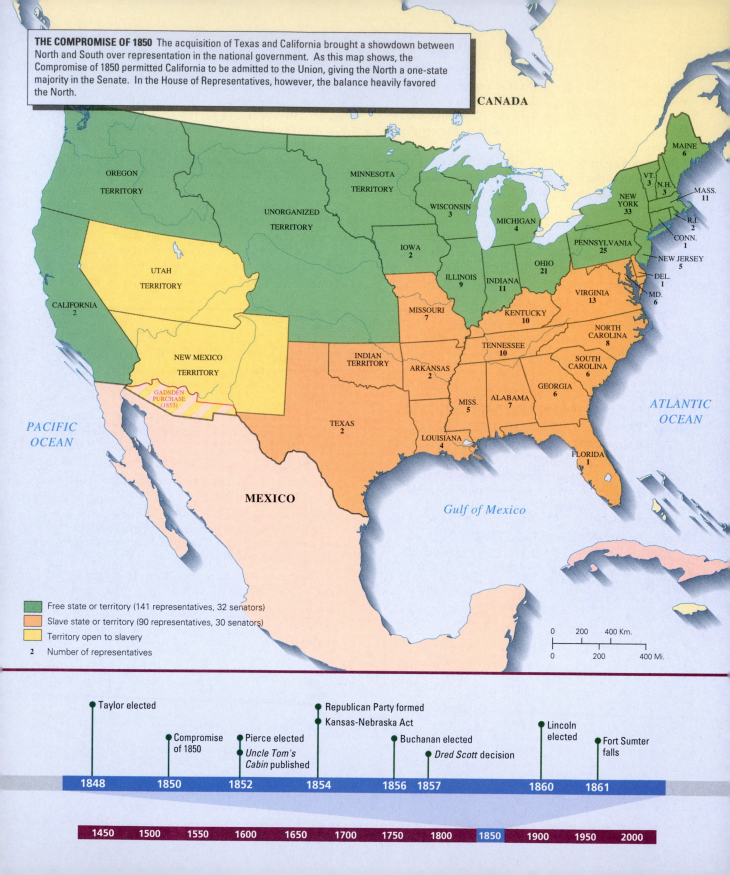

CHAPTER 13

Sectional Conflict and Shattered Union, 1850–1861

New Political Choices

- What constraints convinced voters to make new political choices during the 1850s?
- What was the outcome for the political party system?

Toward a House Divided

- What did Stephen A. Douglas expect when he proposed to organize the Nebraska Territory?
- What choices and constraints influenced the outcome of this proposal?

The Divided Nation

- What did northerners and southerners expect to happen in the presidential election of 1860?
- What choices did they make as a result, and what was the outcome?

The Nation Dissolved

- What choices were available to Abraham Lincoln and Jefferson Davis in March 1861?
- What political factors constrained their choices?

INTRODUCTION

Expectations
Constraints
Choices
Outcomes

The United States entered a period of major growth and transition during the 1850s. Wealth and population grew dramatically as technology and industry continued to advance rapidly. After the successful military adventure against Mexico, the future seemed to hold infinite promise. Many Americans *expected* that their nation's growing wealth and vitality would open great opportunities for them. The nation simply needed to chart a correct course to claim its destiny.

But achieving the national destiny meant *choosing* particular goals and specific methods. Sharp disagreements *constrained* Americans seeking the correct national course. Most agreed that railroad development was good, but not everyone agreed on where the rail lines should run, how development should be funded, or what should be carried on the rails. Technological advances and industrial development brought new *constraints,* altering the nation's social structure and adding to disagreement. Social disruption occurred as unskilled immigrant factory laborers displaced native-born artisans. Disruption also occurred as commercial cotton growing and slave labor expanded farther into the American continent.

These problems quickly became the subject of political debate. Old-line northeastern and southern political interests continued to clash over traditional matters like tariffs and currency control. But rising immigration and westward migration brought new voters and new interests into play, particularly regarding the expansion of slavery. Reformers continued their efforts to restore order and virtue, and to fight for moral reform. All of these voter groups had extremely diverse *expectations* about the correct course for the nation.

The *outcome* of these diverse *expectations* was a changing political environment. Both the Whigs and the Democrats attempted to direct and exploit the events of the 1850s. But both faced new *constraints* in the changing social, economic, and political climate. The total number of voters grew significantly, but so did the diversity of the electorate. Building a coalition strong enough to win a national election became increasingly difficult as regional, ethnic, and social distinctions influenced voters.

In this fragmented climate, the expansion of slavery into the territories became the dominant political issue. Political leaders *chose* either to seek compromise or to ignore the slavery question. In reality, they could do neither. Through all the debates, political platforms, and confrontations, two separate societies attempted to control the course of national destiny.

As the nation's leaders wrestled with a host of new issues amid political fragmentation, the confrontation between those two societies peaked. Although many people wanted peace and favored reconciliation, the political structure thwarted that desire. *Constrained* by the regional interests that had given birth to them, the new political coalitions proved incapable of compromise. The *outcome* was the end of the Union.

CHRONOLOGY

Toward a Shattered Union

1848	Zachary Taylor elected president Immigration to the United States exceeds 100,000 for the first time
1850	Compromise of 1850
1852	First railroad line completed to Chicago Publication of *Uncle Tom's Cabin* by Harriet Beecher Stowe Franklin Pierce elected president Destruction of the Whig party begins American party emerges
1853	Gadsden Purchase
1854	Kansas-Nebraska Act Ostend Manifesto Formation of the Republican party
1855	Sack of Lawrence, Kansas Pottawatomie massacre
1856	James Buchanan elected president
1857	*Dred Scott* decision Proslavery Lecompton constitution adopted in Kansas
1858	Lincoln-Douglas debates
1859	John Brown's raid on Harpers Ferry
1860	Abraham Lincoln elected president Crittenden compromise fails
1861	Formation of the Confederate States of America Shelling of Fort Sumter

New Political Choices

The presidential election in 1848 had celebrated American expansion and nationalism, but the flow of Americans into California soon created a crisis. It began when newly elected president Zachary Taylor ordered Californians to draw up a state constitution and apply for statehood. California produced a document that barred slavery in the state. Taylor then recommended that California be admitted as a free state and that Utah and New Mexico be organized as territories without reference to slavery.

Taylor's proposal frightened and angered southerners, for they had assumed that California would be open to slavery. Southerners also pointed out with alarm that another free state would unbalance sectional representation in the Senate. John C. Calhoun stated, "I trust we shall persist in our resistance until restoration of all our rights, or disunion, one or the other, is the consequence."

The Politics of Compromise

Henry Clay, who had crafted the Missouri Compromise, believed that any successful agreement would have to address all sides of the issue. He proposed an **omnibus** bill—a package of separate proposals—to the Senate early in 1850. California would enter the Union as a free state, but the slavery question would be left to popular sovereignty in all other territories acquired from Mexico. Clay then called for an end to the slave trade in the District of Columbia to appease abolitionists and for a new, more effective **fugitive slave law** to ensure southern support of his proposed legislation.

omnibus Including or covering many things.

fugitive slave law Law providing for the return of escaped slaves to their owners; a 1793 law was replaced with a stiffer version as part of the Compromise of 1850.

♦ This painting shows Henry Clay attempting to convince his fellow senators to support his omnibus compromise bill in 1850. Clay failed, but Illinois senator Stephen Douglas was able to get the compromise passed by breaking up the complicated bill, calling for a vote on each separate provision. *Library of Congress.*

Congress debated the bill for six months, then finally defeated it in July 1850. However, **Stephen A. Douglas** of Illinois revived the compromise by submitting each component of Clay's omnibus package as a separate bill. Using persuasion and backroom political arm-twisting, he steered each bill through Congress. President Taylor's sudden death on July 9 also made passage of the compromise package easier because his successor, **Millard Fillmore,** obtained northern Whig support for the bills. Finally, in September, Congress passed the Compromise of 1850.

The **Compromise of 1850** did little to settle underlying regional differences. Many northerners resented the fact that slaveowners could pursue runaway slaves into northern states and return them back into slavery. Nor did southerners find reason to celebrate. They had lost the balance of power in the Senate and gained no protection for slavery, either in the territories or at home. Still, the compromise created a brief respite from the slavery-extension question.

Stephen A. Douglas Illinois senator who tried to reconcile northern and southern differences over slavery through the Compromise of 1850 and sponsor of the Kansas-Nebraska Act.

Millard Fillmore Vice president who succeeded Zachary Taylor when he died in office and who tried to occupy a middle ground on slavery.

Compromise of 1850 Plan intended to reconcile North and South on the issue of slavery; it recognized the principle of popular sovereignty and included a strong fugitive slave law.

The compromise soon took its toll on the political system, particularly the Whigs. They passed over Millard Fillmore in 1852 in favor of Mexican War hero General Winfield Scott as their presidential nominee. The Democrats tapped the virtually unknown **Franklin Pierce** of New Hampshire. Despite the fact that Scott was a national figure and a distinguished military hero, he was overwhelmed by Pierce. Pierce gathered 254 electoral votes to Scott's 42. Although no one knew it at the time, the election of 1852 marked the end of the Whig party. It was the casualty of a changing political environment.

A Changing Political Economy

During the 1850s, industrial growth accelerated. By 1860, fewer than half of all northern workers made a living from agriculture. Steam began to replace water as the primary power source, and factories were no longer limited to locations along rivers and streams. The use of interchangeable parts became more sophisticated and intricate. For example, in 1851, Isaac Singer began mass-producing sewing machines. As industry expanded, the North became more reliant on the West and South for raw materials and for the food that northeastern factory workers consumed.

Railroad development stimulated economic and industrial growth. Between 1850 and 1860, American railroad trackage jumped from 9,000 to more than 30,000 miles. Most of these lines linked the Northeast with the Midwest, carrying produce to eastern markets and eastern manufactures to western consumers. In 1852, the Michigan Southern Railroad completed the first line into Chicago from the East, and by 1855 that city had become a major transportation hub.

Railroads quickly reshaped the expanding American economy. Western farmers, who had previously shipped their products downriver to New Orleans on slow and undependable barges and boats, now sent them much more rapidly by rail to eastern industrial centers. Warehouses and **grain elevators** sprang up to accommodate such shipments. Reliable transportation and storage facilities induced farmers to cultivate more land. Mining boomed, particularly the iron industry, as the rail lines not only transported ore but became a major consumer.

Government actively supported railroad development and expansion, particularly in sparsely settled areas where returns on investment were expected to be meager. State and local governments loaned money directly to rail companies, financed them indirectly by purchasing stock, or extended state tax exemptions. The most crucial aid to railroads, however, was federal land grants. These were given to railroad developers who then leased or sold plots along the proposed route to finance construction. In 1850, a 2.6-million-acre land grant went to a railroad between Chicago and Mobile. Congress also invested $150,000 in 1853 to survey routes for a transcontinental railroad.

Railroads and improved farm technology opened up many parts of the Midwest to commercial farming. The steel plow, devised in 1837 by **John Deere,** allowed farmers to cultivate more acres with greater ease, and the mechanical reaper, invented in 1841 by **Cyrus McCormick,** could harvest more than fourteen field hands could. The combination of greater production and speedy transportation prompted westerners to increase farm size and concentrate on cash crops. It also greatly increased the economic and political power of the West.

The Midwest developed as America's breadbasket as food shortages and poverty were driving millions from Europe. Beginning in the 1840s, a potato blight in Ireland caused extensive crop failures and increasing numbers of people to flee. Total immigration to the United States exceeded

Franklin Pierce New Hampshire lawyer and politician who was chosen as a compromise candidate at the 1852 Democratic convention and became the fourteenth president of the United States.

grain elevator A building equipped with mechanical lifting devices and used for storing grain.

John Deere American industrialist who pioneered the manufacture of steel plows especially suited for working prairie soil.

Cyrus McCormick Virginia inventor and manufacturer who developed a machine for harvesting crops in 1841 and built a factory to mass-produce the McCormick reaper in 1847.

100,000 for the first time in 1848. In 1851, 221,000 immigrants arrived from Ireland alone. Crop failures and political upheavals also pushed large numbers of Germans toward the United States. In 1852, German immigrants reached 145,000. Many newcomers, particularly the Irish, were unskilled and settled in the industrial cities of the Northeast. The concentration of immigrants there played a significant role in the unraveling of antebellum American politics.

Decline of the Whigs

During the 1850s, many unemployed artisans were forced to accept factory work at a time when the flood of immigrants was driving wages down. Such artisans wanted a political party that would address their most pressing problems: loss of status, income, and jobs.

The Whig party had been their voice in politics during the party's glory days. During the elections in 1848, however, the Whigs had tried to win Catholic and immigrant voters away from the Democrats. Not only did the Whigs fail to attract immigrant voters, but they alienated two groups of supporters. One group was artisans, who saw immigrants as the main source of their economic and social woes. The other was Protestant evangelicals, to whom Roman Catholic immigrants symbolized all that was threatening to the American republic. As a result, increasing numbers abandoned the Whig party to form coalitions more in tune with voters' hopes and fears. Between 1852 and 1856, the Whig party dissolved and was replaced by two emerging parties: the Know-Nothing, or American, party, and the Republican party.

The anti-Catholic, anti-immigrant, **Know-Nothings** traced their origins back to secret **nativist** societies that had come into existence during the 1830s. These secret fraternal organizations entered politics by endorsing candidates who shared their views about immigration. They told their members to say "I know nothing" if they were questioned about the organization or its political intrigues, hence the name Know-Nothings. After the election of 1852, the societies began nominating and voting for their own candidates under the banner of the American party. The party charged that immigrants were part of a Catholic plot to overthrow democracy in the United States. The party advocated a twenty-one-year naturalization period, a ban against naturalized citizens holding public office, and the use of the Protestant Bible in the public schools.

Know-Nothings disagreed about many issues, but they agreed that the Whig and Democratic parties were corrupt and that the only hope for the nation lay in scrapping traditional politics. As Ohio governor Rutherford B. Hayes noted, the people were expressing a "general disgust with the powers that be."

Local antislavery coalitions also deserted the Whigs. Sectional tensions doomed all Whig attempts to formulate a national policy. Those tensions were heightened in 1852 with the publication of *Uncle Tom's Cabin* by **Harriet Beecher Stowe.** Stowe portrayed the darkest inhumanities of southern slavery in the first American novel to include African Americans as central characters. *Uncle Tom's Cabin* sold three hundred thousand copies in its first year and became one of the most popular plays of the period. It drew attention to the new fugitive slave law and its harsh provisions for individuals caught helping runaway slaves. The work of Stowe and the lectures of people like **Harriet Tubman,** a former slave who rescued hundreds from slavery, made northerners increasingly aware of the plight of slaves (see Individual Choices: Harriet Tubman). When Free-Soilers and "conscience" (antislavery) Whigs saw that the party was incapable of addressing the slavery question, they began to look for other political options.

Know-Nothings Members of secret organizations that aimed to exclude Catholics and "foreigners" from public office; members' "I know nothing" response to questions about the organizations produced their nickname.

nativist Favoring native-born inhabitants of a country over immigrants.

Harriet Beecher Stowe American novelist and abolitionist whose novel *Uncle Tom's Cabin* fanned antislavery sentiment in the North.

Harriet Tubman Antislavery activist who escaped from slavery and led many others to freedom on the Underground Railroad.

Increasing Tension Under Pierce

The Democrats were not immune to the problems caused by a changing electorate and by the issue of slavery. In May 1853, only two months after assuming office, Franklin Pierce inflamed antislavery forces by sending James Gadsden, a southern railroad developer, to Mexico to purchase a strip of land lying south of the Arizona and New Mexico territories. Pierce and his southern supporters wanted to buy this land because any southern transcontinental rail route would have to pass through it to go to California. The **Gadsden Purchase,** ratified by Congress in 1853, added 29,640 square miles to the United States for a cost of $10 million and set the southwestern border of the United States.

The Gadsden Purchase led to a more serious sectional crisis. It prompted advocates of a southern transcontinental railroad to push for government sponsorship of the project. They found themselves blocked, however, by Illinois senator Stephen A. Douglas.

A consummate politician, Douglas wanted a national railroad that would pass through Chicago and the Midwest, strengthening that region's economic and political strength and furthering his own career. Using his position as chairman of the Senate Committee on Territories, Douglas thwarted efforts to build a southern transcontinental railroad. Because the northern route that Douglas favored would have to pass through territory that had not yet been organized, Douglas introduced a bill in January 1854 that called for incorporating the Nebraska Territory.

Douglas knew that he would need northern and southern support to get his bill through Congress. Hoping to avoid yet another debate over slavery, Douglas proposed that the issue of slavery be settled by popular sovereignty within the territory. Southerners pointed out, however, that Congress might prohibit popular sovereignty in the Nebraska Territory because it was north of the Missouri Compromise line. Douglas finally supported an amendment to his original bill that divided the territory in half: Nebraska in the north and Kansas in the south (see Map 13.1). He assumed that popular sovereignty would lead to slavery in Kansas and a system of free labor in Nebraska.

Toward a House Divided

The Kansas-Nebraska bill angered northern Democrats, "conscience" Whigs, and Free-Soil advocates. All of them feared that without the Missouri Compromise limitations, slavery would spread throughout the territories. Once again, slavery threatened national political stability. In the North, opponents of the bill formed local coalitions to challenge its passage. On January 24, 1854, a group calling itself the Independent Democrats, who included Salmon P. Chase, Gerrit Smith, Joshua Giddings, and Charles Sumner, denounced the bill as an "atrocious plot" to make Nebraska a "dreary region of despotism, inhabited by masters and slaves." On February 28, other opponents of the bill met in Ripon, Wisconsin, and recommended the formation of a new political party. Similar meetings elsewhere in the North led to the emergence of the **Republican party.**

A Shattered Compromise

Despite strong opposition, Douglas and Pierce secured passage of the **Kansas-Nebraska Act** in 1854. Its passage crystallized northern antislavery sentiment. As Senator William Seward of New York stated, "We will engage in competition for the virgin soil of Kansas, and God give the victory to the side which is stronger in numbers as it is in right."

Southerners were determined to prevail in this struggle. They had come to believe that the expansion of slavery was necessary to prevent northern

Gadsden Purchase A strip of land in present-day Arizona and New Mexico that the United States bought from Mexico in 1853 to secure a southern route for a transcontinental railroad.

Republican party Political party that arose in the 1850s and opposed the extension of slavery into the western territories.

Kansas-Nebraska Act Law passed by Congress in 1854 that allowed residents of the Kansas and Nebraska territories to decide whether to allow slavery.

INDIVIDUAL CHOICES

To Free Others

Harriet Tubman

Fearful of being torn from her family in Maryland and sold to a cotton plantation in the Deep South, Harriet Tubman chose to run away from slavery. Seeking to reunite her family, she returned to the South to help them escape. Despite personal danger to herself, she chose to continue her efforts, finally conducting as many as 300 slaves along the Underground Railroad to freedom. She is seen here (on the left) with some of the slaves whom she helped free. Sophia Smith Collection.

Resisting slavery seemed second nature to Harriet Tubman. Born a slave on a Maryland plantation in 1820, she quickly developed a fiery spirit and was not shy about protesting bad treatment. One such incident so angered the plantation overseer that he hit her over the head with a lead weight, inflicting a permanent brain injury that would cause her to suddenly lose consciousness several times a day for the rest of her life. To overcome this disability, she worked on building herself up physically, becoming an uncommonly strong woman. It was said that she could single-handedly haul a boat fully loaded with stones, a feat deemed impossible for all but the strongest men.

Although Tubman dreamed about freedom after learning of Nat Turner's Rebellion in 1831, her disability and fear of being caught prevented her from acting. But in 1849, all that changed when the owner of her plantation died. Rumors began circulating that the man's estate was going to be liquidated and that the slaves were to be sold "down the river" to cotton plantations in the Deep South. The thought of being taken so far away from any avenue to freedom forced Tubman to choose.

Leaving the plantation, she slowly made her way northward by land, stopping at places she had heard about where free blacks or sympathetic whites would provide food and shelter. After a harrowing flight, she finally arrived in Philadelphia. She was free but was not content with winning freedom just for herself. Tubman had left a large family behind in Maryland and would not be happy until she had won their freedom as well.

Soon after arriving in Pennsylvania, Tubman met William Still, a black clerk for the Pennsylvania Anti-Slavery Society. Still had worked since 1847 as a "conductor" on the Underground Railroad. Every so often, he and others like him made their way secretly into the South, contacted slaves who wanted to escape, and led them northward, stopping at prearranged stations—homes and businesses owned by free blacks or white abolitionists—for food and shelter. With the passage of the Fugitive Slave Act in 1850, Tubman decided that the only way she could win freedom for her family was to become a conductor herself. She chose to risk her freedom—even her life—to bring her parents, her brother and his family, and her own two children out of slavery.

It took Tubman several trips into the South to accomplish her aim of reuniting her family. In the course of her adventure, what began as a commitment to her immediate kin became a mission to her entire people. In all, Tubman made nineteen trips back into the slave South between 1850 and the outbreak of the Civil War in 1861. It was said that she was personally responsible for conducting three hundred slaves to freedom. In between trips she, like Frederick Douglass, Sojourner Truth, and other escaped slaves, told her story to northern audiences, seeking support for her efforts to free individual slaves and for the larger effort to free all slaves. Her activities as a speaker and as an underground agent brought her acclaim and notoriety. John Brown consulted her while planning his raid on Harpers Ferry, and authorities in the South acknowledged her impact by posting a $40,000 reward for her capture.

Tubman continued her activities after the war broke out. Like other black women who had either been born into or had won freedom, she volunteered to go into the South with Union forces to serve as a nurse and cook and to help evacuate slaves from areas won by Federal troops. She also continued speaking out in the interest of her people. To beat the South, she admonished, President Lincoln must set the slaves free.

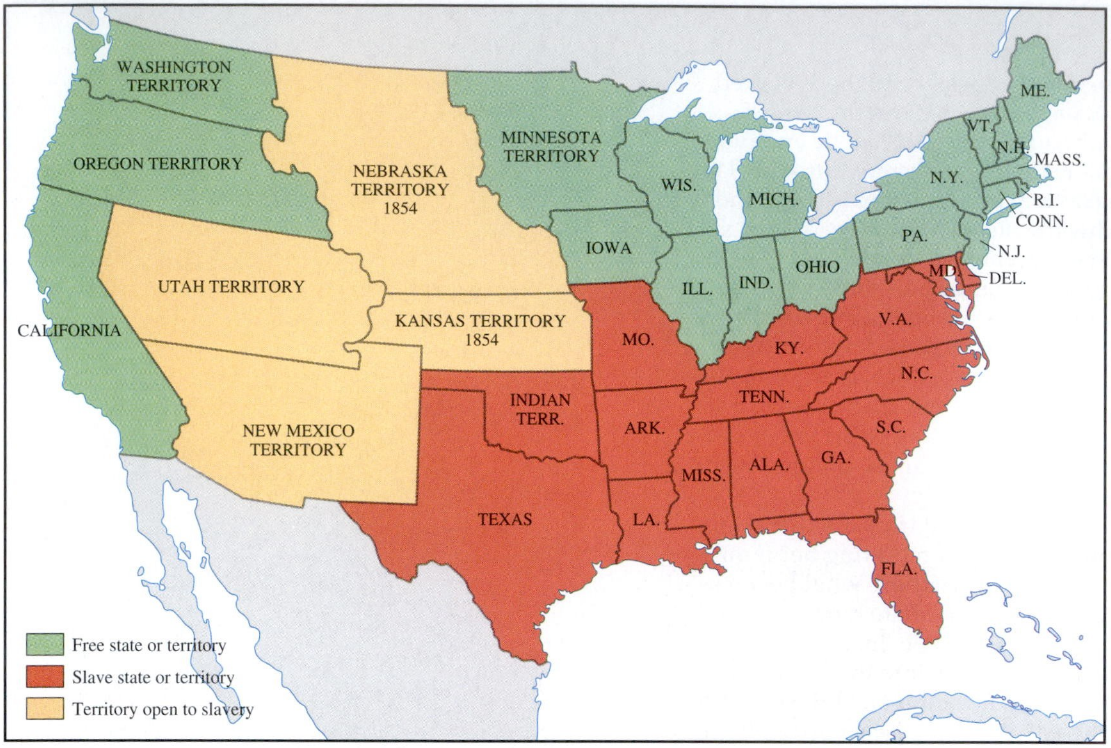

♦ **MAP 13.1 The Kansas-Nebraska Act** This map shows Stephen Douglas's proposed compromise to the dilemma of organizing the vast territory separating the settled part of the United States from California and Oregon. His solution, designed to win profitable rail connections for his home district in Illinois, stirred a political crisis by repealing the Missouri Compromise and replacing it with popular sovereignty.

domination. They saw northern industrial and commercial power as a threat to reduce the South to a "colony" controlled by northern bankers and industrialists. The South needed to expand to survive.

Some southerners attempted to expand slavery by mounting private expeditions into the Caribbean and Central America. They believed that places such as Cuba and Nicaragua could be added to the list of slaveowning states. Although these expeditions were the work of a few power-hungry individuals, many northerners believed them to be part of the Slave Power conspiracy.

President Pierce perhaps unintentionally aggravated this sentiment. In October 1854, three of Pierce's European ministers, including future president James Buchanan, met in Ostend, Belgium, and secretly drafted a statement outlining conditions that might justify taking Cuba from Spain by force. When the so-called **Ostend Manifesto** became public in 1855, many northerners feared that Pierce and the Democratic party secretly approved of adventurism to expand slavery. These perceptions stirred antislavery anxieties and fueled the growth of the newly formed anti-Democratic coalitions.

Bleeding Kansas

Meanwhile, frictions were producing sparks in the Kansas Territory. In April 1854, Eli Thayer of

> **Ostend Manifesto** Declaration by American foreign ministers in 1854 that if Spain refused to sell Cuba, the United States might be justified in taking it by force.

Worcester, Massachusetts, organized the New England Emigrant Aid Society to encourage antislavery supporters to move to Kansas. He hoped to "save" the region from slavery by flooding it with right-minded emigrants. The society eventually sent two thousand settlers to Kansas and equipped them with rifles and ammunition. Proslavery southerners, particularly those in Missouri, also encouraged settlement of the territory. Like their northern counterparts, these southerners came armed and ready to fight for their cause.

As proslavery and abolitionist settlers vied for control of Kansas, the region became a testing ground for popular sovereignty. When the vote came on March 30, 1855, armed slavery supporters from Missouri—so-called border ruffians—crossed into Kansas and cast ballots. These unlawful ballots gave proslavery supporters a large majority in the legislature. They promptly expelled all antislavery legislators and passed laws meant to drive all antislavery forces out of the territory. Antislavery advocates, however, refused to acknowledge the validity of the election or the laws. They organized their own free-state government at Lawrence and drew up an alternative constitution.

Bloodshed soon followed when a proslavery judge, Samuel LeCompte, sent a **posse** of about eight hundred armed men to Lawrence. There they "arrested" the antislavery forces and sacked the town. With that, civil war erupted in Kansas. **John Brown,** an antislavery zealot, took his four sons and three others to exact "an eye for an eye" for the five antislavery settlers who had been killed in Kansas. Brown murdered five proslavery men living along the Pottawatomie River. (The victims had not been involved in the sack of Lawrence.) The Pottawatomie massacre triggered a series of reprisals that killed over two hundred men.

The Kansas issue also led to violence in Congress. During the debates over the admission of the territory, **Charles Sumner,** a senator from Massachusetts, delivered an abusive speech against the proslavery elements in Congress. In "The Crime Against Kansas," he insulted South Carolina senator Andrew Butler by contending that Butler was a "Don Quixote" who had "made his vows" to "the harlot, slavery." Three days later, Representative Preston Brooks, Butler's nephew, beat Sumner unconscious with a cane to avenge his uncle's honor. Sumner was badly hurt and needed almost three years to recover. Though **censured** by the House of Representatives, Brooks was overwhelmingly reelected and openly praised by his constituents for his actions. He received canes as gifts from admirers all over the South. Northerners were appalled by Brooks's action and by southern responses to it.

As the presidential election of 1856 approached, Kansas and slavery dominated the agenda. The Know-Nothings had split over slavery at their initial national convention in 1855. Disagreement over the Kansas-Nebraska Act caused most northerners to bolt from the convention and to join Republican coalitions. In 1856, the remaining Know-Nothings nominated former president Millard Fillmore as the American party's standard-bearer.

John C. Frémont, a moderate abolitionist who had achieved fame as the liberator of California, got the Republican nomination. The few remaining Whigs endorsed Fillmore at their convention. The Democrats rejected both Pierce and Douglas and nominated **James Buchanan** from Pennsylvania, believing that he would be less controversial than the other two.

The election became a contest for the right to challenge Democratic occupancy of the office of president rather than a national referendum on slavery. Buchanan received 45 percent of the popular vote and 163 electoral votes. Frémont finished second with 33 percent of the popular vote and 114 electoral votes. Fillmore received 21 percent of the popular vote but only 8 electoral votes. Frémont's surprising showing demonstrated the appeal of

posse A group of people usually summoned by a sheriff to aid in law enforcement.

John Brown Abolitionist who fought proslavery settlers in Kansas in 1855; he was hanged after seizing the U.S. arsenal at Harpers Ferry in 1859 as part of an effort to liberate southern slaves.

Charles Sumner Massachusetts senator who was brutally beaten by a southern congressman in 1856 after delivering a speech attacking the South.

censure To issue an official rebuke, as by a legislature to one of its members.

James Buchanan Pennsylvania senator who was elected president in 1856 after gaining the Democratic nomination as a compromise candidate.

the newly formed Republican coalition to northern voters. The Know-Nothings, fragmented over slavery, disappeared.

Bringing Slavery Home to the North

Two days after Buchanan assumed office in March 1857, the Supreme Court issued a ruling that sent shock waves through the already troubled nation. **Dred Scott,** a slave formerly owned by an army officer, sued his current owner for his freedom. Although he resided in Missouri, Scott had accompanied his former master to Illinois and to a part of the Wisconsin Territory west of the Mississippi River, where slavery was outlawed by the Missouri Compromise. Scott's attorney argued that living in free territory made Scott a free man. When Missouri courts rejected this argument, Scott, with the help of abolitionist lawyers, appealed to the Supreme Court.

In a 7-to-2 decision, the Court ruled against Scott. Chief Justice Roger B. Taney, a Maryland slaveowner, argued that slaves were not people but property, could not be citizens of the United States, and had no right to petition the Court. Taney then ignited a political powder keg by stating that Congress had no constitutional authority to limit slavery in a federal territory, thus totally negating the Missouri Compromise. The Court's ruling marked the first time since its 1803 decision in *Marbury v. Madison* that it had declared a federal law unconstitutional.

Antislavery forces and northern evangelical leaders called the *Dred Scott* decision a mockery of justice. Some radical abolitionists, harking back to the Hartford Convention's threat of secession (see page 180), argued that the North should separate from the Union. Others advocated impeaching the Supreme Court. Antislavery leaders contended that the next move of the Slave Power would be to get the Supreme Court to strike down antislavery laws in northern states.

While debates raged over the *Dred Scott* decision, the Kansas issue simmered. Although very few slaveholders had actually moved into the territory, proslavery leaders meeting in Lecompton in June 1857 drafted a state constitution favoring slavery. Antislavery forces protested by refusing to vote on this constitution, so it was easily ratified. But when the constitution was submitted to Congress for approval, northern Democrats such as Stephen Douglas joined Republicans in denouncing it. Congress ultimately returned the **Lecompton constitution** to Kansas for another vote. This time Free-Soilers participated in the election and defeated the proposed constitution. Kansas remained a territory.

The Kansas controversy and the *Dred Scott* case figured prominently in the 1858 contest in Illinois for the Senate between Douglas and **Abraham Lincoln,** a small-town lawyer and moderate antislavery Republican. Born in Kentucky in 1809, Lincoln as a young man had worked odd jobs as a farm worker, ferryman, flatboatman, surveyor, and store clerk. In 1834, he was elected to the Illinois legislature and began a serious study of law. Lincoln had steered a middle course between the "cotton" and "conscience" wings of the Whig party. He acknowledged that slavery was evil but contended that it was the consequence of black racial inferiority. The only way to escape the evil, he believed, was to prevent the expansion of slavery into the territories.

Lincoln challenged Douglas to a series of seven debates about slavery that were to be held throughout Illinois. During the debate at Freeport, Lincoln asked Douglas to explain how the people of a territory could exclude slavery in light of the *Dred Scott* ruling. Douglas's reply became known as the **Freeport Doctrine.** Slavery, he said, needed the protection of "local police regulations." In any ter-

Dred Scott Slave who sued for his liberty in the Missouri courts, arguing that four years on free soil had made him free; in 1857 the Supreme Court ruled against him.

Lecompton constitution State constitution written for Kansas in 1857 at a convention dominated by proslavery forces, which tried to slant the document in favor of slavery; Kansas voters rejected it in 1858.

Abraham Lincoln Illinois lawyer and politician who argued against popular sovereignty in his debates with Stephen Douglas in 1858; he lost the senatorial election to Douglas but was elected president in 1860.

Freeport Doctrine Stephen Douglas's belief, stated at Freeport, Illinois, that a territory could exclude slavery by writing local laws or regulations that made slavery impossible to enforce.

ritory, citizens could elect representatives who would "by unfriendly legislation" prevent the introduction of slavery "into their midst." Voters apparently found Douglas's position more attractive than Lincoln's. They elected a majority of Douglas supporters to the state legislature, which then returned Douglas to his Senate seat.

Radical Responses to Abolitionism and Slavery

Southerners reacted with fear to the threat of limitations on the extension of slavery. Because intensive agriculture had depleted the soil in the South, expansion seemed necessary for economic survival. Although Republican leaders maintained that they had no intention of outlawing slavery where it already existed, their commitment against expansion appeared to sentence slavery to death.

Southern apologists defended their system against northern charges that it was immoral and evil. Charles C. Jones and other southern evangelicals offered a religious defense of slavery. They claimed that the Bible condoned slavery, pointing out that the Israelites practiced slavery and that Jesus walked among slaves but never mentioned freedom. The apostle Paul even commanded slaves to obey their masters.

Northern radicals such as John Brown, however, were developing plans that called for slaves to overthrow their masters. In 1857, Brown came east to convince prominent antislavery leaders to finance a daring plan to raise an army of slaves against their masters. Brown and twenty-one followers, including four free blacks, attacked the federal arsenal at **Harpers Ferry,** Virginia, on October 16, 1859, attempting to seize weapons.

Brown's force seized the arsenal but could not convince any slaves to join the uprising. Local citizens surrounded the building until federal troops, commanded by Colonel Robert E. Lee, arrived. On October 18, Lee's forces battered down the barricaded entrance and arrested Brown. He was tried, convicted of treason, and hanged on December 2, 1859.

John Brown's raid on Harpers Ferry captured the imagination of radical abolitionists and terrified southerners. Although Republican leaders denounced it, other northerners proclaimed Brown a martyr. Church bells tolled in many northern cities on the day of his execution, and radical evangelicals offered eulogies to Brown's cause. Brown's raid and the perception that Republicans had secretly sponsored it caused many moderate southerners to consider **secession.** The Alabama, Mississippi, and Florida legislatures resolved that a Republican victory in the upcoming presidential election would provide justification for such action.

The Divided Nation

The Republicans were a new phenomenon on the American political scene: a purely regional political party. The party drew its strength and ideas almost entirely from the North. The Republican platform—"Free Soil, Free Labor, and Free Men"—stressed the defilement of white labor by slavery. By taking up a cry against "Rum, Romanism, and Slavery," the Republicans drew former Know-Nothings and temperance advocates alike into their ranks.

Democratic Divisions and Nominating Conventions

During the Buchanan administration, Democrats found it increasingly difficult to achieve national party unity. Northern Democrats realized that any commitment to slavery would cost them votes at home. Southern Democrats, however, believed that protecting slavery was absolutely necessary. In April 1860, these conflicting views on slavery met when the party convened in Charleston, South Carolina.

The fight began over the party platform. Douglas's supporters championed a popular sovereignty

Harpers Ferry Town in present-day West Virginia and site of the U.S. arsenal that John Brown briefly seized in 1859.

secession Withdrawal from the United States.

position. Southern radicals countered by demanding the legal protection of slavery in the territories. After heated debates, the Douglas forces carried the day on this issue. Disgusted delegates from eight southern states walked out of the convention, thereby denying Douglas the two-thirds majority required for nomination. Shocked, the remaining delegates adjourned the convention and reconvened in Baltimore in June. A boycott by most southern delegates allowed Douglas to win the presidential nomination easily. The party's final platform supported popular sovereignty and emphasized allegiance to the Union, hoping to attract moderate voters from both North and South.

The southern Democratic contingent met one week later and nominated John C. Breckinridge of Kentucky as its presidential candidate. The southern Democrats' platform vowed support for the Union but called for federal protection of the right to own slaves in the territories and for the preservation of slavery where it already existed.

In May 1860, a group of former Whigs, Know-Nothings, and some disaffected Democrats from the Upper South formed the **Constitutional Union party.** They nominated John Bell, a wealthy slaveholder from Tennessee, for president. This group had no hope of winning but believed it could gather enough support to throw the election into the House of Representatives. The party resolved to take no stand on the sectional controversy and pledged to uphold the Constitution and the Union.

The front runner for the Republican nomination was William Seward of New York. A former Whig, Seward had actively opposed the extension of slavery. Abraham Lincoln emerged as Seward's main challenger at the party's Chicago convention. Many delegates considered Seward too radical and doubted his honesty. Lincoln, by contrast, had a reputation for integrity and had not alienated any of the Republican factions. Lincoln won the nomination on the third ballot.

The Election of 1860

The 1860 presidential campaign began as two separate contests. Lincoln and Douglas competed for northern votes, and Breckinridge and Bell vied for the South. The Republicans were not even on the ballot in the **Deep South.** Breckinridge and the southern Democrats expected no support in the North. Douglas proclaimed himself the only national candidate. Bell and the Constitutional Unionists attempted to campaign in both regions but at-

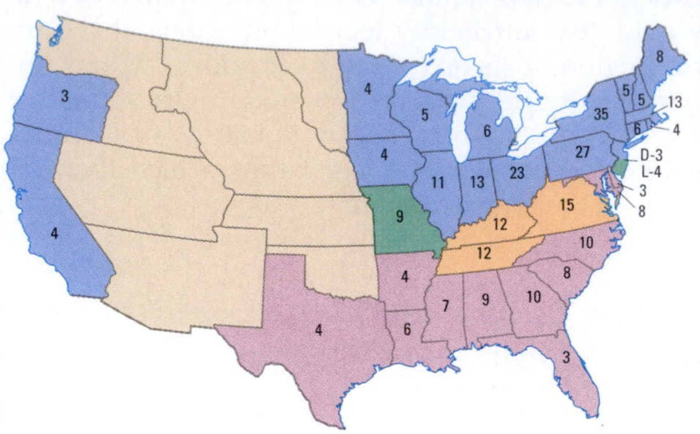

	Electoral Vote		Popular Vote	
Lincoln (Republican)	180	59.4%	1,865,593	39.8%
Douglas (Northern Democratic)	12	3.9%	1,382,713	29.5%
Breckinridge (Southern Democratic)	72	23.8%	848,356	18.1%
Bell (Constitutional Union)	39	12.9%	592,906	12.6%

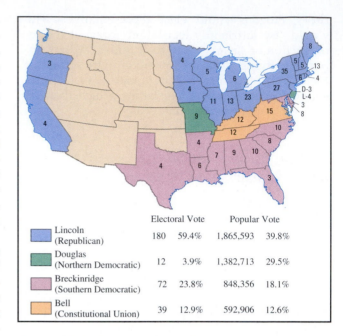

♦ **MAP 13.2 Election of 1860** The election of 1860 confirmed the worst fears expressed by concerned Union supporters during the 1850s: changes in the nation's population made it possible for one section to dominate national politics. As this map shows, the Republican and southern Democratic parties virtually split the nation, and the Republicans were able to seize the presidency.

Constitutional Union party Political party that organized on the eve of the Civil War with no platform other than the preservation of the Constitution, the Union, and the law.

Deep South The region of the South farthest from the North; usually said to comprise the states of Alabama, Florida, Georgia, Louisiana, Mississippi, and South Carolina.

tracted mostly southern voters who wanted to avoid the crisis of disunion.

Sensing that Lincoln would win the North, Douglas launched a last-ditch effort to hold the Union together by campaigning in the South. Douglas tried unsuccessfully to form a coalition between moderate Democrats and Constitutional Unionists. Already in poor health, he exhausted himself trying to prevent disunion.

As the election drew near, rumors of slave uprisings incited by Yankee strangers led to hysteria in the South. Reports of violence, arson, and rape in faraway places filled southern newspapers. Although supported by no hard evidence, these rumors contributed to the climate of gloom in the South. Even moderate southerners started to believe that the Republicans intended to crush their way of life.

To improve the party's image, Republican leaders forged a platform promising not to interfere with slavery in areas where it already existed but opposing its expansion. Particularly in the Midwest, party leaders worked hard to portray themselves as "the white man's party" rather than as "black Republicans," as their opponents contemptuously called them. These tactics alienated a few abolitionists but appealed to many northerners and westerners.

On November 6, 1860, Abraham Lincoln was elected president of the United States with a clear majority of the electoral votes but only 40 percent of the popular vote. He carried all the northern states, California, and Oregon (see Map 13.2). Douglas finished second with 29 percent of the popular vote but only 12 electoral votes. Bell won in Virginia, Kentucky, and Tennessee. Breckinridge carried the Deep South but won only 72 electoral votes and 18 percent of the popular vote nationwide. For the first time in American history, a purely regional party held the presidency. The Republicans also swept congressional races in the North and had a large majority in Congress for the upcoming term.

The First Wave of Secession

After the Republican victory, southern sentiment for secession intensified, especially in the Deep South. The Republicans were a "party founded on a single sentiment," stated the *Richmond Examiner:* "hatred of African slavery." The *New Orleans Delta* agreed, calling the Republicans "essentially a revolutionary party." To a growing number of southerners, the Republican victory was proof that secession was the only alternative to political domination.

Most Republicans did not believe that the South would actually leave the Union. Calls for secession had been heard in the South for a decade. Seward had ridiculed threats of secession as an attempt "to terrify or alarm" the northern people. Lincoln himself believed that the "people of the South" had "too much sense" to launch an "attempt to ruin the government." He continued to urge moderation.

In a last-ditch attempt at compromise, **John J. Crittenden** of Kentucky introduced several proposals in the Senate on December 18, 1860. He suggested extending the Missouri Compromise line westward across the continent. Crittenden's plan also called for compensation to slaveowners who were unable to recover fugitive slaves from northern states.

Lincoln did not like Crittenden's plan. The extension of the Missouri Compromise line, he warned, would "lose us everything we gained by the election." He let senators and congressmen know that he wanted no "compromise in regard to the extension of slavery." The Senate defeated Crittenden's proposals by a vote of 25 to 23.

Meanwhile, on December 20, 1860, delegates in South Carolina voted 169 to 0 to dissolve their ties with the United States. Seceding from the Union, they proclaimed, was the sovereign right of a state. Other southern states followed South Carolina's lead. During January 1861, Mississippi, Florida, Alabama, Georgia, and Louisiana voted to secede from the Union.

John J. Crittenden Kentucky senator who made an unsuccessful attempt to prevent the Civil War by proposing a series of constitutional amendments protecting slavery south of the Missouri Compromise line.

On February 4, 1861, delegates from the six seceding states met in Montgomery, Alabama, and formed the **Confederate States of America,** or the Confederacy. Shortly afterward, Texans voted to leave the Union and join the Confederacy. The Confederate congress drafted a constitution, and the Confederate states ratified it on March 11, 1861. The Confederate constitution created a government modeled on the government of the United States—but with a few notable differences. It emphasized the "sovereign and independent character" of the states and guaranteed the protection of slavery in any new territories. The document limited the president and vice president to a single six-year term. A bicameral legislative body and six executive departments whose heads served as the cabinet rounded out the government. The U.S. Constitution, excluding provisions in conflict with the Confederate constitution, would remain in force in the Confederacy.

Responses to Disunion

Even as late as March 1861, not all southerners favored secession. John Bell and Stephen Douglas together had received over 50 percent of southern votes in 1860, winning support from southerners who desired compromise and had only limited stakes in upholding slavery. Nonslaveholders constituted the majority in many southern states. The border states, which had numerous ties with the North, were not strongly inclined toward secession. In February, Virginia had even called for a peace conference in Washington. Like Crittenden's efforts, this attempt failed.

The division in southern sentiments was a major stumbling block to the election of a president of the Confederacy. Many moderate delegates to the constitutional convention refused to support radical secessionists. The convention remained deadlocked until Mississippi moderate **Jefferson Davis** was put forward as a compromise candidate.

Davis appeared to be the ideal choice. A West Point graduate, he had served during the Mexican War and as secretary of war under Franklin Pierce. He had twice been elected to the Senate, resigning immediately after Lincoln's victory in 1860. Although Davis had long championed southern interests, he was no romantic, fire-eating secessionist. Before 1860, he had been a strong Unionist. He had supported the Compromise of 1850. Like many of his contemporaries, however, Davis had become increasingly alarmed as he watched the South's political power decline.

To moderates like Davis, the presidential election of 1860 demonstrated that the South could no longer control its own affairs. It had no other option than to withdraw from the nation. Shortly after his inauguration as president of the Confederate States of America on February 9, 1861, Davis asserted: "The time for compromise has now passed. The South is determined to maintain her position, and make all who oppose her smell Southern powder and feel Southern steel."

Northern Democrats and Republicans alike watched developments in the South with dismay. Lame-duck president Buchanan argued that any state leaving the Union did so unlawfully. But he also believed that the federal government had no constitutional power to "coerce a State" to remain in the Union. Buchanan accepted no responsibility for the situation and did little to alleviate the tension.

During the four months between the election and Lincoln's inauguration, the Republicans could do nothing about secession. But Lincoln quickly defined his position: "My opinion is that no state can, in any way, lawfully get out of the Union, without the consent of the others." He tried to reassure southerners that his administration would not interfere with their slaves, but he refused to consider any compromise on the extension of slavery.

Confederate States of America Political entity formed by the seceding states of South Carolina, Georgia, Florida, Alabama, Mississippi, and Louisiana in February 1861.

Jefferson Davis Former U.S. Army officer, secretary of war, and senator from Mississippi who resigned from Congress when Mississippi seceded and became president of the Confederacy.

Black abolitionist Frederick Douglass assessed the crisis this way: "Much as I value the current apparent hostility to Slavery, I plainly see that it is less the outgrowth of high and moral conviction against Slavery, as such, than because of the trouble its friends have brought upon the country." Many northerners, as Douglass correctly perceived, were much more concerned about the breakup of the nation than they ever had been about slavery.

The Nation Dissolved

Lincoln's inaugural address on March 4, 1861, repeated themes that he had been stressing since the election: no interference with slavery in existing states, no extension of slavery into the territories, and no tolerance of secession. "The Union," he contended, was "perpetual," and no state could withdraw from it. Lincoln pledged "that the laws of the Union be faithfully executed in all the States." This policy, he continued, necessitated "no bloodshed or violence, and there shall be none, unless it is forced upon the national authority."

Lincoln, Sumter, and War

Lincoln's first presidential address drew mixed reactions. Most Republicans found it firm and reasonable. Union advocates in both North and South thought the speech held promise for the future. Even former rival Stephen Douglas stated, "I am with him." Moderate southerners believed the speech was all "any reasonable Southern man" could have expected. Confederates, however, branded the speech a "Declaration of War." Lincoln had hoped the address would foster a climate of reconciliation, but it did not.

Even before Lincoln assumed office, South Carolina officials had ordered the state militia to seize two federal forts and the federal arsenal at Charleston. In response, Major Robert Anderson moved all federal troops from Charleston to **Fort Sumter,** an island stronghold in Charleston harbor. The Confederate congress demanded that President Buchanan remove all federal troops from Confederate territory. Despite his sympathy for the southern cause, Buchanan announced that Fort Sumter would be defended "against all hostile attacks." On January 3, 1861, a Charleston harbor **battery** fired on a supply ship as it attempted to reach the fort. Buchanan denounced the action but did nothing.

Immediately after taking office, Lincoln received a report from Fort Sumter that supplies were running low. Under great pressure from northern public opinion to do something without starting a war, he informed South Carolina governor Francis Pickens of his peaceful intention to send unarmed boats to resupply the besieged fort. Lincoln thus placed the Confederacy in the position of either accepting the resupply of federal forts and losing face or firing on the unarmed supply ships and starting a war. From Lincoln's perspective, the plan could not fail. If no shots were fired, he would achieve his objective by holding the fort. But if armed conflict evolved, he could blame the Confederates for starting it.

Confederate officials determined not to allow Sumter to be resupplied. Jefferson Davis ordered the Confederate commander at Charleston, General P. G. T. Beauregard, to demand the evacuation of Sumter and, if the Federals refused, to "proceed, in such a manner as you may determine, to reduce it." On April 12, Beauregard demanded that Anderson surrender. When Anderson refused, shore batteries opened fire. After a thirty-four-hour artillery battle, Anderson surrendered. Neither side had inflicted casualties on the other, but civil war had officially begun.

Public outcry over the shelling of Fort Sumter was deafening. Newspapers across the North

Fort Sumter Fort at the mouth of the harbor of Charleston, South Carolina; it was the scene of the opening engagement of the Civil War in April 1861.

battery An army artillery unit, usually supplied with heavy guns.

♦ In this vivid engraving, South Carolina shore batteries under the command of P. G. T. Beauregard shell Fort Sumter, the last federal stronghold in Charleston harbor, on the night of April 12, 1861. Curious and excited civilians look on from their rooftops, never suspecting the horrors that would be the outcome of this rash action. *Library of Congress.*

rallied behind the Union cause. In New York, where southern sympathizers had once vehemently criticized abolitionist actions, a million people attended a Union rally. Even northern Democrats rallied behind the Republican president. Stephen Douglas proclaimed, "There can be no neutrals in this war, only patriots—or traitors." Spurred by the public outcry, Lincoln called for seventy-five thousand militiamen to save the Union. Northern states responded immediately and enthusiastically. Across the Upper South and the border regions, however, the call to arms meant that a choice had to be made between the Union and the Confederacy.

Choosing Sides in the Upper South

As of April 12, 1861, seven slaveholding states had seceded, but eight remained in the Union. The Upper South, consisting of Virginia, North Carolina, and Tennessee, and the Border States of Missouri, Kentucky, Maryland, and Delaware were critical to the hopes of the Confederacy, for they contained over two-thirds of the South's white population and possessed most of its industrial capacity. If the Confederacy were to have any chance, the human and physical resources of the Upper South were essential.

After Lincoln's call to mobilize the militia, Virginia initiated a second wave of secession. On May 23, the state's voters overwhelmingly ratified an ordinance of secession. The Confederate congress accepted Virginia's offer of **Richmond** as the new Confederate capital. Not all Virginians were flattered by becoming the seat for the Confederacy. Residents of the western portion of the state had strong Union ties and long-standing political differences with their neighbors east of the Allegheny Mountains. They called mass **Unionist** meetings to protest the state's secession and, at a June convention in Wheeling, elected their own governor and drew up a constitution.

For many individuals in the Upper South, the decision to support the Confederacy was not an easy one. No one typified this dilemma more than Virginian **Robert E. Lee,** the son of Revolutionary War hero Henry ("Light Horse Harry") Lee. Lee had strong ties to the Union. A West Point graduate and career officer in the U.S. Army, he had a distinguished record in the Mexican War and as superintendent of West Point. General Winfield Scott, commander of the Union forces, called Lee "the best soldier I ever saw in the field." Recognizing his military skill, Lincoln offered Lee field command of the Union armies. Lee agonized over the decision but told a friend, "I cannot raise my hand against my birthplace, my home, my children." He resigned his U.S. Army commission and accepted command of Virginia's defenses in April 1861.

Influenced by the Virginia convention and by the events at Fort Sumter, North Carolina and Tennessee joined the Confederacy. Tennessee, the eleventh and final state to join the Confederacy, remained divided between eastern residents, who favored the Union, and westerners, who favored the Confederacy. East Tennesseans attempted to divide the state much as West Virginians had done, but Davis ordered Confederate troops to occupy the region, thwarting the effort.

Trouble in the Border States

The start of hostilities brought political and military confrontation in three of the four slave states that remained in the Union. Delaware, which had few slaveholders, quietly stayed in the Union. Maryland, Missouri, and Kentucky, however, each contained large, vocal secessionist minorities and appeared poised to bolt to the Confederacy.

Maryland was particularly vital to the Union, for it enclosed Washington, D.C., on three sides. If Maryland had seceded, the Union might have been forced to move its capital. Because southern sympathizers controlled the legislature, Governor Thomas Hicks, a Unionist, refused to call a special legislative session to consider secession.

Even without a secession ordinance, prosouthern Marylanders caused trouble. On April 6, a mob attacked a Massachusetts regiment that was passing through Baltimore on its way to the capital. The soldiers returned fire. When the violence subsided, twelve Baltimore residents and four soldiers lay dead. Secessionists subsequently destroyed railroad bridges to keep additional northern troops out of the state and effectively cut Washington, D.C., off from the North.

Lincoln ordered the military occupation of Baltimore and declared **martial law.** He then had the army arrest suspected southern sympathizers and hold them without formal hearings or charges. When the legislature met again and appeared to be planning secession, Lincoln ordered the army to surround Frederick, the legislative seat. With southern sympathizers suppressed, new state elections were held that resulted in an overwhelmingly Unionist legislature.

Kentucky had important economic ties to the South but was strongly nationalistic. Kentuckian

Richmond Port city on the James River in Virginia; it was already the state capital and became the capital of the Confederacy.

Unionist Loyal to the United States of America during the Civil War.

Robert E. Lee A Virginian with a distinguished career in the U.S. Army who resigned from that army to assume command of the army of the Confederate States of America.

martial law Temporary rule by military authorities, imposed on a civilian population in time of war or when civil authority has broken down.

Henry Clay had engineered compromises between the regions, and John Crittenden had made the only significant attempt to resolve the current crisis. Most Kentuckians favored compromise. The governor refused to honor Lincoln's call for troops, but the state legislature voted to remain neutral. Both North and South honored that neutrality. Kentucky's own militia, however, split into two factions, and the state became a bloody battleground of brother against brother. In Missouri, Governor Claiborne F. Jackson, a former border ruffian, pushed for secession. When Unionists frustrated the secession movement, Jackson's forces seized the federal arsenal at Liberty. Union sympathizers fielded their own forces and fought Jackson at every turn. Jackson's secessionist movement sent representatives to the Confederate congress, but Union forces controlled the state and drove prosouthern leaders into exile.

SUMMARY

Expectations
Constraints
Choices
Outcomes

As social and economic change heightened Americans' *expectations* during the 1850s, individuals made a variety of *choices*, creating a new political environment. New political allegiances changed party composition and platforms. As the Compromise of 1850 failed to alleviate regional tensions, the Whig party disintegrated. Two completely new groups, the American and Republican parties, replaced the Whigs. Events such as the Kansas-Nebraska Act and the *Dred Scott* decision intensified regional polarization, and radicals on both sides fanned the flames of sectional rivalry.

The *constraints* imposed by regional interests left the new parties with far less ability to achieve compromise than their more nationally oriented predecessors. Even the Democratic party could not hold together, splitting into northern and southern wings. By 1859, the young Republican party, committed to containing slavery, seemed poised to gain control of the federal government. Southerners *expected* that a Republican victory would doom their way of life.

With the election of Abraham Lincoln in 1860, seven southern states *chose* to withdraw from the Union. Last-minute efforts at compromise failed, and on April 12, 1861, five weeks after Lincoln's inauguration, Confederate forces fired on federal troops at Fort Sumter in Charleston harbor.

Lincoln's call to arms forced wavering states to *choose* sides. Virginia, Tennessee, Maryland, Kentucky, and Missouri had to make painful *choices* that frequently brought violence and military action. A second wave of secession and conflict over the Border States solidified the lines between the two competing societies. The sides were quickly drawn, the stakes were set, the division was completed. The nation now faced the bloodiest war in its history.

SUGGESTED READINGS

Fehrenbacher, Don E. *Slavery, Law, and Politics: The Dred Scott Case in Historical Perspective* (1981).

An excellent interpretive account of this landmark antebellum legal decision, placing it firmly in historical context.

Fehrenbacher, Don E. *Prelude to Greatness* (1962).

A well-written and interesting account of Lincoln's early career.

Gienapp, William E., et al. *Essays in American Antebellum Politics, 1840–1860* (1982).

A collection of essays by the rising generation of new political scholars. Exciting and challenging reading.

Holt, Michael F. *The Political Crisis of the 1850s* (1978).

Arguably the best single-volume discussion of the political problems besetting the nation during this critical decade.

Oates, Stephen B. *To Purge This Land with Blood* (1984).

The best biography to date on John Brown, focusing on his role in the emerging sectional crisis during the 1850s.

Potter, David. *The Impending Crisis, 1848–1861* (1976).

An extremely long and detailed work but beautifully written and informative.

Rawley, James. *Race and Politics: "Bleeding Kansas" and the Coming of the Civil War* (1969).

An interesting look at the conflicts in Kansas, centering on racial attitudes in the West. Insightful and captivating reading.

Stowe, Harriet Beecher. *Uncle Tom's Cabin* (1852; reprint, 1982).

This reprint includes notes and a chronology by noted social historian Kathryn Kish Sklar, making it especially informative. See also the one-hour film version produced by the Program for Culture at Play, available on videocassette from Films for the Humanities.

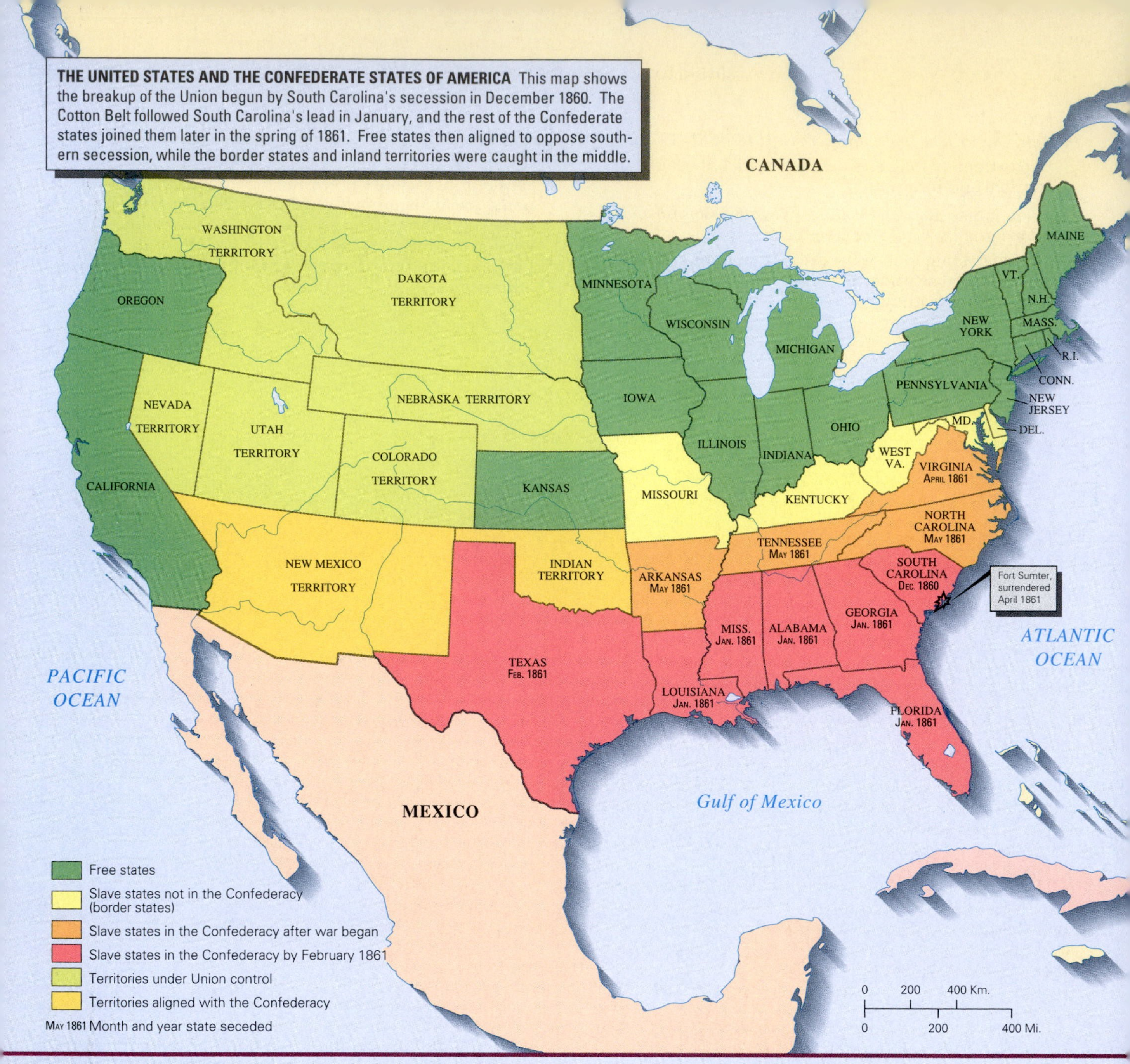
CANADA
WASHINGTON TERRITORY
OREGON
DAKOTA TERRITORY
MINNESOTA
WISCONSIN
MICHIGAN
MAINE
VT.
N.H.
MASS.
R.I.
CONN.
NEW YORK
PENNSYLVANIA
NEW JERSEY
DEL.
MD.
NEVADA TERRITORY
UTAH TERRITORY
NEBRASKA TERRITORY
IOWA
ILLINOIS
INDIANA
OHIO
WEST VA.
VIRGINIA April 1861
CALIFORNIA
COLORADO TERRITORY
KANSAS
MISSOURI
KENTUCKY
NORTH CAROLINA May 1861
TENNESSEE May 1861
NEW MEXICO TERRITORY
INDIAN TERRITORY
ARKANSAS May 1861
SOUTH CAROLINA Dec. 1860
Fort Sumter, surrendered April 1861
MISS. Jan. 1861
ALABAMA Jan. 1861
GEORGIA Jan. 1861
TEXAS Feb. 1861
LOUISIANA Jan. 1861
FLORIDA Jan. 1861
ATLANTIC OCEAN
PACIFIC OCEAN
Gulf of Mexico
MEXICO
Free states
Slave states not in the Confederacy (border states)
Slave states in the Confederacy after war began
Slave states in the Confederacy by February 1861
Territories under Union control
Territories aligned with the Confederacy
May 1861 Month and year state seceded
0 200 400 Km.
0 200 400 Mi.

THE UNITED STATES AND THE CONFEDERATE STATES OF AMERICA This map shows the breakup of the Union begun by South Carolina's secession in December 1860. The Cotton Belt followed South Carolina's lead in January, and the rest of the Confederate states joined them later in the spring of 1861. Free states then aligned to oppose southern secession, while the border states and inland territories were caught in the middle.

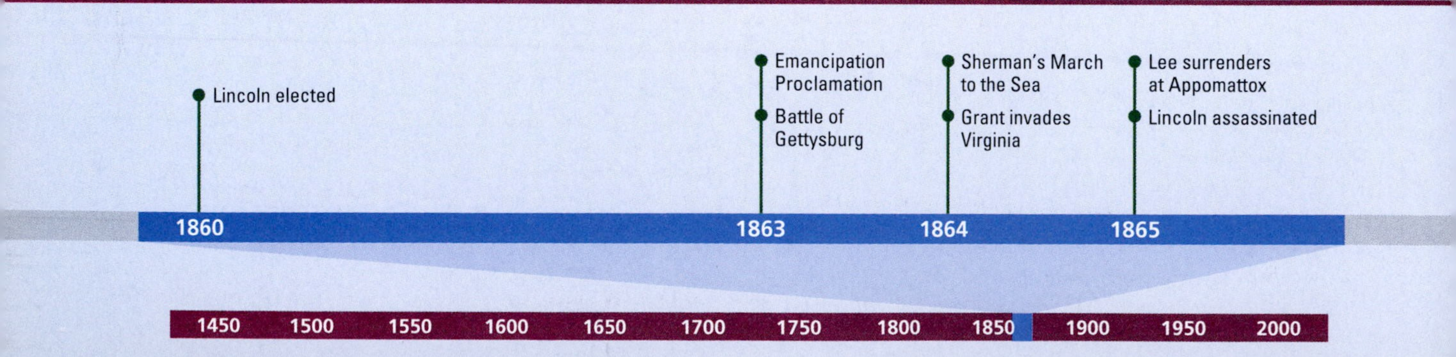
Lincoln elected
Emancipation Proclamation
Battle of Gettysburg
Sherman's March to the Sea
Grant invades Virginia
Lee surrenders at Appomattox
Lincoln assassinated
1860
1863
1864
1865
1450
1500
1550
1600
1650
1700
1750
1800
1850
1900
1950
2000

CHAPTER 14

A Violent Solution: Civil War, 1861–1865

The Politics of War

- What constraints did Abraham Lincoln and Jefferson Davis face as they led their respective nations into war?
- How did they choose to deal with those constraints?

From Bull Run to Antietam

- How did military action during the opening years of the war affect the expectations of people in the North and South?
- How did the Emancipation Proclamation change expectations for the war's outcome?

The Human Dimensions of War

- How did constraints created by the war affect society during the course of the fighting?
- What choices did individuals and governments make to meet those constraints?

Waging Total War

- What expectations contributed to military choices on both sides after 1862?
- What were the outcomes of those choices?

INTRODUCTION

E xpectations
C onstraints
C hoices
O utcomes

Union president Abraham Lincoln and Confederate president Jefferson Davis faced serious political, economic, and military *constraints* as they mobilized for war. Lincoln felt *constrained* by an aged army, a tiny navy, and a sluggish economy, yet even that was more than Davis had to work with. Both presidents also had to contend with political disagreements and demands. These *constraints* combined to shape their *expectations* and *choices*. Davis *chose* to pursue a defensive strategy, *expecting* that the North would soon tire of war. Lincoln, blessed with superior manpower, manufacturing capability, and natural resources, *chose* to use the military to squeeze the South economically, *expecting* that the Confederacy would soon sue for peace. When disastrous losses early in the war and political pressure from radicals in the Republican party upset Lincoln's plan, he *chose* a more aggressive approach. Davis was forced to *choose* a more aggressive course also. The *outcome* was total war as Union and Confederate armies clashed across the better part of a continent.

The economy in the North actually grew as industry moved into high gear to supply the troops. The Union Army kept Confederates from disrupting northern production, and the Union Navy kept international commerce flowing. Meanwhile, the southern economy deteriorated. *Expecting* sales of cotton overseas to keep money flowing in for the war effort, southerners were disappointed when Britain stopped buying cotton and remained neutral. Southerners also had to face the unpleasant reality of invading troops' marching across their land and pitched battles being fought where corn, beans, and cotton once grew. The *outcome* was economic chaos. Many southern people—black as well as white, loyal as well as rebel—went hungry; some even starved.

In the fall of 1862, Lincoln boldly *chose* to change the direction of the war by announcing the Emancipation Proclamation. Knowing that the South would not sue for peace after that development, Lincoln pressed his generals to deal a death blow to southern resistance. In the summer of 1864, Ulysses S. Grant and William Tecumseh Sherman *chose* military strategies that took a terrible human toll. While Sherman slashed his way through the Deep South, Grant sacrificed tens of thousands of his men's lives to contain the Confederate forces under Robert E. Lee. The *outcome* was Lee's surrender on April 9, 1865.

Lincoln then began planning how to bring the defeated South back into the Union. But the man who had led the nation through the war did not survive to pursue his plans for peace. Lincoln was shot by an actor sympathetic to the South. The president died, leaving the nation in mourning, uncertain what the final *outcome* would be.

The Politics of War

Running the war posed complex problems for both Abraham Lincoln and Jefferson Davis. At the outset, neither side had the experience, soldiers, or supplies to wage an effective war. Foreign diplomacy and international trade were vital to both sides. The Union needed to convince the rest of the world that this conflict was a **rebellion** against legitimate authority, the Confederacy that this was a war between nations. The distinction was important. International law permitted neutral nations to trade, negotiate, and communicate with nations engaged in a war. International law forbade neu-

rebellion Open, armed, and organized resistance to a legally constituted government.

CHRONOLOGY

War Between the States

1860	Lincoln elected
1861	Lincoln takes office Fort Sumter falls First Battle of Bull Run George McClellan organizes the Union army Union naval blockade begins
1862	Grant's victories in the Mississippi Valley U.S. Navy captures New Orleans Battle of Shiloh Peninsular Campaign Battle of Antietam African Americans permitted in Union army
1863	Emancipation Proclamation takes effect Union enacts conscription Battle of Chancellorsville and death of Stonewall Jackson Union victories at Gettysburg and Vicksburg Draft riots in New York City
1864	Grant invades Virginia Sherman captures Atlanta Lincoln reelected Sherman's March to the Sea
1865	Sherman's march through the Carolinas Lee abandons Petersburg and Richmond Lee surrenders at Appomattox Lincoln proposes a gentle reconstruction policy Lincoln is assassinated

trals from having any dealings with rebels against a legally constituted government.

Perhaps the biggest challenge confronting both Davis and Lincoln, however, was internal politics. Lincoln had to contend not only with northern Democrats and with **Copperheads**—northerners who sympathized with the South—but also with divisions in his own party. Davis too faced internal political problems. The Confederate constitution guaranteed considerable autonomy to the Confederate states, and each state had a different opinion about war strategy.

Union Policies and Objectives

Lincoln's first objective was to rebuild an army that was in disarray. When hostilities broke out, the Union had only sixteen thousand men in uniform. Nearly one-third of the officers had resigned to support the Confederacy. The remaining military leadership was aged: General in Chief Winfield Scott was 74 years old. The only two Union officers who had ever commanded a brigade were in their seventies. Weapons were old, supplies were low, and personnel was limited. On May 3, acting on his executive authority because Congress was not in session, Lincoln called for regular army recruits to meet the crisis.

Lincoln then ordered the U.S. Navy to stop all incoming supplies to the states in rebellion. In 1861, the navy had few resources, but Navy Secretary Gideon Welles quickly turned that situation around. Starting with almost nothing, he built an effective navy that could both blockade the South and support land forces. By 1862, the Union navy had 260 warships on the seas and a hundred more under construction.

Winfield Scott drafted the initial Union military strategy. He advised that the blockade of southern ports be combined with a strong Union thrust

Copperheads Derogatory term (the name of a poisonous snake) applied to northerners who supported the South during the Civil War.

down the Mississippi River. This strategy would split the Confederacy in two, separating Confederate states and territories west of the river from the rest of the Confederacy. It also would cut the Confederacy off from trade with the outside world. Scott believed that economic pressure would bring southern moderates forward to negotiate a return to the Union. The northern press sneered at this **Anaconda Plan,** noting that Scott intended to "squeeze the South to military death." A passive strategy did not appeal to war-fevered northerners who hungered for complete victory.

When Congress convened in a special session on July 4, 1861, Lincoln explained the actions he had taken in Congress's absence and outlined his plans. He said that he had no intention of abolishing slavery. Rebellion, not slavery, had caused the war, he said, and the seceding states must be brought back into the Union. On July 22 and 25, 1861, Congress passed resolutions validating Lincoln's actions.

This seemingly unified front lasted only briefly. **Radical Republicans** regarded vengeance as the primary objective of the war. Radical leader **Thaddeus Stevens** of Pennsylvania pressed for and got a law promoting severe penalties against individuals in rebellion. Treason was punishable by death, and anyone aiding the rebellion was to be punished with imprisonment, confiscation of property, and the emancipation of slaves. All persons living in the eleven seceding states, whether loyal to the Union or not, were declared enemies of the Union.

The Radicals splintered any consensus Lincoln might have achieved in his own party, and northern Democrats railed against his accumulation of power. Lincoln attempted to appease both factions and used military appointments to smooth political feathers. Still, his attitudes frequently enraged radical abolitionists. Lincoln maintained his calm in the face of their criticism. Nevertheless, ongoing divisiveness hindered efforts to run the war.

Confederate Policies and Objectives

At the start of the war, the Confederacy had no army, no navy, no war supplies, no government structure, and no foreign alliances. It had less than half the people of the Union (9 million as opposed to 23 million) and almost none of the Union's manufacturing capabilities. After the attack on Fort Sumter, the Confederate government's main task was amassing supplies, troops, ships, and war materials.

The Union naval blockade posed an immediate problem. The Confederacy had no navy and no capacity to build ships. Nevertheless, Secretary of the Navy Stephen Mallory converted river steamboats, tugboats, and **revenue cutters** into harbor patrol gunboats. He also developed explosive mines that were placed at the entrance to southern harbors and rivers. Commander James D. Bulloch purchased boats from the British. On one occasion, he bought a fast merchant ship, loaded it with military supplies, maneuvered through the Union blockade at Savannah, and then equipped it to ram Union vessels. The C.S.S. *Sumter* captured or burned eighteen Union ships during the first months of the war.

The Confederates pinned their main hope of winning the war on the army. Southerners strongly believed they could "lick the Yankees" despite being outnumbered. Southern boys rushed to enlist to fight the northern "popinjays." By the time Lincoln issued his call for seventy-five thousand militiamen, the Confederates already had sixty thousand men in uniform.

Despite this rush of fighting men, the South faced major handicaps. Even with the addition of the four Upper South states, Confederate industrial capacity and transportation systems were still

Anaconda Plan Winfield Scott's plan (named after a snake that smothers prey in its coils) to blockade southern ports and take control of the Mississippi River, thus splitting the Confederacy, cutting off southern trade, and causing an economic collapse.

Radical Republicans Republican faction that tried to limit presidential power and enhance congressional authority during the Civil War.

Thaddeus Stevens Pennsylvania congressman who was a leader of the Radical Republicans, hated the South, and wanted to abolish slavery.

revenue cutter A small, lightly armed boat used by government customs agents to look for merchant ships violating customs laws.

outstripped by the North. The southern states built only 3 percent of all firearms manufactured in the United States in 1860. The North produced almost all of the country's cloth, **pig iron,** boots, and shoes. Early in the war, the South produced enough food but lacked the means to transport it where it was needed.

Josiah Gorgas worked miracles as the Confederate chief of **ordnance.** Gorgas purchased arms from Europe while his ordnance officers bought or stole copper stills to make **percussion caps,** bronze church bells to make cannon, and lead to make bullets. He built factories and foundries to manufacture small arms. But despite all his skill, he could not supply all the Confederate troops. In 1861, more than half of the enlistees were turned away because of lack of equipment.

Internal politics also plagued the Davis administration. Despite the shortage of arms, state governors hoarded weapons seized from federal arsenals for their own state militias. Powerful state politicians with little military experience, such as Henry A. Wise of Virginia, received appointments as generals. Davis contributed to the political problems by constantly interfering with the war department and squabbling with everyone.

Davis favored a defensive war. He thought that by counterattacking and yielding territory, the Confederacy could prolong the war and make it so costly that the Union would finally relent. State leaders, however, demanded that their state's borders be protected. In any case, most southerners preferred an aggressive policy. As one editor put it, "Waiting for blows, instead of inflicting them is altogether unsuited to the genius of our people."

The Diplomatic Front

Perhaps the biggest challenge facing the Confederacy was gaining international recognition and foreign aid. The primary focus of Confederate foreign policy was Great Britain. For years, the South had been exporting large amounts of cotton to Britain. Many southerners felt that Britain would recognize the Confederacy immediately following the organization of a government. Such was not the case. Although the British allowed southern agents to purchase ships and goods, they remained neutral and did not recognize the Confederacy. Not convinced that the Confederacy could make good on its bid for independence, the British steered a safe course. They set the tone for other European responses.

Lincoln had to take care not to provoke the British while trying to prevent aid to the Confederacy. Despite his best efforts, an incident at sea nearly scuttled British-American relations. In November 1861, the U.S. warship *San Jacinto* stopped the *Trent,* a British merchant ship carrying two Confederate diplomats, James Mason and John Slidell. The Confederates were then taken to Boston for confinement.

The British were not pleased. They viewed the Trent affair as a violation of international law. President Lincoln calmed the British by arguing that the *San Jacinto's* captain had acted without orders. He ordered the release of the prisoners and apologized to the British.

The Union's First Attack

Confident that the Union could end the war quickly, General Irvin McDowell moved his troops into Virginia in July 1861 (see Map 14.1). McDowell's poorly trained troops ambled along as though they were on a country outing. Their dawdling allowed Confederate General P. G. T. Beauregard enough time to defend a vital rail center near Manassas Junction along a creek called **Bull Run.**

pig iron Crude iron, direct from a blast furnace, that is cast into rectangular molds called pigs in preparation for conversion into steel, cast iron, or wrought iron.

ordnance Weapons, ammunition, and other military equipment.

percussion cap A thin metal cap containing gunpowder that explodes when struck.

Bull Run A creek in Virginia not far from Washington, D.C., where Confederate soldiers forced federal troops to retreat in the first major battle of the Civil War, fought in July 1861.

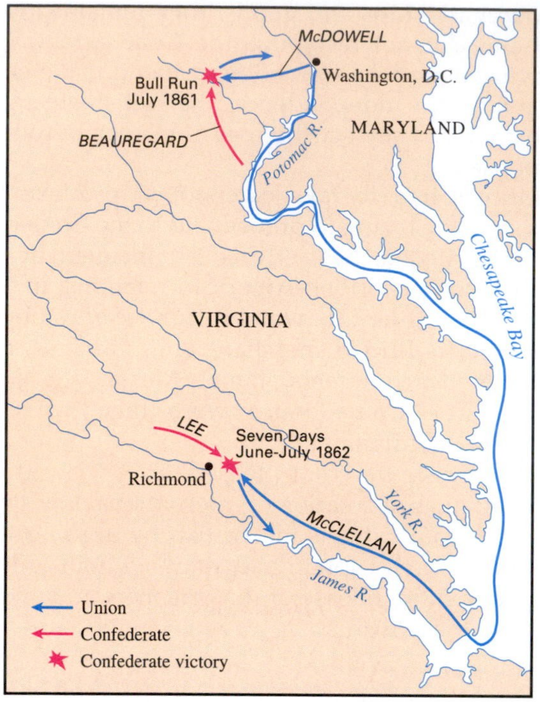

♦ **MAP 14.1 Union Offensives into Virginia, 1861–1862** This map shows two failed Union attempts to invade Virginia: the Battle of Bull Run (July 1861) and the Peninsular Campaign (April–July 1862). Confederate victories embarrassed the richer and more populous Union.

McDowell attacked on Sunday, July 21. He seemed poised to overrun the Confederates until southern reinforcements under **Thomas J. Jackson** took a position on a hill and, fighting furiously, stalled the Union advance. Jackson's stand at Bull Run turned the tide for the Confederacy and earned him the nickname "Stonewall." Under intense cannon fire, Union troops panicked and began retreating pell-mell toward Washington. The Confederates were also in disarray, and they made no attempt to pursue the fleeing Union forces.

This battle profoundly affected both sides. In the South, the victory stirred confidence that the war would be short. Northerners, disillusioned and embarrassed, pledged that no similar retreats would occur. Lincoln replaced General Scott with **George B. McClellan.**

General McClellan's strengths were in organizing and in inspiring his troops. Both were sorely needed. After Bull Run, the army's confidence was badly shaken. Under McClellan, months of training turned the 185,000-man army into a well-drilled and efficient unit. Calls to attack Richmond began anew, but McClellan continued to drill the troops and remained in the capital.

The new year began with Lincoln's taking a much more aggressive stance. On January 27, 1862, he called for a broad offensive, but McClellan ignored the order. Frustrated, Lincoln removed McClellan as general in chief on March 11 but left him in command of the Army of the Potomac.

From Bull Run to Antietam

After Bull Run and McClellan's rebuilding of the Union army, it became clear that the war would be neither short nor glorious. Military, political, and diplomatic strategies became increasingly entangled as both the North and the South struggled for ways to end the war.

The War in the West

Both the United States and the Confederacy coveted the western territories. In 1861, Confederate Henry Hopkins Sibley led an expedition in an attempt to gain control of New Mexico and Arizona. Sibley recruited thirty-seven hundred Texans and marched into New Mexico. Although he defeated a Union force at Valverde and Santa Fe, lack of provisions forced Sibley and his troops to retreat to Texas.

Confederate leaders also sought to gain western territory by making alliances with Indian tribes,

Thomas J. Jackson Confederate general nicknamed "Stonewall" who commanded troops at both battles of Bull Run and who was mortally wounded by his own troops at Chancellorsville in 1863.

George B. McClellan U.S. general who replaced Winfield Scott as general in chief of Union forces; a skillful organizer, he was slow and indecisive as a strategist.

particularly those in the newly settled Indian Territory south of Kansas. Indians who had endured removal to the West had no particular love for the Union. If these tribes aligned with the Confederacy, they not only could supply troops but could form a buffer between Union forces in Kansas and the thinly spread Confederate defenses west of the Mississippi.

Although one Cherokee leader, Stand Watie, became a Confederate general and distinguished himself in battle, Confederate Indian troops never provided the kind of assistance hoped for. They disliked army discipline and became disgusted when promised supplies failed to materialize. Many Indian troops defected when ordered to attack other Indians. Still, several battles, such as the 1862 Battle of Pea Ridge in Arkansas, pitted Indian troops against each other. The divisions between Indian groups allied with the North and with the South often reflected long-standing tribal animosities.

Struggle for the Mississippi

While McClellan stalled in the East, one Union general finally had some success in the western theater. **Ulysses S. Grant** moved against southern strongholds in the Mississippi valley in 1862. On February 6, he took Fort Henry along the Tennessee River and ten days later captured Fort Donelson on the Cumberland River (see Map 14.2). Grant's army suffered few casualties and took more than fifteen thousand prisoners of war. As Union forces approached Nashville, the Confederates retreated to Corinth, Mississippi. In this one stroke, Grant brought Kentucky and most of Tennessee under Federal control.

At Corinth, Confederate general Albert Sidney Johnston finally reorganized the retreating southern troops. Early on April 6, to Grant's surprise, Johnston attacked at Pittsburg Landing, Tennessee, near a small country meetinghouse called Shiloh Church. Union forces under General **William Tecumseh Sherman** were driven back, but the Confederate attack soon lost momentum. The **Battle of Shiloh** raged until midafternoon. When Johnston was mortally wounded, General Beauregard took command. Believing the enemy defeated, he ended the action at the end of the day. Union reinforcements who arrived during the night enabled Grant to counterattack the next morning and to push the Confederates back to Corinth.

Losses on both sides were staggering, by far the heaviest to date in the war. The Union had 13,047 men killed, wounded, or captured, while the Confederacy suffered a loss of 10,694 men. The Battle of Shiloh made the reality of war apparent to everyone. After Shiloh, one Confederate wrote: "Death in every awful form, if it really be death, is a pleasant sight in comparison to the fearfully and mortally wounded." The number of casualties at Shiloh stunned people in the North and South alike.

Farther south, Admiral David G. Farragut's fleet of U.S. Navy gunboats captured New Orleans on April 25. Farragut then sailed up the Mississippi. He scored several victories until he reached Port Hudson, Louisiana, where Confederate defenses and shallow water forced him to halt. Meanwhile, on June 6, Union gunboats destroyed a Confederate fleet at Memphis, Tennessee, and brought the upper Mississippi under Union control. **Vicksburg,** Mississippi, remained the only major obstacle to Union control of the entire river (see Map 14.2).

Grant launched two attacks against Vicksburg in December 1862, but Confederate cavalry and the cannon defending Vicksburg thwarted his offensives. Grant had to come up with a new strategy for taking the city. Union efforts along the Mississippi stalled, but by the close of 1862, Union forces

Ulysses S. Grant U.S. general who became commander in chief of the Union army in 1864 after the Vicksburg campaign; he later became president of the United States.

William Tecumseh Sherman U.S. general who captured Atlanta in 1864 and led a destructive march to the Atlantic coast.

Battle of Shiloh Battle in Tennessee in April 1862 that ended with an unpursued Confederate withdrawal; both sides suffered heavy casualties for the first time, and neither side gained ground.

Vicksburg Confederate-held city on the Mississippi River that surrendered on July 4, 1863, after a siege by Grant's forces.

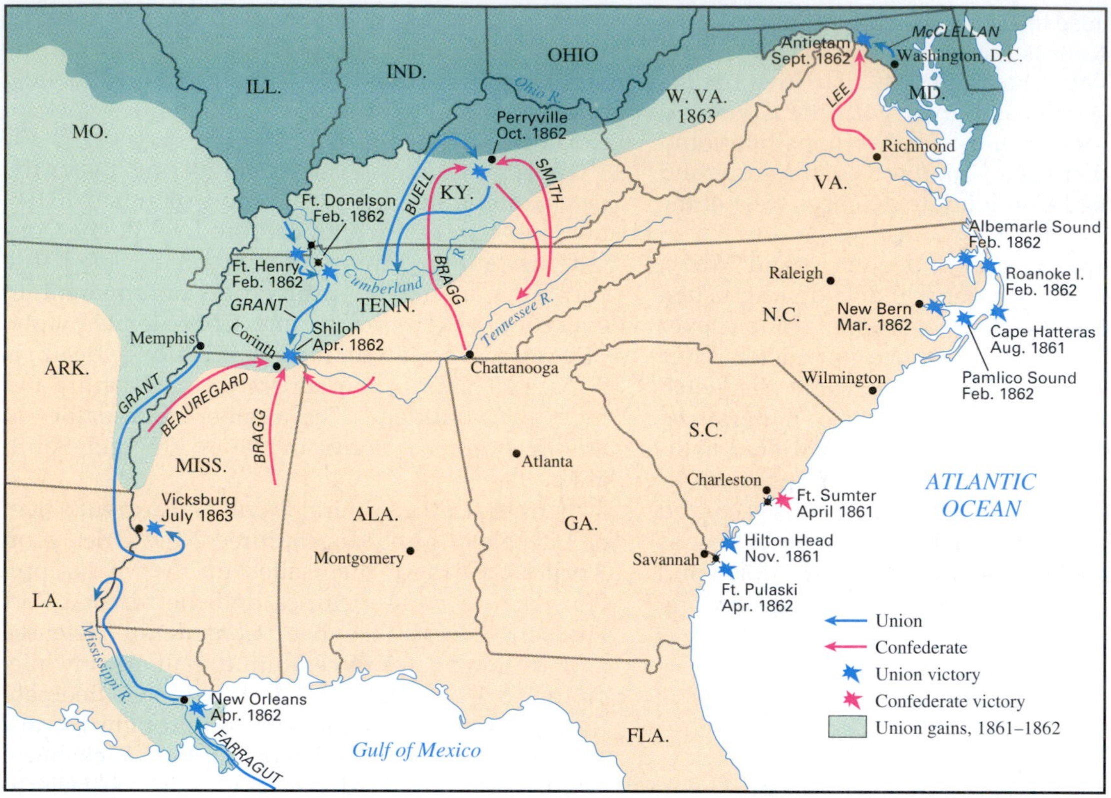

♦ **MAP 14.2 The Anaconda Plan and the Battle of Antietam** This map illustrates the Anaconda Plan at work. The Union navy closed southern harbors while Grant's troops worked to seal the northern end of the Mississippi River. The map also shows the Battle of Antietam (September 1862), in which Confederate troops under Robert E. Lee were finally halted by a Union army under General George McClellan.

had wrenched control of the upper and lower ends of the river away from the Confederacy.

Lee's Aggressive Defense of Virginia

Although Winfield Scott's Anaconda Plan was well on its way to cutting the Confederacy in two, the northern public thought that the path to victory led to Richmond, the Confederate capital. To maintain public support for the war, Lincoln needed victories over the Confederates in the East. Confederate leaders responded by making the defense of Richmond the South's primary military goal. More supplies and men were assigned to Virginia than to defending Confederate borders elsewhere.

A naval battle early in 1862 cleared the way for a Union offensive against Richmond. Early in the war, Confederate forces had captured a Union ship, the *Merrimac.* Hoping to break the Union naval blockade around Norfolk, Virginia, Confederate naval architects redesigned the *Merrimac* in a revolutionary way. They encased the entire ship in iron plates and renamed it the *Virginia.* Operating out of Norfolk, the Confederate ironclad sank several nearly defenseless wooden Union blockaders in a single day. The Union navy countered with the *Monitor,* a low-decked ironclad vessel with a revolving gun turret. In March, the *Virginia* and the *Monitor* shelled each other for five hours in the first battle between ironclad ships. Both were badly damaged but still afloat when the *Virginia* with-

♦ Desperate to break the grip of the Union anaconda, the Confederate navy captured the U.S.S. *Merrimac* and converted it into the ironclad C.S.S. *Virginia*. Virtually immune to any weapon carried by Union frigates, the *Virginia* dominated the sea-lanes out of Norfolk. Eager to launch an invasion up the Chesapeake, Union officials commissioned their own ironclad, the U.S.S. *Monitor,* and sent it into battle against the *Virginia.* After five hours of repeated ramming and artillery pounding, the *Virginia* was so badly damaged that it retreated to Norfolk and never saw action again. *"Engagement Between Monitor and Merrimac" by J. G. Tanner. National Gallery of Art, Gift of Edgar William and Bernice Chrysler Garbisch.*

drew, and limped back to Norfolk, never to leave harbor again. Nevertheless, the age of wooden battleships was over.

Taking advantage of the *Monitor's* success and Union naval superiority, McClellan transported the entire **Army of the Potomac** by ship to Fort Monroe, Virginia. The army then marched up the peninsula between the York and James rivers to begin what became known as the **Peninsular Campaign.** McClellan expected to surprise the Confederates by attacking Richmond from the south (see Map 14.1). In typical fashion, he proceeded cautiously. The outnumbered Confederate forces bluffed McClellan into thinking that he was facing a whole army and slowly retreated to Richmond. On May 31, General Joseph E. Johnston, commander of the Confederate Army of Northern Virginia, attacked at Seven Pines, hoping to surprise his opponent. Johnston was severely wounded, forcing Jefferson Davis to find a replacement.

Davis named Robert E. Lee as that replacement. Lee had previously advised Davis and helped organize the defense of the Atlantic coast. Daring, bold, and tactically aggressive, he enjoyed combat, pushed his troops to the maximum, and was well liked by those serving under him. Lee had an uncanny ability to read the character of his opponents, predict their maneuvers, and turn their mistakes to his advantage.

As McClellan worked his way toward Richmond, Stonewall Jackson staged a brilliant diversionary thrust up the Shenandoah Valley toward Washington. Jackson seemed to be everywhere at once. In thirty days, he and his men marched 350 miles, defeated three Union armies in five battles, captured a fortune in provisions and equipment, inflicted twice as many casualties as they received, and confused and immobilized Union forces in the region.

Following Jackson's brilliant campaign, Lee launched a series of attacks to drive McClellan away from the Confederate capital. Over a seven-day period in late June and early July, he forced McClellan to abandon the Peninsular Campaign.

Army of the Potomac Army created to guard the U.S. capital after the Battle of Bull Run in 1861; it became the main Union army in the East.

Peninsular Campaign McClellan's attempt in the spring and summer of 1862 to capture Richmond by advancing up the peninsula between the James and York rivers.

Fed up with McClellan, Lincoln gave command of the Army of the Potomac to General John Pope. In the **Second Battle of Bull Run,** fought on August 30, 1862, Lee soundly defeated Lincoln's new general. Thoroughly disappointed with Pope's performance and not knowing whom else to turn to, Lincoln once again named McClellan commander of the Army of the Potomac.

Lee's Invasion of Maryland

Feeling confident after the victory at Bull Run, Lee devised a bold offensive against Maryland. His plan had three objectives: (1) to move the fighting out of war-torn Virginia so that farmers could harvest food, (2) to acquire volunteers from Maryland, and (3) to gain diplomatic recognition of the Confederacy by Europe. He hoped to force the Union to sue for peace. On September 4, Lee crossed the Potomac into Maryland, dividing his army into three separate attack wings. McClellan learned of Lee's plans when Union soldiers found a copy of Lee's detailed instructions wrapped around some dropped cigars.

If McClellan had acted swiftly on this intelligence, he could have crushed Lee's army piece by piece, but he waited sixteen hours before advancing. By then Lee had learned of the missing orders. After bitter fighting at Fox's Gap, Lee reunited some of his forces at Sharpsburg, Maryland, near **Antietam Creek** (see Map 14.2). There, on September 17, the Army of the Potomac and the Army of Northern Virginia engaged in the bloodiest single-day battle of the Civil War.

The casualties in this one battle were more than double those suffered in the War of 1812 and the Mexican War combined. One Union soldier said of the Battle of Antietam, "The whole landscape turned red." Both armies were exhausted by the bitter fighting, which ended in a virtual draw. After a day of rest, Lee retreated across the Potomac. For the first time, Lee had been stopped.

Nevertheless, Lincoln was displeased with the performance of his army's leadership. He felt that Lee's force could have been destroyed if McClellan had attacked earlier or pursued the fleeing Confederate army. He fired McClellan again, this time for good, and placed Ambrose E. Burnside in command of the Army of the Potomac.

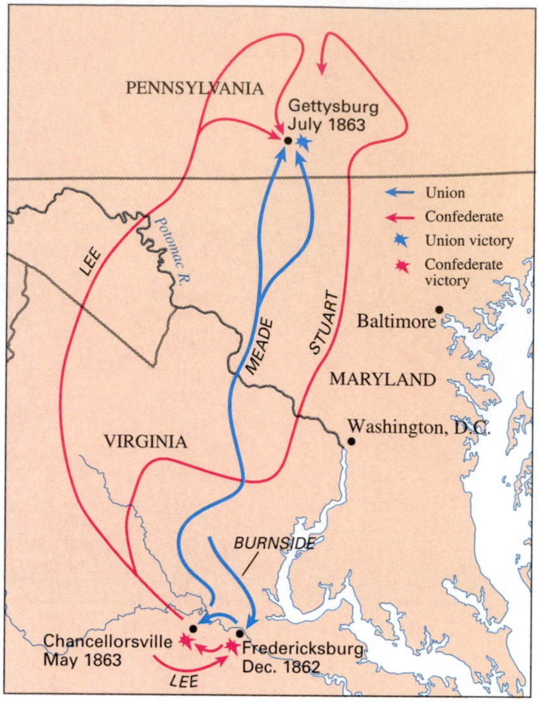

♦ **MAP 14.3 Fredericksburg, Chancellorsville, and Gettysburg** This map shows the campaigns that took place during the winter of 1862 and spring of 1863, culminating the Battle of Gettysburg (July 1863). General Meade's victory at Gettysburg may have been the critical turning point in the war.

Burnside moved the army to the east bank of the Rappahannock River overlooking **Fredericksburg,** Virginia (see Map 14.3). On December 13, in one of the worst mistakes of the war, Burnside ordered a daylong frontal assault against Lee's heavily

Second Battle of Bull Run Union defeat near Bull Run in August 1862; Union troops led by John Pope were outmaneuvered by Lee.

Antietam Creek Site of a battle that occurred in September 1862 when Lee's forces invaded Maryland; both sides suffered heavy losses, and Lee retreated into Virginia.

Fredericksburg Site in Virginia of a Union defeat in December 1862, which demonstrated the incompetence of the new Union commander, Ambrose E. Burnside.

fortified positions. Federal troops suffered tremendous casualties, and once again the Army of the Potomac retreated to Washington.

Diplomacy and the Politics of Emancipation

The year 1862 ended with mixed results for both sides. Union forces in the West had scored major victories, taking Memphis and New Orleans. But the failure of the Army of the Potomac outweighed the Union's success in the West. Lee's victories, however, carried heavy casualties. A long, drawn-out conflict favored the Union unless Jefferson Davis could secure help for the Confederacy from abroad.

The Confederacy still expected British aid, but nothing seemed to shake Britain's commitment to neutrality. The brilliant diplomacy of Charles Francis Adams, Lincoln's ambassador in London, and the fact that Britain possessed a surplus of cotton helped prevent British recognition of the Confederacy. Finally, any prospects the Confederacy had of recognition disappeared with Lee's failure at Antietam.

Five days after the battle, Lincoln unveiled the **Emancipation Proclamation.** The proclamation, which went into effect on January 1, 1863, abolished slavery in rebellious areas. Ironically, the proclamation actually freed no slaves. The four slave states that remained in the Union and Confederate territory under Federal control were exempt from its terms. Moreover, Lincoln had no power to enforce emancipation in areas still controlled by the Confederacy. Lincoln's wording of the proclamation, however, was quite deliberate. He knew that he could not afford to antagonize the slaveholding border states and drive them into the Confederacy. For that reason, the proclamation was not a resounding moral denunciation of slavery.

Still, many northerners considered it a monumental step forward. Frederick Douglass wrote, "We shout for joy that we live to record this righteous decree." Others, however, thought it carried little significance. Confederate leaders argued that the proclamation merely demonstrated Lincoln's hypocrisy. Conservative British newspapers pointed to the paradox of the proclamation: it declared an end to slavery in areas where Lincoln could not enforce it, but it had no effect on slavery in areas under Lincoln's control. British abolitionists, however, applauded the document, as did Radical Republicans.

Lincoln's new general in chief, Henry Halleck, understood the underlying significance of the proclamation. He explained to Grant that the "character of the war has very much changed within the last year. There is now no possible hope of reconciliation." The war was now about slavery as well as secession. As Lincoln told one member of his cabinet, the war would now be "one of subjugation."

The Human Dimensions of War

The Civil War placed tremendous stress on American society, both North and South. As men marched off to battle, women faced the task of caring for families and property alone. As casualties increased, the number of voluntary enlistments decreased. The armies consumed vast amounts of weapons, ammunition, food, clothing, and hardware. Government spending was enormous, hard currency was scarce, and inflation soared as both governments printed paper money to pay their debts. Society in both North and South changed to meet an array of constraints as individuals attempted to carry on their lives in the midst of the war's devastation.

Instituting the Draft

By the end of 1862, heavy casualties, massive desertion, and declining enlistments had depleted both armies. Although the North had a much larger population than the South, military fortunes sagged during 1862 and enlistments were low.

Emancipation Proclamation Lincoln's order abolishing slavery in states "in rebellion" but not in border territories still loyal to the Union as of January 1, 1863.

Over a hundred thousand Union soldiers were absent without official leave. State drafts netted few replacements because the Democrats, who made tremendous political gains in 1862, at times refused to cooperate. In March 1863, Congress passed the **Conscription Act** to ensure enough manpower to continue the war. The law declared all single men between the ages of 20 and 45, and married men between 20 and 35, eligible to be drafted. Draftees were selected by a lottery.

The conscription law offered two ways for draftees to avoid military service. They could hire an "acceptable substitute" or pay a $300 fee to purchase exemption. In effect, the wealthy were exempt from the law. The burden of service thus fell on farmers and urban workers who were already suffering from high taxation and inflation. Together, conscription and emancipation, which touched on long-standing racial resentments, created a sense of alienation among the urban poor that exploded in the summer of 1863.

Some of the worst urban violence in American history began on July 13 in New York City. Armed demonstrators protesting unfair draft laws rioted for five days, during which many blacks were beaten and six were lynched. Businesses owned by blacks and by people who employed African Americans were ransacked. Thousands of poor Irish Americans and other groups who competed for jobs with blacks joined in the riot.

The rioters vented their rage against Republican spokesmen and officials as well. They hanged Republican journalist **Horace Greeley** in **effigy** and sacked the homes of other prominent Republicans. After five days of chaos, a rain of rifle fire from Federal troops put an end to the riots, during which at least 105 people had died. Fearful of more violence, the New York City Council voted to pay the $300 exemption fee for all poor draftees who chose not to serve in the army.

Conscription in the South also met with considerable resentment and resistance. Believing that slaves would not work unless directly overseen by masters, Confederate officials in 1862 exempted planters owning twenty or more slaves from military service. Like Union exemptions, the southern policy fostered the feeling that the poor were going off to fight while the rich stayed safely at home.

♦ Angered by the fact that rich men were virtually exempt from the draft, frightened by the prospect of job competition from freed southern slaves, and frustrated by the lack of resolution on the battlefield, workingmen took to the streets in New York City during the summer of 1863 to protest against the war. Well-dressed men, African Americans, and leading war advocates were the main targets of mob violence during five days of uncontrolled rioting. Many homes and businesses and the Colored Orphan Asylum were burned. At least 105 people died and many more were injured. *Library of Congress.*

Conscription Act Law passed by Congress in 1863 that established a draft but allowed wealthy people to escape it by hiring a substitute or paying the government a $300 fee.

Horace Greeley Journalist and politician who helped found the Republican party; his newspaper, the *New York Tribune,* was known for its antislavery stance.

effigy A likeness or image, usually three-dimensional.

Confederate conscription laws also ran afoul of states'-rights advocates. Southerners developed several forms of passive resistance to the draft laws. Thousands of draftees simply never showed up, and local officials, jealously guarding their political autonomy, made little effort to enforce the draft.

Wartime Economy in the North and South

Although riots, disorder, and social disruption plagued northern cities, the economy of the Union actually grew stronger as the war progressed. Manufacturers of war supplies benefited from government contracts. Textiles and shoemaking boomed as new laborsaving devices improved efficiency and increased production. Congress stimulated economic growth by means of railroad subsidies and land grants to support a transcontinental railroad and higher tariffs to aid manufacturing.

The South began the war without an industrial base and in desperate need of outside help if it was to have any chance of winning. In addition to lacking transportation, raw materials, and machines, the South lacked managers and skilled industrial workers. The Confederate government intervened more directly in the economy than did its Union counterpart, offering generous loans to companies that would produce war materials. Josiah Gorgas started government-owned production plants in Alabama, Georgia, and South Carolina. These innovative programs, however, could not compensate for inadequate industrialization.

The supply of money was another severe problem in the South. The South printed paper money, eventually issuing more than $1 billion in unbacked currency. The outcome was runaway inflation. By 1865, a pound of bacon cost $10.

Southern industrial shortcomings severely handicapped the military. Many Confederate soldiers went barefoot because shoes were in such short supply. Ordnance was always in demand. Northern plants could produce over five thousand muskets per day; Confederate production never exceeded three hundred. The most serious shortage, however, was food. Although the South was an agricultural region, most of its productive farmland was devoted to commercial agriculture. Supplies of corn and rice, the primary food products, were continually reduced by military campaigns and Union occupation. Southern cattle were range stock grown for hides and tallow rather than for food. Hog production suffered because of the war. Hunger became part of daily life for the Confederate armies. Before the war ended, many Union soldiers referred to their opponents as "scarecrows."

Southern civilians suffered from shortages as well. Distribution of goods became almost impossible as invading Union forces cut the few Confederate rail lines. The flow of cattle, horses, and produce from the West diminished when Union forces gained control of the Mississippi. Although some blockade runners made it through, their number decreased as the war continued. The fall in 1862 of New Orleans, the South's major port, was devastating to the southern economy. Cities faced food shortages, newspapers were printed on wallpaper, clothes were made from carpet, and pins were made from dry thorns. Cut off from the outside world, the South consumed its existing resources and found no way to obtain more.

Women in Two Nations at War

Because the South had fewer men than the North, a larger proportion of southern families were left in the care of women. Some women worked farms, herded livestock, and supported their families. Others found themselves homeless. Some tried to persuade their husbands to desert. The vast majority, however, fully supported the war effort despite the hardships at home. Women became responsible for much of the South's agricultural and industrial production. As one southern soldier wrote, women bore "the greatest burden of this horrid war."

Women in the North served in much the same capacity as their southern counterparts. They maintained families and homes alone, working to provide income and raise children. Although they did not face shortages of goods or the ravages of battle, they did work in factories, run family businesses, teach school, and supply soldiers. Women assumed new roles that helped prepare them to become more involved in social and political life after the war.

Women from both sections actively participated in the war. In addition to serving as nurses, they served as scouts, **couriers,** and spies. More than four hundred even disguised themselves as men and served as active soldiers until they were discovered. General William S. Rosecrans expressed dismay when one of his sergeants was delivered of "a bouncing baby boy." Army camps frequently included officers' wives, female camp employees, and camp followers. One black woman served the 33rd U.S. Colored Troops for years without pay. She taught the men to read and write and bound up their wounds.

Free Blacks, Slaves, and War

The Civil War opened new choices and imposed new constraints for African Americans, both free and slave. At first, many free blacks attempted to enlist in the Union army but were turned away. In 1861, General Benjamin F. Butler began using runaway slaves, called contrabands, as laborers. A few other northern commanders also adopted the practice.

After the Emancipation Proclamation, however, Union officials began recruiting former slaves, forming them into regiments known as the U.S. Colored Troops. Some northern state governments sought free blacks to fill state draft quotas. Agents offered generous bonuses to those who signed up. By the end of the war, about 180,000 African Americans had enlisted in northern armies, and over 200,000 had served in the armed forces. By the end of the war, African Americans accounted for about 10 percent of the Union's military manpower.

Army officials discriminated against African-American soldiers in many ways. Units were segregated, and until 1865 blacks were paid less than whites. All black regiments had white commanders, for the government refused to allow blacks to lead blacks. Only one hundred were commissioned as officers, and no African-American soldier ever received a commission higher than major.

At first, African-American regiments were used as laborers or kept in the rear. But when they were finally sent into battle, they performed so well that they won grudging respect. These men fought in every theater of the war and had a casualty rate 35 percent higher than that of white soldiers. Still, acceptance by white troops was slow, and discrimination was the rule.

As the war progressed, the number of African Americans in the Union army increased dramatically. By 1865, almost two-thirds of Union troops in the Mississippi valley were black. Some southerners violently resented the Union's use of these troops. African-American soldiers suffered atrocities because some Confederate leaders refused to take black prisoners. At Fort Pillow, for example, Confederate soldiers massacred more than a hundred black soldiers who were trying to surrender.

Probably no other unit acquitted itself better than the **54th Massachusetts.** On July 18, 1863, it led a frontal assault on Confederate defenses at Charleston harbor. Despite sustaining heavy casualties, the black troops gained the parapet and held it for nearly an hour before being forced to retreat. Their conduct in battle had a large impact on changing attitudes toward black soldiers.

The war effort in the South relied heavily on the slave population, mostly as producers of food and as military laborers. Slaves constituted over half of the work force in armament plants and military hospitals. The use of slave labor freed southern whites for battle.

Life and Death at the Front

Many volunteers on both sides had romantic notions about military service. Most were disappointed. Life as a common soldier was anything but glorious. Letters and diaries written by soldiers tell of long periods of boredom in overcrowded camps, punctuated by furious spells of dangerous action and long marches when they had to carry 50- to 60-pound packs.

courier A messenger carrying official information, sometimes secretly.

54th Massachusetts Regiment of black troops from Massachusetts commanded by Robert Gould Shaw; it led an assault on Fort Wagner in Charleston harbor.

♦ The 54th Massachusetts Regiment was an all-black volunteer unit raised, in part, by Frederick Douglass. This Currier & Ives print shows the daring charge that took the parapet of Fort Wagner, South Carolina. Such bravery won grudging respect for African-American soldiers during the war. *Collection of William Gladstone.*

Although life in camp was tedious, it could be nearly as dangerous as time spent on the battlefield. Problems with supplying safe drinking water and disposing of waste constantly plagued military leaders. Dysentery and typhoid fever frequently swept through unsanitary camps. And in the overcrowded conditions that often prevailed, smallpox, pneumonia, and malarial fevers passed rapidly from person to person. At times, as many as a quarter of the uninjured people in camps were disabled by these diseases.

Lacking in resources, organization, and expertise, the South did little to upgrade camp conditions. In the North, however, women drew on the organizational skills they had gained as antebellum reformers and created voluntary organizations to address the problem. Mental health advocate Dorothea Dix (see page 229) was one of these crusaders. In June 1861, President Lincoln responded to their concerns by creating the **United States Sanitary Commission,** a government agency responsible for advising the military on public health issues. "The Sanitary," as it was called, put hundreds of nurses into the field, providing much-needed relief for overburdened military doctors.

Nurses on both sides, most of whom were women, showed bravery and devotion. Often working under fire at the front and with almost no medical supplies, these volunteers nursed sick and wounded soldiers and offered as much comfort and help as they could. **Clara Barton,** a famous northern nurse known as the "Angel of the Battlefield," called the soldiers her "boys." Unlike Barton, most nurses labored in relative obscurity.

United States Sanitary Commission Government commission established by Abraham Lincoln to improve public health conditions in military camps and hospitals.

Clara Barton Organizer of a volunteer service to aid sick and wounded Civil War soldiers; she later founded the American branch of the Red Cross.

Hospitals were unsanitary, overflowing, and underfunded. One northern nurse noted that the daily food allowance was a mere "eight cents per day" per man.

The problem of dealing with the wounded was unprecedented. New rifled muskets had many times the range of the old smooth-bore weapons used during earlier wars. The effective range of the Springfield rifle used by many Union soldiers was 400 yards, and a stray bullet could still kill a man at 1,000 yards. Waterproof cartridges, perfected by gunsmith Samuel Colt, made these weapons much less prone to misfire and much easier to reload. And at closer range, the revolver, also perfected by Colt, could fire six shots without reloading. Rifled artillery also added to the casualty count, as did exploding artillery shells, which sent deadly shrapnel ripping through lines of men. Many surgeons on the frontlines could do little more than amputate limbs to save lives.

The war exacted a tremendous emotional toll on everyone, even on those who escaped physical injury. As one veteran put it, soldiers had seen "so many new forms of death" and "so many frightful and novel kinds of mutilation."

Conditions were even worse in prison camps. Throughout much of the war, an agreement provided for prisoner exchanges, but as the war dragged on, the exchange system broke down. The major reason was the refusal by Confederate officials to exchange African-American prisoners of war. Those who were not slaughtered like the men at Fort Pillow were enslaved. Also, late in the war, Union commanders suspended all prisoner exchanges in hopes of depriving the South of much-needed replacement soldiers.

The most notorious of the Civil War prison camps was **Andersonville** in northern Georgia, where thousands of Union captives languished in an open stockade with only a small creek for water. Designed to house 10,000 men, Andersonville held more than 33,000 prisoners during the summer of 1864. As many as 100 men died of disease and malnutrition there each day, and estimates put the death toll at that one prison at nearly 14,000 during the war. In the North, a camp at Elmira, New York, had a similar record for atrocities.

Death became all too familiar to Americans between 1861 and 1865. Eight percent of the white male population in the United States between the ages of 13 and 43 died in those years. "Death does not seem half so terrible as it did long ago," one Texas woman reported. "We have grown used to it."

Waging Total War

As the war entered its third year, Lincoln faced severe challenges on several fronts. The losses to Lee and Jackson in Virginia and the failure to catch Lee at Antietam had eroded public support. Many northerners resented the war, conscription, and abolitionism.

Lincoln's Generals and Northern Successes

Lincoln had replaced McClellan with Burnside, but the results had been disastrous. Lincoln then elevated General Joseph Hooker. Despite Hooker's reputation for bravery in battle, Lee soundly defeated "Fighting Joe" Hooker at **Chancellorsville** in May 1863 (see Map 14.3). Lincoln replaced Hooker with General George E. Meade.

Chancellorsville was a devastating loss for the North, but it was perhaps more devastating for the Confederates. On the evening after the battle, Confederate troops mistook Stonewall Jackson's party for Union cavalry and opened fire, wounding Jackson. Doctors amputated Jackson's arm. "He has lost his left arm," said Lee, "but I have lost my right." Eight days later, Jackson died of pneumonia.

In the West, Union forces were mired during the first half of 1863. General Rosecrans was bogged down in a campaign to take Chattanooga, Tennessee. Grant had settled in for a long, drawn-out siege at Vicksburg (see Map 14.4). Nowhere did

Andersonville Confederate prisoner-of-war camp in northern Georgia where some fourteen thousand Union prisoners died of disease and malnutrition.

Chancellorsville Site in Virginia where, in May 1863, Confederate troops led by Lee defeated a much larger Union force; Stonewall Jackson was mortally wounded in this battle.

there seem to be a prospect for the dramatic victory Lincoln needed.

The summer of 1863, however, turned out to be a major turning point in the war. When Confederate leaders met in Richmond to weigh their options, Davis and his cabinet considered sending troops to relieve Vicksburg. Lee, however, advocated another major invasion of the North. Such a maneuver, he believed, would allow the Confederates to gather supplies and encourage the northern peace movement. Confederate leaders agreed and approved Lee's plan.

Confederates met only weak opposition as they marched into Maryland and Pennsylvania, where they seized livestock, supplies, food, clothing, and shoes (see Map 14.3). Then, on June 30, a Confederate brigade searching for shoes encountered a Union cavalry unit west of **Gettysburg,** Pennsylvania. Meade, who had been trailing behind Lee's army, moved his forces into Gettysburg. On July 1, Lee forced the Union army to fall back.

Meade took up an almost impregnable defensive position on Cemetery Ridge. The Confederates hammered both ends of the Union line on July 2 but could gain no ground. On the third day, Lee ordered a major assault on the middle of the Union position. Over thirteen thousand men, led by Major General George E. Pickett, tried to cross open ground and take the hills held by Meade. Pickett's charge was one of the few tactical mistakes Lee made during the war. Meade's forces drove off the attack. The whole field was "dotted with our soldiers," wrote one Confederate officer. Losses on both sides were high, but Confederate casualties during the three-day battle exceeded twenty-eight thousand men, more than a third of Lee's army. Lee retreated, his invasion of the North a failure.

On the heels of Gettysburg came news from Mississippi that Vicksburg had finally fallen. Union forces had been shelling the city continuously for nearly seven weeks, driving residents into caves and shelters, but it was starvation and disease that finally laid waste to the city. On July 4, Vicksburg surrendered. Then on July 9, **Port Hudson** followed suit. The Mississippi River was now totally under Union control. The "Father of Waters," said Lincoln, "again goes unvexed to the sea."

The losses at the battles of Gettysburg and Vicksburg devastated the Confederates. Cut off from almost any hope of foreign intervention and low on food, munitions, uniforms, shoes, and weapons, Confederate morale plummeted. As Josiah Gorgas wrote in his diary after the battles of Gettysburg and Vicksburg, "The Confederacy totters to its destruction." But the Confederacy proved more resilient than many expected.

Meade, like McClellan, failed to pursue Lee and his retreating troops, allowing them to escape into Virginia. When he learned of Lee's escape, Lincoln grumbled, "Our Army held the war in the hollow of their hand and they would not close it."

Nor was General Meade Lincoln's only source of irritation. In Tennessee, Rosecrans had moved no closer to Chattanooga. The war, which had appeared to be nearly over, was, in Lincoln's words, "prolonged indefinitely." Lincoln needed a general with killer instincts.

Grant, Sherman, and the Invention of Total War

Two generals rose to meet Lincoln's needs: Ulysses S. Grant and William Tecumseh Sherman. These two men invented a new type of warfare—**total war**—that brought the South to its knees. Both were willing to wage war not only against the government and armed forces of the Confederacy but also against the civilian population. Their goal was to destroy the South's means and will to continue the struggle.

Lincoln placed Grant in charge of all Union forces in the West on October 13. Grant's immediate goal was to relieve Union forces that had captured Chattanooga but had then been besieged by Confederate forces under Braxton Bragg. Grant

Gettysburg Site of a major battle that occurred in Pennsylvania in July 1863 when Lee led Confederate forces in an unsuccessful invasion of the North.

Port Hudson Confederate garrison on the Mississippi River that surrendered to Union forces in July 1863, thus giving the Union unrestricted control of the Mississippi.

total war War waged not only against enemy troops but also against the civilian population to destroy morale and economic resources.

♦ Disliked by most of his fellow officers because of his coarse behavior and unfounded rumors of binge drinking, Ulysses S. Grant had the right combination of daring, unconventionality, and ruthlessness to wear down Robert E. Lee's forces in Virginia and finally defeat the Confederate army. *National Archives.*

first relieved the pressure on Chattanooga by sending Sherman's troops there. Troops under Sherman and General George H. Thomas then stormed the Confederate strongholds that overlooked the city and drove Bragg's forces out of southern Tennessee. Confederate forces also withdrew from Knoxville in December, leaving the state under Union control. Delighted with Grant's successes, Lincoln promoted him again on March 10, 1864, this time to general in chief. Grant immediately left his command in the West to prepare an all-out attack on Lee and Virginia. He authorized Sherman to pursue a campaign into Georgia.

Grant also suspended prisoner-of-war exchanges. Realizing that the Confederates needed soldiers badly, he understood that one outcome of this policy would be slow death by starvation for Union prisoners. Cruel though his policy was, Grant reasoned that victory was his primary goal and that suffering and death were unavoidable in war. Throughout the remainder of the war, this single-mindedness pushed Grant to make decisions that cost tens of thousands of lives on both sides but led to Union victory.

On May 4, 1864, Grant marched toward Richmond. The next day, Union and Confederate armies collided in a tangle of woods called **The Wilderness** near Chancellorsville. Two bloody days of fighting followed, broken by a night during which hundreds of wounded burned to death in brushfires between the two lines. Grant decided to skirt Lee's troops and head for Richmond, but Lee anticipated the maneuver and blocked Grant's route at Spotsylvania. Twelve more days of fighting brought neither side a victory.

Casualties on both sides at Spotsylvania were staggering, but Union losses were especially high. As one Confederate officer put it, "We have met a man, this time, who either does not know when he is whipped, or who cares not if he loses his whole army."

Grant withdrew and attempted to move around Lee, but again Lee anticipated his approach. On June 1, the two armies met once again at **Cold Harbor,** Virginia. Grant ordered a series of frontal attacks against the entrenched Confederates. Lee's veteran troops waited patiently as Union soldiers marched toward them. Many of the young attackers had pinned their names on their shirts so that they might be identified after the battle. The Confederates fired volley after volley until dead Union soldiers lay in piles. One southerner described Grant's assaults as "incredible butchery."

The Wilderness Densely wooded region of Virginia that was the site, in May 1864, of a devastating but inconclusive battle between Union forces under Grant and Confederates under Lee.

Cold Harbor Area of Virginia, about 10 miles from Richmond, where Grant made an unsuccessful attempt to drive his forces through Lee's center and capture Richmond.

During the three campaigns, Grant lost sixty thousand troops, more than Lee's entire army. In a single day of frontal assaults at Cold Harbor, Grant lost twelve thousand men. Said Lee, "This is not war, this is murder." But Grant's seeming wantonness was calculated, for the Confederates lost over twenty-five thousand troops. And Grant knew, as did Lee, that the Union could afford the losses but the Confederacy could not. He also saw no other way to end the conflict. Despite diminished manpower and resources, Lee refused to surrender. And so the killing continued.

Now near Richmond, Grant guessed that Lee would expect him to assault the city. Instead, he swung south of Richmond and headed for Petersburg. His objective was to take the vital rail center and cut off the southern capital. Shaken by devastating losses, Grant's generals advanced cautiously, allowing Lee time to respond. Lee rapidly shifted the **vanguard** of his troops and occupied Petersburg. Grant bitterly regretted the indecision of his generals, feeling that he could have ended the war. Instead, the campaign settled into a siege.

The Election of 1864 and Sherman's March to the Sea

Lincoln was under fire from two directions. On May 31, 1864, a splinter group of Radical Republicans, concerned that Lincoln would be too soft on southerners after the war, nominated John C. Frémont as their presidential candidate. Lincoln's wing of the party, which began calling itself the Union party, renominated Lincoln in June. To attract Democrats who still favored fighting for a victory, Union party delegates dumped Vice President Hannibal Hamlin and chose **Andrew Johnson,** a southern Democrat, as Lincoln's running mate.

In August, the Democratic National Convention selected McClellan as its presidential candidate. The Democrats included a peace plank in their platform. Thus Lincoln sat squarely between one group that criticized him for pursuing the war and another group that rebuked him for failing to punish the South vigorously enough.

Confederate president Jefferson Davis also had political problems. As military losses mounted, resistance to the war increased. Several states refused to comply with the Confederate congress's call for a new draft. Governors in Georgia, North Carolina, and South Carolina kept troops at home and defied Davis to enforce conscription. Like Lincoln, Davis was under growing pressure to end the war.

The two sides did have several conversations about negotiating a settlement. Lincoln stated his terms: reunion, abolition, and amnesty for Confederates. Davis responded that "amnesty" implied criminal behavior, which he categorically denied, insisting that "independence" or "extermination" was the only possible outcome for the South.

Sherman gave Lincoln the push he needed to win the election. During the summer of 1864, he advanced his army slowly toward Atlanta, one of the South's few remaining industrial centers (see Map 14.4). Only General Joseph E. Johnston's skillful retreats kept Sherman from annihilating his army. But the continuous retreats prompted President Davis to replace Johnston with the more aggressive John Bell Hood. Hood attacked, but Sherman inflicted such serious casualties that Hood had to retreat to Atlanta.

For days, Sherman shelled the city. When a last-ditch southern attack failed, Hood evacuated Atlanta on September 1. Union troops occupied the city the following day. This victory caused despair among Confederates and gave great momentum to Lincoln's re-election campaign.

Lincoln's re-election efforts were also given a boost by General Phil Sheridan's campaign in the Shenandoah Valley. In June, Confederate commander Jubal Early led a raid into Maryland. Sheridan headed off Early's offensive and then pursued him down the Shenandoah. Sheridan's men lived off the land and destroyed both military and civilian supplies whenever possible. Sheridan drove Early from the region in October and laid waste to much of Lee's food supplies.

These victories proved the decisive factor in the election of 1864. They defused McClellan's

vanguard The foremost position in any army advancing into battle.

Andrew Johnson Tennessee senator who became Lincoln's running mate in 1864 and who succeeded to the presidency after Lincoln was killed.

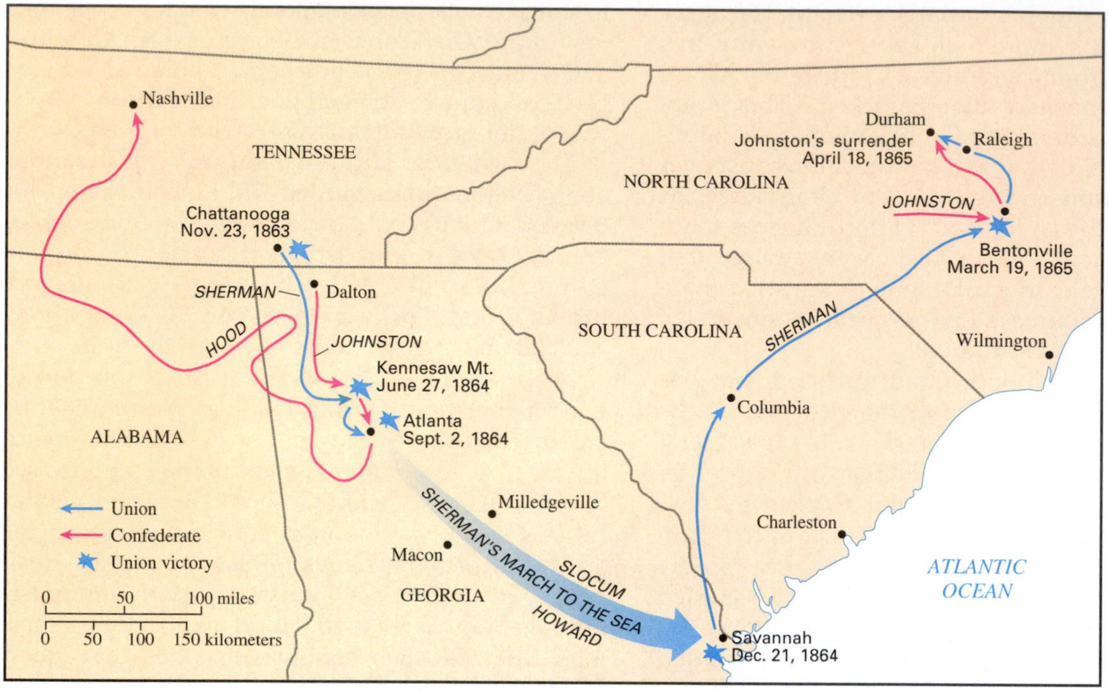

♦ **MAP 14.4 Sherman's Campaign in the South** This map shows how William Tecumseh Sherman's troops slashed through the South, destroying both civilian and military targets and reducing the South's will to continue the war.

argument that Lincoln was not competent to direct the Union's military efforts and quelled much antiwar sentiment in the North. These victories also caused the Frémont candidacy to disappear before election day. Lincoln defeated McClellan by half a million popular votes but won in the Electoral College by an overwhelming margin of 212 to 21.

The southern peace movement had viewed a Democratic victory as the last chance to reach a settlement. Now all hope of negotiation appeared lost. Despite the bleak prospects, Lee's forces still remained in Petersburg, as did Hood's in Georgia. Southern hopes were dimmed but not extinguished.

Sherman grew frustrated with the occupation of Atlanta and posed a bold plan to Grant. He wanted to ignore Hood, leave the battered Confederates loose at his rear, go on the offensive, and "cut a swath through to the sea." "I can make Georgia howl," he promised. Despite some misgivings, Grant agreed and convinced Lincoln.

A week after the election, Sherman began preparing for his 300-mile **March to the Sea** (see Map 14.4). His intentions were clear. "We are not only fighting hostile armies, but a hostile people," he stated. By devastating the countryside and destroying the South's ability to conduct war, he intended to break down southerners' will to resist. "We cannot change the hearts of those people of the South," he concluded, but we can "make them so sick of war that generations would pass away before they would again appeal to it." With that, he burned most of Atlanta and then set out for Savannah. His troops plundered and looted farms and

March to the Sea Sherman's march from Atlanta to Savannah from November 16 to December 20, 1864, during which Union soldiers carried out orders to destroy everything in their path.

towns on the way, foraging for food and supplies and destroying everything in their path.

As Sherman began moving toward Savannah, Hood seized the opportunity by drawing on Nathan Bedford Forrest's Confederate cavalry for reinforcements to attack General George H. Thomas's Union force at Nashville. Hood struck at Franklin, Tennessee, on November 30, but Thomas's troops shattered the attacking force, leaving the Confederate Army of Tennessee in fragments.

Sherman entered Savannah unopposed on December 20. The March to the Sea completed, Sherman turned north toward Columbia, South Carolina. Sherman's "bummers," so called because they lived off the land, took special delight in ravaging the countryside of South Carolina, which they regarded as the seat of the rebellion. When they reached Columbia, flames engulfed the city. Whether Sherman's men or retreating Confederates started the blaze is not clear.

With the capital in flames, Confederate forces abandoned South Carolina and moved north to join Joseph E. Johnston's army in North Carolina. Union forces quickly moved into abandoned southern strongholds, including Charleston. Major Robert Anderson, who had commanded Fort Sumter in April 1861, returned to raise the Union flag over the fort that he had surrendered four years earlier.

The Fall of Lee and Lincoln

Sherman's marches were the centerpiece of a Union strategy that was a brutal variation on Winfield Scott's Anaconda Plan. In concert with Sherman's efforts, other Union armies attacked various southern strongholds. Admiral Farragut had already closed the port of Mobile, Alabama. The primary target, however, was Lee. Grant maintained the siege at Petersburg while Sherman moved north. His goal was to join Grant in defeating Lee and ending the war.

Hoping to keep the Confederacy alive, Lee made a desperate move in early April 1865. Fearing encirclement by Grant's forces, Lee advised Davis to evacuate Richmond. Lee then abandoned his stronghold in Petersburg and moved west as rapidly as possible, toward Lynchburg. From Lynchburg, Lee hoped to use surviving rail lines to move his troops south to join Johnston's force in North Carolina.

Grant ordered an immediate assault as Lee's forces deserted Petersburg. Lee had little ammunition, almost no food, and only thirty-five thousand men. As they retreated westward, hundreds of Confederates collapsed from hunger and exhaustion. By April 9, Union forces had surrounded Lee's broken army. Saying, "There is nothing left for me to do but go and see General Grant, and I would rather die a thousand deaths," Lee sent a note offering surrender.

The two generals met at the courthouse in Appomattox, Virginia. Grant offered generous terms, allowing Confederate officers and men to go home "so long as they observe their paroles and the laws in force where they reside." This guaranteed them immunity from prosecution for treason and became the model for surrender. Grant sent the starving Confederates rations and allowed them to keep their horses.

Lee's surrender did not end the war. Joseph E. Johnston's forces did not surrender until April 18, at Durham Station, North Carolina. Even then, Jefferson Davis remained in hiding and called for continued resistance. But one by one, the Confederate officers surrendered to their Union opponents. On May 10, Davis and the Confederate postmaster general were captured near Irwinville, Georgia. The last Confederate general to lay down his arms was Cherokee leader Stand Watie, who surrendered on June 23, 1865.

The price of victory was high for both the winner and the loser. Over 360,000 Union soldiers were killed in action, and at least 260,000 Confederates died in the failed cause of southern independence. The war wrecked the economy of the South. Union military campaigns wiped out most southern rail lines, destroyed the South's manufacturing capacity, and severely reduced agricultural productivity. Both sides had faced rising inflation during the war, but the Confederacy's actions had bled the South of most of its resources and money.

Soldiers and civilians on both sides had faced tremendous adversity. The war exacted a tremendous emotional toll on everyone, even on those who escaped physical injury. Perhaps Carl Schurz, a Union general who fought at Chancellorsville,

Gettysburg, and Chattanooga, best summed up the agony of the Civil War: "There are people who speak lightly of war as a mere heroic sport. They would hardly find it in their hearts to do so, had they ever witnessed scenes like these, and thought of the untold miseries connected with them that were spread all over the land."

But the nation had one more horror to face. On April 11, Lincoln addressed a crowd outside the White House about his hopes and plans for rebuilding the nation, urging a speedy reconciliation between the two sections. Three days later, he joined his wife and some friends for a relaxing evening at the theater. At about ten o'clock, an actor and southern sympathizer named **John Wilkes Booth** entered the president's box and shot him behind the ear. Lincoln died the next morning, leaving the nation with no clear sense of what to expect next.

John Wilkes Booth Actor and southern sympathizer who on April 14, 1865, five days after Lee's surrender, fatally shot President Lincoln at Ford's Theater in Washington.

SUMMARY

Expectations
Constraints
Choices
Outcomes

Both the Union and the Confederacy entered the war in 1861 with glowing *expectations.* Jefferson Davis *chose* to pursue a defensive strategy, certain that northerners would soon tire of war and let the South withdraw from the Union. Abraham Lincoln *chose* to use the superior human, economic, and natural resources of the North to strangle the South into submission. But many *constraints* frustrated both leaders during the first year of the war.

For Lincoln, the greatest *constraint* was military leadership. Union forces seemed unable to win any major battles despite their numerical superiority. Although Ulysses S. Grant scored victories in the Mississippi valley, Robert E. Lee and "Stonewall" Jackson defeated every Union general that Lincoln sent to oppose them.

The war's nature and direction changed after the fall of 1862. Lee *chose* to invade Maryland and was defeated at Antietam. After that Union victory, Lincoln *chose* to issue the Emancipation Proclamation, *expecting* that it would undermine southern efforts and unify northern ones. After the proclamation, there could be no *choice* for either side but total victory or total defeat.

Union forces turned the tide in the war by defeating Lee's army at Gettysburg and by taking Vicksburg after a long siege. With an election drawing near, Lincoln spurred his generals to deal the death blow to the Confederacy, and two rose to the occasion. During the summer and fall of 1864, William Tecumseh Sherman made Georgia howl. And Grant, in a brutal campaign in northern Virginia, drove Lee into a defensive corner. In November, buoyed by Sherman's victories in Georgia, Lincoln was re-elected.

In the spring of 1865, Lee made a desperate *choice* to keep the Confederacy alive, racing to unify the last surviving remnants of the once-proud southern army. But Grant surrounded Lee's troops, forcing surrender. Lincoln's assassination a short time later left the nation in shock and a southern Democrat, Andrew Johnson, as president. In North and South, the *outcome* of the Civil War was uncertainty about what would follow.

SUGGESTED READINGS

Abel, Annie Heloise. *The Slaveholding Indians,* 3 vols. (1919–1925; reprint, 1992–1993).

This long-ignored classic work focuses on Indians as slaveholders, participants in the Civil War, and subjects of Reconstruction. Its three volumes have been updated by historians Theda Purdue and Michael

Green. Each volume can stand on its own and will reward the patient reader.

Catton, Bruce. *This Hallowed Ground: The Story of the Union Side of the Civil War* (1956).

Catton is probably the best in the huge company of popular writers on the Civil War. This is his most comprehensive single-volume work. More detailed, but still very interesting, titles by Catton include *Glory Road: The Bloody Route from Fredericksburg to Gettysburg* (1952), *Mr. Lincoln's Army* (1962), *A Stillness at Appomattox* (1953), and *Grant Moves South* (1960).

Escott, Paul D. *After Secession: Jefferson Davis and the Failure of Confederate Nationalism* (1978).

An excellent overview of internal political problems in the Confederacy by a leading Civil War historian.

Josephy, Alvin M. *The Civil War in the American West* (1991).

An excellent overview of an often forgotten chapter in the Civil War. A former editor for *American Heritage,* Josephy writes an interesting and readable story.

McPherson, James. *Battle Cry of Freedom: The Civil War Era* (1988).

Hailed by many as the best single-volume history of the Civil War Era; comprehensive and very well written.

Thomas, Emory M. *The Confederate Nation* (1979).

A classic history of the Confederacy by an excellent southern historian.

Wills, Garry. *Lincoln at Gettysburg: The Words That Remade America* (1992).

A prizewinning look at Lincoln's rhetoric and the ways in which his speeches, especially his Gettysburg Address, recast American ideas about equality, freedom, and democracy. Exquisitely written by a master biographer.

Gettysburg

Ronald Maxwell directed this four-hour epic detailing one of the Civil War's most famous battles. Based on Michael Shaara's Pulitzer Prize–winning novel *The Killer Angels,* this ambitious film seeks to capture not only the historical events but also the atmosphere and personalities of the era.

The Choice for Emancipation

The Context

When Abraham Lincoln became president in 1861, he swore to the nation that he had no intention of interfering with the institution of slavery. But the pressure of war and of politics made that promise difficult to keep. By March 1862, the president was asking Congress to pass a bill compensating slaveholders for the value of their human property if the war brought the institution down. Over the next several months, he discussed various approaches to the thorny problem with members of his cabinet, but publicly he resisted any suggestion of a unilateral presidential order emancipating slaves. Finally, on September 22, 1862, he made an official announcement that shook the nation. The southern states had one hundred days to put down their weapons, or he would use his powers as commander in chief of the U.S. Army and Navy to free every slave in every region of the country that was still at war with the United States. This announcement was the Emancipation Proclamation. (For further information on the context, see page 301.)

The Historical Question

During the years following the Civil War, Republicans heralded the Emancipation Proclamation as the ultimate expression of their party's commitment to American principles and Abraham Lincoln's commitment to liberty. But many questions surround Lincoln's choice to issue the proclamation. If this was a long-standing commitment, why did he wait so long? Why did he choose to free only some slaves and not all slaves? Was there another agenda beyond a commitment to freedom?

The Challenge

Using the sources provided, along with other information you have read, write an essay or hold a discussion on the following question. Cite evidence in the sources to support your conclusions.

What were Abraham Lincoln's purposes for issuing the Emancipation Proclamation when and in the form that he did?

The Sources

1 In his first inaugural address, Abraham Lincoln swore that he would not threaten the institution of slavery where it existed. He even denied that he had the legal right to do so. Here is what he said:

I do but quote from one of those speeches when I declare that "I have no purpose, directly or indirectly, to interfere with the institution of slavery in the States where it exists. I believe I have no lawful right to do so, and I have no inclination to do so. . . ."

I now reiterate these sentiments; and, in doing so, I only press upon the public attention the most conclusive evidence of which the case is susceptible, that the property, peace and security of no section are to be in any wise endangered by the now incoming administration.

2 On August 19, 1862, the *New York Tribune* published an open letter to President Lincoln claiming that 20 million people in the United States were "sorely disappointed and deeply pained by the policy you seem to be pursuing with regard to the slaves of rebels." Lincoln replied:

My paramount object in this struggle is *to save the Union, and is* not *either to save or destroy Slavery. If I could save the Union without freeing* any *slave, I would do it; and if I could save it by freeing* all *the slaves, I would do it; and if I could do it by freeing some and leaving others alone, I would also do that. What I do about Slavery and the colored race, I do because I believe it helps to save this Union; and what I forbear, I forbear because I* do not *believe it would help save the Union. I shall do* less *whenever I shall believe what I am doing hurts the cause, and I shall do* more *whenever I shall believe doing more will help the cause. I shall try to correct errors when shown to be errors; and I shall adopt new views so fast as they shall appear to be true views. I have here stated my purpose according to my view of* official *duty.*

3 Less than a month later, Lincoln received a delegation representing Christian interests in Chicago, who echoed the *Tribune*'s earlier complaint. Lincoln explained:

What good would a proclamation of emancipation from me do, especially as we are now situated? I do not want to issue a document that the whole world will see must necessarily be inoperative. . . . Would my word free the slaves, when I cannot even enforce the Constitution in the rebel states? Is there a single court, or magistrate, or individual that would be influenced by it there? And what reason is there to think it would have any greater effect upon the slaves than the late law of Congress, which I approved, and which offers protection and freedom to the slaves of rebel masters who come within our lines? Yet I cannot learn that that law has caused a single slave to come over to us. . . .

I admit that slavery is the root of the rebellion, . . . I will also concede that emancipation would help us in Europe, and convince them that we are incited by something more than ambition. I grant, further, that it would help somewhat at the North, though not so much, I fear, as you and those you represent imagine. . . .

4 Four days after Lincoln told the Chicago delegation that an emancipation proclamation would be futile, the Union won a major victory at Antietam. Five days after that, Lincoln issued the preliminary draft of the Emancipation Proclamation, giving the southern states one hundred days to stop the war. When the South refused to surrender, Lincoln made the following statement:

Now, therefore, I, Abraham Lincoln, President of the United States, by virtue of the power in me vested as Commander-in-Chief of the Army and Navy of the United States, in time of actual armed rebellion against the authority and government of the United States, and as a fit and necessary war measure for suppressing said rebellion, so, on this first day of January, in the year of our Lord one thousand eight hundred and sixty-three, and in accordance with my purpose to do so, publicly proclaimed for the full period of one hundred days from the day first above mentioned, order and designate [the following] as the States and parts of States wherein the people thereof, respectively, are this day in rebellion against the United States. . . .

And by virtue of the power, and for the purpose aforesaid, I do order and declare that all persons held as slaves within said designated States, and parts of States, are, and hence-forward shall be free. . . .

And upon this act, sincerely believed to be an act of justice, warranted by the Constitution, upon military necessity, I invoke the considerate judgment of mankind, and the gracious favor of Almighty God.

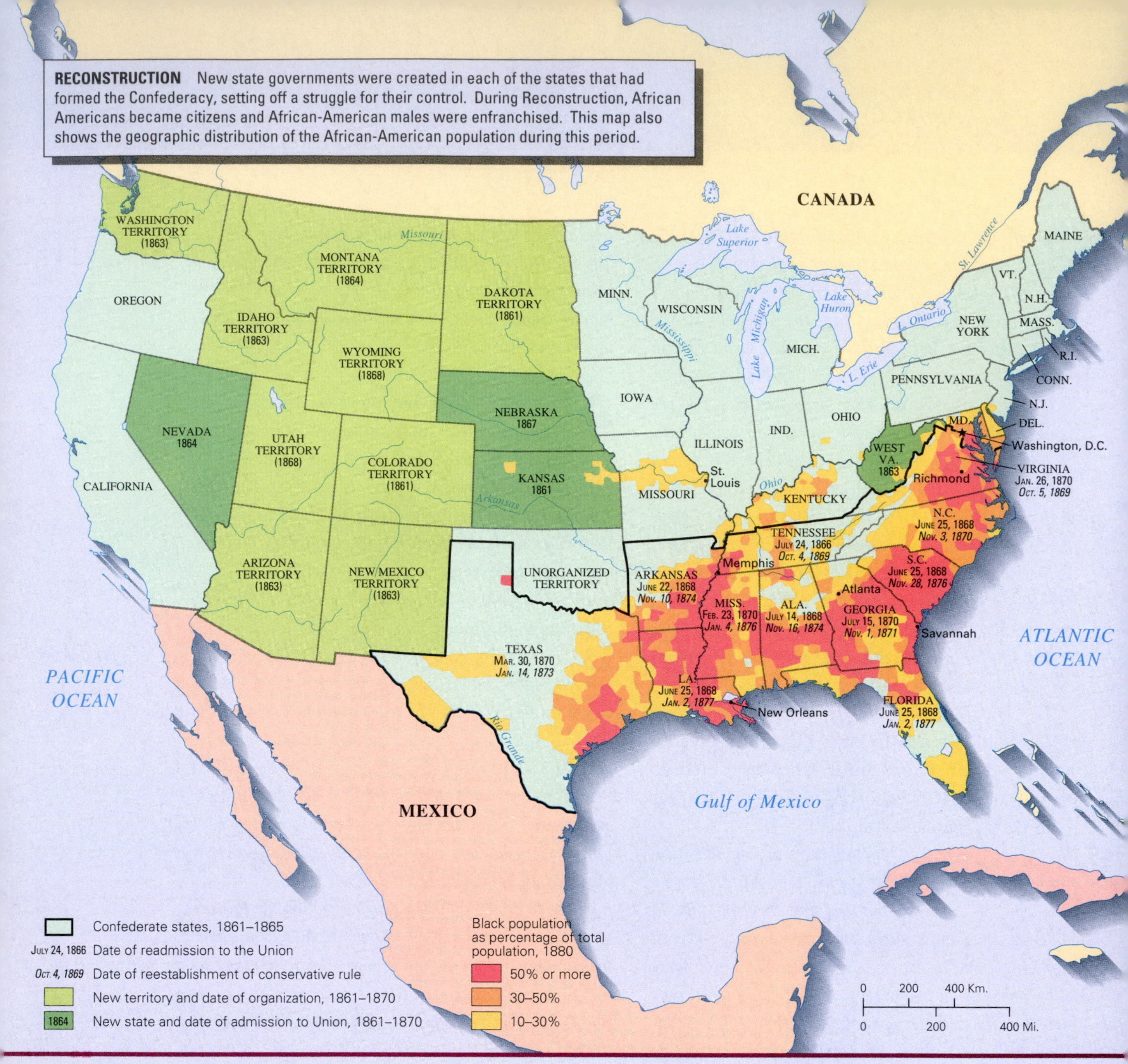

CANADA
MAINE
VT.
N.H.
MASS.
R.I.
CONN.
N.J.
DEL.
MD.
Washington, D.C.
NEW YORK
PENNSYLVANIA
St. Lawrence
Lake Superior
Lake Huron
Lake Michigan
L. Ontario
L. Erie
WASHINGTON TERRITORY (1863)
OREGON
IDAHO TERRITORY (1863)
MONTANA TERRITORY (1864)
Missouri
DAKOTA TERRITORY (1861)
MINN.
WISCONSIN
Mississippi
MICH.
WYOMING TERRITORY (1868)
NEBRASKA 1867
IOWA
OHIO
IND.
ILLINOIS
NEVADA 1864
UTAH TERRITORY (1868)
COLORADO TERRITORY (1861)
KANSAS 1861
Arkansas
MISSOURI
St. Louis
Ohio
KENTUCKY
WEST VA. 1863
VIRGINIA JAN. 26, 1870 OCT. 5, 1869
Richmond
CALIFORNIA
N.C. JUNE 25, 1868 NOV. 3, 1870
TENNESSEE JULY 24, 1866 OCT. 4, 1869
Memphis
ARIZONA TERRITORY (1863)
NEW MEXICO TERRITORY (1863)
UNORGANIZED TERRITORY
ARKANSAS JUNE 22, 1868 NOV. 10, 1874
S.C. JUNE 25, 1868 NOV. 28, 1876
Atlanta
MISS. FEB. 23, 1870 JAN. 4, 1876
ALA. JULY 14, 1868 NOV. 16, 1874
GEORGIA JULY 15, 1870 NOV. 1, 1871
Savannah
TEXAS MAR. 30, 1870 JAN. 14, 1873
ATLANTIC OCEAN
PACIFIC OCEAN
LA. JUNE 25, 1868 JAN. 2, 1877
New Orleans
FLORIDA JUNE 25, 1868 JAN. 2, 1877
Rio Grande
Gulf of Mexico
MEXICO
Confederate states, 1861–1865
JULY 24, 1866 Date of readmission to the Union
OCT. 4, 1869 Date of reestablishment of conservative rule
New territory and date of organization, 1861–1870
1864 New state and date of admission to Union, 1861–1870
Black population as percentage of total population, 1880
50% or more
30–50%
10–30%
0 200 400 Km.
0 200 400 Mi.

RECONSTRUCTION New state governments were created in each of the states that had formed the Confederacy, setting off a struggle for their control. During Reconstruction, African Americans became citizens and African-American males were enfranchised. This map also shows the geographic distribution of the African-American population during this period.

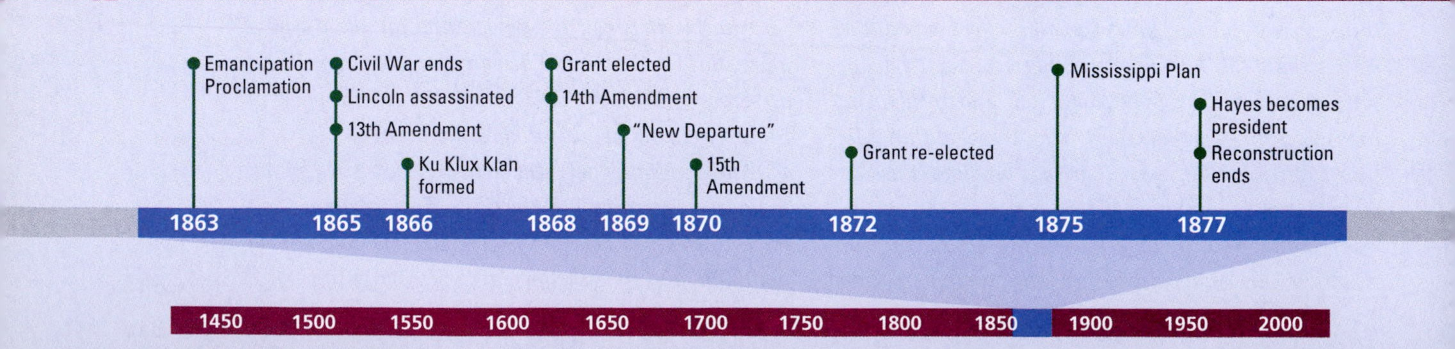

Emancipation Proclamation
Civil War ends
Lincoln assassinated
13th Amendment
Ku Klux Klan formed
Grant elected
14th Amendment
"New Departure"
15th Amendment
Grant re-elected
Mississippi Plan
Hayes becomes president
Reconstruction ends
1863
1865
1866
1868
1869
1870
1872
1875
1877
1450
1500
1550
1600
1650
1700
1750
1800
1850
1900
1950
2000

CHAPTER 15

Reconstruction: High Hopes and Broken Dreams, 1865–1877

Presidential Reconstruction

- What did President Lincoln and President Johnson expect to accomplish through their reconstruction plans?
- At first, how did white southerners choose to respond to Lincoln's and Johnson's efforts at reconstruction? What were the initial outcomes of the presidents' choices?

Freedom and the Legacy of Slavery

- What expectations did freed people hold for freedom? What choices did they make based on those expectations?
- What expectations did southern whites hold at the end of the Civil War? What initial choices did they make to define the legal status of the freed people?

Congressional Reconstruction

- What did Republicans in Congress expect to accomplish by taking control of Reconstruction? What choices did they make to accomplish those goals?
- How did the Fourteenth and Fifteenth Amendments transform the nature of the federal Union?

Black Reconstruction

- Who made up the Republican party in the South during Reconstruction? Why did each major group choose to be Republican?
- What important choices did Republican state administrations make during Reconstruction? How effective were their actions?

The End of Reconstruction

- What was the Mississippi Plan, and how was it related to the end of Reconstruction?
- What were the final outcomes of Reconstruction?

INTRODUCTION

Expectations
Constraints
Choices
Outcomes

By 1865, the war had touched the life of nearly every American. When the last Confederate military resistance collapsed, some 2.6 million men had served in the Union or Confederate army since 1861—about 40 percent of the male population ages 15 to 40 in 1860. More than six hundred thousand had died. Women made important contributions to the war effort as civilians and even as soldiers.

Except for Gettysburg, the major battles in the Civil War had occurred in the South or the border states. Toward the end of the war, Union armies swept across the South, leaving devastation behind them: burned and shelled buildings, ravaged fields, twisted railroad tracks. This destruction, and the collapse of the region's financial system, posed significant *constraints* on economic revival in the South.

More devastating for many white southerners than the property damage and destruction was the emancipation of four million slaves. In 1861, fearful *expectations* about the future of slavery had caused the South to *choose* secession. The *outcome* of the war made those fears a reality. The end of slavery forced southerners of both races to reconsider their *expectations* and to make a series of *choices* about social, economic, and political relations between the races.

Reconstruction, the period between 1865 and 1877, was a time of physical rebuilding throughout the South. The term "Reconstruction," however, refers primarily to the rebuilding of the federal Union and to the political, economic, and social changes that came to the South after the war. Reconstruction involved *choices* about some of the most momentous questions in American history. How was the defeated South to be treated? What was to be the future of the former slaves? Were key decisions to be made in Washington or in the state capitals? Was Congress or the president to establish policies?

As the Republicans reconstructed the Union, they redefined the very nature of the Union. They made *choices* about the terms on which the South might rejoin the Union and about the rights of the former slaves. They also permanently changed the definition of American citizenship.

These changes conflicted with the *expectations* of most white southerners. *Choices* over the future of the South and of the freedmen also produced conflict between the president and Congress. A lasting *outcome* of these *choices* was a significant increase in the power of the federal government and new *constraints* on state governments. In the end, however, the *outcome* of Reconstruction failed to fulfill African Americans' *expectations* for freedom and equality.

Presidential Reconstruction

On New Year's Day, 1863, President Abraham Lincoln began the process by which all people in the nation became free by signing the Emancipation Proclamation. Although the proclamation abolished slavery only in territory under Confederate control, where it could not be enforced, every subsequent advance of a Union army brought the reality of **emancipation** to the Confederacy.

Republican War Aims

The Emancipation Proclamation established the destruction of slavery as a war aim second in importance only to preserving the Union. Freedom for the slaves became a central concern in part be-

emancipation Release from bondage; freedom.

CHRONOLOGY

Reconstruction

1863 Emancipation Proclamation
Ten-Percent Plan

1864 Abraham Lincoln reelected

1865 Freedmen's Bureau created
Civil War ends
Lincoln assassinated
Johnson becomes president
Thirteenth Amendment (abolishing slavery) ratified

1866 Ku Klux Klan formed
Congress begins to assert control over Reconstruction
Civil Rights Act of 1866
Riots by whites in Memphis and New Orleans

1867 Military Reconstruction Act
Tenure of Office Act

1868 Impeachment of President Johnson
Fourteenth Amendment (defining citizenship) ratified
Ulysses S. Grant elected president

1869–1870 Victories of "New Departure" Democrats in some southern states

1870 Fifteenth Amendment (guaranteeing voting rights) ratified

1870–1871 Ku Klux Klan Acts

1872 Grant re-elected

1875 Civil Rights Act of 1875
Mississippi Plan ends Reconstruction in Mississippi

1876 Disputed presidential election: Hayes vs. Tilden

1877 Compromise of 1877
Hayes becomes president
End of Reconstruction

cause **abolitionists** were an influential element within the Republican party. This powerful Republican **faction** developed a third objective: citizenship for the former slaves and the equality of all citizens before the law. The people who held what were then considered extreme views on black rights were called Radical Republicans or simply **Radicals.**

Thaddeus Stevens, the Radical leader in the House of Representatives, had argued as early as 1838 that voting rights should be extended to Pennsylvania's free African Americans. He became an uncompromising advocate of equal rights for African Americans. So did Charles Sumner of Massachusetts, the leading Radical in the Senate. He had argued for **racial integration** of Massachusetts schools in 1849 and won election to the U.S. Senate in 1851. A defender of slavery

abolitionist Someone who condemned slavery as morally wrong and believed that it should be abolished.

faction A group of people with shared opinions and goals who split off from a larger group.

Radicals A faction of the Republican party that advocated citizenship for former slaves; Radical Republicans believed the South should be forced to meet congressional goals for reform.

racial integration The bringing together of people of different racial groups into unrestricted and equal association in a society or organization.

♦ This engraving celebrating the Emancipation Proclamation first appeared in 1863. Although it places a white Union soldier in the center, it also portrays the important role of African-American troops and emphasizes the significance of education and literacy. *The Library Company of Philadelphia.*

had caned Sumner severely on the Senate floor in 1856 because of his outspoken views against slavery.

Most Radicals demanded a drastic restructuring not only of the South's political system but also of its economy. They had opposed slavery on moral grounds, but they also believed that free labor was crucial to democracy itself. "The middling classes who own the soil, and work it with their own hands," Stevens once proclaimed, "are the main support of every free government." The Radicals concluded that free labor would have to be elevated to a position of honor for the South to be fully democratic.

Not all Republicans accepted the proposals of the Radicals. All Republicans had objected to the expansion of slavery, but not all Republicans had been abolitionists, and not all Republicans wanted to extend citizenship rights to the former slaves. Some moderate Republicans were undecided about the proper course to take. Other **moderates** favored rapid restoration of the South so that the federal government could concentrate on stimulating economic growth and developing the West.

Lincoln's Approach to Reconstruction: "With Malice Toward None"

President Lincoln and congressional Radicals agreed that emancipation had to be a condition for the return of the South to the Union. However, major differences appeared over other terms for reunion when Lincoln issued a Proclamation of **Amnesty** and Reconstruction (the "Ten-Percent Plan") in December 1863.

The proclamation offered a full pardon to those who swore their loyalty to the Union and accepted the abolition of slavery. Only high-ranking Confederate leaders were not eligible. When those who took the oath amounted to 10 percent of a state's voters in the 1860 presidential election, the pardoned voters were to write a new state constitution that abolished slavery. They were then to elect state officials. Lincoln hoped such leniency would encourage prominent southerners to abandon the Confederacy and to accept emancipation.

Many Republicans thought that Congress should be more involved in restoring the southern states to the Union. Two leading Radicals, Benjamin F. Wade and Henry W. Davis, proposed that 50 percent of a state's white males be required to swear loyalty to the Union before a new civil government could be formed. Congress passed the Wade-Davis bill in

moderates Those whose views are midway between two more extreme positions; in this case, Republicans who favored some reforms but not all the Radicals' proposals.

amnesty A general pardon granted by a government, especially for political offenses.

July 1864. Lincoln, however, killed it with a **pocket veto.**

Lincoln continued to hope that his Ten-Percent Plan might hasten the end of the war. New state governments were established in Arkansas, Louisiana, and Tennessee during 1864 and early 1865. In Louisiana, the new government denied voting rights to black males, and it maintained restrictions on plantation laborers. Radicals complained loudly, but Lincoln urged patience. The Radicals became convinced that freed people were unlikely to receive equitable treatment from state governments formed under the Ten-Percent Plan. Moderate Republicans moved toward the Radicals' position that only **suffrage** could protect the freedmen's rights and that only federal action could secure suffrage for blacks.

All Republicans could agree by 1865 that slavery had to be destroyed permanently. The Emancipation Proclamation had not affected slavery in states such as Delaware and Kentucky, where it remained legal. To destroy slavery forever throughout the Union, Congress in early 1865 approved the **Thirteenth Amendment.**

By December 1865, only nineteen of the twenty-five Union states had ratified the amendment; however, eight of the reconstructed southern states had ratified it, bringing the total to twenty-seven, the number needed for ratification. Thus the abolition of slavery was accomplished by reconstructed state governments in the South.

♦ Radical Republicans initially hoped that Andrew Johnson would be their ally. Instead he proved to be unsympathetic to most Radical goals. His self-righteous and uncompromising personality led to conflict that eventually produced an unsuccessful effort to remove him from office in 1868. *Library of Congress.*

Andrew Johnson and Reconstruction

After the assassination of Lincoln in mid-April 1865, Vice President Andrew Johnson became president. A Tennessee Democrat who had been born into poverty, Johnson was the only southerner who did not resign from his U.S. Senate seat after **secession.** Lincoln had appointed him military governor of Tennessee early in the war. Johnson had harsh words for Tennessee secessionists, especially the wealthy planters whom he blamed for secession. Radical Republicans applauded Johnson's verbal assaults on these Confederates. He received the Republican nomination for vice president in 1864 because Lincoln wanted to appeal to Democrats and to Unionists in border states.

pocket veto The veto that occurs when Congress adjourns before the end of the ten-day period that the Constitution gives the president for considering whether to sign a bill and the president's decision is to "pocket" the bill—that is, not to sign it and let it expire.

suffrage The right to vote.

Thirteenth Amendment Constitutional amendment ratified in 1865 that abolished slavery in the United States and its territories.

secession The withdrawal of eleven southern states from the United States in 1860–1861, giving rise to the Civil War.

The Radicals hoped that Johnson as president would join in their plans for transforming the South. Johnson, however, soon made it clear that he opposed the Radicals. "White men alone must manage the South," Johnson told one visitor. He did recommend that a few freedmen be given limited political roles. But Johnson saw the major task of Reconstruction as empowering the region's white middle class and keeping the planters from regaining power.

In practice, Johnson's approach to Reconstruction differed little from Lincoln's. Like Lincoln, he relied on his power to grant pardons. Despite his bitterness toward the southern elite, he granted amnesty to most former Confederates who pledged loyalty to the Union and support for emancipation.

Johnson appointed provisional governors for the southern states that had not already been reconstructed and instructed them to call constitutional conventions. Some provisional governors, however, appointed former Confederates to state and local offices, outraging those who expected that Unionists would be appointed to these offices.

Johnson expected the state constitutional conventions to abolish slavery within each state, to ratify the Thirteenth Amendment, and to renounce secession and the state's war debts. The states were then to hold elections and resume their place in the Union. State conventions during the summer of 1865 usually complied with these provisions. Nearly all ratified the Thirteenth Amendment. They renounced secession. However, they all rejected black suffrage.

Freedom and the Legacy of Slavery

After the war, African Americans throughout the South set about creating new, free lives for themselves. Slaves and most free blacks in the South had previously led lives tightly constrained by law and custom. They had been permitted few social organizations of their own. Now freed, they faced enormous changes in almost every aspect of their lives. They quickly developed hopes for a future free from the old constraints.

The central theme of the black response to emancipation was "a desire for independence from white control," historian Eric Foner observes. This desire for **autonomy** affected every aspect of life: family, churches, schools, newspapers, and a host of other social institutions.

Defining the Meaning of Freedom

Freedom was not something that Lincoln or the Union armies gave to enslaved blacks. It came, instead, when individual slaves stopped working for a master and claimed the right to be free. Nor did freedom come to all slaves at the same time. For some, freedom had come before the Emancipation Proclamation, when they had walked away from their owners, crossed into Union-held territory, and asserted their freedom. Toward the end of the war, many slaves simply declared their freedom and left their former masters. Owners were surprised when even their most favored slaves left them. For Kentucky slaves, freedom did not come until ratification of the Thirteenth Amendment.

Across the South, the approach of Yankee troops set off a joyous celebration that the slaves called a Jubilee. One Virginia woman remembered that "when they knew that they were free they, oh! baby! began to sing. . . . Such rejoicing and shouting you never heard in your life." A man recalled that with the appearance of the Union soldiers, "We was all walking on golden clouds. Hallelujah!" Black historian **W. E. B. Du Bois** described it this way: "A great human sob shrieked in the wind, and tossed its tears on the sea,—free, free, free."

autonomy Self-government or the right of self-determination.

W. E. B. Du Bois American historian and civil rights activist who helped found the National Association for the Advancement of Colored People and wrote several influential studies of black life in America.

♦ Before emancipation, slaves typically made their own simple and rough clothing, or they received the cast-off clothing, of their owners and overseers. With emancipation, those freed people who had an income could afford to dress more fashionably. The Harry Stephens family probably put on their best clothes for a visit to the photographer G. Gable in 1866. *Gilman Paper Company, New York.*

The freed people expressed their new freedom in many ways. Some chose new names. Many changed their style of dress. Some acquired guns. A significant benefit of freedom was the ability to travel without a pass. Many freed people took advantage of this new opportunity. Most, however, traveled only short distances to find work, to seek family members separated from them by slavery, or to return to homes that war had forced them to leave.

Many African Americans felt they had to leave the site of their enslavement to experience full freedom. One woman explained that she left the plantation where she had been a slave because "if I stay here I'll never know I'm free." Many freed people did not return to their former homes because of the poor treatment they had suffered there.

The towns and cities of the South attracted many freed people. The presence of Union troops seemed to offer protection from the random violence that occurred in many rural areas. The cities and towns also offered black churches, schools, and other social institutions begun by free blacks before the war. Urban wages were usually better than those on the plantations. Cities and towns, however, had little housing for the influx of former slaves. Most crowded into black neighborhoods of hastily built shanties where sanitation was poor and disease common.

Creating Communities

During Reconstruction, African Americans created their own communities with their own social institutions. Freed people hoped to strengthen family ties. Some families were reunited after years of separation caused by the sale of children or spouses. Some spent years searching for lost family members.

The new freedom to conduct religious services without white supervision was centrally important. Churches became the most prominent social organization in African-American communities. Black ministers advised and helped to educate congregation members as they adjusted to the changes brought by freedom. Ministers emerged as important leaders within developing African-American communities.

Freed people understood the importance of education. Setting up a school, said one, was "the first proof" of independence. Many of the new schools were not just for children but also for adults who

♦ During Reconstruction, freed people gave a high priority to the establishment of schools, often with the assistance of the Freedmen's Bureau and northern missionary societies. This photograph of a newly established school, showing both the barefoot students and the teacher, was taken around 1870. *Library of Congress.*

had previously been barred from learning by state laws. The desire to learn was widespread and intense. One freedman in Georgia wrote: "The Lord has sent books and teachers. We must not hesitate a moment, but go on and learn all we can."

Public school systems had not existed in much of the South before the war. In many places, freed people created the first public schools. The region faced a severe shortage of teachers, books, and schoolrooms. Northern reformers assisted the transition to freedom by focusing on education.

In March 1865, Congress created the **Freedmen's Bureau,** an agency run by the War Department to assist the freed people. The nation's first welfare agency, it helped them find employment or become farmers. Its most lasting contribution, however, was helping to establish a black educational system. Northern aid and missionary societies, together with the Freedmen's Bureau, also established schools to train black teachers. By 1870, the Bureau supervised more than 4,000 schools, with more than 9,000 teachers and 247,000 students. Still, in 1870, the schools had room for only one black child in ten.

African Americans also developed political organizations. In politics, their first objective was recognition of their equal rights as citizens. Frederick Douglass insisted that "slavery is not abolished until the black man has the ballot." Political conventions of African Americans in 1865 attracted hundreds of delegates. In calling for equality and voting rights, these conventions pointed to black contributions in the Civil War as evidence of patriotism and devotion. They also appealed to the Declaration of Independence's assertion that "all men are created equal."

Land and Labor

Former slaveowners reacted to emancipation in a variety of ways. Some tried to keep their slaves from learning of their freedom. A very few, like Mary Chesnut of South Carolina, actually welcomed an end to slavery. Few provided any compensation to assist their former slaves. One freedman stated, "I do know some of dem old slave owners to be nice enough to start der slaves off in

Freedmen's Bureau Agency established in 1865 to aid former slaves in their transition to freedom, especially by administering relief and sponsoring education.

freedom wid somethin' to live on . . . but dey wasn't in droves, I tell you."

Many freed people looked to Union troops for assistance. When General Sherman led his army through Georgia in 1864, thousands of African Americans followed. They told Sherman that what they wanted most was to "reap the fruit of our own labor." In January 1865, Sherman responded by issuing Special Field Order No. 15. It set aside forty acres of land in the Sea Islands and coastal South Carolina and provided for the loan of an army mule for each family who settled there. By June, some forty thousand freed people had settled on 400,000 acres of "Sherman land."

Sherman's action encouraged many African Americans to expect that the federal government would order a similar redistribution of land throughout the South. "Forty acres and a mule" became a rallying cry. Land, Thaddeus Stevens proclaimed, would give the freed people control of their own labor. "If we do not furnish them with homesteads," he once said, "we had better left them in bondage."

The Freedmen's Bureau took the lead in the efforts to assist the freed people toward landownership and free labor. At the end of the war, the Bureau controlled more than 850,000 acres of land abandoned by former owners or confiscated from leading Confederates. In July 1865, General Oliver O. Howard, head of the Bureau, directed agents to divide this land into 40-acre plots.

The widespread expectation of "forty acres and a mule" came to an end when President Johnson issued pardons to the former owners of the confiscated land and ordered Howard to return the land to them. Johnson's order displaced thousands of African Americans who had already taken their 40 acres. They and others who had hoped for land now felt disappointed and betrayed. One recalled years later that they had expected "a heap from freedom dey didn't git."

Sharecropping slowly emerged across the South once expectations of **land redistribution** evaporated. Sharecropping grew out of the realities of the southern agricultural economy. Landowners owned large tracts but had no one to work them. Both black and white families wanted to raise their own crops but had no land, supplies, or money. The entire region was short of **capital.** Under sharecropping, an individual signed a contract with a landowner to rent land. The rent was typically a share of the annual harvest, ranging from a quarter to a third. If the landlord also provided mules, tools, seed, and fertilizer, however, the rent might be half or even two-thirds of the crop. Landowners preferred sharecropping because it encouraged tenants to be productive. Tenants preferred sharecropping to wage labor because they had more control over their work.

♦ Sharecropping gave African Americans more control over their labor than did labor contracts. But sharecropping also contributed to the South's dependence on one-crop agriculture and helped perpetuate widespread rural poverty. Notice that the child standing on the right is holding her kitten, probably to be certain it is included in this family photograph. *Library of Congress.*

sharecropping Agricultural system in which tenant farmers give landlords a share of the crops as rent rather than cash.

land redistribution The division of land held by large landowners into small plots that are turned over to people without property.

capital Money needed to start a commercial enterprise.

Sharecroppers nevertheless often found themselves in debt to a local merchant who had advanced supplies on credit until the harvest came. Many landlords required tenants to patronize the stores they ran. All too often, the debt owed the store exceeded the value of the tenant's share of the harvest. Many southerners, black and white alike, became trapped by sharecropping and debt.

Until the 1890s, the act of casting a ballot on election day was an open process, and any observer could see how an individual was voting. Thus the power of the landlord and the merchant often extended to politics. When a landlord or merchant advocated a particular candidate, the unspoken message was often an implicit threat to cut off credit at the store or to evict a farmer from his plot if he did not vote as directed. Such forms of economic coercion had the potential to undercut voting rights.

The White South: Confronting Change

The slow spread of sharecropping was just one of many ways that the end of slavery transformed the lives of white southerners. For some, the changes were nearly as profound as for the freed people. With Confederate money worthless, savings vanished. Some found their homes and other buildings destroyed. Thousands sold their landholdings and left the South.

Southern whites were unprepared for the extent of change facing them. Their early response to emancipation suggests that, apart from the abolition of slavery, they expected conditions to return to what they had been before the war. The newly reconstructed state legislatures passed **black codes** in 1865 to define the new legal status of African Americans. Black codes placed significant restraints on the freedom of black people. They required all African Americans to have an annual employment contract, restricted them from moving about the countryside without permission, forbade them from owning guns or carrying weapons, restricted ownership of land, and required those without a job to perform forced labor. The black codes clearly represented an effort by white southerners to define a legally subordinate place for African Americans.

Other white southerners used violence to coerce the freedmen into accepting a subordinate status. Violence and terror became closely associated with the **Ku Klux Klan,** a secret organization formed in 1866. Most Klan members were small-scale farmers and workers, but the leaders were often prominent citizens. Former Confederate general Nathan Bedford Forrest became a leader of the Klan. Klan groups throughout the South aimed to restore **white supremacy** and to end Republican rule.

Klan members covered their faces with hoods, wore white robes, and rode horses draped in white. So attired, they set out to intimidate leading black Republicans and their white Radical allies. Klan members also attacked African Americans accused of not showing deference to whites. Nightriders burned black churches and schools. The Klan devastated Republican organizations in many communities.

In 1866, two events dramatized for the nation the violence routinely inflicted on African Americans. In May, a three-day riot by whites in Memphis, Tennessee, left forty-five blacks and three whites dead. In New Orleans, some forty people died in July, most of them African Americans attending a black suffrage convention, in an altercation with police. "It was not a riot," insisted General Philip Sheridan, the military commander of the district. "It was an absolute massacre by the police."

Congressional Reconstruction

By early 1866, most congressional Republicans had concluded that Johnson's Reconstruction policies

black codes Laws passed by the southern states after the Civil War to limit the freedoms of African Americans and force them to return to agricultural labor.

Ku Klux Klan A secret society organized in the South after the Civil War to resurrect white supremacy by means of violence and intimidation.

white supremacy The racist belief that whites are inherently superior to all other races and are therefore entitled to rule over them.

had encouraged the white South to expect that it would be able to govern the region as it saw fit. The black codes, violence against freed people, and the failure of southern authorities to stem the violence turned opinion in Washington against the president's approach to Reconstruction. Increasing numbers of moderate Republicans now joined the Radicals in concluding that southern whites must be constrained.

Challenging Presidential Reconstruction

In December 1865, the Thirty-ninth Congress (elected in 1864) met for the first time. In both houses of Congress, Republicans outnumbered Democrats by more than three to one. The president's annual message proclaimed Reconstruction complete and the Union restored, but few Republicans agreed. Radical Republicans especially had been angered by Johnson's lack of support for black suffrage. To accomplish black suffrage, they needed to assert congressional power over Reconstruction. Most Republicans agreed with the Radicals' commitment to defining and protecting basic rights for the freed people. Most also agreed that Congress had the right to withhold representation from the South until state governments there met these conditions.

When the Thirty-ninth Congress first met, the newly elected congressmen from the South were excluded. Republicans were outraged that such high-ranking former Confederates as Alexander Stephens, the vice president of the Confederacy, stood ready to take his place in Congress. Republicans set up the Joint Committee on Reconstruction to determine whether the southern states were entitled to representation. Thaddeus Stevens, head of the committee, announced that he intended to investigate the whole question of Reconstruction. While the committee worked, the former Confederate states were to have no representation in Congress.

At the same time, Republicans extended the life of the Freedmen's Bureau. Congress also passed a civil rights bill that gave citizenship to African Americans and defined the rights of all citizens. Johnson vetoed both measures, but Congress passed them over his veto. Congress had asserted its control over Reconstruction.

The Civil Rights Act of 1866

The Civil Rights Act of 1866 defined all persons born in the United States (with the exception of certain Indians) as citizens. It also listed certain rights of all citizens, including the right to testify in court, own property, make contracts, bring lawsuits, and enjoy "full and equal benefit of all laws and proceedings for the security of person and property." It authorized federal officials to bring suit against violations of civil rights.

The Civil Rights Act of 1866 was the first effort to define some of the rights of American citizenship. It stipulated that the rights of national citizenship were to take precedence over the powers of the states. By expanding the power of the federal government in unprecedented ways, the law not only challenged traditional concepts of states' rights but did so on behalf of African Americans.

When President Johnson vetoed the civil rights bill, he argued that it violated states' rights. Johnson may have hoped to generate enough political support to elect a more cooperative Congress in 1866. Instead, the veto led most moderate Republicans to give up all hope of cooperation with him. Congress's passage of the Civil Rights Act over Johnson's veto in April 1866 marked the first time that Congress had overridden a veto of major legislation.

Defining Citizenship: The Fourteenth Amendment

Leading Republicans worried that the Civil Rights Act could be repealed by a later Congress or declared unconstitutional by the Supreme Court. Only a constitutional amendment could permanently safeguard the freed people's rights as citizens.

The Fourteenth Amendment, approved by Congress in June 1866, defined American citizenship in much the same way as the Civil Rights Act of 1866. It then specified:

> *No State shall make or enforce any law which shall abridge the privileges or immunities of citizens of the United States; nor shall any State deprive any*

person of life, liberty, or property, without due process of law; nor deny to any person within its jurisdiction the equal protection of the laws.

The Constitution and Bill of Rights prohibited federal interference with basic civil rights. The Fourteenth Amendment extended this protection against action by state governments. The amendment penalized states that did not **enfranchise** African Americans by reducing their congressional and electoral representation.

Some provisions of the amendment stemmed from Republicans' fears that a restored South might try to undo the outcome of the war. One section barred from public office anyone who had sworn to uphold the federal Constitution but then "engaged in insurrection or rebellion against the same." Only a two-thirds vote of both houses of Congress could counteract this provision. (In 1872, Congress pardoned nearly all former Confederates.) The amendment also prohibited either federal or state governments from assuming any of the Confederate debt or compensating slaveowners.

Although Congress adjourned in the summer of 1866, the nation's attention remained fixed on Reconstruction. The bloody riots in Memphis and New Orleans kept northern attention focused on the South. Johnson, who opposed the Fourteenth Amendment, also undertook a speaking tour in which he urged voters to turn the fall election into a **referendum** on Reconstruction policies. His reckless tirades alienated many who heard him. Republicans swept the 1866 elections, outnumbering Democrats 143 to 49 in the new House of Representatives, and 42 to 11 in the Senate.

Radicals in Control: Impeachment of the President

By March 1867, it was clear that the Fourteenth Amendment had fallen short of ratification. The amendment had been rejected by twelve states: Delaware, Kentucky, and all the Confederate states except Tennessee. Moderates became more receptive to other proposals put forth by the Radicals.

The Military Reconstruction Act of 1867, passed on March 2 over Johnson's veto, divided the Confederate states (except Tennessee) into five military districts, each governed by a military commander. The act established a military occupation of the South—the only such episode in American history. The ten states were to hold constitutional conventions, and all adult male citizens were to vote, except former Confederates barred from office under the proposed Fourteenth Amendment. The constitutional conventions were to create new state governments that permitted black suffrage and that ratified the Fourteenth Amendment. Then, perhaps, Congress might recognize those state governments as valid.

On March 2, Congress also limited some of Johnson's constitutional powers. The Tenure of Office Act specified that officials appointed with the Senate's consent were to remain in office until the Senate approved a successor. This measure was intended to prevent Johnson from replacing federal officials who opposed his policies.

Some Radicals soon began to consider **impeaching** Johnson for his obstruction of their policies. The House Judiciary Committee initially found no convincing evidence of misconduct. Johnson, however, confronted Congress over the Tenure of Office Act by removing Edwin Stanton, a Lincoln appointee, from his cabinet post as secretary of war. This action provided the Radicals with grounds for impeachment. On February 24, 1868, the House approved a recommendation for impeachment based on charges stemming from the Stanton affair. The actual motivation was that the Radicals disagreed with Johnson's actions and disliked him.

Johnson remained president after the Senate voted on his impeachment in May 1868 by the narrowest of margins. Thirty-five senators voted in favor of conviction, one vote short of the required two-thirds majority. Moderate Republicans who

enfranchise To grant the right to vote to a person or group of people.

referendum The submission to the public for its approval or disapproval of a law passed or proposed by the legislature.

impeach To formally charge a public official with improper conduct in office and to bring the official to trial for that offense.

regarded the charges against Johnson as dubious thus saved his presidency.

Political Terrorism and the Election of 1868

Shortly after the impeachment vote, the Republicans nominated Ulysses S. Grant for president. Grant seemed the right person to end the conflict between the White House and Congress. During the war, he had fully supported Lincoln and Congress in implementing emancipation. By 1868, he had committed himself to the congressional view of Reconstruction. The Democrats nominated Horatio Seymour, a former governor of New York, and focused most of their campaign against Reconstruction.

In the South, the campaign stirred up fierce activity by the Ku Klux Klan and similar groups. **Terrorists** assassinated an Arkansas congressman, three members of the South Carolina legislature, and several delegates to state constitutional conventions. Mobs attacked Republican newspaper offices and campaign meetings. Such coercion had its intended effect. In St. Landry Parish, Louisiana, where two hundred blacks were killed, not a single Republican vote was cast on election day.

Despite such violence, many Americans probably expected a calmer political future. In June 1868, Congress had readmitted seven southern states that met its requirements, which included ratifying the Fourteenth Amendment. In July, the Fourteenth Amendment was declared ratified. In August, Thaddeus Stevens died. In November, Grant won the presidency, taking twenty-six of the thirty-four states and 53 percent of the vote.

Voting Rights and Civil Rights

Grant's election confirmed that Reconstruction was not likely to be overturned. Radical Republicans now addressed voting rights for all African Americans. As of 1869, voting rights were still defined by the states, and only seven northern states allowed blacks to vote. To guarantee the voting rights of blacks everywhere, Congress approved the **Fifteenth Amendment** in February 1869. Widely considered to be the final step in Reconstruction, the amendment prohibited states from denying the right to vote because of a person's "race, color, or previous condition of servitude." Democrats condemned the amendment as a "revolutionary" change in the rights of states.

Susan B. Anthony and other advocates of woman suffrage opposed the amendment for a different reason: it ignored restrictions based on sex. Before emancipation, supporters of woman suffrage had been among the staunchest opponents of slavery. Now many woman-suffrage advocates urged that the vote be extended to women and black men at the same time. The break between the women's movement and the black movement was patched over somewhat once black suffrage was accomplished, but the wounds never completely healed.

Despite such opposition, within thirteen months the proposed amendment had been ratified by the states. Success came in part because Republicans who had been reluctant to impose black suffrage in the North recognized that the party's future success required black suffrage in the South.

The Fifteenth Amendment did nothing to reduce the violence that had become almost routine in the South. When Klan activity escalated in 1870, southern Republicans turned to Washington for support. In 1870 and 1871, Congress enacted the so-called Ku Klux Klan Acts to enforce the rights specified in the Fourteenth and Fifteenth Amendments.

The prosecution of Klansmen began in 1871. Hundreds were indicted in North Carolina, and many were convicted. In Mississippi, federal officials indicted nearly seven hundred. In South Carolina, President Grant declared martial law and sent federal troops to occupy the region. Hundreds

terrorists Those who use threats and violence, often against innocent parties, to achieve ideological or political goals.

Fifteenth Amendment Constitutional amendment ratified in 1870 that prohibits states from denying the right to vote because of a person's race or because a person used to be a slave.

of arrests followed. By 1872, federal intervention had broken the strength of the Klan.

Congress passed one final Reconstruction measure, largely because of the persistence of Charles Sumner. Passed after Sumner's death, the Civil Rights Act of 1875 prohibited racial **discrimination** in the selection of juries, in public transportation, and in **public accommodations.**

Black Reconstruction

Congressional Reconstruction set the stage for new developments throughout the South, as newly enfranchised black men organized for political action. **Black Reconstruction** began with the efforts of African Americans to take part in politics as early as 1865 and lasted until 1877.

The Republican Party in the South

Nearly all blacks who took an active part in politics did so as Republicans. Throughout Reconstruction, they formed a large majority of the Republican party's supporters in the South. The southern wing of the party also included transplanted northerners and some native white southerners.

Suffrage made politics important in African-American communities. In Louisiana and South Carolina, more than half of the delegates to state constitutional conventions were black. With suffrage established, African Americans began to be elected to public office. Between 1869 and 1877, fourteen black men served in the national House of Representatives and two in the U.S. Senate.

At the state level, blacks were most likely to be elected to the relatively unimportant offices of lieutenant governor and secretary of state. More than six hundred black men served in southern state legislatures during Reconstruction, three-quarters of them in just four states: South Carolina, Mississippi, Louisiana, and Alabama. Only in South Carolina did African Americans ever have a majority in the state legislature.

Most African-American officeholders had some education and had been born free. Of the eighteen who served in statewide offices, only three had been slaves. Blanche K. Bruce was one of these. He had been educated, however, and after the war he attended Oberlin College in Ohio. He then moved to Mississippi, where he was elected U.S. senator in 1875.

Black Republicans achieved power only by securing at least some support from whites. Opponents referred to white Republicans as either **carpetbaggers** or **scalawags.** Both groups included idealists but also included some opportunists who hoped only to fatten their own purses.

Southern Democrats used the term "carpetbagger" to suggest that northerners who came to the South after the war were second-rate opportunists, with their belongings packed in a cheap bag made of carpet. In fact, most northerners who came south were well-educated people from middle-class backgrounds. Most men had served in the Union army and moved South soon after the war to pursue financial opportunities, not politics. Some had left behind prominent roles in northern communities. Others hoped to transform the South by creating new institutions based on free labor and free schools. Carpetbaggers made up a sixth of the delegates to the state constitutional conventions but often took key roles in the conventions and the state legislatures.

discrimination Treatment based on class or racial category rather than on merit; prejudice.

public accommodations Places such as hotels, bars and restaurants, and theaters set up to do business with anyone who can pay the price of admission.

Black Reconstruction The period of Reconstruction when African Americans took an active role in state and local government.

carpetbagger Derogatory southern term for the northerners who came to the South after the Civil War to take part in Reconstruction.

scalawag Derogatory southern term for white southerners who aligned themselves with the Republican party.

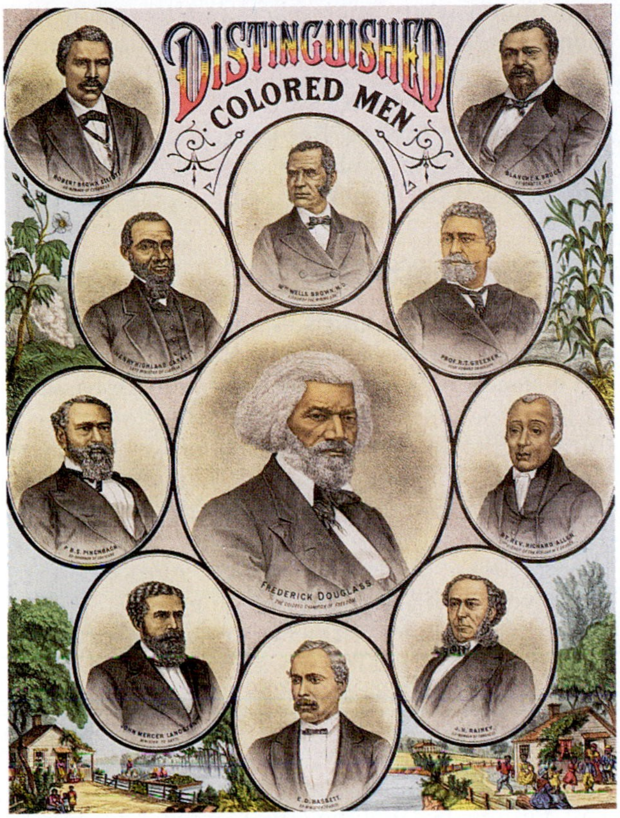

♦ This lithograph from 1883 depicts prominent African-American men, several of whom had leading roles in Black Reconstruction. *Library of Congress.*

Southern Democrats reserved their greatest contempt for scalawags—a term used to describe completely unscrupulous and worthless people. Scalawags were white southerners who became Republicans. Many had been political foes of the Democrats before the war. They made up the largest single category of delegates to the state constitutional conventions. Scalawags included many southern Unionists and others who thought the Republicans offered the best hope for economic recovery. Scalawags included small-town merchants, artisans, and professionals. Others were small-scale farmers from the backcountry, who had traditionally opposed plantation owners. For them, Reconstruction promised an end to political domination by the plantation counties. Still others had been Whigs before the Civil War.

Despite differences, freedmen, carpetbaggers, and scalawags used the Republican party to inject new ideas into the South. Throughout the South, Republican governments extended the role of state and local government and expanded public institutions. They established or expanded schools, hospitals, orphanages, and penitentiaries.

Creating an Educational System and Fighting Discrimination

Free public education was perhaps the most permanent legacy of Black Reconstruction. Reconstruction constitutions required tax-supported public schools. Implementation, however, was expensive and proceeded slowly. By 1875, only half of southern children attended public schools.

The Reconstruction state governments debated whether white and black children should attend the same schools. Most blacks probably favored **integrated** schools. Southern whites, however, warned that integration would drive whites away. Only Louisiana and South Carolina did not mandate that schools be segregated. Most blacks probably agreed with Frederick Douglass that separate schools were "infinitely superior" to no public education.

Funding for the new schools was rarely adequate. They had to be funded largely through **property taxes,** and property tax revenues declined during the 1870s as property values fell. Creating and operating two educational systems, one white and one black, was expensive. Black schools almost always received less support than white schools.

Reconstruction state governments moved toward equal rights in other areas. The new state constitutions prohibited discrimination and protected

integrated Open to people of all races and ethnic groups without restriction.

property taxes Taxes paid by property owners according to the value of their property; often used in the United States to provide funding for local schools.

civil rights. Some states guaranteed **equal access** to public transportation and public accommodations. White Republicans, however, often opposed such laws. Such conflicts pointed up the internal divisions within the southern Republican party. Even when equal access laws were passed, they were often not enforced.

Railroad Development and Corruption

Republicans nationally sought to use the power of government to stimulate economic growth. They typically encouraged railroad construction. In the South, Reconstruction governments granted state land to railroads, loaned them money, or helped to **underwrite** bonds. Sometimes they promoted railroads without finding out whether companies were financially sound. Such efforts often failed. During the 1870s, only 7,000 miles of new track were laid in the South, compared to 45,000 miles in the North.

Railroads sometimes tried to secure favorable treatment by bribing public officials, and all too many accepted their offers. The post–Civil War period saw the ethics of public officials reach a low point. From New York City to Mississippi, revelations and allegations of corruption became staples in political campaigning.

Conditions in the South were especially ripe for political corruption. Opportunities abounded for the ambitious and unscrupulous. Reconstruction governments included many whites and blacks who had only modest holdings but aspired to better things. One South Carolina legislator bluntly said: "I was pretty hard up, and I did not care who the candidate was if I got two hundred dollars." Corruption seemed especially prominent among Republicans only because they held the most important offices. Still, some Reconstruction Republicans remained scrupulously honest. In fact, Mississippi's government under Republican rule was far more honest than it had been under prewar Democratic rule.

The End of Reconstruction

Most white southerners resisted the new social order imposed on them. They created the black codes to maintain white supremacy and to restore elements of a bound labor system. They used terrorism against the advocates of black rights. Such resistance, however, had caused Congress to pass more severe terms for Reconstruction. This backlash drove some southern opponents of Reconstruction to rethink their strategy.

The "New Departure"

By 1869, some leading southern Democrats had abandoned their resistance to change and had chosen instead to accept key Reconstruction measures. At the same time, they also tried to restore the political rights for former Confederates. The **New Departure** Democrats believed that continued resistance would only prolong federal intervention in state politics.

Sometimes southern Democrats supported conservative Republicans. The outcome of this strategy was to dilute Radical influence in state government. Democrats first tried this strategy in Virginia. There William Mahone, a leading Democrat, forged a political **coalition** that accepted black suffrage. Mahone's organization then elected a northern-born, moderate Republican banker as governor. In this way, Virginia became the only Confederate state to avoid Radical Republican rule.

Similar coalitions won in Tennessee in 1869 and in Missouri in 1870. Leading Democrats elsewhere also endorsed the New Departure. They attacked Republicans more for raising taxes and increasing state spending than for their racial policies. Whenever possible, they added charges of corruption.

equal access The right of any group to use a public facility such as streetcars as freely as all other groups.

underwrite To assume financial responsibility for; in this case, to guarantee the purchase of bonds so that a project can go forward.

New Departure A policy of cooperation with key Reconstruction measures that leading southern Democrats adopted in the hope of winning compromises favorable to their party.

coalition An alliance, especially a temporary one of different people or groups.

Such campaigns brought a positive response from many taxpayers because southern tax rates had risen dramatically to support the new schools, subsidies for railroads, and other new programs.

The victories of New Departure Democrats coincided with terrorist activity aimed at Republicans. In Colfax, Louisiana, whites killed 280 African Americans in 1872 in the bloodiest racial incident of the Reconstruction era. A few southern Republicans responded by proposing to create black militias. Most Republicans, however, feared that this might provoke a race war. In most of the South, the suppression of Klan terrorism came only with federal action.

The 1872 Election

The New Departure movement coincided with a division within the Republican party. The Liberal Republican movement began in 1870 as a revolt against corruption in the Grant administration. Liberal Republicans found allies among Democrats when they came out against the Radicals.

Horace Greeley, editor of the *New York Tribune*, won the Liberal nomination for president. Although Greeley had long opposed the Democrats, the Democrats also nominated him. The Liberal Republicans and Democrats were united almost solely by their opposition to Grant and the Radicals. Few Republicans found Greeley an attractive alternative to Grant, and Greeley alienated many northern Democrats by calling for the prohibition of alcohol. Grant won convincingly in 1872 (see Map 15.1). He carried 56 percent of the vote and captured every northern state.

Redemption by Terror: The "Mississippi Plan"

After 1872, southern whites began to abandon the Republicans. The region became polarized largely along racial lines, and the elections of 1874 proved disastrous for Republicans. Democrats won over two-thirds of the South's seats in the House of Representatives and "redeemed" Alabama, Arkansas, and Texas—meaning they regained political control of these states.

Republican candidates in 1874 lost in many parts of the North because of the economic **depression** that began in 1873. After the 1874 elections, Democrats outnumbered Republicans in the House by 169 to 109. Southern Republicans could no longer look to Congress for assistance.

Terrorism against black Republicans and their remaining white allies played a role in the victory of the **Redeemers** in 1874. The Klan had worn disguises and ridden at night, but Democrats now openly formed rifle companies and marched and drilled in public. In some areas, armed whites prevented African Americans from voting.

Political violence reached such an extreme in Mississippi in 1875 that the use of terror to overthrow Reconstruction became known as the Mississippi Plan. Democratic rifle clubs operated freely, attacking Republican leaders in broad daylight. When Mississippi's carpetbagger governor, Adelbert Ames, requested federal help, President Grant declined to give it. The president had grown weary of the continuing costs of Reconstruction and the seemingly endless bloodshed that it occasioned. The Democrats swept the Mississippi elections. When the legislature convened, it removed the black Republican lieutenant governor from office. The legislature then brought similar impeachment charges against Governor Ames. Ames resigned and left the state.

The Compromise of 1877

In 1876, the nation stumbled through a potentially dangerous presidential election. As revelations of corruption grew nationally, the issue of reform took center stage. The Democratic party nominated Samuel J. Tilden, governor of New York, as

depression A period of drastic decline in a national or international economy, characterized by decreasing business activity, falling prices, and unemployment.

Redeemers Southern Democrats who hoped to bring the Democratic party back into power and to suppress Black Reconstruction.

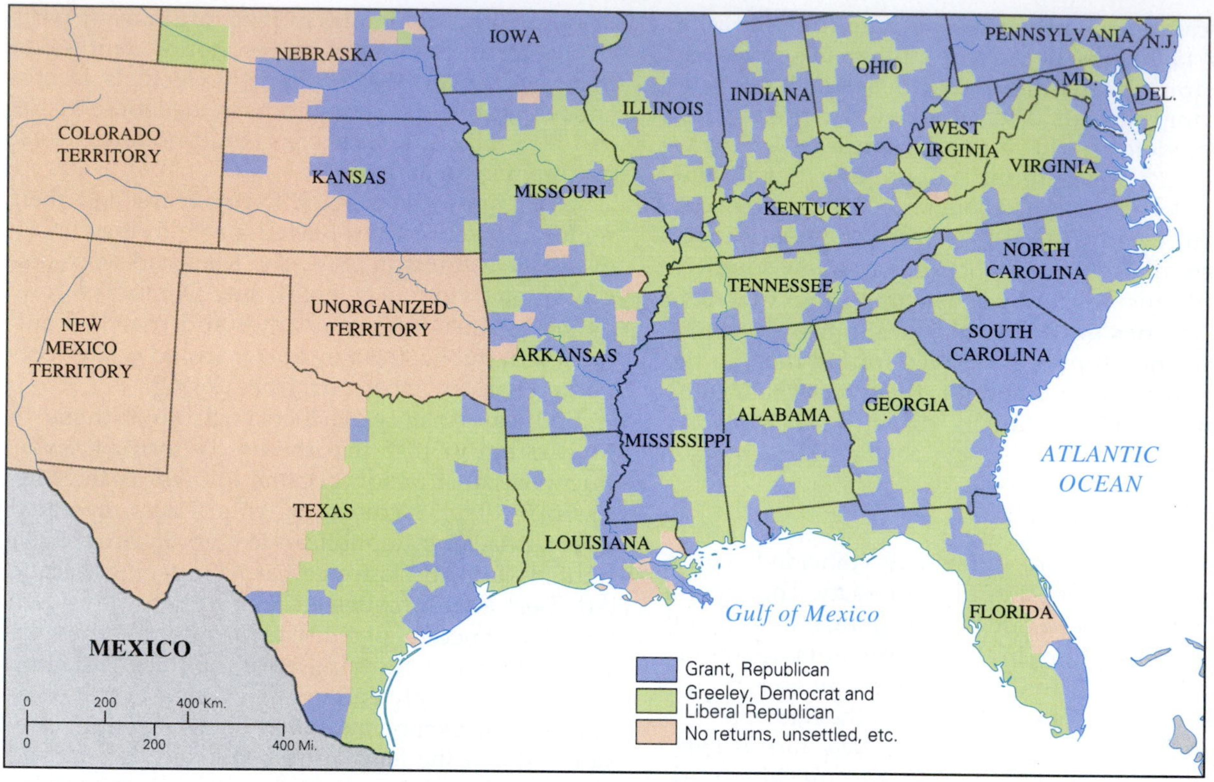

♦ **MAP 15.1. Popular Vote for President in the South, 1872** This map shows which candidate carried each county in the southern United States in 1872. Looking at both this map and the chapter opener map, you can see the relationship between Republican voting and African-American population, as well as where the southern Republican party drew strong support from white voters.

its presidential candidate. Tilden had earned a reputation for reform by opposing the Tweed Ring, the corrupt Democratic political machine that ran New York City government. The Republicans also selected a reform candidate, Rutherford B. Hayes, a Civil War general and governor of Ohio. Hayes's unblemished reputation proved to be his greatest asset.

First election reports indicated a close victory for Tilden, who carried most of the South and crucial northern states such as New York and Indiana. But in South Carolina, Florida, and Louisiana, Republicans still controlled the counting of ballots. Republican election boards in those states rejected enough ballots to give Hayes those three states and thus a one-vote margin of victory in the Electoral College.

The Democrats cried fraud. Some vowed to see Tilden inaugurated by force if necessary. For the first time, Congress had to face the problem of disputed electoral votes that could decide an election. To resolve the problem, Congress created a commission consisting of five senators, five representatives, and five Supreme Court justices. Eight Republicans and seven Democrats sat on the commission.

The nation braced itself for a potentially violent confrontation. However, as commission hearings droned on into February 1877, informal discussions took place among leading Republicans and Democrats. The result was a series of informal agreements usually called the **Compromise of 1877.** Southern Democrats demanded **home rule,** by which they meant an end to federal intervention in southern politics. They also called for federal subsidies for railroad construction and waterways in the South. In return, southern Democrats were willing to abandon Tilden's claim to the White House if the commission ruled for Hayes.

Most of the agreements that were part of the Compromise of 1877 were kept. By a straight party vote, the commission confirmed the election of Hayes. Soon after his peaceful inauguration, he ordered the last of the federal troops withdrawn from the South. The Radical era of a powerful federal government pledged to protect "equality before the law" for all citizens was over. Without federal protection, the last three Republican state governments fell in 1877. The party of white supremacy held sway in every southern state.

The Compromise of 1877 marked the end of Reconstruction. The war was more than ten years in the past, and the passions it had stirred had slowly cooled. Many who had yearned to punish the South for its treason turned to other matters. Some reformers concentrated on civil service or currency issues. A major depression in the mid-1870s, unemployment and labor disputes, the growth of industry, the emergence of big business, and the economic development of the West focused public attention on economic issues.

After Reconstruction

Southern Democrats read the events of 1877 as their permit to establish new systems of politics and race relations. Most Redeemers set out to reduce taxes, to dismantle Reconstruction legislation and agencies, to take political influence away from black citizens, and eventually to reshape the South's legal system to establish African Americans as subordinate. They also began the process of turning the South into a one-party region.

Although voting and officeholding by African Americans did not cease in 1877, the political context changed profoundly once they lost federal enforcement of their rights. The threat of violence from nightriders and the potential for economic retaliation sharply reduced independent action by African Americans. Black political leaders increasingly recognized that efforts to mobilize black voters posed dangers to both candidates and voters. The public schools remained, segregated and underfunded, but important as both a symbol and a real opportunity to learn. Many Reconstruction era laws remained on the books.

Not until the 1890s did black disfranchisement and thoroughgoing racial segregation become widely embedded in southern law (see page 396). From the mid-1870s to the late 1890s, the South lived an uneasy compromise: African Americans had certain constitutional rights, but they exercised their rights at the sufferance of the dominant whites. Such a compromise bore the seeds of future conflict.

For generations after 1877, Reconstruction was held up as a failure. The southern version of Reconstruction—that conniving carpetbaggers and scalawags had manipulated ignorant freedmen—appealed to the racial bias of many white Americans in the North and South alike, and it gained widespread acceptance among novelists, journalists, and historians. Thomas Dixon's popular novel *The Clansman* (1905) inspired the highly influential film *The Birth of a Nation* (1915). Historically inaccurate and luridly racist, the book and the movie portrayed Ku Klux Klan members as heroes who rescued the white South, and especially white southern women, from domination and debauchery at the hands of depraved freedmen and carpetbaggers. Although black historians such as W. E. B. Du Bois challenged this picture of Reconstruction, it was not until the civil rights movement of the 1950s and 1960s that large numbers of American historians began to reconsider Reconstruction.

Compromise of 1877 Compromise in which southern Democrats agreed to allow the Republican candidate the victory in the disputed presidential election in return for the removal of federal troops from the South.

home rule Self-government; in this case, an end to federal intervention in the South.

Historians today recognize that Reconstruction was not the failure that had earlier been claimed. The creation of public schools was but one of the important changes in southern life. At a federal level, the Fourteenth and Fifteenth Amendments eventually were used to restore the principle of equality before the law. Historians also recognize that Reconstruction collapsed not so much because of internal flaws as because of the political terrorism that was unleashed in the South against blacks and Republicans.

SUMMARY

Expectations
Constraints
Choices
Outcomes

At the end of the Civil War, the nation faced difficult *choices* regarding the future of the defeated South and the future of the freed people. Committed to an end to slavery, President Lincoln *chose* a lenient approach to restoring states to the Union. When Johnson became president, he continued Lincoln's approach.

The end of slavery brought new *expectations* for all African Americans. Taking advantage of the *choices* that freedom opened, they tried to create independent lives for themselves and developed social institutions that helped to define black communities. Few were able to acquire land of their own. Most became either wage laborers or sharecroppers. White southerners *expected* to keep African Americans subordinate through black codes and violence.

In reaction against the black codes and violence, Congress *chose* to wrest control of Reconstruction from President Johnson. An attempt to remove Johnson from the presidency was unsuccessful. Reconstruction measures included the Fourteenth and Fifteenth Amendments, the Civil Rights Act of 1866, and the Civil Rights Act of 1875. One *outcome* of these measures was to strengthen the federal government at the expense of the states.

Enfranchised freedmen, transplanted northerners, and some southern whites created a southern Republican party that governed most southern states for a time. The most lasting contribution of these state governments was the creation of public school systems. Like government officials elsewhere, however, some southerners fell prey to corruption.

In the late 1860s, many southern Democrats *chose* a "New Departure": they grudgingly accepted some features of Reconstruction and sought to recapture control of state governments. The 1876 presidential election was hotly disputed, but key Republicans and Democrats *chose* to compromise. The Compromise of 1877 permitted Hayes to take office and brought Reconstruction to an end. Without further federal protection for their civil rights, African Americans faced severe *constraints* in exercising their rights. Sharecropping consigned most to a subordinate economic status. Terrorism, violence, and even death confronted those who *chose* to challenge their subordinate social role. The *outcome* of Reconstruction was white supremacy in politics, the economy, and social relations.

SUGGESTED READINGS

Donald, David. *Charles Sumner and the Rights of Man* (1970).

A good account not just of this important Radical leader but of important Reconstruction issues.

Du Bois, W. E. B. *Black Reconstruction in America: An Essay Toward a History of the Part Which Black Folk Played in the Attempt to Reconstruct Democracy in America, 1860–1880* (1935; reprint, 1969).

Written more than a half-century ago, Du Bois's book is still useful for both information and insights.

Foner, Eric. *Reconstruction: America's Unfinished Revolution, 1863–1877* (1988).

The most thorough recent treatment, incorporating insights from many historians who have written on the subject during the past forty years. Also available in a condensed version.

Litwack, Leon F. *Been in the Storm So Long: The Aftermath of Slavery* (1979).

Focuses on the experience of the freed people.

Woodward, C. Vann. *Reunion and Reaction: The Compromise of 1877 and the End of Reconstruction*, rev. ed. (1956).

The classic account of the Compromise of 1877.

INDUSTRIALIZATION, 1865–1900 After the Civil War, manufacturing expanded significantly, especially in the Northeast. This map indicates major types of manufacturing as of 1900 and the location of natural resources that contributed to industrialization. Some of these natural resources were not exploited until after 1900.

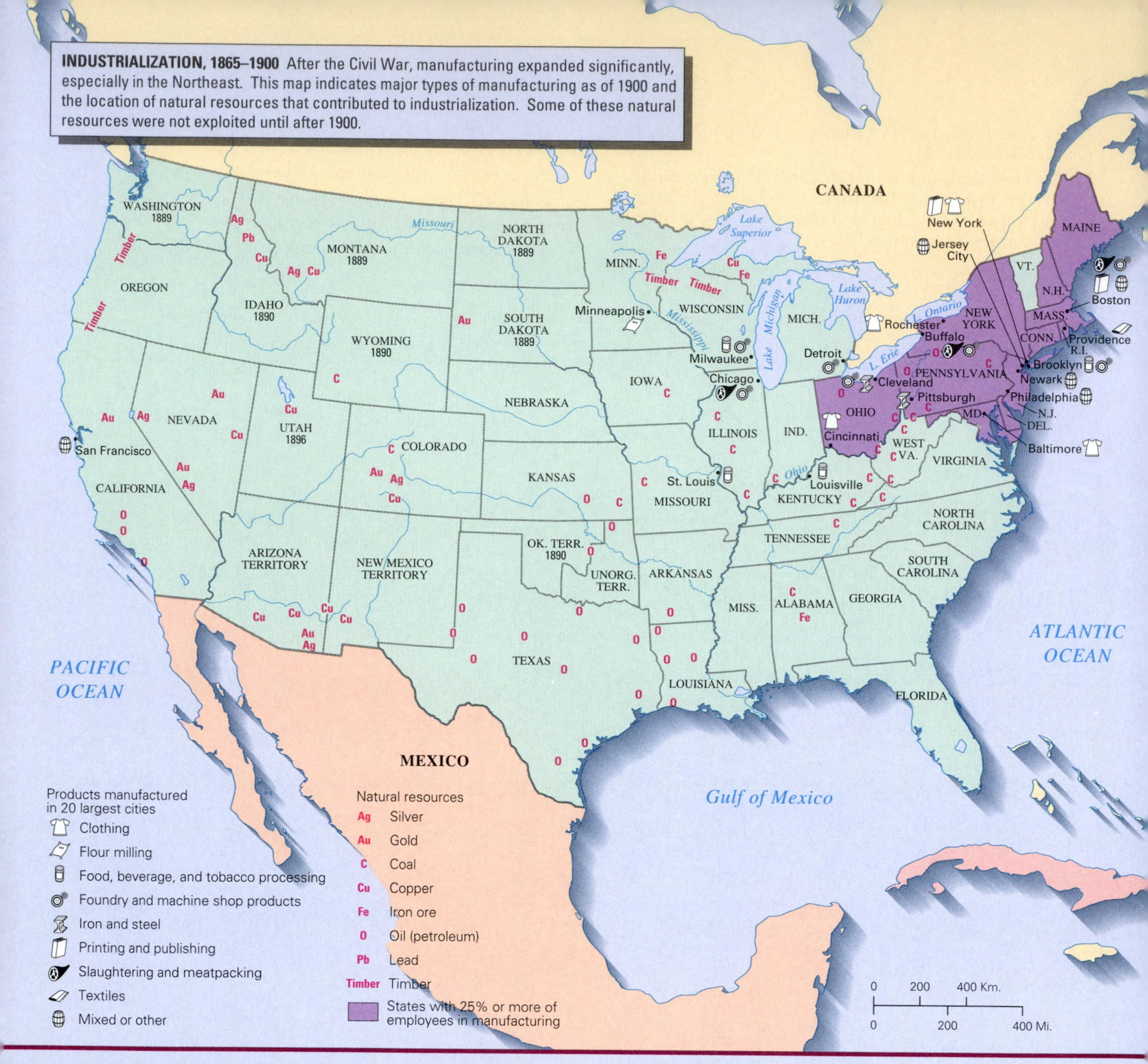

CANADA
MEXICO
PACIFIC OCEAN
ATLANTIC OCEAN
Gulf of Mexico
WASHINGTON 1889
OREGON
CALIFORNIA
NEVADA
IDAHO 1890
MONTANA 1889
WYOMING 1890
UTAH 1896
COLORADO
ARIZONA TERRITORY
NEW MEXICO TERRITORY
NORTH DAKOTA 1889
SOUTH DAKOTA 1889
NEBRASKA
KANSAS
OK. TERR. 1890
UNORG. TERR.
TEXAS
MINN.
IOWA
MISSOURI
ARKANSAS
LOUISIANA
WISCONSIN
ILLINOIS
MICH.
IND.
OHIO
KENTUCKY
TENNESSEE
MISS.
ALABAMA
GEORGIA
FLORIDA
SOUTH CAROLINA
NORTH CAROLINA
VIRGINIA
WEST VA.
PENNSYLVANIA
NEW YORK
VT.
N.H.
MAINE
MASS.
CONN.
R.I.
N.J.
DEL.
MD.
Missouri
Mississippi
Ohio
Lake Superior
Lake Michigan
Lake Huron
L. Ontario
L. Erie
San Francisco
Minneapolis
Milwaukee
Chicago
St. Louis
Louisville
Detroit
Cleveland
Pittsburgh
Cincinnati
Buffalo
Rochester
New York
Jersey City
Boston
Providence
Brooklyn
Newark
Philadelphia
Baltimore
Timber
Products manufactured in 20 largest cities
Clothing
Flour milling
Food, beverage, and tobacco processing
Foundry and machine shop products
Iron and steel
Printing and publishing
Slaughtering and meatpacking
Textiles
Mixed or other
Natural resources
Ag Silver
Au Gold
C Coal
Cu Copper
Fe Iron ore
O Oil (petroleum)
Pb Lead
Timber Timber
States with 25% or more of employees in manufacturing
0 200 400 Km.
0 200 400 Mi.

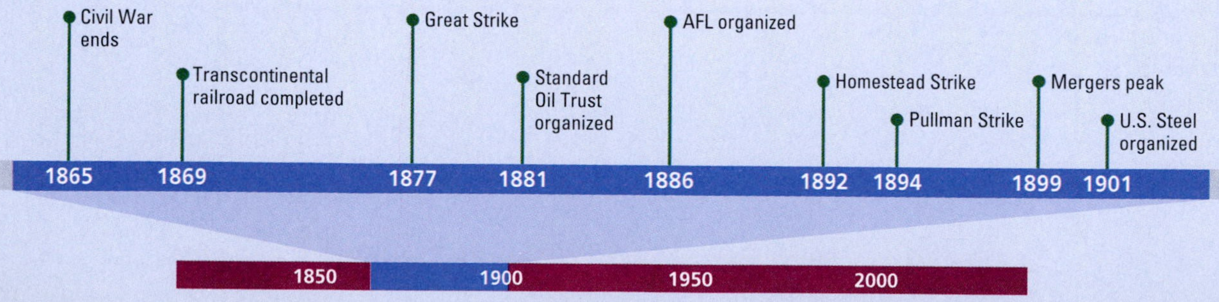

Civil War ends
Transcontinental railroad completed
Great Strike
Standard Oil Trust organized
AFL organized
Homestead Strike
Pullman Strike
Mergers peak
U.S. Steel organized
1865
1869
1877
1881
1886
1892
1894
1899
1901
1850
1900
1950
2000

CHAPTER 16

Survival of the Fittest: Entrepreneurs and Workers in Industrial America, 1865–1900

Foundation for Industrialization

- What expectations encouraged economic growth in the late nineteenth century?
- How did federal policymakers choose to encourage economic growth after the Civil War?

Railroads and Economic Growth

- In the post–Civil War era, what constraints did railroad entrepreneurs and investment bankers face? What was the outcome of their choices?

Entrepreneurs and Industrial Transformation

- How did technology and prevailing business practices define entrepreneurs' expectations in the late nineteenth century?
- How did Carnegie and Morgan choose to deal with competition?

Workers in Industrial America

- What were Americans' expectations regarding economic mobility in the late nineteenth century?
- What constraints did workers face in seeking mobility, and what choices were they able to make?

The Varieties of Labor Organization and Action

- How did the expectations of American workers who joined craft unions compare with those who joined the Knights of Labor?
- What were some outcomes of labor unrest in the late nineteenth century?

The Nation Transformed

- How did Americans respond to the transformation of the economy?

INTRODUCTION

E xpectations
C onstraints
C hoices
O utcomes

In January 1901, 65-year-old Andrew Carnegie used a blunt pencil to write several lines on a sheet of paper. After receiving this paper, J. P. Morgan glanced at it and murmured, "I accept this price." Thereby did Carnegie sell the nation's largest steel company for $480 million. Thereby did Morgan, the nation's most prominent banker, acquire the central element for his plan to create the United States Steel Corporation, the first corporation in the world to be capitalized at more than a billion dollars.

By the time Morgan accepted Carnegie's offer, the U.S. economy had been dramatically transformed from what it had been during the Civil War. Back then, more than half of all American workers had toiled in agriculture. And anyone contemplating the prospects for manufacturing would have noted many potential *constraints:* a partially developed transportation system, limited amounts of capital, an unsophisticated system for mobilizing capital, and a potential shortage of workers. Some, however, would have pointed to the great potential evident in America's vast natural resources and skilled workers.

A generation later, much of that potential had been realized, and the United States stood as a major industrial power. The changes in the nation's economy far exceeded the wildest *expectations* of Americans living in 1865. Few could have imagined that steel production would increase a thousand times by 1900, or that railroads would operate nearly six times as many miles of tracks, or that farms would triple their harvests. Few could have *expected* the torrent of inventions that transformed many people's lives: adding machines, telephones, electric lights, electric streetcars, electric sewing machines, automobiles, motion pictures. By the 1890s, rapid and far-reaching change had become an ingrained part of Americans' expectations.

These economic changes were the result of *choices* made by many individuals: where to seek work, where to invest, whether to expand production, how to react to a business competitor, whom to trust. Among the many economic *choices* Americans made, however, two general areas stand out: competition and cooperation.

As the industrial economy took off, many entrepreneurs found themselves in a love-hate relationship with competition. Carnegie loved it, expressing the *expectation* that it "insures the survival of the fittest." Morgan, by contrast, saw competition as the single most unpredictable factor in the economy and as a serious *constraint* on economic progress. Carnegie's zeal for competition was, in fact, unusual. Although many entrepreneurs paid lip service to competition, most thought more like Morgan than Carnegie.

Other Americans found themselves making *choices* regarding cooperation. Individualism was deeply entrenched in the American psyche, yet the increasing complexity of the economy presented repeated opportunities for cooperation. Entrepreneurs sometimes *chose* to cooperate by dividing a market rather than competing in it. Wage earners sometimes *chose* to join with other workers in demanding better wages or working conditions. In the process, some workers not only cooperated in a union but questioned capitalism, the economic system that paid their wages. The *outcome* of these *choices* was the industrialization of the nation and the transformation of the economy.

CHRONOLOGY

The Growth of Industry

1850s	Development of Bessemer and Kelly steel-making processes
1861	Protective tariff
1862	Homestead Act Land-Grant College Act Pacific Railroad Act
1865	Civil War ends
1869	First transcontinental railroad completed Knights of Labor founded
1870	Standard Oil incorporated Patent Office registers the first trademark
1872	Montgomery Ward opens its mail-order business
1873–1878	Depression
1875	Andrew Carnegie opens J. Edgar Thomson Works
1876	Invention of the telephone
1877	Great Strike Reconstruction ends
1879	Invention of the electric light bulb Henry George's *Progress and Poverty*
1880s	Railroad expansion and consolidation
1881	Standard Oil Trust organized
1882–1885	Recession
1886	Last major railroad converts to the standard gauge First Sears and Roebuck catalogue Peak membership in Knights of Labor Haymarket Square bombing American Federation of Labor founded
1892	Homestead strike
1893–1897	Depression
1894	Pullman strike
1901	United States Steel organized
1902	International Harvester organized

Foundation for Industrialization

By 1865, conditions in the United States were ripe for rapid industrialization. A wealth of natural resources, a capable work force, an agricultural base that produced enough food for a large urban population, and favorable government policies laid the foundation.

Resources, Skills, and Capital

At the end of the Civil War, entrepreneurs could draw on vast and virtually untapped natural resources. Americans had long plowed the fertile farmlands of the Midwest and the South. They had just begun to farm the rich black soil of Minnesota, Nebraska, Kansas, Iowa, and the Dakotas, as well as the productive valleys of California. The Pacific Northwest, the western Great Lakes region, and the South all held extensive forests untouched by the lumberman's saw.

The nation was also rich in mineral resources. Pennsylvania had vast iron ore and coal deposits. It was also the site of early efforts to tap underground pools of crude oil. California had gold. Vast reserves of other minerals lay undiscovered in

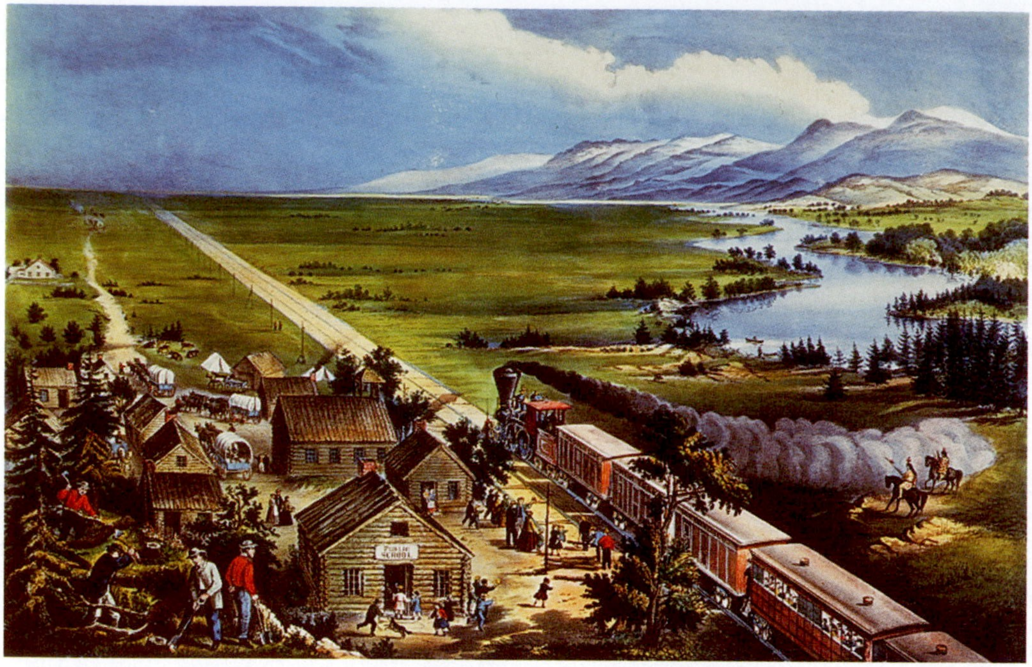

◆ In the popular imagination of most Americans in the late nineteenth century, the West was a vast and unpopulated storehouse of riches—fertile agricultural land, timber waiting to be cut, minerals there for the taking. Popular prints such as this lithograph by Currier & Ives, titled *Westward the Course of Empires Takes Its Way* (1868), which depicts ambitious pioneers moving west, encouraged such attitudes. In such imaginative depictions, there was rarely any indication that the West was already home to many American Indians and Mexican Americans. *Museum of the City of New York.*

1865: iron ore in Michigan, Minnesota, and Alabama; coal throughout the Ohio Valley and in Wyoming and Colorado; oil in the Midwest, Oklahoma, Texas, Louisiana, and California; gold or silver in Nevada and Colorado; and copper in Michigan, Montana, Utah, and Arizona.

Like natural resources, the work force and the skills and experience of workers were important for economic growth. In the early nineteenth century, New Englanders had developed manufacturing systems based on **interchangeable parts** and factories for producing cotton cloth. Their talents and inventiveness gave them a reputation for "Yankee ingenuity." Such skills, however, were not limited to New England.

Another crucial element for industrialization was capital. During the years before the war, capital became centered in the northeastern seaport cities of Boston, New York, and Philadelphia. Banks and **stock exchanges** capable of mobilizing capital had also appeared before the Civil War.

The Transformation of Agriculture

The expanding economy of the nineteenth century rested on a productive agricultural base. Improved transportation helped expand agriculture by mak-

interchangeable parts Parts that are identical and can be substituted for each other.

stock exchange A place where people meet to buy and sell stocks and bonds.

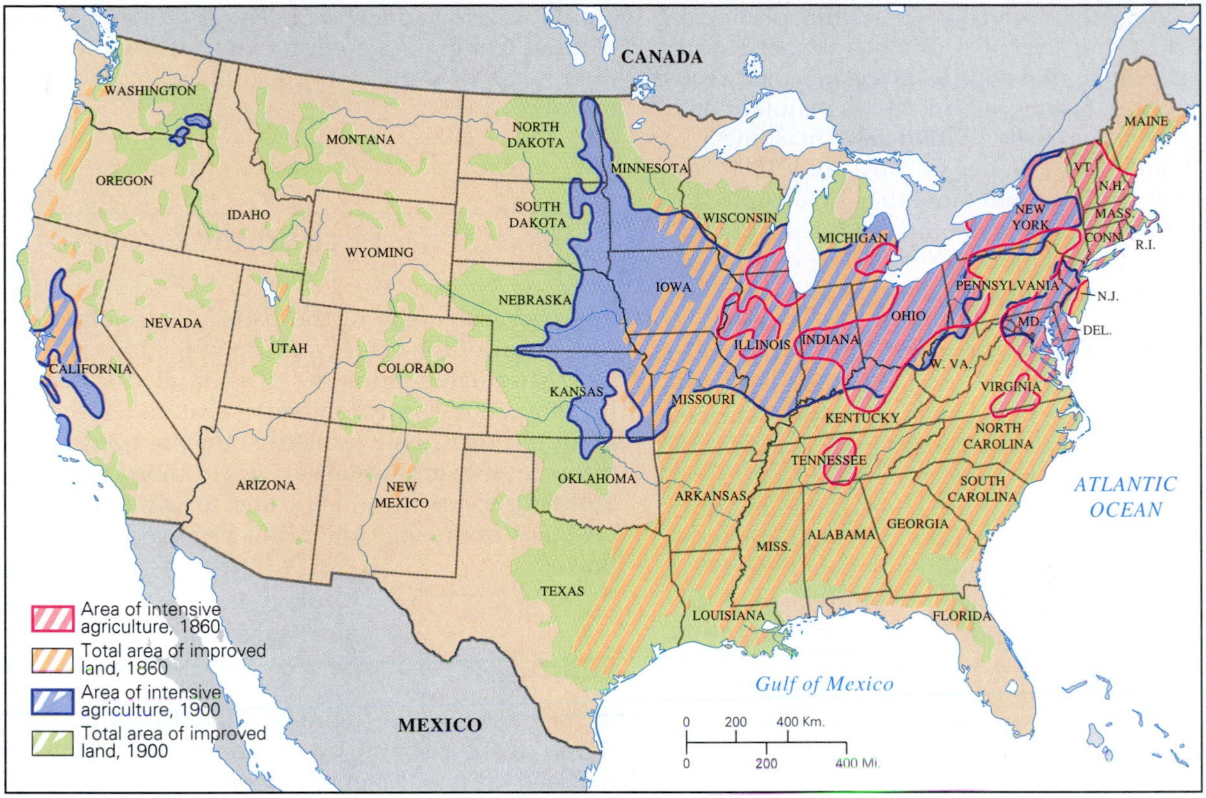

♦ **MAP 16.1 Expansion of Agriculture, 1860–1900** The amount of improved farmland more than doubled during these forty years. This map shows two ways in which agricultural expansion came about: first, western lands were brought under cultivation; second, in other areas, especially the Midwest, land was cultivated much more intensively than before.

ing it possible to move agricultural produce long distances. Up to 1865, farmers had developed 407 million acres. During the next thirty-five years, this acreage more than doubled (see Map 16.1).

The federal government contributed to the rapid settlement of Kansas, Nebraska, the Dakotas, and Minnesota through the **Homestead Act of 1862.** Under this act, any person could receive 160 acres of free land from the government by building a house, living on the land for five years, and farming it. Between 1862 and 1890, 48 million acres passed into private hands in this way. Even more land was purchased from the government for as little as $1.25 per acre.

As production of major crops rose, prices for them fell. Corn sold for 66 cents per bushel in 1866 but fell steadily thereafter, hitting a low of 21 cents in 1896. Wheat dropped from $2.06 per bushel in 1866 to a low of 49 cents in 1894. Cotton followed the same trend. It sold for 9.7 cents per pound in 1876 but only 4.6 cents in 1894.

Homestead Act of 1862 Law passed by Congress in 1862 promising ownership of 160 acres of public land to any citizen who lived on and cultivated the land for five years.

Several factors contributed to the decline in farm prices, but the most obvious is that supply grew faster than demand. As prices for their crops fell, American farmers attempted to maintain their income by using fertilizer and new machinery to grow more crops. Between 1870 and 1890, the amount of fertilizer sold more than quadrupled.

New machinery spurred the production of grain crops. Steel-bladed plows, seed **drills,** reapers, and threshing machines all greatly increased the amount of land one person could farm. For example, a farmer with a hand-held scythe and cradle could harvest only two acres of wheat in a day. Using the McCormick reaper, first produced in 1849, a farmer and a team of horses could harvest two acres in an hour.

The growth of agriculture affected other parts of the economy. It stimulated the farm equipment industry and, in turn, the iron and steel industry. It motivated the development of railroads and sustained them. Throughout the nineteenth century, agricultural products (cotton, tobacco, wheat, and meat) constituted more than two-thirds of American exports. Thus hefty exports spurred oceanic shipping and shipbuilding.

The Impact of War and New Government Policies

In the short run, the Civil War, by diverting labor and capital into war production, probably slowed an expansion of manufacturing already under way. But the war did bring about important changes in the experience and expectations of some entrepreneurs, who began to think in terms of national markets. New government policies also quickened the rate of growth after the war.

Even in the midst of the Civil War, Republicans attempted to stimulate economic growth. They first passed a new **protective tariff** in 1861 to protect American products from foreign competition and to stimulate investment in manufacturing. Next, they used the billion acres of government-owned land to encourage economic development. The Homestead Act stimulated western settlement. The **Land-Grant College Act** (1862) gave land to states to fund public universities that would provide education in engineering and agriculture. Congress also approved the Pacific Railroad Act, a land grant for the first transcontinental railroad, in 1862.

Railroads and Economic Growth

Railroads set much of the pace for economic expansion after the Civil War. Growth of the rail network stimulated industries that supplied materials for railroad construction and operation, especially steel and coal, and industries that needed long-distance transportation to reach their markets. Railroad companies also came to symbolize big business, and some Americans began to fear their power.

Railroad Expansion

In 1865, the lack of a national rail network posed a significant constraint on economic development. Railroad companies operated on tracks of varying **gauges,** making it impossible to transfer railcars between lines. Few bridges crossed major rivers. Until 1869, no railroad connected the eastern half of the country to the Pacific coast.

By the 1880s, the final elements had fallen into place to create a national rail network. The first transcontinental rail line was completed in 1869,

drill A machine for planting seeds in holes or furrows.

protective tariff Tax on imported goods intended to make them more expensive than similar domestic goods, thus protecting the market for items produced at home.

Land-Grant College Act Law passed by Congress in 1862 that gave public land to each state; income from the land was to provide funding for engineering and agricultural colleges.

gauge The distance between the rails in a railroad track.

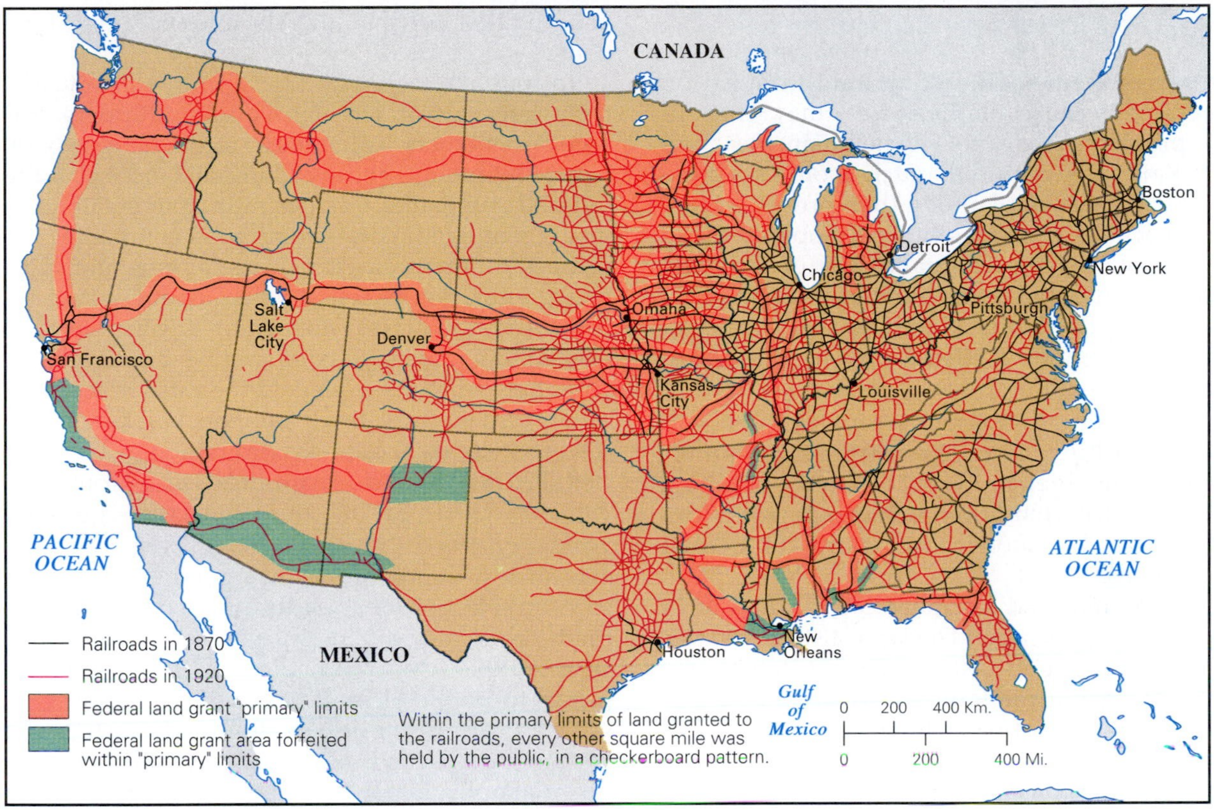
CANADA
Boston
Detroit
Chicago
New York
Pittsburgh
Omaha
Salt Lake City
Denver
San Francisco
Kansas City
Louisville
PACIFIC OCEAN
ATLANTIC OCEAN
MEXICO
Houston
New Orleans
Gulf of Mexico
Railroads in 1870
Railroads in 1920
Federal land grant "primary" limits
Federal land grant area forfeited within "primary" limits
Within the primary limits of land granted to the railroads, every other square mile was held by the public, in a checkerboard pattern.
0 200 400 Km.
0 200 400 Mi.

♦ **MAP 16.2 Railroad Expansion and Railroad Land Grants** Post–Civil War railroad expansion produced the transportation base for an industrial economy. In the West, federal land grants encouraged railroad construction. Within a grant, railroads received every other square mile. Land could be forfeited if construction did not meet the terms of the grant legislation.

connecting Sacramento, California, to Omaha, Nebraska. By 1893, four more transcontinental lines had been built. Between 1865 and 1890, railroads grew from 35,000 miles of track to 167,000 miles (see Map 16.2). By the mid-1880s, most major rivers had been bridged. Companies had replaced many iron rails with steel ones, making it possible to haul heavier loads. New inventions increased the speed, carrying capacity, and efficiency of trains. In 1886, the last major lines converted to a standard gauge, making it possible to transfer railcars from one line to another simply by throwing a switch. This rail network enabled entrepreneurs to ship raw materials and goods easily from one region to another.

Western railroads expanded with generous assistance from the federal government. Congress provided the Union Pacific and Central Pacific railroads, the first companies to build a transcontinental line, not only with sizable loans but also with 10 square miles of the public domain for every mile of track laid. Congress doubled this amount in 1864. By 1871, Congress had authorized some seventy railroad land grants, involving 128 million acres, an area the size of Colorado and Wyoming together. Most railroads sold their land to farmers and companies to raise capital for railroad operations. This practice guaranteed that the railroads would have customers and business along their tracks.

Railroads: Models for Big Business

Railroad companies differed in kind from earlier businesses. Because of their size, they encountered problems that no other businesses had faced. Railroads required much more coordination and long-range planning than previous businesses. Earlier companies typically operated at a single location, but railroads had to provide freight stations, passenger stations, and repair facilities along the entire length of their lines. Financial transactions carried on over hundreds of miles by scores of employees required a centralized accounting office. One result was the development of a bureaucracy of clerks, accountants, managers, and agents. Railroads became training grounds for the first administrators in American business and the models for many subsequent large businesses.

Railroads required far more capital than most manufacturing concerns. The largest steel furnaces in the world cost $741,000 in 1875, but in the same year the Pennsylvania Railroad was capitalized at $400 million. The railroads' huge appetite for capital made them the first American businesses to seek investors on a nationwide and international scale. By the Civil War, the New York Stock Exchange had emerged as the leading place where brokers sold railroad stocks.

Railroads faced higher **fixed costs** than most previous companies. These costs included equipment, property, and commitments to investors. To pay their fixed costs, railroad companies operated at full capacity whenever possible. Doing so sometimes proved difficult. Where two or more lines competed for the same traffic, rate wars often resulted. Competition between railroad companies sometimes became so intense that no line could show a profit. A railroad that could not cover its fixed costs faced bankruptcy.

Some railroad operators attempted to eliminate competition by forming **pools.** The most famous was the Iowa Pool, made up of the railroads operating between Chicago and Omaha. Formed in 1870, the Iowa Pool operated until 1874. Few pools lasted very long. Typically a railroad broke the pool arrangement in an effort to expand, thereby starting a new price war. Customers complained loudly when a pooling arrangement became known; they believed that they paid higher rates because of the pool.

To compete more effectively, railroads adjusted their rates to attract high-volume shippers. Favored customers sometimes received a **rebate.** Large shipments sent over long distances cost the railroad companies less per mile than small shipments sent over short distances, so companies developed different rate structures for long and short hauls. Thus the largest shippers could secure rebates and low rates, and small businesses and farmers operated at a comparative disadvantage. Although railroads explained the rates in terms of differences in costs, small shippers still saw themselves as victims of rate discrimination.

Railroads viewed government as a source of valuable subsidies, but they constantly guarded against efforts to have government regulate their enterprises. Companies campaigned openly to secure the election of friendly politicians and **lobbied** public officials in Washington, D.C., and in state capitals. Most railroad companies issued free passes to public officials, a practice reformers attacked as a form of bribery. Railroads such as the Southern Pacific in California became the most influential political power in the state. Stories of railroad officials bribing politicians became commonplace after the Civil War.

Investment Bankers and "Morganization"

The rapid railroad expansion of the 1880s led to excessive competition, which caused some lines to earn little or no profit. Railway executives at-

fixed costs Costs that a company must pay even if it closes down all its operations—for example, interest on loans, dividends on bonds, and property taxes.

pool An agreement among businesses in the same industry to divide up the market and charge equal prices instead of competing.

rebate The refund of part of the amount given in payment for something.

lobby To try to influence the thinking of public officials for or against a specific cause.

tempted to solve the problem by consolidating small carriers into a large regional railway. The Santa Fe and the Southern Pacific, for example, emerged in the Southwest, and the Great Northern and the Northern Pacific held sway in the Northwest. The Pennsylvania and the New York Central controlled much of the Northeast. Railway executives expected consolidation to lead to fewer price wars and higher profits.

To raise the enormous amounts of capital necessary for construction and consolidation, railroads turned increasingly to investment bankers. **John Pierpont Morgan** had emerged as the most prominent investment banker by the late 1880s. Morgan was the son of a successful Connecticut merchant who turned to investment banking and relocated the family to London when Morgan was 17. After working in his father's London bank, Morgan moved in 1857 to New York, where his father's connections and his own abilities enabled him to become a major banking figure.

Morgan's access to capital in the United States, London, and Paris soon led to his involvement in efforts to stabilize the railroad industry. His price for investing in financially ailing railroads was the consolidation of small lines into larger systems. He often insisted that he or one of his partners be seated on the board of directors to guard against risky decisions in the future. This process became known as "Morganization." "Morganized" lines by 1900 included some of the largest in the country: the Reading, the Baltimore & Ohio, the Chesapeake & Ohio, the Santa Fe, the Erie, the Northern Pacific, and the Southern. A few other investment bankers followed similar patterns.

By 1900, railroad entrepreneurs and investment bankers had twelve large railroad systems that controlled more than half of the nation's track mileage. Twenty other railroads operated most of the rest.

Entrepreneurs and Industrial Transformation

Despite the emergence of large railroad corporations, most American businesses were relatively small. Even as late as 1899, nearly 60 percent of all manufacturing establishments were so small that they averaged only two production workers. Such businesses typically operated in a single shop, were run by the owner, and produced one item for local sale. For example, a wheelwright turned out wheels one at a time. Although a few textile factories employed a hundred workers as early as the 1820s, these companies made only one product in one location. Entrepreneurs in the late nineteenth century challenged all these patterns.

Andrew Carnegie and the Age of Steel

Steel defined the new industrial economy that emerged after the Civil War. This superior metal was difficult and expensive to make until the 1850s, when Henry Bessemer in England and William Kelly in Kentucky independently discovered ways of making it inexpensively and quickly.

In 1875, just south of Pittsburgh, Pennsylvania, **Andrew Carnegie** opened the nation's largest steel plant, the J. Edgar Thomson Works. From then until 1901, Carnegie held central place in the steel industry. Born in Scotland in 1835, Carnegie came to the United States with his penniless parents in 1848. He soon became a messenger in a telegraph office and then a telegraph operator. Because of his great skill at the telegraph key, Carnegie became the personal telegrapher for a high official of the Pennsylvania Railroad. Carnegie rose rapidly and became a superintendent at the age of 25. At the end of the Civil War, he left railroading to devote full attention to his investments in the iron and steel industry. He quickly began to apply to his iron companies the management lessons he had learned with the railroad.

John Pierpont Morgan American banker and industrialist who used investments in railroads and steel to turn his family fortune into a colossal financial empire.

Andrew Carnegie Scottish-born industrialist who made a fortune in steel and believed the rich had a duty to act for the public benefit.

Carnegie followed this basic rule: "Cut the prices; scoop the market; run the mills full." An aggressive competitor, he took every opportunity to cut costs so that he could charge less than his rivals. In 1864, steel rails sold for $126 per ton; by 1875, Carnegie was selling them for $69 per ton. Driven by improved technology and Carnegie's competitiveness, steel prices continued to fall, reaching less than $20 per ton in the late 1890s. By then, the nation produced nearly 10 million tons of steel each year.

Carnegie's success in reducing costs also stemmed from **vertical integration.** Like other entrepreneurs, Carnegie chose to control everything from the supply of raw materials to the distribution of finished products. Vertical integration guaranteed a reliable flow of supplies at predictable prices.

Steel plants stood at one end of the long chain of vertically integrated operations that Carnegie owned or controlled: iron ore mines in Michigan and Wisconsin, a fleet of ships that transported iron ore across the Great Lakes, hundreds of miles of railway lines, tens of thousands of acres of coal lands, ovens to produce **coke,** and plants for turning iron ore into bars of crude iron. Carnegie Steel was vertically integrated from the point where the raw materials came out of the ground through the production of steel rails and beams.

Standard Oil: Model for Monopoly

As Carnegie provided a model for other steel companies and for heavy industry, **John D. Rockefeller** revolutionized the petroleum industry. Born in 1839, Rockefeller became a partner in a grain and livestock business in Cleveland that earned large profits during the Civil War. In 1863, Rockefeller invested these profits in a refinery that had been built to process oil from northwestern Pennsylvania, where oil had been discovered in 1859. After the war, he bought more refineries and incorporated them as Standard Oil in 1870.

The refining business was highly competitive. Recognizing that improved technology could offer a decisive advantage, Rockefeller recruited engineers to make Standard the most efficient refiner. He secured reduced rates or obtained rebates from the railroads. He usually sought to persuade his competitors to join the **cartel** he was creating. Failing in that, he would drive them out of business.

Between 1879 and 1881, Rockefeller centralized decision making among the forty companies that he and his associates controlled by creating the Standard Oil Trust. The **trust** was a new organizational form designed to get around state laws that prohibited one company from owning stock in another. To create the trust, Rockefeller and other shareholders in the individual companies exchanged their stock for trust certificates issued by Standard Oil. Standard Oil thus was able to control all the individual companies, though technically it did not own them. The creation of Standard Oil meant that one company controlled about 90 percent of the nation's refining capacity.

Standard Oil consolidated its operations by closing more than half of its refineries and building several larger plants that incorporated the newest technology. One outcome was greater efficiency. The price of fuel and lighting products fell by more than half from 1866 to 1890. In the 1880s, Standard moved to vertical integration by gaining

vertical integration The bringing together of a wide range of business activities—such as acquiring raw materials, manufacturing, and marketing and selling finished products—into a single organization.

coke Coal from which most of the gases have been removed by heating; it burns with intense heat and is used in making steel.

John D. Rockefeller American industrialist who amassed great wealth through the Standard Oil Company and donated much of his fortune to promote learning and research.

cartel A group of independent business organizations that cooperate to control the production, pricing, and marketing of goods by group members; another term for *pool.*

trust A combination of firms or corporations for the purpose of reducing competition and controlling prices throughout an industry.

control of existing oil fields, building its own pipelines and oceangoing tankers, and creating its own marketing operations. By the early 1890s, Standard Oil had achieved a near **monopoly** over an entire industry. The monopoly proved to be short-lived, however, because of the discovery of new oil fields in Texas and elsewhere. New companies emerged and quickly followed the path of vertical integration.

Technology and Economic Change

By the late nineteenth century, most American entrepreneurs had joined Rockefeller in viewing technology as an important competitive device. Railroads wanted more powerful locomotives, larger freight cars, and stronger rails. Steel companies demanded larger and more efficient furnaces. Ordinary citizens as well as entrepreneurs were infatuated with technology. One invention followed another: an ice-making machine in 1865, the air brake for trains in 1868, the vacuum cleaner in 1869, the telephone in 1876, the phonograph in 1878, the electric light bulb in 1879, and the first American-made gasoline-engine automobile in 1895. By 1900, many Americans had come to expect a steady flow of new and astounding creations.

Thomas A. Edison, born in 1847, stood out in the field of electrical inventions. In 1869, Edison secured the first of the thousand-plus **patents** that he would obtain over his lifetime. In 1876, in Menlo Park, New Jersey, Edison set up the first modern research laboratory. There he and his staff worked at improving electrical technology. Sometimes building on the work of others, Edison's laboratories invented or significantly improved electric lighting, electric motors, the storage battery, the electric locomotive, the phonograph, the mimeograph, and many other products.

Investment bankers played an important role in the development of the new companies that generated and distributed electricity, manufactured electrical equipment, and sold light bulbs and other electrical devices to consumers. General Electric, for example, came about through a series of **mergers** arranged by J. P. Morgan.

Selling to the Nation

Large, vertically integrated manufacturers of consumer goods often produced goods that differed little from each other and cost virtually the same. Such companies sometimes chose not to compete on the basis of price but instead to use advertising to differentiate their products.

Most advertising in the mid-nineteenth century promoted **patent medicines** and books. By 1890, however, large-scale advertising also featured packaged foods, clothing, soap, and petroleum products. After the federal Patent Office registered the first **trademark** in 1870, companies rushed to develop logos that would distinguish their products from nearly identical rivals.

Advertising popularized new ways of selling goods. Previously, most people had purchased goods from small specialty stores, **general stores,** artisans, or door-to-door peddlers. After the Civil War, the appearance of department stores made available a wide range of choices in ready-made products such as clothing and shoes. Such stores relied heavily on newspaper advertising to attract customers. The variety presented by department stores paled, however, when compared to the goods available through the mail-order catalogues

monopoly Exclusive control by one group of the means of producing or selling a product.

Thomas A. Edison American inventor, especially of electrical devices, among them the microphone (1877), the phonograph (1878), and the light bulb (1879).

patent A government grant that gives the creator of an invention the sole right to produce, use, or sell that invention for a set period of time.

merger The union of two or more organizations.

patent medicine A medical preparation that is advertised by a brand name and can be bought without a physician's prescription.

trademark A name or symbol that identifies a product and is officially registered and legally restricted for use by the owner or manufacturer.

general store A store, common in rural areas, that sells a lot of different goods but is not divided into departments.

first offered by Montgomery Ward in 1872 and Sears and Roebuck in 1886. Aimed at rural America, these catalogues offered a wider range of choices than most country-dwellers had ever before seen. Department stores and mail-order houses were possible because manufacturers now produced all sorts of ready-made goods.

Economic Concentration and the Merger Movement

Carnegie and Rockefeller redefined the expectations of other entrepreneurs and provided models for the organization of business. One outcome was that large, complex companies appeared relatively suddenly in the 1880s. At first, they were concentrated in consumer-goods industries.

James B. Duke, for example, used efficient machinery, extensive advertising, and vertical integration to become the largest manufacturer of cigarettes. In 1890, he merged with his four largest competitors to create the American Tobacco Company, which dominated the cigarette industry. Gustavus Swift in the early 1880s began to ship fresh meat from his slaughterhouse in Chicago to the East using his own refrigerated railcars. He eventually added refrigerated storage plants in each city. Other meatpacking companies followed Swift's lead. By 1890, a half dozen firms, all vertically integrated, dominated meatpacking. Monopolies like Standard Oil were fairly rare. More typical was the situation in meatpacking, in which an **oligopoly**—a small number of firms—dominated an industry.

Many new manufacturing companies in the 1870s and early 1880s did not sell stock or use investment bankers to raise capital. Standard Oil and Carnegie Steel expanded by merging with other companies, adding partners, or purchasing companies from retained profits. Rockefeller and Carnegie, for example, concentrated ownership and control in their own hands. The same held true for many other industrial companies until late in the nineteenth century. In 1896, the New York Stock Exchange sold stock in only twenty manufacturing concerns.

At the turn of the century, however, a second phase of vertical and horizontal integration created the need for more capital, and investment bankers began to turn their attention from railroads to heavy industry. In the late 1890s, J. P. Morgan started combining companies in the steel business to create a vertically integrated operation that might challenge Carnegie's dominance. Carnegie had never carried vertical integration to the point of making final products such as wire, barrels, or tubes. He seemed at first to relish the prospect of no-holds-barred competition with what he called "the Trust." When Morgan offered to buy him out, however, he agreed, allowing Morgan in 1901 to create United States Steel, the nation's first billion-dollar corporation.

Other large mergers followed. In 1902, competition between the two largest companies making harvesting machines became so intense that each considered creating its own steel plant. Realizing that this strategy would hurt United States Steel's business, Morgan intervened. Morgan merged the two largest and three smaller harvester firms into International Harvester in 1902, creating a company that dominated 85 percent of the market.

United States Steel and International Harvester were just two of the many new combinations in manufacturing created in a relatively short time at the turn of the century. Between 1898 and 1902, the nation witnessed an astonishing number of mergers. The high point came in 1899, when 1,208 mergers involving $2.3 billion in capital occurred.

Investment bankers sought two primary objectives in reorganizing an industry: to make the industry stable, so that investments would yield predictable **dividends;** and to make the industry efficient, so that dividends would be high. Toward that end, investment bankers placed their representatives on the boards of directors of the new companies. By 1912, the three leading New York banks held 341 directorships in 112 major companies.

Thus, by 1900, many of the characteristics of modern business had emerged. Many industries were

oligopoly A market or industry dominated by a few firms.

dividend A share of profits received by a stockholder.

oligopolistic, dominated by a few vertically integrated companies. **Product differentiation** through advertising had begun. The stock market had moved beyond the sale of railroad securities to play an important role in raising capital for industry.

With the passing of the first generation of industrial empire builders, ownership grew apart from management. Many new business executives were simply hired managers. Ownership rested with hundreds or thousands of stockholders, all of whom wanted a reliable return on their investment. The huge size of the new companies also meant that most managers rarely saw or talked with employees not involved in management or accounting. Many companies treated their employees as expenses to be increased or cut as necessary, with little regard to the impact of their decisions on people.

Workers in Industrial America

The rapid expansion of railroads, mining, and manufacturing created a demand for labor to lay the rails, dig out the ore, tend the furnaces, operate the refineries, and carry out a thousand other tasks. The new workers required to perform these tasks came from across the nation and around the world. Despite the lure of a rags-to-riches triumph like that of Andrew Carnegie, very few became wealthy.

Labor and Mobility

Horatio Alger emerged as one of America's most popular novelists after the success of *Ragged Dick* (1868), the story of an orphaned shoeshine boy who achieves financial success. Alger's books, which sold nearly a hundred million copies, had but one refrain: a poor but hardworking youth, through some unusual opportunity to do good, attracts the attention of a wealthy, powerful person and thereby achieves success, wealth, and happiness. Alger's name became a symbol of the expectation that in America anyone who worked hard and saved could succeed.

The reality of life in industrial America bore little resemblance to Alger's tales. Nearly all successful business leaders came from middle-class or upper-class families. Few workers could expect to move more than a step up the economic scale. An unskilled laborer might become a semiskilled worker, or a skilled worker might become a foreman, but few wage earners moved into the middle class. If they did, it was usually as the owner of a small business.

In industrial America, the treatment of labor differed little from that of the raw materials that went into a finished product. During boom periods, companies advertised for labor and ran their operations at full capacity. When the demand for manufactured goods fell, companies reduced production and laid off workers, cut wages, or reduced hours. Unemployed workers had little to fall back on but their savings or the earnings of other family members. Some churches and private charities gave out food, but state and federal government provided no unemployment benefits. Families that failed to find work might become homeless and go hungry. In a depression, jobs of any sort were scarce, and competition for them was intense.

Workers for Industry

Between the Civil War and 1900, the labor force more than doubled. The largest increases occurred in industries undergoing the greatest changes (see Figure 16.1). Agriculture continued to employ the largest share of the labor force (40 percent in 1900), but the growth of agricultural workers was the smallest of all major categories of workers.

Workers for the rapidly expanding economy came from within the nation and from abroad. Throughout rural New England and the Middle Atlantic states, large numbers of people moved to

product differentiation The use of advertising to distinguish one product from similar products.

Horatio Alger American writer of rags-to-riches stories about impoverished boys who become wealthy through hard work, virtue, and luck.

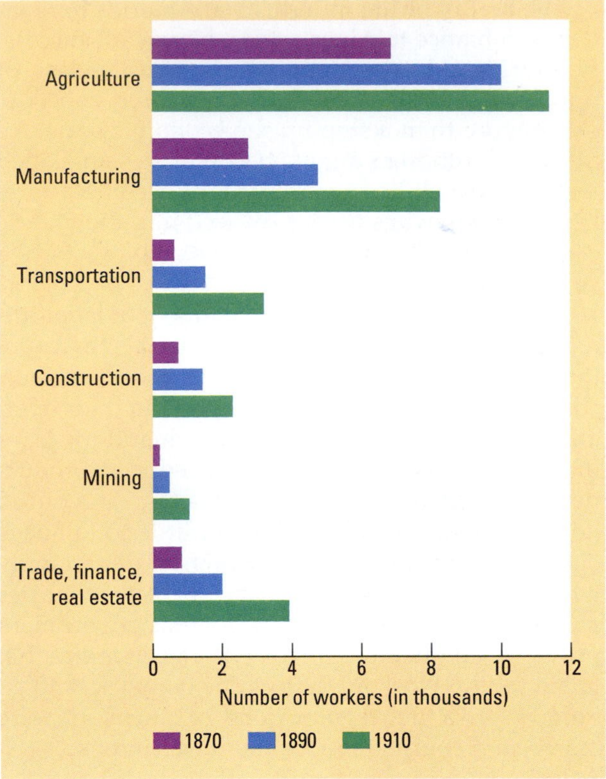
Agriculture
Manufacturing
Transportation
Construction
Mining
Trade, finance, real estate
0
2
4
6
8
10
12
Number of workers (in thousands)
1870
1890
1910

♦ **FIGURE 16.1** Distribution of the Work Force, 1870, 1890, 1910

urban or industrial areas. Owners abandoned small and unproductive farms to take jobs in nearby factory towns or to move west. Many country towns also lost population.

The expanding economy, however, needed more workers than the nation could supply. As a result, the period between 1865 and 1914 witnessed the largest influx of immigrants in American history: more than 26 million people. By 1910, immigrants and their children made up more than 35 percent of the population.

The expanding economy pulled children as well as adults into the ranks of industrial wage earners. In 1910, nearly two million children worked for wages, some as young as 10 years old. More children were employed in the textile industry than in any other kind of manufacturing. Mostly girls, they worked seventy-hour weeks for between 10 and 20 cents per day. Children also worked in tobacco and cotton fields in the South, operated sewing machines in New York, assisted glass blowers in West Virginia factories, and sorted vegetables in Delaware canneries. Most working children turned over all their wages to their parents.

Women as well as children found employment outside the home. Between 1890 and 1910, nearly half of all single women worked for wages, along with a third of widowed or divorced women. Among married women, only 5 to 10 percent did so. Black women were employed at much higher rates in all categories.

Children and mothers worked for wages primarily because the head of the family earned a meager income. One 1875 study showed that the average male factory worker in Lawrence, Massachusetts, earned $500 per year. The average family in Lawrence, however, required at least $600 annually to provide sufficient food, clothing, and shelter. In such circumstances, a family needed two or more incomes.

By 1900, women held a majority of jobs in some occupations. They made up more than 70 percent of the workers in textile factories, more than 70 percent of the nation's secretaries, and 80 percent of telephone operators. Office work usually paid less than factory work but was considered safer and of higher status. Women almost always earned less than their male counterparts. In most industries, the jobs commanding the best pay were reserved for adult males. Even when men and women did the same work, there was usually a pay differential. Not all women worked as wage earners. Some took in laundry, did sewing for neighbors, or rented a room to a boarder. In one eastern factory town in 1912, 90 percent of the families where the husband was the only wage earner took in boarders.

The Transformation of Work

Whether native- or foreign-born, most industrial workers had been born into a rural society. They found industrial work quite different from the work they had done previously. Farm families

♦ The coal mines of Pennsylvania employed more than ten thousand boys under the age of 16. Known as "breaker boys," they sorted coal. Such work was dangerous and sometimes fatal, as this 1911 headline attests. *Library of Congress.*

might work from sunrise to sunset, but they worked at their own speed. Self-employed blacksmiths, carpenters, dressmakers, and other skilled workers also controlled the speed and intensity of their work. Like farmers, they could pace themselves to avoid exhaustion.

People from rural settings expected to work long hours, but they found that industrial work controlled them. The speed of the machines set the pace of the work. If managers ordered a speedup, operators worked faster. Ten- or twelve-hour days at a constant, rapid pace drained the workers. A woman textile worker in 1882 said, "I get so exhausted that I can scarcely drag myself home when night comes." During times of high demand, most steel companies required a seven-day workweek and twelve hours a day. A 27-year-old steelworker in 1910 was blunt: "It's simply a killing pace in the steel works." This was often the literal truth, as exhausted workers were much more likely to be killed in accidents.

Some factory managers saw their dependence on skilled workers as a constraint on their control of production. Such workers set the pace of work, earned more than other workers, and were difficult to replace. Industrial engineer Frederick W. Taylor built a national reputation by redesigning work so that unskilled workers could replace skilled workers. Taylor broke complex tasks down into simpler ones that required few skills to perform. The replacement of skilled workers was intended to increase managers' control over the work process.

The Varieties of Labor Organization and Action

Some workers reacted to the far-reaching changes in the nature of work by choosing to join other workers in efforts to maintain or regain control over their working conditions. They experimented with a variety of organizations. **Craft unions** drew their strength from skilled workers. Some organizations sought reform, hoping to use the power of government to assist workers. Others proposed alternatives to capitalism itself. European immigrants sometimes brought union experience or a commitment to socialism with them. Strikes erupted on an unprecedented scale. Entrepreneurs responded by calling on government to protect property, to maintain order, and to suppress strikes.

Craft Unionism and Its Limits

Skilled workers in many fields outside manufacturing often remained indispensable. In construction, only an experienced carpenter could build

craft union Labor union that organizes skilled workers engaged in a specific craft or trade; also called a trade union.

stairs or hang doors properly. In railroading, only a highly trained engineer could operate a locomotive. In publishing, only a skilled typesetter could transform handwritten copy into lines of lead type. Such workers took pride in the quality of their work and knew that their skill was crucial to their employer's success.

Skilled workers formed the first unions, which were called craft or trade unions because membership was limited to skilled workers in a particular craft or trade. Before the Civil War, workers in most American cities had created local trade unions in attempts to regulate the quality of work, wages, hours, and working conditions for their craft. Local unions eventually formed national trade organizations after 1865.

If most craftworkers within a city belonged to the local union, a strike could be a powerful weapon in the effort to define working conditions. Strikes most often succeeded in prosperous times, when the employer wanted to continue operating and was able to make financial concessions to workers. When the economy experienced a serious downturn, craft unions usually disintegrated because they could not strike effectively. Only after the 1880s did local and national unions develop strategies that permitted them to survive depressions.

Because craft unions limited membership to skilled workers, they were of little help to most industrial workers. Craft unions also frequently restricted their membership to white males. Membership restrictions based on gender or ethnicity were major obstacles to the economic advancement of women and ethnic minorities.

The Great Strike of 1877

In 1877, the nation witnessed widespread labor strife for the first time. When a depression began in 1873, railroad companies reduced operating costs by repeatedly cutting wages. Railroad workers' pay fell by more than a third between 1873 and early 1877. Union leaders talked of organizing a strike but failed to bring one off.

Railway workers took matters into their own hands in 1877 when companies announced additional pay cuts of 10 percent. Baltimore & Ohio Railroad workers in Maryland and West Virginia were the first to strike. Federal troops ultimately restored service on the B & O, but the strike spread to other lines. Strikers shut down the trains in Pittsburgh. When the local militia refused to act against the strikers, the governor of Pennsylvania ordered in militia units from Philadelphia. The troops killed twenty-six people. Strikers and their sympathizers then attacked the militia, forced the troops to retreat, and burned and looted railroad property throughout Pittsburgh.

Strikes and demonstrations of support for strikers erupted across Pennsylvania, New York, and the Midwest. Everywhere, the strikers drew support from their local communities. Coal miners, factory workers, owners of small businesses, farmers, black workers, and women demonstrated their support. State militia, federal troops, and local police eventually broke up the strikes, but not before hundreds had lost their lives and the railroads had suffered property damage of $10 million, half of it in Pittsburgh.

The **Great Strike of 1877** revealed widespread dislike for the new railroad companies and significant community support for strikers. The strike also deeply worried some Americans. They saw in it a forecast of future labor unrest and even revolution. They called for better training for state militia units to suppress such domestic disorders.

The Knights of Labor

The Great Strike suggested that working people could unite across lines of occupation, race, and gender. No organization drew on that potential, however, until the early 1880s, when the **Knights of Labor** emerged as an alternative to craft unions.

Great Strike of 1877 A series of strikes in American cities triggered by railroad wage cuts; the strikes showed widespread support for the demands of workers but were put down by government troops.

Knights of Labor Labor organization founded in 1869; membership, open to all workers, peaked in 1886.

Founded in 1869, the Knights directed their appeals to members of what they called "the producing class." The "producers" included all those who produced value by their labor—the blacksmith whose labor produced tools, the farmer whose labor produced crops, the garment-factory worker whose labor produced clothing. Thus self-employed artisans and farmers were welcome along with wage-earning factory workers. The organization excluded professional gamblers, stockbrokers, lawyers, bankers, and liquor dealers. The Knights accepted African Americans and women as members and helped to provide members of both groups, including the legendary **Mary Harris ("Mother") Jones** (see Individual Choices: "Mother" Jones), with experience in labor organizing.

Terence V. Powderly, a machinist, led the Knights from 1879 to 1893. Under his leadership, they promoted organization, education, and cooperation as their chief objectives. Powderly generally opposed strikes. A lost strike, he argued, often destroyed the local union organization and thereby delayed the more important tasks of education and cooperation. The Knights' endorsement of cooperation was related to the labor theory of value. A major objective of the Knights was "to secure to the workers the full enjoyment of the wealth they create." Toward that end, they promoted a system of producers' and consumers' **cooperatives,** which they hoped would supersede the wage system. The Knights saw cooperatives as an alternative to a capitalistic system based on the payment of wages. They established some 135 cooperatives by the mid-1880s, but few lasted very long. Some folded because of lack of capital, some because of opposition from businesses with which they competed, some because of poor organization.

By the mid-1880s, the Knights of Labor was the most prominent labor organization in the country. Membership jumped from 9,000 in 1879 to 703,000 in 1886. This startling increase in membership came about primarily because local Knights' organizers won strikes against prominent railroads in 1884 and 1885. The Knights' meteoric growth suggested that many working people would band together against the emerging corporate behemoths.

1886: Turning Point for Labor?

The Great Strike of 1877 and the rise of the Knights of Labor were signs of a sense of common purpose among many working people. After 1886, however, labor organizations often found themselves on the defensive and were divided between those trying to make the best of the new realities of industrial capitalism and those seeking to change it.

On May 1, 1886, some eighty thousand Chicagoans marched through the streets in support of an eight-hour workday. Three days later, Chicago police killed several strikers at the McCormick Harvester Works. Hoping to build on the unity demonstrated by the May Day parade, a group of Chicago **anarchists** called a protest meeting for the next day at Haymarket Square. When police tried to break up the rally, someone threw a bomb into the police ranks. The police opened fire on the crowd, and some of the protesters fired back. Eight policemen died, along with an unknown number of demonstrators. About a hundred people, including sixty policemen, suffered injuries.

The Haymarket bombing sparked antiunion feelings. Employers who had opposed unions before now tried to discredit them by playing on

Mary Harris ("Mother") Jones A labor organizer who, beginning in the 1890s, traveled from region to region organizing strikes and protests among coal miners.

Terence V. Powderly Leader of the Knights of Labor who called for cooperative production instead of a wage system.

cooperative A business enterprise in which workers and consumers share ownership and take part in management.

anarchist A person who believes that all forms of government are oppressive and should be abolished.

INDIVIDUAL CHOICES

Choosing to Serve Labor

Mother Jones

Mary Harris Jones, known as Mother Jones, faced many difficult choices in her long career as a union organizer, sometimes involving threats to her personal safety. This picture is from a protest march in 1910, when she was nearly 80 years old. Archives of Labor & Union Affairs, Wayne State University.

In 1891, a white-haired woman more than 60 years old stepped down from a train in an Appalachian mining town. A man anxiously asked her name, and she told him. Thirty years later, she still recalled his response: "The superintendent [manager for the coal-mining company] told me that if you came down here he would blow out your brains. He said he didn't want to see you 'round these parts." The threat had no effect, for she had long since chosen her life's direction. "You tell the superintendent that I am not coming to see him anyway. I am coming to see the miners." For almost fifty years, Mary Harris Jones chose "to see the miners" and to bring them the message of unionism in the face of hostility and threats from mining companies and the local officials who did the companies' bidding.

According to her own account, Mary Harris was born in Ireland in 1830 and came to the United States as a child, with her father. As a young woman, she taught school and worked as a dressmaker or seamstress, then married George Jones, an iron molder and union activist. Her expectations as a wife and mother were shattered, however, when she lost her entire family—her husband and their four children—in a yellow-fever epidemic in 1867.

fears of radical-inspired terrorism. Some people who supported what they saw as legitimate union goals shrank back in horror. In Chicago, eight leading anarchists stood trial for inciting the bombing and, on flimsy evidence, were convicted. Four were hanged, one committed suicide, and three remained in jail until they were released in 1893 by a sympathetic governor, John Peter Altgeld.

Uniting the Craft Unions: The American Federation of Labor

Two weeks after the Haymarket bombing, trade union leaders met in Philadelphia to propose an agreement between the trade unions and the Knights: trade unions would recruit skilled workers, and the Knights would limit themselves to unskilled workers. When the Knights refused to go

On her own, she opened a dressmaking shop in Chicago. Her clients included those she called "the aristocrats of Chicago," and she witnessed "the luxury and extravagance of their lives." The contrast between the opulent expectations of her wealthy clients and tightly constrained lives of the poor left her deeply disturbed.

"Often while sewing for the lords and barons who lived in magnificent houses on the Lake Shore Drive," she recalled in her autobiography, "I would look out of the plate glass windows and see the poor, shivering wretches, jobless and hungry, walking along the frozen lake front. The contrast of their condition with that of the tropical comfort of the people for whom I sewed was painful to me."

In 1871, her shop burned in the great fire that swept much of the city. Thereafter, she chose to give much of her time to helping workers, first through the Knights of Labor. In 1882, she first took part in a strike by coal miners.

As the Knights of Labor began to disintegrate after 1886, some of its trade assemblies (organizations limited to workers in one trade) chose to affiliate with the American Federation of Labor (AFL). In 1890, one received an AFL charter as the United Mine Workers of America (UMW), but it remained an industrial union that admitted both white and black members. Until her death in 1930, Jones fought for the UMW. She became a familiar figure throughout the sooty valleys of Appalachia, where miners' families lived in wretched, company-owned shacks, their lives closely constrained by the power of the mining companies, the often brutal company guards, and compliant local officials.

Jones's white hair, grandmotherly appearance, and deep loyalty to those she called "her boys" earned her the nickname "Mother." Others called her the "miners' angel." One county attorney, however, labeled her "the most dangerous woman in the country" in recognition of her ability to inspire men and women to oppose the mining companies. Her admirers recounted stories of her bravery in the face of danger. One insisted that "she wasn't afraid of the devil."

Mother Jones's talents lay in public speaking and in organizing demonstrations to capture public attention and sympathy. In one strike in 1900, she organized miners' wives to protest against strikebreakers by pounding on pots and pans and frightening the mules that pulled the mine carts. In 1903, she took up the cause of the children who worked in textile mills. By organizing a march of mill children to the home of President Theodore Roosevelt, she captured headlines with her living, walking display of the children's deformities and injuries caused by mill work.

Mother Jones made an unusual choice in her decision to spend the last half of her life as a labor organizer and agitator. But she apparently held traditional expectations about the role of women in society, arguing that their place was in the home. She seems to have seen her own work as an extension of her role as mother. Deprived of her own family, she sought to nurture and protect a much larger family of workers.

along with this plan, the trade unions formed the **American Federation of Labor (AFL).** The combined membership of the thirteen founding unions amounted to only 140,000.

Samuel Gompers became the first president of the new organization. Born in London in 1850, he learned the cigarmaker's trade before coming to the United States in 1863. He became president of the Cigarmakers' Union in 1877. Gompers contin-

American Federation of Labor (AFL) National organization of trade unions founded in 1886; it used strikes and boycotts to improve the lot of workers.

Samuel Gompers First president of the American Federation of Labor; he eventually argued to divorce labor organizing from political theory and stressed practical demands involving wages and hours.

ued as president of the AFL from 1886 until his death in 1924. Gompers opposed labor involvement with radicalism or politics. Instead, he focused on higher wages, shorter hours, and improved working conditions.

Most AFL leaders defined their task as the limited one of winning immediate struggles over wages and hours rather than the radical one of changing capitalism. Unlike the Knights of Labor, they did not try to transform the lives of all workers as a class. Instead, trade union leaders argued that unions should focus solely on their own members.

After the 1880s, the AFL suffered little competition from the Knights of Labor. By 1890, the Knights could claim only 100,000 members. This collapse stemmed only in part from the opposition of the trade unions. The failure of several strikes in the late 1880s cost the Knights many supporters.

Labor on the Defensive: Homestead and Pullman

In the late 1880s and 1890s, even highly skilled workers often found that craft unions could not withstand the power of the new industrial companies. A major demonstration of this reality came in 1892 in Pennsylvania, at Carnegie's **Homestead steel plant,** a stronghold of the Amalgamated Association of Iron, Steel, and Tin Workers. One of Carnegie's partners, Henry Clay Frick, managed the Homestead plant. When the union refused major wage cuts, Frick locked union members out of the plant and prepared to hire replacements.

Frick's first step was to bring in three hundred agents of the Pinkerton detective agency. They came by riverboat, but ten thousand strikers and community supporters resisted when they tried to land. Shots rang out. In the ensuing gun battle, seven Pinkertons and nine strikers were killed. The Pinkertons surrendered, leaving the strikers in control of the town and the plant. Soon after, the governor of Pennsylvania sent in the state militia to take control from the strikers. The militia did its job. The Amalgamated Association never recovered. This crushing defeat of the nation's largest craft union indicated that no union could stand up to the new industrial companies.

A similar fate befell the most ambitious organizing drive of the 1890s. In 1893, under the leadership of **Eugene V. Debs,** railway workers launched the American Railway Union (ARU). Within a year, the ARU claimed 150,000 members and was the largest single union in the nation. The ARU did not affiliate with the AFL.

The twenty-four railway companies that entered Chicago had formed the General Managers Association (GMA) to combat unions. The GMA decided to challenge Debs's union when the ARU supported a strike of Pullman car workers in 1894. When the ARU disconnected **Pullman cars** from every train, the GMA insisted that only railway managers had the authority to determine which cars would make up a train. The managers promised to fire any worker who observed the boycott of Pullman cars.

Within a short time, all 150,000 ARU members were on strike. Rail traffic in Chicago came to a halt, affecting railways across the country. The GMA found an ally in U.S. Attorney General Richard Olney, a former railroad lawyer. Olney convinced President **Grover Cleveland** to use thousands of federal troops to protect trains operated by strikebreakers. Mobs lashed out at railroad property, especially in Chicago, burning trains and buildings. ARU leaders condemned the violence, but a dozen people died before it ended. Union leaders, including Debs, were jailed, and the union was destroyed.

Homestead steel plant Carnegie steel plant in Pennsylvania where state troops in 1892 put down a strike after a violent clash between striking workers and Pinkerton detectives.

Eugene V. Debs American Railway Union leader who was jailed after the Pullman strike; he converted to socialism and later ran for president.

Pullman car A railroad car with private compartments or seats that can be made up into berths for sleeping.

Grover Cleveland New York politician and advocate of clean government who was president of the United States from 1885 through 1889 and again from 1893 through 1897.

♦ This drawing of the administration building for Chicago's Columbian Exposition in 1893 emphasizes the planners' dramatic use of classical architecture and modern electric lighting. Because its buildings were all white, the exposition was called the "White City." *Culver Pictures.*

The depression that began in 1893 further weakened the unions. Many union members were unemployed. Nevertheless, the AFL hung on. By 1897, the organization claimed a membership of nearly 270,000. By then, working people had repeatedly demonstrated their discontent with the constraints they faced in the new economic order.

The Nation Transformed

By 1900, Americans could be excused if they seemed anxious about the economic changes of the previous thirty years. While some celebrated the outcomes of the economic transformation, others argued whether competition or cooperation was the best choice for achieving and maintaining progress.

Survival of the Fittest?

The concentration of power and wealth during the late nineteenth century generated comment and concern at the time. The most prominent statement on the subject was known as **Social Darwinism.** Charles Darwin's work on evolution had concluded that only the toughest, strongest, or cleverest creatures survived in competition against other creatures.

Herbert Spencer in England and William Graham Sumner, a professor of political economy at Yale, adapted Darwin's reasoning to the human situation, producing Social Darwinism. Social Darwinists contended that competition among people produced "progress" through "survival of the fittest." Further, they argued, efforts to ease the harsh impact of competition only protected the unfit. Conversely, powerful entrepreneurs constituted "the fittest" and benefited all humankind by their accomplishments.

Andrew Carnegie enthusiastically embraced Spencer's arguments. "Civilization took its start from that day that the capable, industrious workman said to his incompetent and lazy fellow, 'If thou dost not sow, thou shalt not reap,'" Carnegie wrote.

Although many Americans subscribed to the Social Darwinism propounded by Spencer, Sumner, and Carnegie, many others did not. One humorist poked fun at the three thousand libraries that Carnegie donated to the public by suggesting that they would serve the community better if they contained a kitchen and beds. Henry George,

Social Darwinism The application of Darwinism to the study of human society; a theory that people who succeed in competition do so because of genetic and biological superiority.

a San Francisco journalist, concluded in *Progress and Poverty* (1879) that "material progress does not merely fail to relieve poverty—it actually produces it." The sociologist Lester Frank Ward refuted Social Darwinism by suggesting that biological competition produced bare survival, not civilization. Civilization, he concluded, represented "a triumph of mind" over "ceaseless and aimless competition."

SUMMARY

Expectations
Constraints
Choices
Outcomes

After 1865, large-scale manufacturing developed quickly in the United States on a foundation of abundant natural resources, a pool of skilled workers, expanding harvests, and favorable government policies. The *outcome* was the transformation of the U.S. economy.

Entrepreneurs made *choices* that improved and extended railway lines, creating a national transportation network. Manufacturers and merchants developed new *expectations* based on a national market for raw materials and finished goods. Railroads were the first businesses to grapple with many problems related to size, and they made *choices* that other businesses imitated. Investment bankers combined separate rail companies into larger and more profitable systems.

Andrew Carnegie and John D. Rockefeller were the best known of many entrepreneurs whose *choices* produced manufacturing operations of unprecedented size and complexity. By 1900, oligopoly and vertical integration characterized many industries. Technology and advertising emerged as important competitive devices.

Workers *chose* to migrate to expanding industrial centers from rural areas in the United States and other countries. The new work force included not only adult males but also women and children. Industrial workers had little control over their work and often faced unpleasant or dangerous working conditions.

Some workers *chose* to form labor organizations to fight the *constraints* of low wages, long hours, and poor conditions. Espousing cooperatives and reform, the Knights of Labor *chose* to open their membership to the unskilled, to African Americans, and to women. The Knights died out after 1890. The American Federation of Labor was formed by craft unions. The AFL *chose* to reject radicalism and to work instead within capitalism to improve wages, hours, and conditions for its members. Major strikes between 1877 and 1894 revealed both the depth of workers' discontent and the strength of their organizations. By the mid-1890s, however, labor organizations were on the defensive.

Social Darwinists acclaimed unrestricted competition for producing progress and survival of the fittest. Critics countered that civilization represented a triumph of rationality and cooperation over competition.

SUGGESTED READINGS

Brody, David. *Steelworkers in America: The Nonunion Era* (1960).

A classic study of the lives of steelworkers and the nature of their work.

Dubofsky, Melvyn. *Industrialism and the American Worker, 1865–1920*, 3rd ed. (1996).

A brief introduction to the topic, organized chronologically.

Jones, Mary Harris "Mother." *The Autobiography of Mother Jones*, ed. Mary Field Parton (1925; reprint, 1980).

A self-portrait of the feisty union organizer; not always precise regarding facts and dates, but fascinating for its account of one woman's activism.

Lamoreaux, Naomi. *The Great Merger Movement in American Business, 1895–1904* (1985).

An impressive study of the merger movement using detailed case histories of particular industries.

Montgomery, David. *The Fall of the House of Labor: The Workplace, the State, and American Labor Activism, 1865–1925* (1987).

Looks at the workplace and develops workers' responses to their situation from that perspective.

Porter, Glenn. *The Rise of Big Business, 1860–1910*, 2nd ed. (1992).

A brief introduction to the topic, including the role of the railroads, vertical and horizontal integration, and the merger movement.

THE WEST, 1865–1902 This map identifies various parts of the West. As you can see, the West had very few cities, and those tended to be located on the edges of the region.

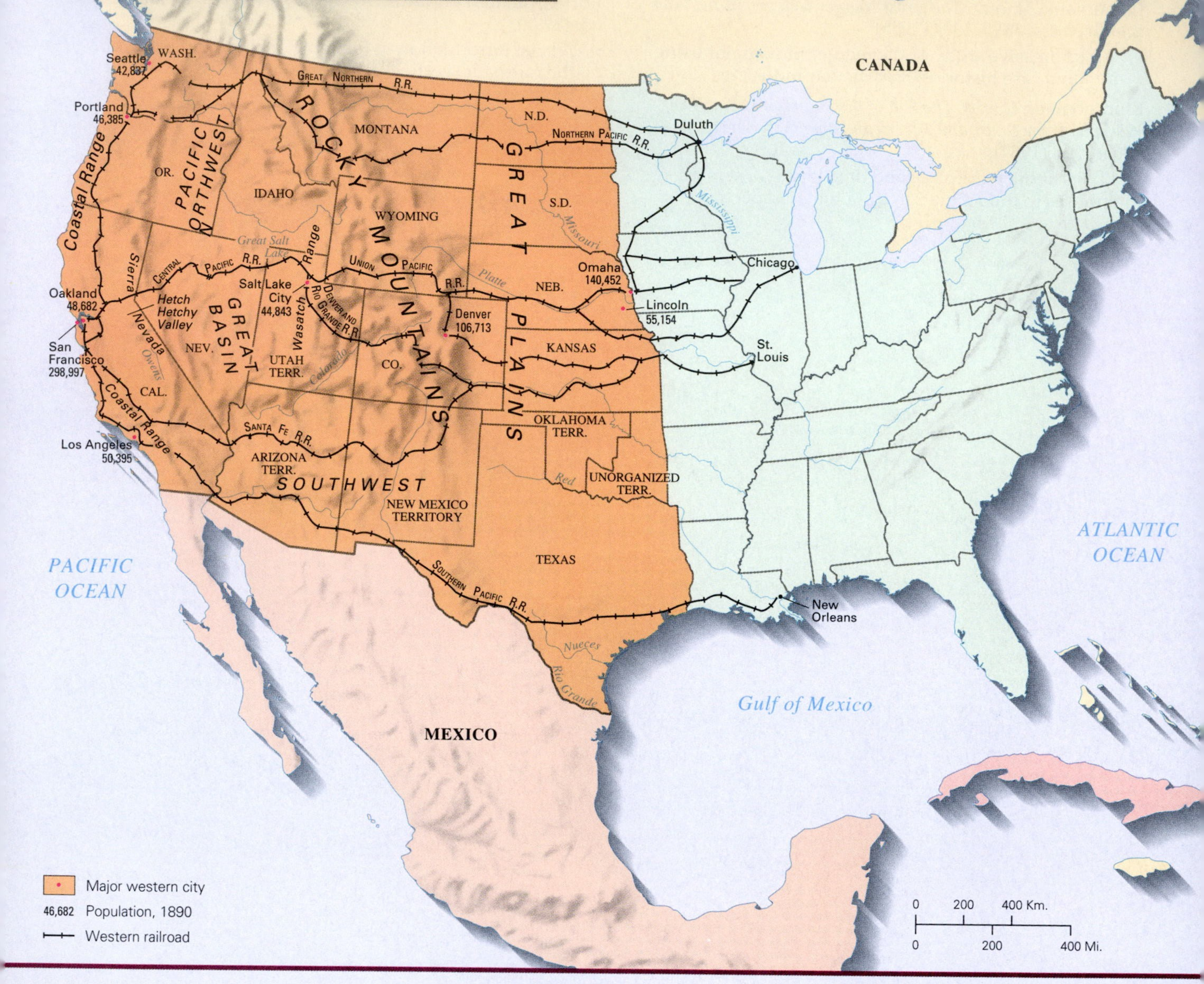
CANADA
WASH.
Seattle
42,837
Portland
46,385
GREAT NORTHERN R.R.
NORTHERN PACIFIC R.R.
N.D.
Duluth
MONTANA
ROCKY MOUNTAINS
GREAT PLAINS
PACIFIC NORTHWEST
OR.
IDAHO
Coastal Range
S.D.
WYOMING
Mississippi
Missouri
Great Salt Lake
Wasatch Range
Sierra Nevada
CENTRAL PACIFIC R.R.
UNION PACIFIC R.R.
Platte
Chicago
Omaha
140,452
NEB.
Oakland
48,682
Hetch Hetchy Valley
GREAT BASIN
Salt Lake City
44,843
DENVER AND RIO GRANDE R.R.
Denver
106,713
Lincoln
55,154
San Francisco
298,997
NEV.
UTAH TERR.
CO.
KANSAS
St. Louis
Owens
Colorado
CAL.
OKLAHOMA TERR.
SANTA FE R.R.
Los Angeles
50,395
ARIZONA TERR.
SOUTHWEST
Red
UNORGANIZED TERR.
NEW MEXICO TERRITORY
TEXAS
PACIFIC OCEAN
ATLANTIC OCEAN
SOUTHERN PACIFIC R.R.
New Orleans
Nueces
Rio Grande
Gulf of Mexico
MEXICO
Major western city
46,682 Population, 1890
Western railroad
0 200 400 Km.
0 200 400 Mi.

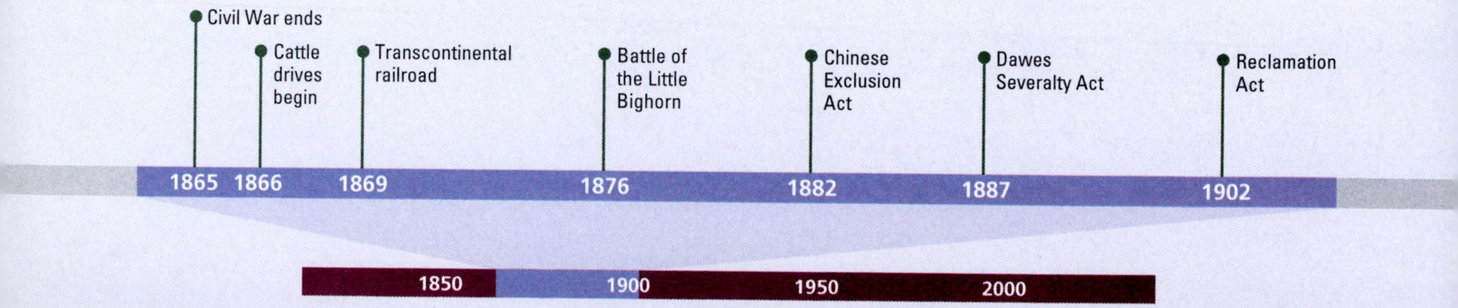
Civil War ends
Cattle drives begin
Transcontinental railroad
Battle of the Little Bighorn
Chinese Exclusion Act
Dawes Severalty Act
Reclamation Act
1865
1866
1869
1876
1882
1887
1902
1850
1900
1950
2000

CHAPTER 17

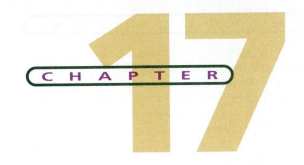

Conflict and Change in the West, 1865–1902

War for the West

- What did federal policymakers hope to accomplish in their choices regarding American Indians after the Civil War?
- How did western Indians choose to respond?
- What expectations probably lay behind their responses? How were the expectations of western Indians different from those of federal policymakers?

Mormons, Cowboys, and Sodbusters: The Transformation of the West, Part I

- How did Mormons, the range cattle industry, and farmers respond to the constraints they faced in the West?
- What were the outcomes of their choices for western development?

Railroads, Mining, Agribusiness, Logging, and Finance: The Transformation of the West, Part II

- What constraints confronted western entrepreneurs engaged in mining, logging, and agriculture?
- How did choices regarding railroads, mining, agribusiness, finance capitalism, and water promote the development of the West?

Ethnicity and Race in the West

- Compare the constraints faced by Indians, Latinos, and Chinese immigrants between 1850 and 1900 and analyze the choices that each group made.

The West in American Thought

- How does the myth of the West compare with the reality?

INTRODUCTION

Expectations
Constraints
Choices
Outcomes

Americans have shown a long-lasting interest in the West of the late nineteenth century. Popular fiction and drama have glorified the West as a land where pioneers overcame great odds. The reality of western life, however, was somewhat different.

At the close of the Civil War, many Americans looked to the West with high *expectations*. Previously, the issue of slavery had *constrained* federal action to develop the West. The secession of the southern states removed that *constraint*, and the Republicans who took charge in Washington in 1861 moved quickly to use federal power to open the West to economic development and white settlement.

As Americans faced west, they held some contradictory *expectations*. On the one hand, prior experience suggested the steady westward extension of family farms. On the other hand, travelers to the West had described it as an area of vast deserts, forbidding mountains, and well-armed, mounted Indian warriors. Potential *constraints* such as these suggested that parts of the West might never be developed like the eastern half of the nation.

In most of the West, rainfall was markedly lower than in the East. This scarcity of water *constrained* development and presented a new set of *choices*. What sort of development was appropriate in a region with little rain? How could western water be harnessed to support development? Who would control the water, and who would benefit from it?

Similarly, the ethnic and racial composition of the West differed significantly from that of the East and South. In 1865, the population of the northeastern and north-central United States was almost entirely of European descent. The South was a biracial society: white and black. But the West was home both to eastern Indians who had been pushed beyond the Mississippi River and to tribal groups who claimed it as their ancestral homeland. It was also home to significant numbers of people who spoke Spanish, who were often of mixed white and Indian ancestry, and whose families had lived in the region long before the arrival of the first Yankees. Finally, the West Coast had attracted immigrants from Asia, especially China, who had *chosen* to cross the Pacific in the *expectation* of making their fortunes in America. In the late nineteenth century, these concentrations of ethnic groups marked the West as a distinctive place.

As individual Americans made *choices* that shaped the development of the West, federal officials also faced important *choices*. The basic *choice* to use the public domain to speed economic development had already been made by 1862. But a related *choice* remained: what to do about the Indians who occupied much of the land. Given the *choices* and *constraints* facing Americans in the West, the *outcome* of efforts to develop the land was sometimes quite different from previous experience and from the *expectations* of those involved. Overall, though, the *outcome* was that the western half of the United States underwent immense change during this period.

CHRONOLOGY

Conflict and Change in the West

1700s	Horse culture spreads throughout the Great Plains
1847	First Mormon settlements near Great Salt Lake
1848	Treaty of Guadalupe Hidalgo
1849	California gold rush begins
1851	New federal Indian policy
1862	Homestead Act
1865	Civil War ends
1866–1880	Cattle drives north from Texas
1867–1868	Treaties establish major western reservations
1868–1869	Army's winter campaign against southern Plains Indians
1869	First transcontinental railroad completed
Early 1870s	Cattle raising begins on northern Plains
1870s	Destruction of buffalo herds Silver mining boom in Nevada
1870s–1880s	Extension of farming to the Great Plains
1871–1885	Anti-Chinese riots across the West
1874	Patent issued for barbed wire
1874–1875	Indian resistance ends on southern Plains
1876	Spring and summer campaign on northern Plains Indian victory in Battle of the Little Bighorn
1877	Army subdues last major Indian resistance on northern Plains Surrender and death of Crazy Horse Chief Joseph and the Nez Perces flee Workingmen's party of California attacks Chinese
1881	Surrender of Sitting Bull
1882	Chinese Exclusion Act
1884	Federal court prohibits hydraulic mining
1886	Surrender of Geronimo
1886–1887	Severe winter damages northern cattle business
1887	Dawes Severalty Act
Late 1880s	Reduced rainfall
1890	Conflict at Wounded Knee Creek
1892	Sierra Club formed
1893	Frederick Jackson Turner presents his frontier thesis
1899	National Irrigation Association formed
1902	Reclamation Act
1907	Japanese immigration ends
1920s	Western movies help make cowboy a mythical figure

War for the West

When Congress chose to use the public domain—western land—to encourage economic development, most white Americans considered the West to be largely vacant. In fact, American Indians lived throughout the West. The most tragic outcome of the development of the West was certainly the experience of the Indians.

The Plains Indians

By the time white Americans began to move west, the acquisition of horses and guns had already transformed the lives of many American Indians. This transformation occurred most dramatically among the tribes living on the **Great Plains,** the vast, relatively flat, treeless region that stretches across the center of the nation. The introduction of the horse to the Great Plains took place slowly, spreading in the late seventeenth century from the Spanish settlements in New Mexico. By the mid-eighteenth century, French and English traders had begun to provide guns to the Indians in return for furs. Thus guns entered the Plains from the east and northeast, and horses entered from the southwest. Together they transformed the culture of many of the Plains tribes.

The Plains Indians were divided into sedentary farmers and nomadic buffalo hunters. The Pawnees, Arikaras, Wichitas, Hidatsas, Mandans, Omahas, Otos, Osages, and similar groups lived a settled life in large, permanent villages located in river valleys. These Indians grew corn, squash, pumpkins, beans, sunflowers, and tobacco. They gathered wild fruits and vegetables and hunted and fished near their villages. Before the arrival of horses, entire villages went on extended hunting trips for buffalo twice a year, once in the early summer after the crops were planted, then again in the fall after the harvest. Horses changed the culture of these Indians only slightly.

By contrast, the horse revolutionized the way of life of some groups who became nomadic hunters. Indians on horseback could kill twice as many buffalo as Indians on foot. Thus the horse substantially increased the number of people the Plains could support. The buffalo provided food (meat), clothing and shelter (made from hides), implements (made from bones and horns), and even fuel (dried dung). Some groups completely abandoned farming and followed the buffalo herds year round. By the early nineteenth century, the horse culture included the Blackfeet, Crows, **Lakotas, Cheyennes,** Arapahos, Kiowas, and Comanches. The Lakotas, the largest of these groups, were often called the Sioux, meaning "enemy," by other Indians.

Whether nomadic buffalo hunters or sedentary farmers, the Plains Indians viewed the land very differently than white settlers did. Europeans be-

♦ In the 1830s, George Catlin painted this buffalo hunt in what is now Montana. The acquisition of horses greatly increased the Indians' ability to kill buffalo. The Cheyennes, an extreme example, abandoned farming and staked their livelihood entirely on hunting. *"Buffalo Chase, Mouth of the Yellowstone" by George Catlin. National Museum of American Art, Washington, DC/Art Resource, NY.*

Great Plains High grassland of western North America, stretching from the Mississippi valley to the Rocky Mountains; it is generally level, treeless, and semiarid.

Lakotas Indian people who lived on the northern Great Plains; hostile tribes called them *Sioux,* which means "enemy."

Cheyennes Indian people who became nomadic buffalo hunters after migrating to the Great Plains in the eighteenth century.

lieved in individual ownership of land. According to Indian tradition, land was to be used but not owned. Horses, weapons, **tipis,** and clothing were all individually owned, but land was not. Among farming peoples, a tribal leader divided farmland among the female heads of each family on the basis of family size.

For the most part, the individual ownership of property was not a pressing goal for Indians. A person achieved high social standing not by accumulating possessions but by sharing. Francis La Flesche, the son of an Omaha leader, received the following advice from his mother: "When you see a boy barefooted and lame, take off your moccasins and give them to him. When you see a boy hungry, bring him to your home and give him food."

The Plains Indians did on occasion seek to gain additional hunting territory, particularly when tribes came under pressure from European westward expansion. But many conflicts stemmed from the desire to seek revenge or to display bravery, not for individual gain.

The Plains Wars

During the 1830s and after, federal Indian policy had focused on removing eastern Indians to land west of the Mississippi River. Federal Indian policy over the next fifty years reduced Indian landholdings west of the Mississippi as farmers, adventurers, and gold seekers made their way west.

In 1851, Congress approved a new Indian policy intended to provide each tribe with a definite territory on which it was to live. Federal officials initially planned large reservations taking up much of the Great Plains. After the Civil War, however, to clear the way for the construction of a transcontinental railroad across the central Plains, they hoped to restrict the Indians to three great reservations in the West—one in the northern Plains, one in the southern Plains, and one in the Southwest. The remainder of the West was to be opened up for development by white settlers. Indians on the reservations were to receive food and shelter from the government and were to be taught how to farm and raise cattle.

At the same time, federal officials encouraged growing numbers of white buffalo hunters to kill the buffalo for meat, hides, and sport. The buffalo's demise came quickly once tanneries in the East began to buy hides. In the mid-1870s, more than 10 million buffalo were killed and stripped of their hides, which sold for a dollar or more each. By 1883, a few hundred animals were left. The Plains Indians' way of life was doomed.

By mid-1868, federal officials thought their new reservation policy had made a promising start. Under treaties signed in 1867, the major southern tribes accepted reservations in Indian Territory (see Map 17.1) after the army presented a show of force. In 1868, the Lakotas agreed to a Great Sioux Reservation in what is now the western half of South Dakota. In the same year, the Crows and Navajos agreed to reservations in Montana and the Southwest, respectively.

Some southern Plains tribes, however, refused to live on reservations. Moreover, they occasionally attacked stagecoach stations, ranches, travelers crossing the Plains, and even military units. After one such attack, General William Tecumseh Sherman, the Civil War general who had become commander of the army on the Plains, declared that all Indians not on reservations "are hostile and will remain so till killed off."

In 1868–1869, Sherman launched a winter campaign on the southern Plains to deal with such "hostile" Indians. The leader of this expedition, General Philip Sheridan, another Union army veteran, directed his men to "destroy their villages and ponies, to kill and hang all warriors, and bring back all women and children." This brutal campaign convinced most southern Plains tribes that further resistance was pointless. Another campaign over the winter of 1874–1875 made all the remaining southern Plains tribes surrender.

Hunting grounds outside the Great Sioux Reservation in the Powder River region of Montana and Wyoming caused conflict on the northern Plains. As the Northern Pacific Railroad prepared to lay track in southern Montana, the government took steps to force all Indians out of the region and onto the reservation.

tipi Tent made from buffalo hide and used as a portable dwelling by Indians on the Great Plains.

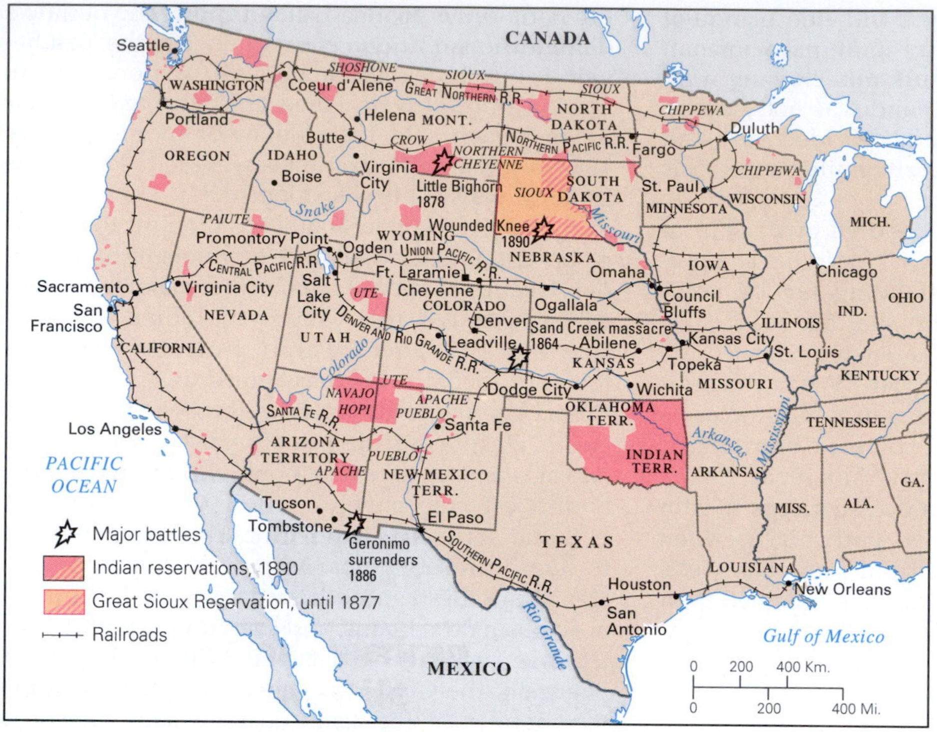

♦ **MAP 17.1 Indian Reservations** This map indicates the location of most western Indian reservations in 1890, as well as the Great Sioux Reservation before it was broken up and severely reduced in size. Note how the development of a few large reservations on the northern Plains and others on the southern Plains opened the central Plains for railroad construction and agricultural development.

The **Great Sioux War** began in 1876 when Sheridan directed troops to converge on Indians in the Powder River area from three different directions. One part of the operation went dreadfully wrong when Lieutenant Colonel George A. Custer, without waiting for the other units, sent his 7th Cavalry against an Indian camp. The encampment on the **Little Bighorn River** proved to be one of the largest ever on the northern Plains, combining several bands of Lakotas and Cheyennes led by **Crazy Horse** and **Sitting Bull.** Custer and nearly three hundred of his men lost their lives in the battle. The Indians then scattered, knowing that their victory would bring massive retaliation.

In the winter of 1876–1877, Sheridan launched another campaign of **attrition.** Troops defeated some Indian bands. Hunger and cold drove most others to surrender. Crazy Horse surrendered only

Great Sioux War War between the tribes that took part in the Battle of the Little Bighorn and the U.S. Army; it ended in 1881 with the surrender of Sitting Bull.

Little Bighorn River River in Montana where in 1876 Lieutenant Colonel George Custer discovered a large Indian encampment and ordered an attack in which he and his men were killed.

Crazy Horse Lakota leader who resisted white encroachment in the Black Hills and fought at the Little Bighorn River in 1876; he was killed by U.S. soldiers in 1877.

Sitting Bull Lakota leader who fought at the Little Bighorn River in 1876 and fled with his people to Canada before surrendering in 1881.

attrition A gradual decrease in number or strength caused by constant stress.

when the government promised that he could live in the Powder River region. Several months later, he was killed when he resisted being put into jail. Sitting Bull and his band escaped to Canada and remained there until 1881, when they finally surrendered. The Great Sioux War had ended. The government then cut up the Great Sioux Reservation to allow for white settlement, taking away the Powder River region and the Black Hills.

The Last Indian Wars

After the Great Sioux War, no Indian group had the capacity for sustained resistance. The last sizable group to refuse to live on a reservation was Geronimo's band of Chiricahua Apaches, who finally gave up in 1886. Small groups occasionally left their reservations but were tracked down by federal troops. One notable instance was the attempted flight to Canada in 1877 of the Nez Perces, led by **Chief Joseph.** They eluded the army for three months as they traveled through Montana toward Canada. More than two hundred died along the way. Joseph surrendered on the specific condition that the Nez Perces be permitted to return to their previous home. Nevertheless, federal officials sent the Nez Perces to Indian Territory.

The last major armed confrontation between the army and the Indians came in 1890, on the Pine Ridge Reservation in South Dakota. There some Lakotas had taken up a new religion, the **Ghost Dance,** that promised to return the land to the Indians, restore the buffalo, and sweep away the whites. Fearing an uprising, federal authorities ordered the Lakotas to stop their dance ritual and called for the arrest of their leader, Sitting Bull (see Individual Choices: Sitting Bull). Sitting Bull was killed when some Ghost Dancers tried to prevent his arrest. A small band of Lakotas then tried to flee, but they were captured and taken to a site near **Wounded Knee Creek.** When an Indian refused to surrender his gun, a brief battle took place that left some 250 Indians and 25 soldiers dead.

The events at Wounded Knee marked the end of armed conflict on the Plains. But the end of the horse culture had been written long before. Once the federal government chose to encourage rapid economic development in the West rather than reserving it for Indians, the outcome was inevitable.

Mormons, Cowboys, and Sodbusters: The Transformation of the West, Part I

Long before the last battles between the army and the Indians, the economic development of the West was well under way. Environmental and other constraints, as well as the cultural expectations of men and women seeking to live in that region, determined the nature of western development. The Mormons' choices in the Great Basin differed significantly from those made by the ranchers and farmers of the Great Plains.

Zion in the Great Basin

By 1865, development of the Great Basin region between the Rocky Mountains and the Sierra Nevada was already well advanced as a result of the **Mormons'** efforts. Led by Brigham Young, the Mormons in 1847 had chosen to settle near the Great Salt Lake. They expected to establish a settlement outside the United States so remote that no one would interfere with them. The Great Basin region, however, was incorporated into the United States after the Mexican War.

Chief Joseph Nez Perces chief who led his people in an attempt to escape to Canada in 1877; after a grueling journey, they were forced to surrender and were exiled to Indian Territory.

Ghost Dance Indian religion centered on a ritual dance; it promised the coming of an Indian messiah who would banish the whites and restore the land to the Indians.

Wounded Knee Creek Site of a conflict in 1890 between Lakota Indians and U.S. troops attempting to suppress the Ghost Dance religion; it was the last major encounter between Indians and the army.

Mormons Members of the Church of Jesus Christ of Latter-Day Saints, founded in New York in 1830.

INDIVIDUAL CHOICES

Choosing to Defend His Homeland

Sitting Bull

After Sitting Bull returned to the United States from Canada in 1881, he became a favorite subject for many photographers. This photo dates to the mid-1880s, when he was about 50 years old. Denver Public Library.

The U.S. Army had high expectations for the great conference of tribes from throughout the northern plains at Fort Laramie in 1868. Federal officials had two major purposes: to end attacks along the Bozeman Trail, which ran through eastern Wyoming, and to secure agreements from the northern Plains Indians to live on a reservation well to the north of the major transportation routes that ran through the new state of Nebraska. At the conference, the army agreed to close the Bozeman Trail and to abandon the forts along it if the Lakotas and their allies agreed to live on the Great Sioux Reservation—the entire western half of what is now South Dakota.

Many of the Lakota leaders were willing to consider the army's proposal. Their battles against the forts along the Bozeman Trail had included both great victories and serious losses. Red Cloud, leader of many of those struggles, was the most prominent of those who agreed to live on the reservation. Most of those who signed the treaty, however, probably had little idea of what they approved.

Sitting Bull chose not to accept any of the treaty's provisions. Instead, he continued to follow the buffalo herd and to defend the territories that his people, the Hunkpapa Lakotas, had wrested from their enemies, the Crows. Anyone—Indian or white—who invaded those regions was in peril. At the same time, he necessarily chose to fight against efforts by the U.S. Army to force the Hunkpapas to live on a reservation and to abandon their traditional way of life. Sitting Bull soon emerged as one of the most significant leaders of opposition to the treaty and to reservation life.

In 1868, Sitting Bull was in his mid-30s and had earned a reputation for fearlessness in battles with the enemies of the Hunkpapas, especially the Crows. He had counted his first coup at the age of 14, when he killed a Crow in a raid and earned the name Tatanka-Iotanka, Sitting Bull, a tribute to his fighting endurance. By 1857, when Sitting Bull was probably 26 years old, the Hunkpapas named him one of the tribal war chiefs in recognition of his many victories in battles with the Crows and other Indian enemies of the Lakotas. He also came to be considered a holy man, whose visions were messages from Wakantanka, the Great Mystery. To his people, Sitting Bull embodied the Lakota virtues of bravery, fortitude, generosity, and wisdom.

Sitting Bull was joined in his rejection of the Fort Laramie Treaty by perhaps a third of all the Lakotas, especially members of the Hunkpapas. The Oglala Lakotas divided, many following Red Cloud to the reservation and some following Crazy Horse to the west of the reservation to live on the "unceded lands" of northwestern Wyoming. In 1869, a group of Sitting Bull's supporters arranged a gathering of Lakotas and Cheyennes at which Sitting Bull was named to an unprecedented position: war chief of the entire Lakota Nation. Given the fluidity of leadership among the Lakotas, the reservation Lakotas did not accept this action, nor did all those who refused to observe the treaty. But it was a signal honor.

Over the next decade, Sitting Bull exercised greater leadership among the various Lakota tribes than any previous leader had. On June 6, 1876, many of the nonreservation Lakotas and Cheyennes had gathered into a very large village, where the Hunkpapas held a sun dance, the most important religious observance among the Plains Indians. Sitting Bull sacrificed a hundred small bits of flesh from his arms to Wakantanka and then danced and sought a vision. His vision was of soldiers falling upside down into the Lakota and Cheyenne village. It was fulfilled when, on June 25, Lieutenant Colonel George A. Custer divided his troops and personally led just over two hundred of them in an attack on a village of Lakotas and Cheyennes that included somewhere between eight hundred and eighteen hundred warriors.

The defeat of Custer was certainly the greatest victory by the Plains Indians in all their battles with the U.S. Army, but it provoked a strong counterattack. As the army attacked and attacked again, Sitting Bull and his followers lost their tipis and their provisions. Finally, they fled to Canada and remained there for several years. Soon, however, the last buffalo disappeared from the Plains, ending the Hunkpapas' traditional way of life more effectively than the army had been able to accomplish. Eventually, they were persuaded to return and to live on a reservation. After his return, Sitting Bull spent a few years touring with William F. ("Buffalo Bill") Cody's Wild West Show, then retired to live in a log cabin on the reservation. There he died at the hands of Indian policemen, some from his own Hunkpapa tribe, in 1890.

Nevertheless, isolated by mountains and deserts, the Mormons created their Zion. The Mormon community was a **theocracy** in which church officials governed every aspect of life. A church-sponsored political party dominated elections for local and territorial officials. Although streams flowed from the nearby Wasatch mountain range, meager rainfall and poor soil constrained farming. Young decreed communal ownership of both land and streams, and church officials made choices about the use of water. Young devised a system for creating farms and irrigation projects based on the right to divert water for irrigation. This system influenced laws on water rights in all the western states. The communal ownership of land ended after 1869.

The Mormon settlement thrived and established satellite communities. By the Civil War, more than twenty thousand Mormons lived in the Utah Territory. After the war, the Mormons came under great pressure to renounce their practice of **polygamy.** Efforts to make Utah a state were blocked repeatedly because of that issue. The Republican party was also concerned about the potential political power of the Mormon church. In 1890, to clear the way for statehood, the Mormon leadership dissolved the church-sponsored political party and disavowed polygamy. Utah became a state in 1896.

Cattle Kingdom on the Plains

As the Mormons were building their centralized and cooperative society in the Great Basin, the more individualistic enterprise of raising cattle was emerging on the western Great Plains. Cattle had first been brought into south Texas in the eighteenth century. Climate encouraged the growth of the herds, and Mexican ranchers developed an open-range system of cattle raising. Vaqueros (cowboys) herded the half-wild longhorns grazing on the unfenced plains. Practices developed in south Texas were subsequently transferred to the range-cattle industry, including **branding** and **roundups.**

At the end of the Civil War, five million cattle ranged across Texas, many unbranded and thus free for the taking. Others could be purchased for a few dollars each. At the slaughterhouses of Chicago, cattle brought ten times or more their price in Texas. To get cattle from south Texas to the Midwest, Texans used the cattle drive. They herded cattle north through Texas and Indian Territory to the railroads then being built westward. A half dozen cowboys, a cook, and a trail boss could drive one thousand to two thousand cattle. Enough animals survived the drive to yield a good profit. Between 1866 and 1880, some four million cattle walked north from Texas.

The first cattle drives went to Sedalia, Missouri. As railroad construction pushed west, it created a series of Kansas cattle towns such as Abilene and Dodge City. Later drives followed more westerly routes. In cattle towns, the trail boss sold his herd and paid off his cowboys, who often spent their earnings at saloons, brothels, and gambling houses. In such towns, eastern journalists and authors discovered and embroidered the exploits of town marshals such as **James B. ("Wild Bill") Hickok** and **Wyatt Earp.** The popular press credited such "town-tamers" with heroic exploits. Usually, though, the most important changes came when a town's middle class, especially the women, organized churches and schools and determined to create a law-abiding community.

Although most Texas cattle were loaded on eastbound trains for slaughtering, some were driven north to vast tracts of land still in the public domain. Thus open-range cattle raising was extended into the northern Great Plains by the early 1870s. Investors could make 50 percent annual profits from cattle raising.

theocracy A state governed by religious authority.

polygamy The practice of having more than one wife at a time.

branding Using a hot iron to burn a unique design on the hide of cattle and other animals; the design, or brand, is used to establish ownership.

roundup A spring event in which cowboys gathered together the cattle, branded newborn calves, and castrated most male calves.

James B. ("Wild Bill") Hickok Western gambler and gunman; in 1876, he was shot in the back and killed while playing poker in Deadwood, Dakota Territory.

Wyatt Earp American frontier law officer and gunfighter involved in 1881 in a controversial shootout at the O.K. Corral in Tombstone, Arizona, in which several men were killed.

By the early 1880s, so many cattle ranches were in operation that beef prices began to fall. The severe winter of 1886–1887 broke the boom. Uncounted thousands of cattle froze or starved to death on the northern Plains. Many investors went bankrupt. Surviving ranchers fenced their ranges and made certain that they could feed their cattle during the winter.

As the cattle industry expanded, so did the romanticizing of the cowboy. Popular fiction created the image of the cowboy as a brave, clean-cut hero, white and often blond, who spent his time defeating villains and rescuing fair-haired white women from danger. In reality, most real cowboys were young and unschooled. Many were African Americans or of Mexican descent. Others were former Confederate soldiers. On a cattle drive, they worked as many as twenty hours a day, faced serious danger if a herd stampeded, slept on the ground, and lived on biscuits, beans, and meager wages. Some tried to form local branches of unions, notably the Knights of Labor.

Plowing the Plains

Farmers entering the Great Plains encountered unfamiliar environmental constraints. Unlike the Indians, whose way of life was in harmony with the Plains environment, the new residents chose to alter the environment. Some succeeded, but others failed and left.

After the Civil War, the land available for new farms stretched from northern North Dakota and Minnesota southward through Oklahoma. Mapmakers in the early nineteenth century had labeled this region the Great American Desert. It was not a desert, however, and some parts of it were very fertile. But west of the line of **aridity,** around the 98th or 100th **meridian,** sparse rainfall was a serious constraint on farming (see Map 17.2). Farmers who expected to follow their usual farming practices ran the risk not only of failing but also of severely damaging the fragile **ecosystem** there.

When the **Kansas-Nebraska Act** (1854) opened up this vast region for development, the first settlers stuck to eastern areas, where the terrain and climate were similar to those they knew. After the Civil War, farmers pressed steadily westward, spurred by the promise of free land under the Homestead Act (1862) or lured by railroad advertising that promised fertile and productive land at little cost.

Those who took advantage of the opportunities for land were quite diverse. Thousands of African Americans left the South, seeking farms of their own. Immigrants from Scandinavia, Germany, **Bohemia,** and Russia flooded in. Most homesteaders, however, moved from areas a short distance to the east, where farmland had become too expensive.

Many single women claimed 160 acres of their own land. Sometimes the wife of a male homesteader did the same. By 1886, women held one-third of all homestead claims in the Dakota Territory. Many single women seem to have viewed homesteading as a speculative venture. They intended to gain title to the land and then sell it to acquire money for other purposes, such as starting a business or creating a nest egg for marriage.

The 160 acres that the Homestead Act provided were sufficient only for farms lying east of the line of aridity. West of that line, most of the land required irrigation or was suitable only for cattle raising, which required much more than 160 acres if a ranch was to be successful. Federal officials were often lax in enforcing the Homestead Act's requirements for establishing ownership. The law required a homesteader to build a house on the land. A husband and wife could each claim 160 acres and then build a house on the boundary between their claims, thereby doubling their land. Cattle ranchers sometimes had all their cowboys file claims and then transfer the land to the rancher

aridity Dryness; the lack of sufficient rainfall to support trees or woody plants.

meridian Any of the imaginary lines representing degrees of longitude that pass through the North and South Poles and encircle the earth.

ecosystem A community of animals, plants, and bacteria, considered together with the environment in which they are found.

Kansas-Nebraska Act Law passed by Congress in 1854 that created the Kansas and Nebraska territories.

Bohemia A region of central Europe now part of the Czech Republic.

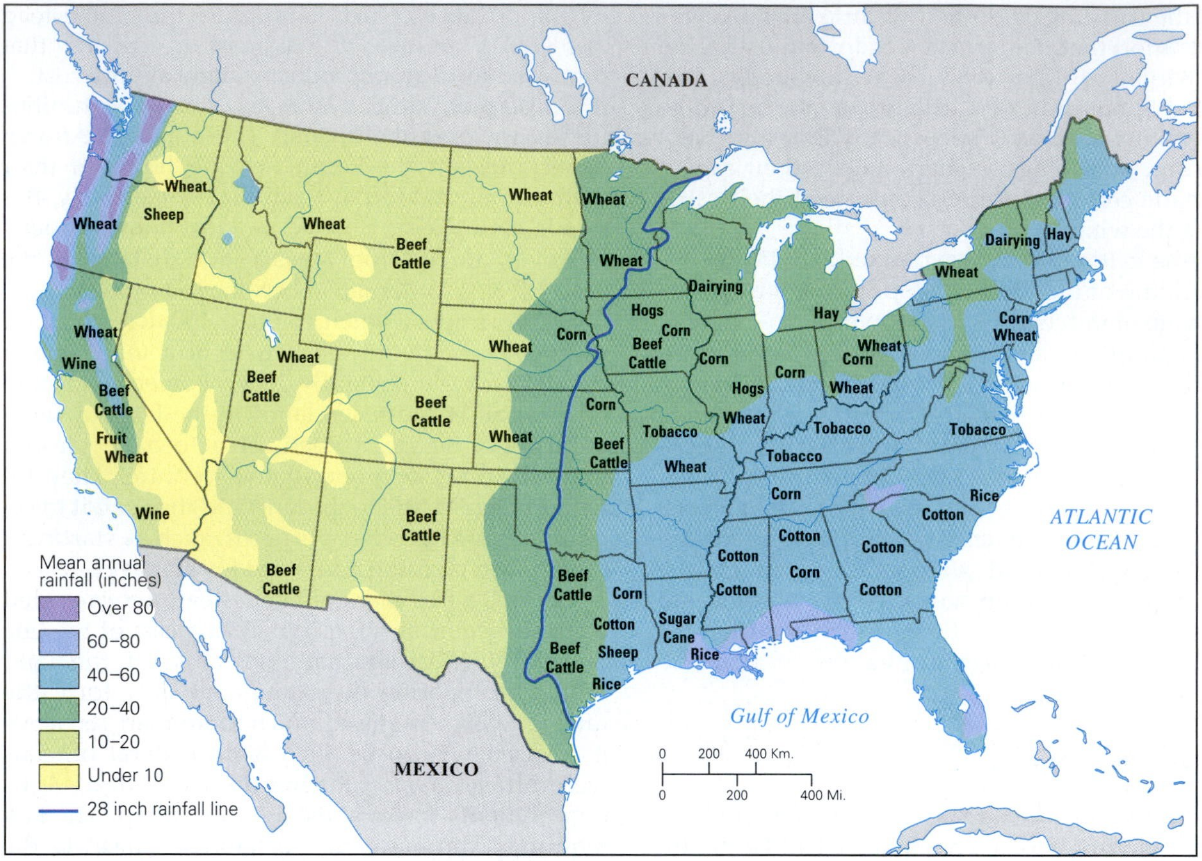

♦ **MAP 17.2 Rainfall and Agriculture, c. 1890** The agricultural prospects of any given area depended on the type of soil, the terrain, and the rainfall. Most of the western half of the nation received relatively little rainfall compared to the eastern half. Crops such as corn and cotton could not be raised in the West without irrigation.

after they received title to it. Thus individuals sometimes acquired a great deal of land by devious means.

People who wished to live on the Plains had to adapt to an environment where water and wood were scarce. The lack of wood led many families to carve homes out of the land itself by tunneling into the sides of low hills. Others cut the tough prairie **sod** into blocks, from which they fashioned one- or two-room houses. Many combined dugout and sod construction. "Soddies" seldom made satisfactory dwellings. The roof usually leaked. Snakes could drop from the ceiling or slither out of the walls. Sod houses were usually so dark inside that sewing, washing clothes, and many other household tasks were done outside whenever possible. Families nevertheless made these sod houses home by placing curtains and potted flowers at the windows.

Plains families looked to technology to meet many of their needs. Barbed wire, first patented in 1874, provided a cheap alternative to wooden fences. The barbs effectively kept ranchers' cattle off farmland. Ranchers eventually used it too.

sod A section of grass-covered surface soil held together by the matted roots of grass.

Much of the Plains had abundant **ground water,** but at depths greater than in the East. Windmills were used to pump water from great depths. Because the sod was so tough, special plows were developed to make the initial cut through it. These plows were so expensive that most farmers hired a specialist (a "sodbuster") to break their sod.

The most serious problem for pioneers on the Plains was lack of rainfall. During the late 1880s, rainfall fell below normal, and crop failures drove many homesteaders off the Plains. Half of the population of western Kansas left between 1888 and 1892. One covered wagon heading east bore the legend, "In God we trusted, in Kansas we busted." Only after farmers learned better techniques of **dry farming,** secured improved strains of wheat (some brought by **Russian-German** immigrants), and began to practice irrigation did agriculture become viable. Even so, farming practices often left exposed soil subject to severe wind erosion.

Railroads, Mining, Agribusiness, Logging, and Finance: The Transformation of the West, Part II

In a region of great distances, relatively few people, and widely scattered population centers, effective transportation was a necessity for economic development. Just as western cattle raisers required rail connections to send their cattle to market, so too did western miners and farmers need railroads to carry the products of their labor to markets. Given the scarcity of water in much of the West, many westerners had concluded by 1900 that water was as important as railroads in the development of the region.

Western Railroads

Railroad promoters understood that building a transcontinental line in the sparsely populated West would be very expensive and that it would not carry sufficient freight to justify the cost of construction. Thus they turned to the federal government for assistance. The Union Pacific and Central Pacific railroads were the first recipients of federal support for transcontinental railroads. The Union Pacific began laying track west from Omaha, Nebraska Territory, and the Central Pacific began building east from Sacramento, California. Construction began slowly, partly because crucial supplies such as rails and locomotives had to be transported long distances. Both lines experienced labor shortages. The Union Pacific solved its labor shortages only after the Civil War, when former soldiers and construction workers flooded west. Many were Irish immigrants. The Central Pacific recruited Chinese immigrant laborers.

Construction proceeded slowly until the end of the Civil War in 1865. The Central Pacific laid only 18 miles of track during 1863, and the Union Pacific laid no track at all until mid-1864. It was not until May 10, 1869, that the tracks of the two companies finally met near **Promontory Point,** north of the Great Salt Lake. Other lines followed during the next twenty years, bringing most of the West into the national market system and speeding the development of western mining, lumbering, and agriculture.

Westerners greeted the arrival of the railroads with joyful celebrations, but some soon wondered whether they had traded isolation for dependence on a greedy monopoly. The Southern Pacific, successor to the Central Pacific, became known as the "Octopus" because its grasping tentacles seemed to reach everywhere. Not all western railroads acquired such bad reputations. James J. Hill of the Great Northern, for example, was called the "Empire Builder" for his efforts to build up the economy and prosperity of the region alongside his rails. Regardless of their reputation, railroads were crucial to the

ground water Water beneath the earth's surface, often between soil and rock, that supplies wells and springs.

dry farming Farming that makes maximum use of available moisture by using techniques such as planting drought-resistant crops and harrowing after a rainfall.

Russian-German Immigrants of German descent who came from Russia, often from farming colonies established in the eighteenth century.

Promontory Point Site in northern Utah where in 1869 the Central Pacific and Union Pacific railroads were linked, thus completing the first transcontinental railroad in the United States.

♦ Only a few of the photographs of the construction of the first transcontinental railroad show the Chinese laborers who were responsible for some of the most dangerous construction on the Central Pacific route through the Sierra Nevada. This photograph was taken, apparently by a photographer from the Union Pacific, when the two lines joined near Promontory Point, Utah Territory. *Denver Public Library.*

economic development of the West. The outcome was the rapid expansion of agriculture and mining.

Western Mining

Between 1848 and 1885, the discovery of gold and silver at many sites scattered throughout the West brought a rush of fortune seekers. **Boom towns** sprang up overnight to meet miners' needs, ranging from picks to groceries. The construction of rail lines to mining towns permitted rapid exploitation of the mineral resources by bringing in supplies and heavy equipment. Once the valuable ore gave out, however, such settlements were likely to become ghost towns.

Many of the first miners collected gold by **placer mining.** The only equipment they needed was a pan. Miners panning for gold simply washed gravel that they hoped contained gold. If present, the gold sank to the bottom of the pan as the gravel was washed away by the water. After the early gold seekers had taken the easily accessible ore, elaborate mining equipment became necessary. Gold-mining companies developed **hydraulic** systems that used great amounts of water under high pressure to demolish entire mountainsides. In the process, they wreaked havoc on the environment downstream. This practice ended only when a federal court outlawed it in 1884.

In most of the West, the exhaustion of surface deposits led to the construction of shafts and tunnels deep underground. Mine shafts in Butte, Montana, eventually reached depths of a mile. Such operations required machinery to move men and equipment and to keep the tunnels cool and dry. By the mid-1870s, the Comstock silver mines in Nevada boasted the most advanced mining equipment in the world. There temperatures soared to 120 degrees in shafts more than 2,200 feet deep. Mighty air pumps circulated air from the surface to the depths, and ice was used to reduce the temperature. Massive water pumps kept the shafts dry. Everywhere, powerful drills speeded the job of removing the ore, and enormous ore-crushing machines operated day and night on the surface.

The mining industry changed rapidly as solitary prospectors panning for gold gave way to large mining companies whose operations were financed by banks in San Francisco and the East.

boom town A town experiencing a sudden increase in prosperity and population.

placer mining Washing minerals from placers—deposits of sand or gravel that contain eroded particles of gold and other valuable minerals.

hydraulic Making use of water under pressure.

Mining companies became vertically integrated, operating not only mines but also ore-crushing mills and railroads. Western miners organized too, forming strong unions. Miners' unions helped secure wages five to ten times higher than those paid to miners in Britain or Germany.

The Birth of Western Agribusiness

Throughout the eastern half of the nation, the family farm was the typical agricultural unit. In California and other parts of the West, however, agriculture sometimes developed into an **agribusiness** involving huge areas, the intensive use of heavy equipment, and wage labor.

Wheat lent itself to large-scale farming because it was the first major crop to be entirely mechanized. By 1880, large wheat farms in the Red River valley of what is now North Dakota and in the San Joaquin Valley of central California measured 100 square miles. Such farming businesses involved major capital investments in land, equipment, livestock, and labor. One Dakota farm required 250 workers at harvest time. California wheat growers were using steam-powered tractors and **combines** in the late 1880s, well before such machinery was used elsewhere.

The huge wheat farms of Dakota proved to be temporary. Most of them were broken into smaller units by the 1890s. In California, however, agriculture continued to flourish on a scale largely unknown in other parts of the country. One California company, Miller and Lux, held more than a million acres. Although wheat raising had declined in significance by 1900, large-scale agriculture became established for a variety of crops. At first, the growers relied on Chinese immigrants for their field labor. When Congress prohibited most Chinese immigration in 1882, growers turned to Japanese and eventually Mexican immigrants.

Logging in the Pacific Northwest

The coastal Pacific Northwest is very different from the remainder of the West. Rainfall is so heavy that the region supports one of the few rain forests outside the tropics. Heavy winter rains and cool, damp summers nurture thick stands of tall Douglas firs and giant redwoods.

At first, in the 1850s and 1860s, the coastal redwoods of California were cut for use in San Francisco and nearby cities. Attention then shifted north to Oregon and Washington, leading to Seattle's development as a lumber town. Some companies quickly became vertically integrated, owning lumber mills in the Northwest, a fleet of schooners to haul logs, and lumberyards in the San Francisco Bay area. The railroads actively promoted the lumber industry by offering cheap rates for log shipments. Lumber production in Oregon and Washington boomed, leaving behind treeless hillsides subject to severe soil erosion.

Water Wars

From the first efforts at western economic development, water was a central concern. Prospectors needed water to separate worthless gravel from gold. Californians worked out a system of **water rights** that closely paralleled the Mormons' system. On the Great Plains, a cattle rancher staked out grazing land by establishing control over a stream. Throughout much of the West, would-be farmers learned that irrigation was vital to their success. Western cities saw lack of water as a major constraint on their ability to grow. Competition for scarce water sometimes led to conflict. Henry Miller, of Miller and Lux, once grumbled that he had spent $25 million in legal fees, mostly to protect his water rights.

Cities also battled for access to water. Beginning in 1901, San Francisco sought federal permission to put a dam on federal land near Yosemite National Park in the Sierra Nevada. Opposition came primarily from the **Sierra Club,** formed in 1892 to

agribusiness Farming that is a large-scale business operation using heavy farm machinery and involving processing and distribution as well as the growing of crops.

combine A power-operated harvesting machine that combines the cutting and threshing of grain.

water rights The right to draw water from a particular source, such as a lake, an irrigation canal, or a river.

Sierra Club Environmental organization dedicated to preserving and expanding the world's parks, wildlife, and wilderness areas.

preserve the Sierra Nevada wilderness. Congressional approval did not come until 1913. Los Angeles resolved its water problems by diverting the water of the Owens River to its use.

The magnitude of the efforts needed to provide enough water led many westerners to look increasingly for federal assistance. The National Irrigation Association, created in 1899, lobbied Congress successfully to secure passage of the **Reclamation Act** of 1902, which promised federal construction of irrigation facilities. To promote family farms rather than agribusiness interests, the law specified that only farms smaller than 160 acres could use this water. However, agribusiness often managed to avoid this limitation.

Ethnicity and Race in the West

In ethnic and racial composition, the West differed significantly from the rest of the nation. In 1900, the western half of the nation included 15 percent of all white Americans and 10 percent of all African Americans, but 81 percent of Americans of Chinese or Japanese ancestry, 82 percent of all American Indians, and 98 percent of immigrants born in Mexico. The West became a racially diverse society long before the rest of the country.

Immigrants to the Golden Mountain

Between 1854 and 1882, drawn initially by the California gold rush, some three hundred thousand Chinese immigrants entered the United States. Most came from southern China, which suffered from periodic famines. The Chinese accounted in 1860 for a third of all miners in California, which they called "the Golden Mountain," and more than half in 1870. They formed a major part of construction labor in the West, especially for railroad building. Chinese immigrants also worked as agricultural laborers and farmers, especially in California.

In San Francisco and in smaller western cities, they established **Chinatowns**—relatively autonomous and largely self-contained Chinese communities. In San Francisco's Chinatown, immigrants formed kinship organizations and district associations to assist and protect each other. A confederation of such associations, the Chinese Consolidated Benevolent Association, eventually exercised great power over the social and economic life in Chinese communities in the West. Such communities were largely male, for immigration officials prevented most Chinese women from entering the country. Gambling and prostitution flourished in these largely male communities, giving Chinatowns reputations as centers for vice.

From the beginning, Chinese immigrants encountered discrimination and violence. In 1854, the California Supreme Court prohibited Chinese from testifying in court against a white person. When the depression of the 1870s set in, white workers blamed the Chinese for causing unemployment. Anti-Chinese riots occurred in Los Angeles in 1871, in San Francisco in 1877 and after, and in many western towns in 1885. White miners in 1885 burned the Chinatown in Rock Springs, Wyoming, killing twenty-eight Chinese.

In these riots, the message was usually the same: "The Chinese Must Go." This slogan first gained popularity in San Francisco in 1877 as part of the appeal of the Workingmen's party of California, which blamed the Chinese for the economic woes of white members. In 1882, Congress responded to repeated pressure from West Coast labor unions by passing the **Chinese Exclusion Act,** prohibiting entry to all Chinese people except teachers, students, merchants, tourists, and officials.

In parts of the West, the Chinese were subjected to segregation similar to that imposed on blacks in the South. Chinese students were barred from the San Francisco public schools from 1871 to 1885, when the city opened a segregated Chinese school.

Reclamation Act Law passed by Congress in 1902 that provided for publicly funded irrigation of western land and created the Reclamation Service to oversee the process.

Chinatown A section of a city that is inhabited chiefly by Chinese people.

Chinese Exclusion Act Law passed by Congress in 1882 that prohibited Chinese laborers from entering the United States; it was extended in 1892 and again in 1902.

Sacramento and a few other towns also established segregated schools. Local custom, enforced occasionally by mob violence, promoted residential segregation. Chinese lived outside Chinatown only as servants or in laundries. Occupational segregation was similarly enforced. Anti-Chinese violence in western small towns in the mid-1880s prompted many Chinese to retreat to the large cities.

In the larger western cities, Chinese merchants took the lead in establishing a strong economic base. Organizations based on kinship, region, or occupation sometimes opposed discrimination and segregation through the courts. When San Francisco passed a city law requiring laundry licenses, the organization of Chinese laundry owners filed suit. In 1886, the U.S. Supreme Court declared the law unconstitutional because local authorities had used it to discriminate on the basis of race. School segregation began to break down shortly before World War I.

When other immigrants began to arrive from Asia, they too concentrated in the West. Significant numbers of Japanese began coming to the United States after 1890. By 1907, nearly 150,000 had arrived. After 1907, immigration of Japanese laborers stopped because of an agreement between the United States and Japan. Whites in the West, especially organized labor, regarded Japanese immigrants in much the same way that they viewed Chinese immigrants.

Forced Assimilation

Federal policy toward American Indians aimed at their rapid assimilation into white society. The final outcome, however, was that federal policies tried to eradicate Indian culture but failed to integrate Indians into the mainstream economy and society.

After 1871, federal policy shifted from treating Indian tribes as sovereign but dependent nations with which the federal government negotiated to viewing them as wards of the federal government. This new policy meant that Indians were to be "civilized." Education was an important element in the "civilizing" process. Federal officials worked with churches and philanthropic organizations to establish schools for Indian children away from the reservations. Teachers at these schools prohibited Indian boys and girls from speaking their own language, practicing their religion, or otherwise displaying their own culture. The teachers' goal was to enable the children to live in white society and to separate them from Indian culture.

Other educational programs aimed to train adult Indian men to be farmers or mechanics. The effort to teach Indian men farming, however, was at odds with traditional gender roles in Indian society: typically women raised crops, and men hunted and fought. Many Indian men viewed farming in the same way as their white male contemporaries viewed housework: as women's work.

The **Dawes Severalty Act** (1887) was intended to make the Indians into self-sufficient, individual farmers. The law committed the government to a policy of **severalty**—that is, individual ownership of land. It divided the reservations into individual family farms of 160 acres each. Once each family had received its allotment, any surplus was to be sold by the government. This policy found support among those who coveted Indian land.

Individual landownership and acquisitiveness, however, were at odds with traditional Indian beliefs and practices. Indians maintained that the land was for the use of all and that sharing was a major obligation. Delegates from the Cherokee, Creek, and Choctaw nations petitioned Congress not to pass the Dawes Act, arguing that "our people have not asked for or authorized this," but to no avail.

The Dawes Act stripped Indians of much of their land. Once all the allotments to Indian families had been made, about 70 percent of the land area of the reservations remained, and much of it was sold outright to settlers. In the end, the Dawes Act did not end the reservation system, nor did it reduce the Indians' dependence on the federal government. Instead it separated the Indians from some of their most valuable land.

Response to the assimilation programs varied widely. Some Indians tried to become part of white

Dawes Severalty Act Law passed by Congress in 1887 that broke up reservations into 160-acre family plots and sought to assimilate Indians into white culture by making them farmers.

severalty The holding of property by individuals.

society; others took a middle way. Susan La Flesche, for example, daughter of an Omaha leader, graduated from medical college in 1889 at the head of her class. She disappointed some of her teachers when she set up her medical practice near the Omaha reservation, treated both white and Indian patients, and took part in tribal affairs. However, Dr. La Flesche also participated in the local white community by taking an active part in the **temperance movement** and sometimes preaching in the Presbyterian church.

Other Indians tried to cling to the old ways, hiding their children to keep them out of school and secretly practicing traditional religious ceremonies. In the late nineteenth century, the peyote cult, based on the hallucinogenic properties of the **peyote cactus,** emerged as an alternative religion. It evolved into the Native American Church by combining elements of traditional Indian culture and Christianity with peyote use. Some Indians also took solace in alcohol.

Mexican Americans in the Southwest

Throughout the Southwest during the late nineteenth century, many Mexican Americans lost their land as large numbers of **Anglos**—English-speaking whites—arrived there. Mexican Americans' landholdings were guaranteed by the Treaty of Guadalupe Hidalgo (1848), which ended the Mexican War, but the vagueness of Spanish and Mexican land grants opened the door to legal challenges. In some instances, Mexican Americans were the victims of outright fraud. In California and Texas, some Mexican-American families with large landholdings kept their land by having a daughter marry a prominent Anglo. Except in New Mexico, however, most found themselves landless laborers.

Although the California gold rush of 1849 attracted fortune seekers from around the world, including Mexico and other parts of Latin America, the vast majority came from the eastern United States and Europe. By the 1880s, the English-speaking majority had pushed aside the Spanish-speaking people of California. By the 1870s, many of the pueblos (towns) created during Mexican or Spanish rule in California had become **barrios** centered around a Catholic church. In some ways, the barrios resembled the neighborhoods of European immigrants in the East. Both had mutual aid societies, political associations, and newspapers published in the language of the community, and both often centered on a church. There was an important difference, however. Neighborhoods of European immigrants consisted of people who had come to a new land seeking opportunity or change. By contrast, the residents of the barrios lived in regions that had been home to Mexicans for generations, but they now found themselves surrounded and dominated by English-speaking Americans who hired them for cheap wages.

Like their counterparts in California, Anglos in Texas used fraud and coercion to obtain land from the Spanish-speaking people born in Texas, the Tejanos. By 1900, much of the land in south Texas had passed out of Tejano hands. But unlike California, Anglo ranch owners usually maintained the social patterns characteristic of Tejano ranchers. A large section of Texas between the Nueces River and the Rio Grande extending west to El Paso remained Mexican culturally. This region was home both to Tejanos and to two-thirds of all Mexican immigrants in the United States before 1900. Most people living there spoke Spanish.

New Mexico presented a third pattern in the late nineteenth century. Hispanos (Spanish-speaking New Mexicans) were clearly the majority of the population in the territory. Although Hispanos were the unquestioned majority and could dominate elections, many who had small landholdings lost their land. Unlike California and Texas, many of those who enriched themselves in New Mexico were wealthy Hispanos.

From 1856 to 1910, the Latino population throughout the Southwest grew more slowly than

temperance movement A movement advocating the avoidance of alcoholic drinks.

peyote cactus A cactus native to Mexico and the southwestern United States that is able to produce a hallucinogenic effect.

Anglo A term applied in the Southwest to English-speaking whites.

barrio A Spanish-speaking community, especially of poor laborers.

♦ In the late nineteenth and early twentieth centuries, Mexican Americans became a major part of the work force for constructing and maintaining railroads in the Southwest. This crew of Mexican-American linemen was working in south Texas when this photograph was taken in 1910. They may have been employed by a railroad to put up and maintain its communication lines or by a telegraph or telephone company. *Texas State Library and Archives Commission.*

the Anglo population. After 1910, however, that situation reversed itself, as political and social upheavals in Mexico prompted massive migration to the United States. Probably a million people—equivalent to one-tenth of the entire population of Mexico as of 1910—arrived over the next twenty years. More than half stayed in Texas, but significant numbers settled in southern California. Inevitably, this new stream of immigrants changed some of the patterns of ethnic relations that had characterized the region since the mid-nineteenth century.

The West in American Thought

The West has long fascinated Americans, and the "winning of the West" has become a national myth that has obscured or distorted the facts. Since at least the 1890s, many Americans have thought of the West in terms of the frontier. According to this way of thinking, to the east of the frontier line lay established society, and to the west of it lay the wild, untamed West. The frontier thus represented the dividing point between savagery and civilization.

The West as Utopia and Myth

During the nineteenth and much of the twentieth century, the West seemed a potential **utopia.** Many Americans could dream of a better life there, even if they never ventured forth. What was the origin of this utopian view of the West? In the popular mind, the West was vacant, waiting to be formed. Nothing was predetermined there. A person or a group such as the Mormons could make a fresh start.

The West appealed as well to Americans who sought to fulfill the American dream of improving their social and economic standing. The presence of free or cheap land, the ability to start over, the idea of creating a place of one's own, all were part of the West's attraction—even for those who never acted on their dreams. Some of those who tried to fulfill their dreams did not succeed, but enough did to provide some justification for the utopian image of the West as a land of promise.

The West achieved mythical status as popular novels, and eventually movies and television, used it as the setting for stories that spoke to Americans' anxieties as well as their hopes. The development of the West gave rise to the myth of the "winning" of the West. The myth begins with the grandeur of wide grassy plains, towering craggy mountains, and vast silent deserts. In most versions, the western Indians face a tragic destiny. They are usually portrayed as a proud, noble people whose demise

utopia An ideal place.

clears the way for the transformation of the land. The starring roles in this drama are played by white pioneers who struggle to overcome natural and human obstacles. These pioneers personify rugged individualism—the virtues of self-reliance and independence—as they triumph through hard work and personal integrity. Many of the human obstacles are villainous characters: greedy speculators, vicious cattle rustlers, unscrupulous moneylenders, selfish railroad barons. Some are only doubters, too skeptical of the promise of the West to take the risks to succeed.

The Frontier and the West

Starting in the 1870s, accounts of the winning of the West suggested to many Americans the existence of an America more attractive than the steel mills and urban slums of their own day. The West was a place where people were more virtuous than the barons of industry and corrupt city politicians. Individual success was possible in the West without labor strife or racial and ethnic discord. This myth has evolved and continues to exert a hold on Americans' imaginations. The cowboy has been the most prominent embodiment of the myth. He is a brave and resourceful loner, riding across the West and dispelling trouble from his path and from the lives of others. A modern version of the medieval knight in shining armor, he rarely does the actual work of a cowboy.

In the 1920s, Hollywood discovered that this image seemed to have special appeal to Americans dissatisfied with the routine of their lives and work. In the 1950s, some found the cowboy symbolic of the American role in the Cold War, as the nation strode across the globe, rescuing grateful nations from the threat of Communist domination.

Like all other myths, the myth of the winning of the West contains elements of truth but also ignores some truths. For example, it usually treats Indians as victims of progress. It rarely considers their fate after they met defeat at the hands of the cavalry. Instead, they obligingly disappeared from the scene. The myth rarely tempers its celebration of rugged individualism by acknowledging the fundamental role government played in the transformation of the West by dispossessing the Indians, subsidizing railroad construction, using the public domain to underwrite economic development, and rerouting rivers. The myth often overlooks the role of ethnic and racial minorities from African American and Tejano cowboys to Chinese railroad construction crews. It overlooks the extent to which these people were exploited as sources of cheap labor. Women typically appear only as helpless victims or noble helpmates. Finally, the myth generally ignores the extent to which the economic development of the West replicated that of the East. If such influences appear in the myth, they are usually as constraints that the hardy pioneers overcame.

Historians have played an important role in shaping this myth of the West. In 1893, **Frederick Jackson Turner,** a young historian, wrote an essay, "The Significance of the Frontier in American History." In that essay, he challenged the prevailing idea among American historians that they should study European societies to discover the origins of American character and institutions. Rather, Turner argued, they should study the American frontier. The western frontier, he claimed, was where America had formed, because it was where individualism and democracy flourished.

Turner's theory about the frontier dominated the thinking of historians for many years. Today, however, historians focus on many elements missing from Turner's analysis. They acknowledge the importance of cultural conflicts among different groups of people; the experiences of American Indians, of the Spanish-speaking **mestizo** peoples of the Southwest, and of Asian Americans; the experiences of women; ecological issues, especially those involving water; and the ways that the western economy resembles and differs from that of the East. If frontier individualism and mobility have been important elements in American history, as Turner suggested, these other elements have been equally important in western history.

Frederick Jackson Turner American historian who argued that the receding frontier and cheap land were dominant factors in creating American democracy and shaping the national character.

mestizo A person of mixed Spanish and Indian ancestry.

SUMMARY

Expectations
Constraints
Choices
Outcomes

The West changed greatly during the forty years following the Civil War. Federal policy toward that region derived from the *expectation* of rapid development, and policymakers often *chose* to use the public domain to accomplish that purpose. The Plains Indians posed *constraints* on development, but most were defeated by the army by 1877.

Patterns of development varied in different parts of the West. In the Great Basin, Mormons created a theocracy and *chose* new approaches to irrigation to meet *constraints* posed by scarce water. A cattle kingdom emerged on the western Great Plains, as railroad construction made it possible to carry cattle east for slaughter. As farming moved west, lack of rainfall *constrained* farmers' expectations. The forests of the Pacific Northwest attracted lumbering companies.

Throughout the West, change was driven by *choices* made in the face of *constraints*. Railroad construction overcame *constraints* posed by vast distances. As western mining became highly mechanized, control shifted to large mining companies able to secure the necessary capital. In California especially, landowners made *choices* that led to the development of large-scale commercial agriculture. Water posed a significant *constraint* on economic development in much of the West.

Asian immigrants, American Indians, and Latino peoples all formed substantial parts of the western population but had significantly different *expectations* and experiences. White westerners *chose* to use politics and, sometimes, terrorism to exclude and segregate Asian immigrants. Federal policies toward American Indians proceeded from the *expectation* that they should be rapidly assimilated and lose their separate cultural identity. Such policies largely failed. American citizens of Mexican descent and subsequent immigrants from Latin America had their lives and cultures *constrained* by Anglo newcomers.

The *outcomes* of the many *choices* made in the late nineteenth century were explosive economic development and population change. Americans have viewed the West as both a utopia and the source of a national myth. Those views overlook important realities in the nature of western development and in the people who accomplished it.

SUGGESTED READINGS

Billington, Ray Allen, and Martin Ridge. *Westward Expansion: A History of the American Frontier*, 5th ed. (1982).

Presents the most detailed treatment of the West and the frontier, largely from a Turnerian perspective.

Brown, Dee. *Bury My Heart at Wounded Knee: An Indian History of the American West* (1971).

One of the first efforts to write western history from the Indians' perspective, drawing on oral histories.

Chan, Sucheng. *Asian Americans: An Interpretive History* (1990).

A good introduction to the history of Asian Americans.

Gomez-Quinones, Juan. *Roots of Chicano Politics, 1600–1940* (1994).

An overview of the political history of Mexican Americans until World War II.

Hundley, Norris, Jr. *The Great Thirst: Californians and Water, 1770s–1990s* (1992).

One of the most recent of a number of studies surveying the role of water in the West.

Limerick, Patricia Nelson. *The Legacy of Conquest: The Unbroken Past of the American West* (1987).

The major recent criticism of the Turner thesis, posing an alternative framework for viewing western history.

Montejano, David. *Anglos and Mexicans in the Making of Texas, 1836–1986* (1987).

An award-winning study of south Texas.

IMMIGRATION AND URBANIZATION, 1865–1900 After the Civil War, many aspects of American life were significantly changed by the growth of cities and a surge in immigration, especially of people from Europe. By 1900, an urban-industrial core region had emerged in the Northeast.

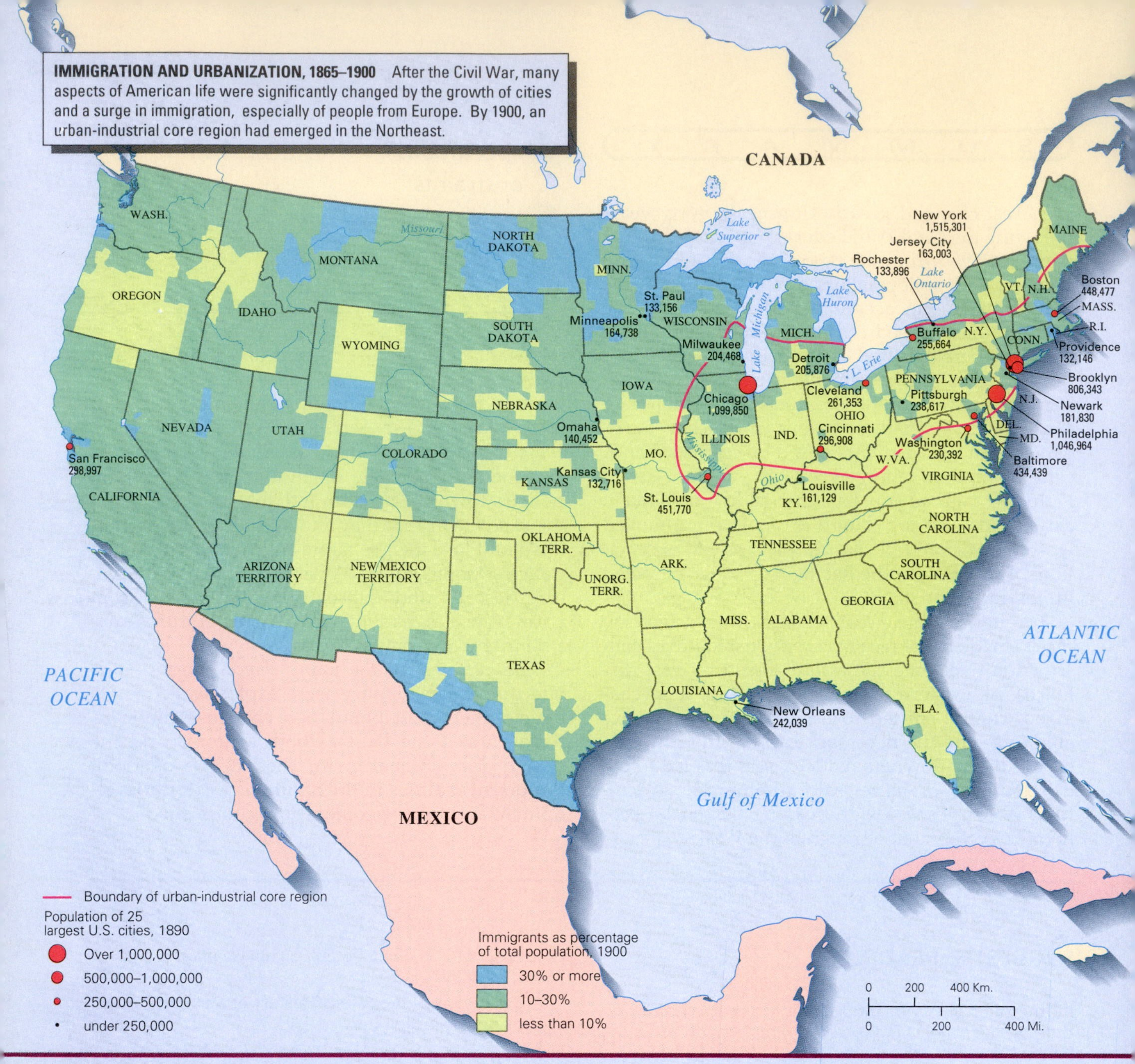

CANADA
MEXICO
PACIFIC OCEAN
ATLANTIC OCEAN
Gulf of Mexico
WASH.
OREGON
IDAHO
MONTANA
WYOMING
NORTH DAKOTA
SOUTH DAKOTA
NEBRASKA
KANSAS
NEVADA
UTAH
COLORADO
CALIFORNIA
ARIZONA TERRITORY
NEW MEXICO TERRITORY
OKLAHOMA TERR.
UNORG. TERR.
TEXAS
MINN.
IOWA
MO.
ARK.
LOUISIANA
WISCONSIN
ILLINOIS
MICH.
IND.
OHIO
KY.
TENNESSEE
MISS.
ALABAMA
GEORGIA
FLA.
SOUTH CAROLINA
NORTH CAROLINA
VIRGINIA
W.VA.
PENNSYLVANIA
N.Y.
N.J.
DEL.
MD.
CONN.
R.I.
MASS.
VT.
N.H.
MAINE
Missouri
Lake Superior
Lake Michigan
Lake Huron
Lake Ontario
L. Erie
Mississippi
Ohio
New York 1,515,301
Jersey City 163,003
Rochester 133,896
Boston 448,477
Providence 132,146
Brooklyn 806,343
Newark 181,830
Philadelphia 1,046,964
Baltimore 434,439
Washington 230,392
Buffalo 255,664
Pittsburgh 238,617
Cleveland 261,353
Cincinnati 296,908
Detroit 205,876
Louisville 161,129
Chicago 1,099,850
Milwaukee 204,468
St. Paul 133,156
Minneapolis 164,738
St. Louis 451,770
Kansas City 132,716
Omaha 140,452
New Orleans 242,039
San Francisco 298,997
Boundary of urban-industrial core region
Population of 25 largest U.S. cities, 1890
Over 1,000,000
500,000–1,000,000
250,000–500,000
under 250,000
Immigrants as percentage of total population, 1900
30% or more
10–30%
less than 10%
0 200 400 Km.
0 200 400 Mi.

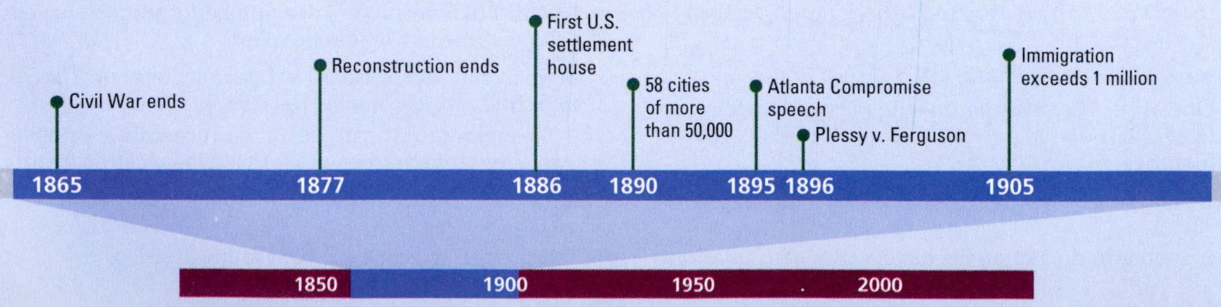

Civil War ends
Reconstruction ends
First U.S. settlement house
58 cities of more than 50,000
Atlanta Compromise speech
Plessy v. Ferguson
Immigration exceeds 1 million
1865
1877
1886
1890
1895
1896
1905
1850
1900
1950
2000

CHAPTER 18

The New Social Patterns of Urban and Industrial America, 1865–1917

The New Urban Environment

- What expectations led many people to move to American cities during the late nineteenth and early twentieth centuries?
- What constraints did urban Americans have to overcome?

Poverty and the City

- What constraints and choices shaped the lives of newcomers to the growing American cities?
- How did different groups analyze the constraints of urban poverty?
- What choices about assisting the poor did their analyses lead them to make?

New Americans from Europe

- What expectations prompted immigrants to leave their homelands for the United States?
- What constraints did they encounter?
- How did immigrants' expectations and choices regarding assimilation compare to those of nativists?

New South, Old Issues

- What outcome did southern officials seek when they wrote new laws on race relations during the 1880s and 1890s?
- What choices did black southerners make in response to the state of race relations in the South?

New Patterns of American Social and Cultural Life

- How did Americans' expectations and choices contribute to important social and cultural trends during the late nineteenth and early twentieth centuries?

INTRODUCTION

Expectations
Constraints
Choices
Outcomes

In 1872, two neighbors in Hartford, Connecticut, concluded they could write a better novel than the ones then in vogue. The first-time novelists, Charles Dudley Warner and Samuel L. Clemens, titled their satire on business and politics *The Gilded Age: A Tale of Today*. The popular novel gave its name to the years from the 1860s through the 1890s: the Gilded Age. The label suggests both the golden gleam of a gilded surface and the cheap nature of the base metal underneath.

Many aspects of late nineteenth-century life justify terming it gilded. The dramatic expansion of business, the technology that typified "progress" for many people, the glittering wealth of the new industrial entrepreneurs, and the rapid economic development of the West all provided the gleaming surface. The grim realities of life for most industrial workers and the plight of racial and ethnic minorities, however, lay uncomfortably just below that golden surface. This chapter examines the *expectations, constraints, choices*, and *outcomes* of the period by looking at social and cultural changes in the late nineteenth and early twentieth centuries. New patterns of life rocked the burgeoning cities. Ethnic and racial groups related to each other in new ways, and new developments revolutionized education, gender roles, creative expression, and cultural participation.

Most of these *choices* and *outcomes* were related to the great transforming experiences of the late 1800s: industrialization, urbanization, immigration, and the development of the West. Together they broke down old *constraints* and created new ones. They fostered new *expectations* among Americans about how people should live and how social groups should relate to one another. Americans' *expectations* sometimes expanded individual *choices* and opportunities. However, some groups tried to impose their values and behaviors on others.

As Americans revised old *expectations* for social relations and forged new ones, the pace of growth created *constraints* that sometimes forced troubling choices. Cities expanded so rapidly that municipal governments faced difficult *choices*. For example, should they use their limited resources to pave streets or build sewers? At the same time, however, the expansion of the educational system removed *constraints* on Americans' opportunities to learn and presented many Americans with new *choices*, such as whether to go to college. Educational opportunities for women helped to expand career *choices*, including such previously all-male professions as medicine and law, or the new profession of social work. In the South, where industrialization lagged, some people made *choices* intended to develop new social and economic patterns.

The expanding industrial economy and rapidly growing cities convinced people throughout Europe to come to America. Such *choices* were often made with the *expectation* of acquiring free land or earning high wages. Some succeeded and turned their dreams into reality. But the hopes of others were dashed by the *constraints* posed by the difficulty of finding available land or steady jobs. The *outcome* of these many *choices* about where to live, how to live, and how to relate to other groups was the transformation of American society and culture during the Gilded Age.

CHRONOLOGY

Social and Cultural Change

1865	Civil War ends 248,120 immigrants enter U.S.
1868	First medical school for women
1870	25 cities exceed 50,000 people
1871	Great Chicago fire Boss Tweed indicted
1872	Clemens and Warner name the Gilded Age
1874	Women's Christian Temperance Union founded
1876	National League (professional baseball) formed
1877	Reconstruction ends
1879	Henry George's *Progress and Poverty*
1882	788,992 immigrants enter U.S.
1883	Civil Rights cases
1885	Mark Twain's *Huckleberry Finn*
1886	First U.S. settlement house
1887	American Protective Association founded Florida segregates railroads
1888	First electric streetcar system
1889	Hull House opens
1890	58 cities exceed 50,000 people Jacob Riis's *How the Other Half Lives* Second Mississippi Plan
1893	Stephen Crane's *Maggie: A Girl of the Streets*
1895	Booker T. Washington delivers Atlanta Compromise
1896	South Carolina adopts white primary *Plessy v. Ferguson*
1897	President Cleveland vetoes immigration restriction First southern steel mill
1899	Scott Joplin's "Maple Leaf Rag"
1901	Frank Norris's *The Octopus* Anarchists barred from U.S. Oil discovered in Texas, Oklahoma, and Louisiana
1903	First World Series
1903–1906	Pogroms against Russian Jews
1907	1,285,349 immigrants enter U.S.
1913	President Taft vetoes immigration restriction Armory Show
1916	Madison Grant's *Passing of the Great Race*
1917	Congress requires literacy test to limit immigration, overriding President Wilson's veto

The New Urban Environment

"The city is the nerve center of our civilization. It is also the storm center." So said Josiah Strong, a leading Protestant minister, pointing up the ambivalence with which many Americans viewed their rapidly growing cities. For recent immigrants and long-time residents, for men and women, for industrial workers and farmers, the ever-expanding cities posed the greatest challenge to their expectations and gave them the widest range of choices.

Surging Urban Growth

What Americans saw in their cities often fascinated them. Cities boasted the technological innovations that many equated with progress. When the journalist William Allen White moved to Kansas City in 1891, the city's streetcars were "marvels" to him and its telephones "a miracle." But the lure of the city stemmed from far more than telephones, streetcars, and technological gadgetry. It also offered theaters, concerts, lectures, fairs, exhibitions, and galleries.

Other visitors were repulsed by what they saw in American cities. A British traveler in 1898 described Pittsburgh as "a most chaotic city. A cloud of smoke hangs over it by day. The glow of scores of furnaces light the river banks by night. . . . All nations are jumbled up here, the poor living in tenement dens or wooden shanties thrown up or dumped down with very little reference to roads." Guillermo Prieto, visiting San Francisco in 1877, was struck by the contrast of luxurious wealth and desperate poverty: "Behind the palaces run filthy alleys, or rather nasty dungheaps without sidewalks or illumination, whose loiterers smell of the gallows."

The odd mixture of fascination and repulsion Americans felt toward cities stemmed in part from the rapidity of urban growth. Cities with more than fifty thousand people grew almost twice as fast as rural areas. The nation had twenty-five cities of that size in 1870 and fifty-eight in 1890, most of them in the Northeast and Midwest. Urban growth came largely through migration from rural areas in Europe and, to a lesser extent, in the United States. The mechanization of farm work meant that fewer workers were required than before. High rural birth rates also contributed to urban growth.

Growth of manufacturing went hand in hand with urban expansion. By the late nineteenth century, the nation had developed a **manufacturing belt** that included nearly all the largest cities as well as the bulk of the nation's manufacturing and finance (see chapter opener map). Some cities began as ports; others developed as industrial centers. Cities often became known for a particular product: iron and steel in Pittsburgh; clothing in New York; textiles in Lowell, Massachusetts; meatpacking in Chicago; flour milling in Minneapolis.

New Cities of Skyscrapers and Streetcars

As the urban population swelled, technological advances permitted cities to expand upward and outward. In the early 1800s, residents got around by foot in cities that measured only a few miles across. Buildings were seldom more than three stories high. In the late nineteenth century, however, new building and transportation technologies removed previous constraints and spelled the end of the "walking city."

Until the 1880s, construction techniques had limited building heights. The higher a building was, the thicker its lower walls had to be. Chicago architects, most notably Louis Sullivan, took the lead in designing taller buildings by using a steel frame to carry the weight of the walls. Economical and efficient, tall buildings created unique city skylines.

Just as steel-frame buildings allowed cities to grow upward, so new forms of transportation allowed cities to expand outward. Electricity transformed urban transit. Frank Sprague, a protégé of Thomas Edison, designed a streetcar driven by an electric motor. Sprague's electric streetcars first appeared in Richmond, Virginia, in 1888, and quickly replaced horse cars and cars pulled by underground cables.

manufacturing belt A region of the country in which an urban population, transportation systems, and other infrastructure support heavy industry.

By the early 1900s, networks of streetcar lines crisscrossed most large cities, connecting neighborhoods to downtown. Some carried middle-class women wearing white gloves and stylish hats to shop at downtown department stores. Skilled workers rode others to their factory jobs. Still other lines carried typists and businessmen to banks and offices. Cities expanded by annexing suburban areas that grew up along the spreading transportation lines. Chicago grew from 17 to 178 square miles between 1860 and 1890.

New railroad lines also brought outlying villages within commuting distance of cities. Wealthier urban residents could now escape the city at the end of the workday. By 1890, commuter lines brought more than 100,000 workers daily into New York City just from its northern suburbs.

The New Urban Geography

Areas within the largest cities became increasingly specialized by economic function. Iron and steel making, meatpacking, shipbuilding, and oil refining had to be established on the outskirts of cities. Land was plentiful and relatively cheap there, and the city center suffered less from the noise, smoke, and odor of heavy industry.

As heavy manufacturing moved to the outskirts of the cities, city centers tended to become more specialized as well. By 1900, a large city usually had a district of light manufacturing that might include clothing and printing. Nearby was usually a **wholesale** trade district with warehouses and offices of wholesalers. **Retail** shopping districts, anchored by department stores, emerged in a central location accessible by streetcar. In the largest cities, banks, insurance companies, and corporation headquarters clustered near one another to form a financial district. A hotel and entertainment district often lay close to both the financial and retail blocks. These areas together made up a central business district.

Residential areas as well as downtowns developed according to economic status. New suburbs ranged outward from the city center in order of wealth. Those who could afford to travel the farthest could also afford the most expensive homes. Those too poor to ride the new transportation lines lived in crowded apartments or small houses within walking distance of work.

Building an Urban Infrastructure

During the rapid urban growth after the Civil War, local governments did little to regulate urban expansion or construction practices. Cities grew with only the most basic planning. Most choices about land use and construction were made by individual landowners, developers, and builders. Everywhere, builders and owners hoped to achieve a high return on their investment by producing the most living space for the least cost. Such profit calculations rarely left room for varied designs or open space.

Private companies sometimes provided gas, electricity, telephone, and public transit under **franchises** from the city. Companies eagerly competed for such franchises, sometimes bribing city officials to secure one. As a result, cities usually found themselves well supplied with franchised utilities. New residential areas sometimes had gas and electric lines before any houses were framed.

The unplanned nature of most urban growth meant that cities could rarely keep up with the demands for fire and police protection, schools, sewage disposal, street maintenance, parks, and water. As a result, city residents sometimes faced contaminated drinking water, inadequate disposal of sewage and garbage, and epidemic disease. By 1900, however, most cities had improved their infrastructure substantially. The quality and quantity of the water supply varied greatly from city to city. To enlarge its water supply, New York City spent seven years and $24 million constructing what was then the largest aqueduct in the world. Baltimore and Boston also undertook huge water projects. Water quality, though, remained a problem. As city officials began to understand that germs caused

wholesale Engaged in the sale of goods in large quantities, usually for resale by a retailer.

retail Engaged in the sale of goods in small quantities directly to consumers.

franchise Government authorization allowing a private company to provide a public service in a certain area.

♦ Monday was laundry day throughout much of America in the late nineteenth and early twentieth centuries. New York tenements were no exception, as is clear from this photograph taken around 1900. Because buildings were so close together, hanging the laundry became a social event, as neighbors leaned out their windows, pinned their clothes to the line, and exchanged greetings. Note the high population density in such areas. *Library of Congress.*

many diseases, cities introduced filtration and **chlorination** of their water to eliminate disease-carrying organisms. Even so, only 6 percent of urban residents received filtered water by 1900.

Cities faced similar constraints in disposing of sewage, cleaning streets, and removing garbage. Even when cities built sewer lines, they usually emptied the untreated sewage into some nearby body of water. One sanitary expert in 1877 called Boston Harbor "one vast cesspool." In most cities, few streets were paved. The rest became mudholes in the rain, threw up clouds of dust in dry weather, and froze into deep ruts in the winter. Chicago counted 2,048 miles of streets in 1890, but only 629 miles were paved. In the late nineteenth century, however, most eastern cities began using asphalt paving, following the lead of Washington, D.C.

Everywhere, urban growth outstripped cities' ability to provide for it. Despite the introduction of uniformed police during the Civil War era, urban crime mushroomed. The **great Chicago fire** of 1871, which devastated three square miles, killed more than 250 people, and left 18,000 homeless, demonstrated the inadequacy of existing fire protection. The Chicago fire spurred efforts to improve fire protection by creating a well-trained and well-equipped staff of firefighters and by regulating construction practices.

Although change came slowly, city utilities and services improved significantly between 1870 and

chlorination The treatment of water with the chemical chlorine to purify and disinfect it.

great Chicago fire The 1871 disaster that destroyed much of the city and spurred national efforts to improve fire protection.

1900. By the early twentieth century, large American cities had more extensive sewer systems and provided more water to each resident than similar cities in Germany. But as late as 1900, no city larger than 150,000 people had a sewage treatment plant.

Poverty and the City

In 1879, in *Progress and Poverty*, Henry George pointed out that the "enormous increase in productive power" had failed to eliminate poverty or to improve the lives of working people. He concluded that progress and poverty went hand in hand: "The 'tramp' comes with the locomotive, and almshouses and prisons are as surely the marks of 'material progress' as are costly dwellings, rich warehouses, and magnificent churches." George was one of many who focused attention on the growing numbers and problems of the urban poor.

"How the Other Half Lives"

In 1890, **Jacob Riis** shocked many Americans with his book *How the Other Half Lives: Studies Among the Tenements of New York*. In a city of a million and a half inhabitants, Riis claimed, half a million had begged for food at some time over the preceding eight years. Of them, only 6 percent were physically unable to work. Most of Riis's book describes the appalling conditions of the **tenements** that housed three-quarters of the city's population. The living space for an entire family often consisted only of a 10-by-12-foot living room and one or two dark, tiny bedrooms. A tenement might house a dozen or more families. Such accommodations, Riis insisted, "make for evil; because they are the hotbeds of the epidemics that carry death to rich and poor alike; the nurseries of pauperism and crime that fill our jails and police courts; . . . above all, they touch the family life with deadly moral contagion."

Crowded conditions in working-class areas developed in part because so many people were constrained by the need to live within walking distance of their work. By dividing buildings into small rental units, landlords packed in more tenants and collected more rent. Rents were high compared to wages, so tenants often took in boarders. Such practices produced alarmingly high population densities. No other American city was as densely populated as New York, but nearly all urban, working-class neighborhoods throughout the United States were crowded.

Few agreed on the causes or cures for the widespread urban poverty. Riis divided the blame among greedy landlords, corrupt officials, and the poor themselves. Henry George pointed to private ownership of property as the culprit. The influential Charity Organization Society (COS), by contrast, argued that individual character defects such as immorality and laziness produced poverty. COS officials expected the recipients of aid to be moral, thrifty, and hardworking.

The Mixed Blessings of Machine Politics

Not everyone blamed the urban poor for their own distress. In most cities, political organizations built loyal followings in poor neighborhoods by addressing desperate needs in a direct and personal way. Instead of repentance, they wanted the votes of the poor.

George W. Plunkitt illustrates the kind of politics such organizations practiced. Born in a poor Irish neighborhood of New York City, Plunkitt became a district leader of **Tammany Hall,** which dominated the city's Democratic party. Plunkitt described how he kept the loyalty of the voters in his neighborhood in a 1905 newspaper interview:

> *Go right down among the poor families and help them in the different ways they need help. . . . It's philanthropy, but it's politics, too—mighty good politics. . . . The poor are the most grateful people*

Jacob Riis New York journalist whose exposure of slum conditions in American cities appalled middle-class Americans and led to calls for slum clearance and new building codes.

tenement An unsafe and often unsanitary apartment building usually occupied by poor families.

Tammany Hall A New York political organization whose "machines" dominated city and sometimes state politics.

in the world, and, let me tell you, they have more friends in their neighborhoods than the rich have in theirs. If there's a family in my district in want I know it before the charitable societies, and me and my men are first on the ground. . . . The consequence is that the poor look up to George W. Plunkitt as a father, come to him in trouble—and don't forget him on election day.

Plunkitt typified many big-city politicians across the country. Neighborhood **saloons** often served as social gathering places, especially for working-class men. Not surprisingly, would-be politicians frequented these saloons and often owned them. They responded to the needs of the urban poor by providing a bucket of coal on a cold winter day, a basket of food at Thanksgiving, or a job on a city crew. In return, they expected recipients to follow their lead in politics. Political organizations based among working-class and poor voters, usually led by men of poor, immigrant parentage, emerged in nearly all large cities. Opponents denounced the leader of the organization as a **boss** and the organization itself as a machine.

One of the earliest city bosses was **William Marcy Tweed,** who became head of the Tammany Hall organization in 1863. Tweed and his associates built public support by spending tax funds on various charities, and they gave to the poor from their own pockets—pockets often lined with public funds or bribes. Under Tweed's direction, city government launched such major construction projects as public buildings and improvements in streets, parks, sewers, and docks. Much of the construction was riddled with corruption. Between 1868 and 1871, the Tweed Ring may have plundered as much as $200 million from the city, mostly in **kickbacks** from contractors. In 1871, evidence of corruption led to Tweed's conviction and imprisonment. Reformers in practically every city subsequently charged officeholders with corruption, but most bosses were more cautious than Tweed.

Perhaps the most important single function the bosses served was to centralize political decision making. As one Boston boss said, "There's got to be in every ward somebody that any bloke can come to—no matter what he's done—to get help." If a pushcart vender needed a permit to sell tinware or a railroad president needed permission to build a bridge, the machine could help him—if he showed the proper gratitude.

Combating Urban Poverty: The Settlement Houses

By the 1890s, young college-educated men and women began to confront urban poverty in an altogether different way. These humanitarians took an environmental approach in assisting the poor. The **settlement house** idea, which originated in London in 1884, involved opening a house in the slums where idealistic university graduates lived among the poor and tried to help them. The first settlement house in the United States opened in New York in 1886.

Jane Addams and Ellen Gates Starr opened **Hull House** in Chicago in 1889. For many Americans, Jane Addams became synonymous with the settlement house movement. Settlement house workers provided a wide range of assistance to slum families: cooking and sewing classes, public baths, childcare facilities, instruction in English, and housing for unmarried working women. Ad-

saloon A place common to middle-class and working-class neighborhoods where patrons could buy and drink alcoholic beverages.

boss Name applied to the head of an urban political organization that based its success on lower-income voters.

William Marcy Tweed New York City political boss who used the Tammany machine to maintain control over city and state government from the 1860s until his downfall in 1871.

kickback A sum of money that a contractor illegally gives "under the table" to the official who awarded the contract.

settlement house Community center operated by resident social reformers in a slum area to help poor people in their own neighborhood.

Jane Addams Illinois social worker who sponsored child labor laws and was a leader in the settlement house movement. She won the Nobel Peace Prize in 1931.

Hull House Settlement house founded by Jane Addams and Ellen Gates Starr in Chicago in 1889 to improve community and civic life in the slums.

dams and other settlement house workers became forces for urban reform, promoting better education, improved public health, and honest government. Settlement houses spread rapidly, with some four hundred operating by 1910. The settlement houses became the first institutions to be created and staffed primarily by college-educated women.

Church-affiliated settlement houses often reflected the **Social Gospel,** a movement initiated by Protestant ministers who were concerned about the social and economic problems of the cities. One of the best known, Washington Gladden of Columbus, Ohio, called for an "Applied Christianity"—the adoption of Christian principles by businesses. By this he meant that businesses should follow Christ's injunctions to love one another and to treat others as you would have them treat you.

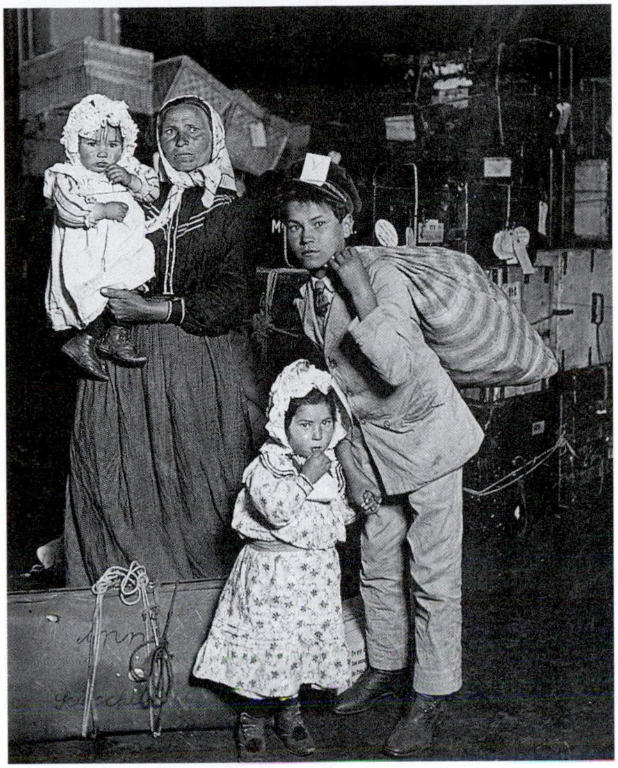

♦ The photographer Lewis Hine took this picture of a family from eastern Europe who arrived in the United States in 1905. After 1890, immigrants came ashore at Ellis Island and were processed by the Immigration Service. For millions of immigrants, Ellis Island was their portal to America. *Courtesy George Eastman House.*

New Americans from Europe

The flood of immigrants that fed the burgeoning cities and industrial labor force from the Civil War to World War I represents the highest level of immigration in American history. In 1865, when the Civil War ended, 248,120 immigrants entered the United States. The number rose to 788,992 in 1882 and peaked at 1,285,349 in 1907.

Most immigrants came from Europe and settled in cities. By 1910, in eighteen of the twenty-five largest cities, immigrants and their children made up more than half the population. Three-fourths of New Yorkers and Chicagoans were first- or second-generation immigrants.

A Flood of Immigrants

Before 1890, most immigrants came from Great Britain, Ireland, Germany, and **Scandinavia.** After 1890, most came from southern and eastern Europe, especially Austria-Hungary, Italy, and Russia.

Most immigrants came because of the United States' reputation as the "land of opportunity," where farms were cheap or free, labor was in demand, and wages were high. Some were attracted by America's reputation for religious toleration and commitment to democracy. Others were recruited by agents sent to Europe by sparsely populated western states or by railroad companies seeking buyers for their land. The reasons for coming varied from country to country, year to year, and person to person.

Groups exhibited distinctive patterns of settlement in the United States. The greatest number of

Social Gospel A moral reform movement of the late nineteenth century led by Protestant clergymen who drew attention to urban problems and advocated social justice for the poor.

Scandinavia The region of northern Europe consisting of Norway, Sweden, and Denmark.

Irish immigrants, many desperately poor, arrived between 1847 and 1854, after the potato blight hit, but Irish immigration continued at high levels until the 1890s. Ninety percent were Catholic. They settled initially in the cities of the Northeast, composing a quarter of the population of New York City and Boston as early as 1860. Although many Irish immigrants worked in the West, the Irish as a group remained urban.

Germans outnumbered all other immigrant groups in the United States before 1900. Rural **overpopulation,** changes in agriculture, and crop failures in the 1840s and 1850s all contributed to the desire to move from Germany. Religious and political persecutions affected some as well. German peasants sold their holdings at home and thus arrived in the United States with the expectation of buying farms. Many did so, especially in the north-central states. Even more German immigrants, however, settled in midwestern towns and cities.

Scandinavian immigration followed the German patterns. The high point of Scandinavian immigration came in the 1880s and 1890s, when Scandinavians accounted for 12 percent of American immigrants. Scandinavian farmers left because of overpopulation and changes in agriculture. Many settled on farms in Minnesota, the Dakotas, Montana, and Nebraska; others landed in Washington State.

Italian immigrants illustrate a different situation. Landless farm laborers from southern Italy and Sicily began to leave in significant numbers in the 1880s. Their numbers increased slowly until, between 1900 and 1915, Italians outnumbered any other single group of immigrants arriving in the United States. At first, many young men worked in construction or agriculture during the summer and returned to Italy during the winter. Eventually, some chose to stay and sent for their families. Large numbers of Italians made the cities of the Northeast their home. In California, Italians became prominent in growing grapes and making wine.

The immigration of Eastern European Jews reveals still a different pattern. In the late nineteenth and early twentieth centuries, one-third of the Jews living in eastern Europe left there, and 90 percent of those came to the United States. The largest number came from Russia, accounting for nearly one-eighth of all immigrants after 1900. Extended **pogroms** occurred in Russia in the early 1880s and from 1903 to 1906. This religious persecution was the most important reason for Jewish migration. Jewish immigration was also different in that entire communities chose to emigrate as a group. They became the most urban of immigrant groups. Half of all the eastern European Jews in America resided in New York in 1914.

Large numbers of Slavic-speaking immigrant groups came only in the 1890s and after, accounting for more than a third of all European immigrants between 1900 and 1914. They immigrated primarily for economic opportunity. The largest single group, Poles, were nearly all Catholic and settled in New York and in the cities of the Midwest. By 1910, Chicago, Milwaukee, Detroit, and Buffalo had large Polish populations. Most Slavic-speaking groups tended to locate in urban and industrial areas.

An Ethnic Patchwork

Immigrant groups tended to congregate in ethnic neighborhoods in American cities. For example, in Manhattan in 1890, the Irish predominated on the West Side and the Germans on the East Side. Neighborhoods of Italians, African Americans, Jews, Chinese, Czechs, Arabs, Finns, Greeks, and Swiss completed the ethnic patchwork. Ethnic patchworks composed of distinctive immigrant communities were not limited to cities. Scandinavians, Dutch, Swiss, Czechs, and Germans were most likely to be farmers, but there were rural farming settlements of many groups. The map at the beginning of the chapter reveals concentrations of immigrants both in the manufacturing belt and in western areas with cheap farmland or mines.

These patterns of settlement reflect the expectations immigrants held about America as well as the opportunities they found when they arrived. The British, Germans, Scandinavians, and Czechs came with capital in the 1870s and 1880s, when good

overpopulation The growth of a population beyond the point where it can be supported by its environment.

pogrom Violent mob attacks on Jewish communities, often resulting in massacres.

farmland could still be acquired relatively cheaply in the north-central states. By contrast, fewer Irish had the necessary capital, and so fewer came with the expectation of becoming farmers. Some post-1900 immigrants, especially Italians and Poles, came without any expectations of staying in America permanently. They planned to work for a time and then return home with full pockets. After 1890, farmland was more difficult to obtain. Newcomers at that point were more likely to find work in the rapidly expanding industrial sectors of the economy.

Hyphenated America

In the nineteenth century, many **old-stock Americans** (sometimes only a generation removed from immigrant forebears themselves) assumed that immigrants should learn English quickly and become citizens resembling themselves. Immigrants from Britain often did assimilate rapidly. They already spoke English and had similar religious values. Most other immigrants, however, resisted rapid assimilation. They held fast to elements in their own culture at the same time that they took up a new life in America. Conscious of being a German or an Italian in America, they often came to think of themselves as **hyphenated Americans:** German-American or Italian-American.

On arriving in America, with its strange language and unfamiliar customs, many immigrants reacted by seeking people who shared their cultural values, practiced their religion, and spoke their language. Ethnic communities thus played significant roles in newcomers' transition from the old country to America. They gave immigrants a chance to learn about their new home with the assistance of those who had come before. At the same time, the newcomers could retain the values and behaviors from their old country that they found most important.

Hyphenated America developed a unique blend of ethnic institutions. Ethnic fraternal lodges sprang up to provide not only social ties but also benefits in case of illness or death. Among them were the Ancient Order of Hibernians (Irish), the Sons of Hermann (German), and the Sons of Italy. Singing societies devoted themselves to the music of the old country. Foreign-language newspapers were vital in connecting the old country to the new, for they provided news from the old country as well as from other similar communities in the United States.

For nearly every group, the church provided the single most important element in ethnic group identity. Immigrant churches shared religion, language, and culture. By 1900, for example, there were separate Lutheran churches speaking German, Norwegian, Swedish, Danish, Finnish, and Icelandic. Catholic services were sometimes conducted in the language of the parish's largest ethnic group and sometimes featured special observances transplanted from the old country.

Nativism

Many old-stock Americans expected that immigrants would embrace the behaviors and beliefs of old-stock Americans and blend neatly into their culture. These expectations came to be identified with the image of the **melting pot.** But the melting-pot metaphor rarely described the reality of immigrants' lives. Most immigrants changed their ways slowly, over their lifetimes.

Few old-stock Americans understood the immigrants' adjustment to their new home. Instead of seeing the ways immigrants changed, many old-stock Americans saw only immigrants' efforts to retain their own culture. They fretted over the multiplication of foreign-language newspapers and feared to go into communities where they rarely heard English. Such fears and misgivings fostered the growth of nativism: the view that old-stock values and social patterns were preferable to those of

old-stock Americans Term used by the Census Bureau to describe people who were born in the United States.

hyphenated Americans Americans with a strong ethnic identity based on their ancestry who felt that they had been shaped by two cultures—Irish-American, for example.

melting pot A phrase describing the vision of American society as a place where immigrants set aside their distinctive cultural identities and were absorbed into a homogeneous culture.

immigrants. Nativists argued that only their values and institutions were genuinely American.

American nativism was often linked to anti-Catholicism because so many immigrant groups were Catholic. The American Protective Association (APA), founded in 1887, noisily proclaimed itself the voice of anti-Catholicism. Its members pledged not to hire Catholics, not to vote for them, and not to strike with them. The APA claimed a half million members by 1894. It dominated the Republican party in parts of the Midwest and occasionally fomented mob violence against Catholics.

Jews, too, faced religious antagonism. Beginning in the 1870s, organizations and businesses began to discriminate against Jews. By the early twentieth century, such discrimination intensified. Some employers refused to hire Jews, many college fraternities and sororities refused to admit them, and **restrictive covenants** constrained them from buying homes in certain areas.

Labor organizations sometimes looked at unlimited immigration as a threat to jobs and wage levels. Anti-Chinese sentiment among Pacific Coast unions contributed to the passage of the Chinese Exclusion Act in 1882 (see page 378). The depression of the 1890s convinced the American Federation of Labor in 1897 to call for a literacy test as a way to reduce the influx of immigrants.

The rise of labor and radical political organizations also contributed to anti-immigrant sentiment. By 1900, a few employers had begun to argue that unions represented foreign, un-American interests. Far more serious was the association of immigrants with radicalism, especially anarchism. Congress banned anarchists from immigrating after Leon Czolgosz, an American-born anarchist with a foreign-sounding name, assassinated President William McKinley in 1901. The link between immigrants and radicalism seemed to be confirmed later when Socialist party candidates received strong support from immigrant voters.

The shift in the sources of immigration from northwestern Europe to southern and eastern Europe also contributed to the rise of nativism in the 1890s. Nativists viewed these **new immigrants** as less desirable than **old immigrants** from northwestern Europe.

The arrival of significant numbers of new immigrants coincided with the glorification of Anglo-Saxons (Germanic ancestors of the English). Relying on Social Darwinism and its argument for survival of the fittest (see page 359), proponents of Anglo-Saxonism were alarmed by statistics that showed old-stock Americans having fewer children than the new immigrants. Some voiced fears of a "race suicide" in which Anglo-Saxons were bred out of existence. Madison Grant, a wealthy New Yorker, epitomized this thinking. Grant claimed in *The Passing of the Great Race* (1916) that all civilization had been created by Nordics—tall, blond, blue-eyed northern Europeans—and that other Europeans had proven themselves unable to sustain civilization.

By the 1890s, these religious, economic, political, and racist strains resulted in demands that the government restrict immigration from Europe. Advocates of restriction initially called for immigrants to pass a literacy test. Opposition came from immigrant organizations and from employers seeking a larger supply of labor. Congress passed literacy measures in 1897, 1913, and 1917, but presidential vetoes prevented the first two from passing. The 1917 law, which did not specify literacy in English, had little impact because most immigrants by then were literate in their own language.

New South, Old Issues

The term **New South** refers to efforts by some southerners to diversify the region's economy and

restrictive covenant Provision in a property title designed to restrict subsequent sale or use of the property, often specifying sale only to a white Christian.

new immigrants Newcomers to America from southern and eastern Europe who began to arrive in large numbers in the 1880s.

old immigrants Newcomers to America from Britain, Germany, Ireland, and Scandinavia who came in waves that peaked during the years 1840–1880.

New South Term first used by southern journalist Henry Grady to promote the image of an industrialized South as the region recovered from the devastation of the Civil War.

to industrialize after Reconstruction. These efforts took place as the South grappled with the legacy of slavery, the Civil War, and Reconstruction. One outcome of these efforts was a modest diversification of the southern economy. Another was that white southerners created a society based on racial segregation that lasted for more than a half-century.

The New South

Following the Civil War, the state of southern railroads was a critical constraint on the region's economic growth. During the 1880s, however, southern railroads more than doubled their miles of track. In the 1890s, J. P. Morgan reorganized southern railroads into three large systems.

The emergence of better transportation led some entrepreneurs to think in terms of new industries, particularly textiles. The 1880s marked a boom era for that industry. New southern mills had more modern equipment and were more productive than the mills of New England. By the 1890s, many New England firms had moved their operations south rather than compete with southern mills. Southern textile mills had cheaper labor costs than those in New England, partly because they relied on child labor. An estimated 70 percent of southern cotton-mill workers were under 21 years of age. A few other industries also developed in the South, including tobacco and cottonseed oil processing, but they did little to transform the regional economy. Nearly all these industries took advantage of the South's cheap, unskilled, and nonunionized labor.

Of greater potential was the iron and steel industry that emerged in northern Alabama. Dominated by the Tennessee Coal, Iron, and Railroad Company, the industry drew on coal from Tennessee and Alabama mines and iron ore from northern Alabama. By the late 1890s, Birmingham, Alabama, had become one of the world's largest producers of pig iron. In 1897, the first southern steel mill opened in Ensley, Alabama, and soon became a serious rival of Pittsburgh's mills. In 1907, J. P. Morgan arranged the merger of the Tennessee Company into his United States Steel Corporation.

The turn of the century also saw the beginning of a southern oil industry near Beaumont, Texas, with the tapping of the Spindletop Pool. The center of petroleum production now shifted from the Midwest to Texas, Oklahoma, and Louisiana, where important discoveries were made in 1901. These discoveries prompted the growth of new companies, notably Gulf and Texaco.

Some southerners tried to diversify the region's agriculture. In doing so, however, they ran up against the cotton textile and cigarette industries. In the end, southern agriculture changed little: owners and sharecroppers farmed small plots, obligated by their rental contracts or **crop liens** to raise cotton or tobacco.

The late nineteenth century also saw the myth of the **Old South** and of the so-called **Lost Cause** blossom. Popular fiction and song, North and South, romanticized the pre–Civil War South as a place of gentility and gallantry, where "kindly" plantation owners cared for "loyal" slaves. The Lost Cause myth portrayed the Confederacy as a heroic effort to retain the life and values of the Old South. Leading southerners, especially Democrats, promoted the Lost Cause myth. Hundreds of statues of Confederate soldiers appeared on courthouse lawns.

The Second Mississippi Plan and the Atlanta Compromise

Dreams of the Old South and the Lost Cause helped fuel the politics of white supremacy that dominated the South after Reconstruction. As long as the Civil Rights Act of 1875 remained in place,

crop lien A claim against a crop, typically held by a storekeeper as the price for extending credit.

Old South Term used to describe the antebellum, or pre–Civil War, South, especially by those who characterized the period as a time of gentility and gallantry.

Lost Cause Term used to describe the Confederate struggle in the Civil War, especially by white southerners who characterized it as a noble but doomed effort to preserve a way of life.

African Americans were theoretically protected against discrimination in public places. Segregation existed, to be sure, but largely without force of law. Restrictions on black political voting and officeholding were also extralegal.

Then, in the **Civil Rights cases** (1883), the U.S. Supreme Court ruled the Civil Rights Act of 1875 unconstitutional. The Court's decision specified that the "equal protection" of the Fourteenth Amendment applied only to state governments, not to individuals and companies. This meant that private businesses need not offer equal access to their facilities. In response, southern lawmakers slowly began to require businesses to practice segregation. In 1887, the Florida legislature required separate accommodations on railroad trains. By 1891, six other states had passed similar laws. Both social custom and local laws began to specify greater racial separation as well.

Mississippi whites took a bolder step in 1890, holding a state constitutional convention to eliminate political participation by African Americans. Shrewdly, the new provisions did not mention the word race. Instead they specified payment of a poll tax, passing a literacy test, and other requirements for voting. Everyone understood that these measures were intended to disfranchise black voters. Those who failed the literacy test could still vote if they could understand a section of the state constitution or law after it was read it to them. This "understanding" clause gave white officials discretion in deciding who passed the test, and they usually permitted white illiterates to vote. The South followed this so-called Second Mississippi Plan with great interest. Except for the **poll tax,** however, no other state imitated its provisions immediately.

Then, in 1895, a black educator signaled his apparent willingness to accept disfranchisement and segregation in a speech at the opening of the Cotton States and International Exposition in Atlanta. Founder of the Tuskegee Institute in Alabama, **Booker T. Washington** seemed to accept an inferior status for blacks, at least for the present: "No race can prosper till it learns that there is as much dignity in tilling a field as in writing a poem. It is at the bottom of life we must begin, and not at the top." He also seemed to condone segregation: "In all things that are purely social, we can be as separate as the fingers, yet one as the hand in all things essential to mutual progress. . . . The wisest among my race understand that the agitation of questions of social equality is the extremest folly." He agreed that equal rights had to be earned rather than belonging to all citizens.

The speech, soon dubbed the **Atlanta Compromise,** earned great acclaim for Washington among whites. His message that blacks were willing to accept segregation and disfranchisement in return for interracial peace and economic opportunity was one that southern whites wanted to hear. Northern whites, too, were receptive to the notion that the South would work out its race relations by itself. Until his death in 1915, Washington held sway as the most prominent black leader in the nation. His message found a mixed reception among African Americans. Some accepted his approach as the best that might be secured at the time. Others criticized his willingness to sacrifice black rights. Henry M. Turner, a bishop of the African Methodist Episcopal church in Atlanta, declared that Washington "will have to live a long time to undo the harm he has done our race."

Separate but Not Equal

Southern lawmakers continued to redefine the legal status of African Americans after Washington's

Civil Rights cases A series of cases that came before the Supreme Court in 1883, in which the Court ruled that private companies could legally discriminate against blacks.

poll tax A tax that many southern states used as a prerequisite to voting to discourage blacks from taking part in the electoral process.

Booker T. Washington A former slave, this educator founded and built the Tuskegee Institute into a leading black educational institution and urged blacks to accept segregation for the time being.

Atlanta Compromise Landmark speech given by Booker T. Washington in 1895, in which he encouraged blacks to accommodate to segregation and work for economic advancement in the available paths.

♦ During the 1890s, Ida B. Wells emerged as the leading opponent of lynching, refusing to be silenced even when threatened herself. She appealed to women especially, through the various women's organizations that developed in the late nineteenth century. *Schomburg Center for Research in Black Culture/New York Public Library/photo by Oscar B. Willis.*

Atlanta speech. State after state followed the lead of Mississippi and disfranchised black voters. In 1898, Louisiana added the infamous **grandfather clause.** Under it, men who would otherwise be prohibited from voting were allowed to vote if their fathers or grandfathers had been eligible to vote in 1867, when the Fourteenth Amendment was enacted. The ruling reinstated whites into the electorate but kept blacks out. Throughout the South, states set up substantial barriers to voting and then carved holes through which only whites could squeeze. South Carolina and other southern states added the white primary as an additional barrier. Southern Democrats, the "white man's party," restricted their primaries and conventions to whites only.

Southern lawmakers also extended segregation by law. The U.S. Supreme Court's decision in ***Plessy v. Ferguson*** (1896), a case involving segregated railroad cars, aided the advocates of such segregation. The Court ruled that "separate but equal" facilities did not violate the equal protection clause of the Fourteenth Amendment. Southern legislators soon applied that reasoning to everything from prisons to restaurants.

Violence against blacks accompanied the new laws. From 1885 to 1900, when the South was redefining race relations, the region witnessed more than twenty-five hundred lynching deaths, almost all of them African Americans. Once the new order was in place, lynchings declined to about eleven hundred between 1900 to 1915.

African Americans fought against lynching in various ways, primarily by publicizing the record of brutality. One of the most prominent opponents was **Ida B. Wells.** In *Free Speech*, the black newspaper that she helped found in Memphis, Tennessee, in 1891, she attacked lynching, arguing that several local victims had been targeted as a means of eliminating successful black businessmen. In response, a mob destroyed her newspaper office. She moved north and spent most of the 1890s crusading against lynching.

grandfather clause Provision in various southern state constitutions restricting suffrage to those whose fathers or grandfathers could vote in 1867, thus depriving blacks of the vote.

Plessy v. Ferguson Case in 1896 in which the Supreme Court upheld a Louisiana law requiring segregated railroad facilities on the grounds that "separate but equal" accommodations were constitutional.

Ida B. Wells Reformer and journalist who crusaded against lynching and advocated racial justice and woman's suffrage. Upon marrying in 1895, she changed her name to Wells-Barnett.

African Americans also sought ways to resist disfranchisement and segregation. Some promoted an exodus from the South to **Liberia,** the nation created in western Africa before the Civil War as a home for free blacks. But few could afford to go to Liberia. Other blacks proposed leaving the South for homestead and railroad land in Kansas. "Kansas Fever" swept through the South in the late 1870s and early 1880s. Perhaps as many as twenty thousand blacks from Louisiana, Mississippi, and Texas moved to Kansas in just a few months in 1879. The 1890s saw another swell in migration. In the 1880s, interest grew in creating all-black communities. A number of such communities were organized, most of them in the South, but others were scattered from New Jersey to California. Between 1892 and 1910, some twenty-five all-black towns were founded in Oklahoma.

New Patterns of American Social and Cultural Life

The decades following the Civil War brought far-reaching social change to Americans in nearly every part of the nation. The educational system, gender roles, sexual relationships, artistic expression, and cultural and leisure activities also changed significantly during this period.

The New Middle Class

The Gilded Age brought substantial changes to the lives of middle-class Americans. In the cities, an army of accountants, lawyers, secretaries, insurance agents, and middle-level managers developed to staff the emerging giant corporations and professional offices. The streetcar made it possible for the middle class to live beyond walking distance of their work. Thus industrialization and urban expansion produced not only sprawling working-class neighborhoods and wealthy enclaves but also distinctively middle-class neighborhoods and suburbs.

Single-family homes set amid wide and carefully tended lawns were common in the new middle-class neighborhoods. Such neighborhoods accelerated the tendency of American urban areas to spread outward and to have lower population densities than their European counterparts. To acquire a single-family house in the leafy suburbs away from urban noise and filth became a part of the American middle-class dream.

Suburban households often followed different patterns than those of working-class or farm families. Middle-class families often hired a servant to assist with household chores, and middle-class women were much more likely to take part in social organizations outside the home. Such families rarely expected their children to contribute to the family's finances but emphasized education instead. Middle-class households were likely to subscribe to daily newspapers and to family magazines such as the *Ladies' Home Journal* and the *Saturday Evening Post*. The new advertising (see page 349) featured in these newspapers and magazines helped create a "consumer culture," particularly among middle-class women, who by 1900 were responsible for nearly all of their families' shopping.

Ferment in Education

The Gilded Age witnessed important changes in education, from kindergarten through the university. Kindergartens, created to provide childcare for working mothers, grew from two hundred in 1880 to three thousand in 1900. Between 1870 and 1900, most northern and western states established school attendance laws, typically requiring children between the ages of 8 and 14 to attend school for a minimum number of weeks annually. School enrollment among those ages 5 to 19 increased significantly, particularly at the secondary level. By 1890, high schools had added a fourth year everywhere but in the South. The high school curriculum changed significantly, including courses such as science, civics, business, home economics, and drafting. The number of high school graduates tripled between 1878 and 1898.

Liberia A nation on the west coast of Africa founded through the efforts of the American Colonization Society and settled mainly by freed slaves between 1822 and the Civil War.

College enrollments also grew, especially in the new state universities created under the Land-Grant College Act of 1862. Still, college students came disproportionately from middle-class and upper-class urban families. The college curriculum changed greatly, from a set of courses required of all students (mostly Latin, Greek, mathematics, rhetoric, and religion) to a system in which students chose a major and electives. New subjects included economics, political science, modern languages, and laboratory sciences. Many universities also began to offer engineering, business administration, and education classes.

Far fewer women than men marched in college graduation processions. **Vassar College** became the first college exclusively for women in 1861. Only one college graduate in seven was a woman in 1870, and this improved only to one in four by 1900. In 1879, fewer than half the nation's colleges even admitted women. Twenty years later, four-fifths did so. Some prestigious private institutions such as Harvard, Princeton, and Yale, however, remained all-male enclaves.

Redefining Women's Gender Roles

Greater educational opportunities for women marked part of a change in social definitions of gender roles. Throughout the nineteenth century, most Americans defined women's social role in terms of the **cult of domesticity.** This held that the proper place for a woman was in the home as wife and mother. Advocates of domesticity conceded that women might also have important roles in the church and the classroom. They contended that women should avoid business and politics, where lax moral standards might corrupt them. Women should occupy a **separate sphere,** immune from such dangers. Widely advocated in the pulpits and journals of the day, the concept of domesticity proved most typical of white middle-class and upper-class women in towns and cities. Farm women and working-class women worked too hard and witnessed too much of the world to fit the model of innocence and daintiness prescribed by advocates of domesticity.

The late nineteenth century saw increasing challenges to domesticity. One challenge came as more women finished college and chose to enter the professions. Important early successes came in medicine. In 1849, Elizabeth Blackwell became the first woman to complete medical school and helped establish the first medical school for women in 1868. By the 1880s, some twenty-five hundred women held medical degrees. About 3 percent of all physicians were women, more proportionately than in most of the twentieth century. After 1900, however, medical schools began to impose enrollment restrictions on women. Access to the legal profession proved surprisingly difficult. Arabella Mansfield was the first woman to be admitted to the bar in 1869, but the entire nation counted only sixty practicing women attorneys ten years later. Most law schools refused to admit women until the 1890s. Women predominated in the new field of social work.

Professional careers attracted relatively few women, but many more became involved outside their homes through women's clubs or in reform activities. Women's clubs became popular among middle- and upper-class women in the late nineteenth century, claiming 800,000 members by 1910. Crusader Ida B. Wells actively promoted the development of black women's clubs. Such clubs often began as forums to discuss literature or art, but they sometimes led women into reform movements. In 1904, Sarah Platt Decker, president of the General Federation of Women's Clubs, bluntly proclaimed, "**Dante** is dead. He has been dead for several centuries, and I think it is time that we dropped the study of his Inferno and turned our attention to

Vassar College The first collegiate institution for women, founded in Poughkeepsie, New York, in 1861.

cult of domesticity The nineteenth-century notion that women's activities were ideally rooted in domestic labor and the nurture of children.

separate sphere The notion that women were meant to pursue occupations having to do with family, church, or school and not those in such traditionally male fields as business and politics, which were considered too competitive and corrupt for women.

Dante Italian poet (1265–1321) best known for his *Inferno,* about a descent into hell.

our own." Female reform organizations often had some link to domesticity: temperance, opposition to prostitution, and abolition of child labor. The **Women's Christian Temperance Union,** one of the most prominent, was formed in 1874.

Women's church organizations, clubs, and reform societies all provided experience in working together under the leadership of women. Through them, women developed networks of working relationships. These experiences and contacts contributed to the effectiveness of women's efforts to establish their right to vote (see page 414).

Emergence of a Gay and Lesbian Subculture

Challenges to domesticity involved women seeking to redefine society's gender roles. A quite different redefinition occurred as gay and lesbian **subcultures** developed in America's burgeoning cities. Homosexuals and lesbians recognized that large cities offered an anonymity not possible in rural areas. Rural communities where practically everyone knew everyone else either prompted people physically attracted to members of their own sex to suppress such tendencies or to exercise them very discreetly. After the Civil War, however, homosexuals and lesbians gravitated toward the largest cities and began to create distinctive subcultures. By the 1890s, one researcher reported that "perverts of both sexes maintained a sort of social set-up in New York City, had their places of meeting, and [the] advantage of police protection." Boston, Chicago, New Orleans, St. Louis, and San Francisco also had clubs, restaurants, and steambaths that catered to homosexuals. Although most homosexuals were secretive about their sexual identity, some flouted their sexuality at "drag balls."

In the 1880s, physicians created medical names for these emerging subcultures, including "homosexual," "lesbian," "invert," and "pervert." Earlier, law and religion had defined particular actions as illegal or immoral. The new medical definitions emphasized not the actions but instead the persons taking the actions. Some theorists proposed that such behavior resulted from a mental disease, but others concluded that homosexuals and lesbians were born that way. The medical definition of *homosexual* stigmatized expressions of deep affection between heterosexuals of the same sex, which became less common as individuals tried to avoid any suggestion that they were anything but heterosexual.

New Patterns in Cultural Expression: From Realism to Ragtime

Shortly after 1900, the director of the prestigious Metropolitan Museum of New York observed "a state of unrest all over the world" in art, literature, music, painting, and sculpture. Unrest meant dramatic changes in American art, literature, and music—many directly influenced by the new urban, industrial, multiethnic society.

Walt Whitman's *Leaves of Grass*, first published in 1855 and reissued in revised editions until his death in 1892, stands as a major work in world literature. Whitman gloried in democracy and in ordinary people. He dealt, too, with topics considered inappropriate for public print, including intimate relationships and the human body:

> *Have you ever loved the body of a woman?*
> *Have you ever loved the body of a man?*
>
> *Do you not see that they are exactly the same to all*
> *In all nations and times all over the earth?*

Emily Dickinson, whose poetry first appeared after her death in 1890, rejected the formal strictures of most previous verse to probe the depths of anxiety and emotion:

> *I can wade Grief—*
> *Whole Pools of it—*
> *I'm used to that—*
> *But the least push of Joy*
> *Breaks up my feet*
> *And I tip—drunken—*

Women's Christian Temperance Union Women's organization founded in 1874 that opposed the evils of drink and supported reforms such as woman's suffrage.

subculture A cultural subgroup, unified by status, interests, or practices, which differentiates its members from the dominant culture on the basis of shared values or loyalties.

American novelists increasingly turned to realistic, critical portrayals of life, rejecting the romantic idealism characteristic of the pre–Civil War period. The towering figure of the era was **Mark Twain** (Samuel Langhorne Clemens). His *Huckleberry Finn* (1885) pokes fun at the social pretensions of the day, scorns the Old South myth, and challenges racial biases against blacks. The novels of William Dean Howells and Henry James, by contrast, present restrained, realistic portrayals of upper-class men and women. After 1890, Stephen Crane, Theodore Dreiser, and Frank Norris sharpened the critical edge of fiction. Crane's *Maggie: A Girl of the Streets* (1893) depicts how urban squalor turned a young woman to prostitution. Norris's *The Octopus* (1901) portrays the abusive power of a railroad. Kate Chopin's *The Awakening* (1899) deals with the repression of a woman's sexual desires.

As American literature moved toward realism, most American painting was moving in the opposite direction. An important exception was Thomas Eakins. Although he received little recognition in the 1870s and 1880s, his work is now considered a major contribution to realism. American painting changed late in the century largely in response to French **impressionism,** which emphasized less an exact reproduction of the world and more the artist's impression of it. James Whistler's work showed impressionist influences. Mary Cassatt was the only American (and the only woman) to rank among the leaders of impressionism, but she lived and painted mostly in France. A prominent American impressionist was Childe Hassam, who often presented urban landscapes.

Robert Henri and his associates in the **Ash Can school** also were preoccupied with urban poverty and ordinary people. The Ash Can adherents faced a challenge from artists influenced by the abstract approach then becoming prominent in France by 1910 or so. In 1913, the so-called Armory Show in New York City presented the art of radical European innovators such as Pablo Picasso, Henri Matisse, and Wassily Kandinsky. Critics dismissed the modernists, but the abstract style caught on.

The most innovative musician at the turn of the century was African-American composer Scott Joplin. Joplin studied piano with a German-born music teacher and then traveled through African-American communities from New Orleans to Chicago. As he traveled, he encountered **ragtime** music and soon began to write his own. In 1899, he published "The Maple Leaf Rag" and soared to fame as the best-known ragtime composer in the country.

The Origins of Mass Entertainment

Better transportation and communication and increased leisure time fostered new forms of entertainment in the late nineteenth century. Companies now organized entertainers into traveling groups and sent them from city to city to perform. Circuses also took advantage of improved transportation to establish regular circuits. Thus mass entertainment had its birth.

Gilded Age booking agencies scheduled traveling dramatic and musical troupes into every corner of the country. Traveling groups of actors, singers, and other performers provided the entertainment mainstay, performing everything from Shakespeare to **slapstick.** In the late nineteenth century, these agencies developed the star system, in which each traveling company had one or two accomplished performers who attracted audiences.

One of the most unusual traveling shows was the **Chautauqua,** a blend of inspirational oratory,

Mark Twain Pen name of Samuel Clemens, an American author who drew on his childhood along the Mississippi River to create novels such as *The Adventures of Huckleberry Finn.*

impressionism A style of painting that developed in France in the 1870s. It emphasized the play of light on surfaces and attempted to convey the impression of observing nature directly.

Ash Can school New York artists of varying styles who shared a dislike of academicism.

ragtime Music blending African rhythms and European form to create a unique style; popularized by Scott Joplin and others in the late nineteenth century.

slapstick A boisterous form of comedy marked by chases, collisions, and crude practical jokes.

Chautauqua Traveling shows offering educational, religious, and recreational activities; part of a nationwide movement of adult education that began in the town of Chautauqua, New York.

education, and entertainment. Thousands of towns held annual Chautauqua assemblies that featured comedians, inspirational orators, opera, glee clubs, lectures, string quartets, or magic-lantern shows on foreign countries.

Professional baseball emerged as a quite different form of mass entertainment after the Civil War. Teams traveled by train from city to city, and urban rivalries built loyalty among hometown fans. The formation of the National League in 1876 established an owners' cartel that monopolized the industry by excluding rival clubs and by controlling the movement of players from team to team. Because African Americans were barred from the National League, separate Negro Leagues emerged. In the 1880s and 1890s, the National League successfully warded off challenges from rival leagues and a players' union. Not until 1901 did another league—the American League—successfully organize. In 1903, the two leagues merged into a new, stronger cartel and staged the first World Series. Other professional sports often adopted baseball's patterns of organization, labor relations, and racial discrimination.

SUMMARY

Expectations
Constraints
Choices
Outcomes

In the Gilded Age, industrialization transformed the economy, while urbanization and immigration challenged many established social patterns. In the midst of economic and social change, Americans developed new *expectations* and faced new *choices* about their relations with each other. The *outcomes* of their many individual *choices* marked a major redefinition of American social and cultural life.

As rural Americans and European immigrants sought better lives in the cities, urban America changed dramatically. New technologies in transportation and communication broke down old *constraints* on individual *choices* about where to live and work. The *outcome* was a new urban geography with separate retail, wholesale, finance, and manufacturing areas and residential neighborhoods defined by economic status.

Many urban Americans struggled under the *constraints* of poverty. To gain support from the poor, political machines like Tammany Hall in New York City helped them in various ways. Social reformers established settlement houses to address the problems of the urban poor in a different way.

Many Europeans immigrated because of their *expectations* of better opportunities in America. Immigrants often formed separate communities, usually centered on a church. The flood of immigrants from southern and eastern Europe spawned nativist reactions among some old-stock Americans.

Some southerners proclaimed the creation of a New South and promoted industrialization. The *outcome* was mixed. The South did acquire some industry, but regional poverty remained. After 1890, white southerners disfranchised African Americans and extended segregation. Booker T. Washington emerged as the best-known African-American leader.

Education underwent far-reaching changes from kindergartens through universities. Challenged in part by the *expectations* of college-educated women, socially defined gender roles began to change as some women *chose* professional careers. Some also *chose* active roles in reform. Urbanization offered new *choices* to gay men and lesbians by permitting the development of urban subcultures. The new *expectations* and *choices* generated by an urban, industrial, multiethnic society contributed to critical realism in literature, new patterns in painting, and ragtime music. Urbanization and changes in transportation and communication also fostered the emergence of an entertainment industry.

SUGGESTED READINGS

Addams, Jane. *Twenty Years at Hull House* (1910; reprint, 1960).

Nothing can convey the complex world of Hull House and the striking personality of Addams as well as her own account.

Ayers, Edward L. *The Promise of the New South: Life After Reconstruction* (1992).

A comprehensive survey of developments in the South during this period.

Clinton, Catherine. *The Other Civil War: American Women in the Nineteenth Century* (1984).

The section on the post–Civil War period surveys the subject, although so many recent works have appeared that no synthesis could cover them all.

Higham, John. *Strangers in the Land: Patterns of American Nativism, 1860–1925* (1965).

This classic of American history played a major role in defining the contours of American nativism and still provides an excellent introduction to the subject.

Kraut, Alan M. *The Huddled Masses: The Immigrant in American Society, 1880–1921* (1982).

A helpful introduction to immigration, especially the so-called new immigration.

McDonald, Terrence J., ed. *Plunkitt of Tammany Hall*, by William L. Riordon (1993).

McDonald provides excellent context for and editing of this classic account of Tammany's relationship with voters.

Mohl, Raymond A. *The New City: Urban America in the Industrial Age, 1860–1920* (1985).

An informative but concise introduction to nearly all aspects of the growth of American cities.

New Choices for Women

The Context

The late nineteenth and early twentieth centuries saw a good deal of public attention given to the emergence of the "New Woman," a consequence of the emergence of a mature industrial economy and a complex, urban society. The era of "separate spheres" was rapidly passing, as women moved out of the home and into the larger society. Young women of upper- and middle-income families attended college, and some of them entered careers. Some women, mostly of middle- and upper-income levels, joined women's associations and sought political changes. Young women of working-class families entered the wage-earning work force as factory or office workers, and some of them became involved in unions. (For further information on the context, see pages 400–402.)

The Historical Question

At the time and since then, some people asked whether the breakdown of separate spheres called into question the concept of domesticity—the expectation that a woman has a special responsibility for the nurturing and protection of the family. Did the emergence of the "New Woman" significantly change expectations about women's roles in American society? Or were the older expectations of domesticity still prominent?

The Challenge

Using the sources provided, along with other information you have read, write an essay or hold a discussion on the following question. Cite evidence in the sources to support your conclusions. **Did the emergence of the "New Woman" significantly change expectations about women's roles in American society?**

The Sources

1 Mrs. Burton Harrison, writing in *Harper's Bazaar* in 1900 on "Home Life as a Profession," had this to say:

Today, when hundreds of young women of our best blood and culture in America are standing within the open doors of schools and colleges, eagerly straining their gaze out into the future, hoping to catch a glimpse of the opportunity for a "career," it seems to behoove the conservative thinkers among us to suggest to some of them the profession of home life. . . . Now, as a matter of historic fact, the cornerstone of the highest civilization has always been the home, and wifehood and motherhood the happiest estate of woman. To my mind, it is a cruel wrong to a young girl to launch her in life unadvised on these points, and imbued with the determination to independence of the other sex. . . .

Far be it from me to suggest a relapse to those dark ages of home life when a girl strummed on the piano or worked in cross-stitch tapestry. . . . On the contrary, I would have her carry back into her home her sheaves of knowledge and accomplishment, and there try to enrich and broaden the domestic sphere. . . . I do not think our homes as they are now a sufficiently satisfying exchange for the broader, more interesting channels for women's work everywhere available. But I earnestly wish they might be made so; and the question of how to accomplish this enormously important result lies largely in the palm of the girl graduate of today.

2 Rena Rietveld Verduin, an Illinois farm wife and mother with only a fifth-grade education, presented these views in 1907 in a community debate sponsored by a local club that organized cultural activities. She spoke in opposition to the proposition "Resolved that women should not enter higher education."

Through an education girls are enabled to become self-supporting and acquainted with the ways of the world. Through an education girls learn to earn a livelihood and are not so liable to throw themselves away in marriage on some worthless man. . . . When [men] discover that the girls don't have to marry—by getting an education and going into some profession—they will be more likely to behave themselves and be at some pains to make themselves worthy of the girl's acceptance. . . . Men seem to think that the women have no business on the face of the earth except to work and slave for them. . . . Girls, get an education and escape slavery.

3 Susan W. Fitzgerald prepared this argument for woman's suffrage in the early twentieth century.

We are forever being told that the place of woman is in the HOME. . . .

SHE is responsible for the cleanliness of her house.

SHE is responsible for the wholesomeness of the food.

SHE is responsible for the children's health.

SHE, above all, is responsible for their morals, for their sense of truth, of honesty and decency, for what they turn out to be.

How Far Can the Mother Control These Things? . . . [The pamphlet then surveys problems of urban life—filthy streets, lack of adequate sanitation, fire hazards, and more.]

It is the MEN and NOT THE WOMEN that are really responsible for the unclean houses, unwholesome food, bad plumbing, danger of fire, risk of tuberculosis and other diseases, immoral influences of the street. In fact, MEN are responsible for the conditions under which the children live, but we hold WOMEN responsible for the results of those conditions. If we hold women responsible for the results, must we not, in simple justice, let them have something to say as to what those conditions shall be? . . . LET THEM VOTE.

Women are by nature and training, housekeepers. Let them have a hand in the city's housekeeping, even if they introduce an occasional house-cleaning.

4 Charlotte Perkins Gilman, who made her living as a writer and lecturer, was largely self-educated. This excerpt is from her article "Are Women Human Beings?" which appeared in *Harper's Weekly* in 1912.

[The] things the women want to do and be and have are not in any sense masculine. They do not belong to men. They never did. They are departments of our social life, hitherto monopolized by men. . . . We find everywhere this same pervasive error, this naïve assumption, which would be so insolent if it were not so absurd, that only men are human creatures, able and entitled to perform the work of the world; while women are only female creatures, able to do nothing whatever but continue in the same round of duties to which they have been so long restricted. . . .

Women will never cease to be females, but they will cease to be weak and ignorant and defenseless. They are becoming wiser, stronger, better able to protect themselves, one another, and their children. Courage, power, achievement are always respected. . . . [As they take] their full place in the world as members of society, as well as their partial places as mothers of it, they will gradually rear a new race of men, men with minds large enough to see in human beings something besides males and females.

REGIONAL BASES OF POLITICAL PARTIES IN THE GILDED AGE After Reconstruction, competition between the Republicans and Democrats settled into distinct regional patterns, as this map showing the party that carried presidential elections in each state reveals.

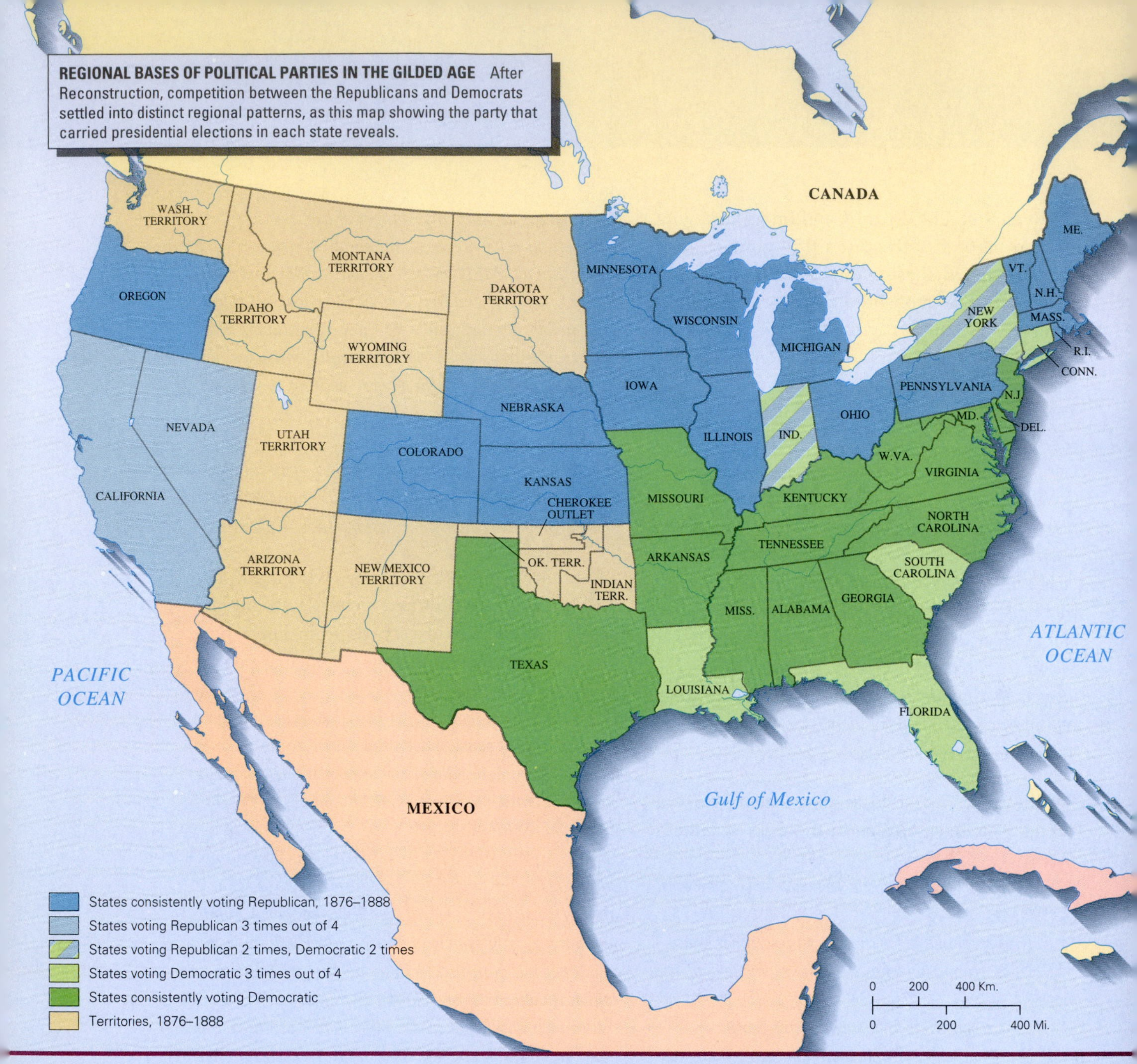
CANADA
WASH. TERRITORY
MONTANA TERRITORY
DAKOTA TERRITORY
IDAHO TERRITORY
WYOMING TERRITORY
OREGON
NEVADA
UTAH TERRITORY
CALIFORNIA
COLORADO
NEBRASKA
KANSAS
CHEROKEE OUTLET
OK. TERR.
INDIAN TERR.
ARIZONA TERRITORY
NEW MEXICO TERRITORY
TEXAS
MINNESOTA
WISCONSIN
MICHIGAN
IOWA
ILLINOIS
IND.
OHIO
MISSOURI
KENTUCKY
ARKANSAS
TENNESSEE
MISS.
ALABAMA
GEORGIA
LOUISIANA
FLORIDA
SOUTH CAROLINA
NORTH CAROLINA
VIRGINIA
W.VA.
MD.
DEL.
N.J.
PENNSYLVANIA
NEW YORK
CONN.
R.I.
MASS.
N.H.
VT.
ME.
PACIFIC OCEAN
ATLANTIC OCEAN
Gulf of Mexico
MEXICO
States consistently voting Republican, 1876–1888
States voting Republican 3 times out of 4
States voting Republican 2 times, Democratic 2 times
States voting Democratic 3 times out of 4
States consistently voting Democratic
Territories, 1876–1888
0 200 400 Km.
0 200 400 Mi.

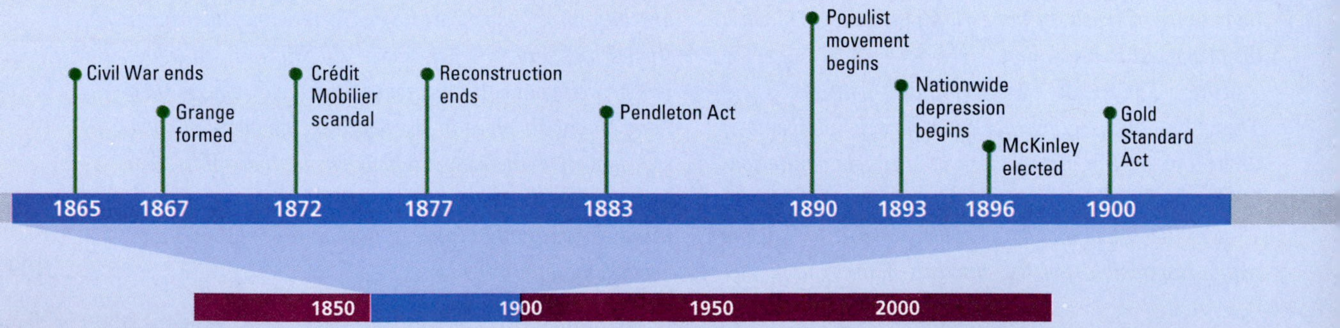
Civil War ends
Grange formed
Crédit Mobilier scandal
Reconstruction ends
Pendleton Act
Populist movement begins
Nationwide depression begins
McKinley elected
Gold Standard Act
1865
1867
1872
1877
1883
1890
1893
1896
1900
1850
1900
1950
2000

CHAPTER 19

Political Stalemate and Political Upheaval, 1868–1900

Parties, Voters, and Reformers

- What were people's expectations about the role of parties in the politics of the Gilded Age?
- What choices did the political parties offer voters?

Political Stalemate

- How did the stalemate that deadlocked politics from 1874 into the 1890s constrain both parties?

Agricultural Distress and Political Upheaval

- Why did farmers choose to take political action outside the major parties?
- What did they expect to accomplish?
- What was the immediate outcome of their choices?

Economic Collapse and Political Upheaval

- What choices did voters face in the 1896 presidential election?
- What were the long-term outcomes of that election?

INTRODUCTION

Expectations
Constraints
Choices
Outcomes

In July 1892, a new political party, the People's party, met in Omaha to *choose* its candidates for president and vice president. The new party, also called the Populists, contended that the *outcome* of industrialization had been material and moral ruin, political corruption, and exploited labor. The Populists also proclaimed their *choices* for dealing with the *outcome* of industrialization. They urged immediate federal action to rescue debtors, break up monopolies, and bring railroads under government ownership. They proposed reforms to increase the power of voters to control the government. And they made clear the *expected outcome* of these changes: that "oppression, injustice, and poverty shall eventually cease in the land."

Most Americans, however, held different *expectations* from the Populists. Most were unwilling to create a vastly more powerful federal government, to place severe *constraints* on the rights of property owners, or to entrust the federal government to self-proclaimed representatives of impoverished farmers and angry workers. In the end, the Populists failed to establish their new party as a major factor in American politics. The *outcome* of their efforts, however, was significant change in the nature of politics in the 1890s—and in the twentieth century as well.

Although most Americans rejected the Populists' remedies, few doubted that there had been a profound transformation of the nation's social and economic life following the Civil War. Congress and the president had grappled with complex *choices* affecting the South and Reconstruction, the future of American Indians, and the role of the federal government in developing the West. But a protracted stalemate gripped national politics from 1875 to 1896, *constraining* those who advocated political changes that would address the issues created by rapid social and economic change.

Throughout those years, men were *expected* to hold intense party loyalties. (Nearly all women were *constrained* from voting throughout this period.) Despite such *expectations*, a few people *chose* to break with the major parties to call for changes in policies or in the nature of politics. Prominent among those demanding change were advocates of woman suffrage. A succession of organizations and parties also spoke out for impoverished farmers and tried, largely unsuccessfully, to forge an alliance among all the disadvantaged—rural and urban, black and white.

The Populist party was the *outcome* of a quarter-century of agrarian radicalism that was fueled by the economic misfortunes of farmers. Eventually, the Populists *chose* to merge with the Democrats in support of the presidential candidacy of William Jennings Bryan in 1896. In the process, the Democratic party shed its deep commitment to minimal government and embraced a more activist role for the government in the economy. In 1896, however, voters *chose* William McKinley, the Republican candidate for president, thereby endorsing a more conservative approach to government. The long-term *outcome*, however, was the transformation of the very nature of American politics.

CHRONOLOGY

Politics

1865 End of the Civil War

1867 First Grange

1868 Grant elected president

1869 National Woman Suffrage Association formed
Wyoming Territory adopts woman suffrage

1870 Utah Territory adopts woman suffrage

1872 Crédit Mobilier scandal
Grant reelected

1872–1874 Granger laws

1875 Whiskey Ring scandal

mid-1870s Grange membership peaks

1877 Reconstruction ends
Munn v. Illinois

1878 Greenback party peaks
Bland-Allison Act

1880 Garfield elected president

1881 Garfield assassinated; Arthur becomes president

1883 Pendleton Act

1884 Cleveland elected president

1886 *Wabash Railway v. Illinois*

1887 Congress disfranchises women in Utah Territory
Interstate Commerce Act

1880s Farmers' Alliances spread

1888 Harrison elected president

1888–1892 Australian ballot adopted

1890 Wyoming becomes a state, with woman suffrage
Idaho becomes a state
McKinley Tariff, Sherman Anti-Trust Act, and Sherman Silver Purchase Act
"Force Bill" defeated
Populist movement begins

1892 Homestead strike
Cleveland elected president

1893 Colorado adopts woman suffrage
Nationwide depression
Sherman Silver Purchase Act repealed

1894 Coxey's Army
Wilson-Gorman Tariff

1895 Morgan stabilizes gold reserve

1896 Utah becomes a state, with woman suffrage
Bryan's "Cross of Gold" speech
McKinley elected president
Idaho adopts woman suffrage

1897 Dingley Tariff

1900 Gold Standard Act

Parties, Voters, and Reformers

Political parties dominated nearly every aspect of the political process from the 1830s until the early 1900s. During those years, Americans expected all meaningful political choices to come through parties. An understanding of politics therefore must begin with an analysis of political parties: what they were, what they did, what they stood for, and what choices they offered to voters.

Republicans and Democrats

Important differences characterized the two parties in their campaign arguments, their actions at state and local levels, and the voters who supported them. Some of those differences appear in the ways the two parties described themselves in their platforms, newspapers, speeches, and other campaign appeals.

Republicans asserted a virtual monopoly on patriotism by pointing to their defense of the Union during the Civil War. They claimed that Democrats had proved themselves disloyal during the conflict. "Every man that shot a Union soldier," one Republican orator proclaimed, "was a Democrat." Republicans exploited the Civil War legacy in other ways too. Republicans in Congress voted generous federal pensions to disabled Union army veterans and to the widows and orphans of those who died. Republican party leaders urged the **Grand Army of the Republic (GAR),** the organization of Union veterans, to "vote as you shot." Republican candidates were frequently Union veterans.

Prosperity formed another persistent Republican campaign theme. Republicans boasted that the economic growth of the postwar era stemmed from their wise policies. They accused the Democrats of endangering prosperity by pledging to reduce the protective tariff. Republicans also claimed to be the party of decency and respectability. Republican campaigners delighted in portraying Democrats as "the old slave-owner and slave-driver, the saloon-keeper, the ballot-box-stuffer, the Kuklux [Klan], the criminal class of the great cities, the men who cannot read or write."

Whereas Republicans defined themselves in terms of what their party did and who they were, Democrats typically explained what they opposed. Most leading Democrats stood firm against "governmental interference" in the economy, especially tariffs and land grants. The Republicans' protective tariff, Democrats claimed, protected manufacturers from international competition at the expense of consumers. Land grants should provide farms for citizens, not subsidies for railroads. Democrats favored a strictly limited role for the government in the economy. This commitment to minimal government went back to the days of Andrew Jackson, who equated governmental activism with privileges for a favored few.

Democrats also opposed governmental interference in social relations and behavior. In the North, especially in Irish and German communities, they condemned **prohibition,** which they called a violation of personal liberty. They defended Catholics against the political attacks of groups like the **American Protective Association (APA).** In the South, Democrats rejected federal enforcement of equal rights for African Americans.

Efforts to mobilize supporters on election day produced all-time records for voter participation. In 1876, more than 80 percent of the eligible voters cast their ballots. At the polling places, party workers distributed lists, or "tickets," of their party's candidates, which voters then used as ballots. Voting was not secret until the 1890s. Before then, everyone could see which party's ticket a voter deposited in the ballot box.

Most voters developed strong party loyalties on the basis of **ethnicity,** race, or religion. Nearly all

Grand Army of the Republic Organization of Union army veterans.

prohibition A legal ban on the manufacture, sale, and use of alcoholic beverages.

American Protective Association An anti-Catholic organization founded in Iowa in 1887 and active during the next decade.

ethnicity Ethnicity, or ethnic background, can include a shared racial, religious, linguistic, cultural, or national heritage.

Catholics and many Irish, German, and other immigrants supported the Democrats as the party that defended them against the APA, nativism, and prohibition. Poor voters in the disproportionately Catholic big cities usually supported the local Democratic machine. Most southern whites supported the Democrats as the party that opposed federal enforcement of black rights. After 1876, the Democrats dominated the South and found pockets of ethnic supporters throughout the North. They comprised a very diverse coalition.

Outside the South, most old-stock Protestants voted Republican, as did most Scandinavian and English immigrants. Most African Americans and former abolitionists supported the Republicans as the party of emancipation. Union veterans supported the Republicans overwhelmingly. Republicans did well in New England, Pennsylvania, much of the Midwest, and among Hispanic voters in the Southwest. The Republicans comprised a more coherent political organization than the Democrats. They agreed that the federal government should encourage economic growth and protect black rights. The Democrats opposed such measures. Neither party advocated government action to regulate, restrict, or tax the developing industrial corporations.

Parties and Patronage

The spoils system, or patronage system, played an important role in Gilded Age politics. Under this system, the winner of an election, whether a mayor or a president, rewarded his loyal followers with appointments to the many government jobs at his disposal. These patronage jobs were considered an appropriate reward for working hard for the candidate during the campaign. Everyone understood that those appointed to such jobs were expected to contribute part of their salaries to the party and to work for that party's candidates. Thus the existence of patronage jobs helped ensure a high voter turnout.

Competition for patronage jobs was always fierce. In 1869, Congressman James A. Garfield grumbled that all "the adult population of the United States" seemed involved in "the rush for office." When Garfield himself became president in 1881, he was so overwhelmed with demands for jobs that he exclaimed in disgust, "My God! What is there in this place that a man should ever want to get into it?"

The government jobs most in demand involved purchasing supplies or handling government contracts. Purchasing and contracts themselves became another form of spoils, awarded to entrepreneurs who supported the party. This system invited corruption. In the 1890s, for example, a Post Office Department official pressured **postmasters** across the country to buy clocks from a political associate. Business owners competing for government contracts sometimes paid bribes to the officials who made the decisions.

Some critics charged that the fundamental defect of the politics of patronage was that it ignored principles and issues. George F. Hoar, a Republican congressman from Massachusetts, complained in 1876 that some of his colleagues believed that the only way to win power was "to bribe the people with the offices" and that these politicians used power primarily for "promotion of selfish ambition." The spoils system did have its defenders. Tammany Hall politician George Plunkitt explained, "You can't keep an organization together without patronage. Men ain't in politics for nothin'. They want to get somethin' out of it."

The most persistent critics of the spoils systems were known as the **Mugwumps.** Centered in Boston and New York, these reformers were largely Republicans who enjoyed high social status. Mugwumps argued that eliminating patronage would drive out the machines and opportunists and restore political decency. Instead of basing appointments on political loyalty, the Mugwumps advocated a **merit system**

postmaster An official appointed to oversee the operations of a local post office.

Mugwumps A group of Republicans who opposed political corruption and campaigned for reform in the 1880s and 1890s, sometimes crossing party boundaries to achieve their goals.

merit system Practice of hiring government workers based on their abilities and their scores on competency tests instead of through patronage.

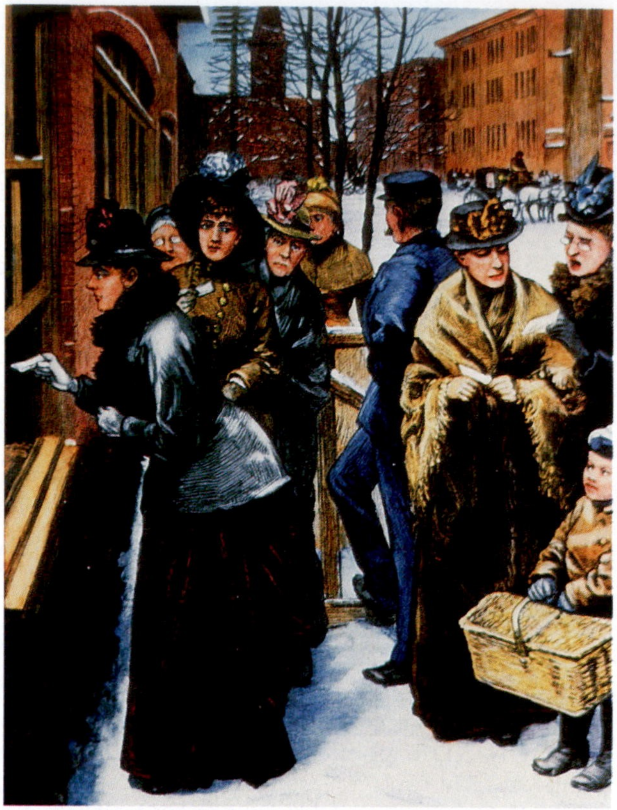

♦ This sketch of women voting in Cheyenne, Wyoming Territory, appeared in 1888. In 1869, Wyoming became the first state or territory to extend suffrage to women. This drawing apppeared shortly before Wyoming requested statehood, a request made controversial by the issue of woman suffrage. *Library of Congress.*

based on a job seeker's ability to pass a comprehensive examination. Educated, dedicated civil servants, they believed, would stand above party politics and provide capable, honest administration. Because the Mugwumps sometimes broke with their party, they drew the contempt of most party politicians.

Challenging the Male Bastion: Woman Suffrage

In the late nineteenth century, some bold women accelerated the efforts to secure the right to vote for women. The struggle for woman suffrage was of long standing. In 1848, Elizabeth Cady Stanton and four other women had organized the world's first Women's Rights Convention, held at Seneca Falls, New York. Stanton was the most prominent leader in the struggle for women's rights, especially voting rights, until her death in 1902. After 1851, Susan B. Anthony became her constant partner in these efforts. They achieved important successes in convincing lawmakers to modify laws that discriminated against women, but all their labor could not change the laws that limited voting to men.

In 1869, Stanton and Anthony formed the **National Woman Suffrage Association (NWSA).** The NWSA sought a constitutional amendment to secure woman suffrage. They built alliances with other reform organizations and worked to improve women's status. For example, members pressed for easier divorce laws and birth control (which Stanton called "self-sovereignty") and promoted women's unions. The major support for the NWSA came from middle-class women—and some men—who were of old-stock American Protestant descent.

The first victories for woman suffrage came in the West. In 1869, the Wyoming territorial legislature extended the **franchise** to women. This action may have been intended to attract women to Wyoming, which had many more males than females. In 1889, when Wyoming asked for statehood, many congressmen balked at admitting a state that permitted women to vote. Congress ultimately relented and approved Wyoming statehood in 1890. In 1893, Colorado became the first state to adopt woman suffrage through a popular vote.

National Woman Suffrage Association New York–based woman-suffrage organization led by Elizabeth Cady Stanton and Susan B. Anthony; it accepted only women as members and worked for related issues such as unionizing female workers.

franchise The right to vote; another word for *suffrage.*

The Utah Territory adopted woman suffrage in 1870. This action strengthened the Mormons' political power, because Mormon women greatly outnumbered non-Mormon women. The Mormons also may have hoped to silence critics who claimed that polygamy degraded women. In an act aimed primarily at the Mormons, Congress outlawed polygamy in 1887 and disfranchised the women in the Utah Territory at the same time. Not until Utah became a state in 1896 did Utah women regain the vote. Neighboring Idaho also adopted woman suffrage in 1896.

Several states began to permit women limited voting rights, especially on matters usually outside party politics, such as school board elections and school bond issues. These concessions reflected the widespread assumption that women's gender roles included child rearing. By 1890, women could vote in school elections in nineteen states and on bond and tax issues in three. But no state passed a suffrage proposal between 1896 and 1910.

Structural Change and Policy Change

The Mugwumps and advocates of woman suffrage were only two of the many groups that identified issues seldom addressed by the two major parties: prohibition, the secret ballot, an end to child labor, and the regulation of business, among others. Most of the reforms these groups called for fall into two categories. *Structural reform* refers to efforts to change the manner in which political decisions are made. Structural issues include the way in which public officials are chosen and eligibility to vote. Thus the Mugwumps and woman suffragettes both advocated structural change. *Policy reform,* by contrast, refers to changes in the way government uses its power. The debate over federal economic policy in the Gilded Age provides an array of contrasting positions. Democrats typically favored laissez faire, believing that federal interference in the economy created a privileged class. Republicans believed in distributing economic benefits to companies and individuals (land, tariff protection) to encourage economic growth. The Grangers (discussed on page 420) wanted federal regulation of corporations.

Although many reform groups had little in common with each other, some formed alliances. The tiny Prohibition party, for example, wanted government to eliminate alcohol, but it also favored woman suffrage because it assumed most women voters would oppose alcohol.

Many political groups supported one important structural change: the **Australian ballot,** which was printed and distributed by the government, not political parties, and marked by voters in the privacy of an enclosed booth. Use of the secret ballot spread rapidly after its introduction in the late 1880s. By 1892, most states had adopted it. This reform had important implications for political parties. It enabled voters to cross party lines and vote a **split ticket.** It also prevented party officials from seeing how a voter cast his ballot. The adoption of the secret ballot and the merit system marked the first significant efforts to limit parties' power and influence.

Political Stalemate

A political stalemate made it difficult for either party to put through major changes in federal policy between 1875 and 1896. Instead, politics often revolved around scandal and spoils rather than issues of policy. When the Republicans briefly broke the stalemate in 1889 and 1890, they found themselves rejected by the voters.

Formula for Stalemate

Competition between Republicans and Democrats at a national level was very close from 1874 to 1896. In the elections of 1880, 1884, and 1888, New York State cast its electoral votes for the winning

Australian ballot A method of voting adopted from Australia, in which the voter's choices of candidates are secret.

split ticket A ballot cast by an individual who has voted for candidates of more than one political party.

candidate. Had it voted for the other candidate, he would have won. Thus a different choice by one or two voters out of every hundred in New York would have changed the result of the national election.

Although most presidential elections during these decades were very close, the Republicans usually won. The Democrats carried only two of the eleven presidential elections between 1860 and 1900. However, from 1877 until 1895, the two parties had nearly equal numbers in the Senate and House of Representatives. The Democrats usually held a slim majority in the House, and the Republicans usually held a similar margin in the Senate. Thus the Republican Senate could block any proposal by a Democratic president, and the Democratic House could block any proposal by a Republican president.

Other factors also made significant changes in policy unlikely. The struggle between Andrew Johnson and the congressional radicals had tipped the balance of power from the presidency to the Congress. Johnson's successors did little to challenge that dominance. Also, both parties held attitudes toward the presidency that made it improbable that a president would seek a leadership role in policy. In the words of John Sherman, a highly influential Republican, the executive "should be subordinate to the legislative department." Virtually no one expected the president to be a major policy initiator, and no president was.

The Grant Administration: Spoils and Scandals

The dogged determination that made Ulysses S. Grant a winning general failed to make him even a satisfactory president. Grant never grasped the potential for presidential leadership. Congress had taken control of domestic policymaking during Andrew Johnson's troubled presidency, and Grant accepted that situation.

Although Grant himself was not involved, his two terms in office (1869–1877) were mired in scandal. Grant all too often named friends or acquaintances to federal posts for which they were unqualified. Many of them saw their positions as little more than a way to enrich themselves. The **Whiskey Ring** provides a prime example. This "ring" of federal officials and distillers, centered in St. Louis, had conspired to evade paying whiskey taxes. In 1875, Treasury Secretary Benjamin Bristow had 230 men indicted for this offense. The indictment included several of Grant's appointees and even his private secretary. Despite the evidence, Grant could not believe his close associates were guilty. He helped his secretary avoid conviction and forced Bristow to resign.

Congress also supplied its share of scandal. In 1868, several prominent congressional leaders had become stockholders in the **Crédit Mobilier,** a construction company created by the chief shareholders in the Union Pacific Railroad. The Union Pacific officers awarded Crédit Mobilier a very generous contract to build the railroad. Thus the company's chief shareholders paid themselves handsomely for constructing their own railroad. To protect this arrangement from congressional scrutiny, the company sold shares cheaply to key members of Congress. Purchasers included many leading Republicans, two of whom later became vice president. Revelation of these arrangements in 1872 and 1873 scandalized the nation.

Hayes, Garfield, and Arthur: The Politics of Faction

Repeated exposures of corruption led Republicans in 1876 to nominate **Rutherford B. Hayes,** whose

Whiskey Ring Distillers and revenue officials in St. Louis who were revealed in 1875 to have defrauded the government of millions of dollars in whiskey taxes, with the collusion of federal officials.

Crédit Mobilier Company created to build the Union Pacific Railroad. It sold shares cheaply to congressmen who approved federal subsidies for railroad construction. The scandalous deal was uncovered in 1872–1873.

Rutherford B. Hayes Reform governor of Ohio who was elected president in 1876 on the Republican ticket.

reputation was unblemished. Hayes helped restore the reputation of the Republican party after the scandals of the Grant administration. In Congress, however, Hayes found few allies when he tried to modify the patronage system. He did not seek reelection in 1880.

The Republicans were badly divided that year. James G. Blaine of Maine, a powerful leader of one Republican faction, sought the presidential nomination. Roscoe Conkling of New York, the leader of the other faction, the **Stalwarts,** promoted the candidacy of former president Grant. The convention ultimately compromised on **James A. Garfield,** a Civil War general and an able congressman from Ohio. The Democrats nominated Winfield Scott Hancock, a distinguished Civil War general. The campaign dealt less with policy issues than with Garfield's minor role in the Crédit Mobilier scandal and with Hancock's Catholic wife. Garfield won by a tiny margin, 48.5 percent to 48.0 percent.

On July 2, 1881, four months after taking office, Garfield was shot by Charles Guiteau, who was mentally unstable. Garfield died in September. Vice President Chester A. Arthur then assumed the presidency. Defying his previous reputation as a loyal Stalwart, Arthur proved that the presidential office can improve the stature of its occupant. He prosecuted Stalwarts involved in post office corruption and even suggested that Congress should reform the spoils system. This suggestion bore fruit in 1883, when Congress passed the **Pendleton Act,** as civil service reformers took advantage of the widespread but false belief that Guiteau was a disappointed office seeker. The act established the merit system for government employment. Competitive examinations became the basis for appointment to **classified positions,** which were removed from the patronage system.

Initially, only 15 percent of federal positions were classified, but the law authorized the president to add positions to the list. The person who held an office when it was first classified was protected from removal on political grounds, so presidents used the law to protect their own patronage appointees. Once those people retired, however, their replacements came through the merit system. In this way, positions were gradually withdrawn from the patronage system. By 1901, the law applied to 44 percent of federal employees. The Pendleton Act laid the basis for the current civil service system.

Cleveland and the Democrats

Because of his failing health, Arthur exerted little effort to win his party's nomination in 1884, allowing Blaine to capture it. The Democrats nominated Grover Cleveland, the governor of New York State, who had earned a reputation for integrity and political courage by attacking Tammany Hall. Tammany voters—many of them Irish—therefore disliked Cleveland.

The campaign quickly turned nasty. Many Mugwumps disliked Blaine and embarrassed him by revealing that he had profited from prorailroad legislation. Blaine supporters gleefully trumpeted the fact that Cleveland had avoided military service during the Civil War and had once fathered a child outside marriage. The election hinged on New York State, where Blaine expected to cut deeply into the usually Democratic Irish vote. A few days before the election, however, a Republican preacher in New York City called the Democrats the party of "rum, Romanism [Catholicism], and rebellion." Blaine ignored this insult to his Irish Catholic supporters until newspapers blasted it the next day. By then the damage was done. Cleveland won New York State by a tiny margin, and New York's electoral votes gave him the victory.

Cleveland was deeply committed to minimal government and to restraining spending. Between

Stalwart Faction of the Republican party led by Roscoe Conkling that was committed wholeheartedly to the spoils system.

James A. Garfield Ohio congressman who was chosen as a compromise candidate at the 1880 Republican convention, elected twentieth president of the United States, and shot to death only four months after taking office.

Pendleton Act Law passed in 1883 that created the Civil Service Commission and the merit system for government hiring and jobs.

classified position Government job filled through the merit system instead of by patronage.

1885 and 1889, he vetoed 414 bills, most of them granting pensions to individual Union veterans. This was twice as many vetoes as for all previous presidents combined. Cleveland provided little leadership but did approve the Dawes Severalty Act (see page 379) and the Interstate Commerce Act.

The Interstate Commerce Act grew out of political pressure from farmers and small businesses that led several states to regulate railroads. In 1871, Illinois had created a railroad and warehouse commission to set maximum rates. Iowa and Wisconsin passed laws regulating railroad freight rates in 1874. In 1877, in *Munn v. Illinois,* the Supreme Court held that businesses with "a public interest," including warehouses and railroads, "must submit to be controlled by the public for the common good." In *Wabash Railway v. Illinois* (1886), however, the Supreme Court put severe limits on the states' power to regulate railroad rates.

The *Wabash* decision prompted Congress in 1887 to pass the Interstate Commerce Act, which created the **Interstate Commerce Commission (ICC),** the first federal regulatory commission. The law prohibited pools, rebates, and different rates for short and long hauls. The prohibitions proved to be largely unenforceable, however, because the law was vague and the ICC had little real power.

Cleveland considered the nation's greatest problem to be the persistent federal budget surplus. Throughout the 1880s, the surplus was often more than $100 million per year. Worried that the surplus encouraged wasteful spending, Cleveland demanded in 1887 that Congress cut tariff rates on raw materials and necessities. Cleveland's action provoked a serious division within his own party. The Democrats could not agree on a bill, and Congress adjourned without voting on the tariff.

In the 1888 presidential election, the Democrats renominated Cleveland. The Republicans nominated **Benjamin Harrison,** senator from Indiana and grandson of former president William Henry Harrison. The Republicans' campaign focused on the virtues of the protective tariff. They raised unprecedented amounts of campaign money by systematically approaching business leaders on the tariff issue. The Republicans also attacked Cleveland's vetoes of pensions for Union veterans.

Harrison won in the electoral voting but received fewer popular votes than Cleveland: 47.9 percent to Cleveland's 48.7 percent. The Republicans also secured majorities in both the House and Senate. In 1889, the Republicans stood poised to create new public policies.

Harrison: Ending the Stalemate?

The new Republican majority's first major task when Congress opened in 1889 was tariff reform. The Republicans wanted to cut the federal surplus without reducing protection. The **McKinley Tariff** of 1890 (named for the congressman chiefly responsible for it, William McKinley) moved some items to the free list (notably sugar, a major source of tariff revenue) but raised tariff rates prohibitively on other items. The House passed the McKinley Tariff in late May 1890 and sent it on to the Senate.

In July, the House approved the Federal Elections Bill, nicknamed the "Force Bill" by its Democratic opponents. The bill proposed federal supervision over congressional elections to prevent disfranchisement, fraud, and violence. The bill did not single out the South, but everyone knew that the South was its target. The measure passed the House and went to the Senate, where approval seemed likely.

Harrison wanted the tariff and election bills passed as a party package. Senate Republicans, however, feared that a Democratic filibuster against the election bill would prevent passage of either measure. Finally, the Republicans agreed to postpone the elections bill if the Democrats would not delay the tariff bill. Over the strong protests of a few New England Republicans, the rest of the

Interstate Commerce Commission Federal commission established in 1887 to oversee railroads.

Benjamin Harrison Indiana Republican senator elected president in 1888 on a platform of high protective tariffs.

McKinley Tariff Tariff law passed in 1890 that sought not only to protect established industries but also, by prohibitory duties, to create new industries; it soon became extremely unpopular.

party sacrificed African Americans' voting rights to gain the revised tariff. (Some seventy years would pass before Congress finally acted to protect black voting rights in the South.) By raising import duties, the McKinley Tariff soon reduced imports, tariff income, and the budgetary surplus.

Another significant law to emerge from the Republican Congress in 1890 was the **Sherman Anti-Trust Act.** Created in response to growing public concern about trusts and monopolies, the law declared that "every contract, combination in the form of trust or otherwise, or conspiracy, in restraint of trade or commerce among the several states, or with foreign nations, is hereby declared to be illegal." The United States thereby became the first industrial nation to regulate business combinations. But the law proved difficult to enforce. Since it did not define "trust," "conspiracy," or "restraint of trade," it was left to courts that were generally sympathetic to business to supply these definitions.

Republicans seemed to have broken the political logjam in 1889–1890. The McKinley Tariff and the Sherman Anti-Trust Act were among a record number of new laws. Other legislation included a major increase in pension eligibility for disabled Union army veterans, admission to statehood for Idaho and Wyoming, and appropriations that laid the basis for a modern navy.

Agricultural Distress and Political Upheaval

Curiously enough, the first strong winds of political change blew not in the industrial cities but in the farm communities of the Great Plains and the South and in the mining camps of the Rocky Mountain region. In the early 1890s, those regions witnessed the birth of a new political party, the People's party or **Populists.**

The Farmers' Complaints

During the Gilded Age, farmers became increasingly dependent on the national railroad network, on fertilizer and laborsaving equipment, on grain and cotton brokers, and on sources of credit in distant cities. At the same time, some began to feel increasingly helpless in the face of the great concentrations of economic power that seemed to be taking over their lives.

Farmers were most distressed by steadily declining crop prices after the Civil War. Many farmers argued that this decline in prices was not attributable to the fluctuations of supply and demand, but rather to the monopolistic practices of grain and cotton buyers. Most agricultural regions were served by only one buyer, who paid the prices set by **commodity markets** in Chicago and New York. Farmers had no choice but to accept the price that was offered. They needed cash to pay their debts. Farmers blamed commodity brokers for the fact that the bushel of corn they sold in Kansas for 10 cents in October brought three or four times that amount in New York in December.

The debts that farmers had contracted to expand production magnified the impact of falling prices. Suppose a farmer borrowed $1,000 for five years in 1881, when corn sold for 63 cents per bushel. The borrowed $1,000 would have been equivalent to 1,587 bushels of corn. In 1886, when the loan came due, corn sold for 36 cents per bushel, requiring 2,777 bushels to repay the $1,000. And this example does not take into account the interest on the loan. Further, the prices of most farm supplies did not fall as rapidly as crop prices. As a result, farmers raised more and more each

Sherman Anti-Trust Act Law passed in 1890 authorizing the federal government to prosecute any "combination" "in restraint of trade"; because of adverse court rulings, it initially proved ineffective as a weapon against monopolies.

Populists Members of the People's party, who held their first presidential nominating convention in 1892 and called for reforms such as the eight-hour workday, direct election of senators, and the secret ballot.

commodity market Financial market in which brokers buy and sell agricultural products in large quantities, thus determining the prices paid to farmers for their harvests.

year just to pay their debts and buy necessities. The more they raised, the lower prices fell.

The railroads also angered farmers. The railroads, farmers claimed, were greedy monopolies that charged them as much as possible. It sometimes cost four times as much to ship freight in the West as in the East. Farmers also protested the railroads' dominance of state politics and distribution of free passes to all manner of politicians.

Crop prices and railroad practices were only two of the farmers' complaints. They protested that bankers charged much higher interest rates in the South and West than in the Northeast. They argued that federal monetary policies contributed to falling prices and thereby compounded their debts. Southern farmers, especially, condemned the tariff for creating artificially high prices on manufactured goods that farmers had to buy. Farmers complained as well that the corporations that made farm equipment and fertilizer overcharged them.

Grangers, Greenbackers, and Silverites

Following the Civil War, farmers joined organizations that they hoped would provide them some relief. Oliver H. Kelley formed the first, the Patrons of Husbandry, in 1867. Usually known as the **Grange,** the new organization included women as well as men. Kelley hoped that the Grange would provide a social outlet for farm families and also educate them about new agricultural methods. It far exceeded his expectations.

The Grange grew rapidly, especially in the Midwest and the central South. In the 1870s, it became a leading proponent of cooperative buying and selling. Many local Granges set up cooperative stores, and some even tried to sell their crops cooperatively. Grangers laid ambitious plans for cooperative factories producing everything from wagons to sewing machines. Some Grangers formed mutual insurance companies, and a few experimented with cooperative banks.

Although the Grange was initially nonpartisan, its membership began talking about political action in the 1870s. "Granger parties" emerged in eleven states. Their most prominent demand was state legislation to prohibit railroad rate discrimination. The resulting state laws were called **Granger laws.**

The Grange reached its zenith in the mid-1870s. Hastily organized cooperatives then began to suffer financial problems because of the nationwide depression. The collapse of cooperatives often pulled down Grange organizations. Political activity brought some successes but also generated bitter disputes within the Granges. The surviving Granges usually avoided cooperatives and politics.

With the decline of the Grange in the late 1870s, some farmers looked to monetary policy for relief. Following the Civil War, the money supply did not grow as rapidly as the economy. The Greenback party argued that the supply of money should be increased through printing more **greenbacks,** the paper money issued during the Civil War. More money in circulation, they believed, would raise prices.

Greenbackers found their most receptive audience among farmers who were in debt. In the congressional elections of 1878, the Greenback party received nearly a million votes and elected fourteen congressmen. However, it proved unsuccessful in attracting votes nationwide. In the 1880 presidential election, the Greenback party endorsed not only inflation but also the eight-hour workday, legislation to protect workers, the abolition of child labor, regulation of transportation, a **graduated income tax,** and woman suffrage. For president, they nominated James B. Weaver of Iowa, a former

Grange Farmers' organization that combined social activities with education on new methods of farming and cooperative economic efforts; officially, known as the Patrons of Husbandry.

Granger laws State laws establishing standard freight and passenger rates on railroads passed because of the lobbying of the Grange.

greenbacks Paper money, not backed by gold, that the federal government issued during the Civil War.

graduated income tax Percentage tax levied on income that varies with income. People who earn more money pay a higher tax rate.

Union general. Weaver got only 3.3 percent of the vote. In 1884, the Greenbackers fared even worse.

A similar monetary analysis motivated those who wanted the government to resume issuing silver dollars. Until 1873, federal mints had accepted gold and silver in unlimited quantities and made them into coins at virtually no charge. Throughout most of the nineteenth century, however, owners of silver made more money selling it commercially than taking it to the mint. Hence, no silver dollars existed for many years. In 1873, Congress dropped the silver dollar from the list of approved coins. Thus the United States joined Britain and Germany on the **gold standard.**

Soon after 1873, silver discoveries in Nevada and elsewhere drove down the price of silver. The rallying cry of farmers and silver miners became "**Free silver** at 16 to 1." This meant that both silver and gold would be coined into dollars in unlimited quantities and that a silver dollar would weigh sixteen times as much as a gold dollar. In 1878, Congress passed the **Bland-Allison Act,** authorizing a limited amount of silver dollars. However, it was not enough to counteract **deflation.** The Sherman Silver Purchase Act of 1890 increased the amount of silver to be purchased and appeased western Republicans, but it did not require free coinage of silver. It satisfied neither silverites nor advocates of the gold standard.

Birth of the People's Party

In the 1880s, three organizations emerged to fill the vacuum left by the Grange's decline. All were called **Farmers' Alliances.** One was centered in the north-central states. Another, the Southern Alliance, began in Texas and spread eastward across the South. Because its membership was limited to white farmers, a third Alliance, the Colored Farmers' Alliance, was formed for black farmers in the South. Like the Grange, the Alliances looked to cooperatives as a partial solution to their problems. The Texas Alliance experimented with cooperative cotton selling, and some midwestern local Alliances built cooperative **grain elevators.**

The alliances worked initially within the framework of the major parties. This was especially important in the South, where any white person who challenged the Democratic party ran the risk of being viewed as a traitor to both race and region. Not until 1890 did widespread farmer support materialize for independent political action in the Midwest. Corn prices had fallen so low by then that some farmers found it cheaper to burn their corn than to buy fuel.

During the summer of 1890, members of the Farmers' Alliance in Kansas, Nebraska, the Dakotas, Minnesota, and surrounding states formed new political parties to contest state and local elections. One leader explained that the political battle they waged was "between the insatiable greed of organized wealth and the rights of the great plain people." Organization of the new party launched a decade of dramatic political change.

The Populist party was launched by parades of farm wagons passing down the hot, dusty main streets of scores of country towns. The festivities ended with a picnic and rally, where speakers decried the plight of the farmer and proclaimed the sacred cause of the new party. Women played a prominent part in Populist campaigning. Mary Elizabeth Lease of Kansas was widely quoted in newspapers as urging farmers to "raise less corn and more hell!"

When the Populists organized a national party in 1892, they emphasized three themes: antimonopolism, government action on behalf of farmers and

gold standard A monetary system based on gold.

free silver The proposal to allow the coinage of all available silver to supplement gold as currency; repeatedly suggested as a solution to the nation's economic troubles.

Bland-Allison Act Law passed in 1878 providing for federal purchase of silver to be coined into silver dollars.

deflation Falling prices, a situation in which the purchasing power of the dollar increases.

Farmers' Alliances Agricultural organizations of the 1880s and 1890s that carried forward the agrarian cause after the decline of the Grange.

grain elevator Storehouse usually located near railroad tracks where farmers stored grain prior to shipping.

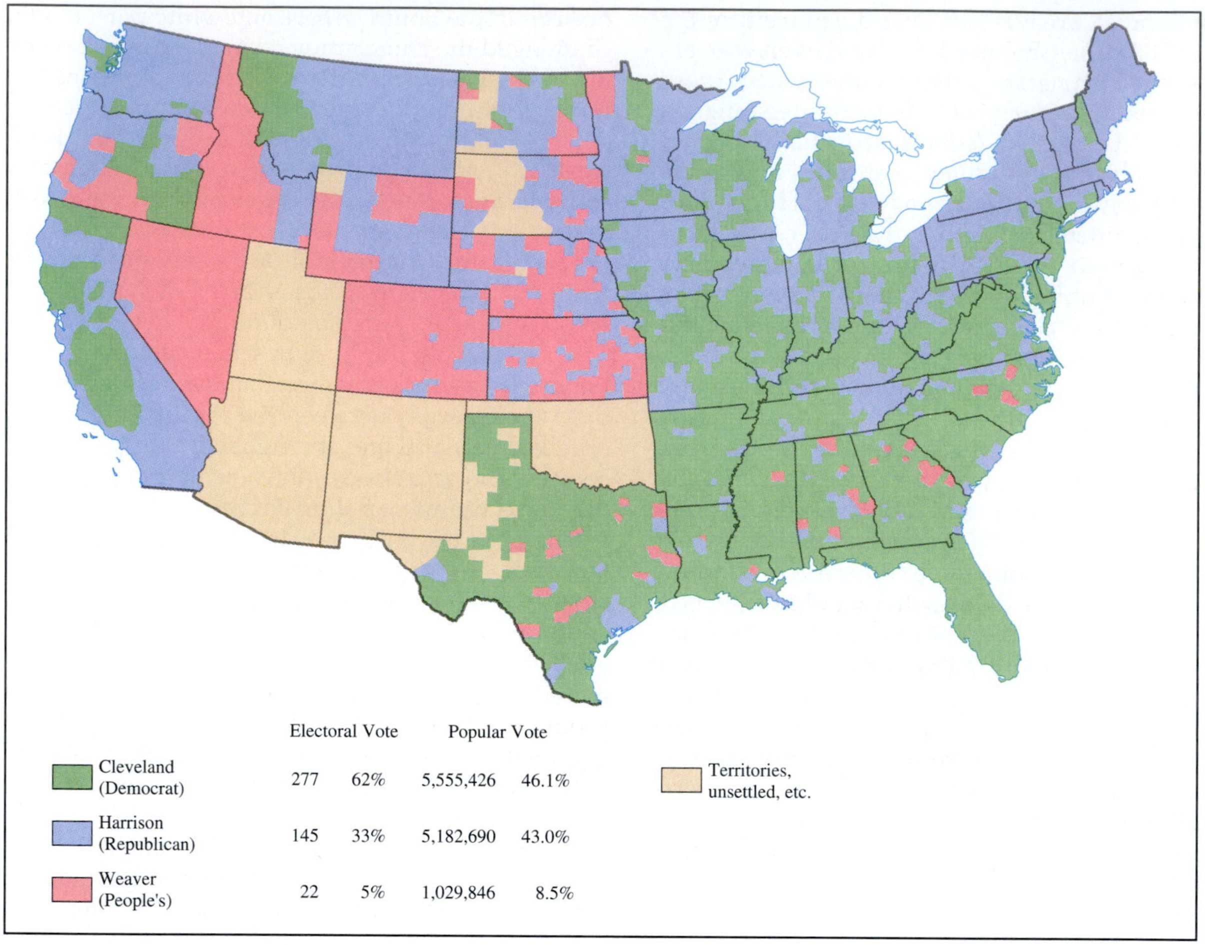
Electoral Vote
Popular Vote
Cleveland (Democrat) 277 62% 5,555,426 46.1%
Harrison (Republican) 145 33% 5,182,690 43.0%
Weaver (People's) 22 5% 1,029,846 8.5%
Territories, unsettled, etc.

♦ **MAP 19.1 Election of 1892** The Populist party's presidential candidate, James B. Weaver, made a strong showing in 1892. This map indicates that his support was concentrated regionally in the West and South and that he had relatively little support in the northeastern states.

workers, and increased popular control of government. Their antimonopolism drew on their own unhappy experiences with railroads, grain buyers, and farm equipment companies. But it derived as well from a long American tradition of opposition to concentrated economic power. Populists often compared themselves to Andrew Jackson in his fight against the Bank of the United States.

The Populists' solution to the dangers of monopoly was government action on behalf of farmers and workers. They proposed federal ownership of the railroads and the telegraph and telephone systems, and government alternatives to private banks. "We believe the time has come," Populists proclaimed in 1892, "when the railroad companies will either own the people or the people must own the railroads." They also demanded inflation (through greenbacks or silver) and a graduated income tax to replace the tariff. They hoped to gain broad support among urban and industrial workers. Their platform called for the eight-hour day for workers and the prohibition of private armies like the one used against the Homestead strikers (see page 358). Some Populists also advocated a proposal called the Sub-Treasury Plan, under which crops stored in government warehouses might be collateral for low-interest loans to farmers.

Finally, the People's party favored a series of changes to make government more responsive to the people: expansion of the merit system for government employees, election of U.S. senators by direct ballot instead of by state legislatures, a one-term limit for the president, the **secret ballot,** and the **initiative** and **referendum.** Many Populists also favored woman suffrage. In the South, they posed a serious challenge to the prevailing politics by seeking to forge a political alliance of the disadvantaged of both races. Thus the Populists wanted to use government to control, even to own, the corporate behemoths that had evolved in their lifetimes, and they wanted to increase the influence of the individual voter in political decision making.

The Elections of 1890 and 1892

The issues in the 1890 elections varied by region. In the West, the Populists lambasted both major parties for ignoring the needs of the people. In the South, Democrats held up the Force Bill as a symbol of the dangers posed by abandoning the party of white supremacy. There the Farmers' Alliance worked within the Democratic party to secure favorable candidates. In the Northeast, Democrats attacked the McKinley Tariff for producing higher consumer prices. In the Rocky Mountain region, nearly all candidates pledged their support for unlimited silver coinage.

The Populists became the most successful new party since the appearance of the Republicans in the 1850s. Populists elected state legislators, representatives in the House of Representatives, and two U.S. senators. Across the South, the Alliance claimed that Democratic candidates owed their victories to its voters. Democrats captured congressional seats across the Midwest and made some gains elsewhere as well. Everywhere, Republicans suffered defeat. In the House of Representatives, the Republicans went from 166 seats in 1889 to only 88 in 1891.

The Republicans renominated Harrison in 1892, but without enthusiasm. The Democrats chose Grover Cleveland as their candidate. The southern Farmers' Alliance joined western Populists to form a national People's party and to nominate James Weaver, the former Greenbacker, for president. Democrats and Populists again earned impressive victories. Cleveland secured 46.1 percent of the popular vote, Harrison 43.0 percent, and Weaver 8.5 percent (see Map 19.1). The Democrats kept control of the House of Representatives and, for the first time in twelve years, also won the Senate. Despite their weak showing nationally, Populist candidates displayed strength in the West and South. The Democrats now found themselves fully able to translate their campaign promises into law.

Economic Collapse and Political Upheaval

After the Democrats swept to power in the 1892 elections, they suddenly faced difficult choices. Could they fulfill their campaign promises for tariff reform? Could they also halt the collapse of the national economy?

Economic Collapse and Depression

Ten days before Cleveland took office, the Reading Railroad declared bankruptcy. A financial panic soon set in as other companies followed it

secret ballot Voting methods in which individual votes are marked in private, so no one knows how an individual is voting.

initiative Procedure allowing any group of people to propose a law by gathering signatures on a petition; the proposed law is then voted on by the electorate.

referendum Procedure whereby a bill or constitutional amendment is submitted to the voters for their approval after having been passed by a legislative body.

INDIVIDUAL CHOICES

Choosing Principle over Party

Grover Cleveland

President Grover Cleveland, confronted with a shattered economy, had to choose between his conservative principles and maintaining the unity of his party. Portrait Grover Cleveland by Anders Zorn. National Portrait Gallery, Smithsonian Institution/Art Resource, N.Y.

Grover Cleveland took the presidential oath of office for the second time on March 4, 1893. Soon after, he faced a series of choices so difficult that he had every reason to expect intense criticism no matter what choice he made or what outcome resulted. He could not escape from making the choices, either, for he was afraid that the economic collapse that had begun shortly before he took office might threaten even the federal government itself.

Like many in his day, Cleveland held a traditional expectation about money. Because money must have intrinsic value, he contended, only precious metals could serve as money. In 1885, during his first term as president, he urged Congress to repeal the silver coinage act passed in 1878, on the grounds that the United States could not, by itself, maintain both gold and silver as money. To attempt to do so, Cleveland feared, would inevitably mean that gold would leave the country. Congress, however, refused to follow his advice in 1885.

When Cleveland's first presidency ended in 1889, the government's gold reserves stood at $197 million. When he took office again in 1893, it seemed that his earlier fears were coming

into bankruptcy. More than fifteen thousand businesses failed in 1893, more than in any previous year.

At the time, no one really understood why the economy collapsed so suddenly. The collapse began when the failure of a major English bank led some British investors to recall their investments in the United States. This recall, combined with the reduction in revenues caused by the McKinley Tariff, resulted in a sharp decline in federal **gold reserves.** Fears about low gold reserves and bank-

gold reserves The stockpile of gold with which the federal government backs up the currency.

true, for the gold reserves had fallen to $103.5 million. This was dangerously close to the $100 million mark that Congress had earlier fixed as the point below which the nation might not be able to maintain the gold standard. The decline in gold reserves was in part the result of cuts in tariff revenues and greatly increased federal expenditures approved by the Republican Congress of 1889–1890. Another factor was widespread anxiety about the economy. Uncertain about the future, many investors chose to liquidate their holdings in return for gold. The shrinking gold reserves alarmed Cleveland.

Because so many business and financial leaders shared the expectation that money must have intrinsic value, they argued that silver coinage (authorized under the Sherman Silver Purchase Act) was dishonest, because it required that silver worth only 53 cents on the open market be made into a dollar coin. The president was pressured from one side by bankers and manufacturers eager to end silver coinage and to restore the gold reserve, and from the other side by members of his own party hostile to banking interests and favorable to silver coinage. Cleveland thus faced a difficult choice. Should he do what he believed to be necessary to maintain the nation's financial integrity? Or should he compromise and thereby preserve the unity of the Democratic party and his own political popularity?

In the midst of these pressures and counterpressures, Cleveland demonstrated his courage when he underwent surgery to remove a cancer from the roof of his mouth and kept his illness secret. Seriously weakened by the surgery and uncertain that he was out of danger, Cleveland labored over a message to a special session of Congress. In his message, he made his choice clear: he asked Congress to repeal the Sherman Silver Purchase Act, knowing his action would divide his own party and bring upon him an avalanche of criticism.

The battle in Congress over repeal of the Sherman Silver Purchase Act was hard fought. Cleveland at times felt depressed about the prospects for success, once writing that "if I did not believe in God I should be sick at heart." But he stubbornly refused all efforts at compromise, and took comfort in the knowledge that he was following his sense of integrity and duty. "I think so often of Martin Luther's 'Here I stand—God help me,'" he told a friend.

The immediate outcome was that Cleveland won in Congress, with the assistance of most Republicans and some Democrats, including some who had previously opposed him. Another outcome was that Cleveland confirmed his personal reputation for integrity, courage, and stubbornness. But the most far-reaching outcome was that the president had splintered the Democratic party and doomed any hopes he may have had for leading it.

ruptcies precipitated a stock market crash in May 1893, which brought on the depression.

Major underlying factors included the end of agricultural expansion and railroad construction. A slow agricultural economy before 1893 produced a decline in sales of farm machinery and, hence, steel. More important were the railroads. Railroad building drove the industrial economy in the 1880s. In the 1890s, however, a number of large lines declared bankruptcy, including the Erie, Northern Pacific, Santa Fe, and Union Pacific. Railroad construction fell by half between 1893 and 1895. The sharp decline in railroad construction produced a domino effect. Production of steel rails fell by more than a third between 1892 and 1894. Thirty-two steel companies closed down as a result. Banks that had invested in railroads and steel companies then collapsed. Nearly five hundred banks failed just in 1893.

These business failures threw at least a third of the wage earners in manufacturing out of work. During the winter of 1893–1894, Chicago counted 100,000 unemployed—roughly two workers out of five. Crowds swarmed at factory gates in response to a rumor that the plant was hiring. Many who kept their jobs received smaller paychecks, as employers cut wages and hours. In 1892, the average nonfarm wage earner received $482 per year. By 1894, this fell to $420.

The depression produced widespread suffering. Many who lost their jobs had little to fall back on except the soup dispensed by charities. Newspapers told of people who committed suicide when faced with starving to death or stealing food. Many men and some women left home desperate to find work. Some walked the roads, but most hopped freight trains. A few found work, but most failed. Some families were never reunited. Those who kept their jobs and homes could not escape the pitiful sight of jobless, homeless men and women walking the streets.

A dramatic demonstration against unemployment began in late January 1894, when Ohio Populist Jacob S. Coxey proposed that the government hire the unemployed to build roads and repair public works. The response to Coxey's call for the unemployed to join him in a march on Washington was electric. All across the country, hundreds of men and a few women tried to join the march. Western groups hijacked some fifty trains and headed east pulling boxcars loaded with unemployed men. (None of the pirated trains traveled far before authorities stopped them and arrested the leaders.) Several thousand people took part in Coxey's march in some way, but most never reached Washington.

When Coxey and his group of several hundred arrived in Washington, he was not permitted to speak at the Capitol. When he tried to do so on May 1, police arrested him for trespassing and dispersed the crowd. The trek of **Coxey's Army** marked the first time that so many protesters had gone to Washington to urge the government to create jobs for the unemployed.

The Divided Democrats

When Congress met in 1893, the majority Democrats faced several divisive issues. Their platform called for cutting the tariff, but the party disagreed over how to do that. The party was also divided over the **Sherman Silver Purchase Act.** Many business leaders believed that the act had caused the depression, but western and southern Democrats disagreed. In addition, the depression and unemployment demanded attention. President Cleveland held to his staunch beliefs in minimal government and **laissez faire.**

Convinced that silver coinage had contributed to the economic collapse, Cleveland asked Congress to repeal the Sherman Act (see Individual Choices: Grover Cleveland). Cleveland won, but at the cost of pitting the northeastern branch of his party against the West and much of the South. This division persisted for the remainder of his term. It plagued discussions of the tariff. The Wilson-Gorman Tariff of 1894 was riddled with so many provisions for special interests that Cleveland refused to sign it. The bill became law without his signature.

In the 1894 elections, voters turned decisively to the Republicans, as the disorganized Democrats lost everywhere but in the Deep South. The Republicans scored their biggest gain in Congress ever, adding 117 seats. The Populists lost support even in their previous strongholds.

To Cleveland's regret, the end of silver purchases did not stop the flow of gold from the treasury. Investors responded to continuing economic uncertainties by converting their securities to gold. Government gold reserves fell dangerously low. In desperation, Cleveland turned for assistance to

Coxey's Army Unemployed workers led by Jacob S. Coxey who marched to Washington to demand relief measures from Congress following the Panic of 1893.

Sherman Silver Purchase Act Law passed in 1890 requiring the federal government to increase its purchases of silver.

laissez faire An economic doctrine under which the free-enterprise system operates with little government interference.

♦ In 1896, William Jennings Bryan (left), candidate of the Democratic, Populist, and Silver Republican parties, traveled some eighteen thousand miles in three months, speaking to about five million people. William McKinley (right), the Republican, stayed home in Canton, Ohio, greeting thousands of well-wishers. *Bryan: Nebraska State Historical Society; McKinley: Ohio Historical Society.*

J. P. Morgan, the symbol of Wall Street and the trusts. Morgan agreed in 1895 to take charge of a bond issue that stabilized the gold reserve, but Cleveland came under heavy criticism for consulting Morgan and for the price that Morgan charged.

The 1896 Election: Bryan Versus McKinley, Silver Versus Protection

In 1896, **William McKinley** garnered the Republican nomination for president. A former Ohio congressman and governor, McKinley billed himself as the "Advance Agent of Prosperity." Although the Republican platform touted the advantages of the gold standard, McKinley focused on the benefits of the protective tariff.

William Jennings Bryan of Nebraska emerged as the Democrats' candidate after delivering a

William McKinley Republican who defeated Bryan in presidential elections in 1896 and 1900; he led the country into the Spanish-American War and was shot by an anarchist in 1901.

William Jennings Bryan Nebraska congressman who advocated free coinage of silver, opposed imperialism, and ran for president unsuccessfully three times on the Democratic ticket.

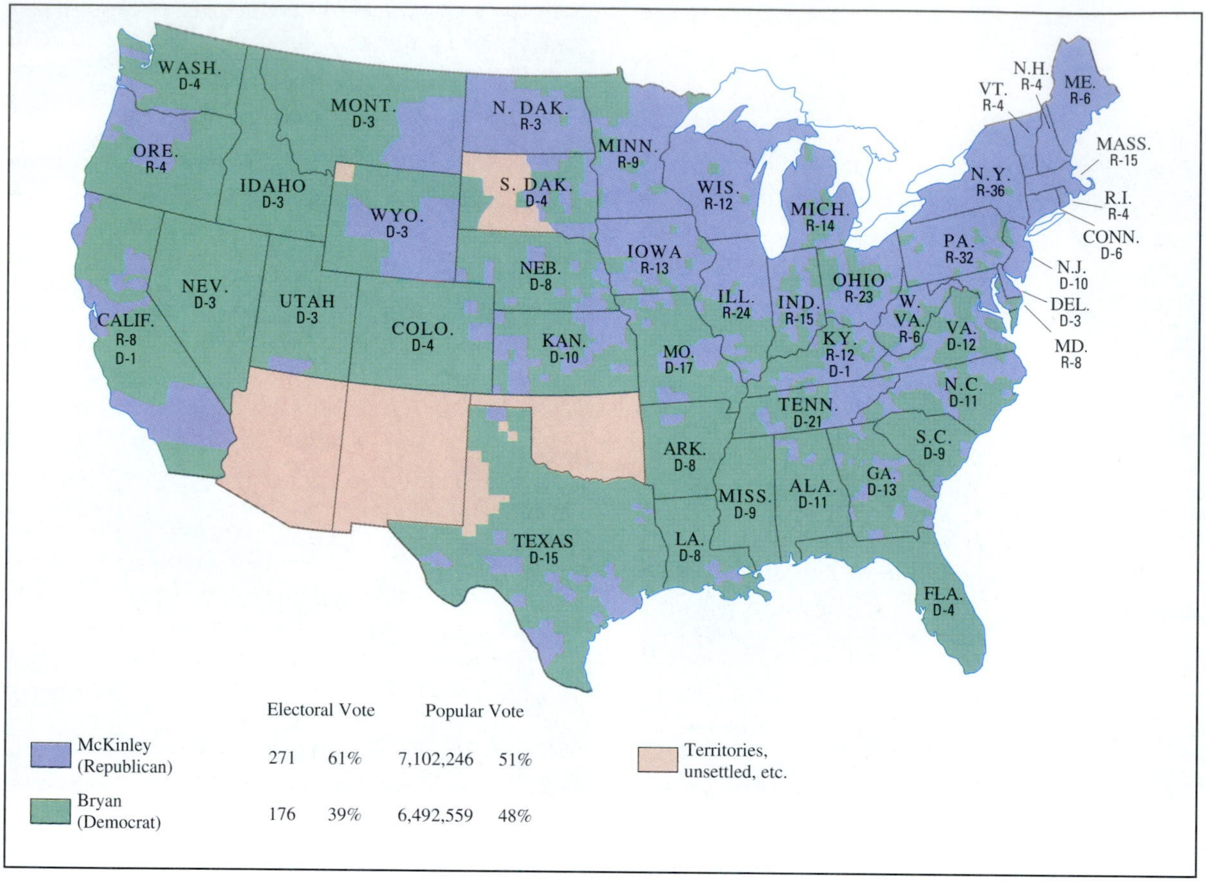

♦ **MAP 19.2 Election of 1896** Bryan could not win with just the votes of the South and West, which had few electoral votes. Even if he had won all the West, South, and border states, he would have needed one or more northeastern states. McKinley won in the urban, industrial core region and the more prosperous farming areas of the Midwest.

masterful speech defending silver at the party's convention. He argued that the conflict between silver and gold was one between "the producing masses" and "the idle holders of idle capital." His closing statement rang defiant: "We will answer their demand for a gold standard by saying to them: You shall not press down upon the brow of labor this crown of thorns. You shall not crucify mankind upon a cross of gold." This "Cross of Gold" speech stunned the convention and secured the Democratic nomination for Bryan. Given his commitment to silver, to the income tax, and to a broad range of other reforms, the Populists felt compelled to give Bryan their nomination too.

Bryan and McKinley both fought an all-out campaign but used sharply contrasting tactics. Bryan, vigorous and young, knew that his speaking voice was his greatest campaign tool. He took his case directly to the voters in four grueling train journeys through 26 states and more than 250 cities. Delivering up to 30 speeches a day and addressing a total of perhaps 5 million people, he stressed that the most important issue was silver.

He found large crowds of enthusiastic supporters nearly everywhere he went.

McKinley campaigned from his front porch in Canton, Ohio. The Republican party carried the campaign to the voters for him. They also chartered trains that brought thousands to hear McKinley. Campaign manager Marcus A. Hanna played on the fears of business leaders that Bryan and silver coinage would bring complete financial collapse to raise an enormous campaign fund of $4 million—more than ten times as much as the Democrats raised.

McKinley scored the largest margin of victory since 1872, taking 51.1 percent of the popular vote and 23 states with 271 electoral votes. Bryan won 22 states and 176 electoral votes. As Map 19.2 indicates, Bryan carried the South and nearly all of the West. McKinley's victory came in the urban, industrial Northeast. Of the twenty largest cities in the nation, only New Orleans went for Bryan.

Bryan's defeat spelled the end of the Populist party. Some Populists moved into the Democratic party; others returned to the Republicans; a few joined the Socialist party; and a few simply ignored politics. The Populists' influence lived on, however, in Bryan's wing of the Democratic party.

After 1896: The New Republican Majority

The presidential election of 1896 stands as one of the most important in American history. The campaigns of 1896 focused on economic issues. Bryan's silver crusade appealed most to debt-ridden farmers and western miners. McKinley forged a broader appeal by emphasizing the gold standard and protective tariff as keys to economic recovery. Many urban residents—workers and the middle class alike—believed that the protective tariff meant manufacturing jobs.

McKinley's victory ushered in a generation of Republican dominance of national politics. The depression and the political campaigns of the 1890s caused a significant number of voters to re-evaluate their partisan commitments and to change parties. After 1896, no one could doubt that the Republicans were the national majority. Republicans ruled in the House of Representatives for twenty-eight of the thirty-six years after 1894 and in the Senate for thirty of those thirty-six years. Republicans won seven of the nine presidential elections between 1896 and 1932. Similar patterns of Republican dominance appeared in state and local government outside the South.

The events of the 1890s also worked significant changes in the party. As Bryan solidified his hold on the party, he moved it away from its commitment to minimal government and laissez faire. While retaining the Jacksonians' distrust of monopoly and their opposition to governmental favoritism toward business, Bryan and other new Democratic leaders now agreed with the Populists that the solution to the problems of economic concentration lay in an active government that could limit monopoly power. "A private monopoly," Bryan never tired of repeating, "is indefensible and intolerable." In other ways, the Democrats changed little. Southern Democrats remained committed to states' rights. Northern Democrats continued to oppose nativism and moral reform.

McKinley provided strong executive leadership and worked closely with leaders of his party in Congress to fulfill Republican campaign promises. In 1897, the **Dingley Tariff** drove tariff rates even higher than the 1890 McKinley Tariff. In 1900, the **Gold Standard Act** wrote that Republican commitment into law. Fabulous gold discoveries in the **Klondike** and Alaska increased the nation's currency supply and stopped the clamor for silver coinage.

Although the majority of American voters considered themselves Republican, many held their

Dingley Tariff Bill passed in 1897 enacting a high protective tariff, averaging 57 percent.

Gold Standard Act Law passed in 1900 that declared gold the nation's monetary standard for all currency issued.

Klondike A region of Canada's Yukon Territory where gold was discovered in 1896, triggering a gold rush that attracted more than 25,000 people to the frozen north.

new party commitments less intensely than before. Before 1890, ethnicity and choice of party went hand in hand. Now voters sometimes felt pulled toward one party by their economic situation and toward the other party by their ethnicity. Such voters sometimes voted a split ticket, supporting Republicans for some offices and Democrats for others. This was much easier than before because most states had adopted the secret ballot by 1892. As more government positions became subject to the merit system, there were fewer rewards for party workers. Voter participation dropped from 79 percent in 1896 to 59 percent in 1912.

American politics in 1888 looked much like American politics in 1876 or even 1844. But in 1896, American politics changed decisively. Political parties would never be as important thereafter.

SUMMARY

Expectations
Constraints
Choices
Outcomes

Americans in the late nineteenth century expected political parties to dominate politics. All elected public officials were nominated by party conventions and elected through efforts of party campaigners. Most civil service employees were appointed in return for party loyalty. Republicans *chose* to use government to promote rapid economic development, but Democrats argued that government is best when it governs least. Voters *chose* between the major parties along the lines of ethnicity, race, and religion.

Some people rejected the *constraints* of party government and sought reform. Mugwumps argued for the merit system in the civil service, accomplished through the Pendleton Act of 1883. By the late nineteenth century, a well-organized woman-suffrage movement had also emerged.

The closely balanced strengths of the two parties contributed to a long-term political stalemate. Republicans broke the *constraints* of stalemate in 1890, passing the McKinley Tariff, Sherman Anti-Trust Act, Sherman Silver Purchase Act, and other measures. But voters subsequently turned against the Republicans.

The 1890s saw important and long-lasting changes in political patterns and people's *expectations* for politics. The political upheaval began when long-suffering western and southern farmers turned to political action. In 1890, members of the Farmers' Alliances *chose* to launch a new political party, usually called the Populists. In 1892, voters rejected the Republicans in many areas, *choosing* either the new Populist party or the Democrats.

President Grover Cleveland proved unable to meet the political challenges of a major depression that began in 1893. In 1896, the Democrats nominated for president William Jennings Bryan, a supporter of silver coinage. The Republicans *chose* William McKinley, who favored the protective tariff as most likely to end the depression. McKinley won, and important long-term *outcomes* were felt well into the twentieth century. First was the beginning of Republican dominance in national politics that lasted until 1930. And second, under Bryan's leadership, the Democratic party discarded its commitment to minimal government and instead adopted a willingness to use government against monopolies and other powerful economic interests.

SUGGESTED READINGS

Bryce, James. *The American Commonwealth,* 2 vols. (1889).
Fascinating firsthand account of the politics of this period.

Cherny, Robert W. *American Politics in the Gilded Age, 1868–1900* (1997).
The most recent survey of the politics of this period.

Lebsock, Suzanne. "Women and American Politics, 1880–1920." In *Women, Politics, and Change.* Ed. Louise A. Tilly and Patricia Gurin (1990).

An overview of women and politics, incorporating summaries of much of the most interesting recent research.

McMath, Robert C., Jr. *American Populism: A Social History, 1877–1898* (1993).

A recent, concise introduction to the populist movement.

Williams, R. Hal. *Years of Decision: American Politics in the 1890s* (1978).

A concise survey of national politics; strongest on congressional decision making.

EXPANSION OF THE UNITED STATES, 1865–1917 As a result of the Spanish-American War, the United States acquired island possessions stretching halfway around the world, from Puerto Rico to the Philippines. These and other acquisitions established the United States as one of the major powers in the Pacific and East Asia, and as the dominant power in the Caribbean.

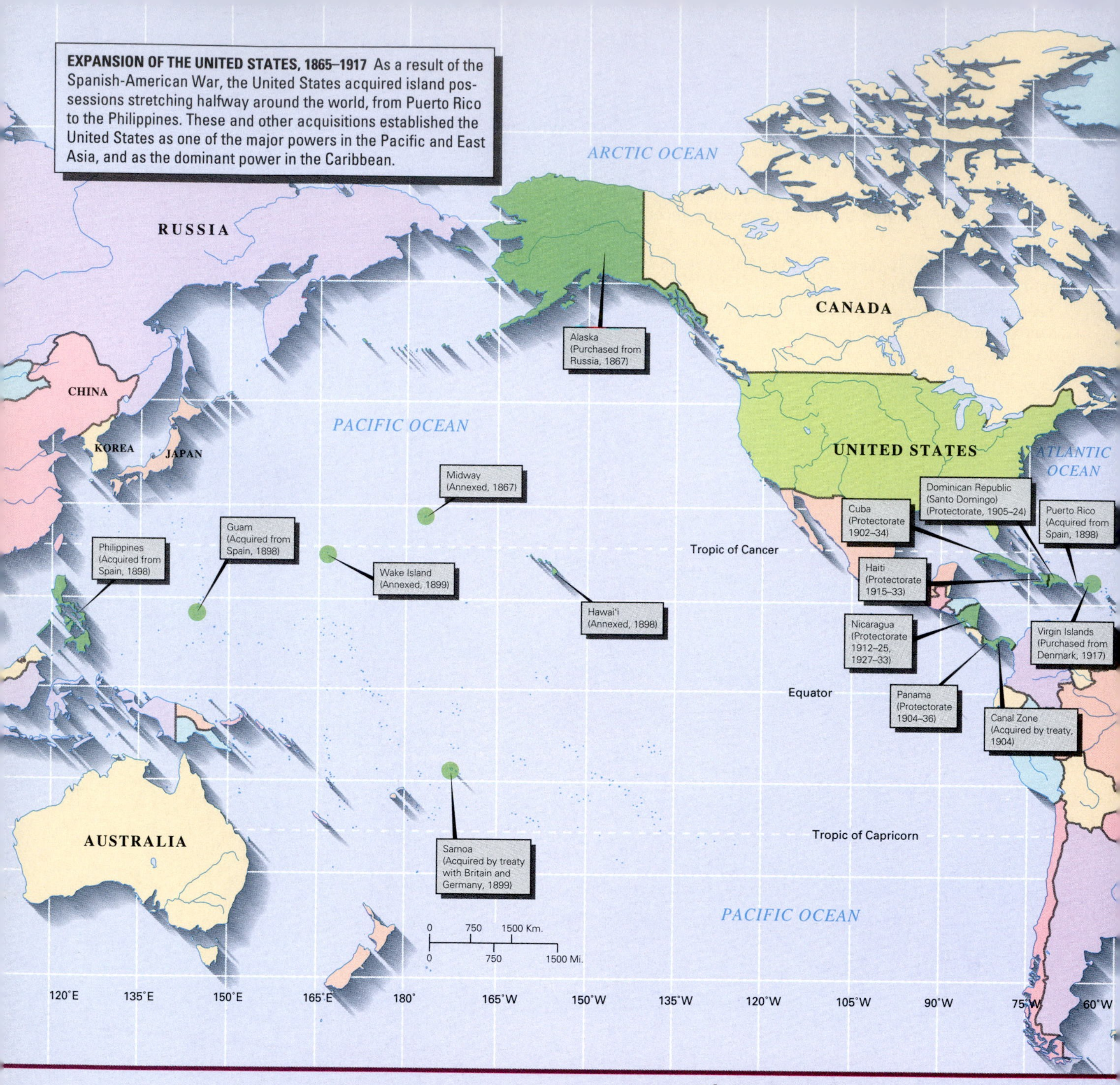
ARCTIC OCEAN
RUSSIA
CANADA
CHINA
KOREA
JAPAN
PACIFIC OCEAN
UNITED STATES
ATLANTIC OCEAN
AUSTRALIA
PACIFIC OCEAN
Alaska (Purchased from Russia, 1867)
Midway (Annexed, 1867)
Guam (Acquired from Spain, 1898)
Philippines (Acquired from Spain, 1898)
Wake Island (Annexed, 1899)
Hawai'i (Annexed, 1898)
Samoa (Acquired by treaty with Britain and Germany, 1899)
Cuba (Protectorate 1902–34)
Dominican Republic (Santo Domingo) (Protectorate, 1905–24)
Puerto Rico (Acquired from Spain, 1898)
Haiti (Protectorate 1915–33)
Nicaragua (Protectorate 1912–25, 1927–33)
Virgin Islands (Purchased from Denmark, 1917)
Panama (Protectorate 1904–36)
Canal Zone (Acquired by treaty, 1904)
Tropic of Cancer
Equator
Tropic of Capricorn
0 750 1500 Km.
0 750 1500 Mi.
120°E
135°E
150°E
165°E
180°
165°W
150°W
135°W
120°W
105°W
90°W
75°W
60°W

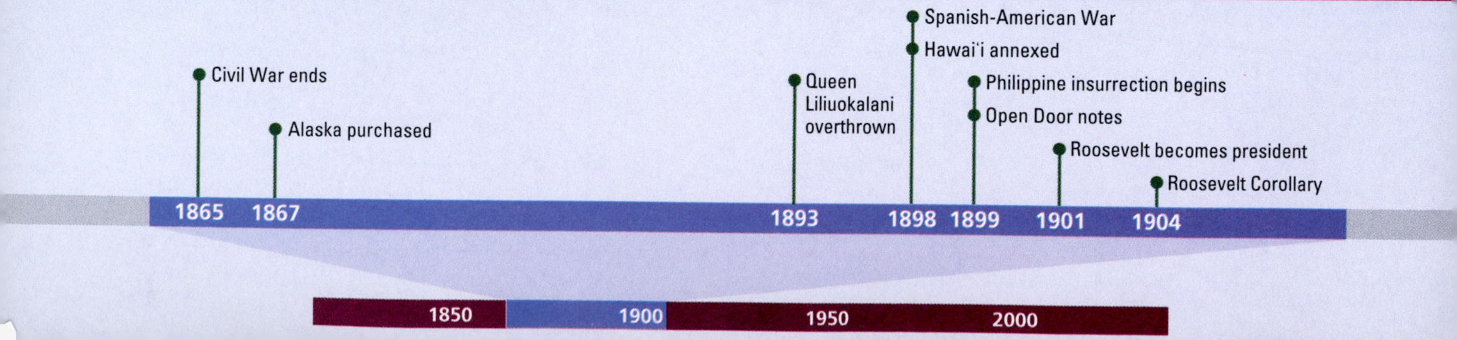
Civil War ends
1865
Alaska purchased
1867
Queen Liliuokalani overthrown
1893
Spanish-American War
Hawai'i annexed
1898
Philippine insurrection begins
Open Door notes
1899
Roosevelt becomes president
1901
Roosevelt Corollary
1904
1850
1900
1950
2000

CHAPTER 20

Becoming a World Power: America and World Affairs, 1865–1913

The United States and World Affairs, 1865–1889

- How did American choices with regard to Alaska, Mexico, and eastern Asia reflect traditional American expectations regarding world affairs?
- How did American choices with regard to eastern Asia and the Pacific reflect new conditions in world affairs?

Stepping Cautiously in World Affairs, 1889–1897

- How and why did some Americans' expectations about the U.S. role in world affairs begin to change between 1889 and 1897?

Striding Boldly: War and Imperialism, 1897–1901

- What were the outcomes of the war with Spain?
- What new expectations about America's role in world affairs were expressed in the debate over the acquisition of new possessions?

"Carry a Big Stick": The United States and World Affairs, 1901–1913

- What were Theodore Roosevelt's expectations about the role of the United States in world affairs?
- What choices did he make to bring about the outcomes he desired?

INTRODUCTION

Expectations
Constraints
Choices
Outcomes

In 1898, the United States went to war with Spain and quickly inflicted a stinging defeat. The *choice* to go to war climaxed a turnabout in American *expectations* regarding foreign affairs. During much of the nineteenth century, the nation's role in world affairs was slight at best, and most Americans *expected* that their nation would stay out of foreign conflicts.

Similarly, Americans had few worries about being pulled into European wars, for Europe remained relatively peaceful. The insulation afforded by the Atlantic and Pacific oceans reinforced Americans' feeling of security, and the powerful British navy provided a protective umbrella for American commercial shipping. Thus George Washington's advice that the nation "steer clear of permanent alliances with any portion of the foreign world" became the cornerstone of American foreign relations for most of the nineteenth century.

In the late nineteenth century, however, the United States took a place among the leading industrial nations of the world. The simultaneous emergence of Germany and Japan as industrial and naval giants contributed to a growing instability in world affairs. Japan joined the European powers in a race for empire in which much of the world seemed fair game for colonial capture. In Africa, major European nations scrambled to claim territory. In eastern Asia, they were joined by Russia and Japan. Britain and Germany sometimes looked toward Latin America as another field for expansion. In eastern Asia, the Pacific, and Latin America, the United States also had long-standing interests, often derived from commerce.

Toward the end of the nineteenth century, some Americans began urging that the nation boldly *choose* to seek a prominent role in world affairs. Most presidents after the Civil War were highly cautious about such a commitment. But a revolution in transportation and communication erased many former *constraints* on foreign relations. American diplomatic representatives abroad had once been connected to Washington only by an occasional memorandum carried by an American ship. Now they could communicate daily by telegraph. Sailing ships had once taken weeks to traverse the Atlantic and Pacific. Now steam-powered, steel-hulled vessels crossed in days and carried many times as much cargo.

Challenges to traditional *expectations* of U.S. isolationism and the dissolving of long-standing *constraints* on action presented American policymakers of the late nineteenth century with more *choices* in foreign relations than their predecessors had faced. One *outcome* of their *choices* was a foreign policy usually described as imperialism. Its foundation was the acquisition of possessions scattered halfway around the world (see chapter opener map). But the emerging U.S. foreign policy resulted in more than just colonies and the navy necessary to maintain and protect them. The larger *outcome* was a redefinition of nearly every aspect of American relations with the rest of the world.

CHRONOLOGY

The United States and World Affairs

1823	Monroe Doctrine
1865	Civil War ends
1867	French troops leave Mexico Alaska purchased from Russia
1872	Arbitration of *Alabama* claims
1887	Constitution forced on Hawaiian monarchy Pearl Harbor granted to U.S. Navy
1889	First Samoa treaty
1890	Mahan's *The Influence of Sea Power upon History* McKinley Tariff
1891	Liliuokalani becomes Hawaiian queen Harrison threatens war with Chile
1893	Queen Liliuokalani overthrown
1894	Wilson-Gorman Tariff
1895–1896	Venezuelan boundary crisis
1896	Reconcentration policy in Cuba McKinley elected
1898	De Lôme letter U.S. warship *Maine* explodes Spanish-American War Hawai'i annexed by joint resolution Treaty of Paris signed
1899	Treaty of Paris ratified Open Door notes Permanent Court of Arbitration created
1899–1902	Philippine insurrection suppressed
1900	Foraker Act McKinley reelected Boxer Rebellion
1900–1901	Hay-Pauncefote Treaties
1901	McKinley assassinated; Roosevelt becomes president
1902	Civil government in the Philippines Cuba becomes a protectorate
1903	Arbitration of Alaska-Canada boundary dispute
1904	Hay–Bunau-Varilla Treaty makes Panama a protectorate, provides for construction of a canal there Roosevelt Corollary
1904–1914	Panama Canal constructed
1905	Dominican Republic becomes a protectorate Roosevelt mediates Russo-Japanese War
1907	Roosevelt's "Great White Fleet"
1912	Nicaragua becomes a protectorate

The United States and World Affairs, 1865–1889

Americans took their first steps toward a new foreign policy following the Civil War, but those steps occurred largely in isolation from each other. Until the 1890s, American foreign policy proceeded largely on a case-by-case basis.

Alaska, Canada, and the *Alabama* Claims

In 1866, the Russian minister to the United States hinted to Secretary of State **William H. Seward** that Russia might sell its holdings in North America if the price were right. Seward made an offer, and in 1867 the two diplomats agreed on a price slightly over $7 million for Alaska. Some journalists derided the new purchase as a frozen, worthless wasteland and labeled it "Seward's Folly." The Senate, however, greeted it with considerable enthusiasm. Charles Sumner, chairman of the **Senate Foreign Relations Committee,** spoke for many in regarding the purchase of Alaska as the first step to the ultimate possession of Canada.

The acquisition of Canada figured prominently in American claims against Great Britain arising out of the Civil War. Several Confederate naval vessels built in British shipyards, notably the *Alabama,* had badly disrupted northern shipping. British ports had also offered refuge, repairs, and supplies to Confederate ships. Although Sumner suggested that Britain should compensate the United States by ceding Canada, Britain proved unresponsive to American demands for any damages. In 1869, however, as relations between Britain and Russia grew tense, the British began to fret that American shipyards might provide similar services for the Russians. In the Treaty of Washington (1871), the two countries agreed to **arbitration.** The 1872 arbitration decision held Britain responsible for the direct claims amounting to $15.5 million in damages.

Testing the Monroe Doctrine: The United States and Latin America

Ever since the formulation of the Monroe Doctrine in 1823, the United States had declared its intentions of preventing further European colonization and meddling in the Western Hemisphere. The first real test of that doctrine came after the Civil War in 1865.

In late 1861, as the United States lurched into civil war, France, Spain, and Britain sent a joint force to Mexico to collect debts that Mexico could not pay. Spain and Britain soon withdrew their contingents, but France remained. Despite resistance led by Benito Juarez, president of Mexico, French troops occupied key areas. Some of Juarez's conservative political opponents cooperated with the French emperor, Napoleon III, to name **Archduke Maximilian** of Austria emperor of Mexico. But Maximilian antagonized many and held power only because of the French army.

During the Civil War, the United States continued to recognize Juarez as president of Mexico but could do little else. As soon as the war ended, however, Secretary of State Seward demanded that Napoleon withdraw his troops. Seward underscored his demand by moving fifty thousand battle-hardened troops to the Mexican border. Thus confronted, Napoleon III withdrew his army

William H. Seward U.S. secretary of state under Lincoln and Johnson; a former abolitionist who had expansionist views and who arranged the purchase of Alaska from Russia.

Senate Foreign Relations Committee One of the standing, or permanent, committees of the Senate; it deals with foreign affairs, and its chairman wields considerable power.

arbitration Process by which parties to a dispute submit their case to the judgment of an impartial person or group and agree to abide by the decision of the arbiter.

Archduke Maximilian Austrian archduke appointed by France to be emperor of Mexico in 1864; he lacked popular support and was executed by Mexican republicans when the French withdrew from the country.

♦ Located on the Hawaiian island of Oahu, Pearl Harbor is one of the finest harbors in the Pacific. This painting was done in 1889, two years after the Hawaiian king granted use of the harbor to the United States. In return, the United States granted preferred status to Hawaiian sugar in the American market. *"Pearl Harbor from the Ocean" by Joseph Strong, 1889. Bishop Museum, Honolulu, Hawai'i.*

in early 1867. Juarez defeated Maximilian in battle and then executed him. The French withdrawal helped create new respect in Europe for the role of the United States in Latin America.

Eastern Asia and the Pacific

Americans had taken a strong commercial interest in eastern Asia since the opening of the China trade in 1784. Following the Civil War, however, American exports to that area made up less than 2 percent of all exports. Some Americans began dreaming of profits from selling to China's hundreds of millions of potential consumers.

Growing trade prospects between eastern Asia and the United States thus fueled American interest in ports in the Pacific that could provide supplies and repairs. Interest focused on two groups of islands with excellent harbors, Hawai'i and **Samoa,** both independent nations. The Hawaiian Islands' location near the center of the Pacific made them an ideal supply depot for ships crossing the ocean. New England missionaries had gone to the islands as early as 1819. By 1842, President John Tyler stated that the United States would not allow the islands to pass under the control of another power.

Hawai'i's relationship to the United States changed significantly after 1875, when the Senate yielded to pressure from ***haole*** sugar growers and exempted Hawaiian imports from the tariff. The outcome was a rapid expansion of the Hawaiian sugar industry, as children of New England missionaries joined American sugar refiners in developing huge sugar plantations. Sugar soon tied the Hawaiian economy closely to the United States. In 1887, a group of *haole* business leaders and plantation owners pressured King Kalakaua into accepting a constitution that limited the monarch's powers and permitted *haoles* to dominate the government. Although the royal family resented *haole* control of the government, they reluctantly granted Pearl Harbor to the American navy in 1887 to secure the renewal of tariff exemptions for Hawaiian sugar.

Samoa A group of volcanic and mountainous islands in the South Pacific.

haole Hawaiian word used to describe persons not of indigenous Hawaiian ancestry, especially whites.

Samoa, in the South Pacific, drew attention not just from the United States but also from Britain and Germany. When German actions in the islands suggested an attempt at annexation, President Cleveland vowed to maintain Samoan independence. All three nations dispatched warships to the vicinity in 1889, and conflict seemed likely until a typhoon scattered and damaged the ships. A subsequent treaty provided for Samoan independence under the protection of the three Western nations.

Stepping Cautiously in World Affairs, 1889–1897

During Benjamin Harrison's administration (1889–1893), the United States began to take its first, cautious steps toward redefining its role in world affairs. One step involved a new role for the U.S. Navy and the commissioning of modern ships able to carry it out. Another involved the emergence of a more coherent set of foreign policy objectives and commitments.

Building a Navy

At the end of the Civil War, the navy, like the army, was rapidly **demobilized.** Unlike the army, which was needed to fight Indians in the West, the navy was largely ignored. Few Americans appreciated the significance of the Civil War experiments with armor-plated, steam-powered ships. Even the navy's wooden sailing vessels deteriorated to the point that some people ridiculed them as fit only for firewood.

Alfred Thayer Mahan played a key role in the emergence of the modern navy. As president of the Naval War College, Captain Mahan exerted a powerful influence, especially during the Harrison administration. In his book *The Influence of Sea Power upon History* (1890), Mahan argued that sea power had been the determining factor in the great European power struggles from the mid-seventeenth to the early nineteenth centuries.

Mahan drew a number of lessons for government policy from his study of history. First, Mahan urged support for a strong **merchant marine.** Second, he advocated a large, modern navy centered on huge, powerful battleships. Third, he stressed a vision for empire. Extend American power beyond the national boundaries, he exhorted, to establish and control a canal through Central America, command the Caribbean, dominate Hawai'i and other strategic locations in the Pacific, and create naval bases at key points in the Atlantic and Pacific.

In 1889, during the Harrison administration, Secretary of the Navy Benjamin F. Tracy urged Congress to modernize and expand the navy significantly. He requested eighteen more battleships, nearly fifty more cruisers, and more smaller vessels. Congress did not give him all that he asked but did begin to create a modern, two-ocean navy centered on battleships that were equal to the world's best.

Revolution in Hawai'i

In 1890, the McKinley Tariff allowed imported sugar to enter the United States without being subject to a tariff. To protect domestic sugar producers, sugar grown within the United States received a subsidy of 2 cents per pound. Hawaiian sugar now encountered stiff competition in the American market, notably from Cuban sugar. Facing economic disaster, many Hawaiian planters craved the 2-cent subsidy and began to talk of annexation to the United States. In 1891, King Kalakaua died and was succeeded by his more assertive sister, **Liliuokalani.** She hoped to restore Hawai'i to the **indigenous** Hawaiians. Fearing that they might

demobilize To discharge from military service.

Alfred Thayer Mahan Lecturer and writer on naval history who stressed the importance of sea power in determining political history and who justified imperialism on the basis of national self-interest.

merchant marine Ships engaged in commerce.

Liliuokalani Last reigning queen of Hawai'i, whose desire to restore land to the Hawaiian people and perpetuate the monarchy prompted *haole* planters to depose her in 1893.

indigenous Original to or belonging in an area or environment.

lose not only their political clout but also their economic holdings, *haole* entrepreneurs set out to overthrow the monarchy. On January 17, 1893, the plotters announced a provisional republican government that would seek annexation by the United States. John L. Stevens, the U.S. minister to Hawai'i, provided crucial assistance for the rebellion by ordering the landing of 150 marines. Liliuokalani surrendered, as she put it, "to the superior force of the United States."

The Harrison administration was unable to annex Hawai'i before Harrison's term of office expired. The succeeding president, Grover Cleveland, withdrew the annexation treaty when he learned how Liliuokalani had been deposed. He asked the new government of Hawai'i to restore the queen. It refused, and Hawai'i became a republic, dominated by its *haole* business and planter community.

Crises in Latin America

Although Harrison and Cleveland acted at cross-purposes regarding Hawai'i, they moved in similar directions with regard to Latin America. Both presidents extended American involvement, and both threatened the use of force.

A rebellion in Chile in 1891 ended with victory for the rebels. Because the American minister to Chile had seemed to side against the rebels, anti-American feelings ran high. In October 1891, a mob in Valparaiso killed two American sailors on shore leave. When the Chilean government failed to apologize, Harrison responded with threats of war. Chile gave in, apologized, and promised to pay damages.

In 1895 and 1896, Grover Cleveland also took the nation to the edge of war over a long-standing boundary dispute between Venezuela and **British Guiana.** Venezuela repeatedly proposed arbitration, but Britain refused. In July 1895, Secretary of State Richard Olney demanded that Britain submit the boundary issue to arbitration. Resting his argument on the Monroe Doctrine, he bombastically proclaimed the United States to be pre-eminent throughout the Western Hemisphere. The British still refused arbitration. Cleveland then asked Congress for authority to determine the boundary and enforce it. Britain faced the possibility of conflict with the United States at a time when it was becoming increasingly concerned about Germany and when tensions were mounting between the British colony in South Africa and the neighboring **Boer republics.** Britain agreed to arbitration.

Cleveland took a more restrained position on Cuba, one of the few vestiges of Spain's New World empire. Cuba had rebelled against the mother country repeatedly. A new rebellion broke out after 1894, when the Wilson-Gorman Tariff placed a high duty on Cuban sugar and sent the Cuban economy into a depression. In 1896, General Valeriano Weyler, the Spanish commander in Cuba, established a **reconcentration** policy to combat guerrilla warfare waged by **insurgents** seeking independence. Weyler ordered the civilian population into fortified towns or camps. Everyone outside these fortified areas was subject to attack. The insurgents responded by ravaging sugar and tobacco plantations, including those owned by Americans.

The U.S. government vehemently protested reconcentration, particularly after disease and starvation swept through the camps, killing an estimated one of every eight Cubans in two years. American newspapers vied with each other in portraying Spanish atrocities and in exaggerating them to attract readers. Such **yellow journalism** swayed many Americans to clamor for action that would rescue the Cubans from Spanish oppression.

British Guiana British colony in northeast South America on the Atlantic coast; its boundary with Venezuela was the source of a long-standing dispute.

Boer republics Self-governing nations established by white South Africans of Dutch descent; they were formed in an effort to escape British rule but were eventually annexed by Britain into its South African colony.

reconcentration Spanish policy in Cuba in 1896 under which the civilian population was ordered into fortified camps as part of a plan to isolate and annihilate Cuban revolutionaries.

insurgents Rebels or revolutionaries.

yellow journalism Journalism that exploits or exaggerates the news to attract readers.

Cleveland reacted cautiously. He proclaimed American neutrality and warned Americans not to support the insurrection. When members of Congress began to push for action to secure Cuban independence, Cleveland ignored the pressure. He did urge Spain to grant concessions to the insurgents, but he considered the insurgents incapable of replacing Spanish rule. Just as he had opposed the annexation of Hawai'i, Cleveland feared that American intervention might lead to annexation regardless of the will of the Cuban people. Nonetheless, by early 1897 he had begun to warn Spain of possible American intervention.

Striding Boldly: War and Imperialism, 1897–1901

In 1898, the United States went to war with Spain over Cuba. Some who promoted American intervention on behalf of the suffering Cubans envisioned a quick war to establish a Cuban republic. Others saw war with Spain as an opportunity to acquire a colonial empire for the United States.

McKinley and War

William McKinley assumed the presidency in 1897 amid increasing demands for action regarding Cuba. McKinley gradually stepped up diplomatic efforts to resolve the crisis. Late that year, Spain responded by recalling General Weyler, softening the reconcentration policy, and offering the Cubans limited self-government but not independence.

In February 1898, however, two events scuttled progress toward a negotiated solution. First, Cuban insurgents stole a letter written by **Enrique Dupuy de Lôme,** the Spanish minister to the United States, and released it to the *New York Journal.* In it, de Lôme criticized President McKinley as "weak and a bidder for the admiration of the crowd." The letter implied that Spain was not seriously committed to reform in Cuba. De Lôme's immediate resignation could not undo the damage. The letter aroused intense anti-Spanish feeling among Americans.

Second, on February 15, a few days after publication of the de Lôme letter, an explosion ripped open the American warship ***Maine,*** anchored in Havana harbor. The *Maine* sank, with the loss of more than 260 American officers and sailors. The yellow press accused Spain of sabotage, claiming that a submarine mine had sunk the ship. Regardless of how the explosion occurred, those advocating intervention now had a rallying cry: "Remember the *Maine!*"

McKinley demanded that Spain put an immediate end to the fighting and submit to his **mediation.** One possible outcome of this mediation was Cuban independence. In reply, the Spanish government consented to end the fighting if the insurgents asked for an **armistice.** Spain was silent, though, on mediation by McKinley and independence for Cuba. On April 11, McKinley asked Congress for authority to stop the war in Cuba. On April 19, Congress passed four resolutions that (1) declared that Cuba was and should be independent, (2) demanded that Spain withdraw "at once," (3) authorized the president to force Spanish withdrawal, and (4) disavowed any intention to annex the island. The first three resolutions amounted to a declaration of war. The fourth has usually been called the **Teller Amendment** for its sponsor, Senator Henry M. Teller of Colorado. In response, Spain declared war.

Nearly all Americans reacted enthusiastically to what they understood to be a war whose purpose was to bring independence to the long-suffering

Enrique Dupuy de Lôme Spanish minister to the United States whose private letter criticizing President McKinley was stolen and made public, increasing anti-Spanish sentiment.

Maine American warship that exploded in Havana harbor in 1898; later investigation suggested an internal explosion.

mediation An attempt to bring about the peaceful settlement of a dispute through the intervention of a neutral party.

armistice An agreement to halt fighting at least temporarily.

Teller Amendment Resolution approved by U.S. Senate in 1898, by which the United States promised not to annex Cuba.

Cubans. From the beginning, however, some voiced distrust of the McKinley administration's motives. This distrust intensified when the McKinley administration defeated efforts to have the Cuban insurgents recognized as the legitimate government of Cuba.

The "Splendid Little War"

Many Americans were taken by surprise when the first engagement in the war occurred not in Cuba but in the **Philippine Islands,** on the other side of the world. A Spanish colony for more than three hundred years, the Philippines, like Cuba, were engaged in a rebellion against Spanish rule.

Assistant Secretary of the Navy **Theodore Roosevelt,** however, was not surprised. In late February 1898, more than six weeks before McKinley's war message to Congress, Roosevelt cabled the American naval commander in the Pacific, George Dewey, and instructed him to crush the Spanish fleet at Manila Bay in the event of war. On May 1, Dewey carried out those orders. His squadron of four cruisers and three smaller vessels steamed into Manila Bay and quickly destroyed or captured ten Spanish cruisers and gunboats. The Spanish lost 381 men; the Americans lost 1, a victim of heat prostration. Dewey became an instant national hero.

Dewey's victory at Manila immediately raised the prospect of establishing a permanent American presence there. This, in turn, revived interest in annexing Hawai'i as a base for supplying and protecting future American involvement in eastern Asia. The annexation of Hawai'i was accomplished on July 7, some five years after the planters had **deposed** Queen Liliuokalani.

Dewey's victory demonstrated that the American navy was clearly superior to that of Spain. By contrast, the Spanish army in Cuba outnumbered the entire American army by more than five to one. The Spanish troops also had years of experience fighting in Cuba. When war was declared, the American army numbered only twenty-eight thousand soldiers. A call for volunteers brought nearly a million—five times as many as the army could take.

The sudden declaration of war caught the army unprepared. Sent to training camps in the South, the new soldiers found chaos and confusion. Food, uniforms, and equipment arrived at one location while the men for whom they were intended stood hungry and idle at another. The heavy wool uniforms were totally unsuited for the climate. Disease raged through some camps, killing many men. Others died from tainted food.

Once in Cuba, American forces concentrated on the port city of Santiago, where the Spanish Atlantic fleet had taken refuge. Inexperienced, poorly equipped, and unfamiliar with the terrain, the Americans doggedly assaulted the fortified hills surrounding the city. At Kettle Hill, Theodore Roosevelt, who had resigned as assistant secretary of the navy to organize a volunteer cavalry regiment, led a successful but costly charge of his **"Rough Riders"** and regular army units. Driving the Spanish from the crest of Kettle Hill cleared a serious impediment to the assault on nearby San Juan Heights and San Juan Hill. Roosevelt's units took a minor part in the attack on those heights. With little regard for accuracy, newspapers declared Roosevelt the hero of the Battle of San Juan Hill.

Once the Americans secured control of the high ground around Santiago Harbor, the Spanish fleet of four cruisers and two destroyers tried to escape from the harbor. A larger American fleet under Admiral William Sampson and Commodore Winfield Schley sank or disabled every Spanish ship. The Spanish suffered 323 deaths, the Americans 1.

Their fleet destroyed and the surrounding hills in American hands, the Spanish in Santiago still waited two weeks before surrendering. A week later, American forces took Puerto Rico. Early in the war, on June 21, an American cruiser had

Philippine Islands A group of islands in the Pacific Ocean southeast of China that came under U.S. control in 1898 after the Spanish-American War.

Theodore Roosevelt American politician and writer who advocated war against Spain in 1898; McKinley's vice president in 1900, he became president in 1901 upon McKinley's assassination.

depose To dethrone or remove from power.

Rough Riders Cavalry volunteers in the Spanish-American War recruited by their lieutenant colonel, Theodore Roosevelt.

◆ Theodore Roosevelt's Rough Riders, on foot because there was not room aboard ship for their horses, are shown in the background of this artist's depiction of the battle for Kettle Hill, a part of the larger battle for San Juan Hill, overlooking the city of Santiago. The artist has put into the foreground members of the 9th and 10th Cavalry, both African-American units that also played a key role in that engagement, but one often overlooked because of the attention usually given Roosevelt and the Rough Riders. *Chicago Historical Society.*

forced Spanish forces on Guam to surrender without a contest. Spanish land forces in the Philippines surrendered when the first American troops arrived in mid-August (see Map 20.1). The "splendid little war," as John Hay, the American ambassador to Great Britain described it, lasted only sixteen weeks. The war cost the United States 385 battlefield deaths and more than 5,000 deaths because of disease and other causes.

The Treaty of Paris

On August 12, the United States and Spain agreed to stop fighting. The truce specified that Spain was to give up Cuba and transfer Puerto Rico and one of the **Ladrone Islands** to the United States. Until a peace conference determined the Philippines' fate, the United States was to occupy Manila.

The only real question remaining was the disposition of the Philippines. McKinley at first seemed inclined to request only a naval base and to leave Spain the remainder of the islands. Spanish authority collapsed everywhere on the islands by mid-August, however, as Filipino insurgents took charge. Britain, Japan, and Germany seemed likely to step in if the United States withdrew. McKinley then apparently decided that defending a naval base on Manila Bay would require control of the entire island group. No one seems to have seriously considered the Filipinos' desire for independence.

McKinley was well aware of the political and strategic importance of the Philippines for establishing an American presence in eastern Asia. He invoked other reasons, however, when he explained his decision to a group of visiting Methodists. He repeatedly prayed for guidance on the Philippine question, he told them. Late one night, he realized that "there was nothing left for us to do but to take them all, and to educate the Filipinos, and uplift and civilize and Christianize them and by God's grace do the very best we could by them, as our fellow men, for whom Christ also died." In fact, most Filipinos had been Catholics for centuries.

Ladrone Islands Islands in the western Pacific now known as the Marianas; they include the island of Guam, which the United States acquired from Spain under the 1898 Treaty of Paris.

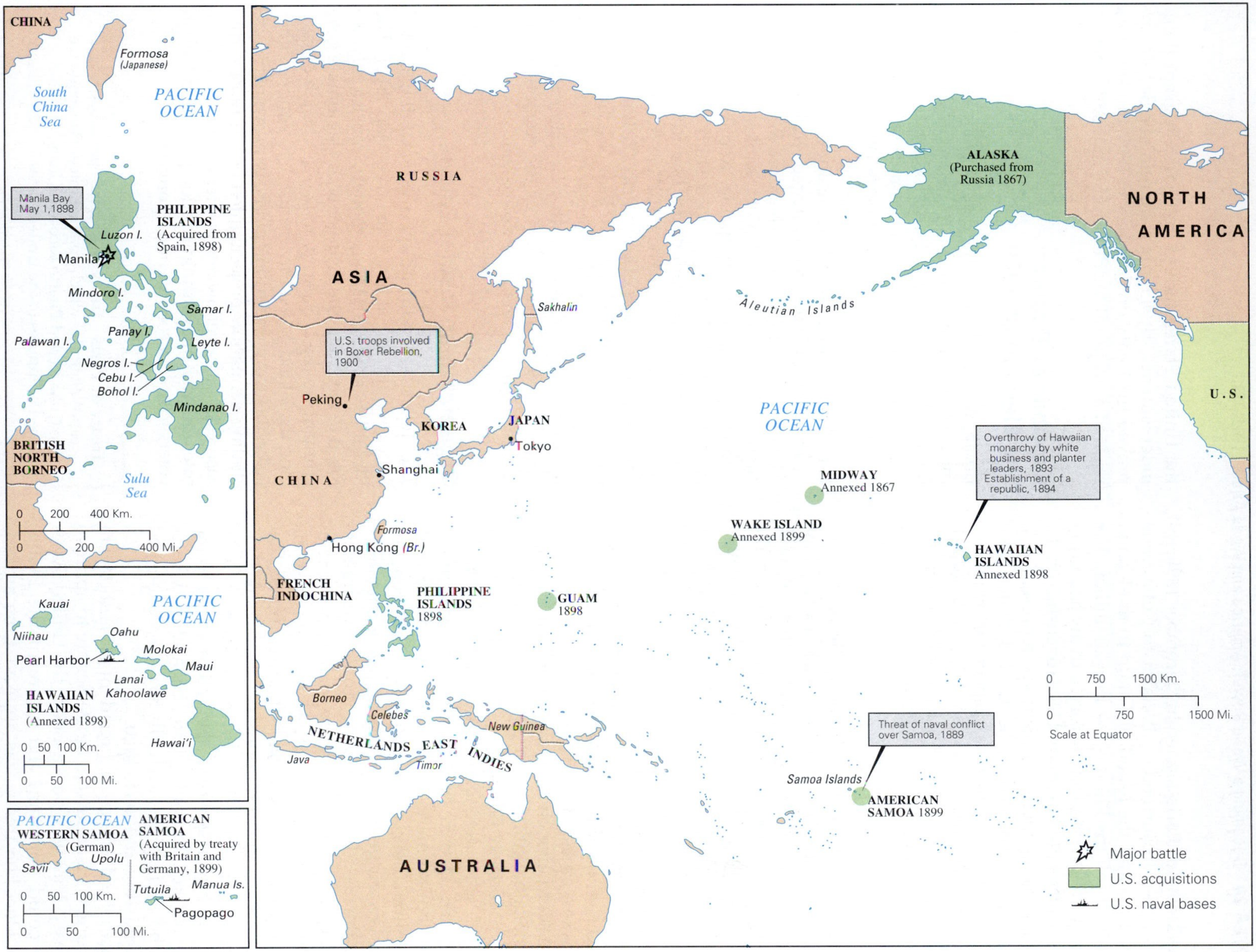
CHINA
Formosa
(Japanese)
South
China
Sea
PACIFIC
OCEAN
Manila Bay
May 1,1898
PHILIPPINE
ISLANDS
(Acquired from
Spain, 1898)
Luzon I.
Manila
Mindoro I.
Samar I.
Panay I.
Palawan I.
Leyte I.
Negros I.
Cebu I.
Bohol I.
Mindanao I.
BRITISH
NORTH
BORNEO
Sulu
Sea
0 200 400 Km.
0 200 400 Mi.
Kauai
PACIFIC
OCEAN
Niihau
Oahu
Pearl Harbor
Molokai
Maui
Lanai
HAWAIIAN
ISLANDS
(Annexed 1898)
Kahoolawe
Hawai'i
0 50 100 Km.
0 50 100 Mi.
PACIFIC OCEAN
WESTERN SAMOA
(German)
Savii
Upolu
AMERICAN
SAMOA
(Acquired by treaty
with Britain and
Germany, 1899)
Tutuila
Manua Is.
Pagopago
0 50 100 Km.
0 50 100 Mi.
RUSSIA
ALASKA
(Purchased from
Russia 1867)
NORTH
AMERICA
ASIA
Sakhalin
Aleutian Islands
U.S. troops involved
in Boxer Rebellion,
1900
Peking
KOREA
JAPAN
Tokyo
PACIFIC
OCEAN
U.S.
CHINA
Shanghai
Overthrow of Hawaiian
monarchy by white
business and planter
leaders, 1893
Establishment of a
republic, 1894
MIDWAY
Annexed 1867
WAKE ISLAND
Annexed 1899
Formosa
Hong Kong (Br.)
HAWAIIAN
ISLANDS
Annexed 1898
FRENCH
INDOCHINA
PHILIPPINE
ISLANDS
1898
GUAM
1898
0 750 1500 Km.
0 750 1500 Mi.
Scale at Equator
Borneo
Celebes
New Guinea
Threat of naval conflict
over Samoa, 1889
NETHERLANDS EAST INDIES
Java
Timor
Samoa Islands
AMERICAN
SAMOA 1899
AUSTRALIA
Major battle
U.S. acquisitions
U.S. naval bases

♦ **MAP 20.1 The United States and the Pacific, 1866–1900** In the 1890s, the United States became a major power in the Pacific and in eastern Asia. This map indicates major acquisitions and activities up to 1900.

The **Treaty of Paris,** signed in December 1898, required Spain to surrender all claim to Cuba, cede Puerto Rico and the island of Guam to the United States, and sell the Philippines for $20 million. For the first time in American history, a treaty acquiring new territory failed to confer U.S. citizenship on the residents. Thus these acquisitions represented a new kind of expansion. The United States now owned territories with no prospect for statehood and whose residents lacked the rights of American citizens. America had become a colonial power.

The terms of the Treaty of Paris dismayed Democrats, Populists, and some conservative Republicans. An active anti-imperialist movement quickly formed, including William Jennings Bryan, Grover Cleveland, Andrew Carnegie, Mark Twain, Jane Addams, and others. The treaty, they argued, amounted to a denial of self-government for the newly acquired territories and therefore violated the Declaration of Independence. For the United States to hold colonies, they claimed, threatened the very concept of democracy. "The Declaration of Independence will make every Filipino a thoroughly dissatisfied subject," Andrew Carnegie warned. Others worried about the perversion of American values. "God Almighty help the party that seeks to give civilization and Christianity hypodermically with 13-inch guns," prayed Senator William Morris of Illinois.

Those who defended the acquisition of the Philippines echoed McKinley's lofty pronouncements about America's solemn duty, along with more mundane claims about economic benefits. Albert Beveridge, senator from Indiana after 1899, stated the need for expansion: "Today, we are raising more than we can consume, making more than we can use. Therefore we must find new markets for our produce." Expansionists also argued that possession of the Philippines would make the United States a leading power in eastern Asia. American business would then have access to the China market. In contrast to the heated debates over the Philippines, virtually no one challenged the acquisition of Puerto Rico.

Bryan, the Democratic presidential candidate in 1896, urged his followers in the Senate to approve the treaty. That way, he reasoned, the United States alone could determine the future of the Philippines. Once the treaty was approved, he argued, the United States should immediately grant them independence. By a narrow margin, the Senate approved the treaty on February 6, 1899, but senators rejected a proposal for Philippine independence.

Republic or Empire: The Election of 1900

Bryan, who easily won the Democratic nomination for a second time, hoped to make independence for the Philippines the central issue in the 1900 presidential election. Bryan found, however, that many conservative anti-imperialists would not support his candidacy because he insisted on silver coinage and attacked big business.

The Republicans renominated McKinley. For vice president, they chose Theodore Roosevelt, the "hero of San Juan Hill." The McKinley re-election campaign seemed unstoppable. Republican campaigners pointed proudly to a short and highly successful war, legislation that had fulfilled party campaign promises on the tariff and the gold standard, and the return of prosperity. Whereas Bryan repeatedly attacked imperialism, McKinley and Roosevelt took pride in expansion. McKinley easily won a second term with 51.7 percent of the vote. He even carried most of the western states where populism had once flourished.

Organizing an Insular Empire

The Teller Amendment specified that the United States would not annex Cuba (see Map 20.2). The McKinley administration, though, consistently refused to recognize the insurgents as a legitimate government, so the U.S. Army took over the job of running the island when the Spanish left. Among other tasks, the army undertook public improvements, including sanitation projects intended to reduce disease, especially yellow fever. After two years of army rule, the McKinley administration permitted Cuban voters to hold a constitutional convention.

Treaty of Paris Treaty ending the Spanish-American War, under which Spain granted independence to Cuba, ceded Puerto Rico and Guam, and sold the Philippines to the United States for $20 million.

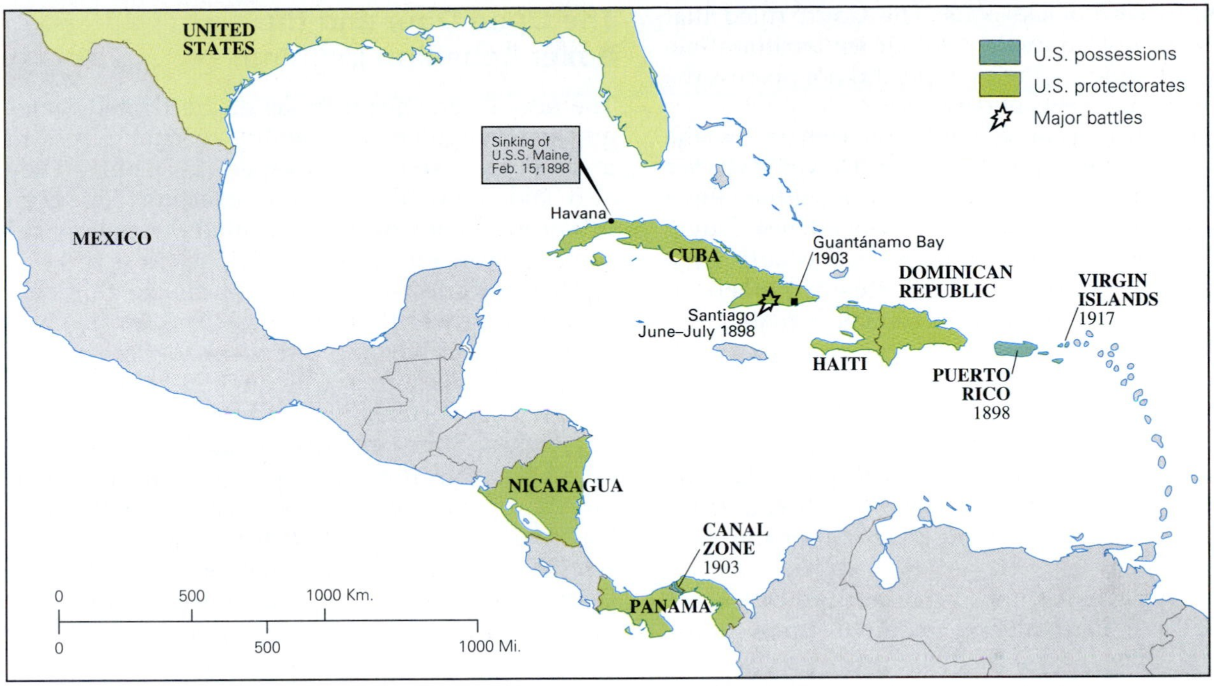

♦ **MAP 20.2 The United States and the Caribbean, 1898–1917** Between 1898 and 1917, the United States expanded into the Caribbean by acquiring possessions and establishing protectorates. As a result, the United States became the dominant power in the region during this time period.

The convention drafted a constitution in 1900 modeled on that of the United States. It did not define relations between Cuba and the United States, however. In March 1901, the McKinley administration specified, and Congress adopted, detailed provisions for Cuba to adopt before the army would withdraw, including these stipulations: (1) Cuba was not to make any agreement with a foreign power that impaired the island's independence, (2) the United States could intervene in Cuba to preserve Cuban independence and maintain law and order, and (3) Cuba was to lease facilities to the United States for naval bases and coaling stations. The Cubans reluctantly accepted the conditions, added them to their constitution, and agreed to a treaty with the United States stating the same conditions. In 1902, Cuba thereby became a protectorate of the United States.

The Teller Amendment did not apply to Puerto Rico. On that island, too, the army provided a military government until 1900, when Congress approved the **Foraker Act.** That act made Puerto Ricans citizens of Puerto Rico but not citizens of the United States. It specified that Puerto Rican voters were to elect a legislature but final authority was to rest with a governor and council appointed by the president of the United States. In 1901, in the **Insular cases,** the U.S. Supreme Court issued a complex decision that, in effect, confirmed the colonial status of Puerto Rico and, by implication,

Foraker Act Law passed by Congress in 1900 that established civilian government in Puerto Rico; it provided for an elected legislature and a governor appointed by the U.S. president.

Insular cases Cases concerning Puerto Rico in which the U.S. Supreme Court ruled in 1901 that people in new island territories did not automatically receive the constitutional rights of U.S. citizens.

the other new possessions. The Court ruled that they were not equivalent to earlier territorial acquisitions and that their people did not possess the constitutional rights of citizens.

Establishment of a civil government in the Philippines took longer. Between Dewey's victory and the arrival of the first American soldiers three months later, a Philippine independence movement, led by **Emilio Aguinaldo,** had established a provisional government. Its forces controlled all the islands except Manila, which remained in Spanish hands until American troops arrived. Aguinaldo and his government wanted independence, not a new colonial master. When the United States decided to keep the islands, many Filipinos resisted and eventually turned to guerrilla warfare. In an ironic turn of events, the United States now found itself in the role that Spain had previously played.

Quelling what American authorities called the "Philippine insurrection" required three years, took the lives of more than forty-two hundred American soldiers (more losses than in the Spanish-American War) and perhaps twenty thousand guerrillas, and cost $400 million (twenty times the price of the islands). In crushing the resistance, U.S. troops resorted to the practice of reconcentration that the American public had so widely condemned when Spain used it in Cuba. Both sides committed atrocities during the conflict. Anti-imperialists saw their fears confirmed that a colonial policy would corrupt American values.

Aguinaldo's eventual defeat and McKinley's reelection ended any prospect for immediate Philippine independence. In 1902, Congress set up a government for the Philippines similar to that of Puerto Rico. Filipinos became citizens of the Philippine Islands, not of the United States. The president of the United States appointed the governor. Filipino voters elected one house in the two-house legislature, and the governor appointed the other. Both the governor and the United States Congress could veto laws passed by the legislature. **William Howard Taft,** governor of the islands from 1901 to 1904, tried to build local support for American control but met with little success. When the first Philippine legislature met in 1907, over half of its members favored independence from the United States.

The Open Door and the Boxer Rebellion in China

The new Pacific acquisitions of the United States greatly strengthened its ability to gain access to markets in eastern Asia, especially China. They also laid a broad basis for asserting American power in eastern Asia. The United States now began to act like a major East Asian power.

The McKinley administration flexed this new American power first in China. By 1899, Britain, Germany, Russia, and France had carved out spheres of influence in China where they claimed special rights—usually a monopoly over trade. The United States claimed no such privileges in China. Fearing the breakup of China into separate European colonies, Secretary of State John Hay in 1899 circulated a letter to Germany, Russia, Britain, France, Italy, and Japan. The Open Door notes asked these countries to permit Chinese authorities to continue to collect tariff duties within their **spheres of influence.** Hay hoped that this measure would preserve some semblance of Chinese sovereignty. He also urged them not to discriminate against citizens of other nations engaged in commerce within their spheres. Thus Hay sought to prevent other nations from carving up China and, at the same time, to make American trade possible throughout China. Although some replies proved less than fully supportive, he announced that the **Open Door policy** was in effect.

The next year, in 1900, a Chinese secret society took up arms to expel foreigners from China. Be-

Emilio Aguinaldo Leader of struggles for Philippine independence, first against Spain and then against the United States.

William Howard Taft Appointed governor of the Philippines from 1901 to 1904; he was elected president of the United States in 1908 and became chief justice of the Supreme Court in 1921.

spheres of influence Areas of a country where foreign nations exercise considerable authority.

Open Door policy Policy advocated by the United States in 1899 under which all nations would have equal access to trading and development rights in China.

U.S
COMMERCIAL
EXPANSIONIST
W.A. Rogers.
A FAIR FIELD AND NO FAVOR!
UNCLE SAM: "I'M OUT FOR COMMERCE, NOT CONQUEST!"

♦ In this 1899 cartoon celebrating the Open Door policy, Uncle Sam insists that the nations of Europe must compete fairly for China's commerce and must not seize Chinese territory. In the background, John Bull (Britain) lifts his hat in approval. *Library of Congress.*

cause the rebels used a clenched fist as their symbol, Westerners called them Boxers. After attacking missionaries, the Boxers laid siege to the foreign **legations** in Peking, the Chinese capital. Hay foresaw that the major powers might use the **Boxer Rebellion** as a pretext to take full control of China. To block such a move, the United States took part in a joint international military expedition to crush the rebellion. Hay insisted that American action was not against the Chinese government but against the rebels.

Although China did not lose territory after the Boxer Rebellion, the intervening nations required it to pay an **indemnity.** After compensating American citizens for losses suffered during the rebellion, the U.S. government returned the remainder of its indemnity to China. As a show of gratitude, the Chinese government used the money to send Chinese students to the United States to develop good will between the two countries.

"Carry a Big Stick": The United States and World Affairs, 1901–1913

In 1901, an assassin's bullet cut down President McKinley and put Theodore Roosevelt in the White House. Roosevelt remolded the presidency, established new federal powers in the economy, and expanded America's role in world affairs. Few other presidents have had so great an impact. He once expressed his fondness for what he described as a West African proverb: "Speak softly and carry a big stick; you will go far." As president, however, Roosevelt seldom spoke softly. Everything he did, it seemed, he did strenuously. Well-read in history and current events, Roosevelt entered the presidency with definite ideas on the proper role for the United States in the world. He envisioned a future in which major powers, particularly the United States, would exercise international police powers.

Taking Panama

Following the American victory over Spain, American diplomats pursued efforts to build a canal through Central America to create a passage between the Atlantic and the Pacific. The considerable time that it took an American battleship stationed on the West Coast to reach Cuba during the Spanish-American War led McKinley to pronounce that an American-controlled canal was "indispensable." The **Hay-Pauncefote Treaties** of 1900 and 1901, in which Britain renounced its interests in an

legation A diplomatic mission in a foreign country.

Boxer Rebellion Uprising in China in 1900 directed against foreign powers; it was suppressed by an international army that included American participation.

indemnity Payment for damage, loss, or injury.

Hay-Pauncefote Treaties Two separate treaties (1900 and 1901) signed by the United States and Britain giving the United States the exclusive right to build, control, and fortify a canal through Central America.

isthmian canal, cleared the way. Experts identified two possible locations for a canal, Nicaragua and Panama (then part of Colombia). In its favor, the Panama route was shorter, and a French canal company had completed some work in the 1870s. **Philippe Bunau-Varilla,** a major stockholder in the French company, did his utmost to sell that company's interests to the United States. Building through Panama, however, meant overcoming both formidable mountains and fever-ridden swamps. Previous studies had shown Nicaragua to be preferable because of fewer natural obstacles. Bunau-Varilla's lobbying led the Senate to approve the Panama route, provided that Colombia agreed to give up land for a canal.

Negotiations with Colombia bogged down over treaty language that significantly limited its sovereignty. Pressure from the United States did lead the Colombian government to accept such limitations—but only in return for more money. Roosevelt, outraged, called it "pure bandit morality." To break the impasse, Bunau-Varilla financed a revolution in Panama. Anticipating such a possibility, Roosevelt had ordered U.S. warships to prevent Colombian troops from crushing the uprising. The revolution succeeded, and Panama declared its independence. The United States immediately extended diplomatic recognition. Bunau-Varilla, named Panama's minister to the United States, promptly signed a treaty that gave the United States much the same arrangement earlier rejected by Colombia.

The **Hay–Bunau-Varilla Treaty** (1904) granted the United States perpetual control over a strip of Panamanian territory 10 miles wide, for a price of $10 million and annual rent of $250,000. The United States also purchased the assets of the French company and in 1904 began construction of the canal. Building the canal proved difficult. Just over 40 miles long, the canal took ten years to build and cost nearly $400 million. Completed in 1914, just as World War I began, the canal was considered one of the world's great engineering feats.

Making the Caribbean an American Lake

Well before the canal was finished, Roosevelt determined to establish American dominance in the Caribbean and Central America to protect the canal. The threat of European intervention in the Caribbean led Roosevelt in 1904 to present what became known as the **Roosevelt Corollary** to the Monroe Doctrine. The corollary stated that the United States would act as the police power in the Western Hemisphere in cases where governments defaulted on their debts or otherwise misbehaved. Roosevelt thus warned European nations against any intervention whatsoever in the Western Hemisphere. If outside authority became necessary in the Caribbean and Central America, Roosevelt insisted that the United States would handle it. He exempted Argentina, Brazil, and Chile from the Roosevelt Corollary as "civilized" powers in their own right.

Roosevelt acted forcefully to establish his new policy. In 1905, the Dominican Republic agreed to permit the United States to supervise government expenditures and thereby became an American protectorate. Roosevelt's successors, William Howard Taft and Woodrow Wilson, expanded his policy of American domination in the Caribbean region. Under Taft, the United States encouraged Americans to invest in the region. Taft hoped that American investment would stabilize and develop the Caribbean economies. Taft supported such **dollar diplomacy** throughout the region, especially in Nicaragua. In 1912, Taft sent marines there to suppress a rebellion against President Adolfo Díaz. Nicaragua, too, became an American protectorate.

Philippe Bunau-Varilla Chief engineer of the French company contracted to build the Panama Canal and later minister to the United States from the new Republic of Panama.

Hay–Bunau-Varilla Treaty Treaty with Panama that granted the United States sovereignty over the Canal Zone in return for a $10 million payment plus an annual rent.

Roosevelt Corollary Extension of the Monroe Doctrine voiced by Theodore Roosevelt in 1904, in which he proclaimed the right of the United States to police Caribbean areas.

dollar diplomacy Policy during the Taft administration of supporting U.S. commercial interests abroad for strategic purposes, especially in Latin America.

The marines remained after the turmoil settled to prop up the Díaz government.

Roosevelt and Eastern Asia

Roosevelt's East Asian policy built on the Open Door notes and American participation in the suppression of the Boxer Rebellion. He found cause for both concern and optimism in Japan's rise as a major industrial and imperial power. His friend Alfred Thayer Mahan, the naval strategist, had warned of the potential danger to the United States posed by Japan. But Roosevelt was also hopeful. He admired Japanese accomplishments and looked forward to Japan's exercising the same degree of international police power in its vicinity that the United States did under the Roosevelt Corollary.

In 1904, Russia and Japan went to war over **Manchuria,** the northern part of China. After the Boxer Rebellion, Russia had pressured China to grant concessions that slowly turned Manchuria into a Russian colony. Russia seemed also to have designs on Korea. Japan responded with force to Russian encroachment on its interests. The Japanese scored smashing naval and military victories over the Russians but lacked the resources to sustain a long war.

Early in the war, Roosevelt indicated some support for Japan. When Japan's resources ran low, Japan asked Roosevelt to act as mediator. The president agreed in hopes of preserving a regional balance of power. The **Treaty of Portsmouth** (1905) recognized Japan's dominance in Korea and gave Japan both the southern half of Sakhalin Island and Russian concessions in southern Manchuria. Russia kept its railroad in northern Manchuria. China was to have responsibility for civil authority in Manchuria. For his mediation, Roosevelt received the 1906 Nobel Peace Prize.

That same year, Roosevelt mediated another significant dispute. The San Francisco school board had ordered children of Japanese parentage to attend the city's segregated Chinese school. The Japanese government regarded this as a serious insult. Roosevelt convinced the board to withdraw the segregation order in return for his efforts to cut off Japanese immigration. Japan agreed informally to limit the departure of laborers to the United States.

In 1908, the American and Japanese governments further agreed to respect each other's territorial possessions and to maintain "the independence and integrity of China" and the Open Door. During the Taft administration, the United States extended the concept of dollar diplomacy to China. Proponents sought Chinese permission for American citizens not just to trade with China but also to invest there, especially in railroad construction. Taft hoped that such investments could head off further Japanese expansion. The effort received Chinese governmental sanction, but little came of it.

The United States and the World: 1901–1913

Before the 1890s, the United States had no clear or consistent set of foreign policy commitments or objectives. After that, its commitments were obvious to all. Acquisition of the Philippines, Guam, Hawai'i, Puerto Rico, eastern Samoa, and the **Canal Zone** represented highly visible components in a new American role in world affairs.

Central to that role was a large, modern, two-ocean navy. Roosevelt was so proud of the navy that, in 1907, he dispatched sixteen battleships—painted white to indicate their peaceful intent—on a fourteen-month world tour. Roosevelt later claimed that his purpose in sending the Great White Fleet "was to impress the American people." But he was clearly interested in impressing other nations too.

Another aspect of America's new role in the world revolved around the principle that the

Manchuria A region of northeast China that the Russians and Japanese fought to control in the late nineteenth and early twentieth centuries.

Treaty of Portsmouth Treaty in 1905 ending the Russo-Japanese War, which was negotiated at a conference in Portsmouth, New Hampshire, through Theodore Roosevelt's mediation.

Canal Zone Territory under U.S. control including the Panama Canal and land extending 5 miles on either side of it.

United States should control an **isthmian** canal. Protecting that canal led the United States to establish **hegemony** in the Caribbean and Central America as a means of preventing any other major power from threatening the canal. The new American role also focused on the Pacific. Captain Mahan had pointed out that the Atlantic Ocean had been the theater of conflict among European nations in the eighteenth century. He looked to the Pacific Ocean as the likely theater of twentieth-century conflict. Again, considerations of commercial enterprise and naval strategy coincided in leading the United States to acquire naval bases at strategic points in the central Pacific (Hawai'i), south Pacific (eastern Samoa), and off eastern Asia (the Philippines).

America's new vision of the world divided nations into two broad categories. On the one hand were all the "civilized" nations. On the other were those nations that Theodore Roosevelt described as "barbarous." American policy toward "civilized" countries—the European powers, Japan, and the large, stable nations of Latin America—focused on finding peaceful ways to realize mutual objectives, especially through arbitration. In eastern Asia, McKinley, Roosevelt, and Taft looked to a balance of power among the contending "civilized" powers as most likely to realize the American objective of maintaining access to the China market.

The conviction that arbitration was the appropriate means to settle disputes among "civilized" countries was widespread. An international conference in 1899 created a Permanent Court of Arbitration in the Netherlands. Housed in a marble "peace palace" built through a donation from Andrew Carnegie, the **Hague Court** functioned as a source of neutral arbitrators for international disputes. Both Roosevelt and Taft tried to negotiate arbitration treaties with major powers, only to find that the Senate was not willing to ratify them. Senators feared that such treaties might diminish their future role in approving agreements with other countries.

The United States and Britain repeatedly used arbitration to settle disputes between themselves. In addition to the *Alabama* claims, they used arbitration in 1903 to settle questions over the boundary between Alaska and Canada and in 1909 to end a dispute over the rights of American fishermen operating off the coast of Canada.

Throughout the late nineteenth and early twentieth centuries, American relations with Great Britain improved steadily. As Germany expanded its army and navy and increasingly challenged Britain, British policymakers sought to improve ties with the United States, the only nation besides Great Britain with a navy comparable to Germany's. During the Spanish-American War, Britain alone among the major European powers sided with the United States and encouraged its acquisition of the Philippines. In signing the Hay-Pauncefote Treaties and reducing its naval forces in the Caribbean, Britain delivered a clear signal: it not only accepted American dominance there but even depended on the United States to protect its own holdings in the region.

isthmian Pertaining to a narrow strip of land connecting two larger landmasses; in this case, the isthmus was Panama.

hegemony The dominance of one over another.

Hague Court Body of delegates from about fifty member nations created in the Netherlands in 1899 for the purpose of peacefully resolving international conflicts; also known as the Permanent Court of Arbitration.

SUMMARY

Expectations
Constraints
Choices
Outcomes

From 1865 to 1889, few Americans *expected* their nation to take a major part in world affairs. The United States did make *choices* to acquire Alaska and to expel the French from Mexico. Other American *choices* brought some involvement in the Caribbean and Central America and in eastern Asia and the Pacific.

The 1890s witnessed the development of enlarged *expectations* and daring *choices* in foreign affairs. During the administration of Benjamin Harrison, Congress approved the creation of a modern navy. Although a revolution presented the United States with an opportunity to annex Hawai'i, President Grover Cleveland *chose* to reject that course. However, Cleveland boldly threatened war with Great Britain over a disputed boundary between Venezuela and British Guiana, and Britain *chose* to back down.

A revolution in Cuba led the United States into a one-sided war with Spain in 1898. The immediate *outcome* of the war was acquisition of an American colonial empire that included Cuba, the Philippines, Guam, and Puerto Rico. Congress annexed Hawai'i in the midst of the war, and the United States acquired Samoa by treaty in 1899. The Filipinos *chose* to resist the imposition of American authority, leading to a three-year war that cost more lives than the Spanish-American War. With the Philippines in hand and an improved navy on the seas, the United States was free of old *constraints* on its influence in East Asia. It now *chose* to assert the principle of the Open Door in China, where American troops helped suppress the Boxer Rebellion.

President Theodore Roosevelt's *choices* played an important role in defining America's status as a world power. He secured rights to build a U.S.-controlled canal through Panama and established Panama as an American protectorate. The Roosevelt Corollary declared that the United States was the dominant power in the Caribbean and Central America. In eastern Asia, by contrast, Roosevelt *chose* to bolster the Open Door policy by maintaining a balance of power.

Roosevelt and many others *expected* that "civilized" nations had no need to go to war. Thus he *chose* to seek arbitration treaties with leading nations, efforts that failed because of Senate opposition. Faced with the rise of German military and naval power, Great Britain *chose* to improve its relations with the United States.

One *outcome* of America's *choices* in foreign affairs was the acquisition of colonies in a foreign policy usually described as imperialism. A larger *outcome* was that the United States took on the role of a world power, thereby redefining its relations with the rest of the world.

SUGGESTED READINGS

Beisner, Robert L. *From the Old Diplomacy to the New, 1865–1900,* 2nd ed. (1986).

A concise introduction to American foreign relations for this period.

Gould, Lewis L. *The Spanish-American War and President McKinley* (1980).

The political decisions involved in war, peacemaking, and the acquisition of Spanish possessions.

LaFeber, Walter. *The New Empire: An Interpretation of American Expansion, 1860–1898* (1963).

A leading treatment, the first to emphasize the notion of a commercial empire.

Langley, Lester D. *The Banana Wars: United States' Intervention in the Caribbean, 1898–1934* (1983; reprint, 1988).

Sprightly and succinct account of the role of the United States in the Caribbean and Central America.

McCullough, David G. *The Path Between the Seas: The Creation of the Panama Canal, 1870–1914* (1977).

Perhaps the most lively, engrossing coverage of its subject.

Miller, Stuart Creighton. *"Benevolent Assimilation": The American Conquest of the Philippines, 1899–1903* (1982).

A thorough account of its subject.

ADOPTION OF PROGRESSIVE REFORMS BY 1915 This map shows the states that had adopted three progressive reforms during the years before 1915. Woman suffrage, long advocated, finally moved toward national adoption during these years. Prohibition was the leading example of moral reform during the period, and the initiative and referendum became popular vehicles for voter expression in some states.

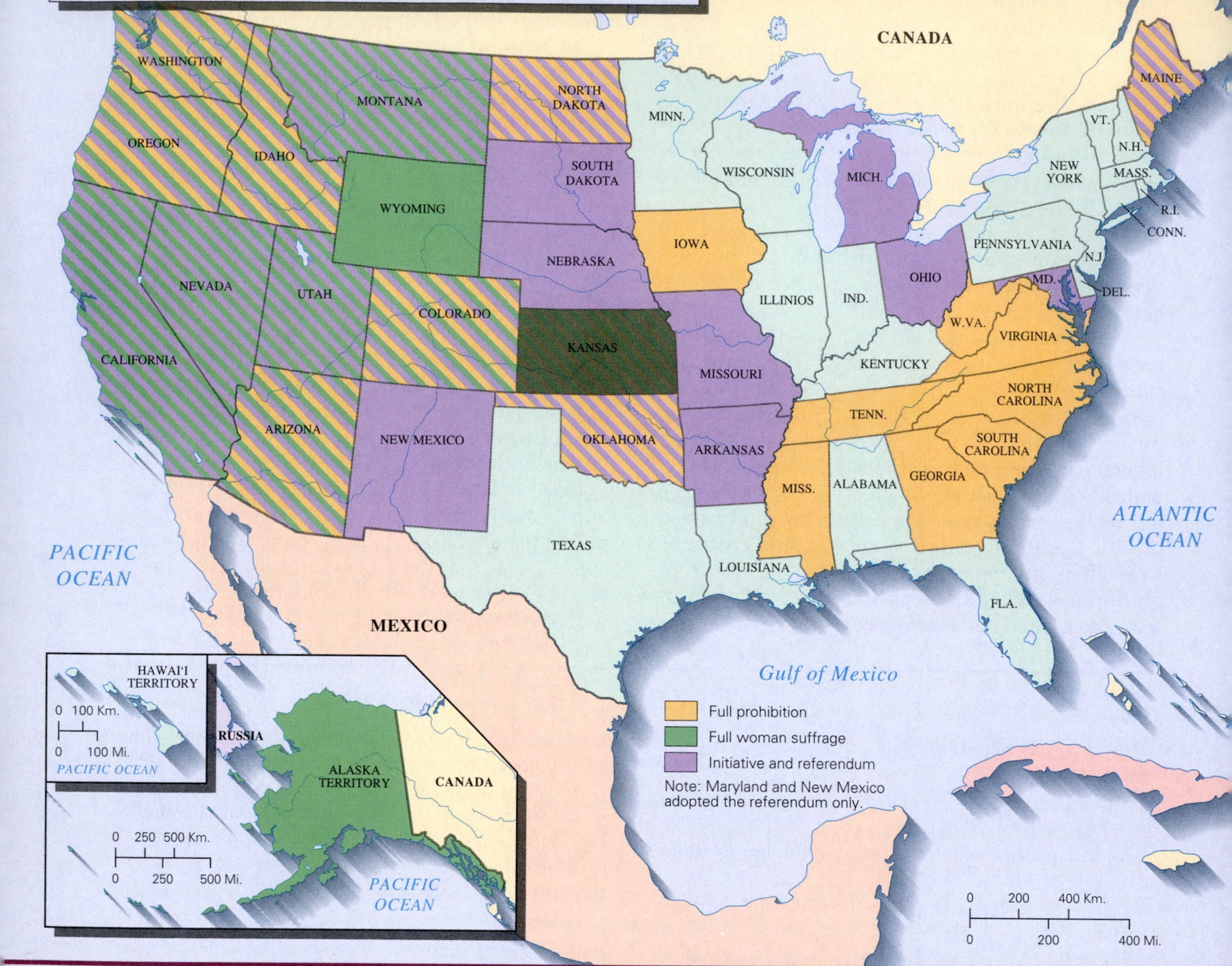
CANADA
WASHINGTON
MONTANA
NORTH DAKOTA
MINN.
OREGON
IDAHO
SOUTH DAKOTA
WYOMING
WISCONSIN
MICH.
NEW YORK
VT.
N.H.
MAINE
MASS.
R.I.
CONN.
NEBRASKA
IOWA
PENNSYLVANIA
N.J.
NEVADA
UTAH
COLORADO
ILLINIOS
IND.
OHIO
MD.
DEL.
W.VA.
VIRGINIA
CALIFORNIA
KANSAS
MISSOURI
KENTUCKY
NORTH CAROLINA
TENN.
ARIZONA
NEW MEXICO
OKLAHOMA
ARKANSAS
SOUTH CAROLINA
MISS.
ALABAMA
GEORGIA
TEXAS
LOUISIANA
FLA.
PACIFIC OCEAN
ATLANTIC OCEAN
MEXICO
Gulf of Mexico
HAWAI'I TERRITORY
0 100 Km.
0 100 Mi.
PACIFIC OCEAN
RUSSIA
ALASKA TERRITORY
CANADA
0 250 500 Km.
0 250 500 Mi.
PACIFIC OCEAN
Full prohibition
Full woman suffrage
Initiative and referendum
Note: Maryland and New Mexico adopted the referendum only.
0 200 400 Km.
0 200 400 Mi.

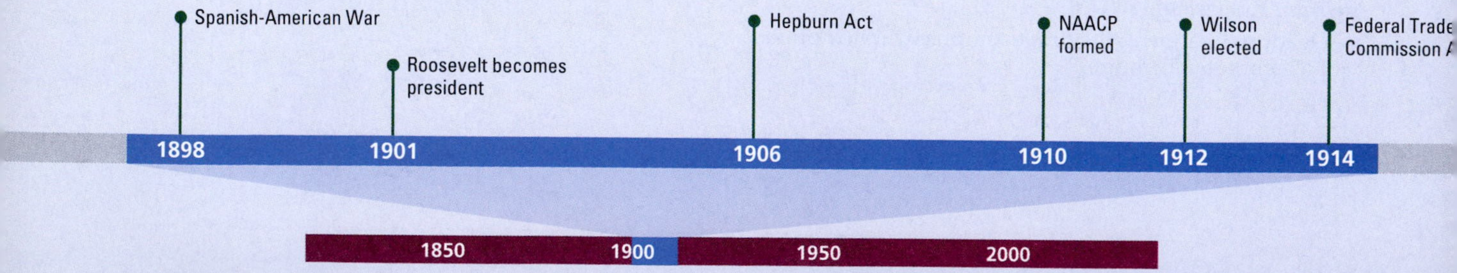
Spanish-American War
Roosevelt becomes president
Hepburn Act
NAACP formed
Wilson elected
Federal Trade Commission A
1898
1901
1906
1910
1912
1914
1850
1900
1950
2000

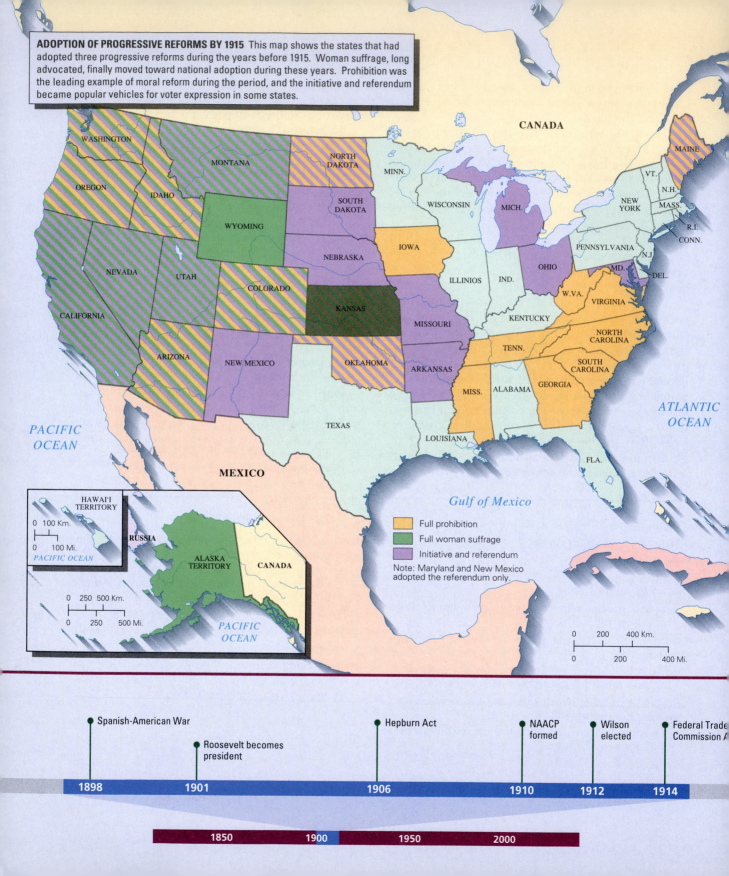

CHAPTER 21

The Progressive Era, 1900–1917

Organizing for Change

- How did progressivism and organized interest groups reflect the changing political expectations of many Americans and their new political choices?
- What choices by women and African Americans produced new organizations devoted to political change?

The Reform of Politics, the Politics of Reform

- How did city and state reforms reflect new expectations for political parties and government?
- How did the rise of interest groups reflect new expectations about politics and government?

Roosevelt, Taft, and Republican Progressivism

- What constraints did Roosevelt face, and how did he choose to deal with them?
- What were the outcomes for the role of the federal government in the economy and for the power of the presidency?

Wilson and Democratic Progressivism

- What choices confronted American voters in the presidential election of 1912?
- How did choices by Wilson and the Democrats influence the role of the federal government in the economy and the power of the presidency?

Progressivism in Perspective

- Were the progressives successful in light of their expectations?
- What lasting outcomes of progressivism affect modern American politics?

INTRODUCTION

Expectations
Constraints
Choices
Outcomes

"Nothing is done in this country as it was done twenty years ago," wrote President Woodrow Wilson in 1913. He exaggerated only slightly. The late 1890s and first twenty years of the twentieth century—the Progressive Era—were a time when "reform was in the air," as one journalist later recalled. In 1912, Walter Weyl, a former settlement house worker, described the state of American politics this way:

> *We are in a period of clamor, of bewilderment, of an almost tremulous unrest. We are hastily revising all our social conceptions. We are hastily testing all our political ideals.*

Weyl's description reflected the widespread popular *expectation* for change. Many different individuals and groups joined the crusade for reform, often with quite different *expectations.* The variety of competing organizations seeking to reform politics produced nearly as much clamor and bewilderment as Weyl described.

At the dawn of the new century, however, few Americans could have anticipated the extent of change that lay ahead. Most probably *expected* a continuation of nineteenth-century political patterns, in which parties dominated politics and government's role in the economy was very limited. Yet many Americans also believed that something should be done to curb the power of the new industrial corporations and to correct the problems of the cities.

Progressivism took shape through many *choices* by voters and political leaders. The basic question in most of these *choices* was this: Should government play a larger role in the lives of Americans? This question lay behind debates over regulation of railroads in 1906 and regulation of banking in 1913, as well as behind proposals to prohibit alcoholic beverages and to limit working hours of women factory workers. Time after time, Americans *chose* a greater role for government. Many times, in fact, all agreed on the need for greater government intervention, and the only *choices* were about the form intervention would take. As they gave government more power, Americans also sought to make it more responsive to ordinary citizens. Americans sometimes impatiently cast former *constraints* aside by putting stricter limits on political parties and by introducing ways for people to participate more directly in politics.

The *constraints* imposed by traditional values of private property and individualism proved more hardy. Although progressives imposed restrictions on the rights of private property, few Americans responded to calls by socialists to eliminate it. Although some reformers proposed to limit individual liberties in the name of morality, a more lasting *outcome* proved to be the breakdown of separate spheres for men and women in politics.

The *outcome* of the political changes of the Progressive Era was a revamped pattern of politics, significantly different from that of the nineteenth century. The long-term changes in the structure and function of government wrought during these decades fundamentally altered American politics and government in the twentieth century. The Progressive Era gave birth to many aspects of modern American politics.

CHRONOLOGY

Reform in the Progressive Era

1889 Pingree elected Detroit mayor

1893 Anti-Saloon League formed

1895 *U.S. v. E. C. Knight*

1896 McKinley elected

1897 Jones elected Toledo mayor

1898 Spanish-American War

1900 First city commission, Galveston, Texas
La Follette elected Wisconsin governor
McKinley re-elected

1901 Socialist Party of America formed
McKinley assassinated; Roosevelt becomes president

1902 Muckraking journalism begins
Oregon adopts initiative and referendum
Antitrust action against Northern Securities Company
Roosevelt intervenes in coal strike
Newlands Act

1903 Women's Trade Union League formed
Du Bois's *Souls of Black Folk*

1904 Steffens's *The Shame of the Cities*
Tarbell's *History of Standard Oil*
Roosevelt elected

1905 Niagara Movement
Industrial Workers of the World organized

1906 Sinclair's *The Jungle*
Hepburn Act
Pure Food and Drug Act
Meat Inspection Act

1907 Financial panic

1908 *Muller v. Oregon*
Race riot in Springfield, Illinois
Taft elected

1909 First "red-light abatement" law
Payne-Aldrich Tariff

1910 Mann Act
National Association for the Advancement of Colored People formed
Johnson elected California governor
Wilson elected New Jersey governor
Taft fires Pinchot

1911 Triangle factory fire

1912 Progressive ("Bull Moose") party formed
Wilson elected president

1913 Sixteenth and Seventeenth Amendments
Underwood Tariff
Federal Reserve Act

1914 Clayton Antitrust Act
Federal Trade Commission Act

1916 Montana elects Rankin first woman in Congress
Wilson reelected
Brandeis appointed to Supreme Court

1917 U.S. enters World War I

Organizing for Change

During the **Progressive Era,** politics dramatically expanded to embrace a much wider range of concerns. And, more than ever before, politics came to reflect the interaction of organized **interest groups.**

The Changing Face of Politics

As the United States entered the twentieth century, the lives of Americans had changed in important ways. The railroad, telegraph, and telephone had transformed concepts of time and space and had fostered the formation of many new organizations. Executives of the new industrial corporations now thought in terms of a national market for their products. Union members allied with others of their trade in distant cities. Farmers studied grain prices in Chicago and Liverpool, England. Physicians organized to establish national standards for medical schools.

Manufacturers, farmers, merchants, carpenters, teachers, lawyers, physicians, and many other occupational groups established national organizations or associations to advance their economic or professional interests. But it was not just occupational groups that formed national associations. So did college graduates, churches, ethnic and racial groups, reformers, humanitarians, and middle-class women. Sooner or later, many of these new organizations sought changes in laws to help them reach their objectives.

The rise of these new organizations transformed American politics. Increasingly, citizens related to politics through organized **interest groups.** At the same time, the typical voter became less and less likely to give his total loyalty to one political party.

Many of these new groups optimistically believed that responsible citizens could achieve social progress and improve the human condition if they acted together and made use of technical know-how. As early as the 1890s, some had begun to call themselves "progressive citizens." By 1910, they were calling themselves simply "progressives."

The term *progressivism* signifies three related developments: (1) the emergence of new concepts of the purpose of government, (2) changes in government policies and institutions, and (3) the political agitation that produced those changes. A progressive can be defined as a person involved in one or more of these activities. The many individuals and groups promoting their own visions of change made progressivism a complex political phenomenon. There was no one progressive movement. Progressivism did, however, reflect the concerns of the urban middle class, especially of urban middle-class women.

Progressivism appeared at the local, state, and federal levels. And progressives promoted a wide range of new government activities: regulation of business, moral reform, consumer protection, conservation of natural resources, educational improvement, tax reform, and more. In all these ways, they brought government more directly into the lives of most Americans.

Women and Reform

Organizations formed or dominated by women burst upon politics during the Progressive era. By 1900, a new ideal for women had emerged from women's colleges and clubs. The "New Woman" stood for self-determination rather than unthinking acceptance of prescribed social roles. By 1910, this fresh attitude, sometimes called **feminism,** was accelerating the transition from the nineteenth-century women's movement for suffrage to the twentieth-century struggle for equality and individualism.

Women's increasing control over one aspect of their lives is evidenced in the birth rate, which fell steadily throughout the nineteenth and early twentieth centuries. They began to challenge laws that banned information about contraception.

Progressive Era A period of reform in the late nineteenth and early twentieth centuries.

interest group A coalition of people working on behalf of a particular cause, such as a change in policy, a particular industry, or a special segment of society.

feminism The conviction that women are and should be the social, political, and economic equals of men.

♦ Margaret Sanger is seen here in 1916 leaving court after being charged with distributing birth-control information illegally. During the Progressive Era, women worked to remove legal barriers to obtaining information on preventing conception. *Smith College Collection, Smith College.*

Margaret Sanger, a nurse practicing among the poor of New York City, became convinced that large families contributed to poverty and damaged the health of women. She saw women die after botched abortions. By 1914, Sanger had concluded, "Women cannot be on an equal footing with men until they have full and complete control over their reproductive function." In 1916, she went to jail for informing women about birth control, a term she originated.

Other women also formed organizations to advance specific causes. The National Consumers' League (formed in 1890) and the Women's Trade Union League (1903) tried to improve the lives of workingwomen. Such efforts received a tragic boost in 1911 when a fire in the Triangle Shirtwaist Company's clothing factory in New York City killed 146 workers—most of them women—who were trapped in a building with no outside fire escapes and with the exit doors locked. The public outcry produced a new state factory safety law.

Some states passed laws specifically to protect workingwomen. In ***Muller v. Oregon*** (1908), the Supreme Court approved the constitutionality of a law limiting women's hours of work. The decision was widely hailed as a vital and necessary protection for women wage earners. By 1917, all but nine states had laws restricting women's working hours.

Support for suffrage grew as more women recognized the need for political action to bring social reforms. Between 1910 and 1915, eight additional western states approved female suffrage. In 1916, **Jeannette Rankin** of Montana became the first woman elected to the House of Representatives. Suffrage, however, scored few victories outside the West.

Convinced that only a federal constitutional amendment would gain the vote for all women, the **National American Woman Suffrage Association (NAWSA)** developed a national organization geared to lobbying in Washington. Despite the predominantly white and middle-class cast of its leaders, the cause of woman suffrage mobilized young, old, rich, poor, black, and white women during the 1910s. Opponents of woman suffrage had long argued that voting would bring women into the

Margaret Sanger Birth-control advocate who believed that birth-control information was essential to help women escape poverty and who disobeyed government laws against its distribution.

Muller v. Oregon Supreme Court case in 1908 in which the Court upheld an Oregon law that limited the hours of employment for women.

Jeannette Rankin Montana social worker who in 1916 became the first woman elected to Congress.

National American Woman Suffrage Association Organization formed in 1890 that united the two major woman suffrage groups at the time.

male sphere and thereby corrupt them. But some suffrage advocates now turned the domesticity argument to their favor, claiming that instead of politics corrupting women, women would purify politics. Feminists took a different approach, arguing that women should vote because they deserved full equality with men.

Moral Reform

Women were prominent as well in organizations intended to bring moral reform, especially those targeting alcohol. By the late nineteenth century, the temperance movement looked increasingly to government to prohibit the sale and consumption of alcohol. Many saw prohibition as a Progressive reform, enlisting government to safeguard the public interest. Few Progressive reforms claimed as many women activists as prohibition.

The drive against alcohol developed a broad base during the Progressive era. Some **old-stock** Protestant churches, notably the Methodists, termed alcohol one of the most significant obstacles to a better society. Many prohibitionists emphasized the need to protect families from the destructive influence of alcohol on husbands and fathers. At the same time, scientists tied alcohol to certain diseases. Sociologists added studies demonstrating unmistakable links between liquor and prostitution, venereal disease, poverty, crime, and broken families.

The **Anti-Saloon League,** formed in 1893, became the model for successful interest group politics. Proudly describing itself as "the Church in action against the saloon," it usually operated through the large old-stock Protestant denominations. The League attacked the saloon for corrupting not only individual patrons but politics as well. Saloons had long been identified with the party machines that dominated many large cities. The League endorsed only politicians who opposed Demon Rum, regardless of their party. As prohibition demonstrated its growing political clout, politicians increasingly lined up against the saloon. At the same time, the League also promoted statewide referendums to ban alcohol. Between 1900 and 1917, voters in nearly half of the states, including most of the West and South, adopted prohibition.

Although prohibitionists had many worthy aims, they also had a hidden agenda. For many, prohibition offered a way to control and "Americanize" immigrants. Factory owners favored the campaign against alcohol because they wanted sober workers. Protestant politicians crusaded against saloons and political machines on moral grounds, but the real stakes were often political control.

Opposition to prohibition came from Irish, German, and southern and eastern European immigrants, who regarded beer or wine as an accepted part of social life. Their churches did not regard the use of alcohol as inherently sinful. These groups regarded prohibition as an infringement on their "personal liberty." Distillers and beer brewers also organized in opposition to the prohibitionists.

The drive against alcohol was by no means the only target for moral reformers. During the Progressive era, they tried to eliminate prostitution completely through legislation. Beginning in Iowa in 1909, states passed "red-light abatement" laws designed to close down brothels. In 1910, Congress passed the **Mann Act,** making it illegal to take a woman across a state line for "immoral purposes."

Racial Issues

Racial issues received little attention during the Progressive era. Only a few white progressives actively opposed disfranchisement and segregation in the South (see page 398). Indeed, southern white progressives often took the lead in enacting discriminatory laws. Journalist Ray Stannard Baker, one of the few white progressives to address the plight of African Americans, asked in his book *Following the Color Line* (1908), "Does democracy really

old-stock People whose families had been in the United States for several generations.

Anti-Saloon League Political lobby for temperance founded in 1893, which organized through churches and offered its endorsement to politicians who favored prohibition.

Mann Act Law passed by Congress in 1910 designed to suppress prostitution. It became illegal to transport a woman across state lines for immoral purposes.

include Negroes as well as white men?" For most white Americans, the answer appeared to be no.

Lynchings and violence continued as facts of life for African Americans. Between 1900 and World War I, lynchings claimed more than eleven hundred victims, mostly in the South, but many in the Midwest. The same years also saw race riots in Atlanta and Springfield, Illinois, that left half a dozen blacks dead and many injured. Little effort was made anywhere to prosecute the leaders of such mobs.

During the Progressive Era, some African Americans challenged the accommodationist leadership of Booker T. Washington. W. E. B. Du Bois, the first African American to receive a Ph.D. from Harvard, argued that blacks should struggle for their rights "unceasingly," and, "if they fail, die trying" (see Individual Choices: W. E. B. Du Bois). In 1905, Du Bois and other black leaders met secretly in Canada, near Niagara Falls, to organize a movement for racial equality. In the wake of the Springfield riot in 1908, some white progressives in 1909 called a biracial conference to seek ways to improve race relations. In 1910, these progressives and the **Niagara Movement** formed the **National Association for the Advancement of Colored People (NAACP).** Du Bois served as the NAACP's director of publicity and research.

Challenging Capitalism: Socialists and Wobblies

Many progressive organizations reflected middle-class and upper-class concerns. Not so the Socialist Party of America (SPA), formed in 1901. Proclaiming themselves the political arm of workers and farmers, the Socialists argued that industrial capitalism had produced "an economic slavery which renders intellectual and political tyranny inevitable." They called for a cooperative commonwealth in which workers would share in the ownership and control of the means of production.

The Socialists' best-known national leader was Eugene V. Debs, leader of the Pullman strike (see page 358). Strong among immigrants, some of whom had become socialists in their native lands, the SPA also took in Christian Socialists (who drew their inspiration from religion rather than from Marx), farmers, and trade union activists. In addition, the party attracted support from some intellectuals such as W. E. B. Du Bois and Margaret Sanger.

In 1905, a variety of radicals, including socialists, organized the Industrial Workers of the World (IWW). The IWW set out to organize the unskilled and semiskilled workers at the bottom of the socioeconomic structure. They aimed at the **sweatshop** workers of eastern cities, **migrant workers,** southern sharecroppers, women workers, African Americans, and the "new" immigrants from southern and eastern Europe. The American Federation of Labor (AFL), which emphasized skilled white males, usually ignored these workers.

IWW members, called Wobblies, had a simple objective: after most workers joined the IWW, they would call a general strike, labor would refuse to work, and capitalism would collapse. The IWW did organize a few dramatic strikes and even scored a few significant victories. A textile strike in Lawrence, Massachusetts, in 1912 gained national attention. But more often, the Wobblies met with brutal suppression by local authorities and rarely made lasting gains.

The SPA counted considerably more victories. Hundreds of cities and towns—including Milwaukee, Wisconsin; Reading, Pennsylvania; and Berkeley, California—elected Socialist mayors or council members. Socialists also won election to state legislatures. Districts in New York City and Milwaukee sent Socialists to Congress. Most Americans, however, had no interest in eliminating private property.

Niagara Movement Civil rights movement that began in 1905 with the meeting at Niagara Falls of W. E. B. Du Bois and others interested in ending segregation and racial inequality in the United States.

National Association for the Advancement of Colored People Biracial civil rights organization founded in New York City in 1910, which worked to end segregation and discrimination in the United States.

sweatshop A shop or factory in which employees work long hours at low wages under poor conditions.

migrant workers Laborers who travel from one area to another in search of work.

INDIVIDUAL CHOICES

Fighting for Equality

W. E. B. Du Bois

A brilliant young intellectual, W. E. B. Du Bois had to choose between leading the quiet life of a college professor and challenging Booker T. Washington's claim to speak on behalf of all African Americans. Schomburg Center for Research in Black Culture; New York Public Library, Astor, Lenox and Tilden Foundations.

In 1904 and 1905, William Edward Burghardt Du Bois moved toward a difficult choice. Should he challenge the leadership of Booker T. Washington, the "Wizard of Tuskegee," the most powerful African American in the nation? In the decade after his Atlanta Compromise address (see pages 397–398), Washington emerged as head of the "Tuskegee Machine." His access to northern white philanthropists made him the chief channel for donations to African-American institutions. And his access to leaders of the Republican party gave him a hand in influencing many, if not most, African-American political patronage appointments, North and South alike. Du Bois, by contrast, was a college professor with few connections to funds or politics, but he was well-known and highly respected among black intellectuals.

Born in Great Barrington, Massachusetts, an area with a very small black population, Du Bois experienced little racial hostility before leaving home. At Fisk University in Nashville, Tennessee, however, he encountered both the constraints of racism and the African-American culture of the South. He completed his undergraduate studies at Harvard, graduated with honors, studied in Germany, and wrote a doctoral dissertation on the suppression of the African slave trade to the United States. In 1895,

The Reform of Politics, the Politics of Reform

In their quest to make politics more honest and to change the structure of government, progressive reformers sometimes found themselves in conflict with the entrenched leaders of political parties. In response, some reformers dedicated themselves to limiting the power of political parties.

Exposing Corruption: The Muckrakers

Journalists played an important role in preparing the ground for reform. In the early 1900s, magazines discovered that their sales boomed when they he became the first African American to receive a Ph.D. from Harvard.

Du Bois then taught at the college level and undertook research and scholarly writing. By the early twentieth century, however, he had chosen to do more than research and teach. In his third book, *Souls of Black Folk* (1903), he challenged Washington's accommodationist approach and insisted that African Americans should never acquiesce in the surrender of their rights. He also presented the concept of *double consciousness,* by which he meant that African Americans had both an African identity and an American identity and needed to be aware of both parts of their cultural heritage. He argued that the "talented tenth"—the African-American intellectual elite—had special leadership obligations. Refuting Washington's claim that African Americans should start at the bottom, Du Bois insisted instead that denial of educational opportunities for the talented tenth constrained all African Americans.

Although the book created a sensation among African-American intellectuals and some white philanthropists, Washington's first response was to invite Du Bois to Tuskegee, apparently to co-opt him into the Tuskegee Machine. Du Bois, however, held back, weighing his choices against the potential for retribution that Washington could bring to bear against his opponents. By late 1904, Du Bois decided to challenge Washington directly, and early in 1905, he charged that Washington had bought and paid for much of the support he had received from the black press.

The next important step, in July 1905, was the formation of the Niagara Movement. This body was to be the organizational vehicle for mobilizing African Americans for an assault both on white supremacy and on Washington's accommodationism. Proclaiming that "persistent manly agitation is the way to liberty," the new organization chose Du Bois as its general secretary. Despite a promising beginning, the movement failed to thrive. In 1910, what was left of the Niagara Movement was transformed into the NAACP, and Du Bois became editor of its journal, *The Crisis.* About the same time, Du Bois briefly joined the Socialist Party of America. He continued to espouse socialist ideas, and the experience of World War I moved him closer to anti-imperialism and pacifism.

Du Bois's uncompromising leadership in the struggle for civil rights and his voluminous writings on both current events and black history made him probably the single most influential African-American intellectual of the twentieth century. By the end of his long life, he concluded that America would never accomplish racial equality. In 1961, he joined the Communist party and accepted citizenship in Ghana, then a socialist nation. There he died during the night of August 27, 1963, the day before one of the greatest civil rights gatherings in American history (see page 647). In announcing Du Bois's death to the huge crowd in Washington, D.C., Roy Wilkins, executive secretary of the NAACP, noted that "at the dawn of the twentieth century his was the voice calling you to gather here today in this cause."

published dramatic exposés of political corruption and corporate wrongdoing. Those who practiced this provocative journalism acquired the name **muckrakers.** *McClure's Magazine* led the surge in muckraking journalism beginning in 1902. *McClure's* readers were treated to **Lincoln Steffens**'s revelations of municipal corruption (published separately in 1904 as *The Shame of the Cities*),

muckrakers Journalists in the Progressive era who wrote investigative articles exposing corruption in city government, business, and industry.

Lincoln Steffens Muckraking journalist and managing editor of *McClure's Magazine* best known for revealing political corruption in city governments.

Ida Tarbell's exposures of Standard Oil's sordid past (published in 1904 as *History of Standard Oil*), and Ray Stannard Baker's discoveries of corruption in labor unions. Sales of *McClure's* soared, and other monthlies soon were detailing the defects of patent medicines, fraud in the insurance industry, the horrors of child labor, and more.

The most famous muckraking exposé, however, was **Upton Sinclair**'s novel *The Jungle* (1906). *The Jungle* exposed in disgusting detail the shortcomings of the meatpacking industry. Sinclair, a socialist, hoped his readers would recognize that the offenses portrayed in his book were the results of industrial capitalism. He described in chilling detail the afflictions of packinghouse workers, from severed fingers to tuberculosis and blood poisoning.

Finley Peter Dunne, a political humorist, claimed that he hadn't "been able to eat anything more nourishing than a cucumber" since reading Sinclair's book. President Roosevelt appointed a commission that confirmed Sinclair's charges. Pressured by Roosevelt and the public, Congress in 1906 passed the **Pure Food and Drug Act,** which banned impure or mislabeled food and drugs, and the **Meat Inspection Act,** which required federal inspection of meatpacking. Sinclair, however, was disappointed that his revelations had not converted readers to socialism. "I aimed at the public's heart," Sinclair later complained, "and by accident I hit it in the stomach."

Reforming City Government

Many municipal reformers argued that corruption and inefficiency were inevitable without major changes in the structure of city government. Usually **city councils** consisted of members elected from neighborhood **wards.** Reformers condemned the ward system for producing city council members unable to see beyond the needs of their own blocks. They concluded that the ward leaders' small favors for neighborhood voters kept the machine in power despite its corruption. Reformers argued that citywide elections, with all city voters choosing from one list of candidates, would result in council members with broader perspectives and would undercut the machines.

James Phelan of San Francisco is one example of an early municipal reformer. Phelan attacked corruption in city government and won election as mayor in 1896. He then led the fight in adopting a new charter that strengthened the office of mayor and required citywide election of supervisors, San Francisco's term for councilmen.

Some municipal reformers proposed new forms of city government, notably the **commission system** and the **city-manager plan.** Both reveal prominent traits of progressivism: a distrust of political parties and a desire for expertise and efficiency.

The commission system first developed in Galveston, Texas, after a hurricane and tidal wave nearly destroyed that city in 1900. The governor appointed five businessmen to run the city. They attracted widespread attention for their efficiency in administering city government. Within two years, more than two hundred communities had adopted a commission system. Typically, all the city's voters elected the commissioners, and each commissioner then took charge of a specific city function.

Ida Tarbell Journalist in the Progressive era whose exposé on the Standard Oil Company revealed its ruthless business ethics.

Upton Sinclair Socialist writer and reformer whose novel *The Jungle* helped bring about government regulation of meatpacking and other industries.

Pure Food and Drug Act Law passed in 1906 that discouraged the use of dyes and preservatives in foods; it forbade the sale of impure or improperly labeled food and drugs.

Meat Inspection Act Law passed in 1906 requiring federal inspection of meatpacking; it was the result of Upton Sinclair's exposé of unsanitary conditions in the industry.

city council A body of representatives elected to govern a city.

ward A division of a city or town, especially an electoral district, for administrative or representative purposes.

commission system System of city government in which all executive and legislative power is vested in a small elective board, usually composed of five members.

city-manager plan System of city government under which a small council, chosen on a nonpartisan ballot, hires a professional to manage the affairs of city government.

The city-manager plan adapted the administrative structure of the corporation to city government. It featured a professional city manager (similar to a corporate executive) who was appointed by an elected city council (similar to a corporate board of directors) to handle much of municipal administration. In 1913, a serious flood led Dayton, Ohio, to adopt a city-manager plan, and other cities then followed.

A few progressives went beyond changing the structure of city government to advocate social reform. Hazen Pingree attracted national attention as mayor of Detroit. Elected in 1889 as an advocate of honest, efficient government, he soon began to criticize the city's gas, electric, and streetcar companies for overcharging customers and providing poor service. His solution was municipal ownership of such utilities. The depression of 1893 led him to address the needs of the unemployed with measures such as work projects and community gardens. Samuel "Golden Rule" Jones, elected mayor of Toledo, Ohio, in 1897, brought the Golden Rule—do unto others as you would have them do unto you—to city government. Under his leadership, Toledo acquired free concerts, free public baths, kindergartens, and the eight-hour workday for city employees.

The Progressive era also saw city governments take up **city planning.** Throughout most of the nineteenth century, urban growth had been driven by a market economy. Cities, however, came to recognize the need to establish separate zones for residential, commercial, and industrial use and to develop efficient transportation systems to reduce traffic congestion. In 1907, Hartford, Connecticut, set up one of the first city-planning commissions. The emergence of city planning represents an important transition in thinking about government and the economy, for it presumed greater government control over use of private property.

Saving the Future

The Progressive Era also saw the development of other professions that were to have an impact on the whole social fabric. In public health, mental health, social work, and education, professionals worked to reshape government to solve the problems of an urban, industrial, multiethnic society. Their objective was to use knowledge to control social forces, to mold society in their own image, and thereby to define the future.

The public schools presented an important arena in which professionals sought change. In the cities especially, graduates of recently established university programs for the preparation of teachers and school administrators began to seek greater control over education. Professional educators pushed for greater centralization in school administration. They particularly pushed to reduce the role of elected **school boards** and school superintendents who had no professional qualifications for their positions.

Advances in medical knowledge and the American Medical Association's efforts to raise the standards of medical colleges and to restrict access to the profession improved the status of physicians. Scientific discoveries helped transform hospitals from charities that provided minimal help for the poor into centers for dispensing the most up-to-date care to all who could afford it. Physicians helped launch public health programs for the eradication of hookworm in the South, **tuberculosis** in the slums, and venereal disease. In the process, public health emerged as a new medical field.

Other emerging professional fields that carried important implications for public policy included mental health and social work. Psychiatrists and psychologists tried to transform the nineteenth-century asylums from places for confining the mentally ill into places where they could be treated and perhaps cured. Social workers often found themselves allied with public health and mental health professionals in their efforts to bring greater governmental control over urban health and safety codes.

city planning The practice of planning urban development by regulating the location of transportation, public buildings, recreational facilities, and zoning.

school board A local board of policymakers that oversees a city or town's public schools.

tuberculosis An infectious disease that attacks the lungs, causing coughing, fever, and weight loss; it was common and often fatal in the nineteenth and early twentieth centuries.

Reforming State Government

As reformers launched changes in various cities, **Robert M. La Follette** pushed Wisconsin state government to the forefront of reform. Elected governor of Wisconsin in 1900, La Follette saw conservative members of his own Republican party defeat his proposals to regulate railroad rates and to replace party nominating conventions with the **direct primary.** He then threw himself into an energetic campaign to elect a state legislature that would support reform. He traveled the state, speaking wherever a crowd gathered. La Follette built a strong political following among Wisconsin's farmers and urban wage earners. The political organization he built not only elected reformers to the state legislature but also re-elected La Follette as governor in 1902 and 1904.

La Follette then led the way to a wide range of reform legislation designed to limit both corporations and political parties. Wisconsin adopted a direct primary, set up a commission to regulate railroad rates, increased taxes on railroads and other corporations, enacted a merit system for hiring and promoting state employees, and limited the activities of lobbyists. La Follette also drew on the expertise of faculty members at the University of Wisconsin. These reforms and reliance on experts came to be called the **Wisconsin Idea.** La Follette won election to the U.S. Senate in 1905 and was re-elected until his death in 1925.

La Follette's success prompted imitators elsewhere. But only in California did progressives produce a volume of reform that rivaled Wisconsin's. Hiram W. Johnson, elected governor in 1910 after revealing widespread bribery in San Francisco government, proved to be an uncompromising foe of corporate influence in politics. At his urging, the legislature regulated railroads and public utilities, placed restrictions on political parties, provided protections for labor and conservation, and adopted woman suffrage. Johnson showed more sympathy for labor than did most other reformers. He appointed union leaders to state positions and supported a variety of measures to benefit working people, including an eight-hour-day law for women, **workers' compensation,** and restrictions on child labor. The sympathies of California progressives, however, did not extend to Asians or Asian Americans. In 1913, California prohibited Asian immigrants from owning land in the state.

California progressives worked to limit the influence of political parties. By 1913, California exceeded all other states in the range of offices that were nonpartisan, including all judges, school administrators, and local and county officials. Only members of the federal Congress, a few statewide officers, and members of the state legislature ran for office as party candidates.

The Decline of Parties and the Rise of Interest Groups

Although California represents the extreme in weakening political parties, nearly all states took steps in that direction. City and state reformers charged that party bosses manipulated nominating conventions, managed public officials, and controlled law enforcement. They claimed too that bosses, in return for payoffs, used their influence on behalf of companies that did business with city or state government. Muckrakers convinced many voters that the reformers were correct. The party organizations that had dominated politics so completely during the nineteenth century now found themselves under attack on every side.

Reformers increased the power of the individual voter and reduced the power of political parties nearly everywhere. State after state adopted the direct primary. Most reformers also sought to introduce or strengthen the merit system to reduce

Robert M. La Follette Governor of Wisconsin at the turn of the century, who instituted a series of reforms including direct primaries, tax reform, and anticorruption measures.

direct primary A primary in which the voters who identify with a party choose that party's candidates directly through an election.

Wisconsin Idea The program of political reforms sponsored by Robert La Follette in Wisconsin, which were designed to decrease political corruption and foster direct democracy.

workers' compensation Payments that employers are required by law to award to workers injured on the job.

the number of patronage positions. Most states made judgeships, school-board seats, and educational offices nonpartisan. A number of states also adopted the initiative and referendum, first approved by Oregon in 1902. Some states adopted the **recall,** under which voters could remove a public official from office. The direct primary, initiative and referendum, and recall are sometimes called "direct democracy" because they remove intermediate steps between the voter and final political decisions.

One outcome of the switch to direct primaries and direct election of U.S. senators was a new style of campaign. Candidates now appealed directly to voters rather than to party leaders and convention delegates. Individual candidates thus ran for office on their records and personal attributes, not their party identification. As campaigns focused more on individual candidates than on party positions, advertising supplanted the armies of party retainers who had mobilized voters previously. Without party efforts to get out the vote, voter turnout began to fall.

Political participation changed not only through the instruments of direct democracy but also through organized interest groups. As the power of political parties faded, organized interest groups became more involved in politics to advance their special concerns. The many groups that advocated change sometimes fought among themselves over which reform goals were most important. Groups increasingly pressured candidates for office to commit themselves to the group's stand on issues. In 1904, for example, the National Association of Manufacturers (NAM) targeted and defeated two key prolabor members of Congress. The American Federation of Labor (AFL) responded in 1906 with a similar strategy and managed to elect six union members to the House of Representatives.

Interest groups also focused greater attention on the legislative process. They began retaining the services of full-time **lobbyists** in Washington. Lobbyists urged congressmen to support their group's position on issues, reminded congressmen of the electoral power of the group, and arranged campaign support for those who favored the group. Lobbyists also appeared at the state level.

Thus, as political parties receded from the dominant position they had once occupied, organized interest groups moved in. Some elected officials came to see themselves less as loyal members of a political party and more as mediators among competing interest groups. Pushed one way by the AFL and the other by the NAM, some politicians responded by counting the number of voters each group could influence in their districts and voted accordingly.

Roosevelt, Taft, and Republican Progressivism

The American public came to identify Theodore Roosevelt with progressivism more than any other single person. Elected vice president in 1900, he became the youngest president in American history in 1901 after the assassination of President William McKinley. In seven years, he changed the nation's domestic policies more than any other president since Lincoln and made himself a legend in the process.

Roosevelt: Asserting the Power of the Presidency

Roosevelt was unlike most other politicians of his day. Independently wealthy, he saw politics as a duty rather than as an opportunity for personal advancement. He defined his political views in terms of character, morality, hard work, and patriotism rather than in terms of party rhetoric. He considered political power a tool to achieve an ethical and socially stable society. Confident in his own personal principles, he did not hesitate to wield the full powers of the presidency. Roosevelt often used the office of the presidency as a "bully pulpit"—a forum for preaching—to gain attention for his message of character and responsibility.

recall Procedure by which voters can seek to remove an elected official from office, submitting a petition to bring the matter to a public vote.

lobbyist A person who tries to influence the opinions of legislators or other public officials for or against a specific cause.

In his first message to Congress, in December 1901, Roosevelt sounded a theme that he was to repeat throughout his political career: the growth of powerful corporations was "natural," but some of them exhibited "grave evils." He set out to remedy those evils. Roosevelt's chief obstacle was the Supreme Court's decision in ***U.S. v. E. C. Knight*** (1895). This decision held that the Sherman Anti-Trust Act did not apply to manufacturing companies because they were not involved in interstate commerce. Roosevelt soon found an opportunity to challenge the *Knight* decision. The creation of the Northern Securities Company set up a railroad monopoly in the Northwest. If any industry qualified as interstate commerce, the railroads did. In February 1902, Roosevelt advised Attorney General Philander C. Knox to seek dissolution of the Northern Securities Company for violating the Sherman Act. For the first time, Americans witnessed a serious federal challenge to the ever-increasing might of powerful corporations. In 1904, the Supreme Court agreed that the Sherman Act applied to the Northern Securities Company and ordered it dissolved.

Bolstered by this confirmation of federal power, Roosevelt launched additional antitrust suits and gloried in his reputation as a **trustbuster.** But he never regarded the trustbusting route as the best way to regulate the economy. He regarded large corporations as natural, inevitable, and potentially beneficial. He thought it made more sense to regulate them than to break them up, so he used trustbusting selectively. Companies that met Roosevelt's standards of public service had no reason to fear antitrust action.

Roosevelt's willingness to take bold action did not stop at reining in the trusts. He interjected himself into a labor dispute in 1902 when **anthracite** coal miners went on strike in Pennsylvania, seeking higher wages and an eight-hour workday. Mine owners refused even to meet with representatives of the **United Mine Workers.** As cold weather approached and coal prices edged upward, public concern grew. In early October, Roosevelt called both sides to Washington to urge them to submit their differences to arbitration. The owners haughtily refused. Roosevelt, now angry, considered their attitude "well-nigh criminal."

Roosevelt began preparations to use the army to dispossess the mine owners and reopen the mines. He also sent Secretary of War Elihu Root to talk with J. P. Morgan, who held a significant stake in the railroads that owned the mines. The threat of military intervention led Morgan to convince the companies to accept arbitration. The arbitration board granted the miners higher wages and a nine-hour workday. No president before had ever intervened in a strike by treating a union as equal to the owners. The coal strike settlement represented what Roosevelt liked to call a **Square Deal,** in which each side received fair treatment.

The Square Deal in Action: Creating Federal Economic Regulation

Roosevelt's trustbusting and settlement of the coal strike brought him great popularity. When he sought election in 1904, he defeated Democratic candidate Alton B. Parker by one of the largest margins up to that time, securing more than 56 percent of the popular vote.

Elected in his own right, Roosevelt now set out to implement meaningful regulation of the railroads, the largest of the nation's big businesses. In 1905, he asked Congress to pass laws regulating railroad rates, opening financial records of railroads to government inspection, and increasing governmental power in strikes involving interstate commerce. Although he had to compromise occasionally with conservative Republicans, Roosevelt accomplished most of his agenda. On June 29,

U.S. v. E. C. Knight Supreme Court ruling in 1895 that the Sherman Anti-Trust Act did not prohibit manufacturing monopolies; it seriously impaired the application of antitrust laws.

trustbuster Label applied to Theodore Roosevelt and others who sought to prosecute or dissolve business trusts.

anthracite Type of coal that contains high levels of carbon and burns with a clean flame; widely used for heating homes and businesses in the early twentieth century.

United Mine Workers Union of coal miners organized in 1890.

Square Deal Phrase used by Theodore Roosevelt to describe the effort to deal fairly with all.

♦ Theodore Roosevelt (left) met with John Muir, a leading advocate for the preservation of wilderness, in 1903 at Yosemite National Park. Although Roosevelt made important contributions to the preservation of parks and wildlife refuges, he was more interested in the careful management of national resources, including federal lands. *Culver Pictures, Inc.*

1906, Congress passed the **Hepburn Act,** which allowed the Interstate Commerce Commission (ICC) to establish maximum railroad rates. The act also limited railroads' ability to issue free passes, a practice reformers had long considered bribery.

Regulating Natural Resources

An outspoken proponent of strenuous outdoor activities, Roosevelt took great pride in establishing five national parks and more than fifty wildlife preserves to save what he called "beautiful and wonderful wild creatures whose existence was threatened by greed and wantonness." Roosevelt, however, deserves to be called a conservationist, not a preservationist. He did not believe that nature should be kept in a pristine condition.

For Roosevelt and Chief Forester **Gifford Pinchot,** conservation involved carefully planning the use of federally owned resources. Pinchot, trained in scientific forestry in Europe, worked to conserve timber and grazing resources by withdrawing large tracts of federal land from public sale or use. They hoped that federal management of these lands would provide for the needs of the present and for the future. While president, Roosevelt more than quadrupled the land under federal protection.

Roosevelt's attitude toward western water clearly reveals his definition of conservation. He strongly supported the National Reclamation Act of 1902, also known as the Newlands Act, which set aside proceeds from the sale of federal lands in sixteen western states to finance irrigation projects. The act established the federal government's responsibility for constructing the dams and canals that made agriculture possible in the arid West. Thus water was to be managed. Far from preserving the western landscape, federal water projects profoundly transformed it.

Taft's Troubles

Soon after Roosevelt won the election of 1904, he announced that he would not seek another term in 1908. He virtually named his successor, William Howard Taft, who had served as governor of the Philippines before joining Roosevelt's cabinet as secretary of war in 1904. William Jennings Bryan faced no serious opposition in winning the Democratic

Hepburn Act Law passed in 1906 that authorized the Interstate Commerce Commission to fix maximum railroad rates and extended ICC authority to other forms of transportation.

Gifford Pinchot Head of the Bureau of Forestry from 1898 to 1910; helped begin the conservation movement.

party's nomination for the third time. Roosevelt's popularity and his endorsement of Taft overcame a lackluster Republican campaign. Taft won just under 52 percent of the vote, and Republicans kept control of the Senate and the House. Soon after turning the reins over to Taft, Roosevelt set off to hunt big game in Africa.

Although Taft's political approach was far more restrained than his predecessor's, he supported Roosevelt's Square Deal. His attorney general initiated some ninety antitrust suits in four years, twice as many as during Roosevelt's seven years. Taft also approved efforts to extend the power of the Interstate Commerce Commission to cover most communication companies.

Taft's administration oversaw the passage of two constitutional amendments. Reformers had long considered the income tax as the fairest means of raising federal revenues. With support from Taft, the **Sixteenth Amendment,** permitting a federal income tax, was ratified in 1913. The **Seventeenth Amendment,** proposed in 1912 and adopted in 1913, changed the method of electing U.S. senators from election by state legislatures to direct election by the voters of the state.

Despite these accomplishments, Taft presided over an increasingly divided Republican party. He alienated the progressive wing of the party in 1909 when he signed the **Payne-Aldrich Tariff,** which retained high rates on most imports. Taft further angered progressives by siding with Joseph Cannon, the highhanded Speaker of the House of Representatives, who used his power to support conservatives. Taft's firing of Roosevelt's friend Gifford Pinchot also greatly annoyed the progressive branch of the party, particularly Roosevelt. By 1912, when Taft faced re-election, he also faced opposition from most progressive Republicans.

Wilson and Democratic Progressivism

In 1912, Theodore Roosevelt bolted the Republican party to run for president as the candidate of the newly formed **Progressive party.** The Democratic presidential candidate that year was Woodrow Wilson, who, like Roosevelt, claimed to be the true voice of progressivism. Roosevelt and Wilson attacked each other's right to claim the title "progressive." They agreed only that William Howard Taft, the Republican candidate, was not a progressive at all.

Debating the Future: The Election of 1912

When Theodore Roosevelt returned from Africa and Europe in 1910, he had already met with the indignant Pinchot, who complained that Taft had betrayed the cause of conservation. He then undertook a speaking tour to propose a broad program of reform that he labeled the **New Nationalism.** Roosevelt did not openly question Taft's re-election, but other Republican progressives began to do so. In the 1910 congressional elections, Republican candidates lost control of the House of Representatives for the first time since 1892.

In February 1912, Roosevelt announced that he would oppose Taft for the Republican presidential nomination. Roosevelt enjoyed great popularity in the thirteen states that had established primaries, winning 278 delegates to 48 for Taft and 36 for La Follette. Taft, however, controlled the party machinery. At the Republican nominating convention, many states sent contesting delegations, one pledged to Taft and the other to Roosevelt. Taft's

Sixteenth Amendment Constitutional amendment ratified in 1913 that gave the federal government the right to establish an income tax.

Seventeenth Amendment Constitutional amendment ratified in 1913 that authorized the direct popular election of U.S. senators.

Payne-Aldrich Tariff Tariff bill in 1909 that began as a Republican attempt to reduce tariffs but that ultimately retained high tariffs on most imports.

Progressive party Party formed in 1912 with Theodore Roosevelt as its candidate for president; it disintegrated when Roosevelt lost the election.

New Nationalism Program of labor and social reform that Theodore Roosevelt advocated in 1910; he made an unsuccessful bid to regain the presidency using this platform in 1912.

supporters controlled the **credentials committee** and gave most of the contested seats to Taft delegates. Roosevelt's delegates walked out, claiming that Taft had stolen the nomination.

Roosevelt's angry supporters regrouped to form the Progressive or "Bull Moose" party. The new party's platform, which was based on the New Nationalism, called for tariff reduction, regulation of corporations, a minimum wage, an end to child labor, and woman suffrage. Women were more prominent at the Progressive convention than at any other presidential nominating session since the Populists'. Jane Addams seconded Roosevelt's nomination.

The hotly contested Democratic nomination went to Woodrow Wilson, the progressive governor of New Jersey. The Democrats' platform attacked monopolies and called for limits on corporate campaign contributions, a single term for the president, and major tariff reductions. Wilson labeled his program the **New Freedom.**

Much of the campaign focused on big business. Roosevelt continued to maintain that the behavior of corporations was the problem, not their size. Wilson depicted monopoly itself as the problem, not the misbehavior of individual corporations. Breaking up monopolies and restoring competition, he argued, would benefit consumers through better products and lower prices. He also pointed out that as long as monopolies faced regulation, they would naturally seek to control the regulator: the federal government. Only antitrust actions, Wilson argued, could protect democracy from this threat.

Taft was clearly the most conservative of the candidates; Eugene V. Debs, the Socialist candidate, was clearly the most radical. The real contest, however, was between Roosevelt and Wilson. In the end, Wilson received most of the usual Democratic vote and won with 42 percent of the total. The Democrats also won sizable majorities in both houses of Congress. Roosevelt and Taft split the traditional Republican vote. Debs, with but 6 percent, did come in first in some counties and in some city precincts (see Map 21.1).

Wilson and Reform, 1913–1914

Born in Virginia in 1856, Woodrow Wilson first gained national attention when he became president of Princeton University in 1902 and initiated educational reforms. In 1910, New Jersey Democrats turned to him when they needed a respectable candidate for governor. Wilson won the election and suddenly embraced reform, shocking the conservatives who had nominated him. In two years, he led the legislature to adopt a direct primary, a corrupt practices act, workers' compensation, and regulation of railroads and public utilities. Many Democratic progressives supported Wilson when he sought the 1912 presidential nomination.

As president, Wilson focused first on tariff reform. Despite the opposition of many manufacturers, Congress passed the Underwood Tariff in 1913, establishing the most significant reductions since the Civil War. To offset the subsequent federal revenue losses, the **Underwood Act** initiated an income tax, recently authorized by the Sixteenth Amendment.

Wilson tackled banking reform next. Although a national banking system had existed since 1863, periodic financial panics such as the one in 1907 had made the system's shortcomings evident. Chief among these was that it had no way to adjust the **money supply** to the needs of the economy. In 1913, a congressional investigation also revealed highly concentrated power in the hands of the few investment bankers. For Wilson and the Democrats in Congress, the crucial question of banking reform was that of control. Conservatives and bankers favored minimal governmental regulation. Progressive Democrats favored strong federal control.

credentials committee Party convention committee that settles disputes arising when rival delegations from the same state demand to be seated.

New Freedom Program of reforms advocated by Woodrow Wilson during his 1912 presidential campaign, including reducing tariffs, revising the monetary system, and breaking up monopolies.

Underwood Act Law passed in 1913 that substantially reduced tariffs and made up for the lost revenue by providing for a small graduated income tax.

money supply The amount of money in the economy, such as cash and the contents of checking accounts.

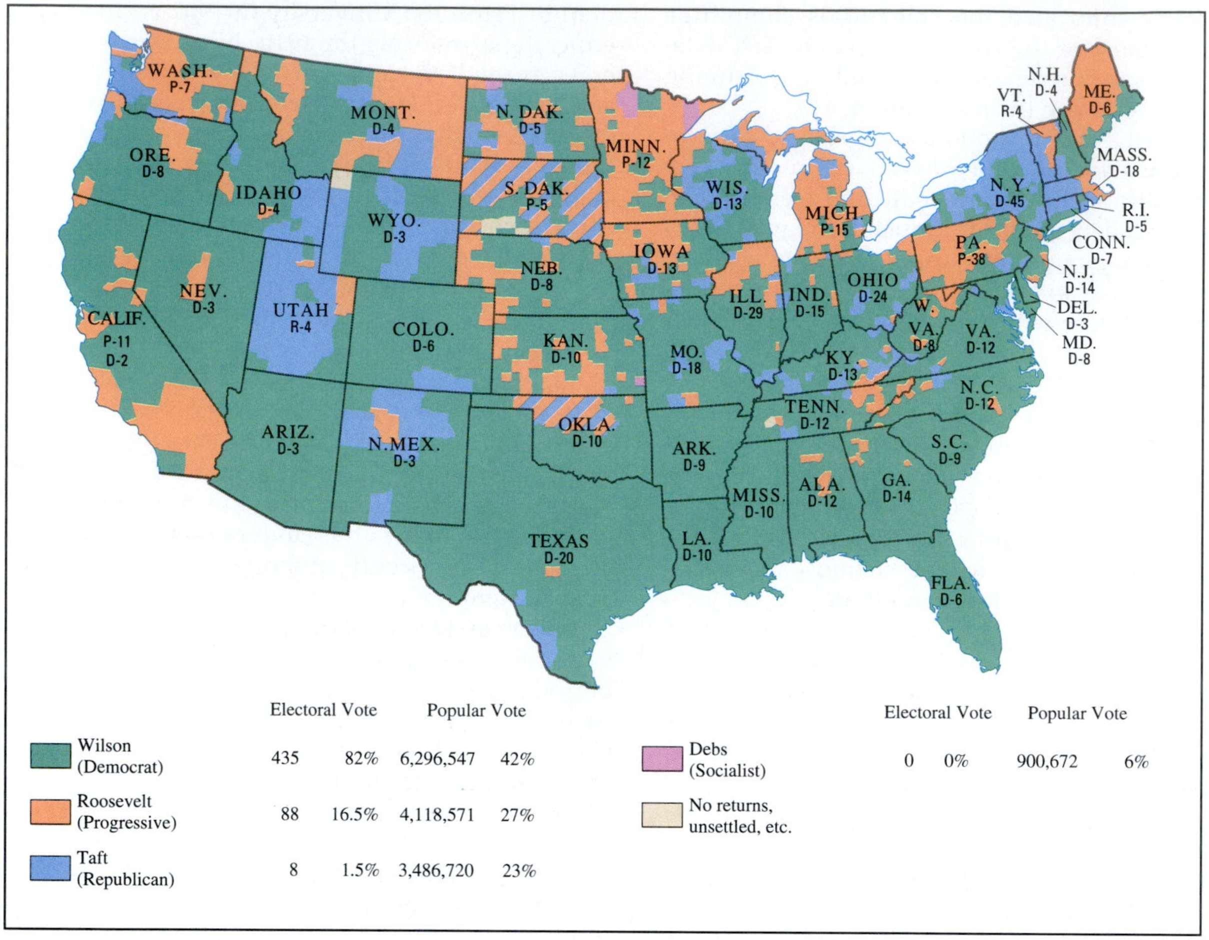

♦ **MAP 21.1 Election of 1912** The presidential election of 1912 was complicated by the campaign of former President Theodore Roosevelt, running as a Progressive. Roosevelt's campaign split the usual Republican vote without taking away much of the usual Democratic vote. Woodrow Wilson, the Democratic candidate, carried many parts of the West and Northeast that Democratic candidates rarely won.

The debate over control ended in compromise. In 1913, the **Federal Reserve Act** established twelve regional Federal Reserve Banks. These were "banker's banks," places where banks kept their reserves. All national banks were required to belong to this Federal Reserve System. The participating banks exercised significant control over the twelve district banks, but the district banks were regulated and supervised by the Federal Reserve Board, a new federal agency with members chosen by the president. In his appointments, Wilson named men sympathetic to banking and thereby reassured the banking community that the "Fed" posed no threat. The Federal Reserve Act created a flexible currency that was no longer solely depen-

Federal Reserve Act Law passed in 1913 establishing twelve Federal Reserve Banks to hold the cash reserves of commercial banks.

dent on the price of gold. It still provides the framework for regulating the nation's banking system.

In 1914, Congress passed the **Clayton Antitrust Act,** which prohibited specified business practices, including **interlocking directorates** among large companies. It also exempted farmers' organizations and unions from the Sherman Act. The antitrust sections of the Clayton Act, however, provided little basis for breaking up big corporations. One senator claimed that the bill started out as "a raging lion with a mouth full of teeth" but ended up as "a tabby cat with soft gums." The weakening of the Clayton Act partly reflected a change of course by Wilson. Instead of breaking up big business, Wilson now moved closer to Roosevelt's position that regulation had more potential for protecting small businesses. Wilson did energetically support passage of the **Federal Trade Commission Act** (1914), a regulatory measure designed to prevent unfair business competition.

Wilson and Social Reform

Apart from establishing a separate department of labor, Wilson did little to appeal to progressives who favored social reform. He considered efforts to outlaw child labor unconstitutional and was not convinced of the need to amend the Constitution for woman suffrage.

Wilson did draw sharp criticism from some northern social reformers in 1913 when his appointees began to institute racial segregation in several federal agencies. A southerner by birth, Wilson believed in segregation. Even though he resisted the most extreme racists in his party, he appointed adamant segregationists to many federal positions. In the South, some Wilson appointees even began to fire African Americans from federal jobs.

Late in 1914, Wilson announced that he was satisfied with the legislation that had been passed and would seek no further reforms. Early in 1916, however, he reversed direction in anticipation of the coming election. Wilson had won the White House in 1912 only because of the split among Republicans. He joined Democratic progressives in Congress, therefore, in pushing measures intended to capture the loyalty of all progressive voters.

As a first step, Wilson nominated **Louis Brandeis** for the Supreme Court. Brandeis's reputation as a staunch progressive and critic of business aroused intense opposition from conservatives. He was confirmed with support from a few progressive Republicans and became the first Jewish member of the Court. Wilson followed up the Brandeis nomination with support for improved credit facilities for farmers, workers' compensation for federal employees, and a law to eliminate child labor.

Wilson's shift toward the social reformers may have been a significant factor in the election. His support for organized labor gave him strong backing among unionists. In states where women could vote, they supported Wilson in disproportionate numbers, probably because he backed issues such as outlawing child labor. Wilson furthermore vowed to keep the United States out of World War I, which had broken out in 1914. In a very close election, Wilson won with 49 percent of the popular vote against Charles Evans Hughes, a moderately progressive Republican.

Progressivism in Perspective

The Progressive Era began with efforts at municipal reform in the 1890s and sputtered to a close

Clayton Antitrust Act Law passed in 1914 banning such monopolistic business practices as price fixing and interlocking directorates; it also exempted farmers' organizations and unions from prosecution under antitrust laws.

interlocking directorate Situation in which the same individuals sit on the boards of directors of various "competing" companies in one industry.

Federal Trade Commission Act Law passed in 1914 that outlawed unfair methods of competition in interstate commerce and created a commission appointed by the president to investigate illegal business practices.

Louis Brandeis Lawyer and reformer who opposed monopolies and defended individual rights; in 1916 he became the first Jewish justice on the Supreme Court.

during World War I. The war diverted public attention from reform, and by the end of the war, political concerns had changed. By the mid-1920s many of the major leaders of progressivism had passed from the political stage.

The Progressive Era transformed American politics and government. Before the Hepburn Act and the Federal Reserve Act, the federal government's role in the national economy consisted largely of instituting land-grant subsidies and protective tariffs. After the Progressive Era, the federal government became a significant player in the economy, regulating a wide range of economic activity. The income tax quickly became the most significant source of federal funds.

The decline of political parties and the emergence of political campaigns based largely on personality and advertising stemmed from progressive reforms. So did the proliferation of organized pressure groups. Women's participation in politics also increased greatly during the era.

The assertion of presidential authority by Roosevelt and Wilson transformed Americans' expectations regarding the presidency. Throughout the nineteenth century, Congress dominated the making of domestic policy. During the twentieth century, however, Americans came to expect forceful executive leadership in the White House.

Perhaps the most instructive legacy from progressivism is the understanding that reforms rarely fulfill all the expectations of their **proponents.** Some advocates of prohibition, for example, predicted that crime and poverty would diminish once alcohol was banned. Prohibition, however, helped give birth to organized crime, as the makers of illegal liquor began to cooperate among themselves rather than engage in cutthroat competition. Those who reduced the power of political parties hoped to destroy political machines and bosses, but instead fostered the growth of interest-group politics. Some machines also proved highly resilient, adapting themselves to new conditions. The Progressive Era taught America that even the most well-intended reforms are not cure-alls.

proponent One who argues in support of something.

S U M M A R Y

Expectations
Constraints
Choices
Outcomes

Progressivism, a phenomenon of the late nineteenth and early twentieth centuries, refers to new concepts of government, changes in government that made those concepts a reality, and the political process by which change occurred. Those years marked a time of far-reaching political transformation, brought about through many *choices* by groups and individuals, who approached politics with fresh but often quite different *expectations.* Organized interest groups became an important part of this process. Women broke through previous *constraints* to take a more prominent role in politics. The Anti-Saloon League was the most successful of a number of organizations that *chose* to reshape government to enforce their moral standards. Some African Americans *chose* to fight the *constraints* of segregation and disfranchisement, looking to W. E. B. Du Bois for leadership. Socialists and the Industrial Workers of the World saw capitalism as the source of many problems, but few Americans *chose* their radical solutions.

Political reform took place at every level, from cities to the federal government. Muckraking journalists exposed corruption, wrongdoing, and suffering. Municipal reformers introduced modern methods of city government in a quest for efficiency and expertise. Some *chose* to use government to remedy social problems by employing the expertise of new professions such as public health and social work. Reformers also *chose* to attack the power of party bosses and machines by reducing the role of political parties.

At the federal level, Theodore Roosevelt set the pace for progressive reform. He challenged judicial *constraints* on federal authority over big business and advocated other forms of economic regulation. The *outcome* was an increase in the federal government's role in the economy. He also *chose* to regulate the use of natural resources.

In 1912, Roosevelt *chose* to form a new political party, the Progressives, calling for the regulation of business. Wilson, the Democrat, favored antitrust action. Wilson won the election but soon *chose* regulation over antitrust action. He presided over the creation of the Federal Reserve System of regulating banking nationwide. Before the 1916 election, Wilson also pushed for social reforms to unify all progressives behind his leadership.

Progressive reforms have had a profound impact on American politics throughout the twentieth century. In many ways, the *outcome* of the Progressive Era was modern American politics.

SUGGESTED READINGS

Chambers, John Whiteclay, II. *The Tyranny of Change: Americans in the Progressive Era, 1890–1920*, 2nd ed. (1992).

A concise overview of American life during the Progressive Era.

Kerr, K. Austin. *Organized for Prohibition: A New History of the Anti-Saloon League* (1985).

A recent treatment of the organization that formed the prototype for many organized interest groups.

Lewis, David Levering. *W. E. B. Du Bois: Biography of a Race, 1868–1919* (1993).

A powerful biography of Du Bois that delivers on its promise to present the "biography of a race" during the Progressive Era.

Link, Arthur S., and Richard L. McCormick. *Progressivism* (1983).

A thorough survey of progressivism, including the views of historians.

Roosevelt, Theodore. *An Autobiography* (1913; abr. ed. reprint, 1958).

Roosevelt's account of his actions sometimes needs to be taken with a grain of salt but nevertheless provides insight into Roosevelt, the person.

Sinclair, Upton. *The Jungle.* With an introduction by James R. Barrett (1988).

This socialist novel about workers in Chicago's packinghouses is a classic example of muckraking.

THE DOMESTIC IMPACT OF WAR World War I had a major impact on the lives of Americans. This map shows two different examples: (1) labor shortages in industry encouraged African Americans to leave the South and move north or, in some cases, west, and (2) increased food demand encouraged more farming, especially of wheat.

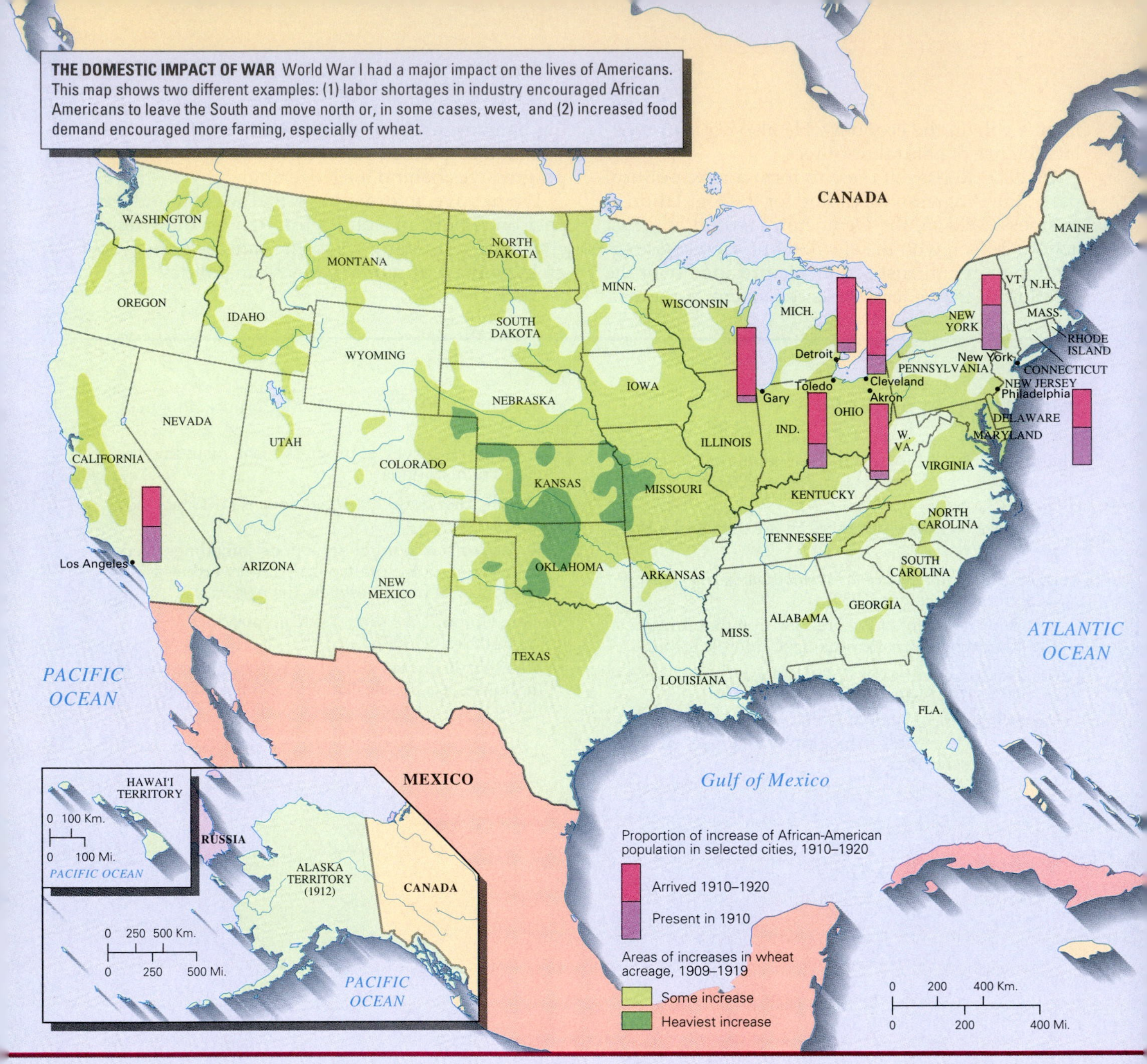

CANADA
WASHINGTON
OREGON
IDAHO
MONTANA
NORTH DAKOTA
SOUTH DAKOTA
WYOMING
NEBRASKA
NEVADA
CALIFORNIA
UTAH
COLORADO
KANSAS
ARIZONA
NEW MEXICO
OKLAHOMA
TEXAS
MINN.
IOWA
MISSOURI
ARKANSAS
LOUISIANA
WISCONSIN
ILLINOIS
MICH.
IND.
OHIO
KENTUCKY
TENNESSEE
MISS.
ALABAMA
GEORGIA
FLA.
SOUTH CAROLINA
NORTH CAROLINA
VIRGINIA
W. VA.
PENNSYLVANIA
NEW YORK
VT.
N.H.
MAINE
MASS.
RHODE ISLAND
CONNECTICUT
NEW JERSEY
DELAWARE
MARYLAND
Los Angeles
Gary
Detroit
Toledo
Cleveland
Akron
New York
Philadelphia
PACIFIC OCEAN
ATLANTIC OCEAN
Gulf of Mexico
MEXICO
HAWAI'I TERRITORY
0 100 Km.
0 100 Mi.
PACIFIC OCEAN
RUSSIA
ALASKA TERRITORY (1912)
CANADA
0 250 500 Km.
0 250 500 Mi.
PACIFIC OCEAN
Proportion of increase of African-American population in selected cities, 1910–1920
Arrived 1910–1920
Present in 1910
Areas of increases in wheat acreage, 1909–1919
Some increase
Heaviest increase
0 200 400 Km.
0 200 400 Mi.

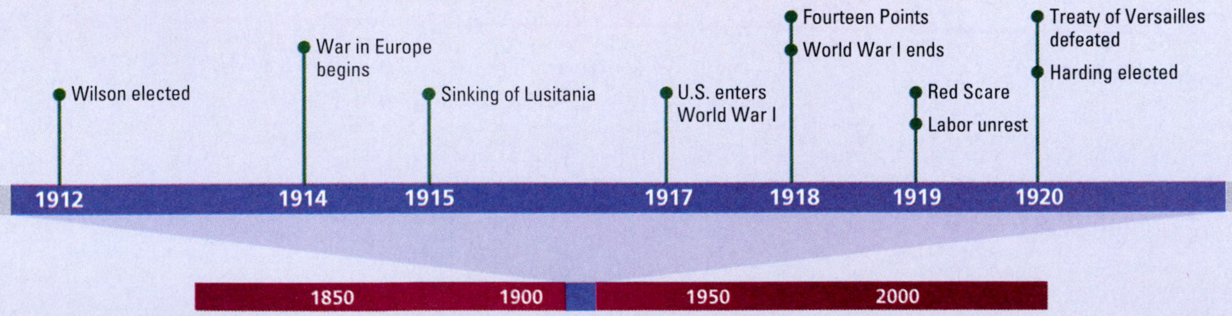

Wilson elected
War in Europe begins
Sinking of Lusitania
U.S. enters World War I
Fourteen Points
World War I ends
Red Scare
Labor unrest
Treaty of Versailles defeated
Harding elected
1912
1914
1915
1917
1918
1919
1920
1850
1900
1950
2000

CHAPTER 22

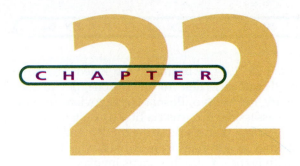

America and the World, 1913–1920

Inherited Commitments and New Directions

- In what ways did existing foreign policy commitments constrain Wilson's choices?
- What major foreign policy choices did Wilson make before the United States entered World War I?

From Neutrality to War: 1914–1917

- What were Wilson's expectations regarding American neutrality?
- What constraints did he face in seeking to maintain neutrality?
- What choices did he make in an effort to do so?
- What was the final outcome?

The Home Front

- What constraints hindered the United States' contribution to the Allied war effort?
- What choices did the federal government make in mobilizing the economy and society?

Americans "Over There"

- What constraints prevented the bulk of the AEF from being sent to Europe until 1918?
- Why did Wilson choose to keep the AEF as separate as possible from the troops of the other Allies?

Wilson and the Peace Conference

- What were Wilson's expectations regarding peace?
- What constraints did he face in realizing those objectives?
- What choices did he make, and what was the outcome?

Trauma in the Wake of War

- How did Americans' expectations change as a result of the outcome of the war and the events of 1919?
- How did these new expectations affect their choice in the 1920 presidential election?

INTRODUCTION

On June 28, 1914, a Bosnian Serb killed Archduke Franz Ferdinand, heir to the throne of Austria-Hungary, in Sarajevo, Bosnia-Herzegovina. To punish the assassination, Austria first consulted with its ally, Germany, then made stringent demands on Serbia. Serbia sought help from Russia, which was allied with France. Tense diplomats invoked elaborate, interlocking alliance systems. Huge armies began to move. By August 4, most of Europe was at war.

Earlier, Theodore Roosevelt had probably voiced the *expectations* of many Americans when he claimed in 1899 that war had become practically obsolete among the world's "civilized" nations. As president, Roosevelt helped shape Americans' *expectations* of security when he argued that the best way to preserve peace was by *choosing* to develop naval strength. Given such *expectations,* many Americans were shocked, saddened, and repelled in August 1914 when the leading "civilized" nations of the world lurched into war.

When Europeans *chose* war in August 1914, the United States had already assumed a major role in world affairs. Since 1898, it had acquired the Philippines and the Panama Canal, come to dominate the Caribbean and Central America, and pursued an active involvement in the balance of power in eastern Asia. All three presidents of the Progressive era—Theodore Roosevelt, William Howard Taft, and Woodrow Wilson—agreed wholeheartedly that the United States should exercise a major role in world affairs. But in 1914, the United States was the only large, industrial nation that had *chosen* not to become part of the elaborate network of treaties and understandings among the powers of Europe and Asia. Woodrow Wilson *chose* to maintain U.S. neutrality.

Expectations
Constraints
Choices
Outcomes

When Wilson entered the White House in 1913, he *expected* to spend most of his time dealing with domestic issues. As a political scientist, he had mostly studied domestic politics, and his winning presidential campaign in 1912 had focused primarily on domestic issues. Although well-read on international affairs, he brought to the White House neither significant international experience nor carefully considered foreign policies. For secretary of state, he *chose* William Jennings Bryan, who had also devoted most of his political career to domestic matters. Both devout Presbyterians, Wilson and Bryan shared a confidence that God had a plan for humankind and that all people shared a basic bond. Both hoped that their foreign policy *choices* might make the United States a model among nations for the peaceful settlement of international disputes. Neither man *expected* that he and the nation were soon to face difficult *choices* over a war so immense and so horrible that its *outcome* would be a profoundly altered world.

Inherited Commitments and New Directions

When Woodrow Wilson entered the White House in 1913, he first fixed his foreign policy attention on Latin America, the Pacific, and eastern Asia. There he tried to balance the anti-imperialist principles of his Democratic party against the **interventionist** commitments of his Republican predecessors. In the end, he not only accepted but actually extended most of these previous Republican commitments.

interventionist Tending to interfere in the affairs of another sovereign state.

CHRONOLOGY

The United States and World Affairs

1912	Wilson elected
1913	Huerta takes power in Mexico Wilson denies recognition of Huerta
1914	U.S. Navy occupies Veracruz War breaks out in Europe U.S. neutrality declared Stalemate on the western front
1915	German U-boat sinks the *Lusitania* United States occupies Haiti
1915–1920	Great Migration
1916	U.S. troops pursue Villa into Mexico National Defense Act Congress promises Philippine independence Sussex pledge United States occupies Dominican Republic Wilson re-elected
1917	Wilson calls for "peace without victory" American troops leave Mexico Germany resumes submarine warfare Czar overthrown in Russia United States declares war on Germany Committee on Public Information War Industries Board Selective Service Act Espionage Act Race riot in East St. Louis Government crackdown on IWW Bolsheviks seize power in Russia Russia withdraws from war Secret treaties published Railroads placed under federal control
1917–1918	Union membership rises sharply
1918	Wilson presents Fourteen Points Germans launch major offensive National War Labor Board Sedition Act Successful Allied counteroffensive Armistice in Europe
1918–1919	Rampant U.S. inflation
1919	Versailles peace conference Seattle general strike Urban race riots Lynchings increase Wilson suffers stroke Boston police strike Senate defeats Versailles treaty
1919–1920	Steel strike Red Scare Palmer raids
1920	Senate defeats Versailles treaty again Harding elected president
1921	Sacco and Vanzetti convictions

Anti-Imperialism and Intervention

Wilson's party had criticized the imperialist foreign policies of McKinley, Roosevelt, and Taft. Secretary of State Bryan was a leading anti-imperialist who had faulted Roosevelt's "Big Stick" approach to foreign affairs. "The man who speaks softly does not need a big stick," Bryan claimed. Wilson shared Taft's commitment to American commercial expansion, but he criticized dollar diplomacy for using the State Department to benefit particular companies.

During the Wilson administration, the Democrats' long adherence to anti-imperialism produced two measures. In 1916, Congress established a bill of rights for residents of the Philippine

Islands and promised them independence at an unspecified date. The next year, Puerto Rico became a U.S. territory, and its residents became U.S. citizens. Thus the Democrats wrote into law a limited version of the anti-imperialism they had proclaimed for more than twenty years.

Yet Wilson was to intervene more in Central America and the Caribbean than any previous president. He sent American marines into Haiti in 1915 after a mob killed the dictatorial president. A subsequent treaty made Haiti a protectorate in which American forces controlled the government until 1933. In 1916, Wilson sent marines into the Dominican Republic, where they remained until 1924.

Wilson and the Mexican Revolution

In Mexico, Wilson similarly engaged in brazen power politics. A rebellion forced dictator **Porfirio Díaz,** who had ruled Mexico for a third of a century, to resign in 1911. Francisco Madero, a wealthy landowner but also a leading reformer, assumed the presidency to great acclaim but proved incapable of uniting the country. Discontent rolled across Mexico, as peasant armies calling for *tierra y libertad* ("land and liberty") attacked the mansions of great landowners. Conservatives feared Madero as a reformer at the same time radicals dismissed him as too timid. Conservative forces led by **General Victoriano Huerta** launched a successful uprising in Mexico City in February 1913 and executed Madero.

Most European governments quickly recognized the Huerta government, but Wilson refused to do so because he considered Huerta a murderer and because Huerta's regime did not rest on the consent of the governed. Telling one visitor, "I am going to teach the South American republics to elect good men," Wilson waited for an opportunity to act against Huerta. In the meantime, anti-Huerta forces in northern Mexico, led by Venustiano Carranza, began to make significant gains.

In April 1914, Wilson found an excuse to intervene when Mexican officials arrested a few American sailors in Tampico. The city's army commander immediately released them and apologized. Wilson, however, used the incident to justify the occupation of **Veracruz,** Mexico's leading port. Veracruz's customs revenue was also the major source of government income. Huerta, facing Carranza's armies and deprived of munitions and customs revenues, fled the country in mid-July. Wilson withdrew the last American forces from Veracruz in November.

Carranza succeeded Huerta as president, and Wilson officially recognized his government. Carranza faced armed opposition, however, from **Pancho Villa** in northern Mexico. When Villa suffered serious defeats, he apparently decided his best hope for defeating Carranza was to incite a war with the United States. Villa's men murdered several Americans in Mexico and then, in March 1916, killed several Americans in New Mexico. After securing reluctant approval from Carranza, Wilson sent an expedition of nearly seven thousand men, commanded by General John Pershing, into Mexico to punish Villa.

Villa deftly evaded the American troops, drawing them ever deeper into Mexico. Carranza then became alarmed about the American expedition. When a clash between Mexican and American forces resulted in casualties, Carranza asked Wilson to withdraw the American troops. Wilson refused. Villa subsequently doubled behind the American army and raided into Texas, killing more Americans. Wilson sent more men into Mexico despite Carranza's insistence that all the American forces be withdrawn. Only in early 1917, when the prospect of war with Germany began to loom large, did Wilson order the troops to withdraw. The episode left a deep reservoir of Mexican resentment toward the United States.

Porfirio Díaz Mexican soldier and politician who became president after a coup in 1876 and governed the country until 1911.

General Victoriano Huerta Mexican general who overthrew the president, Francisco Madero, in 1913, and established a military dictatorship until forced to resign in 1914.

Veracruz The major port city of Mexico, located on the Gulf of Mexico; in 1914, Wilson ordered the U.S. Navy to occupy the port.

Pancho Villa Mexican bandit and revolutionary who led a raid into New Mexico in 1916, which prompted the U.S. government to send troops into Mexico in unsuccessful pursuit.

From Neutrality to War: 1914–1917

At first, Americans paid only passing attention to the assassination of Franz Ferdinand in Sarajevo in 1914. But when Europe plunged into war, Wilson and all Americans faced difficult choices.

The Great War in Europe

Europe's great powers had avoided armed conflict with each other since the Franco-Prussian War ended in 1871. Since then, however, competition for world markets and colonies had encouraged nations to accumulate arms and seek allies. European diplomats had constructed two major alliance systems by 1907. The **Triple Entente** linked Britain, France, and Russia. The **Triple Alliance** of Germany, Austria-Hungary, and Italy stood in opposition. As European nations formed their alliance networks, nationalism fueled aspirations for independence among the various cultural or linguistic groups of central and eastern Europe. These aspirations were especially powerful in the **Balkan Peninsula** (see Map 22.1), where Austro-Hungarian and Serbian interests clashed.

The primary point of conflict involved Bosnia, a territory annexed by Austria-Hungary in 1908. The Slavs in Serbia had previously eyed Bosnia, which contained a substantial Slavic population, as a candidate for Serbian annexation. Ironically, the Serbian nationalists who plotted the Austrian archduke's assassination did so because they feared that his liberal policies toward Bosnian Slavs would dampen their desire to break way from Austria.

After the assassination, Austria first assured itself of Germany's backing, then declared war on Serbia. In turn, Russia confirmed France's support and began slowly mobilizing in support of Serbia. Rather than wait for Russia to marshal its army, Germany declared war on Russia on August 1 and on France two days later. German strategists planned to bypass French defenses along the Franco-German border by moving through neutral Belgium (see Map 22.1). The Germans expected to knock France out of the war quickly and then turn their full power against Russia. Britain entered the conflict in defense of Belgium on August 4. Eventually, Germany and Austria-Hungary combined with Bulgaria and Turkey to form the Central Powers. Italy abandoned its Triple Alliance partners and joined Britain, France, Russia, Romania, and Japan to make up the Allies.

Instead of the quick knockout blow the Germans had anticipated, the armies settled into defensive lines over the **western front:** 475 miles of French countryside extending from the English Channel to the Alps (see Map 22.1). By the end of 1914, the troops had dug elaborate networks of trenches, separated from each other by a desolate **no man's land** filled with coils of barbed wire, where any movement brought a burst of machine-gun fire. As the war progressed, terrible new weapons—poison gas, aerial bombings, tanks—took many thousands of lives but failed to break the deadlock.

American Neutrality

Wilson's initial reaction to the European conflagration was to announce American neutrality. On August 19, he urged Americans to be "neutral in fact as well as in name . . . impartial in thought as well as in action." He hoped not only that America would remain outside the conflict but that he might serve as the peacemaker.

Wilson's hopes for peace proved unrealistic. Most of the warring nations wanted to gain territory, and only a decisive victory could deliver such a prize. The longer they fought, the more territory they coveted to satisfy their losses. As long as they

Triple Entente Informal alliance that linked France, Great Britain, and Russia in the years before World War I.

Triple Alliance Alliance that linked Germany, Italy, and Austria-Hungary in the years before World War I.

Balkan Peninsula Region of southeast Europe bounded by the Adriatic, Aegean, and Black seas; once ruled by Turkey, it included a number of relatively new and sometimes unstable states.

western front The line of battle between the Allies and Germany in World War I, which was located in French territory.

no man's land The field of battle between the lines of two opposing, entrenched armies.

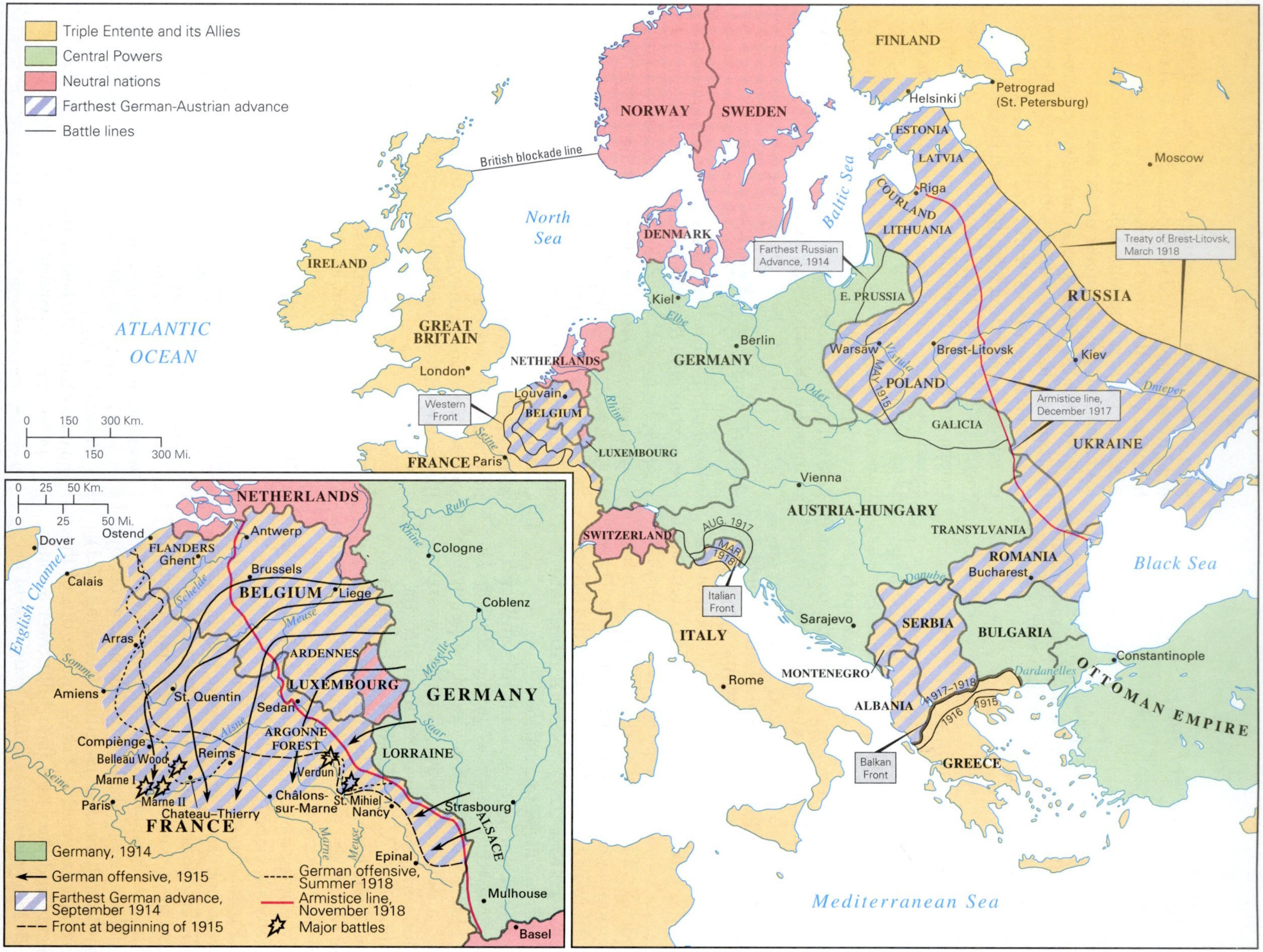
Triple Entente and its Allies
Central Powers
Neutral nations
Farthest German-Austrian advance
Battle lines
0 150 300 Km.
0 150 300 Mi.
ATLANTIC OCEAN
North Sea
Baltic Sea
Black Sea
Mediterranean Sea
IRELAND
GREAT BRITAIN
London
British blockade line
NORWAY
SWEDEN
DENMARK
FINLAND
Helsinki
Petrograd (St. Petersburg)
Moscow
ESTONIA
LATVIA
Riga
COURLAND
LITHUANIA
Farthest Russian Advance, 1914
E. PRUSSIA
Treaty of Brest-Litovsk, March 1918
RUSSIA
Kiel
Elbe
Berlin
GERMANY
Oder
Warsaw
Vistula
MAY 1915
Brest-Litovsk
Kiev
POLAND
Dnieper
Armistice line, December 1917
GALICIA
UKRAINE
NETHERLANDS
Louvain
BELGIUM
Rhine
LUXEMBOURG
Western Front
Seine
FRANCE
Paris
Vienna
AUSTRIA-HUNGARY
TRANSYLVANIA
SWITZERLAND
AUG. 1917
MAR. 1918
Italian Front
ROMANIA
Bucharest
Danube
Sarajevo
SERBIA
BULGARIA
ITALY
Rome
MONTENEGRO
Constantinople
Dardanelles
OTTOMAN EMPIRE
ALBANIA
1917–1918
1916
1915
Balkan Front
GREECE
0 25 50 Km.
0 25 50 Mi.
NETHERLANDS
Dover
Ostend
FLANDERS
Ghent
Antwerp
English Channel
Calais
Brussels
BELGIUM
Liege
Scheldte
Cologne
Ruhr
Rhine
Coblenz
Meuse
Arras
Somme
ARDENNES
Moselle
Amiens
St. Quentin
LUXEMBOURG
GERMANY
Sedan
Aisne
ARGONNE FOREST
Saar
Compiègne
Belleau Wood
Reims
LORRAINE
Verdun
Seine
Marne I
Marne II
Paris
Chateau–Thierry
Châlons-sur-Marne
St. Mihiel
Nancy
Strasbourg
FRANCE
ALSACE
Marne
Meuse
Epinal
Mulhouse
Basel
Germany, 1914
German offensive, 1915
Farthest German advance, September 1914
Front at beginning of 1915
German offensive, Summer 1918
Armistice line, November 1918
Major battles

♦ **MAP 22.1 The War in Europe, 1914–1918** This map identifies the members of the two great military coalitions: the Central Powers and the Allies. Notice how much territory Russia lost by the Treaty of Brest-Litovsk as compared to the armistice line (the line between the two armies when Russia sought peace with Germany).

saw a chance of winning, they had no interest in Wilson's appeals.

Wilson's hope that Americans could remain impartial was also unrealistic. Most Americans sided with the Allies. Britain had cultivated American friendship since the mid-1890s. A shared language and culture joined the upper classes in both countries, and trade and finance united many members of their business communities. Memories of French assistance during the American Revolution fueled enthusiasm for France. The German invasion of neutral Belgium aroused American sympathy as well. Allied propagandists worked hard to generate anti-German sentiment in America, portraying the war as a conflict between civilized peoples and brutal **Huns.**

Not all Americans sympathized with the Allies. Nearly 8 million of the 97 million people in the United States had one or both parents from Germany or Austria. Not surprisingly, many of them disputed the depictions of their cousins as bloodthirsty barbarians. Ethnic loyalties also influenced some 5 million Irish Americans, who disliked the English and held no sympathy for them.

Neutral Rights and German U-Boats

Wilson and Bryan agreed on the need to keep American interests separate from those of the parties to the European conflict. However, they developed different approaches for carrying out that policy. Bryan proved willing to sacrifice neutral rights if insistence on those rights posed the prospect of war. Wilson stood firm on maintaining all traditional rights of neutral nations. Bryan initially opposed loans to **belligerent** nations as incompatible with neutrality. Wilson first agreed, but once it became clear that the ban hurt the Allies more than the **Central Powers,** Wilson modified it to permit buying goods on credit. Finally, he dropped the ban on loans altogether.

Traditional neutral rights also included the freedom of neutrals to trade with all belligerents. However, European powers saw the war as a struggle for survival. Wilson soon found himself in conflict with both sides as they turned to naval warfare to break the deadlock on the western front.

Britain began to redefine neutral rights by announcing a blockade not only of German ports but also of neutral ports. Britain also expanded traditional definitions of **contraband** to include anything that might give even indirect aid to an enemy, including food. Germany responded by declaring a blockade of the British Isles, to be enforced by its submarines, called **U-boats.** U-boats were relatively fragile, and even a lightly armed merchant ship stood a reasonable chance of sinking one that surfaced and ordered a ship to stop. Consequently, submarines struck from below the surface, without warning. When Britain began disguising its ships with neutral flags, Germany countered that neutral flags no longer guaranteed protection from U-boat attacks. Whereas Wilson issued token reprimands over Britain's practices, he strongly denounced those of Germany.

On February 10, 1915, Wilson warned that the United States would hold Germany to "strict accountability" for its actions. On May 7, 1915, a German U-boat torpedoed the British passenger liner ***Lusitania,*** which sank with the loss of 1,198 passengers, including 128 Americans. Americans reacted with horror. When Bryan learned that the *Lusitania* carried rifle cartridges and other contraband, he urged restraint. Wilson, however, prepared a protest message that stopped just short of demanding an end to submarine warfare against unarmed merchant ships. When the German response was noncommittal, Wilson composed an even stronger ultimatum. Bryan feared the words would lead to war, and he resigned as secretary of state.

Huns Disparaging term used to describe Germans during World War I; the name came from a warlike tribe that invaded Europe in the fourth and fifth centuries.

belligerent A nation formally at war.

Central Powers In World War I, the coalition of Germany, Austria-Hungary, Bulgaria, and the Ottoman Empire.

contraband Goods prohibited by law or treaty from being imported or exported.

U-boat A German submarine (in German, *Untersee-boot*).

Lusitania British passenger liner torpedoed by a German submarine in 1915; more than 1,000 drowned, including 128 Americans, bringing the United States closer to war with Germany.

As other U-boat attacks followed, Wilson continued to protest. But after the sinking of the unarmed French ship *Sussex* in March 1916, which injured several Americans, Wilson warned Germany that if unrestricted submarine warfare did not stop, "the United States can have no choice" but to sever diplomatic relations. Germany responded with the **Sussex pledge,** promising that U-boats would no longer strike merchant vessels without warning.

America's economic ties to the Allies grew as the war progressed. The British blockade stifled Americans' trade with the Central Powers, which fell from around $170 million in 1914 to almost nothing two years later. Meanwhile, trade with Britain and France more than offset this decline. American companies sent $756 million in exports to those two nations in 1914 and $2.7 billion in 1916. And by April 1917, American bankers had loaned more than $2 billion to the Allied governments.

Deeply convinced that the best way to keep the United States neutral was to end the war, Wilson sent his close adviser Edward M. House to London and Berlin early in 1916 to sound out the British and Germans on the possibility for peace. House concluded that neither side wanted a negotiated end to the war. Discouraged, Wilson yielded to the increasing numbers of Americans who sought "preparedness"—a military buildup. In the summer of 1916, Congress passed the **National Defense Act,** more than doubling the size of the army, and appropriated the largest naval expenditures in the country's peacetime history.

The Decision for War

After the 1916 election, Wilson tried again to end the war by asking the belligerents to state their terms for ending the fighting. Hoping to cultivate Wilson, Germany announced its support for a peace conference but refused to specify terms. The Allies likewise refused to state their terms.

Still hoping to secure a peace conference, Wilson presented his views on the best way to achieve peace to the Senate in late January 1917. He urged that the only lasting peace would be a "peace without victory" and a "peace among equals" in which neither side exacted gains from the other. The speech received an enthusiastic welcome from most Democrats and progressives. But the British, French, and Germans had no interest in "peace without victory."

In Germany, the initiative passed to those who wanted to resume unrestricted submarine warfare. By denying the Allies American food and supplies, they hoped to achieve a decisive advantage and a quick victory. Germany announced it would resume submarine attacks effective February 1, 1917. Germany knew this move was likely to bring the United States into the war but gambled on being able to win the war before American troops could arrive in large numbers. Wilson accordingly broke off diplomatic relations with Germany on February 3, 1917.

Revelation of the Zimmermann Telegram on March 1 caused a further deterioration in U.S. relations with Germany. In January 1917, **Arthur Zimmermann,** the German foreign secretary, proposed to the German minister in Mexico that Mexico ally itself with Germany. If war broke out between Germany and the United States, Mexico should attack the United States. The incentive for Mexico would be the recovery of its "lost provinces" in the American Southwest. The British intercepted Zimmermann's message and passed it to American representatives on February 24. A public outcry followed the release of the telegram, but Wilson still hesitated to ask for war.

The Germans' sinking of five American ships between March 12 and March 21 removed all doubts from Wilson's mind. On April 2, 1917, Wilson asked Congress for a declaration of war. In asking for war, Wilson tried to unite Americans in a righteous, progressive crusade. He condemned German U-boat attacks as "warfare against mankind" and defined

Sussex pledge German promise in 1916 to stop sinking merchant ships without warning if the United States would compel the Allies to obey "international law."

National Defense Act Law passed in 1916 enlarging the army, strengthening the National Guard, and providing for an officers' reserve corps.

Arthur Zimmermann German foreign minister who proposed in 1917 that if the United States declared war on Germany, Mexico should become a German ally and win back Texas, Arizona, and New Mexico.

American war aims idealistically. "The world must be made safe for democracy," he pleaded. He promised that the United States would fight for democracy, self-government, "the rights and liberties of small nations," and a league of nations.

Not all members of Congress agreed that war was necessary. Senator George W. Norris, a progressive Republican from Nebraska, claimed that the nation was going to war to "preserve the commercial right of American citizens to deliver munitions of war to belligerent nations." Only five other senators, however, joined Norris in opposing the declaration of war on Germany. The House voted 373 to 50 for war.

The Home Front

The war altered nearly every aspect of the American economy, as the progressive emphasis on expertise and efficiency produced unprecedented centralization of economic decision making. Mobilization extended beyond war production to the people themselves, their attitudes toward the war, and their response to the need for labor.

Mobilizing the Economy

In the United States, shortages of military supplies, railway transportation snarls, and serious delays in military equipment deliveries proved to be major constraints for the war effort. As a result, federal direction over manufacturing, food and fuel production, and transportation increased dramatically. The extent to which the federal government exercised control over the economy during World War I has never since been matched.

Much of the nation welcomed government intervention. Business enlisted as a partner with government and supplied its cooperation and expertise. Prominent entrepreneurs volunteered their full-time services for a dollar a year. The wartime centralization of economic decision making came about through new agencies composed of government officials, business leaders, and prominent citizens.

The **War Industries Board (WIB),** established in 1917, oversaw the production of war materials. It did little to improve industrial productivity until Wilson appointed Bernard Baruch, a successful Wall Street investor, to head the board in early 1918. By pleading, bargaining, and sometimes threatening, Baruch usually persuaded companies to set and meet production quotas, to allocate raw materials, and to make the entire economy more efficient. Baruch accomplished most WIB goals without coercing corporate America, and industrial production increased by 20 percent.

Efforts to conserve fuel included the first use of **daylight-saving time.** To make rail transportation more efficient, the federal government ran the railroads as a single system, although it left them under private ownership. The government similarly took over the telegraph and telephone systems and launched a huge shipbuilding program.

The National War Labor Board, created in 1918 to mediate labor disputes, endorsed **collective bargaining** and gave some support for an eight-hour workday in return for a no-strike pledge from labor. Many unions secured contracts that brought significant wage increases. Union membership boomed from 2.7 million in 1916 to more than 4 million by 1919. Most established labor leaders, such as Samuel Gompers, president of the American Federation of Labor (AFL), fully supported the war.

One crucial American contribution to the Allies was food, for the war severely disrupted European agriculture. Food Administrator **Herbert Hoover** promoted increased production and conservation of food. He urged American families to observe

War Industries Board Board headed by Bernard Baruch that coordinated American production during World War I, setting production quotas, fixing prices, and allocating raw materials.

daylight-saving time Setting clocks one hour or more ahead of standard time to provide more daylight at the end of the workday during late spring, summer, and early fall.

collective bargaining Negotiation between the representatives of organized workers and their employers to determine wages, hours, and working conditions.

Herbert Hoover U.S. food administrator during World War I known for his proficient handling of relief efforts; he was elected president in 1928, only to see the country enter a major depression.

Meatless Mondays and Wheatless Wednesdays and to plant "war gardens." Farmers also brought large areas under cultivation for the first time (see chapter opener map). As a result, food shipments to the Allies tripled.

Mobilizing Public Opinion

Not all Americans fully supported the war. Some German Americans were reluctant to see their sons sent to war against their cousins. Some Irish Americans took little interest in saving Britain, especially after the brutal suppression of an attempt at Irish independence in 1916. The Socialist party voted to oppose American participation in the war. This stance greatly increased the Socialists' share of the vote in several cities in 1917.

To mobilize public opinion in support of the war, Wilson in 1917 created the Committee on Public Information, headed by George Creel. Once a muckraker, Creel set out to sell the war to the American people. The **Creel Committee** eventually counted 150,000 lecturers, writers, artists, actors, and scholars championing the cause and whipping up hatred of the "Huns." Most of those serving with the Creel Committee did so as "Four-Minute Men"—ready to make a four-minute speech anywhere a crowd gathered.

The fierce patriotism fanned by the Creel Committee sometimes sparked harsh measures against those considered "slackers" and "Kaiserites." "Woe to the man or group of men that seeks to stand in our way in this day of high resolution," warned Wilson. Zealots across the country took up the cry. Some states prohibited the use of foreign languages in public. Some communities removed German books from libraries and publicly burned them; others banned the music of Bach and Beethoven. Even words with German connections became objectionable: sauerkraut became "liberty cabbage," German measles were renamed "liberty measles," and dachshunds trotted as "liberty pups." Mobs even lynched people suspected of antiwar sentiments.

Civil Liberties in Time of War

German Americans suffered the most from the wartime hysteria, but pacifists, socialists, and other radicals also became targets for government and vigilantes. Congress passed the **Espionage Act** in 1917 and the **Sedition Act** in 1918, prohibiting interference with the draft and outlawing criticism of the government. Some fifteen hundred people were arrested for violating the Espionage and Sedition acts, including Eugene V. Debs, leader of the Socialist party.

Those who voiced dissenting opinions found they could not rely on the courts for protection. When opponents of the war challenged the Espionage Act, the Supreme Court ruled that freedom of speech was never absolute. Just as no one has the right to shout "Fire" in a crowded theater, said Justice Oliver Wendell Holmes, Jr., so in wartime no one has a constitutional right to say anything that might endanger the nation. The Court also upheld the Sedition Act in 1919.

The IWW came under relentless attack. In July 1917, in Bisbee, Arizona, managers of local copper mines, law enforcement officials, and deputized citizens rounded up more than eleven hundred IWW members, marched them at gunpoint into railroad boxcars, transported them over one hundred miles into the desert, and abandoned them. In September 1917, Justice Department agents arrested IWW leaders throughout the West, who were then sentenced to jail terms of up to twenty-five years. Deprived of its leaders and virtually bankrupt, the IWW never recovered.

A few Americans protested the abridgment of civil liberties. One group formed the Civil Liberties Bureau, forerunner of the American Civil Liberties Union. Most Americans, however, did not object to

Creel Committee The U.S. Committee on Public Information (1917–1919), headed by journalist and editor George Creel, which used films, posters, pamphlets, and news releases to mobilize American public opinion in favor of World War I.

Espionage Act Law passed in 1917 that mandated severe penalties for anyone found guilty of interfering with the draft or encouraging disloyalty to the United States.

Sedition Act Law passed in 1918 that supplemented the Espionage Act by extending the penalty to anyone deemed to have abused the government in writing.

the repression. Others who were sympathetic to the victims kept silent. Jane Addams, who had been maligned for expressing her pacifist views before the war, would not sign the Civil Liberties Bureau's appeal for funds, explaining, "I am obliged to walk very softly in all things suspect."

Changes in the Workplace

Intense activism and remarkable productivity characterized American labor's wartime experience. Union membership almost doubled, and a significant number of women became new cardholders. In addition, unions benefited from the encouragement that the **National War Labor Board** gave to collective bargaining between unions and companies. The board also helped settle labor disputes through mediation. Never before had a federal agency interceded this way.

Demands for increased production at a time when millions of men were marching off to war opened opportunities for women. Employment of women in factory, office, and retail jobs had increased before the war, but the war accelerated those trends. Most women who worked outside the home were young and single. Some middle-class women who now entered the paid labor force not only gave up their homebound roles but also rejected their parents' standards of morality and behavior. They adopted instead the less restricted lifestyles that had long been experienced by many wage-earning, working-class women. One commentator observed, "For the first time in the memory of man, girls from well-bred, respectable middle-class families broke through these invisible chains of custom and asserted their right to a nonchalant, self-sustaining life of their own."

The Great Migration and White Reactions

The war also had a great impact on African-American communities. Until the war, about 90 percent of all African Americans lived in the South. By 1920, perhaps as many as 500,000 had moved north in what has been called the **Great Migration.** The largest proportional increases in the African-American population came in the industrial cities of the Midwest. Gary, Indiana, showed one of the greatest gains: 1,284 percent between 1910 and 1920. New York City, Philadelphia, and Los Angeles also attracted many blacks (see chapter opener map). Several factors combined to stimulate this migration. "Every time a lynching takes place in a community down South," T. Arnold Hill of Chicago's Urban League pointed out, "colored people will arrive in Chicago within two weeks." Economic disaster in the South in the form of drought, floods, and the **boll weevil** in 1915 and 1916 was another impetus.

The sharp decline in European immigration caused by the war also spurred the Great Migration. The wartime labor needs of northern cities attracted hundreds of thousands of African Americans seeking better jobs and higher pay. Many industrial jobs paid $3 a day, compared to 50 cents for picking cotton. The impact on some southern cities was striking. Jackson, Mississippi, for example, lost half of all working-class African Americans and a quarter to a third of black business owners and professionals.

The war heightened racial tensions in the South because some whites resented the new options available to blacks. For example, black women who received money from their men in uniform or in wartime jobs sometimes found that they no longer needed farm work. Pine Bluff, Arkansas, officials tried to extend the nation's "work or fight" rule, under which anyone not aiding the war effort by either working or fighting could be arrested, to black women who refused to work in the cotton fields.

Severe wartime racial conflicts erupted in several cities on the northern end of the Great Migration trail. The worst race riot in American history swept through East St. Louis, Illinois, on July 2, 1917. Thousands of African Americans had settled in the city during the previous two years. At least

National War Labor Board Board appointed by President Wilson in 1918 to act as the court of last resort for labor disputes.

Great Migration Mass movement of black people from the rural South to the urban North during World War I; about a half million people relocated.

boll weevil Small beetle of the southern United States that infests cotton plants and whose larvae hatch in and damage cotton bolls.

thirty-nine perished in the riot, and six thousand found themselves homeless. Incensed that such brutality could occur so soon after the nation's moralistic entrance into the war, W. E. B. Du Bois charged, "No land that loves to lynch 'niggers' can lead the hosts of Almighty God."

Americans "Over There"

With the declaration of war, the United States needed to mobilize quickly for combat. The navy was already large and powerful after nearly three decades of shipbuilding. The army, however, was tiny. Millions of men had to be enlisted or drafted, trained, supplied, and transported to Europe.

Mobilizing for Battle

The navy was able to strike back quickly at the German fleet. The convoy technique, in which several ships traveled together under the protection of destroyers, helped cut shipping losses in half by late 1917. By the following spring, the U-boat ceased to pose a significant danger.

The army, however, with only 372,000 men, was not ready for action in April 1917. Many men volunteered but not enough. Congress therefore passed the **Selective Service Act** in May, requiring men ages 21 to 30 to register with local boards to determine who was to be called to duty. For the most part, Americans accepted the draft. Eventually, 24 million men registered, and 2.8 million were drafted. By the end of the war, the combined army, navy, and marine corps counted 4.8 million members.

No women were drafted, but some women chose to serve in the military. Almost thirteen thousand women joined the navy and marines, mostly in clerical capacities. They were permitted to hold full military rank and status for the first time. The army, however, considered enlisting women a "most radical departure" and refused to do it. Women could serve in the Army Corps of Nurses, which enrolled nearly eighteen thousand women but denied them army rank, pay, or benefits. At least five thousand civilian women served in various capacities in France, sometimes near the frontlines, most through the Red Cross, which helped staff hospitals and rest facilities.

Nearly 400,000 African Americans served during World War I. Almost 200,000 served overseas, nearly 30,000 on the frontlines. Most black soldiers were treated as second-class citizens. They marched in segregated **Jim Crow** units in the army, were limited to food service duties in the navy, and were excluded from the marines altogether. Only about 600 African Americans earned commissions as officers. White officers commanded most black troops.

"Over There"

As the first troops of the **American Expeditionary Force (AEF)** trickled into France in June 1917, the Central Powers seemed close to victory. French offensives in April 1917 had failed, and a British summer effort in Flanders had resulted in enormous casualties but little gain. A Russian drive in midsummer proved disastrous, and in November, following the triumph of the **Bolsheviks,** Russia withdrew from the war. Hoping to win the war before many American troops arrived, the Germans planned a massive spring offensive for 1918.

The German offensive came in Picardy at the point where the French and British lines joined. AEF units were hurried to the front to block the German advance. By late May, the Germans had moved to within 50 miles of Paris, which French officials considered evacuating. AEF units fought bravely and effectively. At Château-Thierry and Belleau Wood, they took eight thousand casualties during a monthlong battle over a single square mile of wheat fields and woods.

Selective Service Act Law passed in 1917 establishing compulsory military service for men ages 21 to 30.

Jim Crow Name for any laws or forms of organization that discriminate against blacks; probably derived from a minstrel-show stock character named Jim Crow.

American Expeditionary Force American army commanded by General John J. Pershing that served in Europe during World War I.

Bolsheviks Communists who seized power in Russia in November 1917.

♦ This painting depicts British troops being sent into the no man's land between their trenches and those of the Germans. The development of the machine gun made such efforts highly dangerous and contributed to the staggering losses of World War I. The artist, one of only twelve survivors of a company of eighty sent against the enemy's trenches, recalled that "it was bitterly cold and we were easy targets in snow and daylight." *"Over the Top" by Paul Nash. Imperial War Museum.*

The Allies launched a counteroffensive in July 1918, as American troops finally began to pour into France. The American command insisted on being assigned its own sector of the front to make the American contribution to victory clear. In September, General John J. Pershing launched a stunning one-day offensive against the St. Mihiel **salient** (see Map 22.1). AEF forces then joined a larger Allied offensive in the Meuse-Argonne region, the last major assault of the war. In the Argonne Forest on October 8, Corporal Alvin York, armed with only a rifle and a pistol, killed 25 German soldiers, eliminated 35 enemy machine guns, and took 132 prisoners, thus becoming the most heroic figure of the war. By the time of his exploits, the German general staff was pleading with its government to seek an armistice. Fighting ended on the eleventh hour of the eleventh day of the eleventh month of 1918. By then, more than 2 million American soldiers were in France.

When the clamor of celebration replaced the din of battle, thirty-two nations had entered the war against the Central Powers. Nearly 9 million men in uniform died: Germany lost 1.8 million, Russia 1.7 million, Austria-Hungary 1.2 million, the British Empire 908,400. France lost 1.4 million, including half of its men between the ages of 20 and 32. American losses of 115,000 men were small in comparison.

Wilson and the Peace Conference

When the war ended, Wilson hoped that the peace treaty would not contain the seeds of future wars. He also hoped to create an international organization to keep the peace. Most of the Allies, however, had more interest in grabbing territory and punishing Germany.

Bolshevism, the Secret Treaties, and the Fourteen Points

In December 1917, the Bolsheviks, who had seized power in Russia only a month earlier, tried to demonstrate that the war was nothing more than a capitalist scramble for imperial spoils. They published secret treaties by which the Allies had agreed to take colonies and territories from the Central Powers. These exposés strengthened Wilson's efforts to impose his war objectives on the Allies.

salient Battle line that projects closest to the enemy.

On January 8, 1918, Wilson directly challenged the secret treaties and tried to seize the initiative in defining a basis for peace in a speech to Congress. Wilson presented fourteen specific objectives, soon called the **Fourteen Points.** Points 1 through 5 provided a general context for lasting peace: no secret treaties, freedom of the seas, reduction of barriers to trade, reduction of armaments, and adjustment of colonial claims based partly on the interests of colonial peoples. Points 6 through 13 addressed particular situations: return of territories France had lost to Germany in 1871 and self-determination in Central Europe and the Middle East. The fourteenth point called for "a general association of nations" that could afford "mutual guarantees of political independence and territorial integrity to great and small states alike."

The major Allies reluctantly accepted Wilson's Fourteen Points as a basis for discussion but expressed little enthusiasm for them. When the Germans asked for an end to the fighting, however, they based their request on the Fourteen Points.

Wilson at Versailles

When Woodrow Wilson toured France, Italy, and Britain in December 1918, huge welcoming crowds paid homage to the great "peacemaker from America." Delegates to the peace conference at **Versailles,** which opened on January 18, 1919, assembled amid far-reaching change. The Austro-Hungarian Empire had crumbled, producing the new nations of Poland, Czechoslovakia, and Yugoslavia and the republics of Austria and Hungary. In Germany, **Kaiser Wilhelm II** had **abdicated,** and a republic was being formed. In Russia, a civil war was raging between the Bolsheviks and their anti-Communist opponents. Amid the ruins of the Russian Empire, Finland, Estonia, Latvia, and Lithuania were asserting their independence. The Ottoman Empire was collapsing too, as Arabs revolted with aid from Britain and France. Throughout Europe and the Middle East, national self-determination and government by the consent of the governed seemed to be becoming a reality.

Although representatives were on hand from all the nations that had declared war against the Central Powers, the Big Four made the major decisions at the conference: Woodrow Wilson of the United States, David Lloyd George of Britain, Georges Clemenceau of France, and Vittorio Orlando of Italy. Germany was excluded. Terms of peace were to be imposed, not negotiated. Russia was also excluded on the grounds that it had made a separate peace with Germany in the Treaty of Brest-Litovsk, signed in March 1918. But the specter of Bolshevism hung over the conference.

Wilson learned at the outset that the European leaders were far more interested in pursuing their own national interests than in implementing his Fourteen Points. Clemenceau carried painful memories of Germany's humiliating defeat of France in 1871 and wanted to disable Germany so that it could never again invade his nation. Lloyd George came to Paris with a mandate from British voters for exacting heavy **reparations** from Germany. Orlando insisted on reaping all the territories promised when Italy joined the Allies in 1915.

Facing the insistent and acquisitive Allies, Wilson had no choice but to compromise. He did secure the creation of the **League of Nations,** but only after threatening to make a separate peace with Germany. Rather than achieving a "peace without victory," however, the treaty imposed harsh terms. A "war guilt" clause forced Germany to accept the blame for starting the war. Other provisions required Germany to pay the Allies $33 billion in

Fourteen Points President Wilson's program for maintaining peace after World War I, which called for arms reduction, national self-determination, and a league of nations.

Versailles Magnificent estate near Paris built by Louis XIV in the seventeenth century; the treaty ending World War I was signed there in 1919.

Kaiser Wilhelm II German emperor who had worked to create the great military machine and system of alliances that precipitated the outbreak of World War I.

abdicate To formally relinquish a high office.

reparations Payments required from a defeated nation as compensation to the victors for damage or injury during a war.

League of Nations A world organization proposed by President Wilson and founded in 1920; it worked to promote peace and international cooperation.

reparations and to surrender Alsace-Lorraine, all its colonies, and other European territories (see Map 22.2). To prevent further aggression, the treaty deprived Germany of its navy and limited its army to 100,000 men. German representatives signed on June 28, 1919.

In the end, Wilson compromised on nearly all of his Fourteen Points. He hoped the League of Nations would resolve future controversies without war and would also solve the problems created by the compromises he had reluctantly accepted. He was especially pleased with Article 10 of the **League Covenant,** which specified that League members would take joint economic and military action against aggressors.

The Senate and the Treaty

While Wilson was in Paris, opposition to his plans was taking shape in the Republican-controlled Senate, which had to approve any treaty. The Senate split into three groups over the treaty. **Henry Cabot Lodge,** chairman of the Senate Foreign Relations Committee, led the largest opposition group, called the *reservationists* after the reservations, or amendments, to the treaty that Lodge had proposed. At least part of Lodge's opposition was personal. He disliked Wilson intensely and had been angered by the president's failure to include any Republicans in the Versailles treaty delegation. Lodge's chief public misgiving was that Article 10 might be used to commit American troops to war without congressional approval. A smaller group, the *irreconcilables,* consisted primarily of Republicans who opposed any American involvement in European affairs. A third Senate group, mostly Democrats, favored the treaty.

Wilson decided to appeal directly to the people to win support for the treaty. In September 1919, he undertook an arduous speaking tour of twenty-nine cities. The effort proved too demanding for his fragile health. He collapsed in Pueblo, Colorado, on September 25, and returned to Washington. Soon after, he suffered a serious stroke. Half-paralyzed, Wilson remained in seclusion and carried on few of his duties.

Lodge proposed that the Senate accept the treaty with his reservations. Wilson, however, refused to compromise. On November 19, 1919, the Senate defeated the treaty with the Lodge reservations and then defeated the original version of the treaty. The treaty with reservations came to a vote again in March 1920 but failed to gain a two-thirds majority. The United States would not join the League of Nations.

Legacies of the Great War

Roosevelt, Wilson, and most other prewar leaders had projected the progressive mood of optimism and confidence. Wilson invoked this tradition in claiming that the United States was going to war to make the world "safe for democracy." In doing so, however, he fostered unrealistic expectations that world politics might be transformed overnight.

Americans who believed that rational, civilized people had outgrown war found the conflict a disillusioning experience. For some, wartime suppression of civil liberties called into question their belief in the inevitability of progress. Many Americans became disenchanted by the contrast between Wilson's lofty idealism and the Allies' cynical opportunism. The war to make the world safe for democracy turned out to be a chance for Italy to grab Austrian territory and for Japan to seize German concessions in China.

In the end, the peace conference left unresolved many problems. Wilson's elevation of self-government and **self-determination** encouraged aspirations for independence throughout the colonial empires retained by the Allies. Above all, the war and the treaty helped produce economic and political instability in much of Europe, making it a breeding ground for totalitarian and nationalistic movements that were eventually to bring on another world war.

League Covenant The constitution of the League of Nations, which was incorporated in the Versailles treaty in 1919.

Henry Cabot Lodge Massachusetts Republican senator who led congressional opposition to the Versailles treaty and the League of Nations.

self-determination The freedom of a given people to determine their own political status.

Boundaries of German, Russian, and Austro-Hungarian empires in 1914
Areas lost by Austro-Hungarian Empire
Areas lost by Russian Empire
Areas lost by German Empire
Areas lost by Bulgaria
Areas lost by Ottoman Empire
Demilitarized Zones
Boundaries of 1926
Areas controlled under mandates from the League of Nations, 1920
FINLAND
NORWAY
SWEDEN
Oslo
Helsinki
Leningrad (St. Petersburg)
Stockholm
Tallinn
ESTONIA
North Sea
GREAT BRITAIN
DENMARK
Copenhagen
Baltic Sea
Riga
LATVIA
Volga
Memel
LITHUANIA
Vilnius
RUSSIAN EMPIRE
(Became Union of Soviet Socialist Republics, 1922)
NETHERLANDS
Amsterdam
Danzig
POLISH CORRIDOR
EAST PRUSSIA
GERMANY
Brussels
BELGIUM
RUHR
Cologne
Berlin
POLAND
Warsaw
Weimar
Paris
LUX.
Frankfurt
Rhine
Elbe
Oder
Vistula
Seine
FRANCE
LORRAINE
ALSACE
Loire
Strasbourg
Prague
CZECHOSLOVAKIA
GALICIA
Kiev
Don
Ural
Dnieper
Geneva
Bern
SWITZ.
Vienna
AUSTRIA
Locarno
S. TYROL
Budapest
HUNGARY
Milan
Po
Venice
SLOVENIA
Rhône
Genoa
Rapallo
Trieste
Zagreb
CROATIA
ROMANIA
Belgrade
Corsica
ITALY
YUGOSLAVIA
BOSNIA AND HERZEGOVINA
Danube
Bucharest
Black Sea
Caspian Sea
Rome
MONTENEGRO
(To Yugoslavia 1921)
SERBIA
BULGARIA
Sofia
Sardinia
Naples
ALBANIA
Batum
Baku
Kars
Istanbul
(Constantinople)
Ankara
TURKEY
Tabriz
GREECE
Sicily
Izmir
(Smyrna)
Athens
PERSIA
(IRAN)
TUNISIA
(French)
Annexed by Turkey 1939
Aleppo
SYRIA
(French Mandate)
Tigris
Euphrates
Mediterranean Sea
Crete
Cyprus
(Gr.Br.)
Baghdad
Beirut
Damascus
IRAQ
(MESOPOTAMIA)
(British Mandate)
Kut el Amara
PALESTINE
(British Mandate)
Amman
Jerusalem
TRANSJORDAN
(British Mandate)
Basra
KUWAIT
(Gr. Br.)
Suez Canal
Cairo
NEUTRAL ZONES
NEJD
(SAUDI ARABIA)
LIBYA
(Italian)
EGYPT
(Independent 1922)
Red Sea
Nile
Riyadh
Medina
0 200 400 Km.
0 200 400 Mi.

♦ **MAP 22.2 Postwar Boundary Changes in Central Europe and the Middle East** This map shows the boundary changes in Europe and the Middle East that resulted from the defeat of the four large multiethnic empires—Austria-Hungary, Russia, Germany, and the Ottoman Empire.

Trauma in the Wake of War

The United States began to demobilize almost as soon as French church bells pealed for the **Armistice.** By November 1919, nearly the entire force of 4 million men and women was out of uniform. Industrial demobilization occurred even more quickly, as officials canceled war contracts with no more than a month's notice. The year 1919 saw not only the return of the troops from Europe but also raging inflation, massive strikes, bloody race riots, widespread fear of radical **subversion,** violations of civil liberties, and passage of Prohibition.

Inflation and Strikes

Inflation was the most pressing single problem Americans faced after the war. Between 1913 and 1919, the average American family saw its cost of living double. Such inflation contributed to labor unrest. When the Armistice ended the no-strike pledge taken by unions, they made wage demands to keep up with the soaring cost of living. In 1919, however, management was ready for a fight.

After the war, some companies determined to return labor relations to prewar patterns. They blamed organized labor for the rise in prices and connected strikes and unions to "dangerous foreign ideas" from Bolshevik Russia. Seattle's mayor claimed that a five-day general strike called by all the city's unions in February 1919 was a Bolshevik plot. Boston's police struck in September 1919 after the city's police commissioner fired nineteen policemen for joining an AFL union. Massachusetts governor **Calvin Coolidge** activated the state guard to maintain order and break the union. "There is no right to strike against the public safety by anybody, anywhere, anytime," he proclaimed. By mid-1919, it was clear that conservative political and business leaders had joined forces to roll back the union gains of the war years.

The largest and most dramatic labor conflict in 1919 came against United States Steel. Most steelworkers had not had a recognized union since the 1892 Homestead strike. Many steelworkers put in twelve-hour days and, when they changed shifts, sometimes slogged through twenty-four hours in the mills without rest. Wages had not increased as fast as inflation. When the AFL launched an ambitious unionization drive in the steel industry in 1919, many steelworkers responded eagerly.

The steel industry firmly refused to deal with the new organization, provoking a strike in late September. United States Steel, however, blamed the strike on radicals. Company guards protected strikebreakers, and military forces commanded by General Leonard Wood moved into Gary, Indiana, to help round up what they called "the Red element." By January 1920, after eighteen workers had been killed and hundreds beaten, the strike was over and the unions ousted.

The Red Scare

The steel industry's charges of Bolshevism to discredit strikers came at a time when many government and corporate leaders decried the dangers of Bolshevism at home and abroad. In late April 1919, the discovery in various post offices of thirty-four bombs addressed to prominent Americans such as John D. Rockefeller lent credibility to these fears. In June, bombs in several cities damaged buildings and killed two people. Although the work of a few anarchists, the explosions set off a panic over a radical conspiracy to overthrow the government.

With President Wilson still bedridden, Attorney General A. Mitchell Palmer organized an anti-Red campaign, hoping to enhance his presidential prospects in 1920. "Like a prairie fire," Palmer claimed, "the blaze of revolution was sweeping over every American institution." In November 1919, Palmer launched the first of what came to be called the **Palmer raids** to arrest suspected radicals.

Armistice An agreement to stop fighting.

subversion Efforts to undermine or overthrow an established government.

Calvin Coolidge Massachusetts governor and conservative Republican who became Harding's vice president in 1921; he served as president from 1923 to 1929.

Palmer raids A series of government attacks on individuals and organizations in 1919 and 1920, carried out in a climate of anti-Communist hysteria to search for political radicals.

Authorities rounded up some five thousand people between November and January 1920, and although they found only a few firearms, they **deported** several hundred aliens.

State legislatures joined in with antiradical measures of their own. In January 1920, the New York state legislature expelled five members solely because they were Socialists. When a wide range of respected public figures denounced the assembly action as undemocratic, public opinion regarding the **Red Scare** began to shift. The Red Scare finally spent itself after Palmer's dire predictions of radical activities on May 1, 1920, the major day of celebration for Socialists and Communists alike, came to nothing.

As the Red Scare sputtered to an end, police in Massachusetts arrested two Italian-born anarchists, **Nicola Sacco and Bartolomeo Vanzetti,** and charged them with robbery and murder. Despite inconclusive evidence and the accused men's protestations of innocence, a jury in 1921 found them guilty, and they were sentenced to death. While appeals delayed their execution, many Americans became convinced that the two had been convicted because of their political beliefs and Italian origins. Further, many doubted that they had received a fair trial. Over loud protests at home and abroad, both men were executed in 1927.

Race Riots and Lynchings

The racial tensions of the war years continued into the postwar period. Black soldiers encountered more acceptance and less discrimination in Europe than they had ever known at home. Some whites, however, were determined to restore the state of race relations that had prevailed before 1917. Southern mobs lynched ten returning black soldiers, some still in uniform. Mobs lynched more than seventy blacks in 1919 and burned eleven victims alive.

Rioting also struck outside the South. In July, violence reached the nation's capital, where white mobs attacked blacks throughout the city for three days, killing several. A few days later, in Chicago, whites apparently caused the death of a young African American swimming in Lake Michigan by throwing rocks at him. The incident sparked two weeks of rioting by racial mobs that left fifteen whites and twenty-three blacks dead. By the end of 1919, race riots had flared in more than two dozen places.

The Election of 1920

Republicans confidently expected to regain the White House in the 1920 election. The Democrats had lost their congressional majorities in the 1918 elections, and the postwar confusion and disillusionment often focused on Wilson. One reporter described the stricken president as the "sacrificial whipping boy for the present bitterness."

The reaction against Wilson almost guaranteed the election of any Republican nominee. Several candidates attracted significant support, but no candidate could muster a majority of the convention delegates. Senator **Warren G. Harding** of Ohio emerged as a compromise candidate. Even some of his supporters characterized him as "the best of the second-raters." The Democrats chose James Cox, the governor of Ohio, as their presidential candidate.

The election was a Republican landslide. Harding won 60 percent of the popular vote, the largest popular majority up to that time. Wilson had hoped the election might be a "solemn referendum" on the League of Nations, but it proved to be more of a response to the disappointments of the Wilson years. Americans, it seemed, had had enough idealism and sacrifice.

deport To expel an undesirable alien from a country.

Red Scare Wave of anticommunism in the United States in 1919 and 1920, which included a government crackdown that focused on foreigners and labor unions.

Nicola Sacco and Bartolomeo Vanzetti Italian anarchists convicted in 1921 of the murder of a Braintree, Massachusetts, factory paymaster and the theft of a $16,000 payroll; in spite of public protests on their behalf, they were electrocuted in 1927.

Warren G. Harding Ohio politician and Republican who was elected president in 1920; his administration was marred by corruption and scandal.

SUMMARY

Expectations
Constraints
Choices
Outcomes

Woodrow Wilson took office *expecting* to focus on domestic policy, not foreign affairs. He fulfilled some Democratic party commitments to anti-imperialism but *chose* to intervene extensively in the Caribbean and in Mexico.

When war broke out in Europe in 1914, Wilson proclaimed the United States to be neutral. German submarine warfare and British restrictions on commerce, however, *constrained* traditional *expectations* for neutrality. Wilson secured a German pledge to refrain from unrestricted submarine warfare. He was re-elected in 1916 on the platform that "he kept us out of war." Shortly after his re-election, however, the Germans violated their pledge, and Wilson *chose* to ask for war against Germany.

The war brought new *expectations* in nearly every aspect of the nation's economic and social life. To overcome *constraints* of inefficiency, the federal government *chose* to develop a high degree of centralized economic planning. Fearing that opposition to the war might pose a *constraint* on full mobilization, the Wilson administration *chose* to secure new laws that *constrained* some civil liberties. When the federal government *chose* to back collective bargaining, unions registered important gains. And when labor shortages threatened to *constrain* the war effort, more women and African Americans *chose* to enter the industrial work force. One *outcome* was that many African Americans *chose* to move to northern and midwestern industrial cities.

Germany *chose* to launch a major offensive in early 1918, *expecting* to achieve victory before American troops could make a difference. However, the AEF was able to play a significant part in breaking the German advance. The *outcome* was the Germans' request for an armistice.

In his Fourteen Points, Wilson expressed his *expectations* for peace. *Constrained* by opposition from the Allies, Wilson *chose* to compromise at the peace conference, but he still *expected* that the League of Nations would be able to maintain the peace. Fearing the *constraints* that League membership might place on the United States, enough senators opposed the treaty to defeat it. The *outcome* was that the United States did not become a member of the League.

In the United States, the immediate *outcome* of the war was disillusionment and a year of high prices, costly strikes, the Red Scare, and race riots and lynchings. In 1920, the nation returned to its usual Republican preference when it sent Warren G. Harding to the White House.

SUGGESTED READINGS

Clements, Kendrick A. *The Presidency of Woodrow Wilson* (1992).

More than half of this recent account of Wilson's presidency is devoted to foreign policy matters and the war.

Friedel, Frank. *Over There: The Story of America's First Great Overseas Crusade,* rev. ed. (1990).

A vivid survey of American participation in the fighting in Europe, with many firsthand accounts.

Lewis, Sinclair. *Main Street* (1920; reprint, 1961).

An absorbing novel about a woman's dissatisfaction with her life and her decision to work in Washington during the war.

Link, Arthur S. *Woodrow Wilson: Revolution, War, and Peace* (1979).

A concise introduction to Wilson's role in and thinking about foreign affairs.

Remarque, Erich Maria. *All Quiet on the Western Front.* Trans. A. W. Wheen (1930; reprint, 1982).

The classic and moving novel about World War I, seen through German eyes.

Tuchman, Barbara W. *The Guns of August* (1962; reprint, 1976).

A popular and engaging account of the outbreak of the war, focusing on events in Europe.

The Choice to Declare War

The Context

On April 2, 1917, President Woodrow Wilson spoke to a joint session of Congress and requested that it declare war on Germany in response to the German government's decision to resume unrestricted submarine warfare. Congress did declare war on April 6, and for the first time, the United States found itself involved in a military conflict in Europe. U.S. involvement in World War I lasted for a year and seven months, during which more than 115,000 Americans died on the battlefields of Europe. Once Wilson decided for war, he had to choose the way he would present his decision to Congress and to the American people.

The Historical Question

In asking Congress to declare war on Germany, President Wilson had to choose between a narrow justification, based on American self-interest, and a broader vision of transforming international politics. Wilson chose the broad approach, but members of Congress did not necessarily agree. In calling for war, to what values did Wilson appeal? On what values did Senator Borah base his decision to vote for war? On what values did Senators La Follette and Norris base their opposition to war?

The Challenge

Using the sources provided, along with other information you have read, write an essay or hold a discussion on the following question. Cite evidence in the sources to support your conclusions. **On what values did Wilson, Borah, La Follette, and Norris base their decisions about going to war? What evidence is there that they all drew on the same values as they came to different conclusions about war?**

The Sources

1 President Woodrow Wilson, in a speech to a joint session of Congress on April 2, 1917, asked for a declaration of war against Germany.

I am not now thinking of the loss of property involved, immense and serious as that is, but only of the wanton and wholesale destruction of the lives of non-combatants, men, women, and children, engaged in pursuits which have always, even in the darkest periods of modern history, been deemed innocent and legitimate. Property can be paid for; the lives of peaceful and innocent people cannot be. The present German submarine warfare against commerce is a warfare against mankind. . . .

We are accepting this challenge of hostile purpose because we know that in such a Government [Germany], following such methods, we can never have a friend; and that in the presence of its organized power, always lying in wait to accomplish we know not what purpose, there can be no assured security for the democratic Governments of the world. . . . We are glad, now that we see the facts with no veil of false pretense about them, to fight thus for the ultimate peace of the world and for the liberation of its peoples, the German people included: for the rights of nations great and small and the privilege of men everywhere to choose their way of life and of obedience. The world must be made safe for democracy. Its peace must be planted upon the tested foundations of political liberty. We have no selfish ends to serve. We desire no conquest, no domination.

2 Senator William E. Borah, progressive Republican from Idaho, spoke in the Senate on April 4, 1917.

There can, to my mind, be only one sufficient reason for committing this country to war, and that is the honor and security of our own people and our own Nation. . . . I join no crusade; I seek or accept no alliances; I obligate this Government to no other power. I make war alone for my countrymen and their rights, for my country and its honor.

3 Senator Robert M. La Follette, progressive Republican from Wisconsin, spoke in the Senate on April 4, 1917.

I had supposed until recently that it was the duty of Senators and Representatives in Congress to vote and act according to their convictions on all public matters that came before them. . . . Another doctrine has recently been promulgated by certain newspapers . . . and that is the doctrine of "standing behind the President," without inquiring whether the President is right or wrong. . . . [President Wilson] says that this is a war "for the things which we have always carried nearest to our hearts—for democracy, for the right of those who submit to authority to have a voice in their own government." . . . [But] the President has not suggested that we make our support of Great Britain conditional to her granting home rule to Ireland, or Egypt, or India. . . .

Will the President and the supporters of this war bill submit it to a vote of the people before the declaration of war goes into effect? Until we are willing to do that, it illy becomes us to offer as an excuse for our entry into the war the unsupported claim that this war was forced upon the German people by their Government. . . . Who has registered the knowledge or approval of the American people of the course this Congress is called upon to take in declaring war upon Germany? Submit the question to the people, you who support it. You who support it dare not do it, for you know that by a vote of more than ten to one the American people as a body would register their declaration against it.

4 Senator George W. Norris, progressive Republican from Nebraska, spoke in the Senate on April 4, 1917.

There are a great many American citizens who feel that we owe it as a duty to humanity to take part in this war. . . . I think such people err in judgment and to a great extent have been misled as to the real history and the true facts by the almost unanimous demand of the great combination of wealth that has a direct financial interest in our participation in the war.

We are taking a step to-day that is fraught with untold danger. We are going into war upon the command of gold. . . . By our act we will make millions of our countrymen suffer, and the consequences of it may well be that millions of our brethren must shed their lifeblood, millions of broken-hearted women must weep, millions of children must suffer with cold, and millions of babes must die from hunger, and all because we want to preserve the commercial right of American citizens to deliver munitions of war to belligerent nations. . . . I feel as though we are about to put the dollar sign upon the American flag. . . .

The troubles of Europe ought to be settled by Europe. . . . [Declaring war will take] America into entanglements that will not end with this war but will live and bring their evil influence upon many generations yet unborn.

IMPROVED HIGHWAYS AND MAJOR CITIES, 1920–1930 During the 1920s, as many Americans became automobile owners, they quickly called for more and better highways. This map shows highway expansion during that decade. The nation also became increasingly urban during the 1920s. This map locates the largest cities.

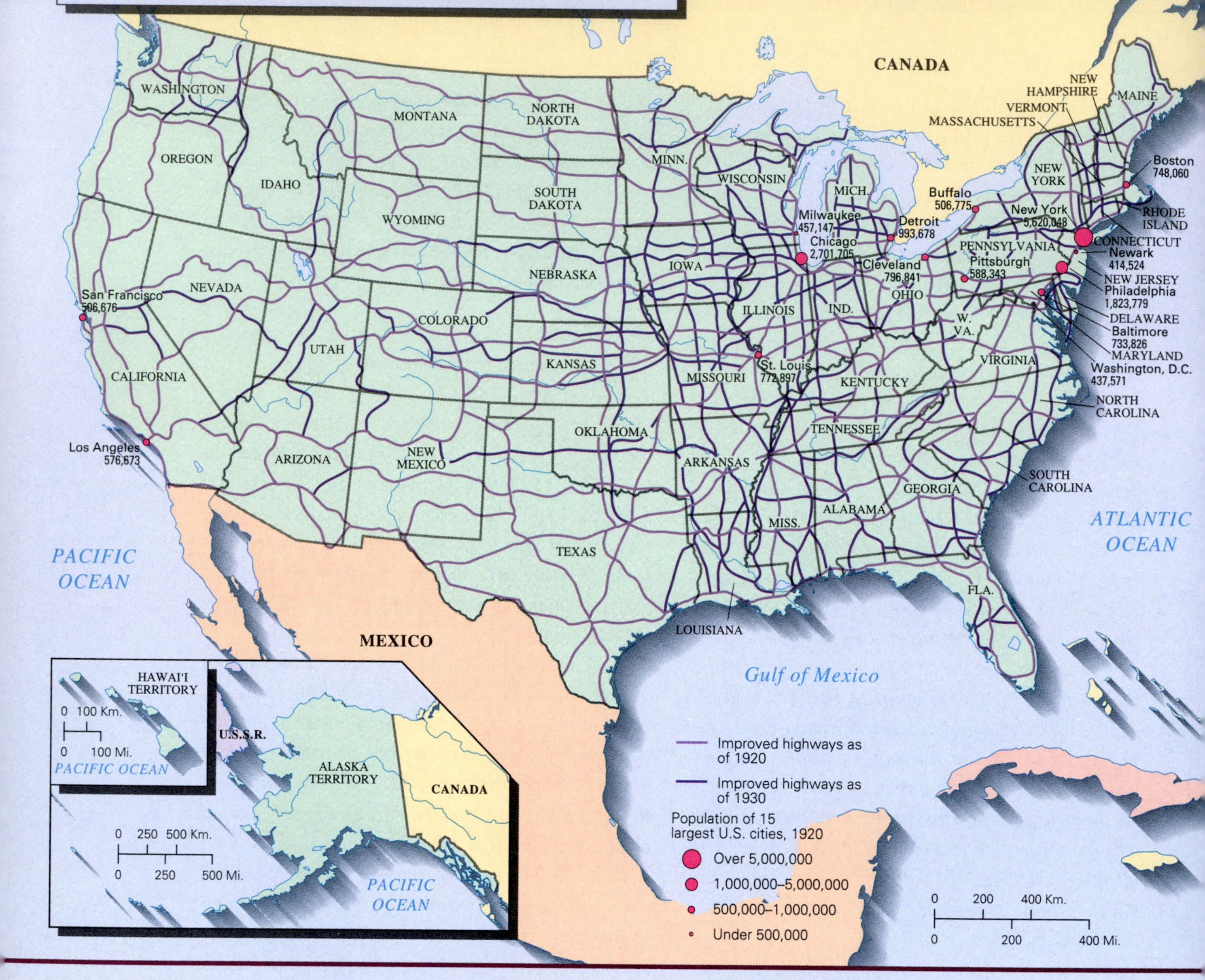
CANADA
WASHINGTON
OREGON
IDAHO
MONTANA
NORTH DAKOTA
SOUTH DAKOTA
WYOMING
NEBRASKA
MINN.
WISCONSIN
MICH.
IOWA
ILLINOIS
IND.
OHIO
NEVADA
UTAH
COLORADO
KANSAS
MISSOURI
KENTUCKY
CALIFORNIA
ARIZONA
NEW MEXICO
OKLAHOMA
TEXAS
ARKANSAS
TENNESSEE
MISS.
ALABAMA
GEORGIA
LOUISIANA
FLA.
NEW HAMPSHIRE
VERMONT
MAINE
MASSACHUSETTS
NEW YORK
PENNSYLVANIA
W. VA.
VIRGINIA
NORTH CAROLINA
SOUTH CAROLINA
RHODE ISLAND
CONNECTICUT
NEW JERSEY
DELAWARE
MARYLAND
Boston 748,060
Buffalo 506,775
New York 5,620,048
Newark 414,524
Philadelphia 1,823,779
Baltimore 733,826
Washington, D.C. 437,571
Pittsburgh 588,343
Cleveland 796,841
Detroit 993,678
Milwaukee 457,147
Chicago 2,701,705
St. Louis 772,897
San Francisco 506,676
Los Angeles 576,673
PACIFIC OCEAN
ATLANTIC OCEAN
Gulf of Mexico
MEXICO
HAWAI'I TERRITORY
0 100 Km.
0 100 Mi.
PACIFIC OCEAN
U.S.S.R.
ALASKA TERRITORY
CANADA
0 250 500 Km.
0 250 500 Mi.
PACIFIC OCEAN
Improved highways as of 1920
Improved highways as of 1930
Population of 15 largest U.S. cities, 1920
Over 5,000,000
1,000,000–5,000,000
500,000–1,000,000
Under 500,000
0 200 400 Km.
0 200 400 Mi.

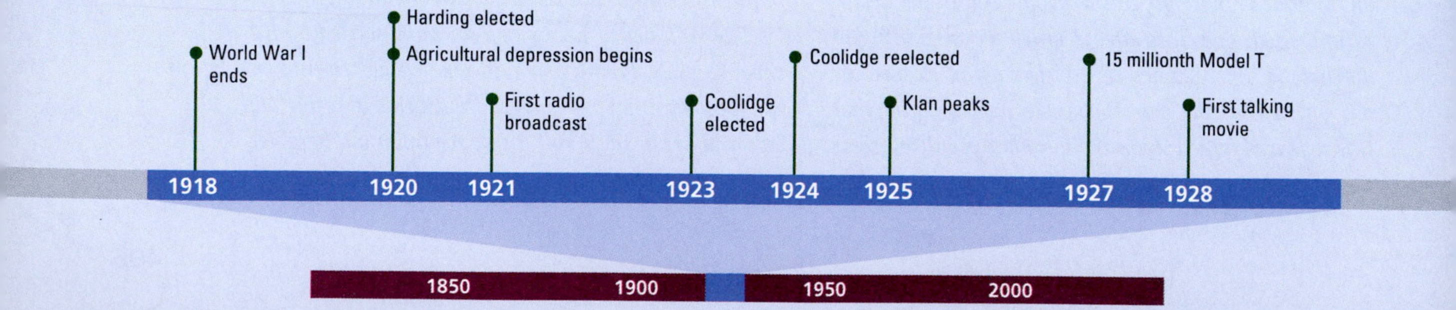
World War I ends
1918
Harding elected
Agricultural depression begins
1920
First radio broadcast
1921
Coolidge elected
1923
Coolidge reelected
1924
Klan peaks
1925
15 millionth Model T
1927
First talking movie
1928
1850
1900
1950
2000

CHAPTER 23

The 1920s, 1920–1928

The Prosperity Decade

- What new economic choices opened for consumers during the 1920s? What new choices opened for business?
- What constraints did farmers face?

The "Roaring Twenties"

- What new expectations and choices shaped American society in the 1920s?
- How did they reflect or contribute to the important social changes of the period?

Traditional America Roars Back

- How did some Americans try to restore traditional social expectations and values during the 1920s?
- What were the outcomes of their choices?

Race, Class, and Gender in the 1920s

- During the 1920s, what expectations and constraints influenced choices faced by American Indians, Mexicans, working people, women, and homosexuals?
- What were the outcomes of their choices?

The Politics of Prosperity

- What were the expectations of the Republican administrations of the 1920s?
- What were their resulting policy choices?

INTRODUCTION

Called the "Jazz Age" and the "Roaring Twenties," the decade of the 1920s sometimes seems to be a swirl of conflicting images. Prohibition attempted to control Americans' drinking habits at the same time the flapper was flaunting the liberation of women from previous *constraints.* The booming stock market promised prosperity to all with money to invest at the same time that thousands of farmers were abandoning the land because they could not survive financially. Business leaders celebrated the expansion of the economy at the same time many wage earners in manufacturing endured the destruction of their unions and their legal protections. White-sheeted armies of the Ku Klux Klan marched as self-proclaimed defenders of Protestant American values and white supremacy at the same time African Americans were creating impressive art, literature, and music. The values of big business reigned supreme in politics at the same time the economy was lurching toward a collapse that few anticipated.

In the 1920s, business turned as never before to focus on the consumer. Americans suddenly found themselves facing a range of consumer *choices* beyond all previous *expectations,* as they were deluged with new products such as automobiles, radios, and electric household appliances of every description. Americans began to purchase on credit as installment-plan buying swept the nation, shattering old *constraints* about paying cash and avoiding debt. By the mid-1920s, it seemed as though much of the nation had *chosen* to borrow money and go on an extended buying binge.

Not everyone shared in the *expectations* bred by the consumer culture of postwar America. The poorest farmers and wage earners were *constrained* from doing so by their economic situations. Some others *chose* not to. Disillusioned with the "war to end war" and scornful of the widespread infatuation with consumer buying, many intellectuals became alienated from American culture. Some *chose* to move to Europe to escape what they saw as the emptiness of American life. For them, modern America had become a spiritual and cultural wasteland.

Expectations
Constraints
Choices
Outcomes

Few other Americans shared the gloom of such intellectuals. For most, the 1920s were a time of glittering *expectations.* Many revealed an unfettered optimism as they picked out their new radio or signed papers to buy a new automobile on the installment plan. For them, the immediate *outcome*—new car, new radio, new styles—seemed to fulfill the rosy *expectations* bred by advertising.

This optimism fed into an expansive popular culture that seemed to reflect a nationwide "age of excess." Radio and movies popularized nationwide tastes, trends, and "heroes" as never before. Led primarily by youths of white, middle-class background, many young people *chose* to flaunt behavior that defied the values of their parents' generation.

Like the shiny new roadsters that filled the advertising in popular magazines, the economy roared along at high speed, fueled by easy credit and consumer spending, virtually unregulated. It carried most Americans with it—until the economic engine sputtered and seemed to die in 1929.

CHRONOLOGY

America in the 1920s

1908 Ford introduces Model T
General Motors formed

1914 Universal Negro Improvement Association founded
War breaks out in Europe

1915 Ku Klux Klan revived

1917 United States enters World War I

1918 World War I ends

1920 Eighteenth Amendment (Prohibition) takes effect
Nineteenth Amendment grants women the vote
Sinclair Lewis's *Main Street*
Harding elected president

1920–1921 Nationwide recession
Agricultural depression begins

1921 Temporary immigration quotas
First commercial radio broadcasts
Bad breath sells Listerine
Farm Bloc formed

1922 Sinclair Lewis's *Babbitt*
T. S. Eliot's *The Waste Land*

1923 Harding dies; Coolidge becomes president
Marcus Garvey convicted of mail fraud
Jean Toomer's *Cane*
American Indian Defense Association formed

1923–1925 Harding administration scandals revealed

1924 National Origins Act
Coolidge elected president
Wheaties marketed as "Breakfast of Champions"
Crossword puzzle fad
Full citizenship for American Indians

1925 Scopes trial
F. Scott Fitzgerald's *The Great Gatsby*
Ku Klux Klan claims 5 million members
Klan leader convicted of murder
One automobile for every three residents in Los Angeles
Chrysler Corporation formed

1926 Railway Labor Act
Florida real-estate boom collapses
Ernest Hemingway's *The Sun Also Rises*

1927 Coolidge vetoes McNary-Haugen bill
Charles Lindbergh's transatlantic flight
15 millionth Model T sold
Duke Ellington conducts jazz at Cotton Club

1928 Coolidge vetoes McNary-Haugen again
Confederacion de Uniones Obreras Mexicanas formed
Ford introduces Model A

1931 Frederick Lewis Allen's *Only Yesterday*
Al Capone convicted and imprisoned

The Prosperity Decade

After World War I ended in 1918, the economy completed an important shift toward consumer goods. Previously, U.S. manufacturing efforts had been dominated by railroads, steel, and heavy-equipment manufacturing, few of which made products for sale to the average consumer. During the 1920s, though, the rise of the automobile industry dramatized the new prominence of **consumer-goods** industries.

The Economics of Prosperity

The 1920s was a prosperous decade for most Americans. Although the economy experienced a sharp recession in 1920–1921, it quickly rebounded. By 1923, unemployment had fallen to 2 percent and remained under 5 percent for the rest of the decade. Manufacturing workers saw their average weekly paycheck grow from $21 in 1922 to $25 in 1929 (see Figure 23.1). Increased productivity meant that prices for most manufactured goods remained stable or even went down. Declining prices for agricultural products brought lower food and clothing prices. Thus many Americans seemed better off by 1929 than in 1920: they earned about the same, and they paid somewhat less for necessities.

Advertisers encouraged Americans to spend their money on more than just necessities. In 1931, journalist Frederick Lewis Allen noted in *Only Yesterday,* a perceptive history of the 1920s, that "business had learned as never before the immense importance to it of the ultimate consumer." Persuading Americans to consume an array of products became crucial to keeping the economy healthy.

The marketing of Listerine demonstrates the rising importance of advertising. Listerine had been devised as a general antiseptic, but in 1921 Gerard Lambert devised a more persuasive approach. Through aggressive advertising, he fostered anxieties about the impact of bad breath on popularity and made millions by selling Listerine to combat the offensive condition. In 1924, General Mills first advertised Wheaties as the "Breakfast of Champions," thereby tying the consumption of cold cereal to success in sports. Americans responded by buying those products and others with similarly creative pitches. "We grew up founding our dreams on the infinite promises of American advertising," wrote Zelda Fitzgerald, wife of F. Scott Fitzgerald.

Changes in fashion also encouraged increased consumption. The popularity of short hairstyles for women, for example, led to the development of hair salons. Cigarette advertisers began to target women. The American Tobacco Company advised women to "Reach for a Lucky instead of a sweet" to attain a slim figure. Technological advances also contributed to the growth of consumer-oriented manufacturing. In 1920, about one-third of all residences had electricity. By 1929, electrical power had reached most urban homes. Advertisers began to stress the time and labor that housewives could save by using vacuum cleaners, washing machines, irons, and toasters. Between 1919 and 1929, consumer expenditures for household appliances grew by more than 120 percent.

This increased consumption contributed to a change in people's spending habits. Before the war, most urban families paid cash for what they bought. But many consumers in the 1920s listened to the advice of retailers: "Buy now, pay later." By the late 1920s, about 15 percent of all retail purchases came through the installment plan. Charge accounts in department stores also became popular.

The Automobile: Driving the Economy

The automobile more than any other single product epitomized the consumer-oriented economy of the 1920s. Automobiles remained a luxury item until **Henry Ford** developed a mass-production system that drove down costs. Other companies jostled with Ford for the patronage of American car buyers. By the late 1920s, America's roadways sported nearly one automobile for every five people.

consumer goods Products such as food and clothing that directly satisfy human wants.

Henry Ford Inventor and manufacturer who founded the Ford Motor Company in 1903 and pioneered mass production in the auto industry.

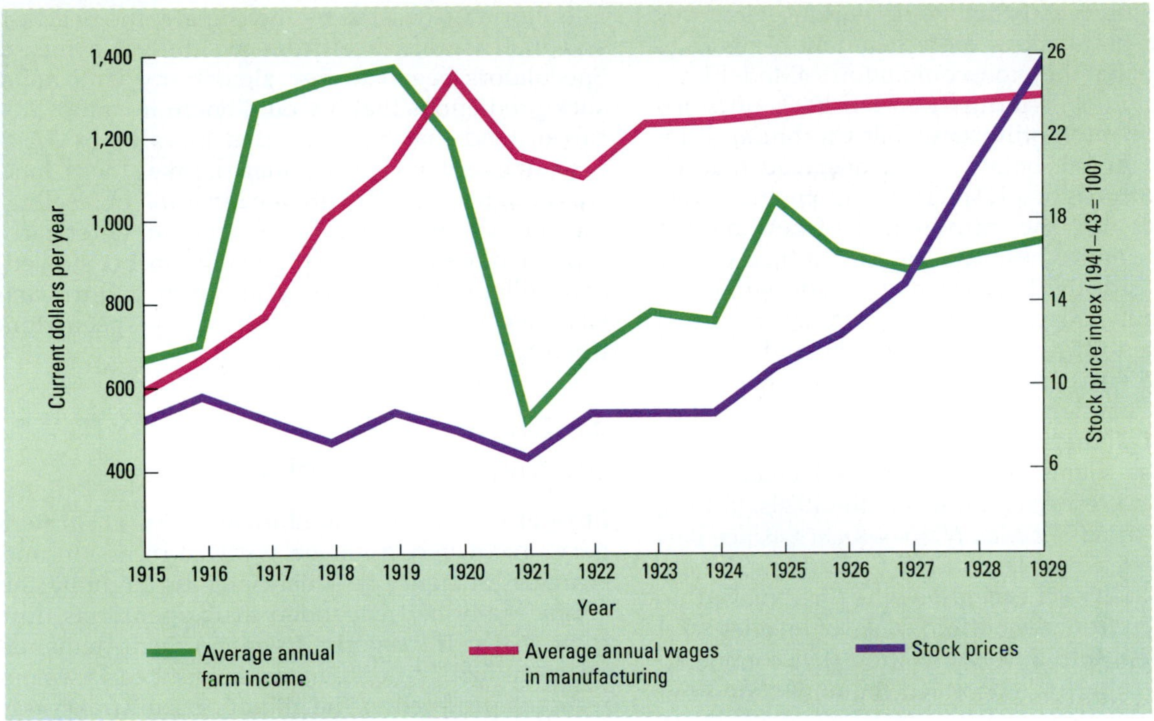

♦ **FIGURE 23.1 Economic Indicators, 1915–1929** This figure presents three measures of economic activity for the period covering World War I and the 1920s. Farm income and wages should be read on the left-hand scale; stock prices should be read on the right-hand scale. *Note:* Incomes are in current dollars, not adjusted for changes in purchasing power. *Source:* U.S. Department of Commerce, Bureau of the Census, *Historical Statistics of the United States, Colonial Times to 1970,* Bicentennial Edition, 2 vols. (Washington, D.C.: U.S. Government Printing Office, 1975), I: 483, 170; II: 1004.

Ford built his success on the **Model T,** introduced in 1908. By 1927, Ford had produced more than 15 million of them, dominating the market by selling at the lowest possible prices. "Get the prices down to the buying power," Ford ordered. His dictatorial management, technological advances, and high worker productivity brought the price of a new Model T as low as $290 by 1927. Cheap to buy and maintain, the Model T made Henry Ford into a wealthy folk hero.

Competition helped keep prices low for middle-class automobile purchasers. General Motors (GM), established in 1908, and Chrysler Corporation, founded in 1925, adopted some of Ford's techniques but also emphasized comfort and style, both missing in the purely functional Model T. Ford finally ended production of the Model T in 1927 and introduced the more stylish Model A the next year.

Ford's company also illustrates how efforts to reduce labor costs by improving labor efficiency caused work on Ford's assembly line to become a thoroughly **dehumanizing** experience. He prohibited his workers from talking, sitting, smoking,

Model T Lightweight automobile produced by Ford from 1908 to 1927 and sold at the lowest possible price, on the theory that an affordable car would be more profitable than an expensive one.

dehumanizing That which deprives of human qualities, such as individuality, by rendering a task mechanical and routine.

singing, or even whistling while working. However, Ford paid his workers more than any of his competitors so that they, too, could afford a Model T.

The automobile industry in the 1920s often led the way in promoting new sales techniques. Installment buying became so widespread that, by 1927, two-thirds of all American automobiles were sold on credit. The introduction of new models every year enticed owners to trade in their cars to keep up with the latest fashions in design, color, and options. Dozens of small automakers closed down when they could not compete with the low prices and yearly models offered by the Big Three. By 1929, Chrysler, Ford, and GM manufactured 83 percent of all the cars in the country.

Business giants like Henry Ford emerged as popular and respected figures in the 1920s. In 1925, in a book titled *The Man Nobody Knows*, Bruce Barton suggested that Jesus Christ could best be understood as a chief executive who "had picked up twelve men from the bottom ranks of business and forged them into an organization that conquered the world." Barton's book led the nonfiction best-seller lists for two years.

"Get Rich Quick": The Speculative Mania

The stock market captured people's fancy in the 1920s as a certain route to riches. Speculation—buying a stock and expecting to make money by selling it at a higher price—ran rampant. Magazine articles proclaimed that everyone could get rich in no time. By 1929, some 4 million Americans, or about 10 percent of American households, owned stock.

Driven partly by real economic growth and partly by speculation, stock prices rose higher and higher. Standard and Poor's index of common stock prices tripled between 1920 and 1929. As long as prices kept going up, it seemed that prosperity would never end.

Although the stock market held the nation's attention as the most popular path to instant riches, other speculative opportunities abounded. One of the most prominent was the Florida land boom. The mania was fed by rapid growth in the population of Florida, especially Miami. People poured into Florida, attracted by the climate, the beaches, and the ease of travel from the chilly Northeast. Speculators began to buy almost any land amid slick predictions that it would boom in value. Stories of land that had increased in value by 1,500 percent over ten years circulated. Like stocks, land was bought on credit with the intention of reselling it at a quick profit. The boom began to falter early in 1926, however, as the population influx slowed, and collapsed later that year when a hurricane slammed into Miami. By 1927, many speculators faced bankruptcy.

Agriculture: Depression in the Midst of Prosperity

Prosperity never extended to agriculture. Farmers never recovered from the postwar recession and struggled to survive financially throughout the 1920s. Many had expanded their operations during the war in response to government demands for more food. After the war, as European farmers resumed production, the glut of agricultural goods on world markets caused prices to fall. Exports of farm products tumbled by half within a few years of the end of the war.

Prices fell as a consequence of this **overproduction.** When adjusted for inflation, corn and wheat prices never rebounded to their prewar levels. The average farm's net income for the years 1917 to 1920 had ranged between $1,196 and $1,395 per year. This fell to a dreadful $517 in 1921, then slowly began to rise. But farm prices did not reach 1917 levels until World War II.

Throughout the 1920s, farmers pressed the government for help. In 1921, the bipartisan congressional **Farm Bloc** formed to promote legislation to assist farmers. Congress passed a few assistance measures in the early 1920s, but none addressed the central problems of overproduction and low prices. In the mid-1920s, proposals to tackle these

overproduction Production that exceeds consumer need or demand.

Farm Bloc Bipartisan group of senators and representatives formed in 1921 to promote legislation to assist farmers.

two key issues invariably met with presidential vetoes. The average farmer saw the value of his land fall by more than half between 1920 and 1928. Hundreds of thousands of people left farms each year in the 1920s. The prosperity decade did not include rural America.

The "Roaring Twenties"

"The world broke in two in 1922 or thereabouts," wrote novelist Willa Cather. She disliked much that came after. F. Scott Fitzgerald, another novelist, agreed with the date but embraced the change. He thought 1922 initiated an "age of miracles" and an "age of art." For most Americans, evidence of sudden and dramatic social change was on all sides, from automobiles, radios, and movies to a new youth culture and an impressive cultural outpouring by African Americans.

The Automobile and American Life

During the 1920s, the automobile profoundly changed American patterns of living. Highways significantly shortened the travel time from cities to rural areas, thereby reducing the isolation of farm life. One farm woman, when asked why her family had an automobile but not indoor plumbing, responded, "Why, you can't go to town in a bathtub." Trucks allowed farmers to take more products to market more quickly and conveniently than ever before. The spread of gasoline-powered farm vehicles also reduced the need for human farm labor and so stimulated migration to urban areas.

If the automobile changed rural life, it had an even more profound impact on life in the cities. Cities continued to grow. The 1920 census recorded more Americans living in urban areas than in rural ones for the first time. The automobile freed suburban developments from their dependence on commuter rail lines. Suburbs mushroomed, sprouting single-family houses. From 1922 through 1928, construction began on an average of 883,000 new homes each year. New home construction rivaled the auto as a driving force behind economic growth.

A look at Los Angeles shows the automobile's pervasive impact on urban life. From 1920 to 1930 the population of Los Angeles County more than doubled, from fewer than 1 million to 2.2 million. Los Angeles became the first large city organized around the auto. By 1925, Los Angeles counted one automobile for every three residents, twice the national average. The auto made it possible for residents to live farther from work than ever before. In the 1920s, Los Angeles developed the lowest urban population density in the United States. By 1930, about 94 percent of all residences in Los Angeles were single-family homes, an unprecedented figure. The first modern supermarket appeared in Los Angeles. So did the first large shopping district designed for the automobile. Los Angeles set the precedent for organizing life around the automobile.

By the late 1920s, the automobile had also begun to demonstrate its ability to strangle urban traffic. Detroit introduced the first traffic lights in 1920. Although they spread rapidly to other large cities, traffic congestion worsened. By 1926, cars in Manhattan's rush hour crawled along at less than three miles an hour—slower than a person could walk.

A Homogenized Culture Searches for Heroes

As the automobile cut travel times, restrictive immigration laws were closing the door to immigrants. These factors, together with the new technologies of radio and film, began to **homogenize** the culture by breaking down cultural differences based on region or ethnicity.

In 1921, the first commercial radio broadcasting station opened. Within six years, 681 were operating. By 1930, 40 percent of all households had radio sets. Movie attendance increased rapidly as well, from a weekly average of 40 million people in 1922 to 80 million in 1929. The equivalent of two-thirds of the nation went to the cinema every week. As Americans across the country tuned into the

homogenize To make something uniform throughout.

same radio broadcast and families laughed or wept at the same movie, radio and film did their part in homogenizing American life, particularly in urban areas.

Radio and film joined newspapers and magazines in prompting national trends, fashions, and fads. In 1923, the opening of the fabulous tomb of the Egyptian pharaoh Tutankhamen led to a passion for things Egyptian. Crossword puzzles captured the attention of many Americans in 1924. Such fads, in turn, created markets for new consumer goods, from Egyptian-style furniture to crossword dictionaries.

The media also contributed to the development of national sports heroes. By the 1920s, as Frederick Lewis Allen observed, sports "had become an American obsession." Radio now began to broadcast baseball games nationwide. Boxing and college football vied with baseball for spectators' dollars. Most Americans were familiar with the exploits of such baseball greats as Lou Gehrig, Ty Cobb, and Babe Ruth, as well as boxers like Jack Dempsey and Gene Tunney and golfers like Bobby Jones.

The rapid spread of movie theaters created a new category of fame: the movie star. Charlie Chaplin, Buster Keaton, Harold Lloyd, and others brought laughter to the screen. Tom Mix was the best-known cowboy of the silver screen. Sex made stars of Theda Bara, the **vamp,** and Clara Bow, the "It Girl," whose publicists not only said she had "it" but also insisted that no one had to ask what "it" was. Rudolph Valentino soared to fame as a male sex symbol in *The Sheik.* Several women committed suicide after Valentino's death in 1926. "Valentino had silently acted out the fantasies of women all over the world," claimed screen star Bette Davis.

The greatest popular hero of the 1920s, however, was neither an athlete nor an actor but a small-town airmail pilot named **Charles Lindbergh.** In 1927, Lindbergh decided to collect the prize of $25,000 offered to the pilot of the first successful nonstop flight between New York and Paris. Flying *The Spirit of St. Louis* for 33½ sleepless hours, Lindbergh earned the $25,000 and the adoration of crowds on both sides of the Atlantic. His accomplishment seemed to proclaim that old-fashioned individualism, courage, and self-reliance could still triumph over adversity.

Alienated Intellectuals

Other Americans went to Paris in the 1920s, but for a different reason. They left to escape what they considered America's dull conventionalism and dangerous materialism. Whether they left for Paris or not, many American writers bemoaned what they saw as the shallowness, greed, and homogenization of American life. **Sinclair Lewis** in *Main Street* (1920) and *Babbitt* (1922) presented small-town, middle-class existence as not just boring but stifling. The title character, George F. Babbitt, is Lewis's version of a typical, narrow-minded suburban businessman who speaks in clichés and buys every gadget on the market. **H. L. Mencken,** the influential editor of the *American Mercury,* relentlessly pilloried the "booboisie," jeered at all politicians, and celebrated only those writers who shared his distaste for most of American life.

Other writers also rejected traditional values in their disillusionment with postwar society and search for self. Edna St. Vincent Millay captured the spirit of rebellion and pleasure seeking in 1920:

My candle burns at both ends;
It will not last the night;
But ah, my foes, and oh, my friends—
It gives a lovely light!

F. Scott Fitzgerald, in *The Great Gatsby* (1925), revealed the dark side of the hedonism of the 1920s, as he portrayed the pointless lives of wealthy pleasure seekers. Ernest Hemingway, in *The Sun Also Rises* (1926), depicted jaded and disillusioned

vamp A woman who uses her sexuality to entrap and exploit men.

Charles Lindbergh American aviator who made the first solo transatlantic flight in 1927 and became an international hero.

Sinclair Lewis Novelist who satirized middle-class America in works such as *Babbitt* (1922) and who became the first American to win a Nobel Prize for literature.

H. L. Mencken Editor and critic who founded the *American Mercury* and who wrote essays of scathing social criticism.

F. Scott Fitzgerald Fiction writer who captured the Jazz Age in novels such as *The Great Gatsby* (1925).

expatriates who go to Spain to see the bullfights in an effort to introduce some excitement into their lives. The novel's dominant tone is one of frustration, futility, and suffering.

Others took the theme of hopelessness even further. **T. S. Eliot,** a poet who had fled America for England in 1915, published *The Waste Land* in 1922, in which he presented a grim view of the barrenness of modern life, where a search for meaning yielded "the empty chapel, only the wind's home." Some writers predicted the end of Western civilization. Joseph Wood Krutch in 1929 concluded that modern civilization was so decadent that it could not rejuvenate itself and would be overthrown by barbarians.

Renaissance Among African Americans

Krutch's fear of the imminent end of Western civilization was limited largely to white intellectuals. Such views were little reflected in the striking outpouring of literature, music, and art by African Americans in the 1920s.

Harlem, a predominantly black neighborhood in New York City, quickly became a symbol of the new, urban life of African Americans. The term **Harlem Renaissance** describes a literary and artistic movement in which black artists and writers insisted on the value of black culture and used African and African-American traditions in literature, painting, and sculpture. Pointing to this renaissance in 1925, the black writer Alain Locke argued that African Americans were "achieving something like a spiritual emancipation" and that henceforth the nation "must reckon with a fundamentally changed Negro." Black actors, notably Paul Robeson (see page 612), began to appear in serious theaters and earn acclaim for their abilities.

Among the movement's poets, **Langston Hughes** became the best known. His poetry rang with the voice of the people, as he sometimes used folk language to convey powerful images (see Individual Choices: Langston Hughes). Zora Neale Hurston began her long writing career with several short stories in the 1920s. Jean Toomer's novel *Cane* (1923) has been praised as "the most impressive product of the Negro Renaissance." In it, Toomer combined poetry and prose to produce sketches and short stories dealing with African Americans in rural Georgia and Washington, D.C.

The Renaissance included **jazz,** which was becoming a central element in distinctly American music. Created and nurtured by African-American musicians in southern cities, especially New Orleans, jazz had been introduced to northern and white audiences by World War I. It became so popular that the 1920s have been called the Jazz Age. Jazz also began to influence leading white composers, notably George Gershwin, whose *Rhapsody in Blue* (1924) brought jazz into the symphony halls. Some attacked the new sound, claiming it encouraged people to abandon their self-restraint, especially with regard to sex. Despite such condemnation, the wail of the saxophone became an integral part of the 1920s.

Louis "Satchmo" Armstrong emerged as the leading jazz trumpeter. Bessie Smith, the "Empress of the Blues," was the outstanding vocalist of the decade. The great black jazz musicians drew white audiences into black neighborhoods to hear them. As increasing numbers of whites went "slumming" to Harlem, the area came to be associated with exotic nightlife and glittering jazz clubs such as the Cotton Club. Edward Kennedy "Duke" Ellington went there in 1927 and began to develop the works that made him a respected composer.

expatriate A person who has taken up residence in a foreign country or renounced his or her native land.

T. S. Eliot American poet who settled in England and whose long poem *The Waste Land* (1922) chronicles the barrenness of modern life.

Harlem Renaissance Literary and artistic movement in the 1920s centered in Harlem, in which black writers and artists described and celebrated African-American life.

Langston Hughes Poet of the Harlem Renaissance whose work, inspired by the rhythms of jazz and the blues, dealt with the joys and sorrows of African Americans.

jazz Style of music developed in America in the early twentieth century, characterized by strong, flexible rhythms and improvisation on basic melodies.

INDIVIDUAL CHOICES

Choosing to Live in Harlem

Langston Hughes

Langston Hughes, an acclaimed author, chose to celebrate black people in his writing and to develop opportunities for other black artists to cultivate their creativity. This portrait by Winold Reiss was made in 1925, when Hughes, in his early twenties, was already a significant figure in the Harlem Renaissance. National Portrait Gallery, Smithsonian Institution/Art Resource, NY.

In the late 1940s, Langston Hughes bought a house on East 127th Street in central Harlem. He could have afforded a house in a wealthy suburb if he had wished, but he chose Harlem. It symbolized other choices he had made throughout his writing career, for he chose to write for and about African Americans.

Born in Joplin, Missouri, in 1902, he lived for a time with his grandmother Mary Langston, from whom he learned lessons in social justice. He began to write poetry in high school, briefly attended college, then chose to work and travel in Africa and Europe. He continued writing poetry, some of which won prizes from African-American journals.

Hughes had become a significant figure in the Harlem Renaissance by 1925, sometimes reading his poetry to the musical accompaniment of jazz or the blues. Some of his work then presented images from black history, like "The Negro Speaks of Rivers" (1921). Other works, like "Song for a Dark Girl" (1927), vividly depicted the constraints of racism.

Way Down South in Dixie
(Break the heart of me)
They hung my black young lover
To a cross roads tree.

The sparkle of the Cotton Club was remote from the experience of most African Americans. But one Harlem leader affected black people throughout the country and beyond. **Marcus Garvey,** born in Jamaica, advocated a form of **black separatism.** His organization, the Universal Negro Improvement Association (UNIA), founded in 1914,

Marcus Garvey Jamaican black nationalist active in America in the 1920s.

black separatism Doctrine of cultural separation of blacks from white society.

Way Down South in Dixie
(Bruised body high in air)
I asked the white Lord Jesus
What was the use of prayer.

Way Down South in Dixie
(Break the heart of me)
Love is a naked shadow
On a gnarled and naked tree.

Other poems looked to the future with an expectation for change and for new choices, as in "I, Too" (1925).

I, too, sing America.

I am the darker brother.
They send me
To eat in the kitchen
When company comes,
But I laugh,
And eat well,
And grow strong.

Tomorrow
I'll sit at the table
When company comes.
Nobody'll dare
Say to me,
"Eat in the kitchen,"
Then.
Besides
They'll see
How beautiful I am
And be ashamed.

I, too, am America.

In the early 1930s, as the Harlem Renaissance waned and the Depression deepened, Hughes, like other American intellectuals, turned to socialism. He traveled again and began writing short stories and plays. Few theaters at that time would stage works by or about African Americans, and few hired African-American actors. Hughes, therefore, chose to use his prestige and his time to create black theater companies in Harlem, Los Angeles, and Chicago.

Hughes's writings poured forth in a near-torrential stream. By the end of his life, in 1967, he had produced ten volumes of poetry; sixty-six short stories; some twenty plays, musicals, and operas; two autobiographical volumes; more than a hundred published essays, both serious and humorous; and several novels, histories, and children's books. The outcome of Hughes's devotion to writing and his choice to focus on the African-American experience was that he established a prominent place for himself among American authors of his time. Also, and perhaps more significant, he helped define the Harlem Renaissance, and he greatly encouraged the development of African-American poetry, fiction, drama, and other writing.

stressed racial pride and solidarity across national boundaries. Garvey argued that whites would always be racist. Therefore blacks from around the world needed to assist Africans in overthrowing colonial rule and building a strong African state. Garvey established a steamship company, the **Black Star Line,** which he hoped would carry

Black Star Line Steamship company founded by Marcus Garvey to carry blacks to Africa; Garvey was convicted of mail fraud in connection with its finances and imprisoned in 1923.

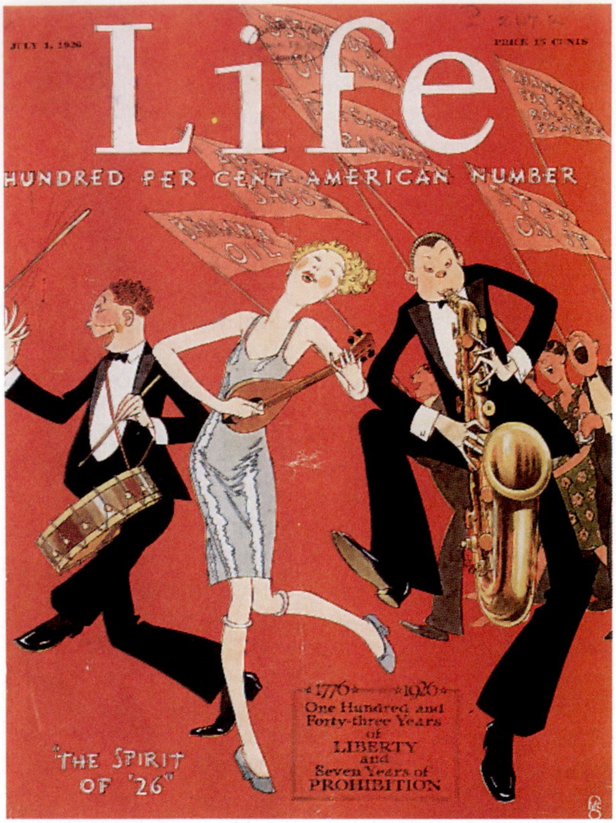

♦ On the one hundred fiftieth anniversary of the Declaration of Independence, *Life* presented this cover parodying the famous painting *The Spirit of '76* by depicting *"The Spirit of '26"*—an uninhibited flapper, a jazz saxophonist and drummer, and banners with the snappy sayings of the day. The caption reads, "One Hundred and Forty-three Years of LIBERTY and Seven Years of PROHIBITION." *Harvard College Library.*

American blacks to Africa. UNIA attracted wide support among urban blacks in the United States.

Black integrationist leaders, however, condemned UNIA for its separatism. The NAACP, especially W. E. B. Du Bois, took the lead in opposing Garvey, arguing that the first task facing blacks was integration and equality in the United States. Garvey and Du Bois called each other traitors.

Federal officials eventually charged Garvey with irregularities in his fundraising for the Black Star Line, and he was convicted of mail fraud in 1923. He spent two years in jail and then was deported to his native Jamaica. Garvey continued to lead UNIA in exile, but most of the local organizations lost members and influence.

"Flaming Youth"

Although African Americans created jazz, those who danced to it, in the popular imagination of the 1920s, were white: a male college student, clad in a swank raccoon-skin coat with a hip flask of illegal liquor in his pocket, and his female counterpart, the uninhibited **flapper** with bobbed hair and a daringly short skirt. This stereotype of "flaming youth" reflected startling changes among many white, college-age youths of middle- or upper-class background.

The prosperity of the 1920s allowed many middle-class families to send their children to college. The proportion of the population ages 18 to 24 enrolled in college more than doubled between World War I and 1930. On campus, students reshaped colleges into youth centers, where football games and dances assumed as much significance as examinations and term papers.

For some college women, the changes of the 1920s seemed particularly dramatic. Young women scandalized their elders by wearing skirts that stopped at the knee, stockings rolled below the knee, short hair often dyed black, and generous amounts of rouge and lipstick. Many observers assumed that the outrageous look reflected outrageous behavior. In fact, women's sexual activity outside marriage had begun to increase before the war, especially among working-class women and radicals. In the 1920s, such changes began to affect middle-class college and high school students. About half of the women who came of age during the 1920s had intercourse before marriage, a marked increase from prewar patterns.

flapper Name given in the 1920s to a young woman with short hair and short skirts, who discarded old-fashioned standards of dress and behavior.

Such changes in behavior were often linked to the automobile. It brought greater freedom to young people, for they could go where they wanted. Sometimes they went to a **speakeasy.** Before Prohibition, few women who valued their reputations entered saloons. Prohibition, however, seemed to glamorize drinking. Now men and women went to speakeasies to drink and smoke together, and to dance to popular music derived from jazz. While some adults criticized the frivolities of the young, others emulated them.

Traditional America Roars Back

Many Americans felt threatened by the upheaval in social values that originated in the cities. Although their efforts to stop the tide of changes that threatened their way of life dated to the prewar era, several movements to preserve traditional values came to fruition in the 1920s.

Prohibition

Prohibition epitomized the cultural struggle to preserve white, old-stock Protestant values and to make immigrants whose values were judged to be quite different conform to "American" standards. Spearheaded by the Anti-Saloon League, prohibition advocates gained strength throughout the Progressive era. They convinced Congress to pass a temporary prohibition measure in 1917 to conserve grain during the war. A more important victory for the "drys" came later that year, when Congress adopted the **Eighteenth Amendment,** prohibiting the manufacture, sale, and transportation of alcoholic beverages. The amendment took effect in January 1920 after three-fourths of the state legislatures ratified it.

Many Americans simply ignored the Eighteenth Amendment from the beginning, and it grew less popular the longer it lasted. By 1926, a poll indicated that only 19 percent of Americans supported Prohibition. Nonetheless, Prohibition remained the law until 1933. Prohibition did reduce drinking and apparently drunkenness. It was most effective among those groups and in those areas that had provided its greatest support. It was never well enforced anywhere, however, and was ignored in most cities. Congress never provided enough money for more than token federal enforcement, and most city police didn't even try because of the immensity of the task. New York State admitted the impossibility of enforcing Prohibition by repealing its enforcement act in 1923.

Prohibition produced unintended consequences. It glamorized drinking. **Bootlegging** flourished. The thirst for alcohol provided criminals with a fresh and lucrative source of income. **Al Capone** and his gang took in more than $60 million from bootlegging in 1927 alone. The scar-faced Capone realized such huge gains in part by systematically eliminating the competition. Gang warfare raged in Chicago throughout the 1920s, producing some five hundred slayings. Despite Capone's undoubted role in murders, bootlegging, and other illegal activities, his extensive political influence kept him immune from local prosecution. Only in 1931 did federal officials finally convict him of income-tax evasion and send him to prison.

The gangs of Chicago had their counterparts elsewhere. Profits from bootlegging not only provided bribes to police and political officials but also led gangsters into gambling, prostitution, and **racketeering.** Through racketeering, they gained power in some labor unions. Some Americans blamed these developments on Prohibition. For other Americans, however, the gangs, killings, and corruption confirmed their long-standing distrust

speakeasy A place for the illegal sale and consumption of liquor during Prohibition.

Eighteenth Amendment Amendment to the Constitution ratified in 1919 forbidding the manufacture, sale, and transportation of alcoholic beverages.

bootlegging Illegal production, distribution, or sale of liquor.

Al Capone Italian-born American gangster who ruthlessly ruled the Chicago underworld until he was imprisoned for tax evasion in 1931.

racketeering Commission of crimes such as extortion, loansharking, bribery, and obstruction of justice in the course of illegal business activities.

of cities and immigrants, and they clung to the vision of a dry America as the best hope for renewing traditional values.

Fundamentalism and the Crusade Against Evolution

Fundamentalist Protestantism also sought to maintain traditional values. **Fundamentalism** emerged from a conflict between Christian modernism and **orthodoxy.** Where modernists tried to reconcile their religious beliefs with modern science, fundamentalists rejected anything incompatible with a literal reading of the Scriptures.

In the early 1920s, some fundamentalists focused on **evolution** as contrary to the Bible. Fundamentalists saw in evolution not just a challenge to the Bible's account of creation, but also a challenge to religion itself. William Jennings Bryan, the former Democratic presidential candidate, provided fundamentalists with their greatest champion. His energy, eloquence, and enormous following guaranteed that the issue received wide attention.

Bryan played a central role in the **Scopes trial,** the most famous dispute over evolution. In March 1925, the Tennessee legislature made it illegal for any public school teacher to teach evolution. Promised the assistance of the American Civil Liberties Union (ACLU), John T. Scopes, a young biology teacher in Dayton, Tennessee, challenged the law. Bryan volunteered to assist the local prosecutors. He claimed that the only issue was the right of the people to regulate public education in the interest of morality. But defense attorney **Clarence Darrow** insisted that he was there to prevent "bigots and ignoramuses from controlling the education of the United States."

Toward the end of the trial, Darrow called Bryan to the witness stand as an authority on the Bible. Under Darrow's withering questioning, Bryan revealed that he knew little about findings in archaeology, geology, and linguistics that cast doubt on biblical accounts. He also admitted that he did not always interpret the Bible literally. "Bryan was broken," one reporter wrote. "Darrow never spared him. It was masterful, but it was pitiful." Bryan died a few days later. Scopes was found guilty, but the Tennessee Supreme Court threw out his sentence on a technicality, preventing appeal. The Tennessee law remained on the books until 1968, although it was not enforced.

Nativism and Immigration Restriction

Since the 1890s, nativists had urged Congress to cut off immigration, but earlier efforts met with either congressional indifference or presidential vetoes. However, the disquieting presence of so many German Americans during World War I, the Red Scare, and the continued influx of poor immigrants from southern and eastern Europe after the war combined in 1921 to convince Congress to approve a temporary act limiting immigration.

The **National Origins Act** of 1924 established permanent restrictions. It limited total immigration to 150,000 people each year and established quotas for each country based on how many Americans came from that country as of 1890. The law thus attempted to freeze the nation's ethnic composition by stopping immigration from southern and eastern Europe. The law completely excluded

fundamentalism An organized, evangelical movement originating in the United States in the early twentieth century in opposition to liberalism and secularism.

orthodoxy Traditional or established doctrine of faith.

evolution The central organizing theorem of the biological sciences, which holds that organisms change over generations, mainly as a result of natural selection; it includes the concept that humans evolved from nonhuman ancestors.

Scopes trial Trial in 1925 in which a high school biology teacher was prosecuted for teaching evolution in violation of Tennessee law; it raised issues concerning the place of religion in American education.

Clarence Darrow Lawyer known for his defense of unpopular causes; his merciless cross-examination of Bryan in the Scopes trial made the argument against evolution look weak.

National Origins Act Law passed in 1924 establishing quotas that discouraged immigration from southern and eastern Europe and encouraged immigration from Scandinavia and western Europe; it also prohibited Asian immigration.

Asians but permitted unrestricted immigration from Canada and Latin America.

Nativism and discrimination flourished throughout the 1920s. In West Frankfort, Illinois, for example, rioting townspeople beat and stoned Italians in 1920 before setting their houses on fire. Nativist-inspired discrimination was more subtle. Exclusive eastern colleges placed quotas on the number of Jews admitted each year. In 1920, Henry Ford, writing in the *Dearborn Independent,* began to accuse international Jewish bankers of controlling the American economy. In 1927, Ford was forced to retract his charges and to apologize when he was sued for libel and challenged to prove his charges.

The Ku Klux Klan

Nativism, anti-Catholicism, anti-Semitism, and fear of radicalism all contributed to the spectacular growth of the Ku Klux Klan in the early 1920s. The original Klan, created during Reconstruction to intimidate former slaves, had long since died out. Formed by William Simmons, the new Klan portrayed itself as a patriotic order devoted to America, Protestant Christianity, and white supremacy.

The new Klan grew spectacularly after 1920, when local organizers were offered $4 of every $10 initiation fee. Membership grew from 5,000 in 1920 to as many as 5 million by 1925. The Klan attacked Catholics, Jews, immigrants, and blacks, along with bootleggers, corrupt politicians, and gamblers in the name of old-fashioned Protestant morality. In rural areas, the Klan's terror was sometimes carried out by **nightriders,** who roved country roads to carry out beatings, kidnappings, torture, brandings, floggings, and even murder.

The Klan was strong not only in the South but also in the Midwest, West, and Southwest. It sometimes exerted a powerful political influence, most notably in Texas, Oklahoma, Oregon, and Indiana. In Oklahoma, the Klan led a successful impeachment campaign against a governor who tried to restrict their nightriding.

Extensive corruption underlay the Klan's self-righteous rhetoric. Some Klan leaders joined primarily for the profits, both legal (from recruiting) and illegal (from political payoffs). And some lived personal lives in stark contrast to the morality they preached. In 1925, D. C. Stephenson, a prominent Klan leader, was convicted of the second-degree murder of a woman who had accused him of raping her. When the governor of Indiana refused to pardon him, Stephenson produced records that proved the corruption of the governor, a member of Congress, the mayor of Indianapolis, and other officials endorsed by the Klan. Thereafter, Klan membership fell sharply.

Race, Class, and Gender in the 1920s

For most people of color, the reality of daily life fell somewhere between the liberation experienced by those in the Harlem Renaissance and the terror felt by those who confronted Klan nightriders. For working people, the 1920s represented a time when many gains from the Progressive Era and World War I were lost. For women, the 1920s opened with a political victory in the form of suffrage, but the unity developed in support of that measure soon broke down.

Race Relations: North, South, and West

Race relations changed little during the 1920s. Terror against African Americans continued after the rioting and bloodshed of 1919. Southern legislators defeated every effort by the NAACP to secure a federal antilynching law. Discrimination and violence were not directed only at blacks. In the West and Southwest, American Indians and those of Asian and Latino descent were frequently the victims of racism.

Californians led the way in passing laws discriminating against Asian immigrants and Asian Americans. In 1920, California voters by a margin of 3 to 1 approved an initiative forbidding Asian

nightriders Bands of masked white men associated with the Ku Klux Klan who roamed rural areas at night, terrorizing and murdering blacks.

immigrants to own or lease land in the state. Some Californians even sought a constitutional amendment to remove citizenship from Asian Americans.

Beginnings of Change in Federal Indian Policy

In the early 1920s, American Indians experienced an intensification of previous assimilationist policies (see page 379). Interior Secretary Albert Fall's attempts to wrest lands along the Rio Grande from the Pueblo Indians, however, did not succeed. In fact, his schemes prompted the formation of the **American Indian Defense Association (AIDA)** in 1923. The AIDA soon emerged as the leading voice for change in federal Indian policy. Its goals were to end land allotments, to improve health and educational services on the reservations, to create tribal governments, and to gain tolerance for Indian religious ceremonies. The AIDA encouraged recognition of Indian cultures and values.

The political pressure applied by the AIDA and by Indians themselves secured several new laws favorable to American Indians. One measure, in 1924, extended full citizenship to all Indians who were still not citizens—about one-third of the total. Some had been reluctant to accept citizenship for fear of losing their tribal rights, so the law included provisions specifically protecting those rights.

Mexicans in California and the Southwest

California and the Southwest attracted growing numbers of Mexican immigrants in the 1920s. Many Mexicans went north to escape the revolution and civil war that devastated their nation from 1910 into the 1920s. Nearly one Mexican in ten may have fled to the United States between 1910 and 1930. More than half went to Texas, but by the mid-1920s, increasing numbers were arriving in California.

Population changes in southern California and south Texas followed change in the agricultural economies of those regions. In south Texas, some cattle ranches were converted to farms, especially for cotton. The 1920s also saw dramatic increases in the commercial production of fruits and vegetables. By 1925, the Southwest produced 40 percent of the nation's fruits and vegetables, crops that were highly labor-intensive. In the late 1920s, Mexicans made up 80 to 85 percent of farm laborers in southern California and south Texas. These changes in population and economy reshaped relations between Anglos and Mexicans.

In south Texas, many Anglo newcomers looked on Mexicans as a "partly colored race" and tried to import sharecropping, disfranchisement, and segregation. Disfranchisement was relatively unsuccessful, but some schools and other social institutions were segregated despite Mexican opposition.

In California, Mexican workers' efforts to organize and strike for better pay and working conditions often sparked violent opposition. In the early 1920s, strikes involving thousands of workers were broken brutally. Workers began organizing on a larger scale in 1928, with the formation of the Confederacion de Uniones Obreras Mexicanas, an umbrella group for various unions in southern California. Local authorities arrested and often beat strikers. Leaders found themselves subject to deportation. But growers adamantly opposed any proposals to restrict immigration from Mexico.

Labor on the Defensive

Difficulties in establishing unions among Mexican workers mirrored a larger failure of unions in the 1920s. When unions tried to recover lost purchasing power by striking in 1919 and 1920, they nearly all failed. After 1921, business took advantage of the conservative political climate to challenge Progressive-era legislation benefiting workers. The Supreme Court responded by limiting workers' rights, voiding laws that eliminated child labor, and striking down minimum wages for women and children.

Many companies undertook anti-union drives. Arguing that unions had become either corrupt or radical, some employers refused to recognize them. At the same time, many companies initiated an approach known as "welfare capitalism." The strat-

American Indian Defense Association Organization founded in 1923 to defend the rights of American Indians; it pushed for an end to allotment and a return to tribal government.

egy was to provide workers with benefits such as insurance, retirement pensions, cafeterias, paid vacations, and stock purchase plans. Such innovations stemmed both from genuine concern about workers' well-being and from the expectation that such improvements would increase productivity and discourage unionization.

Only the railroad unions made significant gains in the 1920s. The **Railway Labor Act** of 1926 established collective bargaining for railroads. But the gains of the railroad unions were unique. The 1920s marked the first period of prosperity since the 1830s when union membership declined. Hostile government policies, welfare capitalism, and lost strikes all contributed to this decline.

Changes in Women's Lives

The attention given to the flapper in the 1920s should not obscure other significant changes in women's gender roles during the decade. Marriage among middle-class couples came to be increasingly valued as a companionship between two partners. Although the ideal of marriage was often expressed in terms of equality, the actual responsibility for the smooth functioning of the family typically fell on the woman.

The 1920s also saw a significant decline in the birth rate. This decline reflected changing social values and the wider availability of birth-control information and devices. More women used diaphragms rather than relying on males to use condoms. Margaret Sanger, the pioneer in the birth-control movement, was able to persuade more doctors to spread birth-control information. As birth control gained the backing of male physicians, it became more respectable. Nonetheless, until 1936, federal law restricted public distribution of information about contraception.

Although the lives of many middle-class women lightened with the introduction of labor-saving devices such as vacuum cleaners, working-class women still spent long days struggling to maintain families. As before, these women often worked outside the home because the family needed the income. The proportion of women working for wages remained quite stable during the 1920s, at about one in four.

Perhaps the most publicized event in women's lives was national woman suffrage. In June 1919, Congress approved the **Nineteenth Amendment** and sent it to the states for ratification. After a grueling state-by-state battle, ratification came in August 1920.

The unity of the suffrage movement quickly disintegrated thereafter. Some suffrage activists joined the League of Women Voters, a nonpartisan group committed to social and political reform. The Congressional Union converted itself into the National Woman's party and, after 1923, focused its efforts on securing an **Equal Rights Amendment** to the Constitution. The League of Women Voters argued that such an amendment would endanger laws that provided special rights and protections for women. In the end, woman suffrage did not dramatically change either women or politics.

Development of Gay and Lesbian Subcultures

In the 1920s, gay and lesbian subcultures became more established and, in places such as New York, Chicago, New Orleans, and Baltimore, relatively open. *The Captive,* a play about lesbians, opened in New York in 1926, and some movies included unmistakable references to gays or lesbians. Novels with gay and lesbian characters circulated in the late 1920s and early 1930s. By the late 1920s, some nightclub acts included material about gays and lesbians in performances intended for largely heterosexual audiences. A relatively open black gay and lesbian community emerged in Harlem.

Railway Labor Act Law passed in 1926 that replaced the Railway Labor Board with a board of mediation only loosely connected with the federal government.

Nineteenth Amendment Amendment to the Constitution in 1920 that prohibited federal or state governments from restricting the right to vote on account of sex.

Equal Rights Amendment Constitutional amendment first proposed by the National Woman's party in 1923, giving women in the United States equal rights under the law.

As many as seven thousand revelers of all races attended the annual Hamilton Lodge drag ball in Harlem, the nation's largest gay and lesbian event.

At the same time, however, more psychiatrists and psychologists were labeling homosexuality a **perversion.** As the work of Sigmund Freud became well known, psychiatrists and psychologists came to regard homosexuality as a sexual disorder that required a cure. Thus Freud may have been a liberating influence with regard to heterosexual relations, but he proved harmful for same-sex relations.

The late 1920s and early 1930s brought increased suppression of gays and lesbians. New state laws gave police greater authority to crack down on them. In 1927, New York police raided *The Captive,* and the New York legislature banned all such plays. In 1929, Adam Clayton Powell, a leading Harlem minister, launched a highly publicized campaign against gays. Motion-picture studios instituted a morality code that prohibited any depiction of homosexuality. The end of Prohibition after 1933 allowed local authorities to use their regulatory power to close businesses with liquor licenses that tolerated gay or lesbian customers. Thus, by the late 1930s, many gays and lesbians were forced to become more secretive about their sexual identities.

The Politics of Prosperity

After 1918, the Republicans returned to the majority role they had played from the mid-1890s to 1912, and they were the unquestioned majority party throughout the 1920s. Progressivism largely disappeared, although Robert La Follette and George Norris persisted in their vigil to limit corporate power. The Republican administrations of the 1920s, however, thought that government should be the partner of business, not its regulator.

Harding's Failed Presidency

Warren G. Harding, elected in 1920, looked like a president—handsome, gray-haired, dignified—but he displayed little intellectual depth below the charming surface. For some cabinet positions, he named the most respected leaders of his party. He chose Charles Evans Hughes for secretary of state, Andrew Mellon for secretary of the treasury, and Herbert Hoover for secretary of commerce. Harding, however, was most at home in a smoke-filled room, drinking whiskey and playing poker with friends. He gave hundreds of government jobs to his cronies. They betrayed his trust and turned his administration into one of the most corrupt in American history. Harding tried to ignore their misdeeds.

The full extent of corruption became clear after Harding died in August 1923. Interior Secretary Albert Fall had accepted huge bribes from oil companies for leases on government oil reserves at Elk Hills, California, and **Teapot Dome,** Wyoming. Attorney General Harry Daugherty had accepted bribes to approve the sale of government property for less than its value. The head of the Veterans Bureau had swindled the government out of more than $200 million. In all, three cabinet members resigned, four officials went to jail, and five men committed suicide.

The Three-Way Election of 1924

Fortunately for the Republican party, the new president, Calvin Coolidge of Vermont, exemplified the honesty, virtue, and sobriety associated with New England. In 1924, Republicans quickly chose him as their candidate for president. The Democratic convention, however, sank into a long and bitter deadlock between its northern and southern wings before turning to John W. Davis, a leading corporate lawyer. The remaining progressives welcomed the independent candidacy of Senator Robert M. La Follette of Wisconsin. La Follette at-

perversion A sexual practice considered abnormal or deviant.

Teapot Dome Government-owned Wyoming oil field that Interior Secretary Albert B. Fall leased to private developers in return for a bribe, causing one of the scandals that disgraced the Harding administration.

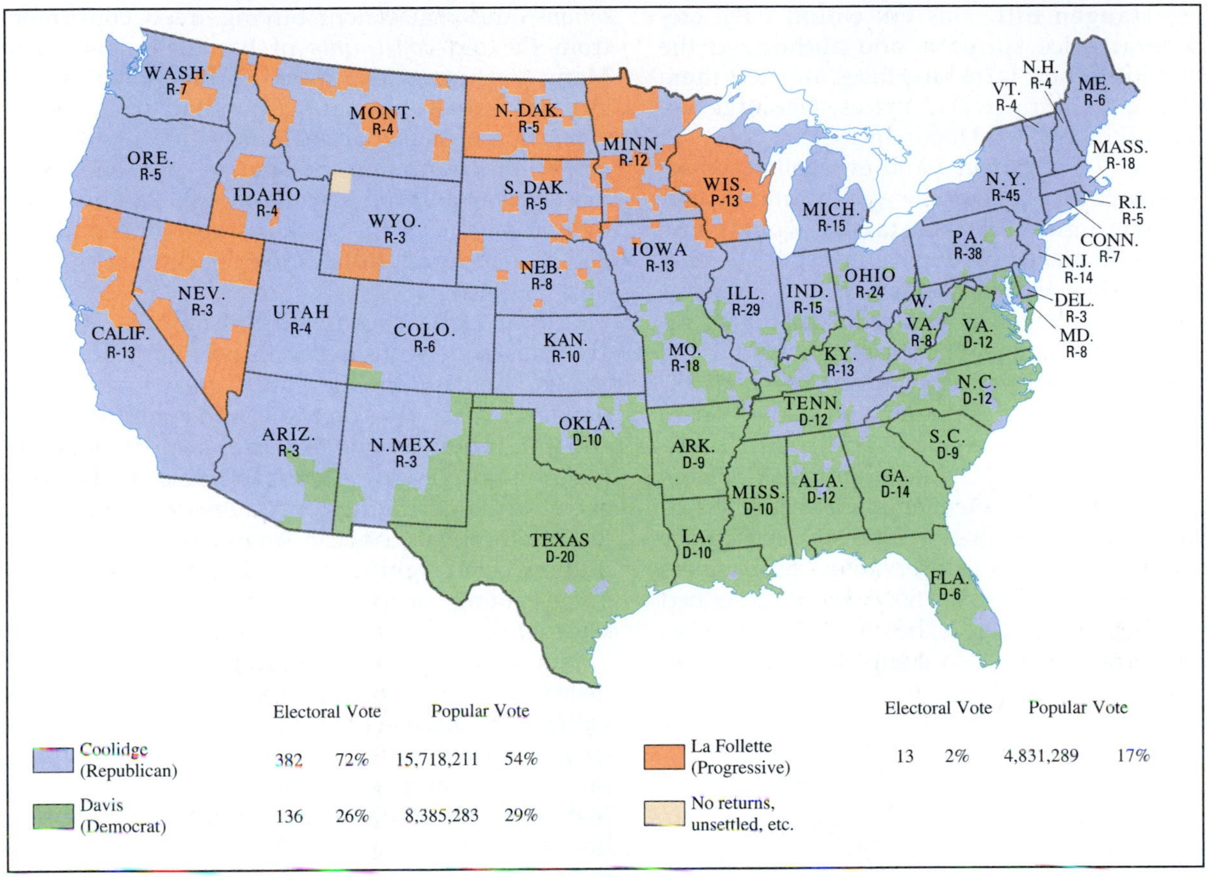

♦ **MAP 23.1 Election of 1924** The presidential election of 1924 was complicated by the campaign of Senator Robert La Follette of Wisconsin, who ran as a Progressive. Much of his support came from Republicans living in the north-central and northwestern regions, where the agricultural economy was most hard hit.

tacked big business, embraced collective bargaining, and advocated public ownership of railroads.

Republican campaigners largely ignored Davis and focused on portraying La Follette as a dangerous radical. Coolidge claimed the key issue was "whether America will allow itself to be degraded into a communistic or socialistic state or whether it will remain American." Coolidge won with nearly 16 million votes and 54 percent of the total. Davis held onto most traditional Democratic voters, especially in the South, receiving 8 million votes. La Follette carried only his home state of Wisconsin but garnered almost 5 million votes nationwide (see Map 23.1).

The Politics of Business

Resolved to limit government, Coolidge tried to reduce the significance of the presidency—and succeeded. Having once announced that "the business of America is business," he believed that the free market would provide economic prosperity for all.

The Coolidge administration's commitment to an unfettered market economy meant it had little sympathy for proposals to assist the faltering farm economy. Congress tried to address the related problems of low prices for farm products and persistent agricultural surpluses with the

McNary-Haugen bill. This bill would have created federal price supports and authorized the government to buy farm surpluses and sell them abroad at prevailing world prices. Coolidge vetoed the bill in 1927 and again in 1928.

Secretary of the Treasury Andrew Mellon did secure substantial tax cuts for the wealthy and for corporations. He argued that these tax cuts would cause the wealthy to make "productive investments" that would benefit everyone. Secretary of Commerce Herbert Hoover, however, was unsuccessful in urging Coolidge to regulate the increasingly wild use of credit, which encouraged stock market speculation.

Coolidge cut federal spending and staffed Washington's agencies with people who shared his distaste for government. Unlike Harding, Coolidge found honest and competent appointees. Like Harding, he named probusiness figures to regulatory commissions and put conservative, probusiness judges in the courts. The *Wall Street Journal* described the outcome: "Never before, here or anywhere else, has a government been so completely fused with business."

McNary-Haugen bill Farm relief bill that provided for government purchase of crop surpluses during years of large output; it was vetoed by Coolidge in 1927 and again in 1928.

SUMMARY

E xpectations
C onstraints
C hoices
O utcomes

The 1920s were a decade of prosperity: unemployment was low, gross national product (GNP) grew steadily, and many Americans fared well. Sophisticated advertising campaigns created bright *expectations,* and installment buying freed consumers from the old *constraints* of having to pay cash. Many consumers did *choose* to buy more and to buy on credit—stimulating manufacturing and an expansion of personal debt. Easy credit and *expectations* of continuing prosperity also helped to loosen *constraints* on speculation. Fueled by many individual *choices,* the stock market climbed higher and higher. Agriculture, however, did not share in this prosperity.

As *expectations* changed during the Roaring Twenties, Americans experienced significant social change. The automobile, radio, and movies broke down old *constraints* on travel and communication and produced, as one *outcome,* a more homogeneous culture. Many American intellectuals, however, *chose* to reject the consumer-oriented culture. During the 1920s, African Americans produced an outpouring of significant art, literature, and music. Some young people *chose* to reject traditional *constraints.*

Not all Americans embraced change. Some *chose* instead to try to maintain or restore earlier cultural values. The *outcomes* were mixed. Prohibition was largely unsuccessful. Fundamentalism grew and prompted a campaign against teaching evolution. Nativism helped produce significant new restrictions on immigration. The Ku Klux Klan, committed to nativism, traditional values, and white supremacy, experienced nationwide growth until 1925, but membership declined sharply thereafter.

Discrimination and occasional violence continued to *constrain* the lives of people of color. Federal Indian policy had long stressed assimilation and allotment, but some groups *chose* to promote different policies based on respect for Indian cultural values. Immigration from Mexico greatly increased the Latino population in California and the Southwest. Nearly all unions faced strong opposition from employers, and only the railroad unions made significant gains during the twenties.

Some older *expectations* and *constraints* regarding women's roles broke down as women gained the right to vote and exercised more control over the *choice* to have children. An identifiable gay and lesbian subculture emerged in cities.

Politics became less prominent. Warren G. Harding and his successor, Calvin Coolidge, both *expected* that government should act as a partner with business, and they made *choices* that minimized regulation and encouraged speculation. Progressive reform largely disappeared from politics, and efforts to secure federal assistance for farmers fizzled. One *outcome* was a federal government that was strongly conservative and probusiness.

SUGGESTED READINGS

Allen, Frederick Lewis. *Only Yesterday: An Informal History of the Nineteen-Twenties* (1931; reprint, 1964).

Filled with anecdotes that bring the decade to life.

Fitzgerald, F. Scott. *The Great Gatsby* (1925).

A fictional portrayal of high living and pleasure seeking among the wealthy of New York.

Huggins, Nathan Irvin. *Harlem Renaissance* (1971).

Thorough and thoughtful, this work places the Harlem Renaissance in the larger context of race relations in the 1920s.

Leuchtenburg, William E. *The Perils of Prosperity, 1914–1932*, rev. ed. (1993).

A comprehensive account of the 1920s by a leading historian.

The Smithsonian Collection of Classic Jazz (1987).

An outstanding collection of compact discs that reflects the development of American jazz, with annotations and biographies of performers.

THE GREAT DEPRESSION AND UNEMPLOYMENT As Herbert Hoover confronted Franklin D. Roosevelt and the Great Depression in the race for the presidency in 1932, the nation was experiencing historically high unemployment. This map shows the percentage of the work force unemployed by state, and how much unemployment jumped in some cities during a ten-month period.

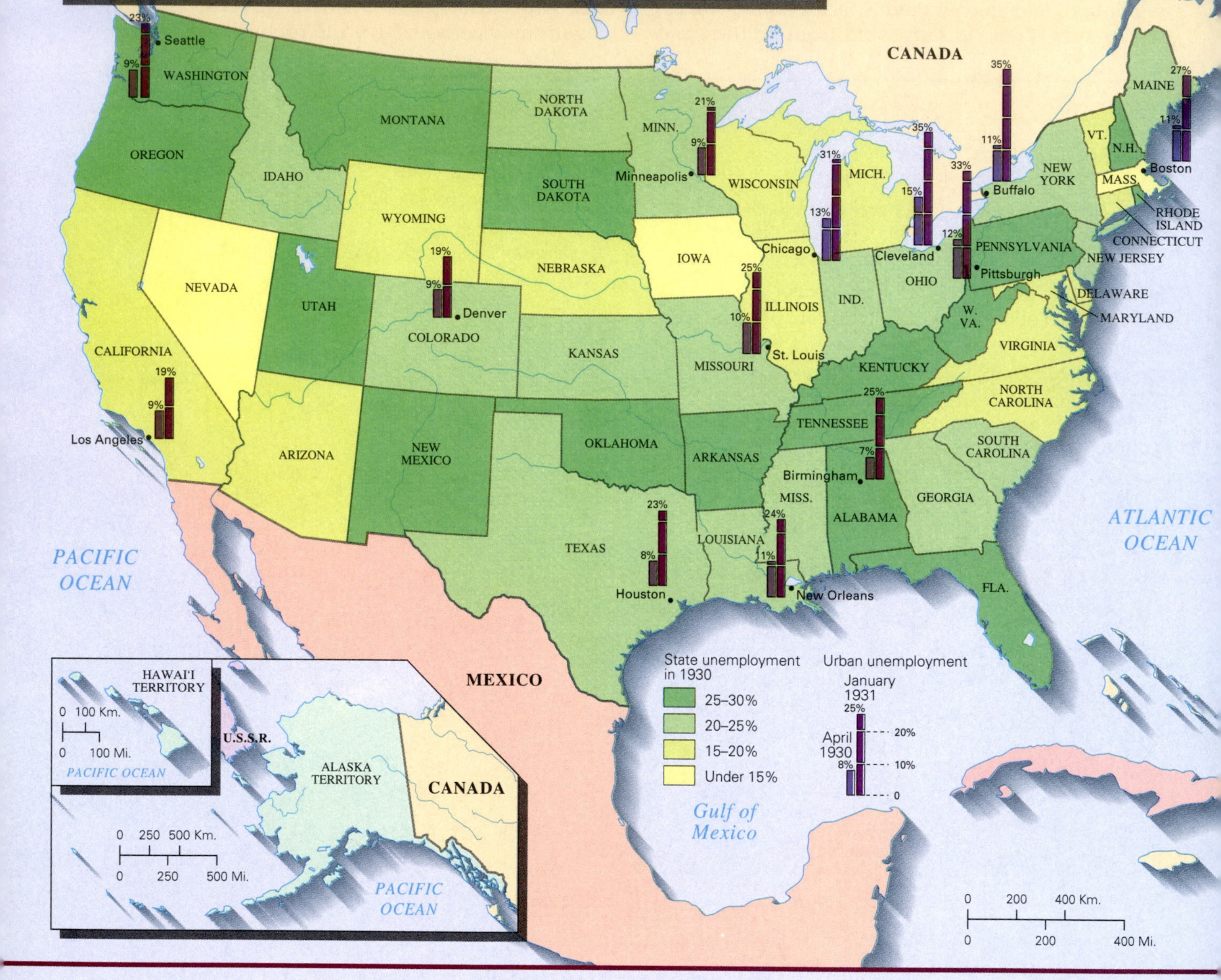
CANADA
WASHINGTON
OREGON
CALIFORNIA
NEVADA
IDAHO
MONTANA
WYOMING
UTAH
ARIZONA
COLORADO
NEW MEXICO
NORTH DAKOTA
SOUTH DAKOTA
NEBRASKA
KANSAS
OKLAHOMA
TEXAS
MINN.
IOWA
MISSOURI
ARKANSAS
LOUISIANA
WISCONSIN
ILLINOIS
MICH.
IND.
OHIO
KENTUCKY
TENNESSEE
MISS.
ALABAMA
GEORGIA
FLA.
SOUTH CAROLINA
NORTH CAROLINA
VIRGINIA
W. VA.
PENNSYLVANIA
NEW YORK
VT.
N.H.
MAINE
MASS.
RHODE ISLAND
CONNECTICUT
NEW JERSEY
DELAWARE
MARYLAND
Seattle 23% 9%
Los Angeles 19% 9%
Denver 19% 9%
Minneapolis 21% 9%
Chicago 31% 13%
St. Louis 25% 10%
Cleveland 35% 15%
Buffalo 35% 11%
Pittsburgh 33% 12%
Boston 27% 11%
Birmingham 25% 7%
Houston 23% 8%
New Orleans 24% 11%
PACIFIC OCEAN
ATLANTIC OCEAN
Gulf of Mexico
MEXICO
HAWAI'I TERRITORY
0 100 Km.
0 100 Mi.
PACIFIC OCEAN
U.S.S.R.
ALASKA TERRITORY
CANADA
0 250 500 Km.
0 250 500 Mi.
PACIFIC OCEAN
State unemployment in 1930
25–30%
20–25%
15–20%
Under 15%
Urban unemployment
January 1931
25%
April 1930
8%
20%
10%
0
0 200 400 Km.
0 200 400 Mi.

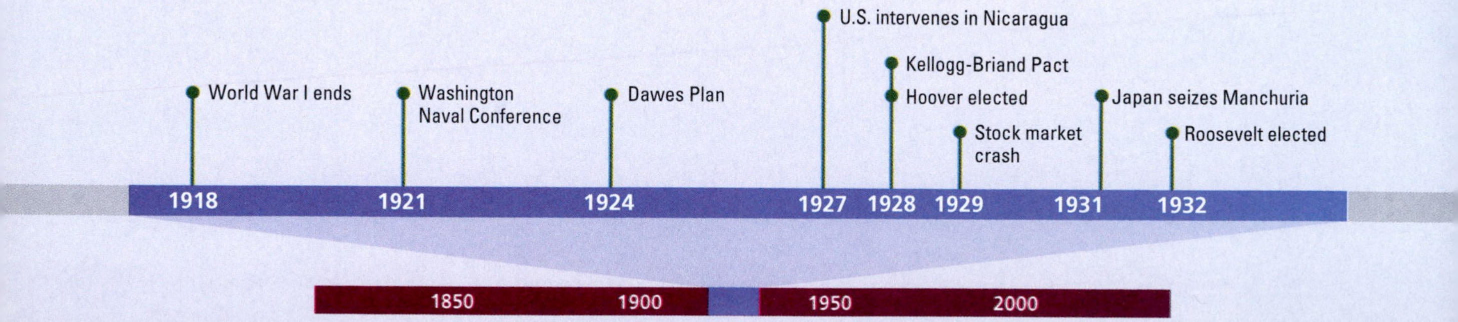
World War I ends
Washington Naval Conference
Dawes Plan
U.S. intervenes in Nicaragua
Kellogg-Briand Pact
Hoover elected
Stock market crash
Japan seizes Manchuria
Roosevelt elected
1918
1921
1924
1927
1928
1929
1931
1932
1850
1900
1950
2000

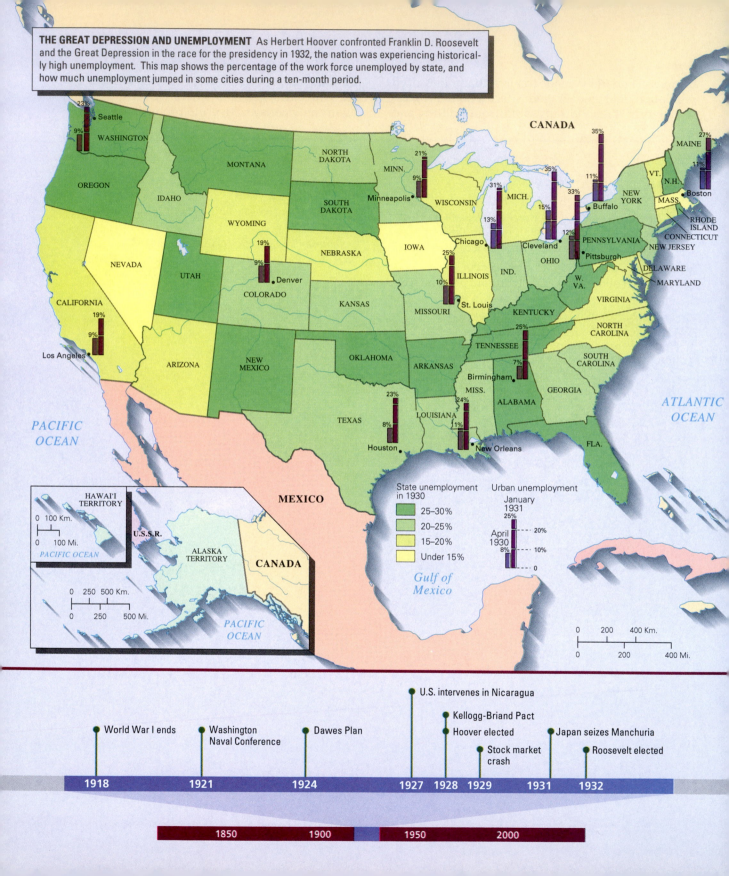

CHAPTER 24

From Good Times to Hard Times, 1920–1932

The Diplomacy of Prosperity

- How did the strength of the American economy, along with America's desire to remain unconstrained in foreign affairs, shape the choices in U.S. foreign policy during the 1920s?

The Failure of Prosperity

- What expectations did Americans have when they chose Herbert Hoover instead of Al Smith to be president?
- What weaknesses constrained the American economy? What expectations caused these constraints not to be clearly seen?

Government and Economic Crisis

- What choices did Hoover make to deal with the Great Depression? How did his expectations about government limit his choices?
- Why were the outcomes of Hoover's efforts to fight the Depression unsuccessful?

Depression America

- What economic and social constraints and choices did the Depression generate for industrial workers, minorities, and women?
- What choices did Americans make during the Depression that reflected the continuity of social and cultural values?

INTRODUCTION

E xpectations
C onstraints
C hoices
O utcomes

As the Roaring Twenties drew to a close, the United States seemed to have reached new levels of success. American prosperity bloomed, fueling much of the world's economic growth. American business interests swept into Europe, Asia, the Middle East, and Latin America. At the same time, the United States government *chose* to avoid a direct role in world politics. Instead, American policymakers from Harding to Hoover *expected* indirect and private means to promote American interests and a stable and peaceful world.

Domestically, the Republican presidents of the twenties *chose* to rely less on governmental supervision and more on unfettered American business to build a prosperous and stable America. For Herbert Hoover, the outlook in 1928 seemed bright. He *expected* to be elected president and to guide the continued growth of American and world prosperity. He was confident that domestic poverty would nearly disappear and international peace would prevail.

This chapter examines the failure of Hoover's *expectations* in the face of the Great Depression. Hoover *chose* to face the decline of the economy with policies that he *expected* would produce continued growth. He found, however, that they only heightened disillusionment and individual hardship. Confronted with dismal realities, Hoover altered policy, but his new *choices* failed to change the course of the Depression. As individuals and society responded to the Depression, many, like Hoover, questioned their long-held values and revised their *expectations,* especially about the role of government. By 1932, it was obvious that the Depression had thwarted Hoover's hopes and ruined his political career. The American people *chose* a president pledged to activism: Franklin D. Roosevelt.

The Depression also revealed the weaknesses of the *expectations* and *choices* that had governed American foreign policy throughout the 1920s. The *constraints* of economic failure dashed hopes of basing peace and international stability on economic growth and voluntary agreements. The *outcome* was an increasingly dangerous world, as nations moved to protect and promote their own economic goals at the expense of others' and, in the case of Japan, of world peace.

The Diplomacy of Prosperity

Two realities shaped American foreign policy in the 1920s: the rejection of Woodrow Wilson's internationalism following World War I and the continuing quest for economic expansion by American business. President Warren Harding, elected in 1920, dismissed any American role in the League of Nations and refused to accept the **Treaty of Versailles.** The administration and Congress simply declared the war to be over. Harding's secretary of state, Charles Evans Hughes, then quickly concluded separate peace treaties with the Central Powers. Hughes also supported efforts by American banks and corporations to expand their business activities around the world. The Great War had made America the world's major industrial producer and banker. Throughout the 1920s, American businesses helped shape the global economy by lending money to other nations.

Because Harding and his successor, Calvin Coolidge, had little interest in foreign affairs, they

Treaty of Versailles Treaty that ended World War I, which was signed at Versailles, France, in 1919.

CHRONOLOGY

A New Era

1918	World War I ends
1920	Harding elected president
1921–1922	Washington Naval Conference
1922	Fordney-McCumber Tariff
1923	France occupies the Ruhr Harding dies in office; Coolidge becomes president
1924	Coolidge elected president Dawes Plan U.S. forces withdraw from Dominican Republic
1927	United States intervenes in Nicaragua Henry Stimson negotiates the Peace of Titiapa Augusto Sandino begins guerrilla war in Nicaragua
1928	Kellogg-Briand Pact Hoover elected president
1929	Agricultural Marketing Act (Farm Board) Stock market crash
1930	Rafael Trujillo seizes power in Dominican Republic Hawley-Smoot Tariff
1931	Japan seizes Manchuria Scottsboro Nine convicted
1932	32,000 U.S. businesses fail U.S. forces begin withdrawal from Nicaragua Reconstruction Finance Corporation (RCF) begins emergency relief Farmers' Holiday Association founded Bonus March Franklin Roosevelt elected president
1933	4,000 U.S. banks fail Unemployment reaches 25 percent Japan withdraws from League of Nations
1934	U.S. forces withdraw from Haiti Sandino murdered by Anastasio Somoza
1936	Somoza becomes president of Nicaragua

deferred to their secretaries of state: Hughes and Frank Kellogg, respectively. Both were capable men interested in developing American business and influence abroad through "independent internationalism." Independent internationalism had two central thrusts: avoiding international responsibilities—sometimes called **isolationism**—and expanding economic opportunities overseas. As secretary of commerce, Herbert Hoover was equally involved in promoting American business activities worldwide. In Asia, the Commerce and State departments encouraged private American investments in Japan and China. In the Middle East, the United States worked hard to overcome British opposition and provide openings for American oil companies seeking drilling rights. Successes in Asia and the Middle East were limited, but efforts to expand the American economic position in Latin America and Europe were quite successful.

isolationism A national policy of avoiding political or economic entanglements with other countries.

♦ **MAP 24.1 The United States and Latin America, 1919–1939** As this map shows, the United States continued to play an active role in promoting its interests throughout Central and South America and the Caribbean between the two world wars. In some cases, as in Nicaragua in the 1920s, this included military intervention, but during the 1920s and the terms of Hoover and Roosevelt, political and economic pressure replaced military force as the primary means to protect U.S. interests.

The United States and Latin America

The 1920s marked a gradual American retreat from direct intervention in Latin America (see Map 24.1). President Harding intended to end the American occupation of Haiti and the Dominican Republic. The withdrawal of American troops proceeded slowly, however, because Harding, Coolidge, and Hoover did not want anti-American governments to seize power. To ensure friendly and stable governments, Americans maintained control over these countries' national finances and trained national guards to act as police forces. With such precautions in place, U.S. troops left the Dominican Republic in 1924, Nicaragua in 1925, and Haiti in 1934.

When American troops withdrew from the Dominican Republic and Haiti, they left better roads and improved sanitary systems. But years of occupation had not advanced educational systems, national economies, or the standard of living. In Haiti, American-imposed segregation and favoritism toward the minority, lighter-colored **mulattos** made social divisions worse. Nor did the United States promote the cause of democracy, favoring stability over freedom, even if that meant dictatorship. In 1930, Rafael Trujillo, an American-trained national guard officer, declared himself dictator of the Dominican Republic. He ruled the country brutally until his death in 1961.

In Nicaragua, civil war broke out when American forces left in 1925. President Coolidge reintroduced American forces in 1927 to protect the pro-American, conservative government and sent special envoy Henry L. Stimson to negotiate a truce. Stimson arranged the **Peace of Titiapa,** which ended most of the fighting. However, **Augusto Sandino,** whose primary goal was to see Nicaragua free of American influence, rejected the truce. Between 1927 and 1932, he carried on a guerrilla war against the government and American forces. Throughout Latin America, his resistance earned him many admirers who saw the United States as an imperial power wielding its might over Latin Americans. The United States withdrew its forces from Nicaragua in 1933. After the U.S. Marines left, the commander of the Guardia Nacional, **Anastasio Somoza,** arranged a peace conference with the rebel. After a farewell dinner, Somoza executed Sandino and his aides. Using the national guard as a political weapon, Somoza was elected president in 1936. He ruled either directly or through puppet presidents until his assassination in 1956. His family would remain in power until 1979, when rebels calling themselves the Sandinistas—after their hero, Sandino—drove the Somozas out of Nicaragua.

Elsewhere in Latin America, the 1920s saw American business interests expand. Throughout Central America, American firms such as the United Fruit Company purchased or pressured governments to give them thousands of acres for plantations on which to grow tropical fruits, especially bananas. In Venezuela and Colombia, American oil companies, with State Department help, successfully negotiated profitable contracts for drilling rights, pushing aside European oil companies. American investment in Latin America rose from $2 billion in 1919 to nearly $3.5 billion by 1929.

Oil also played a key role in American relations with Mexico. American businessmen objected strongly when Mexico began to **nationalize** its oil (see Map 24.1). By 1925, American oilmen were calling for military action to protect their interests in northern Mexico. Coolidge, however, instructed ambassador Dwight W. Morrow "to keep us out of war with Mexico." Morrow understood Mexican nationalism and pride and clearly appreciated

mulatto A person of mixed black and white ancestry.

Peace of Titiapa Agreement negotiated by U.S. Secretary of State Henry L. Stimson in 1927 that sought to end factional fighting in Nicaragua.

Augusto Sandino Rebel who sought to rid Nicaragua of American influence; he was murdered by his rival, Anastasio Somoza.

Anastasio Somoza General who established a military dictatorship in Nicaragua in 1934, deposed his uncle to become president in 1936, and ruled the country for two decades, amassing a personal fortune and suppressing all opposition.

nationalize To convert an industry or enterprise from private to governmental ownership and control.

Mexico and its people. He cultivated a personal relationship with Mexican president Plutarco Calles. Together they reached a compromise that recognized Mexican sovereignty over its oil but delayed nationalization of existing oil properties until 1938.

America and the European Economy

World War I had shattered most of Europe physically and economically, while the United States had climbed during wartime to unprecedented economic heights. After the war, the United States sought to expand exports and restrict imports. High tariffs inched higher throughout the 1920s. In 1922, the **Fordney-McCumber Tariff** set records in protective rates for most imported industrial goods. The effect was not only to limit European imports but also to weaken Europe's ability to acquire the dollars needed to repay its war debts to the United States.

While the tariff was shutting off the entry of European goods into the American market, Secretary of State Hughes and Secretary of Commerce Hoover worked to expand American economic interests in Europe, especially Germany. They believed that if Germany recovered economically and was able to pay its $33 billion war reparations to the victors of World War I, those nations would be able to repay their war debts to the United States. Over $4 billion in American investments flowed into Europe during the decade, doubling American investment there. General Motors purchased Opel, a German automobile firm. Ford built the largest automobile factory outside the United States in England.

Even with the infusion of American capital, Germany could not keep up with its reparations burden by 1923. France responded by sending troops to occupy the industrial **Ruhr Valley** of Germany, igniting an international emergency. Hughes sent Chicago banker Charles G. Dawes to Europe to negotiate a plan to resolve the crisis. Under the **Dawes Plan,** passed in 1924, American bankers loaned $2.5 billion to Germany for economic development, while the Germans promised to pay $2 billion in reparations to the Europeans. The Europeans, in turn, paid $2.5 billion in war debts to the United States. The remedy worked fairly well until 1929, when the Depression ended nearly all loans and payments.

In Europe and the United States, the destruction caused by World War I spurred postwar pacifism and calls for disarmament. In the United States, support for arms cuts was widespread and vocal. In November 1921, Harding invited the major naval powers to Washington for discussions on reducing "the crushing burdens of military and naval establishments."

Pacifism was not the only American motive for hosting the **Washington Naval Conference.** Harding and Hughes were worried about continued Japanese naval expansion and growing Japanese pressures on China. Disarmament suggested a way of dealing with this Japanese threat without expanding the American navy. Hughes shocked conference delegates with a radical proposal that called for scrapping more than 200 tons of warships, primarily battleships. He also called for a ten-year ban on naval construction and for limits to the size of navies, based on a ratio of existing tonnage, that would keep the Japanese behind the British and American navies. Hughes put forth a ratio of 5 to 5 to 3 for the United States, Britain, and Japan. Lesser naval powers like Italy and France would receive even smaller ratios. Most of the nations attending applauded Hughes's

Fordney-McCumber Tariff Law passed in 1922 that raised tariff rates to record levels, fostering the growth of monopolies and provoking foreign tariff reprisals.

Ruhr Valley Region surrounding the Ruhr River in northwestern Germany, which contained many major industrial cities and valuable mines.

Dawes Plan Plan for collecting World War I reparations from Germany, which scheduled annual payments and stabilized German currency by reorganizing the Reichsbank under Allied supervision.

Washington Naval Conference International conference held in Washington, D.C., in November 1921 through February 1922; it produced a series of agreements to limit naval armaments and prevent conflict in the Far East.

proposal, but not Japan, which called the ratio a national insult. The conference dragged on for more than two months, but finally the Japanese agreed—as Hughes had known they would. Prior to the conference, the United States had broken the Japanese **diplomatic code** and had intercepted secret messages instructing the Japanese delegates to concede if Hughes held firm on his ratio.

Many Americans and Europeans applauded the achievements of the Washington conference but wanted to go even further. They sought total disarmament and a repudiation of war. In 1923, Senator William E. Borah of Idaho introduced a resolution in the Senate to outlaw war. It failed, but the idea remained active. In 1927, French foreign minister Aristide Briand suggested a French-American pact to outlaw war between them, privately hoping that such an agreement would commit the United States to aid France if attacked. Secretary of State Kellogg wanted to avoid any such American commitment and deflected the proposal by suggesting a multinational statement opposing war. Kellogg thereby removed any hint of an American commitment to aid any nation under attack. On August 27, 1928, the United States and fourteen other nations, including Britain, France, Germany, Italy, and Japan, signed the **Kellogg-Briand Pact.** Each country renounced war "as an instrument of national policy" and promised to settle disputes by peaceful means. The pact included no enforcement provisions.

By the end of 1928, American independent internationalism seemed to be a flourishing success. American business investments and loans were fueling an expansive world economy and adding to American prosperity. Avoiding entangling alliances, the United States had acted to protect its Asian and Pacific interests against Japan while promoting world disarmament and peace. In Latin America, it had moderated its interventionist image by withdrawing American troops in the Caribbean and trying to mediate a peace among warring factions in Nicaragua (see Map 24.1). It appeared that foreign policies based on economic expansion and noncoercive diplomacy were establishing a promising era of cooperation and peace in world affairs.

The Failure of Prosperity

In August 1927, Calvin Coolidge called reporters from his vacation spot in South Dakota and told them, "I do not choose to run in 1928." Coolidge's announcement stunned the country and his party. Secretary of Commerce Herbert Hoover immediately declared his candidacy.

He seemed the ideal person for the job. A Quaker farm boy from Iowa, Hoover had grown up among thrifty, self-sufficient farmers who believed that hard work was the only way forward. He worked his way through Stanford University. He formed his own mining engineering company in 1908, and by 1914 he had offices in London, Petrograd, Paris, New York, and San Francisco. *Fortune* estimated that he and his wife were worth more than $4 million. Having reached the top in business, Hoover wanted to apply his belief in hard work and sound planning to public service. When the Great War broke out, he offered to help provide relief to Belgium. Hoover traveled across war-torn Europe, seeking funds and materials for Belgium, and earned a reputation as "the Great Humanitarian." When the United States entered the war, President Wilson named him to head the U.S. Food Administration. By war's end, Hoover was an international hero.

The 1928 Election

The theme of Hoover's candidacy in 1928 was American prosperity. "We in America today are nearer to the final triumph over poverty than ever before," he boldly announced. The Democrats nominated Al Smith, four-time governor of New York. Like Hoover, Smith was a self-made man. Smith had entered politics as part of Tammany

diplomatic code Secret code in which diplomatic messages are transmitted.

Kellogg-Briand Pact Treaty signed in 1928 by fifteen nations, including Britain, France, Germany, the United States, and Japan, renouncing war as a means of solving international disputes.

Hall, the Democratic machine that ran New York City, and quickly proved to be an able politician. As a reform-minded, progressive governor, Smith had streamlined government, improved governmental efficiency, and supported legislation to set a minimum wage and maximum hours of work.

Despite his progressive record, Smith had a number of liabilities. Opponents attacked his Catholicism, his big-city background, his opposition to Prohibition, and his Tammany connections. Anti-Catholic sentiment burned hotly in many parts of the country, often fanned by the remnants of the Klan. Evangelist Billy Sunday called Smith supporters "damnable whiskey politicians, bootleggers, crooks, pimps and businessmen who deal with them." For many voters, the choice seemed to be between a candidate who represented hard work and the pious values of small-town, old-stock, Protestant America and one who represented urban upheaval, machine politics, foreigners, and Catholics.

Hoover won easily, with 58 percent of the popular vote. He owed his victory in large part to the prosperity that Republicans claimed as their accomplishment. Also, Smith's religion and position against Prohibition cost him substantial support in the South.

Unlike his predecessors, Hoover came to the White House with the intention of being an active president. He wanted to create a "New Day" for America. Hoover's goal was to encourage economic and social growth by using government to promote cooperation among business and other parts of society. Hoover did not want the federal government to step in to solve society's problems directly. He feared that such governmental involvement would cause the people to give up their freedom. The government should help people solve their problems, not solve their problems for them.

Origins of the Depression

When Herbert Hoover took office, ever-rising stock prices, shiny new cars, and rapidly expanding suburbs seemed to verify Hoover's observation about "the final triumph over poverty." But behind the rush for radios, homes, and vacuum cleaners lay several economic weaknesses. The prosperity of the 1920s depended in large part on a few major industries such as construction, automobiles, and household appliances. Other important sectors of the economy—textiles, railroads, steel, and iron—barely made a profit, while farming and mining suffered steady losses. Farmers saw their income and property values decline to about half their wartime highs. Hundreds of thousands of people left farms throughout the twenties.

Agriculture's troubles were only part of a growing economic distress. By 1929, even the boom industries were showing signs of weakness. New construction starts fell from 11 million to 9 million units between 1926 and 1929. Furniture companies cut their labor force in 1928 after huge inventories piled up. A similar story held for many makers of household appliances. Only the automobile industry was strong in 1928 and 1929.

The economic slowdown in 1929 stemmed from overproduction, poor distribution of income, and too much credit buying. Although the 1920s was a prosperous decade for the upper and middle classes, minorities and those living in rural areas enjoyed no increase in wages or savings. As Hoover assumed the presidency, over 70 percent of all American families lived on less than the $2,500 a year that the Brookings Institute considered an adequate standard of living. Few people, however, took notice of this vast majority of Americans who spent all they earned and for whom missing a single paycheck meant economic hard times.

The Stock Market Plunge

When Americans awoke on Thursday, October 24, 1929, no one realized they would experience one of those days that would change their lives. It was business as usual as men and women prepared to go to work. In the Midwest, people braced themselves against a frigid, unseasonable ice and snow storm. Across the country, Americans followed the lurid story of millionaire theater owner Alexander Pantangas, on trial for assaulting a 17-year-old dancer. Most Americans hardly noticed the rise and fall of stock prices on Wall Street.

Despite the lack of public concern, the activity on the New York Stock Exchange that day would have profound consequences for all Americans. On **Black Thursday,** the bottom suddenly fell out of the stock market. By noon, millions of stocks had been sold as the stock exchange became a frenzied sea of waving arms, raised fists, and screaming voices. In brokerage offices across the country, brokers rushed to place sell orders.

As the exchange closed for lunch, New York's financial leaders hurriedly met to deal with the panic. They concluded that they needed to support stock prices. Twenty-two years earlier, in 1907, New York bankers had stopped a panic and thwarted a possible depression by pooling funds to buy stocks. Now they hoped to repeat history. Led by the bank of J. P. Morgan, financial leaders put together a fund of nearly $50 million. The bankers then told Richard Whitney, vice chairman of the exchange, to use the fund to buy stocks as soon as the market reopened.

At 1:30, Whitney jauntily announced that he was buying ten thousand shares of steel at 205—ten points higher than the existing market price. Amid cheers, others quickly joined the buying drive. By the end of the day, nearly half of the $6 billion lost in the morning had been recovered. Confidence seemed to have been restored.

On Monday, October 28, prices dropped again. But this time no rescuer appeared. Bankers and Wall Street leaders, having already committed $50 million, were hesitant to add to their bailout. On Black Tuesday, October 29, prices plunged drastically and continued to fall throughout November. Between early September and mid-November, the *New York Times* **industrials** fell from 469 to 221. RCA plummeted from 101 to 28, Montgomery Ward from 138 to 49, Union Carbide from 138 to 59. Hundreds of brokers and speculators were ruined.

The stock market crash that began in October 1929 was not solely responsible for the **Great Depression.** Rather, it pushed an already weakened economy into a steep decline. Since 1927, the overall economy had been slowing down and consumption had been declining. Like much of the public, many corporations were in debt. When the market crashed, brokers and banks found their resources dwindling and began demanding repayment of loans. Many borrowers could not meet this demand, and as a result, lenders found themselves unable to meet the demands of depositors. Banks failed, and a substantial portion of the savings of the upper and middle classes vanished.

The crash undermined economic confidence throughout the country. Americans had viewed the soaring stock market as a symbol of the vigor of the economy and of the nation. Now investors were wary. Corporations cut production and laid off workers. Consumers hesitated to spend money. Coupled with the weaknesses of the economy, the stock market crash resulted in the worst and longest depression in American history.

The plummeting domestic economy had international repercussions as well. American banks cut their European loans, and American corporations reduced their purchases. To protect American business from foreign competition, Congress in 1930 passed the **Hawley-Smoot Tariff,** which drastically raised tariffs. It proved to be a catastrophe for world trade. Angered by American actions, twenty-three foreign governments raised their tariffs on American goods, further stifling trade. By 1932, American exports had fallen to their lowest level since 1905. Rather than protect national economies, the high tariffs only spread the global depression. With fewer goods being sold, businesses faced declining profits and slashed production and payrolls.

Stock prices continued downward until 1932. The *New York Times* industrials sank to 58 by

Black Thursday October 24, 1929, when the stock market fell dramatically in what proved to be the beginning of the crash.

industrials Industrial stocks chosen as indicators of trends in the economy.

Great Depression The years 1929 to 1941 in the United States, during which the economy was in a severe decline and millions of people were out of work.

Hawley-Smoot Tariff Law passed in 1930 in response to the Depression, setting the highest tariff rates in U.S. history and thus undermining world trade.

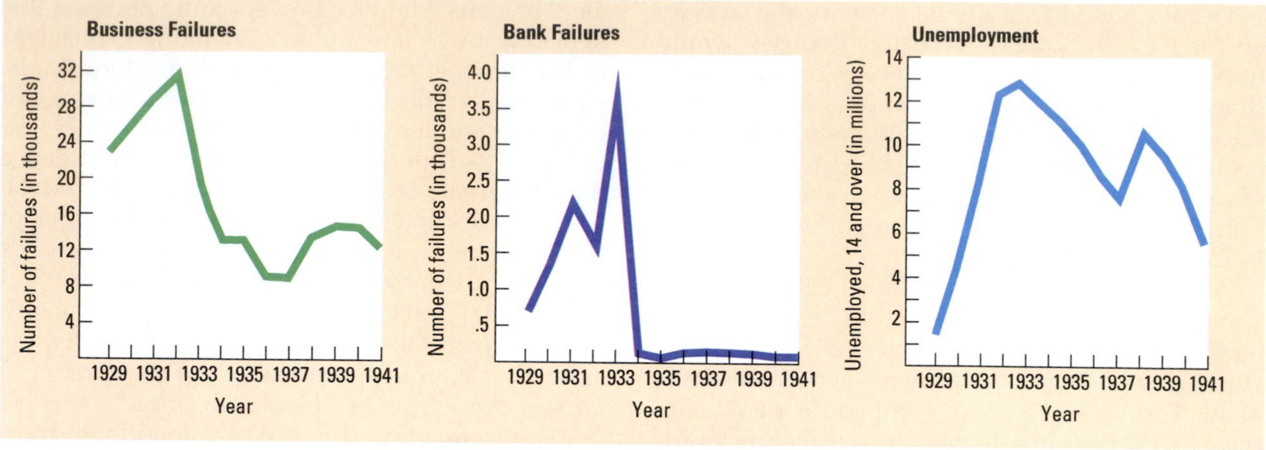

♦ **FIGURE 24.1 Charting the Economics of the Depression** Between 1929 and 1933, there was an expanding number of unemployed people seeking work, and more and more banks and businesses were closing their doors. By 1933, over 4,000 banks had failed, unemployment had reached 24.9 percent, and over 100,000 firms had closed. As the New Deal began, not only did the statistics improve, but for most Americans there was also a feeling of hope.

mid-1932. United States Steel fell from a precrash high of 262 to a low of 22. Many companies did not survive. Between 1929 and 1933, ninety thousand businesses failed, and nine thousand banks closed (see Figure 24.1). As banks collapsed, depositors lost $2.5 billion. The money supply shrank by a third between 1930 and 1933, and expenditures for goods plummeted 45 percent. Purchases of automobiles dropped 75 percent. Unemployment rose from 3 percent in 1929 to 25 percent in 1933 (see chapter opener map). As the downward economic spiral continued, nearly everyone in the nation felt the effects of what was becoming the Great Depression.

Government and Economic Crisis

Shortly after the stock market crash, Hoover called together leaders of banking, industry, and labor. He pleaded with employers not to cut wages or production or to lay off workers. He exhorted unions not to demand higher wages. At the same time, he assured the public that the economy was sound and would soon improve. These efforts worked for only a short time.

When cheerleading failed, public pressure grew for the federal government to take more direct action. Hoover also began to lean toward more direct government involvement. In December 1929, he asked Congress to increase spending for the construction of **public works** projects, including highways, government facilities, and **Boulder Dam.** Federal, state, and local governments doubled their spending on public works, but the economy continued to worsen. Increasingly, Americans blamed Hoover and his admin-

public works Construction projects such as highways and dams, financed by public funds and carried out by the government.

Boulder Dam Dam on the Colorado River between Nevada and Arizona, which was renamed in honor of Hoover.

istration for the hardships they faced. A popular jingle went:

Mellon pulled the whistle
Hoover rang the bell
Wall Street gave the signal
And the country went to hell.

By the end of 1932, workers' income had dropped 40 percent and unemployment had risen to an alarming 25 percent. Small industrial towns were especially hard hit. Donora, Pennsylvania, had only 277 jobs for its population of over 14,000. Many, like Donora's future baseball great Stan Musial, left home seeking greener pastures. Most were unsuccessful. Even rumors of jobs drew thousands to factory gates. Ed Paulson, who roamed the country looking for work, recalled that he developed a "coyote mentality." "You were a predator," he said. "You had to be. The coyote is crafty. . . . We were coyotes in the Thirties, the jobless." Private, state, and local charities and relief agencies vainly tried to meet the needs of the millions out of work. Bread lines and soup kitchens did their best to feed the growing army of hungry and displaced Americans, but the numbers were overwhelming. Across the country, shantytowns bitterly named **Hoovervilles** housed the homeless.

When the stock market crashed, agriculture was already in a depression. Drought in the Mississippi valley soon spread throughout the South and Midwest. It would last a decade. Adding to the misery of farmers, swarms of grasshoppers ate their way across the nation's midsection. The region became known as the **Dust Bowl** (see Map 24.2) in the 1930s, when winds whipped up clouds of dust, sometimes stretching more than 200 miles across and 7,000 to 8,000 feet high. In 1938, the worst year for dust storms, erosion claimed over 850 million tons of **topsoil.** Dust hung in the air and filtered into homes, covering clothing, furniture, food, everything.

Even before the Crash, Hoover had responded to the crisis on American farms by proposing the creation of a national farm board. The board would help stabilize prices by buying agricultural products on the open market. Congress passed the **Agricultural Marketing Act** in May 1929. The Farm Board was initially successful in supporting

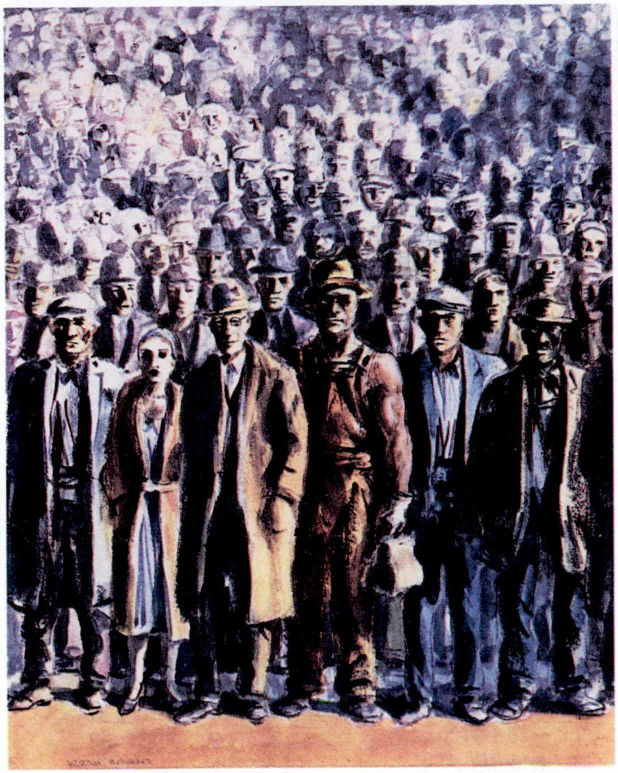

♦ The Great Depression produced large-scale unemployment, which reached 25 percent in 1933. This picture by Reginald Marsh, titled *Unemployed*, effectively captures the despair of men and women seeking jobs. *"Unemployed" by Reginald Marsh, 1932. Library of Congress.*

Hooverville Crudely built camp set up by the homeless on the fringes of a town or city during the Depression.

Dust Bowl Name given to the Great Plains region devastated by drought and dust storms during the 1930s.

topsoil Surface layer of the soil, in which crops grow.

Agricultural Marketing Act Law passed in 1929 that created the Farm Board to stabilize farm prices by buying crop surpluses; the price support program ended in 1931.

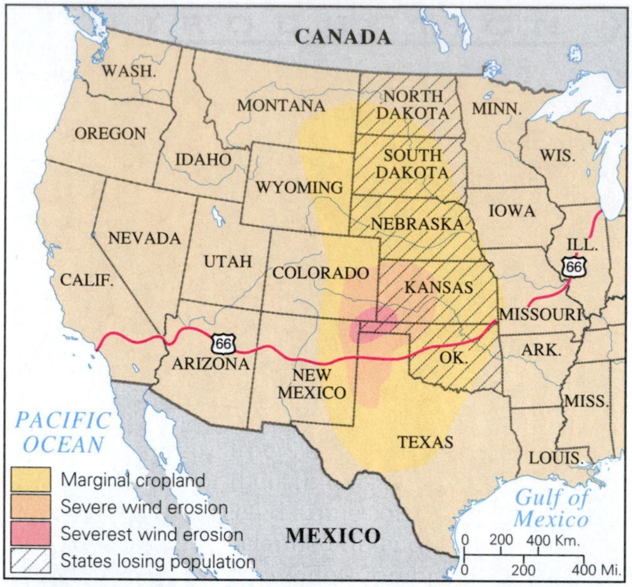
CANADA
WASH.
MONTANA
NORTH DAKOTA
MINN.
OREGON
IDAHO
SOUTH DAKOTA
WIS.
WYOMING
IOWA
NEBRASKA
NEVADA
ILL.
66
UTAH
COLORADO
CALIF.
KANSAS
MISSOURI
66
ARIZONA
NEW MEXICO
OK.
ARK.
MISS.
PACIFIC OCEAN
TEXAS
LOUIS.
Marginal cropland
Severe wind erosion
Severest wind erosion
States losing population
MEXICO
Gulf of Mexico
0 200 400 Km.
0 200 400 Mi.

♦ **MAP 24.2 The Dust Bowl** Throughout the 1930s, wind eroded millions of acres of cropland, sending tons of topsoil into the air and generating tidal waves of dust. This map shows the regions most affected by the Dust Bowl and the loss of population. Many chose to travel Route 66, hoping that it would lead to a better life in California.

farm prices. The world price of wheat sank to $.55 a bushel in February 1931, but Farm Board purchases held the American price steady at $.80 a bushel. By the end of 1931, however, the Farm Board had run out of funds. Agricultural prices then tumbled downward, forcing more farmers into bankruptcy.

As declining farm prices, drought, and dust destroyed farmers' hopes, many turned to direct action. The **Farmers' Holiday Association,** founded in 1932 by Milo Reno, called on midwestern farmers to destroy their products and to resist **foreclosures** (see Individual Choices: Milo Reno). Angry and frequently armed, farmers used their numbers and threats of violence to ensure that foreclosed properties were sold at auction to their previous owners for a fraction of their value. One such "penny auction" returned Walter Crozier's farm in Haskins, Ohio, for a high bid of $1.90. Critics linked the protests with "international Jews, the IWW, Socialists, and Communists." In fact, the protesters were homegrown and simply wanted government support for the farmer.

Hoover's Final Efforts

By December 1931, confronted with a still-worsening economy, Hoover moved in a new direction. He asked Congress for banking reforms, financial support for home mortgages, and the creation of the **Reconstruction Finance Corporation (RFC).** Congress approved all three proposals.

Hoover's primary weapon in fighting the Depression was the RFC, through which he intended to pump money into the economy. Using federal funds, the RFC was to provide loans to banks, savings and loans, railroads, insurance companies, and large corporations to keep them operating. Hoover believed that the money would "trickle down" to workers and the unemployed through higher wages and new jobs. It was an unprecedented effort by the federal government to intervene in the private sector and stimulate the economy. Conservatives called it "an experiment in socialism." Within five months, the RFC had loaned over $805 million to large businesses, but little money trickled down to workers. Liberal critics labeled the program "welfare for the rich" and insisted that Hoover do more for the poor and unemployed through **direct relief** payments and more public works projects.

Farmers' Holiday Association Farmers' organization led by Milo Reno of Iowa that led a strike in the summer of 1932 to protest the drastic decline in farm income.

foreclosure Confiscation of a property by the bank when mortgage payments are delinquent.

Reconstruction Finance Corporation Organization to promote economic recovery established at Hoover's request in 1932; it provided emergency financing for banks, life insurance companies, railroads, and farm mortgage associations.

direct relief Payments directly to the poor and unemployed.

Hoover opposed direct federal relief, or the "dole," for several reasons. He believed that it would be too burdensome for the federal budget and that relief should instead be distributed by private organizations and local government. "Where people divest themselves of local government responsibilities," he explained, "they at once lay the foundation for the destruction of their liberties." He was also convinced that the dole would erode the work ethic and bring about a class of idle Americans.

In 1932, Hoover finally relented and agreed to create the Emergency Relief Division within the RFC and lend $300 million to states for relief. Like other RFC efforts, actual relief spending did not match the potential. Headed by a conservative board of directors, the RFC loaned money cautiously. Further, states whose budgets were already overstrained hesitated to borrow more money. By the end of 1932, the RFC had spent only 10 percent of its relief fund.

The patience of many Americans seemed at an end by the summer of 1932. The Farmers' Holiday movement was spreading across the Midwest, and thousands of veterans, the Bonus Expeditionary Force, were making their way toward Washington. The **Bonus Army,** twenty thousand unemployed veterans of the Great War, headed to the capital to lobby for the Wright-Patman bill, which stipulated early payment of their veterans' bonus, originally scheduled to be paid in 1945. Against his advisers' warnings, Hoover allowed the Bonus Marchers to set up their Hooverville across from Congress in Anacostia Flats.

Hoover respected the veterans' right to assemble, but when the Senate rejected the Patman bill, the president thought the marchers should go home. Nearly half of them, however, stayed in Washington. When the police attempted to clear condemned buildings of marchers, nearly five thousand veterans and eight hundred police clashed, resulting in the deaths of two Bonus Marchers. Hoover then turned to the army to evict the squatters. Using sabers, rifles, tear gas, and fixed bayonets, the army, led by Army Chief of Staff General Douglas MacArthur, drove the veterans from the abandoned buildings. Hoover had given orders to leave the Bonus Marchers at Anacostia Flats alone, but MacArthur ignored these orders. To the horror of most Americans, the army drove off the veterans and their families and set their huts and tents afire. Over one hundred veterans were injured in the melee. What slim chance Hoover had for re-election died at the "Battle of Anacostia Flats."

The Diplomacy of Depression

When Hoover entered the presidency, the world appeared stable and peaceful. Like his predecessors, Hoover intended to use economic and noncoercive means to protect American interests and promote world prosperity. Hoover promised not to intervene in Latin American affairs and continued the process of removing troops. During Hoover's administration, relations between Latin America and the United States improved greatly.

Elsewhere, however, Hoover's efforts to promote prosperity and peace abroad came to little. As the Depression became entrenched, so did isolationism. Most Americans were far more concerned about keeping their jobs and homes than about international affairs. Republican senator George W. Norris of Nebraska urged the United States to look out for its own interests and let Europe be damned. Unfortunately, like the Depression, world problems would not go away.

If most Americans reacted to the Depression by spurning foreign involvements, the opposite was true in Japan. Japan relied heavily on international trade for its economic growth and its food supply. As declining world trade weakened their economy, the Japanese called for their government to protect their national interests. Japanese nationalists began to look hungrily toward Manchuria, a Chinese province. Rich in iron and coal, Manchuria accounted for 95 percent of Japanese

Bonus Army Unemployed World War I veterans who marched to Washington in 1932 to demand early payment of a promised bonus; Congress refused, and protesters who remained were evicted by the army.

INDIVIDUAL CHOICES

Choosing Confrontation

Milo Reno

In 1918 Milo Reno chose to become a spokesman for the farmer and organized the Farmers' Holiday Association. In 1933, he chose to reject Roosevelt's agricultural recovery program, and lost the support of most farmers, who backed the president. State Historical Society of America.

Born in 1866, Milo Reno was raised in the heartland of Populism and enthusiasm for William Jennings Bryan. Ordained as a Cambellite minister by Oskalossa College, Reno chose to give up the ministry to pursue his true calling—organizing farmers for political action. He joined the Farmers' Union in 1918, dominating it until his death in 1936, and was the driving force behind the Farmers' Holiday Association. Wearing a ten-gallon hat and a flaming red necktie, Reno captured farmers' hearts with evangelical-style speeches that combined simple explanations, personalized enemies, biblical quotes, and farm wisdom.

In 1932, he claimed that Hoover's farm policies were driving hardworking, decent people from the land, and in August he called for a farmers' strike. "Stay home, buy nothing, sell nothing," he commanded the farmers in an effort to force change and break "the grip of Wall Street and international bankers on government." Farmers across Iowa and neighboring states heeded his call, refusing to sell their products. Others erected barricades across highways to prevent farmers' products from reaching processors. Outside Sioux City and other midwestern towns, farmers armed with clubs and pitchforks clashed with truck drivers

overseas investment and supplied vital foodstuffs to the island nation.

In September 1931, a small group of young, anti-Western Japanese army officers in Manchuria executed a plan to establish Japanese rule over the region. They blew up a section of track of the Southern Manchurian Railroad and blamed the Chinese. Then, without informing the civilian government of Japan, they used this as an excuse to attack Chinese forces and take control of the province.

World reaction was one of shock and eventual condemnation, but little else. The League of Nations sheepishly called for peace and appointed a committee to investigate the conflict. Neither the United States nor Great Britain, the two major Pa-

and hastily dispatched sheriff's deputies. By mid-August, over eighty picketers had been arrested, and fearful of further violence and arrests, Reno called a "temporary halt" to the strike.

With the barricades, the strike had received national news coverage focused on the distress of farmers, and politicians had responded. Midwest governors listened to Farmers' Holiday spokesmen and pushed Hoover for increased support for farmers. Presidential candidate Franklin D. Roosevelt emphasized that Democrats promised farm prices "in excess of cost." Reno, like millions of other Americans, saw in Roosevelt a chance for hope, cheered his election, and waited anxiously for the New Deal to begin.

As Roosevelt assumed office, Reno and the Farmers' Holiday movement—now claiming ninety thousand members—continued to attract national attention by stopping farm foreclosures and forcing "penny auctions." Again, direct action seemed to work, as many companies halted foreclosures and ten states even passed foreclosure "moratorium laws." But with Roosevelt in office, farmers were also receiving less and less public support for their activism. Many politicians and journalists now linked their movement with communism. Reno was faced with a hard choice. Should he continue direct action or support Roosevelt's agriculture program?

Responding to negative public opinion, Reno asked farm activists to pull back from confrontation and give Roosevelt time to implement his farm programs. Still, Reno had doubts. He considered Roosevelt an "enigma," and was angry when the New Deal's agriculture program—the Agricultural Adjustment Act—did not include cost-of-production provisions. He told a friend, "I have no faith whatever in the gestures that are being made by the administration. It is simply the same old tactic to hand the people a little measure of relief to suppress rebellion, with no intention of correcting a system that is fundamentally wrong."

In October 1933, Reno made a difficult decision, but one he believed necessary. Roosevelt, he was sure, was taking the nation down the wrong path, which would eventually "crush all . . . independence and liberty . . . setting up a bureaucratic, autocratic, dictatorial government." He renewed the call for a strike and stated that a third political party was the only possible solution "to clean up the stinking mess" in Washington. The strike call was largely ignored by farmers, who had begun to trust Roosevelt's promise of federal support. The momentum of the farmers' protest had vanished, consumed by the spread of the federal government into agricultural affairs.

Increasingly out of touch with most farmers, Reno fell into periods of depression and heavy drinking until, stricken with influenza in March 1936, he checked into a sanitarium. "Tell them I'm really sick," he said. Milo Reno died on May 5, 1936.

cific naval powers, wanted to become involved in an Asian war. Invoking the **Stimson Doctrine,** the United States refused to recognize Japan's newly created puppet state of **Manchukuo.** In American eyes, Manchuria remained a part of China.

The Japanese had violated the Kellogg-Briand Pact and principles of the League of Nations, but the ensuing barrage of protests did nothing to

Stimson Doctrine Declaration by the U.S. secretary of state in 1932 that the United States would not recognize Manchukuo or any other arrangement that threatened China's independence.

Manchukuo Puppet state established by Japan in 1932 and not recognized by the United States.

deter their aggression. In Japan, the conquest of Manchuria magnified the power of pro-imperial and anti-Western groups. In 1933, Japan withdrew from the League of Nations.

At the end of Hoover's presidency, the world was a much different place than in 1928. The cheery optimism of a prosperous world at peace had dissipated.

Depression America

Few Americans in November 1932 were concerned about Japanese militarism in distant Manchuria. Their concerns were much closer to home. The Depression had touched every American, forcing changes in lifestyle, thought, and politics. Poverty was no longer reserved for those viewed as lazy or unworthy; it was no longer relegated to remote areas and inner cities. Now poverty dragged down blue- and white-collar workers, and even a few of the once-rich.

Families in the Depression

The 35 percent drop in average annual income between 1929 and 1933 caused many people to worry about basic survival during the Depression. Some also worried that the Depression was causing a decline in family values and morality. Pointing to the drifters uprooted by hard times, to families without fathers, and to reports of increasing abortions and premarital and deviant sexual activities, they forecast the end of American civilization.

Their fears were unfounded. The vast majority of Americans clung tightly to traditional family values and emphasized family unity. Church attendance actually rose during the Depression, and the number of divorces declined. The percentage of people getting married did drop slightly, but marriages were only delayed, not put off entirely. Moralists decried an increasing abortion rate, but in fact the estimated number of abortions remained steady. Studies also indicated that sexual activity, rather than becoming more varied and promiscuous, actually decreased.

The Depression did tear many families apart, but ironically it brought many others closer together. Economic necessity kept families at home playing board games and cards, reading, and listening to the radio. The game of Monopoly allowed players to fantasize about becoming a millionaire and laugh about going broke.

The Middle and Working Classes and Hard Times

For many of the American middle class and most of the working class, the most common fear was economic insecurity. Would the next day bring a reduction in wages, the loss of a job, or the closing of a business? Some saw their businesses go bankrupt and found new careers. Harry S Truman closed his haberdashery and turned to politics. E. Y. Harburg lost his family's hardware store, borrowed $500 from a friend, and started writing songs. One of them, "Brother, Can You Spare a Dime?" became one of the most famous songs of the Depression era. Other people worked for less, lost and found other jobs, or, disheartened, accepted relief.

Observers in Muncie, Indiana, noted that middle-class neighborhoods during the Depression looked much as they had in the mid-1920s. Clean, neatly kept houses stood behind green lawns. But closer examination showed the growing impact of harder and harder times. Newspapers carried more pages of tax delinquencies, evictions, and foreclosures. Signs appeared in yards and windows announcing a variety of services—household beauty parlors, kitchen bakeries, rooms for boarders. A Milwaukee wife recalled, "I did baking at home to supplement our income. I got 9 cents for a loaf of bread and 25 cents for an apple cake. . . . I cleared about $65 a month."

In Muncie and across the country, families adopted the motto "Use it up, wear it out, make it do, or do without." To save money, many women sewed, baked bread, and canned, reaffirming traditional female roles. A Singer sewing machine salesman commented that he was selling machines to people who in the past would not have sewn. Feed sacks became a source of material.

During the 1920s, the automobile had pulled families away from their porches and backyards. They returned during the Depression. Men tended backyard grills, and entire families looked after vegetable and flower gardens. A "mania for flower gardens," and flower shows struck the middle class. Away from the house, use of the local park and library, dances, and movies provided inexpensive entertainment. Family togetherness was praised as one positive outcome of the Depression. An Indiana newspaper editorialized, "All . . . are hoping for a quick return of prosperity . . . but in the mean time millions of Americans already have a kind of prosperity that includes strengthening the family."

Working-class Americans confronted the same challenges as did Middle America but more often faced the prospect of losing a job and being evicted. In Gary, Indiana, nearly the entire working class was out of a job by 1932. Approximately one-sixth of all urban families, having lost their homes, "doubled up" with relatives. Don Blincoe remembered that most households seemed like his, "where father, mother, children, aunts, uncles and grandma lived together" and pooled their earnings.

Living with relatives, however, did not always help. Unemployed males, especially fathers, often felt shamed by their economic problems. A social worker wrote, "I used to see men cry because they didn't have a job. . . . They were belittled before the eyes of their families and they couldn't take it." John Boris, a Slavic immigrant, was devastated by being laid off by Ford after having worked loyally for the company for fourteen years. "Last July, I was a good man," he lamented. "I ain't a man now."

Many former breadwinners deserted their families and took to the road. Some, called hoboes, rode the rails, hitching rides in boxcars, living in shantytowns, and begging and scrounging for food along the road. Estimates in 1932 placed the number of homeless migrants at between 1 million and 2 million. Suicides increased, as did the number of people admitted to state mental hospitals and the number of children placed in orphanages.

Included in the so-called migration of despair were thousands from rural areas, especially parts of Texas, Arkansas, and Oklahoma. Many **"Arkies" and "Okies,"** like those characterized in John Steinbeck's novel *The Grapes of Wrath* (1939), were forced from their farms by insects, dust, debt, and landlords. They loaded their meager possessions into their jalopies and headed for California. By the end of the decade, California's population had jumped by over a million. Some migrants found jobs, but most continued to wander.

Discrimination in the Depression

The Depression intensified the economic and social difficulties of minorities. For the majority of African Americans who lived in the rural South, the Depression started in the 1920s with the decline of agricultural prices. By 1930, few were making more than $200 a year. As agricultural prices continued to shrink, black sharecroppers, farm hands, and tenant farmers either left or were forced from the farm. Nearly 400,000 left the South. Most headed north to urban centers like Harlem. Those who stayed behind were unemployed or worked for extremely meager wages. In some parishes of Louisiana, cotton pickers earned only 40 cents a day, some only $40 a year.

Racial violence and injustice increased as whites used violence and intimidation to drive blacks from jobs and maintain social dominance. Nowhere was racial bigotry more glaring than in the celebrated Scottsboro case. In 1931, nine black men were arrested in Alabama for raping two white prostitutes. Without any physical evidence, an all-white male jury quickly found the **Scottsboro Nine** guilty. Eight were sentenced to death. Years of appeals and retrials followed. The Supreme Court twice ordered a new trial. Though

"Arkies" and "Okies" Names applied to dispossessed farmers and sharecroppers from Arkansas and Oklahoma, both black and white, who migrated to California during the Depression.

Scottsboro Nine Nine African Americans convicted of raping two white women in a freight train in Alabama in 1931; their case became famous as an example of racism in the legal system.

never acquitted, all nine defendants were free by 1950.

Generally, African Americans living in the North found that white racial attitudes there were much like those in the South. As jobs grew scarce, whites demanded and got the jobs previously held by minorities. Unemployment among urban blacks ran 20 to 50 percent higher than among urban whites. Nationally, 50 percent of the black population was out of work or on relief. In Harlem, low wages, limited relief funds, and racial tensions sparked a race riot in 1935 that cost four lives and millions of dollars in damage.

African-American women, especially in northern cities, also saw significant drops in employment, even though they held low-paying jobs. In Chicago, Cleveland, and Philadelphia, the decline in employment among black women averaged 22.6 percent between 1929 and 1940, as white women and men pushed them out of the labor force.

Like African Americans, Latinos found that the Depression aggravated Anglo hostility and made a hard life harder. Between 1914 and 1929, the Mexican population in California, the Southwest, and the Midwest had grown rapidly. Most Mexican nationals and Mexican Americans squeezed out a meager living. They filled menial jobs, worked in the fields, and farmed small plots of land. The Depression forced many into deeper poverty.

Racial hostility intensified as Anglos demanded that Latino workers be fired to provide jobs for whites. In Tucson, Arizona, Anglos accused Mexicans of "taking the bread out of our white children's mouths." Across the country, by 1937 the lack of jobs, together with Anglo pressure and the Mexican government's encouragement, had convinced more than half a million Mexicans to leave the United States. Those who remained found jobs scarce and pay pitiful.

On the farms in California, the average wage was $289 a year, about a third of what the government described as a subsistence budget. As farm wages dropped and working conditions deteriorated, Mexican-American agricultural unions organized strikes. In a few cases, the unions won small pay raises, but usually the growers, supported by local authorities and public opinion, easily broke the strikes.

Asians, too, faced hardships and growing hostility. In San Francisco, nearly one-sixth of the Asian population was on relief. They received about 10 to 20 percent less than whites because relief agencies concluded that Asians could subsist on a less expensive diet. Some second-generation Japanese hoped that by assimilating, by becoming "200 percent American," they could remove economic and social barriers. The Japanese-American Citizens League was organized in 1930 and worked to overcome discrimination and to repeal anti-Asian legislation. By 1940, it had six thousand members but had made little headway. Asians remained isolated in ethnic enclaves.

Women in the Depression

While African Americans and Latinos found their already low status declining, some women discovered new opportunities. More white women entered the work force than ever before, primarily at the bottom of the occupational ladder. But in the professions, gender worked against women. The number of women in the professions declined from 14.2 to 12.3 percent during the Depression. Public opinion polls consistently found that most people, including women, believed that men, not women, should have the available jobs. Women were accused of stealing jobs from men. Opinion was especially hostile toward married women who worked. A survey of fifteen hundred school districts found that 77 percent did not hire married women as teachers and 63 percent fired women when they married. In 1932, 2 million women were out of work, and by 1933, an estimated 145,000 women were homeless.

For many rural women, the Depression took away a major avenue to new status: migration to the city. Throughout the 1920s, an increasing number of rural women, white and black, had moved to urban areas, taking domestic and other service jobs. But during the 1930s, such jobs in the cities became scarce, and many women were forced to remain on the farm. Too frequently, foreclosures and drought destroyed farm life. Rural women like

Ma Joad, heroically depicted in *The Grapes of Wrath,* had to adapt to life on the road, as over 2.5 million farm families were forced to migrate.

Among women who did enter the work force, few found that bringing home the paycheck changed either their status or their role within the family. Husbands still maintained authority and dominance in the home. Unemployed husbands rarely helped with household chores. One husband agreed to help with the laundry but refused to hang the wash outside for fear that neighbors might see him doing woman's work. Still, as wives and mothers, women were praised as pillars of stability in a changing and perilous society.

Franklin D. Roosevelt

As Americans sought to adapt to the economic crisis, many looked to the Democratic party for leadership and a change. Throughout early 1932, **Franklin D. Roosevelt** had campaigned for the Democratic presidential nomination, saying that government needed to be concerned about the "forgotten man," who, through no fault of his own, suffered from the Depression.

Born into wealth and privilege, Roosevelt had attended elite schools: Groton Academy, Harvard University, and Columbia Law School. The popular Roosevelt entered New York politics in 1910, winning a seat in the legislature. Tall, handsome, charming, glib, and willing to work with Tammany Hall, Roosevelt moved up the political ladder quickly. In 1920, he was selected as James Cox's running mate. Roosevelt came off well in a losing campaign.

The climb seemed suddenly over in 1921, however, when Roosevelt was stricken with polio and paralyzed from the waist down. But he and his wife, Eleanor, were determined to overcome his disability. For two years, Roosevelt worked hard to advance from bedridden invalid to barely mobile. He was never able to walk except with the aid of heavy steel leg braces and crutches. At the same time, Eleanor Roosevelt toiled tirelessly to keep his political career alive. Making his return to the political battlefield in 1928, Roosevelt ran for governor of New York and won.

♦ In the 1932 election, Roosevelt campaigned across the nation, always appearing confident and cheerful. Some said that his smile was the biggest political weapon he had—not only against Hoover but also against the Depression. *FPG.*

As governor, Roosevelt saw nothing wrong with governmental activism to deal with economic disaster. He was one of the few governors to mobilize his state's limited resources to help the unemployed and the poor. Although he made little

Franklin D. Roosevelt New York governor elected president in 1932 with the promise of a "new deal for the American people"; he would lead the country through the Depression and World War II.

headway against the Depression, his efforts projected an image of a caring and energetic leader. His brave struggle to overcome polio, combined with his effectiveness as governor and his cheery disposition, made him the logical candidate for the presidency.

The 1932 Election

In accepting the Democratic nomination, Roosevelt emphasized two points: he was a man of action who promoted change, and his paralysis in no way hindered his capacity for work. Roosevelt also established the theme for the coming campaign by promising a "new deal for the American people." Although Roosevelt offered no concrete solutions to the problems plaguing the country, he stirred people's hopes.

The election was a huge success for the Democratic party and Roosevelt. Across the nation, people voted for Democrats: for state and local officials, for Congress, and, most important, for president. Roosevelt won in a landslide, garnering 57.4 percent of the popular vote. Hoover carried only six states.

S U M M A R Y

Expectations
Constraints
Choices
Outcomes

In the period from 1928 to 1932, the United States underwent major changes of lasting impact. Hoover assumed the presidency in 1929 a heroic figure. *Expectations* were high that further growth in the economy would enhance the quality of American life. The onslaught of the Depression, however, quickly changed Hoover's and the nation's fortunes. The economic flaws that had remained hidden during the apparent prosperity of the 1920s were soon exposed as banks and businesses closed. The economic collapse originated in part from internal weaknesses in the economy and the government's *choices* to promote easy money and to encourage speculation.

More than any previous president, Hoover *chose* to expand the role of the federal government to meet the economic crisis. He initiated a series of measures, including the Reconstruction Finance Corporation, by which the federal government tried to stimulate the economy. But Hoover's philosophy of limited government *constrained* the effort. The outcome was that the economy continued to worsen.

The Depression forced Americans to adjust their values and lifestyles to meet the economic and psychological crisis. Industrial workers and minorities faced extra burdens of discrimination and loss of status. Although many Americans had to make difficult *choices* that disrupted their lives, the *outcome* was that society generally remained stable as most people learned to cope with the Depression.

The Depression also made a mockery of Hoover's *expectations* about a prosperous and peaceful world. During the 1920s, the United States had *chosen* a path of independent internationalism that stressed voluntary cooperation among nations, while at the same time enhancing private American economic opportunities around the world. Although relations with Latin America improved under Hoover, elsewhere an *outcome* of the worldwide depression was international instability, as symbolized by Japan's invasion of Manchuria. *Constrained* by economic worries, however, more and more Americans withdrew into isolationism.

By 1932, most Americans had lost their faith in Hoover, the Republicans, and American business. Voters *chose* to put their faith instead in Franklin D. Roosevelt.

SUGGESTED READINGS

Bernstein, Michael A. *The Great Depression* (1987).

A detailed economic examination of the causes and effects of the Depression.

Bird, Carolyn. *The Invisible Scar* (1966).

An excellent study of how people responded to the impact of the Depression.

Macaulay, Neill. *The Sandino Affair* (1985).

An examination of Nicaraguan affairs and the American role in Central America through the eyes of Augusto Sandino.

Nash, Gerald D. *The Crucial Era: The Great Depression and World War II, 1929–1945* (1992).

A comprehensive and straightforward history of the period.

Terkel, Studs. *Hard Times: An Oral History of the Great Depression* (1970).

A classic example of how oral histories can give a human dimension to history.

Thomas, Gordon, and Max Morgan-Witts. *The Day the Bubble Burst: The Social History of the Wall Street Crash of 1929* (1979).

A view of the American economy and the stock market crash as experienced by selected individuals.

Wilson, Joan Hoff. *Herbert Hoover: Forgotten Progressive* (1970).

A positive evaluation of the life of Herbert Hoover that stresses his accomplishments as well as his limitations.

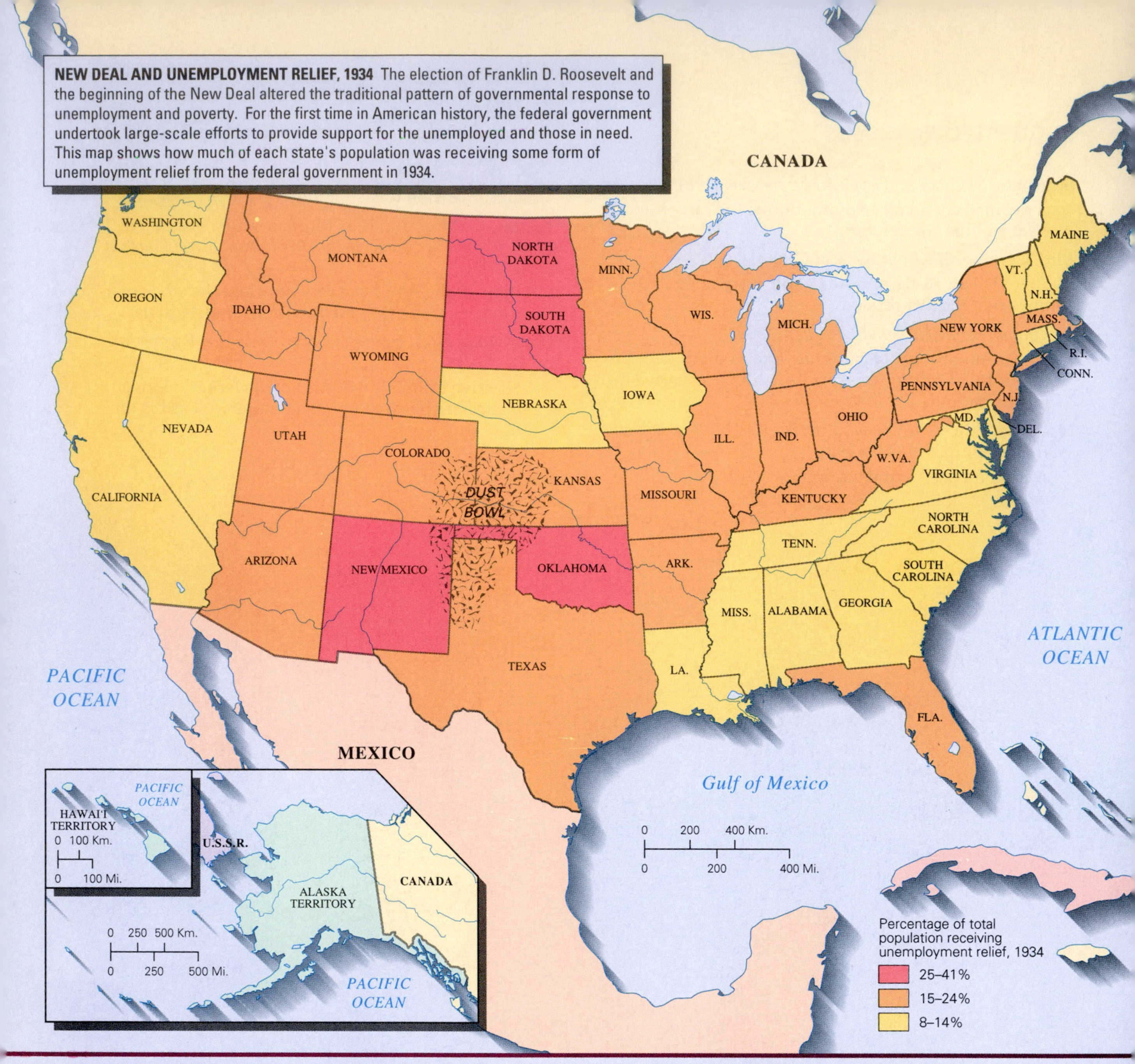
CANADA
WASHINGTON
OREGON
IDAHO
MONTANA
NORTH DAKOTA
SOUTH DAKOTA
MINN.
WIS.
MICH.
WYOMING
NEBRASKA
IOWA
NEVADA
UTAH
COLORADO
CALIFORNIA
KANSAS
DUST BOWL
MISSOURI
ILL.
IND.
OHIO
ARIZONA
NEW MEXICO
OKLAHOMA
ARK.
TEXAS
LA.
MISS.
ALABAMA
GEORGIA
TENN.
KENTUCKY
W.VA.
VIRGINIA
NORTH CAROLINA
SOUTH CAROLINA
FLA.
PENNSYLVANIA
NEW YORK
MAINE
VT.
N.H.
MASS.
R.I.
CONN.
N.J.
MD.
DEL.
PACIFIC OCEAN
ATLANTIC OCEAN
Gulf of Mexico
MEXICO
0 200 400 Km.
0 200 400 Mi.
HAWAI'I TERRITORY
0 100 Km.
0 100 Mi.
U.S.S.R.
ALASKA TERRITORY
0 250 500 Km.
0 250 500 Mi.
Percentage of total population receiving unemployment relief, 1934
25–41%
15–24%
8–14%

NEW DEAL AND UNEMPLOYMENT RELIEF, 1934 The election of Franklin D. Roosevelt and the beginning of the New Deal altered the traditional pattern of governmental response to unemployment and poverty. For the first time in American history, the federal government undertook large-scale efforts to provide support for the unemployed and those in need. This map shows how much of each state's population was receiving some form of unemployment relief from the federal government in 1934.

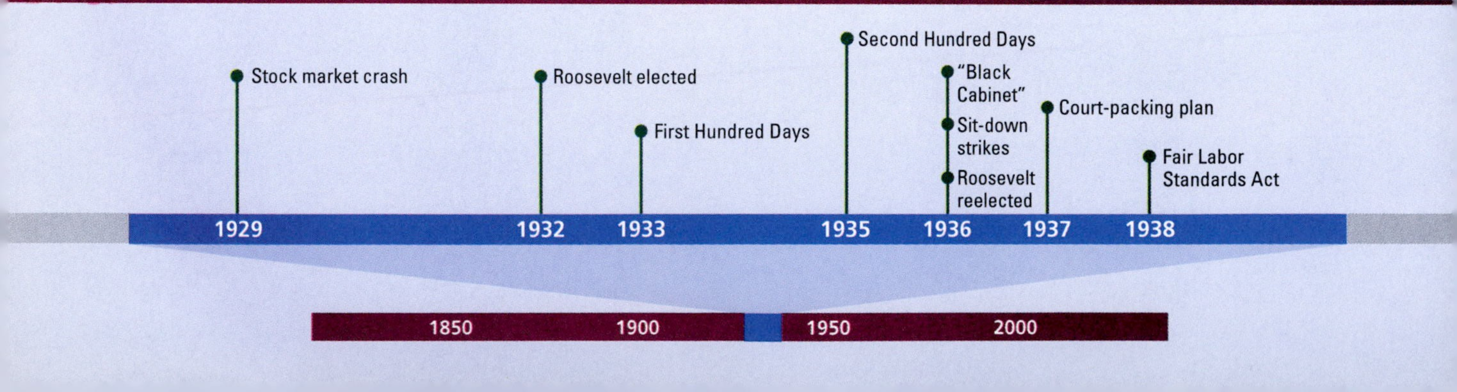
1929 Stock market crash
1932 Roosevelt elected
1933 First Hundred Days
1935 Second Hundred Days
1936 "Black Cabinet"
Sit-down strikes
Roosevelt reelected
1937 Court-packing plan
1938 Fair Labor Standards Act
1850
1900
1950
2000

CHAPTER 25

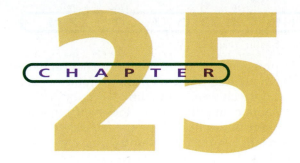

The New Deal, 1933–1940

A New President, a New Deal

- How did public and political expectations and constraints shape Roosevelt's choices during the First Hundred Days?
- How well did the NRA and the AAA meet the expectations of Roosevelt and his advisers?
- How did political and social constraints shape the outcomes of New Deal relief efforts?

The Second Hundred Days

- What were the sources of opposition to Roosevelt's First Hundred Days?
- What was the outcome of Roosevelt's response to his critics?

The New Deal and Society

- What were the outcomes of the New Deal for cities across America?
- What were Roosevelt's expectations regarding civil rights? How did the New Deal affect the choices of women, African Americans, Latinos, and American Indians?

The New Deal Winds Down

- Why did Roosevelt choose to pack the Supreme Court? What was the outcome of this effort?
- What was the outcome of the New Deal for the structure of government and Americans' expectations about government?

INTRODUCTION

The Depression brought to the presidency an individual who would dominate American history for the next thirteen years: Franklin D. Roosevelt. The dire economic situation gave Roosevelt unparalleled opportunities to reshape the federal government's relationship to the country. Roosevelt had few qualms about using the power of the government to combat the Depression.

Americans' *expectations* created opportunities for Roosevelt, but he faced serious *constraints* as well. Crisis or not, there were political and ideological limits on how much the president could change. To many on the political left, Roosevelt's election offered the perfect chance to reform society, to achieve social justice for all, and to restructure American capitalism to make it more humane. But Roosevelt had no intention of abandoning capitalism or restructuring American society. Eleanor Roosevelt, more socially liberal than her husband, reflected, "I'm the agitator; he's the politician." As a politician, Roosevelt knew that the nature of two-party politics loomed as a *constraint* to any significant shift toward the political left. Indeed, many conservatives *chose* to oppose any form of government activism and expansion of federal power. Another obstacle was the lack of precedent: no one knew what kinds of intervention would work on the reeling economy. Even among Roosevelt's advisers, there was disagreement on the nature of programs and the extent and type of governmental activism.

Roosevelt's *choices* were thus shaped by both public and political *expectations* and *constraints*. The *outcome* was the New Deal, which witnessed a barrage of legislation along three paths: economic recovery, relief for the victims of the Depression, and reforms to regulate the economy. This *outcome* was to change the responsibilities and power of the federal government. Roosevelt would be revered and hated, but no one could deny his impact.

In 1933, riding a wave of popular support, Roosevelt faced few political *constraints* as he initiated the First Hundred Days of the New Deal. A year later, that tide had changed. Many who had given Roosevelt a free hand in 1933 were now beginning to oppose him and his programs. Conservatives condemned economic and business controls and excessive federal spending. Liberals called for fewer compromises with business, increased spending, and more programs for workers, minorities, the poor, and the unemployed. With his popularity confirmed by the 1934 elections, Roosevelt *chose* to consider new approaches that placed a stronger emphasis on people than on business. The *outcome* was a Second Hundred Days of legislation passed in 1935 and 1936.

The New Deal expanded not only the functions of government but also the ranks of those voting Democrat. New Deal programs attracted women, minorities, and blue-collar workers. The president's overwhelming victory in 1936 verified the party's increased strength and raised the possibility of further expansion of government social programs. Such *expectations* quickly evaporated, however, as new *constraints* appeared after Roosevelt's unsuccessful challenge to the Supreme Court. By 1938, the New Deal had achieved its final shape. It had not promoted a full economic recovery, but it had restored Americans' faith in the economic and political system. The New Deal had rescued American capitalism. It also had profoundly changed the role and function of government. The long-term *outcome* of the New Deal was that the federal government emerged as the most powerful and important level of government in the nation. Before the 1930s, people looked to local, county, and state government for help. After the New Deal, people looked to Washington for assistance. Government and politics would never be the same.

Expectations
Constraints
Choices
Outcomes

CHRONOLOGY

Out of Depression

1929	Stock market crash
1932	Roosevelt elected president Milo Reno forms Farmers' Holiday Association 32,000 U.S. businesses fail
1933	Dust bowl begins 4,000 U.S. banks fail Bank Holiday First Fireside Chat 12 million Americans (25 percent) unemployed First Hundred Days: AAA, TVA, NIRA, CCC Twenty-first Amendment Home Owner's Loan Corporation formed
1934	Huey Long's Share the Wealth plan Father Coughlin forms National Union for Social Justice Indian Reorganization Act Securities and Exchange Commission formed American Liberty League established Townsend movement begins
1935	Second Hundred Days: WPA, Social Security Act, Wagner Act Rural Electrification Administration formed National Youth Administration created Long assassinated Committee for Industrial Organizations established NRA ruled unconstitutional in *Schechter* case
1936	AAA ruled unconstitutional in *Butler* case Roosevelt re-elected "Black Cabinet" established Sit-down strikes begin
1937	Court-packing plan "Roosevelt's recession"
1938	Fair Labor Standards Act AAA re-established 10.4 million Americans unemployed Republican victories in congressional elections
1939	Marian Anderson's concert at Lincoln Memorial John Steinbeck's *The Grapes of Wrath*
1940	Richard Wright's *Native Son*

A New President, a New Deal

During the long winter of despair between the November 1932 election and the March 1933 inauguration, Roosevelt and his advisers debated what course of action to take against the Depression. His advisers, often called the **Brain Trust** because of the many professors who joined the administration, were deeply divided. One group led by Columbia professors Rexford Tugwell and Raymond Moley believed that the concentration of American business in fewer and fewer hands was inevitable and favorable. Like Theodore Roosevelt, they applauded big business as efficient, economical, and, with the proper controls, beneficial. Their solution to the economic crisis was corporate regulation and public planning.

Brain Trust Group of specialists in law, economics, and social welfare who, as advisers to President Roosevelt, helped develop the social and economic principles of the New Deal.

Felix Frankfurter represented another faction within the Brain Trust. He disagreed about the benefits derived from the concentration of business and the centralization of planning. Frankfurter distrusted big business and wanted more competition, along with social programs to help those most harmed by the Depression. Despite their differences, the Brain Trust agreed on the necessity of federal action to combat the Depression.

Roosevelt relished his advisers' debates, but in the end he made up his own mind about what to include in the **New Deal.** He would do what seemed expedient and would discard whatever did not work and whatever cost too much, politically or socially.

Bank Holiday

As Roosevelt's inauguration approached, the nation faced a severe banking crisis. Many banks had gone out of business since the Crash, leaving depositors penniless. In 1932, 1,456 banks had failed. The public's dwindling confidence in banks caused a growing number of **runs** on banks as depositors demanded their money. Most banks had no money and were forced to close their doors. By March 4, 1933, Inauguration Day, nearly all the country's banks were either closed or operating under severe restrictions. With the banks unable to operate, the economy of the United States was stiffening with paralysis.

On Inauguration Day, Roosevelt reassured the American public that he was going to take action. Millions listened to the radio as the president calmly stated that Americans had "nothing to fear but fear itself." The American economy was sound and would revive, but the nation would not revive by merely talking about it. "We must act quickly," he cautioned, adding that he intended to ask Congress for sweeping powers to deal with the crisis.

On March 6, Roosevelt announced a national **Bank Holiday** that closed all the country's banks. Three days later, as freshmen congressmen were still finding their seats, the president presented Congress with a request for an emergency banking bill. Without even seeing the written bill, Democrats and Republicans gave Roosevelt what he wanted in less than four hours. The **Emergency Banking Act** allowed the Federal Reserve to examine banks and to certify those that were sound. It also allowed the Federal Reserve and the Reconstruction Finance Corporation to support the nation's banks by providing funds and buying stocks of preferred banks.

On Sunday evening, March 12, in the first of his so-called **Fireside Chats,** Roosevelt confidently told Americans that the federal government was solving the banking crisis. Federal banking officials were going to inspect banks, he announced, and those banks determined to be sound would be allowed to reopen. Banks would be safe again. "I can assure you," he joked, "it is safer to keep your money in a reopened bank than under the mattress."

Most of the 60 million Americans who listened to the speech believed the president. When banks in the twelve Federal Reserve cities reopened on Monday, customers deposited rather than withdrew money. Within a month, nearly 75 percent of the nation's banks were operating again. Roosevelt's quick and effective action established a positive national mood. The New Deal was under way. Over the next one hundred days, the new president

New Deal Roosevelt's program for attacking the problems of the Depression, which included relief for the poor and unemployed, efforts to bring about economic recovery, and reform of the nation's financial system.

run A panic during which depositors fearful of bank failure demand to withdraw their money, thus forcing the bank to close.

Bank Holiday Temporary shutdown of banks throughout the country by executive order of President Roosevelt in March 1933, until government authorities could examine each bank's condition to determine its soundness.

Emergency Banking Act Law passed in 1933 that permitted sound banks in the Federal Reserve System to reopen and allowed the government to supply funds to support private banks.

Fireside Chats Radio talks in which President Roosevelt promoted New Deal policies and reassured the nation.

would sign fifteen major pieces of legislation. The legislation, Roosevelt explained, had three different objectives: relief, recovery, and reform.

As the legalization of beer and wine sales in March 1933 illustrates, actual legislation often addressed several of these objectives. Legalizing their sale put people to work. It was also a reform measure aimed at curbing bootlegging. Similar motives informed Roosevelt's support for the repeal of Prohibition, accomplished by passage of the **Twenty-first Amendment** in December 1933.

Primary targets for reform included the banking and stock market industries. In June 1933, Congress passed the Glass-Steagall Banking Act, which reorganized the banking and financial system, gave new powers and responsibilities to the Federal Reserve System, and created the **Federal Deposit Insurance Corporation (FDIC).** The FDIC provided federal insurance for bank accounts of less than $5,000 and thus provided safety to millions of customers. Reforms for the stock market came in May 1933 with the Federal Security Act, which required companies to provide information about their economic condition to stock buyers. The **Securities and Exchange Commission (SEC),** created in June 1934, regulated stock market activities. Public approval for the reforms was widespread.

Seeking Agricultural Recovery

As Roosevelt assumed office, the plight of farmers appeared near disaster. The Farmers' Holiday Association threatened to call a farmers' strike across the nation unless Congress acted to restore farm profits. Roosevelt responded sympathetically because he believed that the family farm was an essential part of American life and needed to be saved. His goal was to raise farm prices through national planning to **parity**—the level of prices that farmers received in the profitable years prior to World War I. Secretary of Agriculture Henry A. Wallace was convinced that the nation's economic problems could not be solved without first resolving the problem of agricultural overproduction and farm profits. The challenge was to convince farmers to cut production. The **Agricultural Adjustment Act (AAA),** passed on May 12, proposed a way to do that.

The act encouraged farmers to reduce production by paying them not to plant. A national planning board determined the amount of land to be removed from production and then allocated specific reductions for wheat, cotton, corn, rice, tobacco, hogs, and dairy products to the states. State boards divided production cuts among participating farmers and compensated them for lost crops and livestock. The money for paying farmers not to plant was generated by a special tax on industrial food processors.

Because the AAA was not approved until May, after spring sowing, hundreds of acres of corn and tobacco crops had to be plowed under. Likewise, farmers had to destroy thousands of hogs and dairy cows and huge quantities of milk. In the Midwest, the continuing drought made it easier for ranchers and farmers to take land out of production. Many shuddered at the waste and pressed for the surplus food to be made available to the needy rather than being destroyed. Others complained that small farmers did not have enough land to remove from cultivation to gain from the program. They also pointed out that sharecroppers and tenant farmers were often evicted when landlords took land out of production to meet AAA quotas. Evictions and the Depression pushed more than 3 million people off the land.

Twenty-first Amendment Amendment to the Constitution in 1933 that repealed the Eighteenth Amendment and thus brought Prohibition to an end.

Federal Deposit Insurance Corporation Created by the Glass-Steagall Banking Act of 1933, it insured deposits up to a fixed sum in member banks of the Federal Reserve System.

Securities and Exchange Commission Bipartisan agency created by Congress to license stock exchanges and supervise their activities, including the setting of margin rates.

parity The fair value of a commodity, as opposed to its market value.

Agricultural Adjustment Act Law passed in 1933 that sought to reduce overproduction by paying farmers to keep land fallow; it was struck down by the Supreme Court in 1936.

Although large amounts of land were left fallow, production did not drop substantially. Farmers took their least productive land out of cultivation and used more scientific farming methods to grow more crops on fewer acres. To ensure crop reduction in 1934, Congress passed the Bankhead Cotton Control Act and the Kerr-Smith Tobacco Control Act. These acts levied special taxes on cotton and tobacco farmers who exceeded their production quotas.

By 1935, recovery in the agricultural sector had clearly started. Farm prices were rising, and the purchasing power of farmers was increasing. Then, in 1936, the Supreme Court declared the AAA unconstitutional in ***Butler v. the United States.*** The Court ruled that the special tax on food processing was illegal. The Roosevelt administration pushed the Soil Conservation and Domestic Allotment Act through Congress quickly to maintain the agricultural recovery. Under this act, the **Soil Conservation Service** paid farmers for cutting back on soil-depleting crops like cotton, tobacco, and wheat and for adopting better conservation methods. Finally, in 1938, Congress approved a second Agricultural Adjustment Act that re-established the principle of federally set commodity quotas, acreage reductions, and parity payments. The second AAA avoided the legal difficulties of the first AAA by using general revenue funds as the source of payments.

The combination of drought and governmental policies stabilized farm prices and saved farms. From 1932 to 1939, farm income more than doubled, and the government provided over $4.5 billion in aid to farmers. Initially regarded as a short-term measure to revitalize agriculture, the second AAA became an accepted solution to farm problems. The policy would contribute to stable agricultural prices for over fifty years. Equally important, Roosevelt's farm programs significantly changed the relationship between agricultural producers and the federal government.

Seeking Industrial Recovery

The **National Industrial Recovery Act (NIRA)** was Roosevelt's answer to the problem of industrial recovery. Approved by Congress in June 1933, the NIRA quickly earned widespread support from business, labor, the unemployed, and community leaders. In a two-part offensive, the **Public Works Administration (PWA)** was given $3.3 billion to put people to work immediately, while the **National Recovery Administration (NRA)** provided programs to restart the nation's industrial engine and create permanent jobs.

The NRA called for business and labor leaders, consumers, and government officials to work together on planning boards to promote industrial growth. The NRA was, Roosevelt explained in a Fireside Chat, a "partnership in planning." To achieve their goals, the boards developed "industrial codes" that set limits on prices, production, and wages. In turn, the government suspended antitrust laws for two years. Roosevelt selected General Hugh Johnson to command the NRA.

Johnson, who had headed the War Industries Board during World War I, relished the opportunity to wage war against the Depression. He immersed himself in forming the planning boards and drafting the codes for the nation's major industries.

Business supported the NRA because it allowed price fixing, which raised prices and profits. Labor

Butler v. the United States Supreme Court ruling in 1936 that declared the Agricultural Adjustment Act invalid on the grounds that it overextended the powers of the federal government.

Soil Conservation Service Agency established by Congress for the prevention of soil erosion; by paying farmers to cut back on soil-depleting crops, the government also addressed the problem of overproduction.

National Industrial Recovery Act Law passed in 1933 establishing the National Recovery Administration to supervise industry and the Public Works Administration to create jobs.

Public Works Administration New Deal agency created in 1933 to increase employment and to stimulate economic recovery.

National Recovery Administration New Deal agency created in 1933 that was responsible for implementing national industrial codes.

was attracted by Section 7a, which gave workers the right to organize and bargain collectively, outlawed child labor, and established minimum wages and maximum hours of work. Although consumers, workers, and government officials were represented on the boards, the boards were dominated by business elements.

Initially, Johnson's zealous efforts were remarkably successful. The blue eagle that was chosen as the NRA's symbol appeared everywhere as Americans promised to do their part. Within six months, the National Recovery Administration had written 557 specific codes covering industries of every size.

But the early enthusiasm for the NRA soon waned. The boards typically emphasized profits rather than market expansion or wage increases. Workers complained that too many codes instituted low wages and that employers frequently violated the wage, hour, and unionization provisions of the codes. Consumers lost faith in the blue eagle as prices rose without any corresponding growth in wages or jobs. Farmers complained that NRA-generated price increases ate up any AAA benefits they received. Businesses complained about mountains of paperwork, criticized Section 7a, and feared further restrictions on their activities.

To nearly everyone's relief, on May 27, 1935, the Supreme Court declared the NRA unconstitutional in *Schechter Poultry Corporation v. the United States.* Noting that the Schechter Corporation was not involved in interstate commerce, the high court ruled that the government could not set wages and hours in local plants. The PWA remained in place, but with the NRA gone, Roosevelt was forced to consider other means to rekindle the economy.

TVA and REA

Perhaps the most innovative and successful recovery program of the New Deal was the **Tennessee Valley Authority (TVA).** The Tennessee River and its **tributaries** ran through some of the nation's most economically disadvantaged areas. The TVA harnessed the river system of the Tennessee Valley through the construction of flood-control and hydroelectric dams (see Map 25.1). The first benefit was new jobs, but the chief outcome was long-term economic development. The TVA's directors used the AAA to improve agriculture while the TVA provided electricity through federally owned hydroelectric systems. Only 2 percent of the homes and farms in the region had electricity in 1933. Twelve years later, the number of electrified homes had reached 75 percent. The TVA's cheap electricity attracted businesses like Monsanto Chemical and American Aluminum to the area.

Although many hailed the TVA's accomplishments, the TVA had its critics. Liberals condemned the agency's practice of segregation. Private utility companies and conservatives opposed the idea of a government-owned agency operating factories and power companies. Such conservative opposition was largely responsible for Congress's failure to approve seven more proposed TVA-like projects in 1937.

The TVA's electrification program nevertheless became a precedent for a nationwide effort. Utility companies had argued that rural America was too isolated and poor to make service profitable. Only about 30 percent of farms had electricity in the early thirties. In 1935, the Roosevelt administration created the **Rural Electrification Administration (REA)** to bring electricity to rural America. Working with rural electrical cooperatives, the REA had electrified 45 percent of rural America by 1945 and 90 percent by 1951. The electrification of rural America was one of the most important social and economic changes that took place as a result of the New Deal. It integrated rural America with the culture of modern, urban America.

Tennessee Valley Authority Independent public corporation created by Congress in 1933 and authorized to construct dams and power plants in the Tennessee Valley region—Tennessee, North Carolina, Kentucky, Virginia, Mississippi, Georgia, and Alabama.

tributary A river or stream that flows into a larger river.

Rural Electrification Administration Government agency established in 1936 for the purpose of loaning money to rural cooperatives to start power plants that would bring electricity to isolated farms.

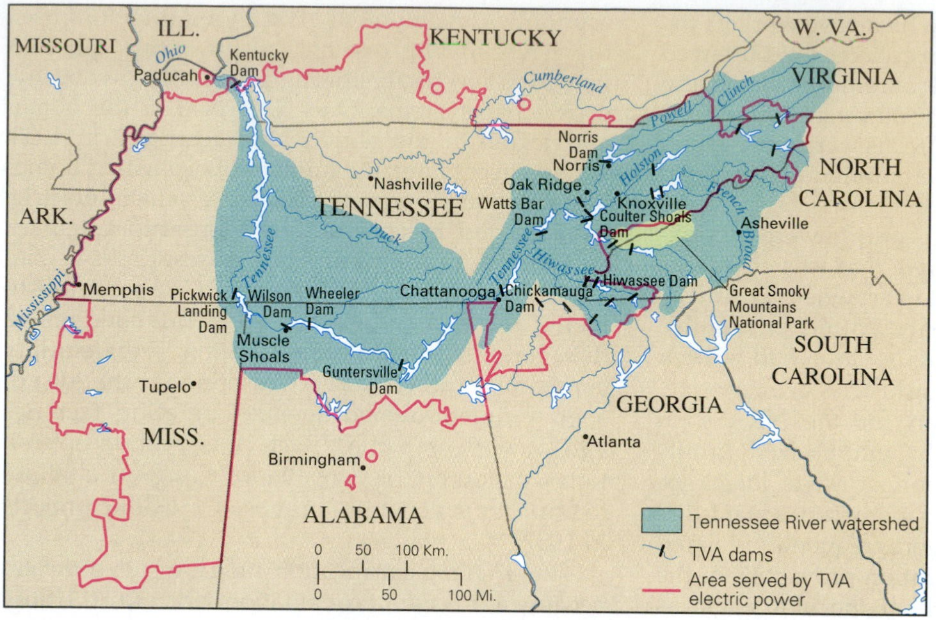

♦ **MAP 25.1 The Tennessee Valley Authority** One of the most ambitious New Deal projects was developing the Tennessee Valley by improving waterways, building hydroelectric dams, and providing electricity to the area. This map shows the various components of the TVA and the region it changed.

Remembering the "Forgotten Man"

Roosevelt did not forget his campaign promises to help the "forgotten man," the 25 percent of the population—nearly 12 million people—who were out of work in March 1933 (see chapter opener map). Recognizing that state and private relief sources were unable to cope with the Depression, Roosevelt proposed four major relief programs during his First Hundred Days.

The **Civilian Conservation Corps (CCC)** established army-style camps to house unemployed urban males ages 18 to 25. Within months, the program had enrolled over 300,000 men, paying them $30 a month, $25 of which they had to send home. By 1941, enrollment was over 2 million men. The "Conservation Army" built national park facilities, cut out roads and **firebreaks,** erected telephone poles, dug irrigation ditches, and planted trees.

The **Federal Emergency Relief Administration (FERA)** and the PWA provided relief for the general population. **Harry Hopkins,** a former social worker, headed the FERA and oversaw a $500 million fund to give to states for their relief efforts. Hopkins soon discovered that some states showed little compassion for the poor. Oregon's governor, for example, opposed payments to anyone able-

Civilian Conservation Corps Organization created by Congress in 1933 to hire young, unemployed men for conservation work, such as planting trees, digging irrigation ditches, and caring for national parks.

firebreak Strip of cleared or plowed land used to stop the spread of a fire.

Federal Emergency Relief Administration New Deal agency created in 1933 to provide direct grants to cities and states to spend on relief.

Harry Hopkins Head of several New Deal agencies, first organizing emergency relief and then public works; he remained a close adviser to Roosevelt during World War II.

bodied enough to work and thought that the feeble-minded and aged should be **chloroformed.** But by 1935, the FERA was spending over $300 million a year on relief measures.

The Public Works Administration, directed by **Harold Ickes,** eventually provided over $4 billion to state and local governments for more than thirty-four thousand **public works** projects, including construction of sidewalks and roads, schools, and community buildings. Ickes wanted PWA projects that were socially and economically desirable, but not all fulfilled his criteria. Urban bosses used PWA monies to make jobs for political supporters, and many communities often ignored their poorest neighborhoods when spending PWA funds.

In November 1933, as high unemployment continued despite the CCC, FERA, and PWA, Roosevelt established the **Civil Works Administration (CWA)** to provide nearly 4 million jobs during the winter of 1933–1934. CWA workers participated in a wide variety of work programs. Critics complained of "make-work" projects that wasted money, but overall CWA funds were well spent. The CWA built over half a million miles of roads and forty thousand schools. It paid the salaries of over fifty thousand rural schoolteachers. Despite its success, Roosevelt ended the CWA in February 1934 when the immediate crisis was over.

Not all relief programs were aimed at the homeless and the poor. Two aided homeowners. The Home Owner's Loan Corporation (HOLC), established in May 1933, permitted homeowners to **refinance** their mortgages at lower interest rates through the federal government. Before it stopped making loans in 1936, the HOLC had refinanced 1 million homes, including 20 percent of all mortgaged urban homes. The National Housing Act, passed in June 1934, created the **Federal Housing Administration (FHA),** which still provides federally backed loans for home mortgages and repairs.

The Second Hundred Days

The New Deal began with almost total support in Congress and among the people. That support did not last. By mid-1933, most Republicans actively opposed New Deal legislation, objecting to relief programs, federal spending, and increased governmental control over business. Conservatives fumed that Roosevelt threatened free enterprise, if not capitalism itself, and that he had betrayed his own class—the rich and privileged. They thought it bad enough when Roosevelt pulled the nation off the **gold standard** in April 1933, but in January 1934 he devalued the gold value of the dollar to $.59. To warn the country about Roosevelt and his "baloney dollars," conservatives became increasingly vocal in their attacks on the president. The Hearst newspaper chain instructed its editors to warn the public that Roosevelt planned to lead the nation into socialism. In August 1934, a coalition of anti–New Deal Democrats, Republicans, and business leaders formed the **American Liberty League (ALL).** By 1935, the ALL was the center of conservative

chloroformed To use the anesthetic chloroform to end a person's life painlessly.

Harold Ickes Secretary of the interior under Roosevelt and Truman and director of the Public Works Administration; he was an efficient administrator who opposed racial discrimination.

public works Construction projects, such as highways or dams, financed by public funds and carried out by the government.

Civil Works Administration Emergency unemployment relief program in 1933 and 1934, which hired 4 million jobless people for federal, state, and local work projects.

refinance To pay off an old mortgage with the proceeds of a new mortgage obtained at a lower interest rate.

Federal Housing Administration Agency created in 1934 to help homeowners finance repairs and to stimulate residential construction through federal mortgages.

gold standard An internationally established value for a nation's currency based on its exchange rate with gold.

American Liberty League Conservative organization that existed between 1934 and 1940 to oppose the New Deal.

opposition to Roosevelt and claimed nearly 150,000 supporters.

Populist Voices

For the majority of the American people, however, Roosevelt and the New Deal still spelled hope and faith in the future. Voters in the 1934 elections gave Democrats friendly to Roosevelt overwhelming victories. They won twenty-six of thirty-five Senate races and nine additional seats in the House. The segment of the Republican party vehemently opposed to the New Deal was virtually wiped out. Those election results made Roosevelt less willing to cooperate with conservatives and business. The president was also aware that economic recovery was not progressing as projected. Unemployment had been reduced, but government work programs still supported nearly 8 million households, or 22 percent of the population. Roosevelt was ready to switch approaches to fighting the Depression. Grassroots criticism that the New Deal was not doing enough to help the "forgotten man" also pushed the president in a new direction.

One of the leading critics was **Father Charles Coughlin,** a Roman Catholic priest who used the radio every Sunday afternoon to reach out to nearly 30 million Americans. Coughlin had lashed out at Hoover and anyone else who opposed relief. "God would have been condemned for giving manna in the desert because it was a dole," he told his audience. Throughout 1933, the "radio priest" of Royal Oak, Michigan, had strongly supported Roosevelt and the New Deal. But by mid-1934, he had turned his influential radio voice first against the National Recovery Administration and then against Roosevelt himself for being too probusiness. In November, he formed the National Union for Social Justice to promote legislation that would help the masses and to peddle his message of blatant anti-Semitism. (Coughlin thought many businessmen and bankers were Jewish.) Coughlin advocated a guaranteed annual income, the redistribution of national wealth, tougher antimonopoly laws, and the nationalization of banking. Within a year, the organization claimed more than 5 million members.

Coughlin was not alone in broadcasting that Roosevelt was not doing enough for the "forgotten man." Senator **Huey Long** of Louisiana, another onetime supporter, hotly criticized the president. Long had achieved power in Louisiana by attacking big money and promising to help poor whites. As governor, he had built roads, schools, and hospitals; provided free textbooks; and imposed new taxes on oil companies and the wealthy. In 1934, he broke with Roosevelt and advocated the **Share the Wealth** plan. The plan called for the federal government to provide every American family with an annual check for $2,000; a home, car, and radio; and a college education for each child. The plan would be funded by having incomes over $1 million taxed at 100 percent and by inheritance laws that would limit inheritances to $5 million. Crying "Soak the Rich!" Share the Wealth societies soon enrolled over 4 million followers.

By 1936, Democratic leaders feared that Long might join forces with Father Coughlin and run for president. Prospects of a third party soared when **Francis Townsend,** a popular spokesman for the elderly poor, appeared willing to join with Long and Coughlin. A doctor in Long Beach, California, Townsend, nearly 70, was well aware of the elderly's plight. Ignored by work programs and frequently denied relief because they owned property,

Father Charles Coughlin Roman Catholic priest whose influential radio addresses in the 1930s at first emphasized social justice but eventually became anti-Semitic and pro-fascist.

Huey Long Louisiana governor, then U.S. senator, who ran a powerful political machine and whose advocacy of the redistribution of income was gaining him a national political following at the time of his assassination in 1935.

Share the Wealth Movement that sprang up around the nation in the 1930s urging the redistribution of wealth through government taxes or programs; its slogan was "Every man a king."

Francis Townsend California physician who proposed the Townsend Plan in 1933, under which every retired person over age 60 would be paid a $200 monthly pension to be spent within the month.

♦ The Works Progress Administration not only built roads and buildings but also provided employment for teachers, writers, and artists. A common theme among WPA artists and writers was the strength and dignity of common people as they faced their difficult lives. Here a Michigan WPA artist sketches WPA workers. *National Archives.*

the elderly were among those most cruelly hit by the Depression. Dr. Townsend advocated a federal old-age pension plan. He wanted the government to provide every American age 60 and over with a monthly $200 pension check. Recipients would be required not to work and to spend the money within the month. Townsend proposed a national sales tax to finance the payments. Several million people joined Townsend Clubs.

The growing popularity of Long, Coughlin, and Townsend reflected the frustration of a large segment of the American population who believed that the New Deal was doing little to help them. Long's and Townsend's programs were attractive because they would aid people, not businesses.

A Shift in Focus

Responding to the growing pressure to modify the New Deal, Roosevelt announced in his 1935 State of the Union address that his administration would adopt a new strategy to combat the Depression. The focus would now be on helping people rather than on helping business increase profits. He asked Congress to provide more work relief, to develop an old-age and unemployment insurance program, and to regulate holding companies and utilities. During the Second Hundred Days, a solidly Democratic and largely liberal Congress responded with a series of acts. In April 1935, Congress allocated nearly $5 billion for relief to be divided among the CCC, the PWA, the FERA, and the newly created **Works Progress Administration (WPA).**

Roosevelt named Harry Hopkins to head the WPA, whose goal was to provide jobs as quickly as possible. Between 1935 and 1938, the WPA

Works Progress Administration Agency established in 1935 and headed by Harry Hopkins, which hired the unemployed for construction, conservation, and arts programs.

employed over 2.1 million people a year. Most performed manual labor, but the WPA employed professional and white-collar workers as well. Teachers, writers, artists, actors, photographers, composers, and musicians were among the professionals who benefited from New Deal programs. The WPA's Writers Project provided future Pulitzer Prize–winning novelist Saul Bellow with a job writing short biographies and allowed African-American author Richard Wright to write his highly acclaimed *Native Son.* Professional theater groups toured towns and cities performing Shakespearean and other plays. By 1939, an estimated 30 million people had watched WPA productions that included known actors such as Orson Welles and John Housman.

The WPA also made special efforts to help women, minorities, and students and young adults. Prodded by Eleanor Roosevelt, the WPA employed between 300,000 and 400,000 women a year. Although some were hired as teachers and nurses, the majority worked on sewing and canning projects. WPA efforts to ensure African-American employment thrived in the northeastern states but stalled in the South. The **National Youth Administration (NYA)** provided aid for college and high school students and programs for young people not in school. In 1936, over 200,000 students were receiving aid. Mary McLeod Bethune, an African-American educator, directed the NYA's Office of Negro Affairs. Through constant pressure, she obtained support for black schools, colleges, and vocational programs.

More dramatic than the WPA was passage of the **Social Security Act** of 1935. Whereas the WPA was a temporary expedient, the establishment of a federal old-age and survivor insurance program was to be a permanent modification of the government's role in society. Previously, only 15 percent of workers had been covered by any sort of pension. The primary force behind the Social Security Act was **Frances Perkins** , the first woman cabinet member (see Individual Choices: Frances Perkins). In 1934, encouraged by the popularity of Dr. Townsend's plan, Perkins chaired the Committee on Economic Security to draft a social security bill. Passed by Congress in August 1935, the Social Security Act had three sections.

The most controversial part of the legislation created the Social Security system. Conservatives insisted that it would remove the incentive to work. Social Security provided a pension plan for retirees 65 or older. They would receive initial payments ranging from $10 to $85 a month, depending on how much they paid into the system. The more a worker paid into the system, the larger his or her pension would be. The program would begin in 1937, when a new tax (mandated by the Federal Insurance Contributions Act, or FICA) would be collected from workers and employers. Not all workers were covered. Many occupations, including domestic and agricultural laborers, were exempt. Compared to Townsend's dream and many existing European systems, U.S. Social Security was limited and conservative. Nonetheless, it represented a major leap in government's responsibility for the welfare of society.

A less controversial section of the bill established a federally supported system of unemployment compensation. Within two years, every state was part of the system, paying the jobless between $15 and $18 a week in unemployment compensation. A third section of the Social Security Act made federal funds available to states for aid to families with dependent children and the disabled. This provision aided nearly 3.8 million female-headed families that had been helplessly impoverished.

The National Labor Relations Act, generally called the **Wagner Act,** strengthened the union

National Youth Administration Program established by executive order in 1935 to provide employment for young people and to help needy high school and college students continue their education.

Social Security Act Law passed in 1935 that created systems of unemployment, old-age, and disability insurance, and provided for child welfare.

Frances Perkins Industrial reformer who, as Roosevelt's secretary of labor from 1933 to 1945, was the first woman cabinet member.

Wagner Act Law passed in 1935 that defined unfair labor practices and protected unions against such coercive measures as the blacklist and company unions.

movement by putting the power of government behind the workers' right to organize. It created the National Labor Relations Board to ensure workers' rights, to conduct elections for union representatives, and to prevent unfair labor practices like firing workers for union activities. Roosevelt's support for the Wagner Act helped clinch labor support for himself and the Democrats.

The combination of the Wagner Act and the Social Security Act reduced the credibility of those who called Roosevelt too conservative. Similar political goals were evident in other acts of the Second Hundred Days. The Revenue Act of 1935 placed higher taxes on inheritance and gifts, raised income-tax rates for the wealthy, and instituted a graduated income tax for corporations. Conservatives, the business community, and the wealthy all blasted the tax changes, but among the not-so-wealthy, the law was clearly popular. The new tax structure actually did little to redistribute wealth. In fact, from 1933 to 1939, the wealthiest 1 percent increased their personal wealth 2.3 percent, controlling 30.6 percent of the nation's wealth. Still, Roosevelt's tax measures further angered business interests and raised conservative cries of a New Deal dictatorship.

Other acts of the Second Hundred Days reasserted Roosevelt's support for the "forgotten man." To help small farmers, sharecroppers, and tenant farmers, the **Resettlement Administration (RA)** and the Farm Mortgage Moratorium Act were passed. The latter allowed federal courts to reduce the debts of farmers to that equal to their property value. It also provided a three-year **moratorium** against farm seizures for farmers who had court permission. The RA tried to resettle marginal farmers on better land.

The New Deal and Society

Just as the Depression had an impact on every segment of society, so too did the New Deal. Newly restored confidence found expression in the popular entertainment of the time. The New Deal encouraged hope for overcoming obstacles that had long limited opportunities for some minorities.

The New Deal and Urban America

As the Depression set in, city governments found that their resources were too few to maintain the city, much less care for the needy. In 1933, 145 of the largest cities collected only 75 percent of the property-tax revenues they were owed. To "save" their budgets, cities cut wages and laid off policemen, firemen, teachers, and other municipal workers. In most cities, relief programs were among those targeted for elimination or reduction. "I am as much in favor of relief for the unemployables as anyone, but I am unwilling to continue this relief at the expense of bankrupting the City of Birmingham," stated the head of the city commission.

The New Deal provided new hope for cities by providing public works projects that eased the burdens of unemployment and relief. In many cities, especially in the West and South, public works projects also improved the existing **infrastructure** by constructing roads, bridges, hospitals, schools, and other public buildings. San Francisco saw the construction of the Golden Gate Bridge. Southern California, especially the Los Angeles basin, drew additional benefits from the water and cheap electrical power supplied with the completion of Boulder Dam in 1935. There were also political gains to be made from federal money and projects. "Roosevelt Is My Religion" was the 1936 campaign slogan of Mayor Edward J. Kelly, who kept Chicago solvent with federal funds.

Other federal programs shaped the growth of urban areas in subtler ways. Agencies like the HOLC and the FHA saved thousands of urban homes

Resettlement Administration Agency established in 1935 to resettle poor families on new farms or in new communities and to make loans enabling sharecroppers to buy their own land.

moratorium Suspension of an ongoing or planned activity.

infrastructure An underlying base for a system or organization; the basic facilities, services, and installations needed for the functioning of a community.

INDIVIDUAL CHOICES

Choosing to Serve

Frances Perkins

Beginning in 1911, Francis Perkins sought to improve working conditions for the nation's men, women, and children. Perkins was the first woman cabinet member, and as secretary of labor, she tirelessly worked to create the Social Security system, establish a minimum wage for workers, and limit the number of hours people could be required to work. New York Historical Society.

On February 1, 1933, responding to a month-long flurry of rumors in the press and among "those in the know" that she was to be chosen secretary of labor, Frances Perkins wrote to President-elect Franklin D. Roosevelt saying that she "honestly" hoped the rumors were wrong. Shortly after the letter, Mary Dewson, director of the Women's Division of the Democratic National Committee, visited Perkins to convince her to take the cabinet position if offered. Dewson, who had recommended Perkins to Roosevelt, reminded Perkins of the many years she had spent fighting to establish unemployment compensation and a minimum wage and to abolish child labor. "You want these things done," Dewson argued. "You have ideas. . . . Nobody else will do it." She told Perkins, "You owe it to the women. . . . Too many people count on what you do."

On February 22, Roosevelt asked Perkins to be secretary of labor. She replied that, if she accepted, she would push for the abolition of child labor and the establishment of unemployment insurance, old-age pensions, a minimum wage, and a limit on maximum hours of work. Roosevelt responded that she would "have to invent the way to do these things" and that she should not "expect too much help from" him. She chose to accept the position. After some opposition from organized labor, she was easily confirmed by the Senate and became secretary of labor—"Madam Secretary," the first woman to serve in a president's cabinet.

She arrived at the position through hard work and a commitment to improving workers' lives. The daughter of a conservative middle-class family, she had been introduced to the lives of workers while taking an economics class at Mount Holyoke College. She quickly immersed herself in the spirit of the Progressive era, participating in the settlement house movement and helping to investigate working conditions as part of the New York Factory Commission that arose after the tragic fire at the Triangle Shirtwaist Company in 1911.

Through her work on the commission and with the Consumers' League, she became involved in New York politics as a supporter of Al Smith. She served Governor Smith as a member of the Industrial Commission, working to improve the circumstances of workers. When Franklin D. Roosevelt replaced Smith as governor in 1929, he named her industrial commissioner, a state cabinet-level position—making her the first woman to hold such a position at the state level. Beginning in 1930, she moved to support legislation that reduced the workweek for women to 48 hours, created a minimum wage, and developed unemployment insurance. Thus, when appointed secretary of labor in 1933, she already was experienced in the politics of improving the life of the worker.

During the First Hundred Days of Roosevelt's administration, Perkins and the Department of Labor helped to create the Civilian Conservation Corps and the Federal Emergency Relief Administration. In 1934, as the chair of the newly created Committee on Economic Security, she began to draft a social security bill. In encouragement, Roosevelt told her: "You care about this thing. You believe in it. Therefore I know you will put your back to it more than anyone else, and you'll drive it through."

The Social Security Act of 1935 was the outcome of many choices, most of which involved Perkins, Harry Hopkins, and Roosevelt. It was decided, for fiscal and political reasons, to have workers pay into the system as opposed to having the government pay for it out of taxes. Perkins wanted to include medical coverage, but it had to be excluded from the Social Security package, in large part because of the hostile reaction of the medical profession. To convince Congress to pass the Social Security program, she made hundreds of public speeches and countless appearances before countless congressional committees. With its passage on August 14, 1935, the relationship between the federal government and the people permanently changed.

Frances Perkins took pride in the passage of the Social Security Act, but she was overjoyed when the Fair Labor Standards Act became law in 1938. "A self-supporting and self-respecting democracy," she testified, "can plead no justification for the existence of child labor, no economic reason for chiseling workers' wages or stretching workers' hours." The bill was attacked by conservatives and union leaders as allowing too much government intrusion. Conservatives called it a form of socialism, while union leaders argued that collective bargaining—not the government—should gain wage and hour benefits for workers. Nevertheless, when the bill became law on June 25, 1938, more than 12 million workers felt its effect. It immediately raised the pay of 300,000 people and shortened the workday for a million more. Together, the Social Security Act and the Fair Labor Standards Act changed the economic and social values of the nation and ushered in a new relationship between the government and the people.

Frances Perkins continued to serve Roosevelt and his successor, Harry S Truman, as an advocate of government support of workers and their families. Retiring in 1953, she wrote, lectured, and joined the faculty at Cornell University. She died in 1965, and her tombstone reflects the fateful choice she made in 1933:

FRANCES PERKINS WILSON
1880–1965
SECRETARY OF LABOR OF U.S.A.
1933–1945

and supported the building of single-family units, rather than high-density multifamily structures. The outcome was to encourage suburbanization rather than the development of central metropolitan areas.

Popular Culture

Movies and radio, the most popular form of entertainment throughout the thirties, provided a break from the worries of Depression life. On average, 60 percent of Americans saw a movie a week. *Gone with the Wind, The Wizard of Oz,* and dozens of musicals like *Top Hat* afforded a brief escape from the daily routine. Movies offered not only escape, though. Some also reflected the social and political changes generated by the Depression and the New Deal. In *Golddiggers of 1933,* unemployed men march across the stage while the lead singer demands,

Remember my forgotten man,
You put a rifle in his hand,
You sent him far away,
You shouted, "Hip Hooray!"
But look at him today.

Cops-and-robbers films remained popular but underwent a slight change. Before the New Deal, famous stars frequently played gangsters. But as the New Deal became part of the American experience, those big names increasingly appeared as brave government officials who brought villains to justice. James Cagney became an FBI agent in *G-Men;* Humphrey Bogart was a crusading district attorney in *Crime School* and *Marked Woman;* and even Edward G. Robinson became a respectable good guy in *Bullets or Ballots.* All three actors had achieved fame playing tough guys, usually convicts or con men. Such character changes reflected a more positive vision of government than ever before.

Like movies, radio provided escape from the "De-repression," as the Depression was frequently called on the "Amos 'n' Andy Show," radio's most popular broadcast from 1928 to 1932. The Depression created a sudden demand for "gloom chasers" like the Marx Brothers, George Burns and Gracie Allen, and Jack Benny. It also sustained crazes like the "Original Amateur Hour," which first aired in 1934. When amateur programs began to fade in 1937, radio turned to quiz shows. Keeping pace in popularity with comedians, amateur shows, and quiz programs were crime fighters like the Shadow, the Green Hornet, Dick Tracy, the Lone Ranger and Tonto, and Sergeant Preston of the Yukon Mounted Police. These heroes proved again and again that truth, justice, honor, and courage always prevailed.

Whereas movies and radio rarely criticized American politics and society, many novelists certainly did. Michael Gold, a young Communist writer, urged other writers and artists to produce works that furthered revolutionary change. Many responded by stressing the immorality of capitalism and the inequities caused by racism and class differences. But few advocated an end to capitalism. Instead they found heroes among those who refused to break under the strain of the Depression. Erskine Caldwell's *Tobacco Road,* John Steinbeck's *The Grapes of Wrath,* and Richard Wright's *Native Son* described "losers" whose misery was not of their own making but society's fault. In these and similar novels, authors assailed the rich and powerful while praising the poor's noble humanitarian spirit.

Still, popular culture typically affirmed traditional American values. Popular themes expressed faith that the long-term effects of democracy would allow the integrity of the nation's people and leaders to emerge.

A New Deal for Minorities and Women

Even more than the president, Eleanor Roosevelt was sensitive to the needs of average Americans. The first truly active First Lady, she crisscrossed the country talking with coal miners, waitresses, farmers, and housewives. Thousands wrote to her to describe their hardships and to ask for help. Although rarely able to provide any direct assistance, Eleanor Roosevelt constantly urged her husband not to neglect the poor, women, and minorities.

♦ In 1935, Mary McLeod Bethune (front center) became the first African-American woman to hold a high-ranking government position, serving as the head of the Office of Negro Affairs in the National Youth Administration. Here she is shown with the Council of Negro Women, which she helped organize in 1935 to focus on the problems faced by African Americans at the national level. *New York Public Library, Schomburg Center for Research in Black Culture.*

Eleanor Roosevelt took the lead in working to reduce discrimination in the government and throughout the country. In 1933, she helped to convene a special White House conference on the needs of women to ensure that women received more than just token consideration from New Deal agencies. Her outspoken support helped Democratic women to organize their own division within the party and to lobby for more important roles in the party and the government. Her efforts resulted in more opportunities for women in government than at any previous time in American history.

Eleanor Roosevelt was just as determined to affirm the equality of African Americans. Working with black educators and administrators like Mary Bethune, she sought to generate new opportunities for blacks. In 1939, she demonstrated her commitment to racial equality when the Daughters of the American Revolution (DAR) refused to allow renowned black opera singer Marian Anderson to sing at their concert hall in Washington, D.C. In protest, Eleanor Roosevelt resigned her membership in the DAR and helped arrange a larger, public concert on the steps of the Lincoln Memorial. Marian Anderson's performance attracted seventy-five thousand people.

Most black leaders complained, however, that the New Deal did little to challenge existing patterns of prejudice, discrimination, and segregation. A political realist, the president recognized the key role of white southern Democrats in Congress, and so he retreated from promoting civil rights legislation, even an antilynching law. When black leaders complained, he admitted, "If I come out for the antilynching bill now, they will block every bill I ask Congress to pass. . . . I just can't take that risk."

Nonetheless, the New Deal brought about some positive changes in favor of racial equality. In August 1936, Mary Bethune organized African Americans within the administration into the

"Black Cabinet," which acted as an unofficial advisory commission on racial relations. Among the most pressing needs for African Americans, the Black Cabinet concluded, was access to relief and jobs. In northern cities, it was not uncommon for state and local agencies to deny African Americans relief. Fortunately, Ickes and Hopkins were proponents of racial equality and used the PWA, CWA, and WPA to provide African Americans with relief and jobs. The WPA alone supported nearly 1 million African-American families and in northern cities, nearly eliminated discrimination from its programs.

Not every New Deal administrator or agency was as committed to equality as Hopkins and the WPA were. The Civilian Conservation Corps and the Tennessee Valley Authority openly practiced segregation and discrimination. African-American skilled workers were almost always given unskilled, lower-paying public works jobs. Even in the best of cases, federal support was not enough to help more than a segment of the black population. In Cleveland, for example, 40 percent of PWA jobs were reserved for African Americans, but black unemployment and poverty still remained high.

Still, most African Americans praised Roosevelt and promised their political support. By 1934, wherever African Americans could vote, blacks were bolting from the Republican party. In the 1936 presidential election, Roosevelt would receive nearly 90 percent of the nation's black vote.

Mexican Americans benefited from the New Deal in much the same way as African Americans. Agencies such as the PWA and WPA not only included Mexican Americans but paid wages that usually exceeded those in the **private sector.** New Deal legislation also helped union organizers trying to assist Latino workers throughout the West and Southwest. San Antonio's Mexican-American pecan shellers, mostly women, were among the lowest-paid workers in the country, earning less than $180 a year. Local union activist "Red" Emma Tenayuca and Congress of Industrial Organizations (CIO) representatives led the pecan shellers in strikes, finally gaining higher wages and union recognition in 1938. In the fields of central California, however, Mexican-American unions had little success in organizing farm workers. Where they were permitted to vote, Mexican Americans deserted the Republican party to vote Democrat.

Unlike most Mexican Americans and African Americans, American Indians benefited directly from the New Deal. Secretary of the Interior Harold Ickes and Commissioner of Indian Affairs John Collier both opposed existing Indian policies, which since 1887 had sought to destroy the reservation system and obliterate Indian cultures. At Collier's urging, Congress passed the **Indian Reorganization Act** in 1934. The act returned land and community control to tribal organizations. It provided Indian self-rule on the reservations and prevented individual ownership of tribal lands. To improve the squalid conditions of most reservations and to provide jobs, Collier organized a CCC-type agency solely for Indians. He also tried to promote American Indian culture. Working with tribal leaders, Collier took measures to protect, preserve, and encourage Indian customs, languages, religions, and folkways. Reservation school curricula incorporated Indian languages and traditions. Collier's New Deal for American Indians did little to improve their standard of living. Funds were too few, and problems created by years of poverty and government neglect were too great.

The New Deal Winds Down

By 1936, the Second Hundred Days had effectively reasserted Roosevelt's leadership and popularity. The prospect of a successful Republican or third-party challenge to Roosevelt was remote. Huey

"Black Cabinet" Members of the Roosevelt administration organized by Mary McLeod Bethune into a semiofficial advisory committee on racial issues.

private sector Businesses run by private citizens rather than by the government.

Indian Reorganization Act Law passed in 1934 that ended Indian allotment and returned surplus land to tribal ownership; it also sought to encourage tribal self-government and improve economic conditions on reservations.

Long had died in 1935, the victim of an assassin's bullet. Another Louisianan, Gerald L. K. Smith, took up Long's populist standard but was no match for the colorful "Kingfish." Smith joined forces with Coughlin and Townsend to form the Union party, but it never posed a threat to Roosevelt. Nor did the Socialist or Communist parties mount any noticeable opposition.

The Republican party, which nominated Kansas governor **Alfred Landon,** was hardly more of a worry. Although Landon accepted most New Deal programs in principle, most Republicans wanted him to attack Roosevelt and the New Deal. Reluctantly, Landon agreed. Roosevelt responded by reminding voters of the New Deal's achievements and stressing his support for the "forgotten man." He attacked big business, the "economic royalists" who wanted to rule like kings over the people. The tactics worked, and Roosevelt won in a landslide. Landon carried only Maine and Vermont.

The Democratic victory in 1936 demonstrated not only the personal popularity of Roosevelt but also the realignment of political forces. Prior to 1930, only two major interest groups successfully influenced government: big business and the South. With Roosevelt and the New Deal, other interest groups—some new, like the CIO, and some old, like agriculture—became integrally involved in the political process. Workers, farmers, women, minorities, and the aged now competed with the South and business for government favor and legislation. Roosevelt recognized the political importance of those who cast their vote for him, and he promised a government intent on seeking "social justice."

His second inaugural address raised expectations that there would be a third one hundred days. "I see millions of families trying to live on incomes so meager that the pall of family disaster hangs over them day by day," he announced. "I see one-third of a nation ill-housed, ill-clad, ill-nourished." The words seemed to promise new legislation aimed at helping the poor and the working class.

Roosevelt and the Supreme Court

Instead of promoting new social legislation, however, Roosevelt pitched his popularity against the Supreme Court— and lost. The president's anger at the Court had been growing since the *Schechter* case. It ruled in the *Butler* case (1936) that the AAA was unconstitutional. The Court also had declared illegal a quota plan for the oil industry, the Railroad Retirement Act, and a New York law establishing a minimum wage for women. As 1937 began, legal challenges to the Wagner Act and the Social Security Act were on the Court's docket. Roosevelt feared that the Court would undo much of the New Deal. He thus proposed to appoint new justices to give the Court a pro–New Deal majority.

Without consulting congressional leaders, Roosevelt presented a plan to reorganize the Court to Congress in early February 1937. Claiming that the Court's elderly judges could not meet the demands of the office, he asked for additional justices to help carry the judicial load. His goal was a new justice for every one over age 70 who had served more than ten years on the Court. Although Congress could change the size of the Supreme Court, many thought that Roosevelt's action threatened the checks and balances of government established by the Constitution. He made a major political miscalculation with his **Court-packing plan.** Many Democrats who had reservations about the New Deal now joined Republicans to say no to Roosevelt.

Roosevelt ignored the growing opposition and pressed on. Roosevelt's case weakened, however, when the Court in a series of 5-to-4 decisions upheld Washington State's minimum wage law, the Wagner Act, and the Social Security system. Even Roosevelt's supporters in Congress now questioned the need to enlarge the Court. The president's position collapsed completely in May when conservative justice Willis van Devanter announced his retirement. By July, Roosevelt had conceded defeat.

Alfred Landon Kansas governor who ran unsuccessfully for president in 1936.

Court-packing plan Roosevelt's unsuccessful proposal in 1937 to increase the number of Supreme Court justices; it was an effort to circumvent the Court's hostility to the New Deal.

He took solace in appointing Hugo Black, a southern New Dealer, to the Court.

Despite the Court's favorable decisions, Roosevelt had lost a great deal. He had lost control over conservative southern Democrats. Having safely broken with Roosevelt on the Court issue, many such Democrats now found it possible to oppose other Roosevelt initiatives. The Court fight had produced a new conservative grouping composed of Republicans, business interests, and southern Democrats. Consequently, a Third Hundred Days was now impossible.

The Resurgence of Labor

Labor strife also dampened many Americans' enthusiasm for the New Deal. During his first administration, Roosevelt had supported unions and workers through the National Recovery Administration and passage of the Wagner Act. "President Roosevelt wants you to join the union," was a common plug that labor organizers used to recruit workers. Mostly, the response was positive, and by mid-1934 unions were growing and becoming more militant.

There were over eighteen hundred strikes in 1934, involving more than 1.5 million workers. Union membership doubled that year. The rise of organized labor was especially pronounced in the mass-production industries. When the leadership of the craft-based American Federation of Labor (AFL) discouraged industry-wide unionization in 1935, a minority element formed the Committee for Industrial Organizations (CIO) to continue organizing industrial unions. Unionization drives were launched in the automobile, rubber, and electrical industries. The CIO also took an active political stance, pushing workers to support only those politicians who were friends of labor. In 1938, the CIO completed its break from the AFL and formed an independent labor organization: the **Congress of Industrial Organizations.**

In March 1936, the CIO supported workers striking against the rubber industry in Akron, Ohio, home of Firestone, Goodyear, and Goodrich. Wanting recognition of their union and higher wages, workers stopped work and refused to leave the factory, launching one of the first major **sit-down strikes** in the United States. With the strikers occupying the factory, the employer could not use **strikebreakers.** When the rubber industry quickly agreed to most of the strikers' demands, the benefits of sit-down strikes seemed clear to labor.

Encouraged by the Akron results, the **United Automobile Workers (UAW)** planned a sit-down strike against General Motors. The UAW focused on plants in Cleveland, Ohio, and Flint, Michigan. Because most General Motors plants received car bodies from Cleveland and Flint, successful strikes in those plants would eventually shut down most of GM's assembly lines. The sit-down strike began on November 30, 1936, when Flint workers took over the factory. Despite cutting off the heat, trying to block deliveries of food, and attacking the plant with company guards and city police, GM was unable to dislodge the strikers. When Michigan Governor Frank Murphy refused to send in state militia units to remove the strikers, the company settled with the UAW. Weeks later, Chrysler gave in to sit-down strikers and also recognized the UAW. In March, United States Steel accepted the steelworkers' union without a strike. Throughout 1937, labor staged more than forty-seven hundred strikes and won 80 percent of them. Union membership soared.

Congress of Industrial Organizations Labor organization established in 1938 by a group of powerful unions that left the AFL to unionize workers by industry rather than by trade.

sit-down strike Strike in which workers refuse to leave their place of employment until their demands are met.

strikebreakers Temporary workers hired by employers to substitute for striking workers.

United Automobile Workers Union of workers in the automobile industry, which used sit-down strikes in 1936 and 1937 to end work speed-ups and win recognition for the fledgling labor organization.

As strikes spread and violent incidents multiplied, unions did not fare well in public opinion. Many people equated strikes and labor militancy with radicalism and communism. Critics also blamed unions for most of the strike-related violence and considered sit-ins illegal. In 1939, the Supreme Court agreed, declaring sit-down strikes unconstitutional.

The End of New Deal Legislation

By 1937, with the economy apparently well on the road to recovery, Secretary of the Treasury Henry Morgenthau argued that the administration should cut relief programs, balance the budget, and allow business a freer hand in shaping the economy. Roosevelt agreed. He cut government spending and closed down many federal job programs. But unemployment rapidly soared to 19 percent, and the recovery collapsed. **Roosevelt's recession** had begun.

Roosevelt's liberal advisers won his ear in calling for a resurrection of the New Deal. The WPA rehired those dropped from the rolls, and Roosevelt attempted to marshal support for new legislation. But the political mood had changed since 1933, and a coalition of conservatives in Congress blocked passage of most of Roosevelt's requested programs.

Prodded by a strong agricultural lobby, Congress did enact a second Agricultural Adjustment Act that paid farmers to reduce production. In June 1938, congressional New Dealers overcame strong opposition to pass the **Fair Labor Standards Act.** The act established an initial maximum workweek of forty-four hours, set a minimum wage of $.25 an hour, and outlawed child labor (under age 16). The act proved to be the last New Deal legislation. In 1938, Roosevelt campaigned unsuccessfully for liberal candidates. The new Congress was more conservative and determined to oppose the president's "socialistic" ideas. Roosevelt recognized political reality and asked for no new domestic programs. By 1939, the economy had recovered to the point where it had been in 1929, and there seemed no reason to expand government programs. The New Deal was over.

The New Deal's Impact

New Deal programs failed to achieve a complete economic recovery largely because Roosevelt never spent enough money to generate rapid economic growth. It was spending connected with the outbreak of another world war that would propel the American economy to new levels of prosperity. Despite the New Deal's failure to promote economic prosperity, it changed the country and its people. It ended the fear generated by the Depression and encouraged a return to a stable and orderly society and economy. Equally important, it altered the basic relationships between government and society and between government and the economy.

Evaluations of the New Deal generally reflect attitudes about the proper role of government in society. Conservatives, during the New Deal and since, argue that the positive legacy of the New Deal is an illusion. Government intervention, they say, was the problem rather than the solution because it undermined individualism and created an expensive and overbearing government. Liberals praise Roosevelt and the New Deal for balancing the needs of the economy with those of society. From the liberal viewpoint, the New Deal promoted stable economic growth and contributed to the overall health of American society. More radical critics of the New Deal focus on what the New Deal failed to accomplish. They point out that the same groups who held power and wealth before the New Deal were still in control afterward and contend that Roosevelt made no effort to combat racism or economic inequalities.

What is indisputable is that the New Deal caused government to play a much larger role in the life of Americans than anyone had previously

Roosevelt's recession Economic downturn of 1937–1938 that was blamed on Franklin D. Roosevelt.

Fair Labor Standards Act Law passed in 1938 that established a minimum wage and a maximum workweek and forbade labor by children under 16.

expected. Before the New Deal, the federal government had remained remote from most Americans. By 1939, it had assumed new and expanded responsibilities. Institutions created by Roosevelt still regulate the nation's banking and financial systems. The economic health of agriculture continues to rely on a series of price-support and loan programs. The Wagner Act remains the overseer of labor-management relations. Social Security continues to provide for the economic welfare of the elderly. The belief in governmental responsibility for the needy has remained part of the American memory and experience. Since the New Deal, the American people have come to look to the federal government and the president for leadership, for legislation, and for solutions to the nation's problems.

SUMMARY

Expectations
Constraints
Choices
Outcomes

The Great Depression brought Franklin D. Roosevelt to power amid widespread *expectations* that he would initiate a major shift in the nature of government. Through a variety of programs, Roosevelt *chose* to use the federal government to regenerate economic growth, to aid millions of Americans in need, and to regulate the economy. Although never a specific overarching plan, the New Deal attacked the Depression on three fronts: recovery, relief, and reform.

The First Hundred Days witnessed a barrage of legislation that dealt with immediate problems of unemployment and economic collapse. In 1935, Roosevelt *chose* to initiate a second burst of legislation that focused on social reform and putting people to work. The overwhelming Democratic victory in 1936 confirmed the popularity of Roosevelt and raised *expectations* of further social and economic regulatory legislation. A Third Hundred Days, however, never materialized. The Court-packing scheme, an economic downturn, labor unrest, and growing conservatism created formidable political constraints against further change. The *outcome* was that the New Deal wound down after 1937.

Although the New Deal failed to restore economic prosperity quickly, it left a lasting imprint on American society. Reforms of the financial and securities systems left a much more secure and stable industry. In the end, the New Deal strengthened capitalism and removed *constraints* for many who had been prevented from achieving the American dream.

The New Deal opened doors for those frequently ignored by government. Farmers, blue-collar workers, women, and minorities all had their New Deal. Each group emerged with stronger *expectations* about government's role in promoting their interests. The New Deal's *outcome* was a profound shift in society's *expectations* about the federal government.

SUGGESTED READINGS

Bergman, Andrew. *We're in the Money: Depression America and Its Films* (1971).

An interesting look at the movie industry and how it reflected the Great Depression.

Blackwelder, Julia Kirk. *Women of the Depression: Caste and Culture in San Antonio, 1929–1939* (1984).

A tightly focused study on Mexican-American, African-American, and Anglo women in the world of San Antonio during the Depression.

Fine, Sidney. *Sit-Down: The General Motors Strike of 1936–1937* (1969).

Using the United Auto Workers' strike against General Motors, Fine examines the industrial union movement and the use of the sit-down strike.

Leuchtenberg, William. *Franklin D. Roosevelt and the New Deal* (1983).

A comprehensive, classic account of how Roosevelt directed the nation from his 1932 election until 1941.

Sitkoff, Harvard. *A New Deal for Blacks* (1978).

A review of how African Americans benefited from and were otherwise affected by the New Deal and the Roosevelts.

Steinbeck, John. *The Grapes of Wrath* (1939).

A classic novel about the survival of the Joad family during the Depression that was later turned into an award-winning film.

Ware, Susan. *Holding Their Own: American Women in the 1930s* (1982).

An examination of the impact of the Depression on the lives and lifestyles of women.

CANADA
MEXICO
PACIFIC OCEAN
ATLANTIC OCEAN
Gulf of Mexico
Seattle
WASHINGTON
OREGON
IDAHO
Minidoka
MONTANA
NORTH DAKOTA
SOUTH DAKOTA
WYOMING
Heart Mountain
MINN.
WIS.
MICH.
Detroit
Chicago
Buffalo
NEW YORK
VT.
N.H.
MAINE
Boston
MASS.
R.I.
CONN.
New York
Philadelphia
N.J.
PENN.
Cleveland
Baltimore
DEL.
MD.
Tule Lake
NEVADA
UTAH
Topaz
San Francisco
CALIFORNIA
Manzanar
Las Vegas
Los Angeles
San Diego
ARIZONA
Posten
Gila River
COLORADO
Denver
Granada
NEBRASKA
IOWA
Des Moines
KANSAS
Kansas City
ILL.
St. Louis
IND.
Indianapolis
OHIO
W.VA.
VIRGINIA
KENTUCKY
MISSOURI
NEW MEXICO
OKLAHOMA
Tulsa
ARK.
Rohwer
Jerome
TENN.
NORTH CAROLINA
SOUTH CAROLINA
GEORGIA
ALABAMA
MISS.
TEXAS
Fort Worth
Dallas
Houston
LA.
New Orleans
FLA.
HAWAII TERRITORY
PACIFIC OCEAN
0 100 Km.
0 100 Mi.
U.S.S.R.
ALASKA TERRITORY
CANADA
0 250 500 Km.
0 250 500 Mi.
PACIFIC OCEAN
0 200 400 Km.
0 200 400 Mi.
Aircraft factories
Other war industries
Shipyards
Japanese relocation centers
Population changes, 1941–1945
Gains
More than 300,000
200,000–300,000
100,000–200,000
Fewer than 100,000
Losses
More than 300,000
200,000–300,000
100,000–200,000
Fewer than 100,000

THE HOME FRONT War-related production finally ended the Great Depression, but it also required many Americans to move, especially to western states where the jobs were. This map shows major war-related industries and the states that gained and lost population. For Japanese Americans, relocation did not mean new jobs, but a loss of freedom as they were assigned to one of ten relocation centers across the country.

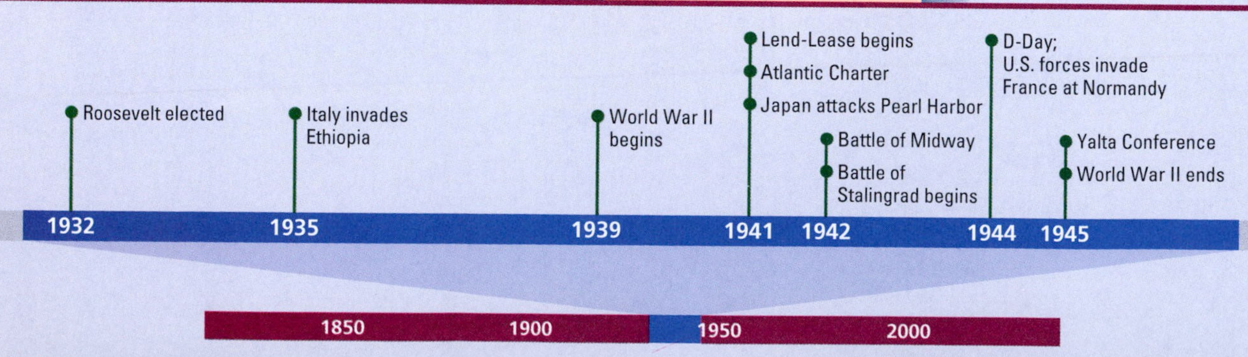
Roosevelt elected
Italy invades Ethiopia
World War II begins
Lend-Lease begins
Atlantic Charter
Japan attacks Pearl Harbor
Battle of Midway
Battle of Stalingrad begins
D-Day; U.S. forces invade France at Normandy
Yalta Conference
World War II ends
1932
1935
1939
1941
1942
1944
1945
1850
1900
1950
2000

CHAPTER 26

America's Rise to World Leadership, 1933–1945

Roosevelt and Foreign Policy

- In what ways did Roosevelt's choices in dealings with Latin America reflect the ideals of the Good Neighbor policy?
- How did isolationism constrain American foreign-policy choices from 1932 to the outbreak of World War II?

The Road to War

- What constraints did Roosevelt face in trying to implement a more interventionist foreign policy?
- In reshaping American neutrality, what choices did Roosevelt make regarding Britain and Japan?

America Responds to War

- What actions did Roosevelt choose to mobilize the nation for war?
- What new social and economic choices did Americans confront as the nation became the "arsenal of democracy"?
- What new opportunities and old constraints did women and minorities encounter on the home front and in their military experiences?

Waging World War

- What choices and constraints did Roosevelt and Truman confront in shaping America's strategy for global conflict?
- What were the stresses within the Grand Alliance?
- What expectations prompted Truman and his advisers to choose to use the atomic bomb?

INTRODUCTION

Expectations
Constraints
Choices
Outcomes

When Roosevelt assumed office in 1933, the cheery optimism of a prosperous world at peace that had greeted Herbert Hoover in 1929 was gone. By then, three nations seemed willing to *choose* military conquest if necessary to achieve their goals. Japan, seeking an empire in Asia, had annexed Manchuria and was threatening China. In Germany, Adolf Hitler and the National Socialist (Nazi) party had gained political dominance amid promises of restoring Germany's military and diplomatic prowess. Having seized power in 1922, Benito Mussolini had used nationalism, imperial designs, and military power to tighten his control over Italy. Roosevelt faced the events in Asia and Europe as an internationalist. He wanted the country to take a more active role in world affairs, but he was *constrained* by strong isolationist views in Congress and among the public. In addition, he understood that American economic recovery was his first priority.

The onslaught of war in 1939, however, allowed Roosevelt to chart a path away from neutrality. He *chose* to help defeat Hitler by providing economic and military assistance to Britain and to *constrain* Japanese expansion by using trade restrictions. Japan's attack on Pearl Harbor in December 1941 drew the United States into World War II.

The war managed to do what the New Deal had not—to restore American prosperity. An *outcome* of America's becoming the "arsenal of democracy" was full recovery and full employment, as 15 million Americans marched off to war. Those remaining at home faced new opportunities and *constraints*. Americans *chose* to move to take war-related jobs, especially on the West Coast. The *outcome* for women and minorities was mixed: they experienced greater opportunities, but they also were *expected* to give up their new opportunities once the war was over.

For Presidents Franklin D. Roosevelt and Harry S Truman, defeating the Axis Powers entailed making strategic decisions that shaped the course of the war. Roosevelt *chose* to allocate most of the nation's resources to defeat Hitler first. By the end of May 1945, Hitler's Third Reich was in ruins and American forces were on the verge of victory over Japan. Roosevelt had died. Truman, facing the prospect of huge casualties with an invasion of Japan, *chose* to use the atomic bomb. The *outcome* was the surrender of Japan, the beginning of a new age of atomic power, and the emergence of the United States as a super power.

Roosevelt and Foreign Policy

Until Franklin Roosevelt ran for the presidency, he was an internationalist who had supported an active American role in world affairs. But as a presidential candidate, he stated his opposition to American participation in the League of Nations and other world organizations. At heart, however, Roosevelt remained an internationalist who believed that international cooperation would create a better world.

The Good Neighbor Policy

In Latin America, Roosevelt built on the improving relations already begun by Hoover. He promised that the United States would be a "good neighbor" and would not interfere in Latin American affairs. His promise was soon tested in Cuba, where President Gerardo "the Butcher" Machado's harsh regime stirred political unrest. In the summer of 1933, Roosevelt sent special envoy Sumner Welles to Cuba to encourage Machado to

CHRONOLOGY

A World at War

1931	Japan occupies Manchuria
1932	Roosevelt elected president
1933	Gerardo Machado resigns as president of Cuba United States recognizes Soviet Union Hitler and Nazi party take power in Germany
1934	Fulgencio Batista assumes power in Cuba
1935	Italy invades Ethiopia Neutrality Act of 1935
1936	Spanish Civil War begins Germany reoccupies the Rhineland Roosevelt reelected president
1937	Japan invades China *Panay* attacked by Japanese aircraft Neutrality Act of 1937
1938	Austria annexed by Germany Munich Conference
1939	Germany invades Czechoslovakia Ribbentrop-Molotov Nonaggression Pact World War II begins as Germany invades Poland Soviets invade Poland and Finland Neutrality Act of 1939
1940	Germany occupies most of western Europe Roosevelt reelected president Burke-Wadsworth Act Destroyers-for-bases agreement
1941	Lend-Lease begins Fair Employment Practices Commission created Atlantic Charter Germany invades Soviet Union U.S. warships attacked by U-boats Japan attacks Pearl Harbor United States enters World War II
1942	War Production Board created Japanese conquer Philippines Japanese Americans interned Battles of the Coral Sea and Midway Manhattan Project begins Congress of Racial Equality founded U.S. troops invade North Africa
1943	U.S. forces capture Guadalcanal Soviets defeat Germans at Stalingrad Detroit race riot U.S. forces invade Italy Tehran Conference
1944	D-day: U.S. forces invade France at Normandy and reach the Rhine Roosevelt reelected president U.S. forces capture Philippines Soviet forces liberate Eastern Europe Battle of the Bulge
1945	Yalta Conference Roosevelt dies; Truman becomes president Soviets capture Berlin Germany surrenders U.S. forces capture Iwo Jima and Okinawa Potsdam Conference Atomic bombs dropped on Hiroshima and Nagasaki Japan surrenders

resign. He succeeded, but Welles considered the new government of Ramón Grau San Martín too radical and recommended using American military force to overthrow Grau. Roosevelt refused to send in the marines. Instead, the United States refused to recognize the Cuban government. Meanwhile, Welles encouraged **General Fulgencio Batista** to overthrow Grau and install a government acceptable to the United States. Batista did so in 1934. As a result, the United States recognized the new government; rescinded the 1902 Platt Amendment, which authorized American intervention in Cuban affairs; and signed a favorable trade agreement. Batista would control the island nation until 1959.

Watching American actions in Cuba, many Latin Americans questioned the reality of Roosevelt's **Good Neighbor Policy.** Secretary of State Cordell Hull raised further doubts when he declared that the United States maintained the right to intervene in Latin America to protect American citizens. At Pan American conferences in 1936 and 1938, however, the United States rejected all reasons for armed intervention.

Roosevelt's commitment to **nonintervention** was tested when, in 1938, Mexico's president, **Lázaro Cárdenas,** nationalized foreign-owned oil properties. American oil interests quickly called on the United States to take action against Mexico. But the American ambassador to Mexico, Josephus Daniels, recommended to Roosevelt that the United States accept Mexico's actions and negotiate a fair settlement with the American companies. Roosevelt took Daniels's advice. By 1940, Roosevelt had vastly improved America's image throughout Latin America.

Roosevelt and Isolationism

While Roosevelt was improving the image of the United States in Latin America, tensions were increasing in Europe and Asia. In Germany, Adolf Hitler by 1935 had ruthlessly instituted a **dictatorship** and expanded the military. The Japanese spoke openly of establishing a larger Japanese sphere of influence and increased pressure on China. Eyeing the Japanese and the Germans uneasily, the Soviet Union, led by Joseph Stalin, sought to improve relations with the United States. Roosevelt also sought improved relations. In November 1933, the United States recognized the Soviet Union.

Within the United States, Roosevelt's decision to establish relations with the Soviets prompted protests that he meant to abandon isolationism. Many voices urged the avoidance of foreign entanglements. A congressional investigation chaired by Senator Gerald P. Nye determined that America's entry into World War I had been the product of arms manufacturers, bankers, and war profiteers— "the merchants of death." Novelists such as Ernest Hemingway (*A Farewell to Arms,* 1929) and John Dos Passos (*Three Soldiers,* 1921) added to antiwar and isolationist sentiments with their powerful stories depicting the senseless horror of war. A Gallup poll revealed that 67 percent of Americans believed that the nation's intervention in World War I had been wrong.

By 1935, tensions in Asia and Europe combined with American isolationism to generate neutrality laws designed to prevent American involvement in future foreign wars. The **Neutrality Act of 1935**

General Fulgencio Batista Dictator who ruled Cuba from 1934 through 1958; his corrupt authoritarian regime was overthrown on New Year's Day, 1959, by Fidel Castro's revolutionary movement.

Good Neighbor Policy Phrase used to describe Roosevelt's Latin American policy, which was based on the belief that the United States had no right to intervene in Latin American affairs.

nonintervention Refusal to interfere, especially in the affairs of another nation.

Lázaro Cárdenas Mexican president from 1934 to 1940, who distributed land to peasants, instituted social reforms, and nationalized foreign-owned oil properties.

dictatorship State or government controlled by a tyrant, or absolute ruler.

Neutrality Act of 1935 Congressional resolution prohibiting arms shipments to nations at war and authorizing the president to warn U.S. citizens against traveling on belligerents' vessels.

prohibited the sale of arms and munitions to any nation at war. Anxious to see the Second Hundred Days successfully through Congress, Roosevelt signed the measure.

Many Americans felt that the Neutrality Act of 1935 came just in time. On October 3, Benito Mussolini's Italian troops invaded the African nation of Ethiopia. Roosevelt immediately announced American neutrality toward the Ethiopian conflict. The arms embargo had little effect on Italy, whose modern army overpowered Ethiopia's antiquated forces. On May 9, 1936, Italy annexed Ethiopia.

International tensions increased in Europe itself in 1936. In March, German troops violated the Treaty of Versailles by occupying the **Rhineland,** and in July, civil war broke out in Spain. Roosevelt proclaimed that the remilitarization of the Rhineland was of no concern to the United States. Most Americans agreed, but public opinion was sharply divided about the conflict in Spain. Liberals and leftists supported the Spanish government's **Republican** forces. Conservatives and most Catholics supported the rebels led by the **fascist** general **Francisco Franco.** However, most Americans agreed when Roosevelt applied the neutrality acts to both sides.

Italy and Germany actively aided Franco, taking the opportunity to test their military capability. German and Italian planes, tanks, and troops augmented Franco's soldiers in attacks on Republican forces and towns. Facing better-equipped and larger armies, the Republican forces fought bravely but were forced to surrender city after city. With the fall of Madrid in March 1939, Franco defeated the last Republican forces.

The Ethiopian War, German militarization, and the Spanish Civil War strengthened American isolationism. The **Neutrality Act of 1937** went beyond the previous act in requiring nations to pay cash for all "nonwar" goods and to carry those goods on their own ships, and in barring Americans from sailing on belligerents' ships. The new act did give the president a small victory by allowing him to determine which nations were at war and which goods were nonwar goods.

Roosevelt used that provision in late July 1937 following a Japanese invasion of northern China. He refused to recognize that China and Japan were at war and allowed American trade to continue with both nations. That fiction did not last long. On December 12, 1937, Japanese aircraft bombed the American gunboat *Panay* and two Standard Oil tankers. Roosevelt wanted to retaliate, but public opinion and Congress insisted otherwise. Within two days of the *Panay* bombing, isolationists in the House had pushed forward a constitutional amendment that would require a public referendum before Congress could declare war. Only after Roosevelt had expended a great deal of political effort did the House return the amendment to committee, effectively killing it. Roosevelt had no choice but to accept Japan's apology and payment of damages for the *Panay*.

The Road to War

World peace was crumbling fast as 1938 began. The fighting in China and Spain raged on. From Berlin, Hitler pronounced his intentions of unifying all German-speaking lands in a new German empire, or Reich. Hitler's first step in creating this

Rhineland Region of western Germany along the Rhine River, which, under the terms of the Versailles Treaty, was to remain free of troops and military fortifications.

Republican In Spain, a left-wing political group that won national elections in 1936 but was prevented from carrying out its programs by a military rebellion and the outbreak of civil war.

fascist Supporter of a political system and dictatorship that glorifies the state, nation, and race over individual liberties and rights.

Francisco Franco Fascist general whose rebel forces defeated the Republicans in the Spanish Civil War (1936–1939); he ruled as dictator of Spain until his death in 1975.

Neutrality Act of 1937 Law that required warring nations to pay cash for "nonwar" goods and barred Americans from sailing on belligerents' ships.

empire was the forced **Anschluss,** or merger, of Austria with Germany.

Hearing only mild protests from other nations, Hitler confidently moved to incorporate other German-speaking areas into the Reich. He next demanded the annexation of the Sudeten region of western Czechoslovakia, which had a substantial German population. The Czechoslovakian government was prepared to resist and appealed for help as German troops massed along the Sudeten border. France, the Soviet Union, and Britain, however, did not want a confrontation with Hitler. On September 30, Britain's prime minister, **Neville Chamberlain,** met with Hitler in Munich and accepted Germany's annexation of the Sudetenland (see Map 26.1). Without British and French support, the Czechs had no option but to concede the loss of territory. Chamberlain returned to England smiling and promising "peace in our time."

Within Germany, Hitler stepped up the persecution of the country's nearly half a million Jews. In 1938, Hitler had Jewish synagogues, businesses, and homes looted and destroyed. Detention centers at Dachau and Buchenwald soon confined over fifty thousand Jews. Thousands of German and Austrian Jews fled to other countries. Many applied to enter the United States, but most were turned away. American anti-Semitism was strong, and the State Department routinely denied entry to German Jews whose property had been seized by the German government. The State Department enforced the immigration laws so strictly between 1933 and 1939 that nearly three-fourths of the 27,400-person quota for Germany and Austria went unfilled.

Convinced that Hitler was a threat to humanity, Roosevelt sounded a dire warning to Americans in his 1939 State of the Union address. "Events abroad have made it increasingly clear to the American people that the dangers within are less to be feared than dangers without," he observed. "This generation will nobly save or meanly lose the last best hope of earth." Events verified Roosevelt's prediction of danger. Hitler ominously concluded a military alliance with Italy, invaded and seized what remained of Czechoslovakia, and demanded that Poland cede the **Polish corridor,** which connected Poland to the Baltic Sea. British and French officials, unwilling to appease Hitler any longer, pledged to protect Poland. Meanwhile, the Soviet Union had reached a secret agreement with Germany—the Ribbentrop-Molotov Nonaggression Pact of August 23, 1939—which divided Poland between them. No longer worried about a Soviet attack, Hitler invaded Poland on September 1, 1939. Two days later, Britain and France declared war on Germany. Within a matter of days, German troops had overrun nearly all of Poland. On September 17, acting under the terms of a nonaggression pact signed with Germany, Soviet forces seized the eastern parts of Poland and subsequently invaded Finland (see Map 26.1). World War II had begun.

Roosevelt and American Neutrality

In the United States, there was little desire to come to the aid of Poland, Britain, or France. Isolationism remained strong. But Roosevelt was determined to do everything possible short of war to help those nations opposing Hitler.

When Germany invaded Poland, the president proclaimed American neutrality. But he also asked Congress to modify the Neutrality Act of 1937 to allow the sale of any goods, including arms, to any nation that paid cash for those goods and carried them away in its own ships. Roosevelt calculated that only Britain and France would be able to take advantage of this cash-and-carry provision, since the British navy denied German ships access to American ports. Although a congressional "peace bloc" argued that the request would drag the nation into the war, Con-

Anschluss Political union, especially the one absorbing Austria into Nazi Germany in 1938.

Neville Chamberlain British prime minister who pursued a policy of appeasement toward the fascist regimes of Europe before World War II.

Polish corridor Territory adjoining the city of Danzig, which connected Poland with the Baltic Sea and which Germany demanded from Poland in 1939.

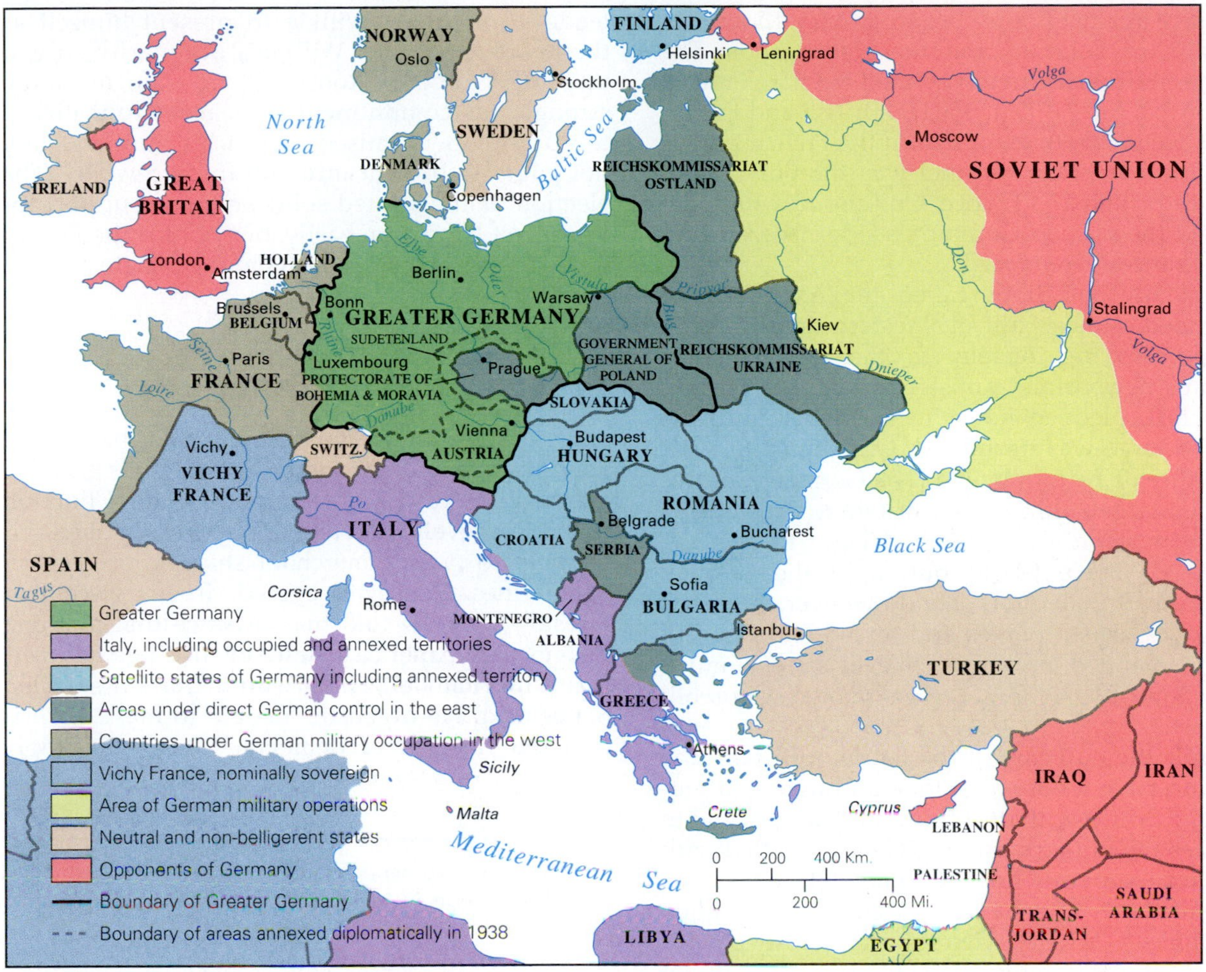

♦ **MAP 26.1 German and Italian Expansion, 1933–1942** By the end of 1942, the Axis nations of Italy and Germany, through conquest and annexation, had occupied nearly all of Europe. This map shows the political and military alignment of Europe as Germany and Italy reached the limit of their power.

gress granted the president's request in the **Neutrality Act of 1939.**

To protect merchant ships approaching American ports, Roosevelt established a 300-mile neutrality zone around American waters. Warships of belligerent nations were forbidden in the zone. If the navy happened to sink any German submarines, Roosevelt joked to his cabinet, he would respond like "the Japs do, 'So sorry. Never do it again.' Tomorrow we sink two."

Roosevelt was even more determined to aid the British after the fall of France in the spring of 1940. Hitler's first attack that spring had been on Denmark and Norway, which fell quickly. The German

Neutrality Act of 1939 Law repealing the arms embargo and authorizing cash-and-carry exports of arms and munitions even to belligerent nations.

offensive against France began on May 10 with an invasion of Belgium and the Netherlands. The German **blitzkrieg** overwhelmed Belgian, French, and British forces. That 350,000 British and French forces were able to escape from the French port of Dunkirk across the channel was the only bright spot for Britain and France. On June 10, Mussolini entered the war on Germany's side. Twelve days later, France surrendered.

Germany and Italy, called the **Axis Powers,** controlled almost all of Western and Central Europe, leaving Britain to face them alone. Britain's new prime minister, the feisty **Winston Churchill,** pledged never to surrender until the Nazi scourge was destroyed. On August 8, 1940, the **Battle of Britain** began. The German air force bombed targets throughout Britain in preparation for an invasion. Outnumbered eight to one, the Royal Air Force (RAF) outfought the German Luftwaffe. British pilots shot down over seventeen hundred German planes and forced Hitler to call off his planned invasion. "Never has so much been done by so few for so many," Churchill declared.

While the outcome of the Battle of Britain was still uncertain, Roosevelt lobbied Congress to provide the British with destroyers and aircraft and to increase the military budget. He argued that with American support, Britain could defeat the Axis without America's having to enter the conflict. Isolationists bitterly denounced Roosevelt for pushing the nation toward war, but Roosevelt got his support for Britain. In September 1940, he signed the **Burke-Wadsworth Act,** creating the first peacetime military draft in American history. By executive order, he exchanged fifty old, mothballed destroyers for ninety-nine-year leases over British military bases in Newfoundland, the Caribbean, and British Guiana. By the end of the year, Congress had approved over $37 billion for military spending.

In 1940, faced with a world becoming more dangerous by the minute, Roosevelt chose to take the unprecedented step of running for a third term in office. The Republicans nominated **Wendell Willkie** of Indiana, a public utilities executive. Initially, Willkie supported aid to Britain and increased military spending. But Republican leaders convinced Willkie to present himself as the peace candidate. Willkie's popularity surged upward, forcing Roosevelt to affirm more strongly his commitment to peace. "Your boys," the president promised American mothers, "are not going to be sent into any foreign wars." The election demonstrated solid personal support for Roosevelt, who won easily, but not for the Democratic party, which lost seats in the Senate and the House.

The Battle for the Atlantic

As Roosevelt knew, the destroyers-for-bases deal was only a temporary solution to Britain's growing shortage of cash. In December 1940, Churchill asked Roosevelt for loans to pay for supplies and for help to protect merchant ships from German submarines. Roosevelt agreed. In his December Fireside Chat, he told his audience that a strong Britain was America's best defense against Germany. If Britain fell, Hitler would attack the United States next. He urged the people to make the nation the "arsenal of democracy" and to supply

blitzkrieg Sudden, swift military offensive that allowed Germany to defeat Poland in a matter of days.

Axis Powers Coalition of nations that opposed the Allies in World War II, first consisting of just Germany and Italy and later joined by Japan.

Winston Churchill Prime minister who led Britain through World War II; he was known for his eloquent speeches and his refusal to give in to the Nazi threat.

Battle of Britain Series of air battles between British and German planes fought over Britain from August to October 1940, during which English cities suffered heavy bombing.

Burke-Wadsworth Act Law passed in 1940 creating the first peacetime draft in American history and providing for the training of 1.2 million troops.

Wendell Willkie Business executive and Republican presidential candidate who lost to Roosevelt in 1940.

Britain with all the material help it needed to defeat Hitler. He then presented Congress with the **Lend-Lease bill,** which would allow the president to lend or lease war materials to any country considered vital to American security. The bill passed easily on March 11, 1941.

For a while, it appeared that Lend-Lease might have been passed too late. German submarines were sinking so many ships that not even Britain's minimal needs were reaching ports. In March 1941, Churchill warned Roosevelt that Germany's foes could not afford to lose the battle for the Atlantic. In response, Roosevelt extended the neutrality zone to include Greenland. By the summer of 1941, the United States Navy's patrol of the neutrality zone overlapped Hitler's Atlantic war zone. It was only a matter of time before American and German ships confronted each other. In May, a German submarine had sunk the American merchant ship *Robin Moor.*

Hitler's attention, however, was focused eastward. During the spring of 1941, he was preparing for an invasion of the Soviet Union. The nonaggression pact of 1939 had served its purpose. Hitler assembled the largest military force ever massed on a single front: 2,700 planes, 3,350 tanks, and 3.3 million men. On June 22, German forces opened the eastern front.

As German armies raced across the vast expanse of Russia toward Moscow, Roosevelt and Churchill met secretly off the coast of Newfoundland in August 1941. They discussed strategies, supplies, and future prospects. For the first time, both leaders sensed some room for optimism. More ships were getting safely across the Atlantic. But Roosevelt's main concern at the meeting was to develop a set of political principles that would support America's entry into the war. He and Churchill produced the **Atlantic Charter.** The charter reaffirmed the Wilsonian goals of self-determination, freedom of trade and the seas, and the establishment of a "permanent system of general security."

Shortly thereafter, on September 4, 1941, the inevitable encounter between an American destroyer and a German submarine took place. Claiming that the attack on the destroyer was totally unprovoked, Roosevelt obtained congressional permission to arm American merchant ships, to use the navy to convoy ships all the way to Britain, and to allow American ships to attack Axis warships. By the fall of 1941, the U.S. Navy was unofficially at war with Germany. On October 17, the U.S.S. *Kearney* was damaged while protecting a convoy. Two weeks later, the U.S.S. *Reuben James* was sunk, with 115 deaths. On November 13, Congress rescinded all neutrality laws. War was imminent, but Roosevelt

♦ From the beginning of World War II, Roosevelt was determined to help defeat the forces of fascism. Meeting with Churchill on board a cruiser off the coast of Newfoundland in August 1941, the two leaders signed the Atlantic Charter as a prelude to America's waging war against Germany. *FDR Library.*

Lend-Lease bill Bill that became a law in 1941, providing that any country whose security was vital to U.S. interests could receive arms and equipment by sale, transfer, or lease from the United States.

Atlantic Charter Joint statement issued by Roosevelt and Churchill in 1941 to formulate the postwar aims of the United States and Britain, including international economic and political cooperation.

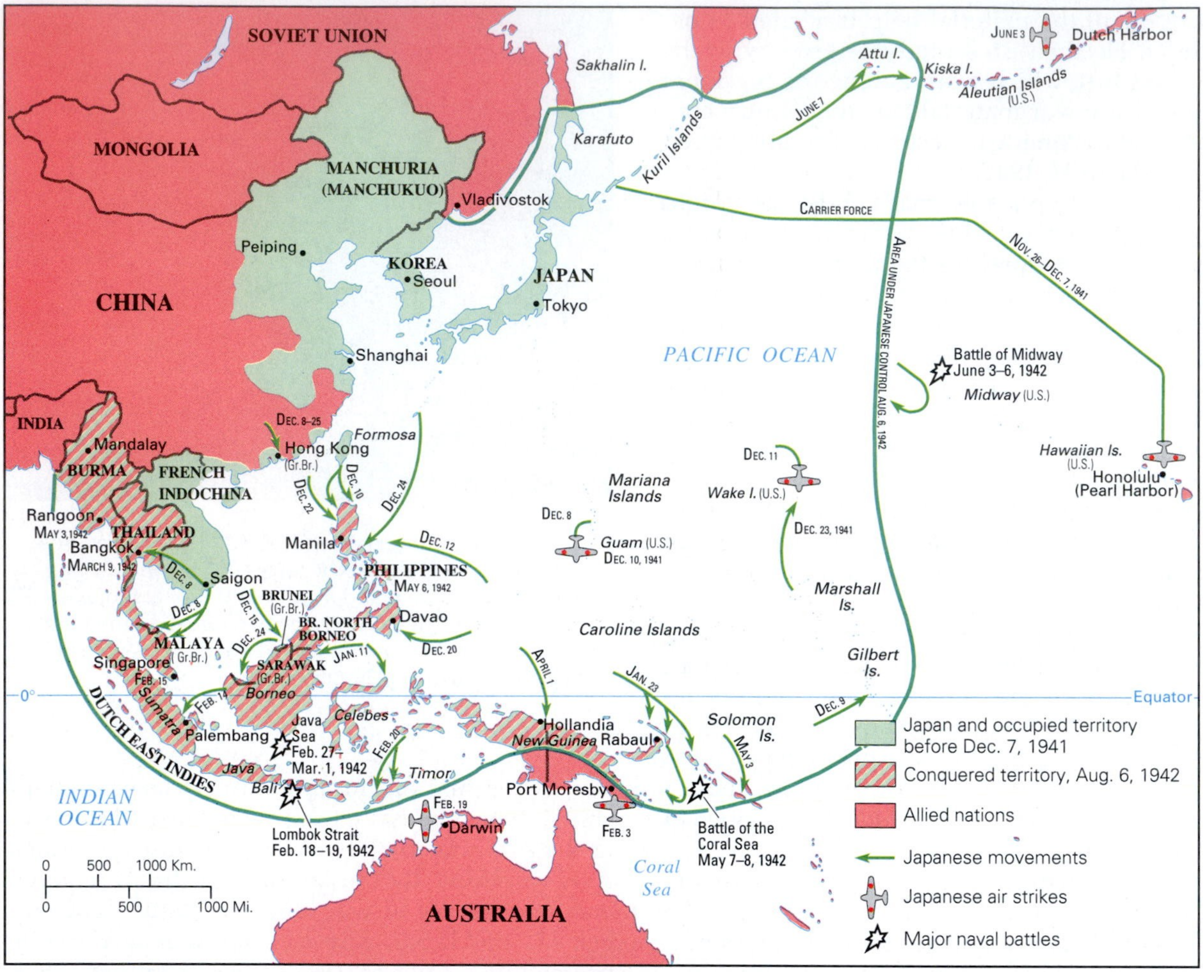

♦ **MAP 26.2 Japanese Advances, December 1941–August 1942** Beginning on December 7, 1941, Japanese forces began carving out a vast empire, the East Asian Co-Prosperity Sphere, by attacking American, British, Dutch, and Australian forces from Pearl Harbor to the Dutch East Indies. This map shows the course of Japanese expansion until the critical naval battles of the Coral Sea and Midway in the spring of 1942 that halted Japanese advances in the Pacific.

envisioned it as a war involving only American naval and air forces.

Facing Japan

Since 1937, Japanese troops had seized more and more of coastal China while the United States did little but protest. In July 1940, Roosevelt responded by forbidding the sale of aviation fuel and scrap iron to Japan.

In September 1941, the situation in East Asia worsened. Japan took over French Indochina (see Map 26.2) and signed a defense treaty with Germany and Italy. Roosevelt promptly increased American forces in the Philippines and added more trade restrictions. Within the Japanese government, there were opposing views on how to react to the American economic sanctions. Those seeking to avoid war hoped that negotiations would settle Japanese-American differences. But those negotiations stalled when Secretary of State Cordell Hull demanded Japan's withdrawal from Indochina and China. Hull's demand played into the hands of Japanese military leaders, who had argued all along that war was unavoidable to break the "circle of force" being created around it.

For Minister of War Hideki Tojo, the choice had become simple: either submit to American demands, giving up the achievements of the past ten years, or safeguard the nation's honor by initiating a war. If negotiations did not produce a more favorable American policy toward Japan by December 1941, the choice was for war. Naval aircraft would target the American fleet at Hawai'i, while the army would invade the Philippines, Malaya, Singapore, and the Dutch East Indies. The negotiations remained stalled.

Pearl Harbor

At 7:49 A.M. (Hawai'i time) on December 7, 1941, Japanese planes struck the American naval base at Pearl Harbor. By 8:12, seven battleships of the American Pacific fleet were aflame, sinking, or badly damaged. Eleven other ships had been hit, nearly two hundred American aircraft had been destroyed, and twenty-five hundred Americans had lost their lives. Fortunately, U.S. aircraft carriers were on maneuvers in the Pacific. Pearl Harbor's repair shops, dry docks, and oil storage tanks also incurred only light damage.

Elsewhere that day, Japanese planes struck Singapore, Guam, the Philippines, and Hong Kong. The Japanese overwhelmed British and American positions throughout the Pacific and East Asia. Roosevelt declared December 7, 1941, "a day which will live in infamy" and asked Congress for a declaration of war against Japan. The December 8 declaration fell one vote short of being unanimous. Three days later, Germany and Italy declared war on the United States.

America Responds to War

The attack on Pearl Harbor unified the nation as no other event had done. Afterward, it was almost impossible to find an isolationist. Thousands of young men rushed to enlist, especially in the navy and marines. On December 8, the navy recruiting station in New York City was besieged by twelve hundred applicants, some of whom had waited outside all night.

The shock of Japan's attack on Pearl Harbor raised fears of further attacks, especially along the Pacific coast. Throughout the week after December 7, West Coast cities reported phantom enemy planes. Rumors circulated that Japanese Americans intended to sabotage factories and military installations. Within a week, the Federal Bureau of Investigation (FBI) had arrested 1,370 Japanese, 1,002 Germans, and 169 Italians.

Japanese-American Internment

The feelings against Japanese Americans were the product of long-standing racist attitudes. Of the nearly 125,000 Japanese Americans in the country, about three-fourths were **Nisei,** those born in the United States. The rest, the **Issei,** were officially citizens of Japan, although nearly all had lived in the United States since 1924, when American law barred them from becoming naturalized citizens.

Echoing its anti-Japanese actions in the 1880s, California moved to "protect" itself. Japanese Americans were fired from state jobs and had their law and medical licenses revoked. Banks froze Japanese-American assets, stores refused service, and loyal citizens vandalized Nisei and Issei homes and businesses. Although some doubted the reality of any threat from the Japanese-American community, no one protested the growing cry that they be relocated away from the coast. On February 19,

Nisei A person born in America of parents who emigrated from Japan.

Issei A Japanese immigrant to the United States.

1942, President Roosevelt signed **Executive Order #9066,** which allowed the military to remove anyone deemed a threat from official military areas. When the entire West Coast was declared a military area, the eviction of the Japanese Americans from the region began. By the summer of 1942, over 110,000 Nisei and Issei had been transported to ten **internment camps** (see chapter opener map). The Supreme Court upheld the internment order twice.

The orders to relocate gave Japanese Americans almost no time to prepare. Families had to pack the few personal possessions they were allowed to take and to store or **liquidate** the rest of their property. Some had two weeks to get ready; others had two days. Most families had to sell their possessions at ridiculously low prices. A twenty-six-room hotel was sold for $500; a pickup truck went for $25; farms sold for a fraction of what they were worth. Japanese-American families lost an estimated $810 million to $2 billion in property and possessions. Decades later, in 1988, the federal government paid $20,000 in compensation to each of the surviving sixty thousand internees.

Internment produced a feeling of helplessness and isolation. Tags with numbers were issued to every family to tie to luggage and coats—no names, only numbers. "From then on," wrote one woman, "we were known as family #10710." Going to the camp, she lost her identity, dignity, and privacy. The Nisei and Issei were surrounded by barbed wire and watched over by guards in towers mounted with machine guns. Photographers were not allowed to take pictures of the wire or the guard towers. In camp, families and individuals were assigned to apartments 20-by-25-foot located in long barracks. An average of eight people were assigned to each apartment. Cots, straw-filled mattresses, and three army blankets were furnished each person.

Some internees were able to leave the camps by working outside, especially on farms. Others volunteered for military service, the other escape route from the camps. Japanese-American units served in both the Pacific and European theaters. The most famous unit was the 442nd Combat Team. The men of the 442nd were among the most decorated in the war.

Aware of rabidly anti-Japanese public opinion, Roosevelt waited until after the 1943 elections to allow internees who passed a loyalty review to go home. A year later, the camps were empty. Returning home, the Japanese Americans discovered that nearly everything was gone. Stored belongings had been stolen. Land, homes, and businesses had been seized by the government for unpaid taxes. Quietly demonstrating their loyalty, Japanese Americans began to re-establish their homes and businesses.

Mobilizing the Nation for War

When President Roosevelt made his first Fireside Chat following Pearl Harbor, "Dr. New Deal" became "Dr. Win the War." He called on factories to run twenty-four hours a day, seven days a week. Gone was every trace of the antibusiness attitude that had characterized much of the New Deal rhetoric. Roosevelt welcomed big business back into the heart of government. Corporate executives left their companies and flocked to Washington to become **dollar-a-year men,** contributing their business skills to help the war effort.

By 1942, one-third of all American production was geared to the war, and the government was allocating millions of dollars to build new plants in vital industries like aluminum and synthetic rubber. By the end of the war, U.S. manufacturers had built over 300,000 aircraft, 88,140 tanks, and 86,000 warships.

As the nation's economy began to retool, Roosevelt acted to provide government direction and

Executive Order #9066 Order of President Roosevelt in 1942 that authorized the removal of "enemy aliens" from military areas and that was used to isolate Japanese Americans in internment camps.

internment camps Camps where over 110,000 Japanese Americans living in the West were isolated on the grounds that they were "enemy aliens" dangerous to U.S. security.

liquidate To convert assets into cash.

dollar-a-year men Corporate executives who volunteered for government jobs to help the war effort.

planning. His first step was to establish the **Office of Price Administration (OPA)** to control prices. In January 1942, Roosevelt established the War Production Board (WPB) and the War Labor Board (WLB). Working together, these boards plus the OPA were to coordinate and plan production, establish the allotment of materials, and ensure harmonious labor relations. Initially, however, they did not create a smoothly working economy. By the fall of 1942, confused priorities and soaring food prices had created a public outcry and labor unrest. To give the government still more control, in September Congress expanded the powers of the OPA and regulated agricultural prices. In turn, Roosevelt created the Office of Economic Stabilization (OES) to coordinate prices, rents, and wages. He appointed former Supreme Court Justice James F. Byrnes as its chief.

Armed with extensive powers and the president's trust, Byrnes became the second most powerful man in the country. "If you want something done, go see Jimmie Byrnes" became the watchword. Almost immediately, Byrnes and the new director of the OPA, Chester Bowles, set maximum prices and froze wages and rents at their March 1942 levels. To deal with scarce commodities, Bowles and Byrnes expanded the existing rationing system, adding gasoline, tires, butter, sugar, cheese, and meat. By the end of 1942, most Americans had a ration book. Despite all government efforts, a strong black market thrived. The right amount of money could buy nearly any item.

By mid-1943, production was booming, jobs were plentiful, wages and family incomes were rising, and inflation was under control. Even farmers were climbing out of debt, as farm income had tripled since 1939. Taxes also went up, especially for businesses and the affluent. Those making $500,000 or more a year paid 88 percent in taxes. Corporate taxes averaged 40 percent, with a 90 percent tax on excess profits. The 1942 Revenue Act also slapped everyone making more than $645 a year with a special "victory tax" of 5 percent, greatly expanding the number of people paying personal income taxes from 13 million to 50 million. The tax changes from 1940 to 1945 moderately altered the basic distribution of wealth by reducing the percentage of income held by the wealthy.

Increased tax revenues funded about half of the total cost of the war. The government borrowed the rest. The national debt jumped from $40 billion to $260 billion by 1945. The most publicized borrowing effort encouraged the purchase of **war bonds.** Movie stars and celebrities asked Americans to "do their part" and buy bonds. The public responded by purchasing over $40 billion of bonds, but the majority of bonds was sold to corporations and financial institutions.

Roosevelt sought to prevent labor disputes while protecting workers through the creation of the War Labor Board. To prevent strikes and keep down labor costs, the WLB allowed workers a maximum 15 percent increase in wages above January 1941 levels. Although most workers accepted this cap on wages as a patriotic duty, some did not. In 1943, John L. Lewis and his United Mine Workers went out on strike. An angry president threatened to seize the mines and jail Lewis. Eventually, the parties reached a compromise that established special circumstances to exceed the cap. Other strikes broke out during the war, but war production was never in jeopardy.

Wartime Politics

As Roosevelt mobilized the nation for war, Republicans and conservative Democrats moved to bury what was left of the New Deal. The congressional elections of November 1942 indicated that Roosevelt and liberal Democrats were facing hard political times. People secure in wartime jobs were no longer as concerned about the social welfare programs of the New Deal. They griped about higher taxes, rents, and prices; about the scarcity of goods, especially gasoline and meat; and about government inefficiency. And they aimed their

Office of Price Administration Agency established by executive order in 1941 to set prices for critical wartime commodities.

war bond Bond sold by the government to finance the war effort.

complaints at Roosevelt and the Democrats. Early military defeats in the Pacific added to the dissatisfaction. Consequently, many Americans who had once supported the New Deal voted Republican in 1942. Business-oriented publications like *Fortune* and the *Wall Street Journal* sounded the attack on remaining New Deal social welfare agendas. Congress axed the CCC, WPA, and NYA and slashed the budgets of several other government agencies.

The Republicans nominated Governor Thomas Dewey of New York as their 1944 presidential candidate. Responding to the conservative tone of the nation, Roosevelt dropped the liberal Henry Wallace as vice president and selected the moderately conservative Harry S Truman from Missouri in his place. Roosevelt campaigned on a strong wartime economy, his record of leadership, and, by November 1944, a successful war effort. Dewey had little with which to attack Roosevelt except suggestions that Roosevelt, at age 62, was too old for the job. Roosevelt's winning totals, though not as large as in 1940, were still greater than pollsters had predicted.

A People at Work and War

Within sixteen days of Pearl Harbor, nearly 600,000 men were in uniform. But still more were needed, and there were not enough volunteers. The United States conscripted over 10 million men during the war. Those drafted were required to serve until the war was over.

At home, the call-up and need to manufacture war-related goods changed everyday life. Cotton, silk, and gasoline became increasingly scarce. The War Production Board established fashion rules to conserve cotton and wool. Garment makers eliminated vests and shirt cuffs and narrowed the lapels on men's suits. The amount of fabric in women's skirts was also reduced. Families collected scrap metals, paper, and rubber to be recycled for the war effort and grew victory gardens. When people complained about shortages, more would challenge, "Don't you know there's a war on?"

One sure sign that there was a war on was that people were moving and taking new jobs as never before. Prior to the war, nearly 3.8 million Americans were unemployed; by the end of 1942, a severe labor shortage existed. To fill the gaps in the work force, employers increasingly turned to women and minorities. Even the Nisei were allowed to leave their relocation camps if their labor was needed. Between 1941 and 1945, 15 million Americans relocated to work in new jobs. Two hundred thousand people, many from the rural South, headed for Detroit, but more went west, where defense industries beckoned. Shipbuilding and the aircraft industry sparked boomtowns that could not keep pace with the growing need for local services and facilities. San Diego, California, mushroomed into a major military and defense industrial city almost overnight. Nearly fifty-five thousand people flocked there each year of the war. Mobile, Alabama; Norfolk, Virginia; Seattle, Washington; and Denver, Colorado, experienced similar rapid growth (see chapter opener map).

Such cities experienced massive problems providing homes, water, electricity, and sanitation for all the newcomers. Crime flourished. Marriage, divorce, family violence, and juvenile delinquency rates soared. The flood of people brought other disturbing social problems. The twelve thousand sailors and soldiers looking for a good time gave Norfolk a reputation as a major sin city. Police estimated that between two thousand and three thousand prostitutes worked in its alleys, taxis, clubs, and restaurants.

New Opportunities and Old Constraints in Wartime

As the wartime labor shortage deepened, employers turned to women and minorities to work the assembly lines. The federal government conducted an emotional campaign suggesting that women could shorten the war if they left the home and went to work. The image of Rosie the Riveter became the symbol of the patriotic woman doing her part. As more jobs opened, women did fill them—some because of patriotism, but most because they wanted the wages. Peggy Terry worked in a munitions plant and

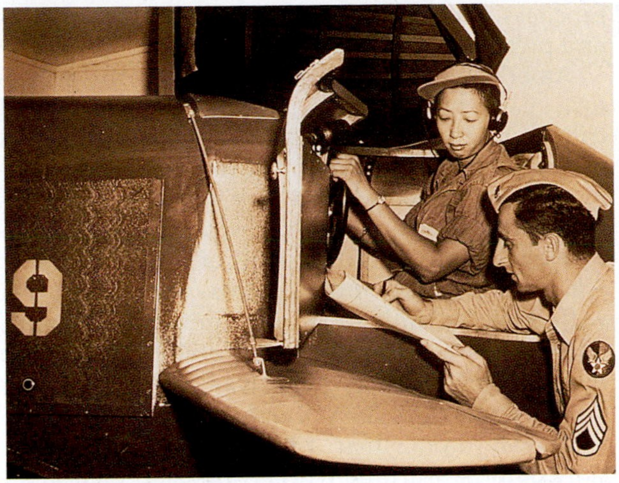

♦ More than 350,000 women served in the military during the war, including Lieutenant Hazel Ying Lee, a Women's Airforce Service Pilot. WASPs flew "noncombat" missions, ferrying planes and supplies across the United States and Canada. Already an experienced pilot in China, Lieutenant Lee is seated here in the cockpit of a trainer. She died in 1943 when her plane crashed. *Texas Woman's University.*

considered it "an absolute miracle. . . . We made the fabulous sum of $32 a week. . . . Before, we made nothing." By 1944, 37 percent of all adult women were working.

But not all was rosy at work. Male workers resented and harassed women. Employers and most men expected that when the war was over, women would happily return to their traditional roles at home. For women, the war experience was a mixed one. They became more aware of their potential and ability. But when the war was over, many were required to sacrifice their newly discovered potential for traditional American values that kept women less than equal.

Like the war experiences of women, those of minorities were mixed. New employment and social opportunities existed, but they were accompanied by increased racial and ethnic tensions. Initially, the war provided few opportunities for African Americans. Shipyards and other defense contractors wanted white workers. The antiblack bias began to change by mid-1942 as the labor shortage worsened. West Coast shipyards were the first to integrate. Lockheed Aircraft then broke the color barrier in August. Word soon spread to the South that blacks could find work in California. Between the spring of 1942 and 1945, over 340,000 African Americans moved to Los Angeles alone.

The growing availability of jobs for African Americans was also the product of increased pressure on government from African-American leaders. In early 1941, **A. Philip Randolph,** leader of the powerful Brotherhood of Sleeping Car Porters union, proposed that African Americans march en masse on Washington to demand equality in jobs and the armed forces. In June, fearing that over 100,000 African Americans would descend on Washington, Roosevelt signed a law that created the Federal Employment Practices Commission (FEPC) and forbade racial job discrimination by the government and companies holding government contracts. Black wages during the war rose from an annual average of $457 to $1,976.

Across the nation, blacks supported the "Double V" campaign: victory over racist Germany and victory over racism at home. Membership in the NAACP and Urban League increased as these organizations took bolder steps to attack segregation, lynching, and discrimination. In 1942, the newly formed **Congress of Racial Equality (CORE)** adopted the sit-in tactic to attempt to integrate public facilities and met with some minor successes. In 1944, the Supreme Court ruled in *Smith v. Allwright* that Texas could not use the "all-white primary" to deny African Americans the right to vote. This decision changed the law, but whites soon found other ways to keep blacks from the polls in Texas.

In the North, patterns of hostility, discrimination, and violence hardened as the population of

A. Philip Randolph African-American labor leader who organized the 1941 march on Washington that pressured Roosevelt to issue an executive order banning discrimination in defense industries.

Congress of Racial Equality Civil rights organization founded in 1942 and committed to using nonviolent techniques such as sit-ins to end segregation.

African Americans increased. White workers went on strike when three black workers were promoted, harping, "We'd rather see Hitler and Hirohito win than work beside a nigger on the assembly line." A violent confrontation in Detroit in June 1943 left twenty-five blacks and nine whites dead.

The opportunities and realities of African Americans in uniform matched those of black civilians. Prior to 1940, blacks served at the lowest ranks and in the most menial jobs in a segregated army and navy. The Army Air Corps and the Marine Corps refused to accept blacks at all. President Roosevelt had made no effort to integrate the military. Blacks and civil rights supporters, including Eleanor Roosevelt, lobbied hard for changes. In 1940, the army began to encourage the recruitment of black officers and promoted **Benjamin O. Davis** from colonel to general. By the beginning of 1942, the Army Air Corps had an all-black unit and eventually would commission six hundred African-Americans as pilots. In April 1942, Secretary of the Navy James Forrestal permitted black **noncommissioned officers** in the U.S. Navy.

Higher ranks for a few did not disguise the fact that for most blacks, military life was often demeaning. In Indiana, over a hundred black officers were arrested for trying to integrate the officers' club. In Salina, Kansas, German prisoners could eat at any local lunch counter, but their black guards could not.

Latinos, too, found new opportunities and continued frustrations during the war. Latinos rushed to enlist as the war started. More than 300,000 Latinos served—the highest percentage of any ethnic community. Unlike African Americans and most Nisei, Latinos served in integrated units and generally faced less discrimination in the military than in society.

For those remaining at home, there were more jobs available, but still most Latinos worked as common laborers and agricultural workers. A serious shortage of farm workers developed during the war. After having deported Mexicans during the Depression, the government had to ask Mexico to supply agricultural workers. Mexico agreed but insisted that the ***braceros*** (Spanish for "helping arms") receive fair wages and adequate housing, transportation, food, and medical care. In practice, ranchers and farmers commonly paid low wages and provided barely livable facilities.

American Indians eagerly supported the war effort, realizing that it offered both individual and tribal opportunities. At least twenty-five thousand Indians served in the military. Among the most famous were three hundred Navajos who served as **code talkers** for the Marine Corps, using their native language as a secure means of communication. American Indians, unlike other minorities, met with little discrimination in the military. For most, military life and wages compared favorably to reservation life. During the war, jobs and higher wages lured over forty thousand American Indians away from their reservations. Mostly unskilled, these wartime workers boosted their families' average income from $400 a month in 1941 to $1,200 in 1945. Many who left the reservation assimilated into American culture and never returned to the old patterns of life.

Waging World War

The Japanese attack on Pearl Harbor convinced most Americans that defeating Japan should be the country's first priority. To Churchill's relief, Roosevelt still considered victory in Europe more important, regarding Hitler as the more dangerous enemy. In late April 1942, Soviet foreign minister V. M. Molotov arrived in Washington to confirm Roosevelt's commitment to the Europe-first strat-

Benjamin O. Davis Army officer who, in 1940, became the first black general in the U.S. Army.

noncommissioned officer Enlisted member of the armed forces, such as a corporal or sergeant, who has been promoted to a rank conferring leadership over others.

braceros Mexican nationals who worked on U.S. farms beginning in 1942 because of the labor shortage during World War II.

code talkers Navajo Indians serving in the U.S. Marines who communicated by radio in their native language so that the enemy could not interpret messages.

egy. Further, Molotov asked for a second front in Western Europe to relieve pressure on the Soviet Union. Roosevelt promised a second front sometime in 1942. His commitment to the European theater of operations cemented the Grand Alliance between the United States, Great Britain, and the Soviet Union to defeat Hitler.

The British, however, vigorously opposed an invasion across the English Channel in 1942, claiming it was too risky. Instead, the British proposed an Allied landing in western North Africa. This would be a safer venture that would also help the British army fighting in western Egypt. Roosevelt agreed to the plan. General **Dwight David Eisenhower** was selected to command American forces in North Africa and Europe.

As planning began for the invasion of North Africa in 1942, the course of the war seemed to darken for the Allies. German forces under General Erwin Rommel were advancing toward Egypt and the Suez Canal. A renewed German offensive was penetrating deeper into the Soviet Union. In the Atlantic, German U-boats were sinking ships at an appalling rate. In the Pacific, Japanese successes continued. In May, commanding general Douglas MacArthur fled by sea as the last American forces in the Philippines surrendered. Japanese forces also captured Singapore and the Dutch East Indies and were establishing bases on New Guinea and the Solomon Islands (see Map 26.2).

Halting the Japanese Advance

The first major American action in the Pacific occurred on May 7, 1942, at the **Battle of the Coral Sea** (see Map 26.3). "Magic," the code name for deciphering Japanese codes, had alerted American forces that Japan was preparing to invade Port Moresby, New Guinea, a step that would threaten Australia. The aircraft carriers *Lexington* and *Yorktown* intercepted the invasion fleet, and in the air-to-ship battle that followed, they turned back the invasion fleet despite the loss of the *Lexington.*

American aircraft carriers also foiled Admiral Yamamoto's plan to seize **Midway Island.** Again alerted by Magic, the carriers *Hornet, Enterprise,* and *Yorktown* lay in wait northeast of Midway (see Map 26.3). The engagement on June 4, 1942, changed the course of the war in the Pacific. Thirty-seven American dive-bombers surprised the Japanese carriers in the middle of rearming and refueling their planes. Four Japanese carriers went down. Although the *Yorktown* sank as well, the air superiority of the Japanese had been destroyed. Hundreds of superb Japanese pilots had perished. The United States, with its greater industrial and population base, now held the upper hand. It was able to launch fourteen new aircraft carriers between 1942 and 1945, whereas Japan launched only six.

With the victories at the Coral Sea and Midway, the next step was to begin retaking lost territory. General MacArthur and the army were given the task of leading an offensive toward the Philippines from the south. The navy, under the direction of Admiral Chester Nimitz, would seize selected islands and atolls and approach the Philippines from the east. Eventually, both forces would join for the final attack on Japan. On August 7, 1942, soldiers of the 1st Marine Division waded ashore on **Guadalcanal Island** in the Solomons. Japan furiously defended the island. Fierce fighting dragged on for the next six months, but in early February 1943, Japan withdrew its last troops from Guadalcanal. By early 1943, American and Australian forces were also

Dwight David Eisenhower Supreme commander of Allied forces in Europe during World War II who planned the D-day invasion; he later became president of the United States.

Battle of the Coral Sea Major U.S. victory in the Pacific in May 1942, which prevented the Japanese from invading New Guinea and thus isolating Australia.

Midway Island Strategically located island in the Pacific that the Japanese navy tried to capture in June 1942; naval intelligence warned American forces of the Japanese plans, and they repulsed the attack.

Guadalcanal Island Pacific island that was the site of the first major U.S. offensive action in the Pacific. In November 1942, U.S. troops finally secured the island from the Japanese.

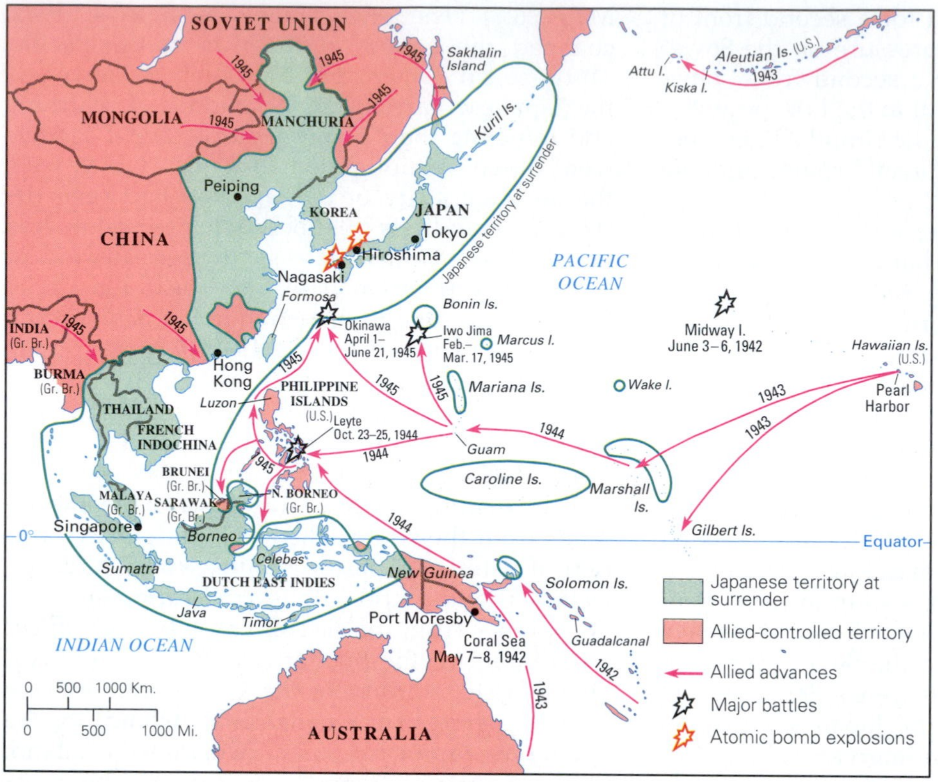

♦ **MAP 26.3 Closing the Circle on Japan, 1942–1945** Following the Battle of Midway, with the invasion of Guadalcanal (August 1942), American forces began the costly process of island hopping. This map shows the paths of the American campaign in the Pacific, closing the circle on Japan. After the Soviet Union entered the war and Hiroshima and Nagasaki were destroyed by atomic bombs, Japan surrendered on August 14, 1945.

driving Japanese forces out of southeastern New Guinea.

The Tide Turns in Europe

In Europe, too, the Allies began to meet with some success. By late 1942, British and American forces were closing in on Rommel's Afrika Corps (see Map 26.4). After halting Rommel's advance at El Alamein, a British offensive led by General Bernard Montgomery drove the German "Desert Fox" westward out of Egypt toward Tunisia. To the west, British and American forces landed in Morocco and Algeria. American forces under General **George S. Patton** overcame stiff resistance to link up with Montgomery. Caught between two Allied armies, the last German forces in North Africa surrendered on May 13, 1943.

German losses in North Africa were light compared to those in Russia. Although Soviet forces had stopped the German advance short of Moscow dur-

George S. Patton American general who commanded troops in North Africa, Sicily, and Europe in World War II and who was known as a brilliant tactician.

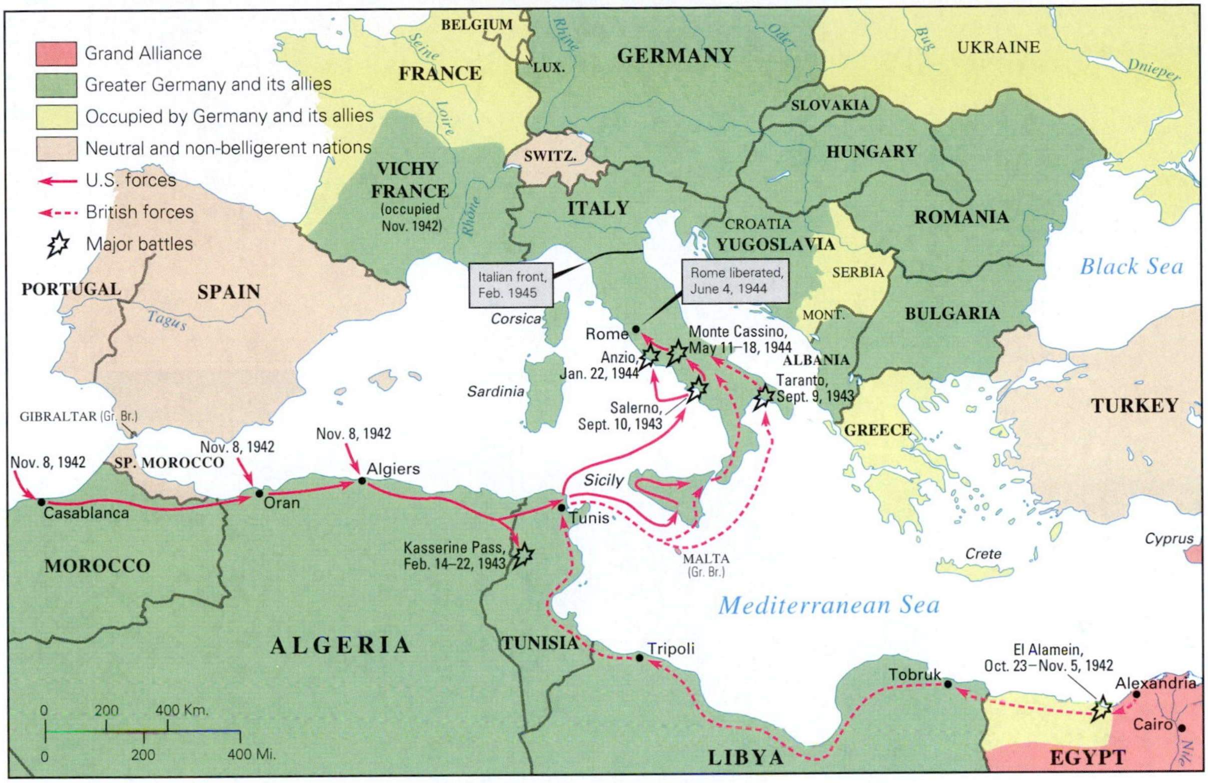
Grand Alliance
Greater Germany and its allies
Occupied by Germany and its allies
Neutral and non-belligerent nations
U.S. forces
British forces
Major battles
BELGIUM
LUX.
GERMANY
FRANCE
UKRAINE
SLOVAKIA
HUNGARY
SWITZ.
VICHY FRANCE (occupied Nov. 1942)
ITALY
ROMANIA
CROATIA
YUGOSLAVIA
SERBIA
MONT.
BULGARIA
ALBANIA
GREECE
TURKEY
PORTUGAL
SPAIN
Black Sea
Seine
Loire
Rhône
Rhine
Oder
Bug
Dnieper
Tagus
Italian front, Feb. 1945
Rome liberated, June 4, 1944
Corsica
Rome
Anzio, Jan. 22, 1944
Monte Cassino, May 11–18, 1944
Taranto, Sept. 9, 1943
Salerno, Sept. 10, 1943
Sardinia
GIBRALTAR (Gr. Br.)
Nov. 8, 1942
SP. MOROCCO
Nov. 8, 1942
Nov. 8, 1942
Algiers
Casablanca
Oran
Sicily
Tunis
Kasserine Pass, Feb. 14–22, 1943
MALTA (Gr. Br.)
Crete
Cyprus
MOROCCO
Mediterranean Sea
ALGERIA
TUNISIA
Tripoli
El Alamein, Oct. 23–Nov. 5, 1942
Tobruk
Alexandria
Cairo
LIBYA
EGYPT
Nile
0 200 400 Km.
0 200 400 Mi.

♦ **MAP 26.4 The North African and Italian Campaigns** Having rejected a cross-channel attack on Hitler's "Atlantic Wall," British and American forces in 1942 and 1943 invaded North Africa and Italy, where victory seemed more assured. This map shows the British and American advances across North Africa and the invasions of Sicily and Italy. German forces fought stubbornly in Italy, slowing Allied advances up the peninsula.

ing the winter of 1941–1942, Germany's 1942 summer offensive had made dramatic gains, especially in southern Russia. But Stalingrad stood in the way of further advances. Bitter fighting quickly reduced the city to rubble, but the Soviets stood fast.

From August through November, the German 6th Army fought to take the city; after November, it fought to survive. On February 2, 1943, the German 6th Army surrendered, having lost over 140,000 men. The number of Soviet losses was probably just as large, but the tide of the war had turned in Europe (see Map 26.5).

In February 1943, however, Stalin knew only that the **Battle of Stalingrad** had cost the Russians dearly. To ease the pressure on his forces, the Soviet leader again demanded that the Allies open up a second front in Europe. Again, he would be disappointed. Churchill had already met with Roosevelt at Casablanca in January 1943 and convinced him to invade **Sicily** and Italy, which

Battle of Stalingrad Battle over the Soviet city of Stalingrad, which was besieged by the German army in 1942 and recaptured by Soviet troops in 1943.

Sicily Large island in the Mediterranean west of Italy, which the Allies conquered in July 1943 as a first step to invading Italy.

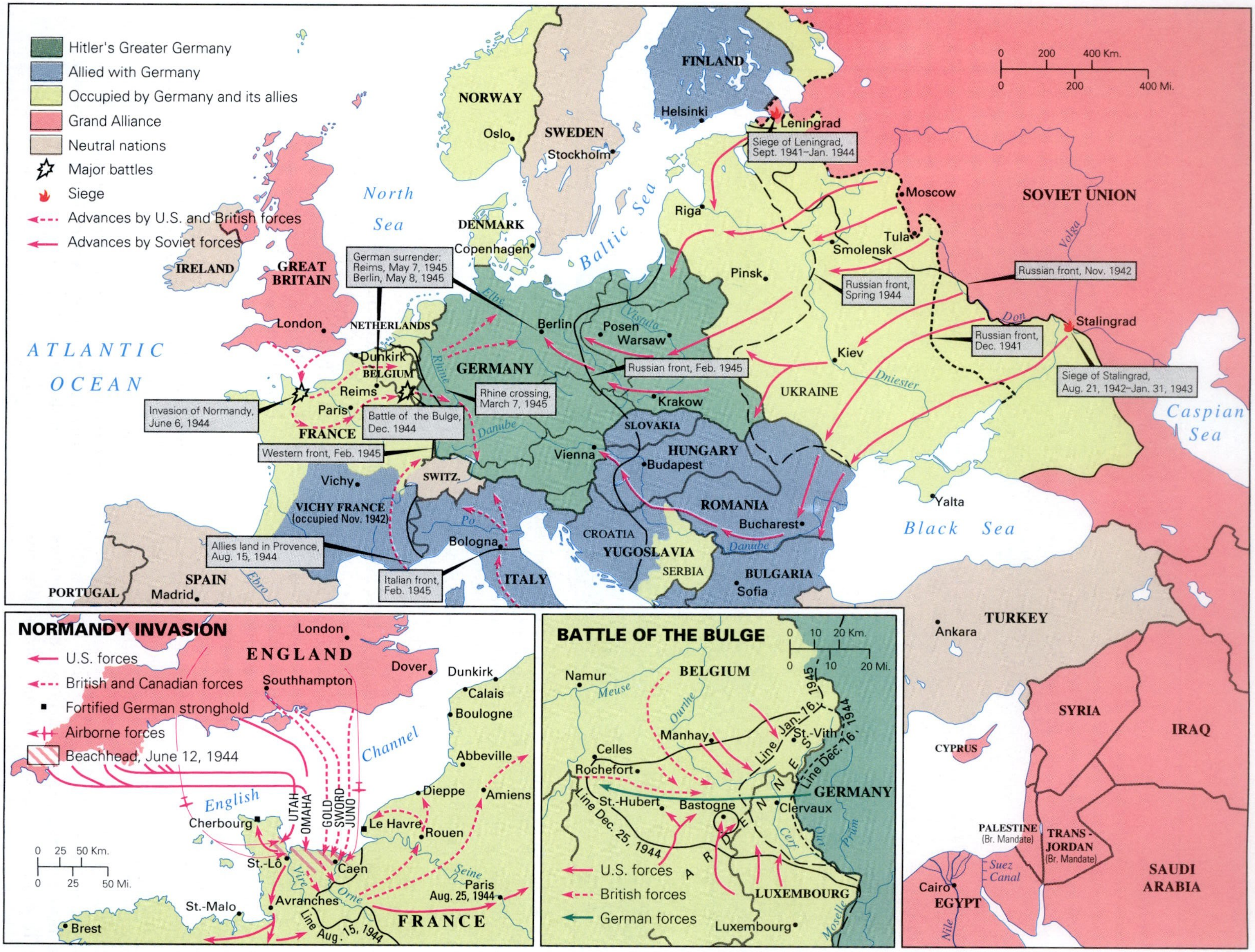

Hitler's Greater Germany
Allied with Germany
Occupied by Germany and its allies
Grand Alliance
Neutral nations
Major battles
Siege
Advances by U.S. and British forces
Advances by Soviet forces
NORWAY
SWEDEN
FINLAND
Helsinki
Leningrad
Siege of Leningrad, Sept. 1941–Jan. 1944
Oslo
Stockholm
North Sea
Baltic Sea
DENMARK
Copenhagen
Riga
Moscow
SOVIET UNION
Tula
Smolensk
Pinsk
IRELAND
GREAT BRITAIN
London
German surrender: Reims, May 7, 1945 Berlin, May 8, 1945
NETHERLANDS
Berlin
Posen
Warsaw
Russian front, Spring 1944
Russian front, Nov. 1942
Stalingrad
Russian front, Dec. 1941
Siege of Stalingrad, Aug. 21, 1942–Jan. 31, 1943
ATLANTIC OCEAN
Dunkirk
BELGIUM
Reims
Paris
FRANCE
GERMANY
Rhine
Elbe
Vistula
Russian front, Feb. 1945
Kiev
UKRAINE
Dniester
Don
Volga
Invasion of Normandy, June 6, 1944
Battle of the Bulge, Dec. 1944
Rhine crossing, March 7, 1945
Krakow
Caspian Sea
Western front, Feb. 1945
Danube
SLOVAKIA
HUNGARY
Vienna
Budapest
SWITZ.
Vichy
VICHY FRANCE (occupied Nov. 1942)
ROMANIA
Bucharest
Yalta
Black Sea
Po
Bologna
CROATIA
YUGOSLAVIA
SERBIA
BULGARIA
Sofia
Allies land in Provence, Aug. 15, 1944
SPAIN
Ebro
PORTUGAL
Madrid
Italian front, Feb. 1945
ITALY
TURKEY
Ankara
CYPRUS
SYRIA
IRAQ
PALESTINE (Br. Mandate)
TRANS-JORDAN (Br. Mandate)
Suez Canal
Cairo
EGYPT
Nile
SAUDI ARABIA
0 200 400 Km.
0 200 400 Mi.
NORMANDY INVASION
U.S. forces
British and Canadian forces
Fortified German stronghold
Airborne forces
Beachhead, June 12, 1944
London
ENGLAND
Dover
Southhampton
Dunkirk
Calais
Boulogne
Channel
English
Abbeville
Amiens
Dieppe
UTAH
OMAHA
GOLD
SWORD
JUNO
Cherbourg
Le Havre
Rouen
St.-Lô
Caen
Vire
Orne
Seine
Paris Aug. 25, 1944
St.-Malo
Avranches
Brest
Line Aug. 15, 1944
FRANCE
0 25 50 Km.
0 25 50 Mi.
BATTLE OF THE BULGE
0 10 20 Km.
0 10 20 Mi.
Namur
Meuse
BELGIUM
Ourthe
Manhay
St.-Vith
Line Jan. 16, 1945
Line Dec. 16, 1944
Celles
Rochefort
St.-Hubert
Bastogne
Clervaux
GERMANY
ARDENNES
Line Dec. 25, 1944
Our
Prüm
Cerf
U.S. forces
British forces
German forces
LUXEMBOURG
Luxembourg
Moselle

♦ **MAP 26.5 The Fall of the Third Reich** In 1943 and 1944, the war turned in favor of the Allies. On the eastern front, Soviet forces drove German forces back toward Germany. On June 6, 1944, D-day, British, Canadian, and American forces landed on the coast of Normandy to begin the liberation of France. This map shows the course of the Allied armies as they fought their way toward Berlin. On May 7, 1945, Germany surrendered.

Churchill called the "soft underbelly of the Axis." To placate Stalin, Roosevelt and Churchill promised an increased flow of supplies and promised they would make no separate peace with Hitler.

The invasion of Sicily—Operation Husky—took place in early July 1943. In a month, the Allies controlled the island (see Map 26.4). In response, the Italians overthrew Mussolini, installed a new government, and changed sides in the war. Italy surrendered unconditionally on September 8, just hours before American troops landed at Salerno. Immediately, German forces assumed the defense of Italy. German troops also freed Mussolini, taking the Italian dictator to German-controlled northern Italy, where they proclaimed him ruler of Italy. The "soft underbelly" turned out to be far from soft. Strong German defenses halted the American advance just north of Salerno. Not until late May 1944 did Allied forces finally break through the German defenses. On June 4, U.S. General Mark Clark's forces entered Rome.

Two days later, the world's attention turned toward Normandy along the west coast of France. The second front demanded by Stalin had at long last begun (see Map 26.5).

Approval for the cross-channel attack had come at the **Tehran Conference** (November 27–December 1, 1943). In the Iranian capital, Roosevelt and Churchill met with Stalin to discuss strategy and to consider a postwar settlement. Roosevelt wanted to establish Soviet support for a new world organization and to obtain a Soviet commitment to declare war against Japan. The three agreed on plans to coordinate a Soviet offensive with the Allied landings at Normandy, and Stalin pledged he would declare war on Japan once the European war was over.

The invasion of Normandy, **Operation Overlord,** was the grandest amphibious assault ever assembled: 6,483 ships, 1,500 tanks, and 176,000 men. Opposing the Allies were thousands of German troops behind the Atlantic Wall they had constructed to stop such an invasion. On **D-day,** June 6, 1944, American forces landed on Utah and Omaha beaches, while British and Canadian forces hit Sword, Gold, and Juno beaches (see Map 26.5). At the landing sites, German resistance varied. The fiercest fighting was at Omaha Beach. By nightfall, all five beaches were secure. After a week, the five beachheads were finally linked, and British and American forces coiled to break through the German positions blocking the road to the rest of France. On July 25, American forces under General Omar Bradley pierced the stubbornly held German defensive lines at St.-Lô and rumbled toward Paris and the German border. The Allies liberated Paris on August 23, and by early November they had taken Aachen on the west side of the Rhine River, the first German city to fall. From November to March, American forces consolidated and regrouped for the final assault on Germany across the Rhine (see Map 26.5).

While the British and Americans advanced across France, Allied bombers were bombing German-held Europe night and day. German cities and civilians were not spared. In one of the worst raids, during the night of February 13–14, 1945, British and American bombers set **Dresden** aflame, creating a firestorm that killed over 135,000 civilians. Nearly 600,000 German civilians would die in Allied air raids.

Stresses Within the Grand Alliance

As Allied forces moved eastward toward the Rhine, the Soviets advanced rapidly westward,

Tehran Conference Meeting in Iran in 1943 at which Churchill, Roosevelt, and Stalin discussed the invasion of Western Europe and plans for a new international organization.

Operation Overload Code name for Allied invasion of France.

D-day Allied invasion of Europe on June 6, 1944, which was carried out by transporting tanks and soldiers from England across the channel to Normandy; *D-day* is short for "designated day."

Dresden Industrial city in eastern Germany, which was almost totally destroyed when it was firebombed by the Allies in 1945.

pushing the last German troops from Russia by the end of June 1944. Behind Germany's retreating eastern armies, the Soviets occupied parts of Poland, Romania, Bulgaria, Hungary, and Czechoslovakia. Following the Red Army came Soviet officials and Eastern European Communists who had lived in exile in the Soviet Union during the war. The Soviet goal was to establish new Eastern European governments that would be friendly to the Soviet Union. A Communist Lublin government (named after the town where the government was installed) was established in Poland, while in Romania and Bulgaria, "popular front" governments, heavily influenced by Communists, took command. Only Czechoslovakia and Hungary managed to establish non-Communist governments as the German occupation collapsed. Britain and the United States eyed the political changes in Eastern Europe with suspicion.

On February 4, 1945, the Big Three met at the Black Sea resort of **Yalta** amid growing apprehension about Soviet territorial goals in Eastern Europe. Roosevelt hoped to secure a Soviet declaration of war on Japan and support for the new **United Nations.** He believed that both were necessary to usher in peace and international stability. He also wanted the Soviets to modify their control over Eastern Europe. Stalin's diplomatic goals were Western acceptance of a Soviet sphere of influence in Eastern Europe, the weakening of Germany, the economic restoration of the Soviet Union, and reassurances that any postwar international system would be based on Big Three cooperation.

Roosevelt and Stalin concurred on Germany. To prevent Germany from ever again posing a military threat to its neighbors, they desired to divide their enemy into smaller, weaker states. Churchill disagreed, saying that the dismemberment of Germany would be too harsh. Unable to agree on the future of Germany, the Big Three postponed further discussions until their next meeting.

The question of which Polish government represented Poland, however, could not be put off. The Soviet Union supported the Lublin government as the only legitimate one. Roosevelt and Churchill, however, hoped to establish a Polish government on the basis of free and honest elections. Their goal matched the ideals of the Atlantic Charter but not the **geopolitics** of the Soviet Union. Stalin argued that Soviet security demanded a friendly government in Poland. The powers agreed on a very ambiguous compromise that called for non-Communist participation in the Polish government but that provided no means of enforcement. On the related issue of Soviet influence throughout Eastern Europe, Roosevelt fared little better. The Yalta Conference left control over Eastern Europe firmly in Soviet hands. Roosevelt did accomplish his two major goals: Stalin promised to enter the war against Japan within three months of Germany's surrender and to support the formation of the United Nations.

Believing that there could be no postwar stability and security without Soviet cooperation, Roosevelt permitted Stalin to keep what he already had or could easily take. Short of ending friendly relations with the Soviet Union, Roosevelt had no means to reduce Soviet power in Eastern Europe. Roosevelt hoped that his good will would encourage Stalin to respond in kind. Both Stalin and Roosevelt were buoyed by the "spirit of Yalta." Only Churchill, who distrusted Stalin, left Yalta in a gloomy mood.

Hitler's Defeat

With his forces crumbling in the east, Hitler approved a last-ditch attempt to halt the American advance. Taking advantage of bad weather that

Yalta Site in the Crimea of the last meeting, in February 1945, between Roosevelt, Churchill, and Stalin; they discussed the final defeat of the Axis Powers and the problems of postwar occupation.

United Nations International organization established in 1945 to maintain peace among nations and foster cooperation in human rights, education, health, welfare, and trade.

geopolitics Government policy based on the influence of geographic and political factors on national interests.

♦ Hitler ordered the "Final Solution"—the extermination of Europe's Jews—soon after the United States entered the war. In this picture, German troops arrest residents of the Warsaw ghetto for deportation to concentration camps. Few would survive the camps, where over 6 million Jews died. *YNO Institute for Jewish Research.*

grounded Allied aircraft, German forces launched an attack in December 1944 through the Ardennes Forest, pushing back the Americans. It was a desperate gamble that failed. The **Battle of the Bulge** delayed Eisenhower's westward assault only briefly and cost Germany valuable reserves and equipment (see Map 26.5). Ultimately, it merely hastened the end of the war. The war was also winding down in Italy. By the end of 1944, British and American forces had taken most of northern Italy. When German armies began to surrender in April 1945, Italian partisans captured Mussolini and hanged him.

On March 7, 1945, American forces crossed the Rhine at Remagen and began to battle their way into the heart of Germany. In Berlin, Hitler and the German High Command waited for the end. American and British troops were moving steadily eastward toward Berlin, while Soviet forces were dangerously close to Berlin's eastern suburbs. Unwilling to be captured, Hitler committed suicide on April 30 and had aides burn his body. Berlin fell to the Soviets two days later. On May 8, 1945, German officials surrendered. The war in Europe was over.

Although Roosevelt had worked since 1939 to ensure Hitler's defeat, he did not live to see it. On April 12, 1945, he died of a massive cerebral hemorrhage at Warm Springs, Georgia. Nor did Roosevelt live to know the full horror of what came to be called the **Holocaust.** No horror could match what advancing Allied armies found as they fought their way toward Berlin. In 1941, the Nazi political leadership had adopted the **Final Solution** to rid Europe of Jews. In concentration camps,

Battle of the Bulge Battle in December 1944 that was the last major Axis counteroffensive against the Allied invasion of Europe; German troops gained territory in France but were eventually driven back.

Holocaust Genocide of European Jews systematically carried out by the Nazis during World War II.

Final Solution German plan to destroy the Jews by isolating them in concentration camps and committing mass executions; by the end of the war, the Nazis had killed 6 million Jews.

Jews, along with homosexuals, Gypsies, and the mentally ill, were brutalized, starved, worked as slave labor, and systematically exterminated. At Auschwitz, the Nazis used gas chambers to execute twelve thousand victims a day. When the camps and their remaining inmates were liberated in 1945, 6 million Jews had been slaughtered, nearly two-thirds of prewar Europe's Jewish population.

Closing the Circle on Japan

Victory in Europe—**V-E Day**—touched off parades and rejoicing in the United States, but Japan still had to be defeated. Japan's strategy was to force the United States to invade a seemingly endless number of Pacific islands before it could attack Japan. The Japanese hoped that pressure would build in the United States for a negotiated settlement. The strategy was based on wrong assumptions. After Pearl Harbor, few Americans would accept anything less than the total defeat of Japan. Equally important, the American military realized that it had to seize only the most strategic islands. With carriers providing air superiority, the Americans could bypass and isolate many Japanese-held islands.

Throughout 1943, General MacArthur advanced up the northern coast of New Guinea, while the navy and marines fought their way through the Solomon Islands. By mid-1944, MacArthur was ready to fulfill his promise to return to the Philippines. At the same time, far to the northeast, the U.S. Navy and the Marine Corps were establishing a foothold in the Gilbert Islands (see Map 26.3).

Next, Admiral Nimitz prepared to take Guam and Saipan in the Mariana Islands. The Japanese rushed a fleet with nine carriers to halt the American invasion of Saipan. Warned of their approach, Admiral Marc Mitscher turned his fifteen carriers to intercept. When the "Great Marianas' Turkey Shoot" ended on June 20, 243 of 373 Japanese planes had been shot down and 3 Japanese carriers had been sunk. All of Saipan's Japanese defenders, including 22,000 Japanese civilians, committed suicide rather than surrender.

By July 1944, the southern and eastern approaches to the Philippines were in American hands. From airfields on Tinian, Saipan, and Guam, long-range B-29 bombers began devastating raids against Japan. In October, American forces landed on Leyte in the center of the Philippine archipelago. Again, the Japanese navy acted to halt the invasion. In the largest naval battle in history, the **Battle of Leyte Gulf** (October 23–25, 1944), American naval forces shattered what remained of Japanese air and sea power. On October 23, General MacArthur returned to the Philippines.

After the Battle of Leyte Gulf, the full brunt of the American Pacific offensive bore down on Okinawa and Iwo Jima in the Ryukyu Islands, only 750 miles from Tokyo. To defend the islands, Japan resorted to kamikaze, or suicide, attacks in explosive-laden airplanes. The American assault on Iwo Jima began on February 19, 1945. Iwo Jima was the worst experience faced by U.S. Marines in the war. Virtually all of the 21,000 Japanese defenders died, and American losses approached one-third of the landing force: 6,821 dead and 20,000 wounded. The battle for Okinawa, begun on April 1, proved even costlier. By the end of June, Okinawa was in American hands, but at a fearful price: 12,000 Americans, 110,000 Japanese soldiers, and 160,000 Okinawan and Japanese civilians dead.

Entering the Nuclear Age

Okinawa proved a painful warning for those planning the invasion of Japan. Fighting for their homeland, the Japanese could be expected to resist until death. American casualties would be extremely high, perhaps as many as a million. But by the summer of 1945, the United States had a new and untried weapon: the atomic bomb. The

V-E Day Official end of the war in Europe on May 8, 1945, following the unconditional surrender of the German armies.

Battle of Leyte Gulf Largest naval battle in history, which occurred in the Philippines in October 1944 as American naval forces crushed Japanese air and sea power.

A-bomb was the product of the **Manhattan Project,** which British and American scientists had been working on since 1942. When the bomb was tested at Alamogordo, New Mexico, on July 16, 1945, the results were spectacular.

President Harry S Truman decided to use the bomb as quickly as possible against Japan. Using the atomic bomb, Truman hoped, would force Japan to surrender without an invasion and perhaps make the Soviets more amenable to American views. Soon after his arrival at Potsdam to meet with Churchill and Stalin in July, Truman informed Stalin that the United States had a new and powerful weapon to use against Japan. The **Potsdam Declaration,** called on Japan to surrender by August or face total destruction.

On July 25, Truman ordered the use of the atomic bombs as soon after August 3 as possible if the Japanese did not surrender. Moral reasons for not using the bomb were not seriously considered. Massive American bombing raids against Japanese cities already had killed tens of thousands of Japanese civilians. The losses at Iwo Jima and Okinawa, along with growing distrust of Stalin, had only strengthened Truman's desire to end the war as quickly as possible.

The first bomb, "Little Boy," was dropped from a B-29 bomber named the *Enola Gay* over **Hiroshima** at 9:15 A.M. on August 6. The atomic blast killed or terribly maimed almost a hundred thousand Japanese. Another hundred thousand would eventually die from radiation. The United States announced that unless the Japanese surrendered immediately, they could "expect a rain of ruin from the air, the like of which has never been seen on this earth."

In Tokyo, peace advocates in the Japanese government sought to use the Soviets as an intermediary. But the Soviet response was to declare war on August 8, exactly as promised, three months after V-E day. On August 9, a second atomic bomb, "Fat Man," destroyed **Nagasaki** and killed nearly sixty thousand people. Emperor Hirohito decided that Japan must "bear the unbearable" and surrender. On August 14, Japan officially surrendered.

World War II was over, but much of the world now lay in ruins. Some 50 million people, military and civilian, had been killed (see Table 26.1). The United States was spared most of the destruction. It had suffered almost no civilian casualties, and its cities and industrial centers stood intact. In many ways, the war had been good to the United

♦ On August 6, 1945, the world entered the atomic age when the city of Hiroshima was destroyed by an atomic bomb. "We had seen the city when we went in," said the pilot of the *Enola Gay,* "and there was nothing to see when we came back." The city and most of its people died. *National Archives.*

A-bomb The first nuclear weapon, which used a chain reaction involving uranium and plutonium to create an explosion of enormous destructive force.

Manhattan Project Scientific research effort to develop an atomic bomb begun in 1942 and carried on in a secret community of scientists and workers near Oak Ridge, Tennessee.

Potsdam Declaration The demand for Japan's unconditional surrender, made after the July 1945 Potsdam Conference attended by Truman, Churchill, Clement Attlee (who replaced Churchill as British Prime Minister just before the meeting) and Stalin.

Hiroshima Japanese city that became the target on August 6, 1945, of the first atomic bomb used in World War II.

Nagasaki City in western Japan devastated on August 9, 1945, by the second atomic bomb used in World War II.

TABLE 26.1 War Dead

Country	Dead
Soviet Union	13.5 million
China	7.4 million
Poland	6.0 million
Germany	4.6 million
Japan	1.2 million
Britain and Commonwealth	430,000
United States	405,000

States. It had decisively ended the Depression. Government regulation and planning took root during the war. And as the war ended, only a few wanted a return to the laissez-faire style government that had characterized the 1920s. Big government was here to stay, and at the center of big government was a powerful presidency ready to direct and guide the nation.

SUMMARY

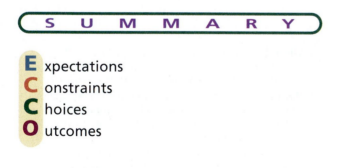

E xpectations
C onstraints
C hoices
O utcomes

At the start of his presidency, Franklin Roosevelt *chose* to promote better relations with Latin America and succeeded. But elsewhere, the international situation grew steadily worse. Japan seized Manchuria in 1931 and invaded China in 1937, while Mussolini and Hitler were seeking to expand their nations' power and territory. In the lengthening shadow of world conflict, the majority of Americans still *chose* isolationism. Wanting to take a more active role in world affairs, Roosevelt found himself *constrained* by isolationist sentiment and by his own *choice* to fight the Depression at home first. Even as Germany invaded Poland in September 1939, the majority of Americans were still anxious to remain outside the conflict. Roosevelt, however, was determined to provide all necessary aid to those nations fighting Germany and Italy.

Roosevelt also *chose* to increase economic and diplomatic pressure on Japan to halt its conquest of China and its occupation of Indochina. But the pressure only convinced the Japanese government that the best *choice* was to attack the United States before it grew in strength. Japan's attack on Pearl Harbor on December 7, 1941, brought a fully committed American public and government into World War II.

Mobilizing the nation for war ended the Depression and increased government intervention in the economy. Another *outcome* of the war was a range of new *choices* for women and minorities in the military and the workplace. For Japanese Americans, however, the *outcome* was internment and the loss of property.

American planners *chose* to give first priority to defeating Hitler. The British and American offensive to recover Europe began in North Africa and expanded to Italy in 1943 and to France in 1944. By the beginning of 1945, Allied armies were threatening Nazi Germany from the west and the east, and on May 8, 1945, Germany surrendered. In the Pacific, the victory at Midway in 1942 gave American forces naval and air superiority over Japan and allowed them to begin tightening the noose around Japan. Worried about casualties if America had to invade Japan, Truman *chose* to use the atomic bomb. The *outcome* of the war was that the United States became economically and militarily stronger than when the war started. Confident Americans *expected* the postwar years to begin "America's Century."

SUGGESTED READINGS

Blum, John Morton. *V Was for Victory* (1976).

A good introduction to society and politics during the war.

Dallek, Robert. *Franklin D. Roosevelt and American Foreign Policy, 1932–1945* (1979).

An excellent, balanced study of Roosevelt's foreign policy.

Daniels, Roger. *Concentration Camps, USA* (1971).

An in-depth and compassionate look at the internment of Japanese Americans.

Gluck, Sherna B. *Rosie the Riveter Revisited: Women, the War, and Social Change* (1987).

An important work examining the changes that took place among women in society during the war.

Jonas, Manfred. *Isolationism in America* (1966).

A solid examination of the varieties of isolationist attitudes in the United States, especially in the 1930s.

Keegan, John. *The Second World War* (1990).

An excellent work that summarizes the military and diplomatic aspects of World War II.

Spector, Ronald. *Eagle Against the Sun* (1988).

One of the best-written general accounts of the war in the Pacific.

Wyman, David. *The Abandonment of the Jews* (1985).

A balanced account of the Holocaust.

The Decision to Drop the Atomic Bomb

The Context

On August 6, 1945, at 8:15 A.M., the *Enola Gay* dropped the first atomic bomb on the Japanese city of Hiroshima. More than 100,000 people died and another 100,000 were injured. Three days later, the United States exploded a second atomic bomb over Nagasaki, killing about 60,000 Japanese. On August 14, Japan surrendered. Within the United States, there was widespread rejoicing—the bomb had ended the war. Many also realized that the development of the atomic bomb and the decision to use it heralded a new age: the atomic era. The bomb was not just a powerful weapon but also a revolutionary development with far-ranging military, ethical, international, and scientific consequences. (For further information on the context, see pages 588–590.)

The Historical Question

Since the detonation of the atomic bomb, historians and others have asked if the choice to destroy the cities was necessary. Did military expediency necessitate dropping the bomb? What other expectations did those involved in building and deciding to use "the gadget" have? Did they consider moral and other aspects of their decision?

The Challenge

Using the sources provided, along with other information you have read, write an essay or hold a discussion on the following question. Cite evidence in the sources to support your conclusions. **What did those involved in planning the use of the atomic bomb consider, and what goals lay behind the final decision?**

The Sources

1 Secretary of War Henry L. Stimson was directly involved in planning the use of the atomic bomb. In an article for *Harper's* in 1947, he explained the military-based decision to use the new weapon. He wrote:

To extract a genuine surrender from the Emperor and his military advisers, they must be administered a tremendous shock which would carry convincing proof of our power to destroy the Empire. Such an effective shock would save many times the number of lives, both American and Japanese, than it would cost. . . . We estimated . . . that such an operation might cost over a million casualties to American forces . . . Enemy casualties would be much larger than our own.

2 A committee of scientists involved in building the atomic bomb met throughout May, June, and July to consider the use of the bomb. In June 1945, the Franck Committee reported:

The military advantages and the saving of American lives, achieved by the sudden use of the atomic bombs against Japan, may be outweighed by the ensuing loss of confidence and wave of horror and repulsion sweeping over the rest of the world, and perhaps dividing even public opinion at home.

. . . If we consider international agreement on total prevention of nuclear warfare as the paramount objective . . . this kind of introduction of atomic weapons to the world may easily destroy all

our chances of success. Russia, and even allied countries which bear less mistrust of our ways and intentions, as well as neutral countries, will be deeply shocked. It will be very difficult to persuade the world that a nation which was capable of secretly preparing and suddenly releasing [such] a weapon . . . is to be trusted in its proclaimed desire of having such weapons abolished by international agreement.

3 Most of the planning to use the atomic bomb was delegated to a special Interim Committee approved by President Harry Truman shortly after he assumed office. It was chaired by Secretary of War Stimson and was composed of three scientists, representatives of the State of War departments, and a special representative of the president. Except for Stimson, none of the committee members knew about the military plans for the invasion of Japan. Another group within the committee also considered which cities made suitable targets for atomic weapons. In May 1945, the committee reported:

We should not give the Japanese any warning. . . . We should seek to make a profound psychological impression on as many of the inhabitants as possible . . . The most desirable target would be a vital war plant employing a large number of workers and closely surrounded by workers' houses.

Hiroshima—This is an important army depot and port . . . in the middle of an urban industrial area. It is a good . . . target and it is such a size that a large part of the city could be extensively damaged . . . Adjacent hills . . . are likely to produce a focusing effect which would considerably increase the blast damage.

4 President Truman told Secretary of War Stimson to move ahead with the plans to drop the atomic bomb. On July 26, 1945, the United States demanded Japan's unconditional surrender and warned that Japan would face total destruction if surrender did not come. Recounting his thoughts on using the bomb, Truman wrote in his diary on July 18, 1945:

This weapon is to be used against Japan between now and August 10th. I have told the Sec. of War, Mr. Stimson, to use it so that military objectives and soldiers and sailors are the target and not women and children. Even if the Japs are savages, ruthless, merciless and fanatic, we as the leader of the world for the common welfare cannot drop that terrible bomb on the old capital or the new.

. . . We will issue a warning statement asking the Japs to surrender and save lives. I'm sure they will not do that, but we will have given them the chance. It is certainly a good thing for the world that Hitler's crowd or Stalin's did not discover this atomic bomb. It seems to be the most terrible thing ever discovered, but it can be made the most useful.

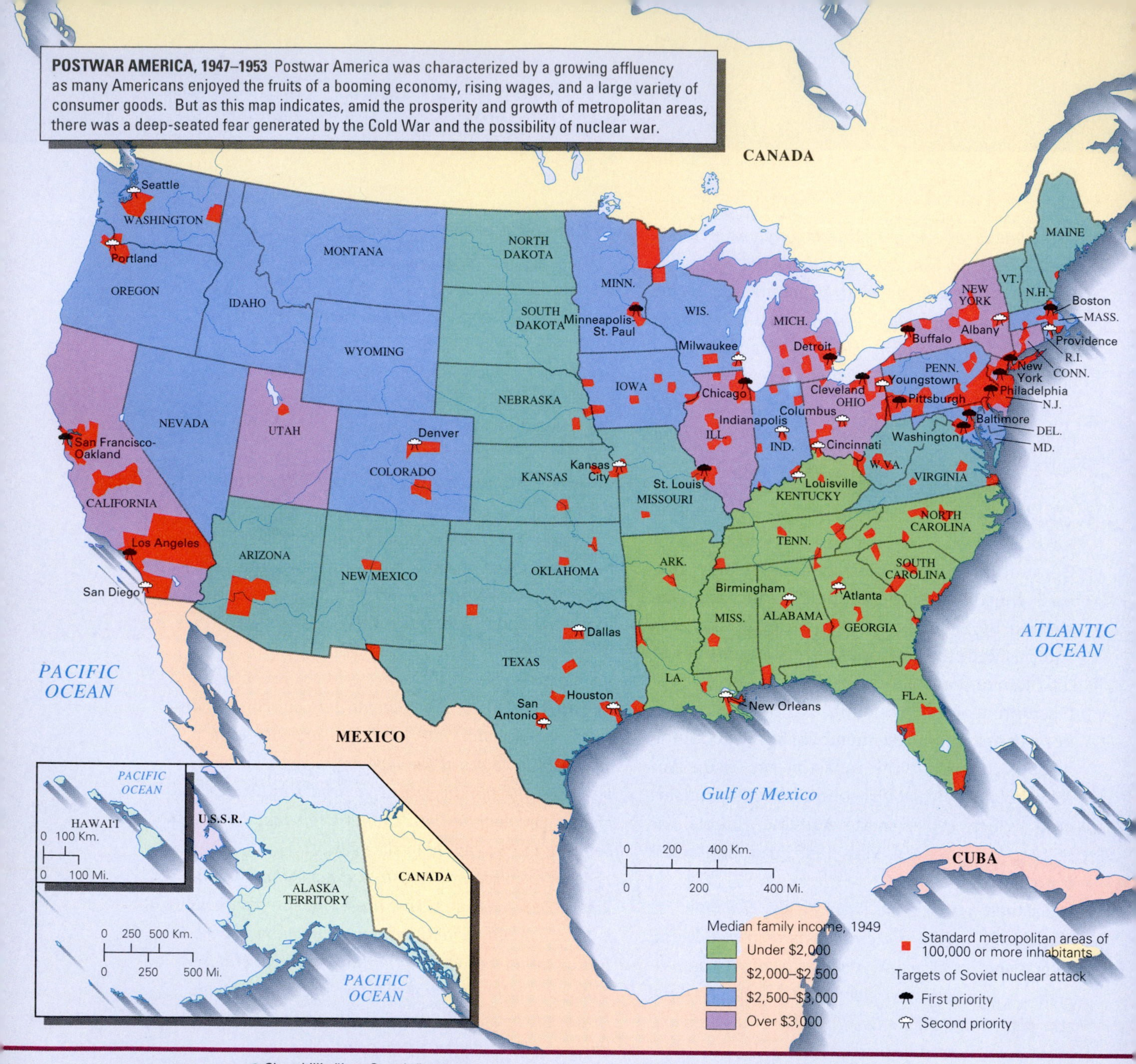
CANADA
MEXICO
PACIFIC OCEAN
ATLANTIC OCEAN
Gulf of Mexico
CUBA
WASHINGTON
OREGON
CALIFORNIA
NEVADA
IDAHO
MONTANA
WYOMING
UTAH
ARIZONA
NEW MEXICO
COLORADO
NORTH DAKOTA
SOUTH DAKOTA
NEBRASKA
KANSAS
OKLAHOMA
TEXAS
MINN.
IOWA
MISSOURI
ARK.
LA.
WIS.
ILL.
MICH.
IND.
OHIO
KENTUCKY
TENN.
MISS.
ALABAMA
GEORGIA
FLA.
SOUTH CAROLINA
NORTH CAROLINA
VIRGINIA
W.VA.
PENN.
NEW YORK
VT.
N.H.
MAINE
MASS.
R.I.
CONN.
N.J.
DEL.
MD.
Seattle
Portland
San Francisco-Oakland
Los Angeles
San Diego
Denver
Minneapolis-St. Paul
Kansas City
St. Louis
Dallas
Houston
San Antonio
Milwaukee
Chicago
Indianapolis
Detroit
Cleveland
Columbus
Cincinnati
Louisville
Youngstown
Pittsburgh
Buffalo
Albany
Boston
Providence
New York
Philadelphia
Baltimore
Washington
Birmingham
Atlanta
New Orleans
HAWAI'I
PACIFIC OCEAN
0 100 Km.
0 100 Mi.
U.S.S.R.
ALASKA TERRITORY
CANADA
0 250 500 Km.
0 250 500 Mi.
PACIFIC OCEAN
0 200 400 Km.
0 200 400 Mi.
Median family income, 1949
Under $2,000
$2,000–$2,500
$2,500–$3,000
Over $3,000
Standard metropolitan areas of 100,000 or more inhabitants
Targets of Soviet nuclear attack
First priority
Second priority

POSTWAR AMERICA, 1947–1953 Postwar America was characterized by a growing affluence as many Americans enjoyed the fruits of a booming economy, rising wages, and a large variety of consumer goods. But as this map indicates, amid the prosperity and growth of metropolitan areas, there was a deep-seated fear generated by the Cold War and the possibility of nuclear war.

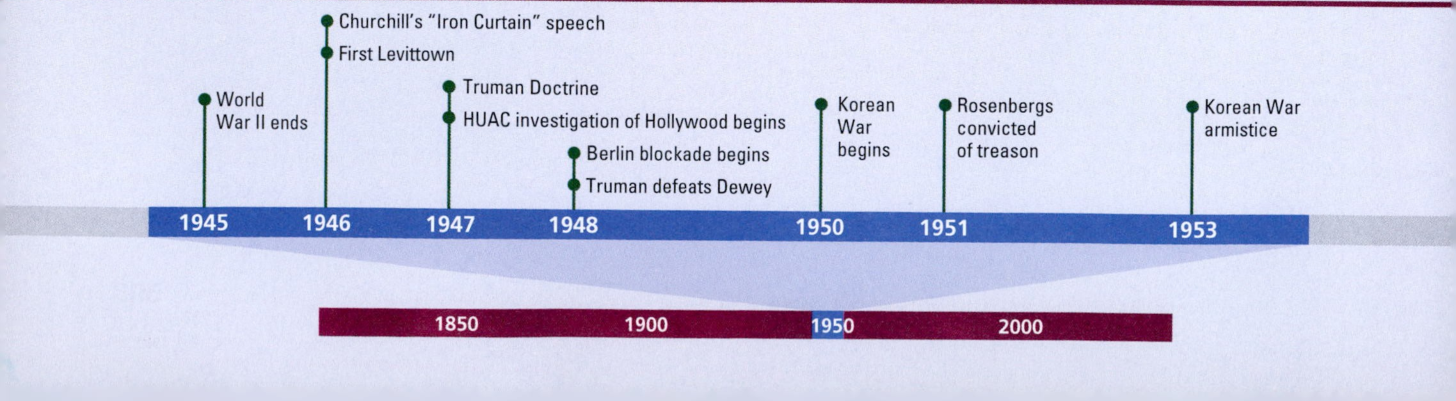
World War II ends
Churchill's "Iron Curtain" speech
First Levittown
Truman Doctrine
HUAC investigation of Hollywood begins
Berlin blockade begins
Truman defeats Dewey
Korean War begins
Rosenbergs convicted of treason
Korean War armistice
1945
1946
1947
1948
1950
1951
1953
1850
1900
1950
2000

CHAPTER 27

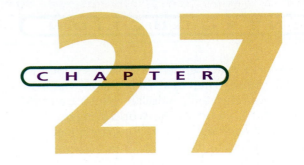

Truman and Cold War America, 1945–1952

The Cold War Begins

- What expectations did Americans have about the postwar world and the Soviet Union?
- How was the containment theory applied to Western Europe between 1947 and 1951?
- Outside Western Europe, what choices did the Truman administration make to promote and protect American interests?

The Korean War

- As the North Koreans invaded South Korea, what choices and constraints did Truman confront when considering policy options?
- What expectations did Truman and General MacArthur have about defeating the North Koreans and unifying Korea? What was the outcome for both leaders?

Homecomings and Adjustments

- What were the social and economic expectations of most Americans as World War II ended? What were the outcomes of these expectations for women and minorities?
- What constraints did proposals to expand New Deal programs encounter as the Cold War developed?
- What constraints did Truman face in implementing his domestic programs? How did they influence his choices?
- Why did Truman win the 1948 election? What choices did members of the New Deal coalition have in 1948, and why did most Democrats vote for Truman?

Cold War Politics

- What fears and events heightened society's fear of internal subversion, and what choices did politicians make in response to them?
- Why and how did Joseph McCarthy become so powerful by 1952?

INTRODUCTION

Expectations
Constraints
Choices
Outcomes

When World War II ended, Americans hoped for a bright future. The Great Depression was over, the war had reignited American industry, and the United States stood as the world's biggest economic and military power. Returning veterans looked forward to living the "American dream," which included owning a home, a car, and a variety of consumer products. More than ever before, women and minorities shared in *expectations* for greater opportunity.

Although everyone hoped for postwar prosperity, political conservatives anticipated the demise of the New Deal. They argued that the New Deal was no longer necessary and that society and the economy should revert to traditional norms. They sought to place *constraints* on the economic and social gains made by minorities, women, and workers. Unions, they asserted, had become too powerful and must be restrained. Women, conservatives argued, should give up their jobs and return full-time to the roles of wife and mother. African Americans and other minorities should return to their customary place in American society.

Which direction would the nation *choose:* the path of the liberal New Deal or a more conservative one? The *outcome* pleased neither ardent liberals nor staunch conservatives. It reflected an acceptance and even some expansion of existing governmental activism but few new programs.

Truman also faced *choices* in shaping a new international order. Isolationism had virtually vanished amid the wreckage of Pearl Harbor and Hiroshima. Truman tried between 1945 and 1952 to seek a lasting peace, but the *outcome* was not what he *expected.* By the end of 1947, American and Soviet leaders had made *choices* that produced a bitter rivalry. The *outcome,* the Cold War, polarized the world, expanded America's global role, and added a new force in American society: the fear of the Soviet Union and communism. When North Korea invaded South Korea, Truman *chose* to commit American troops to halt Communist aggression. At home, the activities of anti-Communists like Senator Joseph McCarthy exposed a dark side of American politics and society.

Despite increased prosperity, American society began to seem less stable and unified, clouding *expectations* for a bright future. Labor unions clashed with employers, many women and minorities found their *expectations* thwarted, and the Korean War dragged on in a stalemate. The *outcome,* by the end of Truman's second term, was widespread political dissatisfaction and a general desire for change.

The Cold War Begins

Germany, Italy, and Japan had been defeated, and the world hoped that an enduring peace would follow. But could the cooperative relationship of the victorious Allies continue into the postwar era without a common enemy to bind them together?

Before 1941, suspicion and distrust had marked the normal relationship between the United States and the Soviet Union. In 1917, when the Soviets seized power, the Wilson administration refused to recognize the new Soviet state and intervened in the civil war between Soviet and anti-Communist forces. The last American troops left in 1920, but Washington refused to recognize the Soviet Union until 1933. Even after President Franklin D. Roosevelt established official ties with Moscow, relations remained frosty. When the Soviets signed their alliance with Nazi Germany in 1939 and claimed parts of Poland for themselves, most Americans saw little real differ-

CHRONOLOGY

From World War to Cold War

1945 Roosevelt dies; Truman becomes president
United Nations formed
Germany surrenders
Potsdam Conference
United States drops atomic bombs
Japan surrenders

1946 George Kennan's "Long Telegram"
Winston Churchill's "Iron Curtain" speech
Iran crisis
Railroad and coal miners' strikes
Construction begins on first Levittown

1947 Truman Doctrine
Truman's Federal Employee Loyalty Program
Taft-Hartley Act
House Un-American Activities Committee begins investigation of Hollywood
Jackie Robinson joins Brooklyn Dodgers
Marshall Plan announced
To Secure These Rights issued

1948 Communist coup in Czechoslovakia
State of Israel founded
Western zones of Germany unified
Berlin blockade begins
Congress approves Marshall Plan
Truman defeats Dewey

1949 North Atlantic Treaty Organization created
Berlin blockade lifted
Peekskill riot
West Germany created
Soviet Union explodes atomic bomb
Communist forces win civil war in China
Alger Hiss convicted of perjury

1950 Hydrogen bomb project announced
Joseph McCarthy's announcement of Communists in the State Department
NSC-68
Korean War begins
Rosenbergs arrested for treason
Inchon landing
North Korean forces retreat from South Korea
U.S. forces cross into North Korea; China enters Korean War

1951 General Douglas MacArthur relieved of command
Korean War armistice talks begin
Rosenbergs convicted of treason

1952 Hydrogen bomb tested

1953 Korean War armistice signed

ence between the brutal totalitarianism of nazism and communism.

American policy toward the Soviets altered in 1941, when Hitler invaded the Soviet Union. Relations with the Soviets improved quickly, as the United States supported the Communists in their war against the Germans. Ideological and other differences were de-emphasized. But even during the war, the two powers viewed each other suspiciously over issues such as the timing of the second European front and the creation of pro-Soviet governments in Eastern Europe.

When Roosevelt died on April 12, 1945, Harry S Truman was left to face the imposing job of finishing the war and creating the peace. Winning the war was mostly a matter of following existing policies, but formulating a new international order required new ideas and policies. In facing this formidable task, the new president counted on his common sense and what he believed would be best for the country. Truman was determined to be a decisive, hard-working president. He had read history; now he would shape it. A plaque on his desk proclaimed, "THE BUCK STOPS HERE."

♦ In July 1945, Truman met with Stalin and Churchill for the first time at Potsdam on the outskirts of Berlin. He was surprised that the Soviet leader was shorter than he and thought that Churchill talked too much, giving him "a lot of hooey." Later Truman wrote, "You never saw such pig-headed people as are the Russians." Here Stalin and Truman *(left)* and advisers Byrnes and Molotov *(right)* pose for photographers. *Truman Library.*

Truman and the Soviets

Truman and other American leaders identified two overlapping paths to peace: international cooperation and **deterrence** based on military strength. They concluded that the United States must continue to field a strong military force with bases in Europe, Asia, and the Middle East. But deterrence alone could not guarantee peace and a stable world. That required the presence of a strong world organization to preserve collective security, a determination not to appease aggressors, and a prosperous world economy.

Not all nations accepted the American vision for peace and stability. Having been invaded twice in the twentieth century, the Soviets advanced different goals. They wanted to have Germany reduced in power and to see "friendly" governments in Eastern Europe. The Soviets were unwilling to allow an open political and economic system to function in neighboring countries. They put little faith in Roosevelt's call for the creation of the United Nations, although they agreed to go along with Roosevelt's idea.

The basic organization of the United Nations was mapped out at the **Dumbarton Oaks** conference in the fall of 1944. The United Nations charter, written at a meeting in San Francisco in April 1945, established a weak **General Assembly** composed of all the world's nations. The smaller **Security Council,** composed of the Big Five (now including France) and six other nations elected for two-year terms, possessed the power to make all real decisions, including taking action against aggressor nations. Each of the Big Five could veto Security Council decisions to ensure that the council could not interfere with their national interests. New York City became the permanent UN headquarters.

When Truman became president, he developed a rapid distrust of the Soviets. He regarded Soviet ac-

deterrence Measures taken by a state, often including a military build-up, to discourage another state from attacking it.

Dumbarton Oaks Conference in Washington, D.C., at which representatives of China, Britain, the USSR, and the United States drew up a blueprint for the charter of the United Nations.

General Assembly Assembly of all members of the United Nations, which debates issues but neither creates nor executes policy.

Security Council Executive agency of the United Nations, which includes five permanent members (China, France, Russia, Britain, and the United States) and six members chosen by the General Assembly for two-year terms.

tions in Poland and Romania as violations of proper behavior, the principles of the Atlantic Charter, and the Yalta agreements. Truman quickly confronted Soviet foreign minister V. M. Molotov over the Soviets' failure to fulfill promises made at Yalta to allow self-determination in Eastern Europe. Truman was less willing to consider Soviet "needs" than Roosevelt had been. In July 1945, Truman had his only face-to-face meeting with Stalin at the Potsdam Conference. The meeting accomplished little. Truman became more convinced than ever before that the Soviets were a major obstacle to world stability.

By early 1946, Truman believed that it was past time for the Soviets to prove their peaceful intentions. In Eastern Europe, every indication suggested that the Soviets were tightening their controls over Poland, Romania, and Hungary. On February 9, 1946, Stalin asserted that future wars were inevitable because of "present capitalist conditions," which most American observers saw as proof of Soviet hostility. Supreme Court Justice William O. Douglas called Stalin's speech "A Declaration of World War III." The Joint Chiefs of Staff agreed and recommended a foreign policy that would support nations threatened by Soviet hostility. The State Department was less alarmed, but it too concluded that the Soviets were following an "ominous course."

George F. Kennan, the **chargé d'affaires** in Moscow, plotted the American response to threatened Soviet expansionism. Asked by the State Department to evaluate Soviet policy, Kennan described Soviet totalitarianism as internally weak. Soviet leaders, he wrote in a report that became known as the "Long Telegram," held Communist ideology secondary to remaining in power. To rule, Soviet leaders relied on fear, repression, and resistance to a foreign enemy. To stay in control, Soviet leaders needed Western capitalism to serve as that enemy, Kennan wrote. Therefore, they could not afford to reach meaningful, long-lasting agreements with the West. He recommended a policy of **containment.** That meant meeting any attempted expansion of Soviet power head-on. Based on Kennan's advice, Truman adopted a policy designed to "set will against will, force against force, idea against idea . . . until Soviet expansion is finally worn down."

Fear of Soviet expansion quickly became a bipartisan issue. Both parties sought to convince the public that the United States must resist Soviet **globalism.** The most sensational warning about the Soviet danger came from Winston Churchill on March 5, 1946, at Westminster College in Fulton, Missouri. With President Truman sitting beside him, the former British prime minister warned that an **"iron curtain"** had fallen across Europe. He called for a "fraternal association of the English-speaking peoples" to halt the Russians. Churchill, *Time* magazine pronounced, had spoken with the voice of a "lion."

As Churchill gave his address, it appeared that an "American lion" was needed in Iran. During World War II, the Big Three had stationed troops in Iran to ensure the safety of lend-lease materials going by that route to the Soviet Union. The troops were to be withdrawn by March 1946, but as that date neared, Soviet troops remained in northern Iran. Britain and the United States sent harshly worded telegrams to the Soviets and petitioned the United Nations to consider an Iranian complaint against the Soviet Union. Soviet forces soon evacuated Iran. The crisis was defused, but it convinced many Americans that the Soviets would retreat only when confronted with firmness.

Throughout the rest of 1946, the United States hardened its resolve in Europe. Postwar credits and loans were determined on the basis of ideology. Thus Britain received a \$3.8 billion loan and France a \$650 million loan, but the Soviet Union and Czechoslovakia received nothing. In Germany, the United States merged its occupation zone with those of the British and French and promised that American troops would remain as long as necessary to protect the German people.

chargé d'affaires A high-ranking member of an embassy, frequently the highest-ranking career diplomat of the mission.

containment Policy of checking the expansion or influence of a hostile power by means such as strategic alliances or the support of weaker states in areas of conflict.

globalism National geopolitical policy in which the entire world is regarded as the appropriate sphere for a state's influence.

"iron curtain" Name given to the military, political, and ideological barrier established between the Soviet bloc and Western Europe after World War II.

The Division of Europe

Throughout western and southern Europe, postwar economic and social turmoil was adding to the popularity of **leftist** and Communist groups. In the eastern Mediterranean, the Soviets were pressuring Turkey to permit some degree of Soviet control over the Dardanelles, the straits linking the Black Sea to the Mediterranean. Nearby, Greece was torn by a civil war between Communist-backed rebels and the British-supported conservative government (see Map 27.1). Communist influence seemed to be growing everywhere.

Truman responded by asserting in a speech to Congress that it was the duty of the United States "to support free people" who resisted subjugation "by armed minorities or by outside pressure." Truman asked Congress for $400 million in aid for Greece and Turkey.

Secretary of State **George Marshall** and Assistant Secretary of State **Dean Acheson** backed Truman's request for aid by warning select Democratic and Republican senators that Greece was on the brink of collapse. A Communist victory there would endanger neighboring states and eventually the entire eastern Mediterranean and Middle East. The Soviets were on the move, Acheson told the senators, and would triumph unless the United States stepped forward and stopped them. Impressed, Senator Arthur Vandenberg said that Truman needed to "scare the hell" out of the country. The president took the advice. In his **Truman Doctrine** speech of March 12, 1947, he blamed almost every threat to peace and stability on an unnamed villain, the Soviet Union. With American support, Turkey resisted Soviet pressure and retained control of the straits, and the Greek government was able to defeat the Communist rebels in 1949.

On June 5, 1947, in a commencement address at Harvard, Secretary of State Marshall uncovered a new weapon in the fight against communism: the **Marshall Plan.** The United States had already loaned nearly $9 billion to Western European nations, but more was needed to ward off a possible European economic collapse. Wartime destruction, drought, and an extremely bitter winter had, by 1947, brought Europe close to social and economic chaos. Millions of people could not heat their homes and were existing on a starvation diet. Communist and Socialist parties were gaining in popularity and strength. Italian Communists represented a third of the electorate, whereas in France nearly a quarter voted Communist. European prosperity had to be restored to preserve democracy and freedom.

For the Truman administration, the question was not whether to aid Western Europe but whether to aid the Soviets and Eastern Europeans as well. To allow the Soviets and their satellites to participate seemed contrary to the Truman Doctrine. If the plan excluded the Soviets, however, the United States might seem to be encouraging the division of Europe. Chaired by George Kennan, the State Department planning staff recommended that the United States offer economic aid to all Europeans. Kennan believed that the Soviets' unwillingness to cooperate with capitalists would keep them from taking part.

Britain and France accepted the American offer within two weeks and called for a meeting in Paris of all interested parties on June 26, 1947. To nearly everyone's surprise, a Soviet delegation arrived. It appeared for a moment that Kennan's gamble had failed. But Soviet foreign minister Molotov rejected a British and French proposal for an economically integrated Europe, joint economic planning, and a requirement to purchase mostly American goods. The Soviets left the conference. Attracted by the

leftist Holding various liberal or radical political beliefs, often resting on a sympathy with the working class and a conviction that government should provide for the basic needs of the people.

George Marshall Chief of staff of the U.S. Army during World War II, who became Truman's secretary of state in 1947 and worked to rebuild the economy of Western Europe.

Dean Acheson Diplomat who took over as secretary of state in 1949; he helped formulate U.S. policy in Korea and advocated a firm stand against Soviet aggression in the Berlin crisis.

Truman Doctrine Anti-Communist foreign policy enunciated by Truman in 1947, which called for military and economic aid to countries whose political stability was threatened by communism.

Marshall Plan Program to foster economic recovery in Western Europe in the postwar period through massive amounts of U.S. financial aid, which began in 1948.

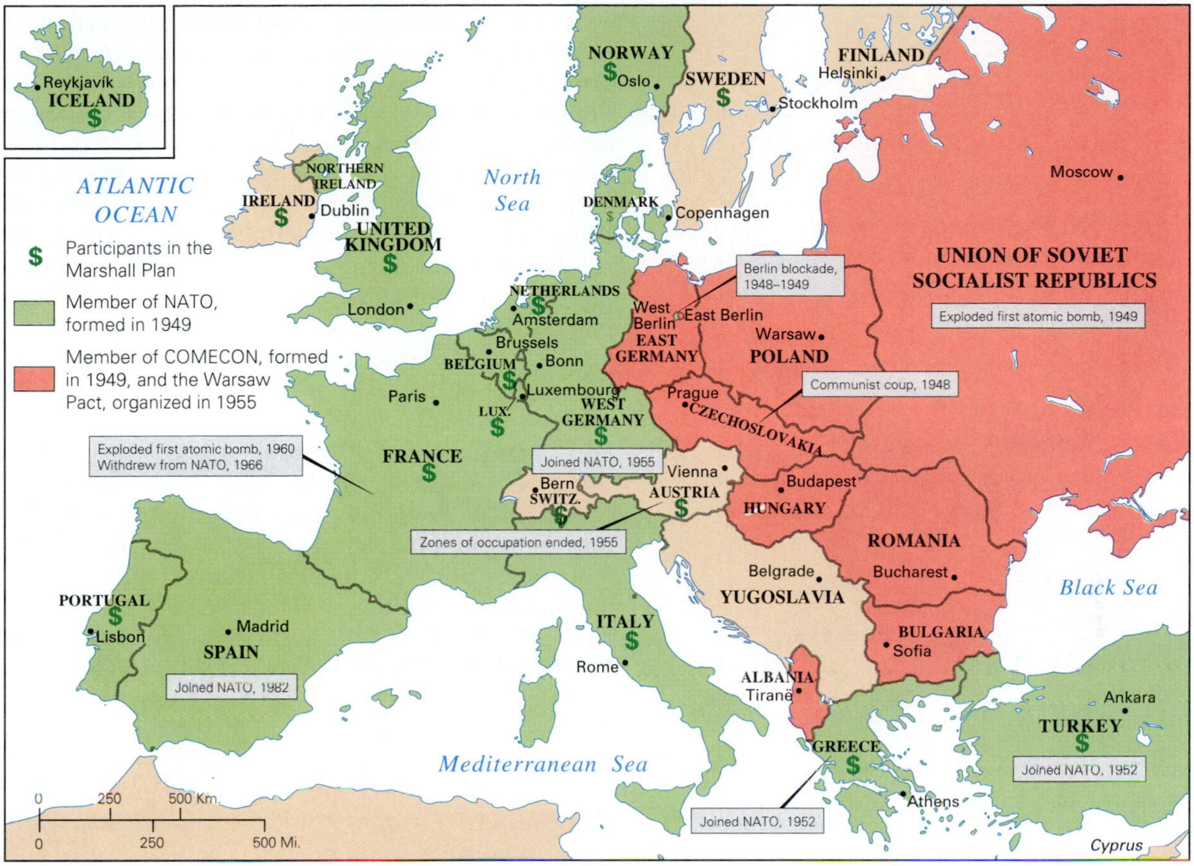

♦ **MAP 27.1 Cold War Europe** Following World War II, Europe was separated by what Winston Churchill called the "iron curtain," which divided most of the continent politically, economically, and militarily into an eastern bloc (the Warsaw Pact) led by the Soviet Union and a western bloc (NATO) supported by the United States. This postwar division of Europe lasted until the collapse of the Soviet Union in the early 1990s.

prospect of American aid, sixteen other nations stayed in Paris and drafted a European recovery program. Completed on September 22, the plan called for four years of American assistance amounting to over $20 billion. Congress consented in 1948 to give $12.5 billion.

The Marshall Plan produced far-reaching consequences east and west of the iron curtain. One condition of the aid was that Western European countries had to purge Communist elements from their governments. The Soviet sphere responded with a hardening of Communist influence and control over Eastern Europe. In September 1947, the Soviet Union formed the Communist Information Bureau (Cominform) to ensure Soviet direction of Europe's Communist parties. And in February 1948, the Soviets engineered a **coup** in Czechoslovakia and installed a Communist government. The death of political freedom in Czechoslovakia proved to many Americans the hostile intent of the Soviets. "We are faced with exactly the same situation with which Britain and France were faced in 1938 and

coup Sudden overthrow of a government by a small group of people in or previously in positions of authority.

THE MAINTENANCE OF INTERNATIONAL STABILITY
SAM, I'LL HAVE TO HAVE HELP OR I'M GOING TO DROP THIS!!
ENGLAND

♦ In many people's views, Truman's decision to support Greece and Turkey and his announcement of the Truman Doctrine (March 1947) represented the transfer of world responsibility from Great Britain to the United States. In Truman's words, "The free peoples of the world look to us for support in maintaining their freedoms."

1939 with Hitler," Truman announced. But Truman was no Neville Chamberlain.

The United States, Britain, and France responded to the "sovietization" of Eastern Europe by unifying their German occupation zones into a West German state. Faced with the prospect of a pro-Western and resurgent Germany, Stalin reacted. On June 24, 1948, the Russians blockaded all land traffic to Berlin and shut off the electricity to the city's western zones. With a population of over 2 million, West Berlin lay isolated 120 miles inside the Soviet zone of Germany. The Soviet goal was to force the West either to abandon the creation of West Germany or to face the loss of Berlin. The Americans were determined not to retreat. Churchill affirmed the American stand. We want peace, he stated, "but we should by now have learned that there is no safety in yielding to dictators, whether Nazi or Communist." The prospect of war loomed.

American strategists confronted the question of how to stand fast without starting a shooting war. Truman chose to use the three air corridors to Berlin from the West that the Soviets had earlier agreed to recognize. British and Americans flew through these corridors to three Berlin airports on an average of one flight every three minutes. To drive home to the Soviets the depth of American resolve, Truman ordered a wing of B-29 bombers, the "atomic bombers," to Berlin. In fact, these planes carried no atomic weapons.

The **Berlin airlift** was a tremendous victory for the United States. The unceasing flow of supplies testified to American resolve to contain Soviet power and to protect Europe. The Soviets ended the blockade of Berlin in May 1949. The crisis ended virtually all congressional opposition to the Marshall Plan and the creation of West Germany.

Truman followed the Berlin action with a call for an American military alliance with Western Europe. By April 1949, negotiations to create the **North Atlantic Treaty Organization (NATO)** were completed (see Map 27.1). Congress approved American entry into NATO in July. Membership in the alliance ensured that American forces would remain in the newly created West Germany and that Western Europe would be eligible for additional American economic and military aid. The Mutual Defense Assistance Act, passed in 1949, provided $1.5 billion in arms and equipment for NATO member nations. By 1952, 80 percent of American assistance to Europe was military aid.

A Global Presence

American foreign policy from 1945 to 1950 focused on rebuilding Western Europe and containing Soviet

Berlin airlift Response to the Soviet blockade of West Berlin in 1948, in which American and British planes made continuous flights to deliver supplies and keep the city open.

North Atlantic Treaty Organization Alliance formed in 1949 that includes most of the nations of Western Europe and North America; its mutual defense agreement was a basic element of the effort to contain communism.

power, but American policy did not ignore the rest of the world. To the south, the Truman administration rejected requests from Latin Americans for a Marshall Plan for the Western Hemisphere. Instead, it encouraged private firms to develop the region through business and trade. The United States did sponsor the creation of the **Organization of American States** to coordinate defense, economic, and social concerns. In the Middle East, fear of future oil shortages led the United States to promote American petroleum interests. In Saudi Arabia, Kuwait, and Iran, the goal was to replace Britain as the major economic and political influence.

Simultaneously, the United States became a powerful supporter of a new Jewish state that was to be created out of **Palestine,** then under British rule. Considering the Nazi terror against the Jews, Truman believed that the Jews should have their own nation. In May 1947, Britain announced that it no longer had the resources to maintain control over Palestine. The United States recognized Israel almost immediately when the United Nations voted to **partition** Palestine into Arab and Jewish states on May 14, 1948. When war broke out between the surrounding Arab states and Israel, Truman and most Americans applauded the victories of Israeli armies.

If Americans were pleased with events in Latin America and the Middle East, Asia provided one bright spot but several disappointments. Under American occupation, Japan's government had been reshaped into a democratic system and placed safely within the American orbit. Success in Japan was offset by reverses in China and Korea. During World War II, the **Nationalist Chinese** government of Jiang Jieshi (Chiang Kai-shek) and the Chinese Communists under Mao Zedong (Mao Tse-tung) had moderated their hostility toward each other to fight the Japanese. Old animosities quickly resurfaced when the war ended. By February 1946, civil war again ravaged China. American supporters of Jiang, most notably his friend, Time-Life publisher Henry R. Luce, recommended that the United States increase its economic and military support for the Nationalist government. Luce and others argued that the civil war in China was as important as the one that threatened Greece. Truman and Marshall disagreed. Although dreading a Communist success in China, they blamed the corrupt and inefficient Nationalist government for China's political and economic turmoil. Truman and Marshall were willing to continue some aid for China but did not want to commit America to an Asian war. Jiang's forces steadily lost the civil war. In 1949, Jiang's army disintegrated, and the Nationalist government fled to the island of Formosa (Taiwan).

Conservative Democrats and Republicans labeled the rout of Jiang as a humiliating American defeat. To quiet critics and to protect Jiang, Truman refused to recognize the People's Republic of China on the mainland and ordered the U.S. 7th Fleet to waters near Taiwan. Increasingly, Truman was feeling pressure to expand the containment policy beyond Europe. The pressure intensified in late August 1949, when the Soviets detonated their own atomic bomb, shattering the American nuclear monopoly. Suddenly, it seemed that the United States was losing the Cold War. From inside and outside the administration came calls for a more aggressive policy against communism. The **National Security Council,** in its Memorandum #68 (NSC-68), called in 1950 for global containment and a huge buildup of American military force.

Truman studied the report but hesitated to implement its recommendations. He worried about the impact of such large-scale military production on domestic goods manufacturing. He eventually agreed to a "moderate" $12.3 billion military budget

Organization of American States An international organization composed of most of the nations of the Americas, including the Caribbean, which deals with the mutual concerns of its members. Cuba is not currently a member.

Palestine Region on the Mediterranean that was a British mandate after World War I; the UN partitioned the area in 1948 to allow for a Jewish and a Palestinian state.

partition To divide a country into separate, autonomous nations.

Nationalist Chinese Supporters of Jiang Jieshi, who fought the Communists for control of China in the 1940s; in defeat they retreated to Taiwan in 1949, where they set up a separate government.

National Security Council Executive agency established in 1947 to coordinate the strategic policies and defense of the United States; it includes the president and four cabinet members.

for 1950 that included building the **hydrogen bomb,** which was first tested in 1952. Supporters of NSC-68, however, won the final argument on June 24, 1950, when North Korean troops stormed across the **38th parallel.**

The Korean War

When World War II ended, Soviet forces occupied Korea north of the 38th parallel, and American forces remained south of it (see Map 27.2). As with Germany, the division of Korea was expected to be temporary. A reunified Korean nation was to appear after the war. But mutual Soviet and American fears soon led to the establishment of an American-supported government in the south, led by **Syngman Rhee,** and a Communist-backed government in the north, headed by **Kim Il-Sung.** By mid-1946, the division of Korea appeared more permanent than temporary.

In 1949, believing Korea to be of little political or strategic importance, the Soviet and American governments withdrew their forces, leaving behind two hostile regimes, each claiming to be Korea's rightful government. Both Koreas launched raids across the border, but neither side gained much ground. Then, on June 25, 1950, Kim Il-Sung launched a full-scale invasion of the south. Truman quickly announced that Korea was, after all, a region vital to American interests and needed American protection. In Truman's mind, Moscow had directed the invasion. The wisdom of NSC-68's recommendations for global containment was undeniably confirmed.

The UN Responds to Communist Aggression

Within days, the South Korean army (ROK) was fleeing before stronger, better-equipped North Korean forces. Immediately, the United States asked the UN Security Council to intervene. The Security Council asked member nations to provide assistance to South Korea. Truman ordered **General Douglas MacArthur** to commit American naval and air units south of the 38th parallel. Two days later, as North Koreans captured the South Korean capital of Seoul, the Security Council approved an international military force to defend South Korea and named MacArthur commander of the United Nations forces. As one of the five permanent members of the Security Council, the Soviet Union could have vetoed the mission to South Korea, but the Russians were boycotting the council for its refusal to recognize the People's Republic of China.

Fearful that a congressional declaration of war against Korea might expand the conflict to involve the Chinese and Russians, Truman never sought one. American troops served in Korea under United Nations resolutions and followed Truman's orders as commander in chief. For the record, the war was called the Korean Conflict or a "police action." Few in Congress objected to Truman's actions.

The infusion of American troops did not halt the North Korean advance. By the end of July 1950, North Korean forces occupied most of South Korea except for the southeastern corner of the peninsula, the **Pusan perimeter.** But in a bold maneuver, MacArthur on September 15 landed some seventy thousand American forces at Inchon, near **Seoul,** nearly 200 miles north of the Pusan perimeter. It

hydrogen bomb Explosive weapon of enormous destructive power fueled by the fusion of the nuclei of various hydrogen isotopes.

38th parallel Negotiated dividing line between North and South Korea, which was the focus of much of the fighting in the Korean War.

Syngman Rhee Korean politician who became president of South Korea in 1948; his dictatorial rule ended in 1960,when he was forced out of office into exile.

Kim Il-Sung Installed by the Soviets as leader of North Korea. He served as premier from 1948 to 1972, when he became president, holding that office until his death in 1994.

General Douglas MacArthur Commander of Allied forces in the South Pacific during World War II and of UN forces in Korea until a conflict over strategy led Truman to dismiss him.

Pusan perimeter Area near the city of Pusan in South Korea, which was the center of a beachhead held by UN forces in 1950.

Seoul Capital of South Korea, which suffered extensive damage during its occupation by Communist forces in 1950 and 1951.

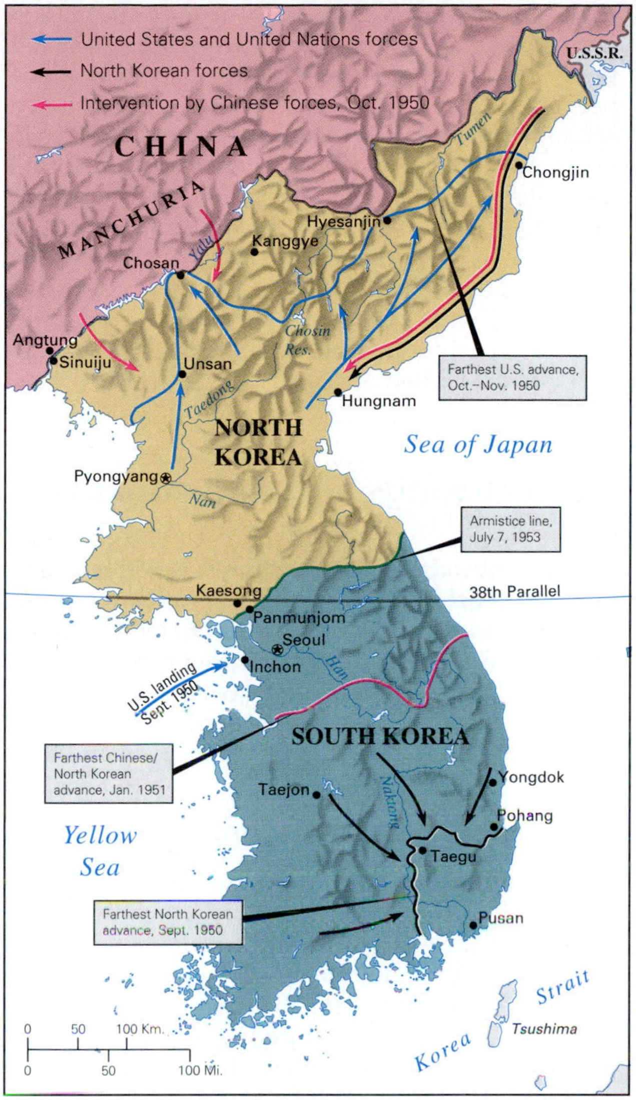

◆ **MAP 27.2 The Korean War, 1950–1953** Seeking to unify Korea, North Korean forces invaded South Korea in 1950. To protect South Korea, the United States and the United Nations intervened. After driving North Korean forces northward, Truman sought to unify Korea under South Korea. But as UN and South Korean forces pushed toward the Chinese border, Communist China intervened, forcing UN troops to retreat. This map shows the military thrusts and counterthrusts of the Korean War as it stalemated roughly along the 38th parallel.

was a brilliant tactical move that surprised the enemy completely. The next day, the United Nations forces along the Pusan perimeter began their advance. The North Koreans fled back across the 38th parallel. Seoul was liberated on September 27. United Nations forces had achieved the purpose of the police action.

Seeking to Liberate North Korea

MacArthur, Truman, and most other Americans now wanted to unify the peninsula under South Korean rule. Bending under American pressure, the United Nations approved the new goal on October 7, 1950. MacArthur had a green light to "liberate" North Korea from Communist rule (see Map 27.2).

An invasion seemed safe. North Korean forces were in disarray, and intelligence sources discounted the possibility of either Soviet or large-scale Chinese involvement. By mid-October, United Nations forces were moving quickly northward toward the Korean-Chinese border at the Yalu River. The Chinese, however, threatened intervention if the invaders approached the border. Some UN units had already encountered Chinese "volunteers." Anxious that the Chinese might move in force, Truman flew to Wake Island to confer with MacArthur. The United Nations commander was supremely confident. If Chinese forces did cross the border, he explained, they could not number more than thirty thousand. American airpower would slaughter them. Unconvinced, Truman ordered MacArthur to use only South Korean forces in approaching the Yalu River. MacArthur violated Truman's orders. On November 24, he moved American, British, and Korean forces to within a few miles of the Yalu. Two days later, nearly 300,000 Chinese soldiers entered the conflict.

In the most brutal fighting of the war, the Chinese attacked in waves, nearly trapping several American and South Korean units. MacArthur had believed that vastly superior American airpower would deal with any Chinese invaders. But his calculations had not foreseen the bitter winter weather or night battles that severely limited the role of American aircraft.

Within three weeks, the North Koreans and Chinese had shoved the United Nations forces back to the 38th parallel. During the retreat, General MacArthur asked for permission to bomb bridges on the Yalu River and Chinese bases across the border. He also urged a naval blockade of China and the use of Nationalist Chinese forces against the mainland. Believing that such an escalation could lead to World War III, Truman allowed only the Korean half of the bridges to be bombed and flatly rejected MacArthur's other suggestions. Truman abandoned the goal of a unified pro-Western Korea and sought a negotiated settlement to end the conflict.

The decision was not popular. Americans wanted victory. MacArthur publicly took exception to the limitations his commander in chief had placed on him. He put it simply: there was "no substitute for victory." Already dissatisfied with MacArthur's arrogance, Truman used the general's direct challenge to presidential power as grounds to fire him and replaced him with General Matthew Ridgway. MacArthur returned to the United States and received a hero's welcome, including a ticker-tape parade down New York's Fifth Avenue. He continued his criticism of Truman's policies at congressional hearings in June 1951, arguing that an expanded war could achieve victory. The administration countered that an expanded war could mean nuclear world war.

In their face-off, neither MacArthur nor Truman won. Truman's public approval rating continued to plummet. At the same time, MacArthur's hopes for a presidential candidacy collapsed as most Americans feared that his aggressive policies might result in another world war. By the beginning of 1952, the vast majority of Americans were weary of the war and wanted it over. The Korean front had meanwhile stabilized along the 38th parallel. Peace talks involving the United States, South Korea, China, and North Korea had begun on July 10, 1951. The negotiations did not go smoothly. For two years, the powers bickered about prisoners, **cease-fire** lines, and a multitude of lesser issues. Over 125,000 UN casualties occurred during the two years of peace negotiations. When the cease-fire finally was concluded by the Eisenhower administration on July 26, 1953, the Korean Conflict had cost over $20 billion and 33,000 American lives.

The "hot war" in Korea had far-reaching military and diplomatic results for the United States. In Europe, Truman moved forward with plans to rearm West Germany in case of a confrontation with the Soviet Communists. Throughout Asia and the Pacific, a large American presence was made permanent. In 1951, the United States concluded a settlement with Japan that kept American forces in Japan and Okinawa. The United States increased its military aid to Nationalist China and French **Indochina.** The containment policy that George F. Kennan had envisioned to protect Western Europe had expanded to include East Asia and the Pacific. According to the philosophy of the day, a Communist victory anywhere threatened the national security of the United States.

Homecomings and Adjustments

By November 1945, 1.25 million GIs were returning home each month wanting to rediscover family, jobs, and the American dream. Armed with the 1944 **G.I. Bill,** which provided low-interest home loans, a year's unemployment compensation, and economic support to attend school or college, returning veterans were eager to begin civilian life.

Adjusting to Peace at Home

Those veterans faced a massive housing shortage in 1945 and 1946. Streetcars were converted into homes in Chicago, grain silos became apartments in North Dakota, and across the country families doubled up. By mid-1946, however, developers like William Levitt were supplying mass-produced, prefabricated houses to meet the demand. Using building techniques developed during the war, Levitt boasted that he could construct a house on

cease-fire A truce that brings an end to fighting.

Indochina French colony in Southeast Asia, which included the present-day states of Vietnam, Laos, and Cambodia; it began fighting for its independence in the mid-twentieth century.

G.I. Bill Law passed in 1944 that provided financial and educational benefits for American veterans after World War II; *G.I.* stands for "government issue."

an existing concrete slab in sixteen minutes. Standardized and with few frills, his homes cost slightly less than $8,000, a very attractive price to many returning soldiers. The first Levittown sprang up in Hempstead, Long Island, in 1946, soon to be followed by others in Pennsylvania and New Jersey.

Most suburban developments were built for the "typical" American family—white, middle-class, and Christian. African Americans, Jews, and other minorities were not welcome. Although the 1948 Supreme Court decision in ***Shelly v. Kraemer*** made it illegal for developers and real-estate agents to restrict housing, the decision did little to integrate most suburbs. Banks rarely made home loans to minorities trying to buy in a white neighborhood.

Cozy homes were only part of the postwar dream. Veterans expected that women who had been hired while they "fought for democracy" would now relinquish their jobs. A fall 1945 *Fortune* poll discovered that 57 percent of women and 63 percent of men believed that married women should not work. Psychiatrists argued that men wanted feminine and submissive wives, not fellow workers. Fashions, like Christian Dior's "New Look," lowered skirts and accented waists and breasts to emphasize femininity.

Not all women accepted the role of contented wife and homemaker. When one ex-GI informed his wife that she could no longer handle the finances because it was not "woman's work," she indignantly reminded him that she had successfully balanced the checkbook for four years. Reflecting such tensions and too many hasty wartime marriages, the divorce rate jumped dramatically. Twenty-five percent of all marriages were ending in divorce in 1946. By 1950, over a million GI marriages had broken apart.

Despite the growing divorce rate, marriage was more popular than ever: two-thirds of the population was married by 1950 and having children. From a Depression level of under 80 per 1,000, the birth rate rose to over 115 per 1,000 within a year of the end of the war (see Figure 27.1). The so-called **baby boom** had arrived and would last for nearly twenty years.

Like women, nonwhites found that "fair employment" vanished as employers favored white males once the war was over. The skilled and industrial jobs that had opened to Latinos and African Americans during the war became scarce by 1946. In 1943, over a million African Americans were employed in the aircraft industry, but by 1950 the number had shrunk to 237,000. The decline was less marked in the automobile, rubber, and shipbuilding industries.

Mexican Americans also found themselves limited to unskilled, menial jobs, despite their rapidly growing numbers in urban areas. Discrimination, denial of educational opportunities, and language barriers combined to trap a majority of Mexican Americans as common laborers. Throughout the Southwest and West, the pattern of Mexican-American migration to urban areas continued to heighten the agricultural labor shortage. Mechanization made up for some of the loss, but more workers were necessary. In 1947, when Mexico pressed for higher wages and better working conditions for Mexicans working in the *bracero* program (see page 580), the United States allowed American farmers to contract directly for Mexican workers with virtually no restrictions on wages and working conditions. Between 1947 and 1950, nearly twice as many undocumented Mexican workers were recruited than had worked under the *bracero* program.

Nonwhite Americans at the end of World War II still lived in a distinctly segregated world. From housing to jobs, from healthcare to education, white society continued to deny nonwhites full participation in the American dream. Still, African Americans and Latinos looked eagerly toward the postwar period. Minorities had achieved social and economic gains during the war, and despite immediate postwar adjustments, it seemed that more progress was possible. One sign of such progress appeared when Jackie Robinson broke the color barrier in professional baseball and played for the Brooklyn Dodgers in 1947. Robinson was voted the National League's Rookie of the Year.

Having fought for democracy, minorities were more determined than ever before not to return to the old ways. Latino and African-American leaders

Shelly v. Kraemer Supreme Court ruling in 1948 that barred developers and real-estate agents from creating whites-only housing but that had little immediate impact.

baby boom Sudden increase in the birth rate that occurred in the United States after World War II and lasted from 1946 to 1964.

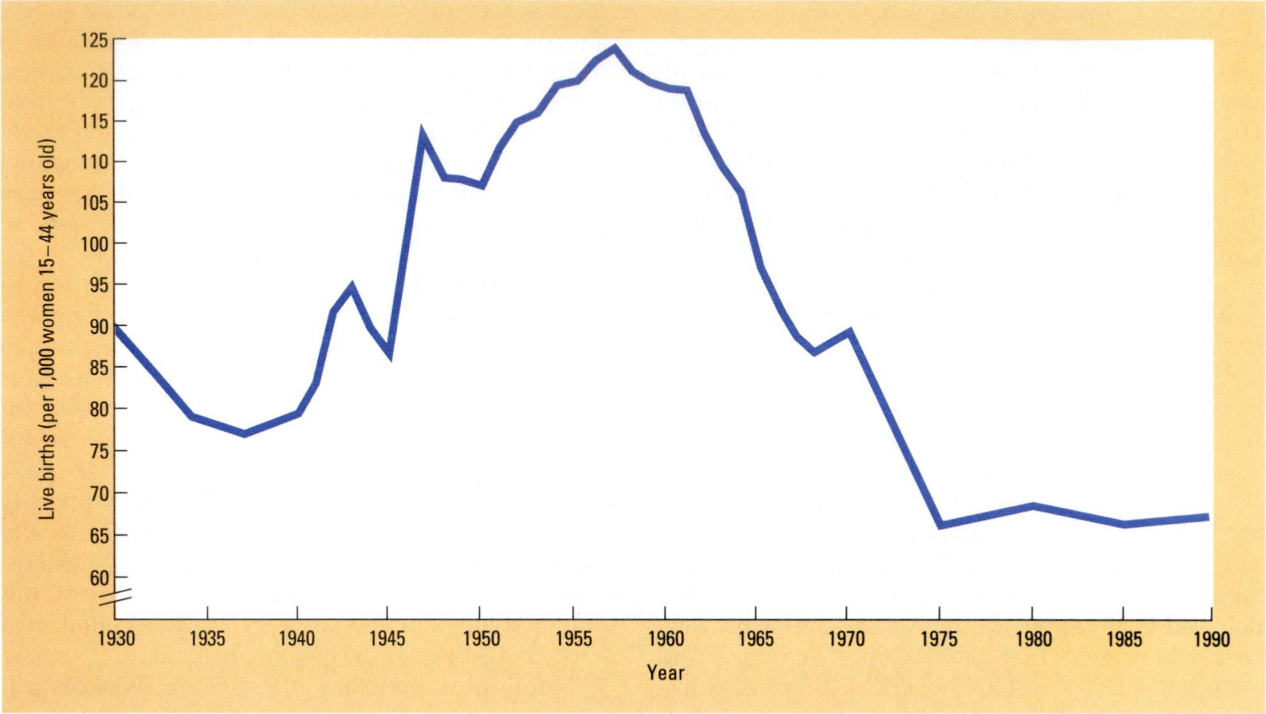

♦ **FIGURE 27.1 Birth Rate, 1930–1990** Between 1946 and 1957, families chose to have more children and the birth rate rebounded from the Depression. This increase is often called the baby boom. During the 1960s, the birth rate slowed down, and since the 1970s, it has remained fairly constant.

insisted that democracy be practiced at home. W. E. B. Du Bois stated that the real problems facing the United States came not from Stalin and Molotov but from racists like Mississippi's Senator Theodore Bilbo and Congressman John Rankin. "Internal injustice done to one's brother," Du Bois warned, "is far more dangerous than the aggression of strangers from abroad."

Truman and Liberalism

When Roosevelt died, many wondered if Truman would continue the New Deal or largely abandon it. Truman ended all speculation when on September 6, 1945, he unveiled a twenty-one-point program. One Republican critic characterized it as an effort to "out–New Deal the New Deal." The president asked Congress to continue governmental controls on the economy, especially on prices, and to renew the **Fair Employment Practices Commission (FEPC).** He recommended an expansion of Social Security coverage and benefits, an increase in the minimum wage to $.65 an hour, and the development of additional housing programs and Tennessee Valley–style projects. Truman also advised Congress that he would soon ask for a national health system to ensure medical care for all Americans.

The expanded New Deal that Truman projected never fully developed. Republicans, conservative Democrats, and business leaders objected to it. They

Fair Employment Practices Commission Commission established by executive order in 1941 to curb racial discrimination in war industries; in 1946, a bill for a permanent FEPC was killed by a southern Democratic filibuster.

argued that Truman's ideas would lead to the development of a socialistic state and destroy private enterprise. Conservatives and big business embarked on a campaign to persuade the American public of the dangers of "New Deal socialism." The National Association of Manufacturers spent nearly $37 million on such propaganda in one year. Conservatives in Congress either killed or significantly modified nearly all of Truman's proposals. FEPC faded away. The full-employment act was revised to eliminate government guarantees of a job for everyone.

The numerous strikes that occurred after the war fed the conservative mood of the country. When prices rose 25 percent but wages remained unchanged during the first eighteen months after the war, nearly 4.5 million workers went on strike to demand better compensation. Congress and state governments responded with measures designed to weaken unions and end strikes. "Right to work" laws banned compulsory union membership and in some cases provided police protection for those crossing picket lines during strikes. Other laws promoted the **open shop** and company-organized workers' associations.

Even Truman squared off against the railroad and coal miners' unions. When locomotive engineers struck in late May 1946, Truman asked Congress for power to draft striking workers into the army. The railroad strike was settled without the bill. Truman responded to a coal strike involving 400,000 United Mine Workers in April 1946 by seizing the nation's coal mines. He applauded when a federal court fined the union $3.5 million and again when the miners finally returned to work on December 7.

The strikes, soaring inflation rates, and divisions within Democratic ranks fit the Republican party's prescription for a 1946 election bonanza. "Had Enough?" Republican candidates asked the voters. Voters responded affirmatively, electing Republican majorities to both houses of the 80th Congress. The new Congress ignored Truman's domestic proposals and instead passed a tax cut and anti-union legislation. The **Taft-Hartley Act,** passed in June 1947 over Truman's veto, was a clear victory for management over labor. It banned the closed shop, prevented industry-wide collective bargaining, and legalized state-sponsored "right to work" laws. The law also empowered the president to use a court injunction to force striking workers back to work for an eighty-day cooling-off period. Truman had cast his veto knowing it would be overridden.

Truman's position on civil rights was cautious but generally supportive. In December 1946, he created the Committee on Civil Rights to examine race relations in the country. In October 1947, the committee's report, *To Secure These Rights,* called on the government to correct the extensive racial imbalances that it had found in American society. The report recommended the establishment of a permanent Commission on Civil Rights, the enactment of antilynching laws, and the abolition of the poll tax. It also called for integration of the U.S. armed forces and support for integrating housing programs and education. Truman asked Congress in February 1948 to act on the committee's recommendations but provided no direction or legislation. Nor did the White House make any effort to integrate the armed forces until black labor leader A. Philip Randolph once again threatened a march on Washington. Truman then issued an executive order to integrate the military forces. The navy and air force complied, but the army resisted until it faced high casualties in the Korean War. Despite his caution, Truman had done more in the area of civil rights than any president since Abraham Lincoln.

The 1948 Election

Republicans had high expectations in 1948. Republican candidates had done well in congressional elections, and Truman's approval rating remained low. To take on Truman, the Republicans chose New York's governor, **Thomas E. Dewey,** who had run a respectable race against Roosevelt in 1944.

open shop Business or factory in which workers are employed without having to join a union; unlike a closed shop, which requires union membership.

Taft-Hartley Act Law passed in 1947 banning closed shops, permitting employers to sue unions for broken contracts, and requiring unions to observe a cooling-off period before striking.

Thomas E. Dewey New York governor who twice ran unsuccessfully for president as the Republican candidate, the second time against Truman in 1948.

Dewey's prospects looked very good in 1948. Not only was the Republican party strong and Truman's popularity weak, but the Democrats were mired in bitter infighting over domestic policy. Dissatisfied Democratic liberals hoped to replace Truman with General Dwight David Eisenhower or Supreme Court Justice William O. Douglas. Neither was willing to run. Grudgingly, minorities and liberals had to settle for Truman. They did secure a party platform that included a civil rights plank.

Many southerners walked out of the Democratic convention to protest the civil rights plank. Unwilling to support a Republican, they organized the **Dixiecrat party** and nominated South Carolina's governor, J. Strom Thurmond, for president. Henry Wallace's supporters also deserted Truman, forming the Progressive party.

With the Democratic party so splintered and public opinion polls showing a large Republican lead, Dewey conducted a low-key campaign. Running for his political life, Truman crossed the nation by train, making hundreds of speeches that stressed the gains made under the Democrats. He attacked the "do-nothing" 80th Congress and its business allies. He told one audience, "Wall Street expects its money to elect a Republican administration that will listen to the gluttons of privilege first and not to the people at all." Truman also emphasized his expertise in dealing with the Soviets. Comparing himself to Dewey, Truman contended that he had the guts to stand up to Stalin.

Confounding the pollsters, Truman defeated Dewey. His margin of victory was the smallest since 1916. Nevertheless, Truman's victory was a triumph for Roosevelt's New Deal coalition. Despite the Dixiecrats, most southerners did not abandon the party; Thurmond carried only four southern states. Wallace did not carry a single state. Truman's victory was made even sweeter when most of the West and Midwest voted Democrat. With Congress once again solidly in Democratic hands, Truman hoped that in 1949 he would succeed with his domestic program, which he called the **Fair Deal.** In his inaugural address, Truman called on government to ensure that all Americans received a "fair share" of the American dream. He asked for increases in Social Security, public housing, and the minimum wage. He also proposed the repeal of the Taft-Hartley Act and the institution of a national health program.

Cold War Politics

Congress responded favorably to Truman's requests for the expansion of programs already well established by the New Deal, such as Social Security. Proposals that went beyond the New Deal, however, failed to gain support. Attacks on the Fair Deal were based on the time-honored objection of too much government intrusion. In 1949, this objection found renewed meaning in the growing national fear of communism. The American Medical Association attacked the idea of a national health system by stressing its "Communistic" nature. Conservatives emphasized the "Communist" nature of government intervention in education. Civil rights legislation was held captive by the southern wing of the party, which called the FEPC part of a Communist conspiracy to undermine American unity. One of Truman's aides wrote that "the consuming fear of communism" fostered a widespread belief that change was subversive and that those who supported change were Communists.

Responding to fears of Communists within the government, Truman moved to beef up the existing loyalty program. In March 1947, the president issued Executive Order #9835, establishing the Federal Employee Loyalty Program. The order specified that, after a hearing, a federal employee could be fired if "reasonable grounds" existed for believing that he or she was disloyal. Attorney General Tom Clark provided a lengthy list of subversive organizations. Between 1947 and 1951, almost three thousand federal employees were forced to resign, and another three hundred were discharged on the basis of disloyalty. In almost every case, the accused had no right to confront the accusers or to refute evidence. Few of those forced to leave government

Dixiecrat party Party organized in 1948 by southern delegates who refused to accept the civil rights plank of the Democratic platform; the party nominated Strom Thurmond of South Carolina for president.

Fair Deal President Truman's plan for legislation on civil rights, fair employment practices, and educational appropriations.

service were Communists. Fewer still were threats to American security. Truman's loyalty program did little to calm internal fears. Instead it intensified a growing hysteria about an "enemy within."

The Second Red Scare

The Second Red Scare reflected the fears and frustrations of many Americans in the immediate aftermath of World War II. America had defeated one set of enemies in the war only to be confronted with another enemy in the form of the Soviet Union and the specter of communism generally. The Soviet domination of Eastern Europe and other Communist advances seemed inexplicable to many Americans—unless America had been betrayed from within. Ironically, the small American Communist party had already declined rapidly since the late 1930s. The end of the Depression and the Nazi-Soviet pact of 1939 had stripped communism of the attraction it had once had for some Americans.

Among those stepping forward to protect the nation from the insidious enemy within, none was more vicious than the **House Un-American Activities Committee (HUAC).** Working with FBI director J. Edgar Hoover, the HUAC announced in 1947 its intention to root out communism within the government and society. HUAC targeted State Department officials, New Dealers, labor activists, entertainers, writers, educators, and those with known liberal philosophies. Hoover proclaimed that there was one American Communist for every 1,814 loyal citizens, while Attorney General Clark warned that Communists were everywhere.

HUAC made its first Cold War splash with its investigation of Hollywood. The committee's goals were to remove leftist viewpoints from the entertainment industry and thus to ensure that the mass media promote American capitalism and traditional American values. With much fanfare, the HUAC called Hollywood notables to testify about Communist influence in the industry. Many of those called used the opportunity to strut their patriotism and denounce communism. Ronald Reagan, president of the Screen Actors Guild, testified that the Conference of Studio Unions was full of Reds. Not all witnesses were cooperative. Some who were or had been members of the Communist party took the Fifth Amendment. Soon labeled "Fifth Amendment Communists," ten were jailed for contempt of Congress and blacklisted by the industry. The president of the Motion Picture Association, Eric Johnson, announced that no one would be hired who did not cooperate with the committee and that there would be no more films like *The Grapes of Wrath* featuring the hardships of poor Americans or "the seamy side of American life."

Anticommunism proved to be a useful weapon for a variety of causes. Manufacturers, including tobacco giant R. J. Reynolds, conducted a massive campaign to inform the nation about the Communistic nature of unions, especially the Congress of Industrial Organizations (CIO). The multimillion-dollar ad blitz successfully harnessed anti-Red hysteria to defeat the CIO's efforts to unionize southern industry. The CIO even expelled eleven unions for having Communist leaders and members. Southerners used anticommunism to fight the civil rights movement. Communities organized "watch groups" to protect themselves from the subversion of communism. These watch groups screened books, movies, and public speakers, and they questioned teachers and public officials, seeking to ban or dismiss those considered suspect. In Peekskill, New York, "loyal" Americans attacked the concert of singer, actor, and activist Paul Robeson, turning it into a riot (see Individual Choices: Paul Robeson).

HUAC's most sensational revelation came from one of the editors of *Time,* a repentant ex-Communist named Whittaker Chambers, shortly before the 1948 election. Chambers accused **Alger Hiss,** a New Deal liberal and former State Department official who had been with Roosevelt at Yalta, of being a Communist. At first Hiss denied even knowing Chambers, but under questioning by Congressman Richard M. Nixon, Hiss admitted

House Un-American Activities Committee Congressional committee created in 1938 that investigated suspected Communists during the McCarthy era and that Richard Nixon used to advance his career.

Alger Hiss State Department official accused in 1948 of being a Communist spy; he was convicted of perjury and sent to prison.

INDIVIDUAL CHOICES

Speaking Out

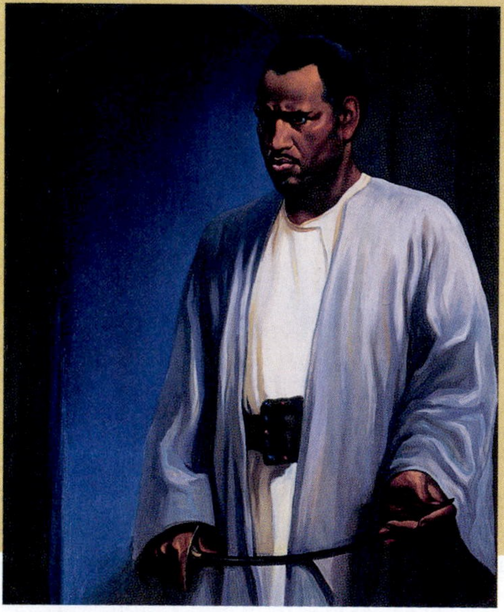

Paul Robeson

Paul Robeson was a brilliant actor, opera singer, and civil rights activist. By choosing to support communism, whose principles he thought would advance the cause of social equality, he sacrificed his career and everything else for which he had worked. National Portrait Gallery, Smithsonian Institute/Art Resource, N.Y.

Paul Leroy Bustill Robeson was exceptional at nearly everything he did. A scholar-athlete, he earned several varsity letters and was named an All-American in football before graduating Phi Beta Kappa from Rutgers in 1919—only its third black graduate. He attended Columbia School of Law and played professional football on weekends to cover his living expenses. In 1922, Robeson took his first acting role in a play staged by the Harlem YMCA. He received his law degree the following year, but believing he could do more for African Americans as an actor than a lawyer, he returned to the theater as an actor and concert singer.

Working with playwright Eugene O'Neill, Robeson was cast as the lead in the Broadway production of O'Neill's *The Emperor Jones* and in his controversial new play about interracial marriage, *All God's Chillun Got Wings.* Critics wrote rave reviews, and Robeson was soon one of the most sought-after actors in the United States and Britain. But more than an entertainer, he was an activist—choosing to advocate equal rights, especially for blacks. "The artist must elect to fight for freedom or for slavery. I have made my choice," he explained.

In fighting for freedom, Paul Robeson walked picket lines for striking workers, demonstrated against lynchings and segregation, and refused to work on any stage that practiced

an acquaintance with Chambers in the 1930s. He denied, however, that he was or had been a Communist. When Hiss sued for libel, Chambers charged that Hiss had passed State Department secrets to him in the 1930s. Chambers even produced rolls of microfilm, hidden in a pumpkin, and showed typed copies of the stolen documents—the notorious Pumpkin Papers. In a controversial trial, Hiss was found guilty of **perjury**

perjury Deliberate giving of false testimony under oath.

segregation. In 1939, he announced that he would no longer act in movies because the film industry did not allow him to show "the life or express the . . . interests, hopes, and aspirations of the struggling people from whom I come." Also in the 1930s, he spoke out loudly against fascism, entertaining Republican troops in Spain and raising money for Jewish refugees from Nazism. In 1934, he visited the Soviet Union and was impressed with Soviet social equality. "I feel like a human being for the first time. . . . Here I am not a Negro but a human being." He told Soviet filmmaker Sergei Eisenstein, "Here . . . I walk in full human dignity."

Despite his activism and his support of the Soviet Union, Robeson's popularity continued to soar, as he performed before thousands in the United States and Europe and broke racial barriers everywhere. In 1942, he became the first African American in modern American theater to be cast as Othello. During World War II, he campaigned for war bonds and toured the European theater in the first integrated United Service Organizations (USO) show. But not everyone was tolerant. Even as he patriotically pushed war bonds, the FBI listed his name on its Detain Communist List (DetComList).

With the onset of the Cold War, Robeson's views, especially his refusal to condemn the Soviet Union and its policies, became unacceptable to most Americans and effectively ended his artistic career. Considering him a Communist, the mayor of Peoria, Illinois, canceled his concert in 1947. And in 1949, over a hundred fans were injured in Peekskill, New York, when an anti-Robeson, anti-Communist mob attacked those who came to hear him. The Peekskill riot was a direct outcome of his statement that blacks would not fight against the Soviet Union "on behalf of those who have oppressed us for generations." From over $100,000 in 1946, his income fell to under $6,000 by 1949.

Considering Robeson an undesirable representative of the country, the State Department took away his passport in 1950. For the next eight years, Robeson was a prisoner in the United States until the Supreme Court upheld his right as a citizen to travel. Free again, he left for Europe. He also published his autobiography, *Here I Stand,* proclaiming that civil rights should become a mass movement, independent of whites, and urging blacks to become aware of their African heritage.

Ill, he returned from Europe in 1963 and retired in virtual seclusion. By the seventies, however, Paul Robeson was again popular, recognized and appreciated for his great talents and—despite great personal costs—his advocacy of civil and social rights. At a Carnegie Hall celebration of his 75th birthday in 1973, Coretta King, widow of slain civil rights leader Martin Luther King, Jr., remarked that Robeson "had been buried alive because . . . he had tapped the . . . wells of latent militancy among blacks." Unable to attend the gala affair, Robeson sent a simple message from the lyrics of "Old Man River," a song he had sung in the 1936 musical *Show Boat:*

You can be sure that in my heart I go on singing:
But I keeps laughin' instead of cryin';
I must keep fightin' until I'm dyin'
And Ol' Man River, he just keeps rollin' along!

in 1949 (the statute of limitations on espionage having expired) and sentenced to five years in prison. Recent research has confirmed that Hiss was in fact a Communist and that he passed secret information to the Soviets.

As the nation followed the Hiss case, news of the Communist victory in China and the Soviet explosion of an atomic bomb heightened American fears. In many people's minds, such Communist successes could have occurred only with help from American traitors. Congressman Harold Velde of Illinois charged that a network of Communists had infiltrated the government. Congress responded by passing, over Truman's veto, the

McCarran Internal Security Act. It required all Communists to register with the attorney general and made it a crime to conspire to establish a totalitarian government in the United States.

Concern about traitors and spies seemed further justified in February 1950, when British authorities arrested nuclear scientist Klaus Fuchs for passing technical secrets to the Soviet Union. Fuchs had worked at Los Alamos, New Mexico, on the American atomic bomb project. Fuchs named an American accomplice, Harry Gold, who in turn named David Greenglass, an army sergeant at Los Alamos. Greenglass claimed that his sister Ethel and her husband, Julius Rosenberg, were part of the Soviet atomic spy ring. The prosecution alleged that the information obtained and passed on by the Rosenbergs was largely responsible for the successful Soviet atomic bomb. The Rosenbergs claimed innocence, but they were convicted of espionage in 1951 and executed in 1953. The Rosenbergs were clearly Communists, but it is doubtful that they provided significant information about the bomb to the Soviets.

Joseph McCarthy and the Politics of Loyalty

Feeding on the furor over the enemy within, Republican Senator **Joseph McCarthy** of Wisconsin emerged at the forefront of the anti-Communist movement. McCarthy entered the public arena following World War II. Running for the Senate in 1946, he invented a glorious war record for himself and even walked with a fake limp. Some regarded him as among the worst senators in Washington—available to lobbyists, without principles, and absent most of the time. In February 1950, looking for an issue on which to get re-elected, McCarthy settled on the internal Communist threat.

The senator tried his gambit first in Wheeling, West Virginia. He announced to a Republican women's group that the United States was losing the Cold War because of traitors within the government. He claimed to know of 205 Communists working in the State Department. In Denver, the senator told reporters that he had a list of "207 bad risks" in the State Department. As he crossed the country, McCarthy changed the number of people on his list but continued to hammer away at security risks. He produced no names and no list for reporters.

A Senate committee quickly refuted most of McCarthy's charges. When the chair of the committee, Democrat Millard Tydings, pronounced McCarthy a fraud, the Wisconsin senator countered by accusing Tydings of questionable loyalty. During Tydings's 1950 re-election campaign, McCarthy worked for his defeat. McCarthy even displayed a faked photograph that depicted Tydings talking to Earl Browder, head of the American Communist party. When Tydings lost by forty thousand votes, McCarthy's stature swelled. The Senate's most powerful Republican, Robert Taft, slapped McCarthy on the back saying, "Keep it up, Joe." The Korean War only increased the senator's popularity. Supported by Republican political gains in the 1950 elections, **McCarthyism** became a powerful political and social force. Politicians flocked to the anti-Communist bandwagon.

By 1952, only 24 percent of Americans polled approved of Truman's presidency. Republicans had a field day attacking "cowardly containment" and calling for victory in Korea. Compounding his problems, a congressional probe of organized crime had found scandal, corruption, and links to organized crime within the government. When Truman lost the opening presidential primary in New Hampshire to Senator Estes Kefauver of Tennessee, he withdrew from the race. As in 1948, Republicans looked to the November election with great anticipation. At last, they were sure, voters would elect a Republican president.

McCarran Internal Security Act Law passed in 1951 requiring Communists to register with the U.S. attorney general and making it a crime to conspire to establish a totalitarian government in the United States.

Joseph McCarthy Senator who began a Communist witch-hunt in 1950 that lasted until his censure by the Senate in 1954.

McCarthyism Attacks on suspected Communists in the early 1950s by Joseph McCarthy and others, which were often based on unsupported assertions and carried out without regard for basic liberties.

SUMMARY

Expectations
Constraints
Choices
Outcomes

People hoped that the end of World War II would usher in a period of international cooperation and peace. This *expectation* vanished as the world entered a period of armed suspicion called the Cold War. To protect the country and the rest of the world from Soviet expansion, the United States *chose* to assume a primary economic, political, and military role around the globe. The *outcome* was Truman's containment policy. First applied to Western Europe, it eventually included Asia as the Cold War became a hot war in Korea. By 1952, with the "loss" of China and the stalemate in Korea, Americans turned against Truman's foreign policy. Many thought that the United States was losing the Cold War and that containment was not a strong enough policy to defeat communism and protect American interests.

At home, the Cold War acted as a *constraint* on liberalism. Moderates and conservatives alike *chose* to use the fear of communism to promote their own political, social, and economic interests. They attacked liberals, unions, and civil rights advocates as radicals, **fellow travelers,** and Communists. Economic prosperity also reduced public support for further growth of the New Deal. Politically, the *outcome* was that although Social Security, a minimum wage, and farm supports grew in scope, new initiatives like civil rights and national healthcare were rejected.

As Americans adjusted to postwar life, one of the major *outcomes* was a re-emphasis on home and family. Women experienced strong social pressure to give up their wartime jobs and take up the "domestic" life. Marriages and births rose. Although jobs and homeownership multiplied for white families, minorities found that the *constraints* of discrimination ended or limited many of the economic and social gains they had made during the war. Although pushed out of the work force or into lesser jobs, many nonwhites, joined by some white women, *chose* to resist being cast in customary roles.

fellow traveler Person who sympathizes with or supports the beliefs of the Communist party without being a member.

SUGGESTED READINGS

Bernstein, Barton. *Politics and Policies of the Truman Administration* (1970).

An excellent collection of essays on the Truman administration from a generally critical point of view.

Gaddis, John L. *The United States and the Origins of the Cold War* (1972).

A comprehensive and balanced view of the origins of the Cold War.

Hastings, Max. *The Korean War* (1987).

A short and readable study of the military dimension of the Korean War.

McCullough, David. *Truman* (1992).

A highly acclaimed, readable biography of Truman.

Reeves, Thomas. *The Life and Times of Joe McCarthy* (1982).

A solid but critical study of Joseph McCarthy and his role in the Second Red Scare.

Theoharis, Athan. *Seeds of Repression: Harry S Truman and the Origins of McCarthyism* (1971).

An examination of the causes of the Second Red Scare and Truman's role in contributing to it.

Tygiel, Jules. *Baseball's Great Experiment: Jackie Robinson and His Legacy* (1983).

Reflections on the life and decisions that brought Jackie Robinson to break the color barrier in professional baseball.

Whitfield, Stephen J. *The Culture of the Cold War* (1991).

A critical account of the impact of the Cold War on the United States.

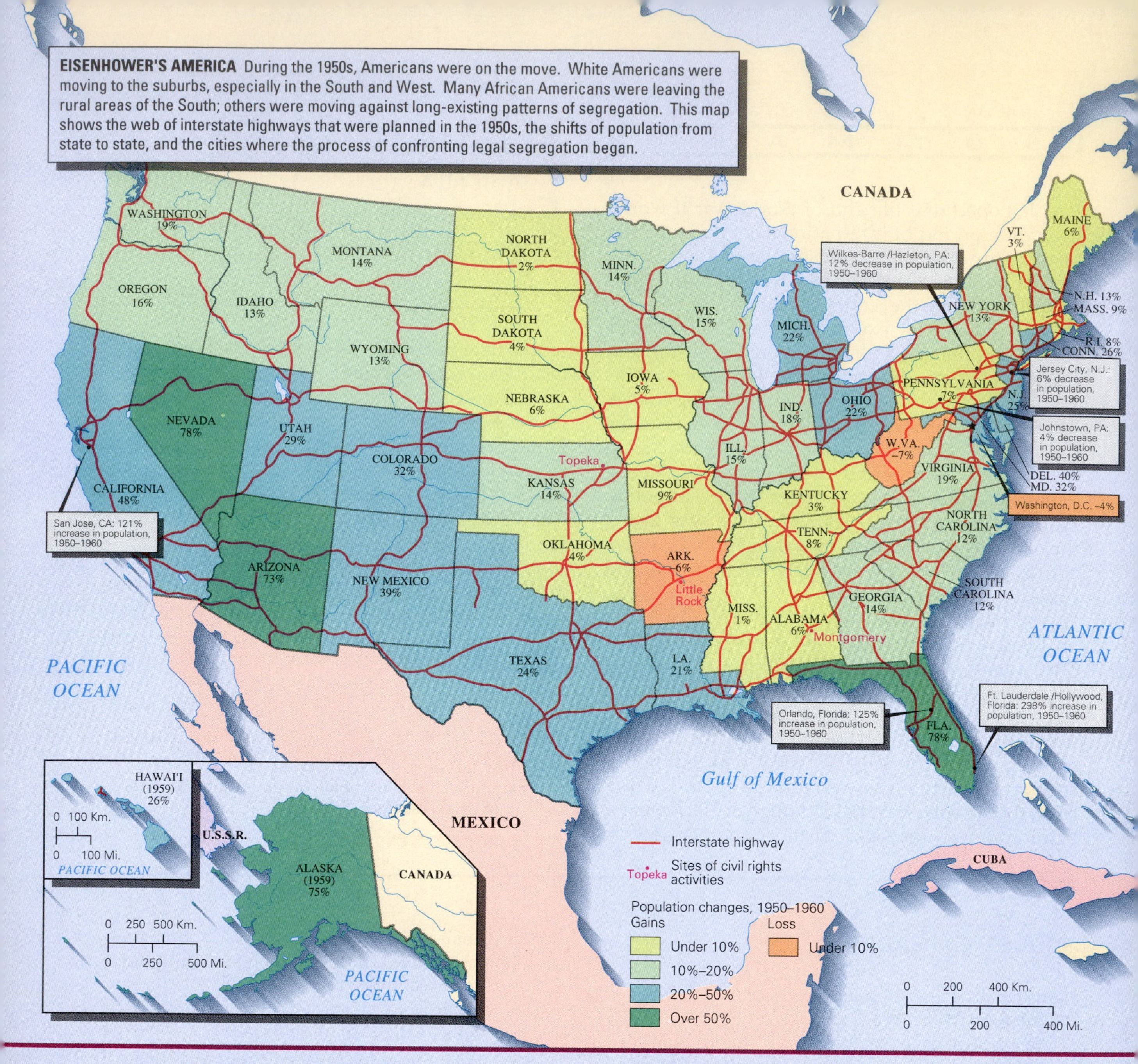

CANADA
WASHINGTON 19%
MONTANA 14%
NORTH DAKOTA 2%
MINN. 14%
OREGON 16%
IDAHO 13%
SOUTH DAKOTA 4%
WIS. 15%
MICH. 22%
WYOMING 13%
IOWA 5%
NEBRASKA 6%
NEVADA 78%
UTAH 29%
COLORADO 32%
Topeka
KANSAS 14%
MISSOURI 9%
ILL. 15%
IND. 18%
OHIO 22%
CALIFORNIA 48%
San Jose, CA: 121% increase in population, 1950–1960
ARIZONA 73%
NEW MEXICO 39%
OKLAHOMA 4%
ARK. 6%
Little Rock
TEXAS 24%
LA. 21%
MISS. 1%
ALABAMA 6%
Montgomery
GEORGIA 14%
TENN. 8%
KENTUCKY 3%
W.VA. –7%
VIRGINIA 19%
NORTH CAROLINA 12%
SOUTH CAROLINA 12%
FLA. 78%
Orlando, Florida: 125% increase in population, 1950–1960
Ft. Lauderdale /Hollywood, Florida: 298% increase in population, 1950–1960
PENNSYLVANIA 7%
NEW YORK 13%
Wilkes-Barre /Hazleton, PA: 12% decrease in population, 1950–1960
Jersey City, N.J.: 6% decrease in population, 1950–1960
Johnstown, PA: 4% decrease in population, 1950–1960
N.J. 25%
DEL. 40%
MD. 32%
Washington, D.C. -4%
VT. 3%
MAINE 6%
N.H. 13%
MASS. 9%
R.I. 8%
CONN. 26%
PACIFIC OCEAN
ATLANTIC OCEAN
Gulf of Mexico
MEXICO
CUBA
HAWAI'I (1959) 26%
0 100 Km.
0 100 Mi.
PACIFIC OCEAN
U.S.S.R.
ALASKA (1959) 75%
CANADA
0 250 500 Km.
0 250 500 Mi.
PACIFIC OCEAN
Interstate highway
Topeka Sites of civil rights activities
Population changes, 1950–1960
Gains
Under 10%
10%–20%
20%–50%
Over 50%
Loss
Under 10%
0 200 400 Km.
0 200 400 Mi.

EISENHOWER'S AMERICA During the 1950s, Americans were on the move. White Americans were moving to the suburbs, especially in the South and West. Many African Americans were leaving the rural areas of the South; others were moving against long-existing patterns of segregation. This map shows the web of interstate highways that were planned in the 1950s, the shifts of population from state to state, and the cities where the process of confronting legal segregation began.

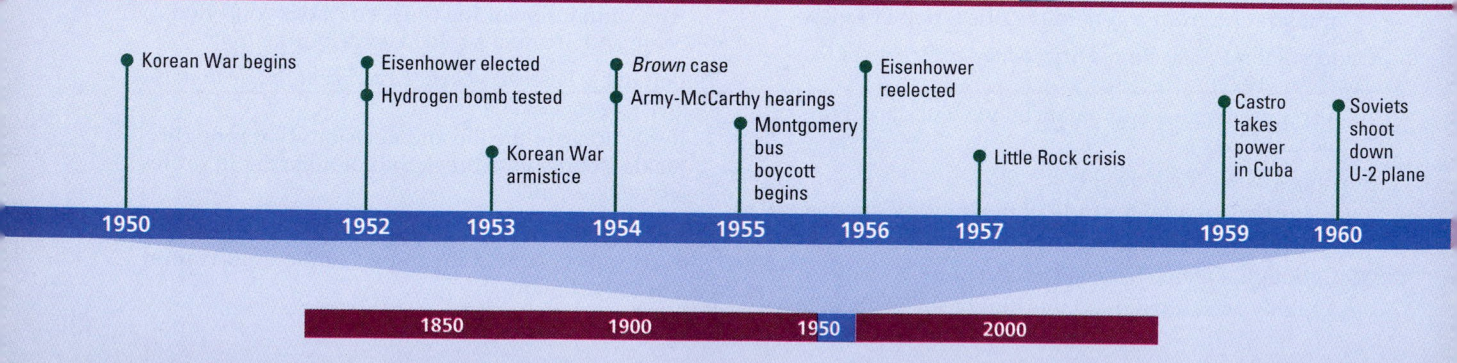

Korean War begins
Eisenhower elected
Hydrogen bomb tested
Korean War armistice
Brown case
Army-McCarthy hearings
Montgomery bus boycott begins
Eisenhower reelected
Little Rock crisis
Castro takes power in Cuba
Soviets shoot down U-2 plane
1950
1952
1953
1954
1955
1956
1957
1959
1960
1850
1900
1950
2000

CHAPTER 28

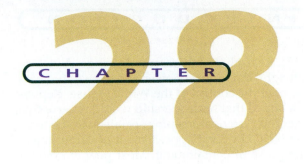

Quest for Consensus, 1952–1960

The Best of Times

- What factors contributed to expectations of prosperity in the 1950s?
- What expectations led American middle-class families to embrace suburban culture? What constraints did the critics of that culture condemn?

The Politics of Consensus

- What constraints did President Eisenhower and other Republicans encounter in trying to roll back the New Deal?
- How did the outcome reflect what Eisenhower called the "middle path"?

Seeking Civil Rights

- How did African-American leaders choose to attack *de jure* segregation in American society during Eisenhower's administration?
- What role did the federal government play in the outcome of civil rights issues during the 1950s?
- What constraints strengthened the strategy of confrontation and litigation in shaping the civil rights movement?

Eisenhower and a Hostile World

- What constraints lay behind the New Look?
- What were the weaknesses of "massive retaliation," and how did Eisenhower choose to address them?

INTRODUCTION

Expectations
Constraints
Choices
Outcomes

In 1952, Republicans represented change. A victory by Dwight David Eisenhower ended twenty years of Democratic control of the White House. Republicans hoped that his leadership would reverse two "dangerous" trends: creeping socialism in the form of the New Deal and appeasement of communism in the guise of containment. Most people *expected* that an Eisenhower presidency would end the Korean War, re-emphasize individual freedoms, and reduce government intervention in social and economic affairs. But most of all, Americans *expected* to enjoy their lives fully, in the strongest, most democratic, and most prosperous nation in the world.

The United States of the 1950s seemed to justify this *expectation.* The country experienced one of the longest periods of sustained economic growth in its history. This affluent America matched the image of a gentle and quiet president who presided over a prosperous nation composed of families that *chose* a stable, suburban life in which the husband worked and the wife raised their children.

For a large segment of the population, this America was real. But prosperity did not touch all Americans. Nor were all Americans, even those in the suburbs, leading happy, stable, or fulfilling lives. Many men and women were dissatisfied with their roles as husband and father, wife and mother, and *chose* other forms of social and personal expression. Many American youths *chose* to reject the values of suburban culture, turning to the driving rhythms of rock 'n' roll and displaying antisocial behavior. At the same time, intellectual and cultural critics condemned the lack of vitality of the suburban culture. The *outcome* was an American society fragmented by differing *expectations.*

For minorities in 1950, the *constraints* against achieving the American dream were formidable. Poverty, prejudice, and segregation remained the norm. But some groups nurtured *expectations* of change. By mid-decade, African Americans were tearing down barriers that blocked their access to the American dream. The *outcome* was a civil rights movement that attacked existing social and legal restrictions and forced white Americans to confront long-standing contradictions in the country's democratic image.

As president, Eisenhower recognized that a political and social consensus accepted much of the New Deal. Faced with this *constraint,* he *chose* to cut spending and reduce government regulations only where possible. In foreign policy, Eisenhower made similar *choices.* He *chose* to maintain the basic strategy of containment. *Constrained* by his desire to balance the budget, he stressed the use of atomic weapons as a cheaper alternative to conventional forces. Eisenhower shaped an *outcome* built on existing patterns of domestic and foreign policy rather than initiating new ones.

CHRONOLOGY

The Fifties

1948 Alfred Kinsey's *Sexual Behavior in the Human Male*

1950 Korean War begins
David Riesman's *Lonely Crowd*

1951 J. D. Salinger's *Catcher in the Rye*
Mattachine Society formed
Allan Freed's "Moondog's Rock 'n' Roll Party"

1952 Eisenhower elected president
Eisenhower visits Korea
Hydrogen bomb tested

1953 Korean War armistice at Panmunjom
Mohammed Mossadegh overthrown in Iran
Joseph Stalin dies
Joseph McCarthy investigates USIA and Voice of America
Alfred Kinsey's *Sexual Behavior in the Human Female*
Termination policy for American Indians implemented
Earl Warren appointed chief justice of Supreme Court
"Father Knows Best" debuts on television
Playboy established

1954 *Brown v. Board of Education*
St. Lawrence Seaway Act
Federal budget balanced
Army-McCarthy hearings
Jacobo Arbenz overthrown in Guatemala
Gamal Nasser assumes power in Egypt
Battle of Dienbienphu
Geneva Agreement (Vietnam)
SEATO founded

1955 Murder of Emmett Till
Montgomery bus boycott begins
Salk vaccine approved for use
AFL-CIO merger
Warsaw Pact
McDonald's opens in California
Geneva Summit

1956 Federal Highway Act
Gayle et al. v. Browser
Southern Christian Leadership Conference formed
Eisenhower re-elected
Suez crisis
Soviets invade Hungary
Allen Ginsberg's *Howl*
Grace Metalious's *Peyton Place*
Elvis Presley's "Heartbreak Hotel"

1957 Little Rock crisis
Civil Rights Act
Baghdad Pact
Sputnik I launched
Jack Kerouac's *On the Road*

1958 Berlin crisis
U.S. troops to Lebanon
Soviet nuclear test moratorium

1959 CENTO formed
Fidel Castro overthrows Batista in Cuba
Nikita Khrushchev visits United States
Cooper v. Aaron

1960 Soviets shoot down U-2 and capture pilot
Paris Summit

The Best of Times

According to the *Reader's Digest,* in 1954 the average American male stood 5 feet 9 inches tall and weighed 158 pounds. He liked brunettes, baseball, bowling, and steak and French fries. In seeking a wife, he could not decide if brains or beauty was more important. The average female was 5 feet 4 inches tall and weighed 132 pounds. She preferred marriage to career, but she wanted to remove the word *obey* from her marriage vows. Both were enjoying life fully, the *Digest* claimed, and buying more of nearly everything.

The nation's "easy street" was a product of big government, big business, and an expanding population. World War II and the Cold War had created military-industrial-governmental linkages that primed the economy through government spending. National security needs by 1955 accounted for half of the U.S. budget, equaling 17 percent of the gross national product. The connection between government and business went beyond spending, though. Government officials and corporate managers moved back and forth in a vast web of jobs. Few saw any real conflict of interests. Frequently, regulatory agencies were staffed by people from the businesses to be regulated. Secretary of Defense Charles E. Wilson had been the president of General Motors and voiced the common view: "What's good for General Motors' business is good for America."

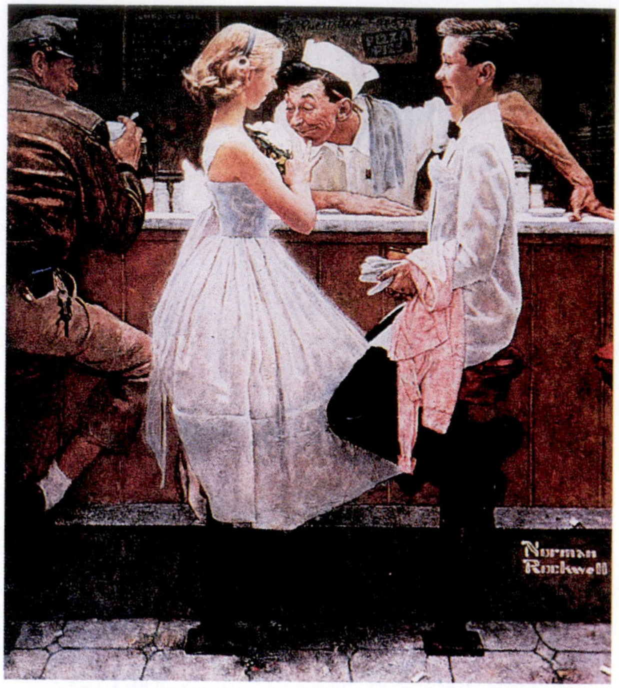

♦ In the popular culture of the 1950s, one of the most memorable events in any young person's life was the high school prom. Here, on this cover of the *Saturday Evening Post* painted in 1957 by Norman Rockwell, a young man in his tuxedo and a young woman in her prom dress have an after-prom milk shake at the local diner. Is that Dad behind the counter? *Courtesy of the Norman Rockwell Family Trust and Curtis Archives.*

Direct military spending was only one aspect of governmental involvement in the economy. Federal research funds flowed into colleges and industries, producing not only new scientific and military technology but a variety of marketable consumer goods such as polyester fabrics and Teflon. On an international level, American foreign-aid programs provided billions of dollars with which other countries bought American goods.

Technological advances also increased profits and productivity. Profits doubled between 1948 and 1958. At the same time, over four thousand mergers took place. In the steel, automobile, and aircraft industries, fewer workers used new technology to produce more goods. Union membership declined slightly. Agricultural and white-collar workers remained unorganized, and unions made little effort to organize the economically booming Sunbelt. Instead, they focused on getting better pensions, cost-of-living raises, and paid vacations. Another consequence of declining union rolls was the merger of the AFL and the CIO in 1955.

For most Americans, jobs and good wages were available. Except for brief **recessions** in 1953 and

recession A decline in the economy that is less severe than a depression.

1958, unemployment remained around 5 percent throughout the 1950s. Industrial wages rose from about $55 a week in 1950 to $72 in 1960. Not everyone benefited from the growing economy. Expanding opportunities in management and sales went almost exclusively to whites. Unemployment for minorities remained at about 10 percent. But for those able to reach the fruits of prosperity, life seemed good.

Suburban and Consumer Culture

During the fifties, the suburb and prosperity formed the heart of popular images of American life. Fourteen million single-family homes were built between 1945 and 1960, most of them in the suburbs. All levels of government helped make the suburbs possible. The Veterans Administration (VA) and Federal Housing Administration (FHA) underwrote thousands of loans. **Zoning laws** were changed to ease construction of tract housing developments. States, counties, and communities spent millions of dollars on roads to connect workplaces, schools, parks, and shopping centers to suburban homes. On the national level, the **Federal Highway Act** of 1956 provided $32 billion over thirteen years to build the interstate highway system.

As Americans sought the pleasant life of suburbia, the urban core deteriorated. Shrinking tax bases made it increasingly difficult for cities to maintain services, buildings, and mass transportation. Increased automobile traffic damaged roads, left railroad stations largely deserted, and added to pollution. Programs to rebuild homes in cities rarely succeeded in meeting the needs of the poor.

The automobile industry helped shape suburbia. By 1960, 75 percent of all Americans had at least one car. Stores had to include parking lots and easy access to roads. Amusement parks like Disneyland, miniature golf courses, drive-in theaters, and fast-food restaurants took advantage of the new availability of the automobile. McDonald's, franchised in San Bernardino, California, in 1955 by entrepreneur Ray Kroc, sold a standardized hamburger for 15 cents and changed the eating habits of America.

To sell automobiles, hamburgers, and all the other products that defined the good life, Madison Avenue continued to use images of youth, glamour, sex appeal, and sophistication. Leading the advertising onslaught was the tobacco industry. When medical reports connected health risks to smoking, the tobacco giants intensified their advertising and stressed that new, longer, filtered cigarettes posed no health hazards. Cigarette advertising increased 400 percent between 1945 and 1960.

Family Culture

Many Americans were sure that the 1950s were the best of all possible times. At the center of those feelings lay the economy, the home, the family, and the church. Religion enjoyed a new popularity. Church attendance rose to 59.5 percent in 1953, a historic high. No one was more esteemed than the Reverends Billy Graham and **Norman Vincent Peale** and Catholic Bishop Fulton J. Sheen. They captivated millions with religious, patriotic, and anti-Communist pronouncements. In spirit with the times, Congress added "under God" to the Pledge of Allegiance in 1954 and "In God We Trust" to all American currency in 1955.

After the disruptions of Depression and war, family took on a renewed importance in the fifties. The divorce rate slowed, and the numbers of marriages and births climbed. The ideal place for women was in the home. Women who avoided wedded bliss were suspected of being homosexual,

zoning laws Local regulations that limit particular types of buildings, such as residences, businesses, or factories, to specified sections of a city or town.

Federal Highway Act Law passed in 1956 appropriating $32 billion for the construction of federal and interstate highways.

Norman Vincent Peale Minister who told his congregations that positive thinking could help them overcome all their troubles in life.

emotionally immature, or just irresponsible. Career women frequently were thought of as neurotic and masculine.

The home was the center of "togetherness," a term defined in 1954 by *McCall's* as the modern partnership of husbands and wives who shared housework and shopping and catered to their children's needs and desires. Popular television shows such as "Leave It to Beaver" (1957) and "Father Knows Best" (1953) reflected the ideal middle-class family. The TV families who lived in all-white neighborhoods featured hardworking fathers and attractive, savvy mothers who always knew how to solve the current week's problem. Their children provided the usually humorous dilemmas that Mom's common sense and sensitivity untangled. Reality, however, rarely matched *McCall's* or television's images.

Another View of Suburbia

Unlike the wives shown on television, more and more married women were working (see Figure 28.1). Some desired careers, but the majority worked to enhance their families' **standard of living.** The percentage of middle-class women working rose from 7 percent in 1950 to 25 percent in 1960. Most found jobs in part-time or clerical positions that paid low wages and provided few benefits. Women filled most secretary, teller, and receptionist slots in banks but held only 15 percent of upper-level positions.

Nor were all homemakers happy. Surveys discovered that more than one-fifth of suburban wives were unhappy with their marriages and lives. Many women complained of the drudgery and boredom of housework and the lack of understanding and affection from their husbands. **Alfred Kinsey's** research on women's sexuality, *Sexual Behavior in the Human Female* (1953), indicated that 25 percent of married women had affairs.

Men also showed signs of being less than satisfied with the popular role of suburban dad. In 1953, Hugh Hefner first published *Playboy,* urging men to break away from the boring middle-class, husband-father image. The growing popularity of *Playboy* and other "men's magazines" signaled that many men were rejecting the ideal of togetherness. Reflecting the shadier side of middle-class life in fiction, the best-selling novel *Peyton Place* by Grace Metalious (1956) set America buzzing over the licentious escapades of the residents of a seemingly placid New England town. Hollywood kept pace with stars like **Marilyn Monroe.** Starting in 1952, movie directors repeatedly cast the "blonde bombshell" in slightly dumb but very sexy roles in which she was usually romanced by slightly older, more worldly men.

Monroe and other sex symbols represented a minor threat to the image of family, community, and nation. Homosexuality, however, appeared to threaten the moral and social fabric of society. Kinsey's 1948 study of male sexuality, *Sexual Behavior in the American Male,* shocked readers by claiming that nearly 8 percent of the population lived a gay lifestyle. According to Kinsey, homosexuality existed throughout American society. The gay bars that could be found in every major city clearly reflected Kinsey's findings.

In a society that emphasized the traditional family and feared internal subversion, homosexuals represented a double threat. The Republican national chairman warned that "sexual perverts . . . have infiltrated our Government" and were "as dangerous as . . . Communists." A Senate investigating committee worried that one homosexual could "pollute a Government office." Responding to such views, the Eisenhower administration barred homosexuals from most government jobs. State and local authorities fol-

standard of living Level of material comfort as measured by the goods, services, and luxuries currently available.

Alfred Kinsey Biologist whose studies of human sexuality attracted great attention in the 1940s and 1950s, especially for his conclusions on infidelity and homosexuality.

Marilyn Monroe American actress who became famous for her blond hair, her sex appeal, and her vulnerability; she died in 1962 at the age of 36.

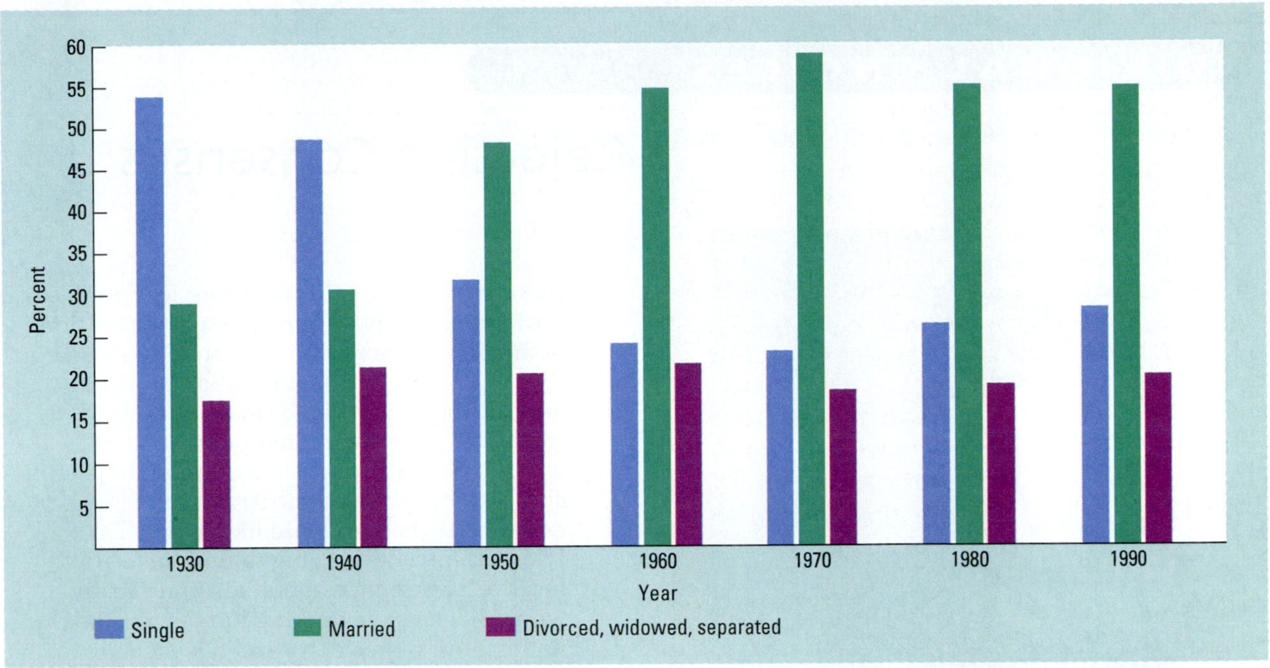

♦ **FIGURE 28.1 Marital Status of Women in the Work Force, 1930–1990** This figure shows the percentage of women in the work force from the Great Depression through 1990. While the number of women who fall into the category of divorced, widowed, and separated remained fairly constant, there was a significant shift in the number of single and married women employed. The number of single women in the workforce declined as the number of married women increased. *Source:* U.S. Department of Commerce, *Historical Statistics of the United States, Colonial Times to 1970,* Vol. I (Washington, D.C.: U.S. Government Printing Office, 1970), pp. 20–21, 131–132; and U.S. Department of Commerce, *Statistics of the United States, 1993* (Washington, D.C.: U.S. Government Printing Office, 1993), pp. 74, 399.

lowed suit. **Vice squads** began making frequent raids on gay and lesbian bars. In response to the virulent attacks, many tried to hide their homosexuality, but some confronted the attacks. In Los Angeles, Henry Hay formed the Mattachine Society in 1951 to fight for homosexual rights. In San Francisco in 1955, Del Martin and Phyllis Lyon organized a similar organization for lesbians, the Daughters of Bilitis.

Most Americans could justify the suppression of gays and lesbians because they appeared to reject the traditional values of family and community. Other critiques of American society were more difficult to reject. A number of respected writers claimed that the suburban and consumer culture stifled diversity and individuality. Mass-produced homes, meals, toys, and fashions created a gray sameness about Americans. Sociologist David Riesman in *The Lonely Crowd* (1950) argued that postwar Americans were overly concerned about fitting into a group. Peer pressure had replaced

vice squad Police unit charged with the enforcement of laws dealing with crimes such as gambling and prostitution.

INDIVIDUAL CHOICES

Rejecting Consensus

Allen Ginsberg

Allen Ginsberg was born in Paterson, New Jersey in 1926. He graduated from Columbia University, then moved to San Francisco. Dissatisfied with his traditional job and lifestyle, he chose to stop working and start writing poetry. Eventually, he became one of the leading Beat poets and voices of his generation.
Robert Kelley, LIFE Magazine, © Time Warner Inc.

In the mid-fifties, Allen Ginsberg left New York for California. "I had passed one session of my life," he remembered, "and it was time to start all over again." In the San Francisco area, he took a job with a small market-research firm and explored poetry, but he was not personally satisfied. He sought psychotherapy, and psychiatrist Philip Hicks asked him what he would like to do. "Doctor, I don't think you're going to find this very healthy," Ginsberg responded, "but I really would like to stop working forever . . . and do nothing but write poetry and have leisure to spend the day outdoors and go to museums and see friends. And I'd like to keep living with someone—maybe even a man—and explore relationships." Hicks said, "Do it."

Making his choice, Ginsberg established a long-term relationship with Peter Orlovsky, retired from work, and wrote his first long-lined poem, *Howl.*

Ginsberg's semiautobiographical cry of outrage and despair against a destructive and abusive society that worships Moloch, the god of materialism and conventionality—exploded on American society in 1956.

Moloch whose mind is pure machinery!
Moloch whose blood is running money!
Moloch whose fingers are ten armies!
Moloch whose heart is a cannibal dynamo!
Moloch whose love is endless oil and stone!
Moloch whose soul is electricity and banks!

At the end of the poem, Ginsberg celebrates his victory over Moloch's control of his conventional identity.

Howl not only rejected traditional American values but immediately became a target of censorship by San Francisco authorities, who claimed that the poem was obscene and pornographic. Almost as soon as it was published, San Francisco police arrested its publisher, Lawrence Ferlinghetti, and sought to confiscate existing copies of the poem. In the obscenity trial that followed, a parade of respected poets and literary critics testified that the poem had merit, forcing the judge to declare that it was not obscene. The poem and the furor over it promptly established a virtually unknown author as a leading Beat poet.

An opponent of social norms, Ginsberg believed that it was necessary to save the nation by rejecting conventionality and calling on the people to discover their true spirits. Interviewed by the *Village Voice* in 1959, Ginsberg argued that recent history was "a vast conspiracy to impose . . . a level of mechanical consciousness" on humankind and that the "suppression of contemplative individuality" was nearly complete. Fortunately, according to Ginsberg, "a few individuals, poets, have had the luck and courage . . . to glimpse something new through the crack of mass consciousness" and "have entered the world of Spirit" to battle "an America gone mad with materialism, a police-state America, a sexless and soulless America."

Ginsberg became the model for Beat writers—writing in the language of the streets about unliterary topics—and fulfilled the popular expectations of the "hipster" Beatnik. As the fifties dissolved into the sixties, Ginsberg and his Haight-Ashbury apartment became a center of the counterculture. He coined the term "flower power," while advocating spirituality and individual freedom induced by using psychedelic drugs and practicing Oriental philosophies and Buddhism. Opposed to the war in Vietnam (see Chapter 30), he asked antiwar protestors to demonstrate peacefully, arguing that flowers, bells, and chants would overcome jeers and oppression. In 1967, he organized the "Gathering of the Tribes for a Human Be-In" in San Francisco, the first of hundreds of counterculture festivals to follow.

As a poet, Ginsberg has chosen to write about his political and social concerns, attacking what he described as the evil forces in society. In 1973, his *Fall of America, 1965–1971* presented Moloch in the guise of the war in Vietnam, nuclear energy, threats to the environment, and America's rampant materialism—and won the National Book Award. From the obscenity trial to prestigious literary awards, the outcome of Allen Ginsberg's choice has been a literary Horatio Alger story, from a "dirty" Beat poet—a hipster predicted to self-destruct—to one of the country's best-known modern poets and "the biographer of his time."

individual thinking. William Whyte's *Organization Man* (1955) found the same lack of individuality and independence. Serious literature also highlighted a sense of alienation from a conformist society. Much of Sylvia Plath's poetry and her novel *The Bell Jar* (1963) depicted women torn between the demands of society and the quest for individual freedom. Contemporary novels such as Saul Bellow's *Henderson the Rain King* (1959), Sloan Wilson's *The Man in the Grey Flannel Suit* (1955), and J. D. Salinger's *Catcher in the Rye* (1951) offered similar themes.

More extreme were the **Beats,** or beatniks, a group of controversial artists, poets, and writers. Allen Ginsberg (*Howl,* 1956) and Jack Kerouac (*On the Road,* 1957) denounced American materialism and glorified a freer, natural life (see Individual Choices: Allen Ginsberg). Although some college students appreciated the beatnik critique of "square America," most Americans rejected their message and condemned their lifestyle. In an article in *Life* (1959), Paul O'Neil described the beatniks as being smelly, dirty people in beards and sandals, who were "sick little bums" and "hostile little females."

The Trouble with Kids

In the 1950s, many observers became alarmed by delinquency among many white, middle-class, suburban teens. What worried most parents was not the violent crime associated with inner-city gangs but teens running amok in cars in pursuit of amusements often involving alcohol and sex. One study of middle-class delinquency concluded that the automobile provided "a private lounge for drinking and for petting or sex episodes."

The problem with kids also seemed wedded to **rock 'n' roll,** a term coined in 1951 by Cleveland disc jockey Alan Freed. He had noticed that white teenagers were buying rhythm-and-blues (R&B) records popular among African Americans. But he also knew that few white households would listen to a radio program playing "black music." Freed decided to change the name to rock 'n' roll and play the less sexually suggestive of the R&B records. His radio program, "Moondog's Rock 'n' Roll Party," was a smash hit.

The barriers between "black music" and "white music" quickly began to blur. White singers such as Pat Boone and Georgia Gibbs sold millions of rock-'n'-roll **cover records** and were heard on hundreds of radio stations that had refused to play the original black artists. By mid-decade, African-American artists like **Chuck Berry,** Little Richard, and Ray Charles were successfully "crossing over" and being heard on "white" radio stations. At the same time, white artists such as **Elvis Presley** were making their own contributions to rock 'n' roll. Presley blended gospel, country, and R&B into an original musical form that quickly rocked the nation. Beginning with "Heartbreak Hotel" in 1956, he recorded fourteen gold records in two years, appeared on the prestigious "Ed Sullivan Show" on television, and drove his audiences of teenage girls into frenzies with sexually suggestive movements. Although an outraged Catholic Youth Center newspaper asked readers to "smash" rock-'n'-roll records, such opponents were waging a losing battle. By the end of the decade, Dick Clark's "American Bandstand," fea-

Beats Group of American writers, poets, and artists in the 1950s, including Jack Kerouac and Allen Ginsberg, who rejected traditional middle-class values and championed nonconformity and sexual experimentation.

rock 'n' roll Style of music that developed out of rhythm-and-blues in the 1950s, with a fast beat and lyrics that appealed to teenagers.

cover record A new version of a song already recorded by an original artist.

Chuck Berry African-American rock musician and composer whose songs chronicled teenage experiences and sentiments and who helped establish rock 'n' roll in the 1950s.

Elvis Presley Rock-'n'-roll musician from a poor white family in Mississippi who gained immense popularity with songs that incorporated the driving beat and frank sexuality of rhythm-and-blues.

turing teenagers dancing to rock-'n'-roll music, had become one of the nation's most watched and accepted programs.

The Politics of Consensus

In 1952, Republicans expected to end the Democrats' twenty-year monopoly on the White House. Crying, "It is time for a change," Republicans chose war hero General Dwight David Eisenhower as their candidate. The Democrats selected Illinois governor **Adlai Stevenson,** whom the Republicans depicted as too intellectual and too liberal. Eisenhower gained many supporters by telling a war-weary public that, if elected, he would go to Korea in pursuit of peace. The Republicans also attacked the Democrats' Cold War and New Deal record. They boasted that there were "no Communists in the Republican Party" and proclaimed that a Republican administration would roll back communism. The liberal spending of the Democrats would be stopped and the New Deal dismantled.

The campaign was almost without drama. The only tense moment came when the Republicans' vice-presidential candidate, Richard M. Nixon, who had risen to prominence because of his outspoken anticommunism, was accused of accepting gifts and a secret cash fund from California business friends. Eisenhower considered dropping him from the ticket. Nixon used television to rally public opinion. In the "Checkers" speech, a teary-eyed Nixon contended that the only gift his family had ever received was a puppy, Checkers. His daughter loved the puppy, Nixon stated, and he would not make her give it back, regardless of his career. It was a sentimental speech, but it worked. Nixon stayed on the ticket.

With a smile as powerful as FDR's grin, Eisenhower buried Stevenson in popular and electoral votes. Ike's broad political coattails ensured a Republican majority in Congress. Eisenhower again swamped Stevenson in 1956, but it was his victory alone, as the Democrats maintained their 1954 majorities in both houses of Congress.

The Middle Path

Eisenhower called himself a modern Republican. He wanted to follow a "middle course" that was "conservative when it comes to money and liberal when it comes to human beings." The president's first priority was a balanced budget. Facing Truman's projected deficits for 1952 and 1953, Eisenhower knew it was necessary to end the war in Korea and to make substantial cuts in the defense budget.

Fulfilling his campaign pledge, President-elect Eisenhower flew to Korea in December 1952 for a three-day visit. Eisenhower wanted to visit the frontline to get a real sense of the war. By the time the commander in chief left Korea on December 5, he was convinced that the war could not be won. The problem was how to persuade the North Koreans and Chinese that a negotiated settlement would be in their best interests.

To prod the Communists, Eisenhower and Secretary of State **John Foster Dulles** implied that the United States would use atomic weapons unless a settlement was soon reached. By July 1953, the "atomic diplomacy" had worked. A truce signed at Panmunjom ended the fighting, brought home almost all the troops, left a divided Korea, and allowed Eisenhower to cut the military budget.

Even as Eisenhower flew home from Korea, he was contemplating other ways to reduce military spending. The answer, he decided, was to reshape the tactics of containment. Eisenhower's **New Look** policy emphasized atomic weapons

Adlai Stevenson Illinois governor who was the Democratic candidate for president in 1952 and 1956 but lost both times to Eisenhower.

John Foster Dulles Secretary of state under Eisenhower who called for massive retaliation with nuclear weapons to deter Soviet aggression.

New Look National security policy under Eisenhower that called for a reduction in the size of the army, the development of tactical nuclear weapons, and the buildup of strategic airpower employing nuclear weapons.

and airpower and thus permitted a reduction of more expensive conventional forces. The policy allowed Eisenhower to balance the federal budget in 1954. Although the New Look represented a change in tactics, it did not change the basic strategy of containment that Truman had initiated.

Eisenhower's second priority was to reverse the "creeping socialism" of the New Deal by eliminating or reducing federal programs. High on his list of government programs to reverse were those involving American Indians. A series of acts between 1953 and 1954 eliminated federal economic support to tribes and liquidated selected reservations. Critics blasted this "termination policy" as an attack on American Indian culture and society. Native Americans increasingly fell under less protective state laws, while economic pressures encouraged them to sell tribal lands. By 1960, nearly one-half of American Indians had abandoned their reservations.

Eisenhower also returned to state and private hands federally owned or controlled energy sources. Although successful in removing many federal controls over energy, Eisenhower faced bitter opposition in trying to modify agricultural policy. The strong bipartisan Farm Bloc ensured that the Agricultural Act of 1954 contained only small modifications of Roosevelt's policy (see page 545). Congress did approve lower payment rates, but because payments were based on production levels, which continued to grow, the total cost of federal subsidies rose steadily.

Eisenhower's "middle path" did not discard New Deal programs altogether or shrink the size of government. Programs such as Social Security had tremendous political support. Eisenhower believed that the Republican party could abolish Social Security only at its own peril. During his two terms, 7 million more Americans became qualified for Social Security, and 4 million more received unemployment payments. The minimum wage rose from $.75 to $1.00 an hour.

But Eisenhower's liberal nature had limits. After the **polio** vaccine developed by **Jonas Salk** was declared effective in 1955, Eisenhower strongly agreed with the American Medical Association that the government should not get directly involved in inoculating the public because it would be socialistic. Eisenhower also vetoed housing projects, public works bills, and antipollution proposals as inappropriate for the federal government.

When Eisenhower increased government spending, his rationale was generally based on national economic and security needs. He pushed the St. Lawrence Seaway project (1954), which connected the Great Lakes with the Atlantic Ocean, on the grounds that it would benefit the nation by increasing trade. He approved the Federal Highway Act (1956) to meet the needs of an automobile-driven nation and to provide the military with a workable transportation network. Following the Soviet launching of the space satellites ***Sputnik I*** (1957) and *Sputnik II* (1958), Eisenhower cited national security needs to support spending more federal money on education.

The successful orbiting of the Soviet satellites created a panic across the nation. Not only was the country vulnerable to missiles and bombs, but *Sputnik* appeared to underscore basic weaknesses in the American educational system. American schools, many critics argued, stressed soft subjects and social adjustment rather than hard subjects: science, languages, mathematics. *Sputnik* spurred Eisenhower and Congress to approve grants to schools for developing strong programs in those subjects. Similarly, Congress cited national defense when it established the **National Defense Student Loans** for college students.

polio Acute viral infection that usually struck children and often caused partial or total paralysis; it was common in the United States until the development of the Salk vaccine.

Jonas Salk American microbiologist who developed the first effective vaccine against polio in 1954.

Sputnik I Satellite launched by the Soviet Union in 1957; the first successful launch of an artificial satellite by any nation, it marked the beginning of the space race.

National Defense Student Loans Loans established by the U.S. government in 1958, designed to encourage the teaching and study of science and modern foreign languages.

The Problem with McCarthy

During the 1952 presidential campaign, Senator Joseph McCarthy had taken a prominent role in attacking Democrats as being soft on communism. With Ike in the White House, many Republicans, including Eisenhower, hoped that the Republican senator would quietly disappear. But McCarthy had no intention of fading from view. He continued his search for subversives in the State Department, the Voice of America, and the **United States Information Agency (USIA).** McCarthy's targets were discharged or pressured to resign. Although few of the individuals McCarthy attacked were guilty of any form of disloyalty, the agitation helped Republicans to rid the government of officials appointed by Democrats. McCarthy's hunt for Communists thus continued to serve partisan purposes.

McCarthy overstepped his bounds, however, when the army drafted his aide David Schine. McCarthy responded by threatening to expose army favoritism toward known Communists. Anti-McCarthy forces in Congress, quietly supported by Eisenhower, concluded that it was time to silence the senator. Charging that he was trying to blackmail the U.S. Army, the Senate investigated McCarthy. The American Broadcasting Company's telecast of the 1954 **Army-McCarthy hearings** allowed over 20 million viewers to see McCarthy's ruthless bullying firsthand. Public and congressional opposition to the senator rose. When the army's lawyer, Joseph Welch, asked McCarthy, who had accused Welch's co-counsel of belonging to a left-wing organization, "Have you no sense of decency?" the nation burst into applause. Several months later, the Senate voted 67 to 22 to censure McCarthy's "unbecoming conduct." Drinking heavily, rejected by his colleagues, and ignored by the media, McCarthy died in 1957. But McCarthyism remained for years a potent political weapon against liberal opponents.

Seeking Civil Rights

African-American leaders became determined during the 1950s to attack the racial inequalities in America. The NAACP had by 1952 won cases permitting African-American law and graduate students to attend white colleges and universities. Yet the concept of "separate but equal," established in 1896 by the Supreme Court ruling in *Plessy v. Ferguson* (see page 399), remained intact. Throughout the country, African Americans still occupied the lowest rungs of the social ladder and worked at the most menial jobs. From the delta of the Mississippi to the White House, African Americans were committed to enlarging their civil and political rights.

The *Brown* Decision

A step toward change came in 1954 when the Supreme Court considered the case of ***Brown v. Board of Education, Topeka, Kansas.*** The *Brown* case had started four years earlier, when Oliver Brown sued to allow his daughter to attend a nearby white school rather than the black school across town. The Kansas courts had rejected his suit, and the NAACP had appealed. In addressing the Supreme Court, NAACP lawyer **Thurgood Marshall** held that the doctrine of "separate but equal" was inherently unequal. He used statistics to show that black schools were

United States Information Agency Agency established by Congress in 1953 to distribute information about U.S. culture and political policies and to gain support for American international goals.

Army-McCarthy hearings The 1954 congressional investigation of allegations that McCarthy had tried to get special treatment from the U.S. Army for an aide; the televised hearings revealed McCarthy's villainous nature and ended his popularity.

Brown v. Board of Education, Topeka, Kansas Supreme Court ruling in 1954 that separate educational facilities for different races were inherently unequal.

Thurgood Marshall Civil rights lawyer who argued thirty-two cases before the Supreme Court and won twenty-nine of them; he became the first African American on the Court in 1967.

unequal when it came to finances, quality and number of teachers, and physical and educational resources. He also read into the record a psychological study indicating that black children educated in a segregated environment suffered from low self-esteem. He stressed that segregated educational facilities could never yield equal products.

In 1954, **Earl Warren,** appointed chief justice of the Supreme Court in 1953, announced for a unanimous court that "separate educational facilities are inherently unequal" and ruled that school segregation was illegal under the Fourteenth Amendment. In 1955, in a second *Brown* decision, the Court provided rather vague enforcement guidelines. The Court did not expect schools to desegregate overnight but wanted them to proceed with "all deliberate speed."

The Court's decision raised a loud cry of protest from white southerners. Virginia passed a law closing all integrated schools. Southern congressmen, in what was called the **Southern Manifesto,** proudly pledged to oppose the *Brown* ruling. Consequently, "all deliberate speed" amounted to a snail's pace. By 1965, only about 2 percent of all southern schools were integrated.

Southern white reactions to the *Brown* case confirmed for African Americans that efforts to undo existing social traditions would encounter strong opposition, even violence. An incident in August 1955 brought home exactly how far some were willing to go to halt threats to "tradition." **Emmett Till,** a teenager from Chicago visiting relatives in Mississippi, broke "tradition" by speaking to a white girl without being asked. For his actions, he was tortured and murdered. Roy Bryant and J. W. Milam were brought to trial and admitted to killing Till. An all-white jury acquitted both men. The verdict was not unexpected. What was a surprise was that black eyewitnesses bravely testified at the trial, despite threats against their lives.

The Montgomery Bus Boycott

In Montgomery, Alabama, African Americans decided to confront another form of white social control: segregation on the city bus line. The bus company practiced "rolling segregation," which required African-American passengers to take seats behind white riders and, if necessary, to give up seats and stand so that whites could sit. In this humiliating game of musical chairs, black Americans always lost.

On December 1, 1955, **Rosa Parks** refused to give up her seat on the bus so that a white man could sit. Mrs. Parks had not boarded the bus with the intention of disobeying the law, although she strongly opposed it. That afternoon, her fatigue and the humiliation of the demand to move were suddenly too much. She refused and was arrested. Local African-American leaders called for a boycott of the buses to begin on the day of Mrs. Parks's court appearance. They submitted proposals to the city and to bus officials calling for the hiring of black drivers and a more equitable system of seating.

On December 5, 1955, the night before the boycott was to begin, nearly four thousand people gathered at Holt Street Baptist Church to hear **Martin Luther King, Jr.,** the newly selected leader of the boycott movement. His words electrified the crowd. "We are here this evening," he announced,

Earl Warren Chief justice of the Supreme Court from 1953 to 1969, under whom the Court issued decisions protecting civil rights, the rights of criminals, and First Amendment rights.

Southern Manifesto Statement issued by one hundred southern congressmen in 1954 after the *Brown* decision, pledging to oppose desegregation.

Emmett Till African-American teenager from Chicago who was killed in Mississippi in 1955 and whose confessed murderers were acquitted by an all-white jury.

Rosa Parks Black seamstress who refused to give up her seat to a white man on a bus in Montgomery, Alabama, in 1955, triggering a bus boycott that stirred the civil rights movement.

Martin Luther King, Jr. Ordained Baptist minister, brilliant orator, and civil rights leader committed to nonviolence, who led many important protests of the 1950s and 1960s; he was assassinated in Tennessee in 1968.

"to say to those who have mistreated us so long that we are tired—tired of being segregated and humiliated, tired of being kicked about by the brutal feet of oppression." He asked the crowd to boycott the buses. He urged his listeners to protest with love and, when confronted with violence, to "bless them that curse you."

On December 6, Rosa Parks was tried, found guilty, and fined $10 plus $4 in court costs. She appealed. Bus and city administrators met with boycott leaders but refused to budge. The boycott, 90 percent effective, stretched into days, weeks, and finally months. Police wrote hundreds of traffic tickets for those involved in the car pools that provided transportation for the boycotters. Insurance companies canceled automobile coverage. On January 30, 1956, a stick of dynamite destroyed King's front porch. Even in the face of personal attack, King urged supporters to avoid violence and to maintain the boycott. As the boycott approached its anniversary, the Supreme Court ruled in *Gayle et al. v. Browser* (1956) that the city's and the bus company's policy of segregation was unconstitutional. "Praise the Lord. God has spoken from Washington, D.C.," cried one boycotter.

The 381-day boycott was tremendously successful in establishing conditions for change. The traditional white view that African Americans accepted segregation had been shattered. In King, a leader had emerged determined to fight segregation throughout American society. Within weeks, he and other black leaders had formed a new civil rights organization, the **Southern Christian Leadership Conference (SCLC).** Across the South, thousands of African Americans took heart from the *Brown* and Montgomery decisions.

Ike and Civil Rights

The White House had little to say about the bus boycott. When asked, Eisenhower gave evasive replies: "I am for moderation, but I am for progress; that is exactly what I am for in this thing." Personally, Eisenhower believed that government, especially the executive branch, had little role in integration. Not all within the administration were so unsympathetic toward civil rights. Attorney General Herbert Brownell drafted the first civil rights legislation since Reconstruction. The Civil Rights Act of 1957 provided for the formation of the U.S. Commission on Civil Rights and opened the possibility of using federal suits to ensure voter rights.

African Americans, meanwhile, made it more difficult for politicians to evade the issue of minority rights. For Eisenhower, the unavoidable finally came over the effort to integrate Central High School in **Little Rock,** Arkansas. Central High was scheduled to be integrated starting in 1957. Governor Orval Faubus, however, ordered National Guard troops to prevent desegregation.

For three weeks, the National Guard prevented nine black students from enrolling. Then, on September 20, a federal judge ordered the integration of Central High School. Faubus complied and withdrew the National Guard. But the crisis was not over. Segregationists were waiting for the black students on Monday, September 23, 1957. When they discovered that the nine had slipped into the school unnoticed, the mob rushed the police lines and battered the school doors, yelling, "Lynch the niggers!" Inside the school, Melba Pattillo Beals thought, "We are trapped. I'm going to die here, in school." School officials loaded the black students into cars and ordered the drivers not to stop: "If you hit somebody, you keep rolling, 'cause [if you stop] the kids are dead." The students escaped to safety.

The following morning, Little Rock's mayor asked for federal troops after angry white throngs began looting and burning part of the city. On September 24, Eisenhower nationalized the Arkansas

Southern Christian Leadership Conference Group formed by Martin Luther King, Jr., and others after the Montgomery bus boycott; it became the backbone of the civil rights movement in the 1950s and 1960s.

Little Rock Capital of Arkansas where Eisenhower sent federal troops in 1957 to protect black students entering an all-white high school and to end rioting by segregationist mobs.

♦ As Elizabeth Eckford approached Little Rock's Central High School, the crowd began to hurl curses, yelling "Lynch her! Lynch her!" and a National Guardsman blocked her entrance into the school with his rifle. Terrified, she retreated down the street away from the threatening mob. A week later, with army troops protecting her, Eckford finally attended—and integrated—Central High School. *Frances Miller, LIFE Magazine © Time Warner Inc.*

National Guard and dispatched a thousand federal troops to Little Rock. The president told the nation that he had sent the federal troops not to integrate the schools but to uphold the law and to restore order. It was a distinction lost on most white southerners.

The following school year (1957–1958), the city closed its high schools rather than integrate them. In response, the Supreme Court ruled in ***Cooper v. Aaron*** (1959) that such evasions of court-ordered integration were illegal. Little Rock's high schools reopened, and integration slowly spread to the lower grades. In Little Rock, as in many other communities, many white students fled the integrated public schools to attend private, segregated schools. Federal power had been used to uphold integration in Little Rock, but meaningful integration of schools was still years away. Although Eisenhower had signed the Civil Rights Act of 1957, critics argued that he had provided little moral or political leadership.

Eisenhower and a Hostile World

Eisenhower and Secretary of State John Foster Dulles believed that the United States had a moral responsibility to protect the world from communism. During the 1952 campaign, Dulles had condemned containment as "appeasement" and promised a global "rollback" of communism. Dulles's language made good campaign rhetoric, but President Eisenhower quickly dismissed liberation and rollback as too provocative. In addition, the death of Soviet Premier Joseph Stalin shortly after Eisenhower assumed office raised the possibility of a less confrontational relationship with the Soviets. The president thus ended up seeking a modification of Truman's containment policy that would be less expensive, move the nation away from confrontation, and weaken the Soviet Union. This modification brought about the New Look policy.

The New Look

The New Look relied on cheaper nuclear deterrence, an enhanced arsenal of nuclear weapons, and the threat of **"massive retaliation"** to protect American international interests (see Map 28.1). In

Cooper v. Aaron Supreme Court ruling in 1959 that barred state authorities from interfering with desegregation either directly or through strategies of evasion.

"massive retaliation" Term used by John Foster Dulles in a 1954 speech implying that the United States was willing to use nuclear force in response to Communist aggression anywhere in the world.

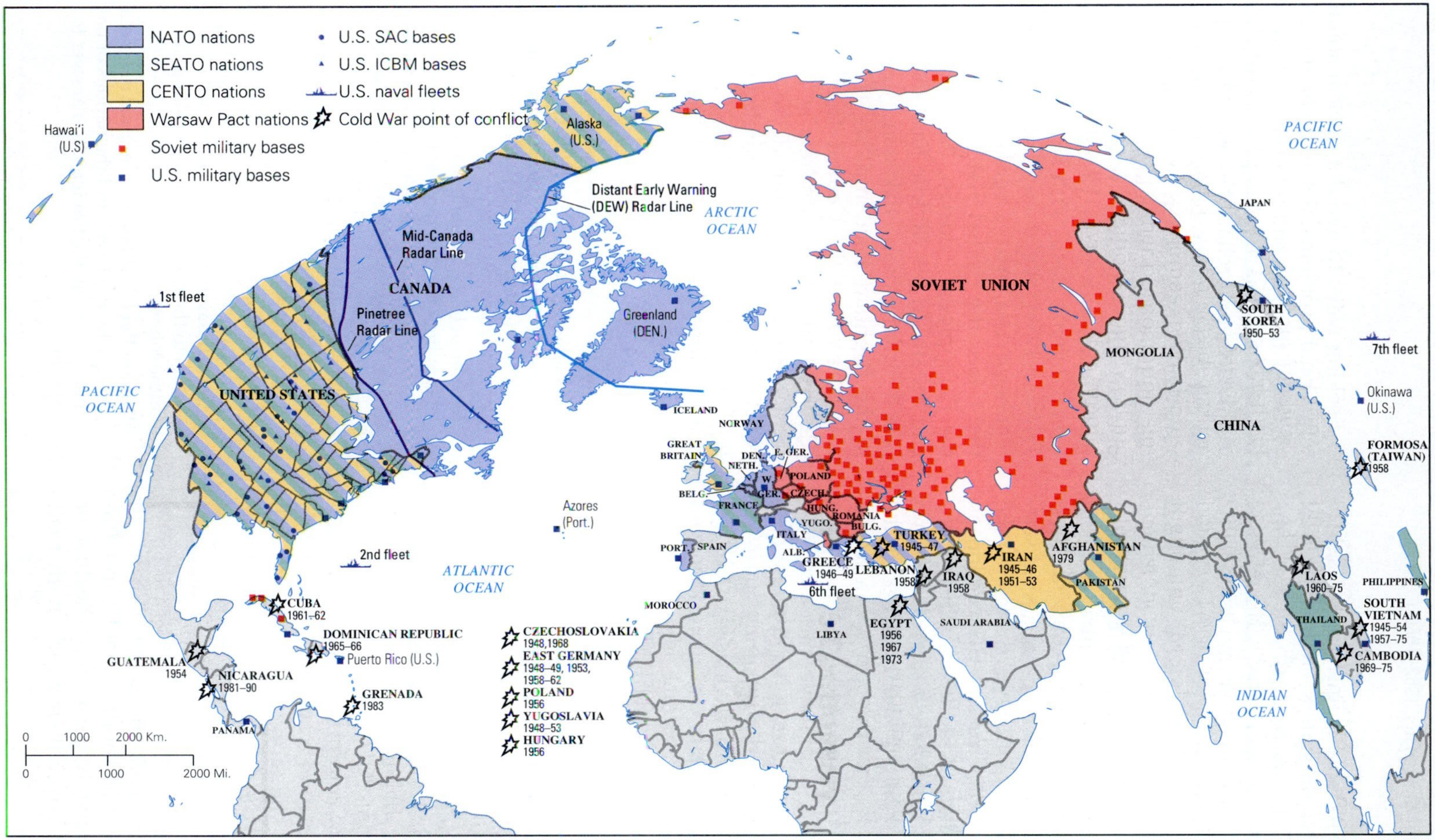
NATO nations
SEATO nations
CENTO nations
Warsaw Pact nations
Soviet military bases
U.S. military bases
U.S. SAC bases
U.S. ICBM bases
U.S. naval fleets
Cold War point of conflict
Hawai'i (U.S)
Alaska (U.S.)
PACIFIC OCEAN
1st fleet
UNITED STATES
CANADA
Mid-Canada Radar Line
Pinetree Radar Line
Distant Early Warning (DEW) Radar Line
Greenland (DEN.)
ARCTIC OCEAN
ICELAND
Azores (Port.)
ATLANTIC OCEAN
2nd fleet
CUBA 1961–62
DOMINICAN REPUBLIC 1965–66
Puerto Rico (U.S.)
GUATEMALA 1954
NICARAGUA 1981–90
GRENADA 1983
PANAMA
CZECHOSLOVAKIA 1948,1968
EAST GERMANY 1948–49, 1953, 1958–62
POLAND 1956
YUGOSLAVIA 1948–53
HUNGARY 1956
0 1000 2000 Km.
0 1000 2000 Mi.
GREAT BRITAIN
NORWAY
DEN.
NETH.
BELG.
E. GER.
W. GER.
POLAND
CZECH.
HUNG.
ROMANIA
BULG.
FRANCE
YUGO.
ITALY
ALB.
PORT.
SPAIN
MOROCCO
GREECE 1946–49
TURKEY 1945–47
LEBANON 1958
6th fleet
LIBYA
EGYPT 1956 1967 1973
IRAQ 1958
IRAN 1945–46 1951–53
SAUDI ARABIA
AFGHANISTAN 1979
PAKISTAN
SOVIET UNION
MONGOLIA
CHINA
JAPAN
SOUTH KOREA 1950–53
PACIFIC OCEAN
7th fleet
Okinawa (U.S.)
FORMOSA (TAIWAN) 1958
LAOS 1960–75
PHILIPPINES
THAILAND
SOUTH VIETNAM 1945–54 1957–75
CAMBODIA 1969–75
INDIAN OCEAN

♦ **MAP 28.1 The Global Cold War** During the Cold War, the United States and the Soviet Union faced each other as enemies. The United States attempted to construct a ring of containment around the Soviet Union and its allies, while the Soviets worked to expand their influence and power. This map shows the nature of this military confrontation—the bases, alliances, and flash points of the Cold War.

explaining the shift to more atomic weapons, Vice President Richard Nixon stated, "Rather than let the communists nibble us to death all over the world in little wars, we will rely . . . on massive mobile retaliation." Demonstrating its nuclear might, the United States exploded its first hydrogen bomb in November 1952. The Soviets tested theirs in August 1953.

Insiders recognized that the New Look policy was marred by several flaws. The central problem was where the United States should draw the massive retaliatory line. The Eisenhower administration's solution was to convince aggressors that the United States would rain nuclear destruction on any threat to its sphere of influence. This policy drew the label of **brinksmanship** because it required the administration to take the nation to the verge of war and trust that the opposition would back down. To convince the world of this daring boldness, Dulles and Eisenhower stressed that atomic weapons were as usable as conventional ones. Eisenhower privately was much more restrained in his willingness to "go nuclear." He recognized that a **thermonuclear** war would have no winners.

To Eisenhower's satisfaction, the nuclear threats seemed to produce immediate results. The North Koreans and Chinese signed a truce ending the Korean War. Although the death of Soviet leader Joseph Stalin now appears to have been the decisive factor, Eisenhower thought the New Look policy had paid off. To lend further credibility to atomic diplomacy, Eisenhower deployed intercontinental bombers carrying hydrogen bombs and dispatched **tactical nuclear weapons** to Europe.

The administration sought to convince the public that surviving an atomic war was possible. Underground **fallout shelters,** well stocked with food, water, and medical supplies, could, it was claimed, provide safety against an atomic attack. Across the nation, civil defense drills were established for factories, offices, businesses, and schools, including "duck-and-cover" drills in schools. Teachers would shout "Drop!" and students would immediately get into a kneeling or prone position and cover their heads with their hands.

Seeking ways to avoid a nuclear solution to international problems, Eisenhower and Dulles emphasized alliances and covert operations. Alliances would clearly mark areas protected by the American nuclear umbrella. They would also protect the United States from being drawn into limited, "brushfire" wars. When small conflicts broke out, the ground forces of regional allies, perhaps supported with American naval and air strength, would deal with them. Eisenhower concluded bilateral defense pacts with South Korea (1953) and Taiwan (1955) and a multilateral agreement, the Southeast Asia Treaty Organization (SEATO, 1954), that linked the United States, Australia, Thailand, the Philippines, Pakistan, New Zealand, France, and Britain. In the Middle East, the United States joined Britain, Iran, Pakistan, Turkey, and Iraq in the Baghdad Pact in 1957. This organization was later called the Central Treaty Organization (CENTO) after Iraq withdrew in 1959. In Europe, the United States welcomed West Germany into NATO. The Soviet bloc responded with the formation of a military alliance between Eastern European nations and the Soviet Union, the **Warsaw Pact,** in 1955.

brinksmanship Practice of seeking to win disputes in international politics by creating the impression of being willing to push a highly dangerous situation to the limit.

thermonuclear Relating to the fusion of atomic nuclei at high temperatures or to weapons based on fusion, as distinct from those based on fission.

tactical nuclear weapons Low-yield, short-range nuclear weapons designed to be used on the battlefield. By contrast, strategic nuclear weapons are used at long-range and intended to destroy large targets, such as cities.

fallout shelter Underground shelter stocked with food and supplies that was intended to provide safety in case of atomic attack; fallout refers to the nuclear particles falling through the atmosphere.

Warsaw Pact Alliance for mutual defense made in 1955 by the USSR and the nations of Eastern Europe; it was the Soviet bloc's answer to NATO.

Turmoil in the Middle East

In the Middle East, Arab nationalism, fired by anti-Israeli and anti-Western attitudes, posed a serious threat to American interests. Egypt and Iran offered the greatest challenges. Egyptian leader Colonel **Gamal Nasser** and Iranian Prime Minister Mohammed Mossadegh were attempting to expel British influence from their nations and grasp control over their valuable resources: the **Suez Canal** in Egypt and oil in Iran.

Although suspicious of Nasser, Eisenhower hoped to woo him with loans, cash, arms, and an offer to help build the **Aswan Dam** on the Nile. Nasser eventually rejected the American efforts, in large part because the United States wanted to promote an Egyptian-Israeli peace. When Nasser bought Soviet bloc weapons, Eisenhower concluded that he was an "evil influence" and canceled the Aswan Dam project in July 1956. Days later, Nasser nationalized the Anglo-French-owned Suez Canal. Israel, France, and Britain resorted to military action to regain control of the canal. On October 29, Israeli forces sliced through the Sinai toward Egypt. The French and British landed their forces in the canal zone on November 3.

Eisenhower was furious. He disliked Nasser, but he could not approve of armed aggression. Joined by the Soviets, Eisenhower sponsored a UN General Assembly resolution (November 2, 1956) calling for the removal of foreign troops from Egyptian soil. Faced with worldwide opposition, France, Britain, and Israel withdrew their forces. Nasser regained control of the canal and emerged as the uncontested leader of those opposing Western influence in Arab countries. The crisis also resulted in a growing Soviet presence in Egypt.

Elsewhere in the Middle East, Eisenhower had better luck. Nasser's actions led the Eisenhower administration to attempt to construct a Middle Eastern anti-Soviet alliance with the northern tier of Middle Eastern states. The major obstacle to such an alliance was Iran, where Prime Minister Mossadegh had nationalized British-owned oil properties and was unlikely to join an anti-Soviet alliance. Eisenhower gave the **Central Intelligence Agency (CIA)** the green light to overthrow the Iranian leader. On August 18, 1953, a mass demonstration funded and orchestrated by the CIA toppled the Mossadegh government. American money flowed into Iran to support the new government. A thankful Iranian government joined the anti-Soviet Baghdad Pact in 1956 and CENTO in 1959 and awarded the United States 40 percent of its oil production.

With Iran safely under American influence, Eisenhower redoubled his efforts to contain Nasser's **Pan-Arab movement** and an expanding Soviet presence in the region. To protect Arab friends from Communist or anti-Western rebellions, Eisenhower asked Congress for permission to commit American forces if their presence was requested. Congress agreed in March 1957 to provide $200 million in military and economic aid to the Middle East.

It did not take long for Eisenhower to use his power. When Jordan's King Hussein was threatened by an internal revolt, the White House announced that Jordan was "vital" to American interests, moved the 6th Fleet into the eastern Mediterranean, and supplied over $10 million in aid. King Hussein put down the revolt, dismissed parliament, and instituted authoritarian rule. In

Gamal Nasser Prime minister and president of Egypt in the late 1950s; he was an Arab nationalist who sought to return valuable foreign-owned resources to Egyptian control.

Suez Canal Canal running through Egypt from the Mediterranean to the Red Sea; it was under French and British control until 1955, when it was nationalized by Egypt.

Aswan Dam Dam on the Nile River in Egypt intended to provide electric power and stop seasonal flooding; construction finally began in 1960.

Central Intelligence Agency Agency established by Congress in 1947 to gather data and organize intelligence operations in foreign countries; it is responsible solely to the president.

Pan-Arab movement Attempts to politically unify the Arab nations of the Middle East, which stressed freedom from Western control and opposition to Israel.

1958, when Lebanon's Christian president, Camile Chamoun, ignored his country's constitution and ran for a second term, nationalistic, anti-West Muslim elements rebelled. Eisenhower committed nearly fifteen thousand troops to protect the pro-American government at Chamoun's request. The American forces left in three months, after Chamoun, with American approval, had stepped down and been replaced by General Faud Chehab. Eisenhower had demonstrated his willingness to protect American interests but had done little to resolve the problems faced by Lebanon and the rest of the Middle East.

A Protective Neighbor

During the 1952 presidential campaign, Eisenhower had charged that Truman had allowed economic problems and popular uprisings to develop in Latin America and that these uprisings had been "skillfully exploited by the Communists." As president, Eisenhower intended to reverse that trend by offering anti-Communist governments economic, political, and military support. He was most concerned about Guatemala, where President Jocobo Arbenz had nationalized thousands of acres owned by the American-based United Fruit Company. These radical actions convinced the administration to use the CIA to remove Arbenz. The CIA supplied Guatemalan colonel Carlos Castillo Armas with "wads of dollar bills" and arms to overthrow the elected government. Colonel Armas launched the effort to "liberate" Guatemala on June 18, 1954, and within two weeks had established a new, pro-American government.

The other major trouble spot in Latin America was Cuba. By the mid-1950s, the corrupt and dictatorial Fulgencio Batista had become an embarrassment to the United States. Many Americans believed that **Fidel Castro,** who was leading a revolt against Batista, could be a pro-American reformer. By 1959, rebel forces had control of the island. But Castro's economic and social reforms soon seemed to endanger substantial American interests. U.S. investors controlled 40 percent of Cuba's sugar industry, 90 percent of Cuba's telephone and electric companies, 50 percent of its railroads, and 25 percent of its banking. Washington tried to push Cuba in the right direction by applying economic pressure. In February 1960, Castro reacted by signing an economic pact with the Soviet Union. Eisenhower termed Castro a "madman." In March, he approved a CIA plan to attack Castro. Actual implementation of that plan, however, would have to be approved by Eisenhower's successor.

The New Look in Asia

When Eisenhower took office, Asia was the focal point of Cold War tensions. Fighting continued in Korea, and in Indochina the Communist **Viet Minh,** led by Ho Chi Minh, were fighting a "war of national liberation" against the French.

Eisenhower continued Truman's policy of supporting French efforts to re-establish colonial rule and defeat communism. By 1954, the United States was paying nearly 78 percent of the war's cost. Articulating the **domino theory,** Eisenhower warned that if Indochina fell to communism, the loss "of Burma, of Thailand, of the [Malay] Peninsula, and Indonesia" would certainly follow, and possibly Australia and New Zealand.

The prospect of the first domino's toppling appeared imminent in 1954. By spring, Viet Minh forces had encircled the French fortress at Dienbienphu. Eisenhower transferred forty bombers to bolster the French in Vietnam. Some advisers wanted a more direct American role, but Eisenhower, believing that "no military victory is possible in that kind of theater," rejected such options. Dienbienphu fell on May 7, 1954, after a fifty-five-day siege.

Fidel Castro Cuban revolutionary leader who overthrew the corrupt regime of dictator Fulgencio Batista in 1959 and established a socialist state.

Viet Minh Vietnamese army made up of Communist and other nationalist groups, which fought the French from 1946 to 1954 to win independence from French rule.

domino theory Notion that if one nation comes under Communist control, then neighboring nations will follow.

Eisenhower was equally unhappy about the results of negotiations held at Geneva between the French and the Viet Minh. The **Geneva Agreement** "temporarily" partitioned Vietnam along the 17th parallel and created the neutral states of Cambodia and Laos. The two Vietnams were to hold elections to unify the nation within two years. American strategists called the loss of half of Vietnam a "disaster." The United States refused to sign the Geneva Agreement. To save South Vietnam, Eisenhower rushed advisers and aid to the government of Prime Minister Ngo Dinh Diem. With American blessings, Diem ignored the Geneva-mandated unification elections, repressed his political opposition, and in October 1955 staged a **plebiscite** that created the Republic of Vietnam and elected him president.

The Soviets and Cold War Politics

Although Eisenhower relied on deterrence to curb Soviet expansionism, he recognized that improved Soviet-American relations might prevent a nuclear confrontation. Negotiating with the Soviets was difficult for him. He questioned the Soviets' commitment to peace. Still, growing Soviet nuclear capabilities and the death of Stalin in 1953 provided the opportunity for reducing tensions. Soon after Stalin's death, the new Soviet leader, Georgii Malenkov, called for "peaceful coexistence." Eisenhower called on the Soviets to demonstrate their willingness to cooperate with the West. Malenkov complied. He agreed to consider some form of on-site inspection to verify any approved arms reductions. Eisenhower responded by asking the Soviets in December 1953 to work toward universal disarmament.

By then, world concern was growing not only about the threat of nuclear war but about the dangers of radiation from the testing of nuclear weapons. Worldwide pressures grew for a summit meeting to deal with the "balance of terror." In 1955, Eisenhower accepted a meeting with the new Soviet leadership of Nikolai Bulganin and **Nikita Khrushchev,** who had replaced Malenkov. Although the Geneva Summit produced no agreement, the meeting did reduce East-West tensions.

The spirit of Geneva quickly vanished when Soviet forces invaded Hungary in November 1956 to put down an anti-Soviet revolt. The Hungarians appealed to the world for help. None came from the United States. Seeing no way to help without risking all-out war, the administration could only watch as the Soviets crushed the revolt.

Eisenhower resumed discussions of a test ban with the Soviets in 1958 after Khrushchev announced a voluntary moratorium on nuclear weapons testing and called for a meeting to discuss the issue. Although the U.S. military said it needed more tests, Eisenhower agreed to hold discussions with the Soviets. Once again, however, the negotiations bogged down over the issue of **verification.** They became even more difficult when another Berlin crisis emerged. The Soviets announced in November 1958 that they intended to sign a treaty with East Germany that would terminate the West's right to occupy West Berlin. For Eisenhower, retreat from Berlin was unthinkable. American and NATO forces made plans for the defense of their zones of the city. Faced with unflinching Western determination, Khrushchev announced a permanent delay in the treaty. The crisis was over.

Khrushchev subsequently sought to smooth relations with the West. In September 1959, he made a twelve-day tour of the United States that included a stop at Camp David, the presidential retreat in Maryland. The Camp David conference produced no agreement, but Eisenhower and the

Geneva Agreement Truce signed at Geneva in 1954 by French and Viet Minh representatives dividing Vietnam along the 17th parallel; the north became Communist and the south had a French-backed government.

plebiscite Special election that allows people to either approve or reject a particular proposal.

Nikita Khrushchev Soviet premier who denounced Stalin in 1956 and improved the USSR's image abroad; he was deposed in 1964 for his failure to improve the country's economy.

verification In disarmament, the methods of inspection that allow each nation to ensure that the others are abiding by agreements.

Soviet premier announced that they would both attend a summit conference in Paris in May and that Eisenhower would later visit the Soviet Union.

The promising thaw in the Cold War proved short-lived once again. On May 1, 1960, an American U-2 spy plane was shot down over the Soviet Union, and its pilot, Francis Gary Powers, was captured. At first, the United States feebly denied the nature of the flight, saying the U-2 was only a weather plane. Khrushchev then showed pictures of the plane's wreckage and presented Major Powers, clearly proving the American spy mission. Eisenhower took full responsibility but refused to apologize for such flights. Khrushchev canceled from the Paris Summit, and Eisenhower canceled his trip to the Soviet Union.

Although Eisenhower was applauded for standing up to Khrushchev, the loss of the U-2, Soviet advances in missile technology and nuclear weaponry, and a Communist Cuba only 90 miles from Florida provided the Democrats with strong reasons to claim that the Republicans had been deficient in meeting Soviet threats. In 1960, turning the Republicans' own tactics of 1952 against them, the Democrats cheerfully accused their opponents of endangering the United States by being too soft on communism.

SUMMARY

Expectations
Constraints
Choices
Outcomes

"Had enough?" Republicans asked voters in 1952. Americans answered by electing Dwight D. Eisenhower. With Ike in the White House, the 1950s spawned popular, if flawed, images of America that reflected the *expectations* of many whose lives centered on affluent suburbs and a growing consumer culture. The images were partially true. Many white, middle-class Americans fulfilled their *expectations* by moving to the suburbs and living the American dream.

Economic realities, social prejudice, and dissatisfaction, however, contradicted the popular imagery. More married women *chose* to enter the work force. Many men and women behaved contrary to the supposed norms of family and suburban culture, while teens and young adults sometimes rejected or criticized established norms and values. The *outcome* was that even affluent suburbia was less stable than it appeared. African Americans *chose* to reshape the nation's social and political agendas. The *outcome* was that racial equality became an issue that neither society nor government could ignore.

Although promising change, Eisenhower *chose* foreign and domestic policies that continued the basic patterns established by Roosevelt and Truman. There were reductions in some domestic programs, but the public *expectations constrained* any large-scale dismantling of the New Deal. The New Look relied on new tactics, but Cold War foreign policies did not change significantly. Eisenhower continued containment and expanded American influence in southern Asia and the Middle East. Meanwhile, relations with the Soviet Union deteriorated with the launching of *Sputnik,* another Berlin crisis, Castro's victory in Cuba, and the U-2 incident.

SUGGESTED READINGS

Ambrose, Stephen E. *Eisenhower: The President* (1984).

A generally positive and well-balanced biography of Eisenhower as president by one of the most respected historians of the Eisenhower period.

Burk, Robert F. *The Eisenhower Administration and Black Civil Rights* (1984).

An insightful examination of federal policy and the civil rights movement.

Devine, Robert A. *Eisenhower and the Cold War* (1981).

A solid and brief account of Eisenhower's foreign policy, especially toward the Soviet Union.

Diggins, John Patrick. *The Proud Decades: America in War and Peace, 1941–1960* (1988).

A short, well-written, and well-researched examination of the postwar period.

Garrow, David J. *Bearing the Cross* (1986).

An in-depth description of the development of the civil rights movement and the role of Martin Luther King, Jr.

Halberstam, David. *The Fifties* (1993).

A positive interpretative view of the 1950s by a well-known journalist and author, especially recommended for its description of famous and not-so-famous people.

Kaledin, Eugenia. *Mothers and More: American Women in the 1950s* (1984).

A thoughtful look at the role of American women in society during the 1950s.

Miller, Douglas T., and Marion Novak. *The Fifties: The Way We Really Were* (1977).

An interesting, useful, and often-quoted description of American society during the 1950s.

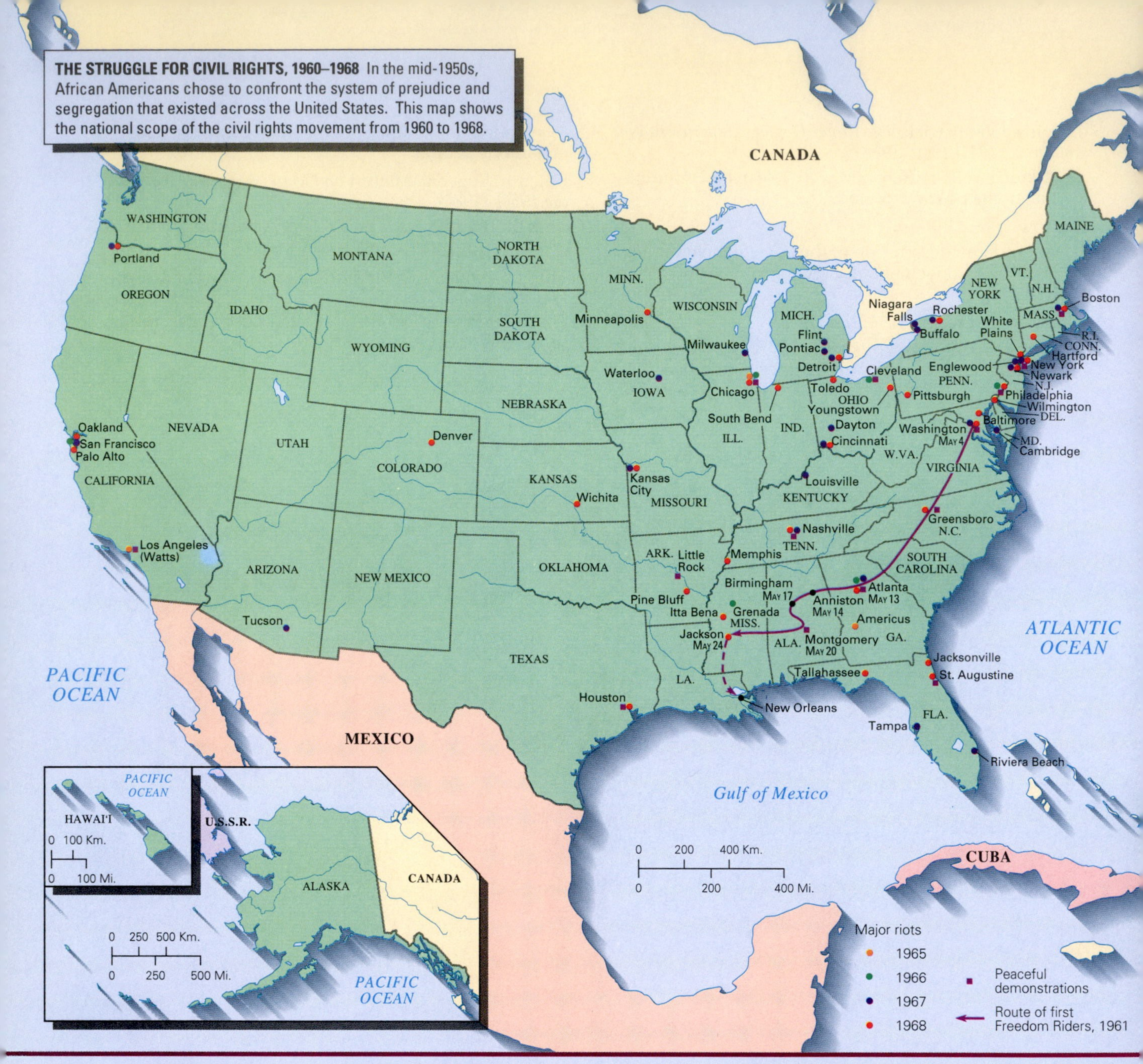
CANADA
WASHINGTON
Portland
OREGON
IDAHO
MONTANA
NORTH DAKOTA
SOUTH DAKOTA
WYOMING
NEBRASKA
MINN.
Minneapolis
WISCONSIN
Milwaukee
MICH.
Flint
Pontiac
Detroit
Waterloo
IOWA
Chicago
South Bend
ILL.
IND.
Toledo
OHIO
Youngstown
Dayton
Cincinnati
Cleveland
Pittsburgh
PENN.
NEW YORK
Niagara Falls
Rochester
Buffalo
White Plains
VT.
N.H.
MAINE
MASS.
Boston
R.I.
CONN.
Hartford
Englewood
New York
Newark
N.J.
Philadelphia
Wilmington
DEL.
Baltimore
MD.
Cambridge
Washington
May 4
W.VA.
VIRGINIA
Oakland
San Francisco
Palo Alto
NEVADA
UTAH
CALIFORNIA
Denver
COLORADO
KANSAS
Kansas City
MISSOURI
Wichita
Louisville
KENTUCKY
Los Angeles (Watts)
ARIZONA
NEW MEXICO
OKLAHOMA
ARK.
Little Rock
Pine Bluff
Memphis
Nashville
TENN.
Greensboro
N.C.
SOUTH CAROLINA
Birmingham
May 17
Anniston
May 14
Atlanta
May 13
Itta Bena
Grenada
MISS.
Americus
Jackson
May 24
ALA.
Montgomery
May 20
GA.
Tucson
TEXAS
LA.
Tallahassee
Jacksonville
St. Augustine
Houston
New Orleans
FLA.
Tampa
Riviera Beach
ATLANTIC OCEAN
PACIFIC OCEAN
MEXICO
Gulf of Mexico
CUBA
0 200 400 Km.
0 200 400 Mi.
PACIFIC OCEAN
HAWAI'I
0 100 Km.
0 100 Mi.
U.S.S.R.
ALASKA
CANADA
0 250 500 Km.
0 250 500 Mi.
PACIFIC OCEAN
Major riots
1965
1966
1967
1968
Peaceful demonstrations
Route of first Freedom Riders, 1961

THE STRUGGLE FOR CIVIL RIGHTS, 1960–1968 In the mid-1950s, African Americans chose to confront the system of prejudice and segregation that existed across the United States. This map shows the national scope of the civil rights movement from 1960 to 1968.

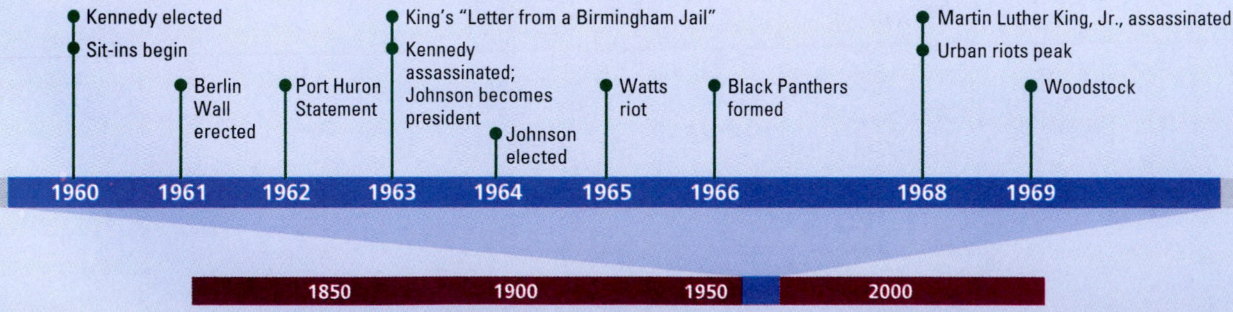
Kennedy elected
Sit-ins begin
Berlin Wall erected
Port Huron Statement
King's "Letter from a Birmingham Jail"
Kennedy assassinated; Johnson becomes president
Johnson elected
Watts riot
Black Panthers formed
Martin Luther King, Jr., assassinated
Urban riots peak
Woodstock
1960
1961
1962
1963
1964
1965
1966
1968
1969
1850
1900
1950
2000

CHAPTER 29

Great Promises, Bitter Disappointments, 1960–1968

Kennedy and the New Frontier

- What expectations did John Kennedy and his advisers have, and how did those expectations run into constraints?
- How did Kennedy's civil rights choices differ from Eisenhower's?
- How did civil rights activists choose to confront those resisting integration in the South?

Flexible Response

- What expectations shaped Kennedy's choices in foreign policy?
- What were some of the outcomes of Kennedy's concerns and interests in the Third World?

Beyond the New Frontier

- How did Lyndon Johnson's Great Society program expand on the expectations of the New Deal?
- How did Johnson choose to attack the constraints that African Americans and other minorities were facing?

New Agendas

- What constraints influenced the civil rights movement in the mid-1960s? What was the outcome?
- What choices did the youth movement explore? How justified were young people's criticisms of traditional American society?

INTRODUCTION

E xpectations
C onstraints
C hoices
O utcomes

John F. Kennedy symbolized a new beginning and promised a better society for all Americans. He energized the nation, raising *expectations,* especially among the poor and minorities, that he would press for solutions to end poverty and discrimination. But Kennedy faced political *constraints* from conservatives in Congress who objected to an expansion of liberal programs and civil rights legislation. As a result, during his three years in office, Kennedy achieved only some of his goals. He *chose* to delay civil rights legislation. The *outcome* was a domestic record of legislation that expanded on existing programs but did not chart new paths of social policy.

Kennedy also vowed to intensify the global struggle against communism. To defeat communism, he *chose* to fund both an arms race and a space race with the Soviet Union. Yet the *outcome* was not a safer and less divided world. The erection of the Berlin Wall, the Cuban missile crisis, and events in Vietnam symbolized heightened tensions.

Building on Kennedy's legacy, Lyndon Johnson *chose* to create the largest expansion of New Deal–style legislation since the Depression. Johnson's Great Society waged a war on poverty and discrimination, promoted education, and created a national system of healthcare for the aged and poor. Johnson, too, faced *constraints.* Conservatives opposed the Great Society's social and political goals, and some moderates objected to its cost and the ineffectiveness of many programs. An expanding war in Vietnam also added *constraints* to Johnson's domestic program.

By 1968, growing social and political turmoil was contributing to the rejection of liberal policies. The optimistic *expectations* Kennedy had inspired were declining amid the divisions of American society. Within the civil rights movement, Black Power leaders *chose* confrontation over compromise. Urban riots and violence drove wedges between African-American leaders and some white supporters. The emergence of a youth-centered **counterculture** that *chose* to reject traditional social and moral values also worked to fragment American society. The *outcome* was that a decade that began with great optimism ended with diminished *expectations* of what the federal government could accomplish.

Kennedy and the New Frontier

Republicans had every reason to worry as the 1960 presidential campaign neared. The last years of the 1950s had not been kind to the Republican party. The Cold War seemed to be going badly as the Soviets downed an American spy plane over the Soviet Union, launched *Sputnik* into space, and supported Castro in Cuba. Domestically, there seemed little or no direction from the White House. The Democrats had gained control of Congress in 1958. The economy also had lapsed into a recession.

On the Democratic side loomed **John Fitzgerald Kennedy,** a youthful, vigorous senator from Massachusetts. Kennedy, a Harvard graduate, came from a wealthy Catholic family. Some worried

counterculture A culture with values or lifestyles in opposition to those of the established culture.

John Fitzgerald Kennedy Massachusetts senator who was elected president in 1960, established the Peace Corps, and forced Khrushchev to remove Soviet missiles from Cuba; he was assassinated in 1963.

CHRONOLOGY

New Frontiers

1960 Kennedy elected president
Sit-ins begin
Boynton v. Virginia

1961 Bay of Pigs invasion
Alliance for Progress
Peace Corps formed
Berlin Wall erected
Vienna Summit
Freedom rides begin
SNCC formed

1962 Cuban missile crisis
James Meredith enrolls at the University of Mississippi
SDS's Port Huron Statement

1963 Martin Luther King, Jr.'s "Letter from a Birmingham Jail"
Limited Test Ban Treaty
Gideon v. Wainright
March on Washington
Ngo Dinh Diem assassinated
Kennedy assassinated; Johnson becomes president

1964 Civil Rights Act
Freedom Summer in Mississippi
War on Poverty begins
Johnson elected president
Escobedo v. Illinois
Griswold v. Connecticut
Berkeley Free Speech Movement

1965 Malcolm X assassinated
Watts riot
Selma march
Voting Rights Act
Medicaid and Medicare established
Elementary and Secondary Education Act

1966 Stokely Carmichael announces Black Power
Black Panther party formed
Miranda v. Arizona

1967 More than seventy-five major urban riots

1968 Martin Luther King, Jr., assassinated
Urban riots in more than 125 cities
Kerner Commission report

about his young age (43) and lack of experience, and others worried about his religion—no Catholic had ever been elected president. To lessen these possible liabilities, Kennedy had added the politically savvy Senate majority leader, **Lyndon Baines Johnson** of Texas, to the ticket, called for a new generation of leadership, and emphasized that those who were making religion an issue were bigots. He challenged the nation to enter a **New Frontier,** to improve the overall quality of life for all Americans, and to reinvigorate American foreign policy against communism.

Facing Kennedy was Eisenhower's vice president, Richard M. Nixon. Trying to distance himself from the image of Eisenhower's elderly leadership, Nixon promised a forceful, energetic presidency and emphasized his executive experience and history of anticommunism. He, too, promised to improve the quality of life, support civil rights, and defeat international communism.

Politics entered a new era in 1960 when the two candidates agreed to hold televised debates. Nixon

Lyndon Baines Johnson Senate majority leader who became Kennedy's vice president in 1961 and president when Kennedy was assassinated in 1963.

New Frontier Program for social and educational reform put forward by John F. Kennedy; though charismatically presented, it was resisted by Congress.

was proud of his debating skills and thought he could score many points against Kennedy. Kennedy recognized, however, that the candidate who appeared calmer and more knowledgeable would "win" the debate. Nixon made a poor impression before the camera. He appeared tired and haggard. He looked at Kennedy and not the camera when answering questions. Worst of all, he sweated. By contrast, Kennedy appeared fresh and confident. The differences in appearance were critical. The radio audience believed that Nixon won the debates, but to the 70 million television viewers, the winner was the self-assured and sweat-free Kennedy.

The televised debates helped Kennedy, but victory rested on his ability to hold the Democratic coalition together. The Texan Johnson used his political clout to keep the South largely loyal even as Kennedy blasted the lack of Republican leadership on civil rights. Kennedy scored the narrowest of victories. Nixon carried more states, 25 to 21, but Kennedy had a narrow margin over Nixon in popular votes and won the electoral count, 303 to 219 (see Map 29.1).

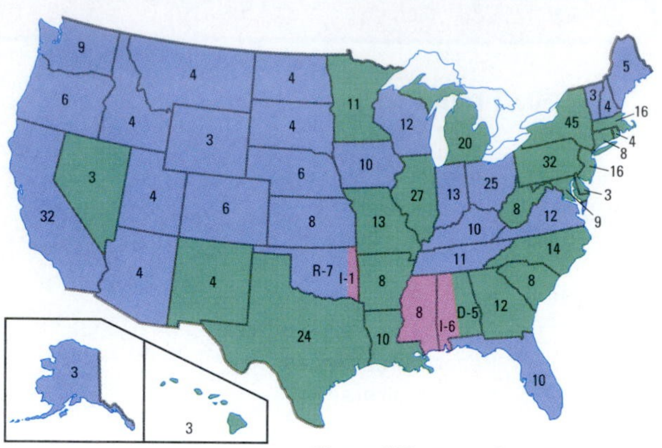

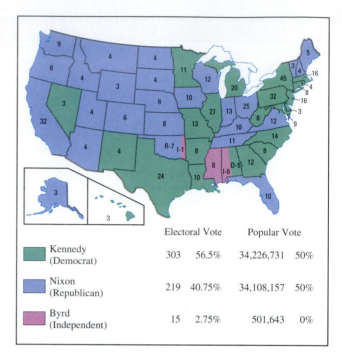

	Electoral Vote		Popular Vote	
Kennedy (Democrat)	303	56.5%	34,226,731	50%
Nixon (Republican)	219	40.75%	34,108,157	50%
Byrd (Independent)	15	2.75%	501,643	0%

♦ **MAP 29.1 Election of 1960** Although Richard Nixon won in more states than John F. Kennedy, Kennedy defeated his Republican opponent by a slim eighty-four electoral votes and fewer than nineteen thousand popular votes in the closest presidential election in the twentieth century.

The New Frontier

Kennedy's inaugural address fired the imagination of the nation. Speaking in idealistic terms, he promised to march against "the common enemies of man: tyranny, poverty, disease, and war itself." He asked all Americans to participate, exhorting them to "ask not what your country can do for you—ask what you can do for your country."

Kennedy's staff and cabinet kept up the image of change and activism. Recruiting from businesses and universities, he appointed men and women whom one reporter dubbed the "best and the brightest." Rhodes scholars and Harvard professors descended on the White House. They included historian Arthur Schlesinger, economist John Kenneth Galbraith (both personal advisers), McGeorge Bundy (national security director), and Dean Rusk (secretary of state). Ford Motor Company's president, Robert McNamara, was tapped for secretary of defense. In a controversial move, Kennedy gave the position of attorney general to his younger brother Robert. John Kennedy praised his choices as men with the "know-how" to solve problems. Not everyone was impressed. Speaker of the House Sam Rayburn remarked that he would "feel a whole lot better . . . if just one of them had run for sheriff once."

Kennedy was politically astute enough to recognize that the new Congress was likely to be an obstacle to substantial innovation. The Democrats lost twenty-two seats in the House in the 1960 elections. Although the Democrats still controlled both houses of Congress, Kennedy could not count on many conservative, southern Democrats to support the New Frontier. Therefore, he opted to push for a limited domestic agenda that included traditional Democratic proposals such as a higher minimum wage and increased Social Security benefits. He decided to delay civil rights and social legislation and instead concentrate on shaping foreign policy and improving the economy.

To spur economic recovery, Kennedy called for more government spending and business- and income-tax cuts. The defense budget was the first beneficiary, growing by almost 20 percent. Meanwhile, the economy rebounded from the "Eisenhower recession," as unemployment fell to 5 percent.

When liberals complained about the lack of civil rights legislation and new social programs, Kennedy pointed to the coalition of Republicans and conservative Democrats. "There is no sense in raising hell and then not being successful," he observed. He promised a civil rights bill and programs to attack poverty in 1963 and 1964.

Civil Rights and the Kennedys

During the campaign, Kennedy had promised "moral leadership" in support of civil rights, but once in office, he moved cautiously. He did appoint several blacks to high office and district courts, including Thurgood Marshall to the United States Circuit Court, but civil rights advocates were far from satisfied. They noted that some judicial appointments went to recognized segregationists, including Harold Cox of Mississippi, who had once referred to African Americans as "niggers" and "chimpanzees" in court. Kennedy did not ban segregation in federal housing until November 1962.

Civil rights activists were resolved, nevertheless, to force an end to segregation. Even as Kennedy assumed office, a new wave of black activism was striking at segregation in the South. The **sit-in** movement began when four freshmen at North Carolina A&T in Greensboro, decided to integrate the public lunch counter at the local Woolworth's store. On February 1, 1960, they entered the store, sat down at the counter, and ordered a meal. A black waitress told them she could not serve them, but still they sat and waited for service. No one tried to remove or arrest them. When the store closed, they were still unserved. They returned to campus as heroes. The next day, twenty A&T students sat at the lunch counter demanding service. By the end of the week, similar sit-ins had spread throughout the South.

In April 1961, the **Student Nonviolent Coordinating Committee (SNCC,** pronounced "snick") was formed to coordinate the increasing number of sit-ins and boycotts of stores, recreational facilities, libraries, bus and train stations, and lunchrooms. Although SNCC professed **nonviolence,** it was much more militant than King's Southern Christian Leadership Conference (SCLC). SNCC spurred more than seventy thousand people to protest for integrated public facilities in more than 140 cities, including some outside the South. Many of those participating in demonstrations were young college students. In some cities, including Greensboro, demonstrators achieved equal service with a minimum of resistance, but particularly in the Deep South, whites reacted violently. Officials in Orangeburg, South Carolina, blasted protesters with high-pressure fire hoses and arrested them.

Sharing headlines with those "sitting in" were the **freedom riders.** Prior to Kennedy's taking office, the Supreme Court had ruled in *Boynton v. Virginia* (1960) that all interstate buses, trains, and terminals be desegregated. James Farmer of the Congress of Racial Equality (CORE) planned a series of "freedom rides" to force integration on southern bus lines and stations. Farmer knew that riders would meet with opposition and hoped to put pressure on the president to uphold the Court's decision. The first buses of freedom riders left Washington, D.C., in May 1961, headed toward Alabama and Mississippi. The freedom riders expected trouble. Governor John Patterson of Alabama had announced that integration would come only over his "dead body." In Anniston, Alabama, a mob of angry whites attacked the buses, setting them on fire and severely beating several freedom riders. The savagery continued at Birmingham. When asked why no police were at the station to protect the

sit-in The act of occupying the seats or an area of a segregated establishment to protest racial discrimination.

Student Nonviolent Coordinating Committee Organization formed to give young blacks a greater voice in the civil rights movement; it initiated black voter registration drives and freedom rides.

freedom riders Civil rights protesters who rode buses throughout the South in 1961 to press for integration in bus terminals.

riders, Birmingham public safety commissioner Eugene "Bull" Connor explained that it was a holiday—Mother's Day.

As Farmer had predicted, the violence forced the federal government to respond. Hoping to avoid further bloodshed, Justice Department official John Seigenthaler obtained state and local protection for the riders through Alabama. But as the buses approached Montgomery, the police and National Guard escorts mysteriously vanished, leaving the freedom riders to face a large and violent crowd alone. A brutal attack left many freedom riders injured, including Seigenthaler, who was beaten unconscious. After an hour of terror, the police finally arrived and restored order.

A livid Attorney General Robert Kennedy deputized local federal officials as marshals and ordered them to escort the freedom riders to the state line, where Mississippi forces took over. Battered and bloodied, the riders continued to the state capital, Jackson. There they were peacefully arrested for violating Mississippi's recently passed **public order laws.** The jails quickly filled as more freedom riders arrived and were arrested. The nation waited for the administration to act. Finally, in September 1961, the Interstate Commerce Commission declared that it would uphold the Court's decision prohibiting segregation. Faced with direct federal involvement, most state and local authorities grudgingly accepted the desegregation of bus and train terminals.

Hoping to steer the activism away from freedom rides and sit-ins, the Kennedy administration argued that efforts should be focused on voter registration drives. There followed the Voter Education Project, a cooperative movement among the major civil rights organizations, which with federal protection would provide the right to vote to many who had been denied since the days of Reconstruction. The results of this effort, which ended in 1964, seemed impressive: the percentage of black voters in the South increased from 29.4 percent to 43.1 percent of blacks eligible to vote. But most of the success came in urban areas, where white opposition was less pronounced than in rural areas. In addition, many of those involved in voter registration were brutally attacked and jailed. The federal government provided minimal protection on the whole.

In some instances, Robert Kennedy hoped to prevent racial violence by a show of federal force, as in the case of **James Meredith,** who integrated the University of Mississippi in 1962. Kennedy sent 500 federal marshals to guard Meredith, hoping that a show of force would prevent violence. The tactic did not work. Thousands of white students and nonstudents attacked Meredith and the marshals. Two people were killed and 166 marshals were wounded before 5,000 army troops arrived. Protected by federal forces, Meredith, who had transferred from a black college, became the University of Mississippi's first African-American graduate in May 1963.

Martin Luther King, Jr., and the SCLC focused their attention next on overturning segregation in Birmingham, Alabama. Organizers planned a series of protest marches demanding the integration of Birmingham's businesses. On Good Friday, 1963, King led the first march and along with others was arrested. From his cell, he wrote a nineteen-page "letter" aimed at those who denounced his activism in favor of patience. The "Letter from a Birmingham Jail" called for immediate and continuous, peaceful civil disobedience. Freedom was "never given voluntarily by the oppressor," King asserted, but "must be demanded by the oppressed." Smuggled out of jail and read aloud in churches and printed in newspapers across the nation, the letter rallied support for King's efforts in Birmingham.

On May 3, young and old alike filled the streets of Birmingham and confronted "Bull" Connor's police, who attacked the marchers with nightsticks, dogs, and high-pressure fire hoses. Television caught it all. Connor's brutality not only horrified much of the American public but caused many Birmingham blacks to reject the tactic of

public order laws Laws passed by many southern communities to discourage civil rights protests; they allowed the police to arrest anyone suspected of intending to disrupt public order.

James Meredith Black student admitted to the University of Mississippi under federal court order in 1962; in spite of rioting by racist mobs, he finished the year and graduated in 1963.

♦ On August 28, 1963, one-quarter of a million people gathered in Washington, D.C., to support racial equality. Martin Luther King, Jr., electrified the crowd by saying, "I have a dream that my four little children will one day live . . . where they will not be judged by the color of their skin but the content of their character." *Francis Miller, LIFE Magazine, © Time Warner Inc.*

nonviolence. The following day, many African Americans fought the police with stones and clubs. Fearing more violence, Birmingham's businessmen met with King on May 10, 1963, and agreed to hire black salespeople. Neither the agreement nor King's pleading, however, halted the violence. Two days later, President Kennedy ordered three thousand troops to Birmingham to maintain order.

Kennedy concluded that the time had come to fulfill his campaign promise to make civil rights a priority. In June 1963, observing that America could not be truly free "until all its citizens were free," he announced that he would send Congress civil rights legislation mandating integration in places of public accommodation.

To pressure Congress to act on the bill, King and other civil rights leaders organized the **March on Washington.** The August 28 march drew the largest crowd in American history, with over 250,000 people attending. King capped the day with an address that electrified the throng. He promised to continue the struggle until justice flowed "like a mighty stream," but he warned about a "whirlwind of revolt" if black rights were denied. "I have a dream," he offered, "that even Mississippi could become an oasis of freedom and justice" and that "all of God's children, black men and white men, Jews and Gentiles, Protestants and Catholics, will be able to join hands and sing . . . 'Free at last! Free at last! Thank God almighty, we are free at last!'"

The march and reactions to white violence against African Americans might have been expected to work in favor of civil rights legislation. But as of November 1963, when Kennedy left for a campaign trip to Dallas, Texas, his bill was still languishing in committee in the House of Representatives.

Flexible Response

If Kennedy was slow to bring federal power to bear on civil rights, he had no reluctance to use

nonviolence Doctrine of rejecting violence in favor of peaceful tactics as a means of gaining political objectives.

March on Washington Meeting of a quarter of a million civil rights supporters in Washington in 1963, at which Martin Luther King, Jr., delivered his "I Have a Dream" speech.

♦ Soviet leader Nikita Khrushchev met with John Kennedy at the Vienna Summit in June 1961. After their first meetings, Kennedy, who had been warned that Khrushchev's style ranged from "cherubic to choleric," was convinced that the Soviet leader had bested him and that he had appeared to be a man "with no guts." Following the Vienna Summit, Kennedy was determined to be tougher with the Soviets. "If Khrushchev wants to rub my nose in the dirt, it's all over," Kennedy stated after their meeting. *Wide World Photos.*

executive power when it came to foreign policy. Kennedy increased military spending to begin a buildup of both nuclear and conventional forces. Space exploration also received a new priority. In April 1961, the Soviets had hurled the first human being, **cosmonaut** Yuri Gagarin, into space. Kennedy informed Congress that funding was needed not only to catch up with the Soviets but to beat them to the moon by the end of the decade. Congress agreed and funded the *Apollo* project.

The country's Cold War challenges were not limited to racing against Soviet arms development and space exploration. An equally important confrontation had been shaping up in the developing regions of the globe. Kennedy employed the strategy of **flexible response** to win the "hearts and minds" of developing nations for the West. This strategy involved special military units like the Green Berets who were trained to deal with Communist insurgency by living off the land and gaining the people's trust. The strategy also featured the use of American economic aid and of the **Peace Corps,** composed of idealistic young men and women who volunteered to help the people of the developing world.

Confronting the Soviets

Kennedy's biggest immediate problem in the Third World lay just to the south of the Florida Keys. The presence of a Communist regime in Cuba was simply intolerable to Kennedy. In January 1961, the newly elected president approved the operation planned by the Eisenhower administration to topple Fidel Castro (see page 636).

The invasion of Cuba began on April 17, 1961. Over fourteen hundred CIA-trained Cuban exiles landed at the **Bay of Pigs.** The predicted uprisings

cosmonaut A Soviet astronaut.

flexible response Kennedy's strategy of considering a variety of military and nonmilitary options when facing foreign policy decisions.

Peace Corps Program established by President Kennedy in 1961 to send young American volunteers to other nations as educators, health workers, and technicians.

Bay of Pigs Site of a 1961 invasion of Cuba by Cuban exiles and mercenaries sponsored by the CIA; the invasion was crushed within three days and embarrassed the United States.

in support of the invaders did not occur, however, and within three days Castro's forces had captured or killed most of the invading force. Kennedy took responsibility for the fiasco but voiced no regrets for his aggressive policy.

To blunt the growing appeal of Castroism in Latin America, Kennedy announced a sweeping foreign-aid package, the **Alliance for Progress.** He proposed over $20 billion in aid to show that "liberty and progress walk hand in hand." In return, Latin American nations were to introduce land and tax reforms. Actions fell short of promises. The United States granted far less than proposed, and Latin American governments implemented few reforms and frequently squandered the aid, much of which ended up in the pockets of government officials. Throughout the 1960s in Latin America, the gap between rich and poor widened.

To try to recapture some of the "can-do" image deflated by the Bay of Pigs disaster, Kennedy sought an opportunity to stand toe to toe with the Soviets. That opportunity came when Soviet leader Nikita Khrushchev agreed to meet Kennedy in Vienna in June 1961 to discuss Berlin, Laos, and a nuclear test ban treaty. After his first private meeting with the Soviet leader, Kennedy was shaken and angry. He thought that Khrushchev had bullied him. In following meetings, Kennedy stood his ground more firmly, stressing that the United States would remain true to its international commitments, especially in Berlin. Khrushchev was unmoved and maintained a December deadline for Allied withdrawal from Berlin.

Returning home, Kennedy asked for large increases in military spending and called fifty-one thousand reservists to active duty. Some advisers advocated the use of force if the Soviets interfered with Western control of West Berlin. To some it appeared that Kennedy and Khrushchev were moving to the brink of war over Berlin. In August 1961, the Soviets added a new point of confrontation by erecting a wall between West and East Berlin to choke off the flow of refugees fleeing East Germany. Although the Berlin Wall challenged Western ideals of freedom, it did not directly threaten the West's presence in West Berlin. The Berlin crisis finally faded when Khrushchev announced that he no longer cared about the December deadline. The wall remained as a stark reminder of where Soviet and American interests collided.

Far more serious than the Berlin crisis was the Cuban missile crisis of October 1962. On October 14, an American U-2 spy plane discovered that medium-range nuclear missile sites were being built in Cuba. Such missiles would drastically reduce the time the United States had to launch a counterattack on the Soviet Union. Kennedy decided on a showdown with the Soviets over the missiles.

Kennedy rejected both an invasion of Cuba and air strikes against the missiles as too dangerous. Instead, he decided on a naval blockade of Cuba until Khrushchev met the U.S. demand to remove the missiles. On Wednesday, October 24, a confrontation seemed imminent as two Soviet freighters and a Russian submarine approached the quarantine line. The Soviet vessels, however, stopped short of the line. Khrushchev had decided not to test Kennedy's will. On October 26, he sent a message that the Soviet Union was ready to remove the missiles from Cuba if the United States publicly announced it would not invade the island. The basis of a solution had been found. The United States publicly pledged not to invade Cuba, and Khrushchev ordered the removal of the missiles. In a nonpublicized, separate agreement, the United States agreed to remove its missiles from Turkey.

Kennedy basked in the victory over Khrushchev, but he also recognized how near the world had come to nuclear war. Kennedy subsequently sought to defuse Soviet-American tensions. A "hotline" telephone link was established between Moscow and Washington to allow direct talks in case of another East-West crisis. In June 1963, Kennedy suggested that the United States would halt its nuclear testing. By July, American-Soviet negotiations produced the **Limited Test Ban Treaty.**

Alliance for Progress Program proposed by Kennedy in 1961 through which the United States provided aid for social and economic programs in Latin American countries.

Limited Test Ban Treaty Treaty signed by the United States, the USSR, and nearly one hundred other nations in 1963, banning nuclear weapons tests in the atmosphere, in outer space, and underwater.

It prohibited nuclear tests in the atmosphere, in space, and under the seas but allowed underground testing. By October 1963, one hundred nations had signed the treaty, although the two newest atomic powers, France and China, refused to participate.

Vietnam

Vietnam represented one of the most significant challenges that Kennedy faced. South Vietnamese president **Ngo Dinh Diem** was losing control of the countryside to the South Vietnamese Communist rebels, the **Viet Cong.** Kennedy rejected arguments that American troops were needed to turn the tide, but he did send more military and civilian "advisers." By November 1963, the United States had committed sixteen thousand advisers to Vietnam—compared with only a few hundred in 1961.

The Viet Cong were only part of the problem. Diem's administration was unpopular. A Roman Catholic whose family had been French officials, Diem did not believe in democracy. He ruled through a handpicked, largely Catholic bureaucracy. Everyone else, including Vietnam's Buddhists, the religious majority, opposed his rule. With American support, Diem cracked down on his opponents. Reformers, rival officers, and protesting Buddhists were jailed, tortured, and killed. In protest, on June 10, 1963, a Buddhist monk set himself on fire. Other **self-immolations** followed. To the shock of many Americans, Diem's sister-in-law, Madame Nhu, referred to the protests as "Buddhist barbecues." To Kennedy and his advisers, Diem had become a liability. The administration secretly informed several Vietnamese generals that it would approve of a change of government. The army acted on November 1, killing Diem and creating a new military government. However, the new government brought neither political stability nor better results against the Viet Cong.

Death in Dallas

In late 1963, Kennedy decided to visit Dallas, Texas, to try to heal divisions within the Texas Democratic party. There he was assassinated on November 22. Police quickly captured the reputed assassin, Lee Harvey Oswald. The next day, a local nightclub owner, Jack Ruby, shot Oswald to death in the basement of the police station. Many wondered if Oswald had acted alone or was part of a larger conspiracy. To dispel rumors, the government formed a commission headed by Chief Justice Earl Warren to investigate the assassination. The commission announced that Oswald had acted alone. Most Americans accepted the findings at the time.

Kennedy's assassination traumatized the nation. Many people canonized the fallen president as a brilliant, innovative chief executive who combined vitality, youth, and good looks with forceful leadership and good judgment. Lyndon B. Johnson, sworn in as president as he flew back to Washington on the plane carrying Kennedy's body, was not cut from the same cloth. Kennedy had attended the best eastern schools, enjoyed the cultural and social life associated with wealth, and liked to surround himself with intellectuals. Johnson, a product of public schools and a state college education, distrusted intellectuals. Raised in the hill country of Texas, his passion was politics. By 1960, his congressional experience was unrivaled: he had served from 1937 to 1948 in the House of Representatives and from 1949 to 1961 in the Senate, where he had been Senate majority leader. Johnson knew how to wield political power and how to get things done in Washington.

Beyond the New Frontier

Five days after Kennedy's death, Johnson asked Congress for "no memorial oration or eulogy" for

Ngo Dinh Diem President of South Vietnam (1954–1963), who jailed and tortured opponents of his rule; he was assassinated in a coup in 1963.

Viet Cong Vietnamese Communist rebels in South Vietnam.

self-immolation Suicide by fire as an act of sacrifice to a cause.

the fallen president other than the passage of Kennedy's civil rights bill. The **Civil Rights Act of 1964** became law on July 2, 1964. The law made it illegal to discriminate for reasons of race, religion, or gender in places and businesses that served the public. Putting force behind the law, Congress established a federal Fair Employment Practices Committee (FEPC) and empowered the executive branch to withhold federal funds from institutions that violated the act.

Johnson wanted to do more, however, than pass legislation that had been initiated by Kennedy. He wanted to create his own legacy. His first step in realizing this ambition was declaring the **War on Poverty** in 1964.

Johnson's assault against the poverty that afflicted at least one-fifth of the American people was to be fought on two fronts: expanding opportunities and improving the social environment. He believed that only the federal government was capable of this task. Therefore, he projected a huge expansion of federal responsibility for social welfare. Special efforts would be made to provide education and job training for the young: "Our chief weapons will be better schools . . . better training, and better job opportunities to help more Americans, especially young Americans, to escape from squalor and misery." The Manpower and Development Training Act, the Job Corps, Head Start, and the Work Incentive Program all aimed at providing new educational and economic opportunities for the disadvantaged. In 1964, the Job Corps enrolled unemployed teenagers and young adults (ages 16 to 21) who lacked employable skills. In 1965, Head Start reached out to disadvantaged preschoolers to give them an opportunity to gain important thinking and social skills.

Conservative Response

Johnson's social programs prompted a reaction from a group of conservatives and ultraconservatives called the New Right. The New Right decried many of the political and social changes taking place in society. According to these conservatives, liberals and a national welfare state were destroying the traditional American values of localism, self-help, and individualism.

The New Right targeted the Supreme Court and Chief Justice Earl Warren as the major causes of what it regarded as the subversion of American life. The rabidly anti-Communist John Birch Society even demanded the impeachment of Warren. From the mid-1950s through the 1960s, the Supreme Court under Warren handed down one decision after another that angered conservatives. To them, the Court seemed to be forcing the liberal agenda of individual rights, social justice, and equality down society's throat. The Court, they believed, had promoted civil rights and the rights of individuals at the expense of society. In *Gideon v. Wainright* (1963) and *Escobedo v. Illinois* (1964), the Court's rulings declared that all defendants had a right to an attorney, even if the state had to provide one. In *Miranda v. Arizona* (1966), the Court held that anyone who was arrested had to be informed of his or her right to remain silent and to have an attorney present during questioning (now called the Miranda warning). The New Right argued that these decisions had tipped the scales of justice in favor of the criminal.

Conservatives believed that the Warren Court's actions also threatened traditional values by allowing the publication of sexually explicit materials and by forbidding prayers and the reading of the Bible in public schools (*Abington v. Schempp*, 1963). The Court's decision in *Griswold v. Connecticut* (1964), which overturned Connecticut's laws forbidding the sale of contraceptives, also disturbed them.

The 1964 Election

The Republican presidential candidate in 1964 offered conservatives a chance to reassert their traditional values and patriotic ideals. Senator Barry Goldwater of Arizona had voted against the Civil Rights Act of 1964 and against censuring Senator

Civil Rights Act of 1964 Law that barred segregation in public facilities and forbade employers to discriminate on the basis of race, religion, sex, or national origin.

War on Poverty Lyndon Johnson's program to help Americans escape poverty through education, job training, and community development.

Joseph McCarthy in 1954 (see page 629). He had opposed "Big Government" and he promised to deal with Communists more forcefully. Whereas Johnson promised not to Americanize the war in Vietnam, Goldwater was willing to commit American troops and even to use nuclear weapons.

In a war of slogans and television spots, Johnson's ads scored more points. Democrats answered one memorable Goldwater slogan, "In your heart you know he's right," by claiming, "In your guts you know he's nuts." Another Johnson ad suggested that a trigger-happy Goldwater would lead the nation into a nuclear holocaust. In a lopsided election, Americans gave Goldwater only 38.4 percent of the popular vote. Over forty new Democratic legislators swelled the Democratic majority in the House of Representatives.

Shaping the Great Society

Having beaten Goldwater, Johnson pushed forward legislation to enact his **Great Society**—his vision of an America freed of racial injustice and poverty. Between 1965 and 1968, more than sixty programs were put in place. Most sought to provide better economic and social opportunities. The Appalachian Regional Development Act (1965), Public Works and Development Act (1965), and Model Cities Act (1966) focused on developing economic growth in cities and long-depressed regional areas. The Omnibus Housing Bill (1965) provided $8 billion for constructing low- and middle-income housing and supplementing low-income rent programs.

Johnson's priorities, however, were health and education. The Elementary and Secondary Education Act (1965) was the first general educational funding act passed by the federal government. It granted more than a billion dollars to public and parochial schools for textbooks, library materials, and special-education programs. Poorer school districts were supposed to receive the highest percentage of federal support, but much of the money went to more affluent suburban school districts.

Passage of the Medical Care Act (1965) represented an even greater achievement to Johnson. This act revolutionized healthcare by providing **Medicare** to help the elderly cover their medical costs. For those on welfare, **Medicaid** provided funds to states to provide free healthcare.

Johnson also was committed to ending racial discrimination. He signed an executive order requiring government contractors to ensure nondiscrimination in jobs. He also appointed the first African-American cabinet member, Secretary of Housing and Urban Development Robert Weaver; the first African-American woman federal justice, Constance Baker Motley; and the first black on the Supreme Court, Thurgood Marshall.

Johnson followed up these appointments with proposals for a voting rights bill. Civil rights leaders had made voting rights their next major issue after passage of the Civil Rights Act of 1964. For nearly one hundred years, most southern whites had viewed voting as a privilege reserved for whites. Led by SNCC's Bob Moses, the **Freedom Summer** of 1964 called for whites and blacks to go to Mississippi to open "Freedom Schools" and to encourage African Americans to register to vote. The Freedom Schools taught basic literacy and black history and tutored African Americans so that they could pass the Mississippi voter literacy test. Prospective black voters in Mississippi had to convince a white registrar that they understood the Constitution and the duties of citizenship. White hostility made the work of registering black voters dangerous. Violence occurred almost daily in Mississippi from June through August 1964. Six Freedom Summer workers were murdered, but the crusade registered nearly sixty thousand new African-American voters. By December 1964, Johnson concurred with

Great Society Social program that Johnson announced in 1965; it included the War on Poverty, protection of civil rights, and funding for education.

medicare Program of health insurance for the elderly and disabled established in 1965; it provides government payment for healthcare supplied by private doctors and hospitals.

medicaid Program of health insurance for the poor established in 1965; it provides states with money to buy healthcare for people on welfare.

Freedom Summer Effort by Civil Rights groups in Mississippi to register black voters and cultivate black pride during the summer of 1964.

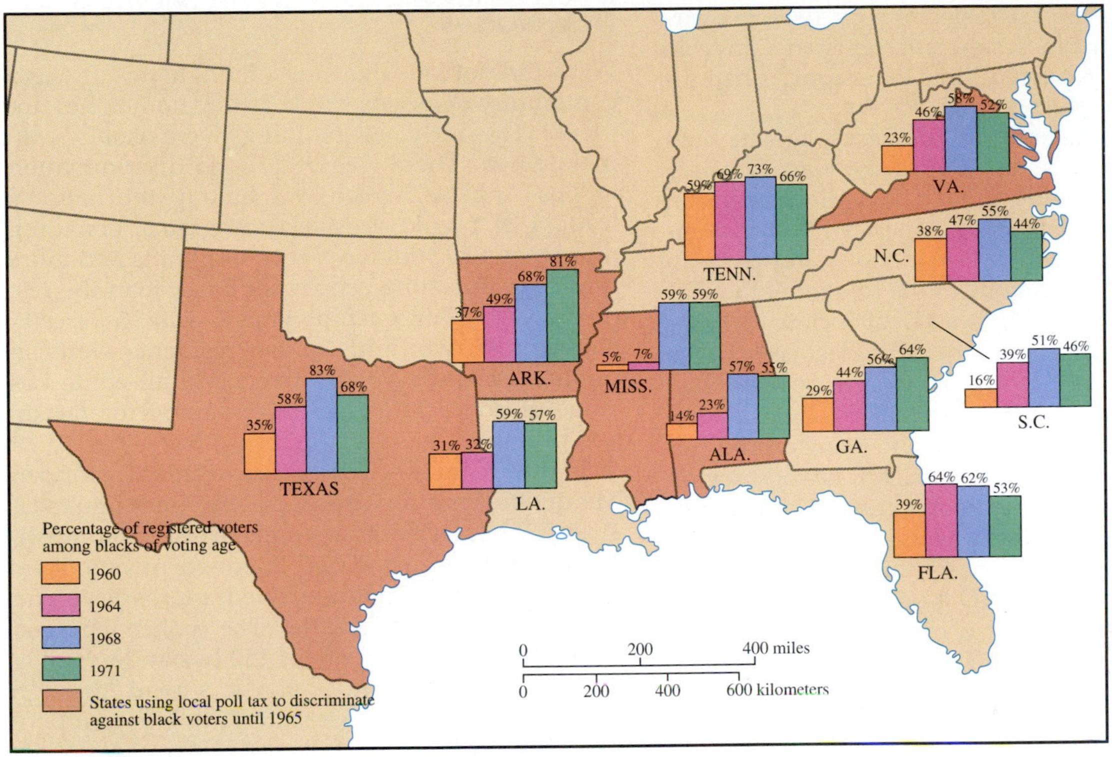

♦ **MAP 29.2 African Americans and the Southern Vote, 1960–1971** An important part of the civil rights movement was to reestablish the African-American vote that had been stripped away in the South following Reconstruction. Between 1960 and 1971, with the outlawing of the poll tax and other voter restrictions, African-American voter participation rose significantly across the South.

Martin Luther King, Jr., on the need for federal voting legislation.

Pointing to the violent response civil rights leaders had met with in Selma, Alabama, in March 1965, Johnson urged Congress to act. King had called for a **freedom march** from Selma to Montgomery because of the former town's adamant and violent opposition to integration. On March 7, 1965, hundreds of freedom marchers faced fifty Alabama state troopers and Sheriff Jim Clark's mounted officers at Selma's Pettus Bridge. After ordering the marchers to halt, the state troopers fired tear gas and charged. As the marchers fled back to Selma, Clark's men chased them down, wielding rubber tubing wrapped with barbed wire. Television coverage of the onslaught stirred nationwide condemnation of Clarks' tactics. Johnson told Governor George Wallace that he would not tolerate any further interference with the march. When twenty-five thousand people resumed the march on March 25, the National Guard escorted them.

In response to Johnson's pressure, Congress passed the 1965 **Voting Rights Act.** It banned a variety of methods, such as literacy tests, that states used to deny blacks the right to vote (see Map 29.2). In Selma, 60 percent of qualified African-American voters registered, voted, and stopped

freedom march Civil Rights march from Selma to Montgomery, Alabama, in March 1965.

Voting Rights Act Law passsed by Congress in 1965 that outlawed literacy and other voting tests and authorized federal supervision of elections in areas where black voting had been restricted.

Sheriff Clark's bid for reelection. By 1968, the percentage of African Americans registered to vote had risen by 30 percent; in Mississippi, it had increased from 7 percent to 67 percent.

Although Johnson's civil rights agenda met with great success, by 1966 many Great Society programs were underfunded and diminishing in popularity. An expanding American war in Vietnam, white backlash to urban riots, and partisan politics forced reductions in the budget of the War on Poverty. Still, by 1970 the Great Society had contributed to nearly a 10 percent decrease in the number of people living below the poverty line. Between 1963 and 1968, African-American unemployment fell nearly 42 percent. Johnson did not totally cure any of society's ills, but he did provide the basis for a more democratic and nondiscriminatory country. In the process, he widened the functions of the federal government more than any president since Franklin D. Roosevelt.

New Agendas

By the end of 1965, federal legislation had confirmed that *de jure* segregation—segregation established by local ordinances or state laws—was illegal in the United States. But equality depended on more than laws. Neither the 1964 Civil Rights Act nor the 1965 Voting Rights Act guaranteed justice, removed oppressive poverty, or provided jobs. *De facto* discrimination—the product of economics, social tradition, and custom—and prejudice remained.

African Americans' frustrations soon changed the nature of civil rights protest. By 1964, more than half of the nation's black population lived in northern cities, and more than a million mostly poor and unskilled blacks left the South during the 1960s. They entered an environment where unskilled jobs were declining and black unemployment was high. Poverty, false hopes, and frustrations led to increased violence and crime. African Americans saw largely white police forces as suppressors rather than protectors. By the mid-1960s, the nation's cities were primed for racial violence. Minor race riots had occurred in 1964, but it was the 1965 **Watts** riot that shook the nation.

New Voices

Watts did not look like most other ghettos. It was a community of largely single-family homes and duplexes. The fairly new buildings were usually well maintained. There was little open discrimination in Los Angeles, which was among the nation's leaders in public assistance programs, spending more than $500 million a year. But Watts had more than four times the people per block than the rest of the city. Male unemployment was 34 percent, and almost two-thirds of the residents were on public assistance. Finally, the nearly all-white Los Angeles police force had a reputation for racism and brutality.

In this climate, Officer Lee Minikus stopped Marquette Frye for drunk driving on August 11, 1965. What started as a simple arrest soon mushroomed into a major riot. A crowd of onlookers gathered as more police arrived and as Frye and Minikus began to scuffle. The police charged through the crowd of about 150 bystanders using nightsticks, and word quickly spread through Watts that the police were attacking innocent people. The Watts riot followed. Many residents pelted the police with stones and bottles and vented their anger by looting and setting fire to cars and stores. When firefighters and police arrived to restore order and to put out the flames, they had to dodge snipers' bullets and **Molotov cocktails.** It took fourteen thousand members of the California National Guard and over one thousand police and eight hundred sheriff's deputies to calm the storm. The costs were high: thirty-four dead, including twenty-eight African Americans, and over $45 million in property destroyed. Four thousand rioters were arrested.

The Watts riot shattered the complacency of many northern whites who had supported civil rights in the South while ignoring the plight of the

Watts Predominantly black neighborhood of Los Angeles where race riots in August 1965 did $45 million in damage and took the lives of twenty-eight blacks.

Molotov cocktail Makeshift bomb made of a bottle filled with gasoline.

inner cities. It also demonstrated a gap between northern blacks and many civil rights leaders. King discovered after the riot that the people of Watts had little use for his "dreams." He was shouted down and jeered. "Hell, we don't need no damn dreams," one skeptic remarked. "We want jobs."

Watts was only the beginning. More deadly urban riots followed, and a new, militant approach to racial and economic injustices erupted: the **Black Power** movement. A change in SNCC's leadership helped usher in a new era of black militancy. By the winter of 1965, Bob Moses had had too much of clubs, dogs, threats, and jails. Emotionally spent, he resigned and moved north. SNCC's new leader, **Stokely Carmichael,** exalted Black Power. "I'm not going to beg the white man for anything I deserve," he announced. "I'm going to take it." SNCC and CORE quickly changed from biracial, nonviolent organizations to Black Power movements.

Among those receptive to a more militant approach were the **Black Muslims** (the Nation of Islam), founded by Elijah Muhammad in the 1930s. The Black Muslims attracted mostly young males and demanded adherence to a strict moral code that prohibited the use of drugs and alcohol. They preached black superiority and independence from an evil white world. By the early 1960s, there were nearly a hundred thousand Black Muslims, but most whites were concerned with only one: **Malcolm X.**

By the age of 20, Malcolm Little's life of hard drugs, pimping, and burglary had put him in prison. Behind bars, his intellectual abilities blossomed. He devoured the prison library, took correspondence courses, and converted to the Nation of Islam, becoming Malcolm X. On his release in 1952, he quickly became one of the Black Muslims' most powerful leaders. A mesmerizing speaker, he rejected integration with a white society that, he said, emasculated blacks by denying them power and personal identity. "Our enemy is the white man!" he roared. But in 1964, he reconsidered the policy of rejecting cooperation with whites. Although still a black nationalist, he recognized that to achieve their goals, Black Muslims needed to cooperate with some whites. He broke with Elijah Muhammad, a defection that cost him his life. On February 21, 1965, three Black Muslims assassinated him in Harlem. After his death, Malcolm X's *Autobiography,* chronicling his personal triumph over white oppression, became a revered guide for many blacks.

Malcolm X represented only one model for urban blacks. Others pursued direct action against white power and advocated violence. Huey P. Newton and Bobby Seale organized the **Black Panthers** in Oakland, California, in 1966. They were primarily noticeable for adopting Mao Zedong's adage that "power flows from the barrel of a gun." Their willingness to use violence frightened many, but others applauded their militance. New SNCC leader H. Rap Brown told listeners to grab their guns, burn the town down, and shoot the "honky." The summer of 1967 seemed to bring Brown's words to life. Over seventy-five major riots took place, the deadliest occurring in Detroit and Newark, resulting in a nationwide total of eighty-seven dead.

After a third summer of urban riots, President Lyndon Johnson created a special commission chaired by Governor Otto Kerner of Illinois to investigate their causes. The committee's report, issued in March 1968, put the primary blame on the racist attitudes of white America. The study

Black Power Movement beginning in 1966 that rejected the nonviolent, coalition-building approach of traditional civil rights groups and advocated black control of black organizations.

Stokely Carmichael Civil rights activist who led SNCC and who coined the term "Black Power" to describe the need for blacks to use militant tactics to force whites to accept political change.

Black Muslims Popular name for the Nation of Islam, an African-American religious group founded by Elijah Muhammad, which professed Islamic religious beliefs and emphasized black separatism.

Malcolm X Black activist who advocated black separatism as a member of the Nation of Islam; in 1963 he converted to orthodox Islam, and two years later he was assassinated.

Black Panthers Black revolutionary party founded in 1966 that accepted violence as a means of social change; many of its leaders were killed in confrontations with police or sent to prison.

described two Americas, one white and one black, and concluded:

> *Pervasive discrimination and segregation in employment, education, and housing have resulted in the continuing exclusion of great numbers of Negroes from the benefits of economic progress.*

The Kerner Commission believed that the solution to America's racial problem was a "compassionate, massive and sustained" commitment "backed by the resources of the most powerful and richest nation on this earth."

Just a month later, the assassination of Martin Luther King, Jr., sparked a new series of riots across the country. King had been in Memphis supporting striking black sanitation workers when, on April 4, 1968, he was gunned down by James Earl Ray, a white racist. African Americans took to the streets in over 125 cities. Sections of Washington, D.C., were engulfed in flames.

As American cities burned and cries of "Burn, Baby, Burn" and "Black Power!" emerged from the smoke, a white backlash occurred. Many Americans backed away from supporting civil rights. Republican politicians were especially vocal. California Governor Ronald Reagan argued the "riff-raff" theory of urban problems: "mad dogs" and "lawbreakers" were the sole cause of the trouble. Governor Spiro Agnew of Maryland blamed activists like H. Rap Brown. Most Americans applauded as police cracked down on the Black Panthers, arresting or killing the party's membership. As the 1968 political campaign began, law and order replaced the Great Society and the War on Poverty as the main issue.

♦ "We're in a time that's divorced from the past," wrote author Norman Mailer, and from Berkeley to Harvard Yard, college campuses were becoming battlegrounds of the social, cultural, and political changes that were sweeping the nation. Whether participating in the counterculture or the Freedom Summer, or opposing the war in Vietnam or college restrictions, America's youth demanded new values and attitudes in the 1960s. *Michael Barson Collection/Past Perfect.*

The Challenge of Youth

As alarming to many Americans as the revolution that was reshaping African-American attitudes was the growing tendency of the nation's white youth to reject traditional values. Although the majority of young people remained quite traditional, an increasing number advocated alternative values. The transformation was particularly noticeable on college campuses.

Many students began to question the goal of education, particularly at huge institutions like the University of California at Berkeley and the University of Michigan. Students complained that concern for individuals was missing from education. Education seemed sterile—more like an assembly line producing a standardized product than an effort to create an independent, thinking individual. In *Growing Up Absurd,* Paul Goodman argued that schools destroyed creativity and replaced it with conformity. Reflecting Goodman's view, many students demanded freedom of expression and a new, more flexible attitude from college administrators and faculty.

Campus activists denounced course requirements and restrictions on dress, behavior, and living arrangements. By the end of the decade, many colleges and schools had relaxed or eliminated dress codes that required the wearing of coats and ties for men and dresses for women. Long hair was accepted for males, and casual clothes like faded blue jeans and shorts became common dress for both sexes on most college campuses. Colleges also lifted dorm curfews and other residence requirements. Some dorms became coed. Academic departments reduced the number of mandatory courses. By the early 1970s, many colleges had introduced programs in fields like African-American, Native American, and women's studies.

Setting their sights beyond the campus community, student activists urged that the campus should be a center for social change. **Students for a Democratic Society (SDS),** organized at the University of Michigan in the early 1960s by Tom Hayden and Al Haber, charged that business and government ignored social inequalities. In 1962, SDS issued its Port Huron Statement, which maintained,

> *The search for truly democratic alternatives to the present, and a commitment to social experimentation with them, is a worthy and fulfilling human enterprise, one which moves us and, we hope, others today.*

Hayden argued that the country should strive to build "an environment for people to live in with dignity and creativeness."

The earliest major confrontation between students and university authorities occurred at Berkeley in 1964. Activists led by Mario Savio protested when the administration tried to prevent students from using a plaza on campus to recruit supporters and solicit funds for various social and political causes. Fresh from the Freedom Summer, Savio demanded freedom of speech on campus. Claiming that the university was not fulfilling its moral obligation to provide an open forum for free thought, Savio asked students and faculty to disrupt the university's activities. Over six thousand students responded, seizing the administration building, boycotting classes, and yelling four-letter words. Although Savio and two other organizers were expelled and sentenced to four months in jail, Chancellor Clark Kerr agreed to allow freedom of expression on campus.

The Berkeley Free Speech Movement encouraged other campus organizers. Student activists in growing numbers focused their attention on civil rights, the environment, and social and sexual norms. By the late sixties, though, their loudest protests opposed American foreign policy, the **military-industrial complex,** and the war in Vietnam. Opposition to the war further expanded the number of student activists.

The youth movement's discontent also found expression in what became known as the counterculture. Many young people came to spurn the traditional moral and social values of their parents. "Don't trust anyone over 30" became the motto of the young generation. The counterculture glorified freedom of the spirit and self-knowledge.

Music was one of the most prominent forms of defiance. Musicians like Bob Dylan and Joan Baez challenged society with protest and antiwar songs. Folk music and protest rock, however, were only a small part of the music challenge. For the majority, rock 'n' roll remained dominant. Performers like the **Beatles,** a British group that exploded on the American music scene in 1964, were among the most popular. The behavior and songs of other British imports such as the Rolling Stones and the Animals depicted a life of pleasure and lack of social restraints. The Grateful Dead and Jimi Hendrix turned rock 'n' roll into a new form of music, psychedelic **acid rock,**

Students for a Democratic Society Left-wing student organization founded in 1962 to criticize American materialism and call for social justice.

military-industrial complex Term first used by Eisenhower to describe the arms industry; in the 1960s, it was used by radicals to describe all those in power who benefited from U.S. militarism.

Beatles English rock group that gained international fame in 1964 and disbanded in 1970; they were known for the intelligence of their lyrics and their sophisticated instrumentation.

acid rock Rock music having a driving, repetitive beat and lyrics that suggest psychedelic drug experiences.

whose swirls of sound and lyrics acclaimed a drug culture and attacked social conventions.

The message of much music of the sixties was wrapped up in drug use—get "high" or "stoned." For many in the sixties generation, marijuana, or "pot," was the primary means to get high. Marijuana advocates claimed that, unlike the nation's traditional drug, alcohol, it reduced aggression and heightened perception. Thus, they argued, marijuana contributed to the counterculture's ideals of peace, serenity, and self-awareness. A more dangerous and unpredictable drug popular with some was LSD, lysergic acid diethylamide. "Acid" was a hallucinogenic drug that altered the user's perceptions of reality. Harvard psychology professor **Timothy Leary** argued for its widespread consumption. He believed that by "tripping" on LSD, people could free themselves from the rat race: "turn on, tune in, and drop out." Drugs offered some within the counterculture a new and liberating experience. But they also proved to be self-destructive and deadly, contributing to the deaths of musicians Jimi Hendrix, Jim Morrison, and Janis Joplin.

Another realm of traditional American values the counterculture overturned was sex. Some young people appalled their parents and society by questioning and rejecting the values that placed restrictions on sexual activities. A new openness about sexuality and a relaxation of the stigma on premarital sex turned out to be a significant legacy of the sixties. But the philosophy of **free love** also had a negative side, as increased sexual activity contributed to a rapid rise in venereal disease.

Perhaps the most colorful and best-known advocates of the counterculture were the **Hippies.** Seeking a life of peace, love, and self-awareness, Hippies tried to distance themselves from conventional society. They flocked in large numbers to northern California, especially to the Haight-Ashbury neighborhood of San Francisco. Elsewhere, some Hippie groups abandoned the "old-fashioned" nuclear family and lived together as extended families in communes. Hippies expressed their nonconformism by favoring long, unkempt hair and ratty blue jeans or long, flowered dresses. Although the number of true Hippie dropouts was small, their style of dress and grooming greatly influenced young Americans.

The influence of the counterculture peaked in the summer of 1969, when an army of teens and young adults converged on **Woodstock,** New York, for the largest free rock concert in history. For three days, through summer rains and deepening mud, more than four hundred thousand came together in a temporary open-air community while popular rock-'n'-roll bands performed day and night. Touted as three days of peace and love, sex, drugs, and rock 'n' roll, Woodstock symbolized for a few fleeting days the power of counterculture values to promote cooperation and happiness.

Timothy Leary Harvard professor and counterculture figure who advocated the expansion of consciousness through the use of drugs such as LSD.

free love Popular belief among members of the counterculture in the 1960s in having sexual activity with as many partners as they liked.

Hippies Members of the counterculture in the 1960s who rejected the competitiveness and materialism of American society and searched for peace, love, and autonomy.

Woodstock Free rock concert in Woodstock, New York, in August 1969, which attracted 400,000 people and was remembered as the classic expression of the counterculture.

SUMMARY

Expectations
Constraints
Choices
Outcomes

The *outcome* of John F. Kennedy's election was a wave of renewed optimism and liberalism. Kennedy's call for a more responsible society and government was at the heart of his New Frontier. Kennedy raised *expectations,* but it was Lyndon B.

Johnson's Great Society that greatly expanded the role of government in social affairs. Heightened *expectations* were clearly visible among the African Americans who looked for legislation to end segregation and discrimination. As Kennedy took office, African-American leaders *chose* to launch a series of sit-ins and freedom marches. Kennedy responded by introducing a civil rights act in 1963 that was finally passed in 1964 after his assassination.

In foreign policy, Kennedy *chose* to expand the international struggle against communism. Confrontations over Berlin and Cuba, a heightened arms race, and an expanded commitment to Vietnam were the *outcomes.*

As president, Johnson *chose* to expand on the slain president's New Frontier. The 1964 Civil Rights Act, the 1965 Voting Rights Act, and Great Society legislation were designed to wage war on poverty and discrimination, to provide federal aid for education, and to create a national system of health insurance for the poor and elderly. But by 1968, growing societal and political divisions *constrained* liberalism. African-American activists *chose* to become more militant in their demands for social and economic equality. The nation's youth, too, seemed unwilling to accept the traditional values of society, and they demanded change. Disturbed by the turmoil, conservatives and many moderate Americans *chose* to oppose government programs that appeared to favor the poor and minorities at their expense. The *outcome* was that a decade that had begun with great promise produced disappointment and disillusionment for many.

SUGGESTED READINGS

Anderson, Terry H. *The Movement and the Sixties* (1995).

A skillful examination of the social and cultural currents of the 1960s.

Bernstein, Irving. *Promises Kept: John F. Kennedy's New Frontier* (1991).

A brief and balanced account of Kennedy's presidency that nonetheless presents a favorable report of the accomplishments and legacy of the New Frontier.

Berschloss, Michael. *The Crisis Years: Kennedy and Khrushchev, 1960–1963* (1991).

A strong narrative account of the Cold War during the Kennedy administration and the personal duel between the leaders of the two superpowers.

Carson, Clayton. *In Struggle: SNCC and the Black Awakening of the 1960s* (1981).

A useful study that uses the development of SNCC to examine the changing patterns of the civil rights movement and the emergence of black nationalism.

Kearns, Doris. *Lyndon Johnson and the American Dream* (1977).

An effective study of how Johnson's background and values shaped his career and the Great Society.

Wolfe, Tom. *The Electric Kool-Aid Acid Test* (1968).

A classic account of the dimensions of the counterculture.

Easy Rider (1969) and *The Graduate* (1967) are two period films that critique traditional social and cultural norms and provide a glimpse of the "values" of the 1960s.

The Debate over Black Power

The Context

By 1965, the civil rights movement had made significant changes in American society. Segregation was illegal under the 1964 Civil Rights Act. Yet many African Americans still were denied equality, were mired in poverty, and felt powerless. The outcome was increasing anger among many African Americans, who replaced the philosophy of nonviolence and passive resistance with aggressive self-defense and a philosophy of "Black Power." Used initially by Paul Robeson following the Little Rock crisis (1957), the phrase burst onto the front pages on June 16, 1966, when Stokely Carmichael renewed the call for Black Power. Quickly, its advocates seemed to drown out calls for "Freedom Now." A white marcher recalled that the "thundering" demands for Black Power seemed to him "chilling . . . frightening." (For further information on the context, see pages 654–656.)

The Historical Question

The phrase "Black Power" grabbed headlines. To many white Americans, it seemed threatening. To many African Americans, it signaled the need to understand the race issue and its resolution in a different way and to make new choices. There was no standard definition of the term. What was Black Power? Was it a call for revolution and racial separation, a pronouncement of racial pride, a cry of desperation?

The Challenge

Using the sources provided, along with other information you have read, write an essay or hold a discussion on the following question. Cite evidence in the sources to support your conclusions. **What meanings did people give to the concept of Black Power? What historical and social experiences shaped these meanings?**

The Sources

1 After Stokely Carmichael called for Black Power, he wrote an essay in the *Massachusetts Review* in which he sought to explain the origins and concerns of the Black Power movement. He said:

Negroes are defined by two forces, their blackness and their powerlessness. There have been traditionally two communities in America. The White community, which controlled and defined the forms that all institutions within the society would take, and the Negro community, which has been excluded from participation in power decisions that shaped the society. . . .

In recent years the answer . . . has been . . . something called "integration." According to the advocates of integration, social justice will be accomplished by "integrating the Negro into the . . . society from which he has been traditionally excluded." . . .

This concept . . . had to be based on the assumption that there was nothing of value in the Negro community . . . so the thing to do was to siphon off the "acceptable" Negroes into the surrounding middle-class white community. . . . Now, black people must look . . . to issues of collective power.

. . . The political and social rights of Negroes have been and always will be negotiable and expandable the moment they conflict with the interests of our "allies." If we do not learn from history, we are doomed to repeat it, and that is precisely the lesson of Reconstruction . . .

. . . To the extent that we are dependent on . . . other groups, we are vulnerable to their influence and domination.

2 Bayard Rustin, long-time civil rights advocate and a past official of CORE, opposed Carmichael's nationalism and separatism. But, as he explained in *Commentary* (1965), African Americans still faced many constraints. He wrote:

The very decade which has witnessed the decline of legal Jim Crow has also seen the rise of de facto *segregation. . . . More Negroes are unemployed today than in 1954. . . . More Negroes attend* de facto *segregated schools today than when the Supreme Court handed down its famous decision. . . .*

. . . Last summer's riots were not race riots; they were outbursts of class aggression in a society where class and color definitions are converging disastrously. . . .

We need allies. The future of the Negro struggle depends on whether the contradictions of this society can be resolved by a coalition of progressive forces which become the effective *political majority.*

3 In 1966, Lerone Bennett, Jr., senior editor of *Ebony*, explained the underlying problems facing black Americans and American society. He wrote:

There is no Negro problem in America. . . .

The problem of race . . . is a white problem . . . white America created, invented the race problem . . . racism is a mask for a much deeper problem involving not the victims of racism but the perpetrators. . . .

It is fashionable . . . to think of racism as a vast impersonal system for which no one is responsible. . . . Racism did not fall from the sky; it was not secreted by insects. No: racism in America was made by man, neighborhood by neighborhood, law by law, restrictive covenent by restrictive covenant, deed by deed.

4 In 1967, President Lyndon Johnson created a commission chaired by Governor Otto Kerner to investigate the causes of racial strife that had swept across America and to recommend possible solutions. In March 1968, the final report provided a bleak image of race relations in the United States.

The events of the summer of 1967 are in large part the culmination of 300 years of racial prejudice. . . . Our nation is moving toward two societies, one black, one white—separate and unequal. . . . Discrimination and segregation have long permeated much of American life; they now threaten the future of every American. . . . This deepening racial division is not inevitable. The movement apart can be reversed. . . .

Violence and destruction must be ended—in the streets of the ghetto and in the lives of people. . . . What white Americans have never fully understood—and what the Negro can never forget—is that white society is deeply implicated in the ghetto. White institutions created it, white institutions maintain it, and white society condones it.

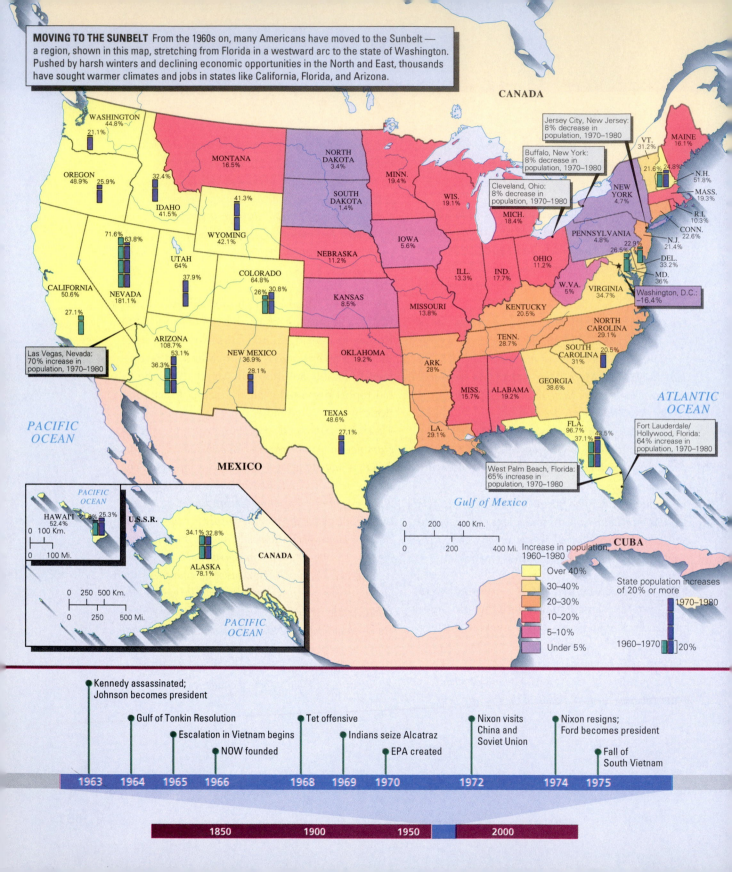

MOVING TO THE SUNBELT From the 1960s on, many Americans have moved to the Sunbelt — a region, shown in this map, stretching from Florida in a westward arc to the state of Washington. Pushed by harsh winters and declining economic opportunities in the North and East, thousands have sought warmer climates and jobs in states like California, Florida, and Arizona.

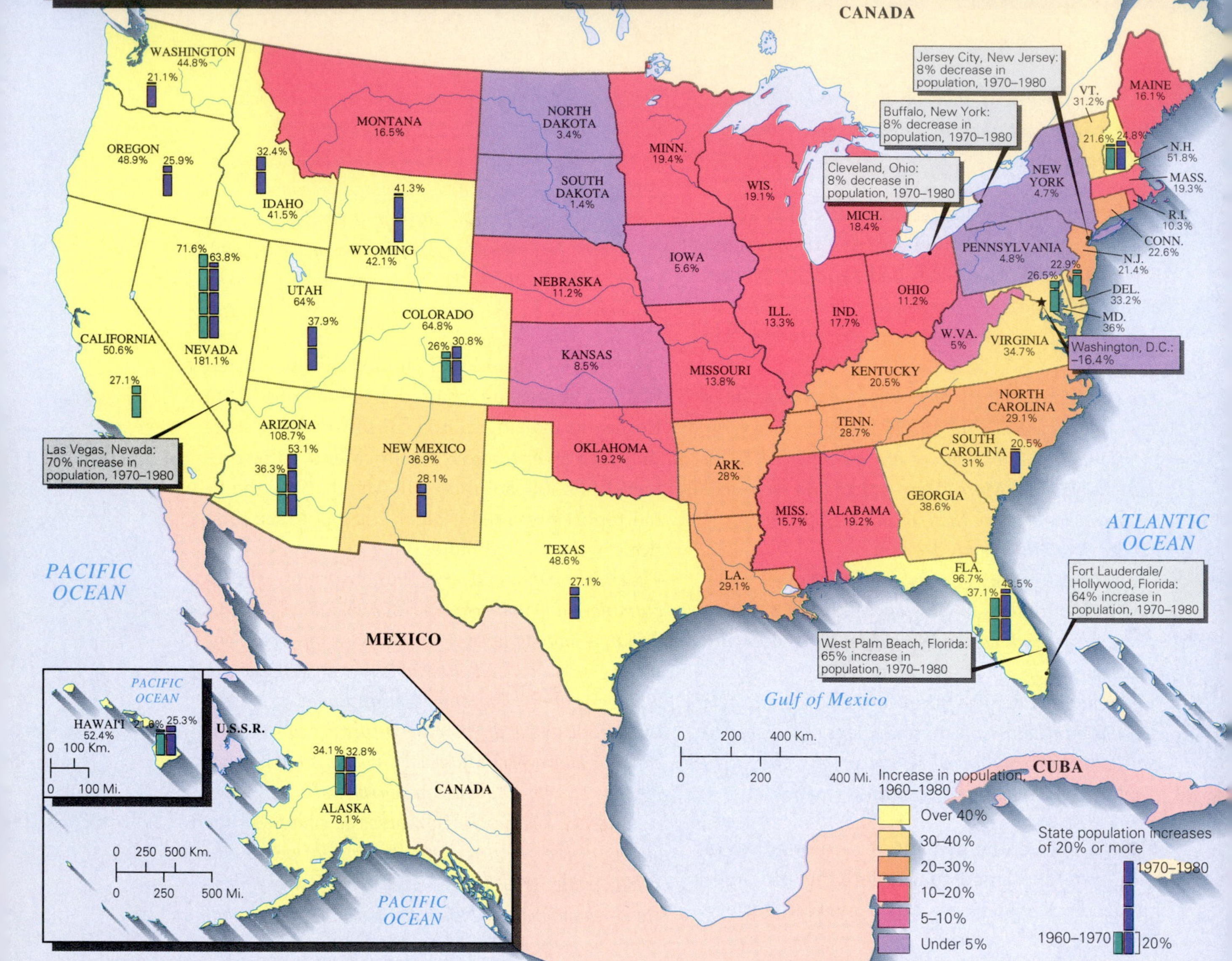

CANADA
WASHINGTON 44.8%
21.1%
OREGON 48.9%
25.9%
IDAHO 41.5%
32.4%
MONTANA 16.5%
WYOMING 42.1%
41.3%
CALIFORNIA 50.6%
27.1%
NEVADA 181.1%
71.6%
63.8%
UTAH 64%
37.9%
COLORADO 64.8%
26%
30.8%
ARIZONA 108.7%
36.3%
53.1%
NEW MEXICO 36.9%
28.1%
NORTH DAKOTA 3.4%
SOUTH DAKOTA 1.4%
NEBRASKA 11.2%
KANSAS 8.5%
OKLAHOMA 19.2%
TEXAS 48.6%
27.1%
MINN. 19.4%
IOWA 5.6%
MISSOURI 13.8%
ARK. 28%
LA. 29.1%
WIS. 19.1%
ILL. 13.3%
MICH. 18.4%
IND. 17.7%
OHIO 11.2%
KENTUCKY 20.5%
TENN. 28.7%
MISS. 15.7%
ALABAMA 19.2%
GEORGIA 38.6%
FLA. 96.7%
37.1%
43.5%
SOUTH CAROLINA 31%
20.5%
NORTH CAROLINA 29.1%
VIRGINIA 34.7%
W.VA. 5%
PENNSYLVANIA 4.8%
NEW YORK 4.7%
VT. 31.2%
MAINE 16.1%
N.H. 51.8%
21.6%
24.8%
MASS. 19.3%
R.I. 10.3%
CONN. 22.6%
N.J. 21.4%
22.9%
DEL. 33.2%
26.5%
MD. 36%
Jersey City, New Jersey: 8% decrease in population, 1970–1980
Buffalo, New York: 8% decrease in population, 1970–1980
Cleveland, Ohio: 8% decrease in population, 1970–1980
Washington, D.C.: –16.4%
Las Vegas, Nevada: 70% increase in population, 1970–1980
Fort Lauderdale/Hollywood, Florida: 64% increase in population, 1970–1980
West Palm Beach, Florida: 65% increase in population, 1970–1980
PACIFIC OCEAN
ATLANTIC OCEAN
Gulf of Mexico
MEXICO
CUBA
0 200 400 Km.
0 200 400 Mi.
PACIFIC OCEAN
HAWAI'I 52.4%
21.6%
25.3%
0 100 Km.
0 100 Mi.
U.S.S.R.
ALASKA 78.1%
34.1%
32.8%
CANADA
0 250 500 Km.
0 250 500 Mi.
PACIFIC OCEAN
Increase in population, 1960–1980
Over 40%
30–40%
20–30%
10–20%
5–10%
Under 5%
State population increases of 20% or more
1970–1980
1960–1970
20%

- **1963** Kennedy assassinated; Johnson becomes president
- **1964** Gulf of Tonkin Resolution
- **1965** Escalation in Vietnam begins
- **1966** NOW founded
- **1968** Tet offensive
- **1969** Indians seize Alcatraz
- **1970** EPA created
- **1972** Nixon visits China and Soviet Union
- **1974** Nixon resigns; Ford becomes president
- **1975** Fall of South Vietnam

1850 1900 1950 2000

CHAPTER 30

America Under Stress, 1963–1975

Johnson and the World

- What expectations led Lyndon Johnson to choose the policy of escalating America's role in Vietnam?
- What were the political, social, and military outcomes of his decision?

Expanding the American Dream

- What constraints did women, Latinos, and American Indians face in American society, and how did they organize to promote change?

Nixon and the Balance of Power

- What choices did Richard Nixon make to achieve an "honorable" peace in Vietnam?
- How did Nixon's choices in shaping Cold War policies differ from those favored by earlier administrations?

Nixon and Politics

- How did Nixon's choices in dealing with the economy and the environment reflect his pragmatic conservatism?
- Why did Nixon achieve such a huge success in the 1972 election? What expectations and constraints led to Watergate?

INTRODUCTION

Expectations
Constraints
Choices
Outcomes

The Sixties began with a wave of optimism and confidence in the ability of the national government to improve society and promote American interests abroad. In 1963, those *expectations* provided the new president, Lyndon Johnson, an opportunity to create his Great Society. In foreign affairs, Johnson had less ambitious *expectations.* He seemed content to continue Kennedy's policies, especially in Vietnam. But he was determined that the United States not be beaten by the Communists of a "two-bit" nation like North Vietnam.

An array of *constraints* blocked any dramatic increase in the American military role in South Vietnam, which many regarded as necessary to defeat the Communists. Sudden escalation would be expensive, could weaken support for Johnson's domestic program, and might drive the Chinese and the Soviets to increase their support of North Vietnam. To the president, the best *choice* seemed to be a carefully controlled, gradual escalation of American force. The administration *expected* the North Vietnamese would then abandon their efforts to conquer South Vietnam.

That strategy failed miserably. North Vietnam *chose* to meet escalation with escalation, until many Americans turned against both the war and Johnson. In 1968, Johnson *chose* to start peace negotiations with North Vietnam. Unexpectedly, he also announced that he would not seek re-election.

The Republicans rallied behind Richard Nixon. He called for a restoration of national prestige and a reassertion of the values that had made the nation strong. Nixon played on the uneasy *expectations* of a society that was fragmented by the Vietnam War and by sharp demands from an array of social groups, from feminists to American Indians, seeking political, economic, and social changes.

Despite their claims of wanting to bring the nation together, Nixon and the Republicans *chose* to inflame social divisions to ensure their victories in 1968 and 1972. They *expected* to construct a solid political base around the Silent Majority: suburban, middle-class, white Americans who were tired of social reform. Promising a new, pragmatic conservatism, Nixon's first administration achieved generally successful *outcomes.* He improved relations with the Soviet Union and the People's Republic of China and gradually withdrew American forces from Vietnam. Domestically, his policy *choices* showed surprising flexibility.

Despite his successes, Nixon was not satisfied. His desire to destroy his political enemies contributed to the illegal activities surrounding the Watergate break-in. Watergate's *outcomes* included not only the unprecedented resignation of a president but a nationwide wave of disillusionment with politics and government.

Johnson and the World

Lyndon Baines Johnson saw the world in black-and-white terms: the free world on one side, the Communist world on the other. In 1964, Johnson perceived a growing Communist menace in Latin America and Vietnam.

Eyeing Castro's presence in Cuba, Johnson resolved that there would be no further erosion of American power in Latin America. Reversing Kennedy's policy, the State Department informed Latin American leaders that social and political reforms were no longer prerequisites for American aid. Johnson wanted order, stability, and pro-American governments. American military equipment and advisers were provided to regimes trying to suppress "Communist" elements. The new policy led to direct military intervention in the Dominican Republic in 1965. There, supporters of

CHRONOLOGY

From Camelot to Watergate

1962 Cesar Chavez forms National Farm Workers Association

1963 Betty Friedan's *The Feminine Mystique*
La Raza Unida formed in Texas
Kennedy assassinated; Johnson becomes president
16,000 U.S. advisers in South Vietnam

1964 Johnson elected president
Civil Rights Act
Gulf of Tonkin Resolution

1965 Voting Rights Act
U.S. air strikes against North Vietnam begin
American combat troops arrive in South Vietnam
Anti-Vietnam "teach-ins" begin
Dominican Republic intervention
National campaign for farm workers

1966 National Organization for Women founded

1967 Antiwar march on Washington

1968 Tet offensive
My Lai massacre
Peace talks begin in Paris
Johnson withdraws from presidential race
Robert Kennedy assassinated
Nixon elected president
American Indian Movement founded

1969 American Indians occupy Alcatraz
Anti-Vietnam march on Washington
First American troop withdrawals from Vietnam
Secret bombing of Cambodia
Vine Deloria's *Custer Died for Your Sins*
Alexander v. Holmes
Warren Burger appointed to Supreme Court

1970 Cambodian invasion
Kent State and Jackson State killings
Clean Air and Water acts
Earth Day observed nationally
Environmental Protection Agency created
Strike-for-Equality Parade
Harry Blackmun appointed to Supreme Court

1971 *Pentagon Papers*
Nixon enacts price and wage controls
Swann v. Charlotte-Mecklenburg
William Rehnquist and Lewis Powell appointed to Supreme Court

1972 Revenue Sharing Act
Watergate break-in
Nixon reelected
Nixon visits China and Soviet Union
SALT I treaty
Bombing of North Vietnam resumes

1973 Watergate hearings
Paris Peace Accords
War Powers Act
"Second battle of Wounded Knee"

1974 Nixon resigns
Gerald Ford becomes president
Jerry Apodaca elected governor of New Mexico
Raul Castro elected governor of Arizona

1975 South Vietnamese government falls to North Vietnamese deposed President Juan Bosch rebelled against a repressive, pro-American regime. Johnson decided that the pro-Bosch coalition was Communist dominated and sent in twenty-two thousand American troops to restore order. The troops left in mid-1966, after Joaquin Balaguer, a conservative, pro-American candidate, was elected president. Johnson claimed to have saved a free nation from communism, but many Latin Americans saw only an example of Yankee arrogance.

The Americanization of Vietnam

Latin America was not the only region where Johnson believed that American interests were threatened by communism. Although the United States had stationed sixteen thousand advisers in South Vietnam by the end of 1963, the Viet Cong, supported by North Vietnam, appeared to be winning the war. American advisers saw little hope for improvement unless American combat troops were committed to the contest. Johnson agreed, but concluded that sending troops to Vietnam in an election year was politically unwise. He decided to delay escalation at least until after the presidential election. Nevertheless, planning began immediately.

The plan that emerged relied heavily on American air power. It would be used against industrial and commercial targets in North Vietnam. Johnson's advisers believed that North Vietnamese leader Ho Chi Minh would end support for the Viet Cong rather than watch his nation's economic future go up in smoke. Without support from the North, the Viet Cong could be defeated by the South Vietnamese army (ARVN). The need for large numbers of American ground forces would consequently be limited. **General William Westmoreland,** commander of American forces in Vietnam, disagreed with that assessment. American ground forces were necessary, he argued, because the ARVN was inept. But Johnson chose not to follow this advice in an election year.

The administration did begin preparing the public for a larger American role in South Vietnam. The White House and the **Pentagon** encouraged newspapers and magazines to stress the Communist threat to South Vietnam and Southeast Asia. The White House waited for an opportunity to ask Congress for permission to use whatever force was necessary to defend South Vietnam.

That chance came in August 1964 off the coast of North Vietnam. On August 1, North Vietnamese torpedo boats skirmished with the American destroyer *Maddox* in the Gulf of Tonkin (see Map 30.1). On August 4, experiencing rough seas and poor visibility, radar operators on the *Maddox* and another destroyer concluded that the patrol boats were making another attack. Confusion followed. Both ships fired wildly at targets shown only on radar screens. Officers on both ships soon concluded that the radar blips had not been attacking vessels. Johnson joked privately that the sailors had probably been shooting at flying fish. Still, he told the nation that the Communists were guilty of "open aggression on the high seas" against the United States. On August 7, he submitted to Congress a resolution asking approval "to take all necessary steps, including the use of armed force," to aid South Vietnam. An overwhelming majority of Congress approved the **Gulf of Tonkin Resolution;** only two senators opposed it.

The Gulf of Tonkin Resolution gave Johnson the freedom to take whatever measures he wanted in Vietnam. Before committing American forces, however, he wanted to wait until after the 1964 election and for another enemy provocation. Johnson got his provocation when the Viet Cong attacked the American base at Pleiku in February 1965, killing eight Americans. Operation Rolling Thunder, the air assault on North Vietnam, began on March 2, 1965. On March 8, the 3rd Marine Division arrived to take up positions around the American base at Da Nang. By July, American planes were flying over nine hundred missions a week and a hundred

General William Westmoreland Commander of all American troops in Vietnam from 1964 to 1968.

Pentagon The U.S. military establishment, so named because its central offices are located in a five-sided building in Arlington, Virginia, called the Pentagon.

Gulf of Tonkin Resolution Resolution passed by Congress in 1964 authorizing the president to take any measures necessary to repel attacks against U.S. forces in Vietnam.

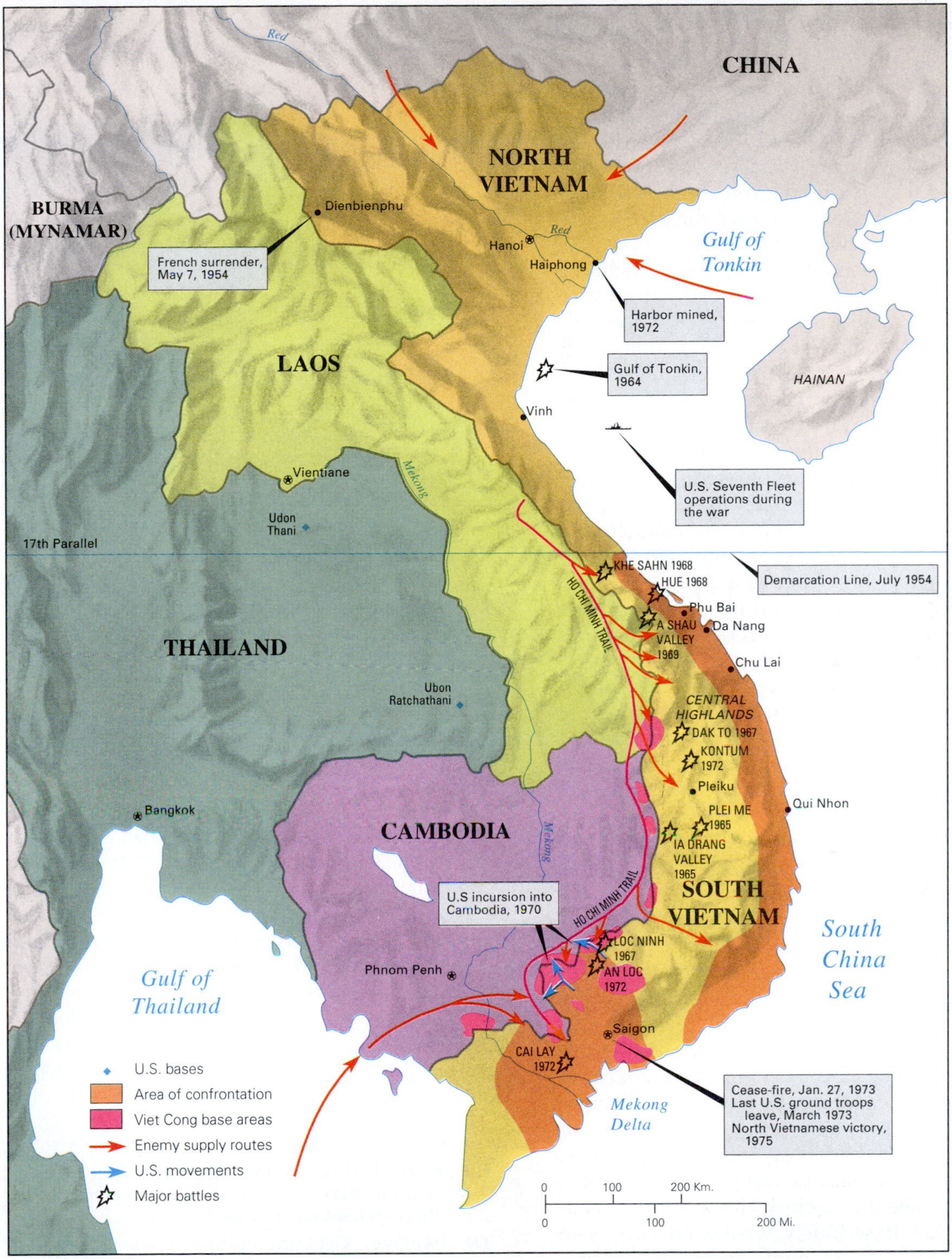
CHINA
NORTH VIETNAM
BURMA (MYNAMAR)
Dienbienphu
French surrender, May 7, 1954
Hanoi
Red
Haiphong
Gulf of Tonkin
Harbor mined, 1972
Gulf of Tonkin, 1964
HAINAN
LAOS
Vinh
U.S. Seventh Fleet operations during the war
Vientiane
Mekong
Udon Thani
17th Parallel
Demarcation Line, July 1954
KHE SAHN 1968
HUE 1968
Phu Bai
A SHAU VALLEY 1969
Da Nang
HO CHI MINH TRAIL
THAILAND
Chu Lai
Ubon Ratchathani
CENTRAL HIGHLANDS
DAK TO 1967
KONTUM 1972
Pleiku
Qui Nhon
PLEI ME 1965
IA DRANG VALLEY 1965
Bangkok
CAMBODIA
SOUTH VIETNAM
U.S incursion into Cambodia, 1970
LOC NINH 1967
AN LOC 1972
South China Sea
Gulf of Thailand
Phnom Penh
Saigon
CAI LAY 1972
Cease-fire, Jan. 27, 1973
Last U.S. ground troops leave, March 1973
North Vietnamese victory, 1975
Mekong Delta
U.S. bases
Area of confrontation
Viet Cong base areas
Enemy supply routes
U.S. movements
Major battles
0 100 200 Km.
0 100 200 Mi.

♦ **MAP 30.1 The Vietnam War, 1954–1975** Following the French defeat at Dienbienphu in 1954, the United States became increasingly committed to defending South Vietnam. This map shows some of the major battle sites of the Vietnam War from 1954 to the fall of Saigon and the defeat of the South Vietnamese government in 1975.

thousand American ground forces had reached Vietnam. Johnson's strategy soon showed its flaws. As the United States escalated the war, so did the enemy. General William Westmoreland now insisted that victory required even more American soldiers. Reluctantly, Johnson gave the green light. Vietnam had become an American war.

Westmoreland planned to use overwhelming numbers and firepower to destroy the enemy. In the first major American offensive, a large-scale sweep of the Ia Drang Valley in November 1965, the 1st Air Cavalry forced North Vietnamese units to retreat into Cambodia. The brutal hand-to-hand fighting left three hundred Americans and an estimated three thousand enemy soldiers dead. Westmoreland and Johnson were pleased. *Time* named Westmoreland "Man of the Year" for 1965.

Throughout 1966 and 1967, both sides continued to escalate. The Viet Cong and North Vietnamese suffered heavy losses of men and supplies, but their determination to continue the struggle remained unbroken. American aircraft rained bombs on North Vietnam and supply routes south, especially the **Ho Chi Minh Trail,** but arms and provisions still moved. In the fall of 1967, Westmoreland informed Washington that half of the enemy's forces were no longer capable of combat. At the same time, he asked to increase the American presence in Vietnam to 542,000.

Unknown to Westmoreland, North Vietnamese leaders were planning an immense offensive for the Vietnamese new year holiday of Tet in January 1968. The Viet Cong struck forty-one cities throughout South Vietnam, including Saigon. In some of the bloodiest fighting of the war, American and South Vietnamese forces recaptured the lost cities and villages.

The **Tet offensive** was a military defeat for North Vietnam and the Viet Cong. It provoked no popular uprising against the South Vietnamese government, the Communists gained no cities or provincial capitals, and they suffered staggering losses. Over forty thousand Viet Cong were killed. Tet was nonetheless a "victory" for the North Vietnamese in that it seriously weakened American support for the war. Coming amid official pronouncements of "victory just around the corner," Tet destroyed the administration's credibility and intensified a growing antiwar movement.

♦ Unlike previous American wars, Vietnam was a war without fixed frontlines. At the isolated outpost of Khe Sahn, fewer than six thousand American marines fought to hold back thirty thousand to forty thousand North Vietnamese regulars for seventy-seven days, killing or wounding more than ten thousand of the enemy. Within weeks after the siege, the United States withdrew from the area. *Robert Ellison/Black Star.*

The Antiwar Movement

Throughout 1964, there was widespread support for an American role in Vietnam. Most Americans accepted the domino theory, which held that a Communist success in one country would lead to the toppling of other "free" governments. A year later, little had changed except that the largely college-based opposition to the war was more outspoken. The University of Michigan held the first Vietnam "teach-in" to mobilize opposition to the war on March 24, 1965. In April, Students for a Democratic Society (SDS) organized a protest march of about fifteen thousand in front of the White House.

Ho Chi Minh Trail Main infiltration route for North Vietnamese soldiers into South Vietnam; it ran through Laos and Cambodia.

Tet offensive Viet Cong and North Vietnamese offensive against South Vietnamese cities in January 1968; a military defeat for North Vietnam, it nevertheless undermined U.S. support for the war.

Those opposing the war fell into two major categories. Pacifists and radical liberals opposed the war for moral and ideological reasons. Others opposed the war for pragmatic reasons: the draft, the loss of lives and money, and the inability of the United States to defeat the enemy. In 1966, high school students hardly mentioned Vietnam or the draft as a problem facing their lives. Three years later, 75 percent of those polled listed both as major worries. By 1967, the possibility of being sent to Vietnam was becoming a concern of many college students. A University of Michigan student complained that if he were drafted and spent two years in the army, he would lose over $16,000 in income. Yet college students were not the most likely to be drafted. Far more often, those who were drafted and sent to Vietnam were poorly educated, low-income whites and minorities.

Nonetheless, it was America's middle class, especially college students, who swelled the antiwar movement and participated in the "Stop-the-Draft Week" in October 1967. That week, over 10,000 demonstrators blocked the entrance to an induction center in Oakland, California, while over 200,000 people staged a massive protest march in Washington against "Lyndon's War."

Until 1967, Johnson displayed little concern about the antiwar movement. Press and television coverage continued to emphasize American successes. Public opinion polls found that the nation stood behind Johnson's efforts to save South Vietnam. But as antiwar numbers increased and as opposition to the war spread beyond students and radicals in 1967, Johnson responded by having federal agents infiltrate, spy on, and try to discredit antiwar groups.

The Tet offensive broadened and intensified antiwar sentiments. The highly respected CBS news anchor Walter Cronkite had supported the war, but Tet changed his mind. Unable to match the administration's claims of impending victory with the fierce Communist offensive, he went on a personal fact-finding tour of Vietnam. On his return, Cronkite announced that there would be no victory in Vietnam. "If I have lost Walter Cronkite, then it's over. I have lost Mr. Average Citizen," Johnson lamented.

Johnson's own circle of advisers began opposing American policy in Vietnam. Secretary of War Robert McNamara left the administration over its policy. Secretary of State Dean Rusk and new Secretary of Defense Clark Clifford argued that military victory was impossible. Clifford concluded that after four years of "enormous casualties" and "massive destruction from our bombing," there was no lessening of "the will of the enemy." Thus, following Tet, when Westmoreland called for more troops, most of Johnson's "wise men" urged sending fewer troops and seeking instead a diplomatic end to the war.

The 1968 Presidential Campaign

As Johnson prepared for the 1968 presidential race, rumors circulated that 200,000 more Americans were being sent to Vietnam. In the New Hampshire primary, Minnesota senator **Eugene McCarthy** challenged Johnson for the Democratic presidential nomination by opposing the Vietnam War. Hundreds of student volunteers knocked on doors and distributed flyers for McCarthy.

Expecting no real challenge to his renomination, Johnson had not entered the New Hampshire primary. But with the furor over Tet, Johnson's political advisers quickly organized a **write-in campaign** for Johnson in New Hampshire. The president beat McCarthy, but by only 6 percent of the vote. Political commentators called McCarthy the real winner of the contest. New York senator **Robert Kennedy** added to Johnson's worries when he proclaimed his candidacy for the presidency and opposition to the war.

On March 31, 1968, a haggard-looking president announced on television that the United States

Eugene McCarthy Senator who opposed the Vietnam War and who made an unsuccessful bid for the 1968 Democratic nomination for president.

write-in campaign An attempt to elect a candidate not registered or listed on the ballot; voters are urged to write in the candidate's name on the ballot themselves.

Robert Kennedy Attorney general during the presidency of his brother John F. Kennedy; he was elected to the Senate in 1964 and was campaigning for the presidency when he was assassinated in 1968.

would negotiate with the Viet Cong and North Vietnamese. The escalation of the ground war was over, and the South Vietnamese would assume a larger role. The bombing of North Vietnam above the 20th parallel would end. Johnson ended his speech with this bombshell: "I have concluded that I should not permit the presidency to become involved in the partisan divisions that are developing in this political year. . . . Accordingly, I shall not seek, and I will not accept, the nomination of my party for another term as president." Listeners were shocked. Lyndon B. Johnson had thrown in the towel. Nearly everyone agrees that the war ended Johnson's political career.

Negotiations with North Vietnam began in Paris in May and went nowhere. The war remained the critical issue within the Democratic political race, which now included Vice President **Hubert H. Humphrey.** McCarthy campaigned against the war and the "imperial presidency." Kennedy opposed the war and called on the government to meet the needs of the poor and minorities. Standing by Johnson's peace efforts, Humphrey relied on party regulars and White House clout to win the nomination. While Kennedy and McCarthy battled for primary victories, Humphrey concentrated on the nonprimary delegations.

By June, Kennedy was winning the primary race. In the critical California primary, he gained a narrow victory over McCarthy, 46 to 41 percent. As Kennedy left his election headquarters, he was shot in the head by Sirhan Sirhan, a Jordanian immigrant. He died the next day.

Kennedy's assassination ensured Humphrey's nomination. McCarthy continued his campaign but was unable to generate much support. By the time of the national convention in Chicago in August, Humphrey had enough pledged votes to ensure his nomination. The convention was nevertheless dramatic. Antiwar and antiestablishment groups demonstrated for McCarthy, peace in Vietnam, and social justice. In the streets of Chicago, radical factions within the SDS promised physical confrontation. The so-called **Yippies** (Youth International party), led by Abbie Hoffman and Jerry Rubin, threatened to contaminate the water supply with drugs. Chicago's mayor, Richard Daley, was determined to maintain order. Inside the convention, delegates argued and screamed support for their positions. Outside, protesters threw eggs, bottles, rocks, and balloons filled with water, ink, and urine at the police, who responded with tear gas and nightsticks. On August 28, the police went berserk before television cameras, viciously attacking protesters and bystanders alike. The violence in Chicago's streets overshadowed Humphrey's nomination.

Many Americans were disgusted by the chaos in Chicago. **George Wallace,** the Democratic governor of Alabama, appealed to this sentiment when he left the Democratic party and ran for president as the American Independent party's candidate. The conservative Wallace, who had opposed federal civil rights legislation, took a dim view of antiwar protesters. He aimed his campaign at southern whites, blue-collar workers, and lower-income white Americans. On the campaign trail, Wallace took special glee in attacking the counterculture and the "rich-kid" war protesters, who avoided serving in Vietnam while the sons of working-class Americans died there. Wallace agreed with his vice-presidential candidate, General Curtis Lemay, that the United States should bomb North Vietnam "back to the Stone Age." Two months before the election, Wallace commanded 21 percent of the vote according to opinion polls.

The Republican candidate, Richard Nixon, also intended to tap this general dissatisfaction. He and Spiro Agnew, his vice-presidential running mate, campaigned on the need for law and order while denouncing pot, pornography, protesters, and permissiveness. He announced that he would "end the war and win the peace" but refused to specify how.

On election day, Nixon won a comfortable margin in the Electoral College, although he received

Hubert H. Humphrey Vice president under Lyndon Johnson who won the Democratic nomination for president in 1968 but lost the election to Richard Nixon.

Yippies Counterculture group that inflamed the protests that disrupted the Democratic National Convention in Chicago in 1968.

George Wallace Conservative Alabama governor who opposed desegregation in the 1960s and ran unsuccessfully for the presidency as an independent in 1968 and 1972.

◆ Violence erupted during the 1968 Democratic National Convention in Chicago. Using nightsticks, police attacked antiwar and anti-establishment protesters who surrounded the convention hotel. The violent confrontations in Chicago did little to quell similar protests, unify the Democratic party, or help Hubert Humphrey's chances for election. *Wide World Photos.*

only 43.4 percent of the popular vote. Conservatives were pleased. Combined, Nixon and Wallace attracted almost 57 percent of the vote, which conservatives said indicated wide public support for an end to liberal social programs and a return to "traditional values." They believed that a major political realignment was taking shape.

Expanding the American Dream

The explosion of the civil rights movement during the 1960s spread African-American activism to all parts of the country. It also contributed to the growth of other groups, such as women, Mexican Americans, and Native Americans, demanding equal rights and access to the American dream.

The Women's Rights Movement

Popular social images during the 1950s showed women happiest at home raising children and running the household. Although this scenario held true for many women, a growing number were dissatisfied with their lives. As the 1960s began, more women were entering the work force, having fewer children, and getting divorced. Many women complained that they were denied access to profitable careers. A 1963 report documented that women worked for less pay (on average, 40 percent that of a man), were more likely to be fired or laid off, and had little success in reaching top career positions. Nor was it just in the workplace that women faced discrimination. Throughout the country, divorce, credit, and property laws generally favored men.

To some women, the role of housewife itself symbolized oppression. **Betty Friedan** was one who concluded that the chores of the housewife amounted to a form of servitude. As a young woman, she had dropped out of a psychology doctoral program to get married, bear children, and keep a suburban home. In her 1963 bestseller, *The Feminine Mystique,* she pondered why she was not satisfied. After reviewing the responsibilities of the housewife (making beds, grocery shopping, driving children everywhere, preparing meals and

Betty Friedan Feminist who wrote *The Feminine Mystique* in 1963 and helped found the National Organization for Women in 1966.

snacks, and pleasing her husband), she asked: "Is this all?" She concluded that it was not enough. Women needed to overcome the "feminine mystique" that promised them fulfillment through the domestic arts. She called on women to set their own goals and seek careers outside the home. Her book contributed to a renewed women's movement.

Title VII of the 1964 Civil Rights Act also produced more activism. Title VII prohibited discrimination on the basis of race, religion, creed, national origin, or sex. Many women and liberals hoped that Title VII would commit the government to gender equality. But when the Equal Employment Opportunity Commission (EEOC) showed little interest in dealing with gender discrimination, proponents organized to press the government to enforce Title VII. Experienced civil rights activists like Mary King and Casey Hayden of the Student Nonviolent Coordinating Committee were anxious to push for women's rights. In "the black movement," one woman wrote, "I had been fighting for someone else's oppression and now there was a way I could fight for my own freedom and I was going to be much stronger than I ever was."

The most prominent women's organization to emerge was the **National Organization for Women (NOW),** formed in 1966 and headed by Betty Friedan. NOW launched an aggressive campaign to draw attention to sex discrimination. It sued the EEOC for not upholding the law and thirteen hundred corporations for gender discrimination. It demanded an Equal Rights Amendment to the Constitution and pushed for easier access to birth-control devices and the right to have an abortion.

NOW's membership grew rapidly, from about 300 in 1966 to 175,000 in 1968. But the movement was larger than NOW's membership. Women in droves attended **consciousness-raising** sessions and other grassroots gatherings to promote women's issues. Calls arose for new social and sexual codes for women. Some women rejected high heels, bras, and other trappings associated with a male-defined image of feminine sexuality. NOW's 1970 Strike-for-Equality Parade demonstrated the growing mass appeal of the women's movement when fifty thousand supporters marched down New York City's Fifth Avenue.

As within the African-American civil rights movement, divisions developed. Many women who supported equal opportunities and rights rejected the feminist label and what they believed was the movement's bias toward career and working women. At the other extreme, some called for a complete redefinition of the traditional institutions of family and marriage. Marriage was "slavery," "legalized rape," and "unpaid labor," according to radical feminist Ti-Grace Atkinson. Still, by the end of the Seventies, a general feminist critique of American society had succeeded in convincing many Americans that women should pursue goals and aspirations beyond the traditional roles of wife, mother, and homemaker.

The Emergence of Chicano Power

Mexican Americans also organized to assert their social and political rights. As the 1960s began, Mexican Americans were largely an invisible minority (see Map 30.2). Outside the Southwest, few Americans were aware of them. Prevailing stereotypes portrayed them as docile, if not lazy, and ridiculed them as poorly educated, unskilled people who spoke English badly. Statistically, Mexican Americans were near society's lowest levels of income and education.

Throughout the 1940s and 1950s, organizations like the League of Latin American Citizens and the G.I. Forum had made minor gains against legal segregation, but little had changed for most Mexican Americans. The New Frontier and the Great Society had revived hope, as organizations began to pressure American society to recognize the needs of the Latino population. In 1963, the Mexican-American majority in Crystal City, Texas,

Title VII Provision of the Civil Rights Act of 1964 that guaranteed women legal protection against discrimination.

National Organization for Women Women's rights organization founded in 1966 to improve educational, employment, and political opportunities for women and to fight for equal pay for equal work.

consciousness-raising Related to achieving greater awareness of the nature of a political or social issue through group therapy or group interaction.

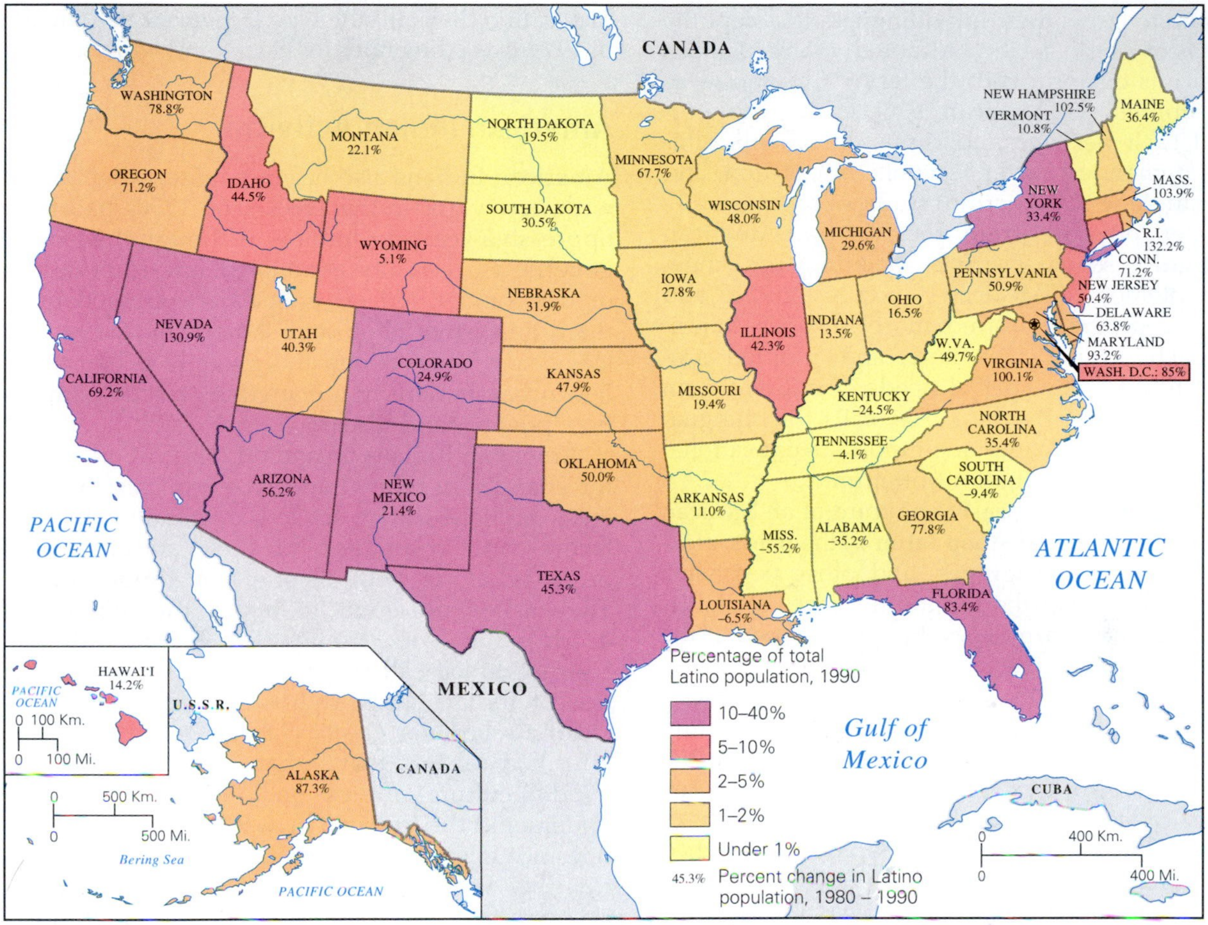
CANADA
WASHINGTON 78.8%
OREGON 71.2%
CALIFORNIA 69.2%
NEVADA 130.9%
IDAHO 44.5%
MONTANA 22.1%
WYOMING 5.1%
UTAH 40.3%
ARIZONA 56.2%
COLORADO 24.9%
NEW MEXICO 21.4%
NORTH DAKOTA 19.5%
SOUTH DAKOTA 30.5%
NEBRASKA 31.9%
KANSAS 47.9%
OKLAHOMA 50.0%
TEXAS 45.3%
MINNESOTA 67.7%
IOWA 27.8%
MISSOURI 19.4%
ARKANSAS 11.0%
LOUISIANA -6.5%
WISCONSIN 48.0%
ILLINOIS 42.3%
MICHIGAN 29.6%
INDIANA 13.5%
OHIO 16.5%
KENTUCKY -24.5%
TENNESSEE -4.1%
MISS. -55.2%
ALABAMA -35.2%
GEORGIA 77.8%
FLORIDA 83.4%
SOUTH CAROLINA -9.4%
NORTH CAROLINA 35.4%
VIRGINIA 100.1%
W.VA. -49.7%
PENNSYLVANIA 50.9%
NEW YORK 33.4%
NEW HAMPSHIRE 102.5%
VERMONT 10.8%
MAINE 36.4%
MASS. 103.9%
R.I. 132.2%
CONN. 71.2%
NEW JERSEY 50.4%
DELAWARE 63.8%
MARYLAND 93.2%
WASH. D.C.: 85%
PACIFIC OCEAN
ATLANTIC OCEAN
Gulf of Mexico
MEXICO
CUBA
HAWAI'I 14.2%
PACIFIC OCEAN
0 100 Km.
0 100 Mi.
U.S.S.R.
ALASKA 87.3%
CANADA
0 500 Km.
0 500 Mi.
Bering Sea
PACIFIC OCEAN
0 400 Km.
0 400 Mi.
Percentage of total Latino population, 1990
10–40%
5–10%
2–5%
1–2%
Under 1%
45.3% Percent change in Latino population, 1980 – 1990

♦ **MAP 30.2 Changing Latino Population** At one time, the great majority of Latinos were Mexican Americans located in the Southwest. In the 1990s, Latinos resided in nearly every major city and included Cubans, Puerto Ricans, and others from throughout the Caribbean and Central and South America. Growing rapidly, the Latino population was projected to become the largest minority in the country by the year 2000, perhaps 12 percent of the total population.

stunned the region by electing an all-Mexican-American slate to the city council. The Crystal City vote was, for many Mexican Americans, a revolutionary act. Across south Texas, Mexican Americans banded together to form El Partido Raza Unida (the United People party) to spread the political "revolution" throughout Texas. The passage of the 1965 Voting Rights Act and Johnson's War on Poverty added more impetus. Throughout the Southwest, the activism of Mexican Americans frightened those supporting the status quo. Texas governor Dolph Briscoe typified conservative sentiment when he denounced the La Raza Unida movement as Communist inspired.

Briscoe was wrong. The Mexican-American movement was a local one, born of poverty and oppressive segregation. Reflecting the grassroots character of the movement was the important role that youths played. Many Mexican-American teenagers and young adults adopted the term

Chicano to stress their unwillingness to accept the dictates of Anglo society. Although many Mexican Americans disapproved, the term "Chicano" was soon applied to Mexican Americans who promoted their heritage and rights. In schools, Chicanos demanded better teachers, integration, and Mexican-American (Latino) studies programs.

Under pressure from the Mexican-American community, school districts, including Los Angeles, implemented Mexican-American studies and bilingual programs, hired more Mexican-American teachers and counselors, and adopted programs to meet the special needs of migrant farm worker children. By the 1970s, calls for bilingual education had become an important educational reform focus for the Latino community.

During the 1960s, nearly one-third of all Mexican Americans worked at **stoop labor** in the fields, picking onions, carrots, grapes, and other perishable crops for less than the minimum wage. Unskilled and uneducated farm laborers were trapped at the bottom of the occupation ladder. They were not covered under minimum wage or labor laws. Established unions made no effort to organize agricultural labor. Finally, in 1962, **Cesar Chavez** created the **National Farm Workers Association (NFWA).** When Chavez called a strike against the grape growers of central California in 1965, the NFWA had reached seventeen hundred members. He demanded a wage of $1.40 an hour and asked the public to support the farm workers by buying only union-picked grapes. With varying degrees of success, the boycott and strike continued for five years until most of the major growers accepted unionization.

As Mexican Americans and other Latinos became more vocal in their demands for a fairer share of the American dream, both political parties began to reach out to moderate Mexican-American leaders. New Mexico's Manuel Lujan, a Republican, was elected to Congress, joining several Mexican-American Democrats in the House of Representatives. In 1974, Democrats Jerry Apodaca and Raul Castro were elected governors of New Mexico and Arizona.

Despite such success stories, the majority of Mexican Americans have not achieved social or economic equality. Economically, the Mexican-American population remains one of the poorest minorities in the United States. Lack of economic success has left few incentives for Latino children to stay in high school. The Latino dropout rate was 45 percent nationwide in 1990, exceeding rates for blacks and whites.

American Indian Activism

American Indians also began to assert their rights with new vigor in the 1960s. The 1950s had been oppressive years for Indians. Although the federal government actually eliminated few reservations or tribal units, federal policies encouraged more than thirty-five thousand American Indians to leave their reservations and move to urban areas. Few urban Indians found anything but discrimination, poverty, and disease.

American Indians on and off reservations called for changes in federal and state policies. Increasingly militant Indian leaders demanded the protection and restoration of their ancient burial grounds, along with fishing and timber rights. They asked museums to return the remains of dead Indians on display. The National Indian Youth Council called for Indians to resist further loss of Indian lands, rights, and traditions. Vine Deloria's popular *Custer Died for Your Sins* (1969) informed readers that Indians asked "only to be freed of cultural oppression." "The white does not understand the Indian," he wrote, "and the Indian does not wish to understand the white." The central issue was not equality and assimilation, Deloria explained, but Indian self-determination. Indians wanted economic prosperity and opportunity,

Chicano Term adopted by many Mexican Americans during the late 1960s to describe their ethnic identity; it was associated with the promotion of Mexican-American heritage and rights.

stoop labor Field labor that involves constant bending, usually to pick fruits and vegetables.

Cesar Chavez Labor organizer who founded the National Farm Workers Association; he believed in nonviolence and used marches, boycotts, and fasts to bring moral and economic pressure to bear on growers.

National Farm Workers Association Migrant workers' union organized by Cesar Chavez in 1962 that used a series of boycotts to force California growers to recognize the union and improve wages and working conditions.

but on terms that would ensure their continued tribal existence.

In the 1960s, Presidents Kennedy and Johnson provided some change, ending the termination program. President Nixon continued the process by placing Indians in top-level positions within the Bureau of Indian Affairs. In 1974, Congress passed the **Indian Self-Determination and Education Assistance Act,** which gave tribes control of many federal programs on their reservations. On the issue of lost land, American Indians pressed their claims, with little prospect of success. Still, some Indian victories have occurred. In 1972, the Passamaquoddy and Penobscot tribes in Maine sued to have over 12.5 million acres, which they claimed had been illegally seized by the state, returned to them. They settled in 1980 for 300,000 acres and the establishment of a $27 million trust fund for the tribes. Also in 1980, the Supreme Court decided that the federal government owed over $106 million to the Sioux for taking the Black Hills of South Dakota in the 1870s.

Although some American Indian leaders turned to Washington and the courts to assert Indian rights, others took more direct action. In 1968, the Chippewas organized the **American Indian Movement (AIM)** to dramatize police brutality toward Indians in Minneapolis. In 1969, a group of San Francisco Indian activists seized **Alcatraz Island,** offering to buy the federally owned island for $24, the same amount that Dutch settlers had paid for Manhattan Island in 1626. They held the island until 1971, when federal authorities, without bloodshed, retook control. In 1973, AIM leaders Russell Means and Dennis Banks organized the armed occupation of Wounded Knee, South Dakota, the site of the 1890 massacre of the Sioux by the army. AIM militants controlled the town for seventy-one days before surrendering to federal authorities. Although the "second battle of Wounded Knee" failed to change federal policy, it did publicize Indian grievances and problems.

Nixon and the Balance of Power

In foreign affairs, Nixon expected to achieve an honorable peace in Vietnam and to reestablish American leadership in world affairs. To realize these goals, he turned to Harvard professor **Henry Kissinger,** his national security adviser and foreign policy expert. Nixon and Kissinger wanted to restructure Cold War policies, particularly with regard to the Soviet Union. They believed that America's military advantage over the Soviets was narrowing rapidly. Because there was little chance that Congress would support efforts to regain clear military superiority, they concluded that it was necessary to improve relations with the Soviet Union. Nixon and Kissinger recognized that the widening split between China and the Soviet Union, which had developed in the 1960s, offered promising possibilities for changing the balance of Cold War power.

Vietnamization

Nixon and Kissinger also knew that Vietnam was the most immediate problem. It dominated and shaped nearly all other issues: the budget, public and congressional opinion, foreign policy, and domestic stability. The Republicans needed a solution to Vietnam before moving ahead on other issues. The central problem was to find a means to protect South Vietnam, to encourage the North Vietnamese to negotiate, and to allow the gradual withdrawal of American forces. Nixon's solution was **Vietnamization:** reducing the American role while strengthening

Indian Self-Determination and Education Assistance Act Law passed in 1974 giving Indian tribes control over federal programs carried out on their reservations and increasing their control of reservation schools.

American Indian Movement Militant Indian movement organized to demand social justice for urban Indians.

Alcatraz Island Rocky island in San Francisco Bay that was occupied from 1969 to 1971 by Native American activists who demanded that it be made available as a cultural center.

Henry Kissinger German-born American diplomat who was national security adviser and secretary of state under President Nixon; he helped negotiate the cease-fire in Vietnam.

Vietnamization Policy announced by Nixon in which the United States scaled back its involvement in Vietnam, returning to its earlier role of helping Vietnamese forces fight their own war.

South Vietnam's military capability. Nixon believed that large-scale opposition to the war would fade once American soldiers started coming home.

Vietnamization began in the spring of 1969. By the end of the year, American forces in Vietnam had declined by over 110,000. The withdrawal of American troops reflected a broader strategy that became known as the **Nixon Doctrine.** This doctrine stipulated that countries confronting communism would have to bear the brunt of the military burden, and that the United States would provide those countries with only economic and political support.

Vietnamization was only a part of Nixon's strategy for ending the conflict in Vietnam. The other element in the "peace plan" was to increase the economic, diplomatic, and military pressure on North Vietnam to end the war. This, Nixon hoped, would be done in two ways: by getting the Soviets and the Chinese to reduce their support for North Vietnam and by bombing enemy bases across the South Vietnamese border in Cambodia and Laos. In March 1969, Nixon ordered the heavy bombardment of Communist sanctuaries inside Cambodia. Fearful of public and political reactions, the administration tried to keep the operation a secret. When Operation MENU ended in 1973, over 383,800 tons of bombs had been dropped on Cambodia. The intense assault was also part of a "madman strategy" Nixon designed to convince the North Vietnamese to negotiate. Nixon said that he wanted Hanoi "to believe that I've reached the point where I might do anything to stop the war."

The strategy did not work. The North Vietnamese appeared unconcerned about Nixon's "madness," the increased bombing, and decreasing support from China and the Soviet Union. They still believed that victory was only a matter of waiting patiently until America was unwilling to continue the war. Consequently, talks between Kissinger and the North Vietnamese in Paris were unproductive.

Nor did American opposition to the war fade away. In November 1969, over 250,000 antiwar protesters paraded past the White House calling for an end to the conflict. News of American atrocities at **My Lai,** which came to light in 1970, added fuel to the antiwar cause. In March 1968, Lieutenant William Calley's platoon had "wasted" the small village, killing more than two hundred men, women, and children. The massacre seemed to offer incontestable proof that the Vietnam War was immoral. The publication of the ***Pentagon Papers,*** a collection of official documents showing government officials had deceived the American public about Vietnam from the 1950s on, furthered public disillusionment with the war.

Still, Nixon refused to change course. In 1970, he ordered American troops to cross the border into Cambodia and destroy North Vietnamese and Viet Cong headquarters and supply areas. He told the public that the incursion was not to widen the war but to hasten its end. The Cambodian invasion, which involved nearly eighty thousand American and South Vietnamese troops, did destroy large amounts of supplies. But it failed to defeat the enemy or to stop the flow of supplies from North Vietnam. It also generated loud protests on college campuses. At Kent State University on May 4, 1970, the Ohio National Guard fired on protesters, killing four and wounding eleven. At Jackson State University in Mississippi, police killed two students during another demonstration. Outraged students responded by shutting down over a hundred campuses. An angry Senate repealed the Gulf of Tonkin Resolution and forbade the further use of American troops in Laos and Cambodia.

By the end of 1971, Kissinger and Nixon were frustrated. They knew that Vietnamization was not progressing well and that there seemed no sign of a settlement in Paris. The North Vietnamese refused to consider any settlement that did not replace South Vietnamese president Nguyan Van Thieu and his government with a coalition that included the Communist National Liberation Front. That condition was unacceptable to the United States. Then, in

Nixon Doctrine Nixon's policy of requiring countries threatened by communism to shoulder the bulk of the military burden, with the United States offering mainly political and economic support.

My Lai Site of a massacre of more than two hundred South Vietnamese villagers by U.S. infantrymen in 1969, an event that added to antiwar sentiment in the United States.

Pentagon Papers Classified government documents on the policy decisions that led to U.S. involvement in Vietnam, which were leaked to the *New York Times* in 1971.

♦ Together, Richard Nixon *(left)* and Secretary of State Henry Kissinger *(right)* sought to refocus American foreign policy by ending the war in Vietnam and improving relations with the Soviet Union and the People's Republic of China. *John Dominis, LIFE Magazine © Time Warner.*

March 1972, Communist forces drove toward Saigon as South Vietnamese forces tottered on the brink of collapse. Livid at the Communist offensive, Nixon ordered massive bombing raids against North Vietnam and Communist forces in South Vietnam. By mid-June 1972, American airpower had stalled the offensive and enabled ARVN forces to regroup and drive back the North Vietnamese. With their cities under almost continuous air attacks, the North Vietnamese became more flexible in negotiations. By October, a peace settlement was ready. "Peace is at hand," Kissinger announced.

Thieu, however, rejected the plan. Reluctantly, Nixon supported Thieu and ordered the Christmas bombing of North Vietnam. Nixon hoped to put additional pressure on Hanoi and to convince Thieu that the United States would protect South Vietnam. After eleven days, Nixon stopped the bombings and advised Thieu that if he did not accept the next peace settlement, the United States would leave him to fend for himself. Thieu thereupon accepted a peace settlement similar to the one offered in October. Following the signing of the Paris Peace Accords in 1973, Nixon and Kissinger proclaimed peace with honor. Kissinger shared the 1973 Nobel Peace Prize with his North Vietnamese counterpart, Le Duc Tho.

The peace accords imposed a cease-fire, required the removal of all American troops (only twenty-four thousand now remained in South Vietnam) but not North Vietnamese troops, and promised the return of American prisoners of war. The peace terms permitted the United States to complete its military and political withdrawal, but the pact did little to ensure the continued existence of South Vietnam. The cease-fire, everyone expected, would be temporary. Kissinger confided privately that the South Vietnamese government might "hold out for a year and a half."

As expected, the cease-fire soon collapsed. North Vietnam continued to funnel men and supplies to the south, but substantial American air and naval support for South Vietnam never arrived. Neither Congress nor the public was anxious to help Thieu's government. Instead, Congress cut aid to South Vietnam. In March 1975, North Vietnam began its final campaign to unify the country, and a month later, its troops entered Saigon. The few remaining Americans and some South Vietnamese were evacuated by helicopter, some from the roof of the American embassy. The Vietnam War ended as it had started, with Vietnamese fighting Vietnamese.

Congress drew one immediate conclusion in the aftermath of American involvement in Vietnam: that limits should be placed on the president's powers to commit American troops to foreign conflicts. The **War Powers Act,** passed in November 1973, required the president to inform Congress within forty-eight hours of deploying troops overseas and to withdraw those troops within sixty days if Congress failed to authorize the action.

Modifying the Cold War

Ending the Vietnam War was essential to Nixon's goal of redefining the Cold War. Nixon hoped that an "era of confrontation" would give way to an "era of negotiation." To this end, he pursued **détente,** a policy intended to reduce tensions with the two Communist superpowers. China was the key to the Nixon-Kissinger strategy. Several bloody border clashes between the Chinese and the Soviets made the Chinese receptive to better relations with the United States. Nixon hoped that American friendship with the Chinese would in turn encourage the Soviets to improve their relations with the United States. Following a secret visit by Kissinger, Nixon flew to Beijing in February 1972 to meet with Communist party chairman Mao Zedong. Suddenly, the "Red Chinese" were no longer the enemy but "hard-working, intelligent and practical" friends. The Cold War was thawing in the East.

Nixon's China policy contributed to improved relations with the Soviet Union. Kissinger followed his secret visit to China with one to Moscow, where he discussed improving relations with President **Leonid Brezhnev.** Nixon flew to Moscow in May 1972 and told Brezhnev that he believed that the two nations should "live together and work together." Needing to reduce military spending, develop the Soviet domestic economy, and increase American trade, Brezhnev agreed. The meeting was a success. Brezhnev obtained increased trade with the West, including shipments of American grain, and the superpowers announced an agreement on the **Strategic Arms Limitation Talks (SALT I),** which established a maximum number of **intercontinental ballistic missiles (ICBMs)** and submarine-launched ballistic missiles (SLBMs) for each side. It seemed as if détente had arrived.

Nixon and Politics

In his foreign policy, Nixon followed new paths in dealing with the Chinese and Soviets that did not reflect traditional Republican views. This was also true of his domestic programs. Nixon believed that Republicans needed to develop a pragmatic and socially responsible conservatism.

Pragmatic Conservatism

Nixon's brand of conservatism, the **New Federalism,** embraced federal power while proposing to make programs more responsive to state and local government. His **Revenue Sharing Act,** passed in October 1972, reflected the new approach. The government would continue to raise revenue through its broad tax base, but it would release more of the money to state and local governments and reduce federal controls on how they spent it.

War Powers Act Law passed in 1973 that set a sixty-day limit on presidential commitment of U.S. troops to hostilities abroad unless Congress authorized continued action.

détente Relaxing of tensions between the superpowers in the early 1970s, which included increased diplomatic, commercial, and cultural contact.

Leonid Brezhnev President of the Soviet Union from 1977 until his death in 1982, who worked to foster détente with the United States during the Nixon era.

Strategic Arms Limitation Talks agreement Agreement between the United States and the USSR in 1972 to limit both offensive nuclear weapons and the anti-ballistic missile systems that protected against them.

intercontinental ballistic missiles Missiles that can travel from one continent to another.

New Federalism Nixon's policy of accepting the existence of government social programs but seeking to trim waste and increase the power of state and local governments.

Revenue Sharing Act Five-year program established in 1972 to distribute large amounts of federal tax revenues to state and local governments to use as they saw fit.

Before the program ended in 1986, state and local governments had received over $83 billion in revenue sharing funds.

Nixon also wanted to redirect the flow of money and responsibility in the welfare system. Unlike many staunch conservatives, Nixon was not opposed to welfare, but he believed that the existing welfare system robbed people of their self-esteem, contributed to the breakup of nuclear families, and punished people for working. His proposal for welfare reform, the Family Assistance Plan (FAP), sought to balance work and welfare but was attacked by conservatives and liberals alike. The Senate defeated it in 1969 and 1971. After its second defeat, Nixon lost interest.

But Nixon did not abandon what he saw as the need for federal social responsibility. Under his administration, food stamps became more accessible; the elderly and the disabled received direct federal support; and Social Security, Medicare, and Medicaid payments were increased. Nixon also supported subsidized housing and expanded the Job Corps. He signed the **Twenty-sixth Amendment** giving 18-year-olds the right to vote, and his administration oversaw the formation of the Occupational Safety and Health Administration (OSHA) and the **Environmental Protection Agency (EPA).**

Nixon believed that the Republican party could not afford to ignore social needs and public concerns in the name of conservatism. The environmental issue was a case in point. When Nixon took office in 1969, the environment was not a major issue. Almost overnight, however, it became one. The ever-present Los Angeles smog, an oil slick off Santa Barbara, California, and the declaration that Lake Erie was ecologically dead provided graphic reminders of the ecological dangers facing the nation. During the second celebration of Earth Day in April 1970, nearly every community in the nation hosted some type of Earth Day activity.

Nixon was not an environmentalist, but he recognized an opportunity. Two days after Earth Day, 1970, he proposed the creation of the EPA. He also signed the Clean Air and Clean Water acts, which limited the amount of pollutants that business and industry could dump into the air and water.

Nixon proved to be flexible in economic matters as well. When he took office, the nation was experiencing a climbing rate of inflation. Nixon's initial response was to cut spending, increase interest rates, and balance the budget. He succeeded in balancing the budget in 1969, but inflation continued to rise even as economic growth slowed, a phenomenon soon dubbed **stagflation.** By 1971, the economy was in its first recession since 1958 and inflation was still climbing. Fearing that the economy would erode Republican support, Nixon radically shifted his approach. "I am now a Keynesian," he announced in April 1971. He asked for increased federal spending to boost recovery and wage and price controls to stall advancing inflation.

Nixon's battle with inflation, however, was a losing one, in part because of economic events over which he had no control. A global drought pushed up farm prices. Following the October 1973 Arab-Israeli Yom Kippur War, Arab nations instituted an oil boycott of the United States for its support of Israel. Gasoline prices nearly doubled. Many Americans were forced to wait in long gas lines. Some areas of the country even instituted fuel oil and gasoline rationing. Increases in food and oil prices pushed the 1974 inflation rate over 10 percent.

Law and Order and Southern Politics

During the 1968 campaign, Nixon had presented himself as the law-and-order candidate, who would use the power of government to combat crime. Once in office, however, Nixon seemed more interested in using the law-and-order theme for political purposes than for attacking street crime. Throughout Nixon's first term, administration officials had waged war against student, antiwar, and

Twenty-sixth Amendment Amendment to the Constitution in 1971 lowering the voting age from 21 to 18.

Environmental Protection Agency Agency created in 1970 to consolidate all major government programs combating pollution.

stagflation Persistent inflation combined with stagnant consumer demand and relatively high unemployment.

civil rights activists. Vice President **Spiro Agnew** denounced antiwar protesters for aiding the enemy. He called for the Silent Majority to reject "the nattering nabobs of negativism" and for authorities to take back the campuses. The White House also employed more direct tactics. The Justice Department, often acting illegally, used **wiretaps** and preventive detention against opponents and infiltrated groups viewed as the administration's enemies.

As part of Nixon's efforts to lock up the once solidly Democratic South for Republicans, the administration worked to slow integration. In response to Mississippi's request in 1969 to postpone the court-ordered integration of several school systems, Attorney General **John Mitchell** petitioned the Supreme Court for a delay. At the same time, the administration lobbied Congress to pass a weaker version of the 1965 Voting Rights Act. Neither effort was successful. Congress rejected changes to the Voting Rights Act, and in October the Supreme Court unanimously decreed in *Alexander v. Holmes* that it was "the obligation of every school district to terminate dual school systems at once." The White House suffered another loss in 1971 when the Court reaffirmed the use of busing to achieve integration in a North Carolina case, *Swann v. Charlotte-Mecklenburg.* The Nixon administration criticized the decisions but agreed to "carry out the law." By 1973, most African-American children in the South attended integrated public schools. Nixon was unable to slow integration, but he did win political support from white southerners.

A second part of Nixon's southern strategy was to alter the ideological composition of the Supreme Court. He wanted a more conservative Court that would interpret the Constitution more narrowly. His first opportunity came in 1969 when Chief Justice Earl Warren retired. Nixon nominated federal judge Warren Burger, a respected conservative who was easily confirmed by the Senate.

Liberal Justice Abe Fortas's resignation soon after gave Nixon a second chance to alter the Court. For political reasons, he wanted to appoint a southerner. Nixon selected Clement Haynesworth of South Carolina to replace Fortas. Haynesworth's record on labor and civil rights raised predictable opposition in the Senate. Democrats and several Republicans joined forces to deny his confirmation. The rejection incensed Nixon, who was determined to force a southerner down the Senate's throat. His second choice was worse than the first. Not only was G. Harrold Carswell of Florida opposed to civil rights and labor, but he was a mediocre judge. A coalition of Republicans and Democrats rejected Carswell. On his third try, Nixon stopped looking for a southerner and selected Harry Blackmun, a conservative from Minnesota, who was confirmed easily. In 1971, Nixon appointed two more justices, Lewis Powell of Virginia (finally a southerner) and William Rehnquist of Arizona, creating a more conservative Supreme Court.

An Embattled President

By the end of Nixon's first term, the Republicans had every reason to gloat. Nearly 60 percent of those polled approved of Nixon's record. Nixon's southern strategy had ensured growing support in what had once been the "solid Democratic South." The law-and-order campaign had proven attractive to Middle America, while protesters and activists were losing strength. The economy, though still a worry, seemed under control. Diplomatically, Nixon had scored major successes in opening relations with China, establishing détente with the Soviets, and reducing American forces in Vietnam.

The continued disarray of the Democratic party only added to Republican confidence. The Democrats nominated **George McGovern** of South Dakota, but he was too liberal for much of the party. George Wallace again bolted the party to

Spiro Agnew Vice president under Richard Nixon, who resigned in 1973 amid charges of illegal financial dealings during his governorship of Maryland.

wiretap Concealed listening or recording device used to monitor communications.

John Mitchell Nixon's attorney general, who eventually served four years in prison for his part in the Watergate scandal.

George McGovern South Dakota senator who opposed the Vietnam War and was the Democratic candidate for president in 1972 defeated by Nixon.

run as a third-party candidate on the American Independent ticket. Wallace's candidacy ended on May 15, 1972, when Arthur Bremer shot and paralyzed him.

Despite almost certain victory, Nixon was plagued by a siege mentality. He was convinced that he was surrounded by enemies: Democrats, social activists, liberals, and much of the press. Repeatedly, he spoke about "screwing" his domestic enemies before they got him. He used the FBI, the Internal Revenue Service, and other government organizations to intimidate and punish his "enemies."

Throughout the campaign, Nixon was obsessed with humiliating the Democrats. To achieve this objective, Nixon's staff and the Committee to Reelect the President (CREEP), directed by John Mitchell, were willing to step outside the normal bounds of election behavior. They turned to a Special Investigations Unit, the "Plumbers," to disrupt the Democrats. The Plumbers had used illegal surveillance and even burglary to investigate sources of suspected leaks of sensitive materials, like the *Pentagon Papers.* Ex-FBI agent G. Gordon Liddy and former CIA operative E. Howard Hunt conducted "dirty tricks" against the Democrats. CREEP approved sending burglars into the Democratic National Headquarters office in the **Watergate** building to copy documents and tap phones.

There on June 17, 1972, a security guard detected the burglars and notified the police, who arrested five men carrying "bugging" equipment. Officials soon determined that they worked for Hunt and Liddy. CREEP and the White House denied any connection to the burglars. As Nixon "categorically" denied that anyone in the White House was involved, Mitchell and White House staffers destroyed incriminating documents and arranged payments to those arrested in return for their silence. The FBI was encouraged to limit its investigation. The furor passed, and the Watergate break-in had little apparent effect on the election. Nixon buried McGovern in an electoral avalanche, winning every state except Massachusetts.

Nixon began his second term by claiming a clear mandate for his policies. From the outside, it appeared that the Nixon administration had a clear field to promote its agenda. But within the White House, concern simmered over the approaching trial of the Watergate burglars. If the truth about Watergate were discovered, the Nixon administration might disintegrate. Although not directly involved in the covert actions against the Democrats, Nixon knew soon after the Watergate break-in that White House officials were implicated and approved of efforts to hide their involvement. "Cover it up," he told John Mitchell.

As the trial approached, the cover-up began to unravel. Before being sentenced, James McCord, who led the burglary team, informed Judge John J. Sirica that key Republicans had been involved in planning the operation and that the burglars had been paid to keep quiet. *Washington Post* reporters Bob Woodward and Carl Bernstein found a trail of suspicious payments that led to the White House, John Mitchell, and CREEP. Amid growing suspicions of White House involvement, the Senate convened a special committee in 1973 to investigate the break-in, chaired by a Democrat, Senator Sam Ervin, Jr., of North Carolina. White House staffer John Dean testified before Sirica and Ervin's committee that top White House officials, including Nixon, were involved in the cover-up. By May 1973, Nixon had fired Dean and watched Bob Haldeman and John Ehrlichman resign.

The cover-up further unraveled with testimony that Nixon had secretly recorded Oval Office conversations, including those with Dean. Responding to public pressure, Nixon appointed Harvard professor Archibald Cox as special Justice Department prosecutor to investigate Watergate. When Cox demanded the Oval Office tapes, Nixon had him fired in October 1973. Calls for Nixon's resignation or impeachment intensified. Adding to Nixon's troubles were accusations that he had improperly taken tax deductions. "I am not a crook," Nixon asserted. Nevertheless, the Internal

Watergate Washington apartment complex that housed the Democratic party's national headquarters; it gave its name to the scandal over the Nixon administration's involvement in a break-in at those headquarters and the president's part in the cover-up that followed.

Revenue Service concluded that Nixon had made errors in his deductions and owed the government half a million dollars. Meanwhile, Vice President Agnew was convicted of income-tax evasion and influence peddling and forced to resign. Nixon named Congressman Gerald R. Ford of Michigan to replace Agnew.

In March 1974, the grand jury investigating the Watergate break-in indicted Mitchell, Haldeman, and Ehrlichman and named Nixon as an "unindicted co-conspirator." Under tremendous pressure, Nixon released transcripts of selected tapes to the House Judiciary Committee. The outcome was devastating. Not only did the transcripts contradict some official testimony, but Nixon's profanity and apparent lack of moral values shocked many Americans. By August, the House Judiciary Committee had charged Nixon with three impeachable crimes: obstructing justice, abuse of power, and denying subpoenas. Once-loyal Republicans told him that he could either resign or face impeachment. Nixon resigned on August 9, 1974, making Ford president. Eventually, twenty-nine people connected to the White House were convicted of crimes related to Watergate and the 1972 campaign.

S U M M A R Y

Expectations
Constraints
Choices
Outcomes

President Johnson *chose* to continue President Kennedy's commitment to save South Vietnam from communism. The *outcome* was an Americanized war in Vietnam. The *expectation* that American superiority would defeat Ho Chi Minh's Communists proved disastrous for the nation. Vietnam cost Johnson his presidency and divided the nation.

It was not just the debate over the war that split the nation. By 1968, the country was aflame with riots in urban centers, and an increasing number of groups was seeking better social, economic, and political *choices.* Those advocating social reforms encountered growing *constraints* generated by a resurgence of conservatism. In 1968, Nixon *chose* to emphasize dissatisfaction with Johnson's war and the Great Society to win the presidency.

As president, Nixon *chose* to escape the quagmire of Vietnam by implementing Vietnamization. He *chose* to promote détente by working to improve relations with the Soviet Union and China. At home, Nixon *chose* an uneven course, switching between maintaining governmental activism and reducing the power of government. Politically, he sought a broader base for the Republican party by pursuing a southern strategy that diminished federal support for civil rights. Despite Nixon's domestic and foreign policy successes, however, his desire to crush opposition eventually led to the Watergate scandal. *Expecting* impeachment, the president *chose* to resign. The *outcome* of the Johnson years and Watergate was a nation with low *expectations* for politics and government, caught in a feeling of drift, disillusionment, and disunity.

SUGGESTED READINGS

Ambrose, Stephen. *Nixon: The Triumph of a Politician, 1962–1972* (1989).

An excellent examination of Nixon and his politics.

Caputo, Philip. *A Rumor of War* (1986).

An excellent personal account of one person's changing perspectives on the war in Vietnam. From his experiences as a young marine officer in Vietnam to an experienced journalist covering the final days in Saigon, Caputo frequently reflected the views of the American public.

Deloria, Vine, Jr. *Behind the Trail of Broken Treaties* (1974).

An examination of U.S. government policies toward Native Americans by a leading Indian activist.

Echols, Alice. *Daring to Be Bad* (1989).

An insightful and interesting account of the radical dimension of the women's movement.

Kutler, Stanley. *The Wars of Watergate* (1990).

A detailed account of the events surrounding the Watergate break-in and the hearings that led to the resignation of Nixon.

McQuaid, Kim. *The Anxious Years: America in the Vietnam-Watergate Era* (1989).

A brief and solid overview of the 1960s.

Roberts, Robert. *Where the Dominoes Fell* (1990).

A brief, well-written history of America's role in Vietnam.

Films

There are many excellent films about the American experience in Vietnam, from the PBS series on Vietnam to feature films like *Platoon, Apocalypse Now,* and *The Deer Hunter*.

INCREASE IN INCOME, 1980–1989 Personal income rose more rapidly in the 1980s than in any other decade, increasing almost 85 percent. As this map indicates, those increases were not uniform. Some regions and states did better than others. Because the inflation rate was approximately 70 percent during this period, the net gain in income was much less than this map appears to show. The graph to the right shows the increase in income with the 70 percent inflation rate both factored in and not factored in.

Range in percent change in income, 1980–1989
122%
30%
NEW HAMPSHIRE
84%
8%
UNITED STATES
33%
–28%
WYOMING
Not adjusted for inflation
Adjusted for inflation
CANADA
WASHINGTON 71.2%
OREGON 70.9%
CALIFORNIA 82.2%
NEVADA 79.6%
IDAHO 70.1%
MONTANA 64.9%
WYOMING 33.1%
UTAH 71.0%
ARIZONA 79.7%
COLORADO 75.1%
NEW MEXICO 67.6%
NORTH DAKOTA 55.1%
SOUTH DAKOTA 75.3%
NEBRASKA 64.9%
KANSAS 65.3%
OKLAHOMA 55.3%
TEXAS 64.5%
MINNESOTA 81.6%
IOWA 65.5%
MISSOURI 81.4%
ARKANSAS 77.5%
LOUISIANA 52.8%
WISCONSIN 76.0%
ILLINOIS 78.9%
MICHIGAN 75.3%
INDIANA 76.6%
OHIO 73.0%
KENTUCKY 80.5%
TENNESSEE 90.3%
MISS. 78.2%
ALABAMA 82.0%
GEORGIA 98.8%
FLORIDA 96.2%
SOUTH CAROLINA 87.6%
NORTH CAROLINA 94.4%
VIRGINIA 101.5%
W.VA. 58.3%
PENNSYLVANIA 83.1%
NEW YORK 105.4%
VT. 109.2%
MAINE 105.0%
N.H. 122.0%
MASS. 119.0%
R.I. 90.1%
CONN. 110.6%
N.J. 117.7%
DEL. 78.8%
MD. 101.9%
Washington, D.C. 95.1%
PACIFIC OCEAN
ATLANTIC OCEAN
MEXICO
Gulf of Mexico
PACIFIC OCEAN
HAWAII 82.9%
0 100 Km.
0 100 Mi.
U.S.S.R.
ALASKA 69.3%
CANADA
0 250 500 Km.
0 250 500 Mi.
PACIFIC OCEAN
Per capita income, 1989
Under $13,000
$13,000–$15,000
$15,000–$17,000
$17,000–$19,000
Over $19,000
11.9% Percent change from 1980 (not adjusted for inflation)
0 200 400 Km.
0 200 400 Mi.

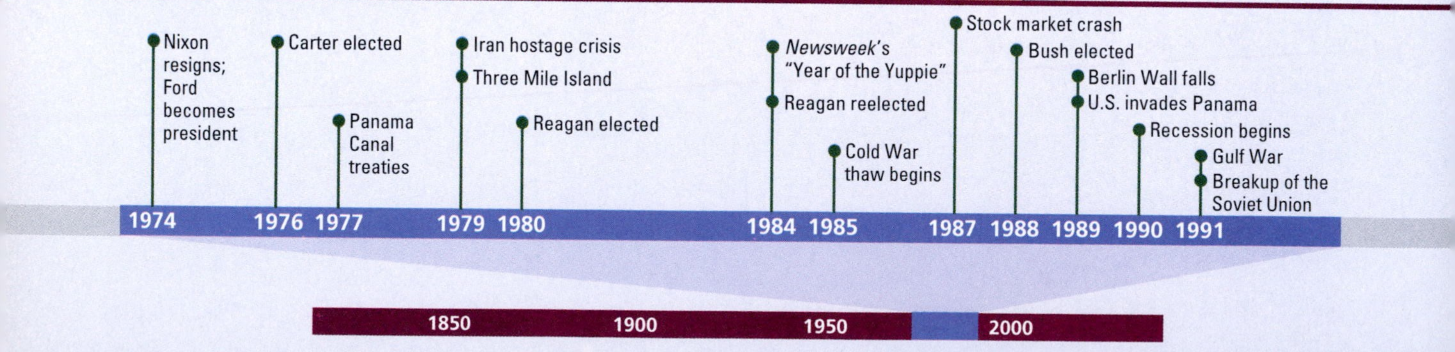

1974 Nixon resigns; Ford becomes president
1976 Carter elected
1977 Panama Canal treaties
1979 Iran hostage crisis
Three Mile Island
1980 Reagan elected
1984 *Newsweek*'s "Year of the Yuppie"
Reagan reelected
1985 Cold War thaw begins
1987 Stock market crash
1988 Bush elected
1989 Berlin Wall falls
U.S. invades Panama
1990 Recession begins
1991 Gulf War
Breakup of the Soviet Union
1850
1900
1950
2000

CHAPTER 31

Facing Limits, 1974–1992

Politics of Uncertainty

- What domestic problems did Gerald Ford and Jimmy Carter face? What were the political and economic outcomes of the choices they made?
- What expectations and constraints did Carter face as a Washington outsider?

Carter's Foreign Policy

- What new directions in foreign policy did Carter take? What were the outcomes of those changes?
- What constraints did Carter face in implementing a policy stressing human rights?

Enter Ronald Reagan—Stage Right

- What expectations influenced Americans who chose to vote for Reagan?
- What was "Reaganomics," and what were the outcomes of Reagan's economic policies for the economy and society?

Asserting World Power

- How did the Reagan administration's expectations about American foreign policy differ from Carter's? How did those views shape the outcomes of Reagan's policies?

In Reagan's Shadow

- What new foreign-policy choices did the United States face as a result of the collapse of the Soviet Union?
- How did the outcome of Reagan's domestic policies shape expectations and outcomes for the Bush administration?

INTRODUCTION

Gerald Ford assumed the presidency after the resignation of Richard Nixon and faced an expanding set of policy *constraints* without Nixon's vision or toughness. The economy continued to flounder, and many of Nixon's foreign-policy initiatives, especially regarding détente, were being questioned by his own party. Also, the political cynicism generated by Vietnam and Watergate operated as a *constraint*. The *outcome* was a presidency with few political or foreign-policy "victories." Nevertheless, the Republican party nominated Ford for the presidency in 1976.

As the nation celebrated its two-hundredth birthday, few Americans *expected* the immediate future to match the success of the past. Limits seemed to loom everywhere. The sluggish economy responded to neither liberal nor conservative policy *expectations.* The liberalism that had attacked racism and poverty was out of vogue, challenged by more conservative *choices.* The Silent Majority seemed to set the tone of the nation, rejecting the idea that a more active government can solve problems and favoring a stronger emphasis on more traditional social values. Even James Earl Carter, the Democratic candidate for the presidency in 1976, argued that the U.S. government could not solve every problem. He urged Americans to sacrifice to overcome problems at home and abroad. As president, however, Carter failed to provide an effective domestic or foreign policy.

The 1980 Republican candidate for president, Ronald Reagan, won popular approval by promoting the *expectation* of a renewed America, powerful and prosperous. He attacked liberal economic and social policies and reemphasized a Cold War foreign policy that would "stand tall" against the Soviet "evil empire." During his administration, the economy seemed revitalized, and government was redirected away from costly social programs. Many Americans felt that business had been freed of many needless government controls, traditional social and family values had been properly reasserted, and the Cold War had been all but won.

E xpectations
C onstraints
C hoices
O utcomes

Not everyone agreed that Reagan's *choices* produced a favorable *outcome.* Critics argued that he placed too much emphasis on wealth and too little on the needs of the poor. Others pointed to a massive national debt and a growing trade deficit as serious economic problems. Despite Reagan's personal popularity, as the Reagan administration ended, more and more Americans were uncertain about the *outcome* of Reagan's economic and social policies.

Running in the shadow of Reagan in 1988, Vice President George Bush seized the Republican presidential nomination in a nation that seemed dissatisfied but unable to pinpoint what was wrong and how to fix it. Responding to the lack of consensus in the polls, Bush offered a "kinder, gentler nation" that would show more concern for minorities, the poor, education, and the environment. Easily defeating Michael Dukakis, the Democratic candidate, Bush assumed the presidency but had little desire to implement domestic policy changes. Instead, he *chose* to focus on foreign policy. Taking office as the Soviet Union shattered, he charted foreign policy in a new international setting: the United States was the only superpower. Bush cautiously supported democratic change in the Soviet Union and Eastern Europe and *chose* to commit American military force in Panama and Kuwait. The *outcome* was that Bush's foreign policy, unlike his domestic policies, generated widespread praise.

CHRONOLOGY

New Directions, New Limits

1974	Nixon resigns; Ford becomes president Ford pardons Nixon
1975	Fall of South Vietnam Helsinki Summit Jackson-Vanik Amendment
1976	Carter elected president
1977	Department of Energy created Panama Canal treaties SALT I treaty expires
1978	Camp David Accords Revolution in Iran topples the shah United States recognizes People's Republic of China
1979	Ayatollah Khomeini assumes power in Iran Nuclear accident at Three Mile Island, Pennsylvania Egyptian-Israeli peace treaty signed in Washington, D.C. Chrysler bailout Hostages seized in Iran Soviet Union invades Afghanistan
1980	Carter applies sanctions against Soviet Union SALT II withdrawn from Senate Iran-Iraq War begins Reagan elected president
1981	Iran releases American hostages Economic Recovery Tax Act
1982	United States sends marines to Lebanon
1983	SDI funded United States invades Grenada Marine barracks in Beirut destroyed
1984	Reagan reelected Withdrawal of U.S. forces from Lebanon Boland Amendment
1985	Mikhail Gorbachev assumes power in Soviet Union Secret arms sales to Iran in exchange for hostages Gorbachev-Reagan summit in Geneva
1986	U.S. bombing raid on Libya Gorbachev-Reagan summit in Iceland
1987	Iran-Contra hearings Stock market crash Intermediate Nuclear Force Treaty
1988	U.S. warship shoots down Iranian passenger jet Terrorists blow up a Pan American jet over Scotland Bush elect president
1989	Communism collapses in Eastern Europe Berlin Wall torn down United States invades Panama Chinese government crushes prodemocracy movement Gorbachev-Bush summit at Malta
1990	Recession begins Free elections in Nicaragua Clean Air Act Iraq invades Kuwait
1991	Breakup of Soviet Union Gulf War Gorbachev resigns

Politics of Uncertainty

When he assumed office in 1974, **Gerald Ford** offered a stark contrast to Richard Nixon. Whereas Nixon was innovative, suspicious, and arrogant, Ford was conservative, trustful, and humble. (He joked that he was a Ford and not a Lincoln.) Responding to Watergate, Ford sought to establish cordial relations with Congress and to restore the people's faith in government. That expectation faded rapidly.

An Interim Presidency

Soon after taking office in 1974, Ford pardoned Nixon for any crimes the former president might have committed. The pardon was widely unpopular. Thereafter, Democrats opposed Ford's policies to deal with the problems of inflation, recession, and the federal deficit. He wanted to cut spending, raise interest rates, and cut business taxes. Democrats instead introduced legislation to create jobs and to increase spending for social and educational programs. Ford in turn vetoed these bills. The consequence of the pardon, rising inflation and unemployment, and the battles with Congress was a political stalemate.

Ford fared only slightly better in his foreign policies. Relying heavily on Henry Kissinger, the national security adviser and secretary of state, Ford continued Nixon's policies, including Vietnamization, arms limitation, and détente (see page 678). Trying to maintain the thaw in the Cold War, Ford met with Soviet Premier Leonid Brezhnev and leaders from thirty-three other nations in Helsinki, Finland, in August 1975. Following these negotiations, the United States officially recognized the boundaries of Europe established after World War II. The Soviets in return agreed to respect an extensive list of **human rights.** The Helsinki agreements quickly came under fire as human rights violations continued in the Soviet Union. Congress responded by passing the Jackson-Vanik Amendment, which required the Soviets to allow more Jewish immigration from the Soviet Union before the United States granted trade agreements. Reading the political climate, Ford backed away from détente.

Ford's efforts to maintain Nixon's pledges of economic and military support for South Vietnam (see page 675) also met with congressional opposition. When North Vietnamese forces seized Saigon in April 1975, Ford blamed Congress for the Communist victory. Most Americans, however, were happy that the conflict was no longer an American war.

Kissinger was far more successful with his diplomacy in the Middle East (see Map 31.1). Following the Yom Kippur War of October 1973, Kissinger flew between the Israeli and Arab capitals seeking to negotiate the removal of Israeli forces from Arab territory. His so-called shuttle diplomacy continued until September 1975, when Israel agreed to withdraw from some occupied areas and Egypt resigned from the anti-Israeli Arab coalition.

The Bicentennial Election and Jimmy Carter

Against the background of the bicentennial celebration of American independence, Ford sought election in his own right. Although he faced a stiff challenge from California governor Ronald Reagan and the Republican right wing, he gained the nomination.

Ford's Democratic opponent, Jimmy Carter, had no national exposure and little political experience apart from being governor of Georgia. But people in 1976 were fed up with politics and politicians. Carter presented himself as a political outsider

Gerald Ford Michigan congressman who became vice president under Nixon in 1973 after Vice President Agnew resigned; Ford became president in 1974 when Nixon resigned.

human rights Basic rights and freedoms to which all human beings are entitled, including the rights to life, liberty, freedom of thought and expression, and equality before the law.

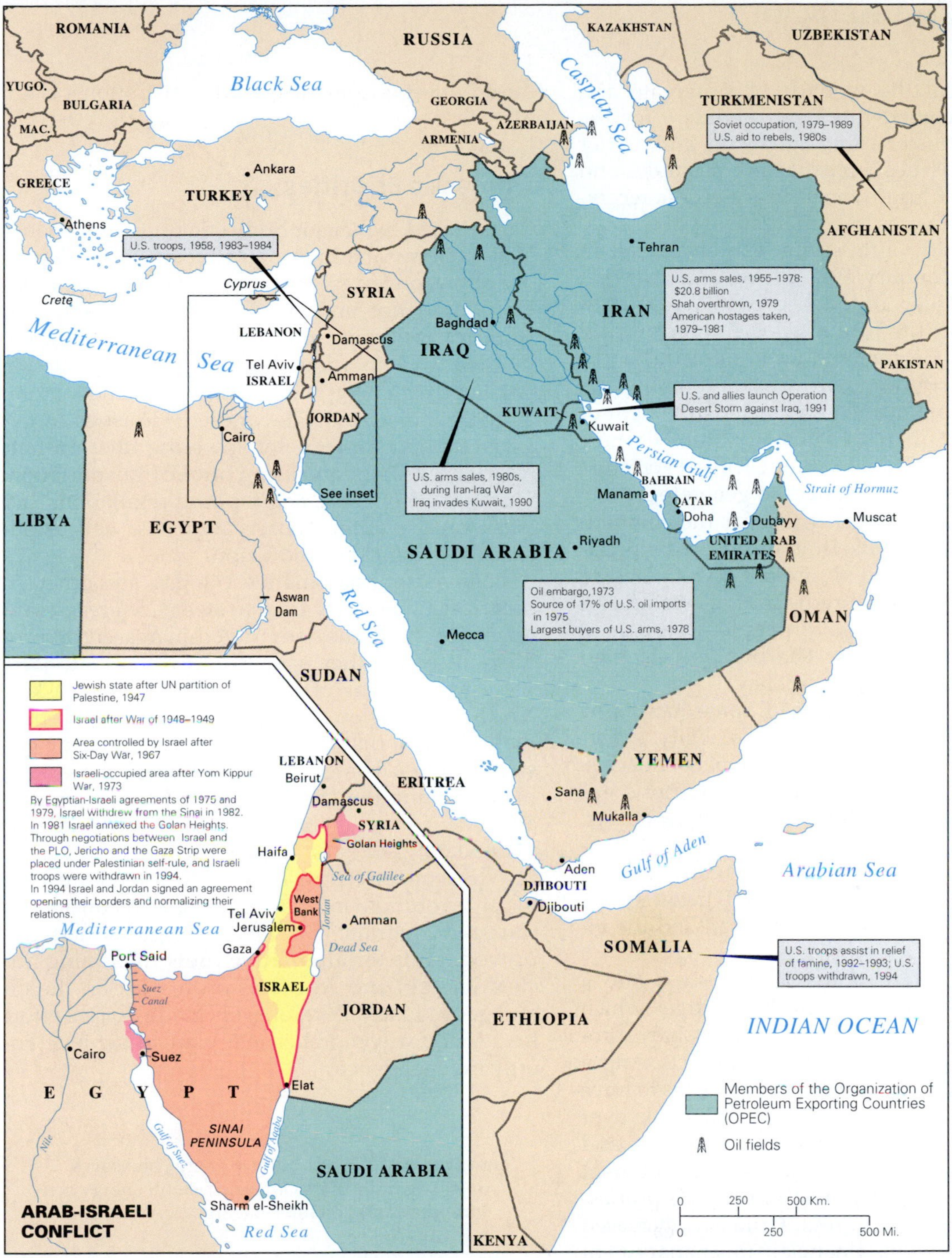
ROMANIA
RUSSIA
KAZAKHSTAN
UZBEKISTAN
Black Sea
Caspian Sea
YUGO.
BULGARIA
GEORGIA
TURKMENISTAN
MAC.
AZERBAIJAN
ARMENIA
Soviet occupation, 1979–1989
U.S. aid to rebels, 1980s
Ankara
GREECE
TURKEY
Athens
AFGHANISTAN
U.S. troops, 1958, 1983–1984
Tehran
Cyprus
SYRIA
U.S. arms sales, 1955–1978:
$20.8 billion
Shah overthrown, 1979
American hostages taken,
1979–1981
Crete
IRAN
Baghdad
LEBANON
Damascus
Mediterranean Sea
IRAQ
Tel Aviv
ISRAEL
Amman
PAKISTAN
U.S. and allies launch Operation
Desert Storm against Iraq, 1991
KUWAIT
Kuwait
JORDAN
Cairo
Persian Gulf
U.S. arms sales, 1980s,
during Iran-Iraq War
Iraq invades Kuwait, 1990
BAHRAIN
Strait of Hormuz
See inset
Manama
QATAR
Doha
Dubayy
Muscat
LIBYA
EGYPT
Riyadh
UNITED ARAB
EMIRATES
SAUDI ARABIA
Aswan
Dam
Red Sea
Oil embargo,1973
Source of 17% of U.S. oil imports
in 1975
Largest buyers of U.S. arms, 1978
OMAN
Mecca
SUDAN
Jewish state after UN partition of
Palestine, 1947
Israel after War of 1948–1949
Area controlled by Israel after
Six-Day War, 1967
Israeli-occupied area after Yom Kippur
War, 1973
By Egyptian-Israeli agreements of 1975 and
1979, Israel withdrew from the Sinai in 1982.
In 1981 Israel annexed the Golan Heights.
Through negotiations between Israel and
the PLO, Jericho and the Gaza Strip were
placed under Palestinian self-rule, and Israeli
troops were withdrawn in 1994.
In 1994 Israel and Jordan signed an agreement
opening their borders and normalizing their
relations.
LEBANON
Beirut
ERITREA
YEMEN
Damascus
SYRIA
Golan Heights
Sana
Mukalla
Haifa
Sea of Galilee
Aden
Gulf of Aden
West
Bank
Jordan
DJIBOUTI
Arabian Sea
Tel Aviv
Djibouti
Amman
Mediterranean Sea
Jerusalem
Dead Sea
Gaza
SOMALIA
Port Said
U.S. troops assist in relief
of famine, 1992–1993; U.S.
troops withdrawn, 1994
Suez
Canal
ISRAEL
JORDAN
ETHIOPIA
INDIAN OCEAN
Cairo
Suez
Elat
E G Y P T
Members of the Organization of
Petroleum Exporting Countries
(OPEC)
SINAI
PENINSULA
Oil fields
Nile
Gulf of Suez
Gulf of Aqaba
SAUDI ARABIA
0
250
500 Km.
ARAB-ISRAELI
CONFLICT
Sharm el-Sheikh
Red Sea
KENYA
0
250
500 Mi.

♦ **MAP 31.1 The Middle East** Since 1946, the United States has tried to balance strong support for Israel with its need for oil from the Arab states. To support U.S. interests in this volatile region, the United States has funneled large amounts of financial and military aid and used overt and covert force to shape regional governments. Agreements signed in Washington in 1993 and 1994 between Israel and the Palestine Liberation Organization and between Israel and the kingdom of Jordan reduced tensions in the region.

who would heal the wounds of Watergate and Vietnam. He seemed the ideal candidate for the time. In a lackluster campaign, Ford and Carter were vague on issues but expansive on smiles and photo sessions. Carter won a close election, receiving 297 electoral votes to Ford's 240.

Brimming with enthusiasm, Carter arrived in Washington in January 1977. He emphasized that he was an outsider, untouched by the politics of Washington and the lure of special interests and political deals. He pledged an administration of honesty, simplicity, and hard work. Promoting his image as a simple farmer, Carter took the oath of office wearing a plain blue business suit. His message to the people was without frills. "We must simply do our best," he stated, to generate a "new spirit . . . of individual sacrifice for the common good." Portraying himself as the people's president, Carter delivered Roosevelt-style "fireside chats" (see page 544) on radio and television and held "phone-ins" that gave people a chance to talk with their president. The public welcomed Carter's open, informal presidency.

But not everyone was charmed. Some questioned whether Carter had the political flexibility, expertise, and muscle to handle congressional politicians. Traditional Democrats also resented Carter's appointments of Georgia friends to government posts. "I busted my butt for Carter," one Democrat complained, "and there's nobody I know who got an appointment." A rift soon developed between the Washington outsiders on Carter's staff and the insiders in Congress.

Democratic congressional leaders flew into a rage when Carter presented his first budget, which axed eighteen pet projects that would have provided jobs and revenue for home districts. Angry Democrats joined with gleeful Republicans to force Carter to restore many of the cuts. The battle over the budget established a pattern. Congress and President Carter frequently marched in different directions. By mid-1977, most of Carter's proposals were buried in Congress. Criticism increased when allegations of financial mismanagement forced the president's close friend Bert Lance to resign as director of the Office of Management and Budget in September 1977. The Lance affair further eroded public trust in Carter's judgment and raised questions about the administration's claim of honesty.

Domestic Priorities

Carter faced two major domestic problems: a sluggish economy and high energy costs due to dependence on foreign oil. He concluded that the economy could not improve until the United States stopped consuming more energy than it produced. It was then importing about 60 percent of its oil. Solving the energy imbalance was the "moral equivalent of war," Carter argued. He asked Americans to save energy by lowering thermostats, wearing sweaters, and using public transportation. Turning to Congress, he proposed regulations and taxes to encourage conservation, as well as increases in domestic production.

Lobbyists for automobile, oil, gas, and other industries immediately tried to steer Congress in another direction. They advocated increased oil production, which they said would also create jobs. The development of large oil fields in Alaska's North Slope region made it difficult for many people to believe that there really was an **energy crisis.** Congress passed only fragments of Carter's plan, creating the Department of Energy in 1977, approving some incentives for conservation, and deregulating the natural gas industry.

When oil prices rose in 1978, forced upward by a revolution in Iran, Congress reconsidered Carter's program. By 1980, Congress had approved funds for **alternative fuels** (including nuclear energy) and an excess-profits tax on the oil and gas industry. But Congress made no real effort to develop a comprehensive plan to achieve energy independence.

energy crisis Vulnerability to energy shortages due to dwindling fossil fuels, wasteful energy consumption, and potential embargoes by oil-producing countries.

alternative fuels Sources of energy other than coal, oil, and natural gas; alternative energy sources include solar, geothermal, hydroelectric, and nuclear energy.

The prospects of using nuclear energy as a substitute for oil dimmed considerably after a nuclear power plant at **Three Mile Island** in central Pennsylvania had a serious accident on March 28, 1979. The plant released a cloud of radioactive gas and nearly suffered a **meltdown.** Over a hundred thousand people were evacuated from the surrounding area. After the accident, more than thirty energy companies canceled nuclear building projects. Thus oil, coal, and natural gas remained the primary sources of American energy.

Carter's economic policies fared even worse than his energy policy. To stimulate the economy, Carter asked for tax reforms, the **deregulation** of transportation industries (trucking, railroads, and airlines), and passage of his energy program. He tried to use tighter credit and higher interest rates to curb inflation. Like Ford, he asked workers and producers to hold the line on wages and prices.

Carter lost the battle with inflation. By 1979, inflation was running at 13 percent, the highest rate since 1947. Unemployment, which stood at nearly 7.6 percent, was also high. Carter assumed part of the blame for the nation's economic troubles. But he also blamed the public for its unwillingness to sacrifice. Most people, however, blamed the president for the nation's difficulties.

The stagflation troubling the American economy was largely the product of a changing world economy over which presidents had little control. The booming economies of West Germany, Japan, Korea, and Taiwan cut into American markets, reducing American profits and prosperity. The new cohesion of the **Organization of Petroleum Exporting Countries (OPEC)** following the Arab-Israeli Yom Kippur War of 1973 caused the price of petroleum products to skyrocket during the rest of the decade. Drastically higher energy costs not only added to inflation and unemployment but threatened the nation's industrial base, which depended on inexpensive fuel. In the new global economy, many American industries were unable to match the production costs, retail prices, or quality of goods produced overseas. Japanese manufacturers, once the joke of international commerce, were gobbling up the electronics industry and cutting deeply into the American automobile market. Korea and Taiwan were taking huge bites out of the American textile markets. Many of the nation's primary industries (iron and steel, rubber, automobiles and their parts, clothing, coal) were forced to cut back production, lay off workers, and even close plants.

In 1978, the giant Chrysler Corporation tottered on the brink of bankruptcy. Carter, facing soaring unemployment, agreed to help Chrysler, and in 1979 Congress underwrote a $1.5 billion private loan for the automobile maker. Critics called the Chrysler bailout welfare for the rich, but supporters argued that the loan saved jobs. With new models, effective advertising, and more efficient production, Chrysler was making more than $2.4 billion in profits by 1984, and Chrysler's chief executive officer, Lee Iacocca, was a national hero. Chrysler's success, however, was the exception. From the Great Lakes to the Northeast, the **Rust Belt** spread over the once-vibrant industrial center of the United States.

Carter's Foreign Policy

Carter's foreign policy was as controversial as his domestic policy. He said that American foreign

Three Mile Island Site of a nuclear power plant near Harrisburg, Pennsylvania; an accident at the plant in 1979 led to a partial meltdown and the release of radioactive gases.

meltdown Severe overheating of a nuclear reactor core, resulting in the melting of the core and the escape of radiation.

deregulation Removal of government regulations from an industry.

Organization of Petroleum Exporting Countries Economic alliance of oil-producing countries, mostly Arab, formed in 1960; in 1973, OPEC members placed an embargo on the sale of oil to countries allied with Israel.

Rust Belt Industrialized region containing older factories that are barely profitable or that have been closed.

policy had been preoccupied by an "inordinate fear of communism." America's recognition of the People's Republic of China in 1978 reflected Carter's beliefs. He advocated a foreign policy that would safeguard human rights, fight poverty, and promote economic and social development, especially in the **Third World.** Yet Carter also pursued traditional East-West power politics.

Carter's foreign-policy advisers reflected the split within his own mind over what American foreign policy should attempt to accomplish. **Zbigniew Brzezinski,** the national security adviser, was an uncompromising Cold Warrior who looked for chances to "stick it to the Russians." He worried that Carter's emphasis on human rights might weaken pro-American but abusive regimes in South Korea, Nicaragua, and the Philippines.

Cyrus Vance, Carter's secretary of state, was more broad-minded than Brzezinski. Vance recognized Cold War constraints but wanted to follow policies that focused on human issues and economic development. Clashes between him and Brzezinski were expected, but Carter believed he could bridge the gap between them.

A Good Neighbor and Human Rights

Latin America seemed to Carter and Vance the best place to sound a new tone in American policy. Carter wanted the United States to abandon its "paternalism" and instead fashion policies that considered each Latin American nation's internal priorities. Carter believed that Panama and the Panama Canal presented an excellent opportunity to chart a new course for U.S. policy in Latin America.

When Carter took office, negotiations to turn control of the canal over to Panama had been stalled for years. Carter assigned the canal a high priority. Within a year, two treaties were written that returned ownership and control of the canal to Panama by 1999 and guaranteed the neutrality of the canal. Carter was pleased, but the American public was not. Nearly 80 percent of those asked opposed giving up the canal. Opponents argued that the canal was built and operated by the United States and should remain that way forever. **Ronald Reagan** labeled the agreement outright appeasement, and conservative Republican senator Jesse Helms of North Carolina promised to kill it in the Senate. He failed, but only barely.

Carter also hoped to promote human rights in Latin America. Conservatives complained that letting human rights drive policy might undermine pro-American governments in Nicaragua and El Salvador. In Nicaragua, the **Sandinista Liberation Front,** a largely Marxist-led organization, was conducting a guerrilla war to oust Anastasio Somoza, who had ruled the country since 1967. Carter considered the corrupt and dictatorial Somoza a liability and stopped all aid to Nicaragua in early 1979. With his national guard disintegrating, Somoza fled to Paraguay in July, taking much of the nation's treasury.

The Sandinistas, led by **Daniel Ortega,** assumed power and promised free elections. Hoping that Ortega would adopt moderate reform programs, Carter asked Congress for $75 million in aid for the new government. Congress agreed, but the Nicaraguan government became more radical and **autocratic.** By 1980, the Sandinistas had canceled

Third World Underdeveloped or developing countries of Latin America, Africa, and Asia.

Zbigniew Brzezinski National security adviser who favored Cold War confrontations with the Soviet Union.

Cyrus Vance Secretary of state who wanted the United States to defend human rights and further economic development in the Third World.

Ronald Reagan Fortieth U.S. president; succeeded Jimmy Carter.

Sandinista Liberation Front Leftist guerrilla movement that overthrew the corrupt regime of Anastasio Somoza in Nicaragua in 1979.

Daniel Ortega Sandinista leader who helped establish the revolutionary government that replaced the Somoza regime in 1979 and who served as president of Nicaragua from 1984 to 1990.

autocratic Having unlimited power or authority; despotic.

elections and established close ties with the Soviet Union.

Conservatives attacked Carter's human rights policy for destroying a pro-American leader and allowing a Communist government to be established in Central America. Republican presidential candidate Ronald Reagan denounced the Communist "takeover" of Nicaragua and the Sandinistas' effort to export revolution to neighboring countries. Reagan called for support for the rebel **Contras** fighting the Sandinistas. Many Contras were former supporters of Somoza and had vowed to overthrow Ortega and restore "democracy." Carter stopped all aid to the Ortega government in early 1981.

Conservatives also called for more American support for El Salvador. There the newly created government of **José Napoleón Duarte** faced threats from both the left and the right. On the left were Farabundo Martí National Liberation Front (FMLN) guerrillas, who occupied more and more territory. On the right were elements within the military who used terrorism to eliminate opposition figures. Carter almost cut off military and economic aid when right-wing death squads murdered reform advocate Archbishop Oscar Romero. But FMLN victories prodded Carter to send millions of dollars in equipment and credit to Duarte.

As the election of 1980 neared, Carter's program for human rights in Latin America lay in ruins. He had been forced to break ties with Nicaragua and disregard murder and torture in El Salvador. His one triumph, the canal treaties, was unpopular at home.

The Camp David Accords

Carter credited his success in Panama to his ability to take a new approach to an old issue. He believed that such a tactic could also be used to achieve a peace settlement between Israel and its Arab neighbors (see Map 31.1). To this end, Carter invited Egypt's president, Anwar Sadat, and Israel's prime minister, Menachem Begin, for talks at the presidential retreat at Camp David in Maryland. Surprisingly, both agreed and arrived in September 1978. Carter smoothed relations between Sadat and Begin, who did not get along well. Carter carefully negotiated agreements by which Egypt recognized Israel's right to exist and Israel returned the Israeli-occupied Sinai Peninsula to Egypt.

Carter had to rescue the **Camp David Accords** several times before they were ratified. But on March 26, 1979, he watched as Begin and Sadat

♦ One of President Carter's greatest triumphs was the signing of the 1978 peace accords between President Anwar Sadat of Egypt *(left)* and Prime Minister Menachem Begin of Israel *(right)*. The agreement followed days of personal diplomacy by Carter at the Camp David presidential retreat. Both Sadat and Begin received the Nobel Peace Prize for their efforts. *Jimmy Carter Presidential Library.*

Contras Nicaraguan rebels, many of them former followers of Somoza, fighting to overthrow the Sandinista government.

José Napoleón Duarte Moderate civilian named to head the government of El Salvador in 1980.

Camp David Accords Treaty signed at Camp David in 1978, in which Israel agreed to return territory captured from Egypt in the Six-Day War in 1967 and Egypt agreed to recognize Israel as a nation.

signed the first peace treaty between an Arab state and Israel. The glow of success was fleeting. Arab leaders and many Egyptians bitterly condemned both the treaty and Sadat and remained committed to the destruction of Israel.

The Collapse of Détente

The most immediate Soviet-American issue that Carter faced was the still-unfinished **SALT II** treaty. Carter decided to negotiate even deeper cuts in nuclear weapons than Ford had proposed. Despite chilly relations, the United States and the Soviet Union were able to reach an agreement on strategic arms limitations in July 1979. Many senators, however, believed that the agreement was too favorable to the Soviets.

The Senate was still debating the treaty in December when the Soviet Union invaded neighboring Afghanistan. Claiming that the Afghan government had asked for help against **Islamic fundamentalist** rebels, Soviet leader Brezhnev sent in eighty thousand troops. Carter called the invasion the "gravest threat to peace since 1945." He withdrew the SALT II agreements from the Senate, halted grain shipments to the Soviet Union, and announced an American boycott of the 1980 Moscow Olympics. The invasion ended Carter's ambiguous Soviet policy. He now called for military superiority and a renewed arms race. He also began providing support for the **mujahedeen,** the Afghan resistance fighters.

The Iranian Revolution

Islamic fundamentalism affected far more than just Afghanistan. It was also behind the 1978 revolution in Iran, which toppled the pro-American ruler, Shah Reza Pahlavi. Since Eisenhower, the United States had supported the shah as a barrier to Soviet influence in the region. The shah had received billions of dollars in American weapons and aid, but his regime had become increasingly repressive. Led by **Ayatollah Ruhollah Khomeini,** a Shiite Muslim sect that condemned the contamination of Iranian culture by Western ideas and values headed the opposition. Khomeini returned to Iran from exile in Paris in February 1979, when the Shiites and the Iranian military forced the shah to flee. The Ayatollah Khomeini then set in motion a repressive fundamentalist Islamic revolution that attacked the United States as the main source of evil in the world.

Carter ended American aid to Iran, ordered Americans home, and reduced the embassy staff in Tehran. After the exiled shah entered a New York hospital to receive cancer treatments, an angry Iranian mob stormed the American embassy in Tehran on November 4, 1979, and took the staff hostage. These Americans were then paraded through the streets and subjected to numerous abuses as the Iranians demanded the return of the shah for trial. The press quickly dubbed the crisis "America Held Hostage."

Carter weighed the conflicting options identified by his advisers. Brzezinski wanted to use military force to free the hostages. Vance argued for negotiation, hoping that Iranian moderates would find a way to free the hostages. Carter sided with Vance and through the **Palestine Liberation Organization (PLO)** was able to negotiate freedom for thirteen hostages, mostly women and African

SALT II Proposal made in 1979 that the United States and the Soviet Union limit the numbers of strategic nuclear missiles in each country; Congress never approved the treaty.

Islamic fundamentalist Member of a movement calling for the replacement of Western secular values and attitudes with traditional Islamic values and an orthodox Muslim state.

mujahedeen Afghan resistance movement, supplied with arms by the United States, that fought the Soviets after the invasion of Afghanistan in 1979.

Ayatollah Ruhollah Khomeini Iranian Shiite leader who was exiled for his opposition to the shah but who returned to Iran in 1979 after the shah's downfall and established a new constitution giving himself supreme powers.

Palestine Liberation Organization Political and military organization of Palestinians originally dedicated to opposing the state of Israel through terrorism and other means.

Americans. As further discussions failed, American frustration and anger grew. In April 1980, Carter agreed with Brzezinski and ordered a military rescue mission. The operation was a disaster. A violent dust storm in the Iranian desert caused three helicopters to malfunction. Carter scratched the mission. Vance, who had opposed the operation, resigned.

Diplomatic efforts through the Canadians and the Algerians eventually resulted in an agreement in late 1980 to release the hostages. By that time, the shah had died of cancer, and Iran was at war with Iraq and needed the assets that Carter had frozen. On January 20, 1981, the last day of the Carter presidency, the hostages were freed, after 444 days of captivity.

Enter Ronald Reagan—Stage Right

According to Republicans in 1980, Carter's failure to free the hostages was typical of his administration's ineptness. Inflation remained at 12.4 percent, and unemployment was near 8 percent. Republicans claimed that Carter was incapable of maintaining either American honor abroad or prosperity at home. Ronald Reagan, a movie actor turned conservative politician, offered voters a clear alternative to Carter. The former California governor easily outran CIA director George Bush in 1980 to become the Republican candidate. Reagan named Bush his running mate. Liberal Republican John Anderson protested his party's turn to the right by running as an independent.

In his campaign for the presidency, Reagan argued that the federal government had grown too large and powerful. He promised to reduce the role of government and to lower taxes, freeing American ingenuity and competitiveness. Across the country, taxes had become a hot issue. In 1978, California had passed **Proposition 13,** which placed a limit on property taxes.

Reagan was a smooth campaigner with a sense of humor. He quipped, "A recession is when your neighbor loses his job. A depression is when you lose yours. A recovery is when Jimmy Carter loses his." Reagan presented himself as the "citizen politician, speaking out for the ideas, values, and common sense of everyday Americans." His conservative agenda called for more power for the individual and less power for the federal government. A vote for Reagan, his supporters claimed, would restore American pride, power, and traditions.

Reagan's message was welcome news not only to Republicans but also to many living in the Sunbelt (see chapter opener map for Chapter 30). By 1980, the region's population exceeded that of the industrial North and East. Politically, the Sunbelt exhibited conservative populism that opposed the power of the federal government. White southerners equated "liberal" government with altering traditional racial norms, and a **"sagebrush rebellion"** in the western Sunbelt opposed federal control and regulation of land and natural resources. Many westerners argued that federal environmental and land-use regulations blocked growth and economic development in the West. Throughout the Sunbelt, Reagan found enthusiastic voters ready to reject liberal, activist government. Further contributing to Republican totals were voters mobilized by the **New Right,** as well as younger voters attracted by the economic goals and social stability Republicans promised. Except for the size of Reagan's majority, the outcome of the election of 1980 was never in doubt.

Reagan emerged with 51 percent of the popular vote, compared to 41 percent for Carter and 7 percent for Anderson. Reagan's electoral count

Proposition 13 Measure adopted by referendum in California in 1978 cutting local property taxes by more than 50 percent.

"sagebrush rebellion" A 1980s political movement in western states opposing federal regulations over land and natural resources.

New Right Conservative movement opposing the political and social reforms that developed in the late 1960s and demanding less government intervention in the economy and a return to traditional values; it was a major political force by the 1980s.

was even more impressive: 489 to 49. Republicans gained a majority in the Senate and narrowed the Democratic majority in the House substantially. It appeared that a new conservative era was beginning.

The Moral Majority and the New Right

Reagan's campaign pulled vital support from the New Right. A loosely knit alliance that combined political and social conservatives, the New Right opposed the social and cultural changes spawned during the 1960s and 1970s. The New Right's social agenda promoted the movement's views of correct family and moral values, condemning abortion, pornography, and homosexuality. To mobilize support, the New Right pioneered the use of direct-mail campaigns that targeted specific segments of the population.

Highly visible among New Right groups were evangelical Christian sects, many of whose ministers were **televangelists.** With donations that exceeded a billion dollars a year, they did not hesitate to mix religion and politics. Jerry Falwell's **Moral Majority** promoted Ronald Reagan on more than five hundred television and radio stations. Falwell called on listeners to wage political war against politicians whose views on the Bible, homosexuality, prayer in schools, abortion, and communism were too liberal. Although many of the television evangelists were sincere, some were susceptible to the lure of wealth and power. In the most publicized scandal, Jim Bakker, whose "Praise the Lord" radio and television shows and enterprises earned millions of dollars, was denounced for forcing women of his church to have sex with him. He was also found guilty of fraud and conspiracy and sentenced to prison in 1987. Other scandals and abuses weakened the electronic ministry by the 1990s.

Reaganism

Reagan brought to the White House a clear and simple vision of the type of America he wanted. Called the "Great Communicator" by the press, he and his staff used imagery and the media expertly. Reagan did not create the policies to realize his vision; instead, he delegated authority to the cabinet and executive staff while he set the grand agenda.

Once in office, Reagan hit hard at the economic crisis of inflation, high interest rates, and unemployment. The administration's economic formula to restore the economy was deceptively simple: increase military spending, reduce taxes, and end government restrictions.

This formula derived from **supply-side economics.** Supply-siders believed that lowering taxes would actually increase tax revenues by increasing the amount of money available for investments. Budget director David Stockman fashioned a tax package and budget that reduced income and corporate taxes and slashed federal spending on social programs. The **Economic Recovery Tax Act,** passed in 1981, cut income and most business taxes by an average of 25 percent. Upper-income levels received the largest tax reduction. Stockman later admitted that the tax act was really a "Trojan Horse" to help the rich. Conservative Democrats joined with Republicans to cut $25 billion from social programs, including food stamps, Aid to Families with Dependent Children, and jobs and housing programs. Reagan also ended Nixon's federal revenue-sharing programs (see page 678) and reduced the amount of federal money paid to the states for Medicare and Medicaid programs. To

televangelist Protestant evangelist minister who conducts television broadcasts; many such ministers used their broadcasts as a forum for defending conservative values.

Moral Majority Right-wing religious organization led by televangelist Jerry Falwell that had an active political lobby in the 1980s on issues such as opposition to abortion and the Equal Rights Amendment.

supply-side economics Theory that reducing taxes on the wealthy and increasing the money available for investment will stimulate the economy and eventually benefit everyone.

Economic Recovery Tax Act Law passed in 1981 that cut income taxes by 25 percent across the board and further reduced taxes on the wealthy.

halt inflation, Federal Reserve chairman Paul Volker pushed interest rates upward.

Cutting taxes and domestic spending was only part of the Reagan agenda for economic growth. Another aim of **Reaganomics** was to free businesses and corporations from restrictive regulations. This aim was most visible in environmental regulations. Interior Secretary James Watt sought to open federally controlled land, coastal waters, and wetlands to mining, lumber, oil, and gas companies. The Environmental Protection Agency under Anne Gorsuch Burford weakened enforcement of federal guidelines for reducing air and water pollution and the cleanup of toxic-waste sites.

Reagan's economic policies were not immediately effective. Although inflation fell from 12 percent in 1980 to 4 percent by 1982, economic growth failed to materialize. Unemployment climbed over 10 percent in one of the worst recessions since World War II, and small businesses and farms faced bankruptcy in increasing numbers. The **trade deficit** skyrocketed from a surplus in 1980 to a $111 billion deficit in 1984, and the federal deficit swelled alarmingly. Reagan called for patience, saying that his economic programs eventually would work.

Suddenly, in 1983, the recession ended. Unemployment dropped to 7.5 percent. Many conservative economists and Republicans praised the administration's policies for the recovery. Others said that the recovery had less to do with Reagan's policies than with increases in world trade and the lowering of oil prices. Critics also pointed out that the national "recovery" was selective. The West Coast was doing well, but the Rust Belt was still rusting. But most Americans simply sought to make the most of renewed prosperity.

The Power of Money

Reagan's support for American business and opposition to government restrictions placed an emphasis on success, profits, and individual gain. While some argued that the new business culture was based on greed, others pointed to the creativity of American capitalism. Developments such as personal computers affected almost every segment of American society. With Apple and IBM leading the way, personal computers restructured the process of handling information and offered new choices for nearly everyone. Bill Gates, who developed software and programs for personal computers, took advantage of these new opportunities to become America's youngest billionaire (see Individual Choices: Bill Gates).

Among the most successful people during the 1980s were financial wizards like Donald Trump, T. Boone Pickens, and Ivan Boesky. Trump, who proclaimed himself the king of the "megadeal," commanded national attention for both his business ventures and his social life. His ghost-written books glorified him as the master of manipulating the economic system for personal gain. Speculators took advantage of government deregulation to sell **junk bonds** to finance **leveraged buyouts.** Riding the crest of the speculative boom, they amassed vast fortunes by arranging to have huge conglomerates gobble up smaller, vulnerable companies. "Buy high, sell higher," *Fortune* proclaimed.

The culture of success filled newspapers, magazines, television, and movies, celebrating people who were making big money and living accordingly. The lifestyle of success captivated young Americans. Those about to enter the work force increasingly considered financial success as their main goal in life. In 1974, only 46 percent of college freshmen and high school seniors listed being "financially successful" as their first priority. In 1986, 73 percent of college freshmen put being "very well off financially" as their priority.

Reaganomics Economic beliefs and policies of the Reagan administration, including the belief that tax cuts for the wealthy and deregulation of industry would benefit the economy.

trade deficit Amount by which imports exceed exports.

junk bond Corporate bond having a high yield and high risk.

leveraged buyout Use of a target company's asset value to finance the debt incurred in acquiring the company.

INDIVIDUAL CHOICES

Leading the Computer Revolution

Bill Gates

In 1974, Bill Gates made an eventful choice. Along with a friend from high school, Paul Allen, the Harvard sophomore decided to create an operating system for a new development in the computer world: the personal computer (PC). The system worked, and Gates left Harvard and formed Microsoft, creating MS-DOS and software packages for what soon became the personal computer revolution. By 1986, his operating system dominated the computer world, and he became the country's youngest billionaire. Corbis-Bettmann.

In December 1974, Bill Gates, a sophomore at Harvard, and his high school friend Paul Allen claimed that they could write a computer program for a new personal computer, the Altair 8080, which came unassembled and cost $397. Neither Gates nor Allen had seen the computer or the microchip that made the Altair run, but they were positive that the advent of personal computing was the beginning of a new era in information processing. "We realized that the revolution" had started, Gates recalled, and "there was no question of where life would focus." Gates and Allen chose to be a part of the revolution.

Having read only sketchy information about the Altair 8080, Gates and Allen invaded the Harvard computer lab and worked day and night for eight weeks. Ignoring his classes and sometimes sleeping at the keyboard, Gates modified the computer language BASIC to fit the Altair. They had no idea if the program would work—"If we had read the book wrong . . . we were hosed," Allen recalled. He then flew to New Mexico to demonstrate the program. Fortunately, it worked, and Gates and Allen were on the cutting edge of the computer revolution. Allen stayed to work for the computer company. Gates finished his academic year at Harvard. Then, over the objections of his parents, he chose to drop out of Harvard and join Allen. At 19, he and Allen formed Microsoft, a company to write software for personal computers. Microsoft made Gates, at age 31, the youngest billionaire in America.

Gates's obsession with computers began in 1968, when his high school in Seattle arranged computer time on a local company's machine.

"We were off in our own world," he remembered. "Nobody quite understood the thing but I wanted to figure out exactly what it could do." At the age of 13, he was "hired" by the company—paid with computer time—to find bugs in the system. Three years later, with Allen, Gates formed a company to analyze automobile traffic data by computer. They made about $20,000 until the government offered to analyze the traffic for no cost.

In 1980, their expectations rising, Gates and Allen agreed to design an operating system to run the software for IBM's entry into the personal computing field. IBM was already a giant in large business and institutional computers, and it was expected that IBM's personal computers would greatly expand the popularity and uses of personal computers. In 1980, each computer company wanted to capture and keep users by having a unique operating system to run software. IBM wanted Microsoft to formulate a new, exclusive system. Gates and Allen began by buying an existing system—QDOS, the "quick and dirty operating system"—and modifying it. Within a year, they had created, in great secrecy, Microsoft DOS (MS-DOS).

IBM's personal computers became the industry's leader and were soon being cloned by other companies. Gates chose to offer MS-DOS to other companies. At first, IBM was reluctant to share "its" system, but both companies benefited. By the 1990s, only two major operating systems still existed for personal computers: Apple and MS-DOS. Microsoft had become the industry giant and Gates the country's richest man.

Looking toward the twenty-first century, Gates continues to seek better and more innovative applications for personal computers, telecommunications, and information processing. His newest challenge is to integrate multimedia and communication systems with an interactive software package more effectively. Still pursuing his choice to be at the forefront of a revolution, Gates looks confidently toward a bright future. "We are going to create the software that puts a computer on every desk and in every home," he said. A billionaire, Paul Allen left Microsoft in 1983 and has since invested in and worked to develop companies in the high-technology, communications, and information delivery fields.

Although new technology and innovative ideas created some millionaires, many others were the beneficiaries of the government. Reagan's tax and economic policies favored the wealthy. The wealthiest 1 percent of Americans saw their slice of the economic pie grow from 8.1 percent to 15 percent during the Reagan years. The majority of American workers and families during the same period lost income. Still, the media spotlighted people making millions. College graduates hoping to become highly paid professionals applied to law, business, and other postgraduate schools in droves.

Not everyone was captivated by the Reagan boom. Social critic Tom Wolfe complained of a "Me Generation" that was self-indulgent and materialistic. Some economists warned that the stock market's climb rested on a weak foundation of shaky credit and fast profits. Such credit and profits, they argued, were related neither to actual economic growth nor to an increase in real buying power and wages.

On "Black Monday," October 19, 1987, their fears came true. The stock market dropped 508 points, the largest single decline in American history. Images of the 1929 Crash and the Great Depression reared up. The Reagan administration was shaken, but the Federal Reserve acted quickly to lower interest rates and to pump money into the economy. The Fed's action stopped the panic selling, and the stock market slowly turned upward again. Some warned, however, that the stock market still did not reflect real economic health and argued that more trouble lay ahead.

They soon had additional evidence when the savings and loan system began edging toward collapse. Until 1982, government regulations permitted **savings and loan associations (S&Ls)** to lend money only for single-family homes. In that year, the Reagan administration lifted nearly all restrictions on lending by S&Ls. Many S&L operators jumped into risky ventures such as office buildings, shopping malls, and junk bonds. Losses were covered by the Federal Savings and Loan Insurance Corporation (FSLIC). It was a no-lose situation for the S&L operators. If they gambled wrong, the government paid for their mistakes.

Corruption, bad loans, poor judgment, and a slowing economy soon pricked the S&L bubble. As real-estate values slumped in 1987, many S&Ls began losing vast sums of money. Some closed their doors. Charles Keating, president of Lincoln Savings and Loan in California, lost more than $2.6 billion of depositors' money. To keep his operation from being investigated, he made sizable "political" contributions to several senators. Eventually convicted of fraud, Keating was not alone in bending and breaking the law. He and scores of others left the S&L industry in ruins. The federal government had to cover more than $500 billion in losses.

By the late 1980s, the financial boom was fading along with the reputations of many who had ridden it. Donald Trump had to sell his airline and most of his real estate to pay creditors. Boesky was arrested for **insider trading** and sentenced to three years in prison.

Reputations fell in the Reagan administration as well. Secretary of the Interior James Watt and Attorney General Edwin Meese resigned following revelations that they had received money and favors for helping some businesses gain lucrative government contracts. They were not alone. Over a hundred members of the Reagan administration were found guilty of illegal behavior. Reagan was untouched by the scandals, however, and his popularity remained high. Some called him the "Teflon President" because no criticism seemed to stick to him.

Reagan's Second Term

Throughout the presidential campaign of 1984, Republicans credited Reagan's leadership and poli-

savings and loan associations Financial institutions originally founded to provide home mortgage loans; deregulation during the Reagan era allowed them to speculate in risky ventures and led to many S&L failures.

insider trading Trading of stocks by someone who has access to confidential information about the companies involved.

cies for renewed prosperity, restored military superiority, and "standing tall" against communism throughout the world. Using the theme "Morning in America," Reagan's re-election campaign projected a new day of economic expansion, morality, and national power. Reagan avoided specific issues while announcing that big-government liberalism was dead.

After a divisive primary season, former vice president **Walter Mondale** won the Democratic nomination. He refused to concede that liberalism was dead. He called for revitalizing social programs. He selected Geraldine Ferraro, a congresswoman from New York, to be his vice-presidential candidate. Although many people applauded Mondale for selecting a woman, others complained that Ferraro was not the best-qualified woman for the job.

Reagan won an overwhelming victory, taking 59 percent of the popular vote and carrying every state except Mondale's Minnesota. Only the poor, African Americans, and Latinos voted Democrat. A majority of organized labor, women, Catholics, white southerners, farmers, and the middle and upper classes voted for Reagan's Republican vision of "Morning in America."

A growing cloud, however, hung over Reagan's American morning: the soaring budget deficit. During his first administration, the annual deficit had gone from $73.8 billion to over $200 billion. Although reducing the deficit had bipartisan support, how to do it remained a partisan issue. Most Democrats took the view that cuts in military spending were needed. They argued that a large part of the deficit came from military spending, which had risen from $164 billion in 1980 to $228 billion in 1985. Republicans countered by blaming the debt on wasteful social programs.

In late 1985, a coalition of Republicans and Democrats passed the Gramm-Rudman-Hollings Act, which established a maximum debt level and ordered across-the-board cuts if the budget failed to match the level set. The plan never worked effectively. By 1989, federal expenditures had climbed to $1,065 billion a year, and the national debt stood at nearly $3 trillion, requiring an annual interest payment of $200 million. The United States had become the world's largest debtor nation. With the deficit seemingly out of control, many advocated a constitutional amendment to require a balanced budget.

Asserting World Power

As a candidate in 1980, Reagan had promised to re-establish the United States as the leader of the world. To accomplish that goal, he believed it was necessary to overcome what he termed the "Vietnam syndrome": the unwillingness to use military force to defend U.S. interests. As president, Reagan promised no lack of resolve to support those interests.

Cold War Renewed

At the center of Reagan's view of the world was his hostility toward the Soviet Union. He believed that the Soviet Union was an "evil empire" that would "commit any crime" to achieve world conquest. America's grand role was to defend global freedom against communism. Large increases in the military budget were necessary, Reagan argued, to close the "window of vulnerability" that Carter had created by allowing the Soviets to pull ahead in the arms race.

With almost no dissent, Congress funded Reagan's military budget. More funds were made available for nuclear weapons and new aircraft, including the B-1 bomber and Stealth fighters and bombers. The navy was enlarged; the army received more tanks and helicopters. The most controversial program called for a new defense system that would use x-ray lasers to blast incoming

Walter Mondale Minnesota senator who was vice president under Jimmy Carter and ran unsuccessfully for president on the Democratic ticket in 1984.

♦ After declaring the Soviet Union an "evil empire" responsible for nearly all the world's problems, President Reagan *(left)* reversed course in 1988 and opened productive discussions with Soviet reformer Mikhail Gorbachev *(right)*. The outcome was an intermediate-range nuclear force treaty that helped end the Cold War, as well as reduce the overall number of nuclear missiles. Here the two leaders pose in front of St. Basil Cathedral in Moscow. *Corbis-Bettmann.*

Soviet missiles. The **Strategic Defense Initiative (SDI),** or Star Wars, as it was soon dubbed, became Reagan's military priority. Between 1983 and 1989, Congress provided over $17 billion for Star Wars research despite criticism that Star Wars owed more to science fiction than to science. By 1989, Reagan had added over $100 billion a year to the military budget.

Numerous defense contractors took advantage of the money being lavished on defense. With billions of dollars available, government and industry officials padded their expense accounts and exchanged bribes and kickbacks on an unprecedented scale. They falsified test results and inflated costs artificially. Billion-dollar cost overruns became commonplace. Critics loudly opposed the military shopping spree but had little effect on Congress or the public.

The Middle East

The Middle East presented the Reagan administration with a complex series of problems that, except for Afghanistan, resisted being explained as Communist aggression. In Afghanistan, the CIA continued to supply the mujahedeen with arms to use against Soviet and Afghan forces. Elsewhere in the Middle East, problems involving Arab nationalism, Arab-Israeli disputes, and terrorism could not be so readily understood in a Cold War context.

As Reagan assumed office, Yassir Arafat's Palestine Liberation Organization had increased its raids against Israel, and shadowy militant Islamic groups had begun a campaign of terrorism against Israel and its Western supporters. Throughout the Mediterranean region, terrorists kidnapped Americans and Europeans, hijacked planes and ships, and attacked airports. Reagan linked the terrorists to Communist organizations, the PLO, and various Arab nations. With American encouragement, Israel invaded neighboring southern Lebanon in 1982 to halt terrorist attacks and to suppress the PLO. As Israeli forces approached the capital city of Beirut, all semblance of internal stability collapsed. A smoldering civil war between Christians and Muslims raged anew.

As part of an international peacekeeping effort, the United States sent nearly two thousand marines

Strategic Defense Initiative Research program designed to create an effective defense against nuclear attack; President Reagan asked Congress to fund SDI in 1983.

to Beirut. They quickly became a target for Muslim terrorists. In October 1983, a suicide driver rammed a truck filled with explosives into the marine barracks at the Beirut airport, killing 241 marines. Reagan denounced the terrorist attack but quietly made plans for the marines' removal. In January 1984, the United States withdrew its forces from Lebanon, where the civil war still raged. In Lebanon, there were no victories.

Nor were there any easy solutions in the **Persian Gulf.** The **Iran-Iraq War,** which started in 1980, created two problems for American foreign policy: protecting vital shipments of oil and ensuring that neither Iran nor Iraq emerged from the war as a dominant power. The Reagan administration provided money and weapons secretly to both sides. When Iranian forces attacked several oil tankers in 1986, American warships began escorting all oil tankers in the gulf. Clashes between American and Iranian forces occurred, one of which mistakenly resulted in the shooting down of an Iranian airliner. When the Iran-Iraq War ended in 1988, it had cost over 2 million lives. American intelligence concluded that neither country could threaten the rest of the region immediately.

To counterbalance Iran and Iraq, the United States supplied Saudi Arabia with sophisticated radar detection planes, tanks, and fighter aircraft. Stores of American military supplies were also buried in the Saudi desert in case of future need.

Farther west, in North Africa, Reagan faced off against **Muammar Qaddafi,** the vehemently anti-American ruler of Libya. Reagan denounced Libya as a "rogue" nation that actively supported the PLO and terrorist groups. In April 1986, terrorists bombed a disco popular among American troops in West Berlin, wounding several and killing an American soldier. Reagan ordered a reprisal raid after American intelligence tied Qaddafi to the terrorists. American planes bombed several targets in Libya, including Qaddafi's quarters, killing a young adopted daughter. The United States had shown Qaddafi "that we could get people close to him," bragged one official.

Although Qaddafi remained in power, what seemed important to most Americans was that the United States had responded to terrorism. The White House continued to call for the economic and political isolation of Qaddafi, particularly after investigations suggested that Libya had aided the terrorists who blew up a Pan American airliner over Lockerbie, Scotland, in December 1988, murdering over 250 people.

Central America and the Caribbean

In Central America and the Caribbean, Reagan thought that any hint of Communist influence justified American action. In the southern Caribbean, Reagan focused on the tiny island of **Grenada,** where a Marxist government had ruled since independence from Britain in 1979.

In October 1983, the radical New Jewel movement took control of Grenada. The Reagan administration immediately expressed concern about the new government, the construction of a large airport runway by Cuban "advisers," and the potential threat to about five hundred Americans attending medical school on the island. (The students did not think they were in any danger.) On October 25, Reagan ordered American forces to invade Grenada. More than two thousand American soldiers quickly overcame minimal opposition, brought home the American students, and installed a pro-American government. The administration basked in the light of public approval.

Determined to uphold his campaign pledge to defeat communism in Central America, Reagan

Persian Gulf Arm of the Arabian Sea that includes the ports of several major oil-producing Arab countries, including Iran, Saudi Arabia, Kuwait, and Iraq.

Iran-Iraq War War between Iran and Iraq that broke out in 1980 over control of a disputed waterway and ended in 1988 with more than 2 million dead.

Muammar Qaddafi Libyan political leader who seized power in a military coup in 1969 and imposed socialist policies and Islamic orthodoxy on the country.

Grenada Country in the West Indies that achieved independence from Britain in 1979 and was invaded by U.S. forces in 1983.

provided billions of dollars in aid to the El Salvadorian government and the Contra "freedom fighters" in Nicaragua. Although the public and Congress strongly supported Reagan's invasion of Grenada, his efforts in Central America stirred considerable opposition. Some critics were disturbed by reports of human rights violations by "death squads" linked to the El Salvadorian military. Many feared that Central America would become another Vietnam. When the press uncovered large-scale American covert aid to the Contras, including the CIA's mining of Nicaraguan harbors in 1984, Congress passed legislation drafted by Representative Edward Boland that allowed only humanitarian aid to the Contras.

Reagan and CIA director William Casey soon sought ways to work around the **Boland Amendment.** In the fall of 1985, the White House believed that it had found a way to do so. National security advisers Robert McFarlane and John Poindexter arranged for the secret sale of arms to Iran. In return, Iran agreed to use its influence with terrorist groups in Lebanon who held American hostages. The cash that Iran paid for the arms was then to be routed to the Contras, allowing them to purchase supplies and weapons.

When the press broke word of the so-called arms-for-hostages deal, a special White House commission and a congressional committee began separate investigations in 1987. Both uncovered evidence that the CIA and the National Security Council had acted without congressional approval and that members of both organizations had lied to Congress to keep their operation secret. McFarlane, Poindexter, and National Security Council aide Oliver North were found guilty and sentenced to prison terms. Although neither investigation uncovered proof that Reagan knew of the operation, some of his closest aides were clearly involved. The scandal damaged his image and that of his presidency.

Reagan and Gorbachev

Reagan made no attempt to improve relations with the Soviet superpower during his first term. He suddenly changed course early in his second term. He called for the resumption of arms limitation talks, and when Soviet leader Konstantin Chernenko died in March 1985, he invited Chernenko's successor, **Mikhail S. Gorbachev,** to the United States.

Gorbachev differed from previous Soviet leaders. He was determined to breathe new life into the Soviet economy, which was stagnating under the weight of military spending and government inefficiency and corruption. He also wanted to institute reforms that would provide more political and civil rights to the Soviet people.

Gorbachev declined Reagan's invitation but agreed to a summit meeting in Geneva in November 1985. The two leaders at first jousted with each other. Reagan condemned the Soviets for human rights abuses, their involvement in Afghanistan, and their aid to Communist factions fighting in Angola and Ethiopia. Gorbachev attacked the proposed development of SDI. But when Gorbachev showed an interest in Hollywood, his relationship with the former movie actor improved. The two leaders left Geneva with a growing fondness for each other.

Gorbachev shocked Reagan when they met again in October 1986 in Reykjavik, Iceland, by proposing a 50 percent reduction in strategic weapons over a five-year period and, less surprisingly, the nondeployment of SDI for ten years. Without consulting his advisers, Reagan responded that the two powers should eliminate all strategic missiles within ten years but allow the development of SDI. The summit ended without an agreement, to the relief of American advisers who considered Reagan's idea of eliminating all nuclear missiles a dangerous one.

Still, Soviet-American negotiations on arms limitations continued with new optimism. By December 1987, negotiators had reached an agreement that eliminated Soviet and American intermediate-range missiles from Europe. Reagan and Gor-

Boland Amendment Motion approved by Congress in 1984 that barred the CIA from using funds to give direct or indirect aid to the Nicaraguan Contras.

Mikhail S. Gorbachev Soviet leader who came to power in 1985; he introduced political and economic reforms and then found himself presiding over the breakup of the Soviet Union.

bachev signed the **Intermediate Nuclear Force Treaty** in Washington during their December 1987 summit. Throughout 1988, Soviet-American relations continued to improve. Gorbachev withdrew Soviet forces from Afghanistan, the Senate approved the Intermediate Nuclear Force Treaty, and Reagan visited Moscow. It seemed that the Cold War was over.

In Reagan's Shadow

As Republicans got ready for the 1988 election, the torch of Reaganism passed to Reagan's vice president, **George Bush.** Bush had devoted many years to public service and had held several important posts under Presidents Nixon and Ford: ambassador to the United Nations, chairman of the Republican National Committee, ambassador to China, and director of the CIA. After gaining the Republican nomination, Bush selected as his running mate a young, conservative, and virtually unknown Indiana senator, J. Danforth Quayle.

Bush Assumes Office

The 1988 campaign proved to be a dull affair. Both Bush and Democratic nominee Michael Dukakis, governor of Massachusetts, lacked flair and style. Dukakis ignored most issues and focused on his personal integrity and success in revitalizing the Massachusetts economy. Bush promised to fight drugs and crime, to take a special interest in education and the environment, and not to raise taxes. "Read my lips, no new taxes," he said. **Negative campaigning,** which aimed at discrediting the opponent rather than addressing issues, dominated the airwaves in 1988. Republican ads were very effective and put Dukakis on the defensive. One focused on Willie Horton, an African-American convicted of murder and imprisoned in Massachusetts, Dukakis's home state. While out of prison on a weekend pass, Horton raped a white woman. Lee Atwater, Bush's campaign manager, said that by the time he was through running the Horton ad, the public would believe that Horton was Dukakis's running mate.

Bush won election easily, gaining 79 percent of the electoral vote and 54 percent of the popular vote. The victory was not as sweet as Bush hoped it would be. His **political coattails** were very short. The Democrats remained the majority party in both houses of Congress.

Bush and a New International Order

Shortly after becoming president, Bush had to respond to unexpected and rapid changes in the Communist world, from Nicaragua to the Soviet Union. Within the Soviet Union, Mikhail Gorbachev's politics of **glasnost** and **perestroika** were producing political and religious freedom, reducing censorship and repression, and starting the development of a capitalist-style economy. Soviet armed forces were being withdrawn from Afghanistan and Eastern Europe (see Map 31.2).

The Bush administration voiced cautious support for Gorbachev's efforts. In December 1989, Bush met with Gorbachev on the island of Malta in the Mediterranean Sea. Gorbachev declared that the Cold War was over. Bush more prudently stated that they were working toward "a lasting peace." Later, Gorbachev visited Washington and signed agreements to improve trade and reduce

Intermediate Nuclear Force Treaty Treaty signed in 1987 by Reagan and Gorbachev that provided for the destruction of all U.S. and Soviet medium-range nuclear missiles and for verification with on-site inspections.

George Bush Politician and diplomat who was vice president under Ronald Reagan and was later elected president of the United States.

negative campaigning Presenting a political opponent as weak, dishonest, or untrustworthy instead of addressing basic political issues.

political coattails The result of voters casting their votes for all members of a political party based on voting for one particular member, generally the highest-ranking candidate on the ticket.

glastnost Policy under Gorbachev that allowed freedom of thought and candid discussion of social problems.

perestroika The restructuring of the Soviet economy and bureaucracy that began in the mid-1980s.

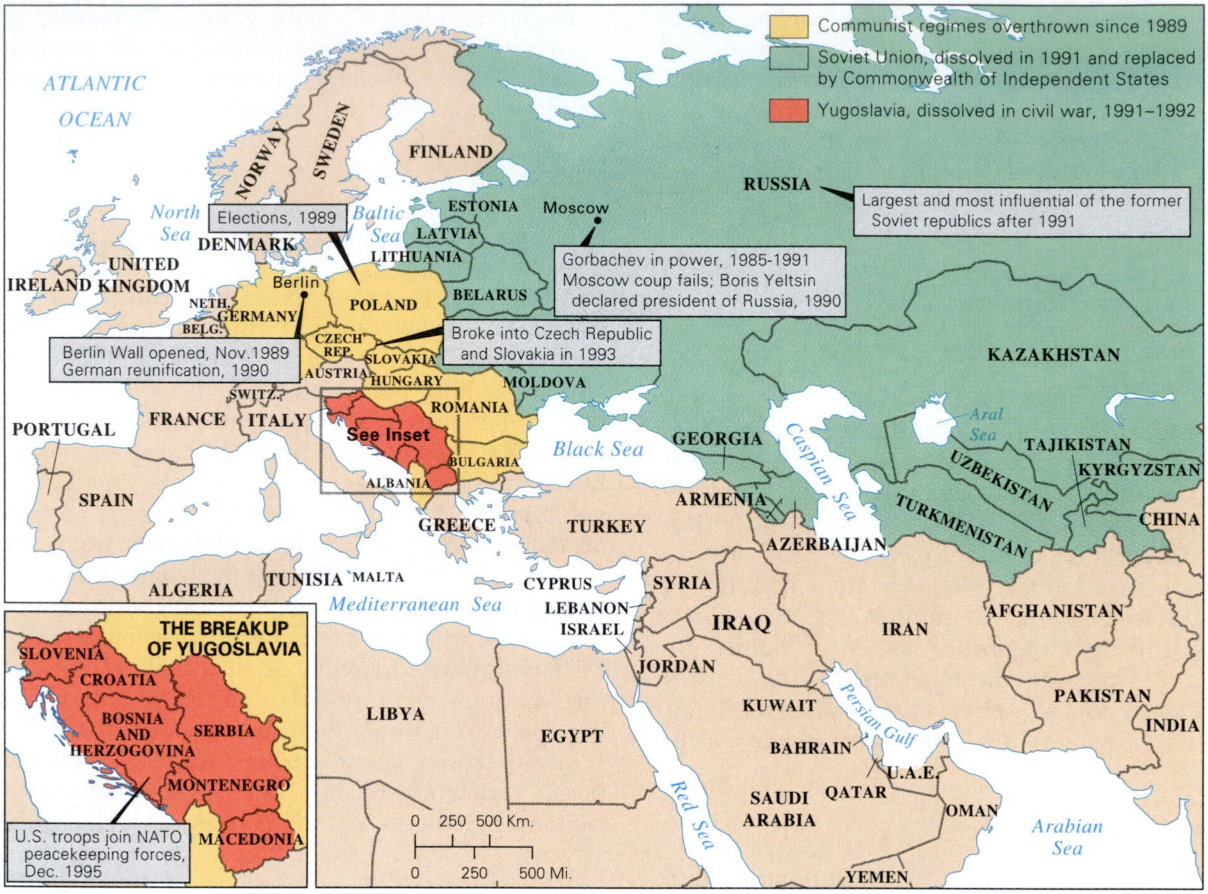

♦ **MAP 31.2 The Fall of Communism** As the Soviet Union collapsed and lost its control over the countries of Eastern Europe, the map of Eastern Europe and Central Asia changed. The Soviet Union disappeared into history, replaced by fifteen new national units. In Eastern Europe, West and East Germany merged, Czechoslovakia divided into two nations, and Yugoslavia broke into five feuding states.

the size of conventional and nuclear arsenals. He was cheered in the United States and around the world. At home, however, his popularity fell as the Soviet economy continued its downward spiral. Attacked by people wanting more reform and by hard-line Communists who feared any reform, Gorbachev asked the United States, Japan, and Western Europe to provide economic support to prevent "chaos and civil wars" in the Soviet Union.

Unable to slow the rush toward reform, the hard-liners on August 19, 1991, attempted a coup. They confined Gorbachev to his vacation home along the Black Sea and outlawed all political parties. In Moscow, **Boris Yeltsin,** leader of the Russian Republic, declared the coup illegal and called on the Russian people to resist. Over 150,000 Muscovites surrounded the Russian parliament building to defend Yeltsin. Faced with popular opposition in Moscow and other cities, the coup collapsed

Boris Yeltsin Russian parliamentary leader who was elected president of the new Russian Republic in 1991 and promised increased democratic and economic reforms.

within seventy-two hours. Released from captivity, Gorbachev announced that he was again in control of the Soviet Union.

By 1992, there was no Soviet Union to command. All that remained was a weak federation, the **Commonwealth of Independent States.** Power rested not with Gorbachev, who soon retired from office, but with the independent republics and especially with Yeltsin.

The collapse of the Soviet Union both simplified and complicated U.S. foreign policy. The threat of war with the Soviet Union was gone, but the new relationship between the United States and the former Soviet Union had not yet been determined. Bush recognized the independent republics and Yeltsin as the spokesman for the Russian Republic and for the Commonwealth. In a June 1992 visit to Washington, Yeltsin announced that Russia was ready to eliminate nearly all of its land-based strategic missiles. Bush applauded the arms reduction proposal, promised increased economic support, and hoped that Yeltsin could bring some stability to what had once been the Soviet Union. Yeltsin, however, could barely provide stability for Russia.

Even before the Soviet Union collapsed, communism was in retreat throughout Eastern Europe. In December 1988, Gorbachev announced that the Soviet Union would no longer intervene in Eastern Europe. Within a year, Poland had a new constitution, a free market economy, and a non-Communist government. In 1989, workers tore down the **Berlin Wall.** As the wall crumbled, so too did the Communist governments of East Germany, Hungary, Bulgaria, Czechoslovakia, and Romania. By the end of 1990, a unified Germany existed, and the Baltic states of Latvia, Estonia, and Lithuania had declared their independence from the Soviet Union.

The Bush administration hoped that free market economies and stable, democratic governments would emerge in the former Soviet bloc. In some nations, there was peaceful movement toward both; in others, there was increased regional and ethnic conflict. Yugoslavia's collapse in 1991 led to a series of bloody conflicts among rival ethnic groups. By 1994, over a hundred thousand people had died, many of them in **Bosnia,** where Muslims fought better-armed Christian Serbs who were trying to dismember the Bosnian republic.

The breeze of democracy was not limited to Eastern Europe. In the People's Republic of China, Central America, and South Africa, similar movements were taking place. Chinese university students sought an end to the authoritarian policies of Deng Xiaoping. Prodemocracy protesters took to the streets in Beijing and other Chinese cities, demanding political, economic, and civil freedoms. They filled **Tiananmen Square** in Beijing, erecting a "Goddess of Liberty" statue that looked like the Statue of Liberty. Rather than relinquishing power, however, China's leaders resorted to force on June 4, 1989. Police and army forces brutally cleared the square and arrested many leaders of the democracy movement. Thousands were killed or injured as the movement for democracy across China was crushed. President Bush condemned the violent repression but resisted demands for sanctions against China. He argued that sanctions would make the Chinese leadership even more brutal.

Bush's policy toward South Africa drew praise for supporting democratic change. In South Africa, the goal was to end **apartheid.** In 1988, after South African president P. W. Botha had brutally repressed anti-apartheid demonstrations, Congress instituted **economic sanctions.** As Bush applauded the willingness of South Africa's new president,

Commonwealth of Independent States Weak federation of the former Soviet republics that replaced the Soviet Union in 1992 and soon gave way to total independence of the member countries.

Berlin Wall Wall that the Communist East German government built in 1961 to divide East and West Berlin; it was torn down in 1989 as the Cold War ended.

Bosnia Region of the former Yugoslavia; its major city is Sarajevo.

Tiananmen Square City square in Beijing where army forces attacked student protesters in 1989, crushing the prodemocracy movement in China.

apartheid Official policy of racial segregation in South Africa; its outcome was political, legal, and economic discrimination against blacks and other people of color.

economic sanctions Trade restrictions that several nations acting together impose on a country that has violated international law.

F. W. de Klerk, to work with Nelson Mandela and other black Africans to end apartheid. Bush lifted the sanctions once it became apparent that substantial progress was being made. In April 1994, South Africa held its first multiracial free elections, electing Mandela president.

In Central America, Bush broke with Reagan's policies (see pages 703–704) by reducing aid to the Contras and encouraging negotiations. His actions contributed to the acceptance of the **Contadora Plan** negotiated by a coalition of Central American nations. Under this plan, the Contras agreed to halt their military operations, and the Ortega government agreed to hold free elections. Opposition candidate Violeta de Chamorro defeated Daniel Ortega in 1990. Although friction between Sandinista and Contra supporters continued, the peaceful change in government effectively ended a bitter struggle.

In El Salvador, American-supported peace negotiations also ended a civil war. Antigovernment rebels agreed to a cease-fire and to participate in future elections. Bush proudly boasted that American efforts in both El Salvador and Nicaragua helped to produce more democratic governments.

Protecting American Interests Abroad

By mid-1991, almost everyone agreed that the Cold War was over. The Soviet Union and Soviet communism had collapsed. The United States stood as the sole superpower. Liberals and moderates called for a "peace dividend," money taken from the military budget and allocated for social programs. But Bush resisted any sizable cuts in the military budget. The world was still a dangerous place, he warned, and needed the military strength of the United States.

One place where Bush exercised that strength was in Panama. During his presidential campaign, he had promised a crackdown on the flow of drugs into the United States. In December 1989, he ordered American forces into Panama to arrest Panamanian dictator **Manuel Noriega** on drug-related charges. Implicated in the torture and murder of his political enemies, Noriega was actively involved in the transshipment of Colombian drugs to the United States.

Within seventy-two hours, American forces were in charge of the country. American casualties were light (twenty-three lost their lives). Some three thousand Panamanians died, almost all civilians. A Miami court found Noriega guilty of drug-related offenses, and he was sentenced to prison in 1992. Panama, however, remained a major route for smuggling drugs into the United States.

By the fall of 1990, President Bush faced a much more serious threat from **Saddam Hussein,** the authoritarian ruler of Iraq. Saddam claimed that the oil-rich sheikdom of Kuwait, which had long been friendly to the United States, was waging economic war against Iraq. Believing that the United States would not intervene, Saddam invaded and quickly overran Kuwait in early August 1990.

Many worried that Saddam intended to control the Persian Gulf region's oil fields, which held over 40 percent of the world's oil. Within hours of the invasion, Bush warned, "This [action] will not stand." Bush helped organize a multinational force of over 700,000, including 500,000 Americans, which was sent to Saudi Arabia in an effort to convince Iraq to withdraw from Kuwait. Many believed that the economic sanctions imposed by the United Nations would force Iraq to leave Kuwait. Bush worked within the United Nations to set a deadline of January 15, 1991, for Iraqi withdrawal from Kuwait.

Eighteen hours after the deadline expired, aircraft of the United Nations coalition began the **Gulf War** with devastating attacks on Iraqi positions in Kuwait and on Iraq itself. For nearly forty days, a

Contadora Plan Pact signed by the presidents of five Central American nations in 1987; it called for cease-fires in conflicts in the region and for democratic reforms.

Manual Noriega Panamanian dictator who was captured by U.S. invasion forces in 1989 and taken to the United States to be tried for drug trafficking.

Saddam Hussein Iraqi ruler who annexed Kuwait in 1990, triggering the Gulf War.

Gulf War War in the Persian Gulf region in 1991 triggered by the Iraqi invasion of Kuwait; a U.S.-led coalition defeated Iraqi forces and freed Kuwait.

high-tech air attack pounded the Iraqis. Saddam had promised, however, that the ground war would be the "mother of all battles." Concern about casualties among the coalition forces was great. Nevertheless, General Norman Schwarzkopf, coalition force commander, was confident of victory and ridiculed the Iraqi leader's military ability: Saddam is "neither a strategist, nor is he schooled in the operational arts, nor is he a tactician, nor is he a general, nor is he a soldier. Other than that he is a great military man."

The ground offensive, called Operation Desert Storm, started the night of February 23. In Kuwait, thousands of demoralized Iraqi soldiers, many of whom had gone without food and water for days, surrendered to advancing coalition forces. Within four days, coalition forces were mopping up the remaining resistance. They liberated Kuwait and humiliated the Iraqi army thoroughly. Estimates of Iraqi losses ranged from 70,000 to 115,000 killed. The United States lost fewer than 150. It was indeed the "mother of all victories," Americans quipped. Some, however, speculated that the offensive should have continued until all of the Iraqi army had been destroyed and Saddam ousted from power.

By the summer of 1991, the United States could claim victory in two wars, the Gulf War and the Cold War. It was clearly the diplomatic and military leader of the world.

A Kinder, Gentler Nation at Home?

Bush entered the White House in 1989 promising a "kinder, gentler nation." Many praised Bush for his apparent rediscovery of social issues. But others concluded from Bush's promise not to increase taxes that substantial action was unlikely.

They were correct. Bush's domestic policy reflected his belief that there was nothing fundamentally wrong with American society or the economy. He saw no reason for extensive new social programs.

Bush did support some social and environmental initiatives. By the end of his first year in office, he could point to legislation that protected disabled Americans against discrimination (the Americans with Disabilities Act) and reduced smokestack and auto emissions and acid rain (the Clean Air Act). Bush also noted that the minimum wage had risen from $3.35 to $4.25 an hour. Only two problem areas seemed to exist: the economy and his broken pledge on taxes.

In mid-1990, in part because of oil-price increases caused by Iraq's invasion of Kuwait, the nation entered into a recession. The recession, plus the growing national deficit, convinced Bush to work with Congress to raise taxes, despite his "no new taxes" pledge. Bush believed that by 1992, the recession would be over, the national debt would be reduced, and voters would happily re-elect him. The recession deepened, however, and lasted into 1992.

The recession lasted longer than Bush expected for several reasons. Fewer American goods were being sold overseas because of a slowdown in the world economy. American firms responded by downsizing to be more competitive. Between July 1990 and July 1993, over 1.9 million people lost their jobs. Sharply rising federal spending and the ever-increasing deficit also contributed to the length of the recession. Despite Bush's pledges to hold down federal spending, during his term the budget skyrocketed, reaching $1.5 trillion in 1992. At the same time, family income dropped below 1980 levels, to $37,300 from a 1980 high of $38,900. Consumers, caught between increasing unemployment, falling wages, and inflation, saw personal savings and confidence in the economy shrink.

Bush did little to halt the economic slide. He responded to Democrats' calls for tax cuts for the middle class, increased and extended unemployment benefits, and other social programs with vetoes and by asking for reductions in **capital gains** taxes. The result was political gridlock. Bush looked increasingly vulnerable as the November 1992 election approached. Unlike Reagan, Bush seemed incapable of projecting the image of a leader who knew where the nation and the world should be going.

capital gains Profits made from selling assets such as securities and real estate.

SUMMARY

Expectations
Constraints
Choices
Outcomes

The years between Nixon's resignation and 1992 were ones of changing *expectations*. During the presidencies of Ford and Carter, the nation seemed beset by *constraints* that limited its domestic prosperity and international status. The policy *choices* that Ford and Carter made neither recaptured people's faith in the nation nor established national goals. In his foreign policy, Carter chose to de-emphasize Cold War relationships and give more attention to human rights and Third World problems. The *outcome*, many believed, was a weakening of America's world position.

Reagan rejected Carter's notion that Americans should sacrifice to overcome the limits facing the nation. He argued that the only *constraint* on American greatness was government's excessive regulation and interference in society. He promised to reassert American power and renew the offensive in the Cold War. As president, Reagan *chose* a conservative program to restore the nation's values, honor, and international prestige. He fulfilled many conservative *expectations* by reducing support for some social programs, easing and eliminating some government regulations, and exerting American power around the world—altering the structure of Soviet-American relations. Supporters claimed that the *outcome* of Reagan's *choices* was a prosperous nation that faced few *constraints*. They applauded Reagan's assessment that his administration had *chosen* to "change a nation, and instead . . . changed a world."

Bush inherited the *expectations* that the Reagan administration had generated. But unlike Reagan, he could not project an image of strong and visionary leadership. Finding fewer *constraints* and more opportunities in the conduct of foreign policy, Bush directed most of his attention to world affairs. As the Soviet Union and communism in Eastern Europe collapsed, Bush gained public approval for his foreign policies, also demonstrating American strength and resolve in Panama and the Persian Gulf. His foreign-policy successes, however, only highlighted his weakness in domestic policy as the nation found itself mired in a nagging recession that sapped the public's confidence in Republican leadership and the economy.

SUGGESTED READINGS

Burroughs, Bryan, and John Helyar. *Barbarians at the Gate: The Fall of RJR Nabisco* (1990).

A novel-like account (also a made-for-television movie) of hostile takeovers, leveraged buyouts, and the politics of greed that revolved around the Nabisco company.

Cannon, Lou. *President Reagan: The Role of a Lifetime* (1992).

The most complete and detailed account of the Reagan presidency from a generally positive perspective.

Duffy, Michael, and Don Goodgame. *Marching in Place: The Status Quo Presidency of George Bush* (1992).

An insightful but critical analysis of the Bush presidency.

Gaddis, John L. *The United States and the End of the Cold War* (1992).

An excellent narrative of events in the Soviet Union and the United States that led to the end of the Cold War, as well as a useful analysis of the problems facing the United States in the post–Cold War world.

Kaufman, Burton. *The Presidency of James Earl Carter, Jr.* (1993).

A well-balanced account and analysis of Carter's presidency and the changing political values of the 1970s.

Schaller, Michael. *Reckoning with Reagan* (1992).

A brief but scholarly analysis of the Reagan administration and the society and values that supported the Reagan revolution.

Sifry, Micah L., and Christopher Cerf, eds. *The Gulf War Reader* (1991).

A collection of essays and documents that provides both insight into and an excellent overview of the Gulf War.

Wolfe, Tom. *Bonfire of the Vanities* (1987).

A best-selling novel (also a movie) about the inside world of financial deals and the quest for power and wealth.

Wall Street (1988).

A movie that provides another example of financial wheeling and dealing and Yuppies in search of wealth and power.

LIVING PATTERNS, 1990 Since the end of the nineteenth century, more and more Americans have migrated to urban areas. As this map shows, as of 1990, only seven states had less than half of their population living in urban areas. In addition, the population density of the nation had risen to an average 70.3 people per square mile.

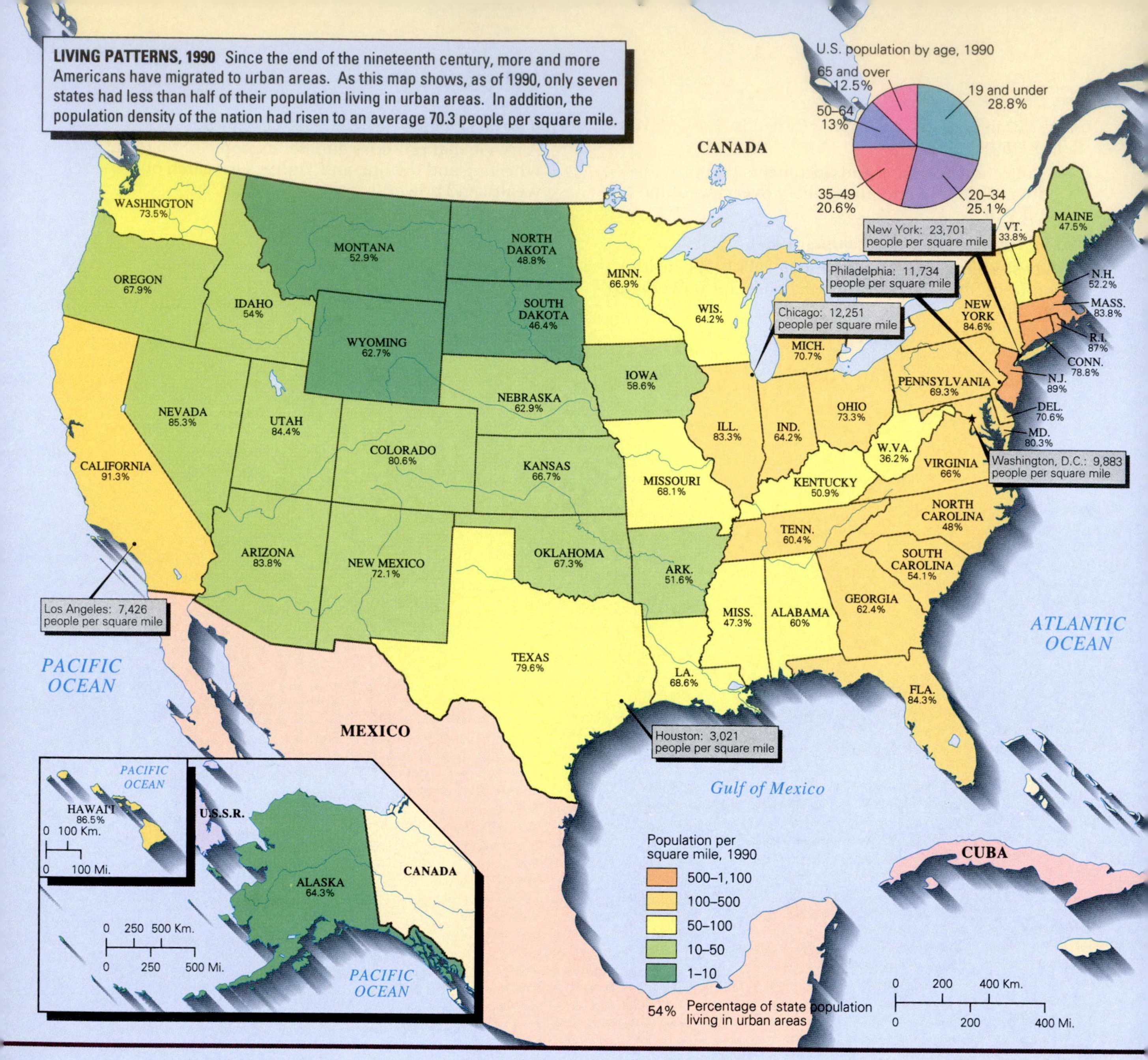

U.S. population by age, 1990
65 and over 12.5%
19 and under 28.8%
50–64 13%
35–49 20.6%
20–34 25.1%
CANADA
WASHINGTON 73.5%
MONTANA 52.9%
NORTH DAKOTA 48.8%
OREGON 67.9%
IDAHO 54%
SOUTH DAKOTA 46.4%
WYOMING 62.7%
MINN. 66.9%
WIS. 64.2%
MICH. 70.7%
IOWA 58.6%
NEBRASKA 62.9%
NEVADA 85.3%
UTAH 84.4%
COLORADO 80.6%
KANSAS 66.7%
CALIFORNIA 91.3%
MISSOURI 68.1%
ILL. 83.3%
IND. 64.2%
OHIO 73.3%
KENTUCKY 50.9%
W.VA. 36.2%
VIRGINIA 66%
PENNSYLVANIA 69.3%
NEW YORK 84.6%
VT. 33.8%
MAINE 47.5%
N.H. 52.2%
MASS. 83.8%
R.I. 87%
CONN. 78.8%
N.J. 89%
DEL. 70.6%
MD. 80.3%
NORTH CAROLINA 48%
SOUTH CAROLINA 54.1%
TENN. 60.4%
GEORGIA 62.4%
ALABAMA 60%
MISS. 47.3%
ARK. 51.6%
LA. 68.6%
FLA. 84.3%
OKLAHOMA 67.3%
TEXAS 79.6%
NEW MEXICO 72.1%
ARIZONA 83.8%
New York: 23,701 people per square mile
Philadelphia: 11,734 people per square mile
Chicago: 12,251 people per square mile
Washington, D.C.: 9,883 people per square mile
Los Angeles: 7,426 people per square mile
Houston: 3,021 people per square mile
PACIFIC OCEAN
ATLANTIC OCEAN
MEXICO
Gulf of Mexico
CUBA
PACIFIC OCEAN
HAWAI'I 86.5%
0 100 Km.
0 100 Mi.
U.S.S.R.
ALASKA 64.3%
CANADA
0 250 500 Km.
0 250 500 Mi.
PACIFIC OCEAN
Population per square mile, 1990
500–1,100
100–500
50–100
10–50
1–10
54% Percentage of state population living in urban areas
0 200 400 Km.
0 200 400 Mi.

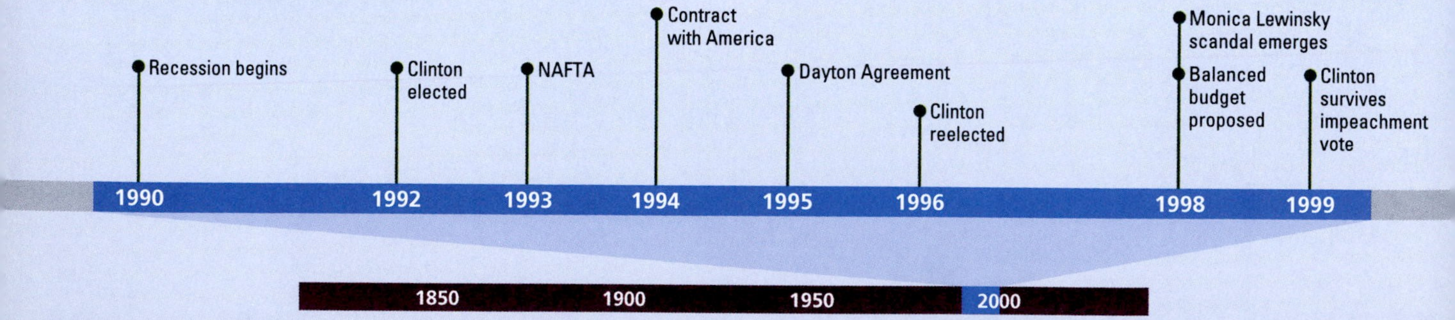

Recession begins
Clinton elected
NAFTA
Contract with America
Dayton Agreement
Clinton reelected
Monica Lewinsky scandal emerges
Balanced budget proposed
Clinton survives impeachment vote
1990
1992
1993
1994
1995
1996
1998
1999
1850
1900
1950
2000

CHAPTER 32

Making New Choices, 1992–1999

An Anxious Society Grows More Confident

- What changes were taking place in the American economy during the 1990s, and how did they affect people's expectations?

The Politics of Morality

- What expectations surrounded the introduction of issues of morality and values into American politics?

Calls for Change

- Given the outcomes occurring during the Clinton presidency, what policy issues seemed most important to Americans in the mid- to late 1990s?
- What was the outcome of the Clinton impeachment trial?

INTRODUCTION

Expectations
Constraints
Choices
Outcomes

Before the election of 1992, many people *expected* the central issue of the campaign and perhaps of the 1990s would be the social and cultural divisions within American society. Liberals and conservatives were bitterly at odds over the values that should guide American society. Liberals believed that government should work to ensure that women, homosexuals, racial and ethnic minorities, and the disadvantaged generally have equal rights and economic opportunities. They supported the Equal Rights Amendment, affirmative action, and bans on antigay legislation. Conservatives, led by the New Right, argued that liberal policies were destroying the basic value system of the country and resulting in crime, violence, immoral behavior, and the breakdown of family life. They campaigned for a return to the traditional values of the two-parent family.

Contrary to *expectations*, the 1992 election seemed to hinge more on economic issues than on social or cultural ones. Since the 1970s, economic growth had slowed. Middle- and lower-class Americans had grown increasingly anxious as their economic circumstances either stagnated or deteriorated. Faced with a lingering recession, voters in 1992 *chose* Bill Clinton, the Democratic governor of Arkansas, over Republican incumbent George Bush and third-party candidate H. Ross Perot. Whereas Bush offered no answers to troubling economic issues, Clinton promised to support social needs while making the choices necessary to control the federal budget and reduce the national debt.

Clinton's efforts to enact major domestic legislation ran into major *constraints*. Faced with strong opposition, he had to abandon his proposed national healthcare plan and modify his goals for other social issues. In addition, the Republicans gained control of Congress in 1994. Clinton proved adept, however, at establishing himself as a centrist while making his Republican opponents appear to be too far to the right. For example, Clinton made the issue of welfare reform his own. He also was successful in foreign policy, helping to bring stability, peace, and democracy to Bosnia and Haiti. These successes and a healthy economy translated into an easy victory for Clinton over Robert Dole and H. Ross Perot in the 1996 elections. The Republicans retained control of Congress.

As Clinton's second term began, both parties promised to cooperate with each other. *Expectations* of cooperation vanished in January 1998 when revelations that Clinton had had a sexual affair with a former White House intern, Monica Lewinsky, surfaced. By a largely partisan vote, the House approved two articles of impeachment charging that Clinton had perjured himself and obstructed justice in dealing with the Lewinsky affair. Although the Senate voted not to remove Clinton from office in February 1999, the *outcome* of the Lewinsky affair was that Clinton's presidency was permanently tainted.

CHRONOLOGY

New Expectations, New Directions

1969	Stonewall Riot
1972	Equal Rights Amendment begins ratification process
1973	*Roe v. Wade*
1974	Busing confrontation in Boston
1976	Hyde Amendment restricts federally funded abortions
1978	*Regents of the University of California v. Bakke*
1981	Beginning of AIDS epidemic in the United States Sandra Day O'Connor appointed to Supreme Court
1982	Equal Rights Amendment fails to win ratification
1986	William Rehnquist appointed chief justice of Supreme Court Antonin Scalia appointed to Supreme Court
1987	Anthony Kennedy appointed to Supreme Court
1988	Bush elected president
1990	Recession begins David Souter appointed to Supreme Court
1991	Clarence Thomas appointed to Supreme Court
1992	Riots in South Central Los Angeles U.S. troops sent to Somalia Clinton elected president *Planned Parenthood of Southeastern Pennsylvania v. Casey*
1993	North American Free Trade Agreement passed Clinton introduces national health package Ruth Bader Ginsburg appointed to Supreme Court
1994	Withdrawal of U.S. troops from Somalia Nelson Mandela elected president of South Africa Violence Against Women Act Contract with America
1995	Dayton Agreement
1996	Welfare reform passed Clinton reelected
1997	Madeleine Albright confirmed as secretary of state *Reno v. ACLU*
1998	Clinton projects balanced budget Monica Lewinsky scandal surfaces House impeaches Clinton
1999	Senate votes not to remove Clinton from office

An Anxious Society Grows More Confident

When Bill Clinton became president in 1993, Americans were worried about their economic future. The largely stagnant economy of the previous two decades made it difficult to maintain their standard of living. Those entering the work force worried that they would not be able to achieve their parents' level of affluence.

Clinton's presidency, however, coincided with the resurgence of the American economy. Sustained economic growth during the 1990s once again made the American economy the envy of the world. By the end of the decade, the unemployment rate had dropped to its lowest level in thirty years, median family income had risen significantly, and the **Dow Jones industrial average** had soared past 11,000.

The Revitalized Economy

During the 1970s, the American economy entered a prolonged period of stagnation. The economy grew at slightly more than 1 percent annually, in contrast to the robust 2.5 percent annual growth rate it enjoyed from the end of World War II through 1970. Although the causes of this slowdown were not clear at the time, what stands out in retrospect is that the basic activity of the economy was shifting from industrial production to providing information and services.

The painful effects of this transition were felt throughout the 1970s and 1980s. Regions that relied on industry saw the closing or moving of plants, the loss of jobs, and economic decline. The Rust Belt continued to decay as steel and coal companies cut back production or closed (see page 691). In addition, for the first time since the Great Depression, white-collar workers felt the effects of downsizing—companies cutting back on their work forces.

Since the early 1990s, American workers however, have been the beneficiaries of a largely successful transition to an information and service economy. American leadership in the computer software, microprocessing, and telecommunications industries, as well as the structure of the country's highly competitive retail markets, has produced a long and sustained economic boom. Between 1992 and 1998, the economy grew at an annual rate of about 3 percent, half a percentage point higher than in the decades after World War II.

During the 1990s, the American economy became the envy of the world, combining low interest, unemployment, and inflation rates. As one after another of the Asian "miracles" such as Japan went bust, the American economy surged forward. Meanwhile, many European countries experienced high unemployment.

The 1990s, like the 1980s, rewarded those at the top very handsomely. In addition, the decade saw a reversal of the long trend of falling real wages for the average American. Whereas the average real wage for men fell about 11 percent between 1979 and 1993, it rose 4 percent between 1997 and 1998. Real wages for the lowest-paid workers rose 6 percent between 1993 and 1998. By the mid-1990s, fast-food restaurants were advertising starting hourly wages that were well above the minimum wage and were offering fringe benefits in an effort to attract workers in the suddenly tight labor market.

Rising wages reflected the trend toward full employment during the decade. The unemployment rate fell from 7.5 percent in 1992 to 4.1 percent in the fall of 1999—the lowest rate since 1968. Minority unemployment rates fell in 1998 to the lowest levels ever recorded—8.9 percent for African Americans and 7.2 percent for Latinos. Even the unemployment rate for blacks ages 16 to 24 fell to a historic low in 1998, although nearly 21 percent of these workers remained unemployed.

During the 1990s, the stock market brought unprecedented returns to investors. The S&P 500, an index of the five hundred largest American companies, averaged unprecedented increases of 33 percent *per year* between 1994 and 1998, about three times the historical average. Americans who bought shares in the initial offerings of America Online, Amazon.com, or any of a number of Internet and high-technology companies saw even greater returns. The boom market of the Nineties made that of the Twenties pale by comparison.

Moreover, a broad spectrum of the American public benefited from this upsurge in the stock market. The percentage of adult Americans who owned stock rose from 10 percent in 1965 to 43 percent in 1999. This increasing stock ownership reflected the wider participation of Americans in pension and 401(k) funds that invest in securities.

The buoyant stock market indicated the fundamental confidence of investors in the American

Dow Jones industrial average New York Stock Exchange index representing stock prices of the thirty largest industrial corporations.

economy. With a few notable exceptions, virtually every economic indicator looked good. Inflation remained under control, averaging less than 3 percent annually. The inflation rate of 1.6 percent for 1998 was the second lowest in thirty years. Low interest rates that had not been seen since the 1960s spurred a construction and building boom. Even the federal budget, which seemed to have been careening out of control in the early 1990s, showed a surplus in 1998 and promised more surpluses in succeeding years.

Most observers were willing to overlook or minimize the few deficiencies of this generally robust economy. One of those deficiencies was that American consumers found many things to buy but had little inclination to save. As a result, the national savings rate fell to its lowest ever, less than 2 percent, and consumer debt rose to record highs. Another problem was the widening trade gap. Whereas in 1980 the United States had a modest trade surplus of $3.7 billion, by 1997 it had a trade deficit of $166 billion.

The Familiar Face of Poverty

For those at the bottom of the economic ladder, even a strong economy did little to ease existing problems. Although the poverty rate fell from 15 percent in 1992 to 13.3 percent in 1997, an estimated 36 million Americans remained mired in poverty. For minorities, the economic picture was worse. Both African Americans and Latinos experienced poverty rates of 27 percent in 1997. Households headed by women also figured prominently in the statistics on poverty. Some 30 percent of women heads of households lived in poverty.

Contributing to what some have called the "feminization of poverty" was the continuing gap between men's and women's income. Women continued to earn roughly 75 percent of the wages earned by men. Alimony was awarded less frequently in the 1990s, and child-support payments, when ordered, were likely to be too small to be of much help. Enforcement of child-support payments was frequently lax. In 1990, for example, more than one-quarter of those who owed child support paid nothing.

The Urban Crisis and Racial Tensions

During the 1980s, the problems of urban Americans seemed beyond solution. Businesses continued to leave the inner cities, taking many well-paying, full-time jobs with them. More and more urban areas came to be peopled by "the underclass," mostly nonwhite, unemployed or underemployed people with little education and even less hope. The only thriving enterprises were gangs and drug sales, especially those of **crack cocaine.**

Violence was a way of life in the inner city. Sections of many cities took on the appearance of war zones. By 1991, one-fourth of all urban school districts had installed metal detectors to prevent students from bringing weapons to school. Murder had become the leading cause of death for black males under the age of 35.

The **Rodney King** affair in Los Angeles illustrates the deeply embedded racism in many urban police departments and the seething racial tensions in many inner cities. A videotape made during the 1991 arrest of King, an African American, showed that four white policemen had clubbed, kicked, and beaten him after he had apparently been subdued. When an all-white jury acquitted three of the policemen (one was found guilty) in April 1992, South Central Los Angeles erupted in violence. For African Americans, the trial was further proof of white racism. The ensuing five-day riot resulted in 53 deaths, 2,300 injuries, 16,000 arrests, and more than $750 million in property damage.

The most famous trial during the 1990s was that of former professional football player O. J. Simpson. The issue of race pervaded the lengthy, televised trial of Simpson, who was accused of murdering his wife, Nicole Brown Simpson, and her friend, Ronald Goldman, on June 12, 1994. Although the prosecution presented the findings

crack cocaine Highly potent form of cocaine that is smoked through a glass pipe and is extremely addictive.

Rodney King African American whose beating by Los Angeles police officers was captured on videotape; the acquittal of the officers in 1992 triggered riots in which fifty-three people were killed.

♦ The April 1992 rioting in Los Angeles that followed the acquittal of three policemen for the beating of motorist Rodney King lasted five days and destroyed much of South Central Los Angeles. Fifty-three people were killed, and property damage exceeded $750 million. Many stores were looted before being set on fire, especially in what was called Koreatown. *Scott Weersing/Enterprise/Gamma Liaison.*

of DNA tests that placed Simpson's blood at the murder scene and his ex-wife's at his residence, Simpson's "Dream Team" of defense attorneys cast doubts on the integrity of police procedures. They scored many points when they showed that Detective Mark Fuhrman, who claimed to have found a bloody glove used in the murders on Simpson's property, had planted evidence in other cases and was a racist. The jury deliberated for less than four hours before proclaiming Simpson innocent in October 1995. The verdict sharply divided Americans along racial lines. Polls showed that more than two-thirds of white Americans believed that Simpson was guilty, whereas a similar proportion of African Americans believed him innocent.

Although Americans remained polarized over racial issues, urban environments improved substantially in the 1990s. Perhaps the most telling statistics concerned violent crimes such as murder, rape, and robbery. Beginning in 1992, the number of violent crimes dropped every year. The homicide rate, which doubled between the mid-1960s and 1980, also declined dramatically. In 1998, the murder rate fell to its lowest level since 1968. Drug use also fell off considerably. Cocaine use, for example, declined by about two-thirds from its peak in 1985.

Safer cities probably reflected a number of factors. First, an expanding economy provided some additional opportunities in the inner cities. Second, more police on the beat served as a deterrent to crime. Third, the enactment of tough "three strikes and you're out" legislation removed many offenders from the streets and swelled prison populations. And finally, aggressive campaigns such as that waged by New York City Mayor Rudolph Giuliani to rid the Times Square area of prostitutes and porn shops led many more urban residents to come out at night.

The Politics of Morality

While liberals continued to espouse government activism as a means to promote social equality and cultural pluralism, conservatives argued that America had become a nation of interest groups clamoring for rights and power and that a sense of national purpose was rapidly fading. They charged that liberal programs and attitudes had made victims of hardworking, thrifty middle-class Americans.

Changing Values

Many conservatives believed that there had been a moral breakdown in American society. They argued that the women's movement, the counterculture, and the **sexual revolution** had caused this breakdown. These movements, they claimed, had undermined the values of work and family by stressing personal fulfillment and advocating "fun, display, and pleasure."

The sexual revolution began with the youth movement of the 1960s (see pages 656–658). By 1970, more than half of those surveyed said that they approved of premarital sex and cohabitation outside marriage. Though still the norm, marriage had lost some of its importance.

By the 1970s, divorce rates were climbing as both men and women became less willing to stay in unsatisfactory marriages. As attitudes toward marriage and divorce changed, divorce laws also changed. **No-fault divorce** allowed spouses to dissolve their marriage because of so-called irreconcilable differences. By the 1990s, half of all those who married eventually divorced.

Divorce, the women's movement, and the sexual revolution also interacted with economic factors to affect the structure of American families. No longer was the American family the image of the typical 1950s family—white, suburban, mother as housewife. Instead, there were increasing numbers of single-parent families and families in which both spouses worked. Television reflected the changing views of American society. By the 1970s, there were few television shows showing families similar to Beaver Cleaver's (see page 622). Some nonwhite families appeared, and many of the situation comedies featured groups of single and divorced people living and working in an urban environment. A week of television in 1997 featured several programs about white and African-American "traditional" households—"Cosby," "Mad About You," "In the House," "The Simpsons"—and several single-parent households—"The Gregory Hines Show" and "Grace Under Fire." But there were also many programs that featured divorced and never-been-married singles—"Seinfeld," "Friends" and "Ellen." The title character in "Ellen" revealed in one episode that she was a lesbian.

A new openness about sex began to pervade society after the 1960s. By the 1980s, sexual content had become standard fare in movies and on television. In 1987, an estimated sixty-five thousand sexual references were broadcast each year in prime-time television programs. During the day, sex and sex-related issues became more daring and numerous on the soaps. Violence, too, became standard. A 1997 study indicated that 44 percent of all network programming had violent content. Sexual and violent content was featured even more on cable and satellite television. One study found that on the premier cable channels, 85 percent of the programming had violent content. Sexually explicit material also could be found in magazines and books, on the Internet, and in X-rated films. Many people called for censorship and ways to limit the amount of sex and violence seen by children. By the 1990s, records, movies, and television all offered rating systems indicating the level of sex and violence in their content. In 1997, however, the Supreme Court ruled in *Reno v. ACLU* that efforts to ban sexually offensive material from the Internet were unconstitutional.

Women and Changing Values

Related to the sexual revolution's effects on American society were demands by women for more personal and economic choices. As the women's movement continued into the 1980s and 1990s, it began, like other social movements, to divide and encounter more opposition. At the center of the

sexual revolution Dramatic change in attitudes toward sex; it began in the 1960s as more and more Americans considered premarital sex acceptable.

no-fault divorce Divorce granted without the need to establish wrongdoing by either party.

divisions and at the heart of the opposition were differences about the meaning and importance of the sexual revolution, home, family, and children.

By the late 1960s, a growing number of women had begun to attack sexism in American society and culture. As unprecedented numbers of women began working, many became angered by the gap between their abilities and their earnings. In August 1970, over fifty thousand women marched in New York to demand better pay and equal access to jobs.

The women's movement began to call for other changes as well. These included abortion rights, the right to reject unwanted sex, and freedom from **sexual harassment.** To help achieve these goals, the National Organization for Women (NOW) and other women's groups in 1967 called for an **Equal Rights Amendment (ERA).**

Many states responded to the changing social values and to pressure from women's groups. They modified laws to reduce or eliminate gender discrimination. Some states legalized abortions. In 1972, Congress drafted the Equal Rights Amendment and sent it to the states for ratification. ERA advocates argued that it was needed to eliminate laws at the state and local levels that blocked women's equality. They pointed out that the ERA also would transfer the responsibility of ensuring equality from individuals and state governments to the federal government.

At first, ratification of the ERA appeared almost certain. Thirty-three of the thirty-eight states needed for ratification had approved it by 1974. But opposition stiffened, and only two more states voted approval before the 1978 deadline. Congress granted an extension of the deadline until 1982, but it did no good.

Conservative forces from more than 130 organizations made the ERA an effective symbol of what they said threatened the traditional family. **Phyllis Schlafly** and other STOP-ERA leaders charged that the ERA would alter the "role of the American woman as wife and mother" and destroy the American family. Their emphasis on the ERA's threat to the traditional family prevented it from being ratified.

The STOP-ERA movement also benefited from the Supreme Court's controversial 1973 decision in the case of ***Roe v. Wade.*** The Court invalidated a Texas law that prevented abortions. Justice Harry Blackmun, writing for the majority, held that "the right to privacy" gave women the freedom to choose to have an abortion during the first three months of pregnancy. The controversial ruling struck down abortion laws in forty-six states that had made it nearly impossible for women to have an abortion. As the number of legal abortions rose from about 750,000 in 1973 to nearly a million and half by 1980, so too did opposition.

Although public opinion polls indicated that a majority of Americans favored giving women the right to choose an abortion, Catholics, Mormons, some Orthodox Jews, and many Protestant churches organized a "Right to Life" campaign to oppose abortion rights. The **Right to Life movement** easily merged with the conservative elements of American society. Responding to conservative and anti-abortion pressure, Congress in 1976 passed the Hyde Amendment, which prohibited the use of federal Medicaid funds to pay for abortions. As President Reagan appointed Sandra Day O'Connor and other conservative justices to the Supreme Court, many people expected the Court eventually to overturn *Roe v. Wade.* But in 1992, in *Planned Parenthood of Southeastern Pennsylvania v. Casey,* the Court confirmed a woman's right to have an abortion. The Court did assert that in some cases the state could modify that right.

sexual harassment Unwanted and offensive sexual advances or sexually derogatory or discriminatory remarks.

Equal Rights Amendment Proposed constitutional amendment giving women equal rights under the law; Congress approved it in 1972, but it failed to achieve ratification by the required thirty-eight states.

Phyllis Schlafly Leader of the movement to defeat the Equal Rights Amendment; Schlafly believed that the amendment threatened the domestic role of women.

Roe v. Wade Supreme Court ruling in 1973 that women have an unrestricted right to abort a fetus during the first three months of pregnancy.

Right to Life movement Anti-abortion movement that favors a constitutional amendment to prohibit abortion; it grew increasingly militant during the 1980s and 1990s.

Sexual harassment became a national issue in 1991 during Clarence Thomas's Senate confirmation hearings for the Supreme Court. Those hearings turned stormy after Anita Hill, a University of Oklahoma law professor, accused Thomas of sexual harassment. Hill testified that a decade earlier, while she was working for Thomas, he had pressured her for dates and told her pornographic stories. Thomas denied her allegations, angrily calling the hearing "a high-tech lynching for uppity blacks." The Senate hearings became a national television spectacle. The predominantly male Senate confirmed Thomas in a close vote, but the hearings focused national attention on the issue of sexual harassment. In response to growing concerns about sexual abuse, Congress passed the **Violence Against Women Act** in 1994.

Gay Rights: Progress and Resistance

Women were not the only group asking society to reconsider America's traditional views of gender. Homosexuals too were demanding equality. In the late 1960s, groups promoting gay and lesbian rights openly demanded an end to laws that discriminated against homosexuals.

The spark for the movement was a police raid in June 1969 on the Stonewall Inn, a gay bar in the Greenwich Village section of New York City. Gays and other members of the community fought back in what came to be called the Stonewall Riot. After the riot, gays and lesbians borrowed tactics from the women's and civil rights movements, formed activist groups, and demanded equality. Because visibility was a major tool and goal of the movement, gays and lesbians demonstrated in support of their lifestyles.

Throughout the 1970s, the gay liberation movement pressured government at all levels to end restrictions against homosexuals in employment, housing, and the military. Success came slowly. One victory came in 1973 when the American Psychiatric Association ended its classification of homosexuality as a mental disorder. Polls indicated that the "straight" public held confusing views. By the mid-1970s the majority of Americans considered homosexuality wrong, but a slight majority opposed job discrimination based on sexual orientation and seemed more tolerant of gay lifestyles.

The growing toleration of gays did not end legal or social discrimination. The Reagan administration equated homosexuality with a disease and denied homosexuals entry into the United States. The New Right and Moral Majority campaigned actively against the rights of homosexuals. Evangelical minister Jerry Falwell called on his followers to "stop gays dead in their perverted tracks." Although 26 states had decriminalized sexual relationships between consenting adults by 1986, only 7 states and about 110 communities had prohibited social and economic discrimination against homosexuals by 1993. In the remaining 43 states and under federal law, no legal recourse existed for those fired from their jobs because of their sexual preference.

The AIDS Controversy

Antigay opposition was strengthened by a growing fear of **acquired immune deficiency syndrome (AIDS),** a disease that was at first regarded primarily as a "gay disease." AIDS was first discovered in the United States in 1981. Within ten years, over 195,700 cases had been reported, and over 97,000 Americans had died of it. Another 1.5 million were estimated to be infected by HIV (human immunodeficiency virus), the virus that causes AIDS. Initially, because most AIDS victims were either homosexuals or intravenous drug users, official and public response to the disease was restrained. But as more and more non-drug-using heterosexuals contracted AIDS, research and educational efforts expanded.

As public fear of AIDS increased, controversy flared about the best means to prevent the spread

Violence Against Women Act Law passed in 1994 that provided federal funds to prevent violence against women, to aid victims, and to punish those convicted of attacks on women.

acquired immune deficiency syndrome Gradual and eventually fatal breakdown of the immune system caused by HIV; AIDS is transmitted by exchanging body fluids through means such as sex or blood transfusions.

of the disease. Claiming to be "realists," many recommended "safe sex," emphasizing the use of condoms as a means to reduce the possibility of getting the disease. Television ads used prominent movie and sports figures to advocate the use of condoms. Some advocated that high schools provide students with free condoms and information about AIDS. Others disagreed. Arguing that free condoms would encourage sexual activity, they promoted abstinence.

Contributing to the public's awareness of AIDS were revelations that Earvin "Magic" Johnson and Arthur Ashe had tested positive for the HIV virus. Ashe, the onetime U.S. Open tennis champion, contracted the disease from HIV-infected blood during a heart bypass operation. Johnson, star of the Los Angeles Lakers basketball team, caught the disease through heterosexual activity. Johnson admitted to being "naive" about AIDS and told the public, "Here I am saying it can happen to anybody." Both became spokesmen for AIDS research and prevention. Ashe died of AIDS in 1993.

By the mid-1990s, some advances had been made in research toward controlling AIDS. Combinations of drugs seemed to have a positive effect in slowing the advance of and death rate from the disease. But there remained no cure for the disease, which by 1996 had claimed more than 280,000 American lives and had infected 20 million people around the world.

Federal Intervention and the Courts

By the 1980s, many Americans who had initially supported civil rights for African Americans and other minorities were rejecting calls for continuing programs to help equalize social and economic relationships. Multiculturalism and federal intervention in support of minority rights, conservatives argued, were weakening American society and undermining traditional values. Among the most disastrous examples of federal intervention, many conservatives held, were requirements for forced busing and **affirmative action.** Both had been largely supported and influenced by the federal court system.

Busing for integration had become a national issue in the early 1970s, when state and federal courts began to order non-Southern school districts to adopt busing to achieve more equally balanced schools. Boston experienced violent protests in 1974 following a busing order, and twenty thousand white students eventually left the school system. In the 1980s, the Reagan and Bush administrations backed away from court-ordered busing. "We aren't going to compel children who don't want to have an integrated education to have one," said one Reagan official. Federal courts also began to take a less favorable view of affirmative action. In part, their rulings reflected the judicial appointments of the Reagan and Bush administrations. By 1992, Reagan and Bush had appointed nearly half of all sitting federal district and appeals court judges. In selecting candidates, they sought individuals who practiced **judicial restraint,** deferring to the views of Congress, the president, and the states on legislation and policy.

Reagan and Bush reshaped the Supreme Court in a conservative bent by appointing six justices. In 1986, five years after appointing Sandra Day O'Connor, Reagan named Justice William Rehnquist to be chief justice and appointed conservative Antonin Scalia to the Court. Anthony M. Kennedy joined the Court in 1987, adding to the conservative majority. The conservative direction of the Court was further reinforced by President Bush's two appointments, David Souter (1990) and Clarence Thomas (1991). In a case involving DeKalb County, Georgia, the Rehnquist Court declared in 1992 that busing should not be used to integrate schools segregated by *de facto* housing patterns.

Affirmative action was already under increasing attack by the time Reagan took office. As the economy slowed, a growing number of middle-class and blue-collar whites had come to believe that affirmative action programs limited their job and ed-

affirmative action Policy that seeks to redress past discrimination through active measures to ensure equal opportunity, especially in education and employment.

judicial restraint Refraining from using the judiciary as a forum for implementing social change but instead deferring to Congress, the president, and the consensus of the people.

ucational opportunities. Believing himself a victim of **reverse discrimination,** Allan Bakke sued the University of California system. Bakke claimed that the School of Medicine at the University of California at Davis had accepted black students less qualified than he and had denied him admission because he was white. In 1978, in *Regents of the University of California v. Bakke,* the Supreme Court ruled that the university should admit him to the medical school. The Court did not totally reject color and gender as considerations for hiring, but the *Bakke* decision weakened many affirmative action programs.

During the Reagan administration, racial and gender preference systems were effectively limited by the Rehnquist Court's 1989 *Croson* decision, which declared state and local government efforts to set aside jobs and contracts for minorities to be illegal. The city of Atlanta and many other municipalities subsequently abolished set-aside programs. In 1997, California voters approved a measure forbidding any consideration of racial or gender preferences in hiring, college admissions, or contracting. Governor Pete Wilson announced that it "began a new chapter in the journey toward a color-blind society."

Calls for Change

In mid-1991, Republicans believed that they had established a new alignment of conservative voters that would continue the shift away from liberalism and big government. President Bush was basking in the glow of Operation Desert Storm and the fall of communism. Most prominent Democrats expected that the president would easily win reelection, so they chose not to compete. As a result, the door was opened for less well-known Democratic candidates. Arkansas governor Bill Clinton emerged as the front-runner and easily won the party's nomination. He selected Senator Albert Gore of Tennessee as his running mate.

Bush campaigned on his presidential experience, his knowledge of world affairs, and Vice President Dan Quayle's call for family values. He blamed the Democratic Congress for the political gridlock. Calling Clinton a "tax-and-spend Democrat," Bush warned that the Arkansas governor's lack of experience, especially in foreign and military affairs, would ruin the country.

Clinton insisted that he was a new kind of Democrat. He called for increased taxes on the wealthy, programs to rebuild the nation's transportation and industrial base, and a strong commitment to a national healthcare program. Unlike Bush, Clinton embraced government activism. Surviving Bush's ads attacking his character, personal life, and avoidance of the draft during the Vietnam War. Clinton steadily emphasized the economy, which was languishing in a recession.

The 1992 campaign also saw the emergence of a third-party candidate. **H. Ross Perot** offered to use $100 million of his own money if supporters could get his name on the presidential ballot in all fifty states. Perot's announcement in February 1992 drew immediate support from many Americans who were disenchanted with both political parties. Perot had a simple message: the politicians had messed up the nation, and control needed to be returned to the people. "It's time to take out the trash and clean up the barn," he told listeners. The deficit was the foremost problem, he said, and he promised to shrink it. By June, one opinion poll showed the feisty Texan leading with 39 percent of the vote. Then, without warning, he withdrew from the race in July. Although Perot later reentered the race, he never regained the momentum he had had in June.

The 1992 campaign culminated in three televised debates between Bush, Perot, and Clinton in September and October. Although both Bush and Perot gained in the public opinion polls following the debates, neither could overtake Clinton, who won the election with 43 percent of the popular vote. Bush received 37.4 percent and Perot 18.9

reverse discrimination Discrimination against members of a dominant group; it results from policies established to correct discrimination against members of minority groups.

H. Ross Perot Texas billionaire who used large amounts of his own money to run as an independent candidate for president in 1992.

percent. Clinton received 370 electoral votes, 100 more than he needed to win.

Political observers wondered if Clinton's success and the success of women and minorities in elections across the nation indicated that the conservative shift in American politics that had begun with Reagan was at its end. Setting a liberal tone, Clinton stated that he wanted a "government that looks like America," and he appointed minorities and women to several posts in the judiciary, the cabinet, and other federal offices. Janet Reno became the first women attorney general, and in 1993 Ruth Bader Ginsburg became the second woman on the Supreme Court. In 1997, Madeleine K. Albright became the first women secretary of state. Clinton's most controversial appointment was his wife, Hillary Rodham Clinton, whom he named to chair the committee to draft a national healthcare plan.

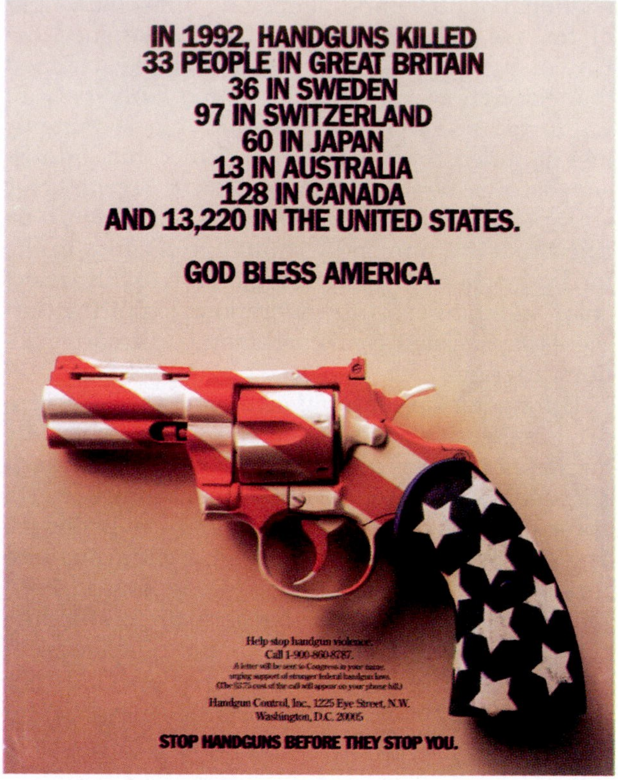
IN 1992, HANDGUNS KILLED
33 PEOPLE IN GREAT BRITAIN
36 IN SWEDEN
97 IN SWITZERLAND
60 IN JAPAN
13 IN AUSTRALIA
128 IN CANADA
AND 13,220 IN THE UNITED STATES.
GOD BLESS AMERICA.
Help stop handgun violence.
Call 1-900-860-8787.
Handgun Control, Inc., 1225 Eye Street, N.W.
Washington, D.C. 20005
STOP HANDGUNS BEFORE THEY STOP YOU.

◆ Throughout the 1980s and 1990s, the issue of gun control sharply divided the nation. This ad strongly asserts the need for control. Opponents argue that the right to bear arms is guaranteed by the Constitution. Advocates for control won a small victory in 1993 when Congress passed the Brady bill, which requires a five-day waiting period and a background check before someone can buy a handgun. *Handgun Control, Inc.*

Clinton, Congress, and Change

Clinton's presidency got off to a slow and shaky start. One of his first actions was to attempt to fulfill a campaign pledge to end discrimination against homosexuals in the military. Faced with substantial opposition in Congress and in the military, Clinton retreated and compromised. The compromise required the armed forces to stop asking about sexual preference as long as gays and lesbians in the service refrained from homosexual activities. The new policy pleased no one. It left even the president's supporters distressed about his willingness to sacrifice principles.

Clinton fared no better with his promise to provide national health insurance for the estimated 35 million Americans who were uninsured. Chaired by his wife, the Task Force on National Health Care Reform in 1993 proposed providing universal insurance primarily by mandating that employers offer health insurance to their employees. A barrage of criticism greeted the task force's report. Businesses objected to providing mandated health insurance. The American Medical Association complained that adopting the recommendations would mean that government would decide how much healthcare an individual could receive and deny an individual's choice of doctors. Such complaints found their mark in a public leery of big changes in medical care. By mid-1994, it was apparent that healthcare reform was a dead issue.

Success did not elude Clinton entirely during his first two years in office. Going against considerable opposition within his own party, he gained congressional approval of the **North American Free Trade Agreement (NAFTA),** which gradually re-

North American Free Trade Agreement Agreement approved in 1993 that eliminated most tariffs and other trade barriers among the United States, Canada, and Mexico.

duced trade barriers between the United States, Canada, and Mexico over a fifteen-year-period. In 1993, Congress also approved the **Brady bill,** which mandated a five-day waiting period before an individual could purchase a handgun. Additionally, Clinton was able in 1993 to secure passage of a budget that he believed would reduce the budget deficit and promote economic growth. Denounced by Republicans as typical liberal "tax and spend" measures, these laws raised taxes on wealthy Americans while making major spending cuts. The failure to achieve significant social reform and Clinton's many compromises, however, more than overshadowed the president's small victories.

As Clinton sank ever lower in public opinion polls in 1994, the Republicans rallied around Newt Gingrich, a conservative member of Congress from Georgia. Some three hundred Republican aspirants to the House of Representatives pledged on September 27, 1994, to support the **Contract with America** that Gingrich promised to enact if Republicans were victorious at the polls. Reflecting Gingrich's philosophy of a minimal federal government, the contract called for various tax cuts and a balanced federal budget by 2002. Apart from specifying cuts in welfare, the contract was vague on how the budget was to be balanced.

Voters responded to Gingrich's call for a political revolution. In the 1994 elections, Republicans picked up nine Senate seats and fifty-two House seats, thereby gaining control of the Senate for the first time since 1987 and of the House for the first time in forty years. In addition, Republicans added fourteen governorships to their total. Democratic mainstays such as Governor Mario Cuomo of New York and Governor Ann Richards of Texas went down to defeat. A conservative revolution even more profound than the one that had elected Ronald Reagan president appeared to be taking shape.

True to his word, Gingrich, the new Speaker of the House, steered virtually all of the Contract with America through the House during its first hundred days in session in 1995. Republicans passed large tax cuts, strong anticrime legislation, and increases in military spending. (Ironically, the only part of the contract that was not fulfilled was the provision calling for term limits for members of Congress.) Euphoria ran high in the Republican ranks.

The contract's pledge to balance the budget by 2002 led to a confrontation between Clinton and Gingrich after the beginning of the new federal fiscal year in October 1995. Since no budget had been agreed on for fiscal year 1995–1996, a continuing resolution was needed to allow the federal government to function and to pay its bills. Gingrich attached specified reductions in Medicare, Medicaid, and welfare spending to the continuing resolution. If Clinton vetoed the resolution because he did not like these reductions, all nonessential services of the federal government would be forced to shut down.

Clinton called Gingrich's bluff and vetoed the resolution. Some 800,000 federal workers were sent home briefly in November and for more than a month beginning in mid-December. National museums, parks, passport offices, and a host of other government offices closed. As the shutdown continued into January 1996, the public increasingly pointed the finger at Gingrich and the Republicans for the budgetary impasse. "It seems like the Republicans have this my-way-or-no-way attitude, and I'm tired of it," a 37-year-old Kansan observed. Senate Majority Leader Robert Dole of Kansas, sensing the damage that the shutdown was doing to his party, finally called for a Republican retreat on the continuing resolution. Government employees went back to work in mid-January, and the leaders of the two parties sat down again to negotiate a budget.

Clinton emerged from the government shutdown with enhanced stature and a new political lease on life. The budgetary battles made him seem a moderate, whereas Gingrich and his supporters came off as extremists.

Following the government shutdowns of 1995–1996, Clinton and the Republican Congress were able to reach substantial agreement on only one major issue, welfare reform. The Republican

Brady bill Law passed in 1993 that established a five-day waiting period for handgun purchases.

Contract with America Pledge taken in September 1994 by some three hundred Republican candidates for the House that promised to reduce the size and scope of the federal government and to balance the federal budget by 2002.

welfare reform bill that Clinton signed late in the summer of 1996 marked a dramatic departure from the federal welfare program that had existed since the New Deal—Aid to Families with Dependent Children. Charging that AFDC payments had created a culture of poverty and dependence because the program did not require recipients to work, Republicans replaced AFDC with block grants to the states. The legislation allowed the states to experiment with a variety of approaches to handling welfare and required adults to work in order to receive welfare. Critics of the measure contended that the end of federal welfare entitlements amounted to a betrayal of the poor.

The 1996 Campaign

Perceiving Clinton as a vulnerable president, a host of Republican candidates emerged in 1995 to compete for the right to carry the party's standard. Despite sharp initial challenges from Steven Forbes, heir to a publishing fortune, and Patrick Buchanan, a conservative columnist, veteran politician Robert Dole secured the nomination easily.

Dole emerged as the Republican nominee only to find himself trailing in the polls by twenty points in June 1996. In an effort to narrow the gap, he resigned his Senate seat. Several factors operated as constraints on his ambitions. First, the economy had grown steadily though not spectacularly during Clinton's presidency. Second, Dole was a moderate Republican who failed to inspire the conservative activists who had energized Reagan's campaigns. Finally, Clinton's handling of the budgetary impasse gave him some credentials as a presidential leader.

Dole's best hopes appeared to rest on further developments in the **Whitewater scandal.** The complicated scandal got its name from the failed Whitewater real-estate development in Arkansas in which the Clintons had invested. On May 28, 1996, a jury convicted Arkansas Governor Jim Guy Tucker and two of the Clintons' other former business partners in Whitewater, James and Susan McDougal, of fraud. The three were found guilty of arranging nearly $3 million in loans from federally backed banks on the basis of falsified appraisals and of using the loans for improper purposes, including the Whitewater development, while Clinton was governor of Arkansas.

Although none of the evidence introduced in the trial implicated the president, that did not absolve him and his wife of suspected wrongdoing in many people's eyes. Hillary Clinton had been a partner in the Rose Law Firm that handled the affairs of the McDougals' failed bank. Vincent Foster, an attorney who followed the Clintons from Arkansas to the White House, committed suicide when the scandal broke in 1993, leading some to speculate that the Clintons had something to hide.

Neither Dole's attempt to question Clinton's character nor the former senator's call for a 15 percent across-the-board cut in income taxes made much of an impression on the electorate. Clinton rolled to an easy victory on November 5, becoming the first Democrat to be re-elected president since Franklin D. Roosevelt. He captured 379 electoral votes and 49 percent of the popular vote. Dole won the remainder of the electoral votes and 41 percent of the popular vote, while Reform party candidate Ross Perot captured 9 percent of the popular vote. Expecting an easy Clinton victory, less than half of all eligible voters cast their ballots. The percentage turnout was the lowest since 1924. Clinton proved to have very short coattails. The Republicans retained control of the Senate and the House.

Clinton's Foreign Policy

When Clinton assumed control of foreign policy, it still was not clear what general policy would replace that of the Cold War. Americans wanted to maintain their power and influence as a super-

Whitewater scandal A scandal involving a failed real-estate development in Arkansas in which President Clinton invested; several of the president's business partners in the Whitewater development were convicted of fraud.

power but were divided over what situations would warrant American intervention. Inexperienced in foreign affairs, Clinton proceeded cautiously and followed the general outline set by President Bush. In economic foreign policy, Clinton completed Bush's effort to pass the NAFTA and General Agreement on Tariffs and Trade (GATT) agreements, to improve trade with China, and to encourage Japan to buy more American goods. Clinton continued to support Russian leader Boris Yeltsin and to work toward agreements with former Soviet countries to destroy nuclear warheads.

Clinton inherited two highly controversial commitments from the Bush administration—in Somalia and in Bosnia. U.S. troops intervened in Somalia in 1992 as part of a United Nations effort to keep the peace between marauding factions in a civil war. But in the absence of any direct U.S. interest in the country, pressure to withdraw the troops grew. By April 1994, Clinton had done so.

Clinton inched forward on the issue of Bosnia amid considerable controversy over whether UN peacekeeping efforts would have any effect. As the carnage increased, however, the Clinton administration agreed to allow American forces to participate in a UN campaign to establish and protect "safe areas" for refugees. In the fall of 1995, the United States sponsored talks between the warring elements—the Serbs, the Muslim Bosnians, and the Croats. The resulting **Dayton Agreement** partitioned the country into a Bosnian-Croatian federation and Serbia and called for UN forces, including 20,000 Americans, to police the peace. By the summer of 1996, when most American forces were withdrawn, much had been accomplished to rebuild the shattered region. In December 1997, Clinton announced, however, that a continued American presence in that nation was necessary to oversee the task of nation building.

The Balkans continued to remain a hot spot during Clinton's second term. The conflict that erupted in 1998 again involved ancient hostilities between Orthodox Christians and Muslims, this time in the Serbian province of Kosovo. Kosovo, 90 percent of whose population consisted of ethnic Albanians, who also were Muslims, had enjoyed considerable autonomy until the breakup of the former Yugoslavia in 1989, when Serbian president Slobodan Milosevic took control of the province. Milosevic ordered a crackdown in Kosovo in 1998 after the emergence of the Kosovo Liberation Army, which sought full independence for the province.

Milosevic's efforts to drive ethnic Albanians from their villages in Kosovo prompted NATO intervention in March 1999 after negotiations to end the conflict failed. NATO launched bombing raids against Serbian targets in Kosovo and Serbia to force a Serb withdrawal from the province. NATO's reluctance to commit troops to the conflict, however, allowed Milosevic to conduct a campaign of **ethnic cleansing** against the Albanians, who began a mass exodus from the province. Milosevic finally capitulated and agreed to sign a UN-approved peace agreement on June 9. British officials sent to investigate mass graves after the conflict ended estimated that some ten thousand ethnic Albanian civilians had been deliberately shot by Milosevic's forces between June 1998 and June 1999.

Iraq remained a problem area as well. Fearful that Saddam Hussein would replenish his chemical and biological weapons after the Gulf War, the United Nations required Iraq to allow UN inspectors access to sites suspected of storing or producing such weapons. From the beginning of these forced inspections, Saddam obstructed the UN efforts. In January 1998, he flatly refused to allow inspectors to visit some sites, including many presidential palaces.

Clinton responded by threatening military action against Iraq. Although Saddam appeared to agree to unrestricted inspections in February 1998, he soon began imposing restrictions on the UN inspections again. Tired of Saddam's delaying tactics, Clinton ordered American warplanes to bomb

Dayton Agreement Agreement signed in Dayton, Ohio, in November 1995 by the three rival ethnic groups in Bosnia, which pledged to end the four-year civil war there.

ethnic cleansing An effort to eradicate an ethnic or religious group from a country or region, often through mass killings.

♦ Following his impeachment by the House of Representatives in December 1998, a determined President Clinton announced that he would not resign his office and vowed to serve out his term to "the last hour." House Minority Leader Richard Gephart *(left)*, Vice President Al Gore, and Hillary Clinton lend support.

Baghdad in December 1998. Saddam soon relented, promising once more to allow inspectors to visit all suspected sites. Few observers, however, expected Saddam's cooperation.

Bridge to the Twenty-first Century

As Clinton began his second term, most Americans were generally pleased with society and the economy and gave the president a high approval rating. The country was at peace, and the economy was growing, providing more jobs while inflation remained low. The previous years of economic growth were broad based, helping to reduce income gaps between men and women and African Americans and whites.

In his State of the Union address in 1998, Clinton focused on the economy's strength as he projected the first balanced budget in thirty years. The budget marked, he stated, "an end to decades of deficits that have shackled our economy, paralyzed our policies, and held our people back." He also suggested that any surplus should be set aside to ensure the future viability of Social Security. "Before we do anything with that surplus," he told Congress, "let's save Social Security first." Stressing "smart government," Clinton called for increased spending on education, daycare, Medicare, and Medicaid, as well as for medical and other scientific research. Republican critics argued that the budget had been balanced through the use of "smoke and mirrors" and represented the Democratic position as a continuation of "big government."

At the time Clinton gave his State of the Union Address, the emerging Monica Lewinsky scandal was rocking the White House and prompting some people to suggest that the president should resign or be impeached. Did the president have a sexual relationship with the former White House intern? Did he ask her to lie about it under oath? Although willing to believe the accusations, most Americans did not seem to care. As the investigation and stories of a cover-up and presidential sexual misconduct continued, Clinton's public approval rose to a record high of 79 percent. Polls suggested that a majority of the public was pleased with Clinton's performance as president and the overall state of the nation and thought that Clinton's private life should be his own business.

The Republican majority in the House of Representatives, however, did not agree with that assessment. On October 8, 1998, for only the third time in American history, the House launched impeachment proceedings against a president. In December, the House approved two articles of impeachment against Clinton. The first article charged that Clinton had perjured himself in his January 1998 testimony in the Paula Jones case. (Jones had filed a sexual harassment suit claiming that Clinton had asked her to perform oral sex on him in 1991 while he was governor of Arkansas. Clinton settled the case in November 1998 by paying Jones $850,000 while admitting nothing.) The second article charged that Clinton had abused the powers of his office and obstructed justice in attempting to cover up the Lewinsky affair.

Although public opinion polls clearly were against Clinton's impeachment, the Senate nevertheless agreed to proceed with the case. After a six-week trial, the Senate acquitted Clinton on both counts on February 12, 1999. Forty-five senators voted in favor of convicting the president of perjury, while fifty voted in favor of the obstruction of justice charge. Since a two-thirds majority was required to remove Clinton from office, he remained president, but with a badly stained reputation.

As Americans neared the new millennium, they appeared to have all but forgotten the high drama and low tragedy of Clinton's impeachment trial. Although some feared computer problems and stocked up on portable generators, canned goods, and extra cash, most awaited the arrival of the year 2000 with quiet confidence and assurance. The American economy was strong and showed no signs of stopping its extraordinary expansion. No great foreign threats loomed on the horizon for the world's remaining superpower. Only time would tell whether those confident expectations would be borne out. But one thing was certain: the making of America would continue.

SUMMARY

E xpectations
C onstraints
C hoices
O utcomes

Americans entered and left the 1990s badly divided over many cultural and social *expectations*. Conservatives and liberals argued heatedly about the morality of the country. From both sides of the political spectrum, activists promoted their point of view. Racial and ethnic minorities, gays, and women were among those insisting that government remove *constraints* in the form of discriminatory laws and practices. Conservatives countered that government programs were already providing too many special programs for minorities and the disadvantaged. Opposed to homosexuality, abortion, and what they considered destructive values, conservatives claimed that American society was too permissive, too preoccupied with sex and violence, and too tolerant of immortality and "alternative lifestyles." They advocated less government interference in economic and social matters and argued for policy choices that stressed "traditional values."

The key issue in the 1992 presidential election proved to be not social issues but economic ones. Reminding voters of the economic recession then facing the country, Bill Clinton was able to outdistance incumbent president George Bush and third-party candidate Ross Perot. The *outcome* of Clinton's efforts to expand the welfare state by proposing national healthcare legislation failed abysmally and encouraged Republican *expectations* of a new era of conservatism. Those *expectations* appeared quite realistic in 1994, when Republicans captured both houses of Congress by proposing the conservative Contract with America.

Clinton chose to steal much of the Republican thunder by successfully proposing budgetary and welfare reforms. The *outcome* of his shift to the political center and of a growing economy was his reelection over Bob Dole in 1996.

The Monica Lewinsky scandal operated as a severe *constraint* on Clinton's political effectiveness during his second term. Although he survived a Senate trial on two impeachment charges, his presidential leadership virtually ended on the day Lewinsky became a household name in January 1998.

As America entered the new millennium, there appeared to be no clear political mandate. During the 1990s, Americans had resoundingly voted against a further expansion of "big government"—at least in the form of national healthcare. But they also had chosen to reject conservatives' calls for a thorough dismantling of the welfare state and to retain Social Security and Medicare. Radical *choices* seemed unnecessary in a country that had enjoyed nearly a decade of prosperity and that had resumed its place as the world's leading economic power.

SUGGESTED READINGS

Campbell, Colin, and Bert A. Rockman, eds. *The Clinton Presidency: First Appraisals* (1995).

An informative and speculative group of wide-ranging essays that explore many aspects of Clinton's first years in office and examine broader political issues.

Congressional Quarterly's Research Reports.

A valuable monthly resource for information and views on issues facing the United States and the world.

Garrow, David J. *Liberty and Sexuality: The Right to Privacy and the Making of Roe v. Wade* (1994).

An in-depth, scholarly account of the origins and impact of *Roe v. Wade* and the legal and political issues dealing with privacy, gender, and abortion.

Shilts, Randy. *And the Band Played On: Politics, People and the AIDS Epidemic* (1987).

A compelling book on the AIDS epidemic and the early lack of action by society; written by a victim of AIDS.

Terkel, Studs. *The Great Divide* (1988).

An interesting and informative collection of oral interviews that provide a personal glimpse of changes taking place in American society.

BIBLIOGRAPHY

Chapter 1 Making a "New" World, to 1558

Robert F. Berkhofer, *The White Man's Indian: Images of the American Indian from Columbus to the Present* (1978); George F. Carter, *Earlier Than You Think: A Personal View of Man in America* (1980); Michael D. Coe, *Mexico* (1984); Alfred W. Crosby, Jr., *The Columbian Exchange: Biological and Cultural Consequences of 1492* (1972); Philip Curtin, *The Atlantic Slave Trade: A Census* (1969); Basil Davidson, *The African Genius: An Introduction to African Cultural and Social History* (1969); John H. Elliott, *The Old World and the New, 1492–1650* (1970); Brian M. Fagan, *Kingdoms of Gold, Kingdoms of Jade: The Americas Before Columbus* (1991); J. D. Fage, *An Introduction to the History of West Africa* (1969); Filipe Fernandez-Armesto, *Columbus* (1991); Morton Fried, *The Notion of Tribe* (1975); Stephen Greenblatt, *Marvelous Possession: The Wonder of the New World* (1991); Christopher Hill, *Society and Puritanism in Pre-Revolutionary England* (1967); Alvin M. Josephy, *America in 1492: The World of the Indian Peoples Before the Arrival of Columbus* (1992); Alice B. Kehoe, *North American Indians: A Comprehensive Account.* (1992); Karen Ordahl Kupperman, ed., *America in European Consciousness, 1493–1750* (1995); Jay A. Levenson, *Circa 1492: Art in the Age of Exploration* (1991); William H. McNeill, *Plagues and Peoples* (1976); Wallace Notestein, *The English People on the Eve of Colonization, 1603–1630* (1954); Anthony Pagden, *European Encounters with the New World: From Renaissance to Romanticism* (1993); J. H. Parry, *The Age of Reconnaissance: Discovery, Exploration, and Settlement, 1450–1650* (1963); William Phillips, and Carla Phillips, *The Worlds of Christopher Columbus* (1992); David Beers Quinn, *North America from Earliest Discovery to First Settlements: The Norse Voyages to 1612* (1977); Ann R. Raminofsky, *Vectors of Death: The Archaeology of European Contact* (1987); A. L. Rowse, *The Elizabethans and America* (1959); Dean Snow, *The Archaeology of North America: American Indians and Their Origins* (1976); Eviatar Zerubavel, *Terra Cognita: The Mental Discovery of America* (1992).

Chapter 2 A Continent on the Move, 1400–1725

Richard Aquila, *The Iroquois Restoration: Iroquois Diplomacy on the Colonial Frontier, 1701–1754* (1997); James Axtell, *The Invasion Within; The Contest of Cultures in Colonial North America* (1985); Lynn Robison Bailey, *Indian Slave Trade in the Southwest; a Study of Slavetaking and the Traffic of Indian Captives* (1966); Jose Antonio Brandao, *Your Fyre Shall Burn No More: Iroquois Policy Towards New France and Its Native Allies to 1701* (1997); Leslie Choquette, *Frenchmen Into Peasants: Modernity and Tradition in the Peopling of French Canada* (1997); Thomas J. Condon, *New York Beginnings; the Commercial Origins of New Netherland* (1968); Charles R. Cutter, *The Protector de Indios in Colonial New Mexico, 1659–1821* (1986); Olive Patricia Dickason, *The Myth of the Savage: And the Beginnings of French Colonialism in the Americas* (1984); W. J. Eccles, *France in America* (1990); Jack D. Forbes, *Apache, Navaho, and Spaniard* (1994); Charles Gibson, *Spain in America* (1966); Ramon A. Gutierrez, *When Jesus Came, the Corn Mothers Went Away: Marriage, Sexuality, and Power in New Mexico, 1500–1846* (1991); Paul Horgan, *Conquistadors in North American History* (1963); Robert H. Jackson, *Indian Population Decline: The Missions of Northwestern New Spain, 1687–1840* (1994); Cornelius J. Jaenen, *Friend and Foe: Aspects of French-Amerindian Cultural Contact in the Sixteenth and Seventeenth Centuries* (1976); Elizabeth Ann Harper John, *Storms Brewed in Other Men's Worlds: The Confrontation of Indians, Spanish, and French in the Southwest, 1540–1795* (1996); Susan Lamb, *Pueblo and Mission: Cultural Roots of the Southwest* (1997); Theda Perdue, *Slavery and the Evolution of Cherokee Society, 1540–1866* (1979); Oliver A. Rink, *Holland on the Hudson: An Economic and Social History of Dutch New York* (1986); Katherine A. Spielmann, ed., *Farmers, Hunters, and Colonists: Interaction Between the Southwest and the Southern Plains* (1991); John Super, *Food, Conquest, and Colonization in Sixteenth-Century Spanish America* (1988); Bruce G. Trigger, *Natives and Newcomers: Canada's "Heroic Age" Reconsidered* (1985); Marce Trudel, *The Beginnings of New France, 1524–1663* (1973); Daniel H. Usner, Jr., *Indians, Settlers, and Slaves in a Frontier Exchange Economy: The Lower Mississippi Valley Before 1783* (1992); David J. Weber, *The Spanish Frontier in North America* (1992).

Chapter 3 Founding the English Mainland Colonies, 1607–1732

Bernard Bailyn, *The New England Merchants in the Seventeenth Century* (1955); Carol Berkin, *First Generations: Women in Colonial America* (1996); Patricia Bonomi, *A Factious People* (1971); Paul Boyer and Stephen Nissenbaum, *Salem Possessed: The Social Origins of Witchcraft* (1974); Timothy Breen, *Puritans and Adventurers* (1980); Jon Butler, *Awash in a Sea of Faith* (1990); William Cronon, *Changes in the Land: Indians, Colonists, and the Ecology of New England* (1983); Andrew Delbanco, *The Puritan Ordeal* (1989); John Demos, *Entertaining Satan* (1982); Philip Gura, *A Glimpse of Sion's Glory* (1984); David Hall, *Worlds of Wonder, Days of Judgment* (1990); James Horn, *Adapting to a New World: English Society in the Seventeenth Century Chesapeake* (1994); Michael Kammen, *Colonial New York* (1975); James Lang, *Conquest and Commerce* (1975); Suzanne Lebsock, *A Share of Honor* (1984); James Lemmon, *The Best Poor Man's Country* (1972); Barry Levy, *Quakers and the*

American Family (1988); H. T. Merrens, *Colonial North Carolina* (1964); Perry Miller, *Errand into the Wilderness* (1956); Edmund Morgan, *American Slavery, American Freedom* (1975); Mary Beth Norton, *Founding Mothers and Fathers: Gendered Power and the Forming of American Society* (1996); Oliver Rink, *Holland on Hudson* (1986); Frederick Siegel, *The Roots of Southern Distinctiveness* (1987); Harry Stout, *The New England Soul* (1986); Alan Tully, *William Penn's Legacy* (1977); Robert Weir *Colonial South Carolina* (1983); Betty Wood, *The Origins of American Slavery: Freedom and Bondage in the English Colonies* (1997).

Chapter 4 The British Colonies in the Eighteenth Century, 1689–1763

Bernard Bailyn, *The Origins of American Politics* (1968); Ira Berlin and Philip Morgan, eds., *Cultivation and Culture: Labor and the Shaping of Slave Life in the Americas* (1993); Patricia Bonomi, *Under the Cope of Heaven: Religion, Society, and Politics in Colonial America* (1986); Richard Bushman, *From Puritan to Yankee* (1967); Jean Friedman, *The Enclosed Garden: Women and Community in the Evangelical South* (1985); Philip Greven, *The Protestant Temperament: Patterns of Childrearing, Religious Experience, and the Self in Early America* (1977); James Henretta, *The Evolution of American Society, 1700–1815* (1982); Rhys Isaac, *The Transformation of Virginia, 1740–1790* (1982); Francis Jennings, *Empire of Fortune* (1988); Joan Jensen, *Loosening the Bonds: Mid-Atlantic Farm Women, 1750–1850* (1986); Charles Joyner, *Down by the Riverside: A South Carolina Slave Community* (1984); Susan Juster, *Disorderly Women* (1988); Michael Kammen, *Spheres of Liberty: Changing Perceptions of Liberty in American Culture* (1986); Peter Kolchin, *American Slavery, 1619–1877* (1993); Allan Kulikoff, *Tobacco and Slaves* (1986); Ned Landsman, *Scotland and Its First American Colony* (1985); Daniel Littlefield, *Rice and Slaves: Ethnicity and the Slave Trade in Colonial South Carolina* (1981); Marcus Rediker, *Between the Devil and the Deep Blue Sea* (1985); Daniel Richter, *The Ordeal of the Longhouse* (1992); Sharon Salinger, *"To Serve Well and Faithfully": Labor and Indentured Servants in Pennsylvania, 1692–1800* (1987); Michael Sobel, *The World They Made Together: Black and White Values in Eighteenth Century Virginia* (1987); Stephanie Wolf, *As Various as Their Land: The Everyday Lives of Eighteenth Century Americans* (1993).

Chapter 5 Choosing Loyalties, 1763–1776

Bernard Bailyn, *The Ideological Origins of the American Revolution* (1967); Carol Berkin, *Jonathan Sewall: Odessey of An American Loyalist* (1974); Timothy Breen, *Tobacco Culture: The Mentality of the Great Tidewater Planters on the Eve of the Revolution* (1985); Edward Countryman, *The American Revolution* (1985); Marc Egnal, *A Mighty Empire: The Origins of the American Revolution* (1988); Eric Foner, *Tom Paine and Revolutionary America* (1976); Robert Gross, *The Minutemen and Their World* (1976); Francis Jennings, *Empire of Fortune: Crowns, Colonies and Tribes in the Seven Years War in America* (1988); Linda Kerber, *Women of the Republic: Intellect and Ideology in Revolutionary America* (1980); Pauline Maier, *American Scripture: Making the Declaration of Independence* (1997); Mary Beth Norton, *Liberty's Daughters: The Revolutionary Experience of American Women, 1750–1800* (1980); Paul Rahle, *Republics Ancient and Modern: Republicanism and the American Revolution* (1992).

Chapter 6 Re-creating America: Independence and a New Nation, 1775–1783

Bernard Bailyn, *The Ordeal of Thomas Hutchinson* (1974); Ira Berlin and Ronald Hoffman, eds, *Slavery and Freedom in the Age of the American Revolution* (1983); Jeremy Black, *War for America* (1991); Colin Bonwick, *The American Revolution* (1991); Andrew Cayton, *The Frontier Republic* (1986); Edward Countryman, *A People in Revolution: The American Revolution and Political Society in New York, 1760–1790* (1981); Jeffrey Crow and Larry Tise, eds., *The Southern Experience in the American Revolution* (1978); John C. Dann, *The Revolution Remembered: Eyewitness Accounts of the War for Independence* (1980); James Flexner, *George Washington in the American Revolution* (1978); Jay Fliegelman, *Prodigals and Pilgrims* (1982); William Fowler and Wallace Coyle, eds., *The American Revolution: Changing Perspectives* (1979); Sylvia Frey, *Water from the Rock: Black Resistance in a Revolutionary Age* (1991); Barbara Graymont, *The Iroquois in the American Revolution* (1972); Robert Gross, *The Minutemen and Their World* (1976); Ronald Hoffman and Peter Albert, eds., *Women in the Age of the American Revolution* (1989); Michael Kammen, *A Season of Youth* (1978); Isaac Kramnick, *Republicanism and Bourgeois Radicalism: Political Ideology in Late Eighteenth Century England and America*; Duncan MacLeod, *Slavery, Race, and the American Revolution* (1974); Mary Beth Norton, *Liberty's Daughters* (1980); Mary Beth Norton, *The British-Americans* (1972); James O'Donnell, *Southern Indians in the American Revolution* (1973); Charles Royster, *A Revolutionary People at War: The Continental Army and American Character, 1775–1783* (1980); John Shy, *A People Numerous and Armed: Reflections on the Military Struggle for American Independence* (1976); James Walker, *The Black Loyalists* (1976).

Chapter 7 Competing Visions of a Virtuous Republic, 1770–1800

Joyce Appleby, *Capitalism and a New Social Order* (1984); Lance Banning, *The Jeffersonian Persuasion: The Evolution of a Party Ideology* (1978); Charles Beard, *An Economic Interpretation of the Constitution* (1913); Walker Bern, *Taking the Constitution Seriously* (1987); Thomas Curry, *The First Freedom* (1986); David B. Davis, *Slavery in the Age of Revolution* (1975); Stanley Elkins and Eric McKitrick, *The Federalist Era* (1993); Joseph Ellis, *American Sphinx: The Character of Thomas Jefferson* (1997); Max Farrand, ed., *Records of the Federal Convention of 1787* (1911–1937); Richard Hofstadter, *The Idea of a*

Party System (1970); Michael Kammen, *A Machine That Would Go of Itself: The Constitution and American Culture* (1986); Allan Kulikoff, *The Agrarian Origins of American Capitalism* (1992); Staughton Lynd, *Class Conflict, Slavery, and the United States Constitution* (1967); Jackson Turner Main, *The Antifederalists* (1961); Drew McCoy, *The Last of the Fathers: James Madison and the Republican Legacy* (1989); Forrest McDonald, *Novus Ordo Seclorum* (1985); William Miller, *The First Liberty: Religion and the American Republic* (1986); Edmund Morgan, *Inventing the People: The Rise of Popular Sovereignty in England and America* (1988); Thomas Pangle, *The Spirit of Modern Republicanism* (1988); Donald Robinson, *Slavery in the Structure of American Politics, 1765–1820* (1971); Gary Wills, *Explaining America* (1981); Gordon Wood, *The Radicalism of the American Revolution* (1992).

Chapter 8 The Triumphs and Trials of Jeffersonianism, 1800–1815

Joyce Appleby, *Capitalism and the New Social Order: The Republican Vision of the 1790s* (1984); James M. Banner, *To the Hartford Convention: The Federalists and the Origins of Party Politics in Massachusetts, 1789–1815* (1970); Lance Banning, *The Jeffersonian Persuasion: Evolution of a Party Ideology* (1978); Irving Brant, *James Madison and American Nationalism* (1968); Roger H. Brown, *The Republic in Peril: 1812* (1964); Andrew Burnstein, *The Inner Jefferson: Portrait of a Grieving Optimist* (1995); Robert Lowry Clinton, *Marbury v. Madison and Judicial Review* (1989); Harry L. Coles, *The War of 1812* (1965); Alexander DeConde, *This Affair of Louisiana* (1976); R. David Edmunds, *The Shawnee Prophet* (1983); R. David Edmunds, *Tecumseh and the Quest for Indian Leadership* (1984); Richard Ellis, *The Jeffersonian Crisis: Courts and Politics in the Young Republic* (1974); William F. Fowler, Jr., *Jack Tars and Commodores: The American Navy, 1783–1815* (1984); Benjamin W. Griffith, Jr., *McIntosh and Weatherford, Creek Indian Leaders* (1988); Donald Hickey, *The War of 1812: A Forgotten Conflict* (1989); Reginald Horsman, *The War of 1812* (1969); Donald Jackson, *Thomas Jefferson and the Stony Mountains: Exploring the West from Monticello* (1981); Linda Kerber, *Federalists in Dissent: Imagery and Ideology in Jeffersonian America* (1970); Ralph Ketcham, *James Madison: A Biography* (1971); Ralph Lerner, *The Thinking Revolutionary: Principle and Practice in the New Republic* (1987); Drew McCoy, *The Elusive Republic: Political Economy in Jeffersonian America* (1980); Forrest McDonald, *The Presidency of Thomas Jefferson* (1976); William G. McLoughlin, *Cherokee Renascence in the New Republic* (1986); John C. Miller, *The Wolf by the Ears: Thomas Jefferson and Slavery* (1977); Gary B. Nash, *Forging Freedom: The Formation of Philadelphia's Black Community, 1720–1840* (1988); John R. Nelson, Jr., *Liberty and Property: Political Economy and Policymaking in the New Nation, 1787–1812* (1987); Julius W. Pratt, *Expansionists of 1812* (1925); Francis Paul Prucha, *The Sword of the Republic: The United States Army on the Frontier, 1783–1846* (1986); Malcolm Rohrbough, *The Trans-Appalachian Frontier; People, Societies, and Institutions, 1775–1850* (1978); James P. Ronda, *Astoria and Empire* (1990); James Ronda, *Lewis and Clark Among the Indians* (1984); Robert Allen Rutland, *The Presidency of James Madison* (1990); Robert Allen Rutland, *James Madison, The Founding Father* (1987); Ronald Schultz, *The Republic of Labor: Philadelphia Artisans and the Politics of Class, 1720–1830* (1993); Bernard W. Sheehan, *Seeds of Extinction: Jeffersonian Philanthropy and the American Indian* (1973); J. C. A. Stagg, *Mr. Madison's War; Politics, Diplomacy, and Warfare in the Early American Republic, 1783–1830* (1983); Robert W. Tucker and David C. Hendrickson, *Empire of Liberty: The Statecraft of Thomas Jefferson* (1990); Anthony F. C. Wallace, *Death and Rebirth of the Seneca* (1970); Steven Watts, *The Republic Reborn: War and the Making of Liberal America, 1790–1820* (1987).

Chapter 9 The Rise of a New Nation, 1815–1836

John M. Belonlavek, *"Let the Eagle Soar!" The Foreign Policy of Andrew Jackson* (1985); Lee Benson, *The Concept of Jacksonian Democracy; New York as a Test Case* (1961); Noble E. Cunningham, Jr., *The Presidency of James Monroe* (1996); George Dangerfield, *The Awakening of American Nationalism, 1815–1828* (1965); Richard Ellis, *The Union at Risk: Jacksonian Democracy, States Rights, and the Nullification Crisis* (1987); Michael Feldberg, *The Turbulent Era: Riot and Disorder in Jacksonian America* (1980); Daniel Feller, *The Public Lands in Jacksonian Politics* (1984); Ronald Formisano, *The Transformation of Political Culture: Massachusetts Parties, 1790s–1840s* (1983); Michael D. Green, *The Politics of Indian Removal: Creek Government and Society in Crisis* (1982); Bray Hammond, *Banks and Politics in America from the Revolution to the Civil War* (1957); Mary W. M. Hargreaves, *The Presidency of John Quincy Adams* (1985); Lawrence Frederick Kohl, *The Politics of Individualism: Parties and the American Character in the Jacksonian Era* (1989); Ernest May, *The Making of the Monroe Doctrine* (1975); William McLoughlin, *Cherokees and Missionaries, 1789–1839* (1984); Marvin Meyers, *The Jacksonian Persuasion: Politics and Belief* (1957); Roger L. Nichols, *Black Hawk and the Warrior's Path* (1992); John Niven, *John C. Calhoun and the Price of Union: A Biography* (1988); Edward Pessen, *Jacksonian America: Society, Personality, and Politics* (1978); Jonathan Prude, *The Coming of Industrial Order; Town and Factory Life in Rural Massachusetts, 1810–1860* (1983); Robert V. Remini, *Henry Clay: Statesman for the Union* (1991); Robert V. Remini, *The Life of Andrew Jackson* (1988); Thomas C. Shevory, *John Marshall's Law: Interpretation, Ideology, and Interest* (1994); William Preston Vaughn, *The Antimasonic Party in the United States, 1826–1843* (1983); Anthony F. C. Wallace, *The Long, Bitter Trail: Andrew Jackson and the Indians* (1993); John William Ward, *Andrew Jackson: Symbol for an Age* (1962); Harry L. Watson, *Liberty and Power: The Politics of Jacksonian America* (1990).

Chapter 10 The Great Transformation, 1815–1840

Ira Berlin, *Slaves Without Masters: The Free Negro in the Antebellum South* (1974);

John Blassingame, *The Slave Community: Plantation Life in the Antebellum South* (1979); Stuart M. Blumin, *The Emergence of the Middle Class: Social Experiences in the American City, 1760–1900* (1989); Marcus Cunliffe, *Chattel Slavery and Wage Slavery: The Anglo-American Context, 1830–1860* (1979); William C. Davis, *A Way Through the Wilderness: The Natchez Trace and the Civilization of the Southern Frontier* (1995); Thomas Dublin, *Women at Work: The Transformation of Work and Community in Lowell, Massachusetts, 1826–1880* (1979); Clement Eaton, *The Growth of Southern Civilization, 1790–1860* (1961); Robert W. Fogel, *Without Consent or Contract: The Rise and Fall of American Slavery* (1991); Elizabeth Fox-Genovese, *Within the Plantation Household: Black and White Women of the Old South* (1988); Karen V. Hansen, *A Very Social Time: Crafting Community in Antebellum New England* (1994); Tamara Herevan, and Maris A. Vinovskis, *Family and Population in Nineteenth-Century America* (1978); Marilynn Wood Hill, *Their Sisters' Keepers: Prostitution in New York City, 1830–1870* (1993); Donald R. Hoke, *Ingenious Yankees: The Rise of the American System of Manufactures in the Private Sector* (1990); David J. Jeremy, *Transatlantic Industrial Revolution: The Diffusion of Textile Technology Between Britain and America, 1790–1830* (1981); Peter R. Knights, *Yankee Destinies: The Lives of Ordinary Nineteenth-Century Bostonians* (1991); Suzanne Lebsock, *Free Women of Petersburg: Status and Culture in a Southern Town, 1784–1860* (1984); Donald G. Mathews, *Religion in the Old South* (1977); Sally McMillen, *Motherhood in the Old South: Pregnancy, Childbirth, and Infant Rearing* (1990); James Oakes, *The Ruling Race: A History of American Slaveholders* (1982); W. J. Rorabaugh, *The Craft Apprentice: From Franklin to the Machine Age in America* (1986); Kenneth A. Scherzer, *The Unbounded Community: Neighborhood Life and Social Structure in New York City, 1830–1875* (1992); Charles G. Sellers, *The Market Revolution: Jacksonian America, 1815–1846* (1991); Ronald E. Shaw, *Canals for a Nation: The Canal Era in the United States, 1790–1860* (1990); Theodore Steinberg, *Nature Incorporated: Industrialization and the Waters of New England* (1991).

Chapter 11 Responses to the Great Transformation, 1815–1840

Michael Barkun, *Crucible of the Millennium: The Burned-Over District of New York in the 1840s* (1986); R. J. M. Blackett, *Building an Antislavery Wall: Black Americans in the Atlantic Abolitionist Movement, 1830–1860* (1983); Jeanne Boydston, *Home and Work: Housework, Wages, and the Ideology of Labor in the Early Republic* (1990); Paul S. Boyer, *Urban Masses and Moral Order in America, 1820–1920* (1978); Richard J. Carwardine, *Evangelicals and Politics in Antebellum America* (1993); Judith Wragg Chase, *Afro-American Art and Craft* (1971); Frances B. Cogan, *All-American Girl: The Ideal of Real Womanhood in Mid-Nineteenth-Century America* (1989); Lawrence A. Cremin, *American Education: The National Experience, 1783–1786* (1980); Jay P. Dolan, *The Immigrant Church: New York's Irish and German Catholics, 1815–1865* (1975); Dena J. Epstein, *Sinful Tunes and Spirituals: Black Folk Music to the Civil War* (1977); Lawrence Foster, *Religion and Sexuality: Three American Communal Experiments of the Nineteenth Century* (1981); Jenny Franchot, *Roads to Rome: The Antebellum Protestant Encounter with Catholicism* (1994); Nathan O. Hatch, *The Democratization of American Christianity* (1990); T. Walter. Herbert, *Dearest Beloved: The Hawthornes and the Making of the Middle-Class Family* (1993); James Oliver Horton, *Free People of Color: Inside the African American Community* (1993); Daniel Walker Howe, *The Political Culture of the American Whigs* (1979); Paul E. Johnson, *A Shopkeepers' Millennium: Society and Revivals in Rochester, New York, 1815–1837* (1978); Carl F. Kaestle, *Pillars of the Republic: Common Schools and American Society, 1780–1860* (1983); Gerda Lerner, *The Grimké Sisters from South Carolina: Pioneers for Women's Rights and Abolition* (1971); Steven Mintz, *Moralists and Modernizers: America's Pre–Civil War Reformers* (1995); Stephen B. Oates, *The Fires of Jubilee: Nat Turner's Fierce Rebellion* (1975); Lewis Perry, *Boats Against the Current: American Culture Between Revolution and Modernity, 1820–1860* (1993); Edward Pessen, *Most Uncommon Jacksonians: The Radical Leaders of the Early Labor Movement* (1967); Merrill D. Peterson, *The Great Triumvierate: Webster, Clay, and Calhoun* (1987); Charles E. Rosenberg, *The Care of Strangers: The Rise of America's Hospital System* (1987); Katherine Kish Sklar, *Catherine Beecher: A Study in American Domesticity* (1973); Ian Tyrrell, *Sobering Up: From Temperance to Prohibition in Antebellum America, 1800–1860* (1979); Major L. Wilson, *The Presidency of Martin Van Buren* (1984); Kenneth H. Winn, *Exiles in a Land of Liberty: Mormons in America, 1830–1846* (1989).

Chapter 12 Westward Expansion and Manifest Destiny, 1841–1849

Paul Bergeron, *The Presidency of James K. Polk* (1987); Ray Allen Billington, *The Far Western Frontier, 1830–1860* (1956); Gene M. Brack, *Mexico Views Manifest Destiny, 1821–1846: An Essay on the Origins of the Mexican War* (1976); Newell. Bringhurst, *Brigham Young and the Expanding American Frontier* (1986); Joan E. Cashin, *A Family Venture: Men and Women on the Southern Frontier* (1991); Malcolm Clark, Jr., *Eden Seekers: The Settlement of Oregon, 1818–1862* (1981); Thomas D. Clark and John D. W. Guice, *Frontiers in Conflict: The Old Southwest, 1795–1830* (1989); Coy F. Cross, II, *Go West Young Man! Horace Greeley's Vision for America* (1995); John Mack Faragher, *Sugar Creek: Life on the Illinois Prairies* (1986); John Mack Faragher, *Women and Men on the Overland Trail* (1979); Paul Wallace Gates, *The Farmer's Age: Agriculture, 1815–1860* (1960); James R. Gibson, *Otter Skins, Boston Ships, and China Goods: The Maritime Fur Trade of the Northwest Coast, 1785–1841* (1992); Richard Griswold del Castillo, *The Treaty of Guadalupe Hidalgo: A Legacy of Conflict* (1990); Neal Harlow, *California Conquered: The Annexation of a Mexican Province, 1846–1850* (1982); Sylvia D. Hoffert, *When Hens Crow: The Woman's Rights Movement in Antebellum America* (1995); Reginald Horsman, *Race and Manifest Destiny: The Origins of American Racial Anglo-Saxonism* (1981); Julie Roy Jeffrey, *Frontier Women: The Trans-Mississippi West, 1840–1880* (1979); Theodore J. Karamanski, *Fur Trade and Exploration: Opening the Far Northwest, 1821–1852* (1983); Timothy M. Matovina, *Tejano Religion and Ethnicity: San Antonio, 1821–1860* (1995); Frederick Merk, *Manifest Destiny and Mission in American History; A Reinterpretation* (1963); Chaplain W. Morrison, *Democratic Politics and Sectionalism: The Wilmot Proviso* (1967); Stanley Noyes, *Los Comanches: The Horse People, 1751–1845* (1993); David Pletcher, *The Diplomacy of Annexation: Texas, Oregon, and the Mexican War* (1973); Catherine Price, *The Oglala People, 1841–1879: A Political History* (1996); Karen Sánchez-Eppler, *Touching Liberty: Abolition, Feminism, and the Politics of the Body* (1993); John H. Schroeder, *Mr. Polk's War: American Opposition and Dissent, 1846–1848* (1973); Henry Nash Smith, *Virgin Land: The American West as Symbol and Myth* (1950); John E. Sunder, *The Fur Trade on the Upper Missouri, 1840–1865* (1993); David J. Weber, *The Mexican Frontier, 1821–1846: The American Southwest Under Mexico* (1982); Albert K Weinberg, *Manifest Destiny: A Study of Nationalist Expansionism in American History* (1958).

Chapter 13 Sectional Conflict and Shattered Union, 1850–1861

Tyler Anbinder, *Nativism and Slavery: The Northern Know Nothings and the Politics of the 1850s* (1992); Stanley W. Campbell, *The Slave Catchers: Enforcement of the Fugitive Slave Law, 1850–1860* (1970); William J. Cooper, *The South and the Politics of Slavery, 1828–1856* (1978); Daniel W. Crofts, *Reluctant Confederates: Upper South Unionists in the Secession Crisis* (1989); Donald Fehrenbacher, *Slavery, Law, and Politics: The Dred Scott Case in Historical Perspective* (1981); Eric Foner, *Free Soil, Free Labor, Free Men; The Ideology of the Republican Party Before the Civil War* (1970); Lacy K. Ford, Jr., *Origins of Southern Radicalism: The South Carolina Upcountry, 1800–1860* (1988); Ronald P. Formisano, *The Birth of Mass Political Parties: Michigan, 1827–1861* (1971); William W. Freehling, *The Road to Disunion* (1990); Lawrence J. Friedman, *Gregarious Saints: Self and Community in American Abolitionism, 1830–1870* (1982); Eugene D. Genovese, *The Slaveholders' Dilemma: Freedom and Progress in Southern Conservative Thought, 1820–1860* (1992); William Gienapp, *Origins of the Republican Party, 1852–1856* (1987); Stanley Harrold, *The Abolitionists and the South, 1831–1861* (1995); Michael Holt, *The Political Crisis of the 1850s* (1970); Robert W. Johannsen, *Stephen Douglas* (1973); Paul Kleppner, *The Third Electoral System, 1853–1892: Parties, Voters, and Political Cultures* (1979); Russell B. Nye, *Fettered Freedom; Civil Liberties and the Slavery Controversy, 1830–1860* (1949); Stephen Oates, *To Purge This Land With Blood: A Biography of John Brown* (1970); James A. Rawley, *Race & Politics: "Bleeding Kansas" and the Coming of the Civil War* (1969); Richard Sewell, *Ballots for Freedom: Antislavery Politics in the United States, 1837–1865* (1976); Joel H. Silbey, *The Partisan Imperative: The Dynamics of American Politics Before the Civil War* (1984); Mitchell Snay, *Gospel of Disunion: Religion and Separatism in the Antebellum South* (1993); Mark W. Summers, *The Plundering Generation: Corruption and the Crisis of the Union, 1849–1861* (1987); John L. Thomas, *The Liberator, William Lloyd Garrison, a Biography* (1963); Larry E. Tise, *Proslavery: A History of the Defense of Slavery in America, 1701–1840* (1987); Wendy Hamand Venet, *Neither Ballots Nor Bullets: Women Abolitionists and the Civil War* (1991); Ronald G. Walters, *The Antislavery Appeal: American Abolitionism After 1830* (1977); Ralph Wooster, *The Secession Conventions of the South* (1962); Bertram Wyatt-Brown, *Yankee Saints and Southern Sinners* (1985); David Zarefsky, *Lincoln, Douglas, and Slavery: In the Crucible of Public Debate* (1990).

Chapter 14 A Violent Solution: Civil War, 1861–1865

David W. Blight, *Frederick Douglass' Civil War: Keeping Faith in Jubilee* (1989); Gabor S. Boritt, *Lincoln and the Economics of the American Dream* (1978); Dudley Taylor Cornish, *The Sable Arm: Negro Troops in the Union Army, 1861–1865* (1966); David P. Crook, *The North, The South, and the Powers, 1861–1865* (1974); Richard N. Current, *Lincoln's Loyalists: Union Soldiers from the Confederacy* (1992); William C. Davis, *Jefferson Davis: The Man and His Hour* (1991); David Herbert Donald, *Lincoln* (1995); David Herbert Donald, *Why the North Won the Civil War* (1960); Robert F. Durden, *The Gray and the Black: The Confederate Debate on Emancipation* (1972); Clement Eaton, *A History of the Southern Confederacy* (1954); Paul D. Escott, *After Secession: Jefferson Davis and the Failure of Confederate Nationalism* (1978); Byron Farwell, *Stonewall: A Biography of General Thomas J. Jackson* (1992); Michael Fellman, *Citizen Sherman: A Life of William Tecumseh Sherman* (1995); James W. Geary, *We Need Men: The Northern Draft in the Civil War* (1991); Joseph T. Glatthaar, *Forged in Battle: The Civil War Alliance, Black Soldiers and White Officers* (1990); Robert W. Johannsen, *Lincoln, The South, and Slavery: The Political Dimension* (1991); Archer Jones, *Civil War Command and Strategy: The Process of Victory and Defeat* (1992); Alvin M. Josephy, Jr., *The Civil War in the American West* (1991); Gerald F. Linderman, *Embattled Courage: The Experience of Combat in the American Civil War* (1989); Ella Lonn, *Desertion During the Civil War* (1928); Mary Elizabeth Massey, *Refugee Life in the Confederacy* (1964); James M. McPherson, *Why the Confederacy Lost* (1992); James M. McPherson, *Abraham Lincoln and the Second American Revolution* (1990); James H. Moorhead, *American Apocalypse: Yankee Protestants and the Civil War, 1860–1869* (1978); Mark E. Neely, Jr., *The Last Best Hope of Earth: Abraham Lincoln and the Promise of America* (1993); Alan T. Nolan, *Lee Considered: General Robert E. Lee and Civil War History* (1991); Frank L. Owsley, *State Rights in the Confederacy* (1925); George C. Rable, *Civil Wars: Women and the Crisis of Southern Nationalism* (1989); James L. Roark, *Masters Without Slaves: Southern Planters in the Civil War and Reconstruction* (1977); Charles Royster, *The Destructive War:*

William Tecumseh Sherman, Stonewall Jackson, and the Americans (1991); Emory M. Thomas, *Robert E. Lee: A Biography* (1995); Emory M. Thomas, *The Confederate Nation, 1861–1865* (1979); Robert M. Utley, *Frontiersmen in Blue: The United States Army and the Indian, 1848–1865* (1981); Garry Wills, *Lincoln at Gettysburg: The Words That Remade America* (1992); Agatha Young, *Women and the Crisis: Women of the North in the Civil War* (1959).

Chapter 15 Reconstruction: High Hopes and Broken Dreams, 1865–1877

Herman Belz, *Emancipation and Equal Rights: Politics and Constitutionalism in the Civil War Era* (1978); Michael Les Benedict, *The Impeachment and Trial of Andrew Johnson* (1973); LaWanda C. Cox, *Freedom, Racism, and Reconstruction* (1997); Laura F. Edwards, *Gendered Strife and Confusion: The Political Culture of Reconstruction* (1997); John Hope Franklin, *Reconstruction: After the Civil War* (1961); John Hope Franklin and Alfred A. Moss, Jr., *From Slavery to Freedom: A History of Negro Americans*, 6th ed. (1988); Herbert G. Gutman, *The Black Family in Slavery and Freedom* (1976); William C. Harris, *With Charity for All: Lincoln and the Restoration of the Union* (1997); Jacqueline Jones, *Labor of Love, Labor of Sorrow: Black Women, Work and the Family, from Slavery to the Present* (1985); William S. McFeely, *Grant: A Biography* (1981); Eric L. McKitrick, *Andrew Johnson and Reconstruction* (1960; reprint, 1988); James M. McPherson, *Ordeal by Fire: Reconstruction* (1982); David Montgomery, *Beyond Equality: Labor and the Radical Republicans, 1862–1872* (1967); Michael Perman, *Emancipation and Reconstruction, 1862–1879* (1987); Roger L. Ransom and Richard Sutch, *One Kind of Freedom: The Economic Consequences of Emancipation* (1977); John David Smith, *Black Voices from Reconstruction, 1865–1877* (1996); Hans Louis Trefousse, *Andrew Johnson: A Biography* (1989); Allen W. Trelease, *White Terror: The Ku Klux Klan Conspiracy and Southern Reconstruction* (1971, reprint 1995); Vernon Lane Wharton, *The Negro in Mississippi: 1865–1890* (1965; reprint, 1974); Forrest G. Wood, *The Era of Reconstruction, 1863–1877* (1975); C. Vann Woodward, *Reunion and Reaction: The Compromise of 1877 and the End of Reconstruction*, rev. ed. (1956); C. Vann Woodward, *Origins of the New South, 1877–1913* (1951).

Chapter 16 Survival of the Fittest: Entrepreneurs and Workers in Industrial America, 1865–1900

Ralph Andreano, ed., *The Economic Impact of the Civil War*, rev. ed. (1967); Paul Avrich, *The Haymarket Tragedy* (1984); Robert V. Bruce, *1877: Year of Violence* (1959); Vincent P. Carosso, *The Morgans: Private International Bankers, 1854–1913* (1987); Alfred D. Chandler, Jr., *The Essential Alfred Chandler: Essays Toward a Historical Theory of Big Business*, ed. by Thomas K. McCraw (1988); Alfred D. Chandler, ed., *The Railroads: The Nation's First Big Business* (1965); Thomas C. Cochran and William Miller, *The Age of Enterprise: A Social History of Industrial America*, rev. ed. (1961); Carl N. Degler, *In Search of Human Nature: The Decline and Revival of Darwinism in American Social Thought* (1991); Melvyn Dubofsky, *Industrialism and the American Worker, 1865–1920*, 3rd ed. (1996); Leon Fink, *Workingmen's Democracy: The Knights of Labor and American Politics* (1983); Robert Fogel, *Railroads and American Economic Growth* (1965); John A. Garraty, *The New Commonwealth, 1877–1890* (1968); Peter George, *The Emergence of Industrial America: Strategic Factors in American Economic Growth Since 1870* (1982); Louis M. Hacker, *The World of Andrew Carnegie: 1865–1901* (1968); Robert L. Heilbroner, *The Economic Transformation of America* (1977); Matthew Josephson, *The Robber Barons: The Great American Capitalists, 1861–1901* (1934; reprint, 1962); Alice Kessler-Harris, *Out to Work: A History of Wage-Earning Women in the United States* (1982); Edward Chase Kirkland, *Industry Comes of Age: Business, Labor, and Public Policy, 1860–1897* (1961); Harold C. Livesay, *Andrew Carnegie and the Rise of Big Business* (1975); David Montgomery, *Workers' Control in America* (1979); Daniel Nelson, *Managers and Workers: Origins of the New Factory System in the United States, 1880–1920* (1975); Allan Nevins, *Study in Power: John D. Rockefeller, Industrialist and Philanthropist*, 2 vols. (1953); Nick Salvatore, *Eugene V. Debs: Citizen and Socialist* (1982); Fred A. Shannon, *The Farmer's Last Frontier: Agriculture, 1860–1897* (1945); Stephan Thernstrom, *Poverty and Progress: Social Mobility in a Nineteenth Century City* (1964).

Chapter 17 Conflict and Change in the West, 1865–1902

Albert Camarillo, *Chicanos in a Changing Society: From Mexican Pueblos to American Barrios in Santa Barbara and Southern California, 1848–1930* (1979); Sucheng Chan, *Asian Californians* (1991); Sarah Deutsch, *No Separate Refuge: Culture, Class, and Gender on an Anglo-Hispanic Frontier in the American Southwest, 1880–1940* (1987); Everett Dick, *The Sod-House Frontier, 1854–1890* (1954); Robert R. Dykstra, *The Cattle Towns* (1968); Juan Gómez-Quiñones, *Roots of Chicano Politics, 1600–1940* (1994); Wesley S. Griswold, *A Work of Giants: Building the First Transcontinental Railroad* (1962); Richard Griswold del Castillo, *The Los Angeles Barrio, 1850–1890* (1979); Frederick E. Hoxie, *A Final Promise: The Campaign to Assimilate the Indians, 1880–1920* (1984); William Issel and Robert W. Cherny, *San Francisco, 1865–1932: Politics, Power, and Urban Development* (1986); Douglas Monroy, *Thrown Among Strangers: The Making of Mexican Culture in Frontier California* (1990); Sandra L. Myres, *Westering Women and the Frontier Experience, 1800–1915* (1982); Victor G. Nee and Brett de Barry Nee, *Longtime Californ': A Documentary History of an American Chinatown* (1972, 1973; reprint, 1986); Donald Pisani, *From the Family Farm to Agribusiness: The Irrigation Crusade in California and the West, 1850–1934* (1984); Leonard Pitt, *The Decline of the Californios: A Social History of the Spanish-Speaking Californians, 1846–1890* (1971); Earl Pomeroy, *The Pacific Slope: A History of California, Oregon, Washington, Idaho, Utah, and*

Nevada (1965); Francis Prucha, *American Indian Policy in Crisis: Christian Reformers and the Indian, 1865–1900* (1975); Glenda Riley, *The Female Frontier: A Comparative View of Women on the Prairie and the Plains* (1988); Joseph G. Rosa, *Age of the Gunfighter* (1995); Fred A. Shannon, *The Farmer's Last Frontier: Agriculture, 1860–1897* (1945); Ronald Takaki, *Strangers from the Different Shore* (1989); Robert M. Utley, *The Lance and the Shield: The Life and Times of Sitting Bull* (1993); Walter Prescott Webb, *The Great Plains* (1931); Donald Worster, *Rivers of Empire: Water, Aridity, and the Growth of the American West* (1985).

Chapter 18 The New Social Patterns of Urban and Industrial America, 1865–1917

Edward L. Ayers, *The Promise of the New South: Life After Reconstruction* (1992); John E. Bodnar, *The Transplanted: A History of Immigrants in Urban America* (1985); Ruth Bordin, *Frances Willard: A Biography* (1986); George Chauncy, *Gay New York* (1994); Lawrence Arthur Cremin, *American Education: The Metropolitan Experience, 1876–1980* (1988); Roger Daniels, *Not Like Us: Immigrants and Minorities in America, 1890–1924* (1997); Allen F. Davis, *American Heroine: The Life and Legend of Jane Addams* (1973); John D'Emilio and Estelle B. Freedman, *Intimate Matters: A History of Sexuality in America* (1988); Peter Gammond, *Scott Joplin and the Ragtime Era* (1975); William H. Gerdts, *American Impressionism* (1984); Lynn D. Gordon, *Gender and Higher Education in the Progressive Era* (1990); David F. Greenberg, *The Construction of Homosexuality* (1988); David C. Hammack, *Power and Society: Greater New York at the Turn of the Century* (1982); Louis R. Harlan, *Booker T. Washington: The Making of a Black Leader, 1856–1901* (1972); Kenneth T. Jackson, *Crabgrass Frontier: The Suburbanization of the United States* (1985); A. T. Lane, *Solidarity of Survival? American Labor and European Immigrants: 1830–1924* (1987); Lawrence W. Levine, *Highbrow/Lowbrow: The Emergence of Cultural Hierarchy in America* (1988); Eric H. Monkkonen, *America Becomes Urban: The Development of U.S. Cities and Towns, 1780–1980* (1988); Regina Markell Morantz-Sanchez, *Sympathy and Science: Women Physicians in American Medicine* (1985); H. Wayne Morgan, ed., *Victorian Culture in America, 1865–1914* (1973); Steven Riess, *Sport in Industrial America, 1850–1920* (1995); Lewis O. Saum, *The Popular Mood of America, 1860–1890* (1990); Thomas J. Schlereth, *Victorian America: Transformations in Everyday Life, 1876–1915* (1991); Louise L. Stevenson, *The Victorian Homefront: American Thought and Culture, 1860–1880* (1991); Jon C. Teaford, *The Unheralded Triumph: City Government in America, 1870–1900* (1984); David Ward, *Cities and Immigrants: A Geography of Change in Nineteenth Century America* (1971); Ida B. Wells-Barnett, *Crusade for Justice: The Autobiography of Ida B. Wells*, edited by Alfreda M. Duster (1970); Mark Wyman, *Round-trip to America: The Immigrants Return to Europe, 1880–1930* (1993).

Chapter 19 Political Stalemate and Political Upheaval, 1868–1900

Walter Dean Burnham, *Critical Elections and the Mainsprings of American Politics* (1970); Paolo E. Coletta, *William Jennings Bryan*, 3 vols. (1964–1969); Carl N. Degler, *The Age of the Economic Revolution, 1876–1900*, 2d ed. (1977); Eleanor Flexner, *Century of Struggle: The Woman's Rights Movement in the United States*, rev. ed., 1996; Milton Friedman and Anna Jacobson Schwartz, *A Monetary History of the United States, 1867–1960* (1963); John A. Garraty, *The New Commonwealth, 1877–1890* (1968); Paul W. Glad, *McKinley, Bryan, and the People* (1964, rpt. 1991); Lewis L. Gould, *The Presidency of William McKinley* (1980); John D. Hicks, *The Populist Revolt: A History of the Farmers' Alliance and the People's Party* (1931); Ari Hoogenboom, *Rutherford B. Hayes: Warrior and President* (1995); Ari Hoogenboom, *Outlawing the Spoils: A History of the Civil Service Reform Movement* (1961); Michael Kazin, *The Populist Persuasion: An American History* (1995); Paul Kleppner, *The Third Electoral System, 1853–1892: Parties, Voters, and Political Cultures* (1979); Suzanne M. Marilley, *Woman Suffrage and the Origins of Liberal Feminism in the United States, 1820–1920* (1996); Richard L. McCormick, *The Party Period and Public Policy: American Politics from the Age of Jackson to the Progressive Era* (1986); Robert C. McMath, Jr., *American Populism: A Social History, 1877–1898* (1993); Horace Samuel Merrill, *Bourbon Leader: Grover Cleveland and the Democratic Party* (1957); H. Wayne Morgan, *William McKinley and His America* (1963); Nell Irvin Painter, *Standing at Armageddon: The United States, 1877–1919* (1987); Norman Pollack, ed., *The Populist Mind* (1967); Carlos A. Schwantes, *Coxey's Army: An American Odyssey* (1985); Theda Skocpol, *Protecting Soldiers and Mothers: The Politics of Social Provision in the United States* (1992); Xi Wang, *The Trial of Democracy: Black Suffrage and Northern Republicans, 1860–1910* (1997); R. Hal Williams, *Years of Decision: American Politics in the 1890s* (1978).

Chapter 20 Becoming a World Power: America and World Affairs, 1865–1913

Robert L. Beisner, *Twelve Against Empire: The Anti-Imperialists, 1898–1900* (1968); Richard H. Collin, *Theodore Roosevelt: Culture, Diplomacy, and Expansion* (1985); John M. Dobson, *Reticent Expansionism: The Foreign Policy of William McKinley* (1988); Justus D. Doenecke, *The Presidencies of James A. Garfield and Chester A. Arthur* (1981); Lewis L. Gould, *The Presidency of Theodore Roosevelt* (1991); David Healy, *U.S. Expansionism: The Imperialist Urge in the 1890s* (1970); Jerry Israel, *Progressivism and the Open Door: America and China, 1905–1921* (1971); Walter LaFeber, *Inevitable Revolutions: The United States in Central America*, rev. ed. (1993); Gerald F. Linderman, *The Mirror of War: American Society and the Spanish-American War* (1974); T. J. McCormick, *China Market: America's Quest for Informal Empire* (1967); Alfred Thayer Mahan, *The Influence of Seapower upon History, 1660–1783* (1890, rpt., 1957); C. Roland Marchand, *The American Peace Movement and Social Reform, 1898–1918* (1972);

Ernest R. May, *American Imperialism: A Speculative Essay* (1968); Ernest R. May, *Imperial Democracy: The Emergence of America as a Great Power* (1961, rpt. 1973); H. Wayne Morgan, *America's Road to Empire: The War with Spain and Overseas Expansion* (1965); H. Wayne Morgan, *William McKinley and His America*, (1963); Thomas J. Osborne, *"Empire Can Wait": American Opposition to Hawaiian Annexation, 1893–1898* (1981); Bradford Perkins, *The Great Rapprochement: England and the United States, 1895–1914* (1968); Dexter Perkins, *A History of the Monroe Doctrine* (1963); Milton Plesur, *America's Outward Thrust: Approaches to Foreign Affairs, 1865–1900* (1971); Julius W. Pratt, *Expanionists of 1898* (1936); Emily S. Rosenberg, *Spreading the American Dream: American Economic and Cultural Expansion, 1890–1945* (1982); E. Berkeley Tompkins, *Anti-Imperialism in the United States: The Great Debate, 1890–1920* (1970); Richard E. Welch, Jr., *The Presidencies of Grover Cleveland* (1988); Richard E. Welch, Jr., *Response to Imperialism: The United States and the Philippine-American War, 1899–1902* (1979); William Appleman Williams, *The Roots of the Modern American Empire* (1969); Marilyn Blatt Young, *The Rhetoric of Empire: American China Policy, 1895–1901* (1968).

Chapter 21 The Progressive Era, 1900–1917

Paula Baker, "The Domestication of Politics: Women and American Political Society, 1780–1920." *American Historical Review* 89 (1984): 620–647; Jack S. Blocker, Jr., *Retreat from Reform: The Prohibition Movement in the United States, 1890–1913* (1976); John Morton Blum, *The Republican Roosevelt*, 2d ed. (1977); Ruth Bordin, *Women and Temperance: The Quest for Power and Liberty, 1873–1900* (1980); H. W. Brands, *T.R.: The Last Romantic* (1997); Kendrick A. Clements, *The Presidency of Woodrow Wilson* (1992); Steven J. Diner, *A Very Different Age: Americans of the Progressive Era* (1998); Louis Filler, *Appointment at Armageddon: Muckraking and Progressivism in the American Tradition*, ref. edn. (1996); Linda Gordon, *Woman's Body, Woman's Right: Birth Control in America*, rev. ed. (1990); Lewis L. Gould, *Reform and Regulation: American Politics from Roosevelt to Wilson*, 3rd ed. (1996); Louis R. Harlan, *Booker T. Washington: The Wizard of Tuskegee, 1901–1915* (1983); Samuel P. Hays, *American Political History as Social Analysis* (1980); Samuel P. Hays, *Conservation and the Gospel of Efficiency* (1959); Ari and Olive Hoogenboom, *A History of the ICC: From Panacea to Palliative* (1976); Arthur S. Link, *Woodrow Wilson*, 5 vols. (1947–1965); Richard Coke Lower, *A Bloc of One: The Political Career of Hiram W. Johnson* (1993); Richard L. McCormick, *The Party Period and Public Policy: American Politics from the Age of Jackson to the Progressive Era* (1986); Michael E. McGerr, *The Decline of Popular Politics: The American North, 1865–1928* (1986); Manning Marable, *W. E. B. Du Bois: Black Radical Democrat* (1986); Sally M. Miller, *Victor Berger and the Promise of Constructive Socialism, 1910–1920* (1973); Daniel Rodgers, "In Search of Progressivism." *Reviews in American History* 10 (Dec. 1982): 113–132; Nick Salvatore, *Eugene V. Debs: Citizen and Socialist* (1982); Melvin I. Urofsky, *Louis D. Brandeis and the Progressive Tradition* (1981); Robert H. Wiebe, *The Search for Order, 1877–1920* (1967); William H. Wilson, *The City Beautiful Movement* (1989).

Chapter 22 America and the World, 1913–1920

Lloyd E. Ambrosius, *Woodrow Wilson and the American Diplomatic Tradition: The Treaty Fight in Perspective* (1987); W. J. Breen, *Uncle Sam at Home: Civilian Mobilization, Wartime Federalism, and the Council of National Defense, 1917–1919* (1984); David Brody, *Labor in Crisis: The Steel Strike of 1919* (1965); Kendrick A. Clements, *William Jennings Bryan: Missionary Isolationist* (1982); Edward M. Coffman, *The War to End All Wars: The American Military Experience in World War I* (1986); Jean Conner, *The National War Labor Board* (1983); John Milton Cooper, Jr., *The Vanity of Power: American Isolationism and World War I* (1969); Patrick Devlin, *Too Proud to Fight: Woodrow Wilson's Neutrality* (1974); Robert H. Ferrell, *Woodrow Wilson and World War I, 1917–1921* (1985); Mark T. Gilderhus, *Diplomacy and Revolution: U.S.-Mexican Relations Under Wilson and Carranza* (1977); Maurine Weiner Greenwald, *War and Work: The Impact of World War I on Women Workers in the United States* (1980); Edward Haley, *Revolution and Intervention: The Diplomacy of Taft and Wilson in Mexico, 1910–1917* (1970); Ellis Hawley, *The Great War and the Search for a Modern Order*, 2nd ed. (1997); D. Clayton James and Anne Sharp Wells, *America and the Great War, 1914–1920* (1998); Robert Johnson, *The Peace Progressives and American Foreign Relations* (1995); David M. Kennedy, *Over Here: The First World War and American Society* (1980); Thomas J. Knock, *To End All Wars: Woodrow Wilson and the Creation of the League of Nations* (1992); David D. Lee, *Sergeant York: An American Hero* (1985); C. Roland Marchand, *The American Peace Movement and Social Reform, 1898–1918* (1972); Ernest R. May, *The World War and American Isolation, 1914–1917* (1959); Joseph A. McCartin, *Labor's Great War: The Struggle for Industrial Democracy and the Origins of Modern American Labor Relations, 1912–1921* (1997); Paul L. Murphy, *World War I and the Origin of Civil Liberties in the United States* (1979); Robert K. Murray, *Red Scare: A Study in National Hysteria, 1919–1920* (1955, rpt. 1964); Ruth Rosen, *The Lost Sisterhood: Prostitution in America, 1900–1918* (1982); William M. Tuttle, *Race Riot: Chicago in the Red Summer of 1919* (1970); Stephen Vaughn, *Holding Fast the Inner Lines: Democracy, Nationalism, and the Committee on Public Information* (1980); James Weinstein, *The Decline of Socialism in America; 1912–1925* (1967, rpt. 1984).

Chapter 23 The 1920s, 1920–1928

Carl Abbott, *Urban America in the Modern Age* (1987); William J. Barber, *From New Era to New Deal: Herbert Hoover, the Economists, and American Economic Policy, 1921–1933* (1985); Daniel H. Borus, ed., *These United States: Portraits of America from the 1920s* (1992); Paul A. Carter, *The Twenties in America*, 2d ed. (1987); E. David Cronon, *Black Moses: The Story of Marcus Garvey and the Universal Negro*

Improvement Association, 2d ed. (1969); Lyle W. Dorset, *Billy Sunday and the Redemption of Urban America* (1991); Martin Bauml Duberman, *Paul Robeson: A Biography* (1989); Lynn Dumenil, *The Modern Temper: American Culture and Society in the 1920s* (1995); Richard Wrightman Fox and T. J. Jackson Lears, eds., *The Culture of Consumption: Critical Essays in American History, 1880–1980* (1983); Linda Gordon, *Woman's Body, Woman's Right: Birth Control in America*, rev. ed. (1990); Edward Jablonski, *Gershwin* (1987); Kenneth T. Jackson, *The Ku Klux Klan in the City, 1915–1930* (1967); Harvey Klehr and John Earl Haynes, *The American Communist Movement: Storming Heaven Itself* (1992); Peter Iverson, *"We Are Still Here": American Indians in the Twentieth Century* (1998); David L. Lewis, *When Harlem Was in Vogue* (1981); Robert S. Lynd and Helen M. Lynd, *Middletown* (1929); Roland Marchand, *Advertising the American Dream: Making Way for Modernity, 1920–1940* (1985); Arnold Rampersad, *The Life of Langston Hughes*, 2 vols. (1986, 1988); Arthur M. Schlesinger, Jr., *The Crisis of the Old Order, 1919–1933* (1957); Arnold Shaw, *The Jazz Age: Popular Music in the 1920's* (1987); Robert Sobel, *The Great Bull Market: Wall Street in the 1920s* (1968); Ferenc Szasz, *The Divided Mind of Protestant America, 1880–1930* (1982); Bernard A. Weisberger, *The Dream Maker: William C. Durant, Founder of General Motors* (1979); Robert H. Zieger, *American Workers, American Unions, 1920–1985* (1986).

Chapter 24 From Good Times to Hard Times, 1920–1932

Francisco Balderrama and Raymond Rodriguez, *Decade of Betrayal: Mexican Repatriation in the 1930s* (1995); David Burner, *Herbert Hoover: The Public Life* (1978); Dan T. Carter, *Scottsboro* (1969); Roger Daniels, *The Bonus March* (1971); Charles DeBenedetti, *Origins of the Modern American Peace Movement, 1915–1929* (1978); Paula Elder, *Governor Alfred E. Smith: The Politician as Reformer* (1983); Ethan Ellis, *Republican Foreign Policy, 1921–1933* (1968); Milton Friedman and Anna Schwartz, *The Great Contraction, 1929–1933* (1965); John Kenneth Galbraith, *The Great Crash, 1929* (1961); Cheryl L. Greenberg, *"Or Does It Explode?" Black Harlem in the Great Depression* (1991); David Hamilton, *From New Day to New Deal: American Farm Policy from Hoover to Roosevelt, 1928–1933* (1991); A. Iriye, *After Imperialism: The Search for New Order in the Far East, 1921–1931* (1965); Neil Macaulay, *The Sandino Affair* (1985); William Mullins, *The Depression and the Urban West Coast, 1929–1933* (1991); James S. Olson, *Herbert Hoover and the Reconstruction Finance Corporation, 1931–1933* (1977); Emily Rosenberg, *Spreading the American Dream* (1982); Louis Schraf, *To Work and to Wed: Female Employment and the Great Depression* (1980); Vicki Ruiz, *Cannery Women, Cannery Lives: Mexican Women, Unionization and the California Food Processing Industry, 1930–1950* (1987); John Shover, *Cornbelt Rebellion: The Farmers' Holiday Association* (1965); Peter Timim: *Did Monetary Forces Cause the Great Depression*? (1976); Susan Ware, *Holding Their Own: American Women in the Thirties* (1982); Joan Hoff Wilson, *American Business and Foreign Policy, 1920–1933* (1968); Donald Worster, *Dust Bowl: The Southern Plains in the 1930s* (1979).

Chapter 25 The New Deal, 1933–1940

Anthony Badger, *The New Deal: The Depression Years, 1933–1940* (1989); Ann Banks, ed., *First Person America* (1980); John Barnard, *Walter Reuther and the Rise of the Auto Workers* (1983); Edward D. Berkowitz, *America's Welfare State: From Roosevelt to Reagan* (1991); Irving Bernstein, *A Caring Society: The New Deal, The Worker, and the Great Depression* (1985); Gary D. Best, *Pride, Prejudice, and Politics: Roosevelt Versus Recovery, 1933–1938* (1990); Roger Biles, *A New Deal for the American People* (1991); Julia Kirk Blackwelder, *No Hiring: The Feminization of Work in the United States, 1900–1995* (1997); Alan Brinkley, *Voices of the Protest: Huey Long, Father Coughlin, and the Great Depression* (1982); William U. Chandler, *The Myth of the TVA: Conservation and Development in the Tennessee Valley, 1933–1983* (1984); Kenneth S. Davis, *FDR: Into the Storm, 1937–1940: A History* (1993); Kenneth S. Davis, *FDR: The New Deal Years, 1933–1937* (1986); Sidney Fine, *Sit-Down: The General Motors Strike of 1936–1937* (1969); Colin Gordon, *New Deals: Business, Labor, and Politics in America* (1994); James Gregory, *American Exodus: The Dust Bowl Migration and the Okie Culture in California* (1989); Lawrence C. Kelley, *The Assault on Assimilation: John Collier and the Origins of Indian Policy Reform* (1983); Roy Lubove, *The Struggle for Social Security* (1968); Robert S. McElvaine, ed., *Down and Out in the Great Depression: Letters from the Forgotten Man* (1983); Patrick J. Maney, *The Roosevelt Presence: A Biography of Franklin Delano Roosevelt* (1992); George McJimsey, *Harry Hopkins* (1987); Jerre Mangione, *The Dream and the Deal: The Federal Writers' Project, 1935–1943* (1972); James T. Patterson, *Congressional Conservatism and the New Deal* (1967); Kenneth Philip, *John Collier's Crusade for Indian Reform, 1920–1945* (1977); Theodore Saloutos, *The American Farmer and the New Deal* (1982); Lois Schraf, *Eleanor Roosevelt: First Lady of American Liberalism* (1987); Harvard Sitkoff, ed., *Fifty Years Later: The New Deal Evaluated* (1985); Patricia Sullivan, *Days of Hope: Race and Democracy in the New Deal Era* (1996); Devra Weber, *Dark Sweat, White Gold: California Farm Workers, Cotton, and the New Deal* (1994); Nancy J. Weiss, *Farewell to the Party of Lincoln: Black Politics in the Age of FDR* (1983).

Chapter 26 America's Rise to World Leadership, 1933–1945

Stephen E. Ambrose, *D-Day, June 6, 1944* (1994); Dorothy Borg and Shumpei Okamoto, eds., *Pearl Harbor as History* (1973); David Brinkley, *Washington Goes to War* (1988); Wayne Cole, *Roosevelt and the Isolationists* (1983); John Costello, *Virtue Under Fire: How World War II Changed Our Social and Sexual Attitudes* (1985); Lyn Crost, *Honor by Fire: Japanese Americans at War in Europe and the Pacific* (1994); Thomas Doherty, *Projections of War: Hollywood, American Culture, and World War II* (1993); Henry L. Feingold, *The Politics of Rescue: The Roosevelt*

Administration and the Holocaust, 1938–1945 (1970); Irwin F. Gellman, *The Good Neighbor Diplomacy: United States Policies in Latin America, 1933–1945* (1979); Susan Hartmann, *The Homefront and Beyond: American Women in the 1940s* (1982); Waldo H. Heinrichs, Jr., *Threshold of War* (1988); Akira Iriye, *Power and Culture: The Japanese-American War, 1941–1945* (1981); Gerald D. Nash, *The American West Transformed: The Impact of the Second World War* (1985); Judy B. Litoff, *We're in This War Too: World War II Letters of American Women in Uniform* (1994); Neil R. McMillen, ed., *Remaking Dixie: The Impact of World War II on the American South* (1997); Verne W. Newton, ed., *FDR and the Holocaust* (1995); William O'Neill, *A Democracy at War: America's Fight at Home and Abroad in World War II* (1993); Richard Polenberg, *War and Society: The United States, 1941–1945* (1972); Richard Rhodes, *The Making of the Atomic Bomb* (1987); Ronald Schaffer, *Wings of Judgment: American Bombing in World War II* (1985); Martin Sherman, *A World Destroyed* (1975); Michael Sherry, *In the Shadow of War: The United States Since the 1930s* (1995); John R. Skates, *The Invasion of Japan: Alternative to the Bomb* (1994); Gaddis Smith, *American Diplomacy During the Second World War* (1965); Mark Stoler, "A Half Century of Conflict: Interpretations of World War II Diplomacy," *Diplomatic History* 18 (Summer 1994): 375–403; Susan C. Taylor, *Jewel of the Desert: Japanese American Internment at Topaz* (1994); Studs Terkel, *The Good War: An Oral History of World War Two* (1984); Jonathan Utley, *Going to War with Japan* (1985); Allen E. Winkler, *Home Front U.S.A.: America During World War II* (1986); David S. Wyman, *The Abandonment of the Jews* (1984); Neil A. Wynn, *The Afro-American and the Second World War* (1975).

Chapter 27 Truman and Cold War America, 1945–1952

William C. Berman, *The Politics of Civil Rights in the Truman Administration* (1970); Paul Boyer, *By the Bomb's Early Light: American Thought and Culture at the Dawn of the Atomic Age* (1985); Kevin Boyle, *The UAW and the Heyday of American Liberalism* (1995); Richard M. Dalfiume, *Desegregation of the U.S. Armed Forces* (1969); Robert J. Donovan, *The Tumultuous Years: the Presidency of Harry S Truman, 1949–1953* (1982); Robert Griffith, *The Politics of Fear: Joseph R. McCarthy and the Senate* (1987); John L. Gaddis, *We Now Know: Rethinking Cold War History* (1997); John L. Gaddis, *Strategies of Containment* (1982); Herbert J. Gans, *The Levittowners* (1967); William S. Graebner, *The Age of Doubt: American Thought and Culture in the 1940s* (1991); John Halliday and Bruce Cummings, *Korea: The Unknown War* (1987); Alonzo Hamby, *Man of the People: A Life of Harry S Truman* (1995); Susan Hartman, *Truman and the 80th Congress* (1971); Gregory Herken, *The Winning Weapon* (1981); Michael Hogan, *The Marshall Plan* (1987); Landon Y. Jones, *Great Expectations: America and the Baby Boom Generation* (1980); Burton Kaufman, *The Arab Middle East and the United States: Inter-Arab Rivalry and Superpower Diplomacy* (1996); Donald Katz, *Home Fires: An Intimate Portrait of One Middle-Class Family in Postwar America* (1992); Melvyn Leffler, *A Preponderance of Power* (1991); Allen J. Matusow, *Farm Policies and Politics in the Truman Years* (1967); Elaine Tyler May, *Homeward Bound: American Families in the Cold War Era* (1988); William O'Neil, *American High: The Years of Confidence 1945–1960* (1986); David M. Oshinsky, *A Conspiracy So Immense: The World of Joseph McCarthy* (1983); James T. Patterson, *Grand Expectations: The United States, 1945–1974* (1996); Arnold Rampersad, *Jackie Robinson* (1997); Gary W. Reichard, *Politics as Usual* (1988); Michael Schaller, *The American Occupation of Japan: The Origins of the Cold War in Asia* (1985); Ellen W. Schrenker, *The Age of McCarthyism* (1994); Athan Theoharis and John S. Cox, *The Boss: J. Edgar Hoover and the Great American Inquisition* (1988).

Chapter 28 Quest for Consensus, 1952–1960

Charles C. Alexander, *Holding the Line* (1985); H. W. Brands, Jr., *Cold Warriors* (1988); Wini Breines, *Young, White, and Miserable: Growing Up Female in the Fifties* (1992); Taylor Branch, *Parting the Water: America in the King Years, 1954–1963* (1988); John D'Emilio, and Estelle B. Freedman, *Intimate Matters: A History of Sexuality in America* (1988); Robert A. Devine, *The Sputnik Challenge* (1993); Robert A. Devine, *Blowing in the Wind: The Nuclear Test Ban Debate* (1978); Barbara Ehrenreich, *Hearts of Men* (1983); Robert Fishamn, *Bourgeois Utopias* (1987); Donald I. Fixico, *Termination and Relocation: Federal Indian Policy, 1945–1970* (1986); Lloyd Gardner, *Approaching Vietnam* (1988); William Graebner, *Coming of Age in Buffalo* (1990); Fred I. Greenstein, *The Hidden-Hand Presidency* (1982); Richard G. Hewlett and Jack M. Hall, *Atoms for Peace and War* (1989); Alice Kessler-Harris, *Out to Work: A History of Wage-Earning Women in the United States* (1982); Nicholas Lemann, *The Promised Land* (1991); Victory Marchetti and John D. Marks, *The CIA and the Cult of Intelligence* (1974); Karal Ann Marling, *As Seen on TV: The Visual Culture of Everyday Life in the 1950s* (1994); Waldo Martin, Jr., *Brown v. Board of Education: A Brief History with Documents* (1998); Martin E. Marty, *Modern American Religion, Vol. 3: Under God, Indivisible, 1941–1960* (1996); Joan Meyerowitz, ed., *Not June Cleaver: Women and Gender in Postwar America* (1994); William Pickett, *Dwight David Eisenhower and American Power* (1995); Stephen G. Rabe, *Eisenhower and Latin America* (1988); Mark H. Rose, *Interstate* (1979); John W. Sloan, *Eisenhower and the Management of Prosperity* (1991); Jane Smith, *Patenting the Sun: Polio and the Salk Vaccine* (1990); John C. Teaford, *The Twentieth Century City* (1993); Mark V. Tushnet, *Making Civil Rights Law: Thurgood Marshall and the Supreme Court, 1936–1961* (1995); Alan Winkler, *Life Under A Cloud: American Anxiety About the Atom* (1993).

Chapter 29 Great Promises, Bitter Disappointments, 1960–1968

Terry Anderson, *The Movement and the Sixties* (1995); Alexander Bloom, ed., *'Takin' It to the Streets: A Sixties Reader* (1995); David Burner, *John F. Kennedy and a New Generation* (1988); Eric Burner, *And Gently He Shall Lead Them: Robert Parris*

Moses and Civil Rights in Mississippi (1994); Claude Andrew Clegg III, *An Original Man: The Life and Times of Elijah Muhammad* (1997); David Farber, *The Age of Great Dreams: America in the 1960s* (1994); Alexander Fursendo and Timothy Naftali, *"One Hell of a Gamble": Khrushchev, Castro, and Kennedy, 1958–1964* (1998); David Garrow, *Protest at Selma: Martin Luther King and the Voting Rights Act of 1965* (1978); Paula Giddings and Cornel West, *Regarding Malcolm X* (1994); James Giglio, *The Presidency of John F. Kennedy* (1991); Hugh Davis Graham, *The Civil Rights Era: Origins and Development of National Policy, 1960–1972* (1990); Allen Matusow, *The Unraveling of America: A History of Liberalism in the 1960s* (1984); James Miller, *"Democracy Is in the Streets"—From Port Huron to the Siege at Chicago* (1987); Charles Murray, *Losing Ground: American Social Policy, 1950–1980* (1984); Thomas Paterson, *Confronting Castro: The United States and the Triumph of the Cuban Revolution* (1994); Thomas C. Reeves, *President Kennedy: Profile of Power* (1994); Theodore Roszak, *The Making of the Counterculture* (1969); Thomas Schoenbaum, *Waging Peace and War: Dean Rusk in the Truman, Kennedy, and Johnson Years* (1988); Bernard Schwartz, *Super Chief: Earl Warren and His Supreme Court* (1983); John E. Schwartz, *America's Hidden Success: A Reassessment of Twenty Years of Public Policy* (1983); Barbara L. Tischler, ed., *Sights on the Sixties* (1992); Irwin Unger, *The Movement: A History of the American New Left, 1959–1972* (1974); Melvin Urofsky, *The Continuity of Change: The Supreme Court and Individual Liberties, 1953–1986* (1991); Robert Weisbrot, *Freedom Bound: A History of America's Civil Rights Movement* (1991).

Chapter 30 America Under Stress, 1960–1975

Stephen Ambrose, *Nixon: The Triumph of the Politician, 1962–1972* (1990); Larry Berman, *Lyndon Johnson's War* (1989); Robert Buzzanco, *Masters of War: Military Dissent and Politics in Vietnam* (1996); Larry Cable, *Unholy Grail* (1991); Peter Caroll, *It Seemed Like Nothing Happened* (1982); Vine Deloria, Jr., *Custer Died for Your Sins* (1969); Robert Devine, *The Johnson Years, Volumes 1–3* (1981, 1987, 1994); Juan Gomez-Quinones, *Chicano Politics: Reality and Promise, 1940–1990* (1990); Richard Griswold de Castillo and Richard A. Garcia, *Cesar Chavez: A Triumph of Spirit* (1995); H. R. Haldeman, *The Haldeman Diaries: Inside the Nixon White House* (1994); Seymour Hersh, *The Price of Power: Kissinger in the Nixon White House* (1983); Troy R. Johnson, *The Occupation of Alcatraz Island: Indian Self-Determination and the Rise of American Activism* (1996); Blanche Linden-Ward and Carol Hurd Green, *American Women in the 1960s* (1993); Kim McQuaid, *The Anxious Years: America in the Vietnam and Watergate Era* (1989); Marguerite V. Marin, *Social Protest in an Urban Barrio: A Study of the Chicano Movement, 1966–1974* (1991); George D. Moss, *Vietnam: An American Ordeal* (1994); Carlos Munoz, Jr., *Youth, Identity, Power: The Chicano Movement* (1989); Richard Nixon, *RN: The Memoirs of Richard Nixon* (1978); James S. Olson and Randy Roberts, *My Lai: A Brief History with Documents* (1998); Herbert Parmet, *The World and Richard Nixon* (1990); Kirkpatrick Sales, *The Green Revolution: The American Environmental Movement, 1962–1992* (1996); Deborah Shapely, *Promise and Power: The Life and Times of Robert McNamara* (1993); Neil Sheehan, *A Bright Shining Lie: John Paul Vann and America in Vietnam* (1988); Melvin Small, *Johnson, Nixon, and the Doves* (1988); Ronald Spector, *After Tet: The Bloodiest Year in Vietnam* (1992); Steven J. Spiegel, *The Other Arab-Israeli Conflict: Making America's Middle East Policy from Truman to Reagan* (1985); Bob Woodward and Carl Bernstein, *All the President's Men* (1974); Daniel Yergin, *The Prize* (1991).

Chapter 31 Facing Limits, 1974–1992

William Berman, *America's Right Turn: From Nixon to Bush* (1994); John A. Booth and Thomas W. Walker, *Understanding Central America* (1989); Peter G. Bourne, *Jimmy Carter: A Comprehensive Biography from Plains to Post-Presidency* (1997); Paul Boyer, ed., *Reagan as President* (1990); Dan Carter, *From George Wallace to Newt Gingrich: Race in the Conservative Counterrevolution, 1963–1994* (1996); Paul Dukes, *The Last Great Game* (1989); John Dumbrell, *American Foreign Policy: Carter to Clinton* (1997); Carol Felsenthal, *The Sweetheart of the Silent Majority* (1981); Lawrence Freedman and Efraim Karsh, *The Gulf Conflict, 1990–1992* (1993); Raymond Gartoff, *The Great Transition: American Soviet Relations and the End of the Cold War* (1994); William E. Griffth, ed., *Central and Eastern Europe: The Opening Curtain* (1989); Samuel P. Hays, *Beauty, Health, and Permanence: Environmental Politics in the United States, 1955–1985* (1987); Haynes Johnson, *Sleepwalking Through History: America in the Reagan Years* (1991); Charles O. Jones, *The Trusteeship Presidency: Jimmy Carter and the United States Congress* (1988); Harold H. Koh, *The National Security Constitution* (1990); Walter LaFeber, *The Panama Canal* (1989); Robert S. Leiken, ed., *Central America: Anatomy of Conflict* (1984); Robert C. Liberman and Robert Wuthnow, eds., *The New Christian Right* (1983); Theodore Lowi, *The End of the Republican Era* (1995); Donald Mabry, ed., *The Latin American Narcotics Trade* (1992); David Mervin, *George Bush and the Guardianship Presidency* (1996); John Palmer and Elizabeth Sawmill, eds., *The Reagan Record* (1984); William B. Quandt, *Camp David* (1986); T. S. Reid, *The Chip* (1985); Robert Scheer, *With Enough Shovels* (1982); Peter Scott and Jonathan Marshall, *Cocaine Politics: Drugs, Armies, and the CIA in Central America* (1991); Allan P. Sindler, *Bakke, DeFunis, and the Minority Admissions* (1978); Philip Slater, *Earthwalk* (1974); Gaddis Smith, *Morality, Reason, and Power* (1986); James B. Stewart, *Den of Thieves* (1991); Strobe Talbot, *Deadly Gambits* (1984); John Kenneth White, *The New Politics of Old Values* (1988); Clyde Wilcox, *Onward Christian Soldiers: The Religious Right in American Politics* (1996); John Woodridge, *The Evangelicals* (1975).

Chapter 32 Making New Choices, 1992–1999

Dan Balz and Ronald Brownstein, *Storming the Gates: Protest Politics and the Republican Revival* (1996); Frank Bean and Marta Tienda, *The Hispanic Population of the United States* (1988); David Bender and Bruno Leane, *Abortion: Opposing Viewpoints* (1997); Susan K. Cahn, *Coming on Strong: Gender and Sexuality in 20th-Century Sport* (1994); Donald T. Crithlow, ed., *The Politics of Abortion and Birth Control in Historical Perspective* (1996); W. Avon Drake and Robert D. Holsworth, *Affirmative Action and the Stalled Quest for Black Progress* (1996); Barbara Ehrenreich, *The Worst Years of Our Lives* (1990); Herbert Gans, *The War Against the Poor: The Underclass and Anti-Poverty Policy* (1995); Nathan Glazer, ed., *Clamor at the Gates: The New American Immigration* (1986); James D. Hunter, *Culture Wars: The Struggle to Define America* (1991); Michael Katz, *The Undeserving Poor: From the War on Poverty to the War on Welfare* (1989); Jonathan Kozol, *Rachael and Her Children: Homeless Families in America* (1988); Elliot Liebow, *Tell Them Who I Am: The Lives of Homeless Women* (1993); John Longone, *AIDS: The Facts* (1988); Manhattan Institute and Pacific Research Institute, *Strangers at Our Gate: Immigration in the 1990s* (1994); David Maraniss, *First In His Class: A Biography of Bill Clinton* (1995); Robert Morris, *Partners in Power: The Clintons and Their America* (1996); Gary Orfield and Susan Eaton, *Dismantling Desegregation: The Quiet Reversal of Brown v. Board of Education* (1996); Robert Reich, *The Work of Nations: Preparing Ourselves for Twenty-First Century Capitalism* (1991); Stanley Renshon, *High Hopes: The Clinton Presidency and the Politics of Ambitions* (1996); Hilda Scott, *Working Your Way to the Bottom: The Feminization of Poverty,* (1985); William Serrin, *Homestead: The Glory and Tragedy of an American Steel Town* (1992); Ruth Sildel, *Women and Children Last* (1986); James Simon, *The Center Holds: The Power Struggle Inside the Rehnquist Court* (1995); Christina Hoff Sommers, *Who Stole Feminism? How Women Have Betrayed Women* (1994); Lawrence Tribe, *Clash of Absolutes* (1992); Melvin Urofsky, *A Conflict of Rights: The Supreme Court and Affirmative Action* (1991); William Wei, *The Asian American Movement* (1993); William J. Wilson, *The Truly Disadvantaged* (1987).

DOCUMENTS

Declaration of Independence in Congress, July 4, 1776

When, in the course of human events, it becomes necessary for one people to dissolve the political bonds which have connected them with another, and to assume, among the powers of the earth, the separate and equal station to which the laws of nature and of nature's God entitle them, a decent respect to the opinions of mankind requires that they should declare the causes which impel them to the separation.

We hold these truths to be self-evident: That all men are created equal; that they are endowed by their Creator with certain unalienable rights; that among these are life, liberty, and the pursuit of happiness; that, to secure these rights, governments are instituted among men, deriving their just powers from the consent of the governed; that whenever any form of government becomes destructive of these ends, it is the right of the people to alter or to abolish it, and to institute new government, laying its foundation on such principles, and organizing its powers in such form, as to them shall seem most likely to effect their safety and happiness. Prudence, indeed, will dictate that governments long established should not be changed for light and transient causes; and accordingly all experience hath shown that mankind are more disposed to suffer, while evils are sufferable, than to right themselves by abolishing the forms to which they are accustomed. But when a long train of abuses and usurpations, pursuing invariably the same object, evinces a design to reduce them under absolute despotism, it is their right, it is their duty, to throw off such government, and to provide new guards for their future security. Such has been the patient sufferance of these colonies; and such is now the necessity which constrains them to alter their former systems of government. The history of the present King of Great Britain is a history of repeated injuries and usurpations, all having in direct object the establishment of an absolute tyranny over these states. To prove this, let facts be submitted to a candid world.

He has refused his assent to laws, the most wholesome and necessary for the public good.

He has forbidden his governors to pass laws of immediate and pressing importance, unless suspended in their operation till his assent should be obtained; and, when so suspended, he has utterly neglected to attend to them.

He has refused to pass other laws for the accommodation of large districts of people, unless those people would relinquish the right of representation in the legislature, a right inestimable to them, and formidable to tyrants only.

He has called together legislative bodies at places unusual, uncomfortable, and distant from the depository of their public records, for the sole purpose of fatiguing them into compliance with his measures.

He has dissolved representative houses repeatedly, for opposing, with manly firmness, his invasions on the rights of the people.

He has refused for a long time, after such dissolutions, to cause others to be elected; whereby the legislative powers, incapable of annihilation, have returned to the people at large for their exercise; the state remaining, in the mean time, exposed to all the dangers of invasions from without and convulsions within.

He has endeavored to prevent the population of these states; for that purpose obstructing the laws for naturalization of foreigners; refusing to pass others to encourage their migration hither, and raising the conditions of new appropriations of lands.

He has obstructed the administration of justice, by refusing his assent to laws for establishing judiciary powers.

He has made judges dependent on his will alone, for the tenure of their offices, and the amount and payment of their salaries.

He has erected a multitude of new offices, and sent hither swarms of officers to harass our people and eat out their substance.

He has kept among us, in times of peace, standing armies, without the consent of our legislatures.

He has affected to render the military independent of, and superior to, the civil power.

He has combined with others to subject us to a jurisdiction foreign to our constitution, and unacknowledged by our laws, giving his assent to their acts of pretended legislation:

For quartering large bodies of armed troops among us;

For protecting them, by a mock trial, from punishment for any murders which they should commit on the inhabitants of these states;

For cutting off our trade with all parts of the world;

For imposing taxes on us without our consent;

For depriving us, in many cases, of the benefits of trial by jury;

For transporting us beyond seas, to be tried for pretended offenses;

For abolishing the free system of English laws in a neighboring province, establishing therein an arbitrary government, and enlarging its boundaries, so as to render it at once an example and fit instrument for introducing the same absolute rule into these colonies;

For taking away our charters, abolishing our most valuable laws, and altering fundamentally the forms of our governments;

For suspending our own legislatures, and declaring themselves invested with power to legislate for us in all cases whatsoever.

He has abdicated government here, by declaring us out of his protection and waging war against us.

He has plundered our seas, ravaged our coasts, burned our towns, and destroyed the lives of our people.

He is at this time transporting large armies of foreign mercenaries to complete the works of death, desolation, and tyranny already begun with circumstances of cruelty and perfidy scarcely paralleled in the most barbarous ages, and totally unworthy the head of a civilized nation.

He has constrained our fellow-citizens, taken captive on the high seas, to bear arms against their country, to become the executioners of their friends and brethren, or to fall themselves by their hands.

He has excited domestic insurrection among us, and has endeavored to bring on the inhabitants of our frontiers the merciless Indian savages, whose known rule of warfare is an undistinguished destruction of all ages, sexes, and conditions.

In every stage of these oppressions we have petitioned for redress in the most humble terms; our repeated petitions have been answered only by repeated injury. A prince, whose character is thus marked by every act which may define a tyrant, is unfit to be the ruler of a free people.

Nor have we been wanting in our attentions to our British brethren. We have warned them, from time to time, of attempts by their legislature to extend an unwarrantable jurisdiction over us. We have reminded them of the circumstances of our emigration and settlement here. We have appealed to their native justice and magnanimity; and we have conjured them, by the ties of our common kindred, to disavow these usurpations, which would inevitably interrupt our connections and correspondence. They, too, have been deaf to the voice of justice and of consanguinity. We must, therefore, acquiesce in the necessity which denounces our separation, and hold them, as we hold the rest of mankind, enemies in war, in peace friends.

We, therefore, the representatives of the United States of America, in General Congress assembled, appealing to the Supreme Judge of the world for the rectitude of our intentions, do, in the name and by the authority of the good people of these colonies, solemnly publish and declare, that these United Colonies are, and of right ought to be, FREE AND INDEPENDENT STATES; that they are absolved from all allegiance to the British crown, and that all political connection between them and the state of Great Britain is, and ought to be, totally dissolved; and that, as free and independent states, they have full power to levy war, conclude peace, contract alliances, establish commerce, and do all other acts and things which independent states may of right do. And for the support of this declaration, with a firm reliance on the protection of Divine Providence, we mutually pledge to each other our lives, our fortunes, and our sacred honor.

JOHN HANCOCK
and fifty-five others

Constitution of the United States of America and Amendments*

Preamble

We the people of the United States, in order to form a more perfect union, establish justice, insure domestic tranquillity, provide for the common defense, promote

* Passages no longer in effect are printed in italic type.

the general welfare, and secure the blessings of liberty to ourselves and our posterity, do ordain and establish this Constitution for the United States of America.

Article I

Section 1 All legislative powers herein granted shall be vested in a Congress of the United States, which shall consist of a Senate and a House of Representatives.

Section 2 The House of Representatives shall be composed of members chosen every second year by the people of the several States, and the electors in each State shall have the qualifications requisite for electors of the most numerous branch of the State Legislature.

No person shall be a Representative who shall not have attained to the age of twenty-five years, and been seven years a citizen of the United States, and who shall not, when elected, be an inhabitant of that State in which he shall be chosen.

Representatives and direct taxes shall be apportioned among the several States which may be included within this Union, according to their respective numbers, *which shall be determined by adding to the whole number of free persons, including those bound to service for a term of years and excluding Indians not taxed, three-fifths of all other persons.* The actual enumeration shall be made within three years after the first meeting of the Congress of the United States, and within every subsequent term of ten years, in such manner as they shall by law direct. The number of Representatives shall not exceed one for every thirty thousand, but each State shall have at least one Representative; *and until such enumeration shall be made, the State of New Hampshire shall be entitled to choose three, Massachusetts eight, Rhode Island and Providence Plantations one, Connecticut five, New York six, New Jersey four, Pennsylvania eight, Delaware one, Maryland six, Virginia ten, North Carolina five, South Carolina five, and Georgia three.*

When vacancies happen in the representation from any State, the Executive authority thereof shall issue writs of election to fill such vacancies.

The House of Representatives shall choose their Speaker and other officers; and shall have the sole power of impeachment.

Section 3 The Senate of the United States shall be composed of two Senators from each State, *chosen by the legislature thereof,* for six years; and each Senator shall have one vote.

Immediately after they shall be assembled in consequence of the first election, they shall be divided as equally as may be into three classes. The seats of the Senators of the first class shall be vacated at the expiration of the second year, of the second class at the expiration of the fourth year, and of the third class at the expiration of the sixth year, so that one-third may be chosen every second year; *and if vacancies happen by resignation or otherwise, during the recess of the legislature of any State, the Executive thereof may make temporary appointments until the next meeting of the legislature, which shall then fill such vacancies.*

No person shall be a Senator who shall not have attained to the age of thirty years, and been nine years a citizen of the United States, and who shall not, when elected, be an inhabitant of that State for which he shall be chosen.

The Vice-President of the United States shall be President of the Senate, but shall have no vote, unless they be equally divided.

The Senate shall choose their other officers, and also a President *pro tempore,* in the absence of the Vice-President, or when he shall exercise the office of President of the United States.

The Senate shall have the sole power to try all impeachments. When sitting for that purpose, they shall be on oath or affirmation. When the President of the United States is tried, the Chief Justice shall preside: and no person shall be convicted with-out the concurrence of two-thirds of the members present.

Judgment in cases of impeachment shall not extend further than to removal from the office, and disqualification to hold and enjoy any office of honor, trust or profit under the United States: but the party convicted shall nevertheless be liable and subject to indictment, trial, judgment and punishment, according to law.

Section 4 The times, places and manner of holding elections for Senators and Representatives shall be prescribed in each State by the legislature thereof; but the Congress may at any time by law make or alter such regulations, except as to the places of choosing Senators.

The Congress shall assemble at least once in every year, and such meeting *shall be on the first Monday in December, unless they shall by law appoint a different day.*

Section 5 Each house shall be the judge of the elections, returns and qualifications of its own members, and a majority of each shall constitute a quorum to do business; but a smaller number may adjourn from day to day, and may be authorized to compel the attendance of absent members, in such manner, and under such penalties, as each house may provide.

Each house may determine the rules of its proceedings, punish its members for disorderly behavior, and with the concurrence of two-thirds, expel a member.

Each house shall keep a journal of its proceedings, and from time to time publish the same, excepting such parts as may in their judgment require secrecy; and the yeas and nays of the members of either house on any question shall, at the desire of one-fifth of those present, be entered on the journal.

Neither house, during the session of Congress, shall, without the consent of the other, adjourn for more than three days, nor to any other place than that in which the two houses shall be sitting.

Section 6 The Senators and Representatives shall receive a compensation for their services, to be ascertained by law and paid out of the treasury of the United States. They shall in all cases except treason, felony and breach of the peace, be privileged from arrest during their attendance at the session of their respective houses, and in going to and returning from the same; and for any speech or debate in either house, they shall not be questioned in any other place.

No Senator or Representative shall, during the time for which he was elected, be appointed to any civil office under the authority of the United States, which shall have been created, or the emoluments whereof shall have been increased, during such time; and no person holding any office under the United States shall be a member of either house during his continuance in office.

Section 7 All bills for raising revenue shall originate in the House of Representatives; but the Senate may propose or concur with amendments as on other bills.

Every bill which shall have passed the House of Representatives and the Senate, shall, before it become a law, be presented to the President of the United States; if he approve he shall sign it, but if not he shall return it with objections to that house in which it originated, who shall enter the objections at large on their journal, and proceed to reconsider it. If after such reconsideration two-thirds of that house shall agree to pass the bill, it shall be sent, together with the objections, to the other house, by which it shall likewise be reconsidered, and, if approved by two-thirds of that house, it shall become a law. But in all such cases the votes of both houses shall be determined by yeas and nays, and the names of the persons voting for and against the bill shall be entered on the journal of each house respectively. If any bill shall not be returned by the President within ten days (Sundays excepted) after it shall have been presented to him, the same shall be a law, in like manner as if he had signed it, unless the Congress by their adjournment prevent its return, in which case it shall not be a law.

Every order, resolution, or vote to which the concurrence of the Senate and House of Representatives may be necessary (except on a question of adjournment) shall be presented to the President of the United States; and before the same shall take effect, shall be approved by him, or being disapproved by him, shall be repassed by two-thirds of the Senate and House of Representatives, according to the rules and limitations prescribed in the case of a bill.

Section 8 The Congress shall have power

To lay and collect taxes, duties, imposts, and excises, to pay the debts and provide for the common defense and general welfare of the United States; but all duties, imposts and excises shall be uniform throughout the United States;

To borrow money on the credit of the United States;

To regulate commerce with foreign nations, and among the several States, and with the Indian tribes;

To establish an uniform rule of naturalization, and uniform laws on the subject of bankruptcies throughout the United States;

To coin money, regulate the value thereof, and of foreign coin, and fix the standard of weights and measures;

To provide for the punishment of counterfeiting the securities and current coin of the United States;

To establish post offices and post roads;

To promote the progress of science and useful arts by securing for limited times to authors and inventors the exclusive right to their respective writings and discoveries;

To constitute tribunals inferior to the Supreme Court;

To define and punish piracies and felonies committed on the high seas and offenses against the law of nations;

To declare war, grant letters of marque and reprisal, and make rules concerning captures on land and water;

To raise and support armies, but no appropriation of money to that use shall be for a longer term than two years;

To provide and maintain a navy;

To make rules for the government and regulation of the land and naval forces;

To provide for calling forth the militia to execute the laws of the Union, suppress insurrections, and repel invasions;

To provide for organizing, arming, and disciplining the militia, and for governing such part of them as may be employed in the service of the United States, reserving to the States respectively the appointment of the officers, and the authority of training the militia according to the discipline prescribed by Congress;

To exercise exclusive legislation in all cases whatsoever, over such district (not exceeding ten miles square) as may, by cession of particular States, and the acceptance of Congress, become the seat of government of the United States, and to exercise like authority over all places purchased by the consent of the legislature of the State, in which the same shall be, for erection of forts, magazines, arsenals, dockyards, and other needful buildings; — and

To make all laws which shall be necessary and proper for carrying into execution the foregoing powers, and all other powers vested by this Constitution in the government of the United States, or in any department or officer thereof.

Section 9 The migration or importation of such persons as any of the States now existing shall think proper to admit shall not be prohibited by the Congress prior to the year 1808; but a tax or duty may be imposed on such importation, not exceeding $10 for each person.

The privilege of the writ of habeas corpus shall not be suspended, unless when in cases of rebellion or invasion the public safety may require it.

No bill of attainder or ex post facto law shall be passed.

No capitation, or other direct, tax shall be laid, unless in proportion to the census or enumeration herein before directed to be taken.

No tax or duty shall be laid on articles exported from any State.

No preference shall be given by any regulation of commerce or revenue to the ports of one State over those of another; nor shall vessels bound to, or from, one State, be obliged to enter, clear, or pay duties in another.

No money shall be drawn from the treasury, but in consequence of appropriations made by law; and a regular statement and account of the receipts and expenditures of all public money shall be published from time to time.

No title of nobility shall be granted by the United States: and no person holding any office of profit or trust under them, shall, without the consent of the Congress, accept of any present, emolument, office, or title, of any kind whatever, from any king, prince, or foreign state.

Section 10 No State shall enter into any treaty, alliance, or confederation; grant letters of marque and reprisal; coin money; emit bills of credit; make anything but gold and silver coin a tender in payment of debts; pass any bill of attainder, ex post facto law, or law impairing the obligation of contracts, or grant any title of nobility.

No State shall, without the consent of Congress, lay any imposts or duties on imports or exports, except what may be absolutely necessary for executing its inspection laws: and the net produce of all duties and imposts, laid by any State on imports or exports, shall be for the use of the treasury of the United States; and all such laws shall be subject to the revision and control of the Congress.

No State shall, without the consent of Congress, lay any duty of tonnage, keep troops or ships of war in time of peace, enter into any agreement or compact with another State, or with a foreign power, or engage in war, unless actually invaded, or in such imminent danger as will not admit of delay.

Article II

Section 1 The executive power shall be vested in a President of the United States of America. He shall hold his office during the term of four years, and, together with the Vice-President, chosen for the same term, be elected as follows:

Each State shall appoint, in such manner as the legislature thereof may direct, a number of electors, equal to the whole number of Senators and Representatives to which the State may be entitled in the Congress; but no Senator or Representative, or person holding an office of trust or profit under the United States, shall be appointed an elector.

The electors shall meet in their respective States, and vote by ballot for two persons, of whom one at least shall not be an inhabitant of the same State with themselves. And they shall make a list of all the persons voted for, and of the number of votes for each; which list they shall sign and certify, and transmit sealed to the seat of government of the United States, directed to the President of the Senate. The President of the Senate shall, in the presence of the Senate and House of Representatives, open all the certificates, and the votes shall then be counted. The person having the greatest number of votes shall be the President, if such number be a majority of the whole number of electors appointed; and if there be more than one who have such majority, and have an equal number of votes, then the House of Representatives shall immediately choose by ballot one of them for President; and if no person have a majority, then from the five highest on the list said house shall in like manner choose the President. But in choosing the President the votes shall be taken by States, the representation from each State having one vote; a quorum for this purpose shall consist of a member or members from two-thirds of the States, and a majority of all the States shall be necessary to a choice. In every case, after the choice of the President, the person having the greatest number of votes of the electors shall be the Vice-President. But if there should remain two or more who have equal votes, the Senate shall choose from them by ballot the Vice-President.

The Congress may determine the time of choosing the electors and the day on which they shall give their votes; which day shall be the same throughout the United States.

No person except a natural-born citizen, *or a citizen of the United States at the time of the adoption of this Constitution,* shall be eligible to the office of President; neither shall any person be eligible to that office who shall not have attained to the age of thirty-five years, and been fourteen years a resident within the United States.

In cases of the removal of the President from office or of his death, resignation, or inability to discharge the powers and duties of the said office, the same shall devolve on the Vice-President, and the Congress may by law provide for the case of removal, death, resignation, or inability, both of the President and Vice-President, declaring what officer shall then act as President, and such officer shall act accordingly, until the disability be removed, or a President shall be elected.

The President shall, at stated times, receive for his services a compensation, which shall neither be increased nor diminished during the period for which he shall have been elected, and he shall not receive within that period any other emolument from the United States, or any of them.

Before he enter on the execution of his office, he shall take the following oath or affirmation:—"I do solemnly swear (or affirm) that I will faithfully execute the office of the President of the United States, and will to the best of my ability preserve, protect and defend the Constitution of the United States."

Section 2 The President shall be commander in chief of the army and navy of the United States, and of the militia of the several States, when called into the actual service of the United States; he may require the opinion, in writing, of the principal officer in each of the executive departments, upon any subject relating to the duties of their respective offices, and he shall have power to grant reprieves and pardons for offenses against the United States, except in cases of impeachment.

He shall have power, by and with the advice and consent of the Senate, to make treaties, provided two-thirds of the Senators present concur; and he shall nominate, and by and with the advice and consent of the Senate, shall appoint ambassadors, other public ministers and consuls, judges of the Supreme Court, and all other officers of the United States, whose appointments are not herein otherwise provided for, and which shall be established by law: but Congress may by law vest the appointment of such inferior officers, as they think proper, in the President alone, in the courts of law, or in the heads of departments.

The President shall have power to fill up all vacancies that may happen during the recess of the Senate, by granting commissions which shall expire at the end of their next session.

Section 3 He shall from time to time give to the Congress information of the state of the Union, and recommend to their consideration such measures as he shall judge necessary and expedient; he may, on extraordinary occasions, convene both houses, or either of them, and in case of disagreement between them, with respect to the time of adjournment, he may adjourn them to such time as he shall think proper; he shall receive ambassadors and other public ministers; he shall take care that the laws be faithfully executed, and shall commission all the officers of the United States.

Section 4 The President, Vice-President and all civil officers of the United States shall be removed from office on impeachment for, and on conviction of, treason, bribery, or other high crimes and misdemeanors.

Article III

Section 1 The judicial power of the United States shall be vested in one Supreme Court, and in such inferior courts as the Congress may from time to time ordain and establish. The judges, both of the Supreme and inferior courts, shall hold their offices during good behavior, and shall, at stated times, receive for their services a compensation which shall not be diminished during their continuance in office.

Section 2 The judicial power shall extend to all cases, in law and equity, arising under this Constitution, the laws of the United States, and treaties made, or which shall be made, under their authority;—to all cases affecting ambassadors, other public ministers and consuls;—to all cases of admiralty and maritime jurisdiction;—to controversies to which the United States shall be a party;—to controversies between two or more States;—*between a State and citizens of another State;*—between citizens of different States;—between citizens of the same State claiming lands under grants of different States, and between a State, or the citizens thereof, and foreign states, citizens or subjects.

In all cases affecting ambassadors, other public ministers and consuls, and those in which a State shall be party, the Supreme Court shall have original jurisdiction. In all the other cases before mentioned, the Supreme Court shall have appellate jurisdiction, both as to law and fact, with such exceptions, and under such regulations, as the Congress shall make.

The trial of all crimes, except in cases of impeachment, shall be by jury; and such trial shall be held in the State where said crimes shall have been committed; but when not committed within any State, the trial shall be at such place or places as the Congress may by law have directed.

Section 3 Treason against the United States shall consist only in levying war against them, or in adhering to their enemies, giving them aid and comfort. No person shall be convicted of treason unless on the testimony of two witnesses to the same overt act, or on confession in open court.

The Congress shall have power to declare the punishment of treason, but no attainder of treason shall work corruption of blood, or forfeiture except during the life of the person attainted.

Article IV

Section 1 Full faith and credit shall be given in each State to the public acts, records, and judicial proceedings of every other State. And the Congress may by general laws prescribe the manner in which such acts, records, and proceedings shall be proved, and the effect thereof.

Section 2 The citizens of each State shall be entitled to all privileges and immunities of citizens in the several States.

A person charged in any State with treason, felony, or other crime, who shall flee from justice, and be found in another State, shall on demand of the executive authority of the State from which he fled, be delivered up, to be removed to the State having jurisdiction of the crime.

No person held to service or labor in one State, under the laws thereof, escaping into another, shall, in consequence of any law or regulation therein, be discharged from such service or labor, but shall be delivered up on claim of the party to whom such service or labor may be due.

Section 3 New States may be admitted by the Congress into this Union; but no new State shall be formed or erected within the jurisdiction of any other State; nor any State be formed by the junction of two or more States, or parts of States, without the consent of the legislatures of the States concerned as well as of the Congress.

The Congress shall have power to dispose of and make all needful rules and regulations respecting the territory or other property belonging to the United States; and nothing in this Constitution shall be so construed as to prejudice any claims of the United States, or of any particular State.

Section 4 The United States shall guarantee to every State in this Union a republican form of government, and shall protect each of them against invasion; and on application of the legislature, or of the executive (when the legislature cannot be convened), against domestic violence.

Article V

The Congress, whenever two-thirds of both houses shall deem it necessary, shall propose amendments to this Constitution, or, on the application of the legislatures of two-thirds of the several States, shall call a convention for proposing amendments, which, in either case, shall be valid to all intents and purposes, as part of this Constitution, when ratified by the legislatures of three-fourths of the several States, or by conventions in three-fourths thereof, as the one or the other mode of ratification may be proposed by the Congress; provided *that no amendments which may be made prior to the year one thousand eight hundred and eight shall in any manner affect the first and fourth clauses in the ninth section of the first article;* and that no State, without its consent, shall be deprived of its equal suffrage in the Senate.

Article VI

All debts contracted and engagements entered into, before the adoption of this Constitution, shall be as valid against the United States under this Constitution, as under the Confederation.

This Constitution, and the laws of the United States which shall be made in pursuance thereof; and all treaties made, or which shall be made, under the authority of the United States, shall be the supreme law of the land; and the judges in every State shall be bound thereby, anything in the Constitution or laws of any State to the contrary notwithstanding.

The Senators and Representatives before mentioned, and the members of the several State legislatures, and all executive and judicial officers, both of the United States and of the several States, shall be bound by oath or affirmation to support this Constitution; but no religious test shall ever be required as a qualification to any office or public trust under the United States.

Article VII

The ratification of the conventions of nine States shall be sufficient for the establishment of this Constitution between the States so ratifying the same.

Done in Convention by the unanimous consent of the States present, the seventeenth day of September in the year of our Lord one thousand seven hundred and eighty-seven and of the Independence of the United States of America the twelfth. In witness whereof we have hereunto subscribed our names.

GEORGE WASHINGTON
and thirty-seven others

Amendments to the Constitution*

Amendment I

Congress shall make no law respecting an establishment of religion, or prohibiting the free exercise thereof; or abridging the freedom of speech, or of the press; or the right of the people peaceably to assemble, and to petition the government for a redress of grievances.

Amendment II

A well-regulated militia being necessary to the security of a free State, the right of the people to keep and bear arms shall not be infringed.

Amendment III

No soldier shall, in time of peace, be quartered in any house without the consent of the owner, nor in time of war, but in a manner to be prescribed by law.

Amendment IV

The right of the people to be secure in their persons, houses, papers, and effects, against unreasonable searches and seizures, shall not be violated, and no warrants shall issue but upon probable cause, supported by oath or affirmation, and particularly describing the place to be searched, and the persons or things to be seized.

Amendment V

No person shall be held to answer for a capital, or otherwise infamous crime, unless on a presentment or indictment of a grand jury, except in cases arising in the land or naval forces, or in the militia, when in actual service in time of war or public danger; nor shall any person be subject for the same offense to be twice put in jeopardy of life or limb; nor shall be compelled in any criminal case to be a witness against himself, nor be deprived of life, liberty, or property, without due process of law; nor shall private property be taken for public use without just compensation.

Amendment VI

In all criminal prosecutions, the accused shall enjoy the right to a speedy and public trial, by an impartial jury of the State and district wherein the crime shall have been committed, which district shall have been previously ascertained by law, and to be informed of the nature and cause of the accusation; to be confronted with the witnesses against him; to have compulsory process for obtaining witnesses in his favor, and to have the assistance of counsel for his defense.

* The first ten Amendments (the Bill of Rights) were adopted in 1791.

Amendment VII

In suits at common law, where the value in controversy shall exceed twenty dollars, the right of trial by jury shall be preserved, and no fact tried by a jury shall be otherwise reexamined in any court of the United States, than according to the rules of the common law.

Amendment VIII

Excessive bail shall not be required, nor excessive fines imposed, nor cruel and unusual punishments inflicted.

Amendment IX

The enumeration in the Constitution, of certain rights, shall not be construed to deny or disparage others retained by the people.

Amendment X

The powers not delegated to the United States by the Constitution, nor prohibited by it to the States, are reserved to the States respectively, or to the people.

Amendment XI

[Adopted 1798]

The judicial power of the United States shall not be construed to extend to any suit in law or equity, commenced or prosecuted against one of the United States by citizens of another State, or by citizens or subjects of any foreign state.

Amendment XII

[Adopted 1804]

The electors shall meet in their respective States, and vote by ballot for President and Vice-President, one of whom, at least, shall not be an inhabitant of the same State with themselves; they shall name in their ballots the person voted for as President, and in distinct ballots the person voted for as Vice-President, and they shall make distinct lists of all persons voted for as President, and of all persons voted for as Vice-President, and of the number of votes for each, which lists they shall sign and certify, and transmit sealed to the seat of government of the United States, directed to the President of the Senate;—the President of the Senate shall, in the presence of the Senate and House of Representatives, open all the certificates and the votes shall then be counted;—the person having the greatest number of votes for President shall be the President, if such number be a majority of the whole number of electors appointed; and if no person have such majority, then from the persons having the highest numbers not exceeding three on the list of those voted for as President, the House of Representatives shall choose immediately, by ballot, the President. But in choosing the President, the votes shall be taken by States, the representation from each State having one vote; a quorum for this purpose shall consist of a member or members from two-thirds of the States, and a majority of all the States shall be necessary to a choice. And if the House of Representatives shall not choose a President whenever the right of choice shall devolve upon them, before the fourth day of March next following, then the Vice-President shall act as President, as in the case of the death or other constitutional disability of the President.

The person having the greatest number of votes as Vice-President shall be the Vice-President, if such number be a majority of the whole number of electors appointed; and if no person have a majority, then from the two highest numbers on the list the Senate shall choose the Vice-President; a quorum for the purpose shall consist of two-thirds of the whole number of Senators, and a majority of the whole number shall be necessary to a choice. But no person constitutionally ineligible to the office of President shall be eligible to that of Vice-President of the United States.

Amendment XIII

[Adopted 1865]

Section 1 Neither slavery nor involuntary servitude, except as a punishment for crime whereof the party shall have been duly convicted, shall exist within the United States, or any place subject to their jurisdiction.

Section 2 Congress shall have power to enforce this article by appropriate legislation.

Amendment XIV

[Adopted 1868]

Section 1 All persons born or naturalized in the United States, and subject to the jurisdiction thereof, are citizens of the United States and of the State wherein they reside. No State shall make or enforce any law which shall abridge the privileges or immunities of citizens of the United States; nor shall any State deprive any person of life, liberty, or property, without due process of law; nor deny to any person within its jurisdiction the equal protection of the laws.

Section 2 Representatives shall be apportioned among the several States according to their respective numbers, counting the whole number of persons in each State, excluding Indians not taxed. But when the right to vote at any election for the choice of Electors for President and Vice-President of the United States, Representatives in Congress, the executive and judicial officers of a State, or the members of the legislature thereof, is denied to any of the male inhabitants of such State, being twenty-one years of age and citizens of the United States, or in any way abridged, except for participation in rebellion, or other crime, the basis of representation therein shall be reduced in the proportion which the number of such male citizens shall bear to the whole number of male citizens twenty-one years of age in such State.

Section 3 No person shall be a Senator or Representative in Congress, or Elector of President and Vice-President, or hold any office, civil or military, under the United States, or under any State, who, having previously taken an oath, as a member of Congress, or as an officer of the United States, or as a member of any State legislature, or as an executive or judicial officer of any State, to support the Constitution of the United States, shall have engaged in insurrection or rebellion against the same, or given aid or comfort to the enemies thereof. Congress may, by a vote of two-thirds of each house, remove such disability.

Section 4 The validity of the public debt of the United States, authorized by law, including debts incurred for payment of pensions and bounties for services in suppressing insurrection or rebellion, shall not be questioned. But neither the United States nor any State shall assume or pay any debt or obligation incurred in aid of insurrection or rebellion against the United States, or any claim for the loss or emancipation of any slave; but all such debts, obligations, and claims shall be held illegal and void.

Section 5 The Congress shall have power to enforce, by appropriate legislation, the provisions of this article.

Amendment XV

[Adopted 1870]

Section 1 The right of citizens of the United States to vote shall not be denied or abridged by the United States or by any State on account of race, color, or previous condition of servitude.

Section 2 The Congress shall have power to enforce this article by appropriate legislation.

Amendment XVI

[Adopted 1913]

The Congress shall have power to lay and collect taxes on incomes, from whatever source derived, without apportionment among the several States, and without regard to any census or enumeration.

Amendment XVII

[Adopted 1913]

Section 1 The Senate of the United States shall be composed of two Senators from each State, elected by the people thereof, for six years; and each Senator shall have one vote. The electors in each State shall have the qualifications requisite for electors of [voters for] the most numerous branch of the State legislatures.

Section 2 When vacancies happen in the representation of any State in the Senate, the executive authority of such State shall issue writs of election to fill such vacancies: Provided, that the Legislature of any State may empower the executive thereof to make temporary appointments until the people fill the vacancies by election as the Legislature may direct.

Section 3 This amendment shall not be so construed as to affect the election or term of any Senator chosen before it becomes valid as part of the Constitution.

Amendment XVIII

[Adopted 1919; Repealed 1933]

Section 1 After one year from the ratification of this article the manufacture, sale, or transportation of intoxicating liquors within, the importation thereof into, or the exportation thereof from the United States and all territory subject to the jurisdiction thereof, for beverage purposes, is hereby prohibited.

Section 2 The Congress and the several States shall have concurrent power to enforce this article by appropriate legislation.

Section 3 This article shall be inoperative unless it shall have been ratified as an amendment to the Constitution by the legislatures of the several States, as provided by the Constitution, within seven years from the date of the submission thereof to the States by the Congress.

Amendment XIX

[Adopted 1920]

Section 1 The right of citizens of the United States to vote shall not be denied or abridged by the United States or by any State on account of sex.

Section 2 The Congress shall have power to enforce this article by appropriate legislation.

Amendment XX

[Adopted 1933]

Section 1 The terms of the President and Vice-President shall end at noon on the 20th day of January, and the terms of Senators and Representatives at noon on the 3rd day of January, of the years in which such terms would have ended if this article had not been ratified; and the terms of their successors shall then begin.

Section 2 The Congress shall assemble at least once in every year, and such meeting shall begin at noon on the 3d day of January, unless they shall by law appoint a different day.

Section 3 If, at the time fixed for the beginning of the term of the President, the President-elect shall have died, the Vice-President-elect shall become President. If a President shall not have been chosen before the time fixed for the beginning of his term, or if the President-elect shall have failed to qualify, then the Vice-President-elect shall act as President until a President shall have qualified; and the Congress may by law provide for the case wherein neither a President-elect nor a Vice-President-elect shall have qualified, declaring who shall then act as President, or the manner in which one who is to act shall be selected, and such persons shall act accordingly until a President or Vice-President shall have qualified.

Section 4 The Congress may by law provide for the case of the death of any of the persons from whom the House of Representatives may choose a President whenever the right of choice shall have devolved upon them, and for the case of the death of any of the persons from whom the Senate may choose a Vice-President whenever the right of choice shall have devolved upon them.

Section 5 Sections 1 and 2 shall take effect on the 15th day of October following the ratification of this article.

Section 6 This article shall be inoperative unless it shall have been ratified as an amendment to the Constitution by the Legislatures of three-fourths of the several States within seven years from the date of its submission.

Amendment XXI

[Adopted 1933]

Section 1 The eighteenth article of amendment to the Constitution of the United States is hereby repealed.

Section 2 The transportation or importation into any State, Territory, or Possession of the United States for delivery or use therein of intoxicating liquors, in violation of the laws thereof, is hereby prohibited.

Section 3 This article shall be inoperative unless it shall have been ratified as an amendment to the Constitution by conventions in the several States, as provided in the Constitution, within seven years from the date of submission thereof to the States by the Congress.

Amendment XXII

[Adopted 1951]

Section 1 No person shall be elected to the office of President more than twice, and no person who has held the office of President, or acted as President, for more than two years of a term to which some other person was elected President shall be elected to the office of President more than once. But this article shall not apply to any person holding the office of President when this article was proposed by the Congress, and shall not prevent any person who may be holding the office of President, or acting as President, during the term within which this article becomes operative from holding the office of President or acting as President during the remainder of such term.

Section 2 This article shall be inoperative unless it shall have been ratified as an amendment to the Constitution by the legislatures of three-fourths of the several States within seven years from the date of its submission to the States by the Congress.

Amendment XXIII

[Adopted 1961]

Section 1 The District constituting the seat of Government of the United States shall appoint in such manner as the Congress may direct:

A number of electors of President and Vice-President equal to the whole number of Senators and Representatives in Congress to which the District would be entitled if it were a State, but in no event more than the least populous State; they shall be in addition to those appointed by the States, but they shall be considered for the purposes of the election of President and Vice-President, to be electors appointed by a State; and they shall meet in the District and perform such duties as provided by the twelfth article of amendment.

Section 2 The Congress shall have the power to enforce this article by appropriate legislation.

Amendment XXIV

[Adopted 1964]

Section 1 The right of citizens of the United States to vote in any primary or other election for President or Vice-President, for electors for President or Vice-President, or for Senator or Representative in Congress, shall not be denied or abridged by the United States or any State by reason of failure to pay any poll tax or other tax.

Section 2 The Congress shall have the power to enforce this article by appropriate legislation.

Amendment XXV

[Adopted 1967]

Section 1 In case of the removal of the President from office or of his death or resignation, the Vice-President shall become President.

Section 2 Whenever there is a vacancy in the office of the Vice-President, the President shall nominate a Vice-President who shall take office upon confirmation by a majority vote of both Houses of Congress.

Section 3 Whenever the President transmits to the President pro tempore of the Senate and the Speaker of the House of Representatives his written declaration that he is unable to discharge the powers and duties of his office, and until he transmits to them a written declaration to the contrary, such powers and duties shall be discharged by the Vice-President as Acting President.

Section 4 Whenever the Vice-President and a majority of either the principal officers of the executive departments or of such other body as Congress may by law provide, transmit to the President pro tempore of the Senate and the Speaker of the House of Representatives their written declaration that the President is unable to discharge the powers and duties of his office, the Vice-President shall immediately assume the powers and duties of the office as Acting President.

Thereafter, when the President transmits to the President pro tempore of the Senate and the Speaker of the House of Representatives his written declaration that no inability exists, he shall resume the powers and duties of his office unless the Vice-President and a majority of either the principal officers of the executive department[s] or of such other body as Congress may by law provide, transmit within four days to the President pro tempore of the Senate and the Speaker of the House of Representatives their written declaration that the President is unable to discharge the powers and duties of his office. Thereupon Congress shall decide the issue, assembling within forty-eight hours for that purpose if not in session. If the Congress, within twenty-one days after receipt of the latter written declaration, or, if Congress is not in session, within twenty-one days after Congress is required to assemble, determines by two-thirds vote of both Houses that the President is unable to discharge the powers and duties of his office, the Vice-President shall continue to discharge the same as Acting President; otherwise, the President shall resume the powers and duties of his office.

Amendment XXVI

[Adopted 1971]

Section 1 The right of citizens of the United States, who are eighteen years of age or older, to vote shall not be denied or abridged by the United States or by any State on account of age.

Section 2 The Congress shall have power to enforce this article by appropriate legislation.

Amendment XXVII

[Adopted 1992]

No law, varying the compensation for the services of the Senators and Representatives, shall take effect, until an election of Representatives shall have intervened.

Territorial Expansion of the United States

Territory	Date Acquired	Square Miles	How Acquired
Original states and territories	1783	888,685	Treaty with Great Britain
Louisiana Purchase	1803	827,192	Purchase from France
Florida	1819	72,003	Treaty with Spain
Texas	1845	390,143	Annexation of independent nation
Oregon	1846	285,580	Treaty with Great Britain
Mexican Cession	1848	529,017	Conquest from Mexico
Gadsden Purchase	1853	29,640	Purchase from Mexico
Alaska	1867	589,757	Purchase from Russia
Hawai`i	1898	6,450	Annexation of independent nation
The Philippines	1899	115,600	Conquest from Spain (granted independence in 1946)
Puerto Rico	1899	3,435	Conquest from Spain
Guam	1899	212	Conquest from Spain
American Samoa	1900	76	Treaty with Germany and Great Britain
Panama Canal Zone	1904	553	Treaty with Panama (returned to Panama by treaty in 1978)
Corn Islands	1914	4	Treaty with Nicaragua (returned to Nicaragua by treaty in 1971)
Virgin Islands	1917	133	Purchase from Denmark
Pacific Islands Trust (Micronesia)	1947	8,489	Trusteeship under United Nations (some granted independence)
All others (Midway, Wake, and other islands)		42	

Admission of States into the Union

	State	Date of Admission		State	Date of Admission
1.	Delaware	December 7, 1787	26.	Michigan	January 26, 1837
2.	Pennsylvania	December 12, 1787	27.	Florida	March 3, 1845
3.	New Jersey	December 18, 1787	28.	Texas	December 29, 1845
4.	Georgia	January 2, 1788	29.	Iowa	December 28, 1846
5.	Connecticut	January 9, 1788	30.	Wisconsin	May 29, 1848
6.	Massachusetts	February 6, 1788	31.	California	September 9, 1850
7.	Maryland	April 28, 1788	32.	Minnesota	May 11, 1858
8.	South Carolina	May 23, 1788	33.	Oregon	February 14, 1859
9.	New Hampshire	June 21, 1788	34.	Kansas	January 29, 1861
10.	Virginia	June 25, 1788	35.	West Virginia	June 20, 1863
11.	New York	July 26, 1788	36.	Nevada	October 31, 1864
12.	North Carolina	November 21, 1789	37.	Nebraska	March 1, 1867
13.	Rhode Island	May 29, 1790	38.	Colorado	August 1, 1876
14.	Vermont	March 4, 1791	39.	North Dakota	November 2, 1889
15.	Kentucky	June 1, 1792	40.	South Dakota	November 2, 1889
16.	Tennessee	June 1, 1796	41.	Montana	November 8, 1889
17.	Ohio	March 1, 1803	42.	Washington	November 11, 1889
18.	Louisiana	April 30, 1812	43.	Idaho	July 3, 1890
19.	Indiana	December 11, 1816	44.	Wyoming	July 10, 1890
20.	Mississippi	December 10, 1817	45.	Utah	January 4, 1896
21.	Illinois	December 3, 1818	46.	Oklahoma	November 16, 1907
22.	Alabama	December 14, 1819	47.	New Mexico	January 6, 1912
23.	Maine	March 15, 1820	48.	Arizona	February 14, 1912
24.	Missouri	August 10, 1821	49.	Alaska	January 3, 1959
25.	Arkansas	June 15, 1836	50.	Hawai`i	August 21, 1959

Presidential Elections

Year	Number of States	Candidates	Parties	Popular Vote	% of Popular Vote	Electoral Vote	% Voter Participation[a]
1789	11	**George Washington**	No party designations			69	
		John Adams				34	
		Other candidates				35	
1792	15	**George Washington**	No party designations			132	
		John Adams				77	
		George Clinton				50	
		Other candidates				5	
1796	16	**John Adams**	Federalist			71	
		Thomas Jefferson	Democratic-Republican			68	
		Thomas Pinckney	Federalist			59	
		Aaron Burr	Democratic-Republican			30	
		Other candidates				48	
1800	16	**Thomas Jefferson**	Democratic-Republican			73	
		Aaron Burr	Democratic-Republican			73	
		John Adams	Federalist			65	
		Charles C. Pinckney	Federalist			64	
		John Jay	Federalist			1	
1804	17	**Thomas Jefferson**	Democratic-Republican			162	
		Charles C. Pinckney	Federalist			14	
1808	17	**James Madison**	Democratic-Republican			122	
		Charles C. Pinckney	Federalist			47	
		George Clinton	Democratic-Republican			6	
1812	18	**James Madison**	Democratic-Republican			128	
		DeWitt Clinton	Federalist			89	
1816	19	**James Monroe**	Democratic-Republican			183	
		Rufus King	Federalist			34	
1820	24	**James Monroe**	Democratic-Republican			231	
		John Quincy Adams	Independent-Republican			1	

Presidential Elections, *Continued*

Year	Number of States	Candidates	Parties	Popular Vote	% of Popular Vote	Electoral Vote	% Voter Participation[a]
1824	24	**John Quincy Adams**	Democratic-Republican	108,740	30.5	84	26.9
		Andrew Jackson	Democratic-Republican	153,544	43.1	99	
		Henry Clay	Democratic-Republican	47,136	13.2	37	
		William H. Crawford	Democratic-Republican	46,618	13.1	41	
1828	24	**Andrew Jackson**	Democratic	647,286	56.0	178	57.6
		John Quincy Adams	National Republican	508,064	44.0	83	
1832	24	**Andrew Jackson**	Democratic	688,242	54.5	219	55.4
		Henry Clay	National Republican	473,462	37.5	49	
		William Wirt	Anti-Masonic	101,051	8.0	7	
		John Floyd	Democratic			11	
1836	26	**Martin Van Buren**	Democratic	765,483	50.9	170	57.8
		William H. Harrison	Whig	739,795	49.1	73	
		Hugh L. White	Whig			26	
		Daniel Webster	Whig			14	
		W. P. Mangum	Whig			11	
1840	26	**William H. Harrison**	Whig	1,274,624	53.1	234	80.2
		Martin Van Buren	Democratic	1,127,781	46.9	60	
1844	26	**James K. Polk**	Democratic	1,338,464	49.6	170	78.9
		Henry Clay	Whig	1,300,097	48.1	105	
		James G. Birney	Liberty	62,300	2.3		
1848	30	**Zachary Taylor**	Whig	1,360,967	47.4	163	72.7
		Lewis Cass	Democratic	1,222,342	42.5	127	
		Martin Van Buren	Free Soil	291,263	10.1		
1852	31	**Franklin Pierce**	Democratic	1,601,117	50.9	254	69.6
		Winfield Scott	Whig	1,385,453	44.1	42	
		John P. Hale	Free Soil	155,825	5.0		
1856	31	**James Buchanan**	Democratic	1,832,955	45.3	174	78.9
		John C. Frémont	Republican	1,339,932	33.1	114	
		Millard Fillmore	American	871,731	21.6	8	
1860	33	**Abraham Lincoln**	Republican	1,865,593	39.8	180	81.2
		Stephen A. Douglas	Democratic	1,382,713	29.5	12	
		John C. Breckinridge	Democratic	848,356	18.1	72	
		John Bell	Constitutional Union	592,906	12.6	39	

Presidential Elections, *Continued*

Year	Number of States	Candidates	Parties	Popular Vote	% of Popular Vote	Electoral Vote	% Voter Participation[a]
1864	36	**Abraham Lincoln**	Republican	2,206,938	55.0	212	73.8
		George B. McClellan	Democratic	1,803,787	45.0	21	
1868	37	**Ulysses S. Grant**	Republican	3,013,421	52.7	214	78.1
		Horatio Seymour	Democratic	2,706,829	47.3	80	
1872	37	**Ulysses S. Grant**	Republican	3,596,745	55.6	286	71.3
		Horace Greeley	Democratic	2,843,446	43.9	[b]	
1876	38	**Rutherford B. Hayes**	Republican	4,036,572	48.0	185	81.8
		Samuel J. Tilden	Democratic	4,284,020	51.0	184	
1880	38	**James A. Garfield**	Republican	4,453,295	48.5	214	79.4
		Winfield S. Hancock	Democratic	4,414,082	48.1	155	
		James B. Weaver	Greenback-Labor	308,578	3.4		
1884	38	**Grover Cleveland**	Democratic	4,879,507	48.5	219	77.5
		James G. Blaine	Republican	4,850,293	48.2	182	
		Benjamin F. Butler	Greenback-Labor	175,370	1.8		
		John P. St. John	Prohibition	150,369	1.5		
1888	38	**Benjamin Harrison**	Republican	5,477,129	47.9	233	79.3
		Grover Cleveland	Democratic	5,537,857	48.6	168	
		Clinton B. Fisk	Prohibition	249,506	2.2		
		Anson J. Streeter	Union Labor	146,935	1.3		
1892	44	**Grover Cleveland**	Democratic	5,555,426	46.1	277	74.7
		Benjamin Harrison	Republican	5,182,690	43.0	145	
		James B. Weaver	People's	1,029,846	8.5	22	
		John Bidwell	Prohibition	264,133	2.2		
1896	45	**William McKinley**	Republican	7,102,246	51.1	271	79.3
		William J. Bryan	Democratic	6,492,559	47.7	176	
1900	45	**William McKinley**	Republican	7,218,491	51.7	292	73.2
		William J. Bryan	Democratic; Populist	6,356,734	45.5	155	
		John C. Wooley	Prohibition	208,914	1.5		
1904	45	**Theodore Roosevelt**	Republican	7,628,461	57.4	336	65.2
		Alton B. Parker	Democratic	5,084,223	37.6	140	
		Eugene V. Debs	Socialist	402,283	3.0		
		Silas C. Swallow	Prohibition	258,536	1.9		
1908	46	**William H. Taft**	Republican	7,675,320	51.6	321	65.4
		William J. Bryan	Democratic	6,412,294	43.1	162	
		Eugene V. Debs	Socialist	420,793	2.8		
		Eugene W. Chafin	Prohibition	253,840	1.7		

Presidential Elections, *Continued*

Year	Number of States	Candidates	Parties	Popular Vote	% of Popular Vote	Electoral Vote	% Voter Participation[a]
1912	48	**Woodrow Wilson**	Democratic	6,296,547	41.9	435	58.8
		Theodore Roosevelt	Progressive	4,118,571	27.4	88	
		William H. Taft	Republican	3,486,720	23.2	8	
		Eugene V. Debs	Socialist	900,672	6.0		
		Eugene W. Chafin	Prohibition	206,275	1.4		
1916	48	**Woodrow Wilson**	Democratic	9,127,695	49.4	277	61.6
		Charles E. Hughes	Republican	8,533,507	46.2	254	
		A. L. Benson	Socialist	585,113	3.2		
		J. Frank Hanly	Prohibition	220,506	1.2		
1920	48	**Warren G. Harding**	Republican	16,143,407	60.4	404	49.2
		James M. Cox	Democratic	9,130,328	34.2	127	
		Eugene V. Debs	Socialist	919,799	3.4		
		P. P. Christensen	Farmer-Labor	265,411	1.0		
1924	48	**Calvin Coolidge**	Republican	15,718,211	54.0	382	48.9
		John W. Davis	Democratic	8,385,283	28.8	136	
		Robert M. La Follette	Progressive	4,831,289	16.6	13	
1928	48	**Herbert C. Hoover**	Republican	21,391,993	58.2	444	56.9
		Alfred E. Smith	Democratic	15,016,169	40.9	87	
1932	48	**Franklin D. Roosevelt**	Democratic	22,809,638	57.4	472	56.9
		Herbert C. Hoover	Republican	15,758,901	39.7	59	
		Norman Thomas	Socialist	881,951	2.2		
1936	48	**Franklin D. Roosevelt**	Democratic	27,752,869	60.8	523	61.0
		Alfred M. Landon	Republican	16,674,665	36.5	8	
		William Lemke	Union	882,479	1.9		
1940	48	**Franklin D. Roosevelt**	Democratic	27,307,819	54.8	449	62.5
		Wendell L. Wilkie	Republican	22,321,018	44.8	82	
1944	48	**Franklin D. Roosevelt**	Democratic	25,606,585	53.5	432	55.9
		Thomas E. Dewey	Republican	22,014,745	46.0	99	
1948	48	**Harry S Truman**	Democratic	24,179,345	49.6	303	53.0
		Thomas E. Dewey	Republican	21,991,291	45.1	189	
		J. Strom Thurmond	States' Rights	1,176,125	2.4	39	
		Henry A. Wallace	Progressive	1,157,326	2.4		
1952	48	**Dwight D. Eisenhower**	Republican	33,936,234	55.1	442	63.3
		Adlai E. Stevenson	Democratic	27,314,992	44.4	89	
1956	48	**Dwight D. Eisenhower**	Republican	35,590,472	57.6	457	60.6
		Adlai E. Stevenson	Democratic	26,022,752	42.1	73	
1960	50	**John F. Kennedy**	Democratic	34,226,731	49.7	303	62.8
		Richard M. Nixon	Republican	34,108,157	49.5	219	

Presidential Elections, *Continued*

Year	Number of States	Candidates	Parties	Popular Vote	% of Popular Vote	Electoral Vote	% Voter Participation[a]
1964	50	**Lyndon B. Johnson**	Democratic	43,129,566	61.1	486	61.7
		Barry M. Goldwater	Republican	27,178,188	38.5	52	
1968	50	**Richard M. Nixon**	Republican	31,785,480	43.4	301	60.6
		Hubert H. Humphrey	Democratic	31,275,166	42.7	191	
		George C. Wallace	American Independent	9,906,473	13.5	46	
1972	50	**Richard M. Nixon**	Republican	47,169,911	60.7	520	55.2
		George S. McGovern	Democratic	29,170,383	37.5	17	
		John G. Schmitz	American	1,099,482	1.4		
1976	50	**Jimmy Carter**	Democratic	40,830,763	50.1	297	53.5
		Gerald R. Ford	Republican	39,147,793	48.0	240	
1980	50	**Ronald Reagan**	Republican	43,899,248	50.8	489	52.6
		Jimmy Carter	Democratic	35,481,432	41.0	49	
		John B. Anderson	Independent	5,719,437	6.6	0	
		Ed Clark	Libertarian	920,859	1.1	0	
1984	50	**Ronald Reagan**	Republican	54,455,075	58.8	525	53.1
		Walter Mondale	Democratic	37,577,185	40.6	13	
1988	50	**George Bush**	Republican	48,901,046	53.4	426	50.2
		Michael Dukakis	Democratic	41,809,030	45.6	111[c]	
1992	50	**Bill Clinton**	Democratic	44,908,233	43.0	370	55.0
		George Bush	Republican	39,102,282	37.4	168	
		Ross Perot	Independent	19,741,048	18.9	0	
1996	50	**Bill Clinton**	Democratic	47,401,054	49.2	379	49.0
		Robert Dole	Republican	39,197,350	40.7	159	
		Ross Perot	Independent	8,085,285	8.4	0	
		Ralph Nader	Green	684,871	0.7	0	

Candidates receiving less than 1 percent of the popular vote have been omitted. Thus the percentage of popular vote given for any election year may not total 100 percent.

Before the passage of the Twelfth Amendment in 1804, the Electoral College voted for two presidential candidates; the runner-up became vice president.

Before 1824, most presidential electors were chosen by state legislatures, not by popular vote.

[a]Percent of voting-age population casting ballots.

[b]Greeley died shortly after the election; the electors supporting him then divided their votes among minor candidates.

[c]One elector from West Virginia cast her Electoral College presidential ballot for Lloyd Bentsen, the Democratic party's vice-presidential candidate.

INDEX